The Fairchild Books
DICTIONARY *of* FASHION

4th edition

The Fairchild Books DICTIONARY of FASHION

4th edition

Phyllis G. Tortora | Sandra J. Keiser

Illustrated by Bina Abling

Fairchild Books
An Imprint of Bloomsbury Publishing Inc.
New York, NY

Fairchild Books
An imprint of Bloomsbury Publishing Inc

1385 Broadway
New York
NY 10010
USA

50 Bedford Square
London
WC1B 3DP
UK

www.fairchildbooks.com

First edition published 1975
Second edition published 1988
Third edition published 2003
This edition first published 2014

Library of Congress Cataloging-in-Publication Data
A catalog record for this book is available from the Library of Congress
2013938689

ISBN: PB: 978-1-60901-489-6

Typeset by Precision Graphics
Cover Design Carly Grafstein
Printed and bound in the United States of America

contents

preface

THIS FOURTH EDITION of *The Fairchild Books Dictionary of Fashion* stands on the foundation of three previous editions, two that were originated and developed by Charlotte Mankey Calasibetta, and a third that was revised by Phyllis Tortora. Since 1975, the work has served as an invaluable reference for students, scholars, authors, designers, those in the fashion business, and anyone with an interest in fashion, past and present. Professor Calasibetta's description of how she created the first edition will provide insight into the formidable task that she undertook:

> *This dictionary evolved from a college course in fashion. In an attempt to teach students a vocabulary of fashion terms that would not become outdated, lists were assembled of collars, necklines, sleeves, skirts, and so on, and each was considered in the light of the existing fashion trends—which were "in," and which were "out." The basic categories for this dictionary grew from these lists. The addition of historical terms and some of the vocabulary of clothing manufacturers rounded out the entries.*

THE FOURTH EDITION

This fourth edition expands on the third with the addition of more than 200 new terms and more than 100 new and updated illustrations. The appendix of designers has been expanded to include nearly 200 designers of fashion apparel and accessories who have become prominent since the publication of the third edition.

Categories

The fourth edition preserves what is best of the earlier editions, but a number of changes make the book even more comprehensive and useful. One of the strengths of the dictionary has been the organization of entries into categories. A reader who is interested in a definition of a "peg-top skirt," for example, will find that entry in the Skirts category and can compare that definition with those for other types of skirts. Illustrations of a variety of skirt types also appear with the category, allowing for visual comparisons.

Should readers not know the category into which an item fits, they can consult the alphabetical listing, where a cross-reference will direct them to the appropriate location. A category for dresses has been added. The table of contents provides a complete list of the categories utilized in this edition.

Kinds of Words Defined in the Dictionary

Contemporary Fashion Terms

As in the earlier editions, a major focus is fashion terms currently in use and those that tend to be revived periodically as well as many terms applied to historic dress. Fashion designers often derive inspiration from the past, and words from earlier decades and even previous centuries may still be in use. For many of the entries, the derivation of the term is noted.

Fashion Terms from Non-Western Cultures and Folk Costume

The focus of this dictionary is fashion in the Western world. To be comprehensive and cover non-Western apparel would require a book far larger than this one. For these reasons, non-Western apparel terms are defined only if they have become part of Western fashion or have some current importance. Folk costume terms are included only if they are used in mainstream fashion.

Historic Fashion Terms

Another important aspect of earlier editions has been the inclusion of historic fashion terms. Historic terms that are no longer in current usage are designated by a special archival symbol, an infinity symbol (∞), as in the following example:

∞**Andalusian casaque** (an-da-loó-zee-an cask) Woman's evening tunic, fastened down center with series of ribbons, with the front of the skirt cut away, and sloping to knee-length in the back. Worn over another skirt c. 1809.

Several unique aspects of historic terms should be noted. One of these is spelling. Before the publication of standardized dictionaries in English in the 18th and 19th c., spelling could be quite erratic. For example, a popular hair and wig style of the 18th c. can be spelled *cadogan, catogan,* or *catagan.* Medieval terms, some of which derive from English and others from French, tend to have many spelling variations. Those with Latin roots tend to be more stable. When these historic terms with many variations are entries, the variations are printed in italics and enclosed in parentheses. For example,

chaussembles (show′-som-bl) (*chausembles, chasembles, cashambles*)

Dictionary users will find many fashion elements from the 19th c. that are named after royalty or famous persons of the past. As fashion changes accelerated and periodicals provided more coverage of fashions, there was a tendency to assign names to styles. Also, historians of costume and dress and other writers of the 19th c. originated many names for styles of earlier centuries. Where possible, definitions of such terms will incorporate a brief explanation of who the historical personage was or note that a particular term was coined at a time long after the costume was worn. In general, where terms derived from proper names are seen by the editors primarily as fashion terms, these are not capitalized.

Merchandising and Retailing Terms

Fashion design, production, and marketing terms were introduced in the revised second edition in an appendix. These and additional entries were incorporated into the alphabetical listing in the third edition, and new industry terms have been added. The terms included are those with specific application to some segment of the fashion industry. General business terms are not included.

Textile Terms

Textile terms are limited to standard textiles that continue to be widely used and to new textile materials that have had a recent impact on fashion. Textile terms are identified by a dagger (†).

†**angora** Soft fuzzy yarn made from the underhair of the angora rabbit that is used for knit wear and for trimmings.

Since the publication of the third edition, an eighth edition of the *Fairchild Books Dictionary of Textiles* has been published. That work provides comprehensive listings of textile terms, both contemporary and historic, and users who require a more complete definition of textile terms designated by the † symbol are advised to consult that work.

Fashion Designers

Like previous editions of *The Fairchild Books Dictionary of Fashion,* this fourth edition includes an appendix of fashion designers and discussion of their work. To manage the size of the dictionary and additions to the appendix, references to fashion designers have been removed from the alphabetical sections. For users who want a fuller discussion of these and other fashion designers, a very thorough examination of the life and work of important fashion designers past and present is to be found in Fairchild Books' publication, *Who's Who in Fashion,* Fifth Edition.

Limitations on Entries Included in the Dictionary

In any book, space imposes some limits on content. The following are some of the kinds of terms not included in this work. Definitions of color terminology have been eliminated because these terms are well defined in a variety of other sources.

As previously noted, non-Western apparel terms and folk costume terms are included only if they have become part of Western fashion. Foreign terms do not appear unless they are used in English in fashion or scholarship about fashion. Foreign words used in English in a fashion context *are* included.

Weapons (e.g., swords, daggers, guns) are not included, even when carried ceremonially. Registered trademark names have been eliminated, in so far as that is possible. The constant addition and deregistration of trademarks makes it very difficult to include such entries and be both up-to-date and accurate. Some trademarks, however, are so significant to fashion that they must be included.

Illustrations

The Fairchild Books Dictionary of Fashion includes some 800 drawings by fashion illustrator Bina Abling. These visual definitions enhance the verbal definitions, showing "anatomical drawings" of various fashion items and identifying the period represented by drawings for items that revive earlier styles. These drawings are based on primary source materials.

Format and Organization of Definitions

The following entries will serve to illustrate the organization and format features of the fourth edition of *The Fairchild Books Dictionary of Fashion.*

abilements/abillements See BILLIMENTS.

Entries are printed in boldface. Where more than one spelling is current, alternate spellings are placed behind a slash in the main entry. Cross-references are in small caps. This cross-reference is to an entry in the alphabetical listing.

baseball cap See under HEADWEAR.

When an entry in the alphabetical listing is to be found in a category under the same name as the entry, the category alone is cross-referenced and the term and definition can be found in that category. If the term is a synonym or is defined within another entry, it is listed as follows:

cadogan net See HEADWEAR: SNOOD.

Category headings are printed in larger type than individual entries. They are set off from the alphabetical text by borders. Cross-references to items in categories are printed in small caps, with the category given first, followed by a colon, and the individual entry listed after the colon. Synonyms are printed in italics. Any cross-reference that does not include a category designation will be found in the alphabetical listing.

ACADEMIC COSTUME

Outfits consisting of caps, called mortarboards (see ACADEMIC COSTUME: MORTARBOARD); gowns; . . . Also called *academic regalia.*

In some entries, closely related terms are defined within the definition of the primary entry. Such terms, like primary entries, are printed in boldface type. When an entry has more than one definition, each definition for the entry is preceded by a number in boldface. Illustrations of terms with numbered definitions indicate by number which definition is shown.

bikini **1.** Two-piece swimsuit introduced in 1946 by designer Jacques Heim, who called it the atom because of its small size. Soon after, a version was advertised as "smaller than the atom." Eventually the name was changed to bikini after Bikini Atoll, a small coral island in the Pacific where atomic tests were made from 1946 to 1956. Bikinis were worn on Riviera beaches, but not accepted on U.S. public beaches until the early 1960s. By the 1980s these suits became still smaller and a number of variations had developed. These were: **string bikini,** consisting of a minimal halter bra with bikini panties, worn low on hips, and made of two triangular-shaped pieces attached to an elastic band or string ties; **teardrop bikini,** made up of bikini pants worn with a bra composed of two tiny triangles with straps at neck and around the body; **tankini** (tan'-kee-nee), a woman's bathing suit with a tank top and a bikini bottom; **corset bikini,** a top that looks like an underwire bra and a bikini bottom; **camikini,** with a camisole top and a bikini bottom. **2.** Man's very brief swim trunks.

When derivations for entries are given, they are preceded by *Der.*

babushka (bah-boosh'-ka) Triangular-shaped scarf or square folded diagonally, worn draped over the head and tied under the chin in the manner of Russian peasant woman. *Der.* Russian, "grandmother." So-called because it was worn by older Russian immigrants to the United States. Also called a *kerchief.*

Pronunciation of the entry, rendered phonetically, follows the main entry. It is printed in parentheses following the boldface entry for the term. Pronunciations are not provided for all terms but are given when pronunciations may not be obvious to the user. These phonetic renderings are, at best, approximations of the actual pronunciation. Many are foreign language words that are nearly impossible to interpret phonetically. Therefore, all terms are rendered in the closest phonetic equivalent in the way that an English-speaker would pronounce the syllables. The accent mark shown in any pronunciation is given after the syllable that should be emphasized.

bandeau (ban-doe')

ACKNOWLEDGMENTS

Many individuals assisted in the preparation of this new edition. We would like to thank them for the expertise they brought to the project.

A number of individuals contributed recommendations for improvements to the third edition of the dictionary. We thank the following fashion scholars for their advice: Audria Gree, IADT Chicago; Jaquee Leahy, Art Institute of California, San Diego; Ellen McKinney, Art Institute of Dallas; Nancy Stanforth, Kent State University; and Svetlana Zakharina, LIM College.

Working with Bina Abling, the illustrator of both the third and fourth editions, was a pleasure. The results of her excellent and illuminating contributions are to be found in the pages of this book. Her ability to interpret our suggestions for revisions of illustrations from earlier editions was much appreciated.

Phyllis Tortora's late husband Vincent's linguistic skills are still reflected in this edition where the pronunciations included in the work are largely those he developed for the third edition.

We offer our special thanks to the staff of Fairchild Books. Olga Kontzias, formerly executive editor, worked through the steps necessary to get the new edition started and provided input to and evaluation of reorganization ideas. Publisher Priscilla McGeehon saw the revision through to completion after Olga's retirement.

Sylvia L. Weber, development editor, was a superb guide in questions of style, and was a most valuable source of advice and encouragement throughout the writing and editing. Without her constant guidance and advice we, the editors, would have had far more difficulty reaching the completion of this project. She made the project enjoyable. She was ably assisted by Sigali Hamberger, who checked the styling of every entry. We thank Carly Grafstein for the attractive designs of the cover and interior of the book.

Working with these professionals was always rewarding; we appreciate all of their help.

Numerous libraries also provided assistance. These were the New York Public Library and the Westchester, New York, Library System and its numerous branches, the library of the Fashion Institute of Technology, the New York Public Library Picture Collection, and the Mount Mary University Library. Internet sources of information and confirmation are too numerous to cite, but without use of the World Wide Web, this project would have required far more time and energy.

Finally, Phyllis Tortora wants to acknowledge the contributions made to this edition by the addition of coeditor Sandi Keiser. She has contributed much as a result of her extensive knowledge about the current fashion scene. It has been a pleasure to work with her. Likewise, Sandi Keiser was honored to be invited to be part of this team. Phyllis Tortora's extensive knowledge of fashion, particularly in the areas of textiles and historic dress, are truly amazing. Her experience and direction on this project made it a labor of love.

abalone See under CLOSURES: ABALONE BUTTON.

abilements/abillements See under HEADWEAR: BILLIMENT.

abstract See under PRINTS, STRIPES, AND CHECKS: ABSTRACT PRINT and HAIRSTYLES: ABSTRACT CUT.

ACADEMIC COSTUME

Outfits consisting of caps, called MORTARBOARDS (see under ACADEMIC COSTUME), gowns, and hoods traditionally worn at commencement exercises or other ceremonial occasions by students and faculty. Although simple gowns and mortarboards may be worn by secondary-school students, those in higher education wear more elaborate regalia consisting of caps, gowns, and hoods that are most often black with color trim on hoods. American academic costume was designed by Gardner Cottrell Leonard of Albany, New York, in 1887, and adopted by the American Intercollegiate Code of 1894, which was subsequently revised in 1932. The code states the style of cap, gown, and hood to be worn by persons with bachelor's, master's, and doctoral degrees along with the colors to be used on the hood. Academic costume originated at the Universities of Oxford and Cambridge more than 600 years ago. Also called *academic regalia* (ak-ah-dem′-ik ree-gale′-ee-yah).

academic hood Decorative drape that comes close to the neck in front and hangs down the back of academic gowns. Made in various lengths and shapes according to the degree held, hoods are usually black with a colored facing indicating the degree granted, while lining colors represent the school colors of the institution conferring the degree; the outer band of velvet indicates the field of study. *Der.* From the cowl cape attached to gowns of undergraduates since end of 15th c. Also see under ACADEMIC COSTUME: BACHELOR'S, MASTER'S, and DOCTOR'S HOODS, and ACADEMIC HOOD COLORS.

academic costume

academic hood colors The lining colors at the back of the academic hood represent the school colors of the college or institution conferring the degree. The outer band of velvet that extends around the front of the neck indicates the different faculties, or fields of study, as follows: Agriculture, maize; Arts and Letters, white; Chiropody, nile green; Commerce and Accounting, drab; Dentistry, lilac; Economics, copper; Engineering, orange; Fine Arts, brown; Forestry, russet; Humanities, crimson; Law, purple; Library Science, lemon; Medicine, green; Music, pink; Nursing, apricot; Optometry, seafoam; Oratory, silver gray; Pedagogy, light blue; Pharmacy, olive green; Philanthropy, rose; Philosophy, blue; Physical Education, sage green; Public Administration, drab; Public Health, salmon pink; Science, golden yellow; Social Science, citron; Theology, scarlet; and Veterinary Science, gray.

bachelor's gown Academic gown, formerly of black worsted or similar fabric, opening in front with two wide box pleats extending to the hem; large flowing sleeves ending in points; back and sleeves set into square yoke with cartridge pleats. Worn with the bachelor's hood and mortarboard at graduation by candidates, or former recipients, of a bachelor's degree. Since the 1970s colored gowns are sometimes worn instead of black. Also see under ACADEMIC COSTUME: BACHELOR'S HOOD, ACADEMIC HOOD COLORS, and MORTARBOARD.

bachelor's hood Black decorative drape, 3′ long in back with a 2″-colored velveteen band around the neck in front and a pendant tail in the back that is turned over to reveal colors of the institution granting the degree. Worn with the bachelor's gown and mortarboard at graduation by candidates or former recipients of bachelor's degree. Also see under ACADEMIC COSTUME: ACADEMIC HOOD COLORS.

doctor's gown Black unclosed academic gown with wide bands of velvet down the front. The full sleeves are set in with cartridge pleats and have three bands of velvet at the upper arm. Worn as part of academic costume by candidates for and holders of doctoral degrees.

doctor's hood Black academic hood with colored velvet band at neck to indicate type of degree. The velvet band extends down the back and is rolled over to show the school colors of the wearer. Square cut at hem and larger than bachelor's and master's hoods. See under ACADEMIC COSTUME: ACADEMIC HOOD COLORS.

master's gown Black open-front gown with a square yoke and long closed hanging sleeves. The arms emerge through slits above elbows of the sleeves, which have crescents cut out near the sleeve hems. In the back cartridge pleats join a full back and sleeves to the yoke. Worn with master's hood and mortarboard by candidates for, and holders of, master's degrees.

master's hood Black cowl drape 3½ feet long in back with band of colored velveteen around the edge that is turned over in back to show a lining identifying the institution granting the degree. Worn with master's gown. Also see under ACADEMIC COSTUME: ACADEMIC HOOD and ACADEMIC HOOD COLORS.

mortarboard Academic headgear consisting of large, square black brim attached horizontally to a cap. A large tassel in center of the flat top is positioned to the right side before graduation, and switched to the left after. Worn all over U.S. today and since 14th c. at universities including Oxford and Cambridge in England. Formerly referred to by various names including *cater cap, corner-cap, cornet, Oxford cap,* and *trencher cap.*

---

accordion bag See under HANDBAGS AND RELATED ACCESSORIES.

accordion pleats See under CLOTHING CONSTRUCTION DETAILS: ACCORDION PLEATS; PANTS: PARTY PANTS; and SKIRTS: ACCORDION-PLEATED SKIRT.

†acetate (as'-uh-tayt) Generic fiber category established by the FTC for manufactured fibers that are chemical variants of cellulose called *cellulose acetate* and are manufactured from cellulose materials, such as wood chips. Also refers to fabrics or yarns made from acetate fibers. Used in a wide variety of apparel, acetate fabrics have a crisp hand and a high luster.

achilles tendon protector See under FOOTWEAR: A.T.P.

acrobatic slipper See under FOOTWEAR.

†acrylic (uh-krihl'-ihk) Generic fiber category established by the FTC for a manufactured fiber primarily composed of a polymer material called *acrylonitrile.* Also refers to fabrics or yarns made from acrylic fibers. Acrylic fabrics have a soft, wool-like hand, good wrinkle resistance, and wash and dry quickly; therefore, they are often used in easy-care apparel products such as sweaters and socks.

action back The extra fullness incorporated into the back of a jacket, coat, or dress that extends from the shoulder blades to the waist in form of pleats or the insertion of a stretch fabric, to permit freedom of movement. See under COATS AND JACKETS: BI-SWING.

action glove See under GLOVES AND GLOVE CONSTRUCTION.

ACTIVEWEAR

Any of a wide variety of apparel items designed to be worn for active sports. Not to be confused with official athletic uniforms worn by professional athletes; although, such uniforms may serve as the inspiration for the design of some activewear. Many consumers wear activewear apparel not only for sports but also as casual dress.

aerobic wear (uh-roh'-bik) Headband, leotards, tights, and leg warmers worn for aerobic dancing. In this costume the headband is usually a brow band of terry cloth; leotards are a tight-fitting, torso-length garment with high or low neck and long or short sleeves; tights are made with or without feet and/or stirrups and are usually made of stretch nylon; leg warmers are knitted leg coverings without feet. Also called *workout suit* or *exercise suit.*

bathing dress See under introduction to SWIMWEAR.

bathing suit See under introduction to SWIMWEAR.

bike suit Tightly fitted, one- or two-piece garment, often worn for bicycling, that extends from the top of the torso to the pant hem, which is located above the knee. The garment fit is achieved by using SPANDEX. Synonym: *bike-tards.* Also see under ACTIVEWEAR: TRI-SUIT and SHORTS.

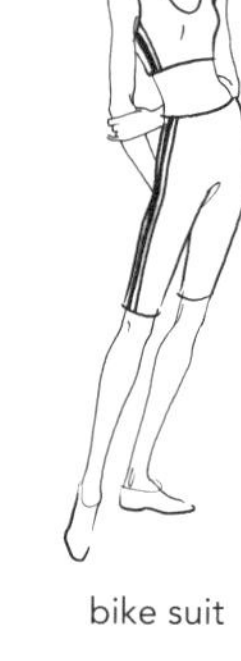

bike suit

bike-tards See under ACTIVEWEAR: BIKE SUIT.

camouflage suit Two-piece suit consisting of a hip-length jacket, tapered pants, and sometimes a matching cap with ear flaps. Made of soft waterproofed duck fabric printed in abstract pattern of greens and browns to blend with surrounding terrain. Used by combat soldiers in World War II. Accepted for sportswear, particularly for duck hunting, in mid-1960s. After the early 1980s accepted for general wear. Also see under PRINTS, STRIPES, AND CHECKS: CAMOUFLAGE.

camouflage suit

cat suit One-piece, skintight, long-sleeved suit with feet; variation of the UNITARD (see under ACTIVEWEAR).

cross-country skiing See under PANTS: KNICKERS #1.

∞cycling suit/cycling costume Any costume worn for bicycling in the late 19th c. Boys: jacket, similar to PATROL JACKET, worn with tight knee pants. Women: RATIONALS (see under ACTIVEWEAR) or a divided skirt with tailored or NORFOLK JACKET, leggings, and a straw sailor hat. Men: KNICKERBOCKERS and NORFOLK JACKET. See under COATS AND JACKETS: NORFOLK JACKET and PATROL JACKET.

exercise suit See under ACTIVEWEAR: AEROBIC WEAR and SAUNA SUIT.

fencing suit Two-piece white suit with close-fitting pants and waist-length jacket made with a standing collar, diagonal closing, and small red heart on left breast. Top is quilted or padded to prevent injury from the fencing foil.

gaiter See under FOOTWEAR.

gymnastic suit Suit worn for gymnastic competitions. Women wear LEOTARDS (see under ACTIVEWEAR). Men wear athletic shirts and long slim tapered pants with a stirrup strap under the instep.

gym suit Suits worn by students for physical education classes, the acceptable style being determined by individual schools. When gym was first introduced, women wore blue serge or sateen pleated BLOOMERS (see under PANTS), white MIDDY BLOUSES (see under BLOUSES AND TOPS), and long black stockings. During the 1930s, ROMPER suits were worn. Since mid-1970s any type of pull-on shorts and T-shirts are acceptable.

hunt breeches Riding breeches with drop front, and legs cut wide from thighs to hips and tight at knees. Usually made in canary or tan cavalry twill with buckskin patches at inside of knees.

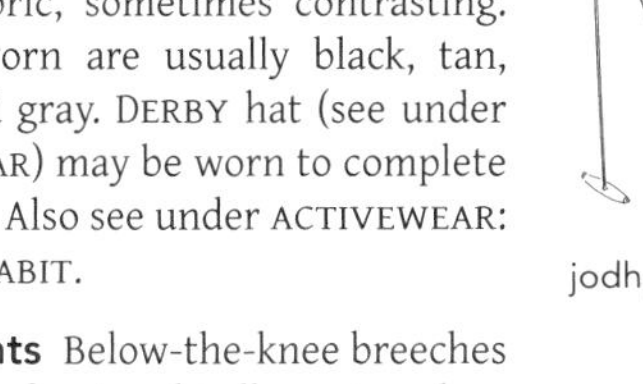

informal habit Suit worn by adults and children for horse shows consisting of a RIDING COAT (see under COATS AND JACKETS) and JODHPURS (see under ACTIVEWEAR), sometimes matched as to fabric, sometimes contrasting. Colors worn are usually black, tan, blue, and gray. DERBY hat (see under HEADWEAR) may be worn to complete costume. Also see under ACTIVEWEAR: RIDING HABIT.

jodhpurs 1930s

jockey pants Below-the-knee breeches with drop front and jodhpur-type legs worn tucked into boots by jockeys in horse races.

jodhpurs (jod′ poors) Riding pants, with drop front or zipper closing, that flare at thighs and have narrow straight-cut legs below knee with cuffs at ankles. Similar to men's breeches worn in India, and popular for men and women horseback riders since 1920s. *Der.* Jodhpur, a city in India. Also see under ACTIVEWEAR: RIDING BREECHES.

jogging suit Suit worn for running or jogging, popular since the 1960s. Examples of different types of jogging suits include the following: (a) sweatsuits; (b) a suit consisting of a zippered jacket, crew-necked sweater, and pants, and (c) warmup suits. Often made of fleece, terrycloth, or velour. See under ACTIVEWEAR: SWEATSUIT and WARMUP.

jogging suit

judo suit Suit, similar in style to karate suit, which is worn for judo, a form of Japanese martial arts. See under ACTIVEWEAR: KARATE SUIT.

jumpsuit #2

jumpsuit 1. First introduced as a combination shirt and ankle-length pants in a one-piece suit with zip-front and long or short sleeves by flyers in World War I and by parachute jumpers and flyers in World War II. 2. Variations adopted for sports and leisurewear by men and women with pants of varying lengths, popular as functional coverups, active sportswear (particularly skiing), and fashionable attire often related to a science fiction or futuristic trend.

karate suit

karate suit Two-piece suit made of white cotton or cotton and polyester, called a *gi* or *ghi* (ghee), that is worn for practicing the martial art of karate. The garment consists of a pair of drawstring pants and a wrap top that ties shut with a belt. As practiced in Asia, the uniform is closed with a white belt (signifying beginners) or a black belt (for advanced practitioners). A belt-ranking system was devised for teaching in Western countries. Different karate systems may have different color-coded ranking designations—beginning with white and progressing through yellow, green, brown, and black to denote each successive level in advancing increments.

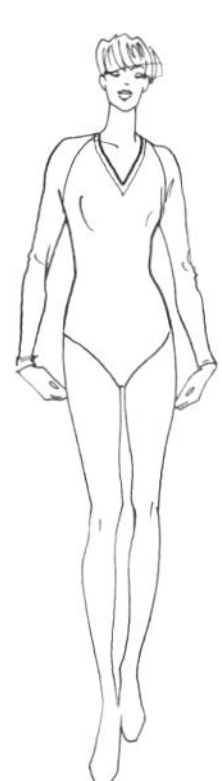

leotard

leotard (lee′-ah-tard′) Originally a two-piece, knit, body-hugging garment worn by the French acrobat Jules Leotard in the 19th c. Now a formfitting one-piece knitted garment with high or low neck, long or short sleeves, and ending in brief panties, which is worn alone or over ankle-length *tights* as practice garment. Adopted by dancers, acrobats, and for exercising. Claire McCardell first introduced it in fashionable dress in 1943; however, it did not catch on until the 1960s.

playsuit Shorts and shirt combined to make a suit with a waistline seam, worn with a coordinating skirt. Introduced in 1930s and fashionable at intervals since.

playsuit and skirt 1930s

∞**rationals** Popular name for full, pleated, serge bloomers or knickerbockers worn by women for bicycling in 1890s.

rationals

riding breeches Pants full-cut at hips and thigh and tightly fitted at knee, sometimes made of stretch fabric, some with zipper closure, and others with buttoned drop front. Worn by men and women with high boots for horseback riding. When made in a yellow fabric, they are called *canary breeches.* Also called HUNT BREECHES (see under ACTIVEWEAR) and *show breeches.* Also see under ACTIVEWEAR: JODHPURS and RIDING SMALLS.

riding habit Any combination of jacket and breeches or jodhpurs worn for horseback riding. The occasion determines the type of costume worn. Also see under ACTIVEWEAR: INFORMAL HABIT. Women's riding costume showed these changes over time. In the early 17th c. composed of long hose, or CALENÇONS, worn with doublet and petticoat, and later in the century, the man's JUSTAUCORPS (see under COATS AND JACKETS). In the 18th and 19th c., a number of named riding-dress styles were worn. See under AMAZONE, BRUNSWICK, EQUESTRIENNE COSTUME, and COATS AND JACKETS: JOSEPH #1. Riding trousers were introduced in the early 1880s for women and worn under the riding dress or skirt. RIDING BREECHES (see under ACTIVEWEAR) without the skirt were worn with a longer jacket about 1914. By the early 1920s, JODHPURS (see under ACTIVEWEAR) were popular.

riding habit

∞**riding skirt** Calf-length wraparound skirt worn by women who rode sidesaddle in late 19th and early 20th c.

∞**riding smalls** Men's RIDING BREECHES worn from 1814 to 1835 and made of light-colored doeskin, with wide hips but tight from knees down.

rodeo suit Suit worn at a Western-type rodeo. Combination of Western shirt, Western pants, neckerchief, cowboy hat, and boots. Some suits are very elaborately trimmed with embroidery, fringe, or beads.

sauna suit Exercise suit made of soft flexible vinyl in either a jumpsuit or two-piece style with zip-front and knitted cuffs at wrists and ankles. Worn around the house, it seals in body heat, acting like a steam bath and encouraging weight loss. An innovation of the late 1960s. Also called an *exercise suit.*

shorts suit 1. Shorts and tops made of matching or contrasting material for sportswear. 2. See under SHORTS.

ski pants Pants or leggings worn for skiing and other winter sports. The styles vary, generally following the trend in trouser leg styles and varying from wide to tight fitting, and often having straps under the feet. First introduced with jodhpur-type legs in the late 1920s; narrow styles in stretch fabrics appeared in 1950s. For downhill racing and jumping competitions. See under ACTIVEWEAR: UNITARD and SKI SUIT.

ski suit Any type jumpsuit or two-piece pants suit worn for winter sports. The first ski pants made their appearance for women in late 1920s and were styled similarly to JODHPURS (see under ACTIVEWEAR). In the 1930s ski suits were made of wool with medium-width trousers and knitted bands at the ankles. Jackets were close-fitting and usually zippered. In the 1968 Winter Olympics, fitted jumpsuits with a contrasting stripe extending down the side were introduced. In the 1984 Winter Olympics, UNITARDS (see under ACTIVEWEAR) were worn. Insulated jackets may be added for extra warmth. While competitive skiers seek to reduce wind resistance as much as possible with close-fitting garments, recreational skiers wear bulkier jumpsuits with high collars and belted waistlines or two-piece pants suits.

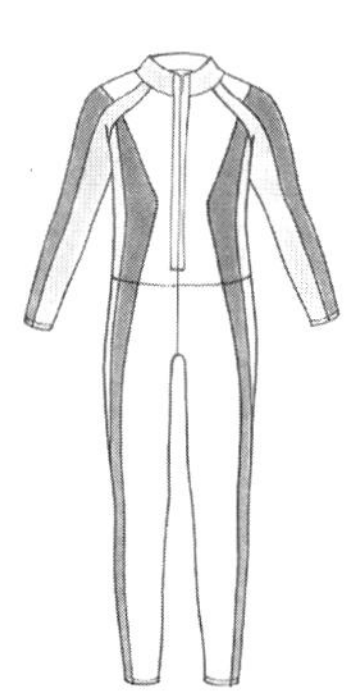
ski suit

snowboarding suit Two-piece pants suit or JUMPSUIT (see under ACTIVEWEAR) worn for the sport of snowboarding. Similar to SKI SUIT (see under ACTIVEWEAR), but more loosely fitted.

snowmobile suit Jumpsuit with attached hood made of wind-resistant nylon and polyester fiberfill insulation. Made with two-way zippers to hips or one-way zipper to knees. Has snap-closed pockets on chest, self-fabric belt, and knitted cuffs at wrists. Some suits have reflective stripes around the sleeves to make the wearer visible to other vehicles. Worn with snowmobile boots and gloves.

snowsuit Two-piece suit, or one-piece jumpsuit, worn by infants up to two years of age. Jumpsuit has a zipper that extends partway up the leg, making access easier. Suits have attached hoods and ribbing at ankles and wrists; some are insulated and waterproofed.

snowsuit 1933

stormsuit Two-piece sport suit made of rubberized nylon consisting of pants and jacket with hood worn for hunting and fishing in inclement weather.

stormsuit

sunsuit Child's or infant's summer playsuit made with romper pants and a bib top.

surfing suit See under ACTIVEWEAR: WETSUIT.

sweatclothes Apparel worn primarily for exercising and jogging. Also worn as leisure wear.

sweatsuit Two-piece suit with fleece lining. Consists of a sweatshirt that pulls over the head or a sweatjacket that zips, plus sweatpants with legs gathered into ribbing or elastic at the ankles. Used by runners and boxers, as well as other athletes, to prevent sore muscles.

swimsuit See under introduction to SWIMWEAR.

tankini See under SWIMWEAR: BIKINI.

teardrop bikini See under SWIMWEAR: BIKINI.

tennis clothes/tennis dress First played in France in the Middle Ages, tennis was introduced in the U.S. as lawn tennis in 1874. The basic rules, height of net, and dimensions of court have remained consistent since that time. For lawn tennis, women wore fitted jackets and full skirts coming to their boot tops. When bustles were in fashion (1870s and 1880s) and when leg-of-mutton sleeves were stylish (1890s), tennis dress reflected the current styles. Men wore long, white flannel trousers and white shirts. For many years it was traditional for players to wear only white. Tailored shorts were worn in 1930s. Player Gussie Moran introduced short dresses with ruffled panties for tennis in 1940s. By the 1960s mini- or micro-skirted dresses, initially white but also made in colors by the 1970s, were worn when playing tennis. Contemporary tennis fashions consist of tennis dresses or shorts and tops for women and shorts and tops for men. These change from season to season with various colors and cuts becoming popular, often based on what professional players have been wearing in tournaments.

tri-suit Tight-fitting suit made with stretch yarns in color-blocked style similar to a TANK SUIT (see under SWIMWEAR) but with mid-thigh length legs. Worn particularly by athletes participating in triathlon competitions, which include swimming, bike riding, and running. *Der.* Shortened form of "triathlon suit."

trunks 1. Loose-legged style men's shorts made with drawstring at waist. Worn from late 19th c. on for boxing and other sports, sometimes over full-length tights. 2. See under SWIMWEAR.

tutu See alphabetical listing.

unitard One-piece BODYSUIT made of knitted fabric. Combines leotards and tights into one suit. Worn for exercising and aerobics, sometimes with small bikini pants on top. See under ACTIVEWEAR: LEOTARD and HOSIERY: TIGHTS. *Der.* From *uni*, meaning "one," and *leotard.*

unitard

warmup 1. *adj.* Describes apparel, most often jackets, pants, or jumpsuits, modeled after those worn by athletes when warming up for sports events. Generally made of knitted fabrics, jackets have raglan sleeves and zipper-front closings; pants have drawstring or elastic waists and elastic or knitted cuffs at ankles. In the 1980s, the types of fabric used expanded to include terrycloth and velour, and the styles were adopted for outdoor sports, beachwear, indoor exercises, and casual wear. 2. Interlined overpants worn for skiing with zippers down the sides for easy removal.

wetsuit Garment made of neóprene, a synthetic rubber, that is used for protection against cold water in sports such as scuba diving, windsurfing, and white-water rafting. It is generally available in one- or two-piece style. One-piece styles may be full wetsuits with arms and legs and sometimes with a hood and boots, or suits may be full length without sleeves. The latter style is called a **farmer John**. A jacket can be worn over farmer Johns or with a high-waisted trouser. One-piece suits with short legs and short sleeves are also available. Some suits close with a **beaver-tail** construction, which is a large flap of material that comes from the back, through the crotch to fasten at the front. Most close with long zippers. Wetsuits are rated according to thickness in millimeters, or "mils," with thicker suits being appropriate for colder water.

workout suit See under ACTIVEWEAR: AEROBIC WEAR.

---

acton See under ARMOR.

adaptation 1. The interpretation of an expensive designer dress reproduced in a less expensive model. Not a direct copy but made with modification of design and fabric. Compare with KNOCKOFF and LINE-FOR-LINE COPY. 2. Costume for a play or film made in a historic period style (e.g., 18th c.), but which differs from the original styles in elements such as design and fabric.

adelaide boot See under FOOTWEAR.

adjustable *adj.* Indicates that some aspect of apparel can be modified to change aspects such as fit, appearance, and size. See under JEWELRY: ADJUSTABLE RING and VESTS: ADJUSTABLE VEST.

adjustments Reductions in the retailer's cost for goods which may be the result of merchandise being returned to the manufacturer or the result of problems with the merchandise.

admiral coat See under COATS AND JACKETS.

adrienne gown See under SACK #1.

∞**aegis** (ee'-jis) In ancient Greek mythology, a garment serving as a piece of armor that was made out of the skin of a goat and worn with the head to the front of the body. In depictions of Zeus, king of the gods, and Athena, goddess of wisdom, the aegis became a shield. In some depictions of Athena, it was a breastplate covered with goat skin that had the image of the head of Medusa in the center bordered with snakes.

aerobic (uh-roh'-bik) *adj.* Describes exercises intense enough to contribute to the strengthening of the vascular system. This adjective is sometimes used with the names of items of apparel intended to be worn for aerobic exercise. See under ACTIVEWEAR: AEROBIC WEAR and FOOTWEAR: AEROBIC SHOE.

aesthetic dress (s-thet'-ik) Styles of dress for men and women adopted by a small group in England who sought reform in the arts in late 19th c. Loosely based on historic costume of the Middle Ages, features of women's dress included elimination of corseting, large sleeves, and softer, more fluid lines than the era's fashionable bustle dresses. The writer Oscar Wilde, a proponent of this movement, wore a velvet suit with knee breeches, a loosely fitted jacket, a soft, wide collar, and flowing tie. His costume was said to serve as the inspiration for the LITTLE LORD FAUNTLEROY SUIT. The Gilbert and Sullivan operetta *Patience* satirized these aesthetic styles, calling them *"greenery yallery, Grosvenor gallery"* (gro'-ven-er) costumes.

aesthetic dress
1880s

Afghanistan-inspired apparel See under COATS AND JACKETS: AFGHANISTAN JACKET; SHIRTS: AFGHANISTAN WEDDING TUNIC; and VESTS: AFGHANISTAN VEST.

afghan stitch See under EMBROIDERIES AND SEWING STITCHES.

african dress See under DRESSES.

Afro hairstyles, clothes, and accessories derived from African or African American cultures. Usually adopted first by African Americans, many Afro styles eventually made their way into mainstream fashion. Beginning in late 1960s, influential examples include garments such as the BUBA (see under DRESSES), DASHIKI, and SELOSO. Also see under HAIRSTYLES: AFRO and AFRO PUFFS; PRINTS, STRIPES, AND CHECKS: AFRICAN PRINT; WIGS AND HAIRPIECES: AFRO WIG; and JEWELRY: AFRO CHOKER.

Afrocentric See under DRESSES: AFRICAN DRESS.

afternoon dress See under DRESSES.

agal See under KAFFIYEH-AGAL.

agate See under GEMS, GEM CUTS, AND SETTINGS.

age See under EDGE #2.

agile manufacturing Technological innovations in apparel manufacturing that allow product developers to be more flexible and faster in responding to consumer demands. With agile manufacturing, special orders can be accommodated more readily. Synonym: *flexible manufacturing.*

aggravators See under HAIRSTYLES.

aglet (egg'-let) **/aiglet/aiguillette** Ornamental metal tag, frequently of gold or silver, similar to modern shoelace tip at end of lacing. Called *points* in the 15th c. and used for joining men's doublet and hose; later used in bunches for a decorative effect.

Agnès Sorel (1422–1450) The mistress of King Charles VII of France who was renowned for her lavish wardrobe. Her name was used as an adjective when describing certain 19th-c. fashion terms. See under AGNÈS SOREL BODICE; HAIRSTYLES: AGNÈS SOREL COIFFURE; AGNÈS SOREL CORSAGE; and DRESSES: AGNÈS SOREL DRESS.

∞**agnès sorel bodice** Woman's dress bodice of 1861 with square neckline front and back, and full bishop sleeves.

∞**agnès sorel corsage** Woman's loose-fitting bodice or a PELISSE-ROBE (see under DRESSES) similar to a jacket, fastened high at neck or worn open, revealing waistcoat. Worn in 1851 and named after Agnès Sorel.

agnès sorel dress See under DRESSES.

∞**agraffe** (ah'-graf) **/agraf/agrafe** **1.** Circular, square, or diamond-shaped clasp, used in pairs to fasten the mantle at the neck in the Middle Ages; made of bronze, gold, or silver embossed in elaborate patterns, set with jewels. **2.** Pin used to fasten slashes in garments in 16th c. Compare with FERMAIL. *Der.* Norman, *aggrape,* "clasp on medieval armor."

aide memoire fan See under FANS.

aiglet See under AGLET.

aigrette See under FEATHERS.

aiguillette (ah-gwel-let) **/aiguille** **1.** Shoulder decoration made of gilt cord, frequently braided, used on military dress uniforms. The cord (aiguillette) has AGLETS at the end. **2.** See under AGLET.

aigulet See under AGLET.

aile de pigeon See under WIGS AND HAIRPIECES: PIGEON-WING.

ajour See under LACES: JOURS.

aketon See under ARMOR: ACTON.

alarm watch See under WATCHES.

Alaska See under FOOTWEAR.

Alaskan seal See under FURS: FUR SEAL.

alb See under CLERICAL DRESS.

albernous/albernoz See under CAPES, CLOAKS, AND SHAWLS: BURNOOSE.

Albert (1819–1861) First name of the husband of Queen Victoria, which was used as an adjective in certain 19th-c. men's fashion terms. He was Prince of Saxe-Coburg-Gotha and, after his marriage, Prince Consort of Great Britain. See under FOOTWEAR: ALBERT BOOT, ALBERT SLIPPER; COATS AND JACKETS: ALBERT DRIVING CAPE, ALBERT JACKET, ALBERT OVERCOAT, ALBERT RIDING COAT, and ALBERT TOP FROCK.

alençon lace See under LACES.

alexandrite See under GEMS, GEM CUTS, AND SETTINGS.

alice in wonderland dress See under DRESSES: PINAFORE DRESS.

A-line Apparel styled close and narrow at the shoulders or waist and flaring gently away from the body to the hem in a line resembling the letter *A*. Introduced in 1955 by Paris couturier Christian Dior, used as an adjective in describing a wide variety of apparel with this shape, including coats, dresses, jumpers, and skirts. See under COATS AND JACKETS: A-LINE COAT; DRESSES: A-LINE DRESS; JUMPERS: A-LINE JUMPER; and SKIRTS: A-LINE SKIRT.

A-line dress See under DRESSES.

A-line shirt See under SHIRTS.

alligator See under LEATHERS.

alligator-grained See under LEATHERS.

alligator lizard See under LEATHERS.

all-in-one 1. Child's full-length knitted garment with legs that may or may not have feet. 2. See under UNDERGARMENTS: FOUNDATION. 3. See under SHOULDERS AND SLEEVES. 4. See under HOSIERY: PANTYHOSE.

all-in-one

allover See under LACES and PRINTS, STRIPES, AND CHECKS.

all-purpose poncho See under CAPES, CLOAKS, AND SHAWLS: PONCHO #3.

all-rounder See under NECKLINES AND COLLARS: DOG COLLAR.

all-sheer pantyhose See under HOSIERY.

all-weather *adj.* Describes clothing and accessories suitable for dry or wet weather and for varying temperatures. See under COATS AND JACKETS: ALL-WEATHER COAT and ALL-WEATHER RAINCOAT; and FOOTWEAR: ALL-WEATHER BOOT.

almain coat/jacket See under COATS AND JACKETS.

almain hose See under TRUNK HOSE.

almandine garnet See under GEMS, GEM CUTS, AND SETTINGS: GARNET.

almoner See under HANDBAGS AND RELATED ACCESSORIES: AULMONIÈRE.

almuce (*amuce, almusse, aunice, aumusse*) 1. See under HEADWEAR. 2. See under CAPES, CLOAKS, AND SHAWLS.

aloe (ahl'-loh) 1. A fiber obtained from the leaves of several tropical plants. 2. See under EMBROIDERIES AND SEWING STITCHES: ALOE THREAD EMBROIDERY. 3. See under LACES.

aloha shirt See under SHIRTS: HAWAIIAN SHIRT.

†alpaca A sheeplike animal of the camel family, related to the llama, native to the Andes in South America. Yarn spun from alpaca fleece is lustrous and shiny.

alpargata See under FOOTWEAR.

alpine *adj.* Describes apparel inspired by or derived from the clothing of the European mountains called the Alps. See under FOOTWEAR: ALPINE BOOT; HEADWEAR: ALPINE HAT; and COATS AND JACKETS: ALPINE JACKET.

alum tanning See under LEATHERS.

amadis sleeve See under SHOULDERS AND SLEEVES.

amazon *adj.* Attached to the names of certain items of women's fashionable apparel as a descriptor. The Amazons were a legendary race of warlike women. The use of the term in the 19th c. was part of a tendency of the period to name fashions for historical or legendary figures. See under NECKLINES AND COLLARS: AMAZON COLLAR; AMAZON CORSAGE; UNDERGARMENTS: AMAZON CORSET; and FEATHERS: AMAZON PLUME.

∞amazon corsage Plain bodice buttoned up front to high neckline and trimmed with small white cambric collar and cuffs; tailored style for women in 1842.

∞amazone Woman's scarlet riding habit with high waistline and full-length skirt worn in early part of 19th c. in U.S., France, and England. *Der.* From legendary Greek women warriors called *Amazons.*

amber See under GEMS, GEM CUTS, AND SETTINGS.

American buskins See under FOOTWEAR.

american coat See under COATS AND JACKETS.

American Fashion Critics' Award Original name for the COTY AWARD.

American Indian One of the names used to refer to the indigenous people of the Americas. Used as an adjective to describe fashion items inspired by or derived from Native American dress. See under BELTS: AMERICAN INDIAN BELT; HAIRSTYLES: AMERICAN INDIAN

HAIRSTYLE; HANDBAGS AND RELATED ACCESSORIES: SQUAW BAG; HEADWEAR: AMERICAN INDIAN HEADBAND; JEWELRY: AMERICAN INDIAN BEADS and AMERICAN INDIAN NECKLACE; and PRINTS, STRIPES, AND CHECKS: AMERICAN INDIAN PRINT.

American Indian beadwork Tiny glass beads in various colors woven to make headbands, necklaces, and used for trimmings—sometimes in shape of medallions—by various North American Indian tribes.

American Indian dress See under DRESSES.

American marten See under FURS.

amethyst See under GEMS, GEM CUTS, AND SETTINGS.

amice See under CLERICAL DRESS.

amorphous See under GEMS, GEM CUTS, AND SETTINGS.

amuce See under ALMUCE.

amulet Small object believed to possess magical powers—a good-luck charm worn as protection against evil by primitive people and surviving to present time in various forms of jewelry. Also see under JEWELRY.

anadem See under HAIR ACCESSORIES.

analog watch See under WATCHES.

anchor store A large, popular retail store usually located at the end of the mall (hence the name "anchor").

andalouse cape See under CAPES, CLOAKS, AND SHAWLS.

∞**andalusian casaque** (an-dah-loo′-zee-an cask) Women's evening tunic fastened down the center with series of ribbons with front of skirt cut away, sloping to knee-length in the back. Worn over another skirt in 1809.

andean shift See under DRESSES.

andradite garnet See under GEMS, GEM CUTS, AND SETTINGS.

androgynous (an-droj′-eh-nus) *adj.* Possessing both male and female characteristics. Styles of various periods may include androgynous elements. Examples for women have included: short boyish bob hairstyles, man-tailored suits of menswear fabrics, tailored trousers, trench coats, slouch hats, neckties, and button-down collars. For men, the adoption of more traditionally feminine styles has included: long hair, makeup, jewelry, and clothes with more color.

androgynous style 1990s

∞**angel overskirt** Woman's short overskirt having two long points on either side used as part of daytime dress in 1894.

angel sleeve See under SHOULDERS AND SLEEVES.

angle bob See under HAIRSTYLES.

angled pocket See under POCKETS: HACKING POCKET.

angled shawl collar See under NECKLINES AND COLLARS.

angle-fronted coat See under COATS AND JACKETS.

anglesea hat See under HEADWEAR.

angleterre, point d' lace See under LACES: POINT D'ANGLETERRE.

∞**anglo-greek bodice** Woman's bodice with wide lapels placed far apart and edged with lace. Worn in 1820s with FICHU-ROBINGS.

anglo-saxon embroidery See under EMBROIDERIES AND SEWING STITCHES.

†**angora** Soft fuzzy yarn made from the under-hair of the angora rabbit; used for knitwear and for trimmings.

angoulême bonnet See under HEADWEAR.

animal print See under PRINTS, STRIPES, AND CHECKS.

anime A style reflecting Japanese cartoons featuring characters that are androgynous in appearance with large eyes, brightly colored streaked hair, and punk-style clothing.

ankh Egyptian symbol for eternal life, somewhat like a cross with vertical bar forming a loop at top. Popular as jewelry motif, especially as necklaces and rings, in late 1960s and 1970s. Also called *ansate cross.* See under JEWELRY: ANKH RING.

ankle boot See under FOOTWEAR.

ankle bracelet See under JEWELRY.

ankle-jack See under FOOTWEAR.

ankle length See under LENGTHS.

ankle-length hosiery See under HOSIERY.

ankle sock See under HOSIERY.

ankle-strap See under FOOTWEAR.

anklet 1. See under JEWELRY: ANKLE BRACELET. 2. See under HOSIERY: ANKLE SOCK.

ankle watch See under WATCHES.

Annette Kellerman See under SWIMWEAR.

Annie Hall The film that popularized a specific style of women's dressing, inspired by clothing worn by actress Diane Keaton, who played the role of Annie Hall in the eponymous film, written and directed by Woody Allen. Typical styles included such elements as baggy pants, men's shirts and

Annie Hall style 1978

vests, and the idea of wearing clothes in an uncoordinated manner.

annular brooch A medieval period metal brooch used to fasten cloaks or capes that consisted of a closed ring and a nail-shaped sharp pin that fastened the fabric in place. Also see PENANNULAR BROOCH.

anorak See under COATS AND JACKETS.

ansate cross See under ANKH.

anslet See under DOUBLET.

antelope See under FURS and LEATHERS.

antelope-finished lambskin See under LEATHERS.

anti-embolism stocking See under HOSIERY.

antigropolis See under FOOTWEAR.

∞**antique bodice** Long-waisted, tight bodice with low décolletage and deep point at front waistline; worn for evening by women in 1830s and 1840s.

antique couching See under EMBROIDERIES AND SEWING STITCHES: ORIENTAL COUCHING.

antique finish See under LEATHERS.

antique lace See under LACES.

antique satin See under SATIN.

†**antique taffeta** Crisp taffeta that may have irregular slubs throughout in imitation of 18th-c. fabrics. Also made in iridescent effects with lengthwise and crosswise yarns of different colors.

antireflective coating See under EYEWEAR.

antoinette fichu See under SCARVES: FICHU #1.

antwerp lace See under LACES.

ao dai Pantsuit consisting of a long-sleeved mid-calf tunic, slashed on side seams (or one side), and full-length pants; worn by men and women in Vietnam.

apache (ah-patch'-ee) **1.** Styles similar to clothes worn by American Southwest tribes of North American Indians from Arizona and New Mexico. **2.** In France, *apache* (ah'-pash) is slang for gangster or thug, especially as depicted by French nightclub dancers. *Der.* The French word was taken from the North American Indian tribe of the same name, which was thought to be very fierce. Also see under HANDBAGS AND RELATED ACCESSORIES: SQUAW BAG; SCARVES; and SHIRTS.

ape drape See under HAIRSTYLES: SHAG.

apex See under HEADWEAR.

apollo corset See under UNDERGARMENTS.

apollo knot See under HAIRSTYLES.

apparel **1.** Any type of clothing worn by men, women, and children. Synonyms include: *attire, clothes, costume, dress, garb, garment, habit, uniform, robe, raiment,* and *vestments,* the last of which is used particularly for clerical dress. **2.** Used since early 14th c. to denote clothing, particularly a suit of clothes. ∞**3.** Late 14th c.: embroidered borders of ecclesiastical garments. ∞**4.** Late 14th c.: embellishment of armor.

apparel industry The suppliers, apparel product developers, manufacturers, and vendors engaged in the production of ready-to-wear clothing for men, women, and children. Also called *cutting-up trade, garment trade, needle trade,* and *rag business.*

apparel price ranges Prices in the apparel industry may be designated as falling into one of the following categories that form a continuum of prices from low to high: **discount, mass market, moderate, better, contemporary, bridge**, and **designer**.

apparel product development All of the processes that are needed to take a garment from inception to delivery to the customer.

apparel supply chain The network of fiber, textile, and findings (trim, thread, labels) suppliers, apparel product developers, manufacturers, vendors, and all the channels of distribution that work together to bring apparel products to the ultimate user.

appenzell See under EMBROIDERIES AND SEWING STITCHES.

applejack cap See under HEADWEAR: NEWSBOY CAP.

applied casing See under CLOTHING CONSTRUCTION DETAILS: CASING.

appliqué (ap-plee-kay') **1.** Surface pattern made by cutting out fabric or lace designs and attaching them to another fabric or lace by means of embroidery or stitching. **2.** See under LACES. **3.** Applied leather designs on shoes and handbags.

appurn See under APRONS: NAPRON.

après ski (ah-pray') *adj.* (French) "After-skiing." In fashion, describes clothing and accessories typically worn when relaxing after skiing. This look first became popular in the 1950s at famous resorts such as Sun Valley, Lake Placid, and San Moritz. As more people began to ski, the look increased in popularity. Elements included colorful, glamorous sportswear items such as vests of fur or embroidery, pants of velvet, printed fabrics, and suede, as well as sweaters in jacquard knits and unusual boots. See under FOOTWEAR: APRÈS-SKI BOOT.

apron checks See under PRINTS, STRIPES, AND CHECKS.

apron dress See under DRESSES.

APRONS

apron **1.** Item of apparel designed to protect clothing or used as a decorative accessory. Historically, aprons were worn from the 13th c. on by men and women. They originated in Middle Ages from an extra piece of cloth tied over skirt by women before sitting down at the table. See under APRONS: BARMECLOTH. This style was later adopted by servants and worn with a bib top. In the 16th to 18th c., color of the apron denoted the trade of workman or artisan. See under CHECKERED APRON MAN, BLUE-APRONED MAN, and GREEN-APRONED MAN. Decorative aprons of lace and embroidery were worn over dresses in the first half of the 17th c., throughout the 18th c., and during the 1870s. *Der.* Old French, *napperon,* and its diminutive *nappe,* meaning "cloth." During the Middle Ages, a *napperon,* or napkin, became apron. (Older spelling *appurn.*) **2.** Dress with a free-hanging panel attached to the front of a skirt, which resembles an apron. **3.** See under TIES.

barber's apron Long circular cape, fastening at the neckline in back, originally made of cotton fabric and now sometimes of plastic, worn to protect clothes while hair is being cut.

∞**barmecloth** Early medieval term for an apron. Gradually replaced by the word apron after the end of the 14th c. Also called *barmhatre.*

∞**barmfell** A leather apron, as it was called from 14th to 17th c. Also called *barmskin.*

∞**belly-chete** 16th-c. slang used for apron.

bib apron First worn in the 17th c., an apron that extends high on chest, held by straps over the shoulders crossing in center back and attached at the waistline.

bib apron

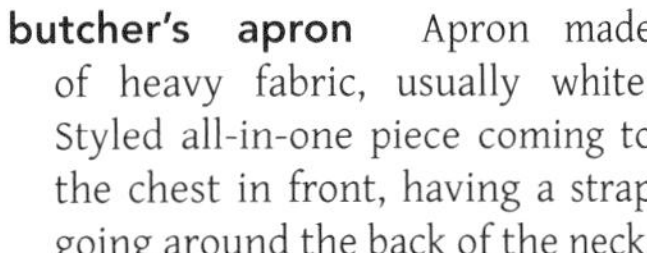

butcher's apron Apron made of heavy fabric, usually white. Styled all-in-one piece coming to the chest in front, having a strap going around the back of the neck, curved under the arms, and tied at center back. *Der.* From apron worn by butchers when cutting meat. Also see under APRONS: CHEF'S APRON.

carpenter's apron Characterized by having a large pocket made of fabric or leather divided into sections and mounted on a belt. Worn to carry nails, small tools, etc.

cartoon apron Usually a butcher's style apron printed with humorous pictures or slogans.

chef's apron Apron of canvas, terrycloth, or other type of fabric, styled like a butcher's apron and worn by cooks for outdoor barbeques as well as in the kitchen. May have a KANGAROO POCKET (see under POCKETS) across the center front and be screen printed with a name or message.

cobbler's apron Hip-length, large-pocketed apron originally worn by shoemakers, carpenters, and other workmen to hold nails. Popular as women's fashion in late 1960s, and usually made of fabric. Also see under APRONS: CARPENTER'S APRON.

cobbler's apron

cocktail apron Tiny half-apron made of net, lace, or fabric.

∞**fig leaf** Small black silk apron worn by women in 1860s and 1870s.

half-apron Bibless apron coming only to waist.

hoover apron Utility wraparound dress with two half-fronts and attached sash that goes through slot at each side seam to tie in back. *Der.* Originated during World War I, when Herbert Hoover was a food administrator in the U.S.

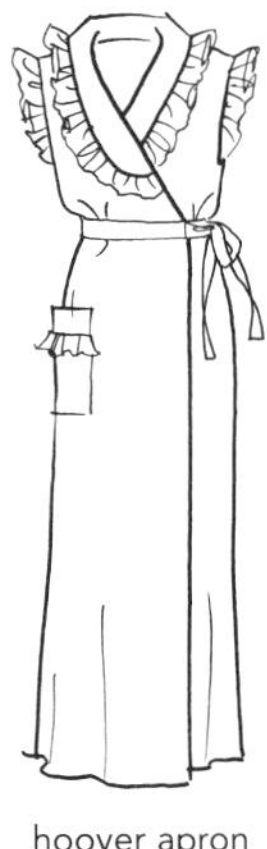
hoover apron 1935

∞**laisse-tout-faire** (le'-zay-too-fare) Long apron worn over the dress for home wear in 17th c.

∞**lawn-tennis apron** Drab-colored bib apron worn for tennis by women in 1880s. The skirt was pulled up on left side and draped at the back where there was a large patch pocket for holding tennis balls. Another pocket was placed low on the right side of the skirt. Both pockets were decorated with embroidery.

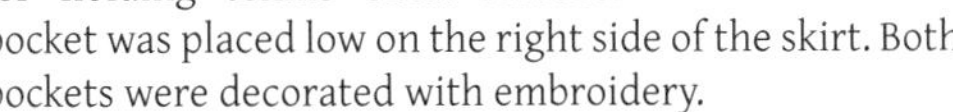

∞**napron** Used in 14th c. and first half of 15th c. for *apron. Der.* Old French, *naperon,* diminutive of *nape* or *nappe,* "tablecloth" or "apron." From about 1460, new spellings *apron* and *appurn* were used.

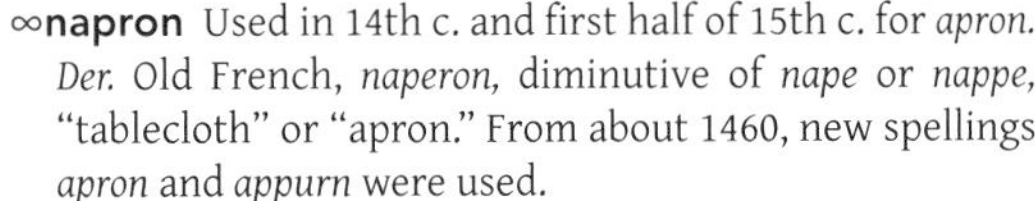

pinafore apron Apron worn by young girls made with a gathered skirt, bib top, and suspender straps. Sometimes made with ruffles over the shoulders extending to waistline.

∞**priscilla apron** Young girl's apron of 1890s, styled with full skirt shirred into waistband. Bib top extended around neck in a broad, lace-trimmed, sailor-collar effect. Had straps from shoulder blades to waistband in back. Frequently made of lightweight cotton fabrics.

∞**safeguard** Man's colored apron worn by bakers and tradesmen from 16th to 18th c.

∞**tea apron** White lawn apron with small pocket, which ties around waist and is trimmed with ruffles, VALENCIENNES LACES (see under LACES), and HEM-STITCHING (see under EMBROIDERIES AND SEWING STITCHES). Used when sewing, or to protect the dress, in early 20th c.

trucker's apron Shaped similar to a butcher's apron with large pockets in front. Has a slit in center front and ties around each leg.

∞**tyes** American term for girl's apron in late 19th c.

work apron Any apron designed to cover the clothes amply while the wearer is working at a job that might soil or harm garments.

---

apron swimsuit See under SWIMWEAR: PINAFORE SWIMSUIT.

apron tongue See under FOOTWEAR: TONGUE.

apron wrap jumper See under JUMPERS: WRAP JUMPER.

aquamarine See under GEMS, GEM CUTS, AND SETTINGS.

Arabian Nights See under HAREM.

araneum lace See under LACES: ANTIQUE LACE.

Aran Isle sweater See under SWEATERS.

arba kanfoth (ar′-ba kan-foth) Undergarment worn by Orthodox Jewish men, consisting of a rectangle of cloth with hole or slit in center for head and tassels or fringe at the corners.

arch cushion See under FOOTWEAR.

arctics See under FOOTWEAR.

argentan lace See under LACES.

argentina borregos lamb See under FURS: LAMB.

argyle See under PLAIDS AND TARTANS and SWEATERS. Also see HOSIERY: ARGYLE SOCKS.

arizona ruby See under GEMS, GEM CUTS, AND SETTINGS: RUBY.

armband bracelet See under JEWELRY.

armenian lace See under LACES.

armenian mantle See under COATS AND JACKETS.

armhole Section of garment through which arm passes or into which sleeve is fitted. Usually round but may be squared underneath the arm. Older synonyms include *armscye* (arm′-sye), *armseye, arm's eye.*

∞ARMOR

Protective garments worn by soldiers and knights from early times, especially those made of CHAIN MAIL and cast metal from Middle Ages through 17th c. See under ARMOR: MAIL.

acton (ak′-tun) (*ackton, acketon, aketon, auqueton, hacketon, haqueton*) **1.** A padded, sleeveless jacket worn under CHAIN MAIL in the 12th and 13th c. Used interchangeably with GAMBESON by experts on medieval costume and armor. **2.** Later applied to a steel-plated jacket worn as armor.

basinet (*bascinet, bacinet, basnet*) Pointed steel helmet worn as armor from 1350 to 1450.

bouchette (boo-shet) Large buckle used in medieval times to fasten breastplate of armor.

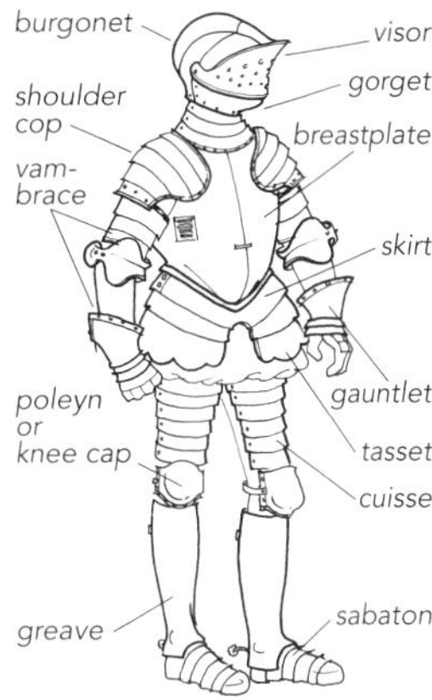

armor with parts labeled

brassart (brass′-are) Piece of armor worn on upper arm for protection from mid-14th to 15th c.

brayette (*braguette*) Metal CODPIECE worn as armor in 16th c.

burgonet (bur′-gon-ay) Metal helmet worn as armor in the 16th c. Has a brim that projects over the eyes, called an *umbril,* and a metal projection to protect the back of the neck. It may have hinged earflaps and one or more standing pieces or *combs* on the crown. Some are decorated with elaborate hammered designs. *Der.* French, of Burgundian origin and adopted by England, Germany, Italy, and France. Compare with ARMOR.

camail (ka-mal′) Shoulder cape of CHAIN MAIL laced to helmet worn as part of armor during first half of 14th c.

cannon Piece of protective plate armor for the upper arm or forearm, cylindrical or semi-cylindrical.

capeline (cap-leen) Iron or steel skullcap worn by foot soldiers in Middle Ages.

cervellière (ser′-vel-yair) Close-fitting steel cap usually worn under helmet during Middle Ages. *Der.* French, *cervelle,* "brains."

chain mail See under ARMOR: MAIL.

chapel de fer (sha-pel de fehr) Armor for head, a skullcap of iron or steel, sometimes with brim; worn by medieval knights. *Der.* French, "cap of iron."

chausse (shos′ez) Stockings of CHAIN MAIL (see under ARMOR: MAIL), worn by knights and soldiers in last quarter of the 13th c.

coat of mail See under ARMOR: HAUBERK.

coiffe de mailles (qwaff de mile) Hood of mail worn by Norman war lords from late 11th to mid-12th c. Later worn under helmet and, in 15th c., by ordinary soldiers. Also called *coif of mail.*

coiffette (kwah-fet′) Iron or steel skullcap worn by soldiers during 14th c.

cointise (kwan-teez′) Lappet or scarf under the crest of helmet worn in late 12th c. Also spelled *quaintise, quintise.*

collaret Armor worn in the Middle Ages to protect the neck.

corselet Originally leather armor; later in 16th c. metal-plate armor worn by pikemen, made of cast metal—lighter than the cuirass. See under ARMOR: CUIRASS.

coutes (koot) Armor for the elbows worn over CHAIN MAIL in early 13th c. Also plate armor for elbows in latter 14th c. *Der.* French, *coude,* "elbow."

cuirass (kew-rass′) 1. Sleeveless leather thigh-length tunic worn as armor by ancient Greeks and Romans. 2. Armor consisting of breastplate and backplates of steel worn either under or over other garments from mid-14th to mid-17th c. At first worn over a mail shirt and *jupel* (see under DOUBLET #1) and under a TABARD, later worn outside with metal TASSETS (see under ARMOR) forming a skirt. Similar to CORSELET (see under ARMOR) or breastplate.

cuisse (qwees) Piece of armor or padding shaped to protect the thigh that was worn during the Middle Ages.

culet (ku′-lit) Piece of armor consisting of a skirt of articulated plate fastened to a backplate to protect the loins worn from mid-16th to mid-17th c.

demi brassard Armor worn in early 14th c. consisting of a metal plate worn to protect the upper arm.

demi-jamb Armor consisting of a metal plate over front of leg from ankle to knee connected to the SOLLERET (see under ARMOR) or shoe. Worn by knights and soldiers in the early 14th c. Also see under ARMOR: GREAVE.

demi-vambrace Armor worn on front of forearm from elbow to the wrist.

épaulière (ep′-ool-yehr) Armor consisting of single piece of unarticulated shoulder plate, first worn about 1300; smaller in size than the pauldron. See under ARMOR: PAULDRON. Also called *epaulet* and *shoulder cop.*

gambeson See under ARMOR: ACTON.

gauntlet Armor of MAIL, or PLATE (see under ARMOR), worn on the hand from 15th to 17th c.

gorget (gorge′-et) Armor worn on throat in Middle Ages.

greave Metal-plate leg covering reaching from ankle to knee. Worn from 11th to 17th c. as armor. Also called *jamb* (*jambe*) (zham). When made of leather in the 14th c., called a *jambeau* (zham-bow′). When worn just on the front of the leg, called a *demijamb* (*jambe*) (dem-ee-zham).

hauberk (ho′-berk) Knee-length shirt made of mail worn as armor in 11th, 12th, and 13th c. Sometimes covering hands ending in mail mittens. Sides were split from waist down in front and back for convenience in riding horseback and worn over quilted gambeson (see under DOUBLET). Sometimes called *coat of mail.* Also see under ARMOR: VAMBRACE.

jamb/jambe See under ARMOR: GREAVE.

jambeau (zham′-bow) Leather armor worn to protect leg in 14th c. See under ARMOR: GREAVE.

jazerant (jazz′-er-ant) Armor worn in 14th c. consisting of a leather or cloth tunic covered with overlapping plates of leather, metal, or horn. Also spelled *jazeran, jazerine, jesseraunt.*

knee-piece Armor worn to protect the knee. Called *poleyn* (pol′-ain) or *knee cop.*

lame (lah-may) Armor composed of thin overlapping plates used for covering the hands. Also see under ARMOR: GAUNTLET.

mail The earliest form in armor consisted of metal rings sewn to foundation of leather in parallel rows. By the Middle Ages, metal rings were interlinked and called *chain mail. Der.* Middle English, *maille,* one of the "rings" from which it was made.

mentonnière (mohn-ton′-yehr) Protective armor for lower part of face or chin that was worn in tournaments in the Middle Ages.

morion Lightweight helmet, with brim forming peaks front and back. Turned down on sides with high comb in center extending from front to back over crown of head. Popular in 16th c. throughout Europe, and associated with Spanish conquistadors in Mexican conquest. Also called *comb morion.* Compare with ARMOR: BURGONET.

pauldron (pol′-drun) Armor worn in late 15th c. consisting of single large, rigid shoulder plate lapping over armor at chest and back. Also called *épaulière* (eh-pol-yair′) and *shoulder cop.*

plastron Iron breastplate worn as armor between HAUBERK and ACTON. See under ARMOR.

plate Armor made from solid sections of metal.

poleyn Piece of armor consisting of a metal plate (originally leather) worn over knee cap, introduced in 13th c. Also called *knee cop* and *genouillière* (zhe-no-yair′).

rerebrace (rer′-bras) Plate armor worn on the upper arm. See under ARMOR: CANNON and VAMBRACE.

sabaton Broad-toed armor of mid-16th c. strapped over top of foot. Also called *bear paw* or *duckbill solleret.* Also spelled *sabatayne.* Also see under ARMOR: SOLLERET.

sallet (sal′-ay) Helmet worn in 15th c. by Germans, French, and British, usually cast in one piece in pot-like shape flaring somewhat at neck in front and sometimes in back. Covered entire face with small slit to see through, sometimes had a moveable visor. Also spelled *celata, salade, salet.*

shoulder cop Small plates covering front of shoulder. Later they were small pieces of articulated metal. Still later consisted of a single large plate called a PAULDRON (see under ARMOR). Also called *épaulière.*

solleret (sol'-er-ay) Piece of armor worn during the Middle Ages to protect the foot. Consisted of jointed flexible pieces of iron. In the 15th c. had a long pointed toe—then called *solleret à la poulaine* (sol'-er-ay ah lah poo-layn'). Also spelled *soleret, solaret.* Also see under ARMOR: SABATON.

tasset Armor for the upper thigh made either of a single plate or of several narrow flexible plates joined together by rivets. Also spelled *tace, tasse.*

tonlet Flaring skirt of metal plates or of solid metal, sometimes fluted with deep vertical folds, worn as armor in 16th c. Also called *lamboy, jamboy,* or *base.*

umbril See under ARMOR: BURGONET.

vambrace 1. Armor consisting of metal plate worn either on the forearm or above or below the HAUBERK, in early 13th c. 2. Later, plate armor for entire arm made up of upper and lower CANNONS and COUTES for the elbow. (See under ARMOR.)

ventail Armor for lower part of the face on helmets used in the 16th c. If face guard is made in three pieces, ventail is middle piece.

visor Movable part of helmet that could be lowered to cover the face.

---

armseye/arm's eye See under ARMHOLE.

armur raccoon See under FUR: USSURIAN RACCOON.

army cap See under HEADWEAR: FATIGUE CAP, OVERSEAS CAP, and SERVICE CAP.

Army/Navy clothes Surplus items of clothing typically worn by men and women of the U.S. Army and Navy that were sold after World War II in special stores called "Army/Navy stores." At present, merchandisers calling themselves army and navy stores can be found online and in some communities.

arrasene See under EMBROIDERIES AND SEWING STITCHES.

Arrow Collar Man® See under NECKLINES AND COLLARS: DETACHABLE COLLAR.

arrowhead See under EMBROIDERIES AND SEWING STITCHES.

Art Deco A nonrepresentational style of art that rose to prominence in 1920s and 1930s, which relies on geometric and stylized forms drawn from diverse sources ranging from Aztec motifs to animal and floral patterns. The term only came into use in 1968 when the author, Bevis Hillier, writing about the style, derived it from the name of a Paris exposition of 1925 that featured designs of this period: Exposition International des Arts Décoratifs et Industriels Modernes. In fashion, the style was most evident in textiles and jewelry. Art Deco design experienced a revival in the late 1960s and has continued to appear since then. Also called *Art Moderne, Modernistic, Jazz Modern, Skyscraper Style.* See under HOSIERY: ART DECO HOSE; JEWELRY: ART DECO EARRING; and PRINTS, STRIPES, AND CHECKS: ART DECO PRINT.

Art Deco design 1920s

artichoke See under HAIRSTYLES.

artificial crinoline See under UNDERGARMENTS: HOOPS.

†artificial silk Used before 1925 to describe rayon and acetate. Also called *art silk.*

†artillery twill Synonym for WHIPCORD.

artist's smock 1. Traditionally a SMOCK used by artists. Usually three-quarter length with full sleeves gathered into bands at wrists and a large round collar and, sometimes, with black tie around the neck. 2. Any smock worn when painting.

Art Moderne See under ART DECO.

Art Nouveau (art noo'-vo) Design style of the period between 1890 and 1910 that represented an attempt by artists and artisans to develop a style that had no roots in the past. Designs emphasized: curved, waving lines; stylized natural forms of plants, animals, and women; and a strong sense of motion. Revived in later periods, especially in jewelry and textiles. The style was known as *stile liberty* (stee'-lay lee-bare-tay') in Italy, as *Jugendstil* (Yu'-gend-stil) in Germany, and as *modernismo* (moh-der-nees'-moh) in Spain. See under HOSIERY: ART NOUVEAU HOSE and PRINTS, STRIPES, AND CHECKS: ART NOUVEAU PRINT.

Art Nouveau design 1898

artois See under CAPES, CLOAKS, AND SHAWLS.

artois buckle See under CLOSURES: BUCKLES D'ARTOIS.

art silk See under ARTIFICIAL SILK.

art to wear See under WEARABLE ART.

Ascot Fashionable horse-racing spot, Ascot Heath, in England, for which a number of fashions have been named. See under COATS AND JACKETS: ASCOT JACKET; NECKLINES AND COLLARS: ASCOT NECKLINE/COLLAR; SCARVES: ASCOT SCARF; and TIES: ASCOT.

A-shirt See under SHIRTS: ATHLETIC SHIRT.

asooch (*aswash*) 17th-c. term meaning "sash-wise" or "scarf-wise"; draped diagonally from shoulder to hip.

aspirational brands See under BRAND.

assembler The worker who joins UPPER and SOLE in shoemaking.

assisi embroidery See under EMBROIDERIES AND SEWING STITCHES.

associated buying office An office that offers consultation services and buys merchandise for a group of independently owned stores. Participating stores are shareholders in the buying office. Synonym: *cooperative buying office.*

assortment The merchandise available in a store at any given time. Assortments are often described in terms of **breadth** (i.e., numbers of styles) and **depth** (i.e., numbers of sizes and colors available for each style).

asterism See under GEMS, GEM CUTS, AND SETTINGS.

†astrakhan/astrakan 1. Fabric with a heavy, curly pile made to imitate karakul lamb fleece. May be woven or knitted. Used as trimming or for men's hats. 2. Wool from the karakul lamb. 4. See under FURS: KARAKUL.

astrolegs hose See under HOSIERY.

astronaut's cap See under HEADWEAR.

aswash See under ASOOCH.

asymmetric/asymmetric balance The principle of informal balance, rather than formal balance; when an imaginary line is drawn vertically down the middle of a garment, each side is different. In women's dresses, examples would include drapery arranged more to one side, a side closing, one shoulder uncovered, or trimming arranged differently on each side of the dress. Other examples include SWIMWEAR: ASYMMETRIC SWIMSUIT; CLOSURES: ASYMMETRIC CLOSING; CLOTHING CONSTRUCTION DETAILS: ASYMMETRIC HEM; NECKLINES AND COLLARS: ASYMMETRIC COLLAR/NECKLINE; and SKIRTS: ASYMMETRIC SKIRT.

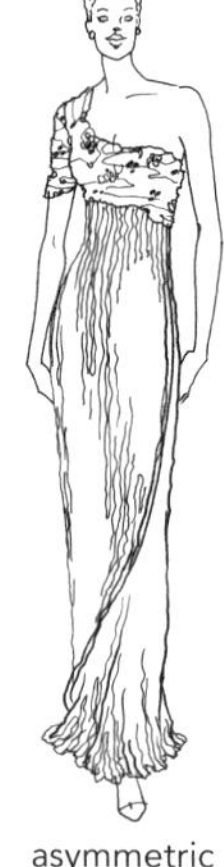
asymmetric dress 1994

Ata See under TALLITH.

atef See under HEADWEAR.

atelier de couture Workrooms in which Parisian haute couture designers and their staff design and produce their COLLECTIONS.

athletic clothes See under ACTIVEWEAR.

athletic pants See under PANTS: SWEATPANTS.

athletic shirt See under UNDERGARMENTS and SHIRTS.

athletic shoes See under FOOTWEAR.

athletic shorts See under SHORTS.

athletic socks See under HOSIERY: SWEATSOCK.

at-home wear Informal clothing worn at home, particularly when entertaining. See under SLEEPWEAR AND LOUNGEWEAR: CAFTAN and HOSTESS ROBE.

atours See under HEADWEAR.

A.T.P. See under FOOTWEAR.

attaché case See under HANDBAGS AND RELATED ACCESSORIES: BRIEFCASE #1.

attached collar See under NECKLINES AND COLLARS.

attifet See under HEADWEAR.

attire 1. Synonym for APPAREL. 2. See under HEADWEAR.

aubusson stitch See under EMBROIDERIES AND SEWING STITCHES: REP STITCH.

Audubon Plumage Law Law passed in early 20th c. prohibiting the use and import of feathers from rare birds, such as the egret, that were used as fashionable trim on women's hats from late 19th to early 20th c. *Der.* Named for John James Audubon, American ornithologist who died in 1851.

aulmoniere See under HANDBAGS AND RELATED ACCESSORIES.

aumusse/aunice See under HEADWEAR: ALMUCE.

au natural See under HAIRSTYLES.

∞auqueton See under ARMOR: ACTON.

aurora borealis crystal See under under JEWELRY.

Australian opossum See under FURS.

Austrian crystal See under JEWELRY.

Austrian seal See under FURS.

automobile *adj.* Describes apparel used by drivers in the early days of automobile use. See under HEADWEAR: AUTOMOBILE CAP and AUTOMOBILE VEIL.

automobile coat See under COATS AND JACKETS: DUSTER.

avant-garde (ah-vant' gard) (French) Used in English to mean new, unconventional, ahead of its time. Used as an adjective to describe apparel that may be provocative or startling.

avatar See under VIRTUAL INTERNET SITE.

aviator *adj.* Applied to apparel or accessories that are copied from or inspired by clothing worn by airplane pilots. See under EYEWEAR: AVIATOR GLASSES and HEADWEAR: AVIATOR'S HELMET.

award sweater See under SWEATERS: LETTER SWEATER.

awning stripe See under PRINTS, STRIPES, AND CHECKS.

ayrshire embroidery See under EMBROIDERIES AND SEWING STITCHES.

aztec *adj.* Describes apparel ornamented with designs and motifs associated with the Aztec civilization of ancient Mexico. See under PRINTS, STRIPES, AND CHECKS: AZTEC PRINT and SWEATERS: AZTEC SWEATER.

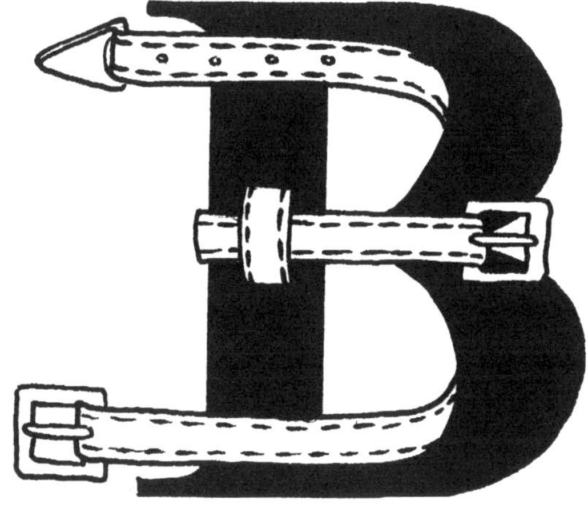

babet bonnet See under HEADWEAR.

babet cap See under HEADWEAR.

babushka See under SCARVES.

baby *adj.* Describes apparel or textiles, implying something of smaller size.

baby beads See under JEWELRY: BABY BRACELET.

∞**baby bodice** Daytime bodice introduced in 1878 with lingerie features similar to a baby's dress, such as vertical pleats down front, a wide sash, basques (see under BASQUE #2) below waistline, and a square neck. Later, in 1897, worn with a high drawstring neckline fastened with ribbon and a wide sash.

baby bonnet See under HEADWEAR.

baby boomers Commonly used to refer to the 76 million Americans born after World War II between the years 1946 and 1964.

baby boot See under FOOTWEAR.

baby bunting Infant's outdoor combination blanket-sack with zipper front and separate or attached hood, frequently made of blanket cloth and bound with satin. Also called *bunting* and *grow bag*. Contemporary baby buntings may be made with legs instead of a sack bottom.

baby bunting
c. 2000

baby-doll dress See under DRESSES.

baby-doll nightgown See under SLEEPWEAR AND LOUNGEWEAR.

baby-doll nightie See under SLEEPWEAR AND LOUNGEWEAR.

baby-doll pajamas See under SLEEPWEAR AND LOUNGEWEAR.

baby-doll shirt See under SHIRTS.

baby-doll shoe See under FOOTWEAR.

baby-doll sleeve See under SHOULDERS AND SLEEVES: PUFFED SLEEVE.

baby dress See under DRESSES.

baby irish lace See under LACES.

baby lace See under LACES.

baby louis heel See under FOOTWEAR: LOUIS HEEL.

baby ribbon Narrow ribbon ⅛″ to ¼″ in width, sometimes made of reversible satin. Originally used for baby clothes and also to thread through insertion, lace, and beading in late 19th and early 20th c.

∞**baby sash** Woman's sash of ribbon tied in bow at back; popular at end of 19th c.

baby skirt See under SKIRTS.

baby stuart cap See under HEADWEAR.

bachelor's gown See under ACADEMIC COSTUME.

bachelor's hood See under ACADEMIC COSTUME.

bachlick See under SCARVES.

bacinet See under ARMOR: BASINET.

back 1. The rear or underside of a fabric or garment, as opposed to the front or upper side. ∞2. 14th-c. term sometimes used to describe any outer garment.

back-combing See under HAIRSTYLES.

backing See under CLOTHING CONSTRUCTION DETAILS.

backless bra See under UNDERGARMENTS.

backless dress See under DRESSES.

backpack See under HANDBAGS AND RELATED ACCESSORIES.

∞**backs** Referred to clothing in general in the 14th c.

backstay See under FOOTWEAR.

back stitch/backstitch See under EMBROIDERIES AND SEWING STITCHES.

back strings 18th-c. synonym for LEADING STRINGS.

back-wrap dress See under DRESSES: WRAP DRESS.

badger See under FURS.

bäffchen See under CLERICAL DRESS: GENEVA BANDS.

bag 1. Any one of various kinds of luggage. 2. Shortened form of the word HANDBAG. See under HANDBAGS AND ACCESSORIES. 3. Shortened form of BAGWIG. See under WIGS AND HAIRPIECES: BAGWIG.

∞**bag bodice** Woman's bodice with PLASTRON (see under PLASTRON #2) cut to blouse over belt or waistband, worn in daytime in 1883.

bag bonnet See under HEADWEAR.

bag cap See under HEADWEAR.

bagge See under POCKETS.

baggies See under PANTS: BAGGY PANTS.

bagging shoe See under FOOTWEAR: STARTUP.

baggy pants See under PANTS.

∞**bag-irons** Iron, bronze, or silver frames with suspension units made of a crossbar and swivel used in medieval pouches worn hanging from belt in 15th and 16th c. Lower section of concentric semicircular rings acted as stiffeners for the opening and the flap that was the closing. Also called *bag-rings*.

bagnolette See under HEADWEAR.

bagpipe sleeve See under SHOULDERS AND SLEEVES.

bag-rings See under BAG-IRONS.

bags Slang that referred to men's trousers in 19th and early 20th c. See under PANTS: OXFORD BAGS.

baguette cut See under GEMS, GEM CUTS, AND SETTINGS.

baguette bag See under HANDBAGS AND RELATED ACCESSORIES.

bag-waistcoat See under VESTS.

bagwig See under WIGS AND HAIRPIECES.

bakelite Trade name of plastic (phenol formaldehyde) that may be clear and uncolored or colored and opaque. Used for jewelry and handbags and/or their fittings. Sometimes bakelite is used as a generic name for this type of plastic. It continues to be used today.

Bakst, Leon Nikolaevich (1868–1924) Russian artist who, after leaving Russia for Paris in 1909, won international fame designing sets and costumes for the Ballets Russes, produced by Diaghilev. Helped to start a wave of Orientalism in women's dresses in the pre–World War I era.

bal/balmoral See under FOOTWEAR.

balaclava See under HEADWEAR.

balas ruby See under GEMS, GEM CUTS, AND SETTINGS: SPINEL.

balayeuse See under DUST RUFFLE.

†**balbriggan** Soft, lightweight tubular knit fabric made of cotton, manufactured, or blended yarns in a plain stitch. It may be slightly napped on the reverse side. Used for pajamas and SNUGGIES (see UNDERGARMENTS). *Der.* Named for Balbriggan, Ireland, where the fabric was first used for a type of unbleached hosiery.

baldric/baldrick See under BELTS.

Balenciaga fisherman hat See under HEADWEAR.

Balfour plaid See under PLAIDS AND TARTANS.

ballantine See under HANDBAGS AND RELATED ACCESSORIES: RETICULE.

ball earring See under JEWELRY.

ballentine See under HANDBAGS AND RELATED ACCESSORIES: RETICULE.

ballerina length See under LENGTHS.

ballerina shoe See under FOOTWEAR.

ballet laces See under FOOTWEAR.

ballet neckline/ballerina neckline See under NECKLINES AND COLLARS.

ballet skirt See under SKIRTS.

ballet slipper See under FOOTWEAR.

ball fringe See under BRAIDS.

ball gown See under FORMAL ATTIRE.

ball heel See under FOOTWEAR.

balloon *adj.* Describes apparel that has the rounded shape of a balloon. See under HEADWEAR: BALLOON HAT; SHORTS: BALLOON SHORTS; SKIRTS: BUBBLE SKIRT; and SHOULDERS AND SLEEVES: BALLOON SLEEVE.

ballpoint embroidery See under EMBROIDERIES AND SEWING STITCHES: LIQUID EMBROIDERY.

ballroom neckcloth See under TIES.

balmacaan coat (bal-má-can) See under COATS AND JACKETS.

Balmoral (bahl-mor'-al) Castle near Braemar, Aberdeenshire, Scotland, purchased by Queen Victoria in 1852. She built another granite castle on this site, using it as a fashionable retreat. The name of the castle was used as an adjective when describing certain fashionable items of Victorian apparel.

∞**balmoral bodice** (bahl-mor'-al) Tight-fitting, jacket-type bodice with long sleeves worn by women in the early 1860s and early 1880s. Made with high neck and a series of double box pleats in back, one over the other to form fullness over hips; or made with long tabs over the bustle in back. Usually worn with contrasting skirt in 1880s, at which time it was also called *postillion corsage*.

balmoral boot See under FOOTWEAR.

balmoral cap/bonnet See under HEADWEAR.

balmoral jacket See under COATS AND JACKETS.

balmoral mantle See under CAPES, CLOAKS, AND SHAWLS.

balmoral petticoat See under UNDERGARMENTS.

Balmoral tartan See under PLAIDS AND TARTANS.

Baltic seal See under FURS.

Baltic tiger See under FURS.

bamberges See under FOOTWEAR.

bambin/bambino hat See under HEADWEAR.

band 1. See under NECKLINES AND COLLARS. 2. See under CLERICAL DRESS: GENEVA BANDS.

†**bandanna** (ban-dan'-nah) 1. Cotton calico fabric usually made by RESIST PRINTING on red or navy-blue with black-and-white designs. 2. See under SCARVES. 3. Silk printed square from India used as neckcloth or snuff handkerchief in 18th and 19th c. 4. See under PRINTS, STRIPES, AND CHECKS. *Der.* From Hindu *bandhnu*, a "method of tie-dyeing cloth."

band bow See under TIES.

∞**bandbox** 1. In the 16th and 17th c., a box in which collars, called bands (see under NECKLINES AND COLLARS: FALLING BAND), were kept. Bandboxes developed for use in Europe from mid-18th c. on. Used in the U.S. for storage and transportation of clothing, hats, etc., during the 19th c. After the Civil War they declined in popularity, and by late 19th c. were replaced by more utilitarian trunks, portmanteaux, and hatboxes. 2. Hatbox, usually round, of cardboard or thin wood covered with stiff paper that by the 1820s in the U.S. was printed with pictorial panoramas. European boxes were plainer. Both were used to carry small items as well as hats.

band briefs See under UNDERGARMENTS.

band cuff See under CUFFS.

bandeau 1. See under HEADWEAR. 2. See under UNDERGARMENTS: BRA. 3. See under SWIMWEAR.

bandeau d'amour See under HAIRSTYLES.

bandeau slip See under UNDERGARMENTS: BRA-SLIP.

banded agate See under GEMS, GEM CUTS, AND SETTINGS: AGATE.

banded bottom sleeve See under SHOULDERS AND SLEEVES.

banded collar See under NECKLINES AND COLLARS.

banded neckline See under NECKLINES AND COLLARS.

banded sleeve See under SHOULDERS AND SLEEVES.

bandelet 1. See under GLOVES AND GLOVE CONSTRUCTION. 2. See under SCARVES.

band-leg panties See under UNDERGARMENTS: BAND BRIEFS.

bandoleer See under BELTS.

bandolier 1. Shoulder bag carried by women of Great Plains Native American tribes. Made in pouch style and used to carry small items, e.g., combs, needle and thread. 2. See under BELTS: BANDOLEER.

bandore and peak See under HEADWEAR.

banging chignon See under HAIRSTYLES.

bangle bracelet See under JEWELRY.

bangle watch See under WATCHES: BRACELET WATCH.

bangs See under HAIRSTYLES.

banian/banjan See under BANYAN.

∞**banyan** (*banian, banjan*) Comfortable, loose-fitted dressing gown worn by men from the late 17th through the early 19th c. Often very decorative, these garments were made from a wide variety of fabrics, including cotton calicos, elaborate silks, and glazed wool. Although this garment was made for indoor wear, it was not unheard of for a man to go outside or have his portrait painted in his banyan. *Der.* From *banian*, a caste of Hindu merchants from the subcontinent of India.

banyan

bar drop pin See under JEWELRY.

barbe See under HEADWEAR.

barber's apron See under APRONS.

barbette/barbet See under HEADWEAR.

barbs See under introduction to FEATHERS.

barbula See under BEARD.

∞**barcelona handkerchief** Colored or black silk handkerchief made in checks or fancy designs in twill weave. Worn around neck or head, or carried in hand, in 18th and 19th c. *Der.* From Barcelona, Spain, where they were first made.

Bardot, Brigitte (bar'-doe) French movie actress who became a sex symbol of the 1950s and 1960s, after starring in the movie *And God Created Woman* (1956). Responsible for a wave of interest in tousled hairstyles, tight jeans, body sweaters, and blue-and-pink–checked gingham little-girl dresses.

Bardot hair See under HAIRSTYLES.

bar drop pin See under JEWELRY.

bare bra See under UNDERGARMENTS.

barège shawl See under CAPES, CLOAKS, AND SHAWLS.

bare midriff *adj.* Describes clothing that exposes the body from under the bust, baring the rib cage, to the waist or hips. Introduced in the U.S. in the late 1920s and early 1930s, made popular by film star Carmen Miranda in the 1940s, and revived in the 1960s and 1980s after interest developed in the fashions of India such as the SARI and the short-waisted blouse worn with it. This style is revived from time to time. See under SLEEPWEAR AND LOUNGEWEAR: BARE-MIDRIFF PAJAMAS and BLOUSES AND TOPS: BARE-MIDRIFF TOP.

bare midriff 1936

bare top See under BLOUSES AND TOPS.

barette See under HAIR ACCESSORIES: BARRETTE.

bargello stitch See under EMBROIDERIES AND SEWING STITCHES.

bark cloth See under TAPA CLOTH.

bark tanning See under LEATHERS: VEGETABLE TANNING.

barmecloth See under APRONS.

barmfell See under APRONS.

barmhatre See under APRONS: BARMECLOTH.

barmskin See under APRONS: BARMFELL.

barn coat See under COATS AND JACKETS: FIELD COAT.

barong tagalog See under SHIRTS.

baroque (bahr′-oke) Art and decorative style popular during the 17th and first half of 18th c. that was characterized by heavy ornate curves and excessive ornamentation. Applied to certain jewelry and embroidery designs that derive from the baroque style.

baroque design

baroque pearl See under GEMS, GEM CUTS, AND SETTINGS: PEARLS.

barouche coat See under COATS AND JACKETS.

bar pin See under JEWELRY.

†barré (ba-ray′) (*barry*) 1. Defect in woven fabric consisting of differences in warps or filling as to color or texture. 2. (French) Fabrics or knits with horizontal stripes in two or more colors. Uses: neckwear.

barred buttonhole See under CLOSURES: WORKED BUTTONHOLES.

barrel *adj.* Describes cylindrically shaped objects. See under CLOSURES: BARREL SNAPS; CUFFS: BARREL; HAIRSTYLES: BARREL CURLS; HANDBAGS AND RELATED ACCESSORIES: BARREL BAG; TIES: OSBALDISTAN TIE; SHOULDERS AND SLEEVES: BARREL SLEEVE; and TRUNK HOSE.

∞barrel-shaped muff Large muff made of or trimmed in fur, sometimes concealing arms to elbows. Illustrated in paintings such as *Madame Molé-Raymond* by Vigée-Lebrun and *Mrs. Siddons* by Gainsborough.

barrette (ba-ret) 1. See under HAIR ACCESSORIES. 2. See under HEADWEAR.

barrister's wig See under WIGS AND HAIRPIECES.

∞barrow 19th-c. covering for infants consisting of a piece of flannel wrapped around the body and covering the feet. By the early 20th c. this had become a LAYETTE item: a long wraparound strapless petticoat set onto a wide underarm band that pinned shut. Generally it was worn with the hem pinned up with large safety pins.

barry See under BARRÉ.

barrymore collar See under NECKLINES AND COLLARS.

bar-shaped tie See under TIES.

bar tack See under EMBROIDERIES AND SEWING STITCHES.

bar tack buttonhole See under CLOSURES: WORKED BUTTONHOLE.

bas de chausses See under CHAUSSE and NETHER STOCKS.

bascinet See under ARMOR: BASINET.

base 1. See under GEMS, GEM CUTS, AND SETTINGS. ∞2. See under ARMOR: TONLET.

baseball *adj.* Used to describe any item of clothing that is derived from or influenced by clothing worn for the American sport of baseball. See under HEADWEAR: BASEBALL CAP; COATS AND JACKETS: BASEBALL JACKET; and SHIRTS: BASEBALL SHIRT.

base coat See under COATS AND JACKETS.

∞bases 1. Man's separate skirt, hung in unpressed tubular pleats, that was worn with a padded doublet or under armor, between the years 1490 and 1540. Sometimes simulated in steel in armor. 2. Skirt of a jacket or jerkin, hanging in unpressed pleats. 3. See under COATS AND JACKETS: BASE COAT.

bases

basic dress See under DRESSES.

basics In retailing, refers to those products for which there is a constant and continuing demand. Examples: hosiery, jeans, T-shirts. Also called *staples.*

basinet See under ARMOR.

basket See under HEADWEAR.

basket bag See under HANDBAGS AND RELATED ACCESSORIES.

basketball shoe See under FOOTWEAR.

basket button See under CLOSURES.

basket stitch See under EMBROIDERIES AND SEWING STITCHES.

†basket weave Variation of plain weave, made by weaving two or more crosswise yarns over and under same number of lengthwise yarns to produce a checkerboard effect.

basket weave

basket-weave stitch See under EMBROIDERIES AND SEWING STITCHES.

∞basque (bask) 1. In the 17th c. originally referred to a part of a man's doublet extending below the waist that was made with a series of vertical slashes forming tabs. 2. By mid-19th c., used for the part of a woman's bodice that extended below the waistline. 3. In the early 20th c., referred to a woman's waist-length jacket or dress that fit tightly through waist and rib cage.

basque #2

basque beret See under HEADWEAR: BERET #1.

∞basque-habit Bodice worn from the 1860s on with square-cut tabs below the waistline.

basque shirt See under SHIRTS.

basque waistband See under BELTS.

basquina See under BASQUINE #2.

∞basquin body Woman's daytime bodice of the 1850s, without a waistline seam that extended below the waistline.

∞basquine (bas'-keen) 1. See under COATS AND JACKETS. 2. Wide underskirt of rich fabric held out by hoops; worn in the 16th c. Also called *basquina* in Spain.

Bass Weejuns See under FOOTWEAR.

baste/basting stitch See under EMBROIDERIES AND SEWING STITCHES.

bateau neckline (ba-toe') See under NECKLINES AND COLLARS.

bathing cap See under HEADWEAR.

bathing dress See under introduction to SWIMWEAR.

bathing slipper See under FOOTWEAR.

bathing suit See under introduction to SWIMWEAR.

bathrobe See under SLEEPWEAR AND LOUNGEWEAR.

bathrobe dress See under DRESSES.

†batik 1. A method of dyeing in which the pattern area is covered with wax and the fabric placed in a dyebath where the uncovered areas take up the color. Additional colors can be added by selectively covering and uncovering areas of the cloth. Because the wax sometimes cracks during handling, and dye leaks through these cracks, fabrics often show fine lines or streaks in the patterns. 2. See under PRINTS, STRIPES, AND CHECKS.

bating See under LEATHERS.

†batiste A plain-weave, lightweight, sheer fabric usually made of cotton or a cotton and polyester blend. Made in a variety of colors and printed designs and used for men's and women's shirts, handkerchiefs, infants' clothing, women's blouses, dresses, nightgowns, and lingerie.

batswing tie See under TIES.

batt See under FOOTWEAR.

battant l'oeil See under HEADWEAR.

battenberg jacket See under COATS AND JACKETS.

battenberg lace See under LACES.

batter's cap See under HEADWEAR.

†batting Matted sheets of fibers used in quilting or stuffing. Fibers used include cotton, wool, kapok, spun rayon, or FIBERFILL.

battle jacket See under COATS AND JACKETS.

∞battlements Trimming consisting of square-cut tabs that were used in same manner as scallops on dresses, skirts, jackets, and basques in the 19th c.

batwing sleeve See under SHOULDERS AND SLEEVES.

baum marten See under FURS.

bautte/bautta See under CAPES, CLOAKS, AND SHAWLS.

bavarian dress See under DRESSES.

bavarian lace See under LACES.

bavolet See under HEADWEAR.

bayadère See under JEWELRY and SCARVES.

bayadère stripe (bah-yah-deer') ∞1. In 1850s, flat velvet trimming used either woven in or applied to dresses. 2. Name of fabric with brilliant contrasting horizontal stripes. 3. See under PRINTS, STRIPES, AND CHECKS. *Der.* Costume of Indian *bayadère*, or "dancing girl."

B-boys See under HIP-HOP.

beach *adj.* Describes clothing for wearing at the beach. See under CAPES, CLOAKS, AND SHAWLS: BEACH PONCHO; HEADWEAR: BEACH HAT; WIGS AND HAIRPIECES: BEACH WIG; and SWIMWEAR: BEACH COAT and BEACH WRAP-UP.

beach coat See under SWIMWEAR.

beach pajamas Full-length culottes, often made of printed fabric, and sometimes worn with matching bolero as sportswear in 1920s and 1930s; revived in 1970s.

beach dress/beach shift Simple cover-up designed to be worn over a bathing suit, often in matching fabric.

beach toga See under SWIMWEAR: BEACH COAT.

beachwear Items of apparel or accessories specifically for use at the beach. See category introduction for SWIMWEAR.

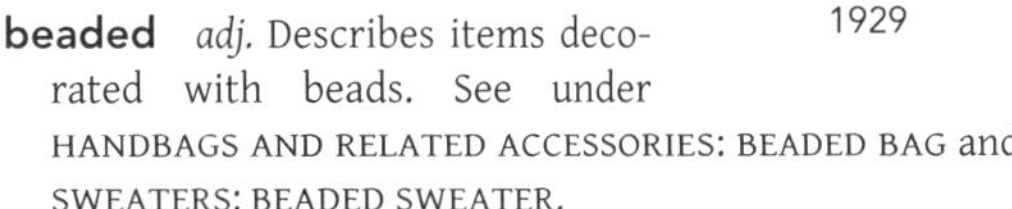

beach pajamas 1929

beaded *adj.* Describes items decorated with beads. See under HANDBAGS AND RELATED ACCESSORIES: BEADED BAG and SWEATERS: BEADED SWEATER.

beaded necklace See under JEWELRY: AMERICAN INDIAN NECKLACE.

beaded velvet See under CUT VELVET.

beading 1. See under EMBROIDERIES AND SEWING STITCHES. 2. See under LACES.

beads See under JEWELRY.

beanie See under HEADWEAR: SKULLCAP.

bear paw See under ARMOR: SABATON.

beard The hair that grows on the lower part of a man's face that, when not shaved off, may be trimmed and shaped around the jaw and chin in various ways that may be given fashion names. The following are some specific types of beards: **bodkin beard** Beard with long point in center of chin; worn by men from early 1520 to early 17th c. **favourite** Small tuft of hair worn on man's chin from 1820 to 1840. **goatee** Small pointed beard similar to tuft of hair on a goat's chin. **imperial** Man's small pointed tuft of hair under lower lip. Fashion set by Emperor Napoleon III of France from 1852 to 1871. **newgate fringe** Colloquial term in 19th c. for men's short whiskers that formed a fringe around the jaw. **pique devant** (peek deh'-vahn) Short pointed beard worn with a moustache by men from 1570s to 1600. Also called *pickdevant* and *barbule.* **soul patch** A type of goatee consisting of a small patch of whiskers just below the lip. Synonyms: *smig, mouche.* An imperial is slightly larger than a soul patch and pointed. **vandyke beard** Small pointed beard. *Der.* Named for the type of beards depicted by Flemish painter Sir Anthony Van Dyke (1599–1641) in his portraits of men.

goatee

vandyke beard

∞**beard box** Early American device made of pasteboard; worn at night over beard to preserve its shape.

∞**beard brush** Small brush used in public to comb the beard; popular during the first half of 17th c.

bearer See under UNDERGARMENTS.

bearskin 1. See under HEADWEAR. 2. See under FURS.

Beatles/Beatle Rock-music group from Liverpool, England, that became very popular in early 1960s. Members were George Harrison, John Lennon, Paul McCartney, and Ringo Starr. They appeared in mod clothing and long hairstyles that launched a style trend for young people in England, the U.S., and throughout the world. Clothing derived from styles associated with the group were often described with the adjective "Beatle." See under HAIRSTYLES: BEATLE CUT and FOOTWEAR: BEATLE BOOT.

beatnik Young, radical bohemians of the 1950s who were influenced by the so-called beat poets and French existentialist writers. Men wore working men's clothes and women wore their hair very long and dressed in black leotards and black skirts with ballet shoes.

Beaton, Sir Cecil (1904–1980) An English-born photographer and illustrator for *Vogue* magazine. In 1928 Beaton started creating drawings of clothes worn at society parties, as well as caricatures of well-known English actresses. As a photographer he did both fashion and portrait photos, becoming a favorite of the British royal family. During World War II he photographed in North Africa, Burma, and China for Ministry of Information. He designed scenery and costumes for ballet, opera, and theater productions in both London and New York. Beaton designed the costumes for stage productions of *My Fair Lady* and the film *Gigi.* Queen Elizabeth II knighted him in 1972.

beau (boh) (pl. *beaux*) *adj.* Used from the 1680s to the mid-19th c. to describe a gentleman who was fastidious about his clothes and accessories, similar to but not as effeminate as *fop.* Also see under DANDY.

Beau Brummell (Boh Brum'-ul) Used in a somewhat derogatory way, a man who takes an unusually strong interest in his appearance and his clothes (*e.g.,* "He's a Beau Brummell"). *Der.* From the nickname of George

"Beau" Brummell (1778–1840), an English dandy who was a court favorite and men's fashion leader during the Regency period (1811–1820). Brummell insisted on impeccable grooming, absence of showy fabrics or excessive decoration, and superb tailoring.

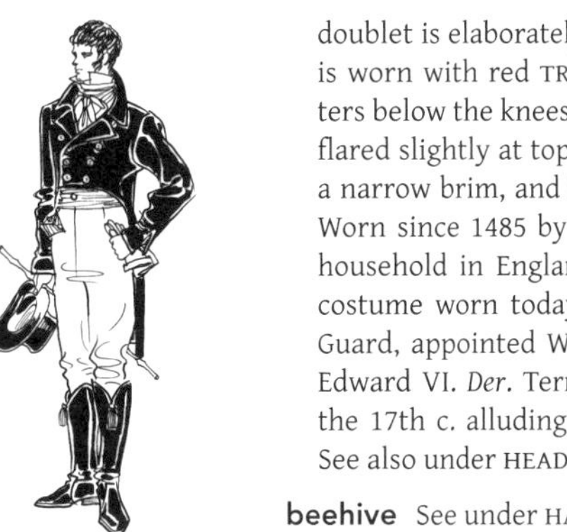
beau of the time of George "Beau" Brummell

beau monde (bow mond) (French) Refers to the world of fashion; literal translation: "the beautiful world."

beaufort coat See under COATS AND JACKETS.

beautiful people Expression coined by writer Rebecca Warfield in *Vogue* magazine in 1962 to describe rich and fashionable people.

beauty spot Mark on the face, either natural (such as small mole) or artificial, drawing attention to a good feature. Also see under PATCH #3.

beauvais embroidery See under EMBROIDERIES AND SEWING STITCHES.

beaux Plural form of BEAU.

beaver See under FURS.

beaverette See under FURS.

beaver hat See under HEADWEAR.

beaver tail See under SWIMWEAR: WETSUIT.

bebe bonnet See under HEADWEAR.

bebop cap See under HEADWEAR: NEWSBOY CAP.

becca See under HEADWEAR: ROUNDLET.

bedale jacket See under COATS AND JACKETS.

†bedford cord Heavyweight cotton or manufactured fiber fabric characterized by heavy lengthwise cords or stripes. The ribs are formed by heavy yarns that are used as backing or stuffer yarns. Carded single- or two-ply yarns are used for the face of fabric. Popular for women's and men's summer suits, in which the abbreviated *cord* is typically used. Also made by knitting and called *cord knit.* Lighter weights are called *warp piqué* (pee-kay').

bedgown See under SLEEPWEAR AND LOUNGEWEAR.

bed head hair See under HAIRSTYLES.

bed jacket See under SLEEPWEAR AND LOUNGEWEAR.

bedroom slipper See under FOOTWEAR.

bed socks See under HOSIERY.

beefeater's uniform Tudor-era uniform consisting of knee-length red DOUBLET with white ruffle at neck. The doublet is elaborately trimmed with gold and black and is worn with red TRUNK HOSE, red stockings with garters below the knees, a black hat with a soft, high crown flared slightly at top that is pleated into headband with a narrow brim, and black shoes trimmed with rosettes. Worn since 1485 by Yeomen of the Guard of the royal household in England, appointed by Henry VII. Same costume worn today by Yeomen Extraordinary of the Guard, appointed Wardens of the Tower of London by Edward VI. *Der.* Term in use from about the middle of the 17th c. alluding to British fondness for roast beef. See also under HEADWEAR: BEEFEATER'S HAT.

beehive See under HAIRSTYLES.

beehive hat See under HEADWEAR.

beer jacket See under COATS AND JACKETS.

beggar beads See under JEWELRY.

beggar's lace See under LACES.

beguin See under HEADWEAR.

belcher handkerchief See under TIES.

∞belette (*bilett*) An ornament or jewel, as it was called from the 13th to 16th c.

Belgian lace See under LACES.

belgrave shoe See under FOOTWEAR.

bell *adj.* Describes a wide variety of apparel details or items that have the approximate shape of a bell. See under CAPES, CLOAKS, AND SHAWLS: BELL; FOOTWEAR: LOUIS HEEL; PANTS: BELL-BOTTOMS; SHOULDERS AND SLEEVES: BELL SLEEVE; SKIRTS: BELL SKIRT; UMBRELLAS: BELL UMBRELLA; and UNDERGARMENTS: BELL HOOP.

bellboy/bellhop/bellman *adj.* Describes garments inspired by or modeled after the clothing worn by hotel employees, called bellboys. Although uniforms worn by these employees now differ from hotel to hotel, at one time most wore a distinctive uniform consisting of waist-length red jacket with high Chinese collar closing diagonally, trimmed with gold braid and buttons, and a small red pillbox hat. See under COATS AND JACKETS: BELLBOY/BELLHOP JACKET.

bellboy hat See under HEADWEAR.

bellied doublet See under PEASCOD-BELLIED DOUBLET.

bellows *adj.* Describes apparel details or items that expand and contract like a bellows, an instrument used to produce a stream of air. See under FOOTWEAR: BELLOWS TONGUE; POCKETS: BELLOWS POCKET; and SHOULDERS AND SLEEVES: BELLOWS SLEEVE.

belly chain See under JEWELRY.

belly-chete See under APRON.

∞**belly piece** At the front of man's DOUBLET, a stiffened triangular ridge lined with buckram, pasteboard, or whalebone. Worn from 1620s through the 1660s.

belt bag See under HANDBAGS AND RELATED ACCESSORIES.

BELTS

belt Decorative or functional item worn circling above, below, or at the natural waistline. Also worn over the shoulder in military fashion. May be made of fabric, leather, plastic, chain, etc. In the past and in poetic writings it was also called a *girdle*. Belts in classical antiquity were mostly of the sash type. In the Middle Ages, as fitted garments were made, belts became important; and a man's or woman's wealth could be determined by the richness of his or her linked, elaborately jeweled belt.

American Indian belt Leather belt decorated with woven North American Indian beadwork in bright colors and motifs.

∞**baldric/baldrick** Wide decorative belt used to hold dagger, worn at hip level. Worn diagonally from right shoulder to left hip, where sword was placed. Used from 13th to 17th c.

bandoleer (*bandolier*) Wide belt having loops to hold cartridges, with one or two straps extending over shoulders.

∞**basque waistband** Belt or waistband decorated with five pointed tabs; worn over afternoon dresses by women in latter half of 19th c.

bikini chain belt Fine gold chain worn with bikini or hip-hugger pants. Introduced in late 1960s.

black belt See under ACTIVEWEAR: KARATE SUIT.

braided belt Belt made by plaiting narrow strips of leather, vinyl, elastic, thong, or fabric that may buckle or tie.

brown belt See under ACTIVEWEAR: KARATE SUIT.

cartridge belt

cartridge belt Webbed or leather belt worn by armed forces and law enforcement officers, with individual spaces for ammunition. The belt may have an attached holster for a gun. This style without a holster but with a row of fake bullet cartridges has sometimes appeared as a fashion fad.

chain belt

chain belt Belt made of various sizes of chain. May be a single chain or a series of chains looped to medallions or imitation jewels at intervals.

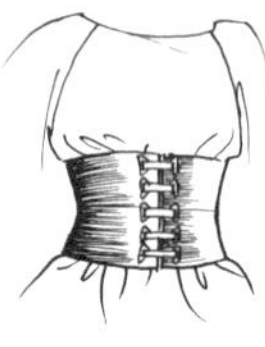
cinch belt

cinch belt Wide belt worn pulled tight, usually of elastic or fabric, either laced or clasped in front; popular during 1940s and 1950s.

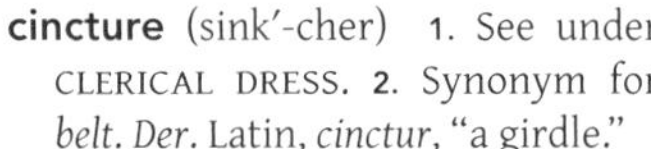

cincture (sink'-cher) **1.** See under CLERICAL DRESS. **2.** Synonym for *belt*. *Der.* Latin, *cinctur*, "a girdle."

∞**cingulum** (sing'-oo-luhm) **1.** Belt or girdle worn under the breasts by women in ancient Rome. **2.** Belt worn by men in Rome on tunic to adjust the length of garment. **3.** Roman sword belt. **4.** See under CLERICAL DRESS.

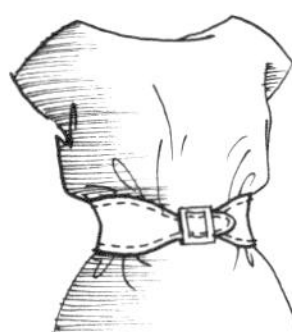
contour belt

contour belt Any belt that is curved so that it conforms to the body shape. It may be wider in the front or the back and various versions have been fashionable periodically. One type, called a dip belt, was usually made out of stiffened fabric and cut wider in the front, with a pointed lower edge. It fastened by strings attached to each end that came from the back around to the front and tied under the belt. It was fashionable in late 19th and early 20th c.

∞**corselet belt** Wide belt, sometimes enclosing the rib cage, frequently laced up front in manner similar to peasant's bodice. Called *swiss belt* in the 19th c.

cowboy belt Wide leather belt, sometimes with tooled designs, worn at top of hipbone by frontier cowboy to hold gun holster. Adapted for women's and men's sportswear.

cross-girdling See under BELTS: GREEK BELT.

cummerbund

cummerbund Wide fabric belt, sometimes pleated lengthwise and fastened in back. Worn with men's semiformal dinner suit; also worn by women. Copied from wrapped cloth belts worn in some Asian countries. *Der. kamarband*, "loin-band."

dip belt See under BELTS: CONTOUR BELT.

D-ring belt A narrow belt closed by pulling the end through two D-shaped rings.

gaucho belt (gow'-cho) Belt made of medallions of leather and metal joined with chain; introduced in the late 1960s. *Der.* Spanish, "cowboy" of South America.

∞**gobelin corselet** Woman's belt in the form of a corselet (see BELTS: CORSELET BELT); worn in mid-1860s; comes up high underneath the bust to form a point in front at waistline, narrows in back, and is trimmed with a ruffle of lace.

greek belt Long narrow sash that crosses over chest and winds around waist, a fashion innovation of the 1960s copied from sash worn in ancient Greece. Also called *cross-girdling*.

∞**half belt** Belt that does not extend around the entire waistline. It may be used in the back only. One such belt is the *martingale belt*, a half belt worn on back of garment, above or below normal waistline. *Der.* Part of horse's harness designed to hold its head down.

judo belt See under ACTIVEWEAR: KARATE SUIT.

karate belt See under ACTIVEWEAR: KARATE SUIT.

kidney belt Extremely wide belt, similar to a POLO BELT (see under BELTS), worn when motorcycling to prevent injury.

marguerite girdle Stiff belt that is laced in back and wider in front, forming two points above and below waistline. Sometimes made with butterfly arrangement in front and with a ruffle, PEPLUM, or bow in back to give a BUSTLE effect (see BUSTLE #2). Popular in 1860s and worn at intervals since.

martingale belt See under BELTS: HALF BELT.

mesh belt Belt made of extremely small metal links fastened together to form a flexible fabric-like band.

money belt Belt worn under or over clothing when traveling, with hidden zippered compartment for money.

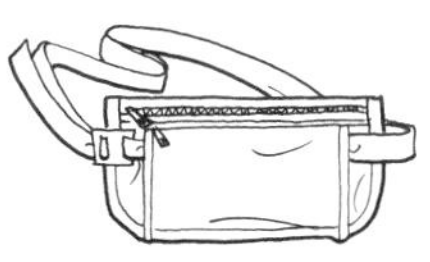
money belt

monk's belt 1. See under CLERICAL DRESS: CINCTURE. 2. Fashion term for a belt of cincture type made of rope, braided rayon, or nylon, with tassels on the ends.

obi See under OBI-STYLED SASH.

obi-styled sash Sash that is approximately 4″ to 5″ wide at the center and tapers to 1″ to 1½″ at the ends. It is worn wrapped around the waist twice and tied, with the ends hanging down the front. The tapered ends may be of contrasting colors or fabrics. Although it is a single piece of fabric, it gives the appearance of a double sash. Adapted in 1980s from the obi, which is a sash approximately 15″ wide and 4 to 6 yards long, and worn by Japanese men, women, and children over a KIMONO. It is folded lengthwise, with the fold toward hem, wrapped twice around waist, and tied in a flat butterfly bow in back. Style of tying and design of fabric vary according to age and sex. Sometimes spelled *obe*.

obi-styled sash

polo belt Wide leather belt covering the rib cage; it fastens in front with three small buckles on narrow leather straps. Originally worn by polo players for protection. Also see under BELTS: KIDNEY BELT.

∞**pompeian silk sash** Wide black silk belt woven with allegorical figures, usually worn by women with a bodice, colored skirt, and white summer jacket in 1860s.

safari belt Wide belt with attached flap pockets in front.

sam browne belt Belt around waist with extension strap over right shoulder, worn by U.S. Army officers, guards, and some policemen. Also called *shoulder belt*. *Der.* Named after British general, Sir Samuel Browne, who, having lost his left arm, couldn't support his sword without this special belt.

sash Any belt of soft material that loops over and ties in a knot or bow rather than buckling.

sash

self-covered belt Any belt cut out of the same fabric as the garment it accompanies; usually stiffened with a liner. Available in kits for the home sewer. If tied, it is called a *self sash*.

self sash See under BELTS: SELF-COVERED BELT.

serpentine belt Belt made in a wavy design, zigzagging around the body.

shoulder belt See under BELTS: SAM BROWNE BELT.

skirt-belt Belt with attached PEPLUM forming a short skirt. Introduced in late 1960s to wear over jumpsuits, body stockings, and pants.

spaghetti sash A sash made of a long narrow piece of fabric, with cording inserted as filler to give a rounded effect, sometimes knotted at the ends.

surcingle belt A webbed belt woven in plain or striped fabric fastened with a metal buckle through which a harness leather tab is pulled. Sometimes has a zippered pocket for money. *Der.* From the girth that fastens a horse's saddle or blanket.

swiss belt See under BELTS: CORSELET BELT.

thong belt 1. Wide leather belt with eyelets at each end through which a piece of rawhide is laced. 2. Belt made of braided rawhide.

tooled leather belt 1. Handmade leather belt, of various widths, embossed with various motifs. May be purchased in kits. 2. Belts imitating the above, stamped out by machine, sometimes imported from Mexico and Central America. 3. Belts from India in intricate designs that are inked in various colors.

webbed belt Belt of heavy canvas webbing, usually wide and fastened with a clip buckle, worn by military. Used in a narrower width on bathing suits in the 1920s.

Adapted for casual wear in various widths and colors by men and women since the 1960s.

weight belt 1. Belt of nylon webbing fitted with approximately twelve-pound weights. Used for scuba diving and underwater swimming. Extra weights may be added. 2. Wide, leather-textured vinyl or fabric belt with eight- to ten-pound weights worn under or over clothing as a reducing aid or figure improver.

white belt See under ACTIVEWEAR: KARATE SUIT.

∞**zone** (zo-knee) Belt worn by ancient Greek women around the hips, usually the lower one of two belts.

---

belt buckle See under CLOSURES.

beluque See under CAPES, CLOAKS, AND SHAWLS.

Ben Casey Television series of the 1950s with physician Ben Casey as the central character. Because of its popularity, some of the clothes worn by the doctor served as the inspiration for fashionable clothes, most notably the *Ben Casey collar* and the *Ben Casey shirt.* See under NECKLINES AND COLLARS: MEDIC COLLAR and SHIRTS: MEDIC SHIRT.

bench coat See under COATS AND JACKETS: BENCHWARMER JACKET.

benchmark brands See under BRAND.

benchwarmer jacket See under COATS AND JACKETS.

bench wig See under WIGS AND HAIRPIECES.

bend 1. See under LEATHERS. ∞2. A band of fabric on a dress, fillet for hair, or a hat band; used from the 11th to the 15th c. 3. See under PRINTS, STRIPES, AND CHECKS.

ben franklin glasses See under EYEWEAR.

†**bengaline** Heavy-weight fabric characterized by large corded effect in the crosswise direction. Often made of lustrous fibers and used for more formal women's apparel such as suits or coats, for millinery, and ribbons.

benjamin See under COATS AND JACKETS.

benjy 1. See under VESTS. 2. See under HEADWEAR.

benny See under COATS AND JACKETS: BENJAMIN.

benoiton coiffure See under HAIRSTYLES.

†**berber** Fabric of moderate weight—similar to CHINCHILLA CLOTH—that is used for skirts and jackets.

berdash See under BURDASH.

beret See under HEADWEAR.

beret sleeve See under SHOULDERS AND SLEEVES.

bergère hat See under HEADWEAR.

berlin gloves See under GLOVES AND GLOVE CONSTRUCTION.

berlin woolwork See under EMBROIDERIES AND SEWING STITCHES.

bermuda collar See under NECKLINES AND COLLARS.

bermuda shorts See under SHORTS.

bernhardt mantle See under CAPES, CLOAKS, AND SHAWLS.

Bernhardt, Sarah (búrn-hart) (1845–1923) Famous French actress known as the "Divine Sarah," whose elaborate costumes, hairstyles, and jewels influenced fashion in Europe and the U.S. in late 19th c. Her name is sometimes used as an adjective to describe styles that were associated with or inspired by her.

Bernhardt sleeve See under SHOULDERS AND SLEEVES.

bernos See under CAPES, CLOAKS, AND SHAWLS: BURNOOSE.

berretino See under HEADWEAR: ROUNDLET #1.

berretta/berrette See under CLERICAL DRESS: BIRETTA.

bertha See under NECKLINES AND COLLARS.

bertha pelerine See under NECKLINES AND COLLARS.

beryl See under GEMS, GEM CUTS, AND SETTINGS.

besom pocket See under POCKETS: WELT POCKET.

bespoke (British) Men's custom-made garments such as suits and coats.

bessarabian lamb See under FURS: LAMB.

betrothal ring See under JEWELRY.

betsie ruff See under NECKLINES AND COLLARS.

better goods See under APPAREL PRICE RANGES.

better market Apparel priced under CONTEMPORARY DESIGNER MARKET and BRIDGE MARKET, but above MASS MARKET and MODERATE GOODS MARKET. Also see under PRICE POINT.

bevel See under GEMS, GEM CUTS, AND SETTINGS.

beveled cut See under HAIRSTYLES.

bewdley cap See under HEADWEAR: MONMOUTH CAP.

bezel See under GEMS, GEM CUTS, AND SETTINGS: CROWN.

biarritz gloves See under GLOVES AND GLOVE CONSTRUCTION.

bias

†**bias** The direction of a fabric that is diagonal to the lengthwise or crosswise direction. When woven fabrics are pulled in the bias direction, they exhibit greater stretch

than in the lengthwise or crosswise directions, unless the fabrics are woven with stretch yarns or given special finishes. See under BIAS CUT.

bias binding Narrow strips of fabric cut on the bias, thus pliable for use in covering raw edges of curved necklines and armholes, or used at trimming. May either be hand-cut or sold in packages.

bias-cut A technique used by designers for cutting clothing to utilize the greater stretch in the bias or diagonal direction of the fabric, thereby causing it to accentuate body lines and curves and drape softly. For example, a full-skirted dress cut on the bias will hang more gracefully or a narrow dress will cling to the figure. Bias-cut garments were an important feature of the designs of Madeleine Vionnet in 1920s and 1930s, and bias-cut styles are revived periodically. In the Middle Ages, before the development of knitting, hose were cut on the bias in order to make them fit better. Old spelling was *byesse*.

bias pleat See under CLOTHING CONSTRUCTION DETAILS.

bias skirt See under SKIRTS.

bias slip See under UNDERGARMENTS.

bib 1. Square, rounded, or otherwise shaped piece of fabric or flexible plastic that is tied around the neck to protect clothing when the wearer is eating. Usually for children, bibs have been worn since the 16th c. When a similar-shaped element is introduced into apparel, the term "bib" may be used in the name. See under NECKLINES AND COLLARS, JEWELRY, and BLOUSES AND TOPS. 2. Extra piece of cloth attached to waist of apron, pants, or skirt extending upward over chest. See under APRONS: BIB APRON; JUMPERS: BIB JUMPER; PANTS: OVERALLS; and SHORTS: BIB SHORTS. 3. See under JEWELRY: BIB NECKLACE.

bib cravat See under TIES.

bibi bonnet See under HEADWEAR.

bicorne/bicorn See under HEADWEAR.

bicycle *adj.* Describes any item of clothing derived from or influenced by clothing worn for bicycling. See under GLOVES AND GLOVE CONSTRUCTION: BICYCLE GLOVE and HEADWEAR: BICYCLE HELMET.

bicycle bal See under FOOTWEAR.

bicycle-clip hat See under HEADWEAR.

bifocals See under EYEWEAR.

bifurcated garments Garments constructed with legs.

big coat See under COATS AND JACKETS.

big easy sweater See under SWEATERS.

biggin/biggonet See under HEADWEAR.

big regular Men's size for pajamas, corresponding to a chest measurement of 48″ or more, and a height of 5′7″ to 5′11″.

big shirt See under SHIRTS: OVERSIZED SHIRT and BIG T-SHIRT.

bike jacket See under COATS AND JACKETS.

biker collar See under NECKLINES AND COLLARS.

bike shorts See under SHORTS.

bike suit See under ACTIVEWEAR.

bike-tards See under ACTIVEWEAR: BIKE SUIT.

bikini 1. See under SWIMWEAR. 2. *adj.* Describes garments, other than swimwear, influenced by the cut of bikini swimwear. See under BLOUSES AND TOPS: BIKINI TOP; BELTS: BIKINI CHAIN; HOSIERY: BIKINI PANTYHOSE; and UNDERGARMENTS: BIKINI PANTIES and BIKINI BRIEF.

bilett See under BELETTE.

bill See under HEADWEAR: VISOR.

billfold See under HANDBAGS AND RELATED ACCESSORIES: WALLET.

billiment/billment See under HEADWEAR: BILLIMENT.

billycock/billicock See under HEADWEAR.

binche (bansh) See under LACES.

bindi A bright dot of red color applied to the middle of the forehead between the eyebrows, worn by women of the Buddhist and Hindu faiths; may represent honor, love, and prosperity.

binding 1. See under CLOTHING CONSTRUCTION DETAILS. 2. See under GLOVES AND GLOVE CONSTRUCTION.

binding off Knitting term for removing stitches from the needles on a hand-knitted article in such a way that the piece of knitting will not ravel.

binette See under WIGS AND HAIRPIECES.

bingle See under HAIRSTYLES.

biot See under FEATHERS.

bird cage See under HEADWEAR.

bird-of-paradise feathers See under FEATHERS.

†bird's-eye 1. Fabric woven in linen or cotton on a loom with a DOBBY ATTACHMENT (see under DOBBY WEAVE) in small diamond design with dot in center. Crosswise yarns are heavier and loosely twisted to make fabric more absorbent to use for diapers. Also called *diaper cloth.* 2. Clear-finished worsted suiting woven with a geometrical design in diamond effect with small dot in center. Used for men's and women's suits.

biretta 1. See under CLERICAL DRESS. 2. See under HEADWEAR.

Birkin bag See under HANDBAGS.

birlet See under HEADWEAR: BOURRELET.

birrus See under CAPES, CLOAKS, AND SHAWLS.

∞**birthday suit** 1. Man's court suit worn in 18th c. for a royal birthday. 2. Slang for naked, as when born.

birthstone See under GEMS, GEM CUTS, AND SETTINGS.

birthstone necklace See under JEWELRY.

birthstone ring See under JEWELRY.

†**bisette** (bee-set') ∞1. Used in Lyons, France, in the mid-16th c. to describe the silver thread trim on apparel. 2. See under LACES.

bishop collar See under NECKLINES AND COLLARS.

bishop sleeve See under SHOULDERS AND SLEEVES.

bi-swing See under COATS AND JACKETS.

bivouac mantle See under CAPES, CLOAKS, AND SHAWLS.

black belt See under ACTIVEWEAR: KARATE SUIT.

black fox See under FURS.

Blackglama® See under FURS.

black opal See under GEMS, GEM CUTS, AND SETTINGS: OPAL.

black tie 1. Abbreviated reference to men's semiformal evening attire. Compare with WHITE TIE. 2. See under TIES.

Black Watch tartan See under PLAIDS AND TARTANS.

blackwork See under EMBROIDERIES AND SEWING STITCHES.

blade jacket See under COATS AND JACKETS.

Blake See under FOOTWEAR: McKAY SHOE CONSTRUCTION.

∞**blanchet** Long white cotton camisole with sleeves, collar, and fur lining; worn over the shirt in the 15th c.

blanket See under FURS.

blanket plaid See under PLAIDS AND TARTANS.

blanket sleepers See under SLEEPWEAR AND LOUNGEWEAR.

blanket stitch See under EMBROIDERIES AND SEWING STITCHES.

blazer See under COATS AND JACKETS.

blazer button See under CLOSURES.

∞**blazer costume** Tailored suit with matching jacket and skirt; worn with a shirtwaist by girls and women in mid-1890s. Jacket usually had wide lapels and did not fasten in front.

blazer sock See under HOSIERY.

blazer stripe See under PRINTS, STRIPES, AND CHECKS.

blazer sweater See under SWEATERS.

bleached jeans See under PANTS: BLUE JEANS.

bleaching The process of removing color from some substance. Among the materials that are sometimes bleached are textiles and furs.

†**bleeding** Tendency of dyed fabric to lose color or run when wet.

bleeding madras See under MADRAS.

blehand/blehant See under BLIAUT.

†**blended yarn** Yarns that are composed of two or more fibers mixed together and then spun to form one yarn (e.g., cotton fibers and polyester staple). When such a yarn is used to make a fabric, the fabric possesses some of the qualities of both fibers.

blending 1. See under BLENDED YARN. 2. See under FURS.

bliaut (blee-o') (*bliaud, bliaunt, blehant, blehand*) ∞1. Overgown worn long or knee-length by men and long by women, from 12th to early 14th c. Made with a tight-fitting bodice that laced up the sides or back; it had a full skirt attached at a low waistline; long sleeves that sometimes had PENDANT CUFFS (see under CUFFS); and was worn with a belt at the hip. 2. For men another variation was narrow-sleeved, slit from hem to knee, and often worn under a coat of chain mail.

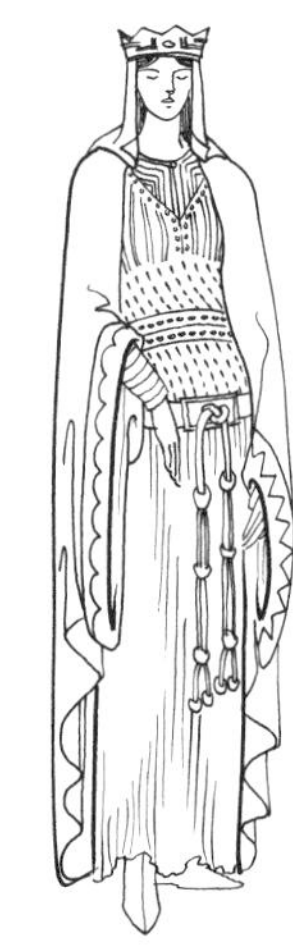
bliaut 12th century

blind eyelet See under CLOSURES.

blind stitch See under EMBROIDERIES AND SEWING STITCHES: SLIP STITCH.

bling See under HIP-HOP.

blistered See under SLASHING.

block/block pattern See under SLOPER.

block heel See under FOOTWEAR.

blocking 1. Process of shaping knitted clothing after completion or washing by drawing its outline on paper and shaping article to conform. 2. Millinery term for placing a felt or straw hood over a block of wood, then using heat or steam for desired shape.

block printing See under PRINTS, STRIPES, AND CHECKS.

blonde de fil See LACES: MIGNONETTE LACE.

blonde lace See under LACES.

bloodstone See under GEMS, GEM CUTS, AND SETTINGS.

Bloomer, Amelia Jenks See under BLOOMER COSTUME.

bloomer costume Knee-length dress worn over pants gathered at the ankle. Costume was modeled after clothing worn in health sanitariums, and adopted by women's rights advocates of the 1850s. Although she did not originate the style, Amelia Jenks Bloomer (1818–1894), writer and lecturer on women's rights, wrote favorably about and wore this costume for her lectures; thus, it was named after her. Although the style did gain acceptance as women's attire, suitable for exercising and athletic activities, it was not widely adopted. Since the 1850s, full pants gathered at the hem are still called BLOOMERS.

bloomer costume

bloomer dress See under DRESSES.

bloomers 1. See under PANTS. 2. Slang for underpants. See under UNDERGARMENTS.

bloomer shorts See under SHORTS.

bloomer swimsuit See under SWIMWEAR.

BLOUSES AND TOPS

blouse Clothing for the upper part of the body, usually softer and less tailored than a *shirt;* worn with matching or contrasting skirt, pants, suit, or jumper. The practice of wearing the same blouse with different skirts was new in the mid-19th c. Prior to then, even if dresses were made in two parts—a bodice and a skirt—both parts were generally of the same fabric and intended to be worn together. Originally, the term blouse was applied to a type of shirt worn by a member of the armed forces of the U.S. (e.g., an Army blouse or Navy middy blouse). *Blouse* first came into civilian use when the middy blouse was adopted for boys in the 1860s. Its usage in reference to women's fashion expanded when women's *shirtwaists* were introduced in the 1890s; however, that garment was more likely to be called a *waist* until the 1920s, when sportswear and suits became more fashionable, and blouses became an essential part of a woman's wardrobe. *Der.* French, *blouson,* "to blouse."

top Clothing worn as a blouse or shirt substitute with pants or a skirt mainly for sportswear, and sometimes for evening. The term comes into use in the 1930s when HALTER TOPS (see under BLOUSES AND TOPS) were popular for both sportswear and evening. A synonym for *blouse.*

bare-midriff top Top that ends below bust and bares the rib cage. Often made with strapless, halter, or tank neckline. Similar to CROPPED TOP. See under BLOUSES AND TOPS.

bare top Strapless evening bodice tightly fitted and boned.

bib blouse Blouse with high collar and an inset of contrasting color or fabric in front that has the appearance of a bib.

bib blouse

bib top Bare-back top, just covering front of body, as in, for example, the top of overalls.

bib top

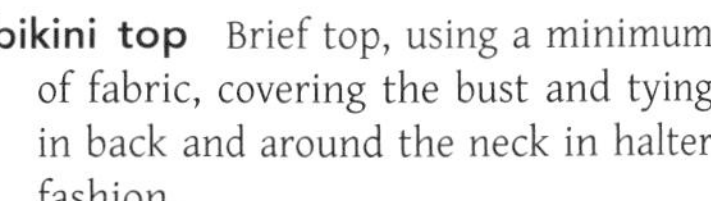
bikini top Brief top, using a minimum of fabric, covering the bust and tying in back and around the neck in halter fashion.

blouse-slip See under UNDERGARMENTS.

blousette (blooz-et′) Sleeveless blouse for wear under cardigans or suits. Popular from the 1930s to 1940s. Also see DICKEY #1.

blouson blouse (blue-zohn′) Type of OVERBLOUSE (see under BLOUSES AND TOPS) with fullness at the waist usually gathered into a band.

blouson blouse

bodyshirt See under SHIRTS: BODYSHIRT #3.

∞**bolero blouse** Long-waisted blouse with attached pieces of fabric forming a false bolero, popular for women during 1920s and 1930s.

bow blouse Blouse with band around neck that has two long ends in front that tie in a bow.

bow blouse

bustier Tight-fitting top sometimes laced similar to a corset or camisole. Used separately or for the top of a dress.

butcher boy blouse Woman's blouse, hip-length or longer, shaped like a smock, usually yoked and buttoned either front or back. Popular in 1940s, and used later for maternity blouse. *Der.* Garment worn by French butchers' delivery boys.

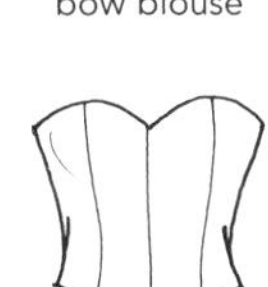
bustier

camisole top 1. Top made with straps over the shoulder, or strapless, cut straight across with elastic drawn through a heading. May hang free or have elastic at waistline. Sometimes made with built-in bra. 2. Top with spaghetti straps and low scoop neckline in front and back. *Der.* From word *camisole,* a lingerie item.

camisole top #2

capelet blouse Blouse with a double-tiered collar in the shape of a cape and sometimes made in bow-tie style with BISHOP SLEEVES (see under SHOULDERS AND SLEEVES).

chemisette Sleeveless blouse worn under a suit in early 20th c.

choli (*cholee, coli*) Blouse worn with an Indian SARI, reaching just to the ribs, made with short tight sleeves and scooped neckline. Frequently made of fine silk and sometimes trimmed with gold braid or embroidery. Worn by Hindu women, and popular in the U.S. since 1968, when bare-midriff styles became a trend. *Der.* Hindu, *coli.*

cossack blouse Long overblouse made with a high-standing collar and full sleeves, fastened asymmetrically in front, and secured with a belt or sash. Embroidery is frequently used for trim on collar, down the blouse's front, and on its cuffs. Same as *Zhivago blouse* and *Russian blouse.*

cossack blouse

cropped top Any top that is cut short to bare the midriff section. Similar to BARE-MIDRIFF TOP (see under BLOUSES AND TOPS); although, not as likely to be fitted. This top may be a cut-off shirt, T-shirt, or sweatshirt, and has been adopted as a style worn by men, as well as women and children since the 1980s.

cropped top

dandy blouse Ruffle-trimmed blouse reminiscent of DANDY styles of early 19th c.

dashiki See alphabetical listing.

diamanté top (dya-mahn-tay') Top made entirely (or partly) of sparkling sequins, beads, or paillettes. Very popular in mid-1980s. *Der.* French, "made of diamonds."

drawstring blouse Blouse that fastens at neckline with drawstring (e.g., see BLOUSES AND TOPS: GYPSY BLOUSE and PEASANT BLOUSE).

dueling/fencing blouse Blouse in the style of a European man's shirt of the 17th c., worn by both men and women, and generally made with white cotton, crepe, or jersey fabric. Tailored with notched collar, dropped shoulder, and long full sleeves gathered into tight cuffs.

flashdance top Knit shirt similar to conventional sweatshirt with sleeves cut short and neckline cut low in various styles. Both are left in unfinished state with seams overcast on right side of shirt. *Der.* From costume designs by Michael Kaplan for the movie *Flashdance,* 1983.

flip-tie blouse See under BLOUSES AND TOPS: STOCK-TIE BLOUSE.

∞**gabrielle waist** (ga-bree-el') Woman's fitted WAIST (see under BLOUSES AND TOPS) of 1870s, buttoned down the center of the front of the garment. Sometimes made with a small, fluted ruff and sleeves in a series of puffs.

∞**garibaldi shirt/blouse** (gar-ih-bawl'-dee) Red merino wool high-necked shirt of 1860s. While some examples had EPAULETS on the shoulders and were trimmed with black braid, bloused, belted, and worn with a black CRAVAT (see under TIES AND NECKCLOTHS), the name was also applied to any red blouse made with full sleeves gathered into wristband and having a small collar. *Der.* Inspired by clothes worn by Italian patriot Giuseppe Garibaldi (1807–1882) and his troops during their campaign to unite Italy in the 1840s and 1850s.

garibaldi blouse 1862

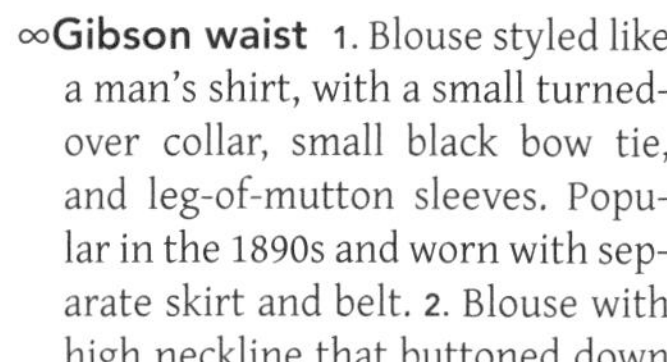

∞**Gibson waist** 1. Blouse styled like a man's shirt, with a small turned-over collar, small black bow tie, and leg-of-mutton sleeves. Popular in the 1890s and worn with separate skirt and belt. 2. Blouse with high neckline that buttoned down the back, had leg-of-mutton sleeves, and Gibson pleats. Made in LAWN, SATIN, BOBBINETTE, and other fabrics; it was elaborately decorated with lace, insertions, and tucks. *Der.* Named after Charles Dana Gibson, who created the "Gibson Girl."

gibson girl blouse, 1899

granny blouse See under BLOUSES AND TOPS: VICTORIAN BLOUSE.

granny waist Fitted bodice of the 1890s, with lace insert in front, large lace ruffles around a low neckline, and optional large lace ruffles falling over the arms from puffed sleeves. *Der.* Named for the styles worn by or associated with grandmothers of the late 19th c.

∞**guimpe** (gamp) Separate blouse worn under a low-necked dress in the 1890s, similar to a CHEMISETTE (see under BLOUSES AND TOPS).

gypsy blouse Full blouse with drawstring neckline and either short puffed or long full sleeves. Popular in the late 1960s. *Der.* Originally worn by gypsies, a nomadic people of Europe, Asia, and North America. Similar to *peasant blouse.*

halter top Top with front supported by narrow ties or straps around the back and neck, leaving the back bare.

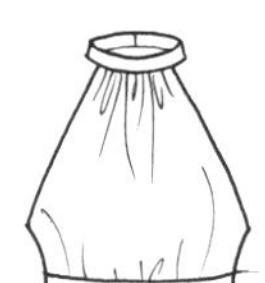
halter top

∞**hubbard blouse** Loose-fitting tunic blouse with ruffles at hem, sleeves, and neck with a cord used to pull in fullness at waist. Worn by young girls in 1880s over kilt-pleated skirt.

Indian wedding blouse Blouse with a neckline like that of a CAFTAN, having long, set-in sleeves flaring at wrist and rounded shirttails. Elaborately embroidered (by machine chain stitch) around the garment's neckline, front, hems of sleeves, and hem. Usually imported from India in a cotton fabric.

jabot blouse (zha-bo′) **1.** Back-buttoned blouse having a standing band collar with attached ruffle or jabot in center front. **2.** Front-buttoned blouse with jabot-like ruffles on either side of opening.

jumper Sailor's OVERBLOUSE or MIDDY BLOUSE (see under BLOUSES AND TOPS).

∞**martha washington waist** V-necked blouse of late 1890s with dickey that has a choker collar. It was made with a surplice front gathered at shoulder seams, draped to one side, and tied in back with a bow. Sleeves varied from full double puff to single puff coming to elbow and fitted to wrist. *Der.* For Martha Washington, wife of first U.S. president, George Washington.

maternity blouse/maternity top Overblouse that is worn by pregnant women. The earlier versions, c. 1940s, were designed to hang loosely from a yoke; by the 1980s maternity tops were styled similarly to any type of blouse, shirt, T-shirt, or top.

matinee See under BLOUSES AND TOPS: TEA JACKET.

middy blouse **1.** Slip-on blouse made with a braid-trimmed SAILOR COLLAR (see under NECKLINES AND COLLARS) and cuffs worn with a SAILOR TIE (see under TIES) slipped through a loop on blouse. Sometimes has an insignia on left sleeve. Worn in blue serge and white duck by members of the U.S. Navy and by civilian boys since the 1860s. By the 1890s it was adopted by women for lawn tennis, canoeing, boating, and yachting. In 1906, it was worn with black sateen or serge-pleated BLOOMERS (see under PANTS) as a GYMNASIUM SUIT (see under ACTIVEWEAR: GYM SUIT). Since World War I, it has been worn with KNICKERS for biking and sportswear. In 1920s, it was worn for gym classes and camping. Also see under DRESSES: PETER THOMSON DRESS. **2.** Any slip-on blouse made with a sailor collar. Also called a *nautical blouse.*

middy blouse #1 1910

nautical blouse See under BLOUSES AND TOPS: MIDDY BLOUSE.

overblouse Any blouse or top worn over the skirt or pants rather than tucked inside.

oversized top Extra-large, slip-on top made in many styles, sometimes hip-length with full sleeves.

peasant blouse Folk-style woman's blouse often referred to by national names (e.g., Romanian, Polish, or Swedish). Usually white with puffed or long raglan sleeves made with embroidered borders. Neckline is sometimes square and trimmed with embroidery, or round and made with elastic or drawstring. Also see under BLOUSES AND TOPS: GYPSY BLOUSE.

peasant blouse

∞**peek-a-boo waist** Woman's waist made of eyelet embroidery; popular in early 20th c.

peplum blouse OVERBLOUSE (see under BLOUSES AND TOPS) made in two ways: (1) with separate seam at waist to which ruffle or bias-cut circular piece is added for fullness, or (2) long and full with elasticized waistline, thus making a ruffle waistline.

pullover/pull-on blouse Any blouse that has no fasteners and pulls on over the head. Also called a *slip-on blouse.*

Russian blouse See under BLOUSES AND TOPS: COSSACK BLOUSE.

screen print top Knit top screen printed with animals, hearts, and other designs—often popular cartoon characters, pop stars, or slogans are used.

see-through blouse Blouse of transparent fabric worn by women with or without a bra or body stocking underneath.

shell Sleeveless or cap-sleeved slip-on, collarless blouse that may have one or several buttons down the back. Made in woven or knitted fabric, this classic style may be dyed to match or contrast in an ensemble with a skirt and jacket.

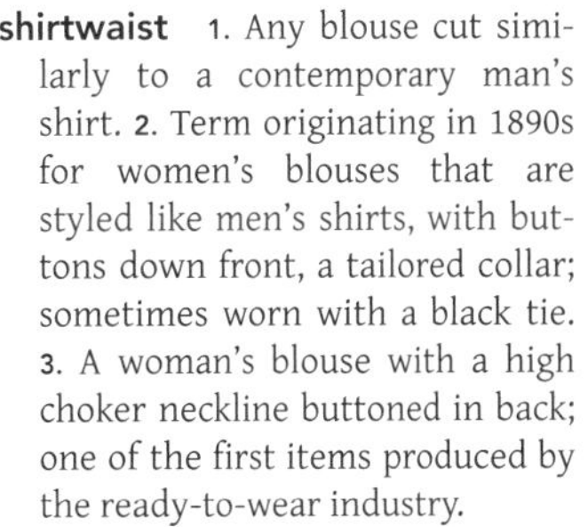

shell

shirtwaist **1.** Any blouse cut similarly to a contemporary man's shirt. **2.** Term originating in 1890s for women's blouses that are styled like men's shirts, with buttons down front, a tailored collar; sometimes worn with a black tie. **3.** A woman's blouse with a high choker neckline buttoned in back; one of the first items produced by the ready-to-wear industry.

shirtwaist #1 1943

sleeveless blouse Any style of blouse without sleeves.

slip-blouse See under UNDERGARMENTS: BLOUSE-SLIP.

slip-on blouse See under BLOUSES AND TOPS: PULLOVER BLOUSE.

smock top Full OVERBLOUSE (see under BLOUSES AND TOPS) with full sleeves, similar to a SMOCK.

squaw blouse Heavily embroidered blouse resembling PEASANT BLOUSE (see under BLOUSES AND TOPS) inspired by North American Indian styles. *Der.* White settlers' name for a North American Indian woman.

stocking bodice Knitted or shirred elastic tube pulled over woman's torso as a *strapless* top to wear with pants, shorts, or an evening skirt. Popular in the 1940s, revived in late 1960s and 1980s. By the 1990s more likely to be called a tube top.

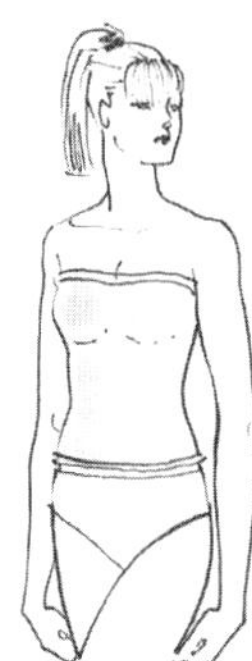
stocking bodice

stock-tie blouse Plain blouse with an ascot neckline (see under NECKLINES AND COLLARS: ASCOT). Also called *flip-tie blouse* and *stock-tie shirt.*

strapless top An elastic or stretch top made without straps. Also see under BLOUSES AND TOPS: STOCKING BODICE.

stretch top Close-fitting blouse made of stretchy knit fabric. Also see under BODY SUIT.

sweater blouse Sweater made of fine yarn and worn as a blouse, sometimes having ruffled details or dressmaker styling and worn tucked inside skirt. Worn intermittently since 1930, and particularly popular in the 1980s.

tailored blouse Any style of blouse with little or no ornamentation or trimming. Similar in style to a men's shirt.

tank top

tank top Similar to men's undershirt, with U-neckline and deep armholes shaped toward shoulder to form narrow straps. Similar to ATHLETIC SHIRT (see under UNDERGARMENTS). *Der.* From TANK SUIT, a bathing suit, known as a "tank" and worn in early indoor swimming pools (see under SWIMWEAR: TANK SWIMSUIT).

∞**tea jacket** Loose informal jacket or bodice with close-fitting back. Sometimes made with tight sleeves and loose-hanging front profusely trimmed with lace. Worn by women from late 1880s to end of 19th c., replacing the tailor-made bodice of the dress for afternoon tea. Also called *matinee.*

top See under introduction to BLOUSES AND TOPS.

torso blouse OVERBLOUSE (see under BLOUSES AND TOPS) that fits snugly and extends to hips.

trapeze top TANK TOP (see under BLOUSES AND TOPS) with a flared bottom.

tube top See under BLOUSES AND TOPS: STOCKING BODICE.

tunic blouse

tunic blouse Thigh-length, sleeved or sleeveless overblouse, worn over a skirt, slacks, or alone as a short dress. Popular in the 1940s and revived in the 1960s.

tuxedo blouse Woman's blouse styled like a man's formal shirt. There are many variations of this blouse: (a) a bib style with contrasting collar; (b) a blouse with tucked front; and (c) a blouse trimmed with vertical ruffles. A black bow tie and black coat styled like a tuxedo jacket are sometimes worn to complete the outfit.

twinset A matched set of blouses designed to be worn together; these may be made of the same or complementary fabric. The outermost blouse is usually long-sleeved with a buttoned front, while foundation blouse is styled like a shell or with a camisole top.

∞**vassar blouse** Woman's blouse worn in 1890s, similar to a peasant blouse. Had a drawstring neckline with upstanding ruffle and bouffant sleeves—either three-quarter or full-length—ending in a ruffle. Sometimes decorated with embroidery, ribbon suspender straps, or clusters of bows on the shoulders.

victorian blouse 1. Blouse inspired by late Victorian era blouses that had yokes, high necklines, and long sleeves. Sometimes trimmed with tucks, lace, insertion, and/or ruffles; they were usually white. Introduced in late 1960s as a version of the SHIRTWAIST (see under BLOUSES AND TOPS) of late Victorian era and also called *granny blouses.* 2. Front-buttoned blouse with lace-edged, high-standing collar, lace-edged yoke, and leg-of-mutton sleeves. Usually made of plaid or printed fabric.

∞**waist** BLOUSE or SHIRTWAIST (see under BLOUSES AND TOPS); term used from 1890 through the 1920s.

wifebeater Slang, originating in the early 1990s, for a plain white ATHLETIC SHIRT (see under UNDERGARMENTS) that became a fashionable women's top. *Der.* From the stereotype of working-class, violent men—as characterized in plays, films, or TV programs—who are often costumed in athletic shirts.

wrap blouse Blouse with two bias-cut front sections extended into long sash ends that are crossed and wrapped around waist. Worn in mid-1960s and revived in 1980s.

wrapped top Diagonal piece of fabric, about 1½ to 2 yards long and 1 yard wide, worn folded in half and wrapped around the body with ends tied in front to make a strapless top. Two long ends hang down at waist. May be stitched to front of shorts to make rompers or attached to pants to make a jumpsuit.

∞**yoke blouse** Woman's waist or blouse, worn from mid-1860s to 1890s, with square yoke in front and back outlined with a ruffle. Also has fullness below yoke, elastic at waist, and a ruffle below waist or a waistband. Also called a *yoke waist* or *yoke shirtwaist.*

Zhivago blouse (zhi-vah'-go) Men's or women's blouse style, inspired by the 1965 film *Dr. Zhivago.* Same as COSSACK or *Russian blouse.* See under BLOUSES AND TOPS.

blouse coat See under COATS AND JACKETS.

∞**blouse dress** Boys' or girls' dress of 1870s and 1880s made with a BLOUSON BLOUSE type top (see under BLOUSES AND TOPS) and a low waistline. Usually the skirt was pleated and short. Also called a *blouse costume*. For later versions, see under DRESSES: FRENCH DRESS.

blouse-slip/blouse-top See under UNDERGARMENTS.

blousette See under BLOUSES AND TOPS.

blouson See under BLOUSES AND TOPS: BLOUSON BLOUSE; COATS AND JACKETS: BLOUSON JACKET; DRESSES: BLOUSON DRESS; and SWIMWEAR: BLOUSON SWIMSUIT.

blouson dress See under DRESSES.

blucher/blucher bal See under FOOTWEAR.

blue-aproned men English tradesmen of 16th to 18th c. who were recognized by their aprons of blue fabric—a color not worn by the upper classes. Also see under BLUE COAT.

blue billy See under SCARVES.

bluebonnet See under HEADWEAR.

∞**blue coat** 1. A bluecoat worn by apprentices and servants from the late 16th c. to late 17th c. Blue garments, typically associated with the lower class, were not generally worn by gentlemen. Also see under BLUE-APRONED MEN and GREEN-APRONED MEN. 2. Slang for a policeman.

blue fox See under FURS.

blue jeans See under PANTS.

blue pelt See under FURS.

boa See under SCARVES.

board shorts See under SHORTS and SWIMWEAR.

boarded finish See under LEATHERS.

boater See under HEADWEAR.

boater tie See under TIES.

boating shoe See under FOOTWEAR.

boat neckline See under NECKLINES AND COLLARS: BATEAU.

bob See under HAIRSTYLES.

bobbinet †1. A machine-made net fabric with hexagonal meshes. 2. See under LACES.

bobbin lace See under introduction to LACES.

bobby pin See under HAIR ACCESSORIES.

bobby's hat See under HEADWEAR.

bobby socks See under HOSIERY.

∞**bobby soxer** (slang) Teenager of the 1940s who followed current fashion trends such as bobby socks and saddle shoes. (See under HOSIERY: BOBBY SOCKS and FOOTWEAR: SADDLE SHOES.)

bobtailed coat See under COATS AND JACKETS.

bob-wig See under WIGS AND HAIRPIECES.

bodice 1. The upper part of a woman's dress, often close-fitting. Synonyms: *body, corsage*. 2. See under UNDERGARMENTS: PAIR OF BODIES.

∞**bodice en coeur** (bod'-ees on cur) Upper part of a woman's evening dress of the mid 19th c. that has a low, heart-shaped neckline. Also called *Marquise bodice* (mar-kees' bod-iss).

bodies Garment silhouettes that are used repeatedly, season after season, minimizing product development costs by allowing manufacturers to modify existing patterns.

bodkin 1. Long, flat needle with blunt end used to string elastic and ribbon through eyelet INSERTION, WAISTBANDS, or HEADINGS (see under CLOTHING CONSTRUCTION DETAILS). ∞2. 16th to 19th c.: long hairpin used by women. 3. Instrument for punching holes in leather or fabric.

bodkin beard See under BEARD.

body 1. *adj.* Describes apparel that fits the body closely. Examples: body stocking, body shirt. 2. See under BODICE #1. †3. *n.* Quality of a fabric implying firmness, both stiffness and flexibility.

body boot See under FOOTWEAR.

body briefer See under UNDERGARMENTS.

body clothes Tightly fitted clothes with built-in comfort, e.g., stretch jeans, leotards, body stockings, bodysuits made of basic yarns combined with elastomeric fibers (see under ELASTOMERS) to give stretch.

body coat See under COATS AND JACKETS.

body hose See under BODY STOCKING.

body jewelry Highly decorative accessories designed to be worn on all parts of the body, face, and head, as well as over body stockings or other clothing. Examples include: items which may be pasted on, and elaborate pieces of metal jewelry and decorative chains that may be attached to a cape, dress, cap, pant, or coat, or a scarf made of loose strands of pearls. Popular in late 1960s. Designed by Bill Smith, Kenneth J. Lane, and Paco Rabanne. Also see under UNDERGARMENTS: CADORO BRA and JEWELRY: BODY PIERCING.

body painting Fad of late 1960s that involved painting face and body with fantasy flowers, geometric shapes, and other designs. See under TATTOO and CASTE MARK.

body piercing See under JEWELRY.

bodyshaper pantyhose See under HOSIERY: PANTYHOSE.

bodyshapers See under UNDERGARMENTS.

bodyshirt See under BODYSUIT and SHIRTS.

body shorts See under SHORTS.

body stocking Introduced in early 1960s as a one-piece, knitted body garment with legs and feet, with or without sleeves. In 1964, Warner's won a Coty Fashion Award for a filmy nude-colored Lycra tricot-knit stretch garment designed with shoulder straps and no legs. Legless variety is also known as *bodysuit, body shirt*, or *body sweater*. When designed as a control undergarment, called BODY BRIEFER (see under UNDERGARMENTS).

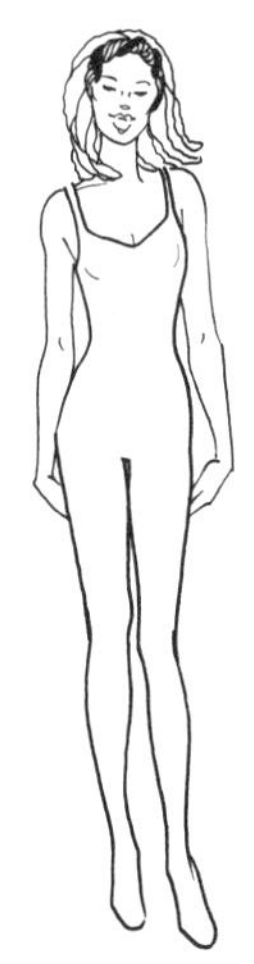
body stocking

bodysuit 1. One-piece, fitted garment without legs and with a snap crotch. Made in a variety of plain, patterned, or ribbed knits. Made sleeveless or with long or short sleeves, and with varying styles of collars and necklines. Sometimes substitutes for a blouse or sweater. Also called a *body shirt* or *body sweater*. 2. See under UNDERGARMENTS. 3. In 1986, Donna Karan changed the concept of the bodysuit silhouette somewhat to include "blouse" or "shirt" styles in a variety of fabrics, as well as suede and leather.

bodysuit #1

body sweater See under BODY STOCKING.

body wave See under HAIRSTYLES: PERMANENT WAVE.

bohemian lace See under LACES.

boho *adj.* Short for *bohemian*. Descriptive of persons having an unconventional lifestyle, such as gypsies in the region of Bohemia (the Western side of the Czech Republic). Styles characterized as boho are made in vibrant colors, softly flowing fabrics, and combinations of variously patterned fabrics.

boiled shirt See under SHIRTS: FORMAL SHIRT #3.

boiled wool Contemporary name for FULLED WOOL.

boiler suit Synonym for COVERALL.

Bokhara shawl See under CAPES, CLOAKS, AND SHAWLS.

bold look Descriptive of menswear style of the late 1940s and 1950s. Not a radical change in style but rather a continuation of the ENGLISH DRAPE SUIT, with greater emphasis on coordination among the shirt, accessories, and the suit.

boldini See under HAIRSTYLES.

bolero (bo-lehr′-o) 1. See under COATS AND JACKETS. 2. *adj.* Describes garments derived from or inspired by an above-the-waist jacket that was named for a dance called the "bolero." See under BLOUSES AND TOPS: BOLERO BLOUSE; CAPES, CLOAKS, AND SHAWLS: BOLERO CAPE; COATS AND JACKETS: BOLERO; HEADWEAR: BOLERO TOQUE; and SWEATERS: BOLERO SWEATER.

bolero costume See under DRESSES.

bollinger See under HEADWEAR.

bolo tie See under TIES.

bolster collar See under NECKLINES AND COLLARS.

bolton thumb See under GLOVES AND GLOVE CONSTRUCTION.

∞**bombast** Stuffing material used in apparel, especially TRUNK HOSE, in the 16th and 17th c. It could consist of such diverse materials as horsehair, wool, rags, flax, cotton, or bran.

bomber jacket See under COATS AND JACKETS: FLIGHT JACKET.

bonaid See under HEADWEAR: BLUEBONNET.

Bonaparte, Napoleon (1769–1821) Napoleon I, Emperor of France, 1804–1815. He encouraged use of French textiles and established military fashions for men, e.g., tight cream-colored breeches, BICORNE hat (see under HEADWEAR), high-rolled, collared jackets. His first wife, the Empress Josephine, influenced dress and accessory styles of the Empire period, most notably cashmere shawls. Also see under NECKLINES AND COLLARS: NAPOLEONIC COLLAR.

bondage apparel Belts, arm binders, blindfolds, body harnesses, chastity belts, collars, gags, hoods, and leashes worn by those who engage in the act of being restrained for pleasure.

bonding The process by which two or more pieces of fabric are joined together to make a composite. Used to increase opacity or insulation or to modify the opposite side of a fabric.

bone lace See under LACES.

boned foundation See under UNDERGARMENTS.

bones See under CLOTHING CONSTRUCTION DETAILS: STAY #1.

bongrace See under HEADWEAR.

bonnaz embroidery See under EMBROIDERIES AND SEWING STITCHES.

bonnet See under HEADWEAR.

bonnet à bec See under HEADWEAR.

bonnet babet See under HEADWEAR: BABET BONNET.

bonnet en papillon See under HEADWEAR: BONNET À BEC.

bonnet rouge See under HEADWEAR.

Bonnie and Clyde The 1967 film that inspired styles that were essentially a revival of the 1930s silhouette, incorporating a late-1960s, above-the-knee skirt length. Characteristic styles included: three-piece suit with V-neck, long waistline, and unbuttoned jacket; pinstriped gangster suits; and the beret worn to side of the head. Costumes were designed by Theadora Van Runkle.

styles inspired by *Bonnie and Clyde* film

book bag See under HANDBAGS AND RELATED ACCESSORIES.

bookbinder print See under PRINTS, STRIPES, AND CHECKS.

boot 1. See under FOOTWEAR. 2. See under HOSIERY.

boot blow-up Plastic or rubber boot form inserted to retain shape when boots are not being worn.

boot bracelet See under JEWELRY.

boot cuff See under CUFFS.

boot-cut pants See under PANTS.

bootee/bootie See under FOOTWEAR.

boot garters See under FOOTWEAR.

boot hook See under FOOTWEAR.

boot hose See under HOSIERY.

boot hose tops See under HOSIERY: BOOT HOSE.

boot jack Device, introduced in the 18th c., that is used to aid an individual in removing his/her boots.

bootlace tie See under TIES: STRING TIE.

boot leg See PANTS: BOOT CUT.

boots See under FOOTWEAR.

boot sleeve See under SHOULDERS AND SLEEVES.

boot stocking See under HOSIERY: BOOT HOSE.

boot strap See under FOOTWEAR: BOOT HOOK #1.

Borazon® See under GEMS, GEM CUTS, AND SETTINGS.

bord See under GLOVES AND GLOVE CONSTRUCTION: BANDELET.

border 1. Trimming at edge, or just above edge, on an item of apparel or an accessory. 2. Decorative woven cords or stripes in handkerchiefs. 3. Decorative edge on fabric or edge used for identification purposes.

border print See under PRINTS, STRIPES, AND CHECKS.

borders See under HEADWEAR: BILLIMENT.

bosom 1. Synonym for the human breast. 2. That part of a garment that covers the breast.

∞**bosom bottles** Tiny bottles holding water, worn by ladies in the latter half of 18th c. to keep small bouquets of flowers fresh. Bottle was formed like a small vial that could be fastened to shoulder or tucked into the neckline of dress.

∞**bosom flowers** Artificial flowers worn by men and women in the 18th c., usually with full evening dress. Also worn by the dandies in daytime. Also see under BOUTONNIERE and CORSAGE.

bosom friends See under FALSIES.

bosom knot See under BREASTKNOT.

bosom shirt See under SHIRTS.

bosses See under HEADWEAR.

boteh See under CAPES, CLOAKS, AND SHAWLS: CASHMERE SHAWL.

botews See under FOOTWEAR: BUSKINS #2.

bottine See under FOOTWEAR.

bottom-up theory of fashion change The idea that some fashion changes result from the adoption by older or more affluent individuals of styles that originated with groups or individuals who are young, less affluent, or from the counterculture. Compare with TRICKLE-DOWN THEORY OF FASHION CHANGE.

†**bottomweight** Fabric suitable for such garments as pants, skirts, winter dresses, and lightweight jackets.

bouchette See under ARMOR.

bouclé (boo-klay') †1. A rough, curly, knotted yarn made by twisting together two fine foundation threads with a thicker yarn that is delivered in such a way as to cause the thick yarn to twist up on the surface. 2. Any fabric made with these yarns. *Der.* French for *buckle* or *curl.*

boudoir cap See under HEADWEAR.

boudoir slipper See under FOOTWEAR.

bouffant (boo-fahn′) (French) Full or puffed. Also used in English (boo-fahnt′) to describe apparel or hairstyles that are full or puffed out. See under DRESSES: BOUFFANT DRESS; HAIRSTYLES: BOUFFANT; SCARVES: BUFFON; SHOULDERS AND SLEEVES: BOUFFANT MÉCANIQUE; SKIRTS: BOUFFANT SKIRT; and UNDERGARMENTS: BOUFFANT PETTICOAT.

bouffant dress See under DRESSES.

boulevard heel See under FOOTWEAR.

boulogne hose See under TRUNK HOSE.

bound See under CLOTHING CONSTRUCTION DETAILS.

bound buttonhole See under CLOSURES.

bound pocket See under POCKETS.

bound seam See under CLOTHING CONSTRUCTION DETAILS.

Bourbon hat See under HEADWEAR.

bourbon lock See under HAIRSTYLES: LOVE LOCK.

bourdon lace See under LACES.

bournouse See under CAPES, CLOAKS, AND SHAWLS: BURNOOSE.

bourrelet (boor-lay′) **1.** See under HEADWEAR. **2.** Stuffed, rolled trimming. **3.** See under UNDERGARMENTS: BUM ROLL.

bourse (boorce) **1.** See under HANDBAGS AND RELATED ACCESSORIES. **2.** See under WIGS AND HAIRPIECES.

boutique (boo-teek′) Small shop selling a variety of merchandise including dresses, jewelry, accessories, antique bibelots, or objets d'art. Ever since Parisian designer Lucien Lelong opened his *Boutique de la Maison Couture* in 1929, haute couture designers have taken up the practice of selling a variety of designer label merchandise in boutiques. The term has been applied to small shops everywhere since the 1950s; now such shops are often contained within large department stores.

boutonnière (boo-ton-yair′) **1.** Flower worn in lapel buttonhole. The practice was initiated by wealthy men about town and has been popular for formal functions since the 19th c. **2.** Small bouquet, or flower, worn by women on left shoulder or lapel. *Der.* French, "buttonhole."

bow **1.** A knot, usually having two loops and two ends—often of a narrow fabric, ribbon, or string—used for sashes, neckties, or decorative trim. Also called a *bow knot*. **2.** *adj.* Applied to garments for which a bow is an important element. See under BLOUSES AND TOPS: BOW BLOUSE; NECKLINES AND COLLARS: BOW COLLAR; and TIES: BOW TIE. **3.** See under EYEWEAR: TEMPLE.

Bow, Clara American film star of 1920s, called the "It Girl" in 1926. A round-eyed beauty with small cupid's-bow lips, she typified sex appeal and inspired several hats of the late 1920s. See under HEADWEAR: CLARA BOW HAT.

bow knot See under BOW #1.

bowl crop See under HAIRSTYLES.

bowl cut See under HAIRSTYLES.

bowler See under HEADWEAR: DERBY.

bowling *adj.* Describes apparel designed for the sport of bowling or influenced by apparel used for bowling, as played in a bowling alley. For examples of special clothing worn, see under SHIRTS and FOOTWEAR.

bowling bag See under HANDBAGS AND RELATED ACCESSORIES.

box bag See under HANDBAGS AND RELATED ACCESSORIES.

∞**box bottoms** Men's close-fitting, below-the-knee breeches made with stiffened lining; worn in 19th c.

box calf See under LEATHERS.

box cape See under CAPES, CLOAKS, AND SHAWLS.

box clutch see under HANDBAGS AND RELATED ACCESSORIES: BOX BAG.

box coat See under COATS AND JACKETS.

boxer *adj.* Describes undergarments or shorts that are styled similarly to those garments worn for sport of boxing. See examples under SHORTS, SWIMWEAR, and UNDERGARMENTS.

boxer bag see under HANDBAGS AND RELATED ACCESSORIES.

boxes See under FOOTWEAR: GALOSHES.

box jacket See under COATS AND JACKETS.

box pleat See under CLOTHING CONSTRUCTION DETAILS and SKIRTS.

boy briefs See under UNDERGARMENTS.

boy coat See under COATS AND JACKETS.

boyfriend jeans/pants See under PANTS.

boyish bob See under HAIRSTYLES.

boy-leg See under LENGTHS.

boy shorts swimsuit See under SWIMWEAR.

boys' sizes Sizes 8 to 20, each size available in slim, regular, and husky. Sizes are determined by height, weight, and circumference of chest and waist.

bra See under UNDERGARMENTS.

∞**bracae** (brak′-ay) Latin word for loose-fitting pants or hose worn by northern European tribes. Adopted for use by Roman soldiers when fighting in cold, northern regions. Called *broc* by Anglo-Saxons. See under BRAIES.

bracelet 1. Ornament usually worn on the arm or wrist. See under JEWELRY. 2. *adj.* Describes elements of apparel that bear some relationship in length, appearance, or function to a bracelet. See under HANDBAGS AND RELATED ACCESSORIES: BRACELET BAG; FOOTWEAR: BRACELET-TIE SHOE; GLOVES AND GLOVE CONSTRUCTION: BRACELET LENGTH; SHOULDERS AND SLEEVES: BRACELET SLEEVE; and WATCHES: BRACELET WATCH.

bracelet ring See under JEWELRY: SLAVE BRACELET.

braces (British usage) Suspenders, first worn about 1787. Also called *gallowses.*

∞**bractiate** Pin used to fasten garments from 6th to mid-8th c.

bra cups See under UNDERGARMENTS.

braguette See under ARMOR: BRAYETTE.

BRAIDS

braid 1. *n.* Narrow woven band for use as trimming, binding, or for outlining lace and embroidery. 2. *v.* To plait or interweave strands of hair, fabric, or straw. 3. See under HAIRSTYLES.

ball fringe Type of braid with little fuzzy balls suspended at regular intervals. Used on beach ponchos and robes in the 1950s and fashionable for dress trimming in the late 1870s and 1880s. Currently, more likely to be used on drapes and other household textiles.

coronation braid Firmly woven mercerized cord braid, alternately wide and narrow, used to outline a pattern in embroidery or lace. Also used for COUCHING (see under EMBROIDERIES AND SEWING STITCHES).

diamanté braid (dya-mahn-tay') Fake sparkling jewels, e.g., rhinestones, sewn on strips of fabric. Used as trimming on dresses, blouses, evening wear, etc. *Der.* French, "set with diamonds."

embroidered braid Tape with decorative motifs embroidered at regular intervals used for trimming.

galloon 1. Narrow tape or braid made of cotton, silk, rayon, wool, or manufactured fibers (sometimes with metallic threads added) used for trimming. 2. Double-edged lace made in various widths. 3. Double-edged, wide braid frequently made of gold or metallic yarn, with jewels which may be spaced at regular intervals. A highly decorative rich braid. *Der.* French, *galon*, "braid."

gimp Braid made from heavy core yarn, arranged in a pattern, and stitched to create a raised effect.

hercules braid Worsted braid, heavily corded, and ½" to 4" in width; several widths often used together.

horsehair braid Permanently stiff, coarse braid originally made from horsehair; now made from nylon. Uses: stiffening bouffant skirts at the hemline and in millinery.

lacet Braid of silk or cotton woven in various widths, frequently with looped edges. Uses: for trimming and edging, and sometimes combined with crochet work or tatting.

ladder braid Braid with open stitches crossed by bars, creating a ladderlike effect, made with a bobbin.

middy braid Narrow, flat, white braid originally used to trim collars and cuffs on middy blouses and sailor collars.

military braid Flat, ribbed, worsted, or gold braid sometimes in twill weave in various widths. Used to designate rank on military uniforms.

rapolin (rap'-o-lin) Swiss millinery braid made in triple rows and having an uneven surface.

rat-tail braid Silk braid of tubular shape used for trimming.

rice braid Firmly woven, highly mercerized braid with wide parts alternating with narrow, to give the appearance of grains of rice. Used for trimming. Similar to a CORONATION BRAID. See under BRAIDS: CORONATION BRAID.

rickrack Braids of varying widths that are usually made of cotton or blends and have a zigzag form.

russian braid See under BRAIDS: SOUTACHE BRAID.

soutache braid (soo-tash') Narrow, flat, decorative braid. Used for borders and for all-over ornamental patterns. Also called *Russian braid. Der.* Hungarian, *sujtas*, "flat trimming braid."

---

braided belt See under BELTS.

braie girdle See under BREECH GIRDLE.

∞**braies** Medieval term, from which the word BREECHES derives, for loose-fitting pants that were either full-, knee-length, or short and were worn by men as an undergarment. Earlier forms were called *bracae* by the Romans and *broc* by the Anglo-Saxons.

braies

brand 1. *n.* A manufacturer or distributor-assigned name, mark, or label assigned to a product in order to encourage consumer-recognition of the product. Some brands are trademarked (see under TRADEMARK) but others are not. **Branding** is the process of planning the direction, inspiration, and energy that a brand represents. Branding has become so much a part of contemporary merchandising that a variety of terms have been developed to describe various types of brands. These include but are not limited to (1) **aspirational brands** Higher-priced labels or looks from which a brand takes inspiration in part because its target audience admires the label or look but for economic reasons they cannot afford to buy it. (2) **benchmark brands** Competing labels and/or stores that share a target customer, particularly those whose goods, services, and processes are the best performing in their class. (3) **exclusive brands** The result of a licensing arrangement between a brand owner and a retail distribution partner, giving the retailer all rights to distribute product under that brand name in a particular product category or categories. (4) **lifestyle brand** A brand offering that goes beyond the initial apparel product line to include other product categories. (5) **brand equity** A corporate asset for the owners of a brand or label that reflects consumers' willingness to pay more for the branded product than a similar generic product and influences strategies related to brand extensions. (6) **brand image** A consumer's set of assumptions and feelings about products and/or services provided under a brand name. (7) **brand extension** Refers to the practice of expanding a brand's reach into the consumer market by launching new product categories under a successful brand name. Other aspects of brand development can include (8) **brand portfolio** A collection of multiple brands managed by a single company but not necessarily recognized by consumers as related (e.g., brands owned by Jones Group, Inc.). (9) **brand umbrella** A collection of multiple brands managed by a single company marketed so that consumers understand that they are related in promise and quality (e.g., Gap, Old Navy, and Banana Republic, or all of the Kohl's house brands). (10) **co-branding** A strategy in which an exclusive collection of products is designed by a branded product developer or designer for a particular retailer, reflecting a partnership between them for a specified length of time. **2.** *adj.* Having an assigned name, mark, or label, as in "brand merchandise."

brand equity See under BRAND.

brand extension See under BRAND.

brand image See under BRAND.

brand portfolio See under BRAND.

brand umbrella See under BRAND.

branding See under BRAND.

brandenburg See under COATS AND JACKETS.

brandenburgs See under CLOSURES: FROGS.

brand loyalty Consumer preference for a particular brand of merchandise.

†**brand-name fiber** Fiber sold under a specific TRADEMARK or TRADE NAME (e.g., Lycra®).

bra-shift See under DRESSES.

bra-slip See under UNDERGARMENTS.

brassart (brass'-are) ∞**1.** See under ARMOR. **2.** See under SHOULDERS AND SLEEVES. **3.** Wide white silk ribbon bow with streamers worn by first communicants. ∞**4.** 19th-c: mourning band of black cloth worn on upper left arm. ∞**5.** Ribbon bow worn in the 19th c. on the elbow of an evening dress.

brass button See under CLOSURES.

brassiere See under UNDERGARMENTS: BRA.

bratt See under CAPES, CLOAKS, AND SHAWLS.

brayette See under ARMOR.

bray girdle See under BREECH GIRDLE.

Brazilian emerald See under GEMS, GEM CUTS, AND SETTINGS.

Brazilian peridot See under GEMS, GEM CUTS, AND SETTINGS.

Brazilian sapphire See under GEMS, GEM CUTS, AND SETTINGS.

breadth See under ASSORTMENT.

breaker pants See under PANTS.

breakfast cap See under MORNING CAP.

breakfast coat See under SLEEPWEAR AND LOUNGEWEAR.

breakfast wrapper See under ROBE DE CHAMBRE.

breakline See under NECKLINES AND COLLARS.

breast See under FOOTWEAR: HEEL.

breasted heel See under FOOTWEAR.

breast hook See under STAY HOOK.

breast kerchief See under SCARVES.

∞**breast knot** Bunch of ribbons or ribbon bow worn at bosom of woman's dress in 18th and early 19th c. Also called *bosom knot.*

breastplate See under JEWELRY.

breast pocket See under POCKETS.

breasts See under CLOSURES.

breech/breeches **1.** Garment that extends from the waist to just below the knee, where it fastens with a buckle or buttons. Traditionally worn by men, breeches were replaced by full-length PANTS in the early 19th c. By the latter part of the 19th c., garments cut like breeches were more likely to be referred to as KNICKERS. **2.** Colloquial term that can refer to any two-legged garment covering the lower half of the body. Sometimes called *britches.* ∞**3.** Derived

breeches #1

from the word BRAIES, and used in the 14th to 16th c. to refer to the upper part of hose that fit the trunk of the body, and in the 16th c. as synonymous with TRUNK HOSE or HOSE.

breech belt Waistband of the BREECH or BREECHES. Also see under BREECH GIRDLE.

breechcloth/breechclout See under LOIN CLOTH.

∞**breech girdle** Belt or string pulled through wide hem at top of breech in drawstring fashion—at waist or a little below. Worn from 13th to 15th c. by men. Also called *braie girdle, bray girdle, bregirdle*.

breeching A ritual carried out in Renaissance in England when a boy of age 5 or 6 was given his first pair of breeches.

bregirdle See under BREECH GIRDLE.

bretelles 1. An ornamental trimming on women's dresses that consists of REVERS (see under NECKLINES AND COLLARS) or ruffles that extend in a diagonal line from the outer edge of the shoulder to the waist at or close to the center of the front and back. Especially popular from 1814 to 1835. Synonym: *suspender trimming*. 2. Decorative bands with the appearance of functional straps or suspenders that extend from the waist in back over the shoulders to the waist in front. *Der.* French, "suspenders."

bretelles #1

breton See under HEADWEAR.

breton costume See under COATS AND JACKETS: BRETON JACKET.

breton jacket See under COATS AND JACKETS.

breton lace See under LACES.

breton work See under EMBROIDERIES AND SEWING STITCHES.

brick stitch/brick work See under EMBROIDERIES AND STITCHES.

bridal Adjective used to describe clothing and accessories worn by a bride at a wedding. See under HEADWEAR: BRIDAL VEIL; LACES: BRIDAL LACE; and JEWELRY: BRIDAL SET.

bridal dress See under DRESSES: WEDDING DRESS.

∞**bride lace** Blue ribbon used in 16th and 17th c. to tie sprigs of rosemary given as wedding favors to the arm; later used on hats.

brides ∞1. In the 1830s and 1840s, name applied to ribbons attached to the inside brim of a bonnet or broad-brimmed hat that were loosely tied or hung free. Sometimes, by extension, refers to the bonnet itself. 2. See under introduction to LACES.

bride's garter See under WEDDING GARTER.

bridesmaid's dress See under DRESSES.

bridge jewelry See under JEWELRY.

bridge line A line at the upper end of the apparel price range that is made with fewer details and less expensive fabrics than designer clothing. See under APPAREL PRICE RANGES.

bridge market A price point that falls between BETTER MARKET and DESIGNER MARKET (similar in price to CONTEMPORARY DESIGNER MARKET), with fabrication and detailing to match that price point.

∞**bridles** Strings attached to mobcap for tying under the chin in the 18th c. Also called *kissing strings*.

bridle bag See under HANDBAGS AND RELATED ACCESSORIES.

briefcase See under HANDBAGS AND RELATED ACCESSORIES.

briefers See under SWIMWEAR.

briefs See under UNDERGARMENTS.

brigadier wig See under WIGS AND HAIRPIECES: MAJOR WIG.

brilliant cut See under GEMS, GEM CUTS, AND SETTINGS.

brim See under HEADWEAR.

britches See under BREECHES #2.

British *adj.* 1. Descriptive of styles originating in Great Britain, and also often referred to by the following names: *London look* and *Savile Row look*. 2. Conservative, elegant look for men reflecting the influence of London tailors of Savile Row, which included narrow shoulders, three-button suit coats with narrow lapels, and narrow trousers without cuffs popular in the 1960s. 3. Contemporary men's wear influenced by London tailors. Many of the finest men's custom tailoring shops are located on Savile Row, a street in London's West End. They have catered to a wealthy international clientele with quality and conservative men's apparel ever since Henry Poole & Co. opened in 1846.

British warm See under COATS AND JACKETS.

brittany work See under EMBROIDERIES AND SEWING STITCHES: BRETON WORK.

broadbrim See under HEADWEAR.

†**broadcloth** 1. Closely woven, plain-weave fabric with a fine rib in the crosswise direction. Usually made from cotton or cotton blends but can also be made of other fibers. 2. Wool or wool-blend fabric made in plain or twill weave with a napped (brushed) surface that is brushed in one direction.

broad-stitched seam See under CLOTHING CONSTRUCTION DETAILS.

broadtail lamb See under FURS.

broc See under BRAIES.

†brocade A heavy fabric with a complex, raised pattern that is woven on a JACQUARD loom. Electronic or mechanical controls in this loom can manipulate yarns to combine many different types of weaves in a single fabric. Often made with decorative and lustrous yarns, the resulting fabric is especially suitable for evening and formal wear.

brocade embroidery See under EMBROIDERIES AND SEWING STITCHES.

†brocatelle Medium-weight dress fabric woven on a jacquard loom with a pattern that stands out in high relief giving a blistered effect. Some fabrics give the appearance of being quilted. Made of filament yarns on its face, with cotton yarns in the backing.

broché See under CAPES, CLOAKS, AND SHAWLS.

brodekin/brodkin/brotiken See under FOOTWEAR.

broderie anglaise See under EMBROIDERIES AND SEWING STITCHES: MADEIRA EMBROIDERY.

broderie russe See under EMBROIDERIES AND SEWING STITCHES: RUSSIAN EMBROIDERY.

brogan See under FOOTWEAR.

brogue See under FOOTWEAR.

broken hat See under HEADWEAR: CHAPEAU BRAS.

broken twill weave See under HERRINGBONE WEAVE.

broker A person—frequently called a *middleman*—who acts as an intermediary in business deals between the retailer and the manufacturer.

bronx jacket See under COATS AND JACKETS: PERFECTO JACKET.

bronzed leather See under LEATHERS.

brooch See under JEWELRY: PIN.

Brooks Brothers A New York specialty store, originally for men, founded in 1818. Known for men's classic styles. Women's classics, including tailored suits, shirts with button-down collars, and tailored skirts, were added to the Brooks Brothers products in 1949. Currently the store and its branches sell classic clothes in stores and online for both men and women.

broomstick skirt See under SKIRTS.

brow band See under HEADWEAR.

brown belt See under ACTIVEWEAR: KARATE SUIT.

brown George See under WIGS AND HAIRPIECES.

Bruce tartan See under PLAIDS AND TARTANS.

bruges lace See under LACES.

Brummell, Beau See under BEAU BRUMMELL.

brummell bodice See under UNDERGARMENTS.

brunch coat See under SLEEPWEAR AND LOUNGEWEAR.

∞brunswick Close-fitting riding coatdress with mannish collar worn by women in 18th c. *Der.* Said to have originated in Brunswick, Germany.

brunswick gown See under SACK #1.

brush See under FURS.

brush cut See under HAIRSTYLES: CREW CUT.

brush-dyeing See under FURS and LEATHERS.

†brushed *adj.* Woven or knitted fabrics that have had fibers pulled or brushed up to the surface to create a soft texture or nap.

brussels lace See under LACES.

brussels net See under LACES.

brutus head/wig See under HAIRSTYLES.

buba See under DRESSES.

bubble 1. *adj.* Describes apparel or hairstyles with a balloon-like shape. See under CAPES, CLOAKS, AND SHAWLS: BUBBLE CAPE; HAIRSTYLES: BUBBLE CURLS; HEADWEAR: BUBBLE HAT; JEWELRY: BUBBLE BRACELET; SLEEPWEAR AND LOUNGEWEAR: BUBBLE COVER-UP; and SKIRTS: BUBBLE SKIRT. 2. *n.* Child's garment with short or long lengths that are slightly balloon-shaped.

bubble #2

bubble beret See under HEADWEAR: BERET.

bubble bob See under HAIRSTYLES: BEEHIVE.

bubble dress See under DRESSES.

bubble-up theory of fashion change See under BOTTOM-UP THEORY OF FASHION CHANGE.

Buchanan tartan See under PLAIDS AND TARTANS.

buck A piece of equipment (for pressing) that is shaped and padded as a base for use in steam-pressing apparel.

bucket bag See under HANDBAGS AND RELATED ACCESSORIES.

bucket hat See under HEADWEAR.

bucket-top boot See under FOOTWEAR: FRENCH-FALL BOOT.

buckingham/buckinghamshire lace See under LACES.

buckle See under CLOSURES.

buckled jumper See under JUMPERS.

buckled wig See under WIGS AND HAIRPIECES.

buckles d'artois See under CLOSURES.

buck oxford See under FOOTWEAR.

†buckram Loosely woven, heavily sized fabric in a plain weave used for stiffening. Similar to crinoline but heavier and much stiffer. Sizing will wash out, making fabric unsuitable for washable garments. *Der.* From costly material made in Bukhara, Uzbekistan.

bucksain See under COATS AND JACKETS.

buckskin/buckskins 1. See under LEATHERS. ∞2. Referred to buckskin gloves, breeches, or riding gaiters between the 15th and 19th c.

buckskin jacket See under COATS AND JACKETS.

buckskin jumper See under JUMPERS.

buckskin vest See under VESTS.

bucky pelts See under FURS.

budget See under HANDBAGS AND RELATED ACCESSORIES.

budget goods See under APPAREL PRICE RANGES.

budget market The low end of the apparel pricing spectrum. Also called MASS MARKET.

buffalo checks See under PRINTS, STRIPES, AND CHECKS.

buff coat See under COATS AND JACKETS.

buffing See under introduction to LEATHERS.

buffins, pair of See under TRUNK HOSE.

buff jerkin See under COATS AND JACKETS: BUFF COAT.

buffon See under SCARVES.

bug-eyed glasses See under EYEWEAR.

bugle beads See under JEWELRY.

bugle chain See under CHAIN.

built-in bra See under UNDERGARMENTS.

built-up heel See under FOOTWEAR: STACKED HEEL.

built-up slip See under UNDERGARMENTS.

built-up straps Shoulder straps constructed in continuous curve as part of garment, usually used for a slip or swimsuit.

∞bulgare pleat (bool'-gar pleet) Double box pleats kept in place with elastic on inside of skirt; used in the mid-1870s.

†bulky 1. *adj.* Describes yarns or fabrics made with yarns that have been crimped, curled, or otherwise treated to make them larger and softer. 2. *adj.* Describes anything that is exceptionally large.

bulldog toe See under FOOTWEAR.

bulletproof jacket See under COATS AND JACKETS.

bull head See under HAIRSTYLE.

bullion See under EMBROIDERIES AND SEWING STITCHES and LACES.

bullion-hose See under TRUNK HOSE.

bully-cocked See under HEADWEAR: COCKED HAT.

bumper See under FOOTWEAR.

bumper/bumper brim See under HEADWEAR.

bumper collar See under NECKLINES AND COLLARS.

bum roll See under UNDERGARMENTS.

bun See under HAIRSTYLES.

bundle See under BUNDLE SYSTEM.

bundle stitch See under EMBROIDERIES AND SEWING STITCHES.

bundle system In the garment trade, a method of garment production that initially involved an unorganized flow of work from one employee to another. Garment pieces are tied together into a bundle. The operator takes the bundle, performs one or more operations, bundles the finished work, and then passes the work to the next employee. In the development bundle system, items move in units or bundles in a more highly organized manner from one operator to another.

bunka embroidery See under EMBROIDERIES AND SEWING STITCHES.

bunny suit See under SLEEPWEAR AND LOUNGEWEAR.

bun snood/bun-warmer See under HEADWEAR: CHIGNON CAP.

bunting See under BABY BUNTING.

Burberry® 1. Originally a trademark for a heavy or lightweight British fabric treated to resist rain, snow, and wind. Used in officers' coats during World War I, the fabric was also made into raincoats and people often referred to raincoats manufactured from this fabric as "Burberrys." The trademark is still registered and as currently described covers a wide variety of apparel produced by this company. 2. See under COATS AND JACKETS. 3. See under PLAIDS AND TARTANS: BURBERRY PLAID.

∞burdash/berdash Fringed sash worn by fashionable young men over their coats in late 17th and early 18th c.

burgonet See under ARMOR.

burka See under BURQA and CHADOR #1.

†burlap Loosely constructed, plain-woven fabric made of jute or other minor bast fibers. Originally considered a utility fabric for bags and sacks. Now sometimes embroidered and used for handbags and items of apparel.

burlet See under HEADWEAR: BOURRELET.

burnet/burnette See under HEADWEAR.

burngrace See under HEADWEAR: BONGRACE.

burnoose/burnouse See under CAPES, CLOAKS, AND SHAWLS.

†burn-out/burnt-out *adj.* Describes fabric or lace that has a patterned effect produced by using yarns of two different fibers and destroying all or part of one of the yarns. Chemicals that dissolve one of the fibers are printed onto the fabric in the design areas. A burn-out pattern effect may be produced on velvet by dissolving parts of the pile but leaving other pile areas and the ground intact. See under PRINTS, STRIPES, AND CHECKS.

burn-out lace See under LACES: PLAUEN LACE.

burnsides Side whiskers and full moustache with clean-shaven chin worn from 1860s to end of 19th c. *Der.* Named for Major General Ambrose Everett Burnside, commander of Army of the Potomac in 1862, under General Grant.

burnsides

burnt-out See under BURN-OUT.

buros See under CAPES, CLOAKS, AND SHAWLS: BIRRUS.

burqa/burka/chadari An all-enveloping garment worn by some Muslim women. Most closely associated with the countries of Pakistan (worn there for more than 400 years) and Afghanistan (worn for 200 or more years), the garment is known by either the name chadari or burqa and may have other spellings such as *chadder, chaddah, chadur, chadar, chudder,* or *chuddar,* and *burqua* or *berka.* In the 21st c. this garment differs somewhat in each country. The Pakistani version of the burqa consists of a cap, a cape-like body covering that includes an eyehole grid, and a separate panel at the front. The fullness of the fabric is gathered into soft pleats or folds or gathered and sewn onto the cap. The Afghan chadri has a cap to which the eye grid panel is attached and has no inserted front panel. Hundreds of fine, pressed pleats are sewn onto the cap. Other countries with large Muslim populations may choose variations of these garments. In some cases, it is worn with a headscarf, or it may cover the wearer from head to toe and have netting over the eyes. See illustration under CHADOR, and see under HEADWEAR: HIJAB for reference to the head scarf worn by some Muslim women.

burqini See under SWIMWEAR.

burr cut See under HAIRSTYLES: INDUCTION CUT.

burse See under HANDBAGS AND RELATED ACCESSORIES.

burunduki See under FURS.

busby See under HEADWEAR.

bush coat/jacket See under COATS AND JACKETS.

bush cut See under HAIRSTYLES: CREW CUT.

∞busheling Formerly used to refer to the alteration or repair of men's clothing.

bush hat See under HEADWEAR.

bush shirt See under SHIRTS: SAFARI SHIRT.

business man's cut See under HAIRSTYLES.

business sheer hose See under HOSIERY: SHEER HOSE.

business suit Man's suit, conservative in style and color, suitable for daytime wear at the office and also worn for other occasions—with exception of formal and semiformal occasions. Cut to distinguish it from a sport suit, which may be made of plaids and brighter colors. May be single- or double-breasted and made in one-, two-, or three-button style. Traditionally worn with a dress shirt and tie; however, in the late 1990s, as casual dress became more common in the business world, some men wore business suits with T-shirts.

business suit

∞busk Long, flat piece of wood, whalebone, steel, and sometimes horn that was inserted into a casing in the front of a woman's bodice or corset to maintain a flat line. Some busks were highly ornamented with low-relief carvings or engravings. Used from the second half of the 16th c. to the 19th c.

buskins See under FOOTWEAR.

bust A woman's breasts.

Buster Brown **1.** See under FOOTWEAR. **2.** See under HAIRSTYLES: BUSTER BROWN. **3.** See under NECKLINES AND COLLARS: BUSTER BROWN.

bustier **1.** See under BLOUSES AND TOPS. **2.** See under UNDERGARMENTS.

bustle **1.** See under UNDERGARMENTS. **2.** General term describing exceptional fullness at the back of the skirt of a woman's dress.

bustle back **1.** See under HEADWEAR. **2.** See under SKIRTS.

bustle curls See under HAIRSTYLES.

bustle dress See under DRESSES.

bust measurement See under CHEST MEASUREMENT.

bust pads See under FALSIES.

butcher boy blouse See under BLOUSES AND TOPS.

†butcher linen **1.** Heavyweight, durable fabric, made in plain weave. Originally of linen for butcher's aprons, later made in cotton. Under current labeling legislation, the fiber from which the fabric is made must be identified. Used for summer suits and sportswear. **2.** Spun rayon fabrics that imitate linen by using yarn of uneven thickness. Term is a misnomer and *butcher rayon* should be used.

butcher rayon See under BUTCHER LINEN #2.

butcher's apron See under APRONS.

butch haircut See under HAIRSTYLES: CREW CUT.

butterfly *adj.* Describes an item or element of apparel that is shaped like a butterfly. See under EYEWEAR: BUTTERFLY GLASSES; FOOTWEAR: BUTTERFLY BOW; HEADWEAR: BUTTERFLY CAP and BUTTERFLY HEADDRESS; NECKLINES AND COLLARS: BUTTERFLY COLLAR; SHOULDERS AND SLEEVES: BUTTERFLY SLEEVE; and TIES: BUTTERFLY BOW TIE.

Butterick, Ebenezer Merchant tailor who is said to have invented the sized, tissue paper pattern. In 1863, he cut out a pattern for his son's trousers using heavy paper similar to cardboard. His wife suggested women would like ready cutout patterns for all clothes. Since the cardboard was too bulky, he next tried a lighter-weight paper and finally tissue paper. By 1890s patterns were available for anything made of cloth, from a wedding gown to a pincushion. There were Butterick designers in New York, Paris, London, Berlin, and Vienna who developed the newest ideas of great modistes. Also see under DELINEATOR.

button **1.** See under CLOSURES. **2.** See under GLOVES AND GLOVE CONSTRUCTION.

button-down See under NECKLINES AND COLLARS and SHIRTS: IVY LEAGUE SHIRT.

button earrings See under JEWELRY.

buttoned shoe See under FOOTWEAR.

buttonhole/buttonholes See under CLOSURES.

buttonhole stitch See under EMBROIDERIES AND SEWING STITCHES.

button hook **1.** Small metal hook attached to long handle formerly used to pull buttons through buttonholes of shoes or gloves. **2.** Small metal hooks first used in the 1860s instead of eyelets on shoes, the laces winding around hooks, crisscrossing to fasten shoes. Used now on skating and other types of boots and called *speed lacing* or *lacing studs*. See under CLOSURES: SPEED LACING.

button shoe See under FOOTWEAR: BUTTONED SHOE.

button-tab sleeve See under SHOULDERS AND SLEEVES.

B.V.D.'s® See under UNDERGARMENTS: ENVELOPE COMBINATION.

buyer An individual authorized to make purchases for a retailer.

buying Making purchases of goods from a manufacturer for a retailer who will sell them to the ultimate consumer. Often done through a RESIDENT BUYING OFFICE.

buying office See under RESIDENT BUYING OFFICE.

buzz cut See under HAIRSTYLES: CREW CUT.

bycocket See under HEADWEAR.

byesse See under BIAS.

byron *adj.* Derived from the name of Lord George Gordon Byron (1788–1824), who was an important English poet of the Romantic period. He became famous not only for his poetry, but also for his behavior, which was considered outrageous at the time. His name was used as a fashion adjective not during his lifetime, but well after his death, to describe apparel that was thought to be "romantic." See under TIES: BYRON TIE and NECKLINES AND COLLARS: BYRON COLLAR.

byrrus See under CAPES, CLOAKS, AND SHAWLS: BIRRUS.

byzance See under JEWELRY.

byzantine embroidery See under EMBROIDERIES AND SEWING STITCHES.

byzantine stitch See under EMBROIDERIES AND SEWING STITCHES.

caban 1. See under COATS AND JACKETS. 2. See under COATS AND JACKETS: GABARDINE.

cabana set See under SWIMWEAR.

cabas See under HEADWEAR.

cabbage ruff See under NECKLINES AND COLLARS: RUFF.

cabin-boy breeches See under PANTS.

∞**cable hatband** Band of gold yarn twisted to resemble a rope or cable; worn in the late 16th c.

cable stitch See under EMBROIDERIES AND SEWING STITCHES.

cable sweater See under SWEATERS.

cable yarn See under CORD YARN.

cabochon See under GEMS, GEM CUTS, AND SETTINGS.

cabretta See under LEATHERS.

cabriole headdress See under HEADWEAR.

cabriolet bonnet See under HEADWEAR.

cache-folies See under WIGS AND HAIRPIECES.

cache-laid See under MASKS.

cache-peigne See under HEADWEAR.

cack See under FOOTWEAR.

CAD See under COMPUTER-AIDED DESIGN.

CAD/CAM See under COMPUTER-AIDED DESIGN/COMPUTER-AIDED MANUFACTURING.

caddie/caddy See under HEADWEAR: BUSH HAT.

cadenette (cad-net′) (French) "Lock of hair." See under HAIRSTYLES: COIFFURE EN CADENETTES.

cadogan See under HAIRSTYLES and WIGS AND HAIRPIECES: CLUB WIG.

cadogan net See under HEADWEAR: SNOOD.

cadoro bra See under UNDERGARMENTS.

caesar haircut See under HAIRSTYLES.

caftan Long, full robe with a slit neckline that is often decorated with embroidery and has long or three-quarter-length sleeves that widen to the end. Based on a North African or Middle Eastern garment, the caftan was adopted by American women in the 1960s and after and worn as at-home or evening dress.

caftan

caftan neckline See under NECKLINES AND COLLARS.

cage 1. Overblouse or dress made out of lattice-like or transparent fabric. 2. See under UNDERGARMENTS: HOOPS.

cage-americaine See under UNDERGARMENTS: HOOPS.

cage dress See under DRESSES.

cage empire See under UNDERGARMENTS: HOOPS.

cage petticoat See under UNDERGARMENTS: HOOPS.

caging See under FURS.

cagoule See under CAPES, CLOAKS, AND SHAWLS.

cainsil (kane-sil) See under CHAINSE.

cairngorm See under GEMS, GEM CUTS, AND SETTINGS.

cake hat See under HEADWEAR.

calamanco See under FOOTWEAR: CALAMANCO SHOES.

calamanco shoes See under FOOTWEAR.

calash See under HEADWEAR.

calasiris See under KALASIRIS.

calcarapedes See under FOOTWEAR.

calceus See under FOOTWEAR.

calculator watch See under WATCHES.

calèche See under HEADWEAR: CALASH.

∞**calençons** (kal′-sen) Worn by women in early 17th c., a type of long drawers or hose worn with doublet and petticoat that later developed into the breeches and trousers of women's contemporary riding habit.

calendar watch See under WATCHES.

†**calender** Passing fabric between two heated rollers in order to produce a smooth, even appearance.

calf length See under LENGTHS.

calfskin See under FURS and LEATHERS.

cagoule See CAPES, CLOAKS, AND SHAWLS.

†calico Plain-weave, light- to medium-weight cotton or cotton-blend fabric, usually printed with very small designs such as flowers or geometric forms. Also see under PRINTS, STRIPES, AND CHECKS: CALICO PRINT.

calico button See under CLOSURES.

california embroidery See under EMBROIDERIES AND SEWING STITCHES.

calisthenic costume See under DRESSES.

calk See under FOOTWEAR.

calligraphic scarf See under SCARVES.

callout An enlarged drawing of a detail area on a technical flat.

calotte 1. See under HEADWEAR. 2. See under CLERICAL DRESS.

calypso chemise See under DRESSES.

calypso shirt See under SHIRTS.

CAM See under COMPUTER-AIDED MANUFACTURING.

camail See under ARMOR.

camargo See under COATS AND JACKETS.

camargo hat See under HEADWEAR.

camauro See under CLERICAL DRESS.

†cambric Fine, closely woven cotton fabric made with mercerized yarns given a calendered finish. May also be made of linen and used for handkerchiefs. *Der.* From Cambrai, France.

cambridge coat See under COATS AND JACKETS.

cambridge paletot See under COATS AND JACKETS.

camelaurion See under HEADWEAR.

cameleons See under FOOTWEAR.

†camel hair 1. Fibers from the crossbred Bactrian camel of Asia, which produces soft, luxurious yarn that is resistant to heat and cold. 2. Cloth made of these fibers.

cameo 1. A small low-relief carving often made from a banded two-layered gemstone such as onyx or sardonyx, which gives a raised design, usually in white with another color left as the background. Most common subject is a woman's head and shoulders. The opposite of INTAGLIO. See under GEMS, GEM CUTS, AND SETTINGS: CAMEO and INTAGLIO. 2. Two-tone shell carved in the same manner as mentioned previously to produce a **shell cameo.** 3. Colored pottery material similar to that used by Josiah Wedgwood molded to produce a WEDGWOOD® CAMEO (see under JEWELRY).

camera bag See under HANDBAGS AND RELATED ACCESSORIES.

Cameron tartan See under PLAIDS AND TARTANS.

cames See under UNDERGARMENTS: CHEMISE.

camikini See under SWIMWEAR: BIKINI.

camise See UNDERGARMENTS: CHEMISE.

camisette See under UNDERGARMENTS.

∞camisia (Medieval English) Chemise. See under UNDERGARMENTS: CHEMISE.

camisole 1. See under UNDERGARMENTS. 2. See under BLOUSES AND TOPS: CAMISOLE TOP. 3. See under NECKLINES AND COLLARS: CAMISOLE NECKLINE. ∞4. Sleeved jacket or jersey, formerly worn by men.

cami-tap set See under UNDERGARMENTS: TAP PANTY.

camouflage pants See under PANTS.

camouflage print See under PRINTS, STRIPES, AND CHECKS.

camouflage suit See under ACTIVEWEAR.

camp 1. Deliberate adoption of styles or behaviors that are generally considered to be vulgar, artificial, or humorous. Often used as an adjective to describe such styles. 2. See under SHIRTS and SHORTS.

campagus See under FOOTWEAR and CLERICAL DRESS.

campaign coat See under COATS AND JACKETS.

campaign hat See under HEADWEAR.

campaign wig See under WIGS AND HAIRPIECES.

camp shirt See under SHIRTS.

camp shorts See under SHORTS.

canadienne See under COATS AND JACKETS.

canary breeches See under ACTIVEWEAR: RIDING BREECHES.

canary diamond See under GEMS, GEM CUTS, AND SETTINGS.

cancan dress See under DRESSES.

candlewick embroidery See under EMBROIDERIES AND SEWING STITCHES.

candy stripe See under PRINTS, STRIPES, AND CHECKS.

cane Staff or walking stick used as a walking aide carried as a fashionable accessory. Canes vary from rough, rustic wood for country use, e.g., **shillelagh** (sha-lay′-lee), to polished woods with elaborately decorated heads. Carried from 16th c. to present by men, and occasionally by women, specific types included: **malacca cane** (mah-lah′-kah), also called a *clouded cane,* carried in 18th c. and made from the mottled stem of the malacca palm; **rattan canes**, carried in 17th and 18th c. and made from an

East Indian palm; **constable**, a small cane with a gold-plated top carried by men in 1830s and 1840s; **penang lawyer**, a walking stick used by men in 19th c. made from a palm stem with a bulbous top.

∞**canezou** (can-zoo′) Refers to any of several types of 19th-c. accessory garments that were sometimes worn as a means of extending the life of an older garment. **1.** A woman's waist-length SPENCER JACKET (see under COATS AND JACKETS) of 1820s without sleeves, this sleeveless overblouse style continued in use until the 1860s. **2.** In 1830s a cape, cut short and pointed, extending down center front and back but not covering the arms. Also called *canezou pelerine.* **3.** By mid-19th c. an elaborate fichu or scarf of muslin, ribbons, and lace covering bodice of dress.

canezou pelerine See under CANEZOU #2.

∞**canions** Tubular garments worn on the thighs as extensions of men's TRUNK HOSE from 1570 to 1620. Frequently of different fabric or color than the trunk hose. Shown at ELIZABETHAN STYLES.

cannetille (can-tee) (*cantile*) **1.** Military braid of gold or silver thread that looks like lace. **2.** Fine spiral-twisted gold or silver thread, used for embroidery.

cannon **1.** See under CANNONS. ∞**2.** See under ARMOR.

∞**cannons** Frills of lace or bunches of ribbons that fell down over tops of wide boots worn by men during 1660s and 1670s. Also called *port canons* or *canons.* Also worn with low shoes and PETTICOAT BREECHES. Shown at PETTICOAT BREECHES.

cannon sleeve See under SHOULDERS AND SLEEVES.

canotier See under HEADWEAR: BOATER.

canteen bag See under HANDBAGS AND RELATED ACCESSORIES.

cantile See under CANNETILLE #1.

canvas embroidery See under EMBROIDERIES AND SEWING STITCHES: BERLIN WOOLWORK.

cap See under HEADWEAR.

capa See under CAPES, CLOAKS, AND SHAWLS.

CAPES, CLOAKS, AND SHAWLS

cape Sleeveless outerwear of various lengths usually opening in center front; cut in a full circle, in a segment of a circle, or on the straight—usually with slits for arms. A classic type of outerwear worn in one form or another throughout history. During the Middle Ages, a cape was more often called a *mantle.* Important from then on during various eras and in various lengths as a separate item or attached to coats. See also under CAPES, CLOAKS, AND SHAWLS: BURNOOSE.

cloak As often referred to in the latter half of the 19th c., loose outer garment not clearly distinguishable from outer garments that might also be classified as *capes, mantles,* or *loose coats* with vestigial sleeves.

shawl Decorative or utilitarian wrap, larger than a scarf, worn draped over the shoulders and sometimes the head. May be oblong, square, or a square folded diagonally. Believed to have originated in Bukhara, Uzbekistan, it was worn in Kashmir as early as the late 16th c. Also worn in Persia and India, and worn by country people for utilitarian purposes. Did not become fashionable in Europe until second half of 18th c. Very popular throughout the 19th c. and worn intermittently since. *Der.* Persian and Hindu, "shal." Also see under CAPES, CLOAKS, AND SHAWLS: SPANISH SHAWL.

all-purpose poncho See under CAPES, CLOAKS, AND SHAWLS: PONCHO #3.

∞**almuce** (*amuce, almusse, aunice, aumusse*) Small fur-lined medieval cape with attached hood that tied under the chin.

∞**andalouse cape** (an′-da-looz′) Cape worn outdoors by women in 1846, made of silk and trimmed with fringe.

∞**artois** (ahr-twah′) Long loose cloak with lapels and several capes, the longest ending near the waistline; worn by men and women in late 18th c.

∞**balmoral mantle** Cloak of velvet, cashmere, or wool styled like an INVERNESS CAPE (see under CAPES, CLOAKS, AND SHAWLS) and popular for outdoor wear in the 1860s. Named for the castle in Scotland purchased by Queen Victoria and Prince Albert.

∞**barège shawl** (ba-rezh′) A printed shawl made in France in the 1850s from fabric with worsted crosswise yarns and silk lengthwise yarns.

∞**bautte/bautta** (bah-oot′-ta) Black cloth wrap of 18th c. with hood that could be drawn down over face to form a half mask.

beach poncho Oblong terrycloth poncho that can be laid flat for use as a towel at the beach.

∞**bell** Circular cape used as traveling cloak, sometimes hooded, sometimes with side and back vents, and worn by men and women from late 13th to early 15th c.

∞**beluque** Woman's cape or mantle worn in the 15th c.

∞**bernhardt mantle** Woman's short outdoor cape with loose front and dolman or sling sleeves that was popular in 1886. *Der.* Named after Sarah Bernhardt, a famous French actress of the period.

∞**birrus** (*byrrus, buros*) Hooded cape of rough cloth, worn in bad weather by Romans of all classes under the last emperors.

∞**bivouac mantle** (biv-oo-wak′) Full-length, loose cape of scarlet cloth, styled with high collar, padded and lined with ermine. Worn by women in 1814.

Bokhara shawl (bo-kar′-a) Shawls made in Bokhara, Uzbekistan, of camel's hair spun into yarn. Dyed with vegetable dyes and woven into 8-inch strips of patterned fabric joined invisibly to form shawls.

∞**bolero cape** Elbow-length cape, worn by women at end of 19th c., cut like a bolero in front and tapered to waistline in back. Also called *bolero mantle.*

box cape Straight cut, elbow- or hip-length cape with broad padded shoulders and square silhouette. Made of fur or wool and fashionable in late 1930s.

∞**bratt** 1. Mantle or cape made of coarse material worn by peasants in Ireland in 9th and 10th c. Also called *Irish mantle.* 2. Used in latter part of 14th c. for wrap or blanket for an infant.

∞**broché** (bro-shay′) Paisley-type shawl, popular in the 1830s, made in Scotland, and woven in alternating stripes of pattern and plain color. See under CASHMERE SHAWL #2.

bubble cape Elbow-length fur cape often made with skins worked in the round. Popular in 1950s and early 1960s.

burnoose

burnoose/burnouse Circular, three-quarter-length wool cape that had a pointed hood or was fashioned with fabric that was cut and sewn to simulate a hood. The hood often had a tassel attached at the point. The garment was derived from capes worn by indigenous people of North Africa. Especially popular from the 1840s to the 1860s, the style is occasionally revived.

∞**cagoule** (ka-gool′) Cloth or fur semicircular cape with attached hood worn by peasants from 11th to 13th c.

∞**capa** 1. Wide, circular, full-length, hooded cape worn by Spanish men from Middle Ages to early 17th c. In the Romantic age in France (c. 1830s and 1840s), it was called *cape a l'espagnole* (les-pan-yol′) and worn by women. 2. Full cape worn by bullfighters in Spain, used to attract bull's attention. *Der.* Latin, *capa,* "hooded cloak."

capelet Any small attached or detachable cape (e.g., a cape collar) on a coat, dress, or suit. Also see under CAPES, CLOAKS, AND SHAWLS: TIPPET.

capote (kah-pote′) (*capot*) 1. Full circular cape with wide cape collar and red lining. Used as a working cape by matadors at Spanish and Mexican bullfights. ∞2. Generic for hooded coat or cloak worn since the Middle Ages.

∞**capuchon** (kap′-oo-shon) Woman's waist-length outdoor evening mantle with wired hood and long tight sleeves worn in 1837. Also called *carmeillette* (kar-may′-yet).

∞**cardinal** 1. In 18th c., three-quarter-length scarlet cloak with hood that resembled the MOZETTA worn by cardinals in Roman Catholic Church. See under CLERICAL DRESS: MOZETTA. 2. Woman's waist-length red cloak without hood or collar, worn in 1840s.

carmeillette See under CAPES, CLOAKS, AND SHAWLS: CAPUCHON.

casaweck See under COATS AND JACKETS.

cashmere shawl 1. Extremely fine, soft shawl, handmade from hair of the Tibetan cashmere goat. The Maharaja has overseen weaving in the Kashmir Valley of northwestern India since c. 1586. For over 200 years shawls were woven for the court and never left India. Two main types were made: (a) Those with woven designs that were made in sections and sewn together in square and oblong shapes. Often they were woven in pairs so that they were reversible. These were called *twin* or *double shawls.* (b) Others woven in a color scheme of white, red, or green, and subsequently embroidered in gold, silver, and silk threads. The characteristic design is a cone or leaf pattern called a **boteh**. Such shawls were extremely popular during French Consulate (1799–1804) and Empire periods (1804–1814). 2. Machine-made sheep's wool imitations of cashmere shawls produced in France and Scotland and popular during the 19th c. Known also as **paisley shawls** (pay′-slee), after the town of Paisley in Scotland, where large numbers of these shawls were manufactured. The characteristic boteh design became known as a *paisley design.*

paisley shawl

∞**cassock mantle** Woman's knee-length short-sleeved cloak, with shirring at shoulders and down the center back, worn in the 1880s.

cawdor cape See under CAPES, CLOAKS, AND SHAWLS: GLENGARRY CAPE.

∞**chambord mantle/chambard mantle** Three-quarter-length hooded woman's cloak of 1850s that resembled a shawl with fullness in back; made of satin or velvet.

chaussee hood See under CAPES, CLOAKS, AND SHAWLS: EPITOGA #2.

∞**chlaine** (klain) Woolen cape worn in Greece during Homeric period by shepherds and warriors.

∞**chlamys** (klay′-mis or klahm′-is) Oblong mantle approximately 5′ × 3′ or 6′ × 3′, fastened in front or on one shoulder with a pin. Worn in ancient Greece by travelers,

chlamys

youths, soldiers, and hunters. In Greek mythology, it is worn by the god Hermes. Chlamys of a more semicircular shape continued to be worn in Byzantium and in later centuries for sports and traveling.

∞**circular** Long cape or mantle of silk, satin, or other fine fabrics in extra-wide widths and frequently lined with rabbit or gray squirrel, combined with bright fabric. Fashionable in late 19th c.

clerical cape See under CLERICAL DRESS.

cloak See under introduction to CAPES, CLOAKS, AND SHAWLS.

∞**colleen bawn cloak** Woman's cloak worn from 1860s to 1890s made of white grenadine, with a large cape pulled up in center back and fastened with rosettes or bowknots. *Der.* After the title of a melodrama by Dion Boucicault.

compass cloak See under CAPES, CLOAKS, AND SHAWLS: FRENCH CLOAK.

cope 1. See under CLERICAL DRESS. 2. Style worn as a coronation robe by English sovereigns. 3. Originally a hooded cloak designed as a rain cape; sometimes made with sleeves and fastened in center front. After its adoption by clergy, it was always sleeveless and richly decorated.

∞**cottage cloak** Woman's hooded cloak of 19th c. tied under chin, similar to those seen in pictures of the fairy-tale character Little Red Riding Hood.

∞**crispin** 1. Cloak without a collar worn by actresses waiting in the theater wings in early 19th c.; later adopted for men, women, and children. First worn in mid-1820s. 2. Man's evening cloak, with full sleeves and quilted lining, worn in late 1830s. 3. Woman's short mantle of early 1840s with close-fitting back and a small PELERINE cape (see under CAPES, CLOAKS, AND SHAWLS)—sometimes with sleeves—made of bias-cut satin, velvet, or cashmere and often padded.

crocheted shawl Fringed shawl made by hand-crocheting, usually in a lacy pattern. Popular in late 1960s and early 1970s in oblong, semicircular, or triangular shapes.

domino #2

domino 1. Originally, a large hood worn by monks. Later, a cloak with attached hood for men and women. 2. A large cloak, usually black, worn with a small mask for traditional carnival and masquerade costume, popular in 18th and 19th c.

∞**dorothy cloak** Wool cape manufactured and sold to the public after 1890 by the Shakers, a religious community. Full length, with a short shoulder cape, and without arm slits, it opened down the front and closed with silk ribbon ties. It had a very full, attached hood and was made in a variety of colors. *Der.* Named after the Shaker designer Eldress Dorothy Durgin.

∞**epitoga** 1. Originally an ancient Roman cloak worn over the toga, often having bell-shaped sleeves. 2. Cloak worn in the 13th c. similar to #1, but cut more like a robe and worn as academic dress. Also called *chausse* or *chaussee hood.* 3. The medieval hood reduced to symbolic form as a part of academic and ceremonial robes.

∞**esmeralda cloak** Waterproof wrap of the late 1860s worn in U.S. Introduced from Paris in both plain and tartan designs. In England, worn only in the rain. In Paris it had two capes, no sleeves, and was ornamented with bows, frills, fringe, satin braid, and rosettes.

∞**eugénia, the** Voluminous woman's cape of early 1860s, seven-eighths length. Usually black with second cape reaching to waist in back and shorter in front. Both capes were edged with fancy box-pleated ribbon.

∞**faldetta** Waist-length colored taffeta women's mantle trimmed with wide lace ruffle; worn in 1850.

fichu-pelerine
1834

∞**fichu-pelerine** Large cape or shawl-like covering for woman's shoulders worn from mid-1820s to 1860s. Usually white and often made with a double cape and turned-down collar, and tied in front with the ends reaching below the waist as far as knee length.

fishnet poncho Square, medium-sized poncho made of fishnet or see-through fabric with a high, large, turtleneck collar. The edge of the collar and the hem is trimmed with ball fringe.

∞**french cloak** Long circular or semicircular cape, sometimes with a square flat collar or shoulder cape worn in 16th and 17th c. One type of french cloak was the **compass cloak**, a full circular cape worn by men. When made in semicircular shape, it was called a **half-compass cloak**. In the 16th c., any of these cloaks was also called a *manteau.*

French policeman's cape Circular-cut, knee-length cape worn by French policemen, made of heavy black wool and rubber. Heavy enough to be swung like a club. Authentic cape was sold as sportswear in boutiques and Army surplus stores in U.S. in late 1960s. Also called *gendarme cape.*

∞**frileuse** Women's cape or pelerine wrap with a fitted back and loose sleeves, made of quilted satin or velvet. Worn indoors or at the theater in 1847.

∞**froufrou mantle** Woman's shoulder cape of late 1890s made in three tiers trimmed with RUCHING. Had a high-standing collar and rosettes and long ribbon streamers in front. Also called *froufrou cape. Der.* From the name of the comedic play *Froufrou,* written by Henri Meilhac and Ludovic Halévy in 1869.

fur stole Waist-length fur cape first worn in the 20th c., with elongated ends in front, sometimes trimmed with tails of animals. Formerly called *pelerine* or *tippet.* Very popular in late 1940s, 1950s, and 1960s, especially in mink.

gendarme cape See under CAPES, CLOAKS, AND SHAWLS: FRENCH POLICEMAN'S CAPE.

genoa cloak See under CAPES, CLOAKS, AND SHAWLS: ITALIAN CLOAK.

∞**glengarry cape** Three-quarter-length cape worn by women in the 1890s, made with a tailored collar and single-breasted closing. A hood, sometimes plaid lined, was attached at neckline under the collar. Also called *cawdor cape.*

glocke (glok'-ka) Medieval poncho-type outer garment made of LODEN CLOTH, with a hole in center of large circle of fabric. Was worn especially in mountainous Alpine regions of Europe. *Der.* German, "bell."

half-compass cloak See under CAPES, CLOAKS, AND SHAWLS: FRENCH CLOAK.

∞**inverness cape** (in-ver-ness) Man's full cape, usually long, and made of wool or worsted. Was close-fitting at neck and fell loose from shoulders—often made in plaid patterned fabric.

Irish mantle See under CAPES, CLOAKS, AND SHAWLS: BRATT.

∞**isabella (the)** Hip-length collarless cape of mid-1850s made with slashes for arms and extra capelets at dropped shoulders to cover arms.

∞**italian cloak** Short, hooded cloak worn by men in the 16th and 17th c. Also called *spanish cloak* or *genoa cloak.*

∞**jocelyn mantle** Knee-length, double-skirted, sleeveless woman's mantle of 1852 made with three capes trimmed with fringe.

∞**lacerna** Semicircular, knee-length cape fastened in center front or on right shoulder by a fibula (pin). Worn by ancient Romans from the 2nd c. B.C. to the 5th c. A.D. Made of wool in white, natural, amethyst, and purple decorated with gold.

lapponica Poncho of plaid wool with fringed edges imported from Finland. Colorful plaids are of all varieties, some being in large squares of color; some being more complicated, similar to the STEWART TARTANS (see under PLAIDS AND TARTANS); and some in smaller checks similar to glen plaid (see under PLAIDS AND TARTANS: GLEN URQUHART PLAID).

∞**limousine** Full-length circular woman's evening cape of late 1880s with shirring around neck so fullness falls in folds over the arms, forming sleeves.

∞**maintenon cloak** (mant-nown') Woman's wide-sleeved, black velvet coat of 1860s sometimes embroidered and usually trimmed with a wide pleated flounce covered with GUIPURE LACE (see under LACES). *Der.* Named for the Marquise de Maintenon, mistress and second wife of Louis XIV of France.

manteau (man-tow') See under CAPES, CLOAKS, AND SHAWLS: FRENCH CLOAK.

∞**mantelet** **1.** A short cape mentioned by Chaucer in *The Knight's Tale* in 1386. **2.** Small cloak worn by women in 18th c. **3.** Scarf of fur, lace, or silk worn around shoulders, crossed over chest, and ends tied in back from 1814 to 1835. **4.** 19th-c. woman's rounded shoulder cape with long end tucked under belt in front. Also spelled *mantelot* or *mantlet.*

mantilla (man-til'-ah) **1.** Shawl or veil worn by Spanish women, usually of black lace; white lace worn for festive occasions. Worn draped over head, sometimes over a high comb placed in hair, wrapped around neck, and falling over shoulders. This shawl has influenced 20th-c. fashions. ∞**2.** Lightweight shawl of silk, velvet, or lace worn by women from 1840s to 1880s. Shawl hung long in back and had long ends in front. Also spelled *mantella.* *Der.* Diminutive of Spanish *manta,* "shawl."

∞**mantle** **1.** Long, loose, cape-like cloak originally cut square, oblong, or as a part of a circle. Worn from 12th through 16th c. by men and women. Mantles could be either **open mantles**, one length of fabric fastened by a pin or clasp on one shoulder, at the center, or tied at the neck, or **closed mantles,** with openings for the head to slip through. **2.** In 14th c. usually a ceremonial cape. Sometimes lined and called a double mantle. **3.** By 19th c., a cape without sleeves. **4.** Wrap for infants in 17th and 18th c. *Der.* Latin, *mantellum,* "covering."

open mantle 13th c.

∞**mantlet matilda/mantlet matilde** Type of shawl-like woman's garment trimmed with fringe or taffeta in front, worn in 1850s.

mantón de Manila See under CAPES, CLOAKS, AND SHAWLS: SPANISH SHAWL.

∞**maud** Woman's fringed wrap of plaid fabric worn in mid-1850s.

maxi cape Any ankle-length cape.

midi cape Any calf-length cape.

∞**moldavian mantle** Full-length woman's mantle of mid-1850s with long capes over the shoulders forming "elephant sleeves."

∞**montpensier mantle** (mon-pon-see'-ay) Woman's cape-like garment of 1840s, long in back, with front ending in a point and slit up sides, leaving arms free.

∞**mother hubbard cloak** Woman's or girl's three-quarter-length cloak of 1880s made of brocade, velvet, satin, or cashmere with quilted lining, high collar tied at neckline, full sleeves—often in DOLMAN (see under SHOULDERS AND SLEEVES) style with shirring over shoulders. Sometimes the back section was draped over a *bustle* and tied with ribbon bow.

∞**mousquetaire mantle** (moose-key-tare') Braid-trimmed, black velvet mantle of mid-19th c. with short, deep cuffs lined with quilted satin. Worn by women in 1847. *Der.* From cape worn by French musketeers or royal bodyguards of Louis XVIII in 17th c.

mozetta See under CLERICAL DRESS.

muleta cape A Spanish-type midi cape made of felt, sometimes scarlet, and trimmed with wool tassels around the neck, down the front, and around hem of the garment. Featured in late 1960s for women.

∞**normandie cape** Lightweight, hip-length woman's cape of late 1890s made with ruffles extended down center front, around the hem, sometimes around yoke, and a standing collar or a double-tiered ruff at the neck.

∞**nurse's cape** Three-quarter-length cape of navy-blue wool trimmed with brass buttons and lined in red. At one time worn by nurses when they wore traditional uniforms.

officer's cape Three-quarter-length cape in navy-blue worsted with small standing collar; part of dress uniform of officers in U.S. Navy.

∞**opera cape** Man's full, circular calf-length black worsted cape, sometimes lined in red satin. Worn for formal occasions with TAIL COAT (see under COATS AND JACKETS) and TOP HAT (see under HEADWEAR). *Der.* In the 19th c., it was fashionable attire with the high silk hat for the opera. Also favored by magicians and circus ringmasters.

∞**opera wrap** Women's full-length opera cape of the early 1900s; usually made of elaborate fabric trimmed with fur or feathers.

∞**paenula** (pay'-new-la) Hooded cape or poncho-shaped garment, made of heavy woolen fabric or leather. Worn by ancient Romans for traveling or inclement weather.

paisley shawl See under CAPES, CLOAKS, AND SHAWLS: CASHMERE SHAWL #2.

palatine See under CAPES, CLOAKS, AND SHAWLS: TIPPET.

∞**palatine royal** A fur cape of 1851 with a quilted hood and short ends in front. Also called a *victorine.*

∞**paletot-cloak** (pal-ah-tow' or pal-tow') Man's hip-length cape of the 1850s made in single- or double-breasted style with armhole slits.

∞**paletot-mantle** (pal-ah-tow' or pal-tow') Woman's three-quarter-length cloak with hanging sleeves and a cape collar worn in late 1860s.

∞**palla** Rectangular shawl-like garment resembling ancient Greek HIMATION. Worn draped around body over a STOLA by Roman women, sometimes with one end draped over head.

palla and stola

∞**pallium** Rectangular shawl worn by Roman men. Also see under HIMATION.

∞**paludamentum** (pa-lu-da-men'-tum) **1.** Purple mantle of rich fabric fastened with clasp at shoulders. Worn by Roman emperors and military officers. **2.** Same item worn by upper-class Byzantine men, the emperor, and the empress, but changed to ankle-length by 5th c. This garment had a large, square decoration called a TABLION at the open edge over the breast.

paludamentum #2

∞**pelerine** (pel-er-reen') **1.** Woman's short shoulder cape of fur, velvet, or other fabric worn from 1740 to end of 18th c. Sometimes worn with long scarf ends crossed and tied around waist. **2.** A wide collar-like cape, sometimes permanently attached, made of lace or fabric worn over a dress or PELISSE (see under COATS AND JACKETS); was especially popular from c. 1820 to 1850.

∞**peplum rotonde** Woman's waist-length circular cloak, made with back vent and fringed border, worn in 1871.

piano shawl See under CAPES, CLOAKS, AND SHAWLS: SPANISH SHAWL.

∞**pierrot cape** (pee-ehr-oh') Woman's three-quarter-length cloak of 1892; included an additional shoulder cape and satin ruff at neckline similar to that worn with PIERROT COSTUME.

∞**polish mantle** Knee-length woman's cloak of mid-1830s; included an attached cape made of satin edged with fur.

∞**polonaise** (pol-on-nays') In 1750s a cape or small hooded cloak drawn back like a polonaise dress (see under POLONAISE #1). Also called *polonaise pardessus* (pol-on-nays' par-de'-soo).

poncho **1.** Fashion item shaped like a square or a small oblong blanket with hole in center for the head. Frequently fringed around the edges. Popular in late 1960s and after. **2.** Utilitarian garment

poncho #1

consisting of waterproof fabric with a slash in the center for the head. When worn, it was used as a rain cape; when not worn it could be used as a tarpaulin or a blanket. **3.** Square of nylon fabric, 54″ × 80″, laminated with polyvinyl chloride, that slips over the head and snaps closed at the sides to make a partial sleeve. One size fits everyone. Usually styled with an attached hood. Originally made of a rubberized fabric and worn by policemen on rainy days. Also called a *rain poncho* or *all-purpose poncho.* ∞**4.** Woman's loose, three-quarter-length cloak worn in the 1860s with buttons from neck to hem, a small standing collar, full sleeves—which are narrower at the wrist—with capes over the sleeves.

rain cape **1.** A lightweight plastic cape that may be folded, placed in a small envelope, and carried for use when it rains. **2.** A cape of any fabric treated for water repellency.

rain poncho See under CAPES, CLOAKS, AND SHAWLS: PONCHO #3.

rebozo (re-bow′-zho) An oblong shawl made of locally produced, traditional fabric, worn originally by South American Indians and introduced as a fashion item in late 1960s.

∞**ripple cape** In the 1890s, a woman's short ruffled cape that extended beyond the shoulder by shirring three layers of fabric or lace onto a yoke trimmed with ribbon.

∞**roquelaure** (roke′-ay-lore) (*roculo, roccelo, rocklo*) Man's knee-length to full-length heavy cloak of 18th c., often trimmed with fur and lined with bright-colored silk. Usually made with a cape collar and back vent for riding horseback. *Der.* From Antoine Gaston Jean-Baptiste, le duc de Roquelaure (1656–1738), minister of wardrobe under Louis XIV.

∞**rotonde** Woman's short or three-quarter-length circular *cape* of 1850s and 1860s made of lace or of same material as a dress.

∞**sagum** (sa′-goom) Red woolen rectangle of cloth worn pinned on the right shoulder as a cape by Roman soldiers and by all Roman citizens in time of war. The phrase "put on the sagum" was synonymous with saying "go to war."

serape (say-rah′-pay) Bright-colored, oblong rectangle worn by Mexicans over the shoulder. Handmade in horizontal-striped patterns, it resembles a small blanket. Usually made with fringed ends.

∞**shale** French shawls, with handspun warp and machine-spun merino wool filling yarns, made in Rheims.

shawl See under introduction to CAPES, CLOAKS, AND SHAWLS.

skoncho A do-it-yourself-style poncho made from a brushed wool plaid blanket or striped with fringe on two ends; similar to a blanket used at a football game. A 16″ slash is cut diagonally in the center. May also be worn as a skirt.

∞**soccus** (*socq*) Ceremonial and coronation cape fastened on the right shoulder and worn during Middle Ages by kings and dignitaries.

∞**sontag** (sonn′-tag) Woman's small cape of 1850s and 1860s worn for warmth, often knitted or crocheted with ends crossed in front and worn under a cloak. *Der.* Named for German opera singer, Henriette Sontag.

∞**sortie de bal** (sor′-tee de bal) Woman's evening *cloak* with attached hood, worn from 1850s to 1870s. Made of silk or cashmere and lined with a quilted fabric.

space blanket Insulated blanket with one side aluminized, the other brightly colored. Worn on one side to insulate from the cold, while the other side protects from the heat of the sun. Folds to pocket size for easy carrying. *Der.* Developed for NASA space program in late 1960s.

spanish cloak See under CAPES, CLOAKS, AND SHAWLS: ITALIAN CLOAK.

spanish shawl Large, embroidered silk shawl that was usually made in China and then shipped to Spain, where the long silk fringe was added. When such a shawl was shipped by way of Manila in the Philippines, it was known as a *mantón de Manila.* When used as a wrap, the shawl was folded diagonally with the point in center at the back and the ends thrown loosely over the shoulders. A fashionable accessory of the early 20th c., it was revived in the late 1960s and early 1970s and becomes fashionable periodically. Also called *piano shawl,* because in the early 20th c. this type of shawl was draped on the top of grand pianos.

spanish shawl 1926

∞**spencer cloak** Woman's cloak of early 19th c. made of embroidered net with elbow-length sleeves.

stole **1.** See under SCARVES. **2.** See under CAPES, CLOAKS, AND SHAWLS: FUR STOLE.

∞**tabard** Short, heavy cape of coarse cloth; worn outdoors in 19th c. by men and women.

∞**tablet mantilla** Watered or plain silk wrap of mid-1850s made with a yoke that falls low on the shoulders. Trimmed with cut-turret (tab-shaped) edging, narrow braid, and fringe.

∞**talma** **1.** Woman's long cape or cloak, frequently hooded, worn in 1860s. **2.** Woman's knee-to-hip-length cape of embroidered satin, lace, or velvet with fringe at hem; used as an outer garment from 1850s to mid-1870s. **3.** In 1890s, a woman's full-length coat with loose sleeves and lace cape or deep velvet collar. **3.** Knee-length man's cape with a turned-over collar and silk lining, worn for evening in 1850s. *Der.* Named for François Joseph Talma (1763–1826), a French tragic actor of Consulate and Empire period. Also called *talma mantle.*

∞**tebenna** (te-bain′-ah) Etruscan semicircular cloak in purple, white, or black (for funerals) worn by a king and important citizens—short at first, later knee-length, and finally full-length. The Roman toga is thought to have developed from this cloak.

templar cloak See under COATS AND JACKETS: CABAN.

tippet ∞1. Shoulder cape of fur or cloth worn by women from 16th c. on. In the 1840s, such a small fur or lace shoulder cape with long, flat ends in front reaching below the waist, was called a **palatine**. 2. See under CAPES, CLOAKS, AND SHAWLS: FUR STOLE.

∞**tudor cape** Woman's short circular cape of 1890s, usually embroidered. Made with pointed yoke front and back, epaulet on each shoulder, and velvet Medici collar.

∞**venetian cloak** Woman's black satin cloak of late 1820s with collar, cape, and wide hanging sleeves.

victorine See under CAPES, CLOAKS, AND SHAWLS: PALATINE ROYAL.

∞**visite** (vee-zeet) Woman's loose, cape-like outdoor garment worn in last half of 19th c.

∞**waterproof cloak** Outer garment with small, tasseled hood worn by women from 1867 to 1870s, made of waterproof fabric. Later became an ankle-length, semi-fitted coat with princess lines buttoned down the front. Also see under CAPES, CLOAKS, AND SHAWLS: ESMERALDA CLOAK.

∞**watteau cape** (wat-toe′) Knee-length woman's cape of the 1890s. Styled with collar fitted on neck, then turned over. Made with single box pleat in back, and gathered to neckline in front. Made with separate pieces gathered over the shoulders to form capes over the arms. *Der.* Named for the artist Antoine Watteau (1684–1721).

∞**witchoura mantle** 1. Woman's cloak, worn from 1808 to 1818, made with long, fur-trimmed cape. 2. In the 1830s, a woman's winter mantle with standing collar, large sleeves, and lined or trimmed with fur.

---

cape à l'espagnole See under CAPES, CLOAKS, AND SHAWLS: CAPA.

cape coat See under COATS AND JACKETS.

cape collar See under NECKLINES AND COLLARS.

cape hat See under HEADWEAR.

capelet See under BLOUSES AND TOPS and CAPES, CLOAKS, AND SHAWLS.

capelet collar See under NECKLINES AND COLLARS: CAPE COLLAR.

capeline See under ARMOR and HEADWEAR.

cape may diamond See under GEMS, GEM CUTS, AND SETTINGS.

cape ruby See under GEMS, GEM CUTS, AND SETTINGS.

capeskin See under LEATHERS.

cape sleeve See under SHOULDERS AND SLEEVES.

Capezio® See under FOOTWEAR: BALLET SLIPPERS.

capless wig See under introduction to WIGS AND HAIRPIECES: WIG.

cap of dignity See under HEADWEAR: CAP OF MAINTENANCE.

cap of estate See under HEADWEAR: CAP OF MAINTENANCE.

cap of maintenance See under HEADWEAR.

capot See under COATS AND JACKETS: CAPOTE.

capote 1. See under CAPES, CLOAKS, AND SHAWLS. 2. See under COATS AND JACKETS. 3. See under HEADWEAR.

capot-ribot See under HEADWEAR.

cappuccio See under HEADWEAR: CHAPERON.

caprice See under COATS AND JACKETS.

capri-length panty-girdle See under UNDERGARMENTS: GIRDLE.

caprioll See under HEADWEAR: CABRIOLE HEADDRESS.

capri pants See under PANTS.

cap sleeve See under SHOULDERS AND SLEEVES.

capuche See under HEADWEAR: CAPUCHE and CAPUCHIN.

capuchin See under HEADWEAR.

capuchin collar See under NECKLINES AND COLLARS.

capuchon 1. See under HEADWEAR: CAPUCHIN. 2. See under CAPES, CLOAKS, AND SHAWLS.

capucine See under HEADWEAR: CAPUCHIN.

capulet See under HEADWEAR.

caraco See under COATS AND JACKETS.

caraco corsage See under COATS AND JACKETS: CARACO #2.

caracul 1. See under FURS: KARAKUL. 2. See under KARAKUL CLOTH in alphabetical listing.

carat See under GEMS, GEM CUTS, AND SETTINGS.

caravan See under HEADWEAR.

caravan bag See HANDBAGS: SAFARI BAG.

carbatina See under FOOTWEAR.

carbuncle See under GEMS, GEM CUTS, AND SETTINGS.

carcaille See under NECKLINES AND COLLARS.

car coat See under COATS AND JACKETS.

†**carded yarn** Yarn made from short fibers, known in the textile industry as staple fibers, that have been subjected to the process of carding. Carding is the first step in making staple fibers into yarns. The fibers are separated, straightened out somewhat, and formed into a weblike mass, after which the web is drawn out and given a greater or lesser degree of twist to form a yarn. Carded yarns have more fibers on the surface and are not as smooth as COMBED YARNS.

cardigan *adj.* Describes collarless garments, with round or V-shaped necklines, that button down the front. The name is derived from that of James Thomas Brudenell, 7th Earl of Cardigan (1797–1868), the lieutenant general in the British Army during the Crimean War who led the famous charge of the Light Brigade. Needing an extra layer of warmth for the cold Crimean winter, he wore a sleeveless knitted woolen vest under his uniform. Present-day cardigans do not resemble the original garment. See under COATS AND JACKETS: CARDIGAN COAT; NECKLINES AND COLLARS: CARDIGAN NECKLINE; SHIRTS: CARDIGAN SHIRT; and SWEATERS: CARDIGAN SWEATER. Shown at SWEATERS: CARDIGAN.

cardinal See under CAPES, CLOAKS, AND SHAWLS.

cardinal pelerine See under NECKLINES AND COLLARS.

carding See under CARDED YARN.

care label Permanently attached label for apparel required by a Federal Trade Commission ruling of 1972. The label must provide care and maintenance directions. Exceptions include hats, gloves, and footwear; articles selling for less than three dollars; items that would be defaced by attaching a label; or items not requiring cleaning.

careless See under COATS AND JACKETS.

cargo *adj.* Apparel that has cargo pockets. See under POCKETS: CARGO POCKET. Also see under PANTS: CARGO PANTS and SHORTS: CARGO SHORTS.

carmagnole See under COATS AND JACKETS.

carmeillette See under CAPES, CLOAKS, AND SHAWLS: CAPUCHON.

carnaby *adj.* Styles adopted first in London in connection with MOD fashions, which were then introduced in the U.S. in 1964. See under NECKLINES AND COLLARS: CARNABY COLLAR.

carnaby cap See under HEADWEAR: NEWSBOY CAP.

carnaby dress See under DRESSES.

Carnaby Street A London backstreet, located behind the grand shopping thoroughfare of Regent Street, where the mod styles first appeared in many small boutiques catering to avant-garde young customers; included such items for sale as miniskirts; capes for men; polka dot shirts with large, flat, white collars; low-slung, bell-bottomed trousers; newsboy caps; and wide vinyl neckties one day—string ties the next. A major factor in the trend for young men to move away from traditional styling, it also influenced skirt lengths for women and styling of children's wear.

carnelian See under GEMS, GEM CUTS, AND SETTINGS.

carnival collar See under NECKLINES AND COLLARS.

carnival lace See under LACES: BRIDAL LACE #2.

∞**caroline corsage** Women's evening bodice of 1830s made with lace ruffles forming a V in front; extended around shoulders into small cape.

Caroline hat See under HEADWEAR.

caroline sleeve See under SHOULDERS AND SLEEVES.

carpenter *adj.* Describes clothing modeled after or influenced by clothing worn by carpenters. See under PANTS: CARPENTER PANTS and APRONS: CARPENTER'S APRON.

carpenter's apron See under APRONS.

carpet bag See under HANDBAGS AND RELATED ACCESSORIES.

carpet slipper See under FOOTWEAR.

carpincho See under LEATHERS.

carriage boot See under FOOTWEAR.

carriage dress See under DRESSES.

carriage parasol See under UMBRELLAS AND PARASOLS.

carriage suit Three-piece set for infant, consisting of jacket, pants, and hat. Worn outdoors in baby carriages since the late 1920s.

carriage trade Coined by merchants (c. 1890–1910) to refer to affluent customers who arrived at the stores in their own carriages. Still sometimes used in reference to upscale customers.

carrick See under COATS AND JACKETS.

carrickmacross lace See under LACES.

carryall See under HANDBAGS AND RELATED ACCESSORIES: TOTE BAG.

carryall clutch See under HANDBAGS AND RELATED ACCESSORIES.

carrying frocks See under LONG CLOTHES.

carryover Apparel styles from one season's line that are repeated the following season. See under COLLECTION.

Cartier Reknown French jeweler with retail stores around the world. Alfred Cartier and his son Louis established the firm in 1898, and by the beginning of the 20th c., they had become the most prestigious jewelers in the world. Among their clients were the king of Portugal, grand dukes and princes of Russia, the Brazilian royal family, and other royalty and celebrities throughout the world.

cartoon apron See under APRONS.

cartoon fashions Apparel imprinted with images of comic strip and cartoon characters. Part of the trend toward LICENSING.

cartoon T-shirt See under SHIRTS.

cartoon watch See under WATCHES.

cartridge belt See under BELTS.

cartridge pleats See under CLOTHING CONSTRUCTION DETAILS.

cartwheel *adj.* Describes apparel that has the shape of a large wheel like those used on carts. For examples see under HEADWEAR: CARTWHEEL HAT; SHOULDERS AND SLEEVES: CARTWHEEL SLEEVES; and NECKLINES AND COLLARS: RUFF.

carwash skirt See under SKIRTS.

casaque See under COATS AND JACKETS: CASAQUE and COATS AND JACKETS: CASSOCK #1.

casaquin See under COATS AND JACKETS: CARACO.

∞**casaquin bodice** Tight-fitting bodice for daytime dress, similar in cut to man's tail coat (see under COATS AND JACKETS: SWALLOW-TAILED COAT), closing with buttons down front and worn in 1878.

casaweck See under COATS AND JACKETS.

cascade **1.** Ruffles, bias cut from fabric in a circular manner, that fall in folds. **2.** Trimming used in the 19th and 20th c., made by cutting a narrow piece of fabric on the BIAS and pleating it to form repeating shell designs. ∞**3.** Jet pendants of beads with a zigzag edge used at waistline or bodice in 1860s. **4.** See under NECKLINES AND COLLARS.

∞**cased body** **1.** Man's sleeveless jerkin worn over DOUBLET in second part of 16th c. **2.** Woman's bodice of early 19th c. with series of horizontal pleats or rows of SHIRRING (see under CLOTHING CONSTRUCTION DETAILS) across the front.

cased sleeve See under SHOULDERS AND SLEEVES.

casentino See under COATS AND JACKETS.

cashambles See under CHAUSSEMBLES.

†**cashgora** Fiber obtained from goats bred in New Zealand that are a cross between female cashmere goats and angora males. The fiber is fine, soft, and strong; has a low-to-medium luster; and dyes well.

†**cashmere** **1.** A fine, soft, downy wool undergrowth produced by the cashmere goat, which is raised in the Kashmir region of India and Pakistan and parts of northern India, Tibet, Mongolia, Turkmenistan, China, Iran, and Iraq. Similar goats are now being raised in the U.S. **2.** Cloth woven from this wool fiber. Synonym: PASHMINA.

cashmere shawl See under CAPES, CLOAKS, AND SHAWLS.

cashmere sweater See under SWEATERS.

cashmere work See under EMBROIDERIES AND SEWING STITCHES.

casing See under CLOTHING CONSTRUCTION DETAILS.

casque See under HEADWEAR.

casquette See under HEADWEAR.

cassock See under COATS AND JACKETS and CLERICAL DRESS.

cassock mantle See under CAPES, CLOAKS, AND SHAWLS.

∞**castellated** (kas-tell-ay′-ted) *adj.* describing a garment with "squared scallops" at edges, particularly the edge of sleeves or hem. Used in 14th and 15th c. Similar to DAGGING. Also see under BATTLEMENT.

caste mark Red mark, usually worn in center of forehead by women of India, that originally symbolized and identified caste or class membership but which now serves a decorative function. Paste-on caste marks were introduced in U.S. as body jewelry for women in 1968. See also under BINDI.

Castle, Irene American ballroom dancer, married to her dancing partner, Vernon Castle. Together they made tea-dancing the rage pre–World War I. By 1914 she had started many fashion fads—earlobe-length hair brushed back off forehead in loose weaves, Dutch lace caps, slashed HOBBLE SKIRTS (see under SKIRTS), and dancing shoes with BALLET LACES (see under FOOTWEAR).

castor See under HEADWEAR.

casual wear Clothing designed to be worn for occasions that do not require more formal dress. Over time, casual wear has been widely accepted for many activities, including some work situations. See under CASUAL FRIDAY. Also see under SPORTSWEAR.

casual work days/casual Friday Working days identified by business or industry when employees can wear casual dress to work. For many companies, the selected day is Friday.

casual Friday style

casula See under CLERICAL DRESS: CHASUBLE.

catagan See under HAIRSTYLES: CADOGAN and WIGS AND HAIRPIECES: CLUB WIG.

catalogue showroom (catalog) Setting like a warehouse in which merchandise is sold from a catalogue or floor samples.

catcher's mask See under MASKS.

catch stitch See under EMBROIDERIES AND SEWING STITCHES.

category killer A product, service, brand, or company that has a competitive advantage that makes it difficult for other companies to compete profitably.

cater cap See under HEADWEAR.

Catherine II Eventual Russian monarch who married Peter III of Russia in 1745; After Peter III ascended the throne in 1762, he was deposed, and his crown usurped by Catherine. A major fashion influence of her time, one of her dresses, worn to receive the Turkish ambassador in 1775, was trimmed with many diamonds and 4,200 magnificent pearls. During her reign, coiffures were limited in height to about 36″.

catherine-wheel farthingale See under FARTHINGALE.

catogan wig See under WIGS AND HAIRPIECES: CLUB WIG.

cat's eye See under GEMS, GEM CUTS, AND SETTINGS.

cat stitch See under EMBROIDERIES AND SEWING STITCHES: CATCH STITCH.

cat suit See under ACTIVEWEAR.

cattlehide See under LEATHERS.

catwalk A runway upon which models walk to show new collections in fashion shows.

caudebec See under HEADWEAR.

caul 1. See under HEADWEAR. 2. See under WIGS AND HAIRPIECES.

cauliflower wig See under WIGS AND HAIRPIECES.

caution fee Fee paid by American designer or manufacturer to attend a showing of a Paris couturier. That fee, which may be equal to cost of one or two items, can be applied to purchases.

cavalier *adj.* Describes apparel derived from or inspired by clothing worn by partisans of King Charles I of England (1625–1649). Among the styles favored by cavalier men were long, curled hairstyles; large-brimmed hats decorated with feathers; wide, flat collars decorated with lace; wide-cuffed boots; and full, hip-length capes. For examples see under HEADWEAR: CAVALIER HAT; NECKLINES AND COLLARS: CAVALIER COLLAR; and SHOULDERS AND SLEEVES: CAVALIER SLEEVE.

cavalier style 1630

cavu shirt See under SHIRTS.

cawdebink See under HEADWEAR: CAUDEBEC.

cawdor cape See under CAPES, CLOAKS, AND SHAWLS: GLENGARRY CAPE.

caxon See under WIGS AND HAIRPIECES.

∞**ceint** (sant) Man's or woman's belt or girdle worn in the 14th and 15th c. Also spelled *seint.*

celata See under ARMOR: SALETT.

cellophane Generic name, once a trademark, for a thin, transparent film made of acetate. Used in ribbon-sized strips to cover paper fibers imitating straw or used alone as synthetic straw for hats, handbags, etc.

celluloid collar See under NECKLINES AND COLLARS.

cellulose Basic substance, a carbohydrate, contained in all vegetable fibers, and certain manufactured fibers, including ACETATE and RAYON.

cervellière See under ARMOR.

ceryphalos See under HEADWEAR.

CFDA See under COUNCIL OF FASHION DESIGNERS OF AMERICA.

CGMM See under COMPUTER GRADING AND MARKER MAKING.

chaconne See under TIES.

chaddah See under CHADOR #1.

chador/chaddar/chadri (*chadder, chaddah, chadur, chadar, chudder, chuddar*) 1. An all-enveloping shapeless cape worn by women in some Muslim countries. Exact cut and how it is worn varies from country to country. It is either worn with a head scarf, or it may cover the wearer from head to toe and have netting over the eyes. In Afghanistan, this garment is called a BURKA. Also spelled BURQA. 2. An Indo-Iranian shawl or mantle about three yards in length. Also called *uttariya.* 3. Indian shawls wrapped around the shoulders or waist by Hindu men.

chador #1

chadur See under CHADOR #1.

chaffers See under HEADWEAR: ENGLISH HOOD.

chain 1. Series of connected loops or links made of metal, plastic, or tortoiseshell used for closings or worn as an ornamental accessory in the form of necklace, bracelet, or belt. Chains are called by various names according to shape of links. **Cobra chain** is composed of two rows of triangular-shaped links that alternate in a flat effect.

chain

Herringbone chain is made of small slanting links, giving a flat effect. **Roped chain** is composed of two (or more) pieces of chain twisted and wound together like rope. 2. *adj.* Used to describe items of apparel that incorporate chains into their design. See under BELTS: CHAIN BELT; CLOSURES: CHAIN CLOSURE; HEADWEAR: CHAIN HAT; FOOTWEAR: LOAFER; and JEWELRY: CHAIN BRACELET and CHAIN NECKLACE.

roped chain

chain mail See under ARMOR: MAIL.

chain store A retail outlet owned by a centralized organization that owns and operates a number of retail outlets in different locations that are similar in the lines of merchandise they sell and in their methods of operation.

∞**chainse** (shens) Medieval garment of the 11th and 12th c. that was worn over a CHEMISE (see under UNDERGARMENTS) and may have been worn as a housedress or perhaps as a summer garment, as it was made of washable, lightweight fabric—probably white linen.

chain stitch See under EMBROIDERIES AND SEWING STITCHES.

chainstitched embroidery See under EMBROIDERIES AND SEWING STITCHES.

chalcedony See under GEMS, GEM CUTS, AND SETTINGS.

chalk stripe See under PRINTS, STRIPES, AND CHECKS.

†**challis** (shal'-lee) Soft, plain-weave fabric made of wool, rayon staple, cotton, or manufactured fiber blends. Supple and lightweight, it is often printed in small floral patterns. Generally used for women's dresses and sportswear, infant wear, and robes.

∞**chamarre** (shah-mar) (*chammer, chymer, samarra, samarre, shamew*) An academic robe made like a long, full coat with sleeves full at the shoulders—usually fur-lined and decorated with braid and passementerie. Introduced around 1490 in England; later referred to a *judge's gown.* Also see under CLERICAL DRESS: SIMAR.

chambord mantle/chambard mantle See under CAPES, CLOAKS, AND SHAWLS.

†**chambray** (sham'-bray) A broad class of plain-weave fabrics made with colored yarns in the lengthwise direction and white yarns in the crosswise direction. May be a plain color, striped, or checked. Usually made of either cotton or manufactured fibers, or a blend of the two.

Chambre Syndicale de la Couture Parisienne (sham'-br san'-dee-kale de lah koo'-ture pah-ree-zee-en) An association of Parisian couturiers founded in 1868 as an outgrowth of medieval guilds that regulates its members in regard to piracy of styles, dates of openings for collections, number of models presented, relations with press, questions of law and taxes, and promotional activities. Formation of the organization was brought about by Charles Frederick Worth. An affiliated school was organized in 1930 called L'École de la Chambre Syndicale de la Couture. Since 1975, this organization has worked within the FÉDÉRATION FRANÇAISE DE COUTURE, DU PRÊT-À-PORTER DES COUTURIERS ET DES CRÉATEURS DE MODE.

Chambre Syndicale de la Mode Masculine (sham'-br san'-dee-kale de lah mode mas'-ku-leen) Organization of couture and men's ready-to-wear designers formed in 1975 as another vehicle for promotion working within the FÉDÉRATION FRANÇAISE DE COUTURE, DU PRÊT-À-PORTER DES COUTURIERS ET DES CRÉATEURS DE MODE.

Chambre Syndicale des Paruriers (sham'-br san'-dee-kale deh pa-roo'-yer) An association comprised of accessory houses in Paris that produce bags, belts, feathers, flowers, gloves, and umbrellas.

Chambre Syndicale du Prêt-à-Porter (sham'-br san'-dee-kale duh pret-ah-por-tay') Organization of couture and women's ready-to-wear designers formed in 1975 as another vehicle for promotion working within the FÉDÉRATION FRANÇAISE DE COUTURE, DU PRÊT-À-PORTER DES COUTURIERS ET DES CRÉATEURS DE MODE.

chameleon fabrics Textiles that can change in color according to external conditions such as temperature, light, and other environmental stimuli.

chammer See under CHAMARRE.

chamois See under LEATHERS.

†**chamois cloth** (sham-wah') Soft cotton fabric that is either knitted or woven. Made with a fine soft nap in imitation of chamois-dyed sheepskin. Should not be shortened or confused with CHAMOIS (see under LEATHERS).

championship ring See under JEWELRY.

chandelier earring See under JEWELRY.

Chanel bag See under HANDBAGS AND RELATED ACCESSORIES.

Chanel jacket See under CHANEL SUIT.

Chanel neckline See under NECKLINES AND COLLARS.

Chanel-style jacket See under CHANEL SUIT.

Chanel-style suit See under CHANEL SUIT.

Chanel suit Classic women's suit style originated by Gabrielle Chanel in the 1920s and revived in the 1960s. It had a collarless, CARDIGAN-style jacket, and the 1960s version was frequently made of plaid fabric with a braid trim. Because the

Chanel suit 1960s

designer's name is a registered trademark of the fashion house she founded, other designers who adapt the design of the Chanel suit or jacket or other Chanel designs must call them *Chanel-style* rather than simply *Chanel.*

changeable earrings See under JEWELRY.

†changeable effect An iridescent effect in fabric that is achieved by using lengthwise and crosswise yarns dyed different colors. Usually made in silk or lustrous manufactured fibers in fabrics such as TAFFETA to achieve the most dramatic effect. Synonyms: *glace* (glahs-ay'), *shot.*

changeable taffeta See under CHANGEABLE EFFECT.

change pocket See under POCKETS: TICKET POCKET.

change purse See under HANDBAGS AND RELATED ACCESSORIES.

channel setting See under GEMS, GEM CUTS, AND SETTINGS.

chantilly lace See under LACES.

chapeau See under HEADWEAR.

chapeau à la charlotte See under HEADWEAR: CHARLOTTE.

chapeau bras See under HEADWEAR.

chapeau claque See under HEADWEAR: OPERA HAT.

chapeau cloche See under HEADWEAR.

chapel cap See under HEADWEAR.

chapel de fer See under ARMOR.

chapel-length train See under LENGTHS.

chapel veil See under HEADWEAR.

chaperon See under HEADWEAR.

chaperone See under HEADWEAR: CHAPERON.

chapiney See under FOOTWEAR: CHOPINE.

chaplet See under HEADWEAR.

chappals See under FOOTWEAR.

chaps See under PANTS.

Charlie Chaplin 1. See under COATS AND JACKETS. 2. See under FOOTWEAR: CHARLIE CHAPLIN TOE.

charlotte See under HEADWEAR.

charlotte corday cap See under HEADWEAR.

charlotte corday fichu See under SCARVES: FICHU #1.

charm See under JEWELRY.

charm bracelet See under JEWELRY.

charm necklace See under JEWELRY.

charro pants See under PANTS.

Chase, Edna Woolman Editor-in-chief of American *Vogue* magazine from 1914 to 1952; also editor of British *Vogue* and French *Vogue,* first published in 1916 and 1920, respectively. Considered one of the most able and competent fashion authorities. One of her outstanding achievements was the introduction in 1914 of a society-sponsored fashion show with live models called "Fashion Fête," the beginning of her long promotion of American designers.

chasembles See under CHAUSSEMBLES.

chasing See under JEWELRY.

chasseur jacket See under COATS AND JACKETS.

chastity belt Belt-like device worn by women in the Middle Ages to ensure marital fidelity.

chasuble See under CLERICAL DRESS.

chatelaine (shat'-eh-lane) 1. Ornamental device of oxidized silver, silver-plated metal, or cut steel, suspended at a woman's waistline or hooked to belt to hold small items such as scissors, thimble case, tape measure, penknife, watch, keys, or buttonhook. Worn in last half of 19th c. See CORDELIÈRE. 2. Antique silver or plated scent bottle worn around neck on a long chain in 1980s. *Der.* French, "lady of the castle." Also see under JEWELRY and WATCHES.

chatelaine #1

chatelaine bag See under HANDBAGS AND RELATED ACCESSORIES.

chatelaine watch See under WATCHES.

chati cat See under FURS: SPOTTED CAT.

chatoyancy See under GEMS, GEM CUTS, AND SETTINGS.

chausembles See under CHAUSSEMBLES.

∞chausons (show-son') (French) Equivalent of the English underpants, called BRAIES (see under UNDERGARMENTS), worn from the 5th through the 13th c.

∞chausse (shos) 1. See under ARMOR. 2. Stockings and trunks cut in one piece, similar to contemporary tights. First worn in Norman period (1066–1154). Later in the Middle Ages, they fastened to the upper garment (a DOUBLET) by means of lacers called POINTS. 3. Around mid-16th c. chausses were divided into two parts—upper part then called haut de chausses, later called TRUNK HOSE and upper stocks. Lower part was called **bas de chausses** (ba deh shos), then hose, and finally stockings. 4. See under CAPES,

chausse #2

CLOAKS, AND SHAWLS: EPITOGA #2. *Der.* French, "bottom of hose." Also see LOWER STOCKS.

∞**chaussembles** (show′-som-bl) (*chausembles, chasembles, cashambles*) Man's cut-and-sewn hose with attached soles of leather or whalebone worn in Middle Ages. Likely cut on the BIAS to provide some degree of stretch, they were somewhat baggy and ill-fitting as compared to later knitted HOSIERY.

∞**chausses en bourse** (shos on boorce) Breeches padded so they were fuller at bottom—making a flattened balloon shape; worn in 17th c. *Der.* French, "bag breeches."

chausses en tonnelet See under TRUNK HOSE.

chaussures à crics See under FOOTWEAR.

∞**cheat** 1. Man's waistcoat or vest of 17th c. with expensive fabric in front and poorer quality in back. 2. 19th-c. man's false shirt front with collar attached, which was worn instead of a full shirt in the 19th c.

chechia See under HEADWEAR.

check/checks See under introduction to PRINTS, STRIPES, AND CHECKS.

checked gingham See under GINGHAM.

checkerboard checks See under PRINTS, STRIPES, AND CHECKS.

checkerboard hose See under HOSIERY.

∞**checkered-apron man** English barbers of 16th c. distinguished by the checked pattern of their aprons. Also see under BLUE-APRONED MEN and GREEN-APRONED MEN.

cheek wrappers See under HEADWEAR: DORMEUSE.

cheeks-and-ears See under HEADWEAR: COIF #3 and ORRELET.

cheetah See under FURS.

chef's apron See under APRONS.

chef's hat See under HEADWEAR.

Chelsea *adj.* Describes apparel in the style of that worn by the Chelsea Set, young people who frequented a London area called Chelsea that was popular with artists and writers. Items chosen by this group had far-reaching influence on general fashion trends, which changed from time to time and were usually copied in other countries. In the late 1940s and 1950s, tight jeans from the U.S. were popular; in the late 1960s, old uniforms—including nurses' or policemen's uniforms, red guardsmen's tunics, and Navy overcoats—were all featured. Also see under NECKLINES AND COLLARS: CHELSEA COLLAR and FOOTWEAR: BEATLE BOOT.

chemise (shem-ees′) 1. See under UNDERGARMENTS. 2. See under DRESSES.

chemise gown See under DRESSES: PERDITA CHEMISE.

chemise slip See under UNDERGARMENTS.

chemisette (shem-ee-zet′) 1. See under SCARVES. 2. See under BLOUSES AND TOPS. 3. See under VESTEE. 4. See under SHIRTS: HABIT SHIRT.

∞**chemisette à jabot** (ah zha′-bo) Embroidered or pleated ruffle of 1850s and 1860s worn as a fill-in at front opening of a REDINGOTE (see under COATS AND JACKETS: REDINGOTE #5), showing from neck to waist.

∞**chemisette garter** Vertical supporter for hose attached to the corset in 1830s and 1840s.

chemise tucker See under SCARVES: CHEMISETTE.

†**chenille** Fabrics made from chenille yarns. These yarns have a fuzzy surface with short fibers projecting on all sides. Chenille fabrics may be woven or knitted. When woven, they are usually made with the chenille yarns in the crosswise direction.

chenille embroidery See under EMBROIDERIES AND SEWING STITCHES.

chenille lace See under LACES.

cheongsam See under DRESSES.

cherusse See under NECKLINES AND COLLARS.

chesterfield See under COATS AND JACKETS.

Chesterfield, 6th Earl of A British fashion leader in the 1830s and 1840s after whom the CHESTERFIELD COAT (see under COATS AND JACKETS) was named.

chest-high boot See under FOOTWEAR: WADERS.

chesticore See under COATS AND JACKETS: JUSTAUCORPS.

chest measurement 1. Men: distance around body at fullest part of upper torso; one of the measurements by which suits are sold. 2. Women: measurement around the body across the back, high up under the arm and above the fullest part of the bust; differs from the **bust measurement,** which is taken at fullest part of bosom.

†**cheviot** (shev′-ee-ott) 1. Rough-surfaced, hairy fabric made in a plain or twill weave from wool, manufactured fibers, or blends. Does not hold a crease well; therefore, it is generally used for casual clothing. 2. Cotton shirting woven with fairly heavy yarns in checked, striped, or small-figured patterns.

chevron 1. Motif consisting of two straight lines meeting to form an inverted V. 2. Badge of these V stripes worn on sleeve by policemen, firemen, and the military to indicate rank.

∞**chevrons** Trimmings for women's clothes introduced in mid-1820s; usually a zigzag band near hem of skirt.

chic 1. *n.* The quality of being very much in style. 2. *adj.* Smart, sophisticated, stylish.

chicken skin See under LEATHERS.

chicken-skin gloves See under GLOVES AND GLOVE CONSTRUCTION.

†chiffon 1. Thin, transparent fabric made in a plain weave. It drapes well and is made from tightly twisted or CREPE YARN. Originally made in silk; now also made in manufactured fibers. Dyed solid colors or printed in floral designs. Uses: sheer dresses, blouses, and scarves. 2. A trifle or bit of feminine finery. *Der.* French, *chiffe,* "rag."

chignon See under HAIRSTYLES.

chignon cap See under HEADWEAR.

chignon strap See under HEADWEAR.

chill mask See under MASKS: HOT MASK.

chimere/chimer See under CLERICAL DRESS.

chimney-pot hat See under HEADWEAR: TOP HAT.

China doll hairstyle See under HAIRSTYLES.

china grass See under RAMIE.

china mink See under FURS.

china ribbon 1. Narrow ribbon, about ⅛″ wide, woven with a plain edge popular in mid-19th c. for China ribbon embroidery. See under EMBROIDERIES AND SEWING STITCHES: ROCOCO.

†china silk Soft, lustrous silk fabric in a plain weave that may have slight texture due to use of irregular yarns; made in China and Japan. Originally handmade in China as early as 1200 B.C., the name is also applied to machine-made fabrics of a similar type.

chinchilla See under FURS.

†chinchilla cloth Thick, heavyweight coat fabric, of wool, or wool and cotton blend, distinguished by curly nubs on the surface. 1. Woven as a double cloth with a plain back and a satin face. Extra crosswise yarns added to the face of fabric are loosely floated over the surface. When napped and rubbed into curled tufts, these yarns form distinctive nubs on the surface. Less expensive fabric is not woven in the same manner and may have a different surface effect. 2. A similar fabric made by knitting and brushing surface yarns into nubs.

chin cloak See under SCARVES.

chiné See under PRINTS, STRIPES, AND CHECKS: WARP PRINT.

Chinese *adj.* Describes apparel that is adapted from or inspired by Chinese styles, including items such as MAO JACKETS and MANDARIN COATS (see under COATS AND JACKETS), CHINESE PAJAMAS (see under SLEEPWEAR AND LOUNGEWEAR), MANDARIN NECKLINES (see under NECKLINES AND COLLARS), and Chinese dresses with side slit called CHEONGSAM (see under DRESSES). When China opened its doors to the West in the early 1970s, there was a revival of interest in Chinese fashions resulting in such styles as the basic worker's suit—or MAO SUIT—quilted jackets, the CHINESE SHOE, and denim workers' coats. Saint Laurent featured Chinese ensembles in 1977 that included small versions of red conical Asian hats; jackets of red and gold brocade with frog closings and mandarin collars; and pants tapered to hem worn with boots having flared tops.

chinese collar See under NECKLINES AND COLLARS.

Chinese design Design composed of motifs such as dragons, lanterns, clouds, and mountains, in style typical of Chinese paintings and embroideries.

Chinese dog See under FURS.

Chinese dress See under DRESSES: CHEONGSAM.

chinese embroidery See under EMBROIDERIES AND SEWING STITCHES.

chinese jacket See under COATS AND JACKETS: CHINESE JACKET and MAO JACKET.

chinese knot Ornamental knot of covered cord used as trimming on apparel. Copied from traditional ornaments on Chinese robes.

Chinese lamb See under FURS: KARACUL.

chinese lounging robe See under SLEEPWEAR AND LOUNGEWEAR.

chinese pajamas See under SLEEPWEAR AND LOUNGEWEAR.

chinese raccoon See under FURS: USSURIAN RACCOON.

chinese shoe See under FOOTWEAR.

chinese slipper See under FOOTWEAR: KAMPSKATCHA SLIPPER.

chinner See under SCARVES: CHIN CLOAK.

†chino (chee′-no) Durable cotton, firmly woven with a fine steep twill and dyed a yellowish-tan or khaki color. Contemporary versions are also dyed in many colors. Originally used for summer uniforms for the U.S. Army, by the 1950s the fabric had been adopted by teenagers for school and general wear, particularly for pants. Now used for a wide variety of casual clothing.

chinoise, à la (shin′-waaz, ah lah) (French) Phrase meaning "from the Chinese." Often used as an English fashion term to describe items of apparel that show Chinese influences.

chinoiserie (shin-waaz-ze-ree′) Those designs in textiles, fashion, and the decorative arts that derive from Chinese styles.

chinos See under PANTS.

chin stays See under HEADWEAR.

†chintz Medium-weight cotton or blended fabric with a glazed or shiny finish that may be a plain color or printed with floral, bird, or other designs. Originally a fabric for slipcovers and draperies; now also used for variety of items such as beachwear, shorts, blouses, skirts, dresses, and rainwear. *Der.* Indian, *chint,* name for a gaudily printed fabric of cotton.

chip See under GEMS, GEM CUTS, AND SETTINGS.

chip bonnet See under HEADWEAR.

chip straw Wood or straw cut in fine strips for hats or baskets. Used for women's hats in 18th c. and for women's CHIP BONNETS (see under HEADWEAR) in the 19th c.

chique-tades See under SLASHING.

∞**chiton** (ki'-tawn) Garment worn in ancient Greece that consisted of a rectangle of fabric wrapped around the body and fastened at the shoulders with one or more pins. A number of variations of this basic style were worn at different points in Greek history. They were as follows: (1) **chitoniskos** (ki-tawn-iss'-kos): Worn by men from about 800 to 550 B.C., usually short, made of patterned wool, and fitted closely to the body; (2) **doric peplos**: Worn by women from about 800 to 550 B.C., usually reaching to the ankles, pinned at the shoulder with a large pin; made of patterned wool and fitted closely to the body; (3) **ionic chiton** (eye-ohn'-ik ki'-tawn): Worn from 550 B.C. to 480 B.C. (and less often from 480 B.C. to 300 B.C.) by men and women, either short (for men) or long, and made of lightweight wool or of linen and pleated. More fully cut than earlier chitons, it had long, full sleeves fastened with many small brooches at the shoulder; (4) **doric chiton**: Worn from 400 B.C. to 100 B.C. by men and from 450 B.C. to 300 B.C. by women and made of wool, linen, or silk; was generally short when worn by men and long when worn by women. More narrowly fitted than the ionic chiton, and sleeveless, it was fastened at each shoulder with a single pin. (5) **helenistic chiton**: Worn by women from 300 to 100 B.C., similar to the doric chiton but narrower, and often belted below the bosom, this chiton was worn long and made of lightweight wool, linen, or silk; (6) **exomis**: Worn by working-class men and slaves in all Greek periods, this chiton was short and fastened over one shoulder and was probably made from sturdy, durable wool fabric.

chitoniskos See under CHITON.

∞**chitterlings** (chit-er-lings) Popular term used in the 18th and 19th c. for frills or ruffles on front of man's shirt.

chlaine See under CAPES, CLOAKS, AND SHAWLS.

∞**chlamydon** (kla'-mee-don) A type of outer garment for women in ancient Greece that was pleated to a band of fabric and worn under the left arm and over the right shoulder.

chlamydon

chlamys See under CAPES, CLOAKS, AND SHAWLS.

chlorspinel See under GEMS, GEM CUTS, AND SETTINGS: SPINEL.

choir-boy collar See under NECKLINES AND COLLARS.

choir robe Ankle-length closed robes, similar to academic gowns (see under introduction to ACADEMIC COSTUME), worn by singers in church choirs.

choker Accessory or item clothing that fits high on the neck. See under NECKLINES AND COLLARS and JEWELRY.

choli See under BLOUSES AND TOPS.

choori-dars See under PANTS.

chitoniskos

doric peplos

ionic chiton worn under a shawl

doric chiton

helenistic chiton

exomis

chopine See under FOOTWEAR.

chou (shoo) (pl. *choux*) **1.** Frilly pouf of fabric used at neckline. **2.** Large rosette used to trim gowns in late 19th and early 20th c. **3.** See under HEADWEAR. **4.** See under HAIRSTYLES: CHIGNON. *Der.* French, "cabbage."

christening dress See under DRESSES.

chrome tanning See under LEATHERS.

chronograph See under WATCHES.

chronometric watch See under WATCHES.

chrysoberyl See under GEMS, GEM CUTS, AND SETTINGS.

chrysolite See under GEMS, GEM CUTS, AND SETTINGS: PERIDOT.

chrysoprase See under GEMS, GEM CUTS, AND SETTINGS.

chubby See under COATS AND JACKETS.

chuddah/chudder See under CHADOR #1.

chukka (chuh′-ka) Periods in the game of polo. Used to describe modern clothes and accessories similar to those worn when playing polo. See under FOOTWEAR: CHUKKA BOOTS; HEADWEAR: CHUKKA HAT; and SHIRTS: POLO SHIRT.

chunky heel See under FOOTWEAR.

chunky shoe See under FOOTWEAR.

chute See under JEWELRY.

chymer See under CHAMARRE.

ciclaton See under CYCLAS.

cigarette pant See under PANTS.

CIM See under COMPUTER INTEGRATED MANUFACTURING.

cinch **1.** See under BELTS. **2.** See under WAISTLINES: CINCHED WAISTLINE.

cinch buckle/cinch closing See under CLOSURES: RING CLOSING.

cincture **1.** See under BELTS. **2.** See under CLERICAL DRESS.

cinglation See under CYCLAS.

cingulum **1.** See under BELTS. **2.** See under CLERICAL DRESS.

circassian round robe See under DRESSES.

∞**circassian wrapper** (ser-kash′-yan) Loose wrap, cut somewhat like a nightgown, worn by women for daytime in Empire Period, 1813. *Der.* Caucasian tribe of Circassia, a historical region west of the Caucasus mountains and north of the Black Sea.

∞**circassienne** Late-18th c. version of *the polonaise* (a draped skirt), worn by women just before French Revolution. *Der.* French, "circassian."

circle/circular *adj.* Describes garments that are shaped like a circle. See under CAPES, CLOAKS, AND SHAWLS: CIRCULAR; SKIRTS: CIRCLE; SHOULDERS AND SLEEVES: CARTWHEEL SLEEVE; and POCKETS: ROUND POCKET.

circular See under CAPES, CLOAKS, AND SHAWLS.

circular hem See under CLOTHING CONSTRUCTION DETAILS.

†**circular knit** Fabric knitted in a tubular shape with no SELVAGE. Made either by hand or machine. Pantyhose knitted in this manner have no seams.

circular ruffle Ruffle cut from circle of fabric rather than straight across the grain, making graceful folds less bulky than a gathered ruffle. Also see under CASCADE #1.

circumfolding hat See under HEADWEAR: OPERA HAT.

†**ciré** (sear-ray′) Finishing process or the fabric produced by the process in which wax or other compounds are applied to the surface of a fabric, after which a hot roller is passed over the surface to produce a high polish. If the fibers in the fabric are heat sensitive, the fibers will fuse and the effect will be permanent.

†**ciselé velvet** (seez-el-ay′) A fabric with a raised pattern of velvet figures on a satin ground formed by cut and uncut loops—with the cut pile being higher.

citrine See under GEMS, GEM CUTS, AND SETTINGS.

city boots See under FOOTWEAR.

city pants/city shorts Coined by the fashion-industry newspaper *Women's Wear Daily* in 1968 for women's pants or shorts suitable for town wear. Also see under PANTS: CITY PANTS and SHORTS: CITY SHORTS.

civet cat See under FURS.

clamdiggers See under PANTS.

claque See under HEADWEAR.

clara bow hat See under HEADWEAR.

clarence See under FOOTWEAR.

clarissa harlowe bonnet/hat See under HEADWEAR.

∞**clarissa harlowe corsage** Evening-dress bodice with an off-the-shoulder neckline, folds caught at the waist by band of ribbon, and short sleeves trimmed with two or three lace ruffles. Worn in late 1840s. *Der.* From heroine in novel *Clarissa, or the History of a Young Lady,* by Samuel Richardson, published in 1747–48.

classic Apparel made in a style that continues to be fashionable over a long period of time, and that may return to high fashion at intervals. When revived, classic fashions retain the basic line of the original style, but are sometimes altered in minor details, e.g., COATS AND JACKETS: CARDIGAN, BLAZER, TRENCHCOAT, and POLO COAT; or DRESSES: CHEMISE and SHIRTWAIST DRESS.

classic look See under BROOKS BROTHERS and PREPPY.

classic pull-back See under HAIRSTYLES.

classification (class) A general type of merchandise that is housed within an individual department. Examples include: sportswear, evening wear, or lingerie.

class ring See under JEWELRY.

claw-hammer coat See under COATS AND JACKETS.

clayshooter's vest See under VESTS.

clean-stitched seam See under CLOTHING CONSTRUCTION DETAILS.

cleats See under FOOTWEAR.

cleavage 1. See under GEMS, GEM CUTS, AND SETTINGS. 2. Separation between a woman's breasts, made more obvious when a low neckline is worn.

clerical cape See under CLERICAL DRESS.

clerical collar See under CLERICAL DRESS.

CLERICAL DRESS

Items of clothing worn by members of the clergy either during rituals being celebrated or as a means of identifying their clerical status within their religion. Also called *ecclesiastical dress* or *clerical vestments.* These entries do not include religious garb or symbols worn by lay members of a religion. Such entries will be found in the alphabetical listing.

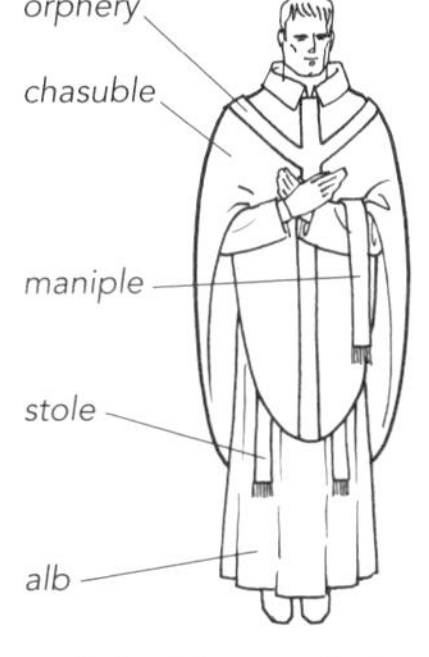

clerical dress: priest

alb Full-length, long-sleeved LITURGICAL ROBE (see under ROBE #2) with drawstring neckline or cowl hood worn by priests at Mass. Originally of white linen, now often of blended cotton and man-made fibers. *Der.* Latin, "white."

amice (am'-ees) A strip of linen placed around the shoulders and tied in position to form a collar worn by priests saying mass.

bäffchen See under CLERICAL DRESS: GENEVA BANDS.

biretta (bi-ret'-tah) **birretta/berrette/barrette** 1. Stiff, square clerical cap with three or four upright projections on top radiating from center, sometimes finished with a pompon. 2. 16th-c.: a round cap that later became square on top when hatters learned to use a rigid frame. Worn by clergy today, e.g., cardinals and bishops.

calotte (ka-loht') **calot/callot** Tiny, close-fitting skullcap cut in shaped gores, often with a tab at center of top; worn by Roman clergy, priests, and monks in early Christian orders—now worn by the pope. Also called *zucchetto* (zook-ket'-toe).

camauro (ka-mao'-row) Red velvet, ermine-trimmed cap slightly larger than a skullcap, formerly worn by pope of Roman Catholic Church.

campagus (kam-pa'-gus) Shoe worn by bishops in Western Church, particularly Roman Catholic, sometimes Episcopal.

capuche See under HEADWEAR.

cassock

cassock 1. Full-length liturgical robe, made like a coat with standing collar, worn by clergy, altar boys, and choirs, sometimes under white SURPLICE or COTTA (see under CLERICAL DRESS). Also called *soutane* (soo-tahn'). 2. Short front-buttoned jacket worn by clerics.

casula (kas-oo'-lah) Latin name for CHASUBLE (see under CLERICAL DRESS).

chasuble (chaz'-yu-behl) Sleeveless clerical garment, shaped somewhat like a PONCHO (see under CAPES, CLOAKS, AND SHAWLS), with round neckline and open sides. Sometimes has a Y-shaped band from neck to hem called the ORPHREY (see under CLERICAL DRESS). Worn as part of vestments at the celebration of Mass in the early Christian church, now worn by priests over the cassock. *Der.* Latin, *casula,* "cloak."

chimere/chimer (she'-mar) Full-length, sleeveless robe, similar to an academic robe worn by Anglican bishops. Extra-full lawn sleeves were attached to armholes.

cincture (sink'-cher) Twisted rayon, silk, or rope belt—approximately eight feet in length—worn by clergy with the ALB (see under CLERICAL DRESS). It is worn doubled, with one end pulled through the loop and the long ends hanging free. With tassels on the end, called **traditional**; when knotted at the end, called **contemporary**. Shown at COPE.

cingulum (sin-goo'-lum) Belt worn with liturgical garments since Middle Ages.

clerical cape Three-quarter-length cape of wool MELTON with satin lining, small velvet collar, and braided frog closing worn by clergy.

clerical collar Stiff, white, standing band collar worn by clergy with suit or with liturgical robes. May be fastened in back as a **roman collar** or have a narrow opening in front. White collar is sometimes half covered by a similar black collar, which may be attached to the CASSOCK or to a bib-like RABAT (see under CLERICAL DRESS). Also see under CLERICAL DRESS: GENEVA BANDS.

clerical front An adjustable shirt front worn by clergymen with a black business suit or under a pulpit robe.

Fits around the neck usually with black collar on top of a white collar. Ties secure the garment at the waist. Usually made in black faille or wool, with or without a center pleat down the front. Also called *shirt front.*

clerical shirt Black or gray shirt with short or long sleeves styled, a fly-front, and standing CLERICAL COLLAR (see under CLERICAL DRESS) worn by clergymen. A second collar of white may be inserted inside the neckline. Frequently has white cuffs. Formerly made of lightweight wool, now made in wash-and-wear fabrics.

colobium (koh-lo′-bee-um) A liturgical garment derived from a Roman secular garment consisting of a long linen tunic, either sleeveless or with short sleeves. It was replaced by the DALMATIC.

cope Ornately embroidered, semicircular mantle, fastened across the chest with an elaborate clasp arrangement worn on ceremonial occasions by the pope and dignitaries of the Roman Catholic Church and by priests offering the Benediction.

cope and cincture

cotta (coat′-tah) Clerical surplice made like a full, short, white overtunic, gathered into a narrow rounded yoke with long, full, bell-shaped sleeves. Worn by clergy over CASSOCK and by choir members over long robes.

dalmatic See under DALMATIC.

ecclesiastical vestments Garments worn by the clergy for religious services.

fanons Two decorative LAPPETS attached to back of miter worn by the pope, which hung down over the shoulders. These may originally have been used to hold the miter on the head. See under CLERICAL DRESS: MITER.

ferraiolo (fair-ay-o′-lo) A full-length, black, circular cape worn as an outer garment by clerics over other vestments for ceremonial occasions such as receptions, academic occasions, or banquets.

fisherman's ring Gold ring used at investiture of the pope of the Roman Catholic Church. The figure of St. Peter in a fisherman's boat is engraved on the ring along with name of the pope.

geneva bands Collar consisting of two short white linen tabs hanging down from the neckline, attached to a string tied around the neck. Worn mainly by clergy. Also called *short bands* and *bäffchen* (bef′-ken). *Der.* Originated by Swiss Calvinist clergy in Geneva, Switzerland.

geneva gown Black clerical gown worn by Calvinists and later by other Protestant clergy; similar to an academic robe and often worn with two vertical white linen bands at the neck called GENEVA BANDS (see under CLERICAL DRESS).

∞geneva hat Wide-brimmed, high-crowned hat worn in late 16th and early 17th c. by Puritan ministers and others.

liturgical robe See under ROBE #2.

maniple Narrow ornamental band about 3″ long, worn by Catholic priests on the left arm near the wrist.

mantelletta (mahn-tell-et′-tah) Sleeveless, thigh-length, circular-cut garment that opens in front and has a small collar. Worn by prelates of Roman Catholic Church over the ROCHET, it is made of silk or wool with two vertical slits for arms. For cardinals it is red, purple, or rose-colored. See under CLERICAL DRESS: ROCHET.

mantellone (mahn-tell-own′-nay) Purple ankle-length ecclesiastical mantle, worn over the CASSOCK (see under CLERICAL DRESS) by lesser prelates of Papal court of the Roman Catholic Church.

miter Tall, ornamental headpiece, worn by Catholic and Episcopal church dignitaries, with high separate pointed arches in front and back.

miter

mozetta (mo-zet′-tah) Elbow-length cape with ornamental hood hanging in back, worn by cardinals and church dignitaries. *Der.* Italian *mozzare,* "to cut short."

orphrey (or′-free) (*orfray, orfrey*) Y-shaped band of embroidery decorating the CHASUBLE (see under CLERICAL DRESS), which extends from each shoulder in both the front and back to meet and form a vertical stripe in center front and back. See illustration at category heading CLERICAL DRESS.

pallium A narrow band of white wool that was worn by popes and archbishops. Prelates wore the band with one end falling to the front and the other to the back.

parament (pa′-ra-ment) Synonym for an ornamental ecclesiastical vestment.

pileolus/pilleolus (pil-eh′-oh-lus) Skullcap worn by Catholic priests and pope under the MITER and TIARA (see under CLERICAL DRESS). *Der.* Latin, "skullcap."

rabat (rab-e; ra-bat) Black dickey or shirt front to which the white CLERICAL COLLAR is attached (see under CLERICAL DRESS). Worn by Catholic and Protestant clergy, with suits or with liturgical robes.

rabat

rochet (rash′-et) Similar to a SURPLICE (see under CLERICAL DRESS) and worn especially by bishops and abbots.

roman collar See under CLERICAL DRESS: CLERICAL COLLAR.

shirt front See under CLERICAL DRESS: CLERICAL FRONT.

short bands See under CLERICAL DRESS: GENEVA BANDS.

simar (si-mar′) Clerical robe, similar to full-length CASSOCK (see under CLERICAL DRESS), but having short button-on false sleeves and a shoulder cape that does not fasten in front. Worn at home or on the street (but not worn for high church services), particularly by prelates of the Catholic church. Made of white wool for the pope, black wool with scarlet trimmings for cardinals, black wool with amaranth red or purple trim for penitential or mourning days for bishops, and ash-gray wool for Franciscans. Also worn by seminarians without the false sleeves (thus indicating inferior dignity). Also see under CHAMARRE.

soutane See under CLERICAL DRESS: CASSOCK #1.

stole Long, narrow scarf, part of clerical vestments worn over the COTTA (see under CLERICAL DRESS) by clergymen.

surplice Loose, white overblouse, either waist- or knee-length, gathered to flat yoke with full open sleeves; worn by clergy, acolytes, and choir singers. Also see under CLERICAL DRESS: COTTA.

tiara (tee-ar′-a) An ancient headpiece, worn by the pope of the Roman Catholic Church, consisting of three coronets placed one on top of the other, each successively smaller.

ventilated collar Stiff, white, standing collar punctured with holes around the sides and back. Used to support the black CLERICAL COLLAR, creating a white trim at center front and around the edge.

vestments See under introduction to CLERICAL DRESS.

zucchetto See under CLERICAL DRESS: CALOTTE.

---

clerical front See under CLERICAL DRESS.

clerical shirt See under CLERICAL DRESS.

clip See under JEWELRY.

clip-back earring See under JEWELRY.

clip closure See under CLOSURES.

clip hat See under HEADWEAR: BICYCLE-CLIP HAT.

clip-on sunglasses See under EYEWEAR.

clip-on tie See under TIES.

cloak See under introduction to CAPES, CLOAKS, AND SHAWLS.

∞**Cloak and Suit Industry** Name given to manufacturers of coats and suits when the first U.S. census of the clothing industry was made in 1860. This category made up half of the total number of manufacturing establishments in the country. Originally called *Cloak and Mantilla Manufacturers,* later called *Coat and Suit Industry.*

∞**cloak bag breeches** Full, oval-shaped man's breeches fastened above or below the knee, with decorative points or bows. Worn in early 17th c. Also see under BREECHES.

cloche See under HEADWEAR.

clock 1. See under HOSIERY: CLOCKED HOSE. 2. Triangular gore inserted into a stocking, cape, or collar to make it wider, with embroidery over the joined seams. Worn since the 16th c.

clog See under FOOTWEAR.

cloisonné (kloi-zeh-nay′) An enameling technique in which small areas of colored enamel separated by thin metal bands form the design. This technique is used in a wide variety of types of jewelry. *Der.* French, "partitioned." Also see under JEWELRY: CLOISONNÉ NECKLACE.

close coat See under COATS AND JACKETS.

closed display/closed back display See under WINDOW DISPLAYS.

closed dress/closed gown See under DRESSES: ROUND DRESS.

closed island displays Display in which merchandise is visible but enclosed behind glass. Often used for especially valuable objects. See under SHOWCASE DISPLAY.

closed seam See under FOOTWEAR.

closeout Merchandise that remains unsold from a seasonal line. Usually all these remaining items are sold at a discount.

closeout store A discount store to which a retailer sends merchandise from its regular-price store that has been slow to sell or has reached the end of its season.

close-plate buckle See under CLOSURES.

close stitch See under EMBROIDERIES AND SEWING STITCHES: BUTTONHOLE STITCH.

closing 1. Manner in which an item of apparel fastens. Early clothing in Europe was draped and held together by belts or pins called FIBULAE. Later, lacing was used, then buttons—with men's clothing buttoning left to right and women's buttoning right to left. 2. The type of device by which a garment or part of a garment is secured. See under introduction to CLOSURES.

CLOSURES

closure A device used to close or fasten shoes or a garment. Synonym: *closing.*

abalone button (ah-bah-low-nee′) Type of pearl button made from shell of a mollusk called an *ear shell,* or *sea-ear,* found off Pacific coast of the U.S.

asymmetric closing Garment closing that fastens at the side or diagonally rather than at the center of the garment.

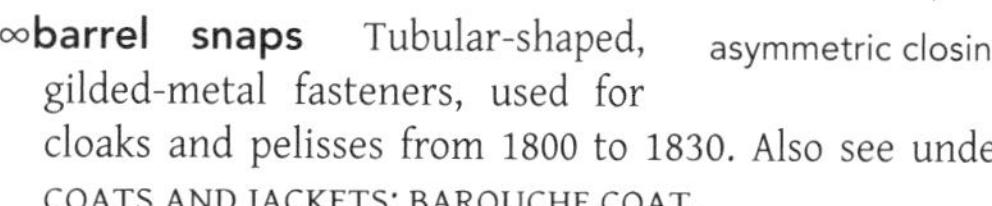

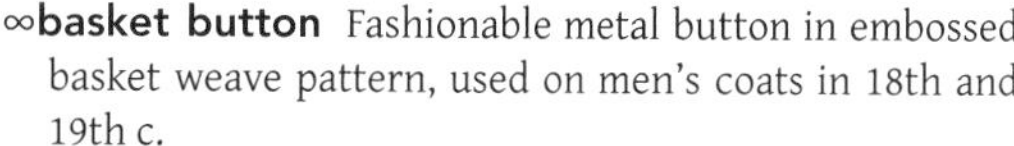

asymmetric closing

barred buttonhole See under CLOSURES: WORKED BUTTONHOLE.

∞**barrel snaps** Tubular-shaped, gilded-metal fasteners, used for cloaks and pelisses from 1800 to 1830. Also see under COATS AND JACKETS: BAROUCHE COAT.

∞**basket button** Fashionable metal button in embossed basket weave pattern, used on men's coats in 18th and 19th c.

belt buckle Any ornamental or functional device, usually plastic or metal, used to fasten a belt.

blazer button Distinctive brass or gold-plated brass button with a monogram, a coat-of-arms, or a crest embossed or engraved on top. Usually sold by the set, which includes three large and four small sleeve buttons. Specifically used on blazers. See under COATS AND JACKETS: BLAZERS.

blind eyelet Shoe-industry term for metal eyelet concealed in the inner surface of leather while the outside layer has a punched hole through which shoestring is pulled.

bound buttonhole Buttonhole with edges finished with separate strips of fabric or leather binding.

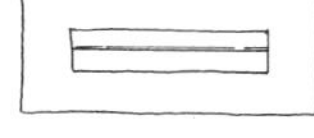

bound buttonhole

brass button Gilt button made of brass or of other metals or plastic gilded to simulate brass. Brass buttons are often used on jackets and coats worn by U.S. military personnel. Brass buttons are also used by civilians on various types of apparel.

∞**breasts** As used by tailors' bills in the 18th c. to refer to waistcoat buttons. Coat buttons were listed as **coats**.

buckle A decorative or functional clasp, usually of metal, wood, or plastic. Consists of a rectangular or curved rim, often with one or more movable tongues. Also a clip device fixed to end of a strap that is used to fasten to other end of belt or to another strap. Used in various periods as a decorative feature for belts, shoes, and knee breeches.

military buckle

∞**buckles d'artois** Shoe buckles of enormous size worn from 1775 to 1788. *Der.* Named after the Comte d'Artois, later Charles X of France.

button 1. A decorative ornament used for trimming or as a functional fastener. Usually made with holes punched in center or a shank on the back, they close by slipping through a buttonhole or loop. First introduced in the 13th c. as trim, buttons became functional by the 14th c.; by the 16th c. buttons of all types were used. *Der.* French, *bouton,* a round object, a bud, a knob. 2. See under GLOVES AND GLOVE CONSTRUCTION.

buttonhole Opening for button to go through in order to secure the garment. Generally classified as either a BOUND or a WORKED buttonhole (see under CLOSURES). Their use dates from about the 15th c.

button hooks See under CLOSURES: SPEED LACING.

∞**calico button** Metal ring covered with calico, sometimes with metal eyelets in center, used mainly for undergarments from 1840s on.

chain closure Laced closing using a metal chain instead of a lacer. Used on vests and blouses, it was a novelty of the late 1960s.

cinch buckle/cinch closure See under CLOSURES: RING BUCKLE.

clip closure Metal fastener with a spring-backed device on one side of garment and a ring, eyelet, or slotted fastener on other side. Used mainly on raincoats, jackets, car coats, and also on jewelry.

∞**close-plate buckle** Shoe buckle of late 1660s to 1680s made of tutania—an alloy of tin, antimony, and copper—cast in a mold by a street peddler in about fifteen minutes.

coats See under CLOSURES: BREASTS.

collar button See under CLOSURES: STUD.

covered button Ball- or disk-type button covered with fabric either matching or contrasting with garment. Kits of various-sized disks to be covered may be purchased by the home sewer. First used in latter part of 16th c. The button industry in the U.S. was started in 1826 by Emily Graves Williston, wife of storekeeper Samuel Williston in East Hampshire, Massachusetts, who first covered wooden buttons by hand. Later she invented a machine for this purpose and her factory was credited with one-half of the world production of buttons.

covered zipper Zipper made with fabric tape covering teeth so that they do not show when zipper is closed.

crocheted button Shank-type buttons made by crocheting over a disk, a ball, or a barrel-shaped object. Sometimes used on sweaters and formerly used on dresses and coats in Victorian era and early 19th c.

cuff button 1. Small button, usually of mother-of-pearl, sewed on shirt cuff to fasten it. Introduced in 19th c. and used in lieu of *cuff links.* ∞2. In the late 17th c., referred to two metal disks connected by links used to replace earlier CUFF STRING (see under CLOSURES).

∞**cuff string** String pulled through eyelets on cuff to fasten it. Used in lieu of a button in the 17th c. Also called *sleeve string.*

cut-steel buckle Popular buckle of early 20th c. made of polished steel with jewel-like facets. Used on silk or moiré afternoon or evening shoes and on belts.

∞**death's head button** Domed 18th-c. button covered with metal thread or mohair, which formed an X on top like the cross of the skull and crossbones.

∞**dorset thread button** Brass wire ring covered with cotton threads radiating from center to form a flat button; used on underwear from about 1700 to 1830.

double-breasted closing See under DOUBLE-BREASTED in alphabetical listing.

D-ring closure 1. See under CLOSURES: RING BUCKLE. 2. D-shaped closings on footwear through which shoelaces are threaded.

fly-front closing Buttonholes, or a zipper, inserted under a placket. Developed in latter half of 19th c. for overcoats, particularly the chesterfield, and used on men's or women's trousers.

∞**foil button** Silk pasted on paper and glued to reverse side of glass button; patented in 1774.

∞**French portrait buttons** Buttons worn around 1790 with profiles of famous people in light color mounted against a black silk background and surrounded with a rim of tin (e.g., profiles of Lafayette, Mirabeau, and Louis XVI).

frog Ornamental fastener using cording or braid through which a soft ball made of cording or a button is pulled. Uses: closing garments, especially military uniforms and some Chinese clothes. When introduced in the West from China in last quarter of 18th c., they were named **Brandenburgs** after braid-trimmed uniforms worn by Brandenburg troops of Prussia during the Napoleonic War. Also called *olivettes.*

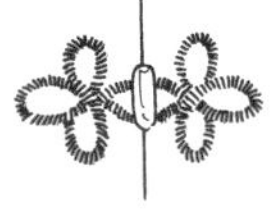
frog

galosh closure Closing with a metal hook on one side that clips into a metal fastener with several slots in order to adjust the degree of tightness. A closing used for such garments as raincoats, coats, and jackets. *Der.* Similar to closings for galoshes in the early 20th c.

glitter button Any type of button set with rhinestones or imitation gems. Also see under CLOSURES: RHINESTONE BUTTON.

glove button Tiny buttons, usually round and often pearlized, used to button long gloves.

gold button Any type of gold-colored button, formerly solid gold or plated. Henry VIII had jeweled gold buttons made to match his rings. A record of the 15th c. notes 25 golden buttons, each set with seven pearls, at a cost of 200 gold pieces. In the 16th c., gold buttons set with diamonds and other precious stones were frequently used.

gripper closure Metal fastener in the shape of a large snap, used on some types of jackets and raincoats. Also used on children's and infants' clothing, particularly at crotch of pajamas, panties, and pants, to enable them to be put on more easily.

∞**hasp** Decorative silver fastening, similar to HOOK AND EYE (see under CLOSURES). Uses: coat fasteners in 17th and 18th c.

∞**hip buttons** As used from late 17th to end of 19th c., a name for a pair of buttons placed on either side of center back pleats of man's suit coat.

hook and eye Closing that employs a small metal hook on one side and either an embroidered loop or a small metal loop or bar on the other side. Used extensively for shirtwaists and dresses with back closings in late 19th and early 20th c. Almost entirely replaced by the zipper on contemporary clothing.

hook and loop closure See under CLOSURES: VELCRO®.

industrial zipper See under CLOSURES: ZIPPER.

laced closing Leather thong or cord laced through small metal or embroidered eyelets. Popular method of fastening garments in Middle Ages and in late 1960s. Also used for shoes from 18th c. on. Also see POINTS in alphabetical listing.

lacing studs See under CLOSURES: SPEED LACING.

latch buckle Round, square, or oblong metal plates attached to each end of a belt and closed over one another. A swivel from one end of the belt slips through a slot in the other end and turns to fasten.

∞**leek button** Shank-type button with metal edge surrounding a metal shell or mold of pasteboard made in Leek, England, and patented in 1842.

loop and button Closing with a series of corded loops on one side and covered or round buttons on the other side. Used for its decorative effect. Sometimes used on wedding dresses.

machine-made buttonhole Buttonhole made on a sewing machine with a zigzag stitch or by a special attachment.

mother-of-pearl button Button made from nacre, the inside shell of the oyster. First manufactured in U.S. in 1885 from imported mollusks and later from domestic oysters found in Chesapeake Bay.

∞**neck button** Decorative button of mid-17th c. worn at neck of doublet and held closed by loop on opposite side to reveal the fine shirt underneath.

olive button Long, oval-shaped, silk-covered button worn from mid-18th c. on.

olivette See under CLOSURES: FROG.

pearl button Classic button for almost any use, originally made from shells. Sometimes called "ocean pearl" until development of plastic in the 1930s, after which imitation pearl buttons were widely used. Also see under CLOSURES: MOTHER-OF-PEARL BUTTON.

piped buttonhole Buttonhole similar to BOUND BUTTONHOLE in which PIPING (see under CLOTHING CONSTRUCTION DETAILS) is used around the opening.

poker chip button Extra-large round, flat button with a shank on the back. *Der.* From size and shape of a poker chip.

rhinestone button Any button set with stones, made of glass or PASTE (see under JEWELRY), that simulates a diamond.

ring buckle Two rings on one end of belt through which opposite belt end threads—first through both, then back through one—and pulls tight. When rings are made in the shape of a "D," called a **D-ring buckle**. Also called *cinch buckle* or *cinch closing.* Borrowed from fastenings on horse bridles and saddle straps and used mainly on belts and cuffs of sleeves.

self-covered button See under CLOSURES: COVERED BUTTON.

shank button Button with metal or plastic loop on the back.

shirt button Small mother-of-pearl or imitation pearl button with four holes and a ridge around the edge. Originally used on men's shirts.

shoe buckle Buckles worn on the shoe were very popular in France and Italy about 1660 and in England during reign of Charles II (1660–1685). Also fashionable in colonial America until about 1770. At first intended to hold shoe in place, the buckle was small in size and worn with a BUTTERFLY BOW (see under FOOTWEAR), it later reached larger dimensions. Also see CLOSURES: BUCKLE and PINCHBECK. Revived in 1870s and at end of 19th and early 20th c., but limited to women's shoes. Revived for both men's and women's shoes in late 1960s.

single-breasted closing See under SINGLE-BREASTED.

sleeve button 1. Button at wrist to close cuff or sleeve. 2. Decorative trim used on sleeves of man's suit coat consisting of two or three buttons placed on outside of cuff. This particular fashion originated in the 18th c. when large cuffs were worn buttoned back to the sleeve.

sleeve string See under CLOSURES: CUFF STRING.

slide fastener See under CLOSURES: ZIPPER.

∞**snail button** Covered button ornamented with FRENCH KNOTS (see under EMBROIDERIES AND SEWING STITCHES) that were used on men's coats and waistcoats in the 18th c.

snap closure Metal fastener used to close a garment at places where there is little strain. Replaced almost entirely in contemporary garments by ZIPPERS and GRIPPER CLOSURES (see under CLOSURES).

speed lacing Closing on boot consisting of metal hooks replacing eyelets for upper part of lacing. Used particularly on ice skates, ski boots, and hiking boots. Also called *button hooks* or *lacing studs.*

storm flap Large flap that covers a zipper and has buttons and buttonholes to keep the flap in place.

stud Small ornamental closure used since the mid-18th c. that is not fastened to the shirt. Consists of a broader section, a short post, and a smaller button-like end that is inserted through an eyelet to fasten a shirt front, neckband, or cuffs. Also called *collar button.*

surplice closing See under CLOSURES: WRAP CLOSING.

tab/tabbed closing An extra flap, strap, or loop of fabric, used with buttonhole, buckle, or snap to close coats, collars, sleeves, and cuffs. Popular closing for car coats in the mid-1960s.

tailored buttonhole See under CLOSURES: WORKED BUTTONHOLE.

tied closing 1. Type of closing used on a wrap-style garment (e.g., a sash used on bath robes, wrap dresses, and skirts) to hold the garment closed. 2. Series of ties used to fasten a garment.

toggle closure Rod-shaped button, usually of wood, attached by rope loop on one side of garment and pulled through similar loop on opposite side. Also see under COATS AND JACKETS: TOGGLE COAT.

Velcro® Trademark for a tape woven with minute nylon hooks that mesh with loops on opposite tape. Used on children's and adults' clothing, sportswear, and shoes. First used by astronauts. Generic term for this type of closure is *hook and loop.*

wooden button Button made of wood that may be made in all sizes and shapes (e.g., a ball shape with shank on back or disk-shaped). In the late 1930s, larger saucer-shaped buttons tied on with matching corded fabric were used on women's coats.

worked buttonhole Buttonhole made by covering the raw edges of a slit in the fabric with hand or machine stitches. In hand-worked buttonholes, first the slit is made, then the raw edges are covered by embroidering them with a buttonhole stitch. Machine-made worked buttonholes are stitched first, then cut open. A stitch similar to the buttonhole stitch is made by the sewing machine. The shapes of worked buttonholes may vary as follows: **bar tack** or **rectangular buttonhole** Worked buttonhole with straight bar, called a bar tack, embroidered across the ends. **oval buttonhole** Worked buttonhole with fan-shaped arrangement of stitches at both ends. **tailored buttonhole** Worked buttonholes

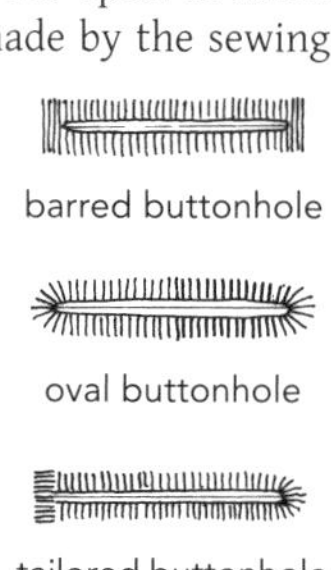
barred buttonhole
oval buttonhole
tailored buttonhole

with a bar tack at one end and a fan-shaped arrangement of stitches at the other end. **keyhole buttonhole** Worked buttonhole with a bar tack at one end and an area of much enlarged fan-shaped stitches at the other so as to allow a place for the button shank to rest.

wrap closing Closing by wrapping one side of garment over the other and holding with a belt, sash, button, or snap. Also called surplice closure.

zipper Although the name "zipper" was coined and registered as a trademark by B. F. Goodrich Co. in 1925, the forerunner of this device was patented in 1893 by Witcomb B. Judson. He called it a *clasp locker.* The design was improved by Gideon Sundback, who manufactured *Hookless Fasteners* used for corsets, gloves, sleeping bags, money belts, and tobacco pouches. Goodrich used zippers in "Zipper boots." By the 1930s zippers were so widely used in garments ranging from handbags to men's trousers that "zipper" became a generic term applied to any toothed, slide fastener. This device consists of parallel rows of metal or nylon teeth on adjacent edges of an opening, interlocked by sliding tab. Teeth may be covered by fabric tape and almost invisible or made in various lengths to use on necklines, skirt plackets, coat and jacket fronts, or handbags and pockets. Large-sized zippers, originally used for upholstery and industrial uses, were adopted for decorative trim on clothing in mid-1960s and were called **industrial zippers**.

---

clot See under FOOTWEAR.

cloth Synonym for TEXTILE FABRIC.

clothe 1. To put on garments. 2. To provide with clothing.

clothes Collective term for all items of apparel worn on the body by men, women, and children. *Der.* Anglo-Saxon, *cläthas,* plural of *cläth,* "cloth." Synonyms: *apparel, attire, clothing, costume, dress, garb, garment, raiment, vestments.*

CLOTHING CONSTRUCTION DETAILS

clothing construction The process of making a garment by hand or machine sewing or both. Mass production generally relies on machine processes, while made-to-order clothing uses more hand sewing. See under EMBROIDERIES AND SEWING STITCHES for specific stitches used.

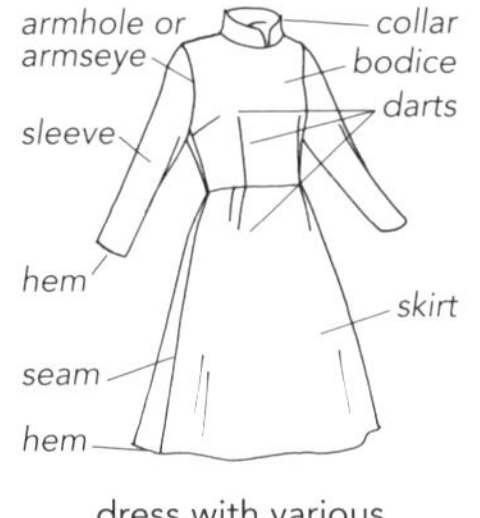

dress with various construction features

details The individual components within the structure of a garment that are combined in order to create the final, functional garment.

accordion pleats Folds in fabrics that are named for their resemblance to the folds of the musical instrument called an accordion. Smaller at the top but larger at the bottom, the lower edge of the hem shows a zigzag pattern. An accordion-pleated skirt takes a full circle of fabric. First used in the late 1880s. Synonyms: *sunburst pleats* and *fan pleats.*

accordion pleats

asymmetric hem Hem of uneven length—may be long in back and short in front or slanted diagonally from one side to the other.

asymmetric hem 1920

backing Layer of fabric placed underneath the outer fabric of a garment. Its function is generally to support the outer fabric.

bar tack buttonhole See under CLOSURES: WORKED BUTTONHOLE.

bias pleats Pressed-down pleats made in fabric cut on the diagonal, usually stitched down a few inches at top to make them hang better.

binding Narrow fabric strips used to cover seams or raw edges of clothing. May be cut on the BIAS or on straight GRAIN.

bound *adj.* Used to describe a raw edge of a garment or part of a garment that has been finished either with band of machine stitching, bias binding, or tape.

bound buttonhole See under CLOSURES.

bound seam Edges of plain seam bound with bias binding (see under CLOTHING CONSTRUCTION DETAILS: BINDING). Used particularly on seams of unlined jackets and around necklines, armholes, and jackets in contrasting color for decoration.

bound seam

box pleat Pleat made by making two folds in fabric, the edges of which face in opposite directions. Sometimes box pleats may be stitched down for some distance before the fullness is released.

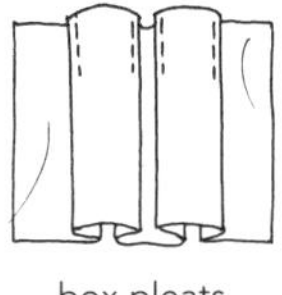
box pleats

broad-stitched seam See under CLOTHING CONSTRUCTION DETAILS: TOPSTITCHED SEAM.

buttonhole See under CLOSURES.

cartridge pleats Small, rounded pleats, like very large gathers. Used quite extensively for gathering skirts in the mid-1800s. *Der.* From their resemblance to cartridge loops on military belts.

casing Fabric stitched in such a way as to form a tunnel through which elastic, a cord, or a drawstring is drawn. Types of casings include: (1) **fold-down casing**, formed by turning down and stitching an extension at the edge of a garment. (2) **applied casing**, formed by folding a separate strip of fabric, stitching it to form a tunnel, and then applying it to some part of a garment.

circular hem Hem used on a full, circular, or gored skirt. If narrow, hem is machine-stitched or hand-rolled. Deeper hems have fullness worked in with tiny DARTS OR GATHERINGS or may have a FACING applied. (See under CLOTHING CONSTRUCTION DETAILS.)

clean-stitched seam Plain seam pressed open on wrong side of garment with the raw edges turned under and stitched so they will not ravel.

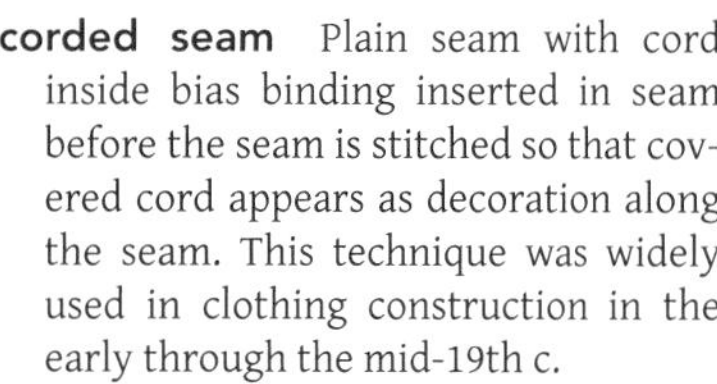

clean-stitched seam

cluster pleats Pressed or unpressed pleats arranged in groups. Usually consisting of a large BOX PLEAT with several small KNIFE PLEATS on either side. See under CLOTHING CONSTRUCTION DETAILS.

corded seam Plain seam with cord inside bias binding inserted in seam before the seam is stitched so that covered cord appears as decoration along the seam. This technique was widely used in clothing construction in the early through the mid-19th c.

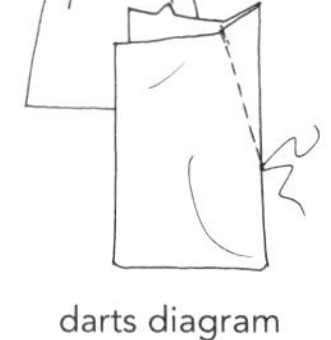

corded seam

crystal pleats Very fine, heat-set ridges usually used in sheer nylon or polyester fabrics. Also see under CLOTHING CONSTRUCTION DETAILS: MUSHROOM PLEAT.

dart Sewing term for V-shaped tuck used to make garment conform to the body. Used frequently at shoulders, waist, or in side seam under the arm.

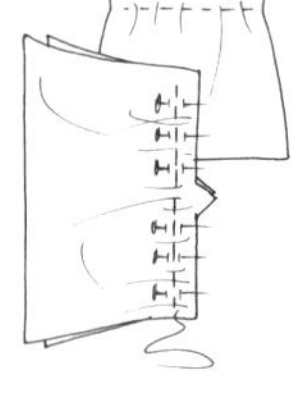

darts diagram

double ruffle Strip of fabric stitched in the center and gathered to form a ruffle on either side of stitching.

double-stitched seam See under CLOTHING CONSTRUCTION DETAILS: TOPSTITCHED SEAM.

ease 1. *v.* The process of joining a slightly larger garment piece to a smaller garment piece by evenly distributing the fullness along the seam where the pieces are joined. 2. *n.* The fullness produced when garment pieces are eased.

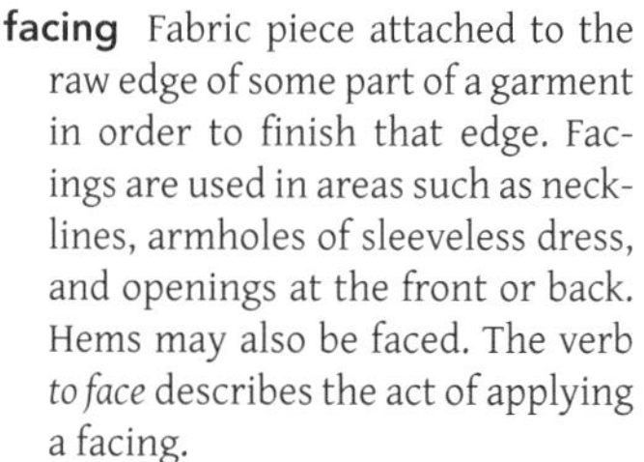

ease

enclosed seam A seam that is hidden on the inside of the garment by folding the edges between other plies of fabric.

envelope pleats Large INVERTED PLEAT (see under CLOTHING CONSTRUCTION DETAILS) placed at the side seam of dress skirt. Reveals a pocket underneath when one edge is pulled aside.

eyelet See in alphabetical listing.

faced hem Hem created by the use of another piece of fabric—usually lighter in weight and bias cut; sewed on at base of hem, turned up, and finished like a plain hem. Usually used when dress or pants are to be made longer or the garment is very flared.

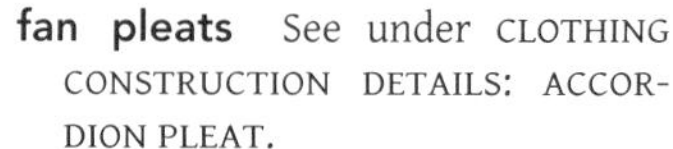

faced hem

facing Fabric piece attached to the raw edge of some part of a garment in order to finish that edge. Facings are used in areas such as necklines, armholes of sleeveless dress, and openings at the front or back. Hems may also be faced. The verb *to face* describes the act of applying a facing.

facings at armhole, neck, and front closing

fan pleats See under CLOTHING CONSTRUCTION DETAILS: ACCORDION PLEAT.

feather boning See under CLOTHING CONSTRUCTION DETAILS: STAY #1.

fell seam See under CLOTHING CONSTRUCTION DETAILS: FLAT-FELLED SEAM.

flat-felled seam Seam created by placing the undersides of garment pieces together and stitching a seam of about $\frac{5}{8}$″ wide that appears on the right sides. One edge of the seam is then cut off to $\frac{1}{8}$″ and the other edge folded over cut edge. Both are then pressed flat in the same direction and the folded edge is topstitched. As a result, two rows of stitching appear on outside. This creates a very durable seam. Also called *fell seam.*

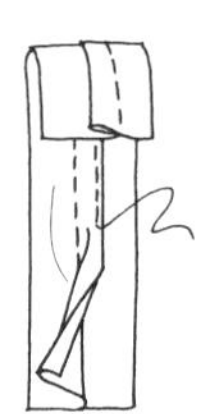

flat-felled seam

flat pleats See under CLOTHING CONSTRUCTION DETAILS: KNIFE PLEATS.

fluted hem Tiny hem finished with picot edge (see PICOT #2) in a sheer nylon fabric, which is set in crystal pleats. The edge gives a serpentine effect winding outward and inward.

french seam Seam created by placing the undersides of garment pieces together and stitching a seam that appears on the right sides. This seam is trimmed; subsequently the fabric is folded so that the outsides of the fabric

french seam

pieces are together. A seam is then stitched that encases the previously stitched seam. This seam is mostly used on transparent and lightweight fabrics that ravel.

fused hem Introduced in the 1960s , a hem created with special tape that, when pressed with a hot iron, melts and adheres to the fabric. Sometimes this type of hem loosens when garment is washed or dry cleaned.

fused seam Seam made in plastic or vinyl by heating edges to be joined. Also called *welded seam.*

gathering Drawing up fullness along several threads in a row of stitching. Also see under CLOTHING CONSTRUCTION DETAILS: SHIRRING.

gathers

gauging See under CLOTHING CONSTRUCTION DETAILS: SHIRRING.

godet (go-day′) Triangular piece, sometimes rounded at top and flaring at the base, set into a skirt or sleeve to give added fullness. See under CLOTHING CONSTRUCTION DETAILS: GORE and GUSSET.

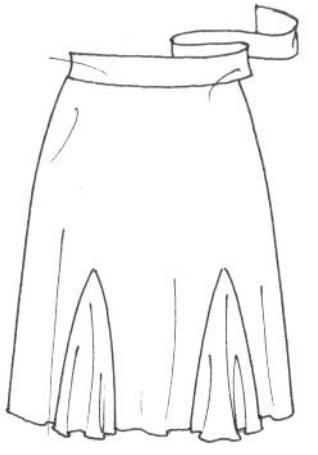
godet

∞**godet pleats** (go-day′) Pleats that hang in a series of rolls forming a gored skirt, popular in 1890s. Also called *pipe-organ pleats.*

gore 1. Skirt section, wider at hem than top, providing fullness and shaping to waist without using darts. A four-gore skirt has seams at sides, center front, and center back; six-gore skirt has side-front and side-back seams as well as side seams. There may be as many as twenty-four gores in a skirt. 2. In sewing, a triangular insert of fabric that creates fullness, greater width, or desired shape. Used in skirts and bell-bottom pants. Also used in gloves at wrist, to make a flared cuff and facilitate opening. Also called *godet.*

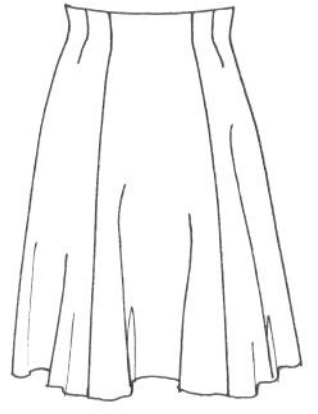
six gored skirt

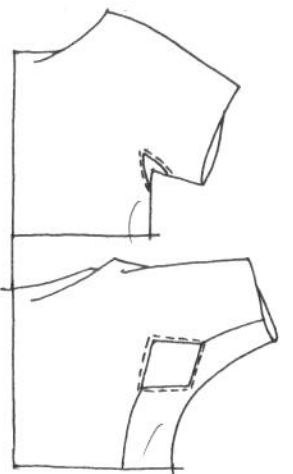
gusset #1

gusset 1. Diamond-shaped piece of fabric inserted under the arm of sleeve or in the crotch seam to permit greater movement. 2. Triangular piece used at sides of handbag, at sides of men's shirttails, and sides of shoes for wider opening.

handkerchief hem Hem that falls in points, creating an appearance similar to the effect when a handkerchief is held in the center and allowed to fall into soft folds.

handkerchief hem

heading Small hem through which elastic is pulled.

hem The lower edge of an item of clothing, such as a skirt or blouse, or sleeves. That edge is turned under and secured, usually by sewing.

inverted pleat Pleat formed by bringing two folds to a center line and pressing them. Reverse side of several inverted pleats will look like box pleats.

inverted pleats

kick pleats Single flat pleat or one KNIFE PLEAT (see under CLOTHING CONSTRUCTION DETAILS) at the back or front of a narrow skirt to make walking easier.

kilt pleats Flat pleat covering half of next pleat, all folded in the same direction as in a Scottish kilt.

knife pleats Pressed-in pleats, usually placed ½″ to 1″ apart. All pleats go in the same direction. Also called *flat* or *side pleats.*

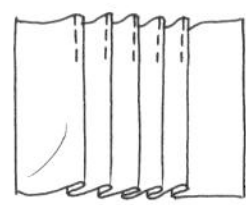
knife pleats

lapped seam/lap seam Simple seam used on interfacing and also in shoe and glove construction. One layer of material is placed on top of another and topstitched. Excess material is trimmed away.

lettuce edging Narrow-hemmed finish for edges of garments that creates the appearance of a curly lettuce leaf.

lingerie hem Rolled hem with overcast stitches at intervals forming minute puffs between stitches. Handmade hem popular in the 1920s and still used occasionally.

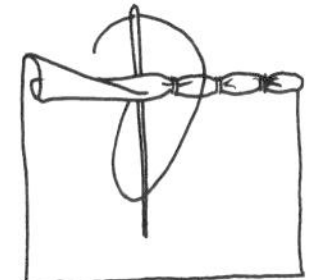
lingerie hem

machine-made buttonhole See under CLOSURES.

miter To finish a square corner with a diagonal seam.

mushroom pleats Very fine, heat-set pleats similar to CRYSTAL PLEATS (see under CLOTHING CONSTRUCTION DETAILS). *Der.* From appearance of the inside cap of the mushroom.

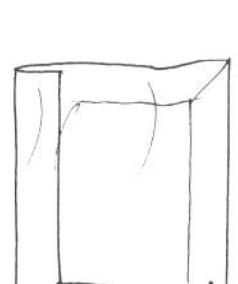
mitered corner

nun's tucks Tucks, usually of 2″ or more in width, placed around the hem of a dress or used on sleeves in a series of three, five, or seven.

open-welt seam See under CLOTHING CONSTRUCTION DETAILS: TUCKED SEAM.

overcast seam 1. Plain seam pressed open on wrong side and each raw edge finished by hand- or machine-overcast

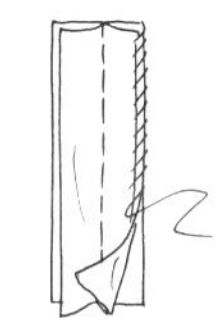
overcast seam

stitches to prevent raveling. **2.** Seam made on inside of garment with both raw edges overcast together either by hand or machine.

overlapped seam See under CLOTHING CONSTRUCTION DETAILS: LAP SEAM.

petal hem Hem that falls in rounded sections similar to petals of a flower.

picot hem A hem made with a two-needle, double chain stitch machine that forms a fagotted insertion that is cut apart, resulting in a picot edge; used on hems or ruffles for decorative effect or to reduce bulkiness. See under EMBROIDERIES AND SEWING STITCHES: HEMSTITCH #2.

pinked *adj.* Describes seams or other fabric areas that have been finished by trimming raw edges with pinking shears, which creates saw-toothed edges that prevent raveling.

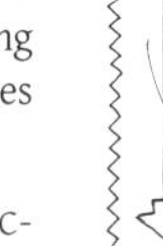
pinking

pin tucks See under CLOTHING CONSTRUCTION DETAILS: TUCK.

piped buttonhole See under CLOSURES.

pipe-organ pleats See under CLOTHING CONSTRUCTION DETAILS: GODET PLEAT.

piping A folded piece of bias binding. Piping may be inserted between two layers of fabric before stitching to create a decorative effect as, for example, in piped seams. Piped seams are similar to corded seams but have a flat rather than a rounded edge.

placket A slit at neck, side, front, back, or wrist in dress, blouse, pants, or skirt to facilitate taking garment on and off that has been used since the 16th c. Fastened in early times by lacings, buttons, or hooks and eyes; since 1930s by zippers; and since 1970s by Velcro®. A **side placket** is an opening placed in the side seam of a dress or blouse to facilitate putting on a fitted dress. It extends about 4″ above and below waistline. Originally fastened with SNAPS (see under CLOSURES), later side plackets closed by a special type of zipper. Most dresses had this type of opening from 1930s to 1950s. Later they were replaced by long back zippers extending from neckline to hips.

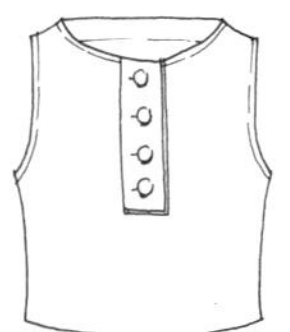
placket

plain hem Hem folded up and hand-sewn. The edge of the hem may be finished to prevent raveling by various means including: turning the hem edge under and machine stitching, pinking (see under CLOTHING CONSTRUCTION DETAILS: PINKED), or sewing tape to the edge by machine, after which hand stitches are used to finish the hem.

plain hem

plain seam Simple seam stitched on wrong side of garment, usually pressed open. Used on a fabric that will not ravel.

pleat/plait **1.** *n.* Fold of fabric usually pressed flat but sometimes left unpressed. When used in a skirt, blouse, or dress, it is sometimes stitched down at the top of the garment to improve the way the pleat falls. In polyester and nylon fabrics, pleats may be put in permanently with a heat-setting process. **2.** *v.* To set in folds.

rolled hem Handmade hem used on sheer and delicate fabrics. First rolled between the fingers, then sewed with tiny stitches. Used for chiffon evening gowns of the 1920s and 1930s, and still used occasionally.

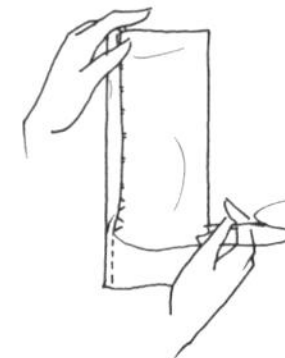
rolled hem

saddle seam See under FOOTWEAR.

saw-toothed hem Faced hem made with pointed edges.

scalloped hem Faced hem made with rounded edges simulating a shell design.

seam The place at which two or more layers of textile material or leather are sewn together. A variety of stitches and techniques can be utilized in creating seams. See individual types of seams listed under CLOTHING CONSTRUCTION DETAILS and GLOVES AND GLOVE CONSTRUCTION.

seam binding Narrow, woven, straight grain tape used at hem of garment to cover raw edge. Also stitched to seams on wrong side to prevent stretching. Sometimes used to bind cut edges of raveled seams.

shirring Three or more rows of *gathers* made by small running stitches in parallel lines. Used to produce fullness at tops of gloves, skirts, sleeves, and swimsuits. May be made by using a large stitch on the sewing machine and then pulling the bobbin thread to form gathers or by using elastic thread on the bobbin. Also called *gauging.*

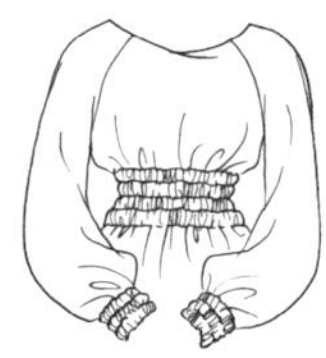
shirring

shoulder dart V-shaped dart, extending from mid-shoulder seam to bust, or from shoulder seam to shoulder blade in back.

side placket See under CLOTHING CONSTRUCTION DETAILS: PLACKET.

side pleats See under CLOTHING CONSTRUCTION DETAILS: KNIFE PLEATS.

slot seam Seam created by folding under the edge of each of two garment pieces, laying the edges facing each other over a tape or strip of fabric, and topstitching the folded edges through the underlying fabric. This technique is often used to create a contrast in color or fabric between the underlying fabric and the top garment fabric.

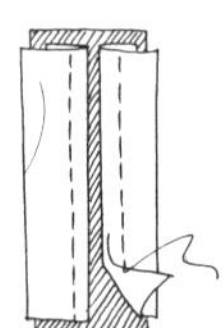
slot seam

stay 1. Strip of material, originally whalebone but now usually thin metal or plastic, placed behind or within seams or darts and used to stiffen such garments as corsets, bodices, collars, or belts. Light boning used particularly at hem of skirt to extend it is called **feather boning.** 2. Piece of fabric stitched under pleats or gathers to hold fullness in place.

strap seam Plain seam stitched with wrong sides together, thereby making the seam on the outside of the garment. The seam is pressed open. Bias tape, with the edges folded under, is laid over the open seam and topstitched into place.

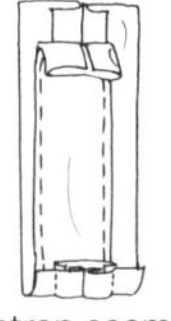
strap seam

stud See under CLOSURES.

sunburst pleats See under CLOTHING CONSTRUCTION DETAILS: ACCORDION PLEAT.

sunburst tucks Used in a series, these are darts that taper to nothing. May be arranged around the neckline of a dress, on the front of the blouse, or at the front of the waistline. Provide a decorative effect and reduce fullness without gathers. Also called *fan tucks.*

tailored buttonhole See under CLOSURES: WORKED BUTTONHOLE.

topstitching Stitching visible from the outer or "top" side of a garment that consists of one or more rows of machine stitching made through all layers of fabric.

topstitched seam Plain seam pressed open and stitched on either side of seam on right side of garment or pressed to one side and stitched on reverse side. Also called *double-stitched seam* or, when double rows of stitching are placed on either side of the seam, *broad-stitched seam.*

topstitched seam

tuck A means of controlling fullness of a garment in which part of the garment piece is made smaller by folding the fabric and stitching a line parallel to the fold. At the place where the tuck ends, fullness is released. Often tucks are arranged in a series and designated by width (e.g., 1″, ½″, ¼″, or **pin tucks**; the latter are only wide enough for a row of stitching).

tucked seam Seam finished with tucks stitched about ¼″ to 1″ from either side of seam and pressed to meet over seam. Also called *open-welt seam.*

umbrella pleats Similar to ACCORDION PLEATS (see under CLOTHING CONSTRUCTION DETAILS) but larger, like the folds of an umbrella.

venetian-blind pleats A pleat formed by a wide-stitched tuck made in the fabric. Each tuck slightly overlaps the previous one in the fashion of Venetian blind slats.

watteau pleats Box pleats hanging free from back shoulder yoke to hem of dress or dressing gown. *Der.* From the name of an 18th-c. French painter who often depicted women wearing dresses with this style pleat. The term was coined in the 19th c. Shown at WATTEAU BACK.

welded seam See under CLOTHING CONSTRUCTION DETAILS: FUSED SEAM.

welt seam Plain seam stitched on underside of the fabric; one edge is trimmed, then both edges are pressed in same direction with the narrower edge under the wider. Finally the seam is topstitched at a point close enough to the seam to catch wider edge. This is a very durable seam finish and may also be used for decorative effects if the color of the topstitching contrasts with the fabric.

welt seam

worked buttonhole See under CLOSURES.

---

clothing industry See under APPAREL INDUSTRY.

clouded cane See under CANE.

clout-shoen See under FOOTWEAR: CLOT.

cloverleaf lapel See under NECKLINES AND COLLARS: LAPEL.

clown suit Popular fancy dress costume for children or adults consisting of a jumpsuit with full pant legs with ruffles at cuffs and ankles. A large unstarched RUFF (see under NECKLINES AND COLLARS) is worn at the neckline. Made of two colors, divided down center front and back, and trimmed with pompons. Worn with tall, tapered DUNCE CAP (see under HEADWEAR).

club bow tie See under TIES.

club wig See under WIGS AND HAIRPIECES.

cluny lace See under LACES.

cluster curls See under HAIRSTYLES.

cluster earring See under JEWELRY.

cluster pleats See under CLOTHING CONSTRUCTION DETAILS.

cluster ring See under JEWELRY.

clutch coat See under COATS AND JACKETS.

clutch purse/bag See under HANDBAGS AND RELATED ACCESSORIES.

CMT See under CUT, MAKE, AND TRIM.

coachman's coat See under COATS AND JACKETS.

coal-scuttle bonnet See under HEADWEAR.

coatdress See under DRESSES.

†coated fabrics Fabrics sometimes made nonporous and water repellent through coating with various substances such as lacquer, varnish, pyroxylin, rubber, polyethylene, or plastic resin.

coatee See under COATS AND JACKETS.

coat-jumper See under JUMPERS.

coat of mail See under ARMOR: HAUBERK.

coats See under CLOSURES: BREASTS.

COATS AND JACKETS

coat Sleeved outerwear that ranges from hip-length to full-length, it is designed to be worn over other clothing either for warmth or as a decorative element of the costume. Although a coat with set-in sleeves was worn in ancient Persia, MANTLES and CAPES (see under CAPES, CLOAKS, AND SHAWLS) were more generally worn as the outermost garment until the end of the 18th c. when the REDINGOTE and PELISSE were introduced (see under COATS AND JACKETS). *Der.* From "cloak," in use by mid-19th c., and not changed to "coat" until the late 19th c.

jacket For men: (English) A garment, often sleeveless, that was worn over a DOUBLET in France and England in 15th c. and into the early 17th c. It was also called a *jerkin.* In 18th c. worn by country people, laborers, seafarers, and apprentices, thus becoming a mark of social inferiority. In mid-19th c. accepted by gentlemen, replacing the suit coat for some occasions. For women: In the 17th c. the jacket referred to a type of BODICE that was more loosely fitted than more formal wear and was also called either a doublet or waistcoat. In the 19th c., when women adopted dresses made up of separate bodices and skirts, the separate bodice was referred to as a **jacket bodice**, whereas the term "jacket" alone as used today (see #1 below) was applied to separate garments such as the ZOUAVE JACKET (see under COATS AND JACKETS). In the 20th c., many styles, for both formal and informal occasions, were introduced for both men and women. Present-day usage defines jackets as follows: **1.** An item of apparel, usually shorter than hip-length, designed to be worn over other clothing, either indoors or outdoors. Some are made with double-breasted or single-breasted closings; others have no closing, and some are closed with a zipper. **2.** Part of a suit that covers the upper part of the body—a *suit jacket. Der.* Old French, *jackquette,* the diminutive of *jacque,* a coat.

admiral coat Double-breasted REEFER-style coat (see under COATS AND JACKETS), frequently with gold buttons. *Der.* Adapted from coats worn by U.S. Navy officers.

Afghanistan jacket Jacket of lambskin, tanned with hair left on, made with leather side out, giving a shaggy border around edge, sometimes embroidered on the smooth side. Popular in late 1960s as part of trend toward ethnic clothes.

∞**albert driving cape** Not a true cape, but a single- or double-breasted, loose, CHESTERFIELD-style coat (see under COATS AND JACKETS) of 1860 usually made with no back seam. It could be used for driving a horse-drawn carriage. Also called *driving sac.*

∞**albert jacket** Man's single-breasted jacket of 1848. It was made with or without waistline seam side pleats and had no breast pocket.

∞**albert overcoat** Man's loose-fitting mid-calf overcoat with fly front, small shoulder cape, flapped hip pockets, long back vent, and vertical slit breast pockets; worn in 1877.

∞**albert riding coat** High-buttoned single-breasted man's coat of 1841 with front cut away in slanted style. Made with broad collar, narrow lapels, and hip pockets.

∞**albert top frock** Men's heavy overcoat styled like a FROCK COAT (see under COATS AND JACKETS), made with wide velvet collar, flap pockets, wide cuffs, and lapels; worn from 1860s to 1900.

A-line coat Coat made close and narrow at the shoulders, flaring gently from under arms to hem; shaped like letter A, made in single- or double-breasted style, with or without a collar. Introduced in 1955 by Paris designer Christian Dior.

all-weather coat Waterproofed or water-repellent coat sometimes made with zip-in lining to adapt to various temperatures.

all-weather raincoat Raincoat that can be worn year-round, as it is made with a zip-out lining, usually of acrylic pile.

∞**almain coat/jacket** (al'-man) Jacket worn by men over DOUBLET in second half of 15th and early 16th c. Made in a close-fitting style with short, flared skirt and long hanging sleeves, and slashed at front seams.

∞**alpine jacket** **1.** Waist-length jacket worn with LEDERHOSEN (see under SHORTS) as part of a Tyrolean mountain climber's costume. **2.** Englishman's jacket similar to a NORFOLK JACKET (see under COATS AND JACKETS), made double-breasted with vertical flap pockets and pleat down center back. Worn buttoned to neck, often without a vest, in 1876.

∞**american coat** (British English) Man's single-breasted full-length coat, usually black, made with narrow lapels, wide collar, and full skirt; worn in 1829.

∞**angle-fronted coat** Variation of man's MORNING COAT (see under COATS AND JACKETS), cut away diagonally on each side to reveal triangles of waistcoat; worn from 1870 to 1880. Also called *university coat.*

anorak (an'-nah-rack) Hip-length jacket made of water-repellent fabric, sometimes lined with fur, which has a zip-front and drawstring hem and is worn for winter sports. Introduced in World War II for pilots. *Der.* Eskimo word for a hooded waist-length jacket of sealskin or printed cotton worn for warmth by Greenland Eskimos.

anorak

∞**armenian mantle** Loose-fitting PELISSE (see under COATS AND JACKETS) without a cape, enriched with PASSEMENTERIE made of braid, worn by women in 1847.

∞**ascot jacket** Loose-fitting man's jacket with rounded hems in front and matching fabric belt pulling in the waistline, worn in 1876.

automobile coat See COATS AND JACKETS: DUSTER.

balmacaan (bal-ma-kan) Raglan-sleeved, loose-fitting–style coat that buttons up the front to the neck and has a small, turned-down collar. Frequently made of tweed or water-repellent fabric. *Der.* Named after Balmacaan, Inverness-shire, Scotland.

balmacaan

∞**balmoral jacket** 1. Woman's jacket of 1867 that buttoned to neck with front and back points below waist. 2. Woman's belted, double-breasted, semi-fitted jacket with lapels and small gauntlet-cuffed sleeves, similar to coat of riding habit, worn c. 1870.

barn coat See under COATS AND JACKETS: FIELD COAT.

∞**barouche coat** (bar-roosh) Woman's tight-fitting, three-quarter-length outdoor coat with full sleeves, fastened in front with gold barrel-shaped snaps and an elastic-type belt with buckle; worn in 1809.

baseball jacket Waist-length zippered or snap-closed jacket with ribbed cuffs and waist styled after those worn by Major League and Little League baseball players. While those used in professional and amateur sports are made in team colors with team name on the front and player's number on the back, those for general wear are made in a wide variety of colors and fabrics and may or may not have team logos or other decorations. Also called *varsity jacket.*

baseball or varsity jacket

∞**base coat** Man's jacket or *jerkin* with short sleeves, square neckline, and skirts, or BASES, hanging in tubular unpressed pleats to just above the knees; worn from 1490 to 1540.

∞**basquine** (bas-keen′) (*basquin, basquine*) 1. Woman's coat with pagoda sleeves, fringed trimming, and long extension below the waistline, worn in 1857. 2. Outdoor jacket worn in 1860s.

∞**battenberg jacket** Woman's loose-fitting outdoor jacket with large buttons and a turned-down collar, worn in 1880s.

battle jacket Waist-length Army jacket worn in World War II, having two breast pockets, fitted waistband, zippered fly-closing, and turn-down collar with REVERS (see under NECKLINES AND COLLARS). Also called *Eisenhower jacket* after Allied forces Commander-in-Chief General Dwight D. Eisenhower, who wore this style.

battle jacket

beach coat See under SWIMWEAR.

∞**beaufort coat** Man's suit jacket of 1880s with single-breasted, four-button closing; narrow, straight sleeves; and seams often double-stitched. Also called *jumper coat.*

bedale jacket A waxed cotton jacket introduced as a water-repellent garment for riding that has become a popular jacket for town or country. Also called *barbour bedale jacket.*

∞**beer jacket** Short, boxy cotton jacket with patch pockets and brass buttons; originally worn by upperclassmen at Princeton University in 1930s, and copied by other students.

bellboy/bellhop jacket Waist-length jacket with standing collar, two rows of brass buttons on front in V-style, frequently connected with gold braid. Originally worn by messenger boys, pages, and bellboys at hotels. Now used mainly for band uniforms and occasionally adapted for men's, women's, and children's wear.

bench coat See under COATS AND JACKETS: BENCHWARMER JACKET.

benchwarmer jacket Hooded knee-length jacket slipped over head and zipped at neck. Copied for young people from jackets worn by football players waiting on the bench. Also called *bench coat.*

∞**benjamin** Overcoat, generally white, worn by working men in the 19th c. Also called *benny* or *lily benjamin.*

big coat Long, full, sometimes ankle-length voluminous coat with long, full sleeves. Worn belted, unbelted, or with a belt in the back to confine the fullness.

bike jacket Waist-length sport jacket. Styling varies but is often similar to a WINDBREAKER or BATTLE JACKET (see under COATS AND JACKETS).

bi-swing Suit or sport jacket with set-in belt in back and deep pleats extending upward to each shoulder to give freedom of movement. Has single-breasted closing and conventional notched collar with lapels. Popular in the 1930s for men and women.

blade jacket Man's business jacket of the 1930s made with extra fullness at upper arm and back or shoulder blades, giving broad-shouldered appearance and freedom of movement.

blazer Sport jacket in a solid color or striped. Originally single-breasted, and with patch pockets, now made double-breasted as well and with

blazer

varying types of pockets. Generally worn with trousers or skirt of contrasting color. *Der.* Earliest uses of this term seem to have been for bright (blazing) red jackets worn for sports.

blouse coat Coat with V-shaped neckline, *dolman* or *kimono* sleeves, and single-button closing at waistline; frequently made with slightly flounced skirt and lavish, high fur collar; popular in the 1920s.

blouson jacket (blue′-zohn) Jacket with a bloused effect at a normal or low waistline, either gathered into knitted waistband or pulled in by drawstring. *Der.* French, "blouse."

∞**bobtailed coat** Short-tailed man's coat with narrow REVERS (see under NECKLINES AND COLLARS) worn at end of 18th and early 19th c.

∞**body coat** In 19th-c. men's tailoring, used to distinguish a suit coat from an outdoor coat or overcoat.

bolero Waist-length or above-the-waist jacket, usually collarless and often sleeveless, with rounded front, and no fastenings. Copied from the Spanish bullfighter's embroidered jacket and worn by women since late 19th c. *Der.* From name of a Spanish dance and also music for the dance.

bolero

bomber jacket See under COATS AND JACKETS: FLIGHT JACKET.

box coat 1. Woman's straight coat with wide shoulders, popular in late 1920s and 1930s. Also see under COATS AND JACKETS: CARRICK. ∞2. Heavy, warm overcoat with single or multiple shoulder capes worn throughout 19th c., particularly by coachmen and travelers riding outside coach on the "box." Also called *driving coat* and *curricle coat* (kur′-eh-kul). ∞3. Hip-length woman's double-breasted jacket styled like a REEFER (see under COATS AND JACKETS), worn in early 1890s. ∞4. Unfitted jacket that ended below the waistline, styled with large sleeves, a standing collar, and a side closing. Worn in mid-1890s. 5. See under COATS AND JACKETS: EMPIRE JACKET #2. ∞6. Three-quarter-length unfitted coat of early 1900s, made with shawl collar, unfastened in front. Sometimes trimmed lavishly with braid. 7. Double-breasted girl's coat sometimes made with shawl collar, or an extra cape, worn in early 20th c.

box jacket Any straight, unfitted jacket, waist-length or longer.

boy coat Double-breasted coat with long, notched collar and set-in sleeves.

∞**brandenburg/brandenbourg/brandenburgh** Man's long, loose winter coat made in military style with frog closings, worn in last quarter of 17th c. *Der.* Named for braid-trimmed uniforms worn by Brandenburg troops of Prussia during the Napoleonic War who fought for a state located in the eastern part of Germany.

∞**breton jacket** (bret-ohn′) Fitted hip-length woman's jacket buttoned on either side to a front panel, with tailored collar and lavishly trimmed with wide braid. Frequently shorter in center back. In the late 1870s, when worn with matching skirt, called a *Breton costume.*

British warm British Army or Navy officers' heavy double-breasted overcoat, knee-length or shorter; copied for civilian wear in 1950s and 1960s.

bronx jacket See under COATS AND JACKETS: PERFECTO JACKET.

∞**bucksain** Man's padded overcoat with wide sleeves, worn in 1850s.

buckskin jacket Western-style jacket of sueded DOESKIN or SHEEPSKIN (see under LEATHERS) trimmed with long fringe. A standard style in the American West from colonial days, it was adapted for city wear in the late 1960s.

∞**buff coat** Man's leather jacket made of ox or buffalo hides. Sometimes with shoulder wings and sleeves of fabric, sometimes sleeveless. Worn in 16th and 17th c. Originally a military garment worn during civil wars in England, adopted by civilians and American Colonists. Also called *buff jerkin* or *leather jerkin.*

bulletproof jacket Any jacket that is constructed with strong, bullet-resistant fiber such as Kevlar® aramid. One example is a lightweight jacket with zipper front and three bulletproof panels—two in front and one in back—that slip into pockets in the lining.

Burberry® Trademark of Burberry's International, Ltd., London that has been applied to an expensive unisex trenchcoat-type raincoat. Made in lightweight polyester and cotton fabric with an optional plaid zip-out lining. Skirts, scarves, and umbrellas are made to match the lining. Details include hand-stitching on collar, handmade buttonholes, and D-rings on belt for holding objects. First used by British officers in 1914. Also see alphabetical listing.

bush jacket/bush coat Jacket originally worn in Africa on hunting expeditions, where it was made of khaki-colored cotton with peaked lapels, single-breasted front, belt, and four large bellows pockets. Adapted for fashion sportswear and made in all types of fabrics and worn by men, women, and children. *Der.* From clothes worn on hunting trip into the African bush country. Also called *bush coat* or **safari jacket**, which is similar in all respects to the bush jacket, but called by this name in the mid- and late 1960s when introduced as a fashion item for women by Dior, the French couturier. Newer versions in 1980s styled with-

bush jacket or safari jacket

out belt, sometimes with epaulets. *Der.* From name of African hunting trip, *safari,* for which similar style jacket is worn.

∞**caban** Man's loose outdoor garment of the 1840s that had wide, bell-like sleeves, sometimes had a small cape at the shoulders, and a hood. Also known as *templar cloak.*

∞**camargo** (ka-mar'-go) A woman's jacket with draped fullness, pannier-style around hips, and worn over waistcoat or vest in late 1870s. *Der.* After Marie Anne de Cupis Camargo (1710–1770), celebrated dancer.

∞**cambridge coat** Three-button, single-, or double-breasted man's suit coat of 1870, made with three seams in back and a center vent.

∞**cambridge paletot** (pal-ah-tow' or pal-tow') Man's knee-length overcoat of mid-1850s cut with wide cape collar, large turned-back cuffs, and wide lapels extending almost to hem.

∞**campaign coat** Originally a long military overcoat worn by the rank and file from about 1667, and later adopted by men for civilian wear in late 17th c.

canadienne (ka-nah'-dee-en) Woman's hip-length, double-breasted, belted coat designed in Paris during the 1940s; copied from coats worn by Canadian soldiers.

cape coat **1.** Coat with sleeves and an attached or separate cape. **2.** Combination of cape and coat with the back falling like a cape, the front having sleeves and looking like a coat. Also see under COATS AND JACKETS: DOLMAN.

∞**capote/capot** (kah-poat) **1.** Man's loose coat with turn-down collar and cuffs, worn in 18th c. **2.** Hooded coat or cloak worn from Middle Ages on.

∞**caprice** (ka-preece) Loose, short, sleeveless woman's evening jacket of mid-19th c. that tapered to rounded point below the waist in back.

caraco (kar'-a-ko) **1.** Fitted hip-length suit jacket with peplum made by French designer Yves Saint Laurent in 1969; said to derive from jackets depicted in Toulouse-Lautrec paintings. ∞**2.** Thigh-length fitted jacket, flaring below waist, made with no waistline seams, and popular for women from late 18th through 19th c. Also called *caraco corsage.*

car coat Sport or utility coat made hip- to three-quarter length, which is comfortable for driving a car. First became popular with the station-wagon set in suburbia in 1950s and 1960s and has become a classic style since then. Some of the styles in which car coats have been made include BENCHWARMER, DUFFEL COAT, RANCH COAT, MACKINAW JACKET, STADIUM COAT, and TOGGLE COAT. See under COATS AND JACKETS.

cardigan coat/cardigan jacket Collarless coat or jacket made with plain, round neckline and buttoned down center front and which may have binding around the neckline and down the front. *Der.* Named for 7th Earl of Cardigan, who needed an extra layer of warmth for his uniform during the Crimean War, 1854.

∞**careless** Man's loose-fitting caped overcoat with spread collar and no seams at waistline, worn in 1830s.

∞**carmagnole** (car'-man-yole) Jacket or short-skirted coat with wide collar, lapels, and rows of metal buttons. Worn with black pantaloons and red LIBERTY CAP (see under HEADWEAR) by French Revolutionaries in 1792 and 1793.

∞**carrick** Man's or woman's full-length duster worn from 1877 on. Styled like a box coat with three capes and similar to an ULSTER. (See under COATS AND JACKETS: ULSTER #1 AND #2.)

∞**casaque** (ka-sack') **1.** Fitted jacket, buttoned down the front, worn by women from mid-1850s to mid-1870s. Early types had extensions of the bodice (see under BASQUE) to the hips or beyond; later types had skirts draped in POLONAISE style. **2.** (French) Jacket worn by jockeys, usually made in bright colors of their respective stables. **3.** Girl's coat cut on princess lines, worn in 1860s. **4.** See under COATS AND JACKETS: CASSOCK #1.

∞**casaweck** (ka-sa'-wek) Woman's short, quilted outdoor mantle made with close-fitting velvet or silk collar and sleeves. Frequently trimmed with fur, velvet, or lace. Worn from mid-1830s to mid-1850s. Also see under COATS AND JACKETS: POLKA and VARENS.

casentino (ca-zen-tee-no) Red overcoat with a green lining worn by coachmen in Casentino, a section of Italy. Later adapted for winter sportswear.

cassock ∞**1.** Long, loose overcoat with a cape collar. Worn from late 16th through 17th c. by men and women for hunting and riding, and by foot soldiers. Also called a *casaque* (ka-sack'). **2.** See under CLERICAL DRESS.

Chanel jacket See under CHANEL SUIT.

Chanel-style jacket See under CHANEL SUIT.

Charlie Chaplin coat Ankle-length, full-shouldered, oversized coat with baggy sleeves ending in wide-buttoned cuffs and huge patch pockets. Introduced by Claude Montana, French couturier, in spring collection of 1985. *Der.* Named after Charlie Chaplin, an early silent-film comedian.

∞**chasseur jacket** Fitted, hip-length, military-inspired women's jacket of 1880s made with standing military collar, slashings at hem, and elaborately trimmed with braid and BRANDENBURGS (see under CLOSURES: FROG).

chesterfield coat

chesterfield coat Semi-fitted, straight-cut, classic man's or woman's overcoat in single- or double-breasted style, with black velvet collar. Single-breasted style usually has a fly-front closing. Originally an overcoat introduced in 1840s for men. Popular in late 1920s through 1940 and worn at intervals since. *Der.* Named after the 6th Earl of Chesterfield, a fashion leader in 1830s and 1840s.

chinese jacket Short, boxy coat reaching slightly below waist with standing collar, KIMONO SLEEVES (see under SHOULDERS AND SLEEVES), and FROG FASTENERS (see under CLOSURES). Worn by Chinese workmen and frequently copied as beach or lingerie coat. Once referred to as a coolie coat, deriving from the Chinese, *kuli,* "unskilled workman." Coolie coat is now considered a derogatory term.

chubby Woman's straight-cut, waist- to hip-length jacket of long-haired fur, made collarless, with straight sleeves. Popular in late 1930s and revived in early 1970s.

∞**claw-hammer coat** Colloquial name for the SWALLOW-TAILED COAT (see under COATS AND JACKETS) named for shape of coattails with ends cut straight across, resembling claws of a hammer.

∞**close coat** *adj.* Used to refer to a buttoned coat in the 18th and 19th c.

clutch coat Woman's coat with no fasteners in front, worn open or held clutched together. Originally introduced in the mid-1920s as a low-waisted evening wrap with bagpipe sleeves and large fur collar. The style also crept into daywear. Revived periodically.

clutch coat

coachman's coat Double-breasted coat with large, wide lapels, a fitted waistline, and a flared skirt. Frequently has a cape collar and brass buttons. Copied from English coachmen's coats of 19th c.

∞**coatee** Short, close-fitting coat with short skirt, flaps, or coattails. Fashionable in mid-18th c. and also in 1860s.

coats See under CLOSURES: BREASTS.

coat set A child's coat made with matching hat or matching pants, sold together since 1940s.

coachman's coat, 1775

coattail Portion of coat below the back waistline, especially the long back portions of a SWALLOW-TAILED coat or a CUTAWAY (see under COATS AND JACKETS).

cocoon Wrap coat with very large shoulders, deep-cuff, batwing sleeves, and standing collar that may be rolled down. Envelops the figure, tapering to the hem, like a cocoon. Used as a *rain or shine coat.* Originally introduced by Yves Saint Laurent in spring 1984 as an evening coat in velvet, it reached to thigh in back and tapered in cutaway fashion in the front.

∞**codrington** Man's loose-fitting, single or double-breasted overcoat resembling a CHESTERFIELD (see under COATS AND JACKETS) worn in 1840s. *Der.* After Sir Edward Codrington, British admiral, who led fleet to victory at Navarino in 1827.

∞**coin de feu** (kwan' de fuh') Short coat with high neck and wide sleeves, made of silk, velvet, or cashmere; usually worn indoors over a dress in mid-19th c.

∞**combing jacket** Woman's loose jacket, usually waist-length, worn in the bedroom when brushing hair or applying makeup in late 19th and early 20th c.

∞**coureur** (koor-er') Tight-fitting CARACO jacket (see under COATS AND JACKETS: CARACO #2) with short PEPLUM or BASQUES, worn by women during French Revolution.

C.P.O. See under SHIRTS.

cubavera jacket White cotton sport jacket with four patch pockets similar to BEER JACKET (see under COATS AND JACKETS). Worn with lightweight slacks for sportswear by men from 1940 to 1950.

∞**curricle coat** (kur'-eh-kul) **1.** Woman's fitted full-length coat with lapels worn in early 19th c. Cut away in front from chest to waist, sloping to the back; sometimes called *gig coat.* **2.** Synonym for *box coat* of the mid-19th c. See under COATS AND JACKETS: BOX COAT #2.

∞**cutaway** 19th c. man's coat style that was known by a number of different names throughout the century. It originated as a **riding coat**, worn from 1825 to 1870s, and had skirt slanting from waist to thigh in back that was made by cutting away the front of a FROCK COAT (see under COATS AND JACKETS) instead of folding the skirts back for horseback riding. From the riding coat the **newmark** or **newmarket coat** evolved. This name, used since 1838, also has a connection to riding, as New Market, England, was a horse racing center. This was a long-tail coat made single- or double-breasted with front skirts cut away and rounded, often with flap pockets and cuffed sleeves. By the 1850s, this basic style was known as a "cutaway" and worn for more formal occasions. It was usually a black, one-button jacket with peaked lapels and skirt cut away from the waist in front, tapering to knees in back, in a slanting line. It had a back vent topped by two buttons and was

cutaway coat c. 1895

worn with a waistcoat and striped trousers in daytime. By the 1870s the same style was more likely to be called a **morning coat**.

∞**cutaway frock** Man's suit coat almost knee-length—similar to a FROCK COAT (see under COATS AND JACKETS)—and cut away from waistline to each side seam in rounded curve. Worn in 1890s and early 1900s. Similar to the **dress frock coat** worn in 1870s and 1880s, this coat was double-breasted and exposed the shirt in front.

∞**cutaway sack** Man's loose-fitting suit jacket reaching to hips, cut away in rounded lines in front to side seams. Worn in 1890s and early 1900s.

cycle jacket See under COATS AND JACKETS: MOTORCYCLE JACKET.

deck jacket Short, hooded, water-repellent jacket, sometimes made with nylon pile lining, which closes with zipper and has attached ribbed, knitted trim at wrists and neck. Worn on board sailboats and other craft.

denim jacket Any jacket made of blue denim fabric.

dinner jacket 1. Man's white, semiformal jacket worn in summer. 2. See under COATS AND JACKETS: TUXEDO.

∞**directoire coat** (dir-eck′-twa) Woman's coat having ankle-length skirt in back and coming only to waistline in front, worn in late 1880s.

∞**directoire jacket** (dir-eck′-twa) Woman's waist-length jacket of late 1880s. Similar to DIRECTOIRE COAT (see under COATS AND JACKETS), worn as top of a daytime dress.

dirndl coat (durn′-dul) Woman's coat cut with fitted torso and skirt gathered at a low waistline, popular in the mid-1960s. *Der.* From gathered skirt and fitted bodice of the Tyrolean peasant dress called a *dirndl.*

dolman (dole′-man) Woman's short mantle or full-length wrap that gives the appearance of a cape from the back, but is sleeved in front. Worn from 1870s through the 1880s, revived in early 20th c., and returns to current fashion frequently in coat collections. The **peplum dolman**, a variation with long points hanging at sides, was worn by women in the early 1870s. A crocheted dolman that fastened at neck with large bow of ribbon worn in the 1890s was called a **dolmanette**.

dolman c. 1882

∞**d'orsay coat** Man's overcoat of late 1830s, similar to a PILOT COAT (see under COATS AND JACKETS), but fitted at waist with darts. Made with a small collar, slashed or flapped pockets, plain sleeves trimmed with three or four buttons, and no pleats or hip buttons in the back. *Der.* Named for Comte d'Orsay, a 19th-c. arbiter of fashion.

∞**d'orsay habit-coat** Fitted, man-tailored, three-quarter-length coat for women, somewhat resembling man's CUTAWAY (see under COATS AND JACKETS) style; made double-breasted with large REVERS (see under NECKLINES AND COLLARS). Introduced in early 1880s.

doublet See in alphabetical listing.

∞**douillette** (do-yeh′) Woman's winter coat worn from 1818 through 1830s. Over this time, the style changed with the current fashions, the earlier form being a quilted PELISSE (see under COATS AND JACKETS) and the later style consisting of a coat of cashmere, merino wool, or figured satin with a pelerine (a short cape) and having very large sleeves. Also spelled *donnilette.*

down jacket 1. Usually a zippered jacket with long sleeves, knitted cuffs, and waistband, interlined with DOWN quilted to the outer fabric and lining. Worn for its warmth, and popular for everyday use and sportswear since the 1970s. 2. A similar jacket with zip-off sleeves can also be worn as a vest.

dress coat See under COATS AND JACKETS: SWALLOW-TAILED COAT.

dress frock coat See under COATS AND JACKETS: CUTAWAY FROCK.

dressmaker jacket A woman's jacket designed with the fit and details of a dress. A dressmaker jacket generally can be worn without a blouse or top underneath and may have a waistline or unusual details.

dressmaker jacket

driving coat See under COATS AND JACKETS: BOX COAT #2.

driving sac See under COATS AND JACKETS: ALBERT DRIVING CAPE.

∞**du barry mantle** Dolman-style (see COATS AND JACKETS: DOLMAN) wrap of early 1880s with smocked yoke front and back, fur collar, and large, full cuffs. Lavishly trimmed with ribbon bows and streamers at neck, below yoke, sleeves, and at center back. *Der.* Named for Comtesse Du Barry, mistress of King Louis XV of France.

∞**duck-hunter** Striped linen jacket worn by English waiters about 1840s.

duffel coat Car coat or a shorter-length coat fastened with toggles rather than buttons, introduced during World War II, and worn by men in British Navy. In 1950s it was adopted as a sport coat. *Der.* From the original fabric used—a heavy napped wool originally made in Duffel, Belgium. Same as *toggle coat* although sometimes toggle coats are made with a hood.

duffle coat or toggle coat

duo-length coat See under COATS AND JACKETS: ZIP-OFF COAT.

duster ∞1. Tan or brown lightweight full-length coat worn when riding in an automobile in early 20th c. to protect clothing from dust. Worn with AUTOMOBILE VEIL (see under HEADWEAR). 2. Big-shouldered, big-sleeved, big-pocketed classic coat with smocked back, treated for water repellency, and introduced in 1984. 3. Lightweight clutch coat with full swing at hem and small rolled collar, usually made in black bengaline or faille, worn in the 1950s. 4. Fitted coat with long skirt slashed up back to waist worn when riding horseback. Has buttons and buttonholes for closing the slashed skirt. 5. See under SLEEPWEAR AND LOUNGEWEAR: DUSTER. ∞6. Man's summer overcoat of 1870s.

duster coat #3

dutch coat See under COATS AND JACKETS: MUFF'S CLOAK.

edwardian coat Man's knee-length, usually double-breasted and black, topcoat or overcoat with large high-rolled, deep-notched collar, nipped-in waistline, and deep vent in back. Worn with a high silk hat and a cane in Edwardian period, 1901–1910. Versions of this style were revived in the 1960s. *Der.* Inspired by coats of Edwardian era in England.

edwardian jacket Fitted jacket made with some flare at back and sides and vents at sides or center back. Styled with double- or single-breasted closing and NAPOLEONIC or REGENCY COLLAR. (See under NECKLINES AND COLLARS.) Introduced in the 1960s, it was similar in cut to jackets of the Edwardian period. *Der.* After Edward VII, King of England, 1901–1910.

edwardian jacket c. 1967

Eisenhower jacket See under COATS AND JACKETS: BATTLE JACKET.

∞**empire coat** (em′-pire or ohm-peer) Woman's three-quarter to full-length coat of early 1900s worn for traveling or evening wear. Made with a full skirt of large unpressed pleats attached to a high waistline. Bodice is cut somewhat like an ETON JACKET (see under COATS AND JACKETS) with large lapels and a standing MEDICI COLLAR (see under NECKLINES AND COLLARS).

empire jacket (em′-pire or ohm-peer) 1. Jacket name coined by *Women's Wear Daily* for a jacket designed by Karl Lagerfeld in 1992 that was banded under the bosom. ∞2. Square-yoked woman's jacket of mid-1890s made with MEDICI COLLAR (see under NECKLINES AND COLLARS), large box pleats in front and back, and large balloon sleeves. Also called a *box coat.*

∞**english coat** 1. Woman's double-breasted, three-quarter-length jacket of 1890s made somewhat like a PEA JACKET (see under COATS AND JACKETS), with lapels and flapped pockets. 2. Full-length coat of 1890s sometimes made with elbow-length cape.

∞**english walking jacket** Woman's jacket of mid-1870s made in single-breasted style with lapels. Unfitted in front but fitted at waistline in back, flaring to form a PEPLUM. Sleeves with large turned-back cuffs.

english wrap See under COATS AND JACKETS: PALETOT.

eton jacket Straight-cut jacket with collar and wide lapels worn unbuttoned or with only top button closed, reaching to waist or a little below. Adapted from jackets worn by underclassmen at Eton preparatory school in England until 1967, popular for women in early 1890s, revived periodically, and a perennial style for small boys. Also see under ETON SUIT.

eton jacket c. 1896

∞**eton jacket bodice** Woman's waist-length jacket similar to boy's ETON JACKET (see under COATS AND JACKETS) worn open in front over a waistcoat in 1889. In the late 1890s, the front was trimmed with braid and frogs and rounded at waistline.

∞**eugénie paletot** (yoo-je′-nee) 1. Tailored three-quarter-length woman's coat of 1860s made in unfitted double-breasted style with notched collar and bell sleeves having false cuffs. The sides of cuffs and rounded patch pockets were decorated with buttons. 2. Shorter-length sack-type jacket, collarless or with a small collar, closing at neck with one button. *Der.* Named for Eugénie, Empress of France from 1853 to 1871.

evening wrap Any coat of fabric or fur intended to be worn primarily for formal occasions. It may be a coat designed to match or contrast with an evening dress. Very popular in the 1920s in clutch style. In 1930s, popular in black velvet in a full-length with leg-of-mutton sleeves and in hip-length with batwing sleeves.

fake fur coat See under COATS AND JACKETS: FUR FABRIC COAT.

∞**fearnothing jacket** Man's jacket similar to a waistcoat with sleeves, worn by sailors, sportsmen, laborers, and apprentices in the 18th and early 19th c. Made of heavy woolen fabric called **fearnaught.**

fencing jacket Close-fitting, waist-length jacket, usually padded or quilted, made with high-standing collar and fastened diagonally to right side as the observer views the fencer. Worn for sport of fencing and sometimes copied for general wear.

field coat Hip-length coat usually made of cotton canvas that buttons down the front. Generally has large pockets on either side of the front near the hem. Often made with corduroy or leather collar in contrasting color. **Barn coat** is similar in style, but made in various types of materials, including suede.

∞**figaro jacket** Variation of the ZOUAVE or BOLERO JACKET (see under COATS AND JACKETS), with or without shoulder epaulets; worn by women in 1860s and again in 1890s.

fishing parka Knee-length, slip-on jacket styled with attached hood and one large KANGAROO POCKET (see under POCKETS) across the chest. Made of waterproof fabric and worn for fishing in inclement weather.

flight jacket Waist-length jacket, sometimes made of leather. First worn by U.S. Army Air Corps pilots in World War II, as part of their uniform, then adapted for sportswear in 1960s. In early 1980s and after, made in a variety of styles, mainly of nylon, with standing collar, ribbed or elastic waistband, patch or slot pockets, and zip front. Also called *bomber jacket.*

flight or bomber jacket

flyaway jacket Very short jacket with a full back, worn by women in the late 1940s and early 1950s.

fold-up raincoat Any raincoat that folds to small size, specifically a lightweight raincoat frequently of clear vinyl which folds to pocket size. Introduced as early as 1850 and then called POCKET SIPHONIA (sih'-foh'-nee-ah). See under COATS AND JACKETS: SIPHONIA.

french frock See under COATS AND JACKETS: FROCK COAT #1.

frock coat ∞1. Suit coat of the 18th c. that was looser and shorter than dress coats. Single- or double-breasted, it buttoned to the waistline. At first it had a full skirt, flapped pockets, and a vent in back with two buttons at waistline, and a flat, turned-down collar and no lapels. Initially considered suitable for country wear, but after 1770 was accepted for more formal wear as well. The **french frock** coat, for example, was worn from 1770 to 1800 for full dress and usually trimmed with gold embroidered buttons. As the silhouette of men's coats grew narrower, the frock coat skirt also narrowed. Less popular during the Empire period, the frock coat was important from 1816 until the end of the 19th c., after which it was worn by dignitaries and older men. The specific cut varied depending on the current fashionable silhouette, but the 19th c. coat always had a fitted waist attached with a waistline seam to a knee-length skirt that fell straight and met at the center front. Among the variations of the frock coat was the **jemmy frock**, described as fashionable in the 18th c., but by the 19th c. the **jemmy** had become a man's shooting coat styled like a many-pocketed short frock coat. 2. Hip-length, fitted, tailored jacket worn by women in 1890s.

frock coat #1 1895

∞**frock greatcoat** Man's coat worn from 1830s on, similar in cut to a FROCK COAT (see under COATS AND JACKETS) but usually double-breasted, longer, and styled for outdoor wear. Also see under COATS AND JACKETS: TOP FROCK.

∞**frock overcoat** Boy's calf-length overcoat, worn in late 1880s and 1890s, made with fitted lines, usually with a large CAPE COLLAR (see under NECKLINES AND COLLARS).

fur fabric coat Coat made of fabric that simulates fur (e.g., MODACRYLIC pile fabric), sometimes colored with stripes to imitate mink; sometimes stenciled to look like leopard, giraffe, tiger, zebra, and other furs. Incorrectly called a *fake fur coat.*

∞**gabardine/gaberdine** (gab-er-deen) Believed to have been the first fitted European coat-like garment with sleeves. Of Arabian origin, it was introduced from the East by way of Vienna in the mid-14th c. and was popular throughout the 15th c. It had a closed front and wide sleeves with the underarm seam open. Sometimes worn with a belt and sometimes made of felt. Worn particularly by fashionable men until 1560, and by commoners until early 17th c. *Der.* Eastern *gaba,* "coat." Also called *caban.*

∞**garibaldi jacket** (gar-ih-bawl'-dee) Woman's square-cut, waist-length jacket of 1860s made of red cashmere and trimmed with black braid. *Der.* Inspired by clothes worn by Italian patriot Giuseppe Garibaldi.

gascon coat See under COATS AND JACKETS: JUPE.

gendarme jacket (zhahn'-darm) Conventional jacket buttoned and adorned with brass buttons on sleeves, pockets, and down center front. Inspired by jackets worn by French policemen. *Der.* French, *gendarme,* "an armed policeman."

∞**gladstone** Man's short, double-breasted overcoat of 1870s made with shoulder cape and borders of Persian lamb. Named for William Gladstone, a British prime minister of the Victorian era. Also see under COATS AND JACKETS: ULSTER.

golf jacket Short, waist-length jacket with zip front, worn for playing golf. Often styled with a pleat in the back to allow for freedom of movement when swinging a golf club.

greatcoat Heavy, voluminous overcoat worn by men and women, originally made with fur lining and styled similarly to an ULSTER (see under COATS AND JACKETS). Term has been used since the 19th c.

guardsman coat Double-breasted, half-belted coat made with inverted box pleat in back, slashed pockets, and wide collar. *Der.* Adapted from coats of British guardsmen. Also called *officer's coat.*

hacking jacket Single-breasted, fitted jacket similar to man's suit coat, made with slanting flap pockets and center back vent. Used for informal horseback riding and for general casual wear.

happi coat See under SLEEPWEAR AND LOUNGEWEAR.

∞**henrietta jacket** Loose three-quarter-length woman's jacket of 1890s with large collar falling over chest in front, frequently lined with quilted satin.

hunt coat See under COATS AND JACKETS: PINK COAT.

∞**hussar jacket** Woman's short jacket of 1880s fastened with FROGS (see under CLOSURES) and trimmed with braid and worn over waistcoat. Inspired by uniforms of British troops returning from a campaign in Egypt.

∞**imperial** Man's coat worn in 1840s, similar to loose-fitting, fly-front PALETOT overcoat (see under COATS AND JACKETS).

∞**incroyable coat** (on-kwai'-abla) Woman's coat of 1889 made with long coattails and wide lapels. Worn with lace *jabot* and waistcoat for afternoons. Adapted from the SWALLOW-TAILED COAT (see under COATS AND JACKETS). *Der.* Copied after styles of INCROYABLES (see under DIRECTOIRE # 2).

inner-vest jacket Short jacket, snapped or buttoned-down front, and sometimes with hood. Attached to the side seams in front is a vest usually similar to a sweater with front zipper.

insulated jacket Lightweight jacket usually made of tightly woven high-count 70 denier nylon, frequently quilted with padding of POLYESTER fiberfill. Usually made with zip front and rib knit at neck and wrists, and frequently given soil-resistant and water-repellent finish.

inverness coat (in-ver-ness) ∞1. Man's loose-fitting overcoat with below-elbow removable cape, introduced in 1859. In 1870s, sometimes had a separate cape over each shoulder. In 1880s, the sleeves were sometimes omitted. In 1890s, armholes were very large and a "sling" was used to support or rest arm. 2. Knee-length coat with long, removable cape or half-capes over the shoulders, like those worn by men in late-19th c. *Der.* From county of Inverness-shire, Scotland.

∞**irene jacket** Short, fitted, collarless woman's jacket of late 1860s cut away in front above waistline and sloping to below waistline in center back. Lavishly trimmed with braid around neckline, on sleeves, and in back.

jemmy See under COATS AND JACKETS: FROCK COAT.

∞**Joseph** 1. Woman's green riding coat worn in the mid-18th c. 2. Woman's outdoor wrap with loose-fitting sleeves worn from 1800 to 1810.

∞**journade** (zhur-naad) (*jornade*) Short, circular jacket with large, full sleeves, or with sleeves long and slit. Worn in 14th and 15th c. for riding.

judo jacket See under ACTIVEWEAR: KARATE SUIT.

∞**jump** 1. Thigh-length 17th-c. soldier's coat, buttoned down front with long sleeves and vent in back, that was adopted by civilians. Also called *jumpcoat* and *jumpe.* 2. (British usage) Women's jacket.

jumper coat See under COATS AND JACKETS: BEAUFORT COAT.

∞**jupe** (zhoop) (British usage) Woman's riding coat worn with protective skirt or *safeguard* in the 16th and 17th c. Also called *gascon coat* and *jupon.*

∞**justaucorps** (zhust-o-kor') (*justacor, juste, justico, just-au-corps*) 1. Man's tight-fitting, knee-length coat worn over waistcoat. Borrowed from a military coat and worn from mid-17th to early 18th c. in England and France. 2. Woman's riding coat, styled like a man's frock coat, worn from mid-17th to early 18th c. Also called *demi-riding coat* and *habit à la française.*

justaucorps c. 1690

karate jacket An indoor jacket styled like a Japanese kimono but short in length. Worn when engaging in sport of karate and also adopted for at-home wear by men and women in late 1960s. *Der.* Named for sport for which it is used. Also see under ACTIVEWEAR: KARATE SUIT.

laboratory coat/smock Single-breasted coat, usually with turned-down collar and REVERS (see under NECKLINES AND COLLARS), made of white cotton or manufactured fiber. Worn to protect street clothes while working in chemical or medical laboratory. Also called *lab coat.*

leather jerkin See under COATS AND JACKETS: BUFF COAT.

∞**leicester jacket** Englishman's suit or lounge jacket with RAGLAN SLEEVES (see under SHOULDERS AND SLEEVES). Worn in 1857.

lily benjamin See under COATS AND JACKETS: BENJAMIN.

Lindbergh jacket Waist-length heavy woolen or leather jacket with large pockets, lapels, and rolled collar. Made with waistband and cuffs of stretchable rib-knit wool. *Der.* Type of jacket worn by Colonel Charles A. Lindbergh, who made the first solo flight from New York to Paris across the Atlantic in 1927.

∞**Louis XV basque** Woman's fitted, tailored jacket of 1890s worn open down center front, revealing waistcoat or vest. Usually hip length with a standing collar and cut tabs extending from waistline to hem. *Der.* Named after Louis XV, who ruled France from 1710 to 1774.

∞**Louis XVI basque** Woman's fitted jacket of late 1890s made with a point in front at waistline. Had a standing lace-edged MEDICI COLLAR (see under NECKLINES AND COLLARS) extending to two squared lapels and moderate-sized leg-of-mutton sleeves with cuffs that fell over the wrists. Skirt flared over hips, had pleats in center back, and was open at center front. *Der.* Named for Louis XVI of France (1754–1793).

lounging jacket See under COATS AND JACKETS: SMOKING JACKET and SACK JACKET.

lumber jacket/lumberjack Waist-length jacket with a bloused effect and rib-knitted bands at waist and cuffs. Made of woven plaid wool fabric. Originally worn by woodsmen in the lumbering trade. Introduced for sportswear in the late 1920s and worn by both adults and children. Reintroduced in early 1980s.

∞**macfarlane** Man's overcoat made with separate cape over each sleeve and side slits to permit access to pockets of inner garment. Worn from 1850s to end of 19th c.

mackinaw jacket/mackinaw coat Hip-length sport jacket of heavy wool, woven in patterns similar to those used for blankets. Improvised in the winter of 1811 when Captain Charles Roberts, a British officer, became stranded with his patrol on St. Martin's Island in the Straits of Mackinac. When reinforcements failed to reach him, warm coats were made from blankets of wide strips and various patterns. Became popular for explorers and woodsmen of the north and continues in popularity to present. *Der.* Named after Mackinaw City, Michigan, located at tip of Michigan, facing the Straits of Mackinac.

mackinaw jacket

mackintosh ∞1. Loose-fitting, waterproof coat made of patented India rubber cloth of olive drab or dark green with waterproof straps over the seams. Introduced in 1836 and named for the inventor Charles Macintosh, who patented fabric in 1823. 2. (British usage) Slang for various types of raincoats, often abbreviated to *mac.* ∞3. Long coat with single or double detachable cape introduced for women at end of 19th c. for a raincoat. Made either of "single texture" with printed or woven fabric on outside and heavy rubber coating on inside or "double texture" with a layer of rubber between two fabrics. *Der.* Named after Charles Macintosh, who first invented the rubberized fabric in 1823.

mandarin coat Straight-lined coat with Chinese neckline.

mandarin jacket Jacket with standing-band collar copied from styles of Chinese Mandarin costume. Shows some similarities to NEHRU JACKET (see under COATS AND JACKETS).

∞**mandilion/mandeville** (man-dill'-yun) Loose hip-length jacket with narrow, long sleeves worn by men from late 16th to early 17th c. Often worn COLLEY WESTONWARD (e.g., worn by soldiers around shoulders as a cape, with sleeves hanging free). Later worn with short sleeves, sometimes slit, for LIVERY.

man-tailored jacket 1. Woman's suit jacket tailored similarly to a man's suit jacket and made in fabrics of pinstripes, tweeds, and other menswear fabrics. Style may be made with one, two, or three buttons or may be double-breasted. 2. First jackets with mannish-type tailoring were introduced for women as suit jackets in the late 19th c., and the suits were called TAILOR-MADE. Continued in various styles as a type of jacket suitable for working women.

∞**mantee** Woman's coat of 18th c. worn open in front showing STOMACHER (#2) and PETTICOAT (#2) underneath.

mantelet See under COATS AND JACKETS: PARDESSUS.

Mao jacket A straight-cut suit jacket with MANDARIN COLLAR designed with political symbolism in mind as a counterpoint to the Western suit; it is based on a jacket worn during the Qing Dynasty (1694–1912). As a symbol of proletarian unity, the four pockets represent the four virtues: honesty, shame, propriety, and justice. The five buttons represent the five branches of Chinese government: legislation, supervision, examination, administration, and jurisdiction. The three cuff buttons represent the three principles of the people: nationalism, democracy, and peoples' livelihood. It was frequently made out of cotton, without a lining, which symbolized unity.

∞**marlotte** 16th-c. woman's outer garment, similar to short *mantle,* open in front with back falling in folds. Made with short, puffed sleeves and a STANDING COLLAR or RUFF (see under NECKLINES AND COLLARS).

∞**marquise mantle** (mar-keez) Short, lace-trimmed, taffeta woman's mantlet of mid-1840s with short sleeves. Made with fitted back and flounce below the waist. Also called *marquise.*

∞**masher dust wrap** Tight-fitting man's INVERNESS COAT (see under COATS AND JACKETS) of 1880s having large armholes with a separate cape over each shoulder.

maxi coat Term for any ankle-length coat first used in 1969 and thereafter. At the time these coats represented a radical change from MINI COAT styles. See under COATS AND JACKETS: MINI COAT.

mess jacket 1.White waist-length jacket made with large REVERS (see under NECKLINES AND COLLARS) in front and no buttons. Back section is cut in three pieces, with center section extending to shoulders in a modified *T* and center waistline pointed in back. Worn by busboys and waiters. Formerly worn in white as a summer semiformal jacket for men. Originally worn as part of naval formal evening dress. *Der.* From naval "mess room."

∞2. Waist-length jacket with standing collar and LEG-OF-MUTTON SLEEVES (see under SHOULDERS AND SLEEVES) worn by women in 1890s.

∞**metternich sack** (mett′-er-nik) Woman's collarless, knee-length wrap of mid-1860s made of black velvet with three BOX PLEATS (see under CLOTHING CONSTRUCTION DETAILS) at center back. Trimmed at neck, front, shoulders, and cuffs with wide velvet ribbon embroidered with white cord. *Der.* Named for Prince Klemens von Metternich, Austrian statesman of the mid-19th c.

Michael Jackson jacket Red leather jacket designed by Claude Montana for Michael Jackson in the video "Beat It." Copied in polyurethane, buttoning down the front in windbreaker style with stand-up collar and as many as twenty-seven short zippers placed in unusual places (e.g., placed diagonally on each side of chest and on shoulder blades in back, vertically at midriff, and at armholes so that sleeves are detachable). Trademarked and licensed for sale by Stadium Management Corp. and introduced in 1984. *Der.* Named for Michael Jackson, popular singer.

midi coat (mid′-ee) Mid-calf-length coat introduced in 1967 in radical contrast to thigh-length MINI COAT (see under COATS AND JACKETS). Made in many styles. *Der.* From term coined by *Women's Wear Daily.*

military coat Any coat that borrows details from military coats and jackets (e.g., braid trim, epaulets, gold buttons, or high-standing collar). Usually a fitted, double-breasted coat with slightly flared skirt.

∞**military frock coat** Man's FROCK COAT (see under COATS AND JACKETS) worn from early 1820s on, made with standing collar and no lapels, and no flaps on pockets. Later styles had rolled collars and lapels.

military tunic ∞1. Long tunic worn first in France around 1670 by soldiers, over a full, sleeved waistcoat. 2. Man's long, tubelike coat with skirts lapped over in front; adopted by British Army in 1855.

mini coat Thigh-length coat introduced in mid-1960s and made in any number of styles.

∞**monkey jacket** Short jacket made of heavy fabric like a PILOT COAT (see under COATS AND JACKETS). Worn by sailors in rough weather from 1850s on.

morning coat See under COATS AND JACKETS: CUTAWAY.

∞**moscow wrapper** Man's loose-fitting overcoat of 1874 with PAGODA SLEEVES (see under SHOULDERS AND SLEEVES), fly front, narrow turned-down collar of astrakhan fur, and other fur trimming.

motorcycle jacket Close-fitting black leather jacket, waist-length, and fastened to one side of center front with zipper, snap fasteners, or buttons. Popular in the 1960s and since then worn by both children and adults. Very similar to the PERFECTO JACKET (see under COATS AND JACKETS). Also called a *cycle jacket.*

∞**muff's cloak** Man's coat of late 16th and early 17th c. Same as *Dutch coat.* (Note: The "Dutch" in this case means "German" and is a mistranslation of the word *Deutsch,* meaning German.)

∞**napoleon coat** Woman's man-tailored, hip-length jacket of mid-1890s with standing MILITARY COLLAR (see under NECKLINES AND COLLARS), full LEG-OF-MUTTON SLEEVES (see under SHOULDERS AND SLEEVES), military braid down the front, and fastened with large BRANDENBURGS (see under CLOSURES: FROG). *Der.* Named for Napoleon, who wore a similar style during his military career.

Nehru jacket/Nehru coat (nay′-roo) Single-breasted jacket or coat, slightly fitted, with a standing band collar introduced in late 1960s. Adapted from type of coat worn by Indian maharajahs. *Der.* From wearing of this type of coat by Jawaharlal Nehru, Prime Minister of India from 1947 to 1964. Shown at NEHRU SUIT.

newmark/newmarket coat See under COATS AND JACKETS: CUTAWAY.

∞**newmarket jacket** Woman's close-fitting, hip-length jacket with turned-down collar, silk-faced lapels, flapped pockets, and cuffed sleeves. Frequently part of the "masculine" TAILOR-MADE fashions of the 1890s.

∞**newmarket overcoat** 1. Man's long, single-breasted overcoat of 1880s similar to a FROCK OVERCOAT (see under COATS AND JACKETS). Usually made with velvet collar and cuffs and frequently made of HOMESPUN. 2. Woman's long, single- or double-breasted winter coat with velvet collar, lapels, tight sleeves, cuffs, and flapped pockets. Made of heavy fabric for winter from mid-1880s to 1890s.

∞**newmarket top frock** Man's overcoat of 1895 similar to a FROCK COAT (see under COATS AND JACKETS), made of rough CHEVIOT fabric with velvet collar, pockets on waist seams, and the lower part lined with checked fabric—upper part with silk or satin.

norfolk jacket Belted hip-length jacket with two box pleats from shoulders to hem, on front and back. Matching fabric belt is either threaded through slots under pleats or worn over them. Worn by men for sport and travel since 1880s and associated with the character Dr. Watson of Sir Arthur Conan Doyle's Sherlock Holmes stories. Popular for young boys from 1890s to about 1920 and revived periodically. See NORFOLK SUIT in alphabetical listing.

norfolk jacket

∞**norfolk shirt** Man's lounging jacket styled like a shirt made of rough tweed, with box pleat down center back and two box pleats on either side of front. Worn with matching belt. Had a tailored collar and bands at wrist. Worn from 1866 to 1880.

officer's coat See under COATS AND JACKETS: GUARDSMAN COAT.

oriental wrapper See under COATS AND JACKETS: ZOUAVE COAT.

overcoat Man's coat, heavier than a topcoat, designed for very cold weather. Sometimes lined with fur or modacrylic pile and made in any of a variety of styles.

∞**oxonian jacket** Two- or three-button single-breasted tweed jacket worn by men in 1850s through 1860s. Made with many pockets and a back shaped by three seams. Also called *oxford coatee.*

paddock coat Man's long, semi-fitted overcoat worn from 1892 on, made with single- or double-breasted fly-front closing, large pockets, and pleat-covered back vent.

∞**paletot** (pal-ah-tow′ or pal-tow′) Generally refers to an outdoor coat or overcoat. Used for a number of different coat styles for men and women from approximately the 1830s to end of century. For men there were these variations. **1.** In 1830s, the paletot was a short overcoat made without a waistline seam and with or without a short back vent. Sometimes pleated at side seams. **2.** The **paletot-sac** was single- or double-breasted, cut short and straight, sometimes made with a collar, sometimes with a hood, and worn in 1840s and 1850s, whereas the **English wrap** was a double-breasted paletot sac worn in 1840s and similar to a loose CHESTERFIELD COAT (see under COATS AND JACKETS). Women's paletots had these variations. **1.** Late 1830s to end of 19th c., a woman's caped three-quarter-length cloak that hung in stiff pleats from the shoulders. By mid-1840s it had three capes and armholes trimmed with flaps. **2.** From 1860s to 1880s, a woman's short paletot was also called a *yachting jacket.* **3.** From mid-1860s to mid-1880s, it was a long, fitted outdoor coat—reaching to below the knees, frequently trimmed with lace and having tight sleeves. **4.** The **paletot-redingote** (red′-in-gote), of late 1860s, was also long and fitted and made in Princess style, with no seam at the waistline. It had buttons down the front and REVERS (see under NECKLINES AND COLLARS) and was sometimes made with circular shoulder capes. **5.** Another paletot worn in 1870s had wide cuffed sleeves and WATTEAU PLEATS (see under CLOTHING CONSTRUCTION DETAILS) in the back. *Der.* Dutch *paltrok,* from *pals,* "palace" and *rok,* "garment."

paletot-redingote See under COATS AND JACKETS: PALETOT.

paletot-sac See under COATS AND JACKETS: PALETOT.

∞**palmerston wrapper** Man's single-breasted, loose-fitting SACK OVERCOAT (see under COATS AND JACKETS) of mid-1850s made with wide collar and lapels. Sleeves were full at wrists with no cuffs and pockets had side flaps. *Der.* Named after British statesman Henry John Temple, 3rd Viscount Palmerston, who was prime minister of England between 1855 and 1865.

∞**pardessus** (par-de′-soo) 1. French term for man's overcoat. **2.** Generic term used from 1840s to end of 19th c. for woman's outdoor garment of half or three quarter length. Made with sleeves, fitted waistline, and frequently with a cape trimmed with lace or velvet. Also called *mantelet* and *paletot. Der.* French, "for on top."

parka Loose-fitting pull-on jacket made with an attached hood that is sometimes trimmed with real or synthetic fur. Worn originally by the Eskimos and introduced during the 1930s for winter sportswear (e.g., skiing and skating). Still worn in all cold climates. *Der.* Russian-Aleutian, "pelt."

parka

∞**patrol jacket** **1.** Men: Jacket of military cut made with five-button single-breasted closing and Prussian collar. Worn in late 1870s with tight knee pants for bicycling. **2.**Women: Tight-fitting hip-length jacket of late 1880s trimmed with military braid across front. Also had a standing collar at neck and tight-fitting sleeves finished with cuffs.

pea jacket/pea coat **1.** Copy of U.S. sailor's hip-length, straight, double-breasted navy-blue wool coat with notched lapels, vertical slash pockets, and vent in back. Inspiration for coats designed by Yves Saint Laurent in Paris in 1960s and a classic coat style for men, women, and children. Also called *pea coat* and formerly called a *pilot coat.* ∞**2.** From 1830s on, man's double-breasted, unfitted, thigh-length jacket with wide lapels and notched collar. Worn either as an overcoat or as a suit jacket. In 1850s had large buttons, usually six. Also called a *pilot coat. Der.* So called because it was made of "pilot cloth." After 1860s to the present this style was known as a *reefer.*

pea jacket #1

peasant coat Mid-length coat lavishly trimmed down front with embroidery, sometimes with fur borders and cuffs, fashionable in late 1960s.

∞**pelisse** (peh-leese′) Meanings and spellings of this term evolved over time. Its earliest forms involve some use of fur. Later it becomes a warm, winter outdoor garment. **1.** In the Middle Ages a **pelice** or **pelicon** (pel′-ees-sohn) referred to any of a number of fur-trimmed garments. **2.** In the 18th c., for women it was a caped, or hooded, three-quarter-length cloak with armhole slits and entire collar, hem, and front usually edged with

pelisse #3, 1819

fur, sometimes with silk or satin. **3.** In the early 19th c. it was generally full-length, often made of handsome silk fabrics, with a padded or quilted lining for warmth. Sometimes it had one or more shoulder capes. It was fitted and followed the current fashionable SILHOUETTE. Out of fashion by 1850. **4.** Revived in the late 1800s, for women it was a full-length winter mantle gathered on the shoulders and having loose sleeves, often made of silk, velvet, or satin. **5.** For men in the late 19th and early 20th c., the term was applied to a heavy, fur-lined coat with fur collar, worn particularly with formal clothes. Also spelled *pellice.*

∞**pembroke paletot** (pal-ah-tow′ or pal-tow′) Man's calf-length, long-waisted overcoat worn in mid-1850s made with wide lapels, double-breasted with eight buttons, and easy-fitting sleeves with turned-back cuffs. Also had flapped side pockets and vertical breast pocket.

perfecto jacket Black leather jacket, originating during World War II; it was worn by Marlon Brando in the 1954 film *The Wild One,* and subsequently became a symbol of rebellious youth and went on to become part of mainstream fashion. Synonym: *bronx jacket.*

perfecto jacket

∞**petersham frock coat** FROCK COAT (see under COATS AND JACKETS) of 1830s with slanted flapped pockets on hips and collar, lapels, and cuffs of velvet. *Der.* Named for Viscount Petersham, Charles Stanhope, described as an English peer and a "man of fashion."

∞**petersham greatcoat** Man's overcoat, with short shoulder cape, worn in 1830s. *Der.* Named for Viscount Petersham.

pilot coat See under COATS AND JACKETS: PEA JACKET.

pink coat Crimson-colored hunting jacket styled like a man's one-button suit coat with peaked lapels, back vent, and black velvet collar. Worn by men and women for foxhunting. Also called *hunt coat.*

pocket siphonia See under COATS AND JACKETS: SIPHONIA.

∞**polish greatcoat** Full-length tight-fitting man's coat with collar, cuffs, and lapels of Russian lambskin. Closed with FROG fasteners (see under CLOSURES) or loops. Worn with evening dress in early 19th c.

∞**polish jacket** Woman's waist-length jacket made with REVERS (see under NECKLINES AND COLLARS) and collar. Sleeves were wide at wrist, squared off, and slit to elbow on inside seam. Usually made of cashmere lined with quilted satin. Worn outdoors for informal occasions in mid-1840s.

∞**polka** **1.** Woman's short outdoor jacket of mid-1840s made with full sleeves, cashmere or velvet fabric, and lined with silk. A variety of CASAWECK (see under COATS AND JACKETS). **2.** Women's knitted close-fitting jacket.

polo coat Double- or single-breasted camel, vicuña, or camel-colored wool coat with notched collar and tied with a sash. Introduced in 1920s for men's spectator sports; for women in 1930s, this became a classic coat style that is made in many colors and fabrics.

polo coat

∞**polonaise** (pol-on-nays′) **1.** Man's jacket of early 1770s, also called a *polonese frock.* **2.** In 1830s a military redingote, usually of blue fabric, worn by civilians. Also called a *redingote.*

∞**pommel slicker** Raincoat worn when riding horseback in early 20th c. Similar to other raincoats but with long vent in back. Also called a *saddle coat.*

∞**postillion coat** (pos-till′-yon) Double-breasted fitted GREATCOAT (see under COATS AND JACKETS) with flap pockets, high REGENCY COLLAR, and broad REVERS (see under NECKLINES AND COLLARS). *Der.* From clothes worn by *postillions,* "men on horseback accompanying carriages."

∞**prince albert coat** **1.** Double-breasted long FROCK COAT (see under COATS AND JACKETS) worn in late 19th c., with flat collar, usually of velvet. Worn for formal occasions (e.g., weddings and funerals) until about 1920. **2.** Adaptation of this coat for women worn in late 1890s—a double-breasted, fitted, knee-length coat with turned-down collar and *revers,* flared skirt seamed at waistline, and two unpressed pleats with button trim at center back. *Der.* Named for Prince Albert of Saxe-Coburg-Gotha, consort of England's Queen Victoria.

∞**prince of wales jacket** Man's jacket of late 1860s similar to REEFER (see under COATS AND JACKETS). Cut in double-breasted style with three pairs of buttons. Named for Edward VII of England before he became king.

∞**prince rupert** Woman's full-length fitted coat of late 19th c. made of velvet or plush, worn with a blouse and skirt. *Der.* Named after Prince Rupert (1619–1682), son of a Bohemian king, who supported Charles I in the English Civil War and became a councilor to Charles II after the restoration of the monarchy. His biography was published in 1899.

princess coat Woman's fitted coat cut in long panels that flare at hem. Has no seam at the waistline and usually made single-breasted. A classic style. *Der.* Style claimed to have been introduced by Charles Frederick Worth around 1860 in a morning dress for Empress Eugénie.

∞**prussian collar coat** Man's coat of 19th c., which had a narrow standing collar with ends nearly meeting in front or worn turned down.

PVC jacket Hip-length simulated leather-look jackets made with conventional styling including a convertible collar, sometimes a yoke, buttoned- or zip-front, long sleeves, and tied or buckled belt. Made of polyvinyl chloride, a leather substitute that is soft and supple, washable, and water resistant.

pyramid coat Tent-shaped woman's coat of late 1940s and early 1950s made with narrow shoulders and wide hem.

raccoon coat Long, bulky coat of raccoon fur with large rolled collar worn originally by college men in the 1920s. Popular again in the mid-1960s and usually purchased from thrift shops.

racing jacket Lightweight two-ply nylon jacket with zip-front and drawstring hem. Made in various official colors, with a wide stripe outlined by two narrow stripes of red running from shoulder to hem on left side. Jacket is wind-resistant and water-repellent. Originally worn for auto stock racing, now available for men and women. Usually has a patch printed on right chest with automobile brand emblems.

raglan cape/raglan coat Fly-front or double-breasted overcoat first worn in 1857. It had slit pockets and wide RAGLAN SLEEVES (see under SHOULDERS AND SLEEVES) that extended in V-shaped form to neck rather than having a seam at the shoulder. The name was subsequently applied to any long, loose coat with raglan sleeves. *Der.* Named for Lord Raglan (see under RAGLAN, LORD).

raincoat Clothing originally designed to be worn in rainy weather, now also worn as *top coat* in fair weather. Made of waterproof material or given a special surface finish to make it water repellent. Raincoats were introduced in 1830 after the perfection of a rubberized fabric by Charles Macintosh in 1823. Original fabric was waterproof but had an objectionable odor. TRENCHCOATS (see under COATS AND JACKETS) were introduced in World War I. Modern technology in the development of water-repellent finishes in recent years has made it possible to use a greater number of fabrics for raincoats. Another innovation is GORE-TEX®. Also see under COATS AND JACKETS: SIPHONIA.

rain or shine coat Fabric coat treated with a water-repellent finish so that it can be worn as an all-purpose coat.

rajah jacket **1.** Men: Similar to NEHRU JACKET (see under COATS AND JACKETS). **2.** Women: Usually a tunic-length jacket, with standing collar that is usually worn with pants. *Der.* Shortened form of "maharajah."

ranch coat Leather car coat or jacket made in western style with leather side uppermost, sometimes made of or lined with SHEARLING (see under LEATHERS).

redingote (red′-in-gote) ∞**1.** Men: A full overcoat having a large collar, worn for riding in France about 1725. ∞**2.** In 1830, a greatcoat of blue cloth cut in a military style; it closed with frogs and had sloping pockets and a fur collar. Also called a *polonaise.* ∞**3.** Women: Coat adapted from man's coat in 1790s in lighter-weight fabrics and worn as part of a dress rather than an outdoor coat. **4.** During the Empire period, it was an outer coat. ∞**5.** From 1820s on, it was a dress cut like a coat either fastening all the way down the front or with the skirt open to show an underskirt. ∞**6.** In 1890s became an ensemble with matching coat and dress, with the coat usually being cut a little shorter than the dress. **7.** Contemporary: A matching or contrasting coat and dress worn together as an ensemble. *Der.* French, "mannish woman's frock coat" or English, "riding coat."

reefer **1.** Man's double-breasted, thigh-length boxy jacket called a *pea jacket* or *pilot coat* from 1830s to 1860s and taking on the name "reefer" about 1860. See under COATS AND JACKETS: PEA JACKET #2. ∞**2.** Women's and children's short jacket of 1890s and early 20th c., frequently worn with matching skirt as a suit. Made with unfitted double-breasted front and fitted back. **3.** Since 1960s, a short double-breasted car coat. **4.** In 1930s and 1940s, a woman's single-breasted fitted coat with large lapels; revived in 1983 and in use as basic coat style after this.

reefer #4

regency coat Double-breasted coat for man or woman made with wide lapels and high-rolled REGENCY COLLAR (see under NECKLINES AND COLLARS). Sometimes has large cuffs. Man's coat has nipped waist and deep vent in back. *Der.* Inspired by coats of the Regency period.

reversible jacket **1.** Any jacket that can be worn on either side. **2.** Short, down-quilted nylon jacket with zip-out sleeves and zip-front made with knitted cuffs and waistband. Reverses to a knitted jacket with removable sleeves.

riding coat **1.** Tailored, fitted jacket worn for horseback riding, similar in cut to PINK COAT, but in other colors or plaids. Also see under COATS AND JACKETS: HACKING JACKET and PINK COAT. **2.** See under COATS AND JACKETS: CUTAWAY.

sack jacket Loose, comfortable man's jacket, introduced in the late 1840s, that had no waistline, a straight front, center vent in back, sleeves without cuffs, and a small collar with short lapels. Called a *lounging jacket* in England, this jacket is a forerunner of tuxedo jackets and contemporary men's sport jackets.

sack jacket 1840s

∞**sack overcoat** Man's above-the-knee, loose-fitting overcoat worn from 1840s to about 1875. Made with sleeves wide at wrist, WELT POCKETS (see under POCKETS), and back cut in one piece with center slit. The edges of coat were double-stitched or bound. In 1860s closed higher and styled with three- or four-button closing, narrow lapels, optional pockets, and sometimes trimmed with velvet at collar, cuffs, and lapels.

saddle coat See under COATS AND JACKETS: POMMEL SLICKER.

safari coat See under COATS AND JACKETS: BUSH JACKET.

∞**sardinian sac** Loose-fitting, single-breasted man's overcoat of mid-19th c. Made with square-cut collar, no lapels, and full, bell-shaped sleeves. Worn flung over shoulders and secured by cord with tassel in front.

∞**scarborough ulster** Caped and hooded man's ULSTER (see under COATS AND JACKETS) without sleeves worn in early 1890s.

∞**señorita** Woman's waist-length, bolero-style jacket of mid-1860s, made with three-quarter- or full-length sleeves and lavishly trimmed with braid, fringe, buttons, or lace. Worn over a blouse with full sleeves. Also called a *spanish jacket.*

shearling jacket Jacket made of a tanned sheepskin with wool attached. Leather side is sueded or buffed and used for the outside of the coat, with woolly side worn inside. Collar is made with wool side out. Also called *sheepskin jacket.*

sheepskin jacket See under COATS AND JACKETS: SHEARLING JACKET.

shirt-jac See under SHIRTS.

∞**shooting coat** A morning coat, as it was called in 1860s to 1890s. See under COATS AND JACKETS: CUTAWAY.

shortie coat Woman's short coat, about finger tip length, made in boxy fitted or semi-fitted styles, worn in 1940s and 1950s. Revived periodically.

show coat Longer-style riding jacket or suit coat with hacking pockets (pockets with flaps placed at an angle), fitted waist, narrow lapels, three-button closing, inverted pleats at sides, and long slash in center back. Worn for semiformal showing of horses.

∞**simar** (si-mar') (*samarre*) Woman's loose-fitting jacket with side flaps, or skirts, extending to knees, sometimes worn over petticoat to make a dress in 17th and 18th c.

∞**siphonia** (sy-fo-ni-a) Long, weather-proof overcoat worn by men in 1850s and 1860s. The **pocket siphonia** was short and thin enough to be rolled up and carried in case of rain.

∞**skeleton waterproof** Woman's full-length, front-buttoned raincoat of 1890s made with large armholes, and instead of sleeves it was covered by a hip-length circular cape.

ski jacket Any type of wind-resistant jacket worn when skiing. Conventional type zips up front and may be made of nylon, wool, fur, or quilted fabric. Frequently has an attached hood. Usually made waist or hip length with zippered pockets.

slicker 1. OILSKIN or similar coat of rubberized fabric, usually bright yellow or other vivid colors; most commonly fastened with clips in front. Originally worn by sailors, now often worn with SOU'WESTER HAT (see under HEADWEAR) by fishermen and children. 2. A type of yellow, rubber raincoat with slash in back to waist and extra insert so that each side can be fastened around legs to form protection when riding horseback in rainy weather.

∞**sling-duster** (British usage) Coat worn by women in mid- and late 1880s. Made with DOLMAN or SLING SLEEVES (see under SHOULDERS AND SLEEVES). Frequently made of black-and-white checked silk.

smoking jacket 1. Man's jacket of velvet or other luxurious cloth, or with velvet or satin shawl collar. May be with or without buttons, sometimes has a sash, and is worn at home for informal entertaining, since 1850. 2. English version of American TUXEDO JACKET (see under COATS AND JACKETS), a short black semiformal dinner jacket made with satin lapels, called by the French "le smoking." Adapted for women by Paris designer Yves Saint Laurent in mid-1960s.

smoking jacket

snorkel jacket Warm hooded parka, made with front-opening zipper extending up over the wearer's chin, giving the hood the look of a "snorkel" (a submarine's air-intake or exhaust tube). Made hip- to knee-length and usually of water-repellent nylon satin or taffeta with quilted or pile lining and fake-fur edging around hood. Characterized by an inside drawstring waistline and knitted inner cuffs. Also has a multiplicity of zippered and snapped pockets, including one for pencils on the sleeve and a flap fastened with buttons and loops to keep snow out of the front zipper. Very popular in early 1970s for men, women, and children.

∞**spanish jacket** 1. See under COATS AND JACKETS: SEÑORITA. 2. Short, sleeveless jacket worn in 1862, somewhat similar to a bolero with no fasteners in front. Sometimes has a collar attached to a low neckline and often has rounded edges at hem in front.

spencer Short, open jacket, usually ending at or above the waistline. A version with lapels and long sleeves was reintroduced in mid-1980s for women. Thought to have been first worn by a British peer, Lord Spencer, and worn by men from 1790 to 1850 and by women from 1790 until about 1820. Three different stories of the origin of the style are told: (1) Lord Spencer burned one of the coattails of his jacket and cut off the other; (2) He was out riding and tore one of the coattails, so tore off the other; and (3) He made a wager he could start a new fashion and proceeded to cut off the coattails of his jacket, thus creating a new popular fashion.

spencer jacket

∞**spencerette** Woman's fitted jacket with low-cut neckline edged with lace, worn at end of Empire Period, about 1814.

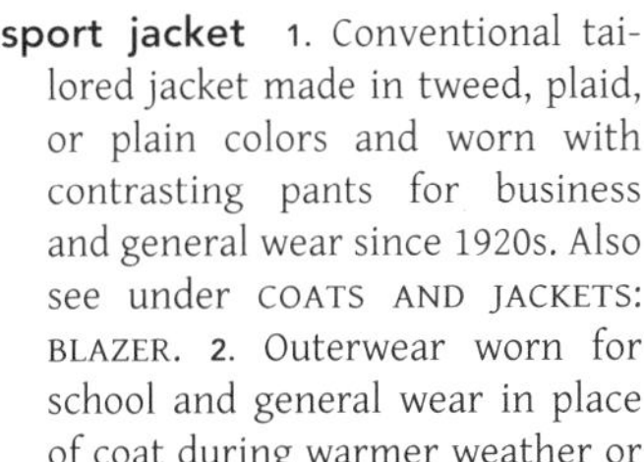

sport jacket #1

sport jacket 1. Conventional tailored jacket made in tweed, plaid, or plain colors and worn with contrasting pants for business and general wear since 1920s. Also see under COATS AND JACKETS: BLAZER. 2. Outerwear worn for school and general wear in place of coat during warmer weather or on informal occasions. 3. Outerwear designed for specific sports (e.g., golf, skiing, and cycling), sometimes accepted for general wear.

stadium coat 1. Car coat of three-quarter length sometimes made with SHEARLING collar (see under FURS and LEATHER) and TOGGLE closing (see under CLOSURES), introduced in early 1960s. By 1980s sometimes made with inner-zipper VEST SWEATER (see under SWEATERS) in front. 2. In early 1980s three-quarter-length reversible jacket made of waterproof vinyl with drawstring hood, two large pockets, and fastened with grippers at sleeves and front. *Der.* Worn at football stadiums.

storm coat Heavy coat sometimes quilted and made with water-repellent finish. May be styled with SHEARLING (see under FURS), pile, or quilted fabric lining and collar. By 1980s entire coat was made of quilted nylon.

∞**stroller jacket** A semiformal man's suit jacket similar to a TUXEDO JACKET, with satin lapels and peaked collar. Also called a SACK JACKET (see under COATS AND JACKETS).

suburban coat Synonym for COATS AND JACKETS: CAR COAT.

∞**sultane jacket** (sul-tane') Very short, sleeveless bolero-type woman's jacket worn in late 1880s. Similar to ZOUAVE JACKET (see under COATS AND JACKETS).

surtout (ser-too') 1. Contemporary French and British term for man's cloak or overcoat. *Der.* French, literally "over all." 2. Synonymous with a number of different overcoat styles in the 17th to the 19th c. See under COATS AND JACKETS for BRANDENBURG, WRAP-RASCAL, GREATCOAT, and WRAPPER #2. 3. Caped coat worn by women in late 18th c.

swagger coat Pyramid-shaped woman's coat with flared bias back. Usually with raglan sleeves and large saucer-shaped buttons attached by fabric cord. Popular in 1930s, revived in 1970s.

swallow-tailed coat c. 1895

swallow-tailed coat Man's formal evening coat that does not button in front, and is cut with peaked lapels trimmed with satin or grosgrain. Made waist length in front with two long tails in back. *Der.* Back resembles the "tail of a swallow." Also called *tails.*

sweater coat Knitted, often cardigan-style, coat.

sweat jacket Garment similar to a sweatshirt but open down the front and closing with buttons or a zipper. Made of cotton knit jersey with cotton fleece lining. Originally gray colored, but now made in any color.

taglioni (tal-yoh-nee') Man's fitted GREATCOAT (see under COATS AND JACKETS) reaching to knees, worn from 1839 to 1845. Usually double-breasted with wide, turned-back lapels; large, flat collar; and cuffs of satin or velvet. Also had a back vent and slit pockets bound with twill fabric. *Der.* Named after Italian ballet master Filippo Taglioni (1777–1871).

taglioni frock coat Man's single-breasted FROCK COAT (see under COATS AND JACKETS) worn from 1838 to 1842, made with short, full skirt, broad notched collar, slashed or flapped pockets, and back vent. *Der.* Named after Italian ballet master Filippo Taglioni (1777–1871).

tail coat/tails See under COATS AND JACKETS: SWALLOW-TAILED COAT.

∞**tallien redingote** (tal-ee-en' red'-in-gote) Outdoor coat worn by women in late 1860s, created by French couturier, Charles Frederick Worth. Matched to dress or made of black silk, coat had a heart-shaped neckline, full back, and a sash tied in large bow with long ends in back. Small bows were tied to ends of sash. *Der.* Named for Theresa Tallien, Princess de Chimay (1773–1835), a fashionable woman who is said to have owned 30 wigs of different colors.

∞**talma lounge** A jacket worn by men in 1898 made with raglan sleeves, straight fronts, and curved or slanted pockets. Worn as an informal jacket. *Der.* Named for François Joseph Talma (1763–1826), a French tragic actor of Consulate and Empire period.

∞**talma overcoat** Raglan-sleeved greatcoat with large armholes worn by men in 1898. *Der.* Named for François Joseph Talma (1763–1826), a French tragic actor of Consulate and Empire period.

∞**teddybear coat** Bulky coat of natural-colored alpaca-pile fabric worn by men, women, and children in 1920s. *Der.* Named after the teddy bear, a child's toy of early 20th c., which was named for President Theodore Roosevelt.

templar cloak See under COATS AND JACKETS: CABAN.

tent coat Woman's pyramid-shaped coat, widely flared at hem, popular in 1930s, 1940s, and in mid-1960s. Revived periodically.

∞**three-decker** Used from late 1870s on for man's or woman's triple-caped ULSTER (see under COATS AND JACKETS).

three-seamer (British usage) A man's jacket with center back seam and two side seams, contrasted with coat having SIDE BODIES and five seams. Term first used among tailor in 1860.

toggle coat See under COATS AND JACKETS: DUFFEL COAT.

topcoat 1. Man's or woman's lightweight coat in any style, designed to wear over suit jacket or dress. See under COATS AND JACKETS: OVERCOAT. ∞2. Woman's tailored, full-length, straight-cut coat worn in 1890s, with moderate LEG-OF-MUTTON SLEEVES (see under SHOULDERS AND SLEEVES), tailored collar, and fly-front closing. Had large flap pockets on hips and small ticket pocket above.

∞**top frock** Man's overcoat cut like a FROCK COAT (see under COATS AND JACKETS) but longer, worn from 1830 on. Usually double-breasted and intended to be worn without a suit coat.

topper coat Woman's hip-length coat, often made with a flared silhouette, popular in early 1940s.

toreador jacket (tor-ay′-ah-dor) Waist-length woman's jacket with epaulet shoulder trimming, frequently braid-trimmed and worn unfastened. Adapted from jackets of bullfighters in Spain and Mexico.

tow coat Three-quarter-length coat similar to a *toggle coat* or *duffel coat,* designed for winter sports.

trench coat Coat made of a chemically finished, water-repellent cotton gabardine, created during World War I for soldiers by Thomas Burberry. After the War the style became an all-purpose civilian coat made of a water-repellent fabric in double-breasted style with a convertible collar, large lapels, epaulets, fabric belt, slotted pockets, and a vent in the back. Over the shoulders in back it had an extra hanging yoke and an extra flap hung from the front right shoulder. In the 1940s women adopted the trench coat, which has become a classic style.

trench coat

tuxedo jacket Man's semiformal jacket made in one-button style with shawl collar usually faced with satin or faille. Until the late 1960s, it was conventionally black or navy for winter and white for summer. Now styled in any color or pattern (e.g., red, green, blue, or plaid fabrics, sometimes with notched collar). Introduced in 1886. *Der.* After Tuxedo Park Country Club, Tuxedo Park, New York, where it was first worn by the well-to-do men who lived there. Also called a *dinner jacket.*

tweed jacket 1. Man's conventional sport jacket of tweed wool fabric or a wool blend usually made with traditional single-breasted styling. 2. Women's jacket of almost any style made out of yarn-dyed wool of a textured nature and usually worn with matching skirt or pants. Popular in the 1920s and 1930s for women as suitable for the "country" rather than town wear.

ulster ∞1. Man's heavy overcoat introduced in late 1860s. Usually made in single- or double-breasted style with a belted back or with a complete belt and detachable hood. By the 1870s, a cape was more usual. About 1875, a TICKET POCKET (see under POCKETS) was placed in left sleeve above cuff, and by 1890 a fly-front closing was used. Length varied, the coat being ankle length in 1870s. ∞2. Woman's coat, similar to man's, worn from late 1870s on. When made with a triple cape, it was called a CARRICK. Sometimes made of waterproof fabric, sometimes with a train. *Der.* Named after a northern province of Ireland in which the cities of Belfast and Londonderry, manufacturing centers for heavy coats, are located. 3. (British usage) A long, loose-fitting overcoat.

∞**varens** Woman's short outdoor jacket of 1847 with loose sleeves. Made of cashmere or velvet with silk lining, a variation of the CASAWECK and POLKA (see under COATS AND JACKETS).

∞**vareuse** (vah-reuz′) Rough woolen overblouse or jacket, similar to the PEA JACKET (see under COATS AND JACKETS).

varsity jacket See under COATS AND JACKETS: BASEBALL JACKET.

vinyl raincoat (vine′-ul) 1. Waterproof raincoat usually made of heavy clear vinyl. Special attention must be paid to sewing the seams, or it will tear where the sewing machine perforates it. 2. Fabric given a vinyl finish and used to make a raincoat.

∞**waistcoat paletot** (pal-ah-tow′ or pal-tow′) Woman's knee-length coat of 1884 in tailored style buttoned only at neckline, made with hip-length waistcoat showing in front.

walking coat Knee-length, single-breasted coat with a notched collar.

wamus (wah′-muss) (*wammus, wampus*) Heavy outdoor jacket or cardigan of coarse cloth, buttoned at collar and wrists worn in the U.S.

watch coat Short, heavy, windproof coat worn by sailors on watch. Also see under COATS AND JACKETS: PEA COAT.

∞**watteau coat** (wat-toe′) Lady's princess-style coat of the 1890s made in fitted unbuttoned style with waistcoat showing in front. Usually had a standing collar, wide lapels, and turned-back cuffs with characteristic single or double box pleat in center back. *Der.* Named for the artist Antoine Watteau (1684–1721).

wellesley wrapper Above-the-knee, double-breasted, sack-like coat, worn in 1853 by men and fastened in front with BRANDENBURGS (see under CLOSURES: FROGS).

western jacket Jacket like those worn by American cowboys, made of buckskin or fabric with breast pockets, a yoke, and sometimes having a fringe of leather on yoke, sleeves, and hem.

windbreaker Formerly a trademark and continues in common usage for a warm, lightweight nylon jacket zipped up front with close-fitting waistband and cuffs, often made with attached hood. Trademark now applies to a wide variety of apparel items.

wraparound coat Woman's coat made without buttons or fasteners in front and held closed with long self-fabric sash. Also called *wrap coat.*

wrapper ∞**1.** Man's loose overcoat, worn in 1840s, either single- or double-breasted. Sometimes used to indicate a CHESTERFIELD (see under COATS AND JACKETS). **2.** In the 1850s, man's loose thigh-length overcoat, with shawl collar, that wrapped in front; sometimes worn with evening dress.

∞**wrap-rascal** Man's loose-fitting overcoat made of heavy fabric, worn from about 1738 to 1850. In the 19th c., it usually referred to coats worn when traveling on the outside of a coach. Also worn in the country.

∞**yachting coat** Woman's hip-length, square-cut jacket worn from 1860s to 1880s. Made single- or double-breasted with large buttons and loose sleeves. Also called *short paletot.* See under COATS AND JACKETS: PALETOT.

yachting jacket Double-breasted four-button man's jacket with lapels and collar, usually styled in navy-blue wool with brass buttons. Made similar to U.S. Naval uniforms with black braid instead of gold, and yacht club buttons instead of Navy buttons; worn on board by yacht club members.

Zhivago coat (zhi-vah'-go) Mid-calf-length coat, lavishly trimmed with fur at neck, cuffs, and hem, sometimes with frog closing. Inspired by costumes worn in *Dr. Zhivago,* 1965 film adapted from eponymous novel by Boris Pasternak, about the 1917 Russian Revolution.

zip-off coat Long coat styled to be used in two or three lengths, achieved by placing zippers at mini and midi lengths. When made to have only two lengths, may be called a *duo-length coat.*

∞**zouave coat** (zoo-ahv') Man's cloak of mid-1840s with velvet collar and cuffs and quilted silk lining. Used for riding, walking, or worn to the opera. Same as the *oriental wrapper. Der.* Arabic, *Zouaova,* a Kabyle tribe, one of the Berbers, living in Algeria or Tunisia.

∞**zouave jacket** (zoo-ahv') **1.** Woman's waist-length, bolero-type jacket fastened at the neck and with curved sides in front. Had relatively full-cut, three-quarter-length sleeves. Showed military influence in the trim inspired by Algerian Zouave troops and American Northern troops of the Civil War. Fashionable 1859 to 1870 and revived in the 1890s. **2.** Similar jacket worn by little boys in the 1860s. *Der.* Arabic, *Zouaova,* a Kabyle tribe, one of the Berbers, living in Algeria or Tunisia.

zouave jacket #1

∞**zouave paletot** (zoo-ahv' pal-ah-tow' or pal-tow') Waterproofed llama-wool coat worn by men with or without a suit coat in 1840s. *Der.* Arabic, *Zouaova,* a Kabyle tribe, one of the Berbers, living in Algeria or Tunisia.

---

coat set See under COATS AND JACKETS.

coat shirt See under SHIRTS.

coat-style pajamas See under SLEEPWEAR AND LOUNGEWEAR.

coat sweater See under SWEATERS.

coattail See under COATS AND JACKETS.

cobbler One who makes or repairs shoes. Synonym: *shoemaker.* Also see under CORDWAINER.

cobbler's apron See under APRONS.

cobra chain See under CHAIN #1.

co-branding See under BRAND.

cocarde See under COCKADE #1.

∞**cock** Used from end of 17th to early 19th c. to refer to action of turning up a hat's brim. Given various names for manner of turn-up. Also see under HEADWEAR: COCKED HAT.

cockade **1.** Ornamental rosette or bow of ribbon, usually made flat around a center button. Sometimes worn as a part of a uniform or badge of office (e.g., tricolor cockade of red, white, and blue worn on side of hat as patriotic symbol during French Revolution). Also called *cocarde.* **2.** Feather trimming. See under FEATHERS. **3.** See under FANS.

cocked hat See under HEADWEAR.

cockers See under FOOTWEAR.

cock feather See under FEATHERS.

cockle See under HAIRSTYLES.

cockle hat See under HEADWEAR.

cockscomb See under COXCOMB.

cocktail *adj.* Describes clothing and accessories worn at cocktail parties and social gatherings where various alcoholic drinks are often served before dinner. See under DRESSES: COCKTAIL DRESS; APRONS: COCKTAIL APRON; GLOVES AND GLOVE CONSTRUCTION: COCKTAIL GLOVES; and JEWELRY: COCKTAIL RING.

cocktail dress See under DRESSES.

coconut straw/coco straw Braided straw, usually tan or light brown, made from coconut-palm leaves.

cocoon See under COATS AND JACKETS and SLEEPWEAR AND LOUNGEWEAR.

cocurs See under FOOTWEAR: COCKERS.

codovec See under HEADWEAR: CASTOR.

∞**codpiece** **1.** Triangular flap at front of crotch of men's trunk hose large enough for a pocket, frequently padded and decorated, worn during 15th and 16th c. Shown at TRUNK HOSE and DOUBLET. **2.** By early 17th c. term applied to front fastening of BREECHES. Also called a *cod placket.* Compare with BRAYETTE.

cod placket See under CODPIECE #2.

codrington See under COATS AND JACKETS.

coffer headdress See under HEADWEAR.

coggers See under FOOTWEAR: COCKERS.

coif (kwaf) **1.** Short for *coiffure.* French, "hairstyle." See under HAIRSTYLES. **2.** To style or dress the hair. **3.** See under HEADWEAR.

coiffe de mailles See under ARMOR.

coiffette See under ARMOR.

coiffure (kwa'-fure) (French) Hairdressing. Adopted from the French for English usage since 18th c. to refer to hairdressing or arrangement of hair. Note: *coiffeur* (m.) (kwa'-fuhr) and *coiffeuse* (f.) (kwa'-fuhz) are the French masculine and feminine forms for hairdresser.

coiffure à l'agnès sorel See under HAIRSTYLES: AGNÈS SOREL COIFFURE.

coiffure à la grecque See under HAIRSTYLES: GREEK COIFFURE.

coiffure à la hérisson See under HAIRSTYLES: HÉRISSON.

coiffure à la indépendance See under HAIRSTYLES.

coiffure à la maintenon See under HAIRSTYLES.

coiffure à la mouton See under HAIRSTYLES.

coiffure à la ninon See under HAIRSTYLES: NINON COIFFURE.

coiffure à la sévigné See under HAIRSTYLES.

coiffure à la titus See under HAIRSTYLES: TITUS.

coiffure à la zazzera See under HAIRSTYLES.

coiffure à l'enfant See under HAIRSTYLES.

coiffure en bouffons See under HAIRSTYLES.

coiffure en bourse See under WIGS AND HAIRPIECES: BAGWIG.

coiffure en cadenettes See under HAIRSTYLES.

coiffure en raquette See under HAIRSTYLES.

coiled bracelet See under JEWELRY: BRACELETS.

coin de feu See under COATS AND JACKETS.

coin dot See under PRINTS, STRIPES, AND CHECKS: DOTS.

coin necklace See under JEWELRY.

coin purse See under HANDBAGS AND RELATED ACCESSORIES: CHANGE PURSE.

coin silver Strong silver alloy, containing 90 percent silver and 10 percent copper. The only silver available to early American colonists, obtained by melting down silver coins. Uses: jewelry.

∞**cointise** (kwan-teez') **1.** See under ARMOR. **2.** Some sources indicate this term may have been used in the Middle Ages to describe very decorative clothing.

cokers See under COCKERS.

colbert embroidery See under EMBROIDERIES AND SEWING STITCHES.

colbertine lace See under LACES.

cold mask See under MASKS: HOT MASK.

cold wave See under HAIRSTYLES: PERMANENT WAVE.

collaborative supply chain Interactive networks of independent manufacturing specialists that join forces operationally to integrate complementary resources in response to a market opportunity through the creation of a particular product.

collar **1.** See under introduction to NECKLINES AND COLLARS. **2.** See under FOOTWEAR: QUARTER.

collar and cuff set Women's separate collar and cuffs usually made of linen, lace, organdy, or other sheer fabrics; often white, trimmed with lace, insertion, embroidery, or tucks. Popular from early 15th c. until 1930s and used occasionally since.

collar button See under CLOSURES: STUD.

collaret **1.** See under NECKLINES AND COLLARS. ∞**2.** See under ARMOR.

collarette à la Lyon See under NECKLINES AND COLLARS: CHERUSSE.

collar necklace See under JEWELRY.

collar pin See under JEWELRY.

collar stay Narrow strip of plastic or metal inserted in point of man's collar from the underside to ensure a crisp unwrinkled look.

collection In the apparel industry, used by couture and ready-to-wear designers, as well as clothing manufacturers, to refer to clothing and accessories offered to customers for a specific season. Originally used only for high-priced couture clothing. Also called **line**.

colleen bawn cloak See under CAPES, CLOAKS, AND SHAWLS.

collegians See under FOOTWEAR: OXONIAN BOOT.

∞**colley-westonward** As used in 16th-c. as slang meaning "worn awry" or "crooked," usually applied to the MANDILION JACKET (see under COATS AND JACKETS), which was worn without putting arms through sleeves and turned sideways so that one sleeve hung in front, the other in back. *Der.* From a Cheshire, England, saying for "anything that goes wrong."

colobium 1. See under UNDERGARMENTS. 2. See under CLERICAL DRESS.

colonial shoe/pump See under FOOTWEAR.

colonial tongue See under FOOTWEAR.

color blocking Use of large geometrical areas of contrasting color in dresses, blouses, jackets. See under DRESSES: MONDRIAN DRESS.

color forecasting Predictions of color preferences developed through research carried out by color forecasting, textile, and apparel companies.

color-graded glasses See under EYEWEAR.

color story 1. A palette of colors, selected for each group in a seasonal delivery, that relates the pieces within that group or delivery to each other, giving visual appeal to a store and encouraging consumers to buy multiple pieces. 2. A palette of colors for materials, prints, and hardware that will be used for an apparel or accessory collection.

colorway The three or four color choices of a solid or printed fabric available for a garment style produced in more than one color.

columnar heel See under FOOTWEAR.

comb 1. An article—often made of tortoiseshell, ivory, plastic, wood, or metal—with a row of narrow teeth that is drawn through the hair or beard to arrange or untangle it. 2. Combs of precious metals or those decorated with jewels are often placed in women's hair to hold it in place and serve as decorations, especially at sides of head or in back when hair is set in a twist. Earliest combs are from late Stone Age.

combat boot See under FOOTWEAR.

combat shorts See under SHORTS.

†**combed yarn** Yarn made from short fibers, known in the textile industry as STAPLE FIBERS, that have been subjected to the process of combing. Combing is an optional step in the spinning of yarns in which fibers that have been carded are subjected to further straightening and alignment, formed into a strand of fibers, and given a greater or lesser amount of twist to form them into a yarn. Combed yarns have fewer fibers on the surface, are smoother, and can be finer yarns than those that have only been carded. See under CARDED YARNS.

combination last See under FOOTWEAR: LAST.

combinations See under UNDERGARMENTS.

combination tanning See under LEATHERS.

combing See under COMBED YARN.

combing jacket See under COATS AND JACKETS.

comb morion See under ARMOR: MORION.

comfort collar See under NECKLINES AND COLLARS.

comforter See under SCARVES.

commander's cap See under HEADWEAR.

commercial match A color match between components of a style provided by a contractor that is satisfactory to the manufacturer.

commissionaire A middleman who operates in foreign countries and buys merchandise for American retailers.

commode See under HEADWEAR.

commodore cap See under HEADWEAR.

commodore dress See under DRESSES.

commonsense heel See under FOOTWEAR.

communion dress Clothing customarily worn by children when taking their first Communion in the Catholic Church. Girls' dress generally consists of a white dress worn with a short white veil. Boys generally wear a white suit. Also see under HEADWEAR: COMMUNION VEIL.

compact Cosmetic container used to hold powder, rouge, eye shadow, and sometimes lipstick. Made of metal or plastic with mirrored lid.

compass cloak See under CAPES, CLOAKS, AND SHAWLS: FRENCH CLOAK.

competition stripes See under SHIRTS: COMPETITION-STRIPED SHIRT and PRINTS, STRIPES, AND CHECKS.

computer-aided design (CAD) Computer hardware and software systems for designing apparel and implementing their manufacture. This technology can significantly decrease errors and save time because the effects of changes in design can be seen on the computer screen without making actual samples.

computer-aided design/computer-aided manufacturing (CAD/CAM) The linking of computer systems for creating designs with those for pattern creation, GRADING, and MARKER making in order to coordinate the steps in production.

computer-aided manufacturing (CAM) Computer hardware and software systems that GRADE and make MARKERS electronically. They may also have the capability to do computer-controlled cutting, use lasers for specialized cutting, and employ robotics in manufacturing. These systems lower the use of manual labor, but because of the initial high capital investment, generally only large manufacturers utilize this sophisticated technology to the maximum.

computer dress See under DRESSES.

computer grading and marker making (CGMM) The computer hardware and software systems that process the pattern grading and marker-making segments of a garment pattern for production.

computer integrated manufacturing (CIM) The production of a finished product by integrating various computer-aided processes (such as CAD, CAM, CGMM) that can link information and equipment throughout the manufacturing process.

concept See under THEME.

concept rig A life-size sample of all apparel and accessories within a concept or THEME so that a complete picture can be created of customers, their lifestyle, and how the items would be worn together.

concept store Buyers and designers shop these stores in major fashion cities in order to quickly identify important seasonal silhouettes and details. Examples include *Colette* and *L'Eclaireur* in Paris.

∞**conch** (conk, consh) Sheer, gauzelike veil of the late 16th c. extending from shoulder to floor and worn cape-like over the shoulders. At the back of the neck, it was attached to a winglike construction that stood up like a high collar behind the head.

conch 16th c.

concierge See under HAIRSTYLES: POMPADOUR.

conductor's cap See under HEADWEAR.

coney/cony See under FURS.

confidants See under HAIRSTYLES.

congress boot See under FOOTWEAR.

conical Asian hat See under HEADWEAR.

considerations See under UNDERGARMENTS: PANIER.

consignment Goods stocked by a retailer but not paid for until they are sold. After selling the goods, the retailer pays the person or firm that provided the goods a price agreed upon at the time of consignment.

conspicuous consumption See under VEBLEN, THORSTEIN.

conspicuous leisure See under VEBLEN, THORSTEIN.

conspicuous outrage See under VEBLEN, THORSTEIN.

constable See under CANE.

Consumer Product Safety Commission (CPSC) A U.S. federal government agency that oversees product safety and, as part of its responsibilities, monitors flammability regulations for apparel and home furnishings.

contemporary designer market A category of fashion with an edgy point of view that targets a younger designer ready-to-wear customer.

continental *adj.* Applied to garments thought to have originated in one of the countries on the continent of Europe. See under CONTINENTAL SUIT; PANTS: CONTINENTAL PANTS; and POCKETS: CONTINENTAL POCKETS.

continental hat See under HEADWEAR: COCKED HAT.

continental heel See under FOOTWEAR.

continental stitch See under EMBROIDERIES AND SEWING STITCHES.

continental suit Man's suit with natural shoulder line, easy-fitting jacket, and narrow, tapered trousers with no belt. Pockets in trousers are slanted from waistline to side seams. Style originated in Italy in 1950s.

†**continuous filament yarn** Manufactured yarns made by pushing the spinning fluid through a spinerette (a type of nozzle), with tiny holes, producing strands of indefinite length. When only one strand is produced, a MONOFILAMENT YARN is formed; when many strands are produced, a MULTIFILAMENT YARN is formed.

contour belt See under BELTS.

contour bra See under UNDERGARMENTS.

contour clutch See under HANDBAGS AND RELATED ACCESSORIES.

contractor A person or firm that agrees to construct apparel for a manufacturer or retailer.

contractual retailer Retailer that has made contractual arrangements with other retailers, with a manufacturer, or with a wholesaler that may be advantageous because it simplifies management and increases market impact. Examples of contractual arrangements include FRANCHISES and LEASED DEPARTMENTS.

control Describes garments such as women's girdles, foundations, or pantyhose made with elastomeric yarns (see under ELASTOMER), which provide support. See under HOSIERY: PANTYHOSE; and UNDERGARMENTS: CONTROL PANTS and GARTER BRIEF.

controls In retailing, refers to the methods used by a retailer to monitor business operations and evaluate the effectiveness of merchandising strategies. Also see under MAZUR PLAN.

convenience goods Products that require relatively little evaluation before their purchase by consumers. Compare with SHOPPING GOODS and SPECIALTY GOODS.

conversation bonnet See under HEADWEAR: POKE BONNET.

†converted goods Textile fabrics processed by a CONVERTER.

†converter In the textile industry, a middleman, either a firm or an individual, that takes woven goods in an unfinished state and applies finishing processes (e.g., dyeing, bleaching, waterproofing). After processing, fabrics are suitable for the clothing manufacturer or the yard-goods retailer.

convertible *adj.* Articles of clothing that can be changed in appearance or form by some means. For examples see under HANDBAGS AND RELATED ACCESSORIES and NECKLINES AND COLLARS.

convertible bra See under UNDERGARMENTS.

convertible swimsuit See under SWIMWEAR.

cookie See under FOOTWEAR: ARCH CUSHION.

coonskin cap See under HEADWEAR: DAVY CROCKETT CAP.

co-op advertising A type of advertising strategy whereby companies share the cost of an advertisement that features a number of companies.

cooperative buying office See under ASSOCIATED BUYING OFFICE.

coordinated group line Apparel items that are organized around color and fabric groups that are intended to be purchased and worn together. Also called *coordinates.*

cope See under CLERICAL DRESS and CAPES, CLOAKS, AND SHAWLS.

copotain See under HEADWEAR.

copped shoe See under FOOTWEAR: CRAKOW.

copper toe See under FOOTWEAR.

copyist Person in the apparel trade who makes replicas of designs—translating a high-priced item to a lower price for a manufacturer.

copyright The set of exclusive legal rights granted to authors or owners of published or unpublished literary, scientific, and artistic works that are fixed in a tangible form. Includes the right to reproduce, distribute, perform, or display the work, and the right to create derivative works. Attempts have been made to provide copyright legal protections to fashion designs.

coq feathers See under FEATHERS.

coquette parasol See under UMBRELLAS AND PARASOLS: MARQUISE.

coral See under GEMS, GEM CUTS, AND SETTINGS.

corazza See under SHIRTS.

†cord **1.** The result of twisting together two or more ply yarns. **2.** A surface effect in fabrics that creates ridges running in the lengthwise direction. **3.** See under LACE: CORDONNET.

cordé handbag See under HANDBAGS AND RELATED ACCESSORIES.

corded seam See under CLOTHING CONSTRUCTION DETAILS.

∞cordelière (kor′-deh-lyare′) (*cordilier*) Long chain, often of gold, that hung from belt or girdle and was used to hold a cross, scissors, or other small items; worn by women in the 16th c. *Der.* French, "cord" or "girdle" worn by Franciscan friars. Also see under CHATELAINE.

cording **1.** Trimming made by inserting a soft, ropelike cord into a strip of bias-cut fabric. **2.** Full-rounded trimming used for frogs and loops, made by pulling the cord through a seamed tube of BIAS fabric to cover cord completely.

cordonnet See under introduction to LACES.

cordovan See under LEATHERS.

cords/corduroys See under PANTS.

†corduroy (kohr′-duh-roy) Strong, durable, woven fabric with vertical stripes of cut pile that are formed by an extra system of crosswise yarns. The lengthwise stripes may be made in various widths. Those that are very narrow are called **pinwale.** Usually made of cotton or a cotton blend. The name is thought to derive from the French *corde du roi,* meaning "cord of the king."

†corduroy knit Knitted fabric made with stripes of cut pile in imitation of woven corduroy fabric.

∞cordwainer Used to refer to a shoemaker. Originally signified one who worked in cordovan leather (from Cordova, Spain), making shoes and other leather items. See under LEATHER: CORDOVAN.

†cord yarn Heavy yarn made by twisting together two or more PLY YARNS. Used in BENGALINE, OTTOMAN, and BEDFORD CORD fabrics. Called *cable yarn* in Great Britain.

cordyback hat See under HEADWEAR: CAUDEBAC.

†core yarn Yarn made with a heavy center cord around which are wrapped finer fiber yarns of different fibers (e.g., synthetic rubber or ELASTOMER core wrapped with yarns made of other fiber) to improve absorption and feel.

cork **1.** Outer bark of oak, *Quercus suber,* grown in Mediterranean countries. Stripped, dried, and boiled to remove sap and tannic acid, then used for fillers in shoes, for clogs, for tropical hats, and for other items that require low weight, resilience, moisture resistance, and insulation against heat. **2.** See under FOOTWEAR: GALOSH #2.

corkies See under FOOTWEAR: WEDGE HEEL.

cork lace See under LACES.

cork rump See under UNDERGARMENTS.

corkscrew curl See under HAIRSTYLES.

corkscrew wig See under WIGS AND HAIRPIECES.

cornalia See under ORALIA.

corned shoe See under FOOTWEAR.

cornercap See under ACADEMIC COSTUME: MORTARBOARD.

cornet **1.** See under ACADEMIC COSTUME: MORTARBOARD. **2.** See under HEADWEAR: HENNIN. **3.** See under HEADWEAR. **4.** See under SKIRTS.

cornet sleeve See under SHOULDERS AND SLEEVES.

cornrows See under HAIRSTYLES.

cornu See under HEADWEAR: ORALIA.

coronal See under CORONET.

coronation braid See under BRAIDS.

coronation robes **1.** Three capes worn by British king or queen for coronation at various times during the ceremony: (a) a red cape lined with white; (b) an ecclesiastical COPE (see under CLERICAL DRESS); and (c) a purple velvet cloak trimmed with ermine. **2.** Ermine trimmed robes worn by British nobility attending the coronation with trains of prescribed lengths according to rank. Worn with various types of CORONETS (see HEADWEAR) according to rank. Also called *robes of state.*

coronet See under HEADWEAR.

corps (cor) (17th-c. French) BODICE.

corps à baleine See under UNDERGARMENTS: CORPS PIQUÉ #2.

corps piqué See under UNDERGARMENTS.

corsage (cor-sahge′) **1.** Small floral arrangement of flowers worn fastened to woman's shoulder or waist, sometimes attached to specially designed wristband and worn on wrist. Worn on special occasions or for formal events. Also see under BOSOM FLOWERS. ∞**2.** A woman's bodice as it was called in the 18th and 19th c.

corsage à la du barry See under DU BARRY CORSAGE.

∞**corsage à la maintenon** (cor-sahge′ ah lah man-teh′-nah) Fitted bodice of 1830s and 1840s trimmed with bow knots down center front. *Der.* For Marquise de Maintenon, second wife of Louis XIV of France.

∞**corsage en corset** (cor-sahge on cor-seh) Tight-fitting evening bodice of 1830s and 1840s, cut in sections with seams similar to those on a corset.

∞**corse** **1.** Tight-fitting underbodice of metal or leather with center-front lacings, worn under tunic by men in 12th and 13th c. **2.** BALDRICK (see under BELTS) for carrying a bugle used by men in 16th c.

corselet ∞**1.** Variant of CORSET, used in 14th and 15th c. **2.** See under BELTS: CORSELET BELT. ∞**3.** See under ARMOR. **4.** See under UNDERGARMENTS. **5.** See under DRESSES: CORSET FROCK. **6.** See under WAISTLINES.

corset **1.** See under UNDERGARMENTS. ∞**2.** In 11th c. a leather bodice stiffened with wood or metal. ∞**3.** From 16th to 18th c., a stiffened bodice called STAYS (see under UNDERGARMENTS). ∞**4.** Woman's gown, laced up back and lined in fur, worn in 14th and 15th c. ∞**5.** Man's surcoat, with or without sleeves, worn in Middle Ages.

corset à la ninon See under UNDERGARMENTS.

corset bikini See under SWIMWEAR: BIKINI.

corset cover See under UNDERGARMENTS: CAMISOLE #1.

corset frock See under DRESSES.

corsican tie See under TIES: NAPOLEON NECKTIE.

corundum See under GEMS, GEM CUTS, AND SETTINGS.

cosmonaut *adj.* Describes apparel that was influenced by public attention paid to the first astronauts in the 1960s. Examples included jumpsuits and helmets. St. Laurent's collection in 1963 showed such influences. These styles helped initiate a trend toward pantsuits and jumpsuits for women. *Der.* Russian, "astronaut." Also see under LUNAR.

cossack *adj.* Pertaining to garments or styles derived from those worn by people inhabiting the Caucasus, an area between the Black and Caspian Seas. Men were particularly noted for their horsemanship and wore distinctive clothing. See under BLOUSES AND TOPS: COSSACK BLOUSE; HEADWEAR: COSSACK FORAGE CAP and COSSACK HAT; NECKLINES AND COLLARS: COSSACK COLLAR; PANTS: COSSACKS; SHIRTS: COSSACK SHIRT; and SLEEPWEAR AND LOUNGEWEAR: COSSACK PAJAMAS.

cosse See under FEATHERS.

cost (wholesale cost or cost to manufacture) The total cost to manufacture a garment. Derived from the total of the costs of materials, FINDINGS, labor, shipping, packaging, and duty, if applicable.

costing marker The layout of the pattern pieces for the PROTOTYPE of a new style in order to ascertain the yardage required.

costume **1.** Dress, coat, or suit with coordinated accessories; an ensemble. **2.** Fancy dress for masquerade parties, Halloween, or costume and masked balls. **3.** Dress from a certain period in history, generally referred to as historic costume. Recently the synonym *historic dress* has been preferred. See under DRESS. **4.** Theatrical dress worn on stage. **5.** Native dress worn for festivals and specific occasions. ∞**6.** In the 1860s, an outdoor day dress or afternoon dress with a long train.

costume à la constitution See under DRESSES.

costume jewelry See under JEWELRY.

∞**cote** (koht) Undertunic worn by men and women during the Middle Ages, as it was called in the 13th c. and after. Spelled *cotte* in France, this garment was worn over a shirt or chemise and under a **surcote** (ser′-koht), or outer tunic. This word is the source of the modern word *coat.* For women, *kirtle* is sometimes used as a synonym.

cote and sideless surcote 1390

∞**cotehardie/cote-hardy/cote-hardie** (coat′-har′-dee) 1. A variant of the *surcote,* or outer tunic, for men. The term seems to have had different applications in different countries. In France, it was identified as either a short garment with long sleeves for outdoor wear, at first simple and later more elegant and fur-trimmed; a gown; or an outer garment open in front and buttoned at the sides. In England, it was a buttoned outer garment fitted through the body to the waist or below where it flared out into a usually knee-length skirt. The sleeves ended at the elbow in front while hanging down at the back in a shorter or longer flap. With time, some versions of the garment became quite decorative. A decorative belt was often worn low on the hip. 2. Woman's close-fitting, dress-like garment of same period, made of rich fabric and laced up back or front. Had long, tight sleeves and slits down the sides of skirt called *fitchets.* Said to have been introduced by Anne, wife of the British Monarch Richard II, who reigned as the King of England from 1377 to 1399.

cotehardie #1

cothurnus See under FOOTWEAR.

cotta See under CLERICAL DRESS.

cottage bonnet See under HEADWEAR.

cottage cloak See under CAPES, CLOAKS, AND SHAWLS.

cottage dress See under DRESSES.

∞**cottage front** Daytime bodice with LACERS in front for decorative effect. Worn over a HABIT SHIRT (see under SHIRTS) or CHEMISETTE (see under SCARVES) in early 19th c.

cotte See under COTE.

†**cotton** Soft, white vegetable fiber from 1/2″ to 2″ long that comes from the fluffy boll of the cotton plant. Grown in Egypt, India, China, and southern U.S. American cottons include *acala, upland, peeler, pima,* and *sea island.* Composed largely of cellulose, cotton fibers are absorbent, comfortable, and washable; therefore, cotton is used alone and in blends with other fibers in a wide variety of apparel items.

cotton batting See under BATTING.

Coty American Fashion Critics Awards Annual awards sponsored by Coty, Inc., international cosmetics and perfume company, from 1942 to 1985, given for outstanding fashion design. Judges were magazine and newspaper fashion editors, broadcasters, and fashion retailers. The *Winnie* was awarded each year to a designer who contributed to American design and had a significant impact on fashion. Originally awards were given to designers of women's fashions. In 1968 the Coty Menswear Fashion Awards were established. A designer receiving a *Winnie* or Menswear Award three times was accepted into the *Hall of Fame.*

couched embroidery See under EMBROIDERIES AND SEWING STITCHES.

couching stitch See under EMBROIDERIES AND SEWING STITCHES.

couel 1. See under HEADWEAR. 2. (British usage) Synonym for COWL (see under NECKLINES AND COLLARS).

Council of Fashion Designers of America A nonprofit organization with a membership of the foremost American designers, founded in 1962 under the leadership of Eleanor Lambert, with Norman Norell as the first president. Membership is by invitation only. Accomplishments include: (a) recognizing American designers both here and abroad; (b) achieving National Endowment of the Arts recognition of fashion as an art form; (c) presenting costume exhibitions annually; (d) hosting the "party of the year" at the Metropolitan Museum of Art in New York City; (e) contributing annually since 1963 to the Costume Institute of the Metropolitan Museum; (f) supporting recognized costume institutes throughout the country, including the costume wing of the Smithsonian; and (g) being instrumental in founding the Fashion Institute of Technology in New York City. Since 1985 an annual awards evening is given to honor individuals who have made an outstanding contribution to fashion and fashion journalism. Acronym: CFDA.

counted cross-stitch embroidery See under EMBROIDERIES AND SEWING STITCHES.

counted thread embroidery See under EMBROIDERIES AND SEWING STITCHES.

countenance See under COUTENANCE.

counter See under FOOTWEAR.

counter book See under PATTERN BOOK.

counterfeit goods Unauthorized illegal copies of goods with registered trade names, trademarks, or logos.

counter fillet See under HEADWEAR.

counter sample See under SEW BY.

countertop display Merchandise shelf or tabletop displays that allow customers to touch and self-select products.

country of origin See TEXTILE FIBER PRODUCTS IDENTIFICATION ACT (T.F.P.IA.).

country-western 1. *adj.* Describes apparel of the style initiated by country-western musicians at the Grand Ole Opry® in Nashville, Tennessee; The style includes a range of apparel, from casual overalls, straw hats, and gingham dresses to ultra-dressy, over-the-top rhinestone- and sequin-studded western garb as worn by Dolly Parton, Barbara Mandrell, and Kenny Rogers. *Der.* From style of music. See also WESTERN as an adjective. 2. Descriptive of the costumes worn by square dancers in the rural U.S. that feature women in dresses and skirts (sometimes gingham) with many petticoats, and men in western pants, plaid or fringed shirts, and neckerchiefs (e.g., as seen on characters in the musical *Oklahoma*). *Der.* Type of dancing originating in rural U.S., usually done to the music of a fiddler.

coureur See under COATS AND JACKETS.

courier bag See under HANDBAGS AND RELATED ACCESSORIES: MESSENGER BAG.

Courrèges boot See under FOOTWEAR.

Courrèges hat See under HEADWEAR.

Courrèges flower sock See under HOSIERY: KNEE-HI SOCK.

Courrèges glasses See under EYEWEAR.

courrier dummies See under MODEL DOLLS.

course See under KNIT.

court dress Items of apparel required to be worn for daily functions and ceremonial occasions in the presence of ruling monarchs. Also see under CORONATION ROBES and COURT HABIT.

∞**courtepye/courtepy** (kor′-tay-pih) Very short overgarment worn in 14th and 15th c. similar to surcoat. Made in a circle with round neckline, high collar, and slashed at the sides. Frequently PARTI-COLORED or embroidered with gems.

∞**court habit** Men's clothing worn only at French court, in 17th and 18th c. Called **grand habit** when referring to the same garment for women.

court plasters See under PATCHES.

court shoe See under FOOTWEAR.

court tie See under FOOTWEAR.

coutenance/countenance Small muff carried in late 16th and early 17th c.

coutes See under ARMOR.

couture (koo′-ture) (French) The business in which original apparel designs are created by designers and the items are manufactured in the couture house using exceptionally fine sewing and tailoring and expensive fabrics. Also see under HAUTE COUTURE.

couture lace See under LACES.

couturier (ko-tour′-ee-ay) (French) Male designer or proprietor of a couture house.

couturière (ko-tour′-ee-air) (French) Female designer or proprietor of a couture house.

coverage See under PRINTS, STRIPES, AND CHECKS.

coverall One-piece jumpsuit worn over other clothes by mechanics and other workmen. Originally worn by gas station attendants in the 1920s. Revised and fashionable for sportswear designs since the late 1960s.

coverall 1942

coverchief See under HEADWEAR.

covered button See under CLOSURES.

covered heel See under FOOTWEAR.

covered placket See under CLOTHING CONSTRUCTION DETAILS.

covered yarn See under CORE YARN.

covered zipper See under CLOSURES.

†**covert cloth** 1. An extremely firm, durable twill-weave fabric with a characteristic mottled look achieved by twisting lengthwise yarns spun from two strands—one dark and the other light. Crosswise yarns are the same or of a dark color. Used for men's and women's suits and coats. 2. Imitated in all-cotton, this fabric is used for work clothes, caps, uniforms, and trousers.

cover-up See under SWIMWEAR: BEACH WRAP-UP.

cowboy/cowgirl Originally used for a man or woman in the western U.S. who herds or tends cattle, usually going about on horseback. In fashion, may be used as an adjective to describe apparel that is derived from styles associated with cowboys or cowgirls. See under BELTS: COWBOY BELT; FOOTWEAR: COWBOY BOOT; HEADWEAR: COWBOY HAT; and SHIRTS: COWBOY SHIRT.

cowboy suit Child's suit worn when playing; an imitation of the regular cowboy's costume. Consists of a shirt, pants, leather bolero, and sometimes CHAPS. Gun belt and a wide-brimmed cowboy hat with chin cord are worn and toy guns are carried. The girls' costume is called a cowgirl's suit and sometimes has a short fringed skirt.

cowhide See under LEATHERS: CATTLEHIDE.

Cowichan sweater See under SWEATERS.

cowl See under NECKLINES AND COLLARS and SWEATERS.

cowpunk An uncoordinated medley of PUNK and WESTERN styles appearing in Los Angeles in 1986. Style includes western fringed jackets or leather jackets worn over miniskirts; chain jewelry; three western belts worn at same time; hats and hairstyles as popularized by pop singer Boy George; ragged-looking shirts; and all types of hairstyles including spiky, mini braids, mohawks, and Indian braids. *Der.* Combination of cowgirl and punk styles.

coxcomb/cockscomb 1. See under HAIRSTYLES. 2. See under HEADWEAR. 3. See under DANDY.

C.P.O. jacket/shirt See under SHIRTS.

CPSC See under CONSUMER PRODUCT SAFETY COMMISSION.

crab-back bathing suit See under SWIMWEAR.

Crafted with Pride in the U.S.A. Council An organization of textile and apparel industry firms (formed in 1984) that promoted domestically manufactured textiles and apparel. Now known as *wearUSA.*

crakow/crakowe/cracow See under FOOTWEAR.

crampons See under FOOTWEAR.

crants See under HEADWEAR.

crapaud See under WIGS AND HAIRPIECES: BAGWIG.

crape See under CREPE #2.

†crash Coarse, loosely woven fabric made in a variety of weights with irregular yarns giving it an uneven texture. Usually made in plain weaves of cotton, cotton blends, or linen.

craunce See under HEADWEAR: CRANTS.

cravat See under TIES.

cravate cocodes See under TIES.

cravat strings See under TIES.

crawcaw See under FOOTWEAR: CRAKOW.

crawlers See under PANTS.

†crease resistance The ability of a fabric to recover from wrinkling. Manufactured synthetic fabrics usually have higher wrinkle recovery than natural fiber fabrics, but special finishes can be applied to natural and regenerated fiber fabrics to aid wrinkle recovery.

creedmore See under FOOTWEAR.

creel backpack See under HANDBAGS AND RELATED ACCESSORIES.

creepalong set Infant's or toddler's two-piece suit usually consisting of a knit shirt with overall-type pants. Also called CRAWLERS (see under PANTS).

creepers 1. See under PANTS: CRAWLERS. 2. See under FOOTWEAR.

∞creeping apron Infant's garment of early 1900s cut long and gathered at hem into a band through which a cord was drawn. Could be pushed up above knees for a romper effect.

cremona cravat See under TIES.

†crepe (krape) (*crape*) 1. A general classification of fabrics made from almost any fiber and characterized by a broad range of crinkled or grained surface effects. 2. In the 18th and 19th c. a heavy crepe fabric dyed black and worn for mourning.

†crepe-back satin (krape) Lightweight fabric with a smooth, lustrous, shiny finish on the face and a dull, crepe appearance on the back. May be used with either side as the exterior. Made in a satin weave with silk, rayon, or manufactured fiber for the lengthwise yarns, and a crepe-twist crosswise yarn. The fabric has twice as many lengthwise as crosswise yarns. Used for dresses, blouses, and lingerie. Also called *satin-back* and sometimes called *satin-faced crepe.*

†crepe de chine (krepp deh sheen) 1. Fine, lightweight silk fabric with a crepe texture that is made by using highly twisted yarns in the crosswise direction and more lengthwise than crosswise yarns. It is piece-dyed or printed and used for dresses and blouses. 2. Crepe-textured fabric made with silk lengthwise yarns and worsted crepe-twisted crosswise yarns. *Der.* French, "crepe of China."

crepe georgette See under GEORGETTE.

crepe-soled shoes See under FOOTWEAR.

†crepe yarn (krape) Yarn that is given a high twist during spinning. The yarn is stiff, wiry, and contracts during finishing giving pebbled surface to fabrics.

crepida See under FOOTWEAR: KREPIS.

crescent Motif copied from shape of moon in its first quarter. Also called a *lunette.* See under FOOTWEAR: CRESCENT TOE.

Crete lace See under LACES.

crève-coeur See under HAIRSTYLES.

crevés (krev-ay) See under SLASHING.

crew cut See under HAIRSTYLES.

crew neckline See under NECKLINES AND COLLARS.

crew-neck shirt See under SHIRTS.

crew-neck sweater See under SWEATERS.

crew sock See under HOSIERY.

crewel work See under EMBROIDERIES AND SEWING STITCHES.

†crewel yarn Two-ply, loosely twisted, fine, worsted yarn used for embroidery.

criardes See under UNDERGARMENTS.

crimmer See under FURS: LAMB.

crimp/crimping †1. *n.* Natural or machine-made bending or waviness in a fiber making yarn resilient, less shiny, bulkier, and suitable for knitting. 2. *v.* To curl the hair with a hot iron. 3. *v.* To shape leather by a machine that uses heat and pressure.

crin (French) Horsehair. See under BRAIDS: HORSEHAIR BRAID.

crinière (cran-yere′) See under WIGS AND HAIRPIECES.

crinkle crepe Synonym for PLISSÉ.

crinolette See under UNDERGARMENTS: BOSTLE.

†**crinoline** (krin′-uh-lyn) 1. Heavily-sized (see SIZING), open-weave cotton fabric. 2. See under UNDERGARMENTS.

crinoline and tournure See under UNDERGARMENTS: BUSTLE.

crinoline era (krin′-uh-lyn) Used by costume historians to designate the period from 1850 to 1870 when crinoline petticoats (see under UNDERGARMENTS: CRINOLINE) or hoops (see under UNDERGARMENTS: HOOPS) were used to support full skirts.

crisp 1. See under HEADWEAR. 2. See under HAIRSTYLES.

crispin See under CAPES, CLOAKS, AND SHAWLS.

crispine See under HEADWEAR.

crispinette See under HEADWEAR: CRISPINE.

crochet (kro-shay′) †1. Fabric made from a continuous series of loops of yarn made with a single hooked needle. Originally developed in the 16th c. as an inexpensive method of creating a lacelike fabric. Modern textile machinery can create fabrics that have the appearance of crochet. 2. *adj.* Describes apparel made by crocheting. See under CAPES, CLOAKS, AND SHAWLS: CROCHETED SHAWL; CLOSURES: CROCHETED BUTTON; and HEADWEAR: CROCHETED CAP. 3. Used from 14th to 17th c. for a hook or fastener (e.g., a hook attached at a woman's waist for suspending a pomander, or a fastener on a shoe).

crochets and loops See under CLOSURES: HOOKS AND EYES.

crocodile See under LEATHERS.

Crocs™ See under FOOTWEAR.

cromwell *adj.* In the 18th c., described clothing inspired by or derived from clothing items worn at the time Oliver Cromwell ruled as Lord Protector of England (1653 to 1658). See under NECKLINES AND COLLARS: CROMWELL COLLAR and FOOTWEAR: CROMWELL SHOES.

cromwell collar See under NECKLINES AND COLLARS.

cromwell shoe See under FOOTWEAR.

crooked shoe See under FOOTWEAR.

crop-doublet See under DOUBLET.

cropped Denoting shortened, or cut off, when referring to clothing or hair. See under BLOUSES AND TOPS: CROPPED TOP and PANTS: CROPPED PANTS.

cropping See under SHEARING.

croquet boot See under FOOTWEAR.

croquis (kro′-key) (French) In fashion illustration, refers to a rough sketch of a figure used as a base on which to show garment design ideas. Also called a *lay figure.*

cross 1. A depiction, stylized or realistic, of an instrument used by Romans for executing individuals. An actual cross would have been made from an upright post of wood with a cross piece near the top, a form that is known as a **Latin cross.** Crosses have been worn by Christians as a symbol of their religious belief from the early days of Christianity and as a badge on the clothing worn by Crusaders during the Middle Ages. Different representations of crosses in badges, jewelry, or as motifs of various kinds have developed and have been given such names as (1) **ansate cross** See under ANKH. (2) **Eastern Orthodox cross** With two cross pieces more than halfway up the central post and a diagonal cross piece a short distance from the bottom. (3) **Greek cross** With the cross piece the same length as the vertical piece and located at its center. (4) **Maltese cross** With four arms of equal length that are shaped like arrowheads, decreasing in size as they approach the center. (5) **St. Andrew's cross** With diagonal arms, like an X. (6) **tau cross** With the cross piece at the top of the post, like the Greek letter *tau.* 2. In European usage means BIAS, or diagonal cut—fabric cut "on the cross."

Latin cross

Eastern Orthodox cross

Greek cross

Maltese cross

St. Andrew's cross

cross-boarded See under LEATHERS.

cross body bag See under HANDBAGS AND RELATED ACCESSORIES.

crosscloth See under HEADWEAR.

crosses See under FURS.

cross-country skiing See under PANTS: KNICKERS #1.

cross fox See under FURS.

cross gaitering See under CROSS-GARTERING.

∞**cross-gartering** 1. Binding or holding the leg coverings (*broc* of Anglo-Saxon, or *braies,* of the French see under BRAIES) close to the leg by crisscrossing strips of leather or cloth around legs on top of stockings or other leg coverings. **2.** Used from mid-16th to early 17th c. to describe the style of gartering hose by using a ribbon around leg below the knee, crossing in back, and tying with bow above knee in front or at side of knee when stockings were worn over CANIONS.

cross-gartering #1

∞**cross girdling** Style of wearing the girdle or sash crossed at the chest and then wrapped around the waist by ancient Greeks. Also see under BELTS: GREEK BELT.

crossover bra See under UNDERGARMENTS.

crossover collar See under NECKLINES AND COLLARS.

crossover neckline See under NECKLINES AND COLLARS: SURPLICE NECKLINE.

crossover thong sandals See under FOOTWEAR: THONG #3.

cross persian lamb See under FURS: LAMB.

cross stone See under GEMS, GEM CUTS, AND SETTINGS: FAIRY STONE.

cross-stitch See under EMBROIDERIES AND SEWING STITCHES.

crotch Area of a garment where the legs meet. British spelling is *crutch.*

crowdsourcing The outsourcing of a job once performed by employees through an open call to a large undefined group of people, generally using the Internet. This technique has been used by young designers to engage their customers in editing their seasonal fashion collections.

crown **1.** See under HEADWEAR. **2.** See under GEMS, GEM CUTS, AND SETTINGS.

crown hats See under HEADWEAR.

crown sable See under FURS: SABLE.

cruches See under HAIRSTYLES.

crusader hood See under HEADWEAR.

crusader's cross See under JEWELRY.

crush hat See under HEADWEAR: CHAPEAU CLAQUE.

crushed leather See under LEATHERS.

crusher hat See under HEADWEAR.

crutch (British usage) CROTCH.

cryptocrystalline See under GEMS, GEM CUTS, AND SETTINGS.

crystal See under GEMS, GEM CUTS, AND SETTINGS.

crystal bracelet See under JEWELRY.

crystalline structure See under GEMS, GEM CUTS, AND SETTINGS.

crystal pleats See under CLOTHING CONSTRUCTION DETAILS.

cuaran See under FOOTWEAR.

cuban heel See under FOOTWEAR.

cubavera jacket See under COATS AND JACKETS.

cube heel See under FOOTWEAR.

cubic zirconia See under GEMS, GEM CUTS, AND SETTINGS.

cue See under HAIRSTYLES.

cue peruke See under WIGS AND HAIRPIECES.

cuff bracelet See under JEWELRY.

cuff button See under CLOSURES.

cuffed Describes the bottom edge of a garment with a wide hem that has been turned back to form a cuff. Examples of garments that are often cuffed are shorts and pants.

cuffed trousers See under PANTS: PRE-CUFFED TROUSERS.

cuff link See under JEWELRY.

CUFFS

cuff **1.** Finish for a sleeve consisting of a separate sewn-on piece or a turned-back extension of a sleeve. **2.** The turned-over or stitched-on piece at the top of a glove. **3.** A turned-back piece at the hem of trousers; a trouser cuff. **4.** A turned-over or stitched-down band at the top of a boot. **5.** See under JEWELRY.

band cuff Simplest type of cuff made from a separate piece of fabric and applied to the bottom of a sleeve. The band is cut from a straight piece of fabric. Such cuffs are made in varying widths and sometimes may have attached ruffles or pieces of elastic pulled through the bands.

barrel cuff See under CUFFS: SINGLE CUFF.

∞**boot cuff** Large turned-back cuff, reaching nearly to elbow. Popular for men's coats from 1727 to about 1740, used on a BOOT SLEEVE (see under SHOULDERS AND SLEEVES).

detachable cuff Cuff cut out of an additional piece of fabric rather than being an extension of the sleeve, and which may be taken off, washed, and reattached to the sleeve.

double cuff See under CUFFS: FRENCH CUFF.

∞**elbow cuff** Turned-back cuff attached to woman's elbow-length sleeves in first half of 18th c., wide on outside of arm and fitting more closely at elbow.

french cuff Large band cuff that doubles back on itself and is usually fastened with a cuff link. Also called *double cuff.*

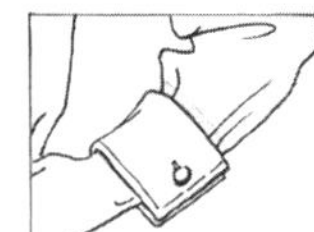
french cuff

fringed cuff Leather band at the wrist that has long, hanging fringe at the end. A fashion innovation of the late 1960s.

gauntlet cuff Wide turned-back cuff that slants away from the arm, flaring wide at top and tapering to wrist.

gauntlet cuff

∞**hand fall/hand cuff** Lace-trimmed, turned-back, flared, starched *cuff* frequently made double. Worn by men and women in 17th c. with FALLING BAND, FALLING RUFF, and STANDING BAND (see under NECKLINES AND COLLARS).

∞**hounds' ears** Large turned-back cuffs with rounded corners used on men's coats from 1660s to 1680s.

knit cuff Cuff made with a rib knit stitch that gives a tight fit but is elastic enough to slip over hand easily.

∞**mariner's cuff** Man's coat cuff, worn in second half of 18th c.; consisted of a small, turned-back cuff decorated on outside with a curved flap, similar to a pocket flap, and three or four buttons that matched those of the coat.

∞**mousquetaire cuff** (moose-ke'-tare) 1. Deep, wide cuff flaring above the wrist, used on men's coats in early 1873. 2. Sleeve of mousquetaire-type worn in late 1880s with flaring top and cuff sometimes trimmed with vandykes (see VANDYKING). *Der.* From uniform of French musketeers or royal bodyguards of Louis XIII in 17th c.

parament (pa-ra'-ment) (*parement*) Ornamental cuff at wrist, turned up over sleeve and stitched.

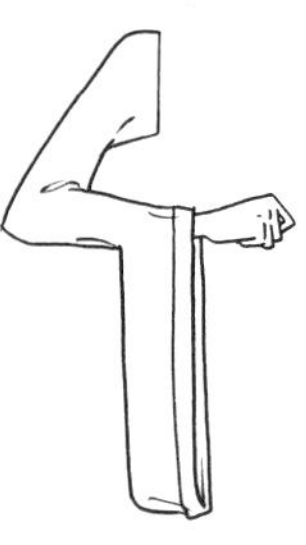
pendant cuff

pendant cuff Style of cuff that hangs down from the sleeve.

roll-up cuff Extension of the sleeve, which is folded over several times to form a cuff. Sometimes fastened with a tab. See under SHOULDERS AND SLEEVES: BUTTON-TAB SLEEVE.

single cuff Band cuff that, in contrast to a French cuff, has no section doubled back on itself. This cuff is stitched to the sleeve and usually closes with one or more buttons.

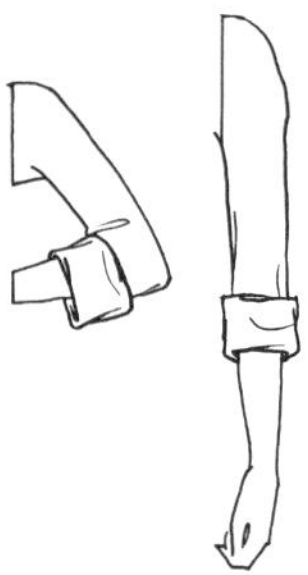
roll-up cuff

turned-back cuff Turned-back extension of the sleeve. Sleeve is cut longer and a section is turned up to form a cuff.

turned-back cuff

---

cuff string See under CLOSURES.

cuff-top girdle See under UNDERGARMENTS: GIRDLE.

∞**cuirass** (kwe-rass') 1. See under ARMOR. 2. Plain, close-fitting waist worn by women in early 1900s. *Der.* French, *cuirasse,* "breastplate."

∞**cuirass bodice/cuirasse bodice** (kwe-rass') Extremely tight, boned women's daytime bodice of mid-1870s extending down over hips to mold the body. Frequently made in fabric different from the dress.

cuirass bodice 1881

∞**cuirass tunic/cuirasse tunic** (kwe-rass') Tight-fitting tunic skirt worn with the cuirass bodice by women in mid-1870s.

cuir savage See under LEATHERS: WET LOOK.

cuisse See under ARMOR.

culet 1. See under GEMS, GEM CUTS, AND SETTINGS: BRILLIANT CUT. ∞2. See under ARMOR.

culotte dress See under DRESSES.

culottes (ku-lotz') 1. Garment that hangs like a skirt, but is actually pants (i.e., a divided skirt). *Der.* French, "breeches, trousers, tights, and knickers." When used as an adjective, indicates a garment with culotte-type construction. See under DRESSES: CULOTTE DRESS; PANTS: CULOTTES; SLEEPWEAR AND LOUNGEWEAR: CULOTTE PAJAMAS; SKIRTS: CULOTTES; and UNDERGARMENTS: CULOTTE SLIP. ∞3. First used for tight, below-the-knee pants worn during reign of Henry III of France, who reigned from 1574 to 1589. ∞4. Synonym for PETTICOAT BREECHES.

cultured pearl See under GEMS, GEM CUTS, AND SETTINGS: PEARL.

cumberland corset See under UNDERGARMENTS: APOLLO CORSET.

cumberland hat See under HEADWEAR.

cummerbund See under BELTS.

cupola coat See under UNDERGARMENTS: BELL HOOP.

†cuprammonium rayon Cellulosic fiber regenerated from wood pulp or from cotton fibers too short to spin into yarns. This fiber is no longer manufactured in the U.S. because it produces high levels of water pollution, but it is manufactured abroad and may be found in imported goods. Used in women's dresses, blouses, and scarves.

curch See under HEADWEAR.

curlyhead See under HAIRSTYLES: POODLE CUT.

curricle coat See under COATS AND JACKETS.

curricle dress See under DRESSES.

curtain drapery (American usage) See under HIP BAGS.

curtains See under HEADWEAR: LAMBALLE BONNET.

cushion cut See under GEMS, GEM CUTS, AND SETTINGS.

cushionet See under UNDERGARMENTS.

cushion headdress See under HEADWEAR.

cushion pad See under UNDERGARMENTS: BUSTLE.

cushion sole 1. See under FOOTWEAR. 2. See under HOSIERY.

cushion-style embroidery See under EMBROIDERIES AND SEWING STITCHES: BERLIN WOOLWORK.

custom designer Designer who creates an original garment that is executed by skilled seamstresses who drape the fabric on a dress form conforming to the customer's individual measurements. Clothes produced by such designers are known as *custom-made* or *made-to-measure.*

customized computer pattern Sewing pattern developed in 1960s, made to fit the individual. Salesperson in store takes customer's measurements, which are then sent to a pattern company and fed into a computer to produce a custom-cut pattern for garment.

custom-made *adj.* Describes garments made by tailor or couture house for an individual customer. The correct size is achieved either by fitting on a dress form adjusted to the customer's measurements or by doing several personal fittings.

customs broker A U.S. agent licensed by U.S. Customs and Border Protection to assist apparel manufacturers in gaining clearance through customs for the importation of goods produced OFFSHORE.

cut and sew construction A method of knit garment construction in which pieces are cut from yardage rather than knit to shape. Ribbings, when used, are sewn on with a seam rather than linked on.

cutaway coat/jacket See under COATS AND JACKETS: CUTAWAY.

cutaway frock See under COATS AND JACKETS.

cutaway sack See under COATS AND JACKETS.

cut-finger gloves See under GLOVES AND GLOVE CONSTRUCTION.

cut, make, and trim (CMT) Apparel contractor that performs the operations necessary to construct, cut, and trim garments for apparel manufacturers.

cut-offs See under SHORTS.

cut order plan Listing of exact style, sizes, and precise quantities that are to be cut from selected materials and ultimately constructed to complete contracted apparel order.

cutout dress See under DRESSES.

cutouts Ornamental holes of different sizes and shapes cut from apparel. See under SWIMWEAR: CUTOUT SWIMSUIT; FOOTWEAR: CUTOUTS; and GLOVES AND GLOVE CONSTRUCTION: ACTION GLOVE.

cut-steel beads See under JEWELRY.

cut-steel buckle See under CLOSURES.

cutter In garment industry, the person who cuts the fabric with an electric knife.

cutting-up trade In the textile industry, used to refer to clothing manufacturers.

cut-up trade Manufacturers who make belts that are added to pants, skirts, and dresses by apparel manufacturers.

cut velvet A fabric that has a fairly complex woven pattern consisting of velvet figures on a background of a relatively sheer fabric. A very decorative fabric, it is used for women's apparel, especially dressy clothing.

cut wig See under WIGS AND HAIRPIECES.

cut work/cut-work 1. See under EMBROIDERIES AND SEWING STITCHES. ∞2. Used in mid-14th through 15th c. to refer to DAGGING, or a dagged border of a garment. Motifs such as leaves, flames, and scallops were used.

cyberfashion A subculture that developed around trance and hardcore electronic music. A mixture of RAVE and GOTH that draws on Japanese ANIME with the use of contrasting colors that reflect ultraviolet light, body piercing, hair extensions, and boots with thick soles that extend up the calf.

cyberpunk See under PUNK.

∞**cyclas** **1.** Sleeveless outer tunic that apparently began as a garment worn over armor in early 14th c.; extended to waist in front and to knees in back, slashed up sides, and then laced. When it became part of civilian clothing, it appears to have been the same as the SURCOTE. Also spelled *ciclaton, cinglaton.* Shown at COTE. **2.** Wrapped garment similar to a toga that was worn in ancient Rome. **3.** Rich, elaborate overgarment, sometimes fur- or silk-lined, made of a large piece of cloth with round opening for head. Worn in medieval times on ceremonial occasions by both men and women (e.g., at the coronation of Henry III of England in the 13th c.).

cycle jacket See under COATS AND JACKETS: MOTORCYCLE JACKET.

cycling suit/cycling costume See under ACTIVEWEAR.

cymophane See under GEMS, GEM CUTS, AND SETTINGS: CAT'S EYE.

czechoslovakian embroidery See under EMBROIDERIES AND SEWING STITCHES.

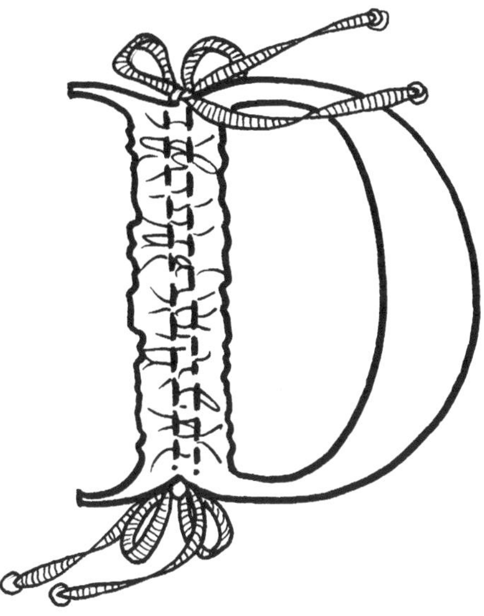

D.A. See under HAIRSTYLES: DUCKTAIL HAIRCUT.

∞**dagging** Ornamental borders cut on garments in shapes of leaves, tongues, and scallops. Originating in the 1340s, these decorations remained fashionable for hems of gowns, sleeves, and garment edges until the end of the 15th c. Also called *cut work, dag, dagges, foliated, jags,* and *jagging.* Also see under CASTELLATED.

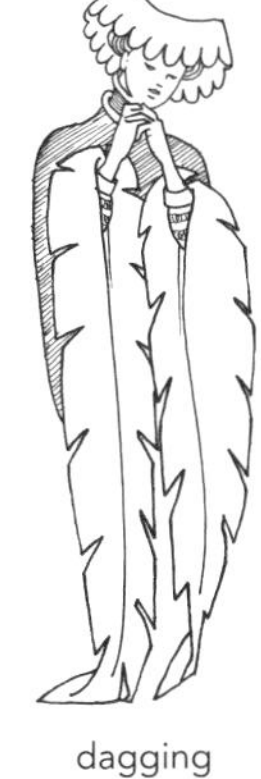
dagging

daisy dukes See under SHORTS.

Dali, Salvador (dah′-lee) (1904–1989) Spanish artist, one of leading exponents of surrealism in painting, noted for his jewelry designs in fantastic shapes. His paintings influenced fashion, display, and advertising.

dalmatic (dal-ma′-tic) Long, extra-wide–sleeved, loose-fitting tunic trimmed with two vertical stripes in front. Worn by men and women in Byzantine period. Later worn as a clerical vestment by cardinals, abbots, and bishops, and as part of the coronation robes of Great Britain. *Der.* From *tunica dalmatica,* worn by Romans in 2nd c., starting in Dalmatia.

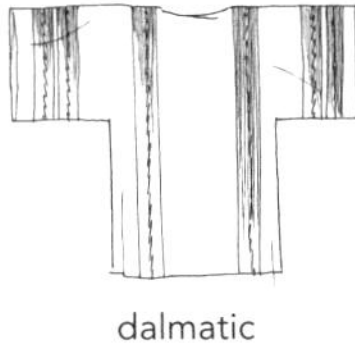
dalmatic

damaging-out Repairing of tears or holes in fur pelts and garments.

damascene/damascening See under JEWELRY.

damascene lace (dam-ah-seen) See under LACES.

†**damask** A broad group of fabrics with elaborate, woven, floral or geometric designs, which are distinguished from the background by contrasting luster and/or color and are also reversible. Woven on a JACQUARD loom, the design of the fabric is often made in a satin weave. Because of their decorative aspects, damask fabrics are often used for evening wear.

dance set See under UNDERGARMENTS: STEP-INS.

dance skirt See under SKIRTS.

∞**dandizette** (dan-dee-zet′) Used from 1816 to 1820 for a female *dandy* conspicuous for her GRECIAN BEND, or the manner in which she walked.

dandy 1. Originating around 1816, a name identifying a man who is excessively fond of and overly concerned with clothes—exemplified by BEAU BRUMMELL, LORD PETERSHAM (see under PETERSHAM), and COUNT D'ORSAY (see under ORSAY, COUNT D')—and who greatly influenced men's fashions in England and France, respectively. Synonyms: *beau,* or, in excessive cases, *fop.* 2. *adj.* Describes apparel and/or styles worn by 19th c. dandies. See BLOUSES AND TOPS: DANDY BLOUSE and SHIRTS: DANDY SHIRT. 3. *adj.* Describes styles similar to those of the EDWARDIAN PERIOD. Characterized by ruffles at neck and wrists. Worn by both men and women in the late 1960s and early 1970s. Complete costume might include an EDWARDIAN SUIT with regency collar (see under NECKLINES AND COLLARS) and shirt with ruffled front and cuffs.

dandy hat See under HEADWEAR.

danish trousers See under PANTS.

darning Method of reweaving threads by hand to repair a hole in a sock or garment, either by hand or with the use of a sewing machine. Also see under EMBROIDERIES AND SEWING STITCHES and LACES: DARNED LACE.

dart See under CLOTHING CONSTRUCTION DETAILS.

dashiki Short- to full-length garment inspired by a central African style. The American version is cut straight and loose-fitting, is collarless, slips on over the head, has bell-shaped or kimono sleeves, and is usually made of an African-inspired distinctive panel or border print. The style was introduced in U.S. during late 1960s for general wear and was particularly popular among African Americans.

dashiki

davy crockett cap See under HEADWEAR.

day cap See under HEADWEAR.

day sheer hose See under HOSIERY: SHEER HOSE.

daywear Apparel that is generally worn during the day, as compared with evening wear or sleepwear.

d.b. (British usage) Slang used among British tailors in the 19th c. to indicate a DOUBLE-BREASTED style (see under CLOSURES).

death's head button See under CLOSURES.

DeBevoise brassière See under UNDERGARMENTS.

∞**debutante slouch** Posture fashionable for young, sophisticated women, starting around 1917 and very popular in 1920s, with shoulders drooping forward giving a flat-chested appearance.

decal Picture or design that can be transferred from specially prepared paper to the skin or other surface such as textile.

decalcomania **1.** The process of transferring a decal to another surface. **2.** Fad for wearing designs from decals of butterflies, flowers, and other motifs on legs and arms, which was especially popular in mid-1960s and after. Also see under TATTOO.

decatur ring See under JEWELRY.

deck *adj.* Describes clothing and accessories derived from or inspired by clothing used for nautical sports. See under COATS AND JACKETS: DECK JACKET; FOOTWEAR: BOATING SHOE; and PANTS: DECK PANTS.

décolletage (deh-coll′-eh-tahzh) (French) The upper part of a woman's torso. In fashion it refers to bare shoulders or a low-cut neckline, or the shoulder and neckline area of a woman's body. Also used as an adjective to describe apparel with a low neckline. See under NECKLINES AND COLLARS: DÉCOLLETÉ NECKLINE and UNDERGARMENTS: DÉCOLLETÉ BRA.

deconstruction A design movement that began in the 1990s with designers who took elements of garment construction and made them more visible in the final garment. For example, putting garment seams on the outside of clothing, leaving edges raw or frayed, dropping knit stitches, and exposing zippers. Designers or brands associated with this movement include Comme des Garçons, Vivienne Westwood, Maison Martin Margiela, and Alber Elbaz for Lanvin.

découpage (deh-coo-pahg′) The art of decorating items with cut-out pictures of paper or fabric pasted to surfaces and shellacked. This technique was especially popular in mid- and late 1960s for decorating handbags. *Der.* French, "cutout."

deep See under ASSORTMENT.

deerskin See under LEATHERS: BUCKSKIN.

deerstalker See under HEADWEAR.

de joinville teck See under TIES.

delhi work See under EMBROIDERIES AND SEWING STITCHES.

Delineator, The Fashion magazine originating in 1872, self-described as a Journal of Fashion Culture and Fine Arts. Associated with the Butterick Pattern Company, this journal had many illustrations of apparel for women and children printed with the pattern number so that a consumer could order tissue paper patterns and make her own clothing. By the 1920s and 1930s the publication had become a more general-interest women's magazine but continued to show fashions from patterns until it ceased publication in 1937.

delphos dress See under DRESSES.

demantoid See under GEMS, GEM CUTS, AND SETTINGS: ANDRADITE GARNET.

demi-boot See under FOOTWEAR.

demi-bra See under UNDERGARMENTS.

demi brassard See under ARMOR.

demi-castor See under HEADWEAR: CASTOR.

demi-coronal See under HEADWEAR: TIARA.

demi-corset See under UNDERGARMENTS.

demi-gigot See under SHOULDERS AND SLEEVES.

demi-habillement See under HALF ROBE.

demi-jamb See under ARMOR.

demi-maunch See under SHOULDERS AND SLEEVES: DEMI-SLEEVE.

demimondaines (demi-mon-dan′) (French) Mistresses of wealthy men who were dressed by famous Parisian couturiers and greatly influenced fashion from the Second Empire in France through the Edwardian era. *Der.* French, "those of the half-world."

demi-riding coat See under COATS AND JACKETS: JUSTAUCORPS.

demi-sleeve See under SHOULDERS AND SLEEVES.

demi-toilette See under HALF DRESS.

demi-vambrace See under ARMOR.

demographic segmentation The practice of identifying markets by demographic characteristics such as age, education, gender, and income on the assumption that certain items and styles will appeal to those who fit into specific segments of the market.

Demorest, Madame Operator of Demorest's Emporium of Fashion from the 1870s to 1890s. Showrooms and a factory were located at Union Square, New York, where ladies came to select home-sewing patterns. From 1865 to 1899 her husband published *Demorest's Monthly Magazine* and *Demorest Fashions,* a weekly newspaper. Both were profusely illustrated with fashions.

†**denier** (den-yer′) International textile and hosiery system used for numbering silk and manufactured filament yarns—the low numbers represent finer yarns, the

higher numbers the heavier yarns. *Der.* From old French *coin*, the weight used as a measure of size and number of silk.

†denim 1. Sturdy, serviceable fabric woven in the TWILL WEAVE, traditionally made with indigo-blue or brown lengthwise yarns and white crosswise yarns; however, it is now made in many color variations and in novelty striped and figured patterns. Uses: sportswear, work clothes, BLUE JEANS and other pants, jackets, and occasionally in high fashion items. *Der.* French, *serge de Nimes,* a fabric made in Nimes, France. Also called *dungaree.* 2. *adj.* Describes garments made of denim fabric. With the acceptance of jeans for daytime and schoolwear in early 1970s, denim fabric was used in matching skirts, jackets, and shorts, as well as men's tailored suits and women's dresses; thus *denim* often preceded the name of the garment as a descriptive adjective. Although denim was originally a cotton fabric, polyester and stretch fibers were combined with cotton to give it a more comfortable feel and make it so that the pants could be worn skintight. *Der.* From name of fabric used. Also see under PANTS: BLUE JEANS and COATS AND JACKETS: DENIM.

denim shirt See under SHIRTS.

denmark cock See under HEADWEAR: COCKED HAT.

dentelle de la vierge See under LACES: DIEPPE POINT LACE.

dentil Greek motif consisting of a series of toothlike scallops used as a border.

department The segment of a retailing establishment that groups together items of merchandise that are complementary to one another, such as a junior department or an active sportswear department.

department store Large retail establishment that organizes its functions and merchandise into departments.

depth See under ASSORTMENT.

derby See under HEADWEAR.

derby shoe See under FOOTWEAR.

desert boot See under FOOTWEAR.

desert fatigue cap See under HEADWEAR.

deshabillé (des-hah-bee') (French) Wrapper, dressing gown, or negligee. (English usage) Refers to the state of being partially dressed or dressed in nightclothes. Also spelled *dishabille* when used in English.

designer Person engaged in creating original clothing and accessories in various areas of the fashion industry. Some designers own their businesses; others are employed by manufacturers to develop collections of merchandise for ready-to-wear, couture, lingerie, millinery, footwear, accessories, and jewelry lines.

designer brand A designer name used as a BRAND name. Also called *signature brand.*

designer collection/designer line See under COLLECTION.

designer jeans See under PANTS.

designer label See under LABEL.

designer scarf See under SCARVES.

Design Industries Foundation Fighting AIDS (DIFFA) Founded in 1984, a U.S.-based fashion industry organization that sponsors AIDS prevention education and raises funds to assist with treatment and care services for those who are at risk of and/or suffering from AIDS.

destination store A type of retailer patronized by a customer because only it provides specific products or services that the customer wants. Customers seek out destination stores.

detachable collar See under NECKLINES AND COLLARS.

detachable cuff See under CUFFS.

detachable pantyhose See under HOSIERY.

detached chain stitch See under EMBROIDERIES AND SEWING STITCHES: LAZY DAISY STITCH.

dettigen cock See under HEADWEAR: COCKED HAT.

development bundle system See under BUNDLE SYSTEM.

deverticalization A strategy for eliminating business divisions that are considered nonessential or not part of a firm's core competencies and outsourcing these tasks to companies that can perform them more efficiently. Also see VERTICAL INTEGRATION.

devotional ring See under JEWELRY.

dhoti See under PANTS.

dhoti shorts See under SHORTS.

diadem See under HEADWEAR.

diadem cap See under HEADWEAR.

diadem comb See under HAIR ACCESSORIES.

diadem fanchon bonnet See under HEADWEAR.

Diaghilev, Sergei Pavlovich (dee-ah-geh-lef) (1872–1929) Russian aristocrat and avant-garde creator of the Ballets Russes, who produced *Scheherazade,* 1910, with costumes by Leon Bakst. The brilliant colors and new concept of stage design started a wave of Orientalism in Paris that affected the whole couture, particularly the work of PAUL POIRET, and banished somber Victorian fashions.

diagonal stitch See under EMBROIDERIES AND SEWING STITCHES.

diagonal weave See under TWILL WEAVE.

diamanté (dya-mahn-tay') *adj.* Indicates a sparkling effect as that of the reflection of gemstones. *Der.* French, "made of diamonds." See under DRESSES: DIAMANTÉ DRESS; BLOUSES AND TOPS: DIAMANTÉ TOP; BRAIDS: DIAMANTÉ BRAID; and HEADWEAR: DIAMANTÉ HEADBAND.

diamanté dress See under DRESSES.

diamond See under GEMS, GEM CUTS, AND SETTINGS.

diamond bracelet/earring/necklace See under JEWELRY.

diamonds by the yard See under JEWELRY.

diamond watch See under WATCHES.

diana vernon hat See under HEADWEAR.

diaper bag See under HANDBAGS AND RELATED ACCESSORIES.

diaper cloth See under BIRD'S-EYE # 1.

dickey (*dicky, dickie*) **1.** Separate fill-in used inside woman's low neckline, with or without an attached collar. May be knitted or woven and may have many types of collars. Also see under BLOUSES AND TOPS: BLOUSETTE. **2.** Man's false shirt front with attached collar, worn over a flannel shirt in the 19th c., not considered proper attire for gentlemen. **3.** Pinafore, or bib, for a child. **4.** See under UNDERGARMENTS.

die cutting Method of cutting a garment piece using a sharp-edged piece of metal (the die), similar to a cookie cutter, which is made in the exact dimensions and shape of the pattern piece. The die is positioned over the fabric to be cut, then a pressurized plate is applied to the die, and this causes it to cut through the fabric layers.

dieppe point lace See under LACES.

Dietrich, Marlene German actress and entertainer, considered the supreme example of a glamorous film star, who was a significant fashion influence in the 1930s and 1940s. She was particularly famous for her legs, arched, plucked eyebrows, and screen wardrobe (designed by Travis Banton, who utilized many clinging chiffons and feather boas). Dietrich was credited with making mannish slacks and fedora hats popular for women.

DIFFA See DESIGN INDUSTRIES FOUNDATION FIGHTING AIDS.

diffusion line A less expensive line produced by a high fashion designer. Examples include Armani X and DKNY. *Der.* A French fashion term that is equivalent to a BRIDGE LINE.

digital watch See under WATCHES.

digitizer A table that enables a pattern to be entered into a computer. The table is embedded with sensors that relate to the *x* (horizontal) and *y* (vertical) coordinates of a grid, allowing the pattern piece to be traced and entered into the computer.

†dimensional stability Ability of a fabric to return to its original shape and size after wear, washing, or dry cleaning.

†dimity A range of lightweight, sheer fabrics usually made of cotton or a cotton blend characterized by lengthwise cords made by bunching or grouping several yarns together. Less often, a checked effect is made by grouping cross-wise yarns together as well.

dink/dinky See under HEADWEAR: SKULLCAP.

dinner dress See under DRESSES.

dinner jacket See under COATS AND JACKETS.

dinner ring See under JEWELRY: COCKTAIL RING.

∞dip Used in 1890s and early 20th c. for the point of a waistline that was lower in front than back.

dip belt See under BELTS: CONTOUR BELT.

dip-dyed hair See under HAIRSTYLES.

dipped bowl/dipped mushroom cut See under HAIRSTYLES: BOWL CUT.

∞diplax Large piece of fabric, nearly square, worn folded double as a mantle by Greek women. It was displayed on Greek and Roman statues as either draped under right arm and pinned together on left shoulder or draped around hips.

∞diploidion (dip-ploy-dion) (pl. *diplois*) Mantle worn by ancient Greeks made out of a square or oblong piece of fabric that has been folded double with the fold placed under the left arm and fastened on the right shoulder. Also see DIPLAX.

dip-top boots See under FOOTWEAR: COWBOY BOOT.

direct marketing Retailing that provides products or services directly to consumers and skips over the retail store; sometimes referred to as *nonstore retailing.*

direct marketing channel See under MARKETING CHANNEL.

Directoire (dir-eck'-twa) **1.** Period in French history from 1795 to 1799, following the French Revolution, when France was ruled by the Directory (in French, *Directoire*), a five-man executive body. **2.** *adj.* Used, especially in the 19th c., to describe apparel styles that were inspired by or derived from styles popular during the Directoire period in France. For women these were high-waisted, narrow-skirted muslin dresses with low necklines that were frequently worn with spencer jackets; flesh-colored stockings; shoes similar to laced ballet slippers; and ostrich plumes in the hair or on turbans. Men were more likely to wear coats cut short in front and with tails in back that were left open in front to show a waistcoat, tightly fitted breeches, stockings, low shoes or high boots, and top hats flaring at

Directoire #2: incroyable and merveilleuse

the crown. Men who affected the most exaggerated of these styles were called **incroyables** (an-kwai′-ab-leh) (meaning "the incredible ones"). They contrived a careless appearance with loosely tied cravats wound high on the neck, unkempt hair, and ridiculously large lapels. Women who were known as **merveilleuses** (mer-vay-use′), or "the marvelous ones," wore few undergarments, extremely low-cut and very sheer dresses, short and shaggy hairstyles, and huge jockey caps or poke bonnets. 3. Styles of late 1880s to 1895 inspired by Sardou's drama *La Tosca* starring Sarah Bernhardt in 1887. Some of these styles have no relationship to the styles of the Directoire period.

directoire bonnet See under HEADWEAR.

directoire coat See under COATS AND JACKETS.

directoire gown See under DRESSES.

directoire jacket See under COATS AND JACKETS.

Directoire skirt See under SKIRTS.

directoire waistline See under WAISTLINES.

dirndl (durn′-del) 1. *adj.* Describes various styles in which a full skirt or pant is gathered into a waistline. See under COATS AND JACKETS: DIRNDL COAT; PANTS: DIRNDL PANTS; SKIRTS: DIRNDL; and UNDERGARMENTS: DIRNDL PETTICOAT. 2. *n.* See under DRESSES.

discharge print See under PRINTS, STRIPES, AND CHECKS.

disco clothes Glittery fashions made in bright, glowing colors, and styled in unrestrained fabrics. Usually made with short skirts for vigorous evening dancing at discotheques. *Der.* French, *discothéque,* "record library," as dancing is done to records rather than live music. See also under FOOTWEAR.

discount See under REDUCTIONS.

discount store Retailer that sells brand name merchandise at below traditional retail prices.

dishabille See under DESHABILLÉ.

dishrag shirt See under SHIRTS.

distressed See under STONE WASHED.

distressing Finishing processes used on denim, leather, and other fabrics to make them look as though they have aged with time and wear. Processes such as stone washing, enzyme washing, acid washing, sandblasting, emerizing (grinding or sueding with an emery-covered roller), and microsanding are used to fade the fabric, create whiskered or ladder effects, fray hems and seams, or actually create rips and tears. Many retailers have recently banned sandblasted products because the process has been linked to an incurable form of lung cancer resulting from inhaling of fiber particles released in processing.

distribution centers Centralized locations used by apparel companies or retailers to prepare merchandise for distribution to retail stores.

distribution channel A business structure that makes products available for consumption by the consumer.

distribution strategy System used by businesses to assure that apparel is placed in stores that sell to the target market for whom the merchandise was designed and manufactured.

∞**ditto suit** Man's suit of the second half of the 18th c. in which the same fabric is used for pants, jacket, vest, and, sometimes, a cap.

ditto suit 18th century

diversification A business growth strategy in which a firm expands its product mix to capitalize on brand recognition, increase sales, and thus enhance efficiencies for greater profit.

divided skirt 1. See under SKIRTS: CULOTTES. 2. See under SKIRTS: DIVIDED SKIRT.

division A breakdown of merchandise in the business organization within a retail store that is the largest unit. Examples of divisions include women's, children's, or men's wear, which are, in turn, subdivided into DEPARTMENTS, CLASSIFICATIONS, and SUBCLASSIFICATIONS.

djellaba/djellabah/jellaba See under SLEEPWEAR AND LOUNGEWEAR. Also see under CAFTAN.

†**dobby attachment** See under DOBBY WEAVE.

†**dobby fabric** Fabric made in the DOBBY WEAVE. *White-on-white broadcloth* is an example of a dobby fabric.

†**dobby weave** Weave forming small repeat geometric patterns that is made on plain loom with **dobby attachment**, a mechanical or electronic device that enables a loom to produce small repeat designs of not more than 8 to 30 rows of crosswise yarns. More complex and larger patterns can be made on a JACQUARD loom.

Dr. Denton's® See under SLEEPWEAR AND LOUNGEWEAR.

Doc Martens® See under FOOTWEAR.

doctor's bag See under HANDBAGS AND RELATED ACCESSORIES.

doctor's gown See under ACADEMIC COSTUME.

doctor's hood See under ACADEMIC COSTUME.

Dr. Scholl's exercise sandals See under FOOTWEAR.

Doctor Zhivago See under ZHIVAGO.

doeskin 1. See under LEATHERS. 2. Misnomer for doeskin fabric.

†doeskin fabric Any of several types of fabric made to simulate the texture and appearance of sueded doeskin leather. The fabrics may be made from napped wool, rayon, manufactured, or cotton fibers and woven or knitted.

doeskin glove See under GLOVES AND GLOVE CONSTRUCTION.

∞dogaline Loose-fitting, straight-cut gown with very wide sleeves—the lower edges of which are turned up and fastened to shoulder—revealing sleeve of the undergown. Worn by men and women during the Middle Ages and 16th c.

dog collar 1. See under NECKLINES AND COLLARS: DOG COLLAR and HALTER NECKLINE. 2. See under JEWELRY.

dog collar scarf See under SCARVES.

dog's-ear collar See under NECKLINES AND COLLARS.

dollar plan A system of planning utilized in some retail establishments in which a forecast of merchandising activities is used to generate a money budget expected to cover purchases of stock to be sold over a specified period.

dollar-round toe See under FOOTWEAR.

dolley madison hood See under HEADWEAR.

doll hat See under HEADWEAR.

dolly See under DOLLY STYLES.

dolly styles (British usage) See under BABY-DOLL STYLES #2.

∞dolly varden polonaise Type of woman's costume—inspired by Charles Dickens's character Dolly Varden in *Barnaby Rudge*—consisting of a fitted bodice and a draped overskirt of chintz, cretonne, or foulard with silk underskirt; either plain, flowered, or quilted (or cashmere in winter). Worn with a wide straw hat that is trimmed with flowers and ribbon and tied under the hair, which was worn in a CHIGNON (see under HAIRSTYLES). Popular in 1870s.

dolman (dole-man) 1. See under COATS AND JACKETS. 2. See under SHOULDERS AND SLEEVES. 3. See under SWEATERS.

dolmanette See under COATS AND JACKETS: DOLMAN.

dolman sweater See under SWEATERS.

dome hat See under HEADWEAR: BUBBLE HAT.

dome ring See under JEWELRY.

dome umbrella See under UMBRELLAS AND PARASOLS: BELL UMBRELLA.

domestic market The sale of goods within the 50 states of the U.S. See under INTERNATIONAL MARKET and REGIONAL MARKET.

domestic sourcing Obtaining of merchandise from sources available within the U.S. See under INTERNATIONAL SOURCE/SOURCING and SOURCING.

domino 1. See under CAPES, CLOAKS, AND SHAWLS. 2. See under MASKS.

dom pedro shoe See under FOOTWEAR.

†donegal tweed 1. Medium- to heavyweight tweed made in Ireland. Originally handwoven in the county of Donegal and made in plain or twill weave, usually of coarse yarns with a single colored warp and a blend of colors in the filling yarn. Uses: coats, suits, skirts, trousers, and jackets. Synonym: *Irish tweed.* 2. Tweeds made from Yorkshire yarns spun and dyed in Donegal, Ireland. 3. Imitations of the original Irish Donegal Tweeds.

donnilette See under COATS AND JACKETS: DOUILLETTE.

don't mentions See under INEXPRESSIBLES.

doo rag See under HEADWEAR.

door-knocker earring See under JEWELRY.

dorelet See under HEADWEAR.

dormeuse/dormouse See under HEADWEAR.

dorm shirt See under SLEEPWEAR AND LOUNGEWEAR.

dorothy cloak See under CAPES, CLOAKS, AND SHAWLS.

d'orsay coat See under COATS AND JACKETS.

d'Orsay, Count See under ORSAY, COUNT D'.

d'orsay habit-coat See under COATS AND JACKETS.

d'orsay pump See under FOOTWEAR.

d'orsay slipper See under FOOTWEAR.

dorset thread button See under CLOSURES.

dots See under PRINTS, STRIPES, AND CHECKS.

†dotted swiss Crisp, lightweight fabric ornamented with regularly spaced dots that are created either by clipped sections of extra crosswise yarns that interlace with lengthwise yarns or flocked dots of fiber glued to the fabric surface.

double besom pocket See under POCKETS: WELT POCKET.

double-breasted *adj.* The front opening of a garment lapped over double and fastening with two rows of buttons. Originally both rows were functional, now one row is usually decorative. Also called *d.b.,* in British English tailors' 19th-c. slang. Shown at COATS AND JACKETS: BLAZER.

double chignon See under HAIRSTYLES.

†double cloth Heavy fabric consisting of two separate fabrics woven at the same time and having a binder yarn that moves from one layer to another to hold them together. Such fabrics are usually reversible, in which case they are referred to as **double-faced.**

double collar See under NECKLINES AND COLLARS.

double cuff See under CUFFS: FRENCH CUFF.

double dress See under DRESSES.

double-entry pocket See under POCKETS.

†**double-faced satin ribbon** Ribbon woven with satin face on both sides.

∞**double-girdled** Describes the ancient Greek fashion of wearing a long, narrow sash, or two separate sashes, wound around waist and crossed over chest to adjust fullness of garment.

†**double knit** Knit fabric in which face and back of the fabric have a similar appearance. Made in a rib knit construction using double sets of needles, the resulting fabric is heavier, has greater dimensional stability, and less tendency to sag or lose its shape than single knit fabrics.

double mantle See under CAPES, CLOAKS, AND SHAWLS: MANTLE #2.

double-needle toe See under FOOTWEAR: NEEDLE TOE.

double ombré stripe See under PRINTS, STRIPES, AND CHECKS.

double-puffed sleeve See under SHOULDERS AND SLEEVES.

doubler See under FOOTWEAR.

double ruffle See under CLOTHING CONSTRUCTION DETAILS.

double-running stitch See under EMBROIDERIES AND SEWING STITCHES.

double stitchdown See under FOOTWEAR: STITCHDOWN SHOE CONSTRUCTION.

double-stitched seam See under CLOTHING CONSTRUCTION DETAILS: TOPSTITCHED SEAMS.

double tee See under SHIRTS.

doublet (dub'-let) ∞**1.** Main garment for upper part of man's body, worn from late 14th c. to 1670, and styled like a close-fitting short jacket of various lengths. Worn with either TRUNK HOSE or BREECHES. This garment seems to have evolved from garments used by the military such as the **gambeson** (gam'-bay-sohn), a sleeveless, padded, and sometimes quilted cloth or leather garment worn under armor in the Middle Ages. By the 14th c. the gambeson had become civilian costume and was more often referred to as a **juppe** or **jupe** (zhup), **jupon**, **gipon** (gee'-pon), or **pourpoint** (poor'-pwan, a French term for the stuffed and quilted jacket worn by men from 14th to 17th c.).

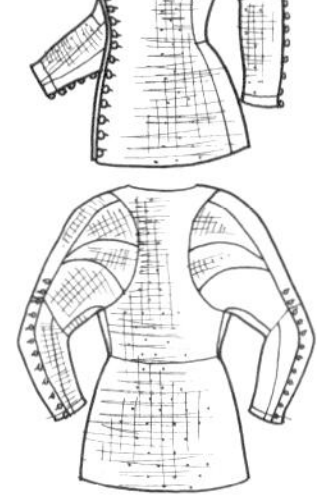
doublet 1300s

The **jack** was a padded, tight-fitting military doublet worn from the late 13th to the late 15th c. that was sometimes made of 30 layers of fabric and worn over the HAUBERK (see ARMOR). As worn by civilians in 14th c., it was a short jacket made of rich fabrics. **Peascod-bellied doublet** had a false front stuffed with cotton into a projection over the waistline that was shaped like the breast of a peacock. It was introduced into France from Spain and popular from 1570 to 1600, though it seems to have originally been a Dutch style. It, too, may have had a military origin and is said to have been in imitation of the CUIRASSE (see under ARMOR) to deflect bullets. Also called *bellied doublet, goose-bellied doublet, kodpeased doublet, long-bellied doublet,* and *shotten-bellied doublet.* Civilian doublets included the **hanseline** (han-sa-lyn) (also spelled *anslet, hanslein, haunseleyns, hense lynes,* and *henselyns*), an extremely short garment, fashionable in late 14th and early 15th c., that some authorities equate with the **paltock**. All that seems to be known with certainty, however, of the paltock is that it was a very short men's garment that served as an anchor for HOSE. The **jerkin** was similar to the doublet with a slightly longer skirt, sometimes with HANGING SLEEVES (see under SHOULDERS AND SLEEVES), and worn from 1450 to 1630. By the 16th and 17th c. the jerkin had become a sleeveless jacket, with WINGS on the shoulders. A **cropdoublet** was short-waisted and popular about 1610. ∞**2.** Part of woman's riding habit from 1650 to 1670. **3.** See under JEWELRY. **4.** Jacket of Scots HIGHLAND DRESS.

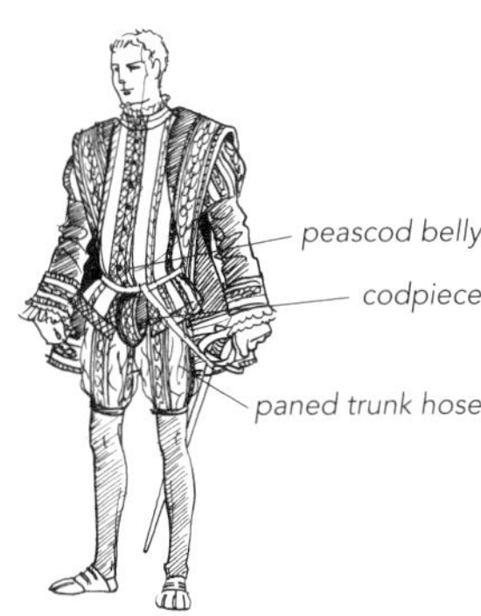

doublet 1542

double welt pocket See under POCKETS: BOUND and BESOM.

double-zipper foundation See under UNDERGARMENTS.

douillette See under COATS AND JACKETS.

†**doupioni** (doop-ee'-on-ee) Yarn or fabric made from silk yarn reeled from double cocoons, or two interlaced cocoons in which the silk is intertwined. Yarn has uneven slubs, rather than being smooth, giving a decorative texture to the fabric. Also spelled *douppioni* and *doppione.*

doup weave See under LENO WEAVE.

down See under FEATHERS.

down jacket See under COATS AND JACKETS.

down vest See under VESTS.

downy calves See under FALSE CALVES.

drag suit See under SWIMWEAR.

drain-pipe trousers See under PANTS.

drape **1.** *n.* The degree to which fabric falls into graceful folds when hung or arranged in different positions. **2.** *v.* The act of creating fashion designs by manipulating, pinning, and cutting muslin or other fabric over a dress form. In this technique, the draped garment is then used to create a pattern from which a garment can be made.

draped collar See under NECKLINES AND COLLARS.

draped heel See under FOOTWEAR.

draped skirt See under SKIRTS.

draping See under DRAPE #2.

drawers See under UNDERGARMENTS.

drawn fabric work See under EMBROIDERIES AND SEWING STITCHES.

drawn thread work See under EMBROIDERIES AND SEWING STITCHES.

drawstring Ribbon or cord inserted through a band of fabric, pulled, and tied to form a closing. See under BLOUSES AND TOPS: DRAWSTRING BLOUSE; HANDBAGS AND RELATED ACCESSORIES: DRAWSTRING BAG; NECKLINES AND COLLARS: DRAWSTRING NECKLINE; PANTS: DRAWSTRING PANTS; SHIRTS: DRAWSTRING SHIRT; SHORTS: DRAWSTRING SHORTS; and WAISTLINES: DRAWSTRING.

Dr. Denton Sleepers® See under SLEEPWEAR AND LOUNGEWEAR.

dreadlocks See under HAIRSTYLES.

dreadnought See under COATS AND JACKETS: FEARNOTHING JACKET.

dresden point See under EMBROIDERIES AND SEWING STITCHES.

dress **1.** *n.* Collective term for all clothing (e.g. the dress of Spain, the dress of an ethnic group). Synonyms: *apparel, clothes, costume.* **2.** *n.* In the field of textiles and apparel, a widely accepted definition of dress is ". . . the total arrangement of all outwardly detectable modifications of the body itself and all material objects added to it" (Roach and Musa, 1980, 11). **3.** *v.* To put on a garment. **4.** *v.* To arrange the hair. **5.** *v.* To tan and finish hides for leather uses. **6.** *adj.* Describes an item of apparel intended to be worn for more formal occasions, e.g., dress shoes, dress shirt.

DRESSES

dress One-piece outer garment that varies in length but extends to at least below the hips and ends in a skirt. In Western costume history, traditionally worn by women. The term *dress* as it is used today did not come into common usage until the late 18th c.; before then the terms *robe* or *gown* or specific names for garments were used (e.g. ropa, kalasiris, mantua). Such words are to be found in the alphabetical listing of terms and definitions. Fashion terms for various dress styles have developed and are generally formed by placing an adjective describing the apparel in front of the word "dress." Examples: coatdress, drop-waist dress, shirt dress, swing dress, sweater dress.

african dress Straight-cut or A-line dress made of African printed fabric (sometimes of raffia) elaborately trimmed with wooden or glass beads or sequins. Made in mini- and full-length styles, some with midriffs, others with see-through midriffs with strands of beads connecting top and skirt. Introduced by Paris couturier Yves Saint Laurent in 1967.

∞**afternoon dress** **1.** Term used during the 19th c. for a type of dress suitable for visiting in the afternoons. **2.** In the early 20th c. indicated a dressy dress, frequently full-length in the 1920s and 1930s, suitable for a garden party or formal tea. Usually worn with a large picture hat.

agnès sorel dress PRINCESS-STYLE dress worn in early 1860s.

A-line dress Dress style that flares gently from under the arms to hem of skirt, resembling the letter *A.* Usually made with narrow shoulders, a high, round neck line, and is similar to a SKIMMER (see under DRESSES). Introduced in 1955 by Paris couturier Christian Dior.

A-line dress 1955

American Indian dress **1.** Dress made of suede or buckskin with simple lines and trimming of beads and fringe, originally worn by North American Indian women. **2.** Modern interpretation of Native American dress in leather, suede, or fabric. Synonym: *Pocahontas dress.*

andean shift Native dress from Peru made in straight-cut style of native fabrics and trimmed with embroidery. Sold in U.S. in late 1960s. Also called an *ocepa. Der.* Dress from Andes Mountains in South America.

apron dress Any dress worn with a decorative apron. Also see under DRESSES: PINAFORE DRESS.

baby-doll dress **1.** Woman's dress cut like a smock, with a high neckline and gathers or pleats hanging from a tiny yoke, similar to children's, infants', and dolls' dresses of the 1930s. Introduced in early 1960s by English designers and used again in late 1970s by French ready-to-wear designers. Shown in MOD DRESS. Elements that made up the entire look included baby-doll shoes with straps over the instep and mini purses on long chains. Also carried over to very short pajamas and nightgowns. Popularity enhanced by movie *Baby Doll* (1956), in which Carroll Baker played the lead. *Der.* Used to refer to clothing and accessories used for children's dolls and infants' clothes in the early 20th c. **2.** Revived in fall 1985 when British designer *Vivienne Westwood* introduced a collection of dresses called by this name. Dresses were similar to children's and dolls' dresses of 1930s and 1940s—some with collars, cuffs, and wide belts, and others with full skirts over crinoline petticoats. Patou, in Paris in the fall of 1986, introduced a style with long sleeves; wrapped, draped bodice; and sometimes worn over petticoats made with ruffles.

baby-doll dress #2

baby dress Dresses popular until mid-20th c. for infants, regardless of gender; usually made of fine white cotton in loose-fitting style and trimmed with tucks, embroidery, and lace. At present such dresses are usually reserved for female infants.

backless dress Dress with extremely low back, sometimes dipping to below the waist, used mainly for evening gowns. Made in many different styles with high front that sometimes has a cutout.

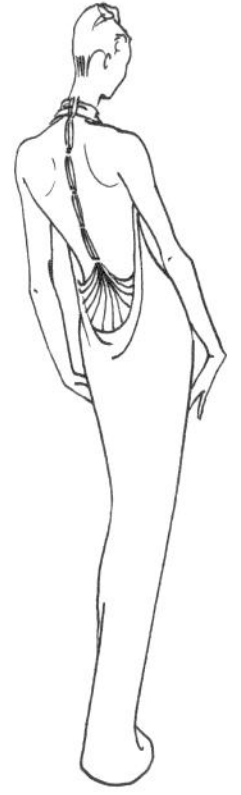
backless dress 1998

basic dress Dress simply cut with no ornamentation, usually colored black. Jewelry, collars, and other accessories can be added to change the appearance. Introduced in the 1930s, worn through 1940s, and revived in early 1970s. Also called "L.B.D." (little black dress), a name that continues to be used in merchandising simple black dresses.

basic dress

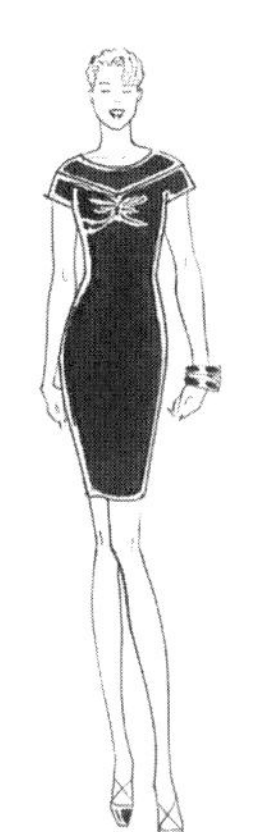
little black dress 2001

bathrobe dress Wraparound dress with shawl collar, no buttons, front lapped over and held in place with a sash. Worn since the mid-1960s.

∞**bavarian dress** Woman's carriage dress, trimmed with bands of fabric down the front, that was worn in the 1820s.

bloomer dress Dress popular for children after World War I worn with matching bloomers underneath.

blouson dress (blue-zohn′) Bloused-top dress with low waistline seam. A style introduced in 1920s and reintroduced in 1950s. *Der.* French "to blouse."

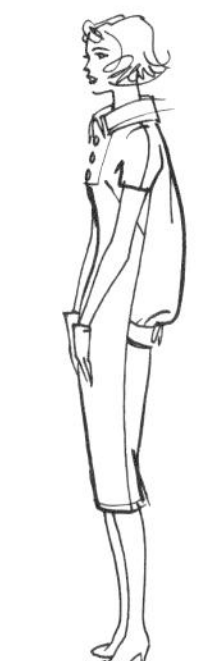
blouson dress

∞**bolero costume** Dress with matching bolero, reaching nearly to the waist, or separate jacket and skirt worn with a shirtwaist. Worn from early 1900s to 1920. Some boleros were fitted, and some had elaborate full-caped sleeves. Also see under COATS AND JACKETS: BOLERO.

bouffant dress (boo-fahnt′) Dress with tight-fitting bodice and full, gathered, pleated, or ruffled skirt. Sometimes skirt is shaped like a bubble, a bell, or a cone, and it may be worn with hoops or petticoats. *Der.* French "full" or "puffed." Also see under DRESSES: BUBBLE and PAPER DOLL DRESSES.

bouffant dress 1949

bra-shift Sleeveless, loose-fitting dress with top of dress fitted to the figure like a bra. An innovation of the mid-1960s.

bridesmaid's dress Any type of dress worn by a bride's attendant(s) at a wedding. May match in style and color with other attendants, and is usually selected to complement the bride's dress.

buba An Afro-inspired dress of 1969 worn by women. Styled in a large panel print and wide decorative borders and with the same design on front and back. Sleeves are usually fitted at armholes, widely flared at wrists, and frequently end in a long point.

bubble dress Dress style of 1959 with fitted bodice, sometimes strapless, with skirt bubbling out at hips and tapering in closely at hem. *Der.* Literally the skirt was shaped like a "bubble." Reintroduced in 1984.

bubble dress

bustle dress Any dress with fullness protruding in back from waist to hips or waist to hem. A style characteristic of 1870 to 1890, which is often called the "Bustle Period" by costume historians. Bustles also appeared in some clothes of the 1940s and were reintroduced in early 1980s. A 1980s version, designed by Christian Lacroix for Jean Patou, consisted of a knee-length dress with large pouf in back and floor-length hanging panel. This style is revived often.

bustle dress 1885

cage dress Woman's garment made in two layers, with inner layer opaque and cut close to body, and outer layer of sheer or latticed fabric hanging loosely. Such dresses, introduced in late 1960s by Paris couturier Yves Saint Laurent, were similar to dresses designed by Spanish couturier Cristobal Balenciaga in Paris in the 1940s. Popular again in the 1990s.

∞**calisthenic costume** Knee-length dress worn with Turkish trousers similar to BLOOMER COSTUME. Worn in late 1850s by women and girls for such sports as archery, ice-skating, and exercising with dumbbells. Later, a version of this dress was called *gymnasium costume.*

∞**calypso chemise** (ca-lip-so) Woman's dress of the 1790s made in two parts: a dress of colored muslin worn under a loose robe.

cancan dress Contemporary version of the traditional costume of Parisian cancan dancers of the 1890s. The bodice has a bustier effect and laces up the back. The skirt has an overskirt with an apron-like effect, which tapers to center back with a large bow, and is worn over underskirt made with rows of ruffles. Designed by Victorine for Karl Lagerfeld of Chanel for fall 1986. *Der.* Similar to dresses worn by music hall dancers in film and stage show *Can-Can* and those shown in paintings by Henri Toulouse-Lautrec.

cancan dress

carnaby dress Simple, beltless dress made in fabrics of unusual color combinations with a large white collar. *Der.* Named for Carnaby Street, in London, England, where "mod" fashions originated in 1960s.

∞**carriage dress** A woman's dress or costume suitable for riding in a carriage. The term was in use from about 1820 to the end of the 19th c. The specific style conformed to current fashions and was frequently trimmed with fur.

chemise (shem-ees′) Dress style that derives from the style of the undergarment called a chemise. Chemise-type dresses are characterized by a loose fit. If they are belted, belts are generally located at hipline or under the bust and the dress is unfitted at the anatomical waistline. Periods in which women wore such styles included the Directoire and Empire periods (c. 1795–1820), the 1920s, the 1960s, and the 1990s. Sometimes called "the sack" in the 1960s by critics of the style. Der. French "shift" or "shirt."

chemise 1959

cheongsam Chinese woman's dress originating in Shanghai, China, in the late 1930s as an attempt to blend traditional Chinese and Western styles. It has a high, close-fitting collar, diagonal front opening that closes with frogs or buttons, short sleeves, a snug fit, and a side slit running from the bottom of the hem and reaching, in more daring versions, as high as the thigh. Used as a basis for Western designs, most notably in housecoats and dresses. Synonyms: *qi pao, Chinese dress,* and *mandarin dress.*

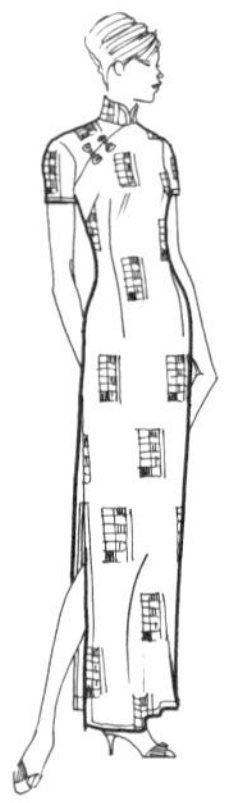

cheongsam

christening dress Any dress or suit worn by infants for their baptism. Until the mid-20th c. both boys and girls wore extremely long white dresses, elaborately trimmed with tucks, lace, and hand embroidery. In recent decades, boys have been dressed either in white suits or in dresses. Dresses for both boys and girls today may be shorter, but would usually cover the feet.

christening dress 1898

∞**circassian round robe** (ser-kash′-yan) Early 1820s evening dress of gossamer gauze made with low, square-cut neckline, short sleeves, high waistline, and skirt elaborately decorated down the front and above the hem with festoons of knotted ribbon. *Der.* Caucasian tribe of Circassia, a historical region between the western end of the Caucasus range and the Kuban River, north of the Black sea.

coatdress Dress fastened down front from neck to hem, like a coat, in single- or double-breasted style, either belted or unbelted. A classic since the 1930s.

cocktail dress Short evening dress with décolleté neckline made in luxury fabrics. Suitable for formal late-afternoon or cocktail parties; popular in the 1950s.

∞**commodore dress** Dress with nautical braid trim worn by girls and young ladies in early 1890s. Typical dress might have a wide, braid-trimmed sailor collar and gathered skirt with braid trim near the hem. Usually worn with a flat SAILOR HAT or a COMMODORE HAT. (See under HEADWEAR.)

computer dress Dress made from discarded computer chips hooked together, sometimes made in one-shoulder style with asymmetric hemlines. Chips are collected from computers, TVs, and other electronic machines. Dresses sold in 1984 by Panages for between $2,000 and $50,000.

∞**corset frock** Dress of late 18th c. made with bodice of three gores of white satin in front and lacing in back, similar to a corset.

costume à la constitution Red, white, and blue striped or flowered dress of muslin or lawn worn with a vivid red sash and helmet-shaped cap. Symbolized the tricolor of the French Revolution and was worn by patriots. Also called *dress à la constitution.*

∞**cottage dress** High-waisted, straight dress of early 1820s with long apron in front made of same fabric. Necklines varied—some low with FICHU (see under SCARVES) and others with white collars either trimmed with frills or V-shaped edging. Sleeves were fitted. Hem of skirt was usually decorated with a tubular-shaped trimming stitched at regular intervals to create puffs of fabric.

culotte dress (ku-lot′) Dress that combines pants and blouse into one garment, usually without a waistline seam, popular in 1967 and after. Also called a *pantdress.*

∞**curricle dress** (kur′-ee-kul) Woman's thigh-length, short-sleeved, open-front tunic usually of net; worn from 1794 to 1803 over a full-length dress.

cutout dress Any dress with cutout portions revealing the body. May have enlarged armholes or be cut out at the midriff, hips, or back. An innovation of the 1960s.

delphos dress Woman's dress made by a new system patented by designer Mariano Fortuny in 1909. The front and back of the dress were laced together, rather than being stitched down the sides. Styles were reminiscent of ancient Greek dresses. Beautiful fabrics were used and the entire dress was minutely pleated, thus molding the body like a Greek statue. Many women wore these dresses, which did not conform to the usual mode of the era, as tea gowns or at-home styles. Fortuny continued to make the same general style until his death in 1949.

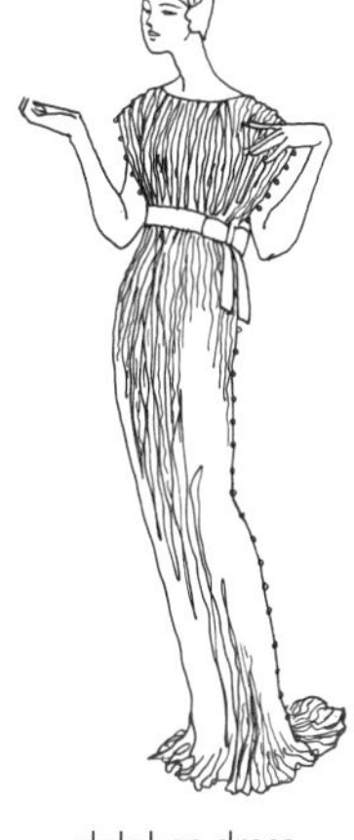
delphos dress c. 1910

diamanté dress (dya-mahn-tay′) Dress made almost entirely of sparkling beads, sequins, or paillettes, giving a glittering effect; very popular in mid-1980s. Although Norman Norell designed dresses in 1968 made entirely of sequins, they were not referred to as diamanté dresses until the mid-1980s. *Der.* French, "made of diamonds."

dinner dress Full-length dress suitable for a formal dinner. Introduced in the 1930s, a dinner dress was distinguished from an evening gown by having the shoulders covered for dinner. Such dresses were frequently made with a coordinated jacket that, when removed, revealed a formal dress.

∞**directoire gown** 1. See under EMPIRE DRESS #1. 2. Slim, coat-style dress with wide lapels, gauntlet-cuffed sleeves, and high-sashed waist. Worn by women in late 19th c.

dirndl Dress with gathers at the waistline that derives from a full-skirted Tyrolean peasant costume originating, and still worn, in Austrian and Bavarian Alps. Specific versions have varied in shape, with those worn in 1980s having a slightly belled shape to the skirt while the 1940s and 1950s version had a fuller skirt with more gathers at the waist to produce a more bouffant effect. The skirt is usually attached to tight-fitted bodice.

double dress

double dress Two dresses designed to be worn one over the other. Often the outer dress may be of sheer fabric while the under dress is of an opaque fabric.

electric dress Novelty dress decorated with electric lights wired to a battery at the waist, designed to be worn to discothèques in the late 1960s.

empire dress (em′-pire or ohm-peer′) 1. Dress with a high waistline located just under the bosom. The waistline is defined by an inserted piece of fabric or a seam. The style derived from the type of dresses that were popular during the DIRECTOIRE and EMPIRE periods in France. Other features included a low-cut neckline in front and back, small puffed sleeves, a

empire dress #1

length to the ankles, and a relatively straight skirt. For court wear, a train usually hung from the shoulders. **2.** Any contemporary dress with high waistline, usually with a narrow skirt. *Der.* From First Empire in France (1804–1814).

∞**empress josephine gown** High-waisted dress with a bodice that closed by wrapping one side over the other, full sleeves, sash ends hanging from inserted belt, and gathered skirt. Worn in the 1890s with a FIGARO JACKET (see under COATS AND JACKETS), the style was inspired by dresses of the First Empire in France (see under EMPIRE STYLES).

∞**eugénie dress** (yoo-je′-nee) Full-skirted dress of 1850s made with three-tiered skirt, tight-fitting waist, and short or pagoda-style sleeves. *Der.* Named for Eugénie, Empress of France.

∞**false gown** **1.** 18th-c. woman's dress style, borrowed from dresses worn by little girls in France, featuring a tight bodice, gathered skirt, and wide ribbon sash. **2.** Dress worn during French Revolution made without PANIERS (see under UNDERGARMENTS) and having a tight bodice with a skirt that was not split in front.

fan-back dress Evening gown with slim-fitting front and back of contrasting fabric made of accordion pleats caught a little below the waistline with a bow. Pleats extend upward and downward in fan shape. Featured by Guy Laroche in black and fuchsia in fall 1986 collection.

∞**fishwife costume** Blouson dress of 1880s made with shawl collar, dickey insert, and full sleeves. Double skirt was gathered at waistline with overskirt turned up revealing a lining of contrasting fabric. Underskirt made of a third fabric, frequently striped to match dickey. Imitated a dress worn with several petticoats by Portuguese fishermen's wives.

flamenco dress Dress with long torso top and skirt made with a series of circular-cut flounces. In the late 1960s adaptations were accepted for general wear. *Der.* Inspired by dresses worn by flamenco dancers in Spain.

flapper dress Short-skirted, unfitted, long-torso dress first worn in the late 1920s and revived in the 1960s and 1990s.

flapper dress 1920s

flip-chip dress Make-your-own dress of colored plastic chips or squares and connecting fasteners put together in any pattern, similar to a LINKED DRESS (see under DRESSES).

∞**florodora costume** (flor-oh′-dora) Dress with tight-fitted, lace-trimmed bodice with bishop sleeves and long, full skirt trimmed with ruffles. Worn with an off-the-face picture hat trimmed with ostrich feathers. *Der.* Worn by chorus of the musical, *Florodora,* a hit of 1900.

flying saucer dress A dress introduced by Issey Miyake in the spring of 1994. Rectangular pieces of polyester fabric, in an array of colors, are stitched together to create horizontally striped yardage. This yardage is gathered, folded, and heat-set; the pleated fabric is stitched into three tubes, one for the body and two for the sleeves, to create a dress that looks like a flying saucer.

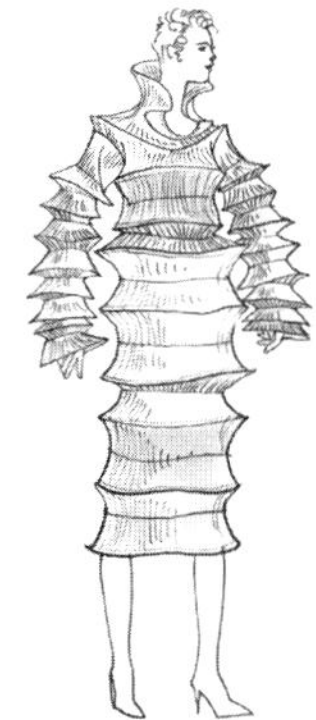
flying saucer dress

foil dress Disposable dress made in various colors of aluminum foil, sometimes quilted. Introduced in 1968 along with PAPER DRESSES (see under DRESSES), and reintroduced in 1986 in creative, imaginative designs.

∞**french dress** Little girl's long-waisted dress, worn in late 19th and early 20th c. Usually made with square or round neckline accented with a large bertha collar. Sleeves may be short, ruffled, or puffed, or of long leg-of-mutton style. Skirt was full with wide ribbon sash at low waistline.

∞**froufrou dress** (froo′-froo′) Daytime dress of 1870 made with low-necked bodice and worn under a short muslin tunic. Skirt was cut away in front, revealing a silk underskirt trimmed with many tiny pinked flounces. *Der.* From the name of the comedy *Froufrou,* written by Henri Meilhac and Ludovic Halévy in 1869.

∞**gabrielle dress** (ga-bree′-el) **1.** Daytime dress of 1865 with bodice and front of skirt cut in one piece. Back was made with two large box pleats on either side and a third in the center. **2.** Girl's jumper-type dress of early 20th c. made in princess style and worn over bracelet-length, full-sleeved, high-necked blouse.

graduation dress White dress worn for graduation. In the early 20th c., young girls were expected to make their graduation dresses in sewing classes. This practice ended after World War II.

granny dress Ankle-length dress styled with a high, round or choker neckline, long or short sleeves, high waistline, and slightly gathered skirt—sometimes with a ruffle at the hem. Frequently made of CALICO fabric in a small print and trimmed with ruffles. Worn by a child or young person and popular in the 1960s. *Der.* Copied from style worn by her grandmother, or "granny."

granny dress

∞**guimpe dress/guimpe costume** Jumper-dress with *guimpe* or blouse under short-sleeved, low-necked dress. Worn from 1880s to early 20th c.—first by children, later by older girls and women. Sometimes took the form of a suspender-type jumper with blouse called GUIMPE (see under BLOUSES AND TOPS) underneath.

∞**habit d'escalier** (ah-beet' des-kahl'-yaye) Late 18th and early 19th c. evening dress made with an overtunic or HALF ROBE. The short sleeves were slit open and trimmed with ribbons tied in ladderlike fashion.

∞**habit-redingote** (red'-ing-gote) Woman's dress of 1879 made in princess style with front closed from neck to knees. Lower front of skirt was cut away and rounded to reveal the underskirt.

∞**handkerchief dress** Dress of the 1880s with a tunic made from, or resembling, a bandanna. Two were arranged diagonally on the front of the dress with one point reaching nearly to the hem of dress. A long-skirted jacket with shaped REVERS (see under NECKLINES AND COLLARS) and waistcoat comprised the bodice of the dress. Also see under DRESSES: HANDKERCHIEF TUNIC.

harem dress 1913

∞**handkerchief tunic** Dress of 1917 with peplum made from large square of fabric, like a handkerchief. Made with center opening for waist and pointed ends hanging down over skirt. Also see under DRESSES: HANDKERCHIEF DRESS.

harem dress Symmetrically or asymmetrically draped dress falling in loose folds to the hem where it is turned under and fastened to a lining giving the hem a draped appearance. Usually made of soft, clinging fabric. In styles of the early 20th c., often made as a harem skirt worn under a tunic overskirt. *Der.* An adaptation of Middle Eastern dress introduced by Paris designers Paul Poiret and Drécoll in 1910 and revived at intervals.

housedress c. 1930s

housedress A simple, inexpensive dress made of washable fabric, worn while doing household chores. In the early 20th c., it was called a *wrapper.* One of the first items made by the garment industry in mass production, the wrapper evolved from a woman's dressing gown.

∞**irish polonaise** (po-lo-nayz) Woman's dress worn from 1770 to 1775 with square-cut neckline, bodice buttoned to waist, fitted at back, and elbow-length sleeves. The skirt is long and pleated, split in front to show shorter underskirt and caught up at waist by buttons or vertical cords into puffed sides. Also called *italian nightgown* or *french* or *turkish polonaise.*

∞**isabeau style dress** (is-ah-bow') Daytime dress of 1860s cut in PRINCESS STYLE and trimmed down front with a row of buttons or rosettes.

jacket dress Dress with a matching or contrasting jacket. The dress is usually sleeveless or bares the shoulders. With the jacket, it is suitable for business or afternoons. Popular since the 1930s.

jacket dress

Jenny Lind dress Hoop-skirted dress of mid-19th c. with three lace ruffles on skirt and off-the-shoulder neckline. *Der.* Copied from style of dress worn by Jenny Lind (1820–1887), coloratura soprano known as the "Swedish Nightingale."

jiffy dress **1.** Sew-it-yourself dress with limited number of pieces that can be stitched together in a short time. **2.** A dress knitted quickly on jumbo needles from a kit or from separately purchased yarn.

∞**juive tunic** (zweeve) Hip-length, princess-style OVERDRESS (see under DRESSES: OVERDRESS #1) of 1875 made with large armholes, V-neck front and back, and overskirt forming a train in back. Worn over regular dress as outdoor costume. *Der.* Probably named for a popular French Opera, *La Juive,* which means "the Jewish woman."

juliet dress Dress in medieval style with high waist line and puffed-topped sleeves that are fitted at the lower arm. *Der.* Inspired by the film of Shakespeare's play *Romeo and Juliet,* made by Franco Zeffirelli in 1968.

jumper dress One-piece dress with sleeves and collar of a contrasting color, giving the appearance of a two-piece blouse and jumper. Also called a *jumper shift.*

kabuki dress (ka-boo'-kee) Collarless wraparound dress with KIMONO SLEEVES (see under SHOULDERS AND SLEEVES), held closed by a sash. *Der.* Copied from traditional dress of actors in Japanese popular *kabuki theater,* which began in early 17th c. with women dancers and actors. In mid-17th c. (1652) the government decreed that there should only be men as actors—doing all the female parts, too. Types fall in three groups: historical plays, domestic plays, and dance dramas performed in stylized acting. Costumes used are elaborate and include exaggerated brocaded KIMONOS; wide, jeweled belts; wigs; and masklike face makeup.

kiltie dress Dress style adapted from the Scottish KILT (see under SKIRTS), in which the front of the skirt is plain with wrapped side closing fastened with a safety pin, and the remainder of skirt is knife-pleated and joined to a simple tailored top. Introduced in the late 1960s.

kimono dress (keh-mo′-no) Wrap-around dress held in place with a sash. Made with *kimono sleeves,* usually cut in one piece with the front and the back of the dress. There are no armhole seams. *Der.* Adapted from the *Japanese kimono,* first used as a dressing robe and adapted for a dress in late 1960s.

kimono dress

Le Canned dress Trade name for a simple shift dress of printed nylon knit packaged for sale in a tin can. Briefly popular in 1967.

Letty Lynton dress Dresses styled by the designer Adrian and worn by Joan Crawford in the 1932 MGM film *Letty Lynton.* One particular style was fitted to the hips with a full skirt, the outstanding feature being very full balloon sleeves covered with ruffles. Another style designed for the movie was a slim SHEATH (see under DRESSES), tight to the knees, with a HALTER neckline (see under NECKLINES AND COLLARS) and flaring TRUMPET SKIRT (see under SKIRTS). *Der. Letty Lynton,* a film from 1932.

Lilly® Trademark for a simple printed-cotton shift dress designed and sold by designer Lilly Pulitzer of Palm Beach, Florida, from late 1960s. Pulitzer began designing these printed dresses after spilling orange juice on her dress. Company was liquidated in mid-1980s; however, the trademark remains active for a wide variety of products ranging from cosmetics to clothing.

Linde Star dress Jeweled full-length evening dress sprinkled with Linde Star sapphires (synthetic sapphires) set at intervals. Novelty dress of the late 1960s.

lingerie dress One- or two-piece woman's dress made of white cotton or linen. Popular in the first decade of the 20th c.; name derived from the similarity to decorative undergarments, both of which were ornamented with lace, embroidery, tucking and frills.

linked dress Dress made by linking geometric-shaped pieces of metal, leather, plastic, or mirror together. Introduced by Paris couturier Paco Rabanne in 1966.

little black dress See under DRESSES: BASIC DRESS.

Little Women dress Child's dress made with plain, fitted, front-buttoned bodice, short or long plain sleeves, small, turned-down collar with ribbon bow tie, and full-gathered skirt. *Der.* Inspired by dresses described in Louisa May Alcott's book *Little Women,* published in 1868.

∞**looped dress** Hoop-skirted dress worn in 1860s, made with skirt in two layers. Outer layer was gracefully looped up in four, five, or six places by fabric tabs called **lyons loops** to show the underskirt.

lyons loops See under DRESSES: LOOPED DRESS.

∞**Manon robe** (man-ohn′) Daytime dress of 1860s with front cut in one piece from neck to hem. Back with double BOX PLEAT or WATTEAU PLEATS (see under CLOTHING CONSTRUCTION DETAILS) hanging from under collar to hem of skirt. *Der.* Named for Manon, heroine of 1733 book by Abbé Prevost.

∞**marguerite dress** Dress of early 1890s with a scarf at the neckline, made with full sleeves gathered into a wide cuff reaching halfway to elbow. Blouse was full and gathered at neckline and worn with full gathered skirt trimmed with bands of braid. Contrasting low-necked sleeveless peasant bodice, laced up the front and back, is worn over the dress.

maternity dress Dress designed for pregnant women following the general style trends but made with more fullness in front. In the late 1990s and after, some maternity clothing fit more tightly.

∞**medici dress** (meh′-dee-chee) Trained PRINCESS DRESS (see under DRESSES) of early 1870s with TABLIER front (see under SKIRTS: TABLIER SKIRT) and short sleeves. *Der.* Inspired by clothes worn by Marie de' Medici, Queen of France (c. 1600).

mermaid sheath Slim, fitted evening gown introduced by designer Norman Norell in late 1960s. Dress was completely covered with SEQUINS (or PAILLETTES), giving a dazzling effect. *Der.* Similar to the way mermaids are pictured (minus the tail).

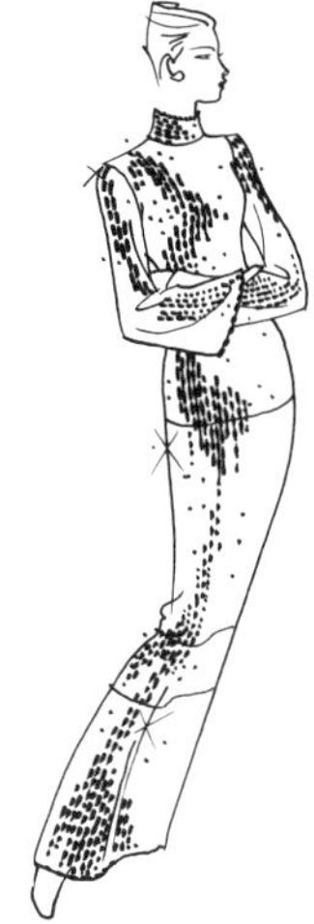
mermaid sheath 1960s

micro dress Shorter version of the MINIDRESS (see under DRESSES), reaching the top part of the thigh like a tunic blouse; introduced in 1966.

midriff dress One-piece dress with a piece of fabric or elastic inserted at waistline, giving the effect of a cinched waist.

mini-crinoline Wide-skirted, short dress style that was popular in the 1980s.

minidress Dress with short skirt coming to mid-thigh or about 6″ above the knee. First introduced in early 1960s by designer Mary Quant in England as part of the "mod" fashions and became mass fashion by end of 1960s. Reintroduced in the mid-1980s and worn since then.

molded dress Dress made with fabric that is heat-set or molded to take on a sculptured geometric form. Introduced by Paris couturier Pierre Cardin in fall 1968 collection.

Mondrian dress 1960s

Mondrian dress (Mohn'-dree-yon) Straight, unconstructed dress made with blocks of color and neutrals heavily banded with black. Introduced by Yves Saint Laurent in fall 1965 collection. *Der.* Inspired by modern linear paintings of Piet Mondrian.

monk's dress Dress styled like a monk's robe with cowl neck, bell sleeves, and cord belt confining fullness.

∞morning dress 1. In the 19th c. applied to any dress suitable for wear in the morning—for visiting, shopping, or at home—as differentiated from a more formal afternoon dress. Also called *morning gown* or *morning robe.* (for women) ∞2. In early 20th c. referred to a HOUSEDRESS (see under DRESSES) of inexpensive fabric.

∞oliver twist dress Young girl's dress worn about 1919. Made with double-breasted, wrap-front and skirt pleated at sides and back and had a fluted frill at neckline and at bottom of three-quarter-length sleeves.

overdress 1. Any dress designed to be worn over another dress. ∞2. Transparent dress worn in late 17th c. constructed with an attached opaque underdress. ∞3. In 1870s, a hip-length bodice worn with a separate skirt. Some were formal in style with low-cut neckline, peplum, and fancy decorative trim of lace and ribbons. See DRESSES: CAGE DRESS.

panel dress A sheath or fit and flare dress that features princess seams originating at the shoulder to create panels that run the length of the dress. Often interpreted in contrasting colors or fabrics.

panel pantdress Dress with free hanging panel in front and back.

∞pannier dress (pan-yehr') Daytime dress of the late 1860s with an overskirt looped up and puffed out at back and sides. Worn over an underskirt with train trimmed with a flounce.

panty dress Girl's dress with matching bloomers, worn in the 1920s. Also called *bloomer dress.*

paper-doll dress style Specific style of dress worn from 1950 to 1960, that had tight bodies, tight waistlines, and very bouffant skirts held out with nylon net and crinoline petticoats. Anne Fogarty designed dresses in this style. *Der.* From the full-skirted paper dolls children played with in the 1930s.

paper dress Classification of dresses made of various types of disposable paper or nonwoven fabrics similar to paper. This fad peaked around 1968. Worn for parties and at the beach, some were hand-painted and very expensive; others were inexpensive and imprinted with funny gimmicks (e.g., Yellow Pages of telephone book, a Heinz soup can, etc.). Revived in 1986 as wedding dress by Susan Lane and made of a nonwoven fabric that resembles paper, selling for $140.00. Also see under DRESSES: FOIL DRESS.

patio dress Gay floral or abstract printed shift suitable for wearing at a backyard barbecue or at the beach.

pearl dress Novelty dress adapted from Asian fashion consisting of draped strands of pearls at the top and long, hanging strands for the skirt, worn over a body stocking. Introduced by a jewelry firm Richelieu Pearls and designed by Bill Smith in 1969.

∞pelisse-robe (pe-leese') Daytime dress in coat style, worn from about 1817 to 1840, fastened down the front with ribbon bows or with hidden hooks and eyes.

peplum dress One- or two-piece dress either fitted or belted at waistline with short ruffle or circular-cut piece of fabric extending below waistline. Popular in 1930s, 1960s, and revived in 1980s.

peplum

∞perdita chemise (per-dee'-tah shem-ees') (British usage) Daytime dress of 1873 made with close-fitting bodice and V-neck with large falling collar, sometimes double. Also had long, tight sleeves, buttons, or ribbon ties down front, and sash at waist tied with long ends in back. Also called *chemise gown. Der.* Named after Perdita Robinson, an actress.

∞Peter Thomson dress One-piece dress with MIDDY COLLAR (see under NECKLINES AND COLLARS) and box pleats from yoke to hem. Worn as uniform by many schoolchildren and older girls (through college) from 1900 to 1920. *Der.* Named for designer Peter Thomson, who was once a tailor for the Navy.

pillow-slip dress Straight-cut CHEMISE dress (see under DRESSES) of 1920s, usually short in length with short *kimono* sleeves.

pinafore dress Dress worn with separate bib-top apron tied in back popular for children. First worn in 1870s and intermittently since. *Der.* Copied from apron worn by children. Also called *Alice in Wonderland* or *apron dress.*

popover Denim wraparound dress with short sleeves, a large patch pocket on the front of slightly flared skirt, and trimmed with decorative double topstitching. Designed by Claire McCardell in 1942 for *Harper's Bazaar.*

Intended as an inexpensive, protective, yet stylish cover-up for household work. Original dress sold for $6.95, and different $30 versions were shown in her collection for several years.

poster dress Any dress imprinted with a blown-up photograph, a brief fad in the mid-1960s. Originally made of paper, later, photographs were printed on fabric. In 1984 called a *toga dress,* which had a wide-shouldered "sandwich board" effect, was sewed up the sides, and printed with posters of animals, motorcycles, and movie stars' faces.

princess dress A dress in which the shape is achieved from seams that extend from either the shoulder or the armhole to the hem with no waistline seam. The fit of a princess dress may resemble a sheath, an A-line or a fit and flare silhouette. Worth claimed to have designed the original style, which was introduced about 1860 for Empress Eugénie. Worn intermittently since. Also called *fourreau dress.*

princess dress

∞promenade dress In last half of 19th c., clothes suitable for walking and shopping, as contrasted with a carriage dress, which was worn for riding in a carriage. Also called *walking costume* or *dress.*

rain dress Dress made of plastic or of fabric treated for water repellency, an innovation of the 1960s.

rhumba dress Bare-midriff dress worn with full-length skirt split up the front, tight through the hips, flaring with a mass of circular-cut ruffles from hips to hem. Popular after it was worn by movie star Carmen Miranda in 1940s, and revived at intervals. *Der.* Named for South American dance.

rhumba dress 1940s

robe de style Evening dress of the 1920s with a dropped waistline and a full skirt. Originated by designer Jeanne Lanvin, this gown was an alternative to the tubular silhouette of the period.

∞robe redingote Dress of 1830s and 1840s with collar and lapels on bodice, and skirt opening in front to show an underskirt.

robe de style 1920s

russian shirtdress Dress with high neckline banded in braid and closed on the side made with slightly full sleeves and banded at the wrist. Also called *Zhivago dress,* from clothes worn in 1965 film version of Russian novel *Dr. Zhivago,* by Boris Pasternak.

∞russian-style dress Two-piece dress of 1890s with knee-length tunic over full-length skirt, high COSSACK COLLAR (see under NECKLINES AND COLLARS), and embroidery trim around neck, cuffs, down side of blouse front, and around hem. Also see under DRESSES: RUSSIAN SHIRTDRESS.

sailor dress Dress with sailor collar or MIDDY BLOUSE (see under BLOUSES AND TOPS) effect trimmed with rows of braid in nautical style. The style was very popular for girls from 1890 to 1930, and for women from 1890 on.

sarong/sarong dress (sar-ong') Long, straight, wraparound skirt made of bright-colored tropical design fabric with deep fold in front, held on by scarf around waist. Worn by men and women of the Malay Archipelago. Adapted as a beach dress style with wraparound skirt draped to one side and strapless top first designed by Edith Head for Dorothy Lamour film *Hurricane* in 1937. Worn by Lamour in many films of the 1930s and 1940s. *Der.* Copied from Indonesian native dress. Also used to describe garments based on the sarong style. See under SWIMWEAR: SARONG SWIMSUIT; SKIRTS: SARONG SKIRT; and UNDERGARMENTS: SARONG®.

sarong

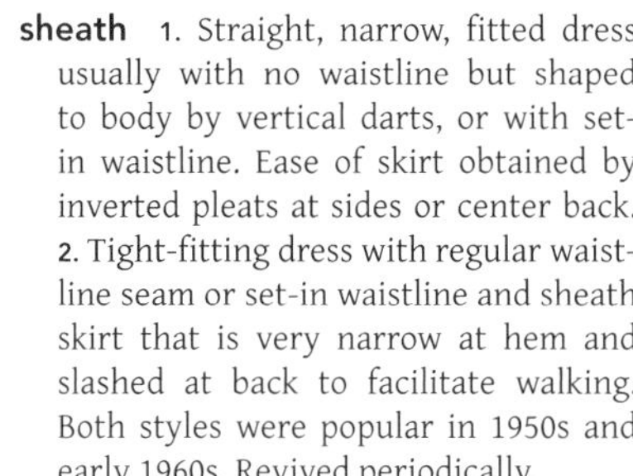

sheath 1. Straight, narrow, fitted dress usually with no waistline but shaped to body by vertical darts, or with set-in waistline. Ease of skirt obtained by inverted pleats at sides or center back. 2. Tight-fitting dress with regular waistline seam or set-in waistline and sheath skirt that is very narrow at hem and slashed at back to facilitate walking. Both styles were popular in 1950s and early 1960s. Revived periodically.

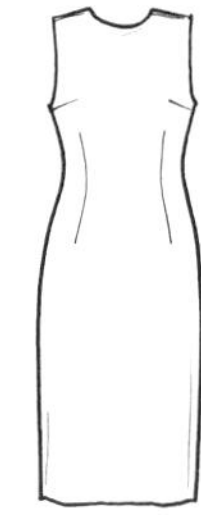

sheath #1

shift 1. Straight-lined basic dress of 1960s, hanging away from body, similar to CHEMISE dress (see under DRESSES) of 1957. The shift dress introduced a diagonal upward dart from the side seam, which improved the fit. 2. See under UNDERGARMENTS: CHEMISE.

shirtdress Straight-lined dress buttoned down the front, cut similar to a man's shirt, and worn with or without a belt. Side seams are often slashed and the hem rounded, similar to the tail of a

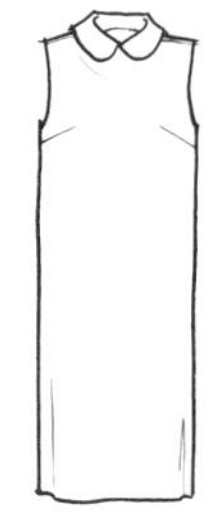

shift #1

man's shirt. Popular in 1967, it was a variation of the classic coatdress or shirtwaist and is revived occasionally.

shirtwaist dress Dress with top styled like a tailored shirt, usually buttoned from neck to waist, and made with either a full or straight skirt. Introduced in the 1930s, very popular in 1940s, and now a classic.

shirtwaist dress

skating dress Originally a close-fitting, long-sleeved bodice with brief thigh-length skirt flaring from a natural waistline, as worn by Norwegian skating star Sonja Henie in films of 1930s. Newer versions with long torsos and flared micro-skirts are worn by current popular figure skaters and Olympic champions.

skating dress

skimmer A-LINE DRESS or SHIFT (see under DRESSES) that hangs away from the body.

slip-dress Simple bias-cut dress with fitted top, straps over shoulders, and no waistline. This style of bias-cut dress of the 1920s and 1930s, as worn by movie star Jean Harlow, was revisited in 1966 and at other times since then.

∞**smock blouse** Child's dress of 1880s with the top bloused below the waistline by gathering with a ribbon pulled through insertion. Knee-length skirt sometimes consisted of two ruffles.

smock dress Dress cut with yoke that comes above the bust and straight hanging skirt attached with slight gathers to the yoke. Usually worn without a belt. Resembles the cut of a smock (see under SMOCK #1); the BABY-DOLL DRESS is similar in cut (see under DRESSES: BABY-DOLL DRESS #1).

square dancing dress Dress with puffed sleeves and a wide, full, circular skirt, frequently finished with a ruffle. *Der.* Worn for square dancing, an American type of country dancing.

squaw dress Full-skirted, minutely pleated dress with elaborate embroidery on long-sleeved bodice and in bands on skirt. *Der.* The word "squaw" is what European settlers called North American Indian women, but the word was not used by North American Indians.

step-in dress Coat-type dress that buttons or zips only three-quarters of the way down the front. Basic dress style since the 1940s.

strapless dress Décolleté dress ending just at top of bosom without shoulders or straps. Top held in place by boning, by shirring with elastic thread, or by using stretch fabric.

suit dress Used in 1960s to refer to a jacket and dress ensemble that resembled a tailored suit.

sundress Dress in strapless or halter style with matching or contrasting jacket, worn in warm weather.

sweater dress 1. Knitted dress styled like a long sweater, with or without knit-in waistline; introduced in 1940s and revived in the 1960s. 2. Two-piece, knitted dress made of matching pull-on sweater and skirt. An innovation of the 1930s, used at intervals since.

sweatshirt dress Extra-large sweatshirt coming almost to knees worn as a tunic over a skirt or pants—or alone as a dress.

∞**swiss dress** Child's two-piece costume worn in mid-1860s with tailored waist-length jacket and full skirt with fitted corselet at waistline.

tent dress Pyramid-shaped dress with broad flaring hem, sometimes made with accordion pleats. Introduced by Pierre Cardin in the spring of 1966.

three-armhole dress An easy-to-make dress promoted by pattern companies. Made in a wraparound style with the left arm going through the first and third armholes, while the right arm goes through the second. An innovation of the 1960s.

thrift-shop dress As it was first referred to in the 1960s, a second-hand dress found in U.S. thrift shops, in Paris flea markets, and in London's Portobello Road antique shops. Popular with the young, this type clothing influenced 1970s fashions for limp fabrics, muted-color prints, and old-fashioned trimmings. In the 1980s, antique dresses of other eras were described as *vintage*. See under VINTAGE FASHIONS.

toga dress 1. Asymmetric dress or at-home robe styled with one shoulder bare, the other covered; an innovation of the 1960s. *Der.* From Roman toga, which covered one shoulder. Also called *one-shoulder dress*. 2. See under DRESSES: POSTER DRESS.

torso dress A dress that follows the line of the body to the hips, where skirt is attached. Sometimes has a belt that sits low on the waistline. May also be made in PANTDRESS style (see under DRESSES).

trapeze dress Unfitted dress made with narrow shoulders that gradually widens, somewhat like a pyramid, to a very wide hem. Designed by Yves Saint Laurent for House of Dior in Paris in 1958. Same style resurfaced in fall of 1986.

trenchdress Shirtwaist dress with snap-front closing and cinch belt at waist. Top features epaulets and free-hanging panel to rib cage, similar to back of trench coat.

trapeze dress

trumpet dress Dress with flared flounce usually starting at knees. Worn in 1930s as tight-fitting dress to knees. Reintroduced in early 1980s as full-length evening gown and shift-type dress with flounce. *Der.* So called because it flares at the hem like a trumpet.

T-shirt dress Simple knit dress styled like an elongated T-shirt, an innovation of late 1950s. Newer versions may have extended cap sleeves, spaghetti sashes, and are often printed with silk screen designs.

tunic dress 1. Two-piece dress with a long overblouse worn over a separate narrow skirt or a one-piece dress designed to give this effect. Originally introduced in the 1850s as a ball dress with the upper skirt trimmed with lace and underskirt with a deep flounce. Popular in slim style in 1880s, 1910 to 1920, and worn intermittently since. 2. Minidress of the late 1960s that could be worn alone or over pants to make a pantsuit.

tunic dress #1

∞**watteau dress** (wa-toe′) Adaptations, especially in the 1850s, 1860s, and 1880s through 1890s. SACK dress (see under SACK #1) similar to those painted by Watteau. One version from the 1860s was styled with a FICHU (see under SCARVES) in front and WATTEAU BOX PLEATS (see under CLOTHING CONSTRUCTION DETAILS) in back and had an overskirt that was looped up at the sides revealing the underskirt. *Der.* Named for the artist WATTEAU, who portrayed such dresses in his paintings.

wedding dress Any dress worn by the bride for a wedding ceremony. Since about the 1840s, brides' dresses have been traditionally white and floor-length, with or without a train. Also called a *bridal dress.*

wedge dress Dress cut with very full, large shoulders and dolman sleeves. Entire dress tapers to hemline in a V or wedge shape.

weskit dress Tailored dress, usually full sleeved, combined with a vest.

wrap dress Dress style characterized by the fabric wrapping either to the front, similar to the kimono dress, or to the back. In either case, it has an extra lap that is approximately equal to the width of the skirt. *Der.* Term shortened from "wraparound" in late 1960s.

wrap dress

X-ray dress "See-through" dress made of transparent fabric worn with an opaque slip in early 20th c.

∞**york wrapper** Back-buttoned, high-necked woman's morning dress made of muslin, worn in 1813. Trimmed with alternate diamond-shaped pieces of needlework in front.

Zhivago dress See under DRESSES: RUSSIAN SHIRTDRESS.

---

dress à la constitution See under DRESSES: COSTUME À LA CONSTITUTION.

dress alikes Women who were friends and wore exactly the same dress or costume, a popular fashion in 1984.

∞**dress clip/dress holder** Device used for holding up woman's skirt, which has been fashionable periodically. In the 1840s a metal hook was attached at the waistline or belt to lift the skirt when walking. In the 1870s this was an elaborate device made with two pendant chains and clips used for holding up skirts. Also see under PAGE.

dress coat See under COATS AND JACKETS: SWALLOW-TAILED COAT.

dress elevator See under PORTE-JUPE POMPADOUR.

dress form Dressmaking form in the shape of human body onto which the designer or home sewer drapes fabrics or clothes while sewing. Also called *dressmaker's dummy, dressmaker's form,* or *model form.*

dress frock coat See under COATS AND JACKETS: CUTAWAY FROCK COAT.

dress holder See under DRESS CLIP.

dress improver See under UNDERGARMENTS: BUSTLE.

dressing gown/robe See under SLEEPWEAR AND LOUNGEWEAR.

dressing sacque See under SLEEPWEAR AND LOUNGEWEAR.

dress lounge (British usage) An early version of the dinner jacket. See under COATS AND JACKETS: DINNER JACKET.

dressmaker 1. Person, usually a woman, who makes clothing for private customers. From 1850 through 1920s, before ready-to-wear lines became available, dressmakers often worked in customers' homes to prepare seasonal wardrobes for the family. Also called a *seamstress.* 2. See under TAILORED.

dressmaker jacket See under COATS AND JACKETS.

dressmaker pin Fine STRAIGHT PIN with head used when sewing on delicate fabrics. Also called *silk pin.*

dressmaker's brim See under HEADWEAR.

dressmaker's dummy See under DRESS FORM.

dressmaker suit Woman's suit made with soft lines and fine details, as contrasted with man-tailored styles that have the sharply defined lines of a man's suit made by a tailor. Fashionable in 1950s and revived in the mid-1980s.

dressmaker swimsuit See under SWIMWEAR.

dress shield Protective device placed inside a dress under the arm to prevent staining of the garment by perspiration. The earliest dress shields (c. 1840s) were made of leather covered by fabric. Later versions were of fabric-covered natural or synthetic rubber.

dress shirt See under SHIRTS.

dress shoe See under FOOTWEAR.

dress sock See under HOSIERY.

dress wellington See under FOOTWEAR.

dressy casual Coined in 2001 to describe clothing appropriate for workers in management positions that was replacing CASUAL WEAR styles that had been accepted in the 1990s. The return to more formal business suits seemed to come as a result of an economic downturn. Also see under CASUAL FRIDAY.

†drill Durable cotton fabric made in a twill weave and similar to DENIM.

D-ring belt See under BELTS.

D-ring closing See under CLOSURES.

drip-dry See under DURABLE PRESS.

driving cape/sac See under COATS AND JACKETS: ALBERT DRIVING CAPE.

driving coat See under COATS AND JACKETS: BOX COAT #2.

driving glove See under GLOVES AND GLOVE CONSTRUCTION.

driving sac See under COATS AND JACKETS: ALBERT DRIVING CAPE.

driving shoe See under FOOTWEAR.

drop earring See under JEWELRY.

drop-front See under PANTS.

dropped shoulders See under SHOULDERS AND SLEEVES.

dropped skirt See under SKIRTS.

dropping See under FURS: LETTING-OUT.

drop waist/dropped waist/dropped waistline See under WAISTLINES: DROPPED WAISTLINE.

drum farthingale See under FARTHINGALE.

drum major's hat See under HEADWEAR.

dual or multichannel distribution System of merchandise distribution in which manufacturers sell their products through manufacturer-owned retail stores and also through other independent retailers.

du barry *adj.* Derived from the name of Marie Jeanne Bécu, Comtesse du Barry (1743–1793) and the last mistress of King Louis XV of France. This adjective was used to describe 19th-c. garments inspired by or derived from clothing items thought to have been worn by Madame du Barry and her contemporaries. See under DU BARRY CORSAGE; COATS AND JACKETS: DU BARRY MANTLE; and SHOULDERS AND SLEEVES: DU BARRY SLEEVE.

∞du barry corsage Bodice with a wide V-shaped front, worn by women from the 1830s to 1850, adapted from the style worn by Comtesse du Barry (1743–1793), last mistress of Louis XV of France. Also called *corsage à la du barry.*

∞du barry costume Style of dress worn by Marie Jeanne Bécu, Comtesse du Barry (1743–1793), last mistress of Louis XV of France. Consisted of a fitted bodice with low décolletage, long V to bodice front filled with lace RUCHING, elbow-length sleeves, and a full skirt.

du barry mantle See under COATS AND JACKETS.

du barry sleeve See under SHOULDERS AND SLEEVES.

Dubinsky, David See under UNION OF NEEDLETRADES, INDUSTRIAL, AND TEXTILE EMPLOYEES.

duchess See under HAIR ACCESSORIES.

†duchesse Lightweight lustrous satin fabric made of silk or rayon and dyed solid colors. Also called *duchesse satin.*

duchesse lace See under LACES.

∞duchesse pleat Used in mid-1870s for back pleats of a skirt, usually two *box pleats* on either side of center-back placket or seam.

duchesse satin See under DUCHESSE.

Duchess of Windsor (1896–1986) The former Wallis Warfield Simpson, an American divorcée who married Edward VIII of England. In order to marry Mrs. Simpson, the king abdicated and assumed the title of Duke of Windsor in 1936. World famous for her impeccable taste and conservative fashion leadership, and usually dressed by French couture, the duchess's wedding gown, designed by designer Mainbocher in Paris, became the most copied dress in the world—available at every price level.

†duck A wide range of strong, firm, plain-weave fabric that is usually made of cotton, linen, or cotton blended with manufactured fibers.

duckbills See under FOOTWEAR.

∞duckbill solleret See under ARMOR: SABATON.

duck-hunter See under COATS AND JACKETS.

ducks See under PANTS.

duck's-foot fan See under FANS.

duck shoe See under FOOTWEAR.

ducktail haircut See under HAIRSTYLES.

dude 1. (American) Used at a Western ranch for someone from the city or the East Coast. Also see under COWBOY/COWGIRL. ∞2. Used in 1890s for a dandy, an affected, or a fastidious man.

dude jeans See under PANTS.

duds Slang for clothes in general.

dueling blouse/shirt See under BLOUSES AND TOPS and SHIRTS.

duet pins See under JEWELRY.

duffel bag See under HANDBAGS AND RELATED ACCESSORIES.

duffel coat See under COATS AND JACKETS.

Duke of Windsor (1894–1972) Edward VIII, king of England, who reigned briefly in 1936 until he abdicated the throne to marry Wallis Warfield Simpson, an American divorcée. He was henceforth known as the Duke of Windsor. As the Prince of Wales he strongly influenced men's fashions in the 1920s and is credited with introducing such styles as the large panama hat, tab collar, windsor knot tie, double-breasted jacket with long roll lapel, Fair Isle sweater, white waistcoat worn as dinner jacket, guard's overcoat, seashore resort-type sportswear, and brown buckskin shoes.

dummy See under DRESS FORM.

dunce cap See under HEADWEAR.

dungarees See under PANTS.

dunstable See under HEADWEAR.

duo-length coat See under COATS AND JACKETS: ZIP-OFF COAT.

duplex print See under PRINTS, STRIPES, AND CHECKS.

duplicate In retailing, a sample copy of the manufacturer's PROTOTYPE that is used by sales representatives in selling styles in the line to retail buyers. Also called *sales sample.*

duppioni See under DOUPIONI.

†durable finish Any fabric finish that will withstand laundering and dry cleaning, and wear for a reasonable period of time.

†durable press (DP) The name given to a special finish that provides garments with shape retention, durable pleats and creases, durably smooth seams, and wrinkle resistance during use and after laundering. Some of the first fabrics that did not require ironing were called **drip-dry** fabrics.

dust cap See under HEADWEAR.

dust cover See under HANDBAGS AND RELATED ACCESSORIES.

duster 1. See under COATS AND JACKETS. 2. See under SLEEPWEAR AND LOUNGEWEAR: BRUNCH COAT.

∞dust gown An overskirt worn by women to protect the dress when riding horseback during the 18th c.

∞dust ruffle Ruffle inside of hem of full-length dress or petticoat to protect dress from becoming soiled when walking outdoors in late 19th and early 20th c. Also called *balayeuse* and *sweeper.*

dutch *adj.* Describes various types of clothing and accessories derived from or inspired by styles worn in the Netherlands.

dutch bob See under HAIRSTYLES: BUSTER BROWN.

dutch-boy cap See under HEADWEAR.

dutch boy heel See under FOOTWEAR.

Dutch cap See under HEADWEAR.

∞Dutch coat Man's short jacket worn in late 14th and 15th c., later called a jerkin. (Note: From 14th to 16th c., "Dutch" usually meant German.) See also under COATS AND JACKETS: MUFF'S CLOAK.

dutchman See under FOOTWEAR.

dutch neckline See under NECKLINES AND COLLARS: SQUARE NECKLINE.

∞dutch waist Woman's bodice without a point in center front worn with the wheel farthingale about 1580 to 1620. See under FARTHINGALE.

duvillier wig See under WIGS AND HAIRPIECES.

∞dux collar Man's narrow standing collar, with front corners turned down, worn from 1860s on.

dyeable shoe See under FOOTWEAR.

dyed sable See under FURS: SABLE.

†dyeing/dyes Coloring of fibers, yarns, fabrics, furs, and leather with natural or synthetic coloring agents, called dyes, that are relatively permanent.

ear band See under JEWELRY.

earclip See under JEWELRY: EARRING.

ear cuffs See under JEWELRY.

earmuffs 1. See under HEADWEAR. 2. See under HAIRSTYLES.

earring See under JEWELRY.

∞**ear string** Black ribbon, or strands of silk, worn through pierced left ear by men from latter part of 16th c. until around 1610.

∞**earthquake gown** Woman's warm gown, suitable for wear outdoors, made in England in 1750 in anticipation of a third earthquake, after two earlier quakes had taken place in London.

ease 1. *n.* Factor taken into consideration when drafting a pattern—allowing extra measure at bust, waist, and hips, so garment will fit comfortably, not skintight. 2. See under CLOTHING CONSTRUCTION DETAILS.

Easter bonnet See under HEADWEAR.

Eastern Orthodox cross See under CROSS #1.

Easter Parade 1. The practice of promenading in new spring clothes on Easter Sunday. A traditional event in New York City and other U.S. cities since the 1880s. People originally rode in carriages and strolled on city streets after church wearing their new clothes in celebration of Easter. In New York activities centered on areas around St. Patrick's Cathedral, at 50th Street and Fifth Avenue extending north to Central Park and south to 42nd Street. The idea of dressing in new spring finery on Easter Sunday dates back to Biblical and Roman times. 2. See under HEADWEAR: EASTER BONNET.

east-west bag See under HANDBAGS AND RELATED ACCESSORIES.

e-broidery See under EMBROIDERIES AND SEWING STITCHES.

ecclesiastical vestments See under CLERICAL DRESS.

écharpe See under SCARVES.

∞**echelles** (eh-shell') Decorative trim on front of woman's bodice made with braid, lace, or ribbon bows arranged in ladder-like effect. Popular from the late 17th c. to the late 18th c. *Der.* From the French, "ladder." Shown at ENGAGEANTES.

Eclipse Tie See under FOOTWEAR.

eco-friendly Apparel made from natural fibers that were grown without pesticides and finished with nonpolluting substances, or from manufactured fibers produced using less polluting processes, or from renewable resources or recycled materials such as plastic bottles. Also called *green clothes.*

écrasé See under LEATHERS.

edge (*neyge, age, oegge, egge*) 1. See under FOOTWEAR. ∞2. An ornamental border of the late 15th and early 16th c., usually made by a goldsmith, used on a headdress.

edge finish See under EMBROIDERIES AND SEWING STITCHES.

edge stitching See under EMBROIDERIES AND SEWING STITCHES.

edging Narrow, decorative border of lace, embroidery, braid, or fringe used for trimming on clothing, particularly at hem, sleeve, or neck.

EDI See under ELECTRONIC DATA INTERCHANGE.

edwardian *adj.* Descriptive of apparel that is in the style of the EDWARDIAN PERIOD (1901 to 1910). Pertaining to fashions based on a revival of such elements of dress of this period, including nipped waistlines, regency collars, capes, and neck ruffles worn by both men and women. These fashions were especially popular in the 1960s. *Der.* From period 1901–1910, when Edward VII was king of England.

edwardian coat/edwardian jacket See under COATS AND JACKETS.

Edwardian period From 1901 to 1910, when Edward VII, first son of Queen Victoria, was king of England. Popular styles that have been revived in later years include fitted frock or suit coats, top hats for men, and HOURGLASS SILHOUETTE in dresses for women, which were often worn with large, decorative hats.

edwardian suit Man's suit with close-fitting, fingertip-length jacket that has high notched lapels and narrow stovepipe pants. Copied from styles of 1900 to 1911, the reign of Edward VII, and popular in exaggerated form by London TEDDY BOYS in late 1950s. Made in velvet for women in late 1960s and early 1970s.

eelskin masher trousers See under PANTS.

eelskin sleeve See under SHOULDERS AND SLEEVES.

eel skirt See under SKIRTS.

egge See under EDGE #2.

egham, staines, and windsor See under HEADWEAR.

egret feathers See under FEATHERS: AIGRETTE.

Egyptian collar See under JEWELRY.

†Egyptian cotton High-quality, long-staple, strong, lustrous cotton produced along the Nile River with staple averaging ⅛″ to 1½″. Imported to make threads, laces, and fine fabrics.

egyptian lace See under LACES.

egyptian sandal See under FOOTWEAR.

Egyptian styles Dress of the ancient Egyptian civilization (c. 3000 to 300 B.C.) was generally draped from rectangles of linen fabric. Although changes in dress can be seen over this time period, styles remained remarkably consistent for almost 3,000 years. Among the basic costume types used throughout Egyptian history were a LOIN CLOTH, a skirt-like garment called a SCHENTI that wrapped around the waist, and a closely fitted, tubular wrapped dress often mistakenly called a KALASIRIS by costume historians but more accurately described as a **sheath dress.** In the period after 1575 B.C., new garments such as tunics and more elaborate garments made of sheer, accordion-pleated fabric were added.

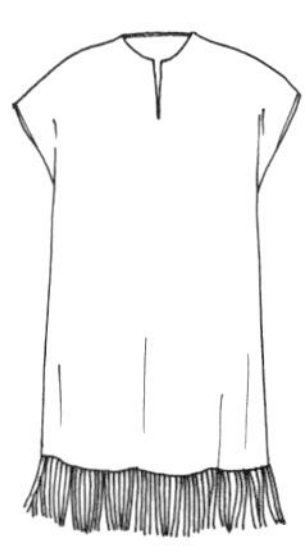

kalasiris

egyptian boy in schenti — sheath dress — pleated robe

Egyptian wig See under WIGS AND HAIRPIECES.

eiderdown See under FEATHERS.

eighths See under FOOTWEAR.

eight-point cap See under HEADWEAR.

Eisenhower jacket See under COATS AND JACKETS: BATTLE JACKET.

†elastic 1. *n.* Stretchable fiber, yarn, or tape. Generally, elastics are made from natural or synthetic rubber or ELASTOMERS such as SPANDEX and frequently are covered with some other fiber, yarn, or fabric. 2. *adj.* Describing any fiber, yarn, fabric, or garment that is stretchable. Synonym: *elasticized.* See under FOOTWEAR: ELASTIC-SIDED BOOT; HEADWEAR: ELASTIC ROUND HAT; JEWELRY: ELASTIC BRACELET; NECKLINES AND COLLARS: ELASTICIZED NECKLINE; UNDERGARMENTS: ELASTIC-LEG BRIEF; and WAISTLINES: ELASTICIZED WAISTLINE.

†elasticity Ability of fabric or yarn to stretch and return to its original shape when tension is released. Especially important for hose and pantyhose. In the years after 2000 many apparel fabrics were made of blends of ELASTOMERS with other fibers in order to improve the fit of the garment made from these fabrics.

elasticized See under ELASTIC.

†elastomer A synthetic material which has the excellent stretchability and recovery of natural rubber. SPANDEX, an elastomeric fiber, is an example.

elbow cuff See under CUFFS.

elbow-length sleeve See under SHOULDERS AND SLEEVES.

electric *adj.* Describes apparel or accessories powered by electricity.

electric dress See under DRESSES.

electric mole See under FURS.

electric-processed rabbit See under FURS: ELECTRIC MOLE and ELECTRIC SEAL.

electric seal See under FURS.

electric sock See under HOSIERY.

electric vest See under VESTS.

electrified sheepskin See under FURS.

electronic data interchange (EDI) Electronic transfer of information from one point to another by way of computers. For example, transmission of purchase orders from retailer to manufacturer, allowing more rapid response to consumer demands.

electronic retailing Sale of merchandise through electronic media. Television sales and shopping on the Internet are examples.

electronic textiles Textiles that have had sensors, power transmission, or other technical devices incorporated in order to create a network within the textile that makes possible the collection of data or transmission of information or generation of power to run electronic devices.

elephant-leg pants See under PANTS.

elephant sleeve See under SHOULDERS AND SLEEVES.

elevator heel See under FOOTWEAR.

Elevator shoe See under FOOTWEAR.

Elizabethan *adj.* Descriptive of clothing styles originating during, or inspired by, the styles of garments and accessories worn during the reign of Elizabeth I of England, from 1558 to 1603. Men's costume usually consisted of SLASHED and PANED TRUNK HOSE, DOUBLET (see under SLASHING. PANES, and TRUNKHOSE) and variations of the RUFF (see under NECKLINES AND COLLARS). Women's dress in the latter part of the period usually had a barrel-shaped skirt, called a FARTHINGALE, and a standing lace collar. Costume of this period is sometimes also called *Shakespearean dress.*

Elizabethan styles: woman wearing a wheel farthingale and man in trunk hose and canions

elkhide See under LEATHERS.

elliptic collar See under NECKLINES AND COLLARS.

embossed leather See under introduction to LEATHERS.

†embossing A process to produce a raised design or pattern in relief on fabrics by passing the cloth between hot, engraved rollers that press the design into the fabric. In heat-sensitive fabrics, embossing is permanent. In other fabrics, resin finishes are used to give fabrics a durable effect. Velvet or plush fabrics are embossed either by shearing or by pressing certain areas flat.

embroidered braid See under BRAIDS.

embroidered sweater See under SWEATERS.

EMBROIDERIES AND SEWING STITCHES

embroidery Fancy needlework or trimming using colored yarn, embroidery floss, soft cotton, silk or metallic thread. Usually done by hand, but may be made on a sewing machine or on mechanized machines, as is SCHIFFLI EMBROIDERY (see under EMBROIDERIES AND SEWING STITCHES). In the Mediterranean world gold embroidery was first made by Assyrians, and later copied by Egyptians, Greeks, and Romans. Each country in Europe developed its own type of embroidery. Needlework has been a popular craft for women since medieval times.

sewing stitches Utilitarian stitches made by hand or by sewing machine in the construction of apparel.

afghan stitch Simple crochet stitch made with a long, hooked needle and yarn in various colors used to make garments and afghans. Also called *tricot stitch* (tree'-co), *Tunisian crochet, railway,* and *idiot stitch.*

aloe thread embroidery Straw-like ALOE fibers satin-stitched, forming a raised effect. Popular in England in the late 19th c.

anglo-saxon embroidery Long surface stitches couched with metal or silk threads in an outline effect. See under EMBROIDERIES AND SEWING STITCHES: COUCHED EMBROIDERY. *Der.* Made by Anglo-Saxons in ancient times.

antique couching See under EMBROIDERIES AND SEWING STITCHES: ORIENTAL COUCHING.

appenzell embroidery (ap-en'-tsell) Fine Swiss DRAWN THREAD WORK (see under EMBROIDERIES AND SEWING STITCHES) used chiefly on handkerchiefs and fine muslin, a cottage industry in Switzerland. *Der.* Named for town in Switzerland where it originated.

appliqué See under alphabetical listing.

arrasene embroidery (ar-a'-seen) Introduced in the 1880s, embroidery with simple stitches using arrasene thread of silk or wool to create a velvetlike effect, which resembles CHENILLE. *Der.* Named for town of Arras, France.

arrowhead stitch/arrowhead Embroidery consisting of two stitches slanted to form an arrow, used singly or filled in with the satin stitch. First seen in Eastern embroideries—and often used as reinforcement or decorative element at top of a pleat or pocket—where it is called an **arrowhead.**

arrowhead stitch

assisi embroidery (ahs-si'-si) Cross-stitch embroidery in which the design image is outlined and the background is worked solidly in cross-stitch. Originated in the Assisi area of northern Italy. See under EMBROIDERIES AND SEWING STITCHES: CROSS-STITCH.

aubusson stitch See under EMBROIDERIES AND SEWING STITCHES: REP STITCH.

ayrshire embroidery Scottish form of embroidery on fine muslin with open filling stitches. Evolved from 18th-c. DRESDEN POINT and TAMBOUR WORK embroidery techniques. See cross-references under EMBROIDERIES AND SEWING STITCHES and also see under EMBROIDERIES AND SEWING STITCHES: MADEIRA EMBROIDERY.

back stitch Stitch used for hand sewing to prevent seam from ripping out; also used for embroidery, where it may serve as a basis for forming BLACKWORK embroidery patterns (see under EMBROIDERIES AND SEWING STITCHES). Each stitch goes back over space left by previous stitch, giving the appearance of a machine stitch.

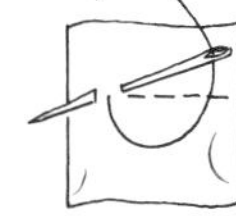
back stitch

backstitch Sewing term for reversing stitch on sewing machine. Used to secure threads at the beginning and ending of seams. Also called *staying a seam* or *stay.*

backstitch embroidery Outline embroidery similar to HOLBEIN work (see under EMBROIDERIES AND SEWING STITCHES), but single-faced rather than double-faced.

ballpoint embroidery See under EMBROIDERIES AND SEWING STITCHES: LIQUID EMBROIDERY.

bargello stitch (bar-gel′-low) Stitch worked vertically on canvas or scrim over a given number of threads to form a zigzag pattern. Visual impact results from color usage and stitch-length variations. Also called *flame* and *florentine stitch.*

bargello stitch

bar tack Embroidery detail used either to reinforce an area, such as the end of a buttonhole, or as a decorative device. Created by taking several parallel stitches of the same size, and then passing another thread around the parallel threads on the surface of the fabric. This latter thread is attached to the fabric only at the ends.

basket stitch Embroidery stitch resembling series of overlapped cross-stitches used to fill in backgrounds.

basket-weave stitch Needlepoint stitch in which a series of diagonal stitches (see under EMBROIDERIES AND SEWING STITCHES: CONTINENTAL STITCH) is most often used to fill background.

baste *v.* To stitch fabrics together either by hand or with large machine stitches to hold in place prior to sewing final seams. After stitching, bastings are removed.

basting *n.* Loose running stitches, often alternating long and short, used to hold sections of garment together before machine stitching.

beading 1. Embroidery in which beads of various kinds are sewn onto dresses, handbags, wedding dresses, sweaters, or blouses. 2. Lines of small embroidered eyelets as seen in WHITE-WORK embroidery (see under EMBROIDERIES AND SEWING STITCHES).

beauvais embroidery (bo-vay′) Tapestry-like embroidery done in many colors. *Der.* Named after city in France where it originated.

berlin woolwork Allover type of needlepoint embroidery (see under EMBROIDERIES AND SEWING STITCHES: NEEDLEPOINT #1) done on canvas, primarily using the cross-stitch. *Der.* Name dates from 1820, when Berlin wool was used. Also called *canvas* or *cushion style* embroidery.

blackwork Embroidery originally done in black silk on white linen, fashionable from 16th to 17th c. Sometimes worked in an all-over, continuous scroll design and used to decorate collars, cuffs, smocks, and handkerchiefs. In modern times the technique has evolved to geometric pattern stitching executed on an even-weave textile. When reversible, called HOLBEIN WORK (see under EMBROIDERIES AND SEWING STITCHES). Also called *spanish blackwork.*

blackwork

blanket stitch Embroidery stitch that looks like a series of connected U letters. Originally used to finish edges of binding on blankets, now for decorative effect. Also called *purl stitch* or *open buttonhole stitch.*

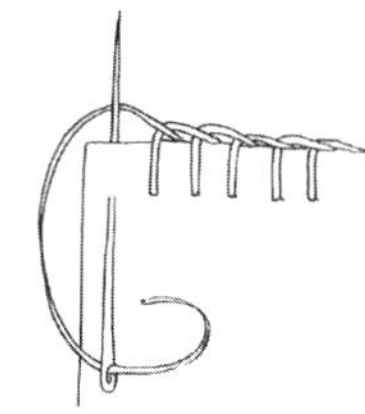
blanket stitch or open buttonhole stitch

blind stitch See under EMBROIDERIES AND SEWING STITCHES: SLIP STITCH.

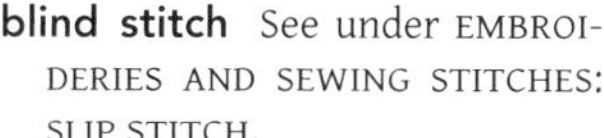

bonnaz (bo-nahz′) Machine embroidery, sometimes worked on canvas-based cloth, with all types of designs possible, since the operator can make the machine go in any direction. Used on sweaters, dresses, hats, gloves, and handbags. *Der.* Named after J. Bonnaz, a French inventor.

breton work Peasant embroidery in colored silk and metallic threads made in floral and geometric designs, largely done in chain stitch. Also called *brittany work. Der.* Originated in Brittany.

brick stitch/brickwork Blanket stitch used on flat fabric in continuous rows resembling brick wall. Also called *long and short stitch, featherwork, Irish stitch, tapestry shading stitch.*

brittany work See under EMBROIDERIES AND SEWING STITCHES: BRETON WORK.

brocade embroidery Embroidery made by needlework done over the designs of brocade fabric.

broderie anglaise See under EMBROIDERIES AND SEWING STITCHES: MADEIRA EMBROIDERY.

broderie russe See under EMBROIDERY AND SEWING STITCHES: RUSSIAN EMBROIDERY.

bullion embroidery (bull-yawn′) Embroidery stitched with fine gold wire. Also, embroidery done with gold or silver threads, or cords, originating in Phrygia (a region of what is now central Turkey) in ancient times.

bundle Embroidery stitch resembling a small bow knot. Made by taking three or four long loose stitches side by side, then placing a small stitch across at the center, drawing them together.

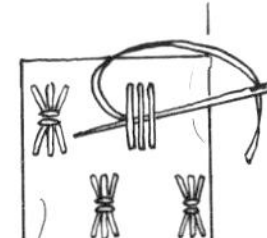
bundle stitch or sheaf stitch

bunka embroidery Japanese embroidery stitched with chain stitch with machine-made knitting yarn (frequently polyester) that is unraveled to reveal its textured effect. This yarn is threaded through a special needle, held like a pencil, and punched into the fabric (similar to making a hooked rug). Usually used to make scenes depicting figures, animals, birds, and floral patterns.

buttonhole stitch Embroidery stitch similar to BLANKET STITCH (see under EMBROIDERIES AND SEWING STITCHES) worked close together with an extra purl at the edge. Used for worked buttonhole. The basic stitch for NEEDLEPOINT LACE (see under LACES) and the most commonly used stitch for edging design areas in cutwork. Also called *close stitch.*

byzantine embroidery Appliqué work combined with decorative stitches done in the 19th c.

byzantine stitch Slanting embroidery stitch, similar to SATIN STITCH (see under EMBROIDERIES AND SEWING STITCHES), worked on canvas as a background filler over three or four vertical and horizontal threads in diagonal pattern.

cable stitch 1. Embroidery stitch, similar to chain stitch, with extra stitch connecting the links. See under EMBROIDERIES AND SEWING STITCHES: CHAIN STITCH #2. 2. Hand-knitting stitch that produces a vertical cable pattern by crossing groups of knitting stitches over each other. 3. Type of stitch used for smocking that consists of extra stitches between the dots.

california embroidery 1. Contemporary term used for leather stitching and braiding. 2. Primitive pre-spanish embroidery made in California by Indians using fishbone needle and animal substance for thread.

candlewick embroidery Tufts made with thick, loosely twisted cotton yarn called *candlewicking* and a large needle. Several stitches are taken in the same place, making loops that are cut to form a fluffy tuft.

canvas embroidery See under EMBROIDERIES AND SEWING STITCHES: BERLIN WOOLWORK and NEEDLEPOINT #1.

carrickmacross See under LACES.

cashmere work Rich, varicolored embroidery, frequently with inlaid APPLIQUÉ done in India, with complicated needlework covering almost entire surface; used for shawls.

catch stitch Loose stitch, like a series of letter Xs crossed near their top, used for bulky hems and for pleats in linings. Also called *cat stitch.*

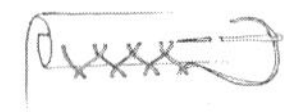
catch stitch

cat stitch See under EMBROIDERIES AND SEWING STITCHES: CATCH STITCH.

chain stitch 1. Embroidery stitch consisting of connected loops that form a chain on the front. 2. Machine stitch made by a commercial sewing machine done with a single thread, forming a chain on the back; used for hems and shoes and easy to remove. 3. Basic crochet stitch.

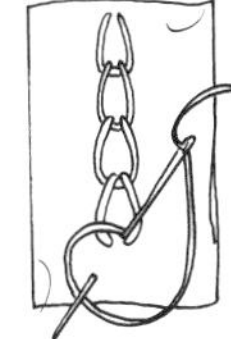
chain stitch #1

chainstitched embroidery Machine embroidery worked in different designs using a chain stitch. Used lavishly at necklines, cuffs, and hems of blouses imported from India in 1980s.

chenille embroidery (shen-neel′) Embroidery originating in France using fine CHENILLE yarn with flat stitches producing a soft, velvetlike pattern.

china ribbon embroidery See under EMBROIDERIES AND SEWING STITCHES: ROCOCO EMBROIDERY.

chinese embroidery Single- or double-faced embroidery that usually covers entire robe or gown with motifs of cherry blossoms, birds, butterflies, and dragons. Created in satin, chain, french knots, feather, and other stitches with silk, gold, or silver threads in an elaborate and intricate design. Originally floss and metal threads were worked over a painted design.

close stitch See under EMBROIDERIES AND SEWING STITCHES: BUTTONHOLE STITCH.

colbert embroidery (col-bare′) Embroidery made with colored threads outlining the designs and background covered with an allover pattern done in the satin stitch.

continental stitch Diagonal stitch on canvas worked over two threads; used to make the pattern or to fill in needlepoint backgrounds. Also called *tent stitch.* Shown at EMBROIDERIES AND SEWING STITCHES: NEEDLEPOINT.

couched embroidery/couching Decorative embroidery made by laying a long piece of yarn or embroidery floss flat while tiny stitches are worked around this yarn at intervals to fasten it tightly. Couching is often used to hold metal threads in place in METAL THREAD EMBROIDERY (see under EMBROIDERIES AND SEWING STITCHES).

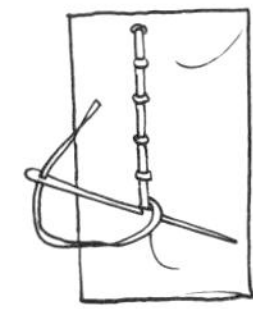
couching

counted cross-stitch embroidery Embroidery stitched on an even weave textile, using cross-stitch and usually worked with embroidery floss. Design is usually executed following a graph pattern.

counted thread embroidery A category of embroidery. For specific types see under EMBROIDERIES AND SEWING STITCHES: COUNTED CROSS-STITCH, BLACKWORK, ASSISI EMBROIDERY, NEEDLEPOINT, and DARNING.

crewel work Embroidery made with heavy, colored, crewel yarns, usually of loosely twisted two-ply worsted, on a linen fabric or ground. Motifs are filled in with many types of stitches.

crochet See under CROCHET #1.

cross-stitch Decorative stitch that forms an *X* worked in various colored yarns on a plain background. Also used in NEEDLEPOINT, CREWEL EMBROIDERY, BLACKWORK, and ASSISI EMBROIDERY (see under EMBROIDERIES AND SEWING STITCHES).

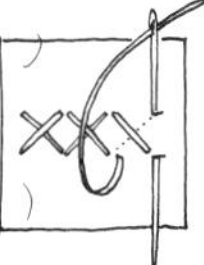
cross-stitch

cross-stitch embroidery Embroidered Xs made in a colored pattern on a plain ground.

cushion-style embroidery See under EMBROIDERIES AND SEWING STITCHES: BERLIN WOOLWORK.

cutwork (***opus scissum***) (oh′-puss siss′-um) Embroidery made by embroidering the edges of a design with BUTTONHOLE STITCHES (see under EMBROIDERIES AND SEWING STITCHES) and cutting out the background fabric around the designs. Threads called BARS or BRIDES (see under category introduction for LACES) are frequently used to connect the larger cut-out areas.

cutwork

czechoslovakian embroidery Bright-colored cotton, silk, or wool threads worked in geometric designs on linen. Made by counting stitches or using a traced pattern.

darning Vertical stitches woven through horizontal stitches in a one-to-one checkerboard pattern to resemble plain woven cloth. Used for mending holes or as an embroidery stitch to fill in backgrounds.

delhi work Chain- and satin-stitch embroidery made in India with metal and silk threads on satin or other fabrics.

detached chain stitch See under EMBROIDERIES AND SEWING STITCHES: LAZY DAISY STITCH.

diagonal stitch Embroidery stitch worked diagonally over double threads of canvas with stitches varying in lengths.

double-running stitch A basic BLACKWORK stitch (see under EMBROIDERIES AND SEWING STITCHES) that is a tiny running stitch, worked and then reversed, so that new stitches fill spaces and make a pattern similar to machine stitch. Also called *line stitch, square stitch, stroke stitch, two-sided stitch, holbein stitch,* and *Italian stitch.*

drawn fabric work Various embroidery stitches are executed with a fine thread and pulled tightly on canvas or an even weave textile, thereby compressing the yarns of the textile together to produce an open lacelike appearance. Also known as *pulled fabric work* or *pulled thread embroidery.*

drawn thread work (*opus tiratum*) (oh′-puss tir-ah′-tuhm) Open, lacelike design resulting from withdrawing yarns from an even woven textile. The remaining yarns are bundled together, stitched over, or folded back on each other to create pattern. For techniques used in drawn threadwork, see under EMBROIDERIES AND SEWING STITCHES: HEMSTITCHING, HARDANGER EMBROIDERY, HEDABO EMBROIDERY, AND NEEDLEWEAVING. Also called *withdrawn thread work* or *withdrawn fabric embroidery.*

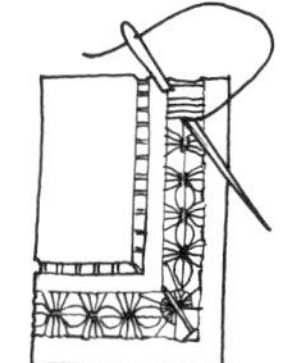
drawn thread work

dresden point German lace of drawn work type on linen, introduced in the late 16th c. Some of the threads are taken out and some left to form a pattern. Others were worked to form square meshes. After the pattern was made, it was embroidered with intricate stitchery. Also called MORAVIAN WORK.

e-broidery The use of yarns and threads with electrical properties to "quilt" electronic circuitry into a garment. Numerically controlled embroidery using conductive thread defines circuits, component connection pads, and sensing surfaces. The commercial embroidery process builds on current technology that allows precise control of the design, layout, and stitch patterns of the circuitry through the use of CAD processes.

edge finish Stitching that completes the edge of a garment to prevent woven fabrics from raveling and knits from curling. May be a turned edge, a hem, a facing, or a stitch such as serging or zigzagging.

edge stitching Machine stitching placed as much as ¼″ away from a garment seam or edge. Also see under EMBROIDERIES AND SEWING STITCHES: TOP-STITCH.

english work Excellent quality of embroidery done by Anglo-Saxon women from 7th to 10th c. Highly prized in England and on the Continent. Also called ***opus anglicum*** (oh′-puss ang′-lee-kum), term usually applied to clerical embroidery done in silk and metal threads.

eyelet embroidery Holes punched out and embroidery worked around the resulting hole, by hand or on a schiffli machine. Also see under EMBROIDERIES AND SEWING STITCHES: MADEIRA EMBROIDERY.

fagoting (*fagotting*) **1.** Stitch, similar to single FEATHER STITCH (see under EMBROIDERIES AND SEWING STITCHES), used to join two edges of fabric together in decorative openwork effect. **2.** Open-work embroidery done by drawing out horizontal threads of a fabric, then tying the vertical threads in groups to produce open spaces. 3. Method of joining two fabric edges together by means of embroidery stitches to produce a lacelike effect. Fagoting is part of a group of techniques known as insertions. Also see under EMBROIDERIES AND SEWING STITCHES: HEMSTITCHING and INSERTIONS.

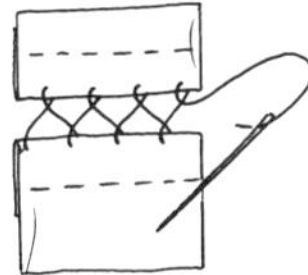
fagoting #1

feather stitch Decorative stitch that looks like a double row of Vs branching out first to one side, then to the other in a continuous line, which is a line stitch based on a buttonhole or chain stitch variation. See under EMBROIDERIES AND SEWING STITCHES: BUTTONHOLE STITCH and CHAIN STITCH #1.

feather stitch

featherwork See under EMBROIDERIES AND SEWING STITCHES: BRICK STITCH.

figure stitch See under EMBROIDERIES AND SEWING STITCHES: ORIENTAL COUCHING.

filling stitch Any type of embroidery stitch used to fill in a design, which may be outlined if desired. Also used to refer to couched grid stitches that are used to fill in a design (see under EMBROIDERIES AND SEWING STITCHES: COUCHED EMBROIDERY).

fishbone stitch Embroidery stitch resembling the backbone of fish, made with a long diagonal stitch crossed at one end with a small diagonal stitch worked in the opposite direction. Stitches usually branch out from a center line. Similar to FEATHER STITCH (see under EMBROIDERIES AND SEWING STITCHES), but worked closer together.

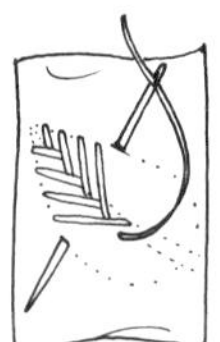
fishbone stitch

flame embroidery See under EMBROIDERIES AND SEWING STITCHES: FLORENTINE EMBROIDERY.

flame stitch See under EMBROIDERIES AND SEWING STITCHES: BARGELLO STITCH.

florentine embroidery Embroidery done on canvas in zigzag patterns and in shaded colors. Also called *flame embroidery,* from the effect it achieved, or *hungarian point embroidery.*

florentine stitch See under EMBROIDERIES AND SEWING STITCHES: BARGELLO STITCH.

free motion machine embroidery Creation of machine embroidery by using decorative thread and dropping the device in the sewing machine that moves the fabric. The embroiderer creates abstract or realistic designs by moving the fabric in various directions.

french knot Decorative stitch used for embroidery. Embroidery floss is looped around the needle, usually twice, after which the needle is pulled through the material, forming a small nub or ball of yarn on the surface.

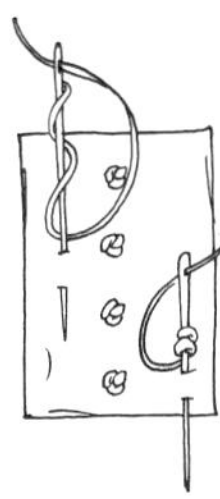
french knot

genoese embroidery Embroidery made by buttonhole-stitching over a cord on muslin and then cutting fabric away from between parts of the design, much like the whitework technique called Madeira work. Formerly used for dress and undergarment trimmings. See under EMBROIDERIES AND SEWING STITCHES: BUTTONHOLE STITCH and MADEIRA WORK.

gimped embroidery Embroidery where the design is achieved by arranging cord or vellum on fabric and covering with silk or gold threads. Obsolete name for this work is *laid embroidery.*

grass embroidery Native American and Caribbean embroidery using colored grasses as threads; usually done on deer skins or textiles.

gros point (groh pwanh) See under EMBROIDERIES AND SEWING STITCHES: PETIT POINT.

ground The base fabric onto which embroidery is applied or stitched.

hardanger embroidery (hard-ahn′-ger) Open form of needlework made in diamond or square patterns on even-weave cotton or linen cloth. The material is stitched with satin stitch–type squares called kosters blocks. This technique is native to the Hardanger region of Western Norway.

hedebo (head-day′-bow) Danish form of whitework that incorporates CUTWORK (see under EMBROIDERIES AND SEWING STITCHES) and NEEDLEPOINT LACE (see under LACES).

hemming stitch Long, loose slanting stitch placed through hem and caught to fabric with a very small stitch.

hemstitch 1. Ornamental stitch made by drawing out several parallel threads, then fastening together groups of vertical threads at regular intervals, making hourglass shapes. Uses: borders on blouses, handkerchiefs, etc. 2. Machine hemstitching done with a special attachment on sewing machines to give the same effect as above. When cut through the middle, each edge forms a PICOT EDGE (see under PICOT #2).

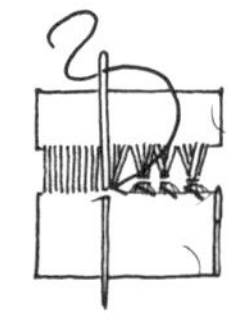
hemstitch #1

hemstitching Embroidery in which several parallel yarns are removed from the fabric and fine stitches used to catch group of three or four cross threads at regular intervals, giving an even openwork arrangement. This type of embroidery, done at the edge of the hem, holds and decorates at the same time.

herringbone stitch Name of the CATCH STITCH (see EMBROIDERIES AND SEWING STITCHES), when used for embroidery work. Also *russian stitch, russian cross-stitch,* and *witch stitch.*

holbein stitch See under EMBROIDERIES AND SEWING STITCHES: DOUBLE-RUNNING STITCH.

holbein work (hole′-bine) Delicate, reversible, outline embroidery, done in double-running stitch using exact geometrical or conventional designs; part of the embroidery technique called blackwork. Popular for trimming in the 16th c. *Der.* Named after the painter Hans Holbein (1465–1524) because design was so frequently shown on his paintings. Also called *romanian embroidery.* Also see under EMBROIDERIES AND SEWING STITCHES: BLACKWORK.

holy work/hollie work Fancy work in lace, cutwork, and embroidery carried out in religious subjects. Used in late 16th c. and by Puritans mainly in the 17th c. to decorate shirts, smocks, wristbands, and neckbands.

honeycomb stitch 1. Similar to BRICK STITCH (see under EMBROIDERIES AND SEWING STITCHES). 2. Machine- or hand-zigzag stitch used for smocking, mending, overcasting, attaching elastic, stretch lace, and blanket binding. Looks like three rows of diamond-shaped stitches.

huckaback stitch/huckaback embroidery Darning stitch worked horizontally on huck toweling, a fabric with ridges at intervals. Stitches are worked underneath the ridges across the fabric to make geometrical motifs. Also called *huck weaving, huck embroidery.*

hungarian embroidery 1. Brightly colored peasant garments and linens embroidered in conventional designs in flat or chain stitch, traditionally used on Hungarian peasant costumes. 2. A type of APPLIQUÉ done on blue, scarlet, or ecru linen.

hungarian point See under EMBROIDERIES AND SEWING STITCHES: FLORENTINE EMBROIDERY.

Indian embroidery Oriental embroidery done by Southeast Asian natives on cloth. May use small glass mirrors decoratively stitched to the fabric. For techniques employed see under EMBROIDERIES AND SEWING STITCHES: CASHMERE WORK, QUILTING, and CHAINSTITCH.

insertions Open, straight-line areas on fabric created either by joining two lengths of fabric with lace-type stitching or by withdrawing threads from fabric and either hemstitching across or drawing ribbon through the voids. Most often found on infants' garments or lingerie.

inverted-T embroidery See under EMBROIDERIES AND SEWING STITCHES: MATHILDE EMBROIDERY.

inverted-Y embroidery See under EMBROIDERIES AND SEWING STITCHES: MATHILDE EMBROIDERY.

irish stitch See under EMBROIDERIES AND SEWING STITCHES: BRICK STITCH.

italian stitch See under EMBROIDERIES AND SEWING STITCHES: DOUBLE-RUNNING STITCH.

janina stitch See under EMBROIDERIES AND SEWING STITCHES: ORIENTAL COUCHING.

japanese embroidery Elaborate embroidery worked with colored silk or metallic threads in satin stitch forming an intricate design or scene. Also includes padded and shaded embroidery.

laid embroidery See under EMBROIDERIES AND SEWING STITCHES: GIMPED EMBROIDERY.

laid stitch Embroidery stitch made by first placing yarn or floss on an area and then working small stitches over it to hold it in place. Similar to filling stitches used in CREWEL EMBROIDERY (see under EMBROIDERIES AND SEWING STITCHES).

lazy daisy stitch Single chain stitch used in embroidery with extra stitch added at outer edge to hold loop in place to form a petal. Also called *detached chain stitch.*

lazy daisy stitch

liquid embroidery Not actually embroidery, but rather a color applied to fabric with ballpoint-shaped paint tubes in special colors. Paint is squeezed from the tube to outline designs on a cloth. Creates a permanent and washable design resembling colored-thread embroidery. When seen at a distance, gives the general effect of embroidery.

lock stitch Machine stitch done with one thread coming across the top of the machine around the tension and through the needle. Other thread comes from a bobbin on the underside of the machine.

long and short stitch See under EMBROIDERIES AND SEWING STITCHES: BRICK STITCH.

madeira embroidery (ma-deer′-a) Eyelet embroidery cut or punched and then overcast. Made with openings arranged in floral or conventional designs on fine lawn or linen. Also called *broderie anglaise* (brod-e′-ree onh-glase′), *ayrshire, english, moravian work,* or *swiss embroidery. Der.* From island of Madeira, where work was originally done by nuns using very pale blue thread on a white ground.

mark stitch See under EMBROIDERIES AND SEWING STITCHES: TAILOR'S TACKS.

mathilde embroidery Wide, vertical band of embroidery used on front of women's dress in early 19th c. Later a band added around hem of dress. The combination with vertical band is called an *inverted-T* or *inverted-Y.*

metal thread embroidery Embroidery stitched in gold, silver, copper, or other metal and metallic threads. Often combined with silk thread embroidery and utilized in

Oriental embroidery, clerical embroidery, and military emblems and badges.

mock safety stitch A category of machine stitches used for seaming similar to the safety stitch but where the stitches are linked on either the underside or both sides of the fabric.

moravian work See under EMBROIDERIES AND SEWING STITCHES: MADEIRA EMBROIDERY.

mountmellick work Irish coarse WHITEWORK that uses cotton thread in raised stitches. For stitches used see under EMBROIDERIES AND SEWING STITCHES: BUTTONHOLE STITCH, CHAIN STITCH #1, CABLE STITCH #1, and PADDING STITCH #1.

needlepoint 1. Allover wool embroidery worked on open canvas or scrim with yarn in a variety of stitches. Used for household articles, fashion items, and decorative art. Regular-sized stitches called *gros point,* small stitches called *petit point.* Also called *canvas work.* 2. Lace made with a needle and thread. See under LACES: NEEDLEPOINT LACE.

needlepoint #1: continental stitch

needle tapestry work Embroidery worked in variety of stitches on canvas to resemble woven tapestries.

needleweaving Figure-eight stitching around the remaining lengthwise yarns of a textile after the crosswise yarns have been withdrawn. The grouping of the stitched threads can form lacelike patterns. Also called *swedish weaving, swedish darning.*

net embroidery See under EMBROIDERIES AND SEWING STITCHES: TULLE EMBROIDERY.

open buttonhole stitch See under EMBROIDERIES AND SEWING STITCHES: BLANKET STITCH.

openwork Embroidery made by drawing, cutting, punching, or pulling aside threads of fabric to form open spaces in the design. For various forms of OPENWORK see under EMBROIDERIES AND SEWING STITCHES: DRAWN FABRIC WORK, HARDANGER, and MADEIRA WORK.

opus anglicum See under EMBROIDERIES AND SEWING STITCHES: ENGLISH WORK.

oriental couching Series of long, straight stitches placed side by side, with each stitch intersected in center by short diagonal stitch. Also called *romanian stitch, janina stitch, figure stitch,* and *antique couching.*

outline stitch Variation of STEM STITCH (see under EMBROIDERIES AND SEWING STITCHES). Used to outline stems, leaves, and other motifs in embroidery.

overcasting 1. By hand: diagonal edging stitch that enters the fabric always from the same side and goes around raw edge to keep it from fraying. 2. By machine: a similar finish for raw edges made by a special sewing-machine attachment or a serger.

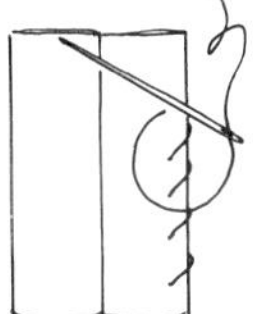

overcasting #1

padding stitch 1. Running stitch sometimes used in rows to provide a base for embroidery stitches (e.g., satin stitch) worked on top. 2. Diagonal rows of basting stitch, often used in tailoring to hold interfacing in place.

petit point Canvas embroidery worked from right to left, working over single threads through large meshes. The same stitch worked over double threads is called **gros point**.

Philippine embroidery Handmade embroidery done in dainty floral motifs by native women in the Philippine Islands. Used on lingerie.

picot stitching 1. See under EMBROIDERIES AND SEWING STITCHES: HEMSTITCH. 2. Stitch used in lacemaking that forms loops of thread extending from the edges.

piqué embroidery (pee-kay') Embroidery worked on firm fabric with white thread using corded outlines and various filling stitches. Used formerly for children's garments.

plain knitting stitch Basic stitch used in knitting. Made by putting one needle through a previous stitch, putting yarn around needle to form a new stitch, and pulling the new stitch through the old.

popcorn stitch Knitting or crocheting stitch that projects like a round pompon.

pulled fabric work/pulled thread embroidery See under EMBROIDERIES AND SEWING STITCHES: DRAWN FABRIC WORK and PUNCH WORK.

punch/punched work Embroidery of openwork type made by pulling certain threads aside with a needle or stiletto and securing them with embroidery stitches. Also called *rhodes work.*

purl stitch 1. Hand-knitting stitch that is the opposite of a knit stitch. Ribs can be formed through the selective use of knit and purl stitches. Making only purl stitches produces a fabric with a nubby surface that is the same on both sides. Alternating rows of knit and purl stitches produce a jersey fabric. See under JERSEY #1. 2. See under EMBROIDERIES AND SEWING STITCHES: BLANKET STITCH. 3. Double purl stitch is used in making buttonholes and is formed by throwing thread over the needle as it crosses.

quilting See alphabetical listing.

raised embroidery/raised work Embroidery done in the satin stitch over padding stitches to give a raised effect in the design. Used for monograms, scallops, etc. If heavily padded, called STUMP WORK (see under EMBROIDERIES AND SEWING STITCHES).

rep stitch Needlepoint half-stitch worked vertically on double thread canvas. Also called *aubusson stitch* (o-buss′-sohn).

rhodes work See under EMBROIDERIES AND SEWING STITCHES: PUNCH WORK.

rococo embroidery (row-cok′-oh) Type of embroidery made with very narrow ribbon, often called *china ribbon embroidery* or *silk ribbon embroidery.*

romanian embroidery See under EMBROIDERIES AND SEWING STITCHES: HOLBEIN WORK.

romanian stitch See under EMBROIDERIES AND SEWING STITCHES: ORIENTAL COUCHING.

running stitch Very tiny even stitches placed close together and used for seams, tucking, gathering, and quilting. Stitches and spaces between them should be equal in length.

russian embroidery 1. Embroidery done mainly in outline designs on holland linen. 2. Cloth and canvas embroidered with wool. Then canvas is removed to leave embroidery on background of cloth. Also called *broderie russe.*

saddle stitch Running stitch made in contrasting or heavy thread. Frequently used for trim on coats, sport dresses, and gloves.

satin stitch Embroidery stitch with straight, usually long, stitches worked very close together either vertically or slanted to fill in a large area (e.g., leaf or flower).

satin stitch

schiffli embroidery A form of shuttle embroidery done by a schiffli machine that can embroider the entire width of fabric at one time, in either elaborate or simple designs. Both eyelet and quilted designs may be made in many colors simultaneously.

seed embroidery Type of german embroidery done with seeds for floral motifs and chenille yarn for stems and leaves, formerly used for handbags.

seed stitch Embroidery stitch consisting of tiny individual back stitches, worked at random to fill background.

shadow embroidery/shadow work Embroidery worked with a catch stitch on the wrong side of transparent fabric.

shell stitch 1. Stitch taken at intervals on a tuck to produce scalloped effect. 2. A crochet stitch forming a shell design.

sicilian embroidery See under EMBROIDERIES AND SEWING STITCHES: SPANISH EMBROIDERY #2.

silk ribbon embroidery See under EMBROIDERIES AND SEWING STITCHES: ROCOCO EMBROIDERY.

slip stitch Small, almost invisible stitches with connecting thread hidden under fabric. Used to join an edge to a single layer (e.g., a hem or facing). Also called *blind stitch, blind hemming,* and *invisible hemming.*

slip stitch

smocking Decorative needlework used to hold gathered cloth together. The stitches catch alternate folds in elaborate honeycombed designs. Used especially on infants' and children's yokes and on waists and sleeves of dresses in late 19th and early 20th c., revived in early 1970s.

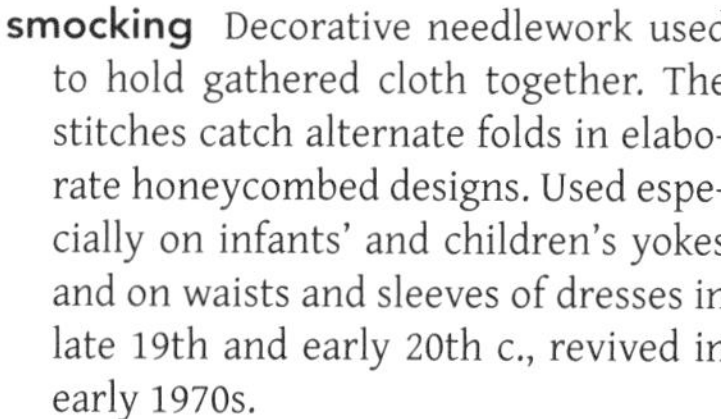

spanish blackwork See under EMBROIDERIES AND SEWING STITCHES: BLACKWORK.

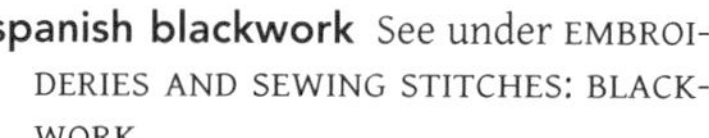

smocking or honeycomb stitch

spanish embroidery 1. Muslin worked with herringbone filling stitches. 2. Lacelike embroidery made on muslin or cambric with braid and closely placed buttonhole stitches. Also called *sicilian embroidery.*

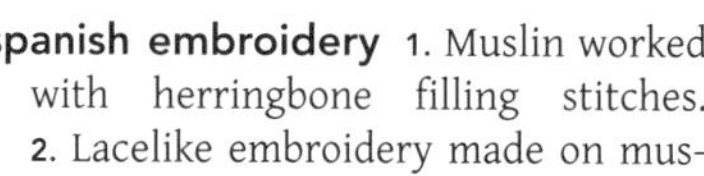

stem stitch 1. Embroidery stitch with overcast stitches placed close together making a rounded, raised, ropelike effect. 2. Outline stitch used in CREWEL WORK (see under EMBROIDERIES AND SEWING STITCHES).

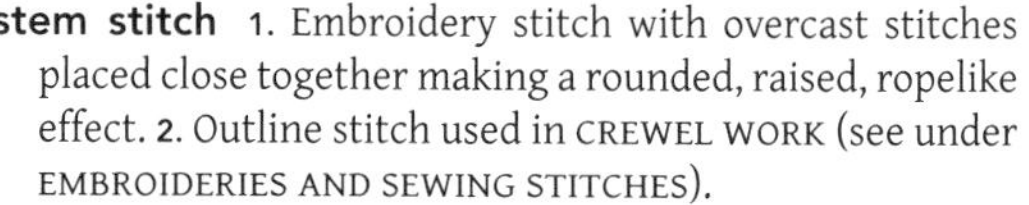

stump work Embroidery in high relief due to much padding, sometimes using horsehair, covered with satin stitches. Subjects are historical, Biblical, or allegorical scenes in grotesque shapes carried out with complicated stitchery. Also called *raised embroidery.*

swedish weaving/swedish darning See under EMBROIDERIES AND SEWING STITCHES: NEEDLEWEAVING.

swiss embroidery See under EMBROIDERIES AND SEWING STITCHES: MADEIRA EMBROIDERY.

tack To sew together lightly with invisible stitches or to join by sewing loosely at just one point.

tailor's tack Large stitch taken through two layers of fabric with a loop left between the layers. The layers are cut apart, leaving tufts in each piece to be used for guide marks in clothing construction. Also called *mark stitch.*

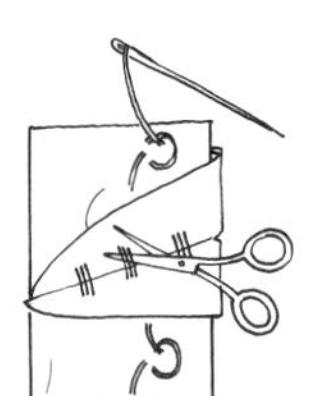
tailor's tacks

tambour work (tam-boor′) Embroidery worked with a hooked needle and a stitch on a double drum-shaped frame. The stitch is similar to the chain stitch. Originally used in Eastern embroideries, replaced by CHAINSTITCHED EMBROIDERY (see under EMBROIDERIES AND SEWING STITCHES).

tapestry shading stitch See under EMBROIDERIES AND SEWING STITCHES: BRICK STITCH.

tapestry stitch Short vertical stitches used in canvas work to imitate tapestry fabric.

tent stitch See under EMBROIDERIES AND SEWING STITCHES: CONTINENTAL STITCH.

top-stitch Machine stitching showing on the right side of the garment (e.g., the edge of a shirt collar).

tricot stitch See under EMBROIDERIES AND SEWING STITCHES: AFGHAN STITCH.

tulle embroidery (tool) Floss silk used on tulle, a netlike fabric, either by darning or by using embroidery stitches on a traced paper design. Formerly used for trimming party dresses. Also called *net embroidery.*

two-sided line stitch See under EMBROIDERIES AND SEWING STITCHES: DOUBLE-RUNNING STITCH.

venetian ladder work Outline embroidery done with two parallel lines of buttonhole stitches connected with cross-stitches at intervals in ladder-style. Used mainly for border work in conventional designs.

whip stitch Short overcast stitch used on rolled or raw edges.

whitework Embroidery executed in white thread on a white textile.

yugoslavian embroidery Bright-colored wool used on coarse linen in geometrical designs, done by counting threads, mainly in cross-stitch, double-purl, slanting, or satin stitch. Also spelled *jugoslavian.*

zigzag stitch Sewing machine stitch giving a saw-toothed effect used to connect 2 flat pieces of fabric together. Also used on edges of fabric to eliminate fraying.

---

emerald See under GEMS, GEM CUTS, AND SETTINGS.

emerald cut See under GEMS, GEM CUTS, AND SETTINGS.

emo One of the style tribes that is described as "deeply emotional." Associated fashions include drainpipe jeans for boys and tight pants, T-shirts, and heavy makeup for girls.

emo hair See under HAIRSTYLES.

emperor shirt See under SHIRTS.

empiecement Trimming effect with outer fabric cut away and edges embroidered to show a sheer fabric underneath. Popular in late 19th and early 20th c.

empire (em′-pire or ohm-peer′) *adj.* Descriptive of styles worn at the time of the First Empire in France (c. 1800–1814) or those derived from or inspired by styles of this period.

∞**empire bodice** (em′-pire or ohm-peer′) Dress bodice of late 1880s giving a short-waisted effect by arranging several silk scarfs around the waist and tying them on one side or in the back.

empire bonnet See under HEADWEAR.

empire coat See under COATS AND JACKETS.

empire coiffure See under HAIRSTYLES.

empire cone hairstyle See under HAIRSTYLES.

empire dress See under DRESSES.

∞**empire house gown** (em′-pire or ohm-peer′) NEGLIGÉE COSTUME of mid-1890s with high collar and tucked yoke, crossed with ribbons tied in a bow at the center front. Floor-length, the gown fell in folds from a yoke and had three-quarter-length sleeves that were trimmed with ruffle at the wrist.

empire jacket See under COATS AND JACKETS.

empire jupon See under UNDERGARMENTS: HOOPS.

Empire period See under EMPIRE STYLES.

empire petticoat See UNDERGARMENTS: HOOPS.

empire skirt See under SKIRTS.

empire stays See under UNDERGARMENTS.

Empire styles (em′-pire or ohm-peer′) France had two Empire periods. The First Empire (1804–1815), under the reign of Napoleon Bonaparte, and the Second Empire, under the reign of Louis Napoleon (1852–1871). **1.** During the First Empire the predominant styles for men consisted of tight-fitting breeches or trousers; double-breasted jackets with high collars; short, single-breasted waistcoats cut straight at hem; and cravats or neck cloths. Women wore dresses like those described under EMPIRE DRESS #1, often with short jackets (see under COATS AND JACKETS: SPENCER), and BONNETS (see under HEADWEAR). **2.** During the Second Empire men wore various types of coats (see under COATS AND JACKETS: FROCK COAT, MORNING COAT, and DRESS COAT) and trousers of a moderately loose fit with TOP HATS (see under HEADWEAR). Women's dresses had a natural waistline, were closely fitted through the bodice, and had extremely full skirts that were supported by hoops after 1857. The styles worn by the Empress Eugénie (see under EUGÉNIE, EMPRESS) were important fashion influences.

empire waistline See under WAISTLINES.

empress eugénie hat See under HEADWEAR: EUGÉNIE HAT.

Empress Josephine See under NAPOLEON.

∞**empress josephine gown** See under DRESSES.

empress petticoat See under UNDERGARMENTS.

†**end** **1.** An individual lengthwise yarn, which may be either SINGLE, PLY, or CORD YARN. **2.** A remnant or short piece of fabric.

enclosed seam See under CLOTHING CONSTRUCTION DETAILS.

endangered species As it relates to fashion, species of animals and birds that are becoming rare because they are being slaughtered for clothing, accessories, adornment, and other reasons. International treaties, federal laws, and state laws have been enacted to protect endangered species. For protective legislation concerning furs, see under introduction to FURS. Also see under AUDUBON PLUMAGE LAW.

endorsement Use of an individual, usually a celebrity, or an organization that states, in an advertisement or in public, approval and preference for a particular product. Generally those making endorsements are paid.

∞**engageantes** (ahn-gahj′-eh-ahnt) 1. (French) Two or three tiers of lace, or sheer-fabric ruffles, used as cuffs on sleeves from end of 17th through 18th c. 2. Detachable undersleeves of white fabric edged with lace or embroidery, worn by women from 1840s until about 1865. Also see under SHOULDERS AND SLEEVES: ISABEAU SLEEVE.

engageantes and echelles on an 18th c. dress

engagement ring See under JEWELRY.

engineered print See under PRINTS, STRIPES, AND CHECKS.

engineer's boot See under FOOTWEAR.

engineer's cap See under HEADWEAR.

english coat See under COATS AND JACKETS.

english cottage bonnet See under HEADWEAR: BIBI BONNET.

english drape 1. Style used for men's single- or double-breasted long suit jacket in 1930s and 1940s. Distinguished by fullness at top of tapered sleeve, width through the chest, and fitted waist. Worn with trousers made with high-rise waistline and pleats at side front. 2. Similar style jacket adopted for women's suits in 1930s and 1940s; revived in 1980s.

english drape suit #1

english embroidery See under EMBROIDERIES AND SEWING STITCHES: MADEIRA EMBROIDERY.

english farthingale See under FARTHINGALE.

english hood See under HEADWEAR.

english rib sock See under HOSIERY.

english thumb See under GLOVES AND GLOVE CONSTRUCTION.

english walking jacket See under COATS AND JACKETS.

english work See under EMBROIDERIES AND SEWING STITCHES.

english wrap See under COATS AND JACKETS: PALETOT.

ensemble (ahn-sahm′-bl) 1. An entire costume, including accessories, that is worn together. 2. More than one item of clothing designed and coordinated to be worn together, such as a dress and coat.

en tablier (ahn tahb′-lee-yeh) Trimming arranged in crosswise rows of lace or ribbon spaced down front panel of dress, sometimes from neck to hem or from waist to hem. Used particularly in 19th c. *Der.* French, *tablier,* "apron."

en tous cas See under UMBRELLAS AND PARASOLS.

entre deux (on′-tray dew) Fine, narrow openwork insertion set into the seams of dainty lingerie used from late 19th c. until mid-1930s.

envelope combination See under UNDERGARMENTS.

envelope bag See under HANDBAGS AND RELATED ACCESSORIES: CLUTCH BAG.

envelope pleat See under CLOTHING CONSTRUCTION DETAILS.

environmental scanning The ongoing process of surveying a variety of resources for economic, political, social, technological, and cultural conditions for insights into how they impact fashion.

environmentally friendly *adj.* Describes products that are manufactured using methods and materials which do not harm the natural environment.

envoy hat See under HEADWEAR.

epaulet/epaulette (ep′-oh-let) 1. Ornamental shoulder trim used on military uniforms, originally consisting of gold braid looped to form fringe around the edge. 2. Shoulder trim used in 19th c., very popular in 1860s. 3. Flat band of fabric, sometimes fastened with a button on shoulders of uniforms; also used on military-style civilian coats and jackets (e.g., trenchcoats). Very fashionable in 1980s on blouses, coats, dresses, shirts, and jackets. ∞4. See under ARMOR: EPAULIÈRE.

epaulets #3

epaulet shirt See under SHIRTS.

∞**epaulet sleeve** See under SHOULDERS AND SLEEVES.

épaulière See under ARMOR.

ephebi (ef-he′-bee) Military cape similar to the CHLAMYS (see under CAPES, CLOAKS AND SHAWLS), worn by Greek soldiers.

epitoga See under CAPES, CLOAKS, AND SHAWLS.

equestrienne costume (ee-kwes-tree-enn′) Riding habits for women, which were called by this name from about the 1840s; consisted of a full-length gathered skirt worn with a tailored jacket, sometimes double-breasted with REVERS and a PEPLUM. Accessories included a tall top hat with veiling hanging down the back, a tailored shirt, and necktie or stock. In the early 20th c., the skirt was uneven in length—shorter on right side, longer on left—looped up when walking, let down when mounted sidesaddle. By 1908 drill breeches and boots were worn under a short skirt. A DERBY, FEDORA, TRICORN, or SAILOR HAT (see under HEADWEAR) was worn over a braided club hairstyle. By 1910 or 1912, women rode astride wearing a divided skirt that buttoned closed in front. Also see under ACTIVEWEAR: RIDING HABIT. *Der.* Latin, "woman skilled in horsemanship."

equipage See under ETUI.

ermine See under FURS.

ermine cap See under HEADWEAR: LETTICE CAP.

erogenous zone theory (e-raj'-ah-nas) Theory expounded by James Laver, noted British authority on historic costume, who believed that emphasis in dress tends to shift from one erogenous zone of the body to another (e.g., when short hemlines are worn, the legs are in focus; when plunging necklines are worn, the bosom or breasts are emphasized). In Laver's theory, the cycle lasts about seven years between shifts of interest from one zone to another and is responsible for fashion change.

∞**escarelle** (es-ka-rel') Pouch or purse attached to a waist or hip belt in the 14th and 15th c. Frequently, this style of belt also had an insertion point for a knife to be attached and worn on the body.

esclavage See under JEWELRY.

esmeralda cloak See under CAPES, CLOAKS, AND SHAWLS.

espadrille See under FOOTWEAR.

etched-out fabric See under BURN-OUT fabric.

eternity bracelet See under JEWELRY: SLAVE BRACELET.

eternity ring See under JEWELRY.

ethnic *adj.* Descriptive of fashionable clothing and accessories derived from or inspired by native or national styles of nations or cultures including: Africans, Asians, South Americans, Europeans, and North American Indians. Became a trend in the 1960s and is periodically a fashion influence for designers.

eton cap See under HEADWEAR.

eton collar See under NECKLINES AND COLLARS.

eton crop See under HAIRSTYLES.

eton jacket See under COATS AND JACKETS and ETON SUIT.

eton jacket bodice See under COATS AND JACKETS.

eton suit Uniform worn by junior schoolboys at Eton College, Eton, Buckinghamshire, England, from 1798 until 1967, that consisted of a waist-length, square-cut jacket with wide lapels and small turned-down collar. It was worn with a white shirt having a white starched collar, narrow, dark tie, and single-breasted vest. The jacket was originally blue or red, and became black in 1820 when England went into mourning for George III. Trousers were usually gray. The basic style was adapted as a dress-up suit for very young boys in the U.S. and England from late 19th through early 20th c. and elements such as the jacket, cap, and tie are revived periodically.

∞**etui** (a-twe) An ornamental case worn hanging from the waist by women in the 17th and 18th c. to hold thimble, scissors, or scent bottle. Also called *equipage.*

EU See under EUROPEAN UNION.

eugénia, the See under CAPES, CLOAKS, AND SHAWLS.

eugénie collarette See under NECKLINES AND COLLARS.

∞**eugénie dress** See under DRESSES.

Eugénie, Empress (yoo-je'-nee) Marie Eugénie de Montijo de Guzmán (1826–1920), Spanish wife of Napoleon III, and Empress of France (1853–1871), who exerted great influence on fashion during the 1850s and 1860s. CHARLES WORTH was her couturier and is credited with designing the PRINCESS-STYLE DRESS for the Empress.

eugénie hat See under HEADWEAR.

eugénie paletot See under COATS AND JACKETS.

eugénie petticoat See UNDERGARMENTS: BUSTLE.

European Union (EU) Major trading bloc consisting of European countries that petition to join and meet specified economic criteria.

even checks See under PRINTS, CHECKS, AND STRIPES: CHECKERBOARD CHECKS.

evening *adj.* Characterizes attire worn primarily in the evening, especially for formal and informal occasions. See under FOOTWEAR: EVENING SHOE/EVENING SLIPPER; SKIRTS: EVENING SKIRT; and UNDERGARMENTS: EVENING PETTICOAT and EVENING SLIP.

evening gown See under FORMAL ATTIRE.

evening wear Used in the retail industry to refer to clothes worn primarily in the evening for formal or informal occasions.

evening wrap **1.** Wrap worn for formal functions, may be styled like a shawl, a cape, a stole, or a coat. **2.** See under COATS AND JACKETS.

even plaid See under PLAIDS AND TARTANS.

even priced Prices for goods that end with an even number. Such endings as .95 or .99 are often assigned to sale merchandise, while .00 or easily divisible numbers are used for nonsale prices.

everett See under FOOTWEAR.

examining gown Simple wraparound gown or one slit up the back and fastened with ties, used by patients in doctors' offices. Originally in coarse muslin, most are now made of disposable, nonwoven materials.

exclusive brand See under BRAND.

exclusive contractor A supplier that contracts to work for just one retail company.

exclusive orders Merchandise orders that, through a special arrangement between vendor and retailer, are sold only to one particular store or buyer.

exercise sandal See under FOOTWEAR: EXERCISE SANDAL and DR. SCHOLL'S EXERCISE SANDALS.

exercise shorts See under SHORTS: ATHLETIC SHORTS.

exercise suit See under ACTIVEWEAR: AEROBIC WEAR and SAUNA SUIT.

expandable bracelet See under JEWELRY.

export agent A representative in a foreign country who assists a U.S. apparel manufacturer with exportation of products produced in that country.

express stripe See under PRINTS, STRIPES, AND CHECKS.

extended marketing channel See under MARKETING CHANNEL.

extended shoulder/extended sleeve See under SHOULDERS AND SLEEVES.

extra large 1. Size range used along with SMALL, MEDIUM, and LARGE for women's sweaters, housecoats, nightgowns, panties, girdles, and panty girdles. 2. Size for men's sport shirts, sport jackets, sweaters, and robes.

extra-long knit shirt See under SHIRTS.

extra small Size designation used along with SMALL, MEDIUM, LARGE, and EXTRA LARGE for men, women, and children in such categories as sweaters, knit and sport shirts, sport jackets, nightgowns and pajamas, robes, gloves, and girdles and panty girdles. Abbreviated XS.

extra-tall Men's size corresponding to a chest measurement of 38″–48″ and a height of 6′3″ to 6′6½″.

eye agate See under GEMS, GEM CUTS, AND SETTINGS: AGATE.

eye candy Something that is visually exciting. In fashion, most often applied to jewelry, lingerie, or other decorative garments.

eyeglass case See under EYEWEAR.

eyeglass chain See under EYEWEAR.

eyeglasses See introduction to under EYEWEAR.

eyelet 1. Circular metal ring clamped on fabric or leather through which a lacer is pulled; first used about 1828. Also see under CLOSURES: BLIND EYELET. 2. Holes punched in fabrics for lacings or as decoration that are embroidered around the edges to keep them from fraying. 3. See under EMBROIDERIES AND SEWING STITCHES: EYELET EMBROIDERY.

eyestay See under FOOTWEAR.

EYEWEAR

eyewear Accessories worn over the eyes to improve the vision or to protect the eyes from the glare of the sun. The most common form of eyewear is called **eyeglasses** or **glasses.** Conventional eyeglasses are made with plastic or glass lenses that fit into metal or plastic frames with TEMPLES (see under EYEWEAR) that extend over top of ears. **Transition lenses,** which darken as the light increases and vice versa, were one of the innovations of the 1980s. Glasses were first introduced in Italy in the late 13th c., where they were an indication of wisdom, as few people could read. During the 17th c. colored lenses were introduced for protection from the sun. In the 1960s glasses suddenly became a fashion item. Originally called *spectacles.*

antireflective coating A coating applied to lenses so that reflection of light from the lens is eliminated, thereby improving vision, reducing eye fatigue, and making the eyes more visible.

aviator glasses Sunglasses with lens wider at sides of face and sloping toward nose. Made in imitation of goggles worn by early airplane pilots. Also called *flyboy glasses. Der.* From style worn by aviator pilots.

ben franklin glasses Small elliptical, octagonal, or oblong lenses with delicate metal frames, worn perched on the middle of the nose. A fad started in 1965 imitating the glasses seen in paintings of Benjamin Franklin, U.S. statesman. Also called *granny glasses.*

ben franklin glasses

bifocals Glasses with lenses divided in two parts for near vision and distance. In the early 1980s customers had the option of purchasing lenses in which the line dividing the two fields of vision was made invisible.

bow See under EYEGLASSES: TEMPLE.

bug-eyed glasses Bulging convex sunglasses shaped like the eyes of an insect. Some glasses are made of a solid piece of plastic shaped to head and face. Unusual colors such as red are sometimes used to give a psychedelic appearance to viewer. An innovation of the late 1960s.

butterfly glasses Large, rimless sunglasses with lenses made in the shape of a butterfly's wings, a fashion of the late 1960s.

clip-on sunglasses Sunglasses without frames made with a clip at the center or on either side that allows them to attach over the top of prescription glasses.

Some, called **flip-up glasses,** have a hinge that permits them to flip up.

color-graded glasses Tinted glasses with the lens color varying from light at the bottom to dark at the top. Designed for use in a car; maps can be read through the clear section at bottom.

Courréges glasses Sunglasses, introduced by Andrè Courréges in 1966, made of a strip of opaque plastic that circled the face extending to the ears. Through the center of the plastic was a tinted horizontal sliver of glass or plastic. Copied widely, they became known by the name of the French couturier who originated the style.

eyeglass case Container for storing eyewear when it is not in use. May be plain or decorative.

eyeglass chain/eyeglass cord Chain or cord that has loops that slip over the temples of glasses so that when glasses are not being used, they can be worn around the neck. May be decorated with crystals, pearls, beads, and the like or left plain.

eyeglasses See under introduction to EYEWEAR.

flip-down glasses Ben Franklin–type glasses with separate hinged lenses that pull down so that eyeshadow or mascara can be applied. Also used for inserting contact lenses.

flip-up glasses See under EYEWEAR: CLIP-ON SUNGLASSES.

flyboy glasses See under EYEWEAR: AVIATOR GLASSES.

folding glasses Glasses with both folding bridge and temples that condense to a 3″ size for easy carrying.

glasses See under introduction to EYEWEAR.

goggles Protective glasses, usually with impact-resistant lenses in wide frames wrapped around temples, held on by strap around head and worn by construction and other types of workers as eye protection when they use power tools, do hammering, drilling, etc., and by auto racers and skiers, and for other sports. Goggles for underwater swimming are watertight.

goggles

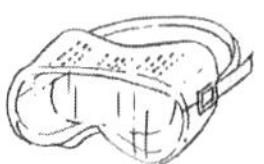

safety goggles

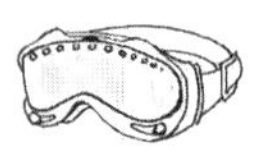

sport goggles

swim goggles

granny glasses See under EYEWEAR: BEN FRANKLIN GLASSES.

half-glasses Glasses for reading that have shallow lenses, allowing wearer to look over top for distance viewing.

half-glasses

harlequin glasses (har′-lee-kwin) Glasses with diamond-shaped lenses. Eyeglasses slanting up to corner peaks.

horn rims/horn-rimmed glasses Eyeglasses with heavy frames of dark horn or mottled brown plastic imitating horn, very popular in the 1940s and 1950s.

instant sunglasses Lightweight, impact-resistant, shaped plastic that is placed behind regular glasses when outdoors.

Lennon specs Sunglasses with circular metal-rimmed lenses and thin metal temples. *Der.* John Lennon, member of the English rock group, The Beatles, made this style popular. Originally English workmen's sunglasses.

lifestyle eyewear Used in retailing eyeglasses to describe frames and lens selections that emphasize personal image and/or specific use such as computer, sports, career, and evening eyewear.

lorgnette (lorn-yet′) A pair of eyeglasses attached to a handle, or a pair of opera glasses, similarly mounted; usually hinged so eyeglasses may be folded when not in use. Used since late 19th c. *Der.* French *lorgner,* "to spy or peep."

louvre sunglasses (loo′-vra) Molded plastic sunglasses made with tilted slats similar to venetian blinds. Introduced from France in mid-1980s.

monocle Men's single eyeglass used for one eye, held in place by cheek and forehead muscles. When not in use, suspended on a ribbon around the neck. Dandies of c. 1820 called this device a **quizzing glass** and had the glass fixed in the head of a cane.

monocle

opera glasses Small binoculars used to provide close-up view at the opera or theater. Usually a fashionable accessory decorated with mother-of-pearl, gold, brocade, etc.

owl glasses Extra-large sunglasses with very wide, heavy rims that give the look of a surprised owl.

pince-nez (pants-nay′) Eyeglasses without ear pieces, kept in place by spring gripping the bridge of the nose. *Der.* French "nose-pincher."

pince-nez

polarized sunglasses Sunglasses with lenses that polarize light, especially effective in cutting down glare. Especially popular with those engaged in outdoor sports such as fishing and hunting.

progressive lens Lens that gradually adds focal power across its surface so that the same lens permits distant, intermediate, and close viewing. No lines are visible at the point where the focus changes.

quizzing glass See under EYEWEAR: MONOCLE.

rimless glasses Lenses attached to metal nose piece and ear pieces but not outlined by a frame. Popular from 1930s to 1940s, and revived in 1960s and after.

safety glasses Glasses made of impact resistant lenses and safety frames worn by industrial and construction workers. Also called GOGGLES (see under EYEWEAR).

shades Slang for sunglasses.

specs Slang for SPECTACLES. See under introduction to EYEWEAR.

spectacles See under introduction to EYEWEAR.

sunglasses Eyeglasses with dark-colored lenses to cut glare and the brightness of the sun; invented about 1885, made popular by movie stars in Hollywood in 1930s and 1940s, and prevalent in fashion from 1960s to the present in various shapes and sizes. Some made with mirrored lenses.

temple Shaft attached to side of glasses, curved at one end to fit over the ear. Also called *bow*.

tortoiseshell glasses Glasses with frames made from imitating tortoiseshell, which is an attractive, brown, speckled material obtained from the shell of the hawksbill turtle. The turtle has been hunted to near extinction, and the use of the natural material has been banned. Heavy tortoiseshell frames became popular in the 1930s, 1940s, and 1950s, replacing metal frames and rimless glasses worn earlier.

transition lenses See under introduction to EYEWEAR.

trifocals Prescription glasses worn to correct vision, made similarly to BIFOCALS (see under EYEWEAR), but with three sections. The lowest section for reading; the middle section for intermediate vision for drawing, playing the piano, playing cards, or using computers; and the uppermost section for distance.

wraparound glasses Sunglasses made of a molded piece of plastic shaped like a headband that is cut out for insertion of the lenses. Similar to COURRÉGES GLASSES (see under EYEWEAR) but with a wider viewing area.

fabala See under FURBELOW.

fabric See under TEXTILE FABRIC.

fabrication The process of selecting fabrics for a seasonal line, groups within a line, and each style within a group.

†**fabric count** In the textile industry, the number of lengthwise (warp) and crosswise (filling) yarns in a square inch of woven fabric. Expressed by first writing the number of warps, then the number of fillings (e.g., 72 × 64 would mean 72 warps and 64 fillings per square inch). Sometimes called THREAD COUNT.

fabric story Related fabrics chosen for a particular group within a seasonal delivery. Like color stories, a well-chosen fabric story helps the retailer in merchandising the sales floor and encourages consumers to buy multiple pieces.

†**face** 1. *n.* Front side of fabric with better appearance—as opposed to back, or reverse side. Some fabrics are reversible and may be used on both sides. 2. *v.* See under CLOTHING CONSTRUCTION DETAILS: FACING.

∞**face cone** Long, megaphone-shaped cone held over face while wig was being powdered; first used in 18th c. Also see under POWDERING JACKET.

faced hem See under CLOTHING CONSTRUCTION DETAILS.

facet See under GEMS, GEM CUTS, AND SETTINGS.

facing See under CLOTHING CONSTRUCTION DETAILS.

factor A business that buys the rights to collect on the invoices of another company that made the sale, delivered the product or service, and generated the invoice for that service or product. Factors provide this service to industries, such as apparel, where long receivables are part of the business cycle; their fee is equal to the face value of the invoice, minus a discount of 2 to 6 percent. A single factor may work in many different industries.

factory outlet A store owned by a manufacturer in which closeouts, overruns, canceled orders, and discontinued and irregular items can be sold.

factory outlet mall A shopping center that houses several FACTORY OUTLET stores.

fad Short-lived fashion that suddenly becomes extremely popular, exists as a trend for a short period of time, and fades relatively quickly.

fade See under HAIRSTYLES.

†**fading** Loss of color in fabrics from exposure to light from washing, dry cleaning, or contact with ordinary household fumes.

fagoting See under EMBROIDERIES AND SEWING STITCHES.

†**faille** (file) Fabric exhibiting a flat-ribbed effect running crosswise that is flatter and less pronounced than GROSGRAIN. Lengthwise yarns are finer and more numerous in order to cover the heavier filling yarns. Originally made in silk—now made of silk, wool, cotton, manufactured yarns, or combinations of yarns. Uses: women's suits and dresses, robes, trimmings, and hats.

Fair Isle sweater See under SWEATERS.

fairy stone See under GEMS, GEM CUTS, AND SETTINGS.

fake fur See under SYNTHETIC FUR.

fake fur coat See under COATS AND JACKETS: FUR FABRIC COAT.

falbala See under FURBELOW.

falbala wig See under WIGS AND HAIRPIECES: DUVILLIER WIG.

faldetta See under CAPES, CLOAKS, AND SHAWLS.

fall ∞1. The front opening of men's breeches or trousers, so called since the 1730s. **Whole falls** were square-shaped flaps that extended across the front to the side seams. **Small** or **split falls** meant a smaller central flap that covered only the center front of the garment. After 1840, the fall was also called a *spair.* 2. See under WIGS AND HAIRPIECES. 3. See under NECKLINES AND COLLARS: FALL.

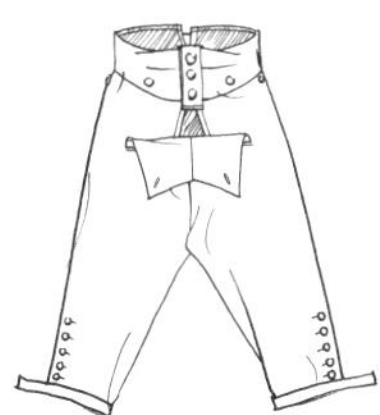

fall closing at the front of men's 18th c. knee breeches (fall #1)

fal-lals Any trifling decoration on a garment or accessory (e.g., ribbons and bows), used since the 17th c.

falling band See under NECKLINES AND COLLARS.

falling ruff See under NECKLINES AND COLLARS: RUFF.

falling tucker See under NECKLINES AND COLLARS: TUCKER.

fall lift Dome-shaped piece of wire mesh placed under the hair, frequently used when wearing a hairpiece called a FALL (see under WIGS AND HAIRPIECES). Much used in the late 1960s.

fallout The fabric remaining in the spaces between pattern pieces after a garment style is cut. These remaining fabric pieces are often recycled.

false bosoms See under FALSIES.

∞**false calves** Padding inserted in men's stockings to make legs more shapely—worn during 17th, 18th, and 19th c. Also called *downy calves.* Called **parchment calves** when the padding was made of parchment.

false calves

false doublet See under JEWELRY.

false eyelashes Eyelashes made of synthetic fibers or animal hair attached to a very narrow band that is adhered to the eyelid with special glue. Each lash may also be glued in place by a skilled technician.

false face See under MASKS: RUBBER MASK.

false gown See under DRESSES.

false hanging sleeve See under SHOULDERS AND SLEEVES: HANGING SLEEVE #2.

false hips See under UNDERGARMENTS: PANIERS.

false rump See under UNDERGARMENTS: RUMP FURBELOW.

falsies Bust pads, usually foam-filled, that are inserted into a bra to give a fuller appearance. They were especially popular in the 1950s, when a large bosom was fashionable. Devices intended to give the bosom a fuller appearance went by different names in different time periods: in the early 1800s, they were called **false bosoms;** in 19th c., some were made of lace ruffles and sometimes called **fluffy ruffles** or **gay deceivers;** and in the late 18th and early 19th c., **bosom friends** made of wool flannel or fur were worn both to protect the chest from cold and to enlarge the bosom.

family ring See under JEWELRY.

fan-back dress See under DRESSES.

fanchon 1. See under HEADWEAR. 2. See under SCARVES: HALF HANDKERCHIEF.

fancies 1. See under HOSIERY. ∞2. Ribbon trimmings used on men's petticoat breeches or other types of open-legged breeches from 1650s to 1670s.

fan collar See under NECKLINES AND COLLARS.

fancy diamond See under GEMS, GEM CUTS, AND SETTINGS.

fancy leather See under LEATHERS.

fancy sapphire See GEMS, GEM CUTS, AND SETTINGS: CORUNDUM.

fancy work See under EMBROIDERIES AND SEWING STITCHES.

fan hoop See under UNDERGARMENTS.

fanny pack See under HANDBAGS AND RELATED ACCESSORIES.

fanny sweater See under SWEATERS.

fanons See under CLERICAL DRESS.

fan parasol See under UMBRELLAS AND PARASOLS: MARQUISE.

fan pleat See under CLOTHING CONSTRUCTION DETAILS: ACCORDION PLEAT.

FANS

fan A hand-held implement for creating a breeze. Some are made rigid—wedge-shaped, round, or flat. Others are pleated, collapsible, and attached to a handle. Made of carved ivory in early Egypt, China, and Japan, fans have been in common use by women in the Western world from mid-16th c. Some materials used include paper, fabric, lace, tortoiseshell, feathers, hand-painted silk, and woven palm. The fan was considered a weapon for coquetry with definite rules for flirtation from 17th through 19th c.

aide memoire fan (ade mem'-whar) Fan, onto the back of which, instructions for dance steps, song lyrics and music, or other useful information was printed. Used in the late 18th and the 19th c.

cockade fan A folding fan, typically mounted on two sticks, that opens to a full, 360-degree circle. A **parasol fan** is similar but generally has a single stick.

cockade or parasol fan

∞**duck's-foot fan** Early folding fan that opened to one-fourth of a circle. Made of alternate strips of mica and vellum with an ivory handle, this fan was introduced to France from Italy by Catherine de Medici, wife of King Henry II of France and queen consort from 1547 to 1559.

folding fan Half- or quarter-circle fan, pleated so as to close narrowly. Introduced to France in mid-16th c. by Catherine de Medici, wife of King Henry II of France and queen consort from 1547 to 1559.

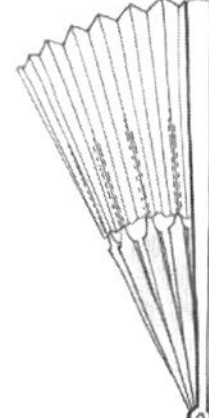
folding fan

parasol fan See under FANS: COCKADE.

---

fantail hat See under HEADWEAR.

fantail wig See under WIGS AND HAIRPIECES.

fan tucks See under CLOTHING CONSTRUCTION DETAILS: SUNBURST TUCKS.

farmer John See under ACTIVEWEAR: WETSUIT.

∞**farthingale/fardingale** A support for 16th- and early-17th-c. women's skirts; may also be used as an adjective to describe the shape of the skirt it supported. The supporting device was variously made of hoops of wood, wire, whalebone, or cane set into a coarse linen fabric. From its introduction in Spain in the second half of the 1400s until it went out of fashion in the first quarter of the 1600s, it changed shapes several times. Its various forms were: (1) **spanish farthingale,** or *verdugado.* The earliest Spanish form consisted of cane hoops sewn to the outside of skirts to maintain a cone-shape to the skirt. By the time it spread to France from Spain, the hoops were worn under the skirt. This shape was variously spelled as *verdugale, verdugalle, verdugado, verdugo.* (2) **drum** or **wheel farthingale** (shown at ELIZABETHAN STYLES), a drum-shaped farthingale produced by using a wheel-shaped piece of whalebone to support the skirt at the waist. The skirt rested on this platelike support, then fell straight to the ground. Also called *italian farthingale, english farthingale, catherine-wheel farthingale, drum-shaped farthingale, tambour farthingale.* (3) **french farthingale** Similar to the wheel farthingale but slightly flatter in front. Sometimes supported by a padded roll, called a **bum roll,** rather than a frame. (4) **roll farthingale** Tubular-shaped skirt supported by means of a BUM ROLL (see under UNDERGARMENTS) tied around the waist. Also see under GUARDINFANTE.

farthingale sleeves See under SHOULDERS AND SLEEVES.

fascinator See under HEADWEAR and SCARVES.

fashion *n.* A sociocultural phenomenon in which a preference is shared by a large number of people for particular styles that change periodically and are replaced by other popular styles. These variations in style can be seen to change with varying speed in different historic periods and cultures. Some styles called classics may remain "in fashion" for long periods of time. Scholars who study fashion often see fashions as reflecting the times and prevailing ideas of society in the periods when they develop. Although fashion is evident in many different kinds of material goods such as home furnishings, architecture, automobiles, literature, and food, it is particularly pronounced and rapid in apparel. By the 20th c., an enormous **fashion industry** had grown up in the United States to design, produce, distribute, and sell fashionable goods both domestically and internationally. Recently scholars who study dress have begun to argue that it is possible to identify fashionable behavior in many non-Western cultures and in early civilizations. They point out that it may be difficult for outside observers to recognize what constitutes fashion in places and times different from their own.

fashion babies See under MODEL DOLLS.

fashion boot See under FOOTWEAR: BOOT.

fashion calendar 1. A schedule for the current year that indicates the market weeks, or dates, when designers' or manufacturers' new lines may be seen by buyers. 2. Retail store schedule listing all fashion promotions for the store, including fashion shows, advertising, and special promotions.

fashion cycle The lifespan of a fashion product or a fashion trend, consisting of five stages: (1) beginning, (2) adoption, (3) rising popularity, (4) peak or saturation, and (5) decline. The first group of consumers to adopt new fashions are generally known as **fashion leaders,** while consumers who adopt a new fashion after the fashion leaders are called **fashion followers** or *fashion emulators.*

fashion director That person in a retailing business who provides buyers with information on current fashion trends so that buyers can select appropriate items.

fashion dolls See under MODEL DOLLS.

fashion followers See under FASHION CYCLE.

fashion forecast Prediction of the colors and styles of apparel and accessories that the majority of people will want to buy at a given time and place.

fashion forward *adj.* Describes designers, retailers, consumers, and merchandise that represent the newest, most fashionable styles.

fashion goods Merchandise that reflects current fashion trends as opposed to BASICS; fashion goods are more risky financially because they are less stable and may have a shorter life span than basics.

Fashion Group International, The An international, professional association of those who work in manufacturing, marketing, retailing, communication, and education of fashion. Founded in 1931 with Mary Brooks Picken as the first president. The organization's archives, which contain data related to the fashion industry since the founding of the organization, are housed at the New York Public Library. Originally formed to promote more careers for women in fashion and serve as a clearinghouse for information and ideas. The Fashion Group circulates information among its members and to students considering fashion careers by means of fashion shows, exhibits, speeches, career courses, and discussion panels, and also sponsors an annual Night of Stars Award Gala.

fashion helmet See under HEADWEAR.

fashion industry See under FASHION.

fashionista A woman who is an avid follower of high fashion.

fashion jewelry See under JEWELRY.

fashion leaders See under FASHION CYCLE.

fashion marks The stitch formation in full fashion, knitted garments—stitches have been increased or decreased to shape the garment. Distinguishes full-fashion knits from cut and sewn knits, in which the garment shape is cut from knitted yard goods and shape is incorporated from traditional shaping devices, i.e., darts and gathers. Fashion marks were once seen in seamed or full-fashioned hosiery, particularly at the back of the leg; modern hosiery techniques make fashion marks in hosiery obsolete. These marks can be seen in some sweaters available at higher price points.

fashion marks

∞**fashion plate** **1.** An illustration depicting the prevailing or new styles in clothing and accessories. First introduced in last quarter of 18th c., hand-colored, engraved fashion plates became important features in women's magazines of the 19th c. **2.** An individual who consistently dresses in the latest fashions.

fashion press Reporters and/or periodicals specializing in reporting news on fashion for trade or consumer magazines, newspapers, broadcast media, and digital media.

fashion promotion Sales promotion of fashion merchandise in a retail store accomplished by newspaper and magazine advertising, window and interior display, publicity, fashion shows, and broadcast media.

fashion season Periods of time that correspond to seasons of the year when specific fashion collections are sold, or that consumers are most likely to wear the merchandise from a specific collection. Examples are: spring, summer, fall, holiday, and resort. Most companies design for between four and six seasons a year.

fashion show An exhibition of fashion merchandise sponsored by a retail store, a designer, or a manufacturer. Apparel is usually shown on live models on a runway or stage, and the show may serve to introduce the clothes for a new season or may be a benefit performance for charity. Synonym: *style show.* The first American fashion show with live models was staged by *Vogue* magazine editor Edna Woolman Chase in November 1914, and introduced the idea of producing a fashion show to benefit a charity. Recent history has seen a rise in the filming of fashion shows for live or future broadcast through various media outlets such as television and the Internet.

fashion trend Direction in which styles, colors, fabrics, and designs are tending to change. Political events, films, personalities, dramas, social, and sports events often influence fashion trends.

fashion victim A person who, in trying to keep up with fashion changes, succeeds only in wearing the most tasteless of available fashions.

fashion watch See under WATCHES.

fashion week A fashion industry event, named after the host city or commercial sponsor, which offers a venue for designers or brands to launch their latest collections. NYC, London, Paris, and Milan, among other cities, have fashion weeks in succession every February for fall collections and September for spring collections. Also see under NATIONAL PRESS WEEK.

†**fast-color** Describes dyed fabric that will not fade when subjected to sunlight, washing, dry cleaning, perspiration, or atmospheric fumes. Also referred to as colorfast.

fastener Synonym for CLOSURES.

fast fashion Apparel that is produced at moderate prices over a very short time frame of weeks instead of months.

†**Fastskin®** Trademark for a variety of products for water sports, including fabric used in swimwear that is designed to reduce drag and turbulence in the water in order to improve athletic performance. Approved for competitive swimming in 1999.

fatigue cap See under HEADWEAR.

fatigues Military clothing worn when doing chores at camp. Some items have been adopted by civilians for general wear. For examples, see under PANTS: FATIGUES; SWEATERS: FATIGUE SWEATER; and HEADWEAR: FATIGUE CAP.

Fauntleroy See under LITTLE LORD FAUNTLEROY SUIT.

∞**fausse montre** (fowss mont-tr') In the late 18th c., an emerging style marked by the appearance of wearing two watches, one of which was actually a snuff box disguised as a watch. *Der.* French, "false watch."

fausse valenciennes See under LACES.

faust slipper See FOOTWEAR: ROMEO.

faux (fo) (French) False or counterfeit; imitation. Used in English to describe gems, pearls, furs, and leathers that are not real or the authentic material that they resemble.

faux jewels See under JEWELRY.

faux Mohawk See under HAIRSTYLES.

favorite/favourites **1.** See under HAIRSTYLES. **2.** See BEARD.

FDA See under FOOD AND DRUG ADMINISTRATION.

fearnaught See under COATS AND JACKETS: FEARNOTHING JACKET.

fearnothing jacket See under COATS AND JACKETS.

FEATHERS

feather Individual unit from a bird's plumage. A feather is composed of a horny stem, the **quill,** which has a smooth front and a grooved back. The flat portion of the feather is called the **vane** and is composed of many individual, small, parallel filaments called **barbs.** At the base of the feather are fluffy, fuzzy filaments called **flues** or **fluff.** Used from earliest times as decorative hair ornaments, necklaces, or body ornaments. Also used for fans or to decorate hats from 16th c. on. In late 1960s and 1970s whole dresses, pants, shawls, and jewelry were made of feathers. Songbird and eagle feathers, as well as other wild bird feathers, are not permitted by law to be used for clothing or accessories in the U.S.

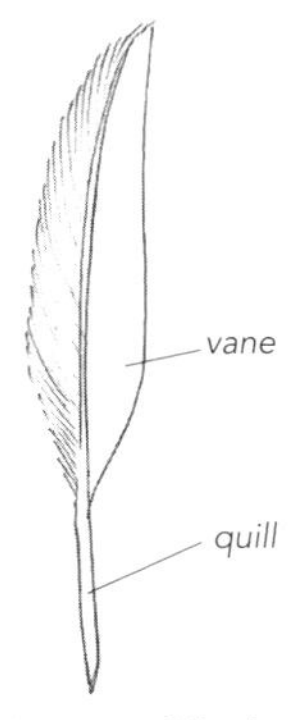

diagram of feather

feather fan

aigrette feather (*aigrette*) (ay-gret') 1. Extremely long, delicate, white feathers with plume at the tip, from the egret, a member of the heron family—a long-legged wading bird that almost became extinct from the demand for these feathers. Popular in the 1920s, it is now illegal in the U.S. to use these feathers on clothes or accessories. 2. Jeweled ornament imitating feathers attached to a headband, worn in the 1920s.

amazon plume Early synonym for an ostrich feather, generally taken from the wing of the bird with the tips of the barbs curled so shaft is concealed.

barbs See under introduction to FEATHERS.

biot (bee-oh) Long strip of short, stiff feathers created by stripping the vane from the stem.

bird-of-paradise feather Long plume, brilliantly colored, often golden-orange. Taken from beneath the shoulder or tail of full-grown male birds of paradise. Used as ornamentation on hats or headdresses. Illegal to import into the U.S. Introduced on evening wear by Yves Saint Laurent in 1969.

cockade Tuft of feathers used as trim.

cock feather Long, curly feathers from the tail of the rooster, often black, blue, and green with iridescent highlights.

coq feather (cok) (French) Cock or chicken feathers

cosse Any short, stiff feather.

down Material used to pad winter jackets and coats to increase warmth. Genuine down comes from fluffy, soft fibers under the feathers of waterfowl (e.g., geese and ducks). Used as interlining for insulation and warmth in vests, jackets, and coats. Often incorrectly used as an adjective to describe garments insulated with synthetic fiberfill.

egret feather See under FEATHERS: AIGRETTE.

eiderdown (eye-der-down') Soft, fine under feathers from the eider duck. Also called *down. Der.* From the feathers of the *eider duck.*

flues See under introduction to FEATHERS.

fluff See under introduction to FEATHERS.

grebe feather Feathers from waterfowl similar to ducks, that are ivory-colored, flecked with brown, and were used for millinery in early 20th c.

guinea feather (gin'-ee) Small, flat feathers from the guinea hen that are characterized by black-, white-, and gray-striated markings. Used in 1960s for pants and stoles.

hackle Rooster feathers, as they are called commercially.

herl Short, delicate, stiff fronds of peacock feather that have been removed from the stem and are bundled together and used as trimming.

jabiru (jab-ih'-roo) Soft, fuzzy plumage from a stork-like South American bird. The white, pale, smoke-colored, and black-and-white feathers were popular for trimming on women's hats, muffs, and collars in early 20th c.

marabou Delicate, fluffy, fine feathers from tail and wing of a species of stork made into trimmings that sell by the yard in black, white, and various other colors. Popular in the 1920s and 1930s for trim on lingerie and boudoir slippers. Also used for trim on dresses or cape collars, sleeves, and hems. Returned to fashion in early 1980s. Because of the expense of these feathers, less costly feathers such as turkey feathers are sometimes substituted.

osprey feather Feathers from the osprey or fish hawk, the breast feathers white, other feathers brown or grayish-brown and crossed by brown bars; used for trimming on hats in early 20th c.

ostrich feather Long, curly, plume feathers from the ostrich, a native African bird. Natural color of the feathers from the female bird is beige, barred with white. Most feathers are dyed in colors. Popular decoration on hats for men and women in time of the Cavaliers, Louis XIV, and in Edwardian era for women, and used in 1960s for whole dresses, capes, stoles, or pants.

paradise feather See under FEATHERS: BIRD-OF-PARADISE FEATHER.

peacock feather Long, thin, dark feather with brilliantly marked "eye" in greenish-blue at the tip, from upper tail of peacock. Individual feathers became a fad of the hippies, carried in the hand, in the late 1960s.

pheasant feather 1. Long, stiff tail feather from the domestic game bird, with striated markings of orange, black, and brown. **2.** Small, soft body feathers of the same bird, sometimes used to cover hats or hatbands.

plumage The mass of feathers that come from the bird's neck and chest area.

plume A single, large feather. Plumes most often used are from ostriches.

quill Long, stiff shaft of a feather with many thin projections called *barbs.* Used as ladies' hat trim, especially in 1940s. Also see under introduction to FEATHERS.

rhea feather (ray'-ah) Either of two South American *ratite* birds, resembling *African ostrich,* having long, draping feathers.

schlappen Rooster tail feathers that are small, narrow, and pointed.

swan's down/swansdown Soft under feathers of swans, used to trim negligées, dresses, and cloaks, especially in late 19th and early 20th c. Compare with MARABOU (see under FEATHERS).

vane See under introduction to FEATHERS.

∞**weepers** Ostrich feathers, worn in late 19th c.

---

feather boa See under SCARVES: BOA.

feather boning See under CLOTHING CONSTRUCTION DETAILS: STAY #1.

feather extensions See under HAIR ACCESSORIES.

featherbrush skirt See under SKIRTS.

feather cut See under HAIRSTYLES.

feathering See under FURS.

feather stitch See under EMBROIDERIES AND SEWING STITCHES.

featherwork See under EMBROIDERIES AND SEWING STITCHES: BRICK STITCH.

Federal Trade Commission (FTC) Regulatory agency that oversees legislation important to the apparel industries including labeling requirements for apparel under the Textile Fiber Products Identification Act, the Permanent Care Labeling Act, and legislation covering fur and wool products labeling. The FTC also monitors the legal aspects of business advertising.

Fédération Française de la Couture du Prêt-à-Porter des Couturiers et des Créateurs de Mode (fed-errats'-yohn fran'seys deh koo'-toor duh pret-ah-por-tay' dey koo'-toor-ee-yair ay dez kre-at'-tuhr de mode) An umbrella organization consisting of three French trade organizations—the CHAMBRE SYNDICALE DE LA HAUTE COUTURE PARISIENNE, the CHAMBRE SYNDICALE DU PRÉT-À-PORTER, and the CHAMBRE SYNDICALE DE LA MODE MASCULINE. It is the governing body of the French fashion industry; it sets industry standards as to quality and use of the term *haute couture.* It also coordinates the dates and locations of the various French fashion weeks. The Federation sponsors the Ecole de la Chambre syndicale de la couture Parisienne, a fashion school, and works closely with the **Union Nationale Artisanale de la Couture et des Activitiés Connexes** (oon-yon' nas'-yon-ee-ahl ar-tiz'-ahn-ahl' deh la koo'-toor ay dey ak-tiv'-ee-tay' kon-eks') (the National Couture Craft Industry and Related Activities Union, composed of couture dressmakers from outside of Paris).

fedora See under HEADWEAR.

feed bag See under HANDBAGS AND RELATED ACCESSORIES.

feldspar See under GEMS, GEM CUTS, AND SETTINGS.

fell seam See under CLOTHING CONSTRUCTION DETAILS: FLAT-FELLED SEAM.

†**felt** Nonwoven fabric made by compressing wool and hair fibers with heat and steam into sheet form. In true felt, no adhesives are used. Some felts are left hard and smooth; others are napped to give a softer hand. When used for hats, the felt is shaped into an object called a HOOD (see HEADWEAR: HOOD #1), which has a crown and a floppy shapeless brim. Hats are made by placing the hood in a metal mold. Steam and pressure are used to achieve desired shape. Felt is also used for apparel, handbags, bedroom slippers, and trimming. *Der.* Anglo-Saxon, *filt,* "filter."

felted wool See under FULLED WOOL.

felts See under FOOTWEAR.

∞**femoralia/feminalia** (fem-or-al'-ah/fem-in-al'-ee-ah) Short pants or drawers, reaching from waist to knees, worn by Roman troops in northern climates; probably imported by Emperor Augustus from Gaul. Also called *Roman leggings.*

fencing Sport of fighting with foils or other types of swords. Special clothing is worn that has sometimes inspired fashionable styles. See under ACTIVEWEAR: FENCING SUIT; COATS AND JACKETS: FENCING JACKET; MASKS: FENCING MASK; and SHIRTS: FENCING SHIRT.

∞**fermail/fermayll/fers** (fer' mail) In 15th c., buckles or pins used to hold slashes (see under SLASHING) of the garments together (e.g., as on sleeves and DOUBLETS).

ferraiolo See under CLERICAL DRESS.

Ferris waist See under UNDERGARMENTS.

ferronnière See under JEWELRY.

fers See under FERMAIL.

festoon Garlands of flowers, braids, or other decorative trimmings arranged in loops.

fetishistic clothing Fashions inspired by styles associated with aberrant sexual practices such as sadomasochism. These include stiletto heels, thigh-high boots, corsets, and garments made of leather, rubber, and PVC plastic. See under BONDAGE APPAREL.

fez See under HEADWEAR.

†**fiber** Basic component from which textile yarns or fabrics are made. These may be either natural materials—such as cotton, wool, or linen, which are short, staple-length fibers; and silk, a long filament fiber—or manufactured materials such as rayon, acetate, or polyester, which can be made in long continuous filaments. See under STAPLE FIBERS and FILAMENT FIBERS. Also see under MONOFILAMENT and MULTIFILAMENT YARNS.

†**fiberfill** Generic for a material consisting of fluffy short fibers. Frequently made of polyester and used between two layers of fabric to make quilted fabrics, padded bras, less expensive coats, and quilted vests.

fiber lace See under LACES.

∞**fibula** (pl. *fibulae*) (fib-you'-lah) Pin or brooch shaped like a long, straight STILETTO, or hinged like a SAFETY PIN. Used by the Greeks and Romans to secure garments, especially at the shoulder.

fibula

fichu 1. See under SCARVES. 2. See under NECKLINES AND COLLARS.

fichu lavalliere See under SCARVES: FICHU #1.

fichu menteur See under SCARVES.

fichu-pelerine See under CAPES, CLOAKS, AND SHAWLS.

∞**fichu-robings** Flat trimming used on the bodice of gown from shoulders to waist to give the effect of a FICHU in the 1820s (see under SCARVES).

field coat See under COATS AND JACKETS.

field pants See under PANTS: FATIGUES #1.

fiesta shirt See under SHIRTS.

fifties *adj*. Descriptive of fashions based on revival of styles popular in the 1950s. Especially notable in the mid-1970s and mid-1980s, when important features included nipped-in waistlines, swing skirts, ruffled petticoats, strapless bodices, high-heeled shoes, and hats. The slim SHEATH silhouette was also popular. Shown at RETRO.

figaro jacket See under COATS AND JACKETS.

fig leaf See under APRONS.

figure improver See under UNDERGARMENTS: BUSTLE.

figure skate See under FOOTWEAR.

figure stitch See under EMBROIDERIES AND SEWING STITCHES: ORIENTAL COUCHING.

filament fiber †1. Long, continuous textile fiber of indefinite length. Silk is the only natural filament fiber. Manufactured fibers can be made in filament lengths or cut into short, STAPLE FIBERS. 2. See under MONOFILAMENT and MULTIFILAMENT YARNS.

filament yarn See under YARN.

filet †1. Net with a square mesh formed by knotting at right angles. 2. Embroidery thread made of fine raw silk fibers twisted together. 3. See under LACES.

filet de bruxelles See under LACES: BRUSSELS NET.

filigree See under JEWELRY.

filigree ring See under JEWELRY.

filled gold See under JEWELRY: GOLD FILLED.

filler See under FOOTWEAR: SOLE.

fillet 1. See under HEADWEAR. 2. See under HAIRSTYLES.

∞**filleting** Narrow tape used as trimming in the 17th c.

filling Crosswise yarn of a woven fabric that runs at right angles to the SELVAGE. Also called *pick, woof,* or *weft.* Opposite of WARP, the vertical yarns.

filling stitch See under EMBROIDERIES AND SEWING STITCHES.

findings In the garment industry or in sewing, all the smaller items and trimmings that complete a garment (e.g., buttons, hooks, bindings, laces).

fine jewelry See under JEWELRY.

fineness †1. A measure of the diameter of yarns or fibers. Also see under DENIER. 2. The purity of gold. 3. Number of sewing machine stitches per inch.

finger band See under HOSIERY.

Finger-Free/fingerless gloves See under GLOVES AND GLOVE CONSTRUCTION.

fingering yarn †1. Combination of woolen and worsted yarn, usually two or more ply, used for hand-knitted garments. 2. Loosely twisted wool yarn used in Great Britain for BERLIN WORK (See under EMBROIDERIES AND SEWING STITCHES).

fingerwave See under HAIRSTYLES.

finish †1. *n*. Any of a number of chemical or mechanical processes that affect the appearance, hand, or performance of textile fibers, yarns, or fabrics. Finishes are generally applied during the manufacturing process to produce fabrics ready for manufacture into apparel or household products. †2. *v*. To apply such a process. 3. *v*. To trim threads, press, or otherwise prepare a garment for shipping after its construction is complete.

†**finished width** Measurement in inches across woven cloth after all operations have been completed.

fins See under FOOTWEAR: FLIPPERS.

fire opal See under GEMS, GEM CUTS, AND SETTINGS.

fishbone braids See under HAIRSTYLES.

fishbone stitch See under EMBROIDERIES AND SEWING STITCHES.

fisher See under FURS.

fishing/fisherman's *adj*. Describes various items of clothing derived from or inspired by clothing worn by fishermen for the sport of fishing. See under COATS AND JACKETS: FISHING PARKA; FOOTWEAR: HIP BOOT and WADERS; SWEATERS: FISHERMAN'S SWEATER; and VESTS: FISHERMAN'S VEST.

fisherman's ring See under CLERICAL DRESS.

fishmouth lapel See under NECKLINES AND COLLARS: LAPELS.

fishmouth toe See under HOSIERY.

fishnet †1. Coarse mesh fabric made in LENO WEAVE. Major uses include dresses, scarves, and trimming. 2. *adj.* Describes apparel made of fishnet fabric. See under CAPES, CLOAKS, AND SHAWLS: FISHNET PONCHO; HOSIERY: FISHNET HOSE; SHIRTS: FISHNET SHIRT; and UNDERGARMENTS: FISHNET UNDERWEAR.

fishtail See under GEMS, GEM CUTS, AND SETTINGS: FISHTAIL SETTING and SKIRTS: FISHTAIL SKIRT.

fishwife costume See under DRESSES.

fit and flare shirt See under SHIRTS: A-LINE and TRAPEZE.

fitch See under FURS.

∞**fitchet** (fich'-ett) (French) Vertical slit made on side front of a skirt or gown to enable woman to reach her pocket, which was a separate undergarment, used from 13th to mid-16th c.

fit The conformance of a garment to the shape and size of the individual who wears it.

fit model A live model whose body dimensions correspond to the company's sample size so that he or she can wear the sample and the designer can assess the fit, styling, and overall look of a new PROTOTYPE.

fitted *adj.* Describing a garment that conforms closely to body lines.

fitted sleeve See under SHOULDERS AND SLEEVES.

fitting *n.* Dressmaker's or tailor's session with customer for altering garment to fit the figure.

fitzherbert hat See under HEADWEAR.

flame embroidery See under EMBROIDERIES AND SEWING STITCHES: FLORENTINE EMBROIDERY.

flamenco dress See under DRESSES.

†**flame resistance** Fabric treated with a flame retardant. Fabric will burn only when placed in a flame, but self-extinguishes rapidly when the ignition source is removed. Also see under FLAMMABLE FABRICS ACT.

flame stitch See under EMBROIDERIES AND SEWING STITCHES: BARGELLO STITCH.

†**Flammable Fabrics Act** Legislation enacted in 1953 that prohibits the sale of highly flammable fabrics or wearing apparel that does not meet established standards, which are revised periodically. Amended in 1967 to include carpets, mattresses, and items of children's sleepwear. The act is enforced by the Consumer Products Safety Commission and has been amended a number of times, including in 2008.

∞**flammeum** (flow-may'-oom) Dark, flame-colored, full-length wedding veil worn by Roman brides. Removed by bridegroom when couple arrived at new home.

flandan See under HEADWEAR.

flange heel See under FOOTWEAR.

flange shoulder See under SHOULDERS AND SLEEVES.

flanging See under HEADWEAR.

†**flannel** Fine, soft fabric made in tightly woven twill or plain weave and finished with a light napping. May be made of wool or other fibers or blends and is often used for women's and girls' coats, suits, and dresses, or men's trousers and sport shirts. *Der.* Welsh, *Gwlanen,* from *Gwlan,* "wool."

†**flannelette** Cotton flannel that is used in sleepwear and sports shirts. See FLANNEL.

flannel nightgown See under SLEEPWEAR AND LOUNGEWEAR.

flannel petticoat See under UNDERGARMENTS.

flannel shirt See under SHIRTS.

flannel skirt See under UNDERGARMENTS: FLANNEL PETTICOAT.

flapped-besom pocket See under POCKETS: WELT POCKET.

flapper 1. *n.* Fashionable young woman in her late teens or early twenties who adopted the unfitted styles, short skirts, and bobbed hair of the 1920s. Suggested origins of this term vary and include: the practice of these young women of wearing open, flapping galoshes or overshoes in bad weather, the hair bows worn by young girls in the post–World War I period, or the flapping of the wings of young birds as they learn to fly. This latter origin is given greatest credence, as the parallel is made between these young women "trying their wings" as young adults, but the usage may have been reinforced by the flapping galoshes they wore. 2. *adj.* Descriptive of revivals of styles inspired by or derived from clothing of the 1920s. Typical dresses were knee-length, long-waisted, blouson and chemise types, often lavishly decorated with beads for evening. Coats were without waistlines or long-waisted, and wrap-style, many with large fur collars. Hair was cut in a short bob, and frequently a brow band and long ropes of pearls were worn. Also called *twenties style.*

flapper dress See under DRESSES.

flap pocket See under POCKETS.

flared-leg pant See under UNDERGARMENTS.

flares See under PANTS.

flashdance *adj.* Descriptive of various items of dancewear designed by Michael Kaplan for the 1983 movie *Flashdance,* and contemporary fashions adapted from these designs. Typical items were loose, oversized, shoulder-baring sweatshirts, tank tops, cardigans, dresses, and exercise pants. Also see under BLOUSES AND TOPS: FLASHDANCE TOP.

flashdance style 1983

flashy nightshirt See under SLEEPWEAR AND LOUNGEWEAR.

flat 1. In fashion sketching, refers to drawings of clothing without a human figure that illustrate all of the construction details of the garment. 2. Two-dimensional garment drawings without bodies that clearly illustrate all construction details. See also under TECHNICAL FLAT.

flat chappals See under FOOTWEAR.

flat collars See under NECKLINES AND COLLARS.

flat felled seams See under CLOTHING CONSTRUCTION DETAILS.

flat front pants See under PANTS.

flat heel See under FOOTWEAR.

flat-knit hose See under HOSIERY: FULL-FASHIONED HOSE.

flat pattern A design process in which a base block, or SLOPER, is used to create a pattern for a new style.

flat pleats See under CLOTHING CONSTRUCTION DETAILS: KNIFE PLEATS.

flats See under FOOTWEAR.

flattop See under HAIRSTYLES: CREW CUT.

†flax Fiber from the stem of the flax plant. Linen fabrics are made from flax fibers.

flea fur See under SCARVES.

flea market 1. *n.* Market held continuously or occasionally in such locations as barns, buildings, or in the open. Flea market shops opened in Paris and England in late 1960s and have been a source of vintage clothing. 2. *adj.* Describes all types of clothing, either used or new, that have the appearance of old or antique clothing and accessories. *Der.* Items of clothing that look as if they might have been purchased in a flea market. See VINTAGE.

fleece †1. Wool sheared from the sheep, usually taken off in one piece. †2. A fabric with a thick, heavy, fleece-like surface; it may be a PILE fabric, or simply one with a NAP, and may be woven or knitted. 3. See under SHEARLING under FURS and LEATHERS.

†fleece-lined fabric Soft fabric with a heavily napped surface on one side. May be woven but more often knitted with floats on back that are brushed to form a NAP. Used for sweatshirts, sweatpants, and jogging suits.

Flemish hood See under HEADWEAR: BEGUIN.

fleshing 1. See under LEATHERS. 2. See under FURS.

fleur-de-lis See under PRINTS, STRIPES, AND CHECKS.

flexible manufacturing system (FMS) "Any departure from traditional mass production systems of apparel toward faster, smaller, more flexible production units that depend upon the coordinated efforts of minimally supervised teams of workers" (AAMA Technical Advisory Committee, 1988, as cited in Hill, 1992, p. 34).

flight *adj.* Describes apparel that is inspired or influenced by clothing or accessories used in flying. Examples: FLIGHT BAG, FLIGHT SUIT.

flight bag See under HANDBAGS AND RELATED ACCESSORIES.

flight deck cap See under HEADWEAR: ASTRONAUT'S CAP.

flight jacket See under COATS AND JACKETS.

flight suit One-piece garment of a design based on suits worn by pilots in the armed forces. Generally made with long sleeves, long legs, and zipping up the front to close. Similar to JUMPSUIT (see under ACTIVEWEAR).

flip See under HAIRSTYLES.

flip-chip dress See under DRESSES.

flip-down glasses See under EYEWEAR.

flip-flops See under FOOTWEAR.

flippers See under FOOTWEAR.

flip-tie blouse See under BLOUSES: STOCK-TIE BLOUSE.

flip-up eyeglasses See under EYEWEAR: CLIP-ON SUNGLASSES.

float †1. *n.* Lengthwise or crosswise yarn in a woven fabric that extends over several rows without being interlaced. †2. *n.* In knitting, a yarn that extends for some distance across back of fabric without being interlaced. 3. A form of fashion illustration that depicts a garment as if it were on a body, but without the body parts that would extend beyond the garment.

floater necklace See under JEWELRY.

floating pedestal wedge See under FOOTWEAR.

floats See under FOOTWEAR: CHUKKA BOOT.

flocked print See under PRINTS, STRIPES, AND CHECKS.

†flocked ribbon Ribbon given a pile-like surface by means of FLOCKING, an electrostatic process, rather than woven in a pile weave like VELVET ribbon.

†flocking 1. Short lengths of fiber that are used in printing designs on fabrics or to cover the surface of a fabric to create surface texture. 2. Method of applying short fibers overall or in a design by first printing fabric with an adhesive and then causing minute pieces of fibers to adhere to the design. When a design is produced the method is known as **flock printing.**

Flohpelzchen See under SCARVES: FLEA FUR.

flokati See under FOOTWEAR.

floor ready merchandise (FRM) Merchandise received by the retailer with hangtags, labels, and price information affixed so that the goods can be placed on the selling floor immediately.

floral print See under PRINTS, STRIPES, AND CHECKS.

florentine embroidery See under EMBROIDERIES AND SEWING STITCHES.

florodora costume See under DRESSES.

florentine neckline See under NECKLINES AND COLLARS.

florentine stitch See under EMBROIDERIES AND SEWING STITCHES: BARGELLO STITCH.

flotation vest See under VESTS.

flounce **1.** Piece of material, either circular or straight-cut, and gathered. Used on hems of skirts, dresses, or jackets, the bottoms of sleeves, or on collars, singly or in series. First introduced in 16th c. **2.** See under FURBELOW.

flounce collar See under NECKLINES AND COLLARS.

flouncing **1.** Decorative lace or embroidered fabric usually gathered at upper edge. **2.** See under LACES.

flower bottle ∞**1.** Fresh flower in small bottle of water worn in buttonhole and held in place under lapel by broad ribbon. Worn by men in the mid-1860s. **2.** See under BOSOM BOTTLES.

flowered mink See under FURS.

flower-pot hat See under HEADWEAR.

∞**flow-flow** Bodice trimming consisting of a graduated cascade of ribbon loops used from 13th to mid-16th c.

flues See under introduction to FEATHERS.

fluff See under introduction to FEATHERS.

fluffy ruffles See under FALSIES.

flush setting See under GEMS, GEM CUTS, AND SETTINGS: CHANNEL SETTING.

fluted hem See under CLOTHING CONSTRUCTION DETAILS.

fluting Tiny pleats in sheer fabrics that give a corrugated effect. Those set in manufactured fabrics may be permanently heat-set. A late 19th-c. trimming popular again in 1960s through 1980s. Also called *goffering*. See under GOFFER 2.

flutter sleeve See under SHOULDERS AND SLEEVES.

flyaway jacket See under COATS AND JACKETS.

flyboy glasses See under EYEWEAR: AVIATOR GLASSES.

fly cap See under HEADWEAR: BUTTERFLY CAP.

∞**fly-fringe** 18th-c. fringe, consisting of strands of silk floss knotted in clumps, used for trimming a gown.

fly-front See under CLOSURES.

flygirls See under HIP-HOP.

flying panel skirt See under SKIRTS.

flying saucer dress See under DRESSES.

FMS See under FLEXIBLE MANUFACTURING SYSTEM.

fob See under WATCH FOB.

fob pin See under JEWELRY: CHATELAINE.

fob pocket See under POCKETS.

∞**fob ribbon** Ribbon attached to watch carried in the FOB POCKET, used from 1740s to 1840s (see under POCKETS). The ribbon end hung outside of pocket and held a fob, seals, or watch key. Worn only with BREECHES or PANTALOONS (see under PANTS: PANTALOONS #2).

foil button See under CLOSURES.

foil dress See under DRESSES.

fold-down casing See under CLOTHING CONSTRUCTION DETAILS: CASING.

folding/fold-up *adj.* Describes an item of apparel that bends over itself in order to become smaller. See under COATS AND JACKETS: FOLD-UP RAINCOAT; EYEWEAR: FOLDING GLASSES; FANS: FOLDING FAN; FOOTWEAR: PULLMAN SLIPPER; HANDBAGS AND RELATED ACCESSORIES: FOLD-OVER CLUTCH; and HEADWEAR: FOLD-UP HAT.

foldover bag See under HANDBAGS AND RELATED ACCESSORIES.

folette See under SCARVES.

foliated See under DAGGING.

follow-me-lads See under HEADWEAR.

∞**folly bells** Tiny bells suspended from chains used to decorate belts, shoulder belts, or neckbands in 15th c.

fontanges See under HEADWEAR.

fontanges hat See under HEADWEAR.

Food and Drug Administration (FDA) A federal agency that is responsible for regulating the safety of cosmetics as well as food and drugs.

fool's cap See under HEADWEAR.

football helmet See under HEADWEAR.

football jersey See under SHIRTS.

footed pajamas See under SLEEPWEAR AND LOUNGEWEAR.

footie See under HOSIERY: FOOTSOCK.

∞**footing** Trimming used on edges of garments (e.g., elaborate ruffles, pleating, lace, net, insertion, and ribbon). Widely used on women's dresses and undergarments in late 19th and early 20th c.

foot-mantle See under SKIRTS.

footsock See under HOSIERY.

foot warmers See under HOSIERY: BED SOCK.

FOOTWEAR

footwear Outermost covering for the foot that serves to protect the foot but frequently is also a decorative element of the costume. The category of FOOTWEAR is often divided among different basic styles of footwear. The definitions of these types of FOOTWEAR may be found under the category of footwear in these entries: BOOT, CLOG, MOCCASIN, MULE, OXFORD, PUMP, SANDAL, and SLIPPER. SHOE has become a general term referring to any footwear that does not extend to above the ankle. Individually named examples of various types (e.g., saddle shoe, loafer, sneaker) of footwear each have a separate entry in the category. Definitions of parts of footwear (e.g., COUNTER, HEEL, QUARTER, SOLE, TOE, TONGUE, UPPER, VAMP) are also included in the FOOTWEAR category.

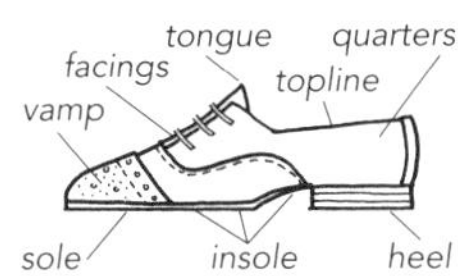

man's oxford shoe with stacked heel

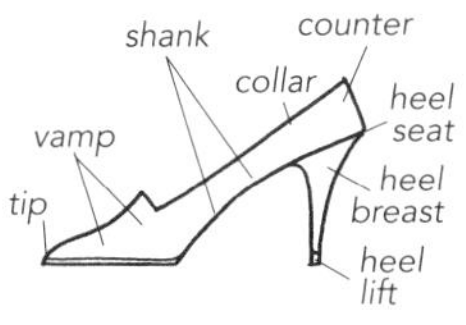

woman's pump with stiletto heel

achilles tendon protector See under FOOTWEAR: A.T.P.

acrobatic slipper Soft, flexible slipper made out of sueded splits of leather (see SUEDED and SPLITS under introduction to LEATHERS). Vamp comes up high in center front and a piece of elastic connects it to the quarter or back of shoe. Worn by dancers and gymnasts and also adopted by avant-garde for streetwear in the 1960s.

∞**adelaide boot** Woman's ankle-high, side-laced boot with patent-leather toe and heel, sometimes with fur or fringed trimming at top. Worn in the U.S. from about 1830s to 1860s.

aerobic shoe Laced shoe of nylon mesh with suede outside counter, toe band, and trim. Somewhat higher cut than a sneaker, with shock-absorbing midsole and non-skid rubber sole.

after-ski boot See under FOOTWEAR: APRÈS-SKI BOOT.

∞**Alaska** In early 20th c., an overshoe or storm rubber with a high tongue over the instep.

∞**albert boot** Man's side-laced boot with fabric top and patent-leather toe, frequently decorated down front with mother-of-pearl buttons; worn from 1840s on. *Der.* From fashion made popular by *Prince Albert,* the consort of England's Queen Victoria.

albert slipper Slipper with a VAMP (see under FOOTWEAR) that extends up to form a tongue that rests on the instep.

all-weather boot Calf-high boot made with fleece-lined upper attached to molded waterproof rubber sole with low heel.

alpargata (ahl-par-gah'-ta) Sandal worn in Spain and South America with rope sole and canvas upper only around the heel. Fastened to foot by cord coming from sole in front, crossing at instep, threaded through holes in upper, and fastened around ankle.

∞**alpine boot** Ankle-high shoe of early 1900s designed with bent nails on a sturdy sole to give mountain climbers a secure footing. Also see under FOOTWEAR: HIKING BOOT.

∞**American buskins** Shoes with stout leather soles and knee-high cloth uppers, or leggings, fastened with lacings, worn by American Colonists. Similar to STARTUPS.

ankle boot See under FOOTWEAR: DEMI-BOOT, GEORGE, and PANTS BOOT.

∞**ankle-jack** Man's ankle-high boot, laced up front with five pairs of eyelets. Popular in East End of London in 1840s.

ankle-strap shoe/sandal Shoe, frequently of the sandal type, having a strap attached at the top of the heel and going around the ankle. Shown at D'ORSAY PUMP. Frequently made with platform sole. Very popular in the 1930s and 1940s, revived in late 1960s, and very popular in 1980s and after.

∞**antigropolis** (an-te-grop'-oh-lis) Man's long GAITER (see under FOOTWEAR), usually leather, coming over thigh in front, but cut away to knee in back; worn in mid-19th c. for walking or riding.

après-ski boot (app-reh-skee) Bulky insulated boot often calf-length and made of long-haired, shaggy fur worn for warmth after skiing. *Der.* French, "after ski." Also called *after-ski boots.*

après-ski slipper Synonym for SLIPPER SOCKS (see under FOOTWEAR).

apron tongue See under FOOTWEAR: TONGUE.

arch cushion Pad for support of the arch of the foot. Also called *cookie.*

arctics 1. Waterproof rubber boot worn over regular shoes, usually with zipper closing; popular in 1940s, revived in 1970s. 2. See FOOTWEAR: GALOSH #1.

athletic shoes A broad category of shoes worn for any of a wide variety of athletic activities. Often used interchangeably with SNEAKERS (see under FOOTWEAR), although it seems to be preferred within the footwear industry over this older term.

A.T.P./achilles tendon protector (a-kil'-ees) Padding placed at the back of the heel collar of some athletic shoes to protect the Achilles tendon. Also called *heel horn.*

∞**baby boot** An infant's soft fabric or leather shoe with a high top, from the second half of 19th c. Usually made of fabric or felt, and elaborately trimmed with embroidery. Also see under FOOTWEAR: BOOTIE #2.

baby-doll shoe Low-heeled shoe with wide, rounded toes similar to MARY JANE shoe (see under FOOTWEAR), sometimes with straps over instep; popular for women in 1960s with miniskirts and little-girl styles. Popularity enhanced by film *Baby Doll* (1956). *Der.* Used to refer to clothing and accessories used for children's dolls and infants' clothes in the early part of the 20th c.

baby louis heel See under FOOTWEAR: LOUIS HEEL.

backstay Reinforcement of the vertical seam at the back of a shoe with a narrow piece of leather.

bagging shoe See FOOTWEAR: STARTUP.

bal/balmoral (bahl-mor'-al) Basic style of OXFORD with the TONGUE cut in a separate piece from the VAMP of the shoe and joined with stitching across the vamp (see cross-references under FOOTWEAR). *Der.* First worn at Balmoral Castle in Scotland in early 1850s.

bal/balmoral shoe

ballerina shoe 1. Soft, low kid shoe with thin sole and flat heel, sometimes made with drawstring throat. Inspired by shoe worn by ballet dancers. Popular in 1940s for schoolgirls. Also see under FOOTWEAR: BALLET SLIPPER. 2. Plain, low-cut pump made with flat or wedge heel and a crepe or synthetic sole, introduced in 1980s.

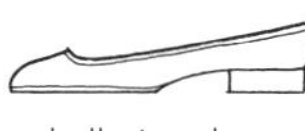
ballerina shoe

ballet laces (bal'-lay) Wide satin ribbons used as lacings for ballet slippers, crisscrossing at intervals around ankle and calf and tied in a bow. Worn in 1870s on bathing slippers and during World War I with high-heeled pumps. Reintroduced in 1980s.

ballet slipper (bal'-lay) 1. Soft, flexible slipper made of kid. Upper is pulled around to form part of the sole, which is very thin and has no heel. Worn by ballet dancers and children for dancing and in late 1940s for streetwear. Most slippers for professional dancers have been made since 1887 by Capezio, trademark of Capezio Ballet Makers, a division of U.S. Shoe Corp. 2. Any similarly styled slipper worn indoors or outdoors usually with a heavier type sole. Reintroduced in 1984 with outer sole for streetwear styled in leather or fabric and sometimes worn with ballet laces.

ball heel Spherical heel made of wood or Lucite®. Popular since 1960s.

ball heel

∞**balmoral boot** (bahl-mor'-al) Short black boot worn by women from 1850s to 1870s with a walking dress. Made with front lacings, sometimes colored. *Der.* Name of Queen Victoria's castle in Scotland that was often used as an adjective when describing certain fashionable items of Victorian apparel.

∞**bamberges** Shin guards worn during Carolingian period, mid-8th to 11th c.

basketball shoe High or low oxford made of canvas or army duck with nonslip molded rubber sole. The shoe laces to the toe and is frequently made with reinforced toe and COUNTER (see under FOOTWEAR). Originally used only for sports, in 1970s accepted for school wear. In 1980s and after, sometimes made in leather with a padded collar added at top.

basketball shoe

Bass Weejun Trademark formerly used for high-quality moccasin-type loafer with tasseled bow in front. Originally copied from a Norwegian-type moccasin. *Der.* Word originally from shortened form of Norwegian-Injun.

bathing slipper Woman's flat fabric shoe, sometimes laced up leg similar to ballet slipper, worn while swimming and popular in late 19th c. After 1920s similar shoes without lacing, frequently of rubber, were worn on beach and in water.

∞**batt** Heavy, laced, low shoe used for country wear in England in 17th c., sent to New England Colonists in 1630s.

Beatle boot Ankle-high boot with pointed toe and side gores of elastic styled for men. Probably the first fashionable ankle-high shoe to be worn by men for general wear in place of oxfords since World War I period. *Der.* Introduced in the 1960s by the Beatles, an avant-garde rock-music group from Liverpool, England. Also called *Chelsea boot.*

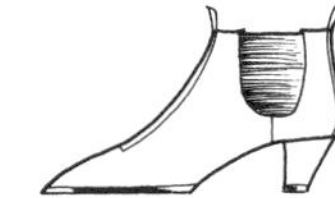
Beatle boot with winkle-picker toe 1964

bedroom slipper Footwear made of fabric, felt, or leather, usually in heelless style and intended for indoor wear.

∞**belgrave shoe** Woman's evening shoe cut like a PUMP, but coming up high in the back, fastened in front with GILLIE lacings; worn in 1870s. See under FOOTWEAR: GILLIE and PUMP.

bell-bottom heel See under FOOTWEAR: LOUIS HEEL.

bellows tongue See under FOOTWEAR: TONGUE.

∞**bicycle bal** Shoe with protective toe cap and a circle stitched over ankle joint. Closed with laces extending toward the toes. Designed for bicycling in latter part of 19th c. and later adopted for other sports.

Blake, Lyman See under FOOTWEAR: MCKAY METHOD.

blind eyelet See under CLOSURES.

block heel See under FOOTWEAR: CUBAN HEEL.

blucher (bloo'-cher or bloo'-ker) 1. Basic oxford type with the tongue and vamp cut in one piece. See FOOTWEAR: OXFORD, TONGUE, and VAMP. 2. Man's ankle-length riding boot that laces up center front through six pairs of eyelets. Worn from 1820 to 1850. *Der.* Named after Field Marshal Gebhard Leberecht von Blücher, Prussian commander at battle of

blucher #1

Waterloo (1815), who devised this type of shoe for army wear in 1810.

blucher bal (bloo′-cher or bloo′-ker) Modified BLUCHER oxford (see under FOOTWEAR) with VAMP stitched over QUARTER at sides, but not stitched over TONGUE (see cross-references under FOOTWEAR).

boating shoe Canvas shoe similar to TENNIS SHOE, but made with a special nonskid rubber sole for walking on slippery boat decks. Also called *deck shoes.* Also see under FOOTWEAR: SPERRY TOPSIDER®.

body boot See under FOOTWEAR: STOCKING BOOT.

∞**boot garters** Worn in the 18th c., straps attached to back of man's boot, which wound around the leg above knee over top of the breeches.

boot hook ∞1. First used in the 19th c., a leather loop attached to back or sides of boot at top, used to aid in pulling on boots. Also called *boot strap.* 2. Long L-shaped piece of metal with a handle used to pull boots on.

∞**bootie/bootee** 1. Bedroom slipper edged with fur or fake fur. 2. Infants' fabric or knitted foot covering. 3. Type of sock worn by astronauts in flight.

boots Shoes that extend to the ankle or above. Boots have been worn since Anglo-Saxon times in various lengths. More popular during some eras such as Louis XIII period and Regency period. From 1820s to 1880s, ankle-high dainty boots were worn outdoors by women. In 1890s, calf-high boots, either buttoned or laced, with medium heel, were worn. In mid-19th c. very fashionable for children. Now classified as **utility boots** and used for various purposes (e.g., skiing, skating, hunting, mountain climbing, etc.), or as **fashion boots**, intended to be worn indoors and out in place of shoes. Made as a fashion item, and not intended to be waterproof, such boots became very fashionable in the mid- and late 1960s and after in all lengths and in many fabrics as well as leather.

utility boot: hiking boot

fashion boot

boot strap See under FOOTWEAR: BOOT HOOK #1.

botews See under FOOTWEAR: BUSKINS #2.

∞**bottine** (bow-teen′) Woman's knee-high riding boot of 16th c.

boudoir slipper (bood-war′) Slippers without backs made in fancy fabrics, and sometimes trimmed with marabou, as they were first called in early 20th c. Also see under FOOTWEAR: MULES.

boulevard heel Sturdy high heel similar to a CUBAN HEEL that is tapered at sides and back, has straight front, and a flange where heel joins with sole.

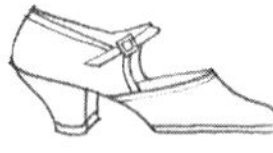

boulevard heel

bowling shoe Soft, supple shoe of oxford or other type with cushioned insole for comfort. Made with hard rubber sole and heel with an added leather tip on the sole of the right shoe (or left, for left-handed bowlers).

bracelet-tie shoe Woman's ankle-strap shoe with loop extending on rim in center back to hold the strap; periodically stylish from the 1930s to the present.

breasted heel Any heel made with a curved section where it attaches to the sole of the shoe at the *shank.*

∞**brodekin/brodkin/brotiken** Lightweight shoe worn in Middle Ages inside boots.

brogan Originally men's ankle-length shoe worn in Scotland. Made of leather and fastened to foot by side flaps either buckled or tied over short tongue.

brogue Heavy walking shoe, a type of OXFORD (see under FOOTWEAR), originally made for men, that usually has a wing tip decorated with heavy perforations and pinkings. Frequently worn for golf but also for city wear. *Der.* From coarse heelless shoe of untanned hide, with hair left on, worn by men in Ireland in 1790.

brogue 1916

bucket-top boot See under FOOTWEAR: FRENCH-FALL BOOT.

buck oxford A BLUCHER-type oxford (see under FOOTWEAR) made with sueded split-leather upper. Typically has a red cushion-crepe rubber sole. When made of white leather, called **white bucks.**

built-up heel See under FOOTWEAR: STACKED HEEL.

bulldog toe Bulbous toe popular on a man's buttoned ankle-high shoe before World War I. Similar to FOOTWEAR: KNOB TOE.

bumper Rubber strip attached across the front of the toe in some athletic footwear.

buskins 1. See under FOOTWEAR: COTHURNUS. ∞2. High, sometimes knee-length, boots often made of patterned silk and worn from 14th to 17th c. Also called *botews* (bot′-toos). ∞3. Leather riding boots worn in 17th c. for traveling. 4. Women's low-cut shoe with elasticized gores at sides of instep worn in the early 20th c. 5. See under FOOTWEAR: AMERICAN BUSKINS.

Buster Brown Comic strip character of the early 20th c. whose haircut, collars, suit, and shoes were widely copied for children's wear. The name became a trademark for children's shoes and is currently a trade name for a wide variety of products.

∞**butterfly bow** Length of stiffly starched lace, resembling outstretched butterfly wings, fastened to front of shoe at end of 17th c.

∞**buttoned shoe** 1. Shoe with a three- or four-button diagonal closing and a BULLDOG TOE (see under FOOTWEAR) or a conventional toe. Worn by men in early 1900s. ∞2. **button shoe** Short boot buttoned up outer side with black glossy or mother-of-pearl buttons. Worn from 1837 to early 20th c. by men, women, and children. When the shoe came to ankle or above and closed to side of center front with a row of small shoe buttons, it was called a **high button shoe.** These were worn by both men and women from late 19th through early 20th c. and have been revived from time to time.

cack Heelless shoe with soft leather sole, made for infants in sizes one to five.

∞**calamanco shoes** (kal-ah-man′-ko) Heavy shoes made from a twilled cotton fabric called *calamanco,* which were worn by American women in Colonial days. Fabric is also spelled *calimanco, callamancoe, calliman, callimanco, calmanco.*

∞**calcarapedes** (kar-kara′-ped-eez) Self-adjusting rubber galoshes worn by men in the 1860s.

∞**calceus** Roman boot coming to below ankle with long straps wrapping around leg, reaching to calf and sometimes the knee. Lower part was slit down each side to permit easy access. When worn by Roman senators, called **calceus patricius.**

calk 1. Device on heel, or sole, of shoe or boot to prevent slipping or give longer wear; may be a metal plate with sharp points. ∞2. In Colonial America, for a CLOG (see under FOOTWEAR) with spiked sole.

∞**cameleons** (ka-me′-le-on) Women's shoes and boots of late 1850s made with cutouts to show colored stockings underneath.

∞**campagus** (kam-pah′-gus) 1. Shoe worn by bishops in Western Church, particularly Roman Catholic, sometimes Episcopal. 2. Shoe worn during Byzantine period and the Middle Ages, high in back to the ankle and fastened with ribbon or strap over instep.

∞**carbatina** (kar-batt′-ee-nah) Ancient Roman sandal made of single piece of untanned hide as sole, overlapping sides of foot, and held on by leather thongs. Copied since 1950s as barefoot summer sandal.

carpet slipper 19th-c. informal slip-on house slipper made of carpeting, cut in pump style with a standing rounded tongue cut in one piece with toe and soft padded leather sole with flat heel made in one piece. Style still made in other fabrics and in felt. Also see under FOOTWEAR: FELTS.

∞**carriage boot** Woman's fur-trimmed winter boot usually of fabric, sometimes of leather, worn over other shoes to keep feet warm in unheated carriages or automobiles in early 20th c.

chain loafer See under FOOTWEAR: LOAFER.

chappals Flat sandals, similar to flip flops, but with a toe ring, which originated in India. Typically made of leather.

Charlie Chaplin toe Wide, round toe used on a mary jane shoe. Featured by Courrèges in his spring 1967 collection. Also see under FOOTWEAR: MARY JANE.

∞**chaussures à crics** (show-sur′ ah kree) Shoes with high heels worn in the 17th c. *Der.* French, "shoes on lifts." Also called *chaussures à Pont-Levis.*

chelsea boot See FOOTWEAR: BEATLE BOOT.

chest-high boot See FOOTWEAR: WADERS.

chinese shoe Fabric, flat-heeled, crepe-soled shoe of MARY JANE type (see under FOOTWEAR) made with one strap and rounded toe. Made in many colors, sometimes with embroidery. The national shoe of China, it was imported by the U.S. and sold first at Asian and later at other stores in late 1970s and 1980s and since.

chinese slipper See under FOOTWEAR: KAMPSKATCHA SLIPPER.

∞**chopine/chopin/chapiney** (sho-peen′) Wooden or cork CLOG, covered with leather, sometimes 18″ high, fitted with toe cap and used as a patten, or overshoe; worn in 16th and 17th c. See under FOOTWEAR: PATTEN.

chopine 16th c.

chukka boot (chuh′-ka) Men's and boys' ankle-high boot laced through two sets of eyelets, made of splits of unlined sueded cowhide. Has thick crepe-rubber sole. Originally worn by polo players and adopted for general wear in 1950s. *Der.* From *chukka,* a period in polo games. A **desert boot,** introduced in 1960s, differs from a chukka boot in that it is usually lined and has a rubber sole. **Floats,** also introduced in early 1960s, have thick crepe soles and a thick pile lining, but are otherwise like chukka and desert boots.

chunky heel High or medium heel that has exaggerated width—a shoe fad of late 1960s and early 1970s.

chunky heel

chunky shoe Shoes of all types made in exaggeratedly heavy shapes with bulbous toes and massive heels, often with very thick platform soles. A fad in late 1960s and early 1970s and fashionable again in the 1990s and after.

chunky shoe

city boots Women's boots of a more tailored or dressy style that are suitable for wear with business or more formal daytime dress.

∞**clarence** Man's laced ankle-high boot of 19th c. made of soft leather with triangular gusset at the side, forerunner of ELASTIC-SIDED BOOT (see under FOOTWEAR).

cleats Projections attached to soles of sport shoes, made of plastic, wood, rubber, or metal. Used particularly on football, golf, and baseball shoes to prevent slipping.

clog 1. See under FOOTWEAR: PATTEN. ∞2. Woman's leather-soled overshoes with instep straps generally matching the shoe, worn outdoors in 17th and 18th c. 3. Wooden shoe. See FOOTWEAR: SABOT. 4. Protective footwear worn in factories before being replaced by steel-toe boots. Variations range from the traditional Dutch klompen, French SABOTS, and Japanese GETA, to the more modern DR. SCHOLL'S EXERCISE SANDALS. Today clogs may be often promoted for gardening; the wood or solid soles also cycle in and out of fashion.

closed seam Shoe seam, similar to a simple fabric seam, stitched on the inside and edges pressed back. Usually used for joining the shoe at center back.

∞**clot** Heavy shoe with thin iron plates on the sole worn by workmen in the 15th c. Also called *clout-shoen.*

cockers (*cokers, cocurs, coggers*) ∞1. High boots, crudely made, worn by laborers, sailors, country people, and shepherds from 14th to 16th c. Also called *okers.* ∞2. In 17th c., boots worn by fishermen. 3. Leggings buttoned or buckled at the side with straps under the instep, as they were called in the 18th c. Word still used today in the north of England.

collar See under FOOTWEAR: QUARTER.

collegians See under FOOTWEAR: OXONIAN BOOTS.

colonial shoe Medium-heeled slip-on shoe with stiffened tongue standing up over instep, frequently decorated with large ornamental buckle. Worn in the 17th and 18th c. in the U.S. and revived often.

colonial tongue Stiffened shoe tongue that extends up from vamp of colonial shoe and is frequently trimmed with ornamental buckle.

columnar heel High circular-styled heel graduating from wide width at sole of shoe to small base.

combat boot Ankle-high laced boot worn by U.S. armed forces and made of special retanned leather designed to be waterproof. Adopted as fashionable footwear in the 1980s and 1990s.

combination last See under FOOTWEAR: LAST.

commonsense heel Low heel used on children's or infants' shoe made by increasing size of OUTSOLE at heel. See under FOOTWEAR: SOLE.

∞**congress boot/congress gaiter** Ankle-high shoe with leather or cloth top and elastic gore inset on each side that was popular from Civil War to early 20th c. Served as the pattern for ROMEO SLIPPERS for men and JULIET SLIPPERS for women (see under FOOTWEAR).

continental heel High, narrow heel made straight in front with square corners at base and slight curve at back. Has a slight edge extending forward where it joins the sole. Exaggeratedly high and narrow version is called a SPIKE HEEL (see under FOOTWEAR).

continental heel

cookie See under FOOTWEAR: ARCH CUSHION.

copped shoe See under FOOTWEAR: CRAKOW.

∞**copper toe** Metal cap placed on children's shoes to keep them from scuffing and wearing out. Used at the turn of the 20th c.

cork See under FOOTWEAR: GALOSH #2.

corkies See under FOOTWEAR: WEDGE HEEL.

∞**corned shoe** Broad-toed shoe worn from 1510 to 1540.

∞**cothurnus** (ko'-thur-nus) Ancient Greek and Roman calf-high boot laced up the front, made of colored leather with thick soles, sometimes of cork if wearer wished to appear taller. Worn by upper classes, huntsmen, and tragedians on stage in ancient Greece. Also called *buskin.* Also spelled *kothornus.*

cothurnus or buskin

counter Extra cup-shaped reinforcement placed at heel of shoe upper, between outer upper and lining, to add stiffness.

Courrèges boot (Koor'-rej) White calf-length, low-heeled fashion boot introduced by French designer André Courrèges in fall of 1963 for wear with miniskirts.

court shoe 1. See under TENNIS SHOE. 2. (British usage) PUMP (see under FOOTWEAR).

court tie 1. (British usage) Man's low-cut oxford, generally of patent leather, worn as part of ceremonial COURT DRESS in England. ∞2. (British usage) Woman's laced oxford of early 20th c. made with two or three pairs of eyelets in blucher style.

covered heel Heel of wood or plastic covered with leather or another plastic.

cowboy boot High-heeled, dip-top, calf-high boot of highly ornate tooled or appliquéd leather, often two-tone. First worn by cowboys of the western U.S., now adapted for women and children. Also called *dip-top boot* and *western boot.*

cowboy boot

∞**crakow/crakowe/cracow/krakow** (kra'-kow) Long-toed shoe of soft material—either a separate shoe or cut in one piece with the hose—introduced from Poland during reign of Richard II in England. During the 14th and 15th c., toes of shoes

crakow

became so long that they were stuffed and fastened by gold and silver chains to bracelets below the knees. Also called *copped, piked,* or *peaked shoe. Der.* After Cracow, Poland. Later called **poulaine** (pooh-lane'). Also spelled *poulain, pullayne.*

crampons Iron plates with spikes on the bottom that fasten onto shoes or boots so as to facilitate walking or climbing on ice.

creedmore **1.** Calf-high, laced work boot with two buckled straps at top. Worn during last part of the 19th and early 20th c. **2.** Ankle-high shoe with buckled strap over instep.

creepers Small plates of metal set with spikes fastened over soles of shoes by straps. Worn when walking on ice and snow to prevent slipping.

crepe-soled shoe Shoe made with crepe rubber sole and heel. Originally worn for sportswear, they were so comfortable that they were adopted for everyday wear, particularly by men and schoolchildren. Fashionable for women since early 1970s.

crepida (pl. *crepidae*) See under FOOTWEAR: KREPIS.

crescent toe Narrow-toed shoe ending with a curved rather than a NEEDLE TOE (see under FOOTWEAR).

Crocs™ Waterproof, no-slip shoes, perforated in the front and with a sling back. Initially marketed as a boating shoe, the shoes became an almost instant fashion, were much copied, and were made in many colors.

∞**cromwell shoe** Woman's shoe with large buckle-trimmed tongue worn in late 1860s for croquet parties. Reintroduced in 1888 with high-cut vamp and large bow trim for daytime wear. *Der.* Named for Oliver Cromwell, Lord Protector of England (from 1653 to 1658).

∞**crooked shoe** Shoe cut specifically to fit left or right foot, first produced in volume about 1850, superseding shoes that were straight-cut and fit either foot.

crossover thong sandal See under FOOTWEAR: THONG SANDAL #3.

∞**croquet boot** Woman's shoe of mid 1860s made of MOROCCAN LEATHER (see under LEATHERS), frequently trimmed with fancy toe-cap, laced with colored ribbon, and trimmed with tassels. *Der.* Named for the game of croquet, a fashionable pastime of this era.

∞**cuaran** (kwar'-ahn) Knee-length boots of horsehide or cowhide held up by thongs—originally "early Scottish bands made of rawhide." Worn by Scots Highlanders around 1500.

cuban heel Medium to high broad heel with slight curve in back, popular in 1930s and 1940s. The **block heel** is a similar straight heel, but set further back and approximately the same width at top and base.

cube heel Square-backed heel made of leather or Lucite®.

cushion sole Cork, felt, or foam rubber used under the insole of shoe as shock absorber when walking.

cutouts In the shoe industry, tiny patterns shaped like diamonds, teardrops, squares, and other shapes cut out of the upper part of shoe to give open-air effect.

deck shoe See under FOOTWEAR: BOATING SHOE.

demi-boot Short boot reaching just to the ankle. Also called *half-boot.*

derby shoe A low-cut leather shoe similar to an OXFORD (see under FOOTWEAR), the major difference being that the tongue and the vamp are cut in one piece. Like the oxford, the quarters are topstitched on the vamp.

desert boot See under FOOTWEAR: CHUKKA BOOTS.

dip-top boot See under FOOTWEAR: COWBOY BOOT.

discotheque shoe A sole with a small heel, fastened to the foot by means of a few narrow straps. Popular for dancing at nightclubs in the mid- and late 1960s. *Der.* French *discotheque,* "record library."

Doc Martens Lace-up boots with air pocket soles to ease pressure on the feet. The boots, first marketed in 1959, were adopted by skinheads and punks in the 1960s and 1970s and subsequently became widely popular among young people.

Dr. Scholl's exercise sandals A simple sandal developed by Dr. Scholl in the late 1960s; its wood sole is characterized by a raised toe and contoured bottom that causes the foot to grip and flex the shoe when walking. The simple leather band across the top of the wood sole comes in a variety of colors.

∞**dollar-round toe** Toe of a shoe whose shape coincided with the rounded edge of half a silver dollar, as it was once referred to in the shoemaking trade.

∞**dom pedro shoe** Ankle-high man's heavy work shoe fastened with laces and one buckled strap over center of lacing, worn in early 1900s. *Der.* Introduced by Dom Pedro of Brazil.

d'orsay pump/d'orsay slipper Pump with closed heel and toe, cut down to the sole at the sides, leaving shank bare. Often made with high heel. Popular in 1940s as evening slipper or at-home shoe. Revived periodically. *Der.* Named for *Count d'Orsay.* See under ORSAY, COUNT D'.

d'orsay pump with ankle strap

double-needle toe See under FOOTWEAR: NEEDLE TOE.

doubler Extra layer of soft fabric placed between the leather and the lining of shoe to make leather look plumper.

double stitchdown See under FOOTWEAR: STITCHDOWN SHOE CONSTRUCTION.

draped heel Heel on woman's shoe with leather or fabric from COUNTER (see under FOOTWEAR) arranged in folds over the back.

draped heel

dress shoe 1. Man's or woman's shoe worn for formal occasions, general wear, and business. Does not include sport shoes or crepe-soled shoes. 2. Girl's shoes worn on Sunday or for special occasions, not for school or sportswear.

∞**dress wellington** Fitted stocking reaching to the knee, attached to a shoe similar to an EVENING SLIPPER (see under FOOTWEAR) and worn under the dress trousers or PANTALOONS (see under PANTS). Worn by men with evening clothes from 1830 to 1850.

driving shoe A casual moccasin or slip-on shoe, ideal for driving because of its flexible grip sole that wraps partway up the heel to protect the back of the shoe. This sole may also be found on sneakers.

∞**duckbills** As they are called today, broad-toed flat shoes worn in England from about 1490 to 1540—shown in paintings of Henry VIII.

duckbills

duck shoe Formerly trademarked oxford or slip-on style shoe usually made in two colors (e.g., brown with tan, navy with yellow) of manufactured waterproof materials with chain-tread rubber soles. Also called *rubber moccasin.*

dutch boy heel Low heel with medium-sized base; its back slants slightly and inside edge is slanted toward front, where it joins the edge.

dutchman Triangular wedge placed between insole and outsole of shoe to improve posture of wearer. Also used between layers of a built-up heel to adjust heel pitch.

dyeable shoe Shoe made of white fabric such as satin, faille, or silk that may be dyed to match a dress, worn primarily for evening parties or weddings.

∞**Eclipse Tie** Trade name for woman's shoe made with one pair of eyelets and a pointed tongue usually coming up high on the instep. Worn in late 19th and early 20th c.

edge In the shoe industry, part of shoe that is visible around outside of front of shoe sole—may be rounded, beveled, or square.

∞**egyptian sandal** Thong-type sandal with T-strap coming up over instep to join two straps attached to both sides of sole. Worn by ancient Egyptians (e.g., sandal found in King Tut's tomb and made entirely of gold).

eighths Height of heels of shoes are measured in eighths of an inch (e.g., a $^{16}/_{8}$ heel is a 2″ heel, a $^{4}/_{8}$ heel is a ½″ heel).

∞**elastic-sided boot** Ankle-high boot, introduced for men and women about 1837, with India-rubber insert on each side, and patented by James Dowie.

elevator heel Man's heel worn to make him appear taller. Inside of shoe is built up at the heel, making the outside of shoe appear lower than it is. Attached heel lift is higher than average.

Elevator shoe Trademark, now expired, for a man's shoe with a wedge inserted inside the shoe toward the heel to make the man appear taller. Usually made to order.

engineer's boot Man's 12″ high, straight-sided boot with low heel and leather strap buckled across the instep. Also has buckle and strap over elastic gore set in the top.

espadrille (ess-pa'-dril) 1. Rope-soled shoe with canvas upper. Some versions tied on with long shoelaces threaded through top of shoe, crossed, and tied around the ankle. Originally worn for bathing shoe and later for sportswear. Popular in 1940s, reintroduced in 1970s, and fashionable periodically since. 2. Restyled in 1980s as an oxford, or pump cut high and straight across instep with medium-high wedge heel covered with jute, made with crepe sole, and no lacers. *Der.* French, shoe made of canvas with cord sole.

espadrille #1

evening shoe/evening slipper Delicate shoe worn with evening clothes. Women's styles include pumps or sandals in gold, silver, or metallic kid, or luxurious fabrics; men's style is usually a patent-leather pump or slipper.

everett Man's house slipper with low back and high tongue curving over instep.

exercise sandal Any of a variety of sandals designed to support the foot properly during exercise. The earliest of these was the trademarked DR. SCHOLL'S EXERCISE SANDALS (see under FOOTWEAR).

eyestay Section of footwear that reinforces the holes used for lacing.

fashion boot See under FOOTWEAR: BOOT.

faust slipper See under FOOTWEAR: ROMEO SLIPPER.

felts Slippers with soft sole and upper frequently made of felt.

figure skate Fancy skating boot with reinforced instep and counter, laces to above the ankle with speed lacing to the top. Color is usually white for woman, black for men.

filler See under FOOTWEAR: SOLE.

fishing boot See under FOOTWEAR: HIP BOOT and WADERS.

flange heel Heel that flares or angles to make a wider base.

flat/flatties See under FOOTWEAR: FLAT HEEL.

flat heel Broad, low heel originally used on children's shoes, now popular on women's shoes. Shoes with this heel are called *flats* or *flatties.*

flat heel

flip-flops Sandal made with sponge rubber sole fastened to the foot by two straps that come up between the first and second toes and fasten to the side of the sole. Copied from the original Japanese *zori,* which is a sandal.

flippers Rubber extensions, shaped like a duck's webbed foot, that fit over the feet and attach with straps around heels. Worn for scuba diving, underwater swimming, and water sports. Also called *fins.*

floating pedestal wedge Medium broad heel similar to a wedge, but cut out under the arch, making it wider at the base of the heel and slanting toward the sole.

floats See under FOOTWEAR: CHUKKA BOOT.

flokati (flow-kat′-ee) Handcrafted Greek slipper sock in above-ankle length, made of fuzzy wool in bright colors and used as after-ski slipper. See FOOTWEAR: SLIPPER SOCKS.

folding slipper See FOOTWEAR: PULLMAN SLIPPER.

foxing 1. Extra fancy-cut piece of leather sewed on at the top of the back seam of the shoe for reinforcement and decoration. 2. Strip of rubber fastened to the upper and the shoe that goes all around the shoe.

∞**french-fall boot** Leather boot of 17th c. with extravagantly wide top crushed down to reveal elaborate lace cannons. Also called *bucket-top boots.* Also see under HOSIERY: BOOT HOSE.

french heel High heel that curves inward at back, then flares slightly outward at base.

french heel

french seam Shoe seam that starts with a simple or closed seam, restitched on either side on the outside. Used for closing back of shoe.

fringed tongue Shoe tongue finished with saw-toothed edge at top.

Frye boot Boot of WELLINGTON type (see under FOOTWEAR), first manufactured in 1863 for Union soldiers. A trade name now used for a variety of boot styles.

gaiter Cloth or leather covering for leg and ankle, buttoned or buckled at side, often held on by straps under foot. Worn by men from end of 18th to early 20th c. and fashionable for women from 1820s to 1840s, and from 1890s to early 20th c. Revived in 1960s in vinyl, leather, or cloth. Fashionable in 1980s and after in water-repellent fabrics for cross-country skiing. Also called *leggings.* Also see under FOOTWEAR: SPATS.

∞**gaiter boots** Woman's buttoned or elastic-sided, ankle-high leather shoes worn from 1835 to 1870. Made with cloth tops and fastened at side—simulating shoe worn with GAITERS (see under FOOTWEAR).

galosh 1. Waterproof ankle-high boot worn over the shoe, fastened with a snap, buckle, or zipper. Rubber galoshes were patented in 1842. Also spelled *goloshe, golosh.* Also called *arctics.* See under CLOSURES: GALOSH CLIP. ∞2. Wooden platform elevating foot above street, worn in 15th and 16th c. Also called a *patten.* Called a **cork** when a man's galosh of 15th c. had a cork rather than wooden sole. ∞3. In the 17th c. also called *boxes.* ∞4. In 16th and 17th c. wooden-soled low overboots. ∞5. In 17th c. became "covers for shoes." ∞6. In 18th c. called CLOGS. Also spelled *galoche, galage, galoss, galossian;* plurals: *gallоses, galloshes, gallotives.*

ganymede sandal (gan-e-meed) Open sandal derived from Ancient Greek style, with vertical straps from the sole extending up the legs and crossed at intervals around the leg with additional straps. Introduced in 1960s to wear with minidresses. *Der.* Named for the beautiful boy who was the cupbearer of the gods in Greek mythology.

george boot Ankle-high boot made with one-buckle fastening similar to JODHPUR BOOT (see under FOOTWEAR). Widely accepted for general wear by men in late 1960s.

geta Japanese sandal elevated by means of wooden blocks under the sole and fastened to foot by two straps, meeting between first and second toes, curved to fasten at sides of sole. Adapted for beachwear in 1960s.

gillie/ghillie (gil′-ee) 1. Laced shoe, usually without a tongue, with rounded lacer pulling through leather loops and fastened around the ankle. Worn with Scottish kilt, therefore also called *kiltie* (see under FOOTWEAR: KILTIE OXFORD). *Der.* Popularized by Edward VIII and sometimes called *prince of wales shoe.* 2. Many adaptations of this style, particularly for women's shoes, include some styles with high heels. *Der.* Scottish, *gille,* "an attendant or personal servant to a Highland chieftain."

gladiator sandal Flat sandal with several wide cross straps holding sole to foot, and one wide strap around ankle. Introduced in late 1960s. *Der.* Copied from sandals worn in Roman arena by "gladiators."

go-go boot Calf-length white boot, similar to COURRÈGES BOOT (see under FOOTWEAR). *Der.* Named because worn by go-go dancers.

golf shoe Oxford-style shoe made of oil-treated leather usually given a water-repellent finish, and having a foam-cushioned inner sole. Original shoes had replaceable golf spikes, located on heel and sole, attached to two metal sole plates. Popular in 1920s in a two-toned black-and-white style that returned to fashion in late 1960s and early 1970s. In the 1980s and after, soles of shoes were made with solid rubber sole with rubber spikes.

granny boot Women's boots laced up the front in imitation of high-topped shoes of 19th c.

Gucci® loafer See under FOOTWEAR: LOAFER.

gumshoe Sneaker or rubber overshoe, as known colloquially. From this comes the slang for a detective or private investigator, alluding to the quiet tread of *sneakers,* which is useful in confidential work.

half-boot See under FOOTWEAR: DEMI-BOOT.

half-jack boot See under FOOTWEAR: JOCKEY BOOT.

harlow pump Sabot-strap pump with high, chunky heel popular in early 1970s. *Der.* Named after shoes worn by Jean Harlow, Hollywood actress of the 1920s and 1930s.

harlow slipper Boudoir slippers, similar to toeless SLIDES (see under FOOTWEAR), with medium to high heel, trimmed with marabou. Copied from slippers worn by Jean Harlow, the Hollywood actress, in the late 1920s and 1930s.

heel Part of the shoe that elevates the back of the foot. Heels may be flat, medium, or high and are measured in one-eighths of an inch (e.g., a 16/8 heel is 2″ high). Inside edge of heel is called the **breast** of the heel. Extra replaceable piece on bottom is called the **heel lift.** Heels may be made of wood, plastic, Lucite®, or metal.

heel horn See under FOOTWEAR: A.T.P.

heel lift See under FOOTWEAR: HEEL.

heely (plural *heelys* or *heelies*) Athletic shoe, trademarked as Heelys Sidewalk Sports™, and also known as *skate shoe* or *roller shoe.* Has one or more removable wheels underneath the heel that allows the wearer to roll as if on skates. Especially popular with children.

∞**hessian boot** (hesh′-an) Man's black leather riding boot, calf-length in back, curving upward to below the knee in front and ending in a point decorated with a tassel. Often made with narrow top border of another color. Worn from 1790s to 1850s.

∞**heuse** (huse) Mid-thigh-length leather riding boot with thick sole, fastened with buttons, buckles, or straps on outer side of leg. Worn by men from 1240s to end of 15th c. Later called *housel* or *huseau.*

high button shoe See under FOOTWEAR: BUTTONED SHOE.

high cut Footwear that extends over the ankle.

hiking boot Above-the-ankle boot with padded collar and soft leather lining. Uppers are made of various materials including leather, GORE-TEX®, or MANUFACTURED FIBER FABRIC. Laced up front through riveted D-RING CLOSURE with SPEED LACING (see CLOSURES) at top. Usually has a cushioned insole and padded quarter and tongue. Heel and lug-type outsole are made of VIBRAM® (a durable synthetic rubber blend—see under FOOTWEAR) welded to upper. Also called *hikers* and *mountain climbing boot.* Shown at FOOTWEAR: UTILITY BOOT.

hip boot Rubber fishing boot, thigh-length, with straps at sides to fasten to belt at waist. Usually insulated and made with a cushioned innersole, steel shank, semihard toe cap, and cleated sole. Also see under FOOTWEAR: WADERS.

hobnailed boot Boot with a sole into which short nails with large heads have been set. The nail heads serve to prevent wear on the soles.

hockey skate Skate rounded in front and attached to boot with reinforced toe. Sometimes has a strap across the instep, worn for ice hockey.

hooded heel Heel slanting into shank of shoe, usually covered in one piece with upper.

housel See under FOOTWEAR: HEUSE.

house slipper Any type of slippers worn indoors.

huarache (wah-rah-chee) Mexican sandal consisting of closely woven leather thongs forming vamp, made with sling back and flat heel. Popular casual shoe in the U.S. for all ages and both sexes.

huseau See under FOOTWEAR: HEUSE.

Hush Puppies® Trade name initially used for casual oxford or slip-on shoes with sueded leather uppers and crepe soles. Popular for men, women, and children. The trademark has now been extended to other shoe styles and products.

∞**hussar boots** (hoo-zar′) Man's calf-length boots coming to a slight point in front, sometimes having turnover tops and iron soles. Style borrowed from the military and worn by men from 1800 to 1820.

ice cube heel Low, square-cut heel of clear Lucite® introduced in 1970. *Der.* The shape and size of an ice cube.

Indian moccasin See under FOOTWEAR: MOCCASIN.

inlay In the shoe industry, a piece of leather or fabric placed underneath a cut-out layer of leather and stitched into place for a decorative effect.

insole Inside of shoe on which sole of foot rests; usually covered by SOCK LINING (see under FOOTWEAR).

instep The inside arch area of the shoe.

insulated boot Any boot with a lining for protection against cold, rain, snow, and bad weather. May be lined with fur, acrylic pile, wool, or foam-bonded fabric.

inverted heel A chunky heel that extends horizontally from the ball of the foot with its length lying on the ground; the back of the shoe, which supports the heel of the foot, seemingly floats in mid air. First introduced by Marc Jacobs in his spring 2008 collection. Also called *reverse heel.*

inverted heel

italian heel Shoe heel worn from 1770s on that curved inward at back, similar to LOUIS HEEL (see under FOOTWEAR). Also had a wedge-shaped extension at top of heel extending under the sole nearly to ball of foot.

jack boot #1
mid-18th c.

∞**jack boot** 1. Man's heavy leather riding boot made with square toes and heels with expanded bucket tops extending over knees. Worn by cavalry and civilians from 1660 to 18th c. **2.** Lightweight boots of 18th c. made of soft leather, sometimes laced or buttoned on outside. Also called *light jack boots.* For HALF-JACK BOOT see under FOOTWEAR: JOCKEY BOOT #3.

jazz oxford Flat-heeled OXFORD made with VAMP line (see under FOOTWEAR) curved and stitched extending downward to arch. The remainder of shoe is cut in one piece with front lacing.

jellies/jelly beans Molded footwear of soft plastic or rubber made in many styles (e.g., wedgies, multistrapped sandals, flat-heeled thongs, high-heeled pumps, and booties). Some have cut-out "portholes" or lattice strips, and are worn with bright-colored contrasting socks. All are made in a great variety of bright colors and were high fashion in 1983–1984. Originally introduced for children, they were imported from Brazil, China, Japan, Greece, and Mexico and were also made in the U.S. The style was basically a practical fisherman's sandal made of soft plastic. *Der.* Named for soft translucent look of jelly in jelly-bean colors.

∞**jemmy boot** Man's lightweight riding boot, a fashionable type of JOCKEY BOOT (see under FOOTWEAR), worn in 18th c.

jockey boot **1.** High leather boot similar to RIDING BOOT (see under FOOTWEAR), worn by jockeys in horse races. ∞**2.** Child's high boot of 19th c. often with cuff of contrasting material trimmed with a tassel. ∞**3.** Man's below-the-knee boot with turned-down top of soft, light-colored leather with loops on either side of top to aid in pulling on. Worn from 1680s to end of 18th c. Also called *half-jack boot.* After 1780s, called *top boot.*

jodhpur boot (jod'-poor) Ankle-high boot fastened with one buckle on the side, worn for horseback riding and for general wear. Similar to GEORGE BOOT (see under FOOTWEAR). *Der.* Named for Jodhpur, a city in India.

juliet slipper Woman's slipper with a high front and back, and V-shaped elastic gores at the sides. *Der.* Named for heroine of William Shakespeare's play *Romeo and Juliet.*

jungle boot Combat boot used for U.S. Army in Vietnam. Made with heavy steel SHANK (see under FOOTWEAR) and tiny drainage holes in sides and heel.

kalso Danish open sandal with platform sole, carved from laminated mahogany, finished with rubber walking sole, and held on with two wide straps—one over instep and one around heel.

∞**kampskatcha slipper** (kamp-skat'-cha) Woman's shoe of late 18th c. with pointed upturned toe, moderately high VAMP, and low curved FRENCH HEEL (see under FOOTWEAR) frequently made of Spanish leather with fur lining. Also called *Chinese slipper.*

Keds® See under FOOTWEAR: SNEAKERS.

kiltie flat A low-heeled shoe with a fringed tongue and shoelace tied over top in a bow usually made with crepe sole. Compare with FOOTWEAR: KILTIE OXFORD.

kiltie oxford Laced shoe with a shawl or fringed tongue projecting over front of shoe through which laces may be tied. Adopted from Scottish-type shoes and popular in 1930s, 1960s, and 1980s.

kiltie oxford with wing-tip toe

kitten heels A short stiletto heel, 1¼″ to 2″ high, with a curve that sets the heel in from the shoe and quickly tapers to a thin base. Also called *trainer heels,* as they are frequently the first heeled shoe worn by a young girl.

kitten heel

knee-high boot Boot that ends just below knee, and fits tightly around the leg and ankle.

knob toe Bulbous toe introduced in the early 1970s. Similar to BULLDOG TOE (see under FOOTWEAR).

kolhapuri sandal/kolhapure/kolhapur (ko'-lap-poor') Leather thong-type sandal imported from India, made of hand-tooled water buffalo hide. When sandals are first worn in the shower, the leather becomes permanently shaped to the sole of the foot. Also spelled *kolhapure, kolhapur.*

kothornus See under FOOTWEAR: COTHURNUS.

krakow See under FOOTWEAR: CRAKOW.

∞**krepis** (kray-pees') Man's toeless sandal with sides and straps crossing in center front, worn in ancient Greece. Similar to Roman sandal called *crepida.*

landlady shoe See under FOOTWEAR: WOOLWORTH SHOE.

∞**landrine/ladrine** (lon-dreen') Louis XIII boot with wide flared cuff reaching halfway up leg with top turned up for riding horseback. Also called *lazarine.*

last Carved wooden or molded plastic form on which a shoe is made. There is a right and left form for each pair in each size. A **combination last** has heel of narrower width than toe.

∞**lasting boots** Late 19th-c. boots made with black wool uppers.

∞**latchet** Strap used to fasten a shoe, as it has been called since the Middle Ages.

lazarine See under FOOTWEAR: LANDRINE.

lift The replaceable part on the bottom of the heel of the shoe. Also called *heel lift.*

lineman's boot High-top or above-the-ankle leather boot, usually black with laces up the center front, made of retanned leather. May have eyelets at the bottom and hooks for SPEED LACING (see under CLOSURES) near the top.

lining Leather or fabric that covers part or all of the interior of footwear.

Littleway shoe construction Process of shoe construction or manufacturing that uses a staple to attach the insole to the upper. The outsole may be sewed on with a lock stitch or cemented to the insole.

loafer Slip-on shoe of moccasin-type construction with a slotted strap stitched to the VAMP (see under FOOTWEAR). Introduced first for wear by college girls in the 1940s, now a classic worn by adults and children. Variations include **chain loafer,** trimmed with metal links or hardware trim over the instep. A classic shoe since the 1960s. A variant of the chain loafer is the **Gucci® loafer** (goo'chee), the most popular of the fine shoes sold by Italian firm Gucci® in the U.S. since early 1960s. It has a distinctive gold-metal harness hardware decoration across vamp. Man's shoe has low heel, woman's, a medium heel. Widely copied throughout the 1960s and early 1970s. The **penny loafer** has a slot in the strap across each vamp into which a coin is sometimes inserted. Pennies were originally inserted, but dimes and quarters are now more generally used. Originally in brown but featured in colors beginning in 1980s. The **tassel-top loafer** has a leather tassel on instep.

penny loafer

louis heel Heel of medium height curved sharply inward around sides and back, then flared slightly at base, similar to heels worn in Louis XV period. Low version is called **baby louis heel,** and a **bell-bottom heel** is an exaggerated version with a chunky medium heel, curved inward and then flaring at the bottom.

louis heel

bell-bottom heel

lounger Pull-on boot for cold weather with full-grain cowhide upper stitched to rubber shoe. Made with cushioned innersole vulcanized to chain-tread crepe outer sole. Sometimes lined and insulated with wool pile and sheepskin innersole.

low cut Footwear cut below the ankle.

lug sole Shoe or boot sole with rubber ridges or cleats to provide additional traction.

lumberman's overboot Man's heavy laced 10″-high boot with oiled-leather top, rubber vamp, and sole worn over felt inner boot. Worn by men in early 20th c., especially when working in lumber industry. *Der.* Boot originally worn in lumbering trade.

Maine hunting boot Waterproof boot consisting of leather uppers sewn to waterproof, vulcanized rubber bottoms. Developed by Leon Bean, owner of L.L. Bean Company of Maine, and first sold by his firm in 1913.

majorette boot Calf-high white boot worn by majorettes or cheerleaders at athletic events since the 1940s. Some have long white tassel attached to front.

mamma shoe Retail store and trade name for shoes worn by older women that stress comfort rather than style. Usually made in an oxford style with medium-high broad heel.

mary jane 1. Low-heeled slipper made of patent leather with blunt toe and single strap over the instep that buttons or buckles at center or side. First used as a trademarked shoe for children in 1927, the style has remained popular ever since, although currently the trademark is applied to a wide variety of apparel. 2. In 1980s a *flattie* or *wedgie* in pump style with buckled strap coming high over the instep. *Der.* Named for shoes worn by character Mary Jane in comic strip *Buster Brown,* drawn by R. F. Outcault in early 1900s. Compare with FOOTWEAR: BABY-DOLL SHOE.

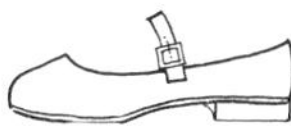
mary jane #1

McKay shoe construction Shoe manufacturing process in which the upper is pulled around the last and fastened to the insole by means of tacks. The outsole may be attached by stitching or by cementing. Invented by Lyman Blake in 1861.

medallion In the shoe industry, an ornamental pattern punched in leather in center of man's wing-tip oxford.

mexican wedding boot Soft, white, leather, above-the-calf boot made in moccasin style fastened down the outside with four large buttons. Colorful embroidery extends from VAMP (see under FOOTWEAR) up to top of boot.

midsole See under FOOTWEAR: SOLE.

military heel Medium to low heel with a broad base. Slants slightly in back and usually has an attached rubber lift. Used on comfort shoes and walking shoes for women.

military heel

miranda pump Platform pump with high, heavy, flared heel worn in 1969. *Der.* Named after Carmen Miranda, a popular movie star of the late 1930s and 1940s.

moccasin Heelless shoe in which the sole is made of leather and comes up to form the QUARTER and part of the VAMP (see under FOOTWEAR). A tonguelike curved piece is hand-stitched to complete the vamp. Thong is threaded around the collar of the slipper and ties on the instep. Frequently is fleece-lined. May have fringe, beadwork, or tassel trim. Sometimes called *Indian moccasin* because this footwear was worn originally by Native Americans.

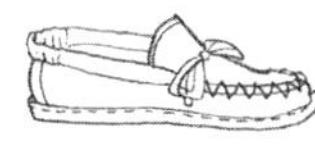
moccasin

moccasin-type shoe Shoe construction based on the MOCCASIN (see under FOOTWEAR), in which the UPPER starts under the sole of the foot and forms the quarter, with the toe stitched to an oval VAMP (see under FOOTWEAR). Hard soles, sometimes of rubber, are added to produce a more durable shoe than the soft Indian moccasin.

mod boot Various types of boots worn by boys and girls in mid-1960s in imitation of English mod fashions (e.g., see under FOOTWEAR: BEATLE BOOT).

moile/moyle/mowle See under FOOTWEAR: MULE.

molded boot A ski boot, sometimes of glass fiber, closed with buckles, made with entire sole and part of shoe molded in one piece. Introduced for skiwear in the late 1960s.

monk shoe Closed shoe with wide buckled strap over tongue at instep rather than lacings. Popular for women in 1940s and for men during World War II when this style was favored by U.S. Army Air Corps officers. Revived in late 1960s and early 1970s.

monk shoe

monster shoe Clumsy, bulky shoe with wide bulbous toe and large clunky heel. Popular in 1968.

motorcycle boots A protective boot worn for riding. Modern versions take advantage of technology, utilizing soft leather to allow for flexing of the ankle and a rugged tread pattern on the sole that dampens vibrations and allows for walking on any kind of turf. Some soles are made with a steel shank.

mountain climbing boot See under FOOTWEAR: HIKING BOOT.

mousers Women's leather stocking-pants reaching to the waist with attached chunky-type shoes made of shiny, wet-appearing leather. Introduced by Mary Quant, British designer, in 1969.

mukluk 1. Boot reaching to lower calf worn by Alaskan Eskimos, made of walrus hide or sealskin in moccasin construction, tanned with the hair left on. Copied for winter wear for men, women, and children in same style since 1960s. 2. Slipper socks made in MOCCASIN construction (see under FOOTWEAR).

mule High-heeled slipper or shoe with vamp but no back, often made of fancy leathers and fabrics. Name has been used since 16th c. Also spelled *moile, moyle, mowle.*

mule

museum heel Medium-height heel with front and back curving inward and then outward to make a flared base. Also called *shepherdess heel.*

∞**napoleons** Long military boots, reaching above knee in front, with piece cut out in back. Worn by civilians on horseback in 1850s. *Der.* Named for Napoleon III, Emperor of France, from 1851 to 1871.

needle toe Long, narrow, extremely pointed toe. Narrower and more pointed variations are called *double-needle* and *triple-needle toes.* Also see under FOOTWEAR: WINKLE PICKERS.

Nike® waffle trainers First true running shoe, developed in 1974 by Bill Bowerman (University of Oregon track coach) who, in seeking a way to get more traction without increasing the weight of shoes, experimented with making the soles in a waffle iron. Subsequently this textured sole was incorporated into a running shoe manufactured by a then-new company called Nike.

oker See under FOOTWEAR: COCKER.

open-back shoe See under FOOTWEAR: SLINGBACK SHOE.

open-shank sandal High-, medium-, or low-heeled sandal shaped like a D'ORSAY PUMP (see under FOOTWEAR) with a strap around the ankle or over the instep; frequently heelless and toeless. Popular style since the late 1930s.

open shank shoe Women's shoe with closed toe and heel portions but open on sides down to sole; sometimes with side straps connecting vamp and quarter. Also see under FOOTWEAR: D'ORSAY PUMP.

open-toed shoe Women's shoe with the toe section cut out.

opera pump Plain, undecorated woman's pump with medium to high heel. Upper is cut from a single piece of leather or fabric. Introduced in 1920s and a basic style since then.

opera slipper Man's bedroom slipper similar to D'ORSAY SLIPPER (see under FOOTWEAR), but front and back sections overlap at shank.

outsole See under FOOTWEAR: SOLE.

oval toe Woman's shoe toe, narrower than a round toe but not an extreme point.

∞**overboot** Crocheted or fabric woman's boot of 1860s worn over the shoes for warmth in carriages in winter. Also used as bedsocks for warmth in winter.

overlay A piece of leather or other material stitched on shoe in decorative manner. Usually made of a contrasting color or a textured leather such as lizard or snakeskin.

overshoe Waterproof fabric or rubber shoe worn over other shoes in inclement weather. Also called *rubbers.* Also see under FOOTWEAR: ARCTICS, GALOSHES, and RAIN BOOTS.

over-the-knee boot Long footwear that ends at some point above the knee.

oxford 1. Originally a shoeman's term to differentiate low-cut shoes from boots. Basic style of low shoe usually fastened with shoelaces, but may be closed with buckles, Velcro®, or other type of fasteners. Shown at definition of FOOTWEAR. ∞2. Historically was a half-boot introduced in England about 1640 and worn by university students. *Der.* Named for Oxford University.

∞**oxford button-overs** Men's shoes of 1860s, covering the instep and closed with buttons instead of laces.

∞**oxonian boots** Man's short black boots worn in 1830s and 1840s often made of patent leather with wedge-shaped portion cut out of either side at top so they pull on easily. Also called *oxonians* or *collegians.*

∞**oxonian shoe** High-laced shoe with seam at instep worn by men in 1848.

pac boot Laced boot coming to the lower calf of the leg, sometimes made with traction-tread for sole and heel. Insulated and pile-lined, sometimes made in rubber. Basic-type boot originally made in MOCCASIN-type construction (see under FOOTWEAR), worn by sportsmen, hunters, and workmen.

paddock boot A less formal type of riding boot that laces to close in order to provide adjustable ankle support.

pantofle (pan-tof′-l) ∞1. Heelless slipper worn from end of 15th to mid-17th c. by men and women. Also spelled *pantoffle, pantoffel.* 2. Overshoe similar to a patten, with a cork sole worn in late 16th c. Also spelled *pantables, pantacles.* 3. Bedroom slippers. *Der.* French, *pantoufle,* "slipper."

pants boot Ankle-high shoe-boot designed to wear with pants.

patten ∞1. Overshoe worn over regular shoes to raise feet above muddy streets. One type had a wooden sole with top portion indented for the heel and was secured by strap fitting over regular shoe. Another consisted of a wooden sole raised about three inches with bands of iron forming the walking surface. Worn by men and women from 14th to mid-19th c. Also called *clog.* Also see under FOOTWEAR: CHOPINE. 2. Shoe fitted with iron blades for skating in Middle Ages.

patten #1 18th c.

peaked shoe See under FOOTWEAR: CRAKOW.

peeptoe See under FOOTWEAR: OPEN-TOED SHOE.

penny loafer See FOOTWEAR: LOAFER.

perforations Small holes punched through leather of shoe to achieve decorative effect. Used particularly for SPECTATOR PUMPS and BROGUES (see under FOOTWEAR). Also called *perfs* in shoe trade slang.

perfs See under FOOTWEAR: PERFORATIONS.

piked shoe See under FOOTWEAR: CRAKOW.

pinafore heel Flat leather or rubber heel made in one piece with the sole having a curve under arch of the shoe. Made in the same manner that rubber heels and soles are joined on SADDLE OXFORDS (see under FOOTWEAR).

pinking Saw-toothed trimming on edges of leather used in contrasting color on extra pieces applied to toes and heels of SPECTATOR PUMPS and GOLF SHOES (see under FOOTWEAR) for a decorative effect.

∞**pinson/pinsnet** Lightweight indoor slipper, often furred, worn from end of 14th to end of 16th c. by men and women. From 17th c. referred to as PUMP (see under FOOTWEAR).

platform sandal Open-type sandal with platform sole usually made with high heel. Popular in 1940s, 1970s, and periodically since.

platform shoe Shoe with thick mid-sole, usually made of cork and covered so that the wearer appears taller. Popular for women in 1940s and revived by Paris designer Yves Saint Laurent in 1960s. Worn by men in 1970s. Revived periodically.

platform shoe

platform sole Mid-sole of shoe, often made of cork or sponge rubber, raising the foot off ground on a platform varying in height from ½″ to 3″. Popular in 1940s for women's shoes, reintroduced in late 1960s by Roger Vivier in Paris, and popular in the U.S. from early 1970s.

platypus toe Squared-off tip of toe shaped like a duck's bill. *Der.* Named for animal with snout shaped in this manner.

plug/plugged oxford Low-laced shoe cut with VAMP and QUARTERS (see under FOOTWEAR) in one piece and a separate lace stay (e.g., FOOTWEAR: SADDLE OXFORDS).

point shoe See under FOOTWEAR: TOE SLIPPER.

police boot Black leather boot reaching to below the knee made in shiny, stiff leather. Similar to a RIDING BOOT (see under FOOTWEAR). Worn by motorcycle police, some state police, and by mounted police in the U.S. and Canada.

∞**polish boot** Woman's high, front-laced boot of 1860s decorated with colored high heel and tassel in front.

poulaine/poulain/pullayne See under FOOTWEAR: CRAKOW.

pre-walkers Infant's shoe with very soft soles, worn before child begins to walk.

prince of wales shoe See under FOOTWEAR: GILLIE.

pullman slipper Man's lightweight, glove leather, flat slipper that folds into small envelope for traveling. Also made in patterned stretch fabrics for women. *Der.* Named for railroad sleeping cars designed by George Pullman and Ben Field in 1858–59 and owned since 1864 by Pullman Palace Car Co.

pump Slip-on shoe with low-cut, rounded, or V-shaped THROAT, a heel that may be of any height and may be covered with the same material as the UPPER. Toes vary from rounded to pointed depending on the current style. Sometimes made with open toe and/or open heel in SLINGBACK SHOE. A classic style for women for day or evening since 1920s. Shown at definition for FOOTWEAR. Also see under SPECTATOR PUMP, COURT SHOE, and OPERA PUMP. See cross-references under FOOTWEAR. *Der.* Pump replaced the word *pinson* used in 17th c.

pyramid heel Medium-high heel with squared base flaring toward the sole—like an inverted pyramid.

pyramid heel

∞quail-pipe boot Man's high, soft leather boot worn pushed down and wrinkled on the leg. Fashionable in late 16th and early 17th c.

quarter Back portion of shoe upper covering the sides and back of the foot. In athletic footwear the top line of the quarter, called the **collar,** is sometimes padded.

racing shoe See under FOOTWEAR: RUNNING SHOE.

∞raglan boot Thigh-length, soft black leather boot worn by men for hunting in late 1850s. *Der.* Named after Lord Raglan. See RAGLAN, LORD.

rain boot 1. Lightweight plastic or rubber stretch galoshes that may be folded and carried in the purse. See under FOOTWEAR: TOTES®. 2. Clear fold-up plastic coverings extending to ankle with zip front. Made with hole at heel through which high-heeled shoe can be worn.

rand A leather strip placed between the shoe UPPER (see under FOOTWEAR) and the sole.

reverse heel See FOOTWEAR: INVERTED HEEL.

riding boot High boot coming to below the knee made of high-quality leather, usually custom ordered to fit leg. Worn with breeches for horseback riding. May have bootstraps at top for ease in dressing.

roller blades An updated version of roller skates, consisting of shoes with wheels attached.

roller skate Above-the-ankle boot made with polyurethane wheels, rubber toe stop, closed with eyelets and speed lacing. Worn for roller skating.

romeo slipper Man's pull-on, boot-type slipper with elastic side gores. Also called *faust slipper. Der.* Named for hero of William Shakespeare's play *Romeo and Juliet.*

rubber boot Molded rubber waterproof boot with or without insulated lining but usually fabric-lined, worn over the shoe (especially by children) or in place of the shoe as protection against rain or snow. In mid-1980s and after made in many colors (e.g., red, yellow, or purple).

rubbers Waterproof lightweight shoes that pull on over regular shoes in inclement weather. Also called *overshoes.* Also see under FOOTWEAR: STORM RUBBERS and TOE RUBBERS.

rubber shoe/rubber moccasin See under FOOTWEAR: DUCK SHOE.

ruby keeler shoe Low-heeled pump tied across instep with ribbon bow similar to tap shoes. Popular for teenagers in early 1970s. *Der.* Named after tap dancer Ruby Keeler, popular star of films in the 1930s who made a stage comeback on Broadway in 1971 in a revival of the 1917 musical *No, No Nanette.*

running shoe Sport shoe with crepe or rubber sole and upper made of two or three colors of contrasting leather or fabric. Sometimes laced to the toe and sometimes styled like a regular oxford. Style inspired by the track shoes worn by athletes, which sometimes have contrasting stripes of colored leather on the sides of the shoe. Also called *racing shoe.*

sabot (sa-bo′) 1. Shoe carved from one piece of wood, worn by peasants in France, Belgium, Spain, and Portugal. Also worn with Dutch national costume. 2. Clog shoe with thick wood sole and open heel, made with closed leather vamp or leather bands across instep.

sabot-strap shoe (sa-bó) Woman's shoe with a wide strap across instep, usually buckling to one side. May be used on a SPECTATOR PUMP (see under FOOTWEAR) type of shoe.

saddle Extra piece of leather sewed over instep of a shoe, usually of contrasting color or texture (e.g., black or brown on white shoes).

saddle oxford/saddle shoe Sport or school shoe usually made of white buck calf with a brown or black leather "saddle"-shaped section over the middle of the shoe. Usually made with rubber soles, it has been a basic style since the 1920s, very popular in the 1940s, and still worn today.

saddle oxford

saddle seam Hand- or machine-stitched seam used on shoes when two raw edges of leather stand up on outside, as on the VAMP of a MOCCASIN (see under FOOTWEAR).

safety shoe Work shoe with a heavy metal reinforced toe, or another protective feature, worn by industrial workers.

safety toe Steel toe box inserted between shoe upper and lining. Used on shoes worn by workmen in industrial plants for protection.

sandal Shoe held on the foot by means of straps or a projection between the toes. Usually made with an open shank and frequently toeless and heelless, or consisting of a sole held to the foot with straps. Worn since earliest times—gold sandals have been found in Egyptian tombs. Greeks and Romans wore many types of sandals. During the Middle Ages, sandals were worn only by peasants. In the 16th c., worn by monks in monastic orders, pilgrims, and by sovereigns at coronations. During the 1920s and 1930s, introduced for evening wear, sportswear, and day wear. *Der.* Greek, *sandalon.*

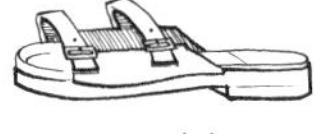
sandal

scuff Open-back, sometimes open-toe, slipper with flat heel. May be of fur, shaggy fabric, lightweight kid, terrycloth, or other fabrics.

sculptured heel Broad, medium-high heel made with a see-through center, introduced in 1960s. Similar to some free-form pieces of sculpture. Used on wooden clogs in late 1970s.

semi cut Shoe cut just to or slightly over the ankle. Also called *three-quarter cut.* Compare with FOOTWEAR: HIGH CUT and LOW CUT.

set-back heel Heel with straight back joined to the sole as far back as possible.

set-back heel

set-under heel Heel with outside edge curving forward under heel.

set-under heel

shandoots Footwear that combines characteristics of the shoe, sandal, and boot. These boot-like shoes with an open toe were introduced in 2012. Also called *sandal-oots* or *sandalboots.*

shank 1. The narrow part of the shoe under the arch of the foot between the heel and the ball of the foot. 2. The narrow strip of metal or other reinforcement inserted under arch of shoe between INSOLE (see under FOOTWEAR) and outer sole to give strength to the arch.

shawl tongue See under FOOTWEAR: TONGUE.

shell See under FOOTWEAR: SKIMMER.

shepherdess heel See under FOOTWEAR: MUSEUM HEEL.

shoe/shoes Outer covering for the foot that does not reach higher than the ankle. Shoes are basically made up of the sole, or part under the foot; the vamp, or front part of the shoe; the quarter or back of the shoe; and the shank or portion under the instep. Shoes may be of the slip-on variety or closed with laces or buckles. VELCRO® (see under CLOSURES) was introduced in the early 1980s for closings.

shower shoe Plain heelless pump with upper of fishnet and sole of rubber or crepe. Worn at home, in the shower, or at the beach.

side-gore shoe Slip-on shoe, usually with high vamp, that has triangular insertions of elastic at sides.

side-laced oxford Oxford laced at side front rather than center front, made with low wedge heel, reinforced counter, side perforations near sole for ventilation, and cushioned arch support. Often made in white and popular with nurses.

skate shoes See under FOOTWEAR: HEELY.

skating boot See under FOOTWEAR: FIGURE SKATE, HOCKEY SKATE, and ROLLER SKATE.

ski boot Waterproof, thick-soled, ankle-high boot of leather or molded plastic, closed with laces or buckles. Sometimes has an inner boot or foam lining. Attaches to ski by clamp that grips the sole. Also see under FOOTWEAR: MOLDED BOOT. Sometimes has a strap and buckle at ankle, tread soles, and removable felt liners of 80 percent wool and 20 percent rayon for warmth. Worn for skiing.

skimmer Very low-cut women's pump with shallow sides set on low or flat heels, usually made of very soft leather. Also called *shell.*

slant/slanted toe Rather wide toe that slants diagonally toward the little toe.

∞slap-sole Woman's or man's high-heeled boot or shoe of the 17th c. that had a flat sole attached at the toe underneath the shoe but not at the heel. This secondary sole kept the heel from sinking into mud. *Der.* From the slapping sound made by the sole while walking.

boot with slap-sole c. 1630

slide Toeless open-back sandal with WEDGE HEEL (see under FOOTWEAR) of various heights or regular heel made of wood or leather in all heights.

slingback shoe Any shoe with an open back and a strap around the heel of the foot to hold it in place. May be made in pump or sandal style.

slingback shoe

slingback thong sandal See under FOOTWEAR: THONG SANDAL #2.

sling pump See under FOOTWEAR: SLINGBACK SHOE.

slip-on shoe Any shoe that stays on the foot without using straps or fasteners (e.g., a PUMP, LOAFER, or MOCCASIN) (see under FOOTWEAR). Also called a *step-in shoe.*

slipper 1. Low shoe usually worn indoors. 2. In 16th c. a low shoe easily slipped on and off as differentiated from BOOTS and OXFORDS (see under FOOTWEAR). 3. Sometimes used to refer to some delicate types of shoes (e.g., evening slipper).

slipper socks Bulky knit socks, frequently handmade with lightweight leather or urethane soles, worn after skiing or around the house. Also called *after-ski slippers, après-ski slippers, mukluk slippers,* and *flokati.*

slip-shoe Man's MULE (see under FOOTWEAR) worn from 16th to mid-18th c. Made with flat heel that produced a shuffling step from which came the word "slip-shod."

∞slop 15th-c. slipper.

sneakers Formerly used to refer to gym shoes or tennis shoes of white canvas. Now refers to a type of low shoe similar to tennis shoes or a high canvas shoe worn by men, women, and boys or girls for school, sportswear, or gym. They originated in 1868 when canvas uppers were added to rubber soles creating "croquet sandals." These were renamed "sneakers" in 1873. In

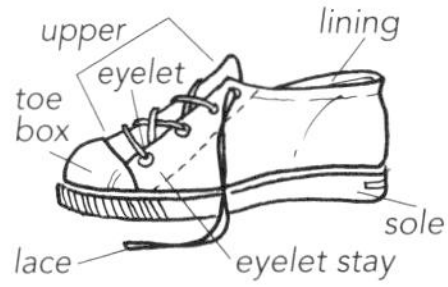

eyelet stay sneaker

1917 U.S. Rubber introduced Keds®. (The name derived from the combination of the words "kids"—for whom the first ones were made—and "ped"—Latin for foot.) See also under FOOTWEAR: ATHLETIC SHOES.

snowmobile boot Waterproof boot with an attached nylon top tightened with drawstring around calf of leg.

∞**soccus** (pl. *socci*) (soke-oos') Light slip-on slipper worn in ancient Greece, especially the low shoe worn by the comic actors on the stage. Compare with COTHURNUS, worn by Greek tragic actors.

sock lining Sole-shaped piece of leather or fabric covering shoe INSOLE (see under FOOTWEAR).

sole Bottom part of the shoe, under the foot, usually consisting of three parts—**outsole,** which touches the ground; **midsole,** also called the *filler,* which fills the space between the outsole and the innersole; and INSOLE (see under FOOTWEAR), which is the part under the foot.

∞**solea** (pl. *soleae*) (sol-eh'-ah) Simple form of sandal worn by the Romans consisting of a wooden sole held on with thongs or a cord.

∞**solers** Early form of slippers used from the 12th c. on. Made of leather or cloth in various unlined styles, worn strapped on the foot. *Der.* Latin, *solea.*

∞**soulette/solette** (soo-let') (early 17th c.) Leather band crossed over instep and under arch of foot to hold the patten to the shoe (see FOOTWEAR: PATTEN #2). Fitted over a **surpied,** a quatrefoil (a four-leafed design motif) of leather, used as trimming on the instep of boot.

Space shoe Formerly trademarked name for side-laced leather orthopedic shoes, with extra moving space for each toe, custom-made over casts of the wearer's feet. Made with thick crepe soles and low wedge heels for comfort.

spanish heel High heel with a curve similar to a FRENCH HEEL (see under FOOTWEAR) but has a straight inside edge.

spats Short cloth or leather GAITER (see under FOOTWEAR) reaching over ankle, buttoned at sides, and held on by strap under instep. First worn by the military, later adopted by civilian men in 1878 to wear with MORNING COAT (see under COATS AND JACKETS) in white, tan, or gray. Also worn by women from 1914 to 1920. Reintroduced at intervals, including the late 1960s for women. Also see under FOOTWEAR: SPATTERDASHES

spatterdashes High leggings worn by men from 1670s on, made mainly of leather or canvas reaching to knees. Fastened down outside of leg with buttons or buckles.

spectator pump Two-toned pump frequently made in contrasting colors of black, navy, red, or brown on white. Extra sewed-on toe and heel pieces of another color sometimes have perforations and are pinked at edges. Introduced in 1920s.

spectator pump

Sperry Topsider Trademark no longer active for shoes with a specially designed rubber sole that provided good traction on a wet boat deck; often made in loafer or sneaker style with canvas upper. This type of shoe is often referred to simply as a **topsider.** The name now applies to a wide variety of footwear.

spiked shoe Shoe with metal appendages on the soles. Used as early as 1861 for playing cricket.

spike heel High, curved, slender heel with tiny base; usually 3″ to 3½″ high. Also see under FOOTWEAR: CONTINENTAL HEEL.

∞**spit-boot** Man's boot combining shoe and GAITER (see under FOOTWEAR), worn in northern England from 18th to mid-19th c. Closed down outside of leg with interlocking fasteners. The last fastener was an iron spike or "spit" that fastened through an iron socket.

sports sandals Sandals for hiking, running, walking, and other forms of exercise. Invented in 1982 by Mark Thatcher, who wanted to devise a shoe that could be used in wading through streams and walking over rough terrain. He used a basic THONG SANDAL (see under FOOTWEAR) with a sturdy rubber sole, and added sturdy nylon straps to hold it on the foot. This sandal was marketed under the trademark **Teva®.** Other companies have adapted the concept to make a wide variety of sports sandals.

spring heel Low, broad heel with extra layer of leather inserted between heel and sole. Used primarily on children's shoes.

squaw boot Below-the-knee boot made of buckskin with fringed, turned-down cuff at top, soft sole, and no heel. Originally worn by North American Indian women, it became a fashion item in late 1960s.

stacked heel Heel built up of horizontal layers of leather. Also called *built-up heel.*

stadium boot Calf-high, sheepskin-lined boot popular to wear to football games in the 1950s. One of the first boots designed to be worn on the foot by women, not over the shoe.

∞**startup** High shoe reaching above the ankle, worn by country men, American Colonists, and sometimes by women in late 16th and early 17th c. Frequently laced or buckled on outside of leg, made of untanned leather, and worn for sports. Sometimes had velvet or silver trim for women. When loose-fitting, it was called a *bagging shoe.* Also spelled *startop, styrtop, stertop.*

step-in shoe See under FOOTWEAR: SLIP-ON SHOE.

stiletto heel (stil-et'-tow) Narrow set-back heel that ends in a tiny rounded base, usually fitted with a metal tip.

As the walking surface is small, there is an enormous amount of weight on the heel. Used mainly from 1950s until mid-1960s and revived in the 1990s. Shown at definition for FOOTWEAR.

stitchdown shoe construction Manufacturing process for shoes that involves turning of the shoe UPPER to the outside rather than around and under the LAST (see cross-references under FOOTWEAR). The outer sole is stitched to the extended edge around the shoe. Simple, flexible, low-cost shoe construction used primarily for infants' shoes, now used for all types of shoes. Sometimes made with two soles and called **double stitchdown.** Sometimes made with three soles and called **triple stitchdown.**

stocking boot Fashion boot made of stretch vinyl, leather, or fabric with no zipper, fitting the leg closely like a stocking. Sometimes reached to thigh with attached panties in late 1960s. Also called *body boot.*

stocking shoe Shoe covered with knitted fabric and attached to a long stocking. Introduced in late 1960s by shoe designer Beth Levine.

storm boot Any type of boot worn in inclement weather. Also see under FOOTWEAR: ALL-WEATHER, RAIN, and RUBBER BOOTS.

storm rubbers Waterproof overshoes with rounded flap coming up over the instep.

straights Soles of shoes that are not shaped to fit right and left feet. This style prevailed from c. 1600 to c. 1825, and can be found even as late as 1900.

stretch boot See under FOOTWEAR: TOTES.

surpied See under FOOTWEAR: SOULETTE.

taj toe Tiny pointed and turned-up, oriental-type toe used on a shoe.

tango shoe A woman's shoe that is cut high in the back with an ankle strap that buckles or ties. Popular from the late 1880s until the 1920s and revived periodically.

tap shoe Any shoe worn by a tap dancer. Made with metal plates at tip of toe and back edge of heel to increase sound when dancing. Men's style is usually a patent-leather pump or oxford; women's is usually a low-heeled patent-leather pump with ribbon tie at instep. Also see under FOOTWEAR: RUBY KEELER SHOE.

tassel-tie Bows ending in tassels on moccasins, wing-tip oxfords, and loafers.

tassel-top loafer See under FOOTWEAR: LOAFER.

tatamis (tah-tahm'-is) Thong-type sandal with nonflexible rubber sole having a slight wedge. Top of sole is made of woven straw matting. Thong straps are made of wide pieces of durable velvet. *Der.* Japanese, *tatami,* "woven straw mat."

tennis shoe Canvas or drill low-cut oxford with a circular-cut vamp. Made with special type of rubber sole for use on tennis courts. Also see under FOOTWEAR: SNEAKERS. Also called *court shoe.*

theo tie An open-throated, tongueless shoe, with ribbon or cord lacings, introduced in early 20th c.

thong sandal 1. Flat, often heelless sandal, held to the foot by narrow strips of leather coming up between first and second toes and attached to sole at either side. Popular for beachwear since 1960s. 2. In early 1980s strap was added around heel, then called **slingback thong.** 3. Thong sandal with complete strap around big toe is called **crossover thong sandal.**

thong sandals #1

three-quarter cut See under FOOTWEAR: SEMI-CUT.

throat The open area at the top of the VAMP in front of the INSTEP. See under FOOTWEAR.

toe Front portion of the shoe covering the toes. In the Middle Ages, toes of shoes became extremely long and pointed. In the 16th c., extremely wide toes were worn on duck-billed shoes. Fashion fluctuates between the extremes.

toe rubbers Overshoes, worn by women, that fit over the toes and have either a strap around the heel or snap together over the instep.

toe slipper Lightweight kid slipper reinforced with a hard shank and toe and usually tied on with satin ribbons crisscrossing across the instep and around the ankle. Worn by ballerinas and toe dancers. Also known as a *point shoe.*

toe spring The distance between the flat surface on which a shoe stands and the toe end of the shoe.

tongue Part of OXFORD shoe (see under FOOTWEAR) under the lacing. A **shawl tongue** is an extra-long tongue folded over the lacing, sometimes made with decorative fringed end, a style made fashionable when Prince of Wales wore it with kilts in Scotland in mid-1920s. Shoe with shawl tongue sometimes called KILTIE SHOE (see under FOOTWEAR). A similar construction consisting of an extra-long leather tongue, often fringed at end, is called an **apron tongue.** It fits behind lacing, then flops over, covering laces completely. A **bellows tongue** is stitched to sides of vamp of shoe and pleated so it expands across instep. In shoes or boots for outdoor wear, it serves to keep out snow.

top boot See under FOOTWEAR: JOCKEY BOOT.

topline The opening in the shoe around the ankle.

topsider See under FOOTWEAR: SPERRY TOPSIDER.

totes Lightweight, fold-up, unlined rubber boots, worn over shoes. Also called *stretch boot* or *rain boot.*

trainer heels See under FOOTWEAR: KITTEN HEELS.

tramezza stitched welting A trade name used by Italian shoe designer Salvatore Ferragamo for footwear made with a hand-crafted welting process. See also under FOOTWEAR: WELT.

triple-needle toe See under FOOTWEAR: NEEDLE TOE.

triple stitchdown See under FOOTWEAR: STITCHDOWN SHOE CONSTRUCTION.

T-strap shoe/sandal Shoe made with a strap coming up from the vamp to join second strap across the instep, forming a T. May have high or low heel with open or closed shank. Popular since 1920s.

T-strap shoe 1928

turned-shoe construction Lightweight shoe, usually in pump style, constructed by stitching sole to upper inside out, then "turning" to right side with seams on inside.

tuxedo pump Low-heeled pump with rounded toe, usually made of patent leather with grosgrain trim around the collar of the shoe and a broad flat grosgrain bow on the vamp. Introduced in mid-1980s.

Ugg boot A trade name for a boot made from sheepskin with a fleece lining and flat sole originating in Australia as a type of slipper to protect against the cold.

upper In the shoe industry, all parts of shoe above the sole. Includes the COUNTER, QUARTER, VAMP, and LINING (see under FOOTWEAR).

utility boot See under FOOTWEAR: BOOT.

vamp Front part of shoe, covering toes and instep. Referred to by this name since 15th c., and was formerly called the *vamprey.*

veldtschoen construction Method of making shoes in which the UPPER (see under FOOTWEAR) is turned out at the bottom edge, cemented, and stitched to the sole.

Vibram® A durable synthetic rubber usually used as a lug-type sole on hiking boots. *Der.* From the first syllables of the name of its inventor, *Vi*tale *Bram*ani, who wanted to make climbing shoes for Alpinists that would be useful not only at lower altitudes but also on the rocky surfaces encountered near the peaks.

vulcanized shoe construction Shoe construction that involves bonding a rubber outsole and heel to a shoe. Upper is tacked or stapled to insole and cement is applied to the shoe bottom. Sole is then inserted into a mold that was previously prepared for individual widths, sizes, and sole pattern. Heat and pressure hold the soling compound to the shoe.

waders Pants and boot in one piece reaching to above waist with suspenders over shoulders. Made of lightweight, flexible vinyl pressed to cotton jersey or rubber, welted to seamless boots with felt liners and cleated nonskid soles. Also called *fishing boot.* Also see under FOOTWEAR: HIP BOOTS.

waist The narrow part of footwear between the toe and heel.

walking shoe Any comfortable shoe with a relatively low heel, sometimes made with a cushion or crepe sole, worn more for comfort than style.

walled toe Deep toe cap with vertical edge at least ¾″ high.

wedge heel Slanted heel made in one piece with the sole of the shoe. Comes in low, medium, and high heights. Introduced in 1930s. Some heels are cut in one piece with a slight platform sole and are usually covered with jute, fabric, urethane, or leather. Some are made of cork and called *corkies.*

wedge heel

wedgie A shoe with a WEDGE HEEL (see under FOOTWEAR) completely joined to soles under arches, made in all styles and heel heights. Popular for women in late 1940s, and periodically revived for women and men. The height of the wedge and style of shoe on which it is placed can vary widely.

wellington boot Calf-length or below-the-knee boot with a seam below ankle making it look like a top has been joined to a men's low shoe with a long, tonguelike projection at vamp. Seams also extend down the sides of the boot to the ankle with boot loops at top. Usually made of water-repellent leather with oak-tanned soles and rubber heels, sometimes leather-lined. *Der.* Named for Duke of Wellington, British military hero who defeated Napoleon in the battle of Waterloo in 1815. Also see under WELLINGTON STYLES in alphabetical listing.

welt Narrow piece of leather stitched to shoe upper lining and INSOLE before being attached to OUTSOLE (see under FOOTWEAR) with seam concealed. A method of shoe construction that permits shoe to be resoled.

western boot See under FOOTWEAR: COWBOY BOOT.

white bucks See under FOOTWEAR: BUCK OXFORD.

wilderness boot Ankle-high laced boot with reinforced rubber toe, reinforced counter, and strap stitched diagonally from arch over ankle to aid in arch support. Made with LUG SOLE (see under FOOTWEAR) and upper of olive-drab cotton duck backed with cotton drill for quick drying. Worn for mild-weather hiking, wading streams, canoeing, or in African bush country.

wing-tip Decorative leather cap sewn to toe of shoe. Sometimes curved with center point and perforated in patterns. Shown at FOOTWEAR: KILTIE OXFORD. See under FOOTWEAR: WING-TIP OXFORD.

wing-tip oxford Laced shoe decorated at toe with wing-shaped overlay perforations, sometimes trimmed with perforations.

winkle pickers British slang for exaggeratedly pointed shoes worn by TEDDY BOYS and Teddy girls in early 1950s. *Der.* From suggestion that the pointed toes can dig out snails, or periwinkles, from the sand. Shown at FOOTWEAR: BEATLE BOOT.

woolworth shoe Shoe sold in millions by Woolworth's stores. Made of cotton canvas, in sandal style, in red, navy, paisley, black, or white. This shoe had sold for fifty years and has been entered in the permanent costume collection in the Metropolitan Museum of Art. Also called *landlady shoe.*

zori See under FOOTWEAR: FLIP-FLOPS.

---

fop A vain man preoccupied with the exquisiteness of his dress or showiness of his person (e.g., affected eccentricities such as the carrying of fans in the late 16th and late 18th c.). *Der.* Middle English *foppe,* "fool." Also see under DANDY.

forage cap See under HEADWEAR.

ford Apparel industry slang for a style that has mass acceptance. *Der.* From the similarity to mass appeal of the inexpensive early Ford automobiles.

fore-and-after cap See under HEADWEAR: DEERSTALKER.

forecasting The predictions of styles and trends that are made to assist retailers in making both long- and short-term merchandising decisions.

forehead cloth See under FRONTLET #2 and HEADWEAR: CROSSCLOTH #2.

∞**forepart** **1.** From 16th c. to 1630: a decorative panel made of expensive or elaborate fabric sewed to an underskirt of coarse fabric. The expensive fabric showed through the split skirt of the gown. **2.** 19th c.: the part of a man's waistcoat extending across the chest.

foresleeve See under SHOULDERS AND SLEEVES.

foretop See under WIGS AND HEADPIECES: TOUPEE #2.

forks See under GLOVES AND GLOVE CONSTRUCTION: FOURCHETTE.

formal attire Clothes worn by men and women at formal social functions. Women's dresses designed for formal occasions are often called *formal gowns, evening gowns,* or *ball gowns.*

formaldehyde tanning See under LEATHERS.

formal shirt See under SHIRTS.

formal suit See under TUXEDO and FULL-DRESS SUIT.

†**foulard** Soft, lightweight silk or manufactured fiber fabric, usually made in a twill weave and surface printed in a small design. Used for scarves, neckties, and dresses. Also see under SCARVES: FOULARD SCARF.

foundation See under UNDERGARMENTS.

foundation pattern See under SLOPER.

foundling bonnet See under HEADWEAR.

fourchette See under GLOVES AND GLOVE CONSTRUCTION.

four-gore slip See under UNDERGARMENTS.

four-in-hand tie See under TIES.

fourragère (foor-ah'-zher) Braided cord worn usually draped around left shoulder as a military award or decoration. Compare with AIGUILLETTE.

fourreau dress See under DRESSES: PRINCESS DRESS.

fox See under FURS.

foxing See under FOOTWEAR.

fraise See under SCARVES.

fraise à la confusion See under NECKLINES AND COLLARS: FALLING RUFF.

frame bag See under HANDBAGS AND RELATED ACCESSORIES.

framing See under HANDBAGS AND RELATED ACCESSORIES: FRAME #2.

france, point de See under LACES: POINT DE FRANCE.

franchise A contractual arrangement between a franchisor (the entity selling its name) and a franchisee (the buyer). In return for using a well-known company name, and sometimes, management assistance, the franchisee, who is an independent owner, pays royalties to the franchisor.

fraternal ring See under JEWELRY.

fraternity pin See under JEWELRY.

Frazer tartan See under PLAIDS AND TARTANS.

free-form ring See under JEWELRY.

free motion machine embroidery See under EMBROIDERIES AND SEWING STITCHES.

freight forwarding company A company that ships goods to the U.S. from the country that produced the goods.

frelan See under HEADWEAR.

French antelope lambskin See under LEATHERS.

french back Back of dress made with three seams—one in center and one on either side curving into the armhole. Fashionable in late 19th and early 20th c. and still used. Also see under SIDE BODIES.

French beret See under HEADWEAR: BERET.

french boa See under SCARVES: BOA.

french bottoms See under PANTS.

french bra See under UNDERGARMENTS.

french braid See under HAIRSTYLES: FISHBONE BRAID.

french cinch See under UNDERGARMENTS.

french cloak See under CAPES, CLOAKS, AND SHAWLS.

∞**french corsage** Woman's BASQUE waist worn in 1860s with wide, tight-fitting CORSELET BELT (see under BELTS), extending to middle of bust and made of different fabric. Bodice had a boat-shaped neckline and double ruffled sleeves. Skirt was of contrasting fabric.

†**french crepe** Originally a silk fabric with a flat smooth surface made in France of crepe-twisted yarns. Now applied to a large group of similar plain-woven fabrics called *lingerie crepes,* made of rayon and other manufactured fibers.

french cuff See under CUFFS.

french drawers See under UNDERGARMENTS.

french dress See under DRESSES.

french-fall boot See under FOOTWEAR.

french farthingale See under FARTHINGALE.

french frock See under COATS AND JACKETS: FROCK COAT #1.

French gigot sleeve See under SHOULDERS AND SLEEVES: LEG-OF-MUTTON SLEEVE.

∞**french gores** Term used in 1807 for panels introduced into skirts to eliminate gathers at the waist.

french heel See under FOOTWEAR.

French hood See under HEADWEAR.

French hose See under TRUNK HOSE.

French jacket See under PETENLAIR.

french kid See under LEATHERS.

french knot See under EMBROIDERIES AND SEWING STITCHES.

french lace See under LACES.

french lock See under HAIRSTYLES: LOVE LOCK.

french maid sleeper See under SLEEPWEAR AND LOUNGEWEAR.

french nightcap See under HEADWEAR: DORMEUSE.

french opening vest See under VESTS.

french panties See under UNDERGARMENTS.

French policeman's cape See under CAPES, CLOAKS, AND SHAWLS.

french polonaise See under DRESSES: IRISH POLONAISE.

French portrait buttons See under CLOSURES.

french purse See under HANDBAGS AND RELATED ACCESSORIES.

French Revolution styles Just before the French Revolution of 1789, styles in dress had simplified somewhat and the conflict did not usher in immediate major style changes; however, certain visible costume symbols were associated with the Revolution. Patriotic Frenchmen and women were expected to wear the Revolutionary colors of red, white, and blue. The red cap of liberty (see under HEADWEAR: BONNET ROUGE), the trousers that replaced knee breeches among the working classes and revolutionaries (their wearers were called SANS CULOTTES or "without knee breeches"), and the CARMAGNOLE (see under COATS AND JACKETS) a short woolen or cloth jacket with a full back were probably the most important symbolic items. Jewelry was made from the stones of the Bastille, the prison that was pulled down at the beginning of the Revolution. Once the worst excesses of the Revolution were over and the DIRECTOIRE period began, styles changed radically from the prewar wide-skirted dresses and elaborate suits to much simpler styles.

man's clothing of the French revolutionary period

french roll See under HAIRSTYLES.

French ruff See under NECKLINES AND COLLARS: RUFF.

∞**french sailor dress** Girl's long-waisted, tailored dress of early 20th c. with BLOUSON effect, short pleated skirt, and SAILOR COLLAR (see under NECKLINES AND COLLARS).

French sailor hat See under HEADWEAR.

french seam 1. See under CLOTHING CONSTRUCTION DETAILS. 2. See under FOOTWEAR.

french skirt See under SKIRTS: CORNET.

French sleeves See under SHOULDERS AND SLEEVES.

french thumb See under GLOVES AND GLOVE CONSTRUCTION.

french twist See under HAIRSTYLES.

french vest See under VESTS.

french wig See under WIGS AND HAIRPIECES: FULL-BOTTOM WIG.

freshwater pearls See under GEMS, GEM CUTS, AND SETTINGS: PEARLS.

fret 1. See under HEADWEAR. ∞2. Trelliswork sometimes used to ornament a garment in a lattice design in the 16th c. *Der.* French, "trelliswork." 3. Greek design consisting of a series of incomplete rectangles in a repeat design. Also called the *Greek key, Greek fret,* or *Grecian border.*

friendship bracelet See under JEWELRY: WOVEN FRIENDSHIP BRACELET.

friendship pin See under JEWELRY.

friendship ring See under JEWELRY.

frigate cap See under HEADWEAR.

frileuse See under CAPES, CLOAKS, AND SHAWLS.

frill Narrow piece of fabric or lace gathered to form a ruffle and attached as trimming to a dress or blouse. Term used since the 16th c.

∞**frilling** Ruffles of gathered, stiff, white muslin worn at the wrist and neck, specifically on widows' dresses of 1870s and 1880s.

fringe 1. Ornamental trim used since medieval times, consisting of loose strands of thread, yarn, or beads, fastened to a band. 2. Fabric or leather slashed into narrow strands, used for trim.

fringed cuff See under CUFFS.

fringed tongue See under FOOTWEAR.

friponne See under SKIRT: JUPE #2.

frisette See under HAIRSTYLES.

frisk See under UNDERGARMENTS.

frizzle See under NECKLINES AND COLLARS: RUFF.

frizz-wig/frizze/frizzle See under WIGS AND HAIRPIECES.

frizzy See under HAIRSTYLES.

FRM See under FLOOR-READY MERCHANDISE.

frock Origin and usage of this term is unclear and it has at various times been applied to such garments as a woman's undergarment, a priest's gown, and a loose-fitting riding coat. Among the specific usages are these: 1. Synonym for a woman's dress. Specific usage has varied. In 16th and 17th c. a general term for an informal gown; by 19th c. usually meant a dress of thin fabric; and in 20th c. was often used for a child's dress as well as to refer to women's dresses generally. 2. From medieval times, a man's loose-fitting, sleeved outer garment of coarse fabric, derived from a monk's HABIT and worn by farm workers or laborers. Also called *smock frock* and in some areas was decorated with smocking. See under SMOCK. 3. See under COATS AND JACKETS: FROCK COAT.

frock coat See under COATS AND JACKETS.

frocked jacket See under COATS AND JACKETS: FROCK #2.

frock greatcoat See under COATS AND JACKETS.

frock overcoat See under COATS AND JACKETS.

frog 1. See under CLOSURES. 2. See under LEATHERS.

front See under WIGS AND HAIRPIECES.

frontayl/frontel See under FRONTLET #2.

front-closure bra See under UNDERGARMENTS.

front hip pocket See under POCKETS.

frontier pants See under PANTS: WESTERN PANTS.

frontlet ∞1. See under HEADWEAR. 2. A brow band covered with face cream, worn at night in the 18th c. to remove wrinkles. Also called *forehead cloth* or *crosscloth* or spelled *frontayl, frontel.*

fronts See under HIP-HOP and under JEWELRY: GRILLS.

front-zipper foundation See under ZIPPER FOUNDATION.

froufrou Fluffy trimmings such as ruffles, ribbons, and laces. *Der.* French, "rustle" or "swish."

froufrou dress See under DRESSES.

froufrou mantle See under CAPES, CLOAKS, AND SHAWLS.

∞**frouting** In the 17th c., process of rubbing perfumed oil into a garment to freshen it.

frouze See under WIGS AND HAIRPIECES.

Frye boot See under FOOTWEAR.

FTC See under FEDERAL TRADE COMMISSION.

full-bottom wig See under WIGS AND HAIRPIECES.

full dress Formal attire consisting of formal evening dress for women and white tie and tails for men.

full-dress suit Man's formal suit consisting of SWALLOW-TAILED COAT (see under COATS AND JACKETS) frequently trimmed with satin lapels, and matching trousers with satin stripes down side of pants. Worn with formal shirt, white vest, and white tie. Also called *white tie and tails.*

†**fulled wool** Woolen or worsted fabrics that have been subjected to the finishing process called **fulling,** which consists of compressing or shrinking the fabric by use of heat, moisture, pressure, and friction to produce a dense appearance somewhat like felt. Contemporary fashion promotions often use the terms *boiled wool* or *felted wool* to refer to these fabrics.

full fashioned Knit garment or garment pieces in which shaping is provided by increasing or decreasing the number of stitches.

full-fashioned hose See under HOSIERY.

full grain See under LEATHER.

fulling See under FULLED WOOL.

full length See under LENGTHS.

full lining Finishing of the inside of the garment with a complete lining, so that no seams of the outer fabric are showing. Used mainly for coats, jackets, and sometimes dresses.

full-piqué/full P.K. seam See under GLOVES AND GLOVE CONSTRUCTION.

full skirt See under SKIRTS.

full tee See under SHIRTS.

full top grain See under LEATHER.

fully let-out See under FURS.

†fume fading Fading of acetate fabrics caused by acid gases in the atmosphere.

fun furs See under FURS.

funky/funk fashion 1. Styles inspired by the funk music played by African Americans that gained popularity in the 1970s. Patchwork leather coats, platform shoes, wide-legged pants, or LAMÉ jumpsuits of satin or gold, large jewelry, and glittery stage makeup worn by performers were imitated by fans. 2. In 1983, the designer Kenzo used "funky factor" to describe hobo styles and baggy oversized suspender pants worn with clown-like makeup.

funnel *adj.* Descriptive of accessories and parts of apparel made in the shape of a flaring cone. See under HEADWEAR: FUNNEL HAT and NECKLINES AND COLLARS: FUNNEL NECKLINE.

funnel sleeve See under SHOULDERS AND SLEEVES: PAGODA SLEEVE.

FURS

fur 1. Pelt of an animal, raw or processed, with the hair attached—as differentiated from leather, which is tanned without the hair. All furs usually have dense short hairs called **underfur,** and much longer, silky hairs called **guard hairs.** Best, or **prime pelts,** are secured in coldest time of year, with the exception of beaver, a water animal, where water is coldest in early spring from melting snow. Furs were used since earliest times for clothing, preceding woven cloth. Popular for trim and linings in the Middle Ages, with certain furs reserved for the nobility. Often used in the latter half of the 19th and early 20th c. for matching collar and cuffs on full-length coats. From 1900 through 1950s fur scarves with head, tail, and feet of animal were fashionable, and in the early 1930s all types of furs were worn. During the 1940s, mink became the most generally used fur, with the fur stole increasing in popularity. In 1964, FUN FURS (see under FURS) were introduced. Later, furs worked in herringbone, grooved, plaid, and tweed patterns were introduced. In the mid-1980s, full-length coats of long-haired furs, e.g., lynx, fox (including silver fox), fisher, fitch, and tanuki were popular, along with mink and sheared beaver. Lightweight KNITTED FURS (see under FURS), made by a laser-cutting technique, were in style in 2002. According to **Federal Fur Products Labeling Act of 1952,** furs must be labeled as to name of fur; proper origin; processing (sheared, dyed, etc.); and a Label Authority Tag must be attached stating that the product was made by a manufacturer who supports code of Fair Labor Standards. In 1969, U.S. Congress passed **Endangered Species Act,** which banned importation and sale of pelts of some animals. Some individual states have also passed laws restricting sale of furs from endangered animals, and in 1975 a Convention on International Trade in Endangered Species of World Fauna and Flora was established. See entries under FURS for definitions of specific furs and fur processing techniques. 2. An item of wearing apparel, accessory, or trimming made from such pelts (e.g., a fur coat, scarf, hat, or muff).

Alaskan seal See under FURS: FUR SEAL.

American marten Least-expensive marten, with long guard hair and underfur ranging in color from blue-brown to dark brown.

antelope Stiff flat hair, similar to calf, in beautiful soft brown color; rarely used for fur as the number of antelopes is very limited.

armur raccoon See under FURS: USSURIAN RACCOON.

Australian opossum Woolly-type fur usually gray in color; best quality comes from Australia and Tasmania.

∞austrian seal Term used in early 20th c. for rabbit fur. Used prior to the Fur Labeling Act, it is no longer correct.

badger Heavy, warm, durable fur with long silvery-gray guard hairs and dense white or tan underfur.

∞Baltic seal/Baltic tiger (early 20th c.) Rabbit fur. Considered incorrect terminology since Fur Labeling Act of 1938.

baum marten Medium-length brown guard hairs and yellow-brown underfur; resembling sable, but guard hairs are coarser, shorter, and not as lustrous. Best pelts are obtained from Europe. Used primarily for jackets, scarves, and trimmings. Fair to good durability; expensive. Also see under FURS: MARTEN and STONE MARTEN.

bearskin Pelt of a bear.

beaver Rich velvety-brown fur that, when sheared, reveals a wide silvery stripe down the center. Preferred color is blue-brown; sometimes left natural or bleached beige for "blonde beaver." Most beaver is sheared and coarse guard hairs are plucked out. Pelts are large, requiring only five to seven for a *let-out* coat (see under FURS: LETTING-OUT). Best qualities from Canada, particularly the Laurentian Valley in Quebec, and the U.S., including Alaska. *Der.* From Middle English *bever,* "brown."

∞beaverette Used in the early 20th c. to mean rabbit fur; considered incorrect since Fur Labeling Act of 1938.

black fox Fur with long silky guard hairs and thick underfur, a color phase of the RED FOX belonging to the same genus. SILVER FOX and PLATINUM FOX are color phases of the black fox. It is possible to raise all types by fur farming with the best qualities obtained from this source as well as from Alaska, eastern Canada, and northern Europe. See cross-references under FURS.

Blackglama® American Legend Cooperative Association trademark for very dark MUTATION MINK (see under FURS).

blanket 1. Fur-industry term for small pieces of fur sewn to form a pattern, making a piece large enough for a fur coat, e.g., mink in brown and white, used to form herringbone, window pane, or checkerboard patterns. Usually imported from Greece. **2.** Fur-industry term for extra-large beaver skins.

blending (Fur industry) Lightly applying dye to tips of hairs of furs, such as mink and sable, to improve the coloring.

blue fox Dark brown fur with a bluish cast, long silky guard hairs, and thick underfur. Some pelts also have silvery hairs. This fox is a color phase of the Arctic WHITE FOX (see under FURS), but its habitat is more southerly. Best qualities from Alaska and Greenland. It is possible to dye the white fox this color.

blue pelt Fur pelt taken in early fall, too soon to be prime, or best, pelt.

broadtail lamb Natural, unsheared, flat moiré pattern, with silky texture. Colors may be natural brown, grays, or black or possibly dyed.

brush Bushy tail of an animal, usually a fox, used as trimming.

bucky pelts Fur pelts taken in spring months when skins are not fully furred and tend to be tough and unyielding. Also called *springy pelts.*

burunduki (bur-oon′-duke-ee) Usually small, lightweight, delicate skins with nine alternating stripes of white and black on a yellow or orangish background. Skin obtained from rodent native to Russia similar to American chipmunk. Frequently imported in PLATES (see under FURS). Used for linings and trimmings.

caging Fur-cleaning process, in which furs are revolved in cage-like wire drums that permit the sawdust, used for cleaning, to fall out through the wire mesh.

calf/calfskin Flat, short, stiff-haired fur from young cattle, usually brown spotted with white, also may be black and white, all black, or brown. Used for trimmings, handbags, belts, shoes, and vests.

caracul See under FURS: KARAKUL.

chati cat See under FURS: SPOTTED CAT.

cheetah Flat fur from the cat family from Africa or Southern Asia, with black spots on a tawny ground. Hair is softer and lighter than leopard. Used for coats, jackets, hats, etc. No longer permitted by law to be used in the U.S.

china mink Yellowish mink found in China dyed to imitate North American mink, which is much more expensive. Also see under FURS: KOLINSKY.

chinchilla Silky-haired fur with a very delicate skin. Best quality has slate-blue underfur and guard hairs that are white and darker at the tips, center back is gray. This small rodent is native to the Andes Mountains in South America. May also be raised on fur ranches. Mutation colors are now available.

Chinese dog Fur with long guard hairs and thick underfur from Mongolia and Manchuria. Used as trimming on inexpensive coats. Sewed into mats for shipment.

Chinese lamb See under FURS: KARACUL.

chinese raccoon See under FURS: USSURIAN RACCOON.

civet cat Spotted fur characterized by elongated black marks against a dark gray background with a greenish cast. Not widely used. Comes from southern China and the Malay Peninsula. The little spotted skunk of South America is sometimes incorrectly called the civet cat.

coney Synonym for RABBIT (see under FURS). The word "rabbit" originally meant "the young of the coney." This term is accepted as a synonym for rabbit for proper fur labeling. Coats may be labeled as beaver-dyed coney or beaver-dyed rabbit.

crimmer See under FURS: LAMB.

crosses (Fur term) Small pieces of fur, such as paws and gills, sewn together to make a large piece that is cross-shaped—used particularly on varieties of lamb.

cross fox Fur with long silky guard hair and dense underfur in a dark reddish color. Named for the marking between the gills in the shape of a "cross" rather than a product of crossbreeding. It is a color phase of the RED FOX (see under FURS).

dropping See under FURS: LETTING-OUT.

dyed sable See under FURS: SABLE.

∞**electric mole** Incorrect terminology used in early 20th c. for RABBIT fur (see under FURS) prior to the Fur Labeling Act of 1938. Correct terminology is *electric-processed rabbit.*

electric-processed rabbit See under FURS: ELECTRIC MOLE and ELECTRIC SEAL.

∞**electric seal** Incorrect terminology for *rabbit* that is sheared and then carved in ridges. Correctly called *electric-processed rabbit.*

electrified sheepskin Sheep or lamb skins tanned with hair intact and given an electrical treatment that gives the hair a silky texture.

ermine Pure white fur from weasel family with short guard hairs and silky soft underfur. Best quality from the far north—Siberia, in particular. As the animal roams further south, it develops protective coloration of light shades of brown. Traditionally used by royalty since Middle Ages and still used on ceremonial robes of British peerage.

feathering Applying extra dye delicately to guard hairs of fur by means of a feather dipped in dye. Used to improve appearance of the fur.

fisher Fur having color shading from brown to blackish tones with long guard hairs and dense underfur. Used primarily for scarves and jackets, usually in its natural state. Best quality pelts come from Labrador. Very good durability; fairly scarce and expensive.

fitch Moderately priced fur, with yellow underfur and black guard hairs with a silky texture; found in Europe. *White fitch,* another type, is found in Ural Mountains of southern Russia. Used for coats, jackets, and trimmings. Durability is very good; relatively inexpensive. Color ranges from ecru with black markings to orange tones.

fleshing Hand process of smoothing reverse side of fur by scraping with a sharp knife.

flowered mink A mink coat worked in a floral design, usually consisting of a six-petal arrangement (e.g., a daisy). Used in color or white against colored background. An innovation of the late 1960s.

fox Fur with long, lustrous guard hairs and deep dense underfur. There are four primary types of foxes and many miscellaneous types. Main groups are: (1) *red fox*—includes black, silver, platinum, and *cross fox* (yellowish with a black cross marking) as color phases; (2) *white fox*—with blue fox a color phase; (3) *gray fox;* and (4) *kit fox.* Northern kit fox is protected by Canadian government. Found in every continent except South America, and also raised on fur farms. Used for coats, jackets, scarves, muffs, jackets, and trimmings. See other fox furs listed separately under FURS: BLACK, BLUE, CROSS, GRAY, PLATINUM, RED, SILVER, and WHITE FOX.

fully let-out Fur-industry term for a fur coat with pelts cut so that one let-out strip goes from neck to hem of coat. Also see under FURS: LETTING-OUT.

fun furs Longhaired and unusual furs worked in an interesting manner into a coat or other garment suitable for sports or informal occasions. Term coined in 1965.

fur farming Raising and scientific breeding of animals for their pelts. Originated in the 1920s with raising of SILVER FOXES; later same method was used to raise RANCH MINK and MUTATION MINK. See under FURS.

fur seal Soft velvety fur from the genuine Alaska seal. All pelts are sheared and dyed either black or brown and other colors. Used for coats, jackets, hats, and muffs. Durability is high. Sealing is controlled by the U.S. government, with pelts coming from the Pribilof Islands, off the coast of Alaska. This fur is expensive because of the limited quantity available. Argentina and Ecuador protect species.

golden muskrat Side portions of the southern muskrat pelt. Also see under FURS: MUSKRAT.

gray fox Long-haired fur with silky guard hairs and dense underfur of a gray color. Used mainly for trimmings; best qualities are from the U.S.

gray muskrat The belly part of the southern muskrat. Also see under FURS: MUSKRAT.

grooving See alphabetical listing.

guanaco (gwa-nak′-ko) Reddish-brown fur from the young guanaco or guanaquito found in Argentina. Inexpensive and not durable, it is used for jackets and trimmings, and is the only member of the llama family used for fur.

guard hairs See under introduction to FURS.

hair seal Stiff, rather short-haired fur with a natural blue-black or blue-and-black mottled effect that may be dyed various other colors. Comes from two varieties of seals, the *harp seal* and the *hooded seal,* whose habitat is the North Atlantic. Baby hair seals are white in color, and used to make sealskin leathers as the fur is slightly woolly.

hamster Small, soft, golden-brown pelts of rodent found in the Rhine River Valley and in Siberia. Similar in appearance to the American muskrat. Used most often for linings. Rarely used in America.

hare Soft short-haired fur, similar to rabbit but with more tendency to mat. Arctic hare from northern Europe and Asia has a long guard hair and is sometimes used to imitate the Arctic fox. Durability is low but higher than rabbit fur.

harp seal See under FURS: HAIR SEAL.

hooded seal See under FURS: HAIR SEAL.

Hudson Bay sable See under FURS: MARTEN.

Hudson seal Proper name is *Hudson seal-dyed muskrat.* Also see under FURS: MUSKRAT.

jaguar Flat, spotted fur with dark rosette markings with two dots in centers against tawny background. Popular for coats and two-piece suits for women in the early 1960s. In comparatively short supply. No longer permitted by law to be used in the U.S.

Jap/Japanese mink Muddy yellow–colored mink from Japan that is always dyed in imitation of more expensive American mink.

Jap fox See under FURS: USSURIAN RACCOON.

Jap raccoon See under FURS: USSURIAN RACCOON.

karakul/caracul (kar′-ah-kul) Lamb pelt with a moiré appearance (see under FURS)—best pelts are the flattest. Majority of skins are white and may be dyed; or may be rusty brown, dark brown, or black. Best quality from Russia. When skins are from China, called *Chinese lamb* or *Mongolian lamb.* Used for coats, jackets, and trimmings. Durability is moderate.

kidskin Short-haired, flat, gray fur with wavy pattern, inexpensive fur with low durability. The best pelts come from young goats of India, China, Ethiopia, and South America.

kit fox See under FURS: FOX.

knitted fur Fur that is cut into quarter-inch strips and the skin sanded to reduce bulk, after which the strips are knitted into fur garments. First done in 1960s by artisans and avant-garde designers; such garments tended to be stiff. New laser-cutting techniques make construction of light, soft, warm garments possible.

knuckle curl Fur-industry term for tight natural curl in *Persian lamb.*

kojah See under FURS: MUTATION MINK.

kolinsky Brownish fur with medium-length silky guard hair and slightly yellowish underfur. Best qualities from Manchuria. Used primarily for scarves and trimmings, and used in imitation of American and Canadian mink. Durability is fair. Also see under FURS: CHINA MINK.

krimmer See under FURS: LAMB.

lamb Many types of lamb are processed for fur, but three main types stand out: *Persian lamb, broadtail lamb,* and *karakul lamb*—differentiated by luster and tightness of the fur curl. Other lamb variations include *Afghan, Astrakhan, Argentine, Bessarabian, Iranian, Kalgan, Soviet Union, India, China,* and *Southwest Africa.* Crimean lamb is called *crimmer* or *krimmer.* Also see under FURS: BROADTAIL, KARAKUL, MOUTON PROCESSED, and PERSIAN LAMB.

lapin (la-pan′) French word for "rabbit." Not used in the U.S. except in a descriptive form (e.g., lapin-processed rabbit).

leathering (Fur industry) Using narrow strips of leather between strips of fur in order to make the fur less bulky and give it a more graceful hang.

leopard Spotted jungle-cat fur judged by: (a) flatness; (b) contrast between spots and background; (c) shape of rosettes or spots. There is no underfur in the best qualities, and better qualities have shorter hair. Best quality is from African Somaliland. Although leopard fur was used as early as Egyptian times, it was not popular for women's wear until after World War I. Good durability; very limited in supply and expensive. No longer permitted by law to be used in the U.S.

∞**lettice** (let′-ees) ERMINE or MINIVER (see under FURS), specifically white ermine or other white or gray fur, in 16th and 17th c.

letting-in Fur-industry term for process of intricate cutting and resewing of a fur skin to make it shorter and broader.

letting-out Fur-industry term for process of intricate cutting and sewing of a fur skin to make it longer and narrower. The pelt is cut down center back, slit into tiny diagonal pieces, and each piece dropped when joined to next pieces. Process makes the pelt long enough that a skin may extend from neck to hem of the garment. Also called *dropping.*

lynx Long, silky-haired, delicately spotted fur. Colors vary from white, blue-gray, pale gray, to brown. Best quality of white comes from the Hudson Bay area and Alaska. Pelts also come from other parts of Canada, Scandinavia, and Siberia. Used for coats, jackets, and trimming. Spain protects the *Spanish lynx.*

lynx cat Differs from lynx, being darker in color with darker spots and shorter guard hairs, similar to the American wildcat. Best qualities are from Nova Scotia, other qualities from Canada and the U.S. Used extensively in coats and jackets and for trimmings.

marguay See under FURS: SPOTTED CAT.

marmot Fur with guard hair and underfur similar to MUSKRAT and MINK (see under FURS). Blue-black color is preferred, other pelts are dyed brown and frequently processed to simulate mink; moderately priced. Marmot comes mainly from the Soviet Union, Manchuria, and China. Used mainly for coats, jackets, and trimmings for cloth coats. No longer permitted by law to be used in U.S.

marten Soft, rich fur with fairly long guard hair and thick underfur similar to sable; blue-black or brown colors preferred, but ranges to canary yellow. Best qualities found in eastern Canada and the Hudson Bay area. Incorrectly called the *Hudson Bay sable.* Also see under FURS: BAUM MARTEN, STONE MARTEN, and AMERICAN MARTEN.

miniver ∞**1.** White or spotted gray and white fur, used for linings and trimmings in the Middle Ages. **2.** White fur, especially ermine, used to trim "robes of state" in various countries. Also see under FURS: LETTICE and VAIR.

mink Fur with silky to coarse guard hairs and dense, soft underfur. Best qualities of the dark pelts are lustrous with the guard hairs giving off a blue reflection. Originally only WILD MINK was available, with best qualities coming from eastern Canada; northeastern U.S. pelts ranked second. Animal also exists in Europe, but pelts are usually of less value. Zoological name is *Mustela vison* and animal is from the weasel family. *Vison* is the European name for mink. Since the 1940s, much mink is raised by fur farming in the U.S. Many color variations are now available due to the development of new strains, or mutations, on ranches (see MUTATION MINK). Most mink is used in the natural color, and the fur is of good durability. In the 1930s, the mink coat became a status symbol. With the growth in popularity of the stole during the 1950s, and the production of more pelts by fur farming, mink became available to the masses. In mid-1960s, patterned and patchwork minks became fashionable. These were made of paws, gills, and small bits pieced together to form *blankets* of flowered, herringbone, plaid, tweed, and windowpane patterns from which a garment was cut. In the late 1960s and early 1970s painted, sheared, hand-screened, and tie-dyed mink became fashionable.

moiré pattern (mwa-ray′) Fur term for appearance of Persian broadtail and American processed broadtail—flat furs with a wavy surface.

mole Extremely soft gray fur, rather flat with a wavy appearance, and a very delicate skin. Best qualities come from Asia. Popular for jackets and trimmings in early 1900s. Poor durability. Always dyed to avoid white skin showing through.

Mongolian lamb See under FURS: KARACUL.

monkey Very long, lustrous black fur with no underfur. Used for trimmings and jackets. Obtained primarily from the colobus monkey on the east and west coasts of Africa.

mouton-processed lamb Woolly fur with a dense pile, made by shearing the merino sheep, rather than "hair" sheep. Used for coats, jackets, and hats. Inexpensive, warm, and durable. Generally dyed brown, frequently water-repellent.

muskrat Fur with long guard hairs and dense underfur, processed three different ways: (1) dyed and striped to resemble mink and sable; (2) sheared and dyed to imitate Alaskan seal and called *Hudson seal-dyed muskrat;* and (3) left natural and finished to improve the coloring. Best qualities of northern muskrat, which is brown or black, are used for Hudson seal-dyed muskrat and come from the Great Lakes region in the U.S. Southern pelts, which vary in color, are used for natural muskrat coats. Durability is moderate to high. Natural muskrat skins are split into five parts, each part used separately as "back coats," "golden sides coats," and "silver belly coats."

mutation mink Strains of mink developed scientifically on fur farms by carefully mating the animals. Original wild pelts were brown. From mating the odd animals, many new colors were produced. Also during the 1960s, mink with longer hair was produced through breeding. A trade name for this type was *kojah.* In order to market pelts, associations of mink breeders were formed.

nailing See under FURS: STAPLING.

natural mink Mink that has not been dyed or colored in any manner.

nutria Fur with a velvety appearance after long guard hairs have been plucked, with colors ranging from cinnamon brown to brown with gray stripes. Fur is similar to beaver although not as thick, lustrous, and rich in color. Animal is a water rodent of northern Argentina. Usually wild but some attempts at breeding were made in 1950s. Used for coats, linings, and trimmings. Durability is moderate. Sometimes kept in natural state with long guard hairs and short underfur in lustrous brown. When produced on a ranch, it is bluish-beige in color and slightly coarser. May also be dyed.

ocelot Spotted fur with elongated dark markings against a tan background. Flatter-haired pelts were the best qualities and came from Brazil and Mexico. Used mainly for coats and jackets. Now on the endangered list and not available.

opossum Long, straight guard hairs and dense underfur that in the natural color is either black or gray. Best qualities come from Australia and the U.S. Used for coats, linings, trimmings, or dyed to imitate other furs such as skunk and fitch; moderately priced. Australian varieties have short, dense, plushlike fur ranging from yellow-gray to blue-gray.

otter Relatively short-haired fur with silky lustrous guard hair and dense underfur—the most durable fur for the weight and thickness. Preferred color has blue-brown guard hairs and underfur slightly lighter with the base being gray to white color. Best qualities come from eastern Canada. Some otter is sheared and plucked. Also see under FURS: SEA OTTER.

paw Fur term for small pieces of fur from paws of animals.

pelt Skin of an animal with the hair attached used for making fur garments and accessories. Also called a *peltry.*

Persian lamb Curly lustrous fur that is usually black but occasionally brown or white. Dark colors are always dyed to color the white skin. Quality is determined by the tightness of the "knuckle" curl and formation of interesting patterns called "flowers." Best quality comes from Bokara, Russia, from Karakul sheep. Others come from Afghanistan, southwestern Africa, and Iran. Popular for coats and trimmings. Durability is high. Available in mutation colors. Also see under FURS: LAMB.

Persian paw Fur of the Persian lamb that is left after a coat is made—the paws, head, and gills. Small pieces are sewed together to make larger pieces called *plates.* Another coat, collar, or garment is then cut from the *plate.*

plates Larger units formed when small pieces of fur are joined together (e.g., Persian lamb plates made from paws and gills that are left over from other garments).

platina See under FURS: PLATINUM FOX.

platinum fox Silvery long-haired fur with long guard hairs and dense black underfur. The reverse of the silver fox, it has much silvery hair and little black hair. First discovered in 1935, and later raised on fur farms in the U.S. and Norway, where the trade name is *Platina.* Originally one of the rarest furs.

plucking (Fur industry) The process of removing some of the longer *guard hairs,* which may mar the beauty of the final product.

pony Short-haired flat fur with a wavy moiré appearance. Used in natural color, bleached, or dyed pale colors. Best quality comes from Poland and Russia. Durability good, but short, bristly fur has a tendency to wear "bald."

prime pelt A best-quality pelt. Animals must be hunted during the season when the pelt is the most fully furred. For most animals, this is during the coldest winter months. *Beaver,* being a water animal, has a fuller pelt in the early spring when the streams are cold with water from melting ice and snow. *Marmot* pelts are best before animal hibernates for the winter.

rabbit Soft, light fur in a variety of colors used in natural state or can be dyed or processed as follows: (a) striped to imitate muskrat, (b) sheared to imitate beaver, and (c) sheared and stenciled to resemble leopard. Best qualities come from Australia and New Zealand. Poor durability; inexpensive. Also see under CONEY.

raccoon Long, light-silvery guard hair and dark-brown underfur. Lighter-weight peltries from the southern part of the U.S. are used for coats. The northern U.S. provides heavy-skinned pelts used primarily for hats and trimmings. Popular for men's and women's coats in 1920s, revived in 1960s. Also see under SHEARED RACCOON.

raccoon dog See under FURS: USSURIAN RACCOON.

ranch mink MINK (see under FURS) in which the color ranges from true rich brown to brownish-black.

red fox Fur with long silky guard hairs and dense underfur, which is red-orange in color. As the fur becomes more yellowish, it is less valuable. A red fox may have different-colored foxes in its litter (e.g., BLACK, SILVER, or CROSS FOX). Best qualities come from Alaska, Siberia, and Labrador.

rosette Spotted marking on leopard fur, resembling a paw mark.

Russian crown sable See under FURS: SABLE.

sable Luxurious fur with lustrous, long, silky guard hairs and soft, dense, fluffy underfur; preferred color, a blue-black-brown. Skins that are light brown in color are tipped, blended, and called *dyed sable.* Used for coats or scarves, with best quality, called *Russian crown sable,* coming from Siberia. Animal is also found in Canada, China, Korea, and Japan. Durability is good and very expensive. Golden sable in amber tone is less expensive.

seal See under FURS: HAIR SEAL and FUR SEAL.

sea otter Fur with silky guard hairs and silky underfur in a deep blue-black or brown with sprinklings of white hairs. Having exceptionally soft, dense, and luxurious pelts, sea otters were hunted almost to extinction for their fur. Now protected in the U.S., these animals can no longer be hunted and their fur cannot be used.

sheared raccoon Velvety-textured fur similar in appearance to beaver, but not as soft or silky and more cinnamon brown in color with lighter stripes. Raccoon is processed by plucking and shearing. Durable fur, much less expensive than beaver.

shearing Process used on furs (e.g., beaver, lamb, muskrat, raccoon, and seal) to cut hairs to same length to give them a velvety appearance.

shearling Pelts from "wool" lambs that have been processed with the hair intact, therefore classifying them as "fur" rather than "leather." Used for jackets, collars, and coats. Usually sueded on the leather side.

silver fox Black long-haired fur with long, silky, silvery guard hairs and dense underfur. Best quality has the greatest amount of "silver" in it. Silver fox may be found in litters of the red fox. Also raised by fur farming.

skin-on-skin process See under FURS: WORKED IN THE ROUND.

skunk Black fur with long guard hairs and thick underfur with characteristic white stripe down back. Quality of fur depends on ability of the underfur to remain black rather than take on a brownish or rust-colored appearance. For an all-black fur, pelts have white streaks removed and are dyed to darken the skin. Used extensively in the 1930s for jackets and coats; best qualities are from the Dakotas and Minnesota. Also found in Canada and South America. Better U.S. types have high durability. Zorina South American skunk is similar, with flatter fur and silky texture.

snow leopard Spotted long silky guard hair with long underfur in a pale yellow-gray color with white belly and markings that are more like spots than rosettes. Found in high altitudes of the Himalaya Mountains of central Asia. No longer permitted by law to be used in the U.S.

spotted cat Variety of spotted fur that comes from three main types of South American cat: the *chati cat,* the *marguay* (mar′-gay), and *long-tailed cats.* Markings are more rounded than those of the OCELOT; fur is less expensive.

springy pelts See under FURS: BUCKY PELTS.

squirrel Very soft gray or brown relatively short fur that takes dye readily and may be made any color or worked into a two-toned pattern. Best qualities come from Europe, Asia, Russia, Poland, Finland, and Canada. Used mainly for jackets, capes, and trimmings. Low durability; moderately priced.

stapling A fur-industry term used for wetting, blocking, and fastening pieces of a fur garment to a board to make them conform to the shape called for in the pattern. Formerly, this process was called **nailing** because nails were used. Now staples are used because of their smaller size.

stone marten Fur with brown guard hairs and grayish-white underfur judged for quality by the contrast of two colors. Best qualities come from Europe, particularly Russia. Used primarily for scarves. Also see under MARTEN.

tanuki Japanese name for raccoon-dog, which must be labeled and sold under name *Ussurian raccoon* in U.S. according to Federal Trade Regulations. Also see under FURS: USSURIAN RACCOON.

tawning The process of finishing furs, making the pelts pliable and water resistant.

tipping Fur-dyeing process in which only the tips of the guard hairs are colored.

underfur/underhair Short fur fiber of animals such as mink, muskrat, and fox as contrasted with the GUARD HAIRS, which are long and silky. Formerly called *fur fiber.* See under introduction to FURS.

Ussurian raccoon Long-haired, yellowish-brown pelt with shoulder and tail tipped with black, slightly coarse guard hair, and long, dense underfur. May be dyed, sheared, or used in natural state mainly for collars and trim. Comes from a species of dog that resembles a raccoon in appearance. The Japanese species, known as TANUKI (see under FURS), has the most silky, fully furred pelt (but is not the largest). Other qualities come from Manchuria, Korea, Siberia, and parts of Europe. Also called *raccoon dog, Armur raccoon, Chinese raccoon, Jap fox, Jap raccoon.* These names cannot be used when merchandising pelts in the U.S. Color is similar to red fox with distinctive cross markings.

∞**vair** Name for highly prized fur worn by kings and magistrates in 13th and 14th c., used for linings and trimmings. Thought to have been a type of squirrel with dark back and white underside.

vertically worked Fur skins that are first let out, and then sewn together so that each skin runs from top of fur coat to hem.

vison See under FURS: MINK.

weasel Soft, silky, short guard hairs and silky underfur similar in texture to ERMINE (see under FURS), a close relative. Color varies with the seasons—winter, white; spring, yellowish; summer, streaked with brown or gray; and brown all year in southern climates.

white fitch See under FURS: FITCH.

white fox Pure white fur with long silky guard hairs and dense underfur. Comes from the *Arctic fox,* which lives north of the timberline and remains white the entire year. The BLUE FOX (see under FURS) is a color phase of this fox living south of the timberline.

wild mink Skins procured from animals that run wild in the forest. Very expensive because skins must be matched in color. Under controlled conditions on a mink farm, color is more uniform and is usually brown.

wolf Long-haired fur with long silky guard hairs and dense underfur. Pale-colored skins are sometimes stenciled to imitate LYNX; others are used in natural state or dyed brown, black, or gray. Quality depends on fluffiness and density of underfur that supports the long guard hairs. The best quality comes from the timber wolf of Canada. Used for coats, capes, jackets, trimmings, and scarves. The red wolf is protected in the U.S.

wolverine Coarse fur with long brown guard hairs and dense gray underfur. Very durable; best qualities found in the Arctic regions, also found in the Rocky Mountains and Siberia. Used mainly for sportswear and trimming. Used in the far north to trim the edges of parkas, as moisture will not condense on it.

worked in the round Method of joining fur skins together horizontally so that skins continue around coat or garment known as the skin-on-skin method.

zebra **1.** Flat, stiff fur with wide, black, irregularly shaped stripes against a light-colored background. Comes from Africa; used infrequently for coats. Calf is sometimes stenciled to imitate zebra. **2.** Pattern that imitates the irregular stripes of a zebra fur.

zorina See under FURS: SKUNK.

---

furbelow (foor′-beh-low) ∞**1.** Skirt ruffles used as trim on women's skirts and scarves in the 18th c. Usually made of same fabric or lace. Also called *falbala* or *fabala.* **2.** In contemporary usage generally refers to useless, ostentatious trimming.

furbelow wig See under WIGS AND HAIRPIECES: DUVILLIER WIG.

†**fur blended yarn** Any yarn made from FUR FIBER blended with other fibers (e.g., wool or nylon, used for knitted or woven clothing).

fur boa See SCARVES: BOA.

fur fabric coat See under COATS AND JACKETS.

fur farming See under FURS.

fur felt Best grade of felt obtained from UNDERFUR (see under FURS) of beaver and rabbit and is used for hats. Also see under HEADWEAR: BEAVER HAT.

fur fiber Fibers obtained from the pelts of fur-bearing animals. See under FURS: UNDERFUR in introduction to category.

Fur Labeling Act See under introduction to FURS.

fur lining Lining a garment with fur for warmth and fashion appeal. If the garment is meant to be reversible, the sleeves are lined; otherwise sleeves are not fur-lined in order to reduce bulkiness.

fur scarf See under SCARVES.

fur seal See under FURS.

fur stole See under CAPES, CLOAKS, AND SHAWLS.

fused collar See under NECKLINES AND COLLARS.

fused hem See under CLOTHING CONSTRUCTION DETAILS.

fused ribbon Ribbon made of acetate or other heat-sensitive manufactured fibers and woven like piece goods. It is then cut with a hot knife, thereby melting the edges enough to keep them from fraying.

fused seam See under CLOTHING CONSTRUCTION DETAILS.

†gabardine (gab′-uhr-deen) Durable, closely woven fabric with diagonal ridges, created by a warp-faced TWILL WEAVE, and made from wool, rayon, or other fibers and blends. Wool gabardine has a firm hand, is made with worsted yarns, and given a clear finish. Used for tailored suits and coats for men and women, pants, sportswear, and riding breeches. *Der.* From word used for a cloak or mantle in the Middle Ages. Also see under COATS AND JACKETS.

gaberdine See under COATS AND JACKETS.

gable bonnet/hat See under HEADWEAR.

gable headdress See under HEADWEAR: ENGLISH HOOD.

∞gabrielle dress See under DRESSES.

gabrielle sleeve See under SHOULDERS AND SLEEVES.

gabrielle waist See under BLOUSES AND TOPS.

gainsborough hat See under HEADWEAR.

gaiter See under FOOTWEAR.

gaiter boots See under FOOTWEAR.

galage See under FOOTWEAR: GALOSH.

galatea fichu See under SCARVES.

galatea hat See under HEADWEAR.

galea Roman soldier's helmet See under HEADWEAR.

∞gallants Small ribbon bows worn in hair or on sleeve, bodice, or skirt in mid-17th c.

∞galligaskins (gal-lee-gas′-kins) 1. See under TRUNK HOSE. 2. Gaiters of leather worn by sportsmen in 19th c.

∞Gallo-Greek bodice Bodice style of 1820s made with narrow, flat trim running diagonally from shoulders to waist in front and back.

galloon See under BRAIDS.

gallowses See under BRACES.

galosh See under FOOTWEAR.

galosh closure See under CLOSURES.

galuchat See under LEATHERS.

gambeson See under DOUBLET and ARMOR: ACTON.

gamin See under HAIRSTYLES.

gaming purse See under HANDBAGS AND RELATED ACCESSORIES.

gamp See under UMBRELLAS AND PARASOLS.

ganges See under LEATHERS.

gangster suit Wide-shouldered, single- or double-breasted suit with wide lapels, inspired by fashions worn in the 1967 film *Bonnie and Clyde.* Usually made of black or gray pinstriped flannel; re-creation of 1930s men's fashion.

ganymede (gan-e′-meed) *adj.* Descriptive of fashions derived from or inspired by styles of ancient Greece that became popular in 1969. Generally consisted of a short tunic with a one-shoulder neckline worn with unusual sandals that reached nearly to the knee. *Der.* From the Greek myth about a Greek boy, named Ganymede, carried off by an eagle to become a cupbearer for Zeus. Also called *Greek boy style.*

ganymede sandal See under FOOTWEAR.

garb See under APPAREL #1.

Garbo, Greta Swedish-born film star of great beauty who gave unforgettable performances from 1925 to 1939 in such movies as *Mata Hari* (1932), *Grand Hotel* (1932), *Anna Karenina* (1935), *Camille* (1936), and *Ninotchka* (1939). At age 36, she retired to a secluded life in New York City. Publicity shy, she was frequently seen in trench coat, slacks, and slouch hat, the latter now called by her name. See under HEADWEAR: GARBO HAT.

garcette See under HAIRSTYLES: COIFFURE EN BOUFFONS.

garçon See under HAIRSTYLES: BOYISH BOB.

∞garde-corps/gardcors (gard′-cor) An outdoor garment worn by men and women in 13th and early 14th c., which consisted of a full, unbelted outer tunic with a hood and long, full hanging sleeves that was frequently worn with the arms passed through slits above elbows. The **herigaut** appears to have been a similar garment.

garde-corps

garden hat See under HEADWEAR.

garibaldi jacket See under COATS AND JACKETS.

garibaldi shirt/blouse See under BLOUSES AND TOPS.

∞**garibaldi suit** (gar-ih-bawl'-dee) 1. Little boy's collarless suit of 1860s consisting of thigh-length overblouse with dropped shoulders, belted at waistline, and worn with calf-length trousers. Trimmed with braid, rickrack, and buttons down center front, around hem of blouse, at sleeves, and down sides of trousers. 2. Little girl's collarless two-piece dress of 1860s with full blouse, sleeves set into dropped shoulders, and a full skirt. Trimmed at neck, down front, around waist, wrists, and hem with bands of leather and steel buttons.

garland Wreath of flowers or foliage. Sometimes worn on the head as ornament or as an honor.

garment See under APPAREL #1.

†**garment dyed** Apparel produced as white or colorless goods, constructed into a garment, then dyed during the finishing process.

garment specification sheet/package Information that includes a technical drawing, specific fabrics for all areas including interfacings (interlinings), all findings (notions), and construction specifications that are essential for the garment style. Size specifications (dimensions) for a full run of sizes, construction requirements, and quality standards for components and finished garment. Also called a garment *spec sheet/package.*

garment purchase agreement (GPA) A contract that describes a quantity of goods to be purchased, along with the price, dates, terms, and conditions of the purchase.

garment standards See under STANDARD SPECIFICATIONS.

garment trade See under APPAREL INDUSTRY.

∞**garnache** Outdoor garment worn from 13th to mid-14th c. that was a long cloak with cape-like sleeves, often lined or collared with fur. Sides were either joined at the waist, from waist to hem, or left open. The garment had two flat, tongue-shaped lapels at the neck. Similar to **housse** (hoos).

garnache

garnet See under GEMS, GEM CUTS, AND SETTINGS.

∞**garniture** Trimmings, as they were called in 19th and early 20th c. (e.g., ruffles, lace, ribbons, and bows).

garrison cap See under HEADWEAR: OVERSEAS CAP.

garter 1. Historically an elastic support attached to girdle or garter belt, used to hold up hose. 2. Since Medieval times through the 18th c., a strip of fabric worn by men that tied around the leg or buckled below knee. 3. Band of elastic worn below the knee to hold up hose. 4. Round elasticized band worn around the sleeve to shorten it. 5. A decorative elasticized band worn under a bridal or prom dress. Bridal garters derived from England and France in the 14th century from the belief that having a piece of the bride's clothing would bring good luck. Today brides who choose to honor this tradition wear a garter mid-thigh on their right leg. The groom removes the garter and tosses it to the single bachelors at the wedding; the bachelor who catches the garter is believed to be the next to be married. A similar tradition has been embraced for proms. The wearing and exchange of a prom garter symbolizes that a young man and woman are together as a couple.

garter belt 1. See under UNDERGARMENTS. 2. See under HOSIERY.

garter briefs See under UNDERGARMENTS.

gascon coat/gaskyn See under COATS AND JACKETS: JUPE.

gaskins See under GALLIGASKINS.

gathered skirt See under SKIRTS.

gathering See under CLOTHING CONSTRUCTION DETAILS.

gaucho (gow'-cho) *adj.* Derived from or inspired by clothing and accessories worn by South American cowboys called gauchos. A gaucho-influenced style consisting of calf-length full CULOTTE-type pants (see under PANTS: GAUCHO) usually worn with a full-sleeved blouse, bolero, and distinctive broad-brimmed GAUCHO HAT (see under HEADWEAR); became popular in the 1960s and 1970s. This style trend was influenced by an Andalusian riding suit worn by Jacqueline Kennedy on her trip to Spain in 1966. *Der.* Spanish, "cowboy" of Argentina, Chile, and Uruguay. Also see under BELTS: GAUCHO BELT.

gaucho style

gaucho suit (gow'-cho) Woman's pantsuit with wide-legged, calf-length CULOTTES (see under PANTS) and a matching BOLERO (see under COATS AND JACKETS), frequently made in leather. A full-sleeved blouse is usually worn under the sleeveless bolero. Introduced in mid-1960s. *Der.* Spanish, "cowboy" of Argentina, Chile, and Uruguay.

†**gauge** (gayj) Knitting measurement of the number of stitches per unit of width and length in a knitted fabric.

gauging See under CLOTHING CONSTRUCTION DETAILS: SHIRRING.

∞**gauntlet** 1. See under ARMOR. 2. See under CUFFS. 3. See under GLOVES AND GLOVE CONSTRUCTION.

†gauze (gawz) **1.** Sheer, open-weave fabric used for trimmings and costumes made in the LENO or PLAIN WEAVE of silk, cotton, rayon, and other MANUFACTURED FIBER fabrics. **2.** Plain open-weave fabric, similar to lightweight muslin, made of loosely twisted cotton yarns. Sometimes given a crinkled finish, used for blouses, and worn unpressed. *Der.* From Gaza, a city in the Middle East.

gauze weave See under LENO WEAVE.

gay deceivers See under FALSIES.

Gay 90s Period from 1890 to 1900 when society began to relax from some of the conservative social conventions of the Victorian era. Socioeconomic trends such as the movement of more women into the workforce, increased participation in active sports by women, and a less formal lifestyle resulted in fashion trends such as tailored clothes for women; divided skirts for bicycling and special clothing for yachting, tennis, canoeing, and swimming; and such as less formal dress for men.

Gay 90s style

Gay 90s swimsuit See under SWIMWEAR.

Gaze, point de See under LACES.

gele See under SCARVES.

gem-cutter See under LAPIDARY.

gemel ring See under JEWELRY.

GEMS, GEM CUTS, AND SETTINGS

gem Mineral that is rare, beautiful, durable, and in demand. It must also be portable and suitable for personal adornment. Divided into PRECIOUS STONES, SEMI-PRECIOUS STONES, ORNAMENTAL STONES, and MARINE GEMS. Gems are classified as TRANSPARENT, SEMITRANSPARENT, or OPAQUE. Also classified as CRYSTALLINE, CRYPTO-CRYSTALLINE, or AMORPHOUS. See definitions of the foregoing cross-references under GEMS, GEM CUTS, AND SETTINGS. Only a qualified gemologist can determine accurately the name of a gem. This is done by testing the gem for hardness, specific gravity, light reflection, and crystalline structure. The **Mohs' scale** is used to rate the degree of hardness of precious gems. The diamond, the hardest gem, has a hardness of 10 and will scratch any gems that rate below it. A set of minerals used to test gems was invented by Friedrich Mohs and is as follows:

Mineral	Hardness
Talc	1
Gypsum	2
Calcite	3
Fluorite	4
Apatite	5
Orthoclass (feldspar)	6
Quartz	7
Topaz	8
Sapphire	9
Diamond	10

gem cut Method of cutting gemstones to be mounted into gold and other metals (e.g., rings, bracelets, necklaces, tiaras). Terminology applied to the shapes of cut gems includes **standard shape,** those that are round, rectangular, or square; and **fancy shape,** any shape that deviates from standard shapes—examples include: heart shape, oval, triangular, and pear. Various cuts have been developed, for example, **shield cut,** which is symmetrical side to side but not top to bottom; **barion cut,** which creates a fountain of light effect; and **portuguese cut**, which scintillates more than most cuts. **Carving** or **incising** a design on the surface of a gem rather than cutting it into facets to reflect light. CABOCHON CUT and CAMEO CUT gems are most often carved (see under GEMS, GEM CUTS, AND SETTINGS).

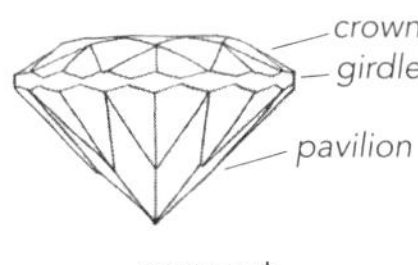

gem cut

gem setting The manner in which a stone is mounted in an article of jewelry. Metals used for genuine jewelry are usually 14k or 18k gold, silver, or platinum. COSTUME JEWELRY (see under JEWELRY) uses any type of metal, sometimes gold-washed or gold-plated.

agate Variety of CHALCEDONY quartz (see under GEMS, GEM CUTS, AND SETTINGS) consisting of bands of color either arranged in curved or wavy parallel bands, and thus called *banded agate,* or in widening circular rings and called *eye agate.* Also with fern or foggy effect called *moss agate* or *mocha stone.*

alexandrite Transparent or translucent variety of the mineral CHRYSOBERYL (see under GEMS, GEM CUTS, AND SETTINGS), which appears one color in daylight and another color under artificial light. May appear emerald green in daylight and columbine-red at night. Named in honor of Czar Alexander II. Said to have been discovered in Russia in 1833 on the same day that the soon-to-be czar celebrated his birthday.

almandite garnet Transparent to opaque semiprecious garnet in varied hues of deep-red, violet-red, and brownish-red to almost black. Includes the CARBUNCLE (see under GEMS, GEM CUTS, AND SETTINGS).

amber An amorphous fossil resin that was exuded from prehistoric trees found in deposits along the southern coast of Baltic Sea in Poland. Also found in marine deposits in Eastern Germany, Romania, Sicily, and Myanmar. Exists in colors and is translucent. Most popular is called "clear" and is yellow; other colors vary from colorless to brownish-red.

amethyst Transparent purple or violet-colored quartz of the crystalline variety. Rated as a semiprecious stone because it exists in large quantities. Best qualities are a clear, even color in the darker tones. The finest qualities come from Uruguay, Ural Mountains, and Brazil. Other sources include Sri Lanka, Japan, South America, and Mexico.

amorphous A property of gems meaning without a crystalline structure. Semiprecious or ornamental gems such as the opal and turquoise are amorphous, as opposed to the diamond, ruby, and amethyst, which are crystalline.

andradite garnet Transparent to opaque garnets called by various names: **topazolite,** yellow, and transparent; **demantoid,** grass-green, and transparent, also known erroneously as *olivine* and as *Ural emerald;* **melanite,** black opaque garnets formerly used for mourning jewelry.

aquamarine Transparent variety of BERYL (see under GEMS, GEM CUTS, AND SETTINGS) from which the emerald comes. Has the same crystalline structure and hardness, but color is aqua rather than green. Comes from Ural Mountains, Brazil, and Madagascar. One large aquamarine found in Minas Gerais, Brazil, weighed 243 pounds.

arizona ruby See under GEMS, GEM CUTS, AND SETTINGS: RUBY.

asterism Ability of a gemstone to project a star-shaped pattern as in rubies and sapphires. Produced synthetically in trademarked LINDE STAR® and HOPE STAR® sapphires.

baguette cut (ba-get') Small stones cut in oblong shape with facets. Usually placed horizontally along the side of a larger center diamond. *Der.* French, "rod."

balas ruby See under GEMS, GEM CUTS, AND SETTINGS: SPINEL.

banded agate See under GEMS, GEM CUTS, AND SETTINGS: AGATE.

base Lower portion of a BRILLIANT-CUT stone (see under GEMS, GEM CUTS, AND SETTINGS).

beryl Mineral from which the EMERALD is obtained (see under GEMS, GEM CUTS, AND SETTINGS).

bevel Slanted cut on gemstone, which reflects light, especially on square-cut gemstones.

bezel See under GEMS, GEM CUTS, AND SETTINGS: CROWN.

birthstone Precious or semiprecious stone assigned to the month of birth, often worn in a ring. Although the breastplate of Jewish high priests (worn first by Aaron) contained 12 stones, and there were, in ancient times, 12 stones for the signs of the Zodiac, the custom of a birthstone for each month is comparatively recent. Became popular among the Hebrews in Poland in the 18th c., reaching its greatest popularity in the 20th c. Popular birthstones are: January—garnet; February—amethyst; March—aquamarine, bloodstone; April—diamond, white sapphire; May—emerald; June—alexandrite, moonstone, pearl; July—ruby; August—peridot, sardonyx; September—sapphire; October—opal, tourmaline; November—citrine (yellow quartz), topaz; December—lapis lazuli, turquoise, zircon.

bloodstone Opaque variety of the mineral quartz characterized by red spots on a dark green background. The early church frequently used it to engrave sacred objects, the red spots simulating the blood of Christ. Found in India and Siberia. Also called *heliotrope.*

Borazon® Trademark for industrial artificial diamonds. First made in 1957. More suitable than natural diamonds for some industrial purposes.

Brazilian emerald Misleading name for a green TOURMALINE (see under GEMS, GEM CUTS, AND SETTINGS) that is used as a gemstone.

Brazilian peridot Misleading name for a yellow-green TOURMALINE (see under GEMS, GEM CUTS, AND SETTINGS) that is used as a gemstone.

Brazilian sapphire Misleading name for a blue TOURMALINE (see under GEMS, GEM CUTS, AND SETTINGS) that is used as a gemstone.

brilliant cut A faceted cut used particularly for diamonds and transparent gems cut with 58 facets, which may be increased to 64, 72, and 80 facets. It usually appears with a flat surface on top, called the **table,** sloping outwardly to the **girdle** or widest point, and tapered to a point at bottom, where a small facet called the **culet** (kue'-lit) is cut. When mounted, only about one-third of gem is visible. The number of facets and the expertise in cutting increase the brilliancy of the stone. It can be round, oval, pear, marquise, or heart-shaped.

cabochon cut (ka-bow-shown') **1.** Type of cut used for gemstones that involves rounding off the top of the stone so that it is higher in the center and slopes to the rim. Used particularly for star rubies and sapphires. **2.** A **high cabochon** cut is a stone with a flat base and a higher elongated top. Also called a *tallow top cut.*

cairngorm Popular stone in Scotland. See under GEMS, GEM CUTS, AND SETTINGS: SMOKY QUARTZ.

cameo cut A raised design carved out of a stone (e.g., onyx or banded sardonyx) that has more than one layer. The foreground color is carved away, leaving a white design exposed on a colored surface, usually of black or orange. Also see under CAMEO.

canary diamond Fancy diamond in a definite yellow color. As differentiated from diamonds that have a yellow tinge, genuine yellow diamonds are rare and expensive.

cape may diamond Misleading name for rock crystal from Cape May, New Jersey.

cape ruby Gem from the GARNET (See under GEMS, GEM CUTS, AND SETTINGS) group, ruby red to black in color and found in deposits with diamonds in Africa. No relationship to genuine ruby.

carat Unit of weight used for gemstones. Fractions of a carat are divided into 10 points. Thus, a 1½ c. stone would be 1.5, or 1 carat and 5 points. In actual weight 1 carat equals 200 milligrams or 2 grams (16 grains). Not to be confused with KARAT, which is related to the quality of gold. (The abbreviation used is c.) See also under GRAIN #2.

carbuncle Variety of ALMANDITE GARNET (see under GEMS, GEM CUTS, AND SETTINGS) that varies from deep red and violet-red to brownish-red and black. Transparent red varieties are used for gems. Before the availability of scientific testing, often believed to be a RUBY or SPINEL.

carnelian Transparent to translucent reddish variety of CHALCEDONY (see under GEMS, GEM CUTS, AND SETTINGS) that may be pale red, deep clear red, brownish-red, or yellow-green. Also called *sard. Der.* Latin, "flesh-colored."

cat's eye **1.** Variety of opalescent, greenish CHRYSOBERYL that is CHATOYANT when cut CABOCHON style. Light seems to fluctuate lengthwise across the stone as it is turned under the light. Also called *cymophane* and *oriental cat's eye.* **2.** Variety of QUARTZ, also CHATOYANT, that is grayish, brownish, or green in color. Not as valuable as #1. See cross-references under GEMS, GEM CUTS, AND SETTINGS.

chalcedony (kal-say-doe′-nee) Transparent to translucent varieties of quartz known by different names for each color: red is called carnelian; apple green called chrysoprase; dark green with red spots is called bloodstone or heliotrope; black-and-white banded is called onyx; and brown banded with white called sardonyx.

channel setting Grooves of metal used to hold stones. Also called *flush setting.*

chatoyancy (sha-toy′-an-see) Optical properties in certain gems produced when stone is cut. As stone turns, a single streak of light reflects from needlelike crystals arranged parallel to one another (e.g., CAT'S EYE or TIGER'S EYE. See under GEMS, GEM CUTS, AND SETTINGS). *Der.* From the French, *chatoyer,* "to change luster," as a cat's eye.

chip **1.** A single-cut MELEE, a small ROSE-CUT diamond, or an irregularly shaped diamond (see under GEMS, GEM CUTS, AND SETTINGS: MELEE and ROSE-CUT). **2.** A break on the edge of a larger diamond.

chlorspinel See under GEMS, GEM CUTS, AND SETTINGS: SPINEL.

chrysoberyl A mineral with a hardness of 8.5 from which the following gems are obtained: ALEXANDRITE, ORIENTAL CAT'S EYE, and CHRYSOLITE (see under GEMS, GEM CUTS, AND SETTINGS).

chrysolite See under GEMS, GEM CUTS, AND SETTINGS: PERIDOT.

chrysoprase Apple-green variety of CHALCEDONY quartz (see under GEMS, GEM CUTS, AND SETTINGS) that comes from California, Oregon, and Silesia.

citrine (sit-reen′) Yellow crystalline quartz that resembles TOPAZ (see under GEMS, GEM CUTS, AND SETTINGS) in color and transparency, sometimes erroneously sold as topaz. Comes from Brazil.

cleavage Ability of gemstone to break along the crystalline structure lines; especially important when cutting valuable diamonds.

coral Translucent substance made up of calcareous skeletons secreted by tiny marine animals found in tropical seas. Precious coral of red or pink "grows" in branchlike formations. Used for necklaces, rosaries, and bracelets; may also be cut into beads.

corundum Extremely hard mineral, rating 9 on Mohs' scale, that produces the precious gems RUBY and SAPPHIRE (see under GEMS, GEM CUTS, AND SETTINGS). Also comes in other colors, but these are not as valuable and are called *fancy sapphires.* All red corundum gems are called *rubies.*

cross stone See under GEMS, GEM CUTS, AND SETTINGS: FAIRY STONE.

crown Upper portion of a brilliant-cut faceted stone (e.g., a diamond). Also called *bezel.* Shown at GEM CUT under introduction to GEMS, GEM CUTS, AND GEM SETTINGS.

cryptocrystalline *adj.* Descriptive of a gem with very fine crystalline structure only visible with X-rays.

crystal **1.** Genuine rock crystal, a mineral. See under GEMS, GEM CUTS, AND SETTINGS: QUARTZ. **2.** Beads or simulated gems of faceted glass resembling rock crystal.

crystalline structure Property possessed by most minerals and thus used as a means of identifying gems under a microscope. Principal systems are variations of hexagonal, cubic, tetragonal, orthorhombic, monoclinic, and triclinic. Minerals with no crystalline structure are called AMORPHOUS (see under GEMS, GEM CUTS, AND SETTINGS).

cubic zirconia Manufactured synthetic stone made to imitate the diamond.

culet See GEMS, GEM CUTS, AND SETTINGS: BRILLIANT CUT.

cushion cut Variation of the BRILLIANT CUT (see under GEMS, GEM CUTS, AND SETTINGS), shaped square with the corners cut off and rounded at the widest part of the stone or girdle. Used particularly for large diamonds and transparent stones.

cymophane See under GEMS, GEM CUTS, AND SETTINGS: CAT'S EYE.

diamond Transparent variety of nearly pure carbon. This is the hardest mineral known and very brilliant when faceted. Colorless stones are most generally known, but diamonds also come in yellow, brown, green, red, and blue. Diamonds are graded according to color, cut, weight, clarity, and brilliance. Originally found only in India, now many come from Brazil and South Africa, with 95 percent coming from the latter.

emerald Precious gem from the mineral BERYL (see under GEMS, GEM CUTS, AND SETTINGS). Hardness is 7½ to 8. Best stones are transparent to translucent green, and large stones of clear color are rare, thus making them very valuable. Predominantly comes from Colombia and Brazil, also found in Ural Mountains and Australia.

emerald cut A type of STEP CUT (see under GEMS, GEM CUTS, AND SETTINGS) with all four square corners cut off diagonally. Used particularly for emeralds and large diamonds. Also see under GEMS, GEM CUTS, AND SETTINGS: CUSHION CUT.

eye agate See under GEMS, GEM CUTS, AND SETTINGS: AGATE.

facet A small plane, cut in a gemstone to enhance its ability to reflect light—the more facets, the more brilliance.

fairy stone Mineral frequently found in the shape of a cross caused by twin crystals. Usually reddish-brown in color and translucent to opaque. Used for crosses for the clergy or for curiosity items. Also known as *staurolite* and *cross stone.*

fancy diamond Any diamond with a distinctive color and high degree of transparency. May be yellow or brown, with green, red, or blue being the most rare.

fancy sapphire See under GEMS, GEM CUTS, AND SETTINGS: CORUNDUM.

feldspar A transparent to opaque mineral with vitreous to pearly luster and a hardness of 6½. Various colors of gem varieties are called by the following names: opalescent called *moonstone* comes from Switzerland, Elba, and Sri Lanka; green, called *amazon stone,* comes from the Urals and Pennsylvania; blue, called *Labradorite,* comes from Labrador; yellow, called *orthoclase,* comes from Madagascar; and reddish, called *sunstone* or *aventurine,* comes from Norway and Siberia.

fire opal Semitransparent to transparent variety of opal that is yellow, orange, or red in color. May show a play of color.

fishtail setting Series of scallops (like fish scales) holding stone in place.

flush setting See under GEMS, GEM CUTS, AND SETTINGS: CHANNEL SETTING.

garnet Gemstone family consisting of 17 different varieties. Hardness ranges from 6½ to 7½. Among those commonly identified by gemologists are almandite (or almandine) garnets and andradite garnets. See under GEMS, GEM CUTS, AND SETTINGS: ALMANDITE GARNET and ANDRADITE GARNET. Garnet exists in all colors but blue and ranges from transparent to opaque.

gem cuts See introduction to GEMS, GEM CUTS, AND SETTINGS.

gem setting See introduction to GEMS, GEM CUTS, AND SETTINGS.

girdle The widest part of a cut gem. Shown at GEM CUT under introduction to GEMS, GEM CUTS, AND GEM SETTINGS.

golden beryl Yellow semiprecious transparent variety of the mineral BERYL (see under GEMS, GEM CUTS, AND SETTINGS).

gold filled Gold of 10 to 22 karats fused to a base metal (e.g., nickel, silver, or brass). Layer of gold should weigh at least one twentieth of the entire metal used. One tenth 18k means that the gold used is 18 karat and that it represents one tenth of the weight of the metal. Compare with JEWELRY: ROLLED GOLD.

goshenite Colorless, transparent variety of the mineral BERYL (see under GEMS, GEM CUTS, AND SETTINGS).

grain Measure used to determine the weight of pearls or to approximate that of diamonds, equal to slightly more than 50 milligrams or ¼ carat. Not the same as the troy grain. Also see under GEMS, GEM CUTS, AND SETTINGS: CARAT.

harlequin opal (har-lay'-kin) White opal that displays uniform patches of colors resembling a mosaic.

heart-shaped cut Variation of the BRILLIANT CUT (see under GEMS, GEM CUTS, AND SETTINGS) in heart shape, used for large diamonds.

heliodor Yellow, transparent variety of the mineral BERYL (see under GEMS, GEM CUTS, AND SETTINGS) from southwest Africa.

heliotrope See under GEMS, GEM CUTS, AND SETTINGS: BLOODSTONE.

hematite Iron mineral that is opaque black, or black with red streaks and metallic luster. Comes from England, Norway, Sweden, and Lake Superior region.

Herkimer diamond Misleading name for ROCK CRYSTAL (see under GEMS, GEM CUTS, AND SETTINGS).

Hope Star Expired trademark for a synthetic star sapphire.

hyacinth Name used for clear transparent zircons of yellow, orange, red, and brown varieties. Also called *jacinth.*

imitation gems Reproductions of fine gemstones in colored glass or other inexpensive material as distinguished from manufactured SYNTHETIC GEMS (see under GEMS, GEM CUTS, AND SETTINGS). The latter, although manufactured, are chemically identical to gems occurring in nature.

intaglio/intaglio cut (in-tal'-yo) Method of cutting gems by engraving design into the surface. Compare with CAMEO carving (see under GEMS, GEM CUTS, AND SETTINGS).

jacinth See under GEMS, GEM CUTS, AND SETTINGS: HYACINTH.

jade Includes two minerals of similar appearance, **nephrite** and **jadeite.** The former is the most common variety, with hardness of 6 to 6½, and color variations from white to leaf green. Often found in China, Turkestan, Siberia, and Alaska. Jadeite is lustrous, transparent to opaque, and more rare, with a hardness of 6½ to 7. Color is white or greenish white to emerald green, translucent to opaque, and found in upper Myanmar (Burma), Yunnan province in southern China, Tibet, Mexico, and South America. In 1965, boulders weighing as much as 10,000 pounds containing gem-quality jade (nephrite) were found in Alaska. Popular in China for centuries either carved into objects or used for jewelry.

jargon See under GEMS, GEM CUTS, AND SETTINGS: ZIRCON.

jasper Form of opaque QUARTZ (see under GEMS, GEM CUTS, AND SETTINGS) available in brown, dark green, grayish-blue, red, or yellow colors.

jet An opaque mineral made largely of carbon, a variety of lignite or coal, that polishes easily. Comes from England, Spain, France, and the U.S. Black varieties of quartz, obsidian, and glass also masquerade as this mineral. All were used for pins, earrings, and beads in mourning jewelry during Victorian era.

Lake George diamond Misleading name for ROCK CRYSTAL (see under GEMS, GEM CUTS, AND SETTINGS).

lapis lazuli Translucent to opaque mineral in tones of blue, deep blue, azure blue, Berlin blue, and greenish-blue. It is a mixture of lazurite and other minerals. Comes from Afghanistan, Siberia, and Chile. Used for beads, brooches, pendants, and cuff links.

Linde Star Trade name for a manufactured synthetic gem that imitates the star sapphire.

malachite Ornamental opaque stone that exists in too large a quantity and is too soft to be a precious or semiprecious gem, mainly from Ural Mountains. May have irregular rings of various tones or be banded. Primary color is green—from emerald green to grass green.

marcasite (mar-ka'-sight) Mineral with a metallic luster having the same composition as iron pyrite, but crystals are different. Cut material sold as marcasite is usually pyrite.

marine gems Gems found primarily in the sea, e.g., PEARLS, AMBER, and CORAL.

marquise cut (mar-keez') Variation of the BRILLIANT CUT (see under GEMS, GEM CUTS, AND SETTINGS), basic shape is oval with pointed ends. Introduced during reign of Louis XV, and named for his mistress Marquise de Pompadour.

mauve diamond (mowv) Fancy diamond of a purplish hue.

melanite See under GEMS, GEM CUTS, AND SETTINGS: ANDRADITE GARNET.

melee (may-lay') Small, brilliant-cut diamonds, usually .20 to .25 carats. *Der.* French, "confused mass."

mocha stone See under GEMS, GEM CUTS, AND SETTINGS: AGATE.

Mohs' scale See under introduction to GEMS, GEM CUTS, AND SETTINGS.

moonstone Opalescent gem variety of FELDSPAR, which is cut CABOCHON style (see under GEMS, GEM CUTS, AND SETTINGS).

morganite Transparent, pink to rose variety of the mineral BERYL (see under GEMS, GEM CUTS, AND SETTINGS). *Der.* Named after J. P. Morgan, financier and collector of gems.

moss agate See under GEMS, GEM CUTS, AND SETTINGS: AGATE.

nephrite See under GEMS, GEM CUTS, AND SETTINGS: JADE.

obsidian Volcanic glass rather than a mineral. Usually black in color, but also comes in red, brown, and greenish black. Attractive colors are cut as gems. Comes from Mexico, Greece, California, and Wyoming.

off-color diamond In the American diamond trade, a diamond with a tinge of an undesirable color, particularly yellow or brown, which is easily discernible.

old mine cut Brilliant cut of the 19th c. that retained much of original stone and had a larger CULET and smaller TABLE when compared to modern cuts. See under BRILLIANT CUT.

olivine PERIDOT as it is called by gemologists (see under GEMS, GEM CUTS, AND SETTINGS).

onyx Variety of CHALCEDONY quartz that consists of parallel straight bands of black and white. Used for cameos and stones for rings. A popular ring for many years is composed of a large onyx with small diamond mounted on it.

opal Transparent to opaque gem that is AMORPHOUS and has a pleasing play of color, or opalescence, when cut CABOCHON (see under GEMS, GEM CUTS, AND SETTINGS). Comes in many colors, including the valuable dark gray, blue, and black colors called *black opal.* Also see under GEMS, GEM CUTS, AND SETTINGS: FIRE OPAL and HARLEQUIN OPAL.

oriental cat's eye See under GEMS, GEM CUTS, AND SETTINGS: CAT'S EYE.

ornamental stones Gems that exist in such large quantities that they are not considered precious or semiprecious gems, e.g., CORAL and TURQUOISE (see under GEMS, GEM CUTS, AND SETTINGS).

oval cut Variation of the BRILLIANT CUT (see under GEMS, GEM CUTS, AND SETTINGS) made in oval shape.

paste See under JEWELRY.

paste setting Stone is glued in place; method used for inexpensive stones.

pavé (pah-vay') A setting of stones placed close to each other so that no metal shows between them.

pavilion Lower portion below the GIRDLE of a brilliant-cut gem. Also called the *base.* Shown at GEM CUT under introduction to GEMS, GEM CUTS, AND GEM SETTINGS.

pear cut Variation of the BRILLIANT CUT, similar to MARQUISE CUT (see under GEMS, GEM CUTS, AND SETTINGS), but with one pointed and one rounded end. Shaped somewhat like a pear. Used particularly for large diamonds.

pearl Divided into three groups: **genuine pearls, cultured pearls,** and **simulated pearls.** 1. **genuine pearls** are secured from oysters that have made a deposit over a grain of sand. The grain of sand is an irritant to the oyster, which secretes a deposit over it, making a pearl. Very expensive and rare, pearls must be matched in size and color. They are translucent to opaque, are most often white or faintly yellowish or bluish, but they may be pink, yellow, purple, red, green, blue, brown, or black. Genuine pearls also include: (a) *baroque pearls,* which are irregular in shape; (b) *freshwater pearls* of chalk-white color found in mussels in freshwater streams in the U.S. and not as lustrous as Oriental pearls; (c) *Oriental pearls,* the most beautiful and expensive natural pearls from Japan, Pacific Islands, Persian Gulf, Australia, Venezuela, and Panama; (d) *seed pearls,* tiny irregular-shaped real pearls. Formerly used in necklaces, now used primarily for embroidery on sweaters or wedding dresses. 2. **cultured pearls** are secured by artificially implanting oysters with a tiny round piece of mother-of-pearl, placing oysters in cages, and lowering them into the ocean. Pearls are formed around the irritant. Pearls formed this way do not have many layers of coating, and can only be distinguished from genuine pearl by X-ray. 3. **simulated pearls** are not gems, but plastic or glass beads coated with a solution called "pearl essence" made from an adhesive combined with fish scales, giving them an iridescent luster.

peridot (pehr'-ee-dot) Transparent gem that is bottle green to olive green in color and comes from Myanmar, Ceylon, and Brazil. Also called *chrysolite.* Called OLIVINE (see under GEMS, GEM CUTS, AND SETTINGS) by minerologists.

precious stone A gem that is not only beautiful, durable, and portable, but also rare, e.g. diamonds, rubies, sapphires, and emeralds.

pronged setting Stone held in place by narrow projecting pieces of metal.

quartz Mineral used for gems that exists in both crystalline transparent varieties, and cryptocrystalline, transparent, or opaque varieties. Crystalline varieties include *rock crystal, amethyst, rose quartz, smoky quartz, citrine, tiger's eye,* and *cat's eye.* Cryptocrystalline quartz appears to the unaided eye to be amorphous, but is revealed as crystalline under the microscope. Usually regarded as chalcedony, although various colors go by different names (e.g., *carnelian* or *sard, chrysoprase, bloodstone* or *heliotrope, agate, onyx, sardonyx, jasper.*)

rhinestone A colorless, transparent, artificial gem made of glass or PASTE (see under JEWELRY) usually cut like a diamond, and used widely for costume jewelry and buttons. *Der.* Originally made in Strasbourg, France, on the Rhine River. Also see under CLOSURES.

rock crystal Clear transparent crystalline variety of the mineral QUARTZ (see under GEMS, GEM CUTS, AND SETTINGS). Exists in such large quantities that it is inexpensive. May be carved for beads. May also be imitated by glass poured into molds to make beads.

rose cut Simple faceted cut, used for inexpensive gems.

rose quartz Transparent crystalline variety of QUARTZ (see under GEMS, GEM CUTS, AND SETTINGS) in rose-pink color.

rubicelle See under GEMS, GEM CUTS, AND SETTINGS: SPINEL.

ruby Transparent precious gem that comes from the mineral CORUNDUM. Pigeon's-blood red is the preferred color. Some stones have an asterism and are called STAR RUBIES. Best quality comes from Burma. *Cape ruby* and *Arizona ruby* are misleading and refer to garnets. *Balas ruby* is misleading and refers to a spinel (see under GEMS, GEM CUTS, AND SETTINGS).

sapphire Any precious, transparent corundum mineral of a color other than red. Preferred color is cornflower blue and called "Kashmir blue." Other sapphires may be white, pink, or yellow. May also be asterated and then called a STAR SAPPHIRE. Rates close to the diamond in hardness.

sapphirine See under GEMS, GEM CUTS, AND SETTINGS: SPINEL.

sard See under GEMS, GEM CUTS, AND SETTINGS: CARNELIAN.

sardonyx Variety of CHALCEDONY quartz that is composed of banded layers of sard or CARNELIAN, and layers of white (see under GEMS, GEM CUTS, AND SETTINGS).

semiprecious gems/stones Gems too plentiful to be considered rare, e.g., TOPAZ, GARNET, TOURMALINE, AMETHYST, and QUARTZ (see under GEMS, GEM CUTS, AND SETTINGS).

simulated gems Copies of precious gems made of PASTE, or other inexpensive materials. See under JEWELRY. Sometimes confused with synthetic gems, which are man-made but chemically identical to natural gems.

smoky quartz Transparent variety of *crystalline quartz* in smoky yellow to dark brown. The national gem of Scotland. Also called CAIRNGORM. Sometimes mistaken for TOPAZ. See cross-references under GEMS, GEM CUTS, AND SETTINGS.

spinel Transparent to opaque semiprecious mineral that closely resembles the ruby. Softer and lighter in weight than a ruby with hardness of 8 on MOHS' SCALE (see in introduction to GEMS, GEM CUTS, AND SETTINGS category). Preferred color is deep ruby red; comes in a great variety of other colors including violet and purple. Misleading terms for the above include: *balas ruby, rubicelle, almandine, sapphirine,* and *chlorspinel.* Properly spinels should be identified by color name. A large red stone on the English Crown, called the Black Prince's ruby, was later proved to be a spinel.

square cut See under GEMS, GEM CUTS, AND SETTINGS: EMERALD CUT.

square setting Four prongs forming corners for EMERALD-CUT stones (see under GEMS, GEM CUTS, AND SETTINGS).

star ruby Genuine ruby from corundum mineral; shows a five- or six-pointed star, or ASTERISM, when cut CABOCHON style (see under GEMS, GEM CUTS, AND SETTINGS).

star sapphire Genuine sapphire from corundum mineral, it shows a five- or six-pointed star, or ASTERISM, when cut CABOCHON (see under GEMS, GEM CUTS, AND SETTINGS). Color varies from blue to gray and transparent to translucent. The 116-carat Midnight Star Sapphire and the 563-carat Star of India, the largest star sapphire in the world, were recovered after a jewel robbery at the Museum of Natural History in New York City in 1965.

staurolite See under GEMS, GEM CUTS, AND SETTINGS: FAIRY STONE.

step cut Rectangular stone cut with facets that are oblong and placed in horizontal positions in steps, or rows, both above and below the girdle, or widest part of the stone.

synthetic gem Gem manufactured in a laboratory having the same physical and chemical properties as genuine gems. Virtually all types of gems can be manufactured, including synthetic diamonds, emeralds, and sapphires. These gems are used in watches and sold for fine jewelry when mounted in necklaces, bracelets, and rings.

table See under GEMS, GEM CUTS, AND SETTINGS: BRILLIANT CUT.

tallow top cut See under GEMS, GEM CUTS, AND SETTINGS: CABOCHON #2.

tanzanite First discovered in the foothills of Mount Kilimanjaro in Tanzania, Africa. In 1968 was confirmed to be blue zoisite by gemologists—the first ever found. Name was changed by Tiffany & Co. of New York to tanzanite, from place where it was found. Not a precious stone, but beautiful when cut. Changes color when held in light to a blue, richer than a sapphire; purple, similar to amethyst; and pinkish salmon brown. One gem found was 2,500 carats and when cut weighed 360 carats.

Tiffany setting High-pronged setting for solitaire stone introduced by Tiffany & Co., New York jewelers, in 1870s and often imitated. In 1971, Tiffany introduced a modernized version of its famous setting.

tiger's eye Semiprecious variety of QUARTZ is CHATOYANT when cut CABOCHON (see under GEMS, GEM CUTS, AND SETTINGS). Yellowish brown, blue, or red in color. Found in South Africa.

topaz Transparent gem of which the most precious is wine-yellow in color. Other colors include colorless, yellowish brown, gray, pale tints of green, blue, lavender, and red. With a hardness of 8, only the diamond, ruby, sapphire, and chrysoberyl are harder; the emerald and spinel are of equal hardness. Found in Europe, South America, Sri Lanka, Japan, Mexico, Utah, Colorado, and Maine.

topazolite See under GEMS, GEM CUTS, AND SETTINGS: ANDRADITE GARNET.

tourmaline Transparent semiprecious mineral that comes in many colors: achroite, colorless; rubellite, rose-red; siberite, violet; indicolite, dark blue, green, blue, and yellowish green. Sometimes erroneously called *Brazilian emerald, Brazilian peridot* (pehr'-ee-dot), *Brazilian sapphire,* and *peridot of Ceylon.*

turquoise Opaque, amorphous, ornamental stone that comes in sky blue, greenish blue, or apple green. Used for jewelry, but exists in too large a quantity to be rare. Popular for jewelry made by North American Indians of Arizona and Mexico; usually set in silver for bracelets, necklaces, pins, and earrings.

Ural emerald See under GEMS, GEM CUTS, AND SETTINGS: ANDRADITE GARNET.

zircon Transparent gem with a luster approaching the diamond when brilliant cut is used. White colorless stones resembling diamonds are sometimes referred to as *matura diamonds,* a misleading term. Yellow, orange, red, and brown zircons are called *hyacinth* or *jacinth;* all other colors, including colorless gray and smoky, are called *jargons,* while blue are called *blue zircon.* A 103-carat zircon is in the Smithsonian Institution in Washington, D.C.

gendarme (john-darm) *adj.* Describes clothing and accessories inspired by or derived from the uniform of a French policeman, a *gendarme.* See under CAPES, CLOAKS, AND SHAWLS: FRENCH POLICEMAN'S CAPE and COATS AND JACKETS: GENDARME JACKET.

generational marketing The study of the values, motivations, and life experiences that drive generational cohorts, influencing how they spend and save their money.

generation X, gen X The population group born following the baby boomers.

†generic fiber categories Common or family name for natural or manufactured fibers as defined by the Federal Trade Commission.

geneva bands See under CLERICAL DRESS.

geneva gown See under CLERICAL DRESS.

geneva hat See under CLERICAL DRESS.

genoa cloak See under CAPES, CLOAKS, AND SHAWLS: ITALIAN CLOAK.

genoese embroidery See under EMBROIDERIES AND SEWING STITCHES.

george See under FOOTWEAR and HAIRSTYLES.

∞genouillère See under ARMOR: POLEYN.

genuine pearl See under GEMS, GEM CUTS, AND SETTINGS: PEARLS.

geometric print See under PRINTS, STRIPES, AND CHECKS.

†georgette/georgette crepe/crepe georgette Fine, sheer, silk fabric made in the plain weave with twisted or creped yarns in both lengthwise and crosswise directions. Used for dresses, evening gowns, blouses, and nightgowns.

German gown See under SACK #1.

German helmet See under HEADWEAR.

German hose See under TRUNK HOSE.

gertrude/gertrude skirt See under UNDERGARMENTS.

geta See under FOOTWEAR.

ghillie See under FOOTWEAR: GILLIE/GHILLIE.

Gibson, Charles Dana (1867–1944) American illustrator, and a master of black-and-white drawings depicting the idealized American girl of the 1890s and early 1900s, which were published in *Scribner's, Harper's,* and *Century* magazines.

Gibson girl (*adj.*) Characterized as derived from or inspired by apparel worn by the Gibson girl, the idealized young woman drawn by Charles Dana Gibson. In subsequent fashion revivals of the styles of the 1890s and 1900–1910, those garments, accessories, and hairstyles were known as Gibson girl styles. Features of these revivals included high-necked collars, tucked and lace-trimmed blouses with LEG-OF-MUTTON SLEEVES (see under SHOULDERS AND SLEEVES), and gathered skirts or hair worn in the POMPADOUR style (see under HAIRSTYLES). *Der.* For Charles Dana Gibson's magazine sketches of fashionable women of the 1895–1910 era. See also under HAIRSTYLES.

Gibson girl

Gibson pleat Wide 2″ pleat at the shoulder of blouse, in front and back, covering the armhole seam and sloping to waistline to give a narrow-waisted effect. *Der.* Named after Charles Dana Gibson, who portrayed "The Gibson girl" in his drawings.

Gibson waist See under BLOUSES AND TOPS.

gibus See under HEADWEAR: OPERA HAT.

gig coat See under COATS AND JACKETS: CURRICLE COAT.

gigot sleeve See under SHOULDERS AND SLEEVES: LEG-OF-MUTTON SLEEVE.

gilet 1. See under VESTS. 2. See under PLASTRON.

gillie See under FOOTWEAR.

∞gills/shirt gills Colloquial term for upstanding points of men's shirt collars in the 19th c.

gimmel ring See under JEWELRY: GEMEL RING.

gimp 1. See under BRAIDS. 2. See HEADWEAR: WIMPLE.

gimped embroidery See under EMBROIDERY AND SEWING STITCHES.

gingham †1. Yarn-dyed, checked or plaid fabric made of cotton or cotton blended with polyester. May be made of coarse yarn or of combed yarns in a high-count fabric. **Checked ginghams** are two-colored effects made by using two colors, or one color and white, for groups of yarns in both the lengthwise and crosswise. **Plaid ginghams** are yarn-dyed designs of several colors. **Zephyr ginghams** are made with fine, silky, mercerized yarns (see MERCERIZATION). Used for dresses, children's wear, sportswear, swimsuits, blouses, and beachwear. 2. See under UMBRELLAS AND PARASOLS.

gingham plaid See under PLAIDS AND TARTANS.

gipcière See under HANDBAGS AND RELATED ACCESSORIES: AULMONIERE.

gipon/gippon See under DOUBLET.

gipser See under HANDBAGS AND RELATED ACCESSORIES: ALMONIERE.

girdle 1. See under UNDERGARMENTS. 2. See under introduction to BELTS. 3. See under GEMS, GEM CUTS, AND SETTINGS.

girls' sizes Size range from 4–6X and from 7–16.

glacé See under LEATHERS.

gladiator sandal See under FOOTWEAR.

gladstone See under COATS AND JACKETS.

gladstone collar See under NECKLINES AND COLLARS.

glam rock/glam 1. Styles worn in the early 1970s by rock stars such as David Bowie. Male singers wore makeup, platform shoes, and glittery silver fabrics. 2. A heavy metal music style of the 1980s performed by either bare-chested macho singers or those of ambiguous sexuality.

glasses See under introduction to EYEWEAR.

glazed kid See under LEATHERS.

glazed leather See under introduction to LEATHERS.

†glazing Process of pressing fabric with heated rollers to give it a high gloss. Finish may be permanent or non-permanent.

glen check/Glen Urquhart check See under PLAIDS AND TARTANS.

glengarry cap See under HEADWEAR.

glengarry cape See under CAPES, CLOAKS, AND SHAWLS.

glen plaid See under PLAIDS AND TARTANS: GLEN URQUHART.

glitter button See under CLOSURES.

glitter hose See under HOSIERY.

globalization The development of worldwide connections among countries and people in specific areas. In the fashion world these relationships may develop in such diverse areas as supplying raw materials, trading, manufacturing, merchandising, research, and/or design of textiles and apparel and other types of dress.

glocke See under CAPES, CLOAKS, AND SHAWLS.

∞glove band/glove string Ribbon or plaited horsehair band tied near elbow to keep a woman's long glove in place. Used from 1640 to about 1700.

glove button See under CLOSURES.

glove length See under GLOVES AND GLOVE CONSTRUCTION.

glover's stitch See under EMBROIDERIES AND SEWING STITCHES: WHIPSTITCH and SADDLESTITCH.

GLOVES AND GLOVE CONSTRUCTION

glove A covering for the hand, usually divided into separate stalls for the thumb and fingers, worn as a decorative accessory, for warmth in cold weather, or as protection for workers. Gloves were known to ancient Egyptians, Greeks, and Romans but did not become an important accessory until the Middle Ages. By the beginning of the 17th c., leather, fabric, and knitted gloves were all available. Throughout the Victorian era and early 20th c., gloves were the mark of a lady or gentleman. In the 1960s, gloves declined in use for social occasions and by 1970s were very seldom worn except for protection from the cold. Also see under GLOVES AND GLOVE CONSTRUCTION: MITTS and MITTENS. *Der.* Origin of the word is disputed, believed to have been from Anglo-Saxon, *glof*, "palm."

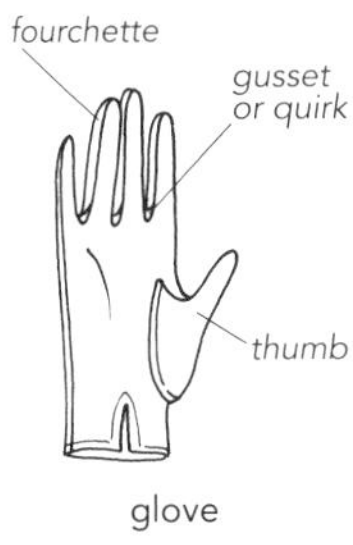

glove

action glove Gloves with cutouts on back of hand or over knuckles to increase flexibility. Originally used for sports such as golf or race car driving, adopted for women's daytime wear in mid-1960s. Also called *cutout gloves* or *racing gloves.*

bandelet/bandelette (ban-day'-lay or ban-day'-let) Wide hem at wrist of a glove. Also called *bord.*

∞berlin glove 1. Sturdy leather gloves produced in Germany. 2. Sturdy white cotton glove worn in the 1830s.

biarritz glove Slip-on glove with no VENT, usually of two- or four-button length.

bicycle glove Wrist-length knitted glove with leather palm padded with two layers of foam for comfort. Mesh knit is used for remainder of glove, leaving the tips of the fingers and thumb exposed.

binding Reinforcement or piping of leather or fabric around wrist and placket of gloves.

bolton thumb See under GLOVES AND GLOVE CONSTRUCTION: ENGLISH THUMB.

bord See under GLOVES AND GLOVE CONSTRUCTION: BANDELET.

bracelet length Gloves ending above the wrist.

button The length of the glove. One button is equal to one French inch (approximately $\frac{1}{12}$ inch longer than American inch), with the measurement starting at base of thumb. A 1-button glove is wrist length, a 6-button glove is about halfway to elbow, and a 16-button glove is a formal length.

∞chicken-skin glove Thin, strong, leather glove treated with almonds and spermaceti, worn at night as cosmetic aid to keep hands soft and white, by women from the end of 17th to early 19th c.

cocktail glove Dressy suede glove with wide, stand-up, accordion-pleated taffeta cuffs. Worn in the 1930s and after.

cut-fingered gloves ∞1. Gloves slashed to show rings on fingers, worn in late 16th c. 2. Women's gloves with tips of fingers cut off, worn in early 18th c. Revived as a fad in 1985.

cutout glove See under GLOVES AND GLOVE CONSTRUCTION: ACTION GLOVE.

doeskin glove **1.** Glove made of suede-finished sheepskin. More precisely it should be "doeskin-finished sheepskin," but the doeskin is permissible. **2.** Glove made from the skin of the female deer, frequently sueded.

driving glove Knitted gloves with leather palms made for a good grip on the steering wheel of the car.

english thumb Glove thumb construction in which the thumb and QUIRK (see under GLOVES AND GLOVE CONSTRUCTION) are cut in a single piece in order to provide freedom of movement. Considered the strongest and best-fitting thumb. Also called *Bolton thumb.*

Finger-Free glove/fingerless gloves Originally a trade name for gloves made with one long strip of material forming all the fourchettes between fingers. Designed by Merry Hull in 1938 for greater flexibility. Currently used by merchandisers to refer to gloves without finger coverings. See under GLOVES AND GLOVE CONSTRUCTION: FOURCHETTE.

forks See under GLOVES AND GLOVE CONSTRUCTION: FOURCHETTE.

fourchette (foor-shet') Narrow piece forming the sides of the fingers of gloves ending in points at tips of fingers and joining the back to the front of the glove. Also called *forks.*

french thumb Glove thumb construction in which a small diamond-shaped piece (the quirk) is inserted in the arch of the thumb, allowing freedom of movement.

full-piqué/full P.K. seam Seam used on expensive kid gloves; all fourchettes are inserted with one piece of leather lapped over the other and stitched on the right side. See under GLOVES AND GLOVE CONSTRUCTION: FOURCHETTE. Also called *kid seam* and *overlapped seam.*

full P.K. seam

gauntlet (gawnt'-let) Above-the-wrist glove with wide flaring cuff. The cuff may be cut in one with the glove or as a separate piece that is sewn to the glove.

gauntlet

glove length Length of a glove, measured in BUTTONS. See under GLOVES AND GLOVE CONSTRUCTION.

glove seam Manner in which gloves are stitched together. Seams must be flexible and sturdy. The body of the glove is cut in one piece and the fourchettes (or pieces for the sides of the fingers) and quirks (small pieces for base of fingers and thumb) are stitched to it by various seams. See under GLOVES AND GLOVE CONSTRUCTION: FOURCHETTE and QUIRK. Various glove seam types are defined in separate entries under GLOVES AND GLOVE CONSTRUCTION.

half-piqué/half P.K. seam Finger seams on the palm side of the hand are stitched with seams turned to the inside while those on the outside of hand are made in piqué manner, with one piece of leather lapped over the other and stitched on the outside, thereby giving the appearance of a more expensive glove.

igloo mitt Shaggy fur mitten, frequently with leather palm, worn for sportswear.

inseam Gloves stitched together inside out and then turned, so that no stitching shows on the right side. Used on sheer nylon, lace, and cotton gloves.

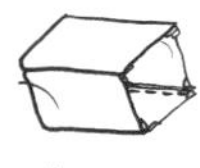
inseam

insert thumb Glove thumb construction in which thumb is cut in one piece and extends all the way to the cuff edge of the glove.

insulated glove Glove lined for protection against cold. Lining may be fur, fleece, wool, or acrylic knit, or laminated foam.

∞jessamy gloves/jasmine gloves Perfumed gloves given by bride and groom as wedding presents in 17th c.; jasmine being most popular scent.

kid glove Gloves made of genuine kidskin and also of sheepskin. Originally all were kid and as the leather became more scarce, other leathers were used. Fashionable from early 19th c. and still used.

kid seam See under GLOVES AND GLOVE CONSTRUCTION: FULL-PIQUÉ.

laying off Final step in the construction of leather gloves in which the glove is placed on a metal hand of the selected size and heated to shape the glove to the correct size.

∞limerick gloves Short or long lambskin gloves made from very young or unborn lambs. Worn by women during latter half of 18th and first half of 19th c.

mittens **1.** Gloves with a thumb and one other compartment for fingers; worn mainly by children and skiers for warmth. So called since 14th c. **2.** See under GLOVES AND GLOVE CONSTRUCTION: MITTS.

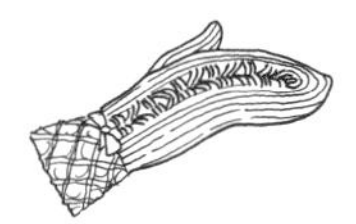
mitten #1

mitts Fingerless gloves, reaching to or above wrist. Often of kid, net, lace, or sheer fabric and sometimes worn with bridal dresses. Also called *mittens* and *finger-free gloves* and used for sports where the fingers need to be unencumbered.

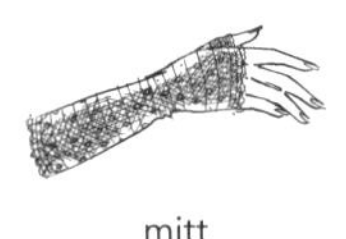
mitt

money mitt Knitted glove with fingers and thumb made with vinyl palm and back. Has zippered slot in center of palm for keys or money.

mousquetaire glove (moos-keh'-tare) Woman's long, loose glove made in pull-on style or with buttoned slit at wrist in 14- or 16-button length. Worn crushed down or with hand out of slit, remainder of glove crushed up to elbow with formal evening dress.

opera glove Long-length glove, sometimes made without a thumb.

outseam Glove seams stitched by machine on the right side, leaving edges exposed. Used on sport gloves (e.g., pigskin and sometimes cotton gloves).

outseam

overlapped seam See GLOVES AND GLOVE CONSTRUCTION: FULL-PIQUÉ.

overseam Gloves stitched on the right side with an OVERCAST STITCH (see under EMBROIDERIES AND SEWING STITCHES) that covers the two raw edges. Also called *round seam.*

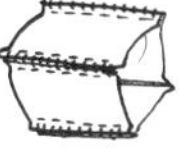
overseam

∞**Oxford glove** Perfumed glove, worn from mid-16th to mid-17th c., scented with Earl of Oxford's favorite perfume.

piqué/P.K. seam See under GLOVES AND GLOVE CONSTRUCTION: FULL-PIQUÉ and HALF-PIQUÉ GLOVE SEAMS.

pointing Ornamental stitching on back of glove, usually in three rows. Same as *silking.*

prix seam/PXM seam (pree) Outseam stitched on a flat machine that moves horizontally instead of vertically. Used on heavier gloves instead of piqué seam. See under GLOVES AND GLOVE CONSTRUCTION: OUTSEAM.

pull-down cutting The process of cutting gloves by die-cutting the pieces.

pull-on Glove that slips easily over the hand and is made without placket or fastening. Also called *slip-on gloves.*

quirk Small triangular insert placed in glove at base of each finger and at thumb. Used to give a close fit yet permit flexibility.

racing glove See under GLOVES AND GLOVE CONSTRUCTION: ACTION GLOVES.

reverse glove Glove thumb construction in which the thumb is set in with a QUIRK (see under GLOVES AND GLOVE CONSTRUCTION) in such a way that the glove is perfectly flat and can be worn on either hand.

round seam See under GLOVES AND GLOVE CONSTRUCTION: OVERSEAM.

saddle-stitched seam Small running stitches visible on the outside of glove that are used to close fingers of the glove.

set-in thumb Glove thumb construction in which the thumb is cut in one piece and set into a round opening.

shorty glove Any two-button glove coming to the wrist.

silking See under GLOVES AND GLOVE CONSTRUCTION: POINTING.

slip-ons See under GLOVES AND GLOVE CONSTRUCTION: PULL-ON GLOVE.

slit trank In glove production, a piece of leather large enough for one glove is called a trank. When a die is pressed on the trank to cut out the glove, the process is called "slitting the trank."

snowmobile glove Similar to SNOWMOBILE MITT (see under GLOVES AND GLOVE CONSTRUCTION) made with fingers.

snowmobile mitt Water-repellent glove with polyester fiberfill or down as insulation. Made with suede-leather palms, rubberized nylon back, knitted cuffs, and leather pull-on tabs.

table-cut glove TRANKS (see under GLOVES AND GLOVE CONSTRUCTION) from which these gloves are cut are hand-pulled to determine the amount of stretch in the leather and then cut. Women's fine kid gloves are made in this manner to ensure proper stretch but no bagginess.

thermal glove Short glove made of glacé leather with silk lining and inner lining of polyfoam. Worn for warmth, especially for riding or driving.

trank Leather piece from which a glove is cut.

wrist-length glove Short glove ending at the wristbone.

wrist-length glove

∞**york-tan gloves** Gloves of soft fawn-colored suede worn mainly by women from 1780 to 1820s.

---

glove seam See under GLOVES AND GLOVE CONSTRUCTION.

glove string See under GLOVE BAND.

goatee See under BEARD.

goatskin See under LEATHER.

gobelin corselet See under BELTS.

gob hat See under HEADWEAR: SAILOR HAT.

godet See under CLOTHING CONSTRUCTION DETAILS.

godet pleat See under CLOTHING CONSTRUCTION DETAILS.

godet skirt See under SKIRTS.

Godey, Louis Antoine See under GODEY'S LADY'S BOOK.

Godey's Lady's Book The first American periodical for women, published by Louis Antoine Godey. Distributed monthly, it contained stories, music, needlecraft, poetry, and fashions. Each month there was a hand-colored engraving showing fashions as well as many black-and-white illustrations. Started in 1830 as the *Lady's Book,* it was later called *Godey's Lady's Book.* Edited by Sarah Josepha Hale from 1837 to 1877. Publication ceased in 1898.

goffer (goff'-er) **1.** An ornamental pleating used for frills and borders as on women's caps. **2.** To press ridges or narrow pleats into a frill.

goffered veil See under HEADDRESS.

goggles See under EYEWEAR.

go-go Coined in late 1960s for a dancer at a discotheque called a go-go dancer, then extended to mean "flashy" or "hip" accessories of this era. Example: FOOTWEAR: GO-GO BOOTS and WATCHES: GO-GO WATCH.

go-go watchband See under WATCHES: GO-GO WATCH.

going frocks See under LONG CLOTHES.

gold **1.** *n.* Precious metal that in its pure state is too soft to be durable. It is usually made into alloys called *karat gold* and used for *plating,* or gold-washed jewelry items. See under JEWELRY. **2.** *adj.* Used to describe anything the color of gold metal.

gold button See under CLOSURES.

golden beryl See under GEMS, GEM CUTS, AND SETTINGS.

golden muskrat See under FURS.

gold filled See under JEWELRY.

gold hose See under HOSIERY: GLITTER HOSE.

gold leaf Pure gold hammered so thin it takes 300,000 units to make a stack 1″ high. Used for jewelry and gold leather.

gold-plated See under JEWELRY.

golds See under JEWELRY: GRILLS.

gold-washed See under JEWELRY.

gole See under HEADWEAR: CHAPERON.

golf bag See under HANDBAGS AND RELATED ACCESSORIES.

golf clothes Apparel that is derived from or inspired by clothing worn for the sport of golf. By 1890s, golf was a sport enjoyed by both men and women. Men wore KNICKERS, a NORFOLK JACKET (see under COATS AND JACKETS), and a cap with a visor; by the 1920s they wore PLUS FOURS (see under PANTS) and a sweater. Women in the early days wore a version of the Norfolk jacket, the GLENGARRY CAP (see under HEADWEAR), and sometimes shorter skirt or a divided skirt. In pre–World War I days, a coat sweater was worn; in the 1930s an ACTION-BACK dress was introduced. See under COATS AND JACKETS: GOLF JACKET; FOOTWEAR: GOLF SHOE; and VESTS: GOLF VEST.

gondolier's hat See under HEADWEAR.

∞**gonel** (gohn'-el) Synonym for GOWN #1 in 14th c.

goose-bellied doublet See under DOUBLET.

gordian knot Decorative square knot used as trimming in the last half of 18th c.—sometimes on bracelets, sometimes a length of false hair used as a CHIGNON (see under HAIRSTYLES). *Der.* From Greek mythological founder of Phrygia (now Turkey) called *Gordius.* An oracle pronounced that he would be master of Asia until the knot he tied was undone. Alexander the Great severed the knot with one blow of his sword.

gore See under CLOTHING CONSTRUCTION DETAILS.

gored skirt See under SKIRTS.

gorge In men's tailoring used to indicate seam where collar meets lapel—may be either high or low.

gorget (gor'-jet) **1.** See under ARMOR. **2.** See under HEADWEAR: WIMPLE. **3.** See HEADWEAR: CHAPERON. **4.** See under NECKLINES AND COLLARS. **4.** See under JEWELRY.

†**Gore-Tex® fabric** Trademark for a porous membrane that repels water but allows for the passage of moisture vapor. Widely used for garments for outdoor sports.

goshenite See under GEMS, GEM CUTS, AND SETTINGS.

goth *adj.* Descriptive of a style, originating in a London club called the Batcave in 1981, that was inspired by the gothic literary works of the 19th c. such as *Dracula.* Followers mixed black, bloodred, and purple colored velvet and lace with fishnet and leather. Hair was dyed black and makeup featured black accents at the eyes and lips.

goth style

Gothic costume Styles of dress that were worn in Western Europe from the 13th to mid-14th c. (early Gothic) and from the mid-14th through mid-15th c. (late Gothic).

gown **1.** From as early as the 11th c., a woman's dress. From the late 18th century, "gown" is most often used to refer to a floor-length, more formal, skirted garment, while "dress" is used for less formal, skirted garments. **2.** Loose-fitting, wide-sleeved outer garment or robe worn by judges, scholars, clergy, and for ceremonial occasions. **2.** See under introduction to DRESSES.

∞**gown à la française** (ah lah frahn'-saiz) Dress, fashionable in 18th c., made with a bodice that fits closely in front and loosely at the back. The front closing was filled in with decorative STOMACHER, and two wide box pleats fell from shoulders to hem in back. *Der.* French, "French gown." Also called *robe à la française* and, in the 19th c., referred to as a *Watteau gown.* Shown at WATTEAU BACK.

∞**gown à la levantine** (ah lah leh-van'-teen) A loose, open robe worn in the last quarter of the 18th c. Fastened at the chest with a pin or ties, the opening revealing a waistcoat and petticoat of contrasting color and fabric. Wrist-length undersleeves matched the petticoat. The overdress had a wide turned-back collar and wide draped sash with long hanging ends, sometimes fur-trimmed. Also called *levite gown.*

∞**gown à l'anglaise** (ah long'-glaze) Dress, close-fitting in both front and back, that was worn in late 18th c. without PANNIERS (see under UNDERGARMENTS). The bodice was shaped to long point in back and closed in front. Skirt was either closed or slashed in front to show matching petticoat. *Der.* French, "English gown." Also called *robe à l'anglaise.*

gown a l'anglaise

gown à la polonaise See under POLONAISE #1.

gown à la sultane See under SULTANE.

∞**gown à la turque** (ah lah toork') Dress, worn c. 1780, with a tight-fitting bodice, turned-down collar, flared sleeves at wrist, and draped large sash knotted on one hip with long hanging ends. Worn over contrasting petticoat. *Der.* French, "Turkish gown."

Grace Kelly bag See under HANDBAGS AND RELATED ACCESSORIES: KELLY BAG.

grading See under PATTERN GRADING.

grade rules Guidelines giving not only the amounts of increase or decrease but also their locations on a pattern in order to create different sizes.

graduation dress See under DRESSES.

graffiti/graffiti (graf-fee'-tee) *adj.* Descriptive of abstract designs used for clothing and accessories made by drawings on fabric, leather or vinyl; piecing bits of fabric, leather, and vinyl together and studding with fake jewels or dabbing with blobs of paint, used for jackets, blouses, shoes, handbags, and belts. Developed from copying street-art forms painted or scratched on buildings. *Der.* Latin, *graffito,* a drawing or writing scratched on a wall or surface.

grain 1. See under LEATHERS. 2. See under GEMS, GEM CUTS, AND SETTINGS. †3. In textile usage, yarn direction, either lengthwise or crosswise.

∞**grande-assiette sleeve** (grawn ahs-ee'-ette) Extra cap sleeve, crescent shape, extending over top curve of shoulder on the DOUBLET from 14th to mid-15th c.

grand habit See under COURT HABIT.

grand vair See under FUR: VAIR.

†**granite weave** Weave characterized by pebbly effect somewhat similar to crepe. Such fabrics are called granite cloth. Also called *momie weave* and *pebble weave.*

granjamer See under SLEEPWEAR AND LOUNGEWEAR.

granny *adj.* Descriptive of types of apparel that might have been worn in the era of one's grandmother. Generally has the connotation of styles worn in the late 19th or early 20th c. See under DRESSES: GRANNY DRESS, EYEWEAR: BEN FRANKLIN GLASSES; FOOTWEAR: GRANNY BOOT; HEADWEAR: GRANNY BONNET; PRINTS, STRIPES, AND CHECKS: GRANNY PRINT; SKIRTS: GRANNY SKIRT; and SLEEPWEAR AND LOUNGEWEAR: GRANNY GOWN.

granny dress See under DRESSES.

granny blouse/granny waist See under BLOUSES AND TOPS: GRANNY WAIST and VICTORIAN BLOUSE.

grass embroidery See under EMBROIDERIES AND SEWING STITCHES.

graundice See under HEADWEAR: CRANTS.

gray flannel See under OXFORD GRAY FLANNEL.

gray fox See under FURS.

†**gray goods/greige goods** Unfinished fabrics, as they come off the loom. Some fabrics may be mill-finished but most are sent to CONVERTERS for the finishing processes. *Der.* French, *grege,* "raw."

gray-market goods Merchandise that, while not exactly illegal, is an unauthorized import. Often such goods are sold at discounters with no warranty or with older dates than those through authorized channels. There is an ongoing campaign to make gray-market goods illegal.

gray muskrat See under FURS.

greaser hair See under HAIRSTYLES.

greatcoat See under COATS AND JACKETS.

greave See under ARMOR.

grebe feathers See under FEATHERS.

∞**Grecian bend** Stance affected by fashionable women from 1815 to 1819 and again from 1868 to 1870 in which the body was tilted forward while a bustle under the skirt emphasized the back.

grecian border See under FRET.

grecian curls See under HAIRSTYLES.

grecian sandal See under FOOTWEAR: GANYMEDE SANDAL.

greek belt See under BELTS.

Greek boy style See under GANYMEDE.

greek coiffure See under HAIRSTYLES.

Greek cross See under CROSS #1.

greek fisherman's cap See under HEADWEAR.

Greek fret See under FRET #3.

greek handbag See under HANDBAGS AND RELATED ACCESSORIES: GREEK BAG.

Greek key See under FRET #3.

greek lace/greek point lace See under LACES: RETICELLA LACE.

Greek lounging cap See under HEADWEAR: LOUNGING CAP.

∞**green-aproned men** London porters of 18th c. distinguished by green aprons worn by members of this trade. Also see under BLUE-APRONED MEN.

Greenaway, Kate See under KATE GREENAWAY COSTUME.

green clothes See under ECO-FRIENDLY.

greenery-yallery See under AESTHETIC DRESS.

gregs See under TRUNK HOSE.

greige goods See under GRAY GOODS.

grey goods See under GRAY GOODS.

grills See under JEWELRY.

gripper closure See under CLOSURES.

grommet See under CLOSURES.

grooving Method of shearing a deep pile of fabric or furs in lines that have a shorter pile than the rest of the surface.

†**grosgrain** (groh′-grayn) Fabric with a large rib that is made by grouping several crosswise yarns together. Made originally in silk, now made mostly with rayon or acetate warp and cotton or rayon filling. Also made entirely of cotton. Used for ribbons, sashes, trim on dresses, bows, neckwear, hatbands, and millinery trimming.

gros point (groh pwanh) See under EMBROIDERIES AND SEWING STITCHES: PETIT POINT and LACES.

gross margin The difference between the net sales and cost of goods sold and usually an indicator of profit.

Grosvenor gallery costume See under AESTHETIC DRESS.

ground 1. Plain base or background part of a decorated textile fabric. 2. In pile fabrics, the lengthwise and crosswise yarns that support the pile. 3. See under LACES. 4. See under EMBROIDERIES AND SEWING STITCHES.

group Items within an apparel COLLECTION that use a limited number of colors and fabrics so that they can be coordinated.

grow bag Synonym for a BABY BUNTING.

grow sleepers See under SLEEPWEAR AND LOUNGEWEAR.

grunge A style of dressing in which clothing items look worn, are either too large or too small, and frequently are purchased from thrift shops. Included among the more popular items of grunge style are heavy work boots and checked shirts.

G-string Narrow band, worn low on the hips, with a decorative ornament on front. Originally worn by striptease dancers.

guanaco/guanaquito See under FURS.

guarantee Issued by a manufacturer, it ensures that a product will perform as it is supposed to. See under WARRANTY.

guard hair See under introduction to FURS.

guardinfante

guardinfante (gard-in-fahn′-tay) Variation of the FARTHINGALE, worn by Spanish royalty in the 17th c. after the style had been given up in the rest of Europe. It was wider from side to side and had a long, wide extension of the bodice below the waistline that extended over the top of the skirt. The bodice shoulderline was horizontal and sleeves were full and slashed, ending in fitted cuffs.

∞**guards** Decorative bands of rich fabrics, plain or embroidered, used to conceal garment seams in the 16th c.

guardsman coat See under COATS AND JACKETS.

guayabera shirt See under SHIRTS.

Gucci® loafer (goo-chee) See under FOOTWEAR: LOAFER.

guepiere See under UNDERGARMENTS.

guiche See under HAIRSTYLES.

guimpe 1. See under BLOUSES AND TOPS. 2. Piece of fabric draped around the face, falling over the neck and chest. Worn by women in the 14th and 15th c., particularly by widows and nuns and still worn by some nuns. Also spelled *guimp.*

∞**guimpe dress/guimpe costume** See under DRESSES.

guimple See under HEADWEAR: WIMPLE.

guinea feathers See under FEATHERS.

guipure/guipure de bruges See under LACES.

guleron See under HEADWEAR: CHAPERON.

gumshoe See under FOOTWEAR.

gun-club checks See under PRINTS, STRIPES, AND CHECKS.

gusset See under CLOTHING CONSTRUCTION DETAILS.

gym bag See under HANDBAGS AND RELATED ACCESSORIES.

gym bloomers See under ACTIVEWEAR: GYM SUITS.

gymnasium costume See under CALISTHENIC COSTUME.

gymnastic suit See under ACTIVEWEAR.

gym sock See under HOSIERY: SWEATSOCK.

gym suit See under ACTIVEWEAR.

gypsy *adj.* Descriptive of colorful garments in bright shades—full skirts, blouses, scarves, boleros, shawls, head scarves, and hoop earrings—characteristic apparel of nomadic tribes called gypsies in Europe. A popular style for Halloween costumes since mid-19th c. and high fashion in late 1960s. *Der.* Originally worn by gypsies, a nomadic people of Europe, Asia, and North America. See under BLOUSES AND TOPS: GYPSY BLOUSE and JEWELRY: GYPSY EARRING.

gypsy stripe See under PRINTS, STRIPES, AND CHECKS: BAYADÈRE STRIPES.

haberdashery A store that sells men's apparel and accessories.

habiliment (heh-bil′-eh-ment) Synonym for clothing, garb, attire, or dress. *Der.* French, *habillement,* "clothing."

habit Characteristic apparel of a calling, rank, or function (e.g., clerical clothes, court dress, or riding habit).

∞**habit d'escalier** See under DRESSES.

∞**habit-redingote** See under DRESSES.

habit shirt See under SHIRTS.

hacking Riding for pleasure, as opposed to "riding to hounds," or fox hunting, for which a specific type of clothing is worn. Sometimes used as an adjective to describe clothing used for riding. See under COATS AND JACKETS: HACKING JACKET; POCKETS: HACKING POCKET; and SCARVES: HACKING SCARF.

hackle See under FEATHERS.

haincelin See under HOUPPELANDE.

HAIR ACCESSORIES

∞**anadem/anademe** (ahn′-ah-dem) Wreath or garland of leaves or flowers, worn on hair by women in late 16th to early 17th c.

barrette (ba-ret′) (*barret, barette*) Clip worn in the hair. May be small and worn one on either side of head, or larger and worn in back or at nape of the neck. Made of plastic, metal, wood or other materials in various shapes (e.g., bar or bow knot). *Der.* French, diminutive of *barre,* "bar."

bobby pin Small, flexible piece of metal bent in half with prongs held together by the spring of the metal; worn to keep hair in place or to set hair in pin curls. See under HAIRSTYLES: PIN CURLS #2.

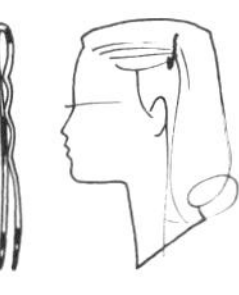

bobby pin

∞**diadem comb** (dye′-ah-dem) High, wide, curved comb with ornamental top worn for evening by women in the 1830s.

∞**duchess** Knot or bow of ribbon worn as part of the FONTANGE hairstyle (see under HEADWEAR) in the late 17th c.

feather extensions Decorative semi-permanent hair accessory consisting of feathers that are attached to strands of hair using special tools that allow attachment and detachment of feathers. A style that gained popularity in 2011.

hairband 1. A ribbon for the hair or fillet, worn from the 15th to 17th c. See under HEADWEAR: FILLET #2. 2. See under HEADWEAR: HEADBAND #1 and #2.

hair extensions See under WIGS AND HAIRPIECES.

hairpin A two-pronged device, typically of plastic or metal, used to hold the hair in place, particularly hair styled in a bun, knot, updo, or French twist. The classic hairpin is a wire bent double with crimps halfway down each side to give flexibility. Pins of very fine wire tinted to match hair are called **invisible hairpins.** Decorated hairpins are worn as jewelry and made of exotic materials or jeweled. Also see under HAIR ACCESSORIES: BOBBY PIN.

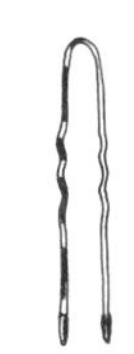

hairpin

hair sticks Long, stiletto-like pieces of wood, plastic, or metal worn for decorative effect. Usually thrust through hair knotted at the back of the head.

hair sticks

∞**papillotte comb** (pahp′-ee-laut) Decorative tortoiseshell comb, 3″ to 4″ long, used on either side of head to puff out hair by women in late 1820s. *Der.* French, *papilloter,* "to flutter," and *papillon,* "butterfly."

∞**peigne josephine** (pahn) Woman's high comb, ornamented with small gilt balls. Worn at the back of head for evening in 1842.

∞**pompon** Hair or cap ornament composed of feathers, tinsel, butterflies, etc., worn in center part of hair by women from 1740s to 1760s, originally called *pompadour* (pohm′-pah-dure).

rat Sausage-shaped, padded roll of nylon mesh (formerly of hair or felt) worn by women under natural hair to create high pompadour effect in early 20th c. and since. Also see under HAIRSTYLES: POMPADOUR #1.

∞**roll/rowle** Pad used to raise the front hair up from forehead in the 16th and 17th c.

scrunchy Elastic band covered with fabric for securing ponytails.

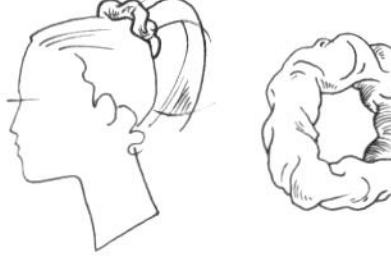

scrunchy

Spanish comb Comb with ornamental top, sometimes 5″ high, worn at crown of head to support a MANTILLA (see under HEADWEAR) or separately for decorative effect.

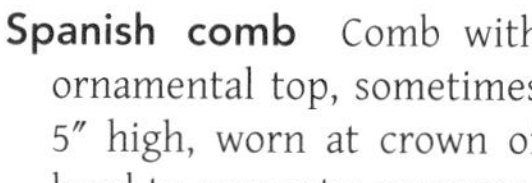

∞**toque** A triangular cushion worn from 1815 to 1820 by women on top of the head to extend the hair.

---

hairband See under HAIR ACCESSORIES.

haircut Trimming and shaping of hair with scissors or razor. See under HAIRSTYLES.

hairdo See under HAIRSTYLES.

hair extensions See under HAIR ACCESSORIES and WIGS AND HAIRPIECES.

†**hair fibers** Fibers obtained from the fleece or pelt of an animal.

hair jewelry See under JEWELRY.

hairline stripe See under PRINTS, STRIPES, AND CHECKS.

hair net See under HEADWEAR.

hairpiece See under introduction to WIGS AND HAIRPIECES.

hairpin See under HAIR ACCESSORIES.

hairpin lace See under LACES.

hair seal See under FURS.

hair sticks See under HAIR ACCESSORIES.

HAIRSTYLES

hairstyle Manner in which the hair is worn. Also called *hairdo, coiffure, coif.* Elaborate hairstyles were popular in ancient times, particularly with the Greeks and Romans. The complexity of hairstyles varied throughout history with some of the most elaborate styles being worn in 18th-c. France. First permanent wave was introduced in about 1909. Hair spray came into general use in the 1950s, thus making possible more elaborate hair arrangements. Hairstyles from the 1960s on revived many old styles as well as introducing totally new ones. Styling gel and mousse were in general use by 1980s.

abstract cut Straight, short, geometric haircut, with one side of hair cut different from other. Introduced by English hairstylist Vidal Sassoon in mid-1960s.

abstract cut

afro Style adopted for African Americans in 1960s in which hair that had a natural tight curl was cut and allowed to assume its natural shape with no attempt made to straighten the hair. The size of the hairstyle varied with the length of hair. There are many interesting variations of this style.

afro

afro puffs Afro hairstyle variation made by parting hair in center, pulling to sides, tying near ears, and teasing to form puffs over ears.

∞**aggravators** Semicurls near the eye or temple, worn by men from 1830s to 1850s.

∞**agnès sorel coiffure** Woman's hairstyle with ribbon bands in front and a knot in back; worn from 1830s to 1850s. Named for AGNÈS SOREL.

American Indian braids See under HAIRSTYLES: AMERICAN INDIAN HAIRSTYLE.

American Indian hairstyle Hair worn straight and long—below shoulder length—and parted in center. A headband worn low on the brow is usually added. The long hair may be tied in two ponytails, made into braids, or hang free. When braided called **American Indian braids.**

angle bob A variation of the blunt cut bob (see under HAIRSTYLES), which is cut short in the back and slightly longer in the front.

ape drape See under HAIRSTYLES: SHAG.

∞**apollo knot** Woman's elaborate evening hairstyle, worn from 1824 to 1832, made with wired loops of false hair, projecting up from crown of head, and finished with decorative comb, flowers, or feathers.

artichoke Short, back-combed, layered hair, not too bouffant, popular in early 1960s.

au natural Hair in its natural wavy or curly state; frequently used to describe African American hair when no chemical agents are used to straighten it.

back-combing Hairdressing technique of lifting each strand of hair and combing or brushing lightly toward the scalp to increase bulk; used widely in 1950s and 1960s for BOUFFANT and BEEHIVE hairdos (see under HAIRSTYLES). Also called *teasing.*

∞**bandeau d'amour** (ban′-doe dahm-moor′) Woman's hairstyle or wig with high slanting and hanging curls, worn in 1770s and 1780s.

∞**banging chignon** (sheen′-yon) Woman's hairstyle of 1770s with wide, flat loop of ribbon-tied hair, hanging from crown of head to nape of neck.

bangs Hair combed forward over forehead and cut straight across, with the remainder left smooth or waved. Called *fringe* in England.

Bardot hair (bar-doe') Long hair, loosely curled and arranged in tousled disarray with loose tendrils around face. Popular after being seen on French film star Brigitte Bardot in 1959.

barrel curls Full, round, large curls frequently grouped at crown or back of the head.

Beatle cut Man's haircut worn full with SIDEBURNS (see under HAIRSTYLES) and well down the neck in back. The first 20th-c. style to revive longer hairstyles for men, it was introduced in the 1960s by the Beatles, an avant-garde rock music group from Liverpool, England.

Beatle cut

bed head hair 1. Either men's or women's hair that is cut in layers and worn naturally, creating a disheveled appearance as if one just got out of bed and had not yet brushed his or her hair. 2. An updo for women that looks as though the hair was done up for a prom or special occasion and then slept in; characterized by a loose chignon or twist and wispy, uncontrolled tendrils.

beehive

beehive High, exaggerated bubble hair shape, achieved by back-combing into a rounded dome. First worn by Teddy girls in London in late 1950s, popular until mid-1960s. Also called *bubble bob.*

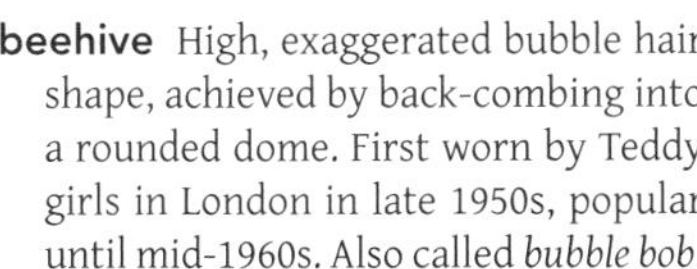

∞**benoiton coiffure** (ben-waa'-tone) Woman's elaborate coiffure of 1866 with hair parted in center, smooth on top, chignon and curls in back. Three gold chains were worn over the top of the head and hung in dangling loops under the chin; sometimes garlands of flowers were used instead of chains. *Der.* Named after *La Famille Benoiton,* a play by Victorien Sardou, 1865.

bingle (British usage) Very short haircut. *Der.* Combination of the words BOB and SHINGLE (see under HAIRSTYLES).

bob Short, blunt-cut hair, either with bangs or bared forehead, introduced in 1920s by Irene Castle. Also called *twenties bob.* Also see under HAIRSTYLES: BOYISH BOB.

boldini (bol'-dee-nee) See under POMPADOUR #1. Also called *Belle Epoque* (bell eh'-puck), *concierge* (cohn'-see-ehrj), and *onion. Der.* For Italian society painter Giovanni Boldini (1845–1931), who often painted women wearing this style.

bouffant (boo-fahnt') Hair exaggeratedly puffed out by means of BACK-COMBING (see under HAIRSTYLES) and held there by use of hair spray. Fashionable in early 1960s for medium-length and long hair. *Der.* French, "full" or "puffed."

∞**bowl crop** Man's hairstyle of 15th c. with hair shaved at back and sides, and longer hair hanging from crown of head in round basin-shaped fashion; a fashion revived in 1970 for young men when it was called a BOWL CUT (see under HAIRSTYLES). Also called *pudding-basin cut.*

bowl crop 15th c.

bowl cut Modern version of the BOWL CROP (see under HAIRSTYLES) that looks as if a bowl was placed over the head and then all the hair that could be seen around the edges of the bowl was cut. As a result, hair on top "under the bowl" is fairly long and hair underneath can range in length from being shaved to being cut very short. Variations of this cut include the **dipped mushroom,** or **dipped bowl cut,** which dips several inches lower at the back of the head and the **under cut,** in which the underneath layer of hair under the bowl is cut with clippers for an additional inch or two. As a result, when the head is shaken, the bowl cut returns to its original shape.

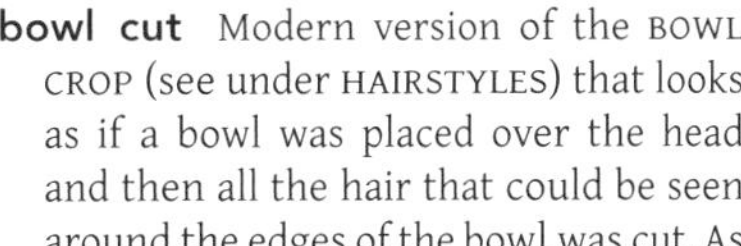

boyish bob Woman's extremely short hairstyle, shingled (see under HAIRSTYLES: SHINGLE) in back and short on sides. Originally popularized by Beatrice Lillie, British actress in the mid-1920s, and worn since at intervals. Also called *Eton crop, gamin,* and *garçon.*

boyish bob or garçon haircut

braids Hairstyle made by plaiting three sections of hair together. Braids may be worn hanging down on shoulders, looped up, tied or pinned together, wound around the head in a coronet, or wound in a BUN (see under HAIRSTYLES) at the nape of the neck. Popular style for children in the early 20th c., also very popular in the 1960s and early 1980s.

brush cut See under HAIRSTYLES: CREW CUT.

∞**brutus head/wig** Man's own hair worn closely cropped or brown unpowdered wig, both worn disheveled. Popular from about 1790 to 1820 and inspired by the French Revolution.

bubble bob See under HAIRSTYLES: BEEHIVE.

bubble curls Very loose curls, back-combed slightly and turned under, appearing on head as series of rounded bumps.

∞**bull head/bull tour** Woman's hairstyle with fringe of thick curls across forehead worn in late 17th c. Also called *taure* (tawr). *Der.* French, *tauteau,* "bull."

bun Large mass of hair confined neatly at crown of the head or at the nape of the neck.

bun

burr cut See under HAIRSTYLES: INDUCTION CUT.

bush cut See under HAIRSTYLES: CREW CUT.

business man's cut Man's moderately short haircut, long enough to be parted or brushed back.

Buster Brown Straight, short hairstyle with bangs over forehead. *Der.* Named for early 20th-c. comic-strip character and popular for little boys. Also called *dutch bob,* especially if worn by girls.

bustle curls Long curls worn dangling at back of head.

butch cut See under HAIRSTYLES: CREW CUT.

buzz cut See under HAIRSTYLES: CREW CUT.

∞cadogan/catagan (ka-do′-gan) **1.** Hairstyle with cluster of ringlets or braids of hair hanging at back of head, tied at nape of neck with wide ribbon. Worn as natural hair or as a wig by men in the 18th c. (see under WIGS AND HAIRPIECES: CATOGAN WIG) and by women in 1870s. **∞2.** Same style worn by women with riding habit in 18th c. Hair usually pulled back, looped up, and tied with a ribbon or the hair itself formed the band. **3.** Hair pulled back with a bow at the nape of neck; a style revived by French couturière Gabrielle Chanel in 1960s. Also see under HAIRSTYLES: GEORGE. *Der.* British General, First Earl of Cadogan (1675–1726).

cadogan #1, 18th c.

caesar cut Contemporary man's haircut in the style shown on Roman busts of Julius Caesar. Moderately short, the hair is layered to about one or two inches and brushed forward to a short bang over the forehead.

chignon (sheen′-yon) Large roll of hair twisted into a circle or figure eight on the back of the head or at the nape of the neck, often enclosed in decorative net or held by fancy hairpins. Classic style in 1860s, in 1920s, 1930s, and revived in 1980s. In the late 17th c., was sometimes called a *chou* (choo).

chignon

China doll hair Typical Chinese hairstyle with short straight hair, sometimes shingled in back, and with bangs at forehead.

chou See under HAIRSTYLES: CHIGNON.

classic pull-back Long hair worn combed neatly to the back and tied with a ribbon. In the 1940s worn with a barrette in the back. Also see under HAIRSTYLES: GEORGE.

cluster curls Groups of false ringlets or sausage curls, mounted on netting to be pinned in place as part of an elaborate coiffure.

∞cockle Woman's curl or ringlet in the 17th c.

coif (kwaf) Another name for hairstyle or shortened form of the *coiffure* (kwaf-foor′).

coiffure See under HAIRSTYLES: COIF.

coiffure à l'agnès sorel See under HAIRSTYLES: AGNÈS SOREL COIFFURE.

coiffure à la grecque See under HAIRSTYLES: GREEK COIFFURE.

coiffure à la hérisson See under HAIRSTYLES: HÉRISSON.

∞coiffure à la indépendance French hairstyle with a sailing-ship model perched on top of wavy locks and curls. Worn in 1778 to honor Benjamin Franklin's appearance at the French court for negotiation of a treaty between the U.S. and France. Also called *Triumph of Liberty.*

∞coiffure à la maintenon (ah la manta-naw′) Woman's coiffure of late 17th and early 18th c. with hair parted in the center, curled, and piled high. *Der.* After the Marquise de Maintenon, second wife of Louis XIV of France.

∞coiffure à la mouton (ah la moo-ton′) Short hairstyle fringed over forehead and crimped on sides. *Der.* French, "sheep."

coiffure à la ninon See under HAIRSTYLES: NINON COIFFURE.

∞coiffure à la sévigné (say-veen′-yay) Woman's hairstyle of 1650 parted in center, puffed out over the ears, hanging in waves and curls to the shoulders with decorated bow at ear level. *Der.* After Marie, Marquise de Sévigné (1626–1696), a witty correspondent and writer of the time.

coiffure à la titus See under HAIRSTYLES: TITUS.

∞coiffure à la zazzera (zatz-zeh′-rah) Man's long hairstyle with ends curled under—originally worn by Romans and revived by Venetians in 15th c.

∞coiffure à l'enfant (ah lon-fon′) Woman's hairstyle of 1780s, bobbed short like a child's.

∞coiffure en bouffons (on buff-on′) Woman's hairstyle with tufts of crimped or curled hair arranged over the temples, and the forehead covered with fringe of hair called *garcette* (gar-cett′). Worn in the Louis XIII period.

∞coiffure en cadenettes (on ka-dey′-net) **1.** A hairstyle worn by men and women of Louis XIII period with two long locks—called **moustaches**—falling on either side of face, wound with ribbons, and tied with bows. **2.** Masculine hairstyle with two long locks pulled back and tied with a ribbon, worn in the 17th c.

∞coiffure en raquette (on ra-ket′) Woman's hairstyle with hair brushed up, puffed over the temples, and supported by a wire hoop. Worn in last quarter of 16th c. *Der.* French, "racket."

cold wave See under HAIRSTYLES: PERMANENT WAVE.

concierge See under HAIRSTYLES: POMPADOUR #1.

∞confidants Woman's clusters of curls placed over the ears in late 17th c.

corkscrew curls Free-hanging curls that appear coiled, frequently lacquered to hold the shape.

corkscrew curls

cornrows Hair braided in horizontal rows by adding more hair after each plait to the braid. *Der.* From African styles worn by African Americans in the South in the 19th c., revived in early 1970s by fashionable African Americans, subsequently copied by others.

cornrows

coxcomb/cockscomb Woman's upswept coiffure with hair brushed to the back and pinned to form a vertical row of ringlets down center back.

∞**crève-coeur** (krev-kur′) Curls at nape of woman's neck worn at the end of the 17th c. *Der.* French, "heartbreaker."

crew cut Man's hair closely cropped so that hair on crown of head stands erect. Front hair is usually a little longer than the back. Originally worn by oarsmen to keep hair out of eyes. Adopted by college men in 1940s and 1950s. At that time it was similar to Army haircuts. Also worn by some women in 1980s and after. When very short and even length all over, called a **butch cut** or a **buzz cut.** Slightly longer versions of the crew cut include the **brush cut,** so named because it stands up like the bristles of a brush, and the **ivy league cut,** with hair longer at the front of the head so it can be brushed up or down or parted. Also see under HAIRSTYLES: FLATTOP.

crew cut

∞**crisp** Curl of hair worn by a woman, as it was called in the 17th c.

∞**cruches** (kroosh) Small curls worn on the forehead, as they were called in the late 17th c.

∞**cue** 18th-c. spelling of QUEUE (see under HAIRSTYLES), the hanging tail of a wig, which first appeared for civilian wear about 1720.

curlyhead See under HAIRSTYLES: POODLE CUT.

D.A. See under HAIRSTYLES: DUCKTAIL HAIRCUT.

dip-dyed hair Hair colored by a technique where the tips of the hair are dipped into hair dye; the dyes used are often bright bold colors.

dipped bowl cut/dipped mushroom cut See under HAIRSTYLES: BOWL CUT.

∞**double chignon** Woman's hairstyle of 1860s, with two large rolls of hair, one above the other, styled at the nape of the neck. Sometimes artificial hair was used.

dreadlocks/rasta dreadlocks Hair arranged in many long hanging twists that was first worn by Rastafarian (a religious sect) reggae musicians from Jamaica. During the 1980s and 1990s some young African American men and women and some Caucasians adopted the style. Sometimes hair spray is used to make locks stand up on top of head in a tousled mass. *Der.* From the style worn by Rastafarians, a religious sect from Jamaica, founded in 1930 when Ras Tafari (Haile Selassie) became emperor of Ethiopia.

dreadlocks

ducktail haircut Short hairstyle combed to come to a point at the nape of the neck. Worn by both men and women in the 1950s. Also called *D.A.,* slang for "duck's ass."

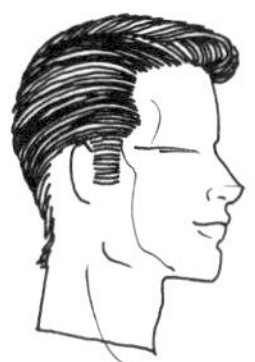
ducktail haircut

dutch bob See under HAIRSTYLES: BUSTER BROWN.

earmuffs Hair parted in center, braided on each side, and wound around to form buns over the ears.

emo hair Hair that is cut unevenly with a razor leaving an asymmetric bang in the front that hangs down to cover one eye.

∞**empire coiffure** (ohm-peer) Hairstyle worn in 1860s with curls in Greek manner around the face, and a band of narrow ribbon wrapped three times around the head. The back is styled in a large CHIGNON (see under HAIRSTYLES) with narrow ribbon wrapped around it several times, ending with two ribbon streamers down the back.

empire cone hairstyle Cone-shaped ornament, frequently wound with braids, and placed on crown of head. Hair is pulled back smoothly from the forehead, brought through the cone, and allowed to hang in a ponytail from top of cone or wound into a cockscomb spike.

eton crop Variation of BOYISH BOB (see under HAIRSTYLES) worn in England.

fade A hairstyle popular in the 1990s that originated with young African American men in which the hair was cut very short on the sides, and long on the top. Sometimes words, names, or designs were shaved on the scalp.

faux Mohawk A variation of a Mohawk where the hair on the sides of the head is not shaved but instead cut shorter than the top strip, which is spiked. See under HAIRSTYLES: MOHAWK.

∞**favourites** Woman's curls worn near the temples from 1690 to about 1720.

feather cut Short, lightly curled woman's bob, cut in layers, popular in 1950s and 1960s.

fillet 19th-c. evening hairstyle made by wrapping a satin band, embroidered with pearls, spirally around the head.

fingerwave Short hair set in flat waves by means of setting lotion and held until dry by bobby pins, or sometimes by combs. Popular in 1930s and revived in early 1970s. Also called *water wave.*

fishbone braid Hair is braided so that the interlacing of hair down center back looks similar to the spine of a fish with small bones on each side. Also called *French braid.*

fishbone or french braid

flattop General category of hairstyles, usually for men, in which the top of the hair is cut to a flat surface. Lengths may vary. The head being round, when the hair is cut flat, the scalp on the top of the head is close to the surface, and may be visible. This is known as a **landing strip.** When the hair is cut so short on top that the only remaining hair forms a horseshoe-shaped ridge on the upper sides and across the front, the cut is called a **horseshoe flattop.** In another version called **white walls,** the back and sides are shaved clean.

flip Medium-length woman's hairstyle with hair turned up on ends to form an incomplete curl. Front is often cut in bangs.

french braid See under HAIRSTYLES: FISHBONE BRAID.

french lock See under HAIRSTYLES: LOVE LOCK.

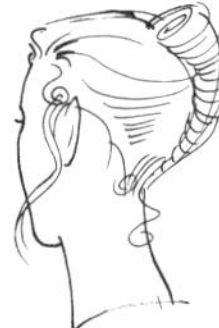
french roll or french twist

french roll/twist Upswept hairstyle with side and back hair combed and twisted in roll at the center back. Popular in 1940s and classic style since.

fringe See under HAIRSTYLES: BANGS.

∞**frisette** (frih-zet') **1.** 19th-c. usage for crimped bangs of hair, either real or false, worn on the forehead. **2.** In the 1860s, a sausage-shaped pad over which back hair was rolled.

frizzy Describing hair in many tight small curls.

gamin (gam'-in) Short boyish cut with shingled back and sides and irregularly cut bangs, popular in 1940s. Also called *urchin* and *garçon. Der.* French, "street urchin." Also see under HAIRSTYLES: BOYISH BOB.

garcette (gar-cett') See under HAIRSTYLES: COIFFURE EN BOUFFONS.

garçon/garçonne (gar-sohn') See under HAIRSTYLES: BOYISH BOB.

george hairstyle

george Long hair pulled back and secured at the nape of the neck with a twist of hair, ribbon, or scarf. Named for hairstyle as seen in 18th-c. portraits of U.S. president George Washington. Classic style for women, adapted by men in early 1970s. Also called a *cadogan* or *catagon.* Also see under HAIRSTYLES: CADOGAN #3.

Gibson Girl Hair worn in high puffy POMPADOUR (see under HAIRSTYLES) with small bun on top of head. Fashionable in 19th c. and early 20th c., made popular in drawings of Charles Dana Gibson. Revived occasionally.

greaser hair A category of hairstyles, including the pompadour and the ducktail, popularized by 1950s rock stars and celebrities such as Elvis Presley and Ricky Nelson. See under HAIRSTYLES: POMPADOUR and DUCKTAIL.

∞**grecian curls** **1.** Hairstyle of the 1860s with rows of curls hanging down the back from the nape of the neck. Sometimes arranged in two rows, one shorter than the other. **2.** Small curls around the face, copied from Napoleonic era, that in turn looked to Greece for inspiration. Used in the 1960s with helmet-style headwear. See under HEADWEAR: HELMET.

greek coiffure Woman's hairstyle of 1860s with center part, hair braided and wrapped around the crown of the head, made to form three hanging loops in back and wound around the loops at nape of neck. Also called *coiffure à la grecque.* Also see under HAIRSTYLES: GRECIAN CURLS.

guiche (gweesh) Few strands of hair made into curl in front of ear. Also called *kiss curl.* When curled back toward the ear instead of forward, called a *reverse guiche.*

hairdo See under introduction to HAIRSTYLES.

∞**hérisson/coiffure à la hérisson** (air-ee'-sonh) For women: Late 18th-c. short hairstyle with loose curls in back and frizzed ends at front and sides. For men: Same cut in front, but worn with a CADOGAN or PIGTAIL (see under HAIRSTYLES) in back. *Der.* French, "bristly, shaggy."

highlights Naturally occurring or artificially dyed lighter areas of the hair that provide a contrast with darker areas.

∞**hurluberlu** (er-loo-bare'-loo) Woman's hairstyle with short curls all over and long ringlets in back, first worn by Madame de Montespan about 1671.

indie fringe A thick style of bangs that are cut long, getting longer toward the sides of the face, creating a grunge appeal.

induction cut An even length of stubble across the head. This is the cut given to male recruits of the U.S. Armed Services. Also called *burr cut.*

∞**irene castle bob** Short bob with hair brushed back off the forehead and hanging in loose waves. *Der.* After Irene Castle, the ballroom dancer who made bobbed hair fashionable prior to World War I.

ironed hair Long straight hair, achieved by placing hair on an ironing board and pressing with a warm iron to remove all waves; a fad with young girls in the late 1960s. Now flat irons are used to achieve super-sleek hairstyles.

ivy league cut See under HAIRSTYLES: CREW CUT.

jumbo curls Very large curls similar to BARREL CURLS (see under HAIRSTYLES).

kiss curl See under HAIRSTYLES: GUICHE.

∞**kolbe** (kol-be′) Man's hairstyle worn in mid-16th c. with bangs in front and hair the same length at sides and back, usually above the ears. Also called *kolbenschmitt*.

La Belle Époque See under HAIRSTYLES: POMPADOUR.

La Goulue See under HAIRSTYLES: POMPADOUR.

landing strip See under HAIRSTYLES: FLATTOP.

layered cut Hair that is cut in graduated lengths in a horizontal fashion around the head.

lion's tail A long piece of hair or a switch, hanging down the back, twined with cord to about 6″ from the bottom, thus appearing like a lion's tail. Also called *queue de lion*.

∞**love lock/long lock** Long lock of curled hair brought forward from nape of neck and worn hanging over chest, popular from 1590 to 1650s for men and sometimes women. Also called a *Bourbon lock, French lock, heart breaker.*

∞**maintenon coiffure** (man-te′-non kwa-foor′) Woman's hairstyle of early 1860s with two long hanging curls at either side of face, tiny curls on the forehead, and a *chignon* at the back of the neck. Filmy lace decorated with foliage and flowers went over the crown of the head and hung down each side to shoulders in form of LAPPETS (see under HEADWEAR). The MAINTENON TOUPET (see under WIGS AND HAIRPIECES) could be added to secure proper effect of curls on the forehead. *Der.* Named for the Marquise de Maintenon, mistress and second wife of Louis XIV of France.

Mandinko Exaggerated MOHAWK-type hairstyle (see under HAIRSTYLES) with sideburns connected to beard and moustache, as worn by Mr. T., television star of early 1980s.

∞**marcel wave** Artificial wave put in woman's hair with heated curling irons, devised by hairdresser Marcel of France in 1907 and popular in the 1920s.

mini-braids/mini-plaits Extremely minute braids introduced in 1968. Natural hair may be styled in this manner or a hairpiece attached.

Mohawk Style in which entire head is shaved except for upstanding fringe of hair, about 3″ high and 2″ or more wide, running from brow to the nape of the neck. Sometimes left long and made to stand up in "spikes" with gel. See under HAIRSTYLES: PORCUPINE. *Der.* Adapted from style worn by Mohawk Indians.

∞**montague curls** (mon′-ta-ghu) Woman's evening hairstyle with a fringe of crescent-shaped curls pasted to the forehead in 1877.

mullet A man's hairstyle that is cut short at the front and sides and left long in the back; it began to appear in the 1960s and 1970s, but became generally well known in the early 1980s.

∞**ninon coiffure** (nee-nonh′ kwa-foor′) Hairstyle with ringlet curls over the forehead, shoulder-length curls at sides (sometimes wired), and back hair pulled into a knot. Introduced in England in mid-17th c. *Der.* Style was later given this name after Anne de Lenclos (1620–1705), known as Ninon de Lenclos, a legendary courtesan and Parisian fashion leader.

onion See under POMPADOUR #1.

∞**oreilles de chien** (or-ray de she-en) Nickname for two long curls worn at either side of face by men from 1790 to 1800. *Der.* French, "dog's ears."

pageboy Straight hair, worn shoulder length or shorter, with ends curled under at back and sides very smoothly. A classic hairstyle. *Der.* From hair of medieval "pages."

pageboy

pannier curls (pann-yeh′) Curls worn at sides of face in front of the ears.

permanent/permanent wave Waves or curls that last until hair is cut off, originally created by chemicals and heated rollers, later by means of chemicals alone. First permanent wave was invented by Charles Nestlé in 1906. First machine wave, introduced in beauty shops, required electrical wiring to each roller. In 1930s, new machineless wave used chemicals and heated rollers. In the early 1940s, the first *cold wave*, in which chemicals curled the hair without heating it, was introduced. This made home permanents possible. In 1960s a soft version called a *body wave* gave hair more fullness for noncurly coiffures. Popular for men in late 1970s. The slang reference for this style is **perm.** Also see under HAIRSTYLES: MARCEL WAVE.

pigeon-wings See under WIGS AND HAIRPIECES.

pigtails 1. Hair worn in two side braids, sometimes with ribbon bow tied on ends. Popular style for young girls since 1940s. 2. Child's hairstyle for short hair with tiny, ribbon-tied braids all over head.

pin curls 1. Curls used on forehead or sides of face made by winding hair around the finger, then setting with bobby pins. When pins are removed, curl is left tightly twisted. 2. Method of setting the hair by making tiny curls all over the head and securing them with bobby pins. May be combed out into either waves or curls.

pixie haircut Short hairstyle cut in layered style close to head and combed in points around forehead and face. Also called *pixie crop*.

pompadour (pohm′-pah-dure) 1. Woman's hair brushed up high and smooth from forehead and temples, sometimes teased or rolled over false stuffing and tucked into a small bun on top of head. Copied from style worn in late 19th and early 20th c. See GIBSON GIRL. Variations of this style called *La Belle Epoque, concierge, onion, Boldini,*

pompadour #1

and *La Goulue* in late 1960s. **2.** Hair rolled up in the front with the back worn straight and curled on ends, popular in 1940s. **3.** Man's hair worn rather long and brushed straight up and back from forehead with no part. Also see under HAIRSTYLES: QUIFF. **4.** See under HAIR ACCESSORIES: POMPON. *Der.* From Marquise de Pompadour, mistress of Louis XV of France.

ponytail **1.** Hair pulled to crown or center back of head and tied with a ribbon or held with an elastic band. Ends left hanging loose like a horse's tail. **2.** Hair parted in the center and two ponytails made—one on either side of the face near the ears.

ponytail #1

poodle cut Allover, short, curled effect similar to hair of a poodle. Also called *curlyhead.*

porc-epic See under HAIRSTYLES: PORCUPINE HEADDRESS.

porcupine hairstyle Man's 1985 hairstyle with center portion from forehead to neck left longer with even longer strands about 8″ in length made to stand up on top of head with gel or mousse.

∞porcupine headdress Man's hairstyle, with short hair standing up like bristles, worn at end of 18th c. Also called *porc-epic.*

pouf See under HAIRSTYLES: BOUFFANT.

∞pouf au sentiment (poof o sont-eh′-mont) Extravagantly high hairstyle elaborately decorated with flowers and other objects, worked over a framework of gauze. Worn by women in 18th c. before the French Revolution.

psyche knot (si-kee) Copy of Greek hairstyle for women with hair pulled back and twisted to form a knot at back of head. *Der.* Named for Greek mythological maiden, Psyche, the lover of Cupid, made immortal by Jupiter.

pudding-basin cut See under HAIRSTYLES: BOWL CROP.

puffs Woman's hair when BACK-COMBED (see BACK-COMBING under HAIRSTYLES) to form bouffant effect at sides of face in early 20th c.

punk hair A variety of unusual hairstyles, including MOHAWK, PORCUPINE, and SPIKY HAIRSTYLES (see under HAIRSTYLES), sometimes dyed a variety of colors.

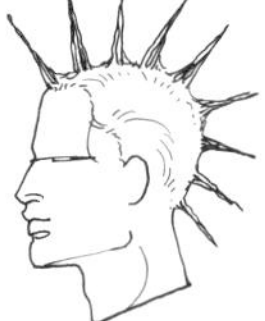
punk hairstyle

queue (kew) Long single braid hanging down the back. Similar to hairstyle worn by Chinese men. Also spelled *cue.*

queue de lion See under HAIRSTYLES: LION'S TAIL.

quiff Hairstyle brushed forward first, then back, giving a somewhat POMPADOUR effect in front (see under HAIRSTYLES). Similar to style worn by Elvis Presley, a rock-music superstar of the 1950s and 1960s.

rasta dreadlocks See under HAIRSTYLES: DREADLOCKS.

razor bob A variation of the bob that is cut with a razor so that the bottom ends are ragged looking.

razor cut Haircut that is done using a razor blade rather than scissors.

∞rècamier hairstyle (ray-cahm′-ee-ay) Hairstyle of 1870s and 1880s arranged with *chignon* high on back of head and curls at neck. *Der.* Named after hairstyle worn by Madame Rècamier.

reverse guiche See under HAIRSTYLES: GUICHE.

ringlets Loose curls that hang in dangling fashion.

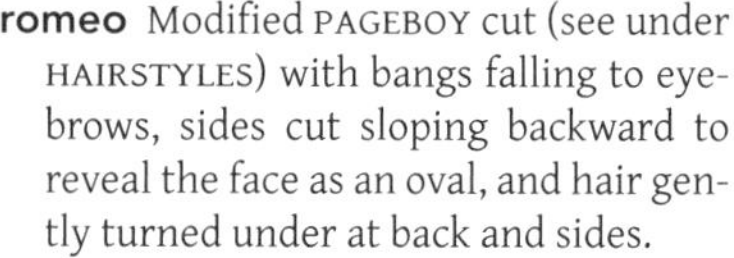

romeo Modified PAGEBOY cut (see under HAIRSTYLES) with bangs falling to eyebrows, sides cut sloping backward to reveal the face as an oval, and hair gently turned under at back and sides.

ringlets

Sassoon Short, straight, boyish hairdo, combed forward from crown, cut in low bangs, shaped to points in front of ears, and shingled in back to deep V. *Der.* First ABSTRACT CUT (see under HAIRSTYLES), designed by British hairdresser Vidal Sassoon in 1964.

sausage curl Tightly rolled horizontal curl usually arranged in layers around sides or back of head from ear level to nape of neck. Popular in late 1930s, early 1940s, and revived in 1980s.

sculptured hair Hair covered with mousse so that it may be arranged in fan-shaped design or brushed straight up from face and cut in scalloped design at top. Styles were introduced by Patti LaBelle, a rock singer in mid-1980s.

shag Longish bob, layered for a shaggy look, with bangs and "shaggy" in front of ears. An innovation of the late 1960s. Also called *ape drape.*

shingle Tapering of hair up back of head, and sometimes around to the sides, in imitation of a man's conventional haircut. Style introduced in 1920s for women, achieving new popularity in the 1960s and 1980s and after. Also see under HAIRSTYLES: BINGLE.

side braid Hair that is SIDE-PARTED and pulled into a braid at the side of the head rather than at the back.

sideburns That part of a man's hair and whiskers that extends from his hairline to below the ears.

side parted The technique of separating the hair on the top of the head at the side rather than in the middle so that most of the hair on the top of the head falls to one side or the other.

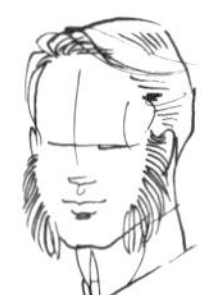
sideburns

slicked-back hair A hairstyle that utilizes product to keep it pulled back away from the face. May be used in combination with a side part.

spiky hair Short or medium-length hair, segmented and twisted to form pointed projections that are stiffened with hair spray, gel, or mousse. Sometimes dyed different colors (e.g., blue, orange, and pink).

spit curls Separate ringlets formed flat against the forehead or cheek often held in place by water, setting lotion, or lacquer. Popular in 1930s, and revived in 1970s and 1980s. Also see under HAIRSTYLES: GUICHE.

Statue of Liberty hair Outré hairstyle of seven spikes of hair, sprayed to stand erect, framing face like Statue of Liberty crown. *Der.* Inspired by the July 4, 1986, celebration of the restoration of the Statue of Liberty in New York harbor.

surfer hair Long, layered hair that is worn shaggy and appears to be bleached blond by the sun.

tapered haircut The hair is cut progressively shorter down the back of the head to nape of the neck. The length of the hair being tapered can vary depending on the style.

taure See under HAIRSTYLES: BULL HEAD.

teasing See under HAIRSTYLES: BACK-COMBING.

teddy boy cut See under TEDDY BOY.

tendrils Long, loosely curled strands of hair worn hanging at the forehead, sides, or nape of neck, popular with the pompadour hairstyle (see under HAIRSTYLES: POMPADOUR #1).

tipping Hand-painting the tips of sections of the hair.

∞**titus** Coiffure, worn in late 18th c., post–French Revolution, that resembled the way a man condemned to the guillotine wore his hair, cut short and brushed forward over forehead. Also called *Titus hairstyle. Der.* From hairstyle of Roman Emperor, Titus, who ruled A.D. 79–81.

topknot Hair twisted into a knot or bun at the crown of the head.

twenties bob See under HAIRSTYLES: BOB.

under cut See under HAIRSTYLES: BOWL CUT.

upsweep/updo Popular 1940s woman's hairstyle with medium-long hair brushed upward from the sides and nape of neck, then secured on top of the head in curls or a pompadour (see under HAIRSTYLES: POMPADOUR #1).

upsweep

urchin See under HAIRSTYLES: GAMIN.

vampire hair Goth-looking hair that is all one length and combed straight back.

Veronica Lake hairstyle Long hair parted on side with heavier section hanging down almost covering one eye. Worn by film star Veronica Lake in 1940s, revived in the 1960s after renewed interest in classic films.

vintage Hollywood hair A medium to long style that is cut in one length and side parted, characterized by big wavy curls. Also called *old Hollywood hair.*

wash-and-wear hair 1. Hair worn in a tousled mass, achieved by washing hair and allowing it to hang uncombed. First popular in early 1980s. 2. Any hairstyle that is cut so as to allow the hair to be washed and worn without any additional styling.

∞**waterfall** Woman's hairstyle of the 1860s and 1870s, usually made with a piece of false waved hair hanging down in back in a confined mass or in form of loose chignon with braid pulled tight at center, making two loops of hair.

water wave See under HAIRSTYLES: FINGERWAVE.

wedge Hair is tapered close to the head at the nape of the neck, almost to a V. Above this the hair is full and all one length. The front and sides are all one length, squared off at middle of ear, and short bangs are informally styled. *Der.* Popular hairstyle after it was worn by Dorothy Hamill, an Olympic figure skating champion in 1976.

white walls See under HAIRSTYLES: FLATTOP.

wind-blown bob Popular 1930s woman's hairstyle that was cut short and shingled so that hair fell softly about the face as if blown by the wind.

Hale, Sarah Josepha See under *GODEY'S LADY'S BOOK.*

half *adj.* Describes smaller or incomplete items of apparel or accessories. The prefix **demi** is a synonym. See under APRONS: HALF-APRON; BELTS: HALF BELT; EYEWEAR: HALF-GLASSES; FOOTWEAR: DEMI-BOOT; HOSIERY: HALF-HOSE; SHIRTS: HALF SHIRT; SHOULDERS AND SLEEVES: HALF SLEEVE; UNDERGARMENTS: DEMI-BRA and HALF-SLIP.

half-compass cloak See under CAPES, CLOAKS, AND SHAWLS: FRENCH CLOAK.

half coronet See under HEADWEAR: DEMI-CORONAL.

∞**half dress** Daytime or semiformal evening dress, as such styles were called in the late 18th c. and 19th c. Also called *half-toilette* or *demi-toilette.*

half gaiters See under FOOTWEAR: SPATS.

half-gown See under HALF ROBE.

half handkerchief See under SCARVES.

half-jack boot See under FOOTWEAR: JOCKEY BOOT.

half kirtle See under KIRTLE.

half lining Lining of only part of the garment (e.g., front completely lined but only the shoulders lined in the back). Frequently used in men's jackets and topcoats.

half-mask See under MASKS: DOMINO.

half-moon pocket See under POCKETS.

half mourning See under MOURNING CLOTHES.

half-piqué/half P.K. seam See under GLOVES AND GLOVE CONSTRUCTION.

∞**half robe** Low-necked, short-sleeved, thigh-length tunic worn over long gown with fullness pulled in at waist by narrow ribbon. Worn from late 18th c. to early 19th c. Also called *half-gown* or *demi-habilliment.*

half sizes Women's garments cut for a fully developed figure: short-waisted in back, larger in waist and hips, height about 5′2″ to 5′8″—usually sized 10½ to 24½.

half-toilette See under HALF DRESS.

Hall of Fame See under COTY AMERICAN FASHION CRITICS AWARD.

halo hat See under HEADWEAR: PAMELA.

halter Strap encircling the neck, used to support front of a garment, leaving shoulders and back bare. Popular in 1930s and 1940s, revived in early 1970s and periodically since then. Used on blouses, dresses, evening wear and swimsuits. See under BLOUSES AND TOPS: HALTER TOP and NECKLINES AND COLLARS: HALTER NECKLINE.

hamburg lace See under LACES.

hamster See under FURS.

†**hand** Characteristics of a fabric that are revealed through sense of touch (e.g., crispness, softness, smoothness, drape, resilience, fineness, and the like).

HANDBAGS AND RELATED ACCESSORIES

handbag Accessory carried primarily by women and girls to hold such items as money, credit cards, and cosmetics. Comes in many styles and made of a variety of materials (e.g., leather, fabric, vinyl, metal, plastic, canvas, straw, and patent leather). The word is often shortened to *bag.* Also called a *purse* or POCKETBOOK. From 13th to 16th c. the AULMONIERE, a small leather pouch, was worn suspended from man's girdle in order to have alms for the poor. From late 19th to early 20th c., women carried a small, elongated bag called a RETICULE. In late 19th c., various types of handbags began to be carried mainly for traveling. By 1920s it was a necessary accessory. In 1968 the MANBAG was introduced for men. See cross-references under HANDBAGS AND RELATED ACCESSORIES.

accordion bag Bag made like an expandable filing envelope that is narrow at the top and pleated at sides and bottom. Usually made with a handle and frequently with a zipper compartment in the center. *Der.* From resemblance to pleats on the musical instrument of this name.

American Indian bag See under HANDBAGS AND RELATED ACCESSORIES: SQUAW BAG.

Apache bag See under HANDBAGS AND RELATED ACCESSORIES: SQUAW BAG.

attaché case See under HANDBAGS AND RELATED ACCESSORIES: BRIEFCASE #1.

∞**aulmoniere** (all-mon-yehr′) (*aumoniere, aulmonier, almoner*) Medieval pouch of silk or leather suspended from girdle, worn by nobles from the 13th c. until the Reformation to carry alms. Also used by women in 14th c. to carry mirrors and tweezers for their hair. **Gipser** was such a bag worn by men in late Middle Ages. Also spelled *gipcière, gypsire.*

backpack Bag with straps fitting over shoulders so that it can be worn on the back. Term *backpack* has largely replaced KNAPSACK (see under HANDBAGS AND RELATED ACCESSORIES) in describing bags worn on the back. Used since 1970s to carry books and sometimes used in place of a handbag in the 1980s and after. Usually made of nylon or other MANUFACTURED FIBERS and sometimes of real or synthetic leather. Variations now include a backpack designed to be carried over one shoulder and called a **one-shoulder backpack.**

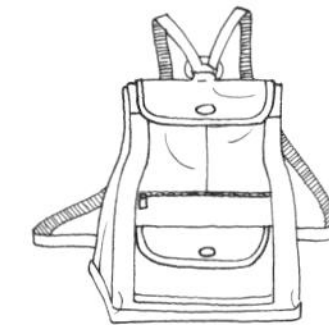
backpack

bag See under HANDBAG in introduction to HANDBAGS AND RELATED ACCESSORIES.

baguette bag (bah-get′) Popular woman's handbag originated by Italian design house of Fendi. An extended oblong shape, the bag closes with a flap over the front and may have both a shoulder strap and handles. It is made in a wide variety of materials. *Der.* Named after a long, narrow loaf of French bread.

ballentine See under HANDBAGS AND RELATED ACCESSORIES: RETICULE.

barrel bag Handbag shaped like a stubby cylinder, with a zipper closing and handles attached to the sides. *Der.* From the shape similar to a small barrel.

barrel bag

basket bag Applies to many types of handbags. Originally woven only of reed in typical basket shapes. Now made of reed, straw, cane, interwoven plastic strips, or other materials such as leather or plastic in the shape of a basket. One popular style resembles a small picnic hamper. Sometimes decorated with shells, beads, sequins, brass, or leather.

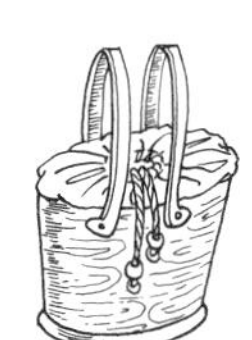
basket bag

beaded bag Any ornate, small bag entirely covered with varicolored pearls or glass beads or a fabric bag, often satin, with a design worked in beads. Beaded bags were used for daytime and evening throughout the 19th c. but were limited to more formal wear by the 20th c. One type popular in the early 1900s was usually hand-crocheted in small, elongated

beaded bag

pouch style with a drawstring top and a beaded tassel at the bottom. Another style, made in France, was oblong in shape with beaded fringe on the bottom and sterling silver frame and handle. This latter type was revived in 1968.

belt bag 1. A small bag worn at waist having slots in the back through which a belt is drawn. Usually has a flap closing and is worn with sportswear. 2. A pouch bag with handle through which a belt is drawn.

billfold See under HANDBAGS AND RELATED ACCESSORIES: WALLET.

Birkin bag A classic two-handle Hermès bag inspired by actress Jane Birkin. The bags continue to be distributed on schedules and in limited quantities, creating ongoing demand through scarcity.

Birkin bag

book bag Slim, oblong bag the size of a notebook cinched around center with strap that forms loop handle; introduced in 1970s.

∞**bourse** (boorce) (*burse*) Large purse or bag worn from 1440 until mid-18th c. Later spelled *burse*.

bowling bag A bag with a domed top (shaped to fit the contour of a bowling ball), a zip or frame top opening and top handle(s).

∞**box bag** Handbag with rigid frame, similar to small suitcase or lunchbox, made in leather, metal, or vinyl.

boxer bag A pouch bag with a drawstring closure made to look like a punching bag.

bracelet bag Type of handbag with one or two BANGLE BRACELETS (see under JEWELRY) as handles. May be a soft pouch bag made of leather or fabric, or it may be made with a frame.

bridle bag A tall bag with a square or rectangular bottom that tapers to a flat top based on a saddle bag.

briefcase 1. Large, usually flat case with a carrying handle, most often made of real or synthetic leather and large enough or can expand sufficiently to hold documents, books, and the like. Also called *attaché case*. 2. Handbag of briefcase size for woman executive that features small outside pockets for personal items.

bucket bag Round handbag made in the shape of a bucket.

budget Wallet or extra pocket hanging from belt used in 17th c.

camera bag A three-dimensional rectangular bag with a zipper top and wrist or shoulder strap. May be a functional bag to hold a camera or a handbag designed to look like a camera bag.

canteen bag Circular-style bag frequently made with a shoulder strap and zipper closing. Made in the shape of a flat canteen used to carry water in dry climates.

caravan bag See under HANDBAGS AND RELATED ACCESSORIES: SAFARI BAG.

carpet bag Handbag made of patterned carpeting or heavy tapestry, in a large satchel style. Popular in 19th c., late 1960s, and revived in mid-1980s in lighter-weight fabrics. *Der.* From carpet valises popular with Northerners for travel just after the Civil War. Southerners alluded to the travelers by the derisive term "carpetbaggers."

carpet bag

carryall See under HANDBAGS AND RELATED ACCESSORIES: TOTE BAG.

carryall clutch Woman's wallet designed to hold coins, bills, photographs and credit cards. Usually the size of U.S. paper money, with snap closing on long edge and purselike sections for coins.

Chanel bag Handbag designed by French couturiere Gabrielle Chanel that has become a classic. Of quilted leather with gold chain handles, it has a gold House of Chanel logo on the front.

Chanel bag

change purse Small purse that closes by a snap clasp on the rigid frame or by a zipper. Usually carried inside handbag to hold coins and made in leather, clear plastic, or matched to the larger handbag. Also called a *coin purse*.

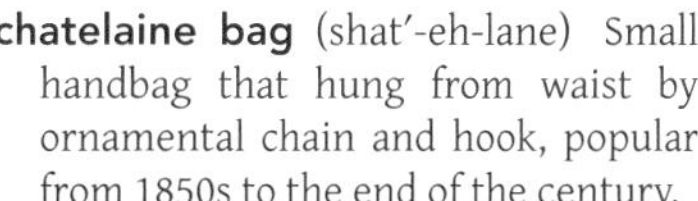

chatelaine bag (shat'-eh-lane) Small handbag that hung from waist by ornamental chain and hook, popular from 1850s to the end of the century.

chatelaine bag

clutch bag/clutch purse 1. Regular-sized handbag without a handle. 2. Type of handbag frequently used for an evening bag. Sometimes has a strap on back through which hand may be inserted, or a fine gold chain attached in such a manner that it is of optional use. Frequently made in envelope style, in which case it is called an **envelope bag.** *Mini-clutch* bags are tiny versions of this style.

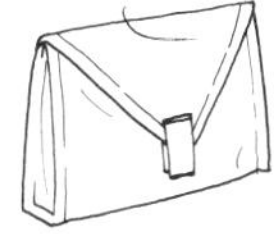
clutch purse

coin purse See under HANDBAGS AND RELATED ACCESSORIES: CHANGE PURSE.

contour clutch WALLET similar to a CLUTCH purse, but curved on top edge, sometimes with attached leather carrying loop at one end. See under HANDBAGS AND RELATED ACCESSORIES: WALLET and CLUTCH BAG. Also called *swinger* or *swinger clutch*.

convertible bag A bag that can be transformed, e.g., from a clutch or tote to a shoulder bag.

cordé bag (kor-day′) Any type of handbag made out of a fabric composed of rows of GIMP (see under BRAIDS) stitched to a background fabric to make a pattern. Popular style in the 1940s and still used.

cordé bag

courier bag See under HANDBAGS AND RELATED ACCESSORIES: MESSENGER BAG.

cross body bag Handbag with long strap designed to be worn with the strap over one shoulder and the bag on the other side of the body, which causes the strap to cross the chest. A variation of the SHOULDER BAG (see under HANDBAGS AND RELATED ACCESSORIES) that developed when women started placing shoulder straps across the body in order to make the bag more secure.

diaper bag/baby bag Handbags that are large enough to carry some of the necessities required when accompanying infants. (These are now widely listed on specialty store websites—real diaper bags by designers such as Armani that look luxurious.)

doctor's bag Large handbag shaped like the bag traditionally carried by a physician. It has two handles, one on either side of hinged top opening.

drawstring bag Any handbag that is closed by pulling a cord, usually of pouch type.

duffel bag **1.** Large barrel-shaped canvas bag with a drawstring top. Used originally by sailors and soldiers to transport their clothing and other items. When used by sailors, called a *sea bag.* **2.** Copied in various sizes for handbags, beach bags, and luggage. May have an extra piece of fabric on outside that forms large pockets around outside of bag. Generally closes with a zipper. **3.** Small, pouch-style, taffeta evening bag with large ruffled top that has tasseled drawstring closure.

duffel bag #2

dust cover A soft cloth bag that is sold with expensive designer bags to protect the bag when it's not in use.

east-west bag A bag that is longer in width than it is in height.

envelope bag See under HANDBAGS AND RELATED ACCESSORIES: CLUTCH BAG.

fanny pack An envelope or pouch-like bag mounted on a strap that fastens around the waist. Intended to be worn with the bag in the back, resting on the hips (or in slang, *fanny*), the bag is made in materials ranging from sturdy nylon to leather and in many sizes. Originally a day pack used for hiking, by the 21st c. it had become acceptable daytime streetwear and is especially popular among travelers.

feed bag Cylindrical leather or canvas bag with flat round bottom and top handles copied from canvas bags used for feeding horses. Forerunner of many open tote bags.

flight bag **1.** Soft canvas satchel with zippered-top closing and two handles, copied from standard carryall issued by airlines to passengers when air travel was less common. **2.** Any handbag used for traveling, larger than a handbag and smaller than a suitcase. Also called a *travel bag.*

fold-over bag Small envelope bag that may be open at the top or with zippered closing. Bag is folded over double and carried in the hand or under arm.

frame bag **1.** *n.* Metal top of handbag around which the bag is constructed. **2. framing** *v.* Securing the frame to the handbag. Material and lining are fitted into frame and secured permanently by machine.

french purse Fold-over wallet for bills. One half incorporates a change purse with metal clasp closing at the top that is actually one end of the wallet.

∞**gaming purse** Drawstring bag of kid, velvet, or embroidered fabric used in 17th c. Made with flat stiffened circular base and pleated sides. *Der.* Used to hold counters and coins when "gaming" (e.g., playing cards for money).

gipser See under HANDBAGS AND RELATED ACCESSORIES: AULMONIERE.

golf bag A tall tubular handbag that mimics the shape of a golfbag.

Grace Kelly bag See under HANDBAGS AND RELATED ACCESSORIES: KELLY BAG.

greek bag Square or rectangular wool open-top bag. Handwoven in Greek-key designs, trimmed around edge with cable yarn that also forms the handle.

gym bag A handbag shaped like a duffel bag.

hatbox bag Handbag made to look like a HATBOX.

hippie bag See under SQUAW BAG.

hobo A soft slouch bag with a top that droops in the middle to form a half-moon shape.

Indian bag See under SQUAW BAG.

indispensible See under HANDBAGS AND RELATED ACCESSORIES: RETICULE.

interchangeable bag Complete handbag with extra covers that snap or button over frame to change colors.

inverted frame Handbag industry term for type of frame covered with fabric or leather so metal frame does not show at top of bag.

Kelly bag Handbag favored by Princess Grace of Monaco (actress Grace Kelly) in the 1950s. After Grace Kelly was seen frequently carrying an alligator TOTE (see under HANDBAGS AND RELATED ACCESSORIES) made by the design house of Hermès, the

Kelly bag

company began to call this bag the Kelly bag. It has since become a classic style, and variations of the bag are now made by many manufacturers.

Kikuyu Open-top, straw tote bag with leather handles. Handwoven of natural sisal in horizontal strips of red and blue alternating with natural color. Made by Kikuyu craftsmen of Kenya.

knapsack A carryall made in heavy fabric that had shoulder straps and was worn by soldiers and hikers to carry necessary gear. Now more likely to be called a BACKPACK (see under HANDBAGS AND RELATED ACCESSORIES) and made in a wide variety of materials for many purposes.

lunchbox bag Identical in shape to the traditional deep lunchbox with a curved lid. Introduced from Italy in 1967, it was first made in papier-mâché and later in metal. Distinctive feature is a collage effect of decorative pictures pasted on the outside and then shellacked. Later do-it-yourself DÉCOUPAGE kits were marketed.

manbag Handbag, typically a shoulder bag or a wrist strap bag, that is carried by a man. A fashion that gained in popularity in early 1970s as an outgrowth of wide use of camera bags by men.

manbag

mesh bag Tiny links of metal joined to make a flexible bag. Popular in early 1900s in small size with sterling silver top and chain with the metal frequently enameled in a floral design. In the 1940s, mesh handbags were made with larger white enameled links and white plastic frames.

messenger bag Large bag with an envelope-like main compartment that usually closes with a zipper and has a large flap over the front that fastens with a buckle or snap. May have either shoulder straps or handles. Inspired by bags typically carried by messengers. A smaller version with a more tailored, square appearance is called a **courier bag.**

minaudiere (min-oh'-dee-yehr') Small, rigid, metal evening bag made in oval, oblong, or square shapes and used to hold cosmetics. Carried in hand or by short chain. Decorated by engraved designs or set with jewels, this expensive jeweler's product gained popularity when sold by Cartier in New York. *Der.* French, feminine of *minaudier*, affected, coquettish, from *minauder*, to "mince."

mini bag Small bags that became important in the 1960s with the introduction of miniskirts. Tiny bags were introduced in all styles. Some had double and triple frames, usually with attached shoulder chains or straps.

mini-clutch bag See under CLUTCH BAG.

∞**miser's purse** Small tubular purse closed at each end, with a slit in center, and two movable rings to keep money at one end or other. Carried from latter half of 17th c. through 19th c. Constructed either by netting, knotting, or knitting, and often beaded, the bags varied in size, with 18th c. and Victorian period purses being larger than those of the early 19th c. Also called *wallet, ring purse, stocking purse,* or *Victorian long purse*.

miser's purse

Moroccan bag 1. Tooled leather handbag made in Morocco of Moroccan leather. Decorated with elaborate designs and color combinations, such as saffron and wine. 2. Handbag made with stitched allover design in saffron on wine-colored leather.

muff bag Basically a muff, an accessory used to keep the hands warm, frequently styled in fur. In the 1930s a zippered compartment to hold small items was added to the muff, and this became a classic item used by little girls.

nameplate A separate piece attached to a bag which identifies the designer or brand; frequently made of metal, but also made of leather, vinyl, and other materials.

newsbag TOTE BAG style (see under HANDBAGS AND RELATED ACCESSORIES) with separate section on the outside to slip in a rolled magazine or newspaper.

north-south bag A bag that is longer in height than it is in width.

one-shoulder backpack See under HANDBAGS AND RELATED ACCESSORIES: BACKPACK.

pannier bag (pan-yeh') A bag with zipper compartment in the center and two open compartments on either side. A single broad handle extends from one side to the other on the outside of the bag at the middle.

pianta bag (pee-ahn'-tah) Small evening bag introduced from Italy in mid-1960s resembling a tiny umbrella made from a square of fabric with four corners folded to the center and a looped center handle.

pocketbook Originally an envelope-like container for written materials and paper money carried by men in the 17th c. and 18th c. Made of leather and often tooled or decorated or of silk or wool worked in colored or metal yarns. Eventually became a synonym for a woman's handbag.

pokey Small drawstring pouch made of sueded leather, sometimes with tiny pocket on front. Popular in the late 1960s. *Der.* Copied from a small leather bag used by '49ers to carry gold nuggets and gold dust.

∞**pompadour bag** Drawstring bag in circular or oblong shape, popular in mid-1880s, made of satin, plush, or velvet with floral embroidery heightened by edgings of gold or silver thread. *Der.* Named after Marquise de Pompadour, mistress of Louis XV of France.

∞**porte-monnaie** (port-mohn'ay) Embroidered handbag carried by women in the 1850s, made with metal frame; sometimes with chain handle, sometimes in clutch styles. *Der.* French, "purse."

∞**pouch** Basic style originally made of soft shirred leather or fabric with a drawstring closing. Now also made with a frame and handles.

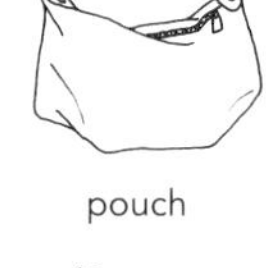
pouch

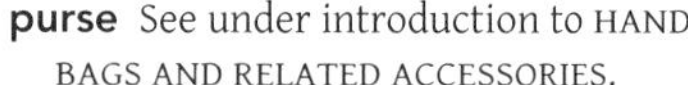

purse See under introduction to HANDBAGS AND RELATED ACCESSORIES.

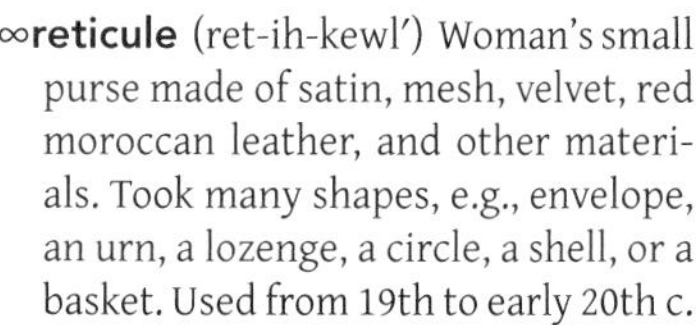

∞**reticule** (ret-ih-kewl′) Woman's small purse made of satin, mesh, velvet, red moroccan leather, and other materials. Took many shapes, e.g., envelope, an urn, a lozenge, a circle, a shell, or a basket. Used from 19th to early 20th c. When first introduced sometimes made fun of and called a *ridicule*. Also called *indispensible, ballantine*.

reticule 19th c.

ring purse See under HANDBAGS AND RELATED ACCESSORIES: MISER'S PURSE.

saddle bags Pair of soft leather bags joined to central strap handle. *Der.* From large bags thrown over horse's saddle to carry provisions.

safari bag Double-handled bag made like a small flight bag with a zippered closing. Characteristic features are the small pockets placed low on the outside of the bag. One of the most popular bags of the late 1960s and now a classic style. Also called *caravan bag.*

safari bag

Sally Jess bag Trademarked by English designer Sally Jess, this bag was a favorite with British younger set in the 1960s. Made of fabric in simple tote design with fabric handle and two cut-out crescent sections at the top.

satchel Leather bag with a rigid flat bottom. The sides slope upward to close on metal frame hinged about halfway down the bag. Often fastened with extra snap locks and with metal reinforcements at corners. Sides are usually recessed. Handle is generally rigid and curved. Similar to a DOCTOR'S BAG (see under HANDBAGS AND RELATED ACCESSORIES).

school bag A rectangular-shaped handbag that mimics a child's bookbag.

sea bag See under HANDBAGS AND RELATED ACCESSORIES: DUFFEL BAG.

shigra Handmade, tote bag–style handbag sold to American tourists or exported to the U.S. from Ecuador, made from fibers taken from the leaves of the cabuya plant. Artisans use a looping system done with a needle to form distinctive patterns with natural and colored yarns. Originally used for storage of grain and flour. Made in patterns characteristic of different communities in Ecuador.

shoulder bag Handbag in any shape or size with long chain or strap to place over the shoulder. Some types of shoulder straps convert to double-chain handles, others may be shortened by unbuckling a section of the strap.

signature bag Handbag of leather or canvas with designer's initials or signature stenciled or printed in an allover repeat pattern. Originating with Louis Vuitton® in Paris, later copied by Hermés, Saint Laurent, Mark Cross, Gucci, etc., and considered a fashion status symbol.

Louis Vuitton® signature bag

∞**sovereign purse** Small, round, half-inch-diameter purse on a curved metal clasp for holding small coins. Carried in the 18th and 19th c.

sporran bag (spo′-an) Adaptation for women of sporran (see HIGHLAND DRESS) as worn by the Scots Highlander. Shoulder bag is made of leather with long strands of horsehair hanging from it. The frame is metal.

squaw bag Handbag inspired by bags used by Native Americans. May be made of genuine doeskin in natural color or made of tiny geometric contrasting patches of colored leather. Most bags are trimmed with fringe. Popular handbag of the late 1960s. Also called *American Indian bag, Apache bag*, and *hippie bag. Der.* Name by which settlers called Native American woman.

stocking purse See under HANDBAGS AND RELATED ACCESSORIES: MISER'S PURSE.

suitcase bag Handbag made of metal and shaped like a miniature suitcase, complete with lock and reinforced corners.

swagger pouch Bag with double handles and two open sections on either side of zippered compartment. Classic style since the 1930s.

swinger bag See under HANDBAGS AND RELATED ACCESSORIES: CONTOUR CLUTCH.

tooled leather bag Typical Western-type handbag made of natural-colored cowhide with hand-stamped pattern. Each individual character is stamped with a metal die.

tote bag 1. Utility bag, large enough to carry small packages, sometimes with an inner zippered compartment for money. Copied from shape of common paper shopping bag. Made with open top and two handles, sometimes with outside loop to hold umbrella. 2. Any large bag with open top and two handles.

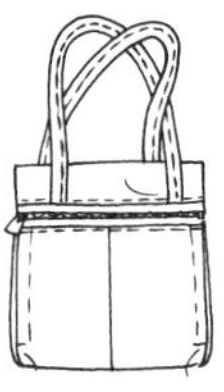
tote bag

travel bag See under HANDBAGS AND RELATED ACCESSORIES: FLIGHT BAG.

∞**travelling bag** Large handbag consisting of two somewhat circular pouches made of fabric fringed around the edges and joined together at the top. Used when traveling in the 1860s.

triplex/triple-framed bag Triple-framed bag with three separate clasps. Each section is an individual compartment. Introduced in 1967, many were styled as tiny MINI BAGS (see under HANDBAGS AND RELATED ACCESSORIES).

umbrella tote 1. TOTE BAG (see under HANDBAGS AND RELATED ACCESSORIES), but with a pocket at side for holding an umbrella. 2. Bag shaped like a briefcase with a zipper around it and the umbrella attached to the side with a plastic loop. 3. Conventional satchel-type bag with zippered compartment at bottom for umbrella.

vanity bag Stiff-framed, box-shaped bag usually fitted with a large mirror and sometimes other grooming accessories.

∞**Victorian long purse** See under HANDBAGS AND RELATED ACCESSORIES: MISER'S PURSE.

wallet 1. Accessory used to carry money, credit cards, and photographs. Sometimes with change purse attached and/or space for checkbook and note pad. Originally used only by men, now also used by women and children. Also called a *billfold* when designed to hold paper money, credit or other cards, and photos, and made to fold in center. 2. In 1980s, smaller sizes, closed with VELCRO®, were introduced to wear on wrist, ankle, or belt, primarily when engaging in sports (e.g., jogging). 3. See under HANDBAGS AND RELATED ACCESSORIES: POCKETBOOK. 4. See under HANDBAGS AND RELATED ACCESSORIES: MISER'S PURSE.

wristlet A small wallet-like bag with a looped strap that dangles from one end allowing it to be carried like a purse or clipped onto the strap of a larger tote.

∞**zouave pouch** (zoo-ahv') Small handbag of various shapes—sometimes rectangular, sometimes triangular—finished with tassels and hung by a hook from the waistband placed underneath the zouave jacket. Worn by women in 1860s. *Der.* Arabic, Zouaova, a Kabyle tribe, one of the Berbers, living in Algeria or Tunisia.

---

hand-blocked print See under PRINTS, STRIPES, AND CHECKS: BLOCK PRINTING.

handcoverchief/hand cloth See under HANDKERCHIEF.

hand cuff See under CUFFS: HAND FALL.

hand fall See under CUFFS.

handkerchief Square of cotton, linen, or silk, sometimes edged with lace or embroidered, carried and used for wiping the face or nose. Men's are usually larger than women's. Often colored for day use, they might be black or black-bordered for mourning. In 1870, plain white cambric was correct for day or evening. In 1890s, it was fashionable to wear in the cuff of the left sleeve, a practice copied from the military. Modern handkerchiefs are made in a wide variety of colors and sizes, although white predominates. Called a *napkin* in 16th c. A handkerchief folded into a square and worn in the breast pocket of a tailored suit is known as a **pocket square.**

∞**handkerchief dress** See under DRESSES. Also see under DRESSES: HANDKERCHIEF TUNIC.

handkerchief hem See under CLOTHING CONSTRUCTION DETAILS.

∞**handkerchief linen** Lightweight, sheer, fine fabric used for handkerchiefs and infant wear.

handkerchief skirt See under SKIRTS.

handkerchief sleeve See under SHOULDERS AND SLEEVES.

handkerchief tunic See under DRESSES.

hand knitting Knitted apparel, accessories, or trimming made entirely by hand, as opposed to machine knitting.

hand-painted print See under PRINTS, STRIPES, AND CHECKS.

hand-screened print See under PRINTS, STRIPES, AND CHECKS: SCREEN PRINTING.

hand sleeve See under SHOULDERS AND SLEEVES.

†**handspun yarn** Yarn made with different types of spindles or hand-spinning wheels—making yarn that is less regular in appearance than machine-made yarns, which adds texture and interest to the woven fabric.

hang 1. The way in which fabric drapes on the figure after it is sewn. 2. Marking the hem of a skirt with pins or chalk so it can be straightened.

hanging sleeve See under SHOULDERS AND SLEEVES.

hank See under SKEIN.

hanseline See under DOUBLET.

happi See under SLEEPWEAR AND LOUNGEWEAR: HAPPI COAT.

happy face Iconic stylized face, made up of a yellow circle with black dots for the eyes and a single black arc-shaped line for the mouth. Used on sweatshirts, buttons, jewelry, and in prints since early 1970s. Also called a *smiley face*.

hardanger embroidery See under EMBROIDERIES AND SEWING STITCHES.

hard goods See under SOFT GOODS.

hard hat See under HEADWEAR.

hare See under FURS.

harem *adj.* Describes clothing styles with characteristics of the costumes of the Near East. Harem styles typically included: full, ankle-length harem pants gathered at the ankle and combined with blouse and bolero that exposed a bare midriff. Sandals are generally worn; jewelry and chains complete the costume. Appeared in the late 1960s to 1980s. Also describes apparel derived from clothing thought to have been worn by Middle Eastern women. See under DRESSES: HAREM DRESS; PANTS: HAREM KNICKERS and PANTS; SKIRTS: HAREM SKIRT; and SLEEPWEAR AND LOUNGEWEAR: HAREM PAJAMAS. Synonym: *Arabian Nights*.

harem dress See under DRESSES.

harlequin (hahr′-leh-kwin) **1.** Traditional theatrical costume made of varicolored diamond-shaped patches on tunic and tights, a flaring brimmed black BICORNE hat (see under HEADWEAR) decorated with pompons, and a black mask. **2.** See under PRINTS, STRIPES, AND CHECKS. **3.** See under EYEGLASSES. **4.** See under HEADWEAR. *Der.* From *Harlequin*, a part played by an actor in 16th- to 18th-c. Italian performances called *commedia dell'arte.* **5.** See under PRINTS, STRIPES, AND CHECKS: HARLEQUIN CHECK.

harlequin #1

harlequin opal See under GEMS, GEM CUTS, AND SETTINGS.

∞**harlot/herlot** Garment, similar to tights, worn by men in England in the late 14th c. Stockings and pants were made in one piece and tied to the upper and outer garments by strings known as points.

harlow *adj.* Descriptive of adaptations of styles of late 1920s and early 1930s, including bias-cut dresses, wide-legged, cuffed trousers for women, shoes, and slippers of this era. These styles were revived in the 1960s. See under FOOTWEAR: HARLOW PUMP and HARLOW SLIPPER, and PANTS: HARLOW PANTS. *Der.* Named for Jean Harlow, platinum-blonde Hollywood star of the late 1920s and 1930s who wore such styles on and off the screen.

Harlow, Jean See under HARLOW.

Harmonized Tariff Schedule for the U.S. (HTSUS) A government resource that identifies tariff classifications and posts current rates for goods imported into the U.S.; it is the responsibility of the U.S. International Trade Commission. Developed to simplify importing by using the same terminology and classifications for all importing countries rather than having different systems for each.

Harper's Bazaar Women's fashion magazine that started in 1867 as a weekly tabloid-style newspaper containing many fashion engravings. It became a monthly magazine in 1901 and was bought by William Randolph Hearst in 1913. Among its best-known editors were Edna Woolman Chase, Carmel Snow, and Diana Vreeland.

harp seal See under FURS: HAIR SEAL.

Harris Tweed® Trademark of Harris Tweed Association for tweed fabric. Defined by the British Board of Trade and Federal Trade Commission as handwoven woolen fabric from the Hebrides Islands, off the coast of Scotland, consisting of Harris, Lewis, Uist, Barra, and other smaller islands. There are two types: (1) made from handspun yarn, and (2) made from machine-made yarn. Used mainly for women's coats styled in a classic manner.

harvest hat See under HEADWEAR.

hasp See under CLOSURES.

hat See under HEADWEAR.

hat à la William Tell See under HEADWEAR: CUMBERLAND HAT.

hatband Decoration, usually of ribbon, around the base of the crown of a hat. In former years, men wore black hatbands for mourning.

hatbox **1.** Initially a circular-shaped item of luggage with a strap handle and flat bottom that was originally made to carry large hats in the 1920s. Now carried by fashion models or used by stores when selling hats. These boxes may be round, oval, hexagonal, or square in shape. **2.** See under BANDBOX.

hatbox bag See under HANDBAGS AND RELATED ACCESSORIES.

hat cap See under HEADWEAR.

hat mask See under MASKS.

hat pin See under HEADWEAR.

hauberk See under ARMOR.

haunseleyns See under DOUBLET.

hausse-cul See under BUM ROLL.

haut de chausses See under CHAUSSES.

haute couture (oat koo′-toor) **1.** As defined by the CHAMBRE SYNDICALE DE LA COUTURE PARISIENNE, firms that create models that may be sold to private customers or to other segments of the fashion industry who also acquire the right to reproduce the designs. Designers show at least two collections a year of original designs to the public. An **original design** is not the only one of its kind, but means only that the garment was designed and made in the atelier of the designer. **2.** As currently used in the United States and in the fashion press, refers to the latest and most advanced fashions; high fashion.

haut ton See under UNDERGARMENTS: BUSTLE.

havelock See under HEADWEAR.

havelock cap See under HEADWEAR: AUTOMOBILE CAP.

Hawaiian shirt See under SHIRTS.

headband See under HEADWEAR.

head cloth See under HEADWEAR: KERCHIEF.

headdress Synonym for HEADWEAR.

heading See under CLOTHING CONSTRUCTION DETAILS.

head rail See under HEADWEAR: COVERCHIEF.

HEADWEAR

headwear Covering for the head, a *headcovering.* Headwear may be decorative or utilitarian or both. It may also serve as a symbol of status, e.g., a CROWN (see under HEADWEAR). The category of headwear is often divided among different-named types of headwear. The definitions of types of headwear are found under the category of HEADWEAR in the following entries: BONNET, CAP, HAT, HELMET, VEIL. It is often difficult to assign a headcovering to one type, so individually named items each have a separate entry. The components of bonnets, caps, hats, and helmets generally include the **brim,** which is the rim of hat and may be narrow to wide—worn level, turned down, up, or to a variety of angles, and the **crown,** which is the portion that covers the top of the head.

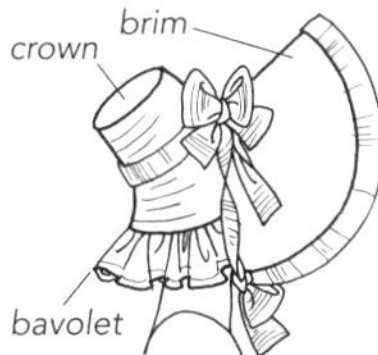

poke-type bonnet

∞**almuce** (al′-mus) A cowl-like hood, frequently of fur or fur lined, introduced in the 13th c., when it was worn by the clergy for church services in inclement weather.

Alpine hat Various types of hats adapted from Bavarian and Austrian Tyrolean hats. **1.** One contemporary version for men is of fur felt, with a slight PILE, a slightly peaked crown with a crease in the center, and an upturned brim in the back. Popular since 1940s as a man's sport hat, it was first introduced in the late 1890s. Also called a *Tyrolean hat.* ∞**2.** Woman's hat with high crown and medium-sized brim worn in 1890s. *Der.* Named for alpine Tyrol region in Austria and Bavaria where this type hat is worn by natives.

Alpine hat #1

American Indian headband Narrow band of leather, fabric, or beadwork placed low on the forehead and tied at side or back, sometimes with feather in back, worn by American Indians and adopted by HIPPIES in the 1960s.

∞**anglesea hat** (angle-see′) Man's hat with flat brim and high, cylindrical-shaped crown, worn about 1830.

∞**angoulême bonnet** (ahn-goo′-lem) Straw bonnet of 1814 made with high pleated crown, broad front brim narrowed at sides, and tied with bow at side. Worn by women in French Empire period, and named for Duchesse d'Angoulême, daughter of Marie Antoinette.

∞**apex** Originally, the spike of olive wood on the peak of a cap worn by a Roman *flamen,* a priest of some particular deity. Later, the entire cap was known by this name.

applejack cap See under HEADWEAR: NEWSBOY CAP.

army cap Caps worn by soldiers of the U.S. Army. See under HEADWEAR: FATIGUE, OVERSEAS, and SERVICE CAPS.

astronaut's cap Cap similar to a BASEBALL CAP (see under HEADWEAR) with elaborately embroidered gold braid on visor, band of gold braid around edge of crown, gold button on top of crown, and adjustable back strap. Copied from caps worn by astronauts and World War II naval commanders, the gold braid is sometimes facetiously called "scrambled eggs." Also called *commander's cap* and *flight deck cap.*

∞**atef** Headdress consisting of tall white cap with two plumes, or feathers, arranged at the sides. Symbolic headdress of certain Egyptian gods, particularly Osiris; also depicted as worn by Egyptian kings.

∞**atours** (a-toor′) Padded, horned headdress worn by women in 14th and 15th c.

∞**attifet** (at-tee′-fet) Woman's headdress of 16th c. arched on either side of forehead to form a "widow's peak" and draped completely with a veil as seen in paintings of Mary Stuart, Queen of Scots. Also see under MARIE STUART BONNET.

attifet 16th c.

∞**attire** Used since the 15th c. for woman's headdress of gold and gems worn on state occasions, later shortened to *tire.*

∞**automobile cap** Cap of waterproof fabric worn by women for automobile riding in early 1900s that consisted of a flat-topped cap with brim rolled down in front and up in back, worn over a tight-fitting hood exposing only the face. Also see under HEADWEAR: HAVELOCK CAP.

∞**automobile veil** Wide, sheer, long veil placed over wide-brimmed hat and tied under chin with ends flowing over front of duster; worn for motoring in early 1900s. Most often made of gauze or chiffon. Also called *motoring veil.*

aviator's helmet **1.** HELMET made of high-impact plastic, sometimes fitted with an oxygen mask, worn by a pilot and crew of planes flying at high altitudes. ∞**2.** World War I helmet fitting the head snugly and fastened under the chin. Made of leather with wool or shearling lining for warmth. Goggles were worn on top. Also called *Red Baron helmet* after a famous World War I ace.

∞**babet bonnet/babet cap** **1.** Small cap for evening worn by women in 1838. Usually made with wide side frills and flattened top, sometimes of tulle. **2.** Woman's morning cap of muslin with ribbon trimming, covering ears and part of cheeks; worn from 1836 to 1840s.

baby bonnet Infant's cap, often made of batiste and lavishly trimmed with lace and ribbons, that is fitted to shape of head and tied under chin.

∞**baby stuart cap** Classic type of infant's close-fitting cap with narrow chin band, illustrated in portrait of Charles II painted by Van Dyck in 1634.

∞**bag bonnet** Woman's bonnet with soft crown fitted loosely over back of head, worn in early 19th c.

∞**bag cap** Man's cloth cap, sometimes made of velvet, shaped like a turban, trimmed with fur or ornamental band; worn in 14th and 15th c.

∞**bagnolette** (ban′-yo-let) Woman's wired hood that stood away from face, covered shoulder; worn in 18th c.

balaclava (bal-ah-kla′-vah) Hood covering the head and shoulders exposing the face, made of knitted wool. Worn by soldiers in 1890s and in World War I and II in cold weather. Now worn by mountain climbers and skiers. *Der.* Named for Crimean War, Battle of Balaklava, fought October 25, 1854.

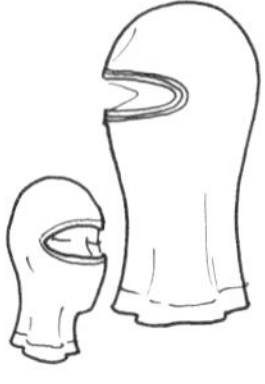
balaclava

Balenciaga fisherman hat A hat introduced by Cristobal Balenciaga in 1967 to accessorize a bride's dress. The slouchy BUCKET HAT (see under HEADWEAR) is characterized by a floppy brim that falls almost over the eyes in front and is longer in the back. It was based on a hat worn by Balenciaga's father, who was a fisherman in Getaria, in the Basque area of Spain.

∞**balloon hat** Woman's hat with wide brim and large puffed-out crown, of gauze over a wire or straw foundation. Fashionable from 1783 to 1785. Inspired by balloon flight of Vincenzo Lunardi. Also called *Lunardi hat* and *parachute hat.*

balmoral cap/bonnet Flat Scottish beret somewhat similar to a TAM-O-SHANTER (see under HEADWEAR: TAM) with wide checked band around head. Usually dark blue with a red or blue pompon on top, with feather and badge of the clan on one side. Worn with *kilts* in Scotland.

bambin/bambino hat (bam-been) Woman's hat with a halo-shaped brim rolling away from the face, worn in the 1930s.

bandeau (band-oh′) Narrow piece of ribbon or fabric, sometimes decorated, worn around head as substitute for a hat.

∞**bandore and peak** Widow's black headdress with heart-shaped brim and black veil, draped in back; worn from 1700 to around 1830.

∞**barbe** Long piece of white linen fabric, pleated vertically, worn encircling the chin with a black hood and long black veil by widows and mourners from 14th to 16th c.

∞**barbette/barbet** (bar-bet′) In the 13th and first half of 14th c., a linen chin band worn pinned on the top or sides of the head, and worn with a small white fillet or COVERCHIEF (see under HEADWEAR). The barbette and coverchief formed the wimple (see under HEADWEAR: WIMPLE #1) in France.

∞**barrette** (ba-ret) 1. Brimless hat with round flat top worn by Jewish men and boys. Clement VII on June 13, 1525, ordered all Jews to wear a yellow barrette. Later revoked, but Pope Paul IV in 1555 ordered all Jews to wear a green barrette. Same style worn by Jewish men for synagogue dress until early 19th c. Also spelled *beret.* 2. See under CLERICAL DRESS: BIRETTA #2.

baseball cap Cap with dome-shaped crown, sometimes made with alternate panels of nylon net for coolness, and an adjustable band or elastic at the back. May have any type of "patch," slogan, or picture on front, e.g, major league football, baseball and Little League team names, makes of cars or trucks, sports insignia, soft-drink brands, cartoon characters, and the like. When first introduced, cap fit more closely to the head like a skullcap. In the 1990s, wearing these caps backward became a fad among the young. Also see under HEADWEAR: BATTER'S CAP.

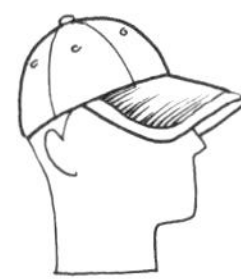
baseball cap

∞**basket** Woman's hat resembling a wicker basket, 1½′ high; worn in second half of 16th c.

basque beret See under HEADWEAR: BERET #1.

bathing cap Tight-fitting cap made of rubber or ELASTOMERS, with or without strap under chin. May be elaborately decorated with rubber flowers, fringe, or other trimmings. Worn to protect hair while swimming.

∞**battant l'oeil** (bah-tan′ loy) Woman's cap, worn in 1770s, with sides projecting forward over temples, eyes, and cheeks in exaggerated fashion.

batter's cap/batter's helmet Duck-bill-visored cap with hard crown for protection worn by baseball players when taking turn at bat.

∞**bavolet** (ba-vo′-lay) A ruffle or piece of cloth extended down from the back of woman's bonnet to shade the neck, worn since 1830.

beach hat Hat used as a sunshade on the beach or at a resort, usually made of bright-colored straw, either natural or synthetic, in a variety of shapes. Frequently has a wide brim, conical crown, and sometimes decorated with felt, sequins, or shells.

beanie See under HEADWEAR: SKULLCAP.

bearskin cap Tall, cylindrical cap of black bearskin with a chain or strap under lower lip or the chin. Worn by some personnel of the British army, also by military guards of Buckingham Palace in London and parliament buildings in Ottawa, Canada. Also see under HEADWEAR: DRUM MAJOR'S HAT.

∞**beaver hat** 1. Hat that was originally made of beaver skins, later with beaver-hair nap felted over wool and rabbit hair base, worn first in 14th c. by men and women. Also see under HEADWEAR: CASTOR. 2. Man's tall hat made of silk in imitation of beaver fur, fashionable in 17th and 18th c. In the 19th c. called *silk hat, opera hat,* and *top hat.*

∞**bebe bonnet** Tiny outdoor bonnet of 1877 trimmed with ribbons, flowers, and tulle and worn with brim turned up showing a cap underneath.

bebop cap See under HEADWEAR: NEWSBOY CAP.

becca See under HEADWEAR: ROUNDLET.

beefeater's hat Distinctive hat worn by Yeomen of the Guard in England, consisting of a narrow brim and soft high crown pleated into headband with crown flaring slightly at the top. Also see under BEEFEATER'S UNIFORM.

∞**beehive hat** 1. Woman's hat with large, bubble-shaped crown and narrow brim trimmed with ribbon tied under chin; worn in 1770s and 1780s. Also called *hive bonnet.* 2. Same style decorated to look like a beehive and fashionable around 1910.

∞**beguin** (bay-gan') Early 16th-c. headdress made from a stiffened rectangle of white linen creased in center over the forehead and draped to form a heart-shaped opening for the face. The back was caught together at nape of neck and remainder was folded symmetrically to form a wide streamer that hung from top of head down the back. *Der.* French, *beguine,* "nun." Also called a *Flemish hood.*

bellboy/bellhop cap Small fabric pillbox, often trimmed with gold braid, sometimes with chin strap, worn by hotel or restaurant bellboys.

∞**benjy** British slang for a straw hat with a wide brim.

beret (beh-ray') 1. General name given to a round, flat hat, usually synonymous with tam (see under HEADWEAR). Some specific types include: **basque beret** (bask beh-ray'), a round, flat, soft woolen cap worn by Basque peasants who inhabit the western Pyrenees region of France and Spain; **pancake beret,** a flat molded felt tam. Worn tilted to one side of the head and associated with the dress of an artist. Also called a *French beret*; **bubble beret,** a large bouffant beret, usually without a brim, worn tilted to side of head in the early 1960s. ∞2. A headcovering with a large flat halo crown with elaborate trim, worn from the 1820s to the 1840s.

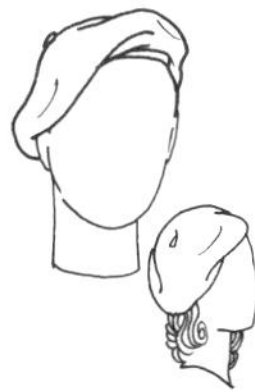
french or pancake beret

bergère hat (ber-zher') Woman's straw hat with low crown and a wide floppy-type brim, sometimes tied under chin. Worn from 1730 to 1800, revived in 1860s and currently used to describe similar hats. Worn by Marie Antoinette (1755–1793), wife of Louis XVI of France, when she played at farming on the grounds of the palace at Versailles. Also called *milkmaid hat* or *shepherdess hat. Der.* French, "shepherdess."

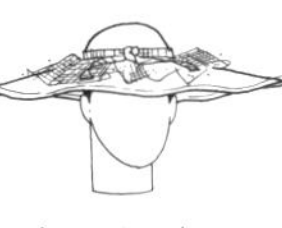
bergère hat

berretino See under HEADWEAR: ROUNDLET #1.

bewdley cap See under HEADWEAR: MONMOUTH CAP.

∞**bibi bonnet** (bee-bee bun-neh) Small woman's bonnet worn in 1830s with sides flaring upward and forward around the face and tied with lace-trimmed ribbons. Also called *English cottage bonnet.*

∞**bicorne/bicorn** (by'-korn) Man's hat of the Napoleonic era in shape of a crescent, with front and back brims pressed against each other, making points on either side. Frequently trimmed with a COCKADE. *Der.* Latin, *bicornis,* "two-horned."

bicorne

bicycle-clip hat Tiny half-hat fastened over crown and side of head by piece of springy metal. Often used for a child's hat of fur. *Der.* From metal clip worn around leg when riding a bicycle to keep trousers from catching in chain or wheel spokes.

bicycle helmet Helmet not covering the ears, with dark adjustable visor and air inlets for ventilating and cooling, held on by a strap under the chin. Shell is high-impact PVC plastic lined with polystyrene, and foam-lined for comfort.

∞**biggin/biggonet/biggon** (big-in/big-on-net) 1. 16th- and 17th-c. term for woman's or child's cap similar to COIF (see under HEADWEAR). 2. Man's nightcap, worn from second half of 16th through 17th c. 3. Large MOB CAP (see under HEADWEAR). Made without chin ties, worn in early 19th c. *Der.* French, *beguine,* "nun."

bill See under HEADWEAR: VISOR.

∞**billiment/billment** (bee-leh-mahn') 1. Decorative jeweled border on French hoods, sometimes made by goldsmiths in the 16th c. 2. Head ornament worn by brides in 16th c. Also called *habillement (habiliment), abillements,* or *borders.*

∞**billycock/billicock** A 19th-c. colloquialism for man's soft, wide, curved-brimmed hat with low crown. *Der.* From either bully-cocked hat of 18th c., or hat first worn by Mr. William (Billy) Coke for shooting parties at Holkham, England.

bird cage Dome of stiff, wide-mesh veiling pinned to crown of head covering face and ears. Worn in place of hat, especially in late 1950s.

biretta (bih-ret'-ah) (*birretta, berrette*) 1. See under CLERICAL DRESS. 2. 16th-c. round cap that later became square on top when hatters learned to use a rigid frame. Worn by clergy today. Also called *barrette.*

birlet See under HEADWEAR: BOURRELET.

bluebonnet Small-sized Scotch TAM (see under HEADWEAR), of blue wool with narrow TARTAN (see under PLAIDS AND TARTANS) band fitting around head, with black streamers in back and colored pompon on top. Originally made in leather for protection when fighting. Also called *bonaid. Der.* Scottish, "bonnet."

boater 1. Man's flat-topped, flat-brimmed straw hat with an oval crown, worn from 1880s to 1930s. Introduced about 1865 for children, later adopted by women. The **henley boater,** popular since 1894, was a blue or gray felt hat of similar shape, named for Henley-on-Thames, England, site of boat races. Used for summer wear until about 1930. Also called *canotier.* 2. Style copied in plastic for wear at political conventions.

boater #1

bobby's hat Hat with domed high crown and narrow turned-down brim worn by English policemen. *Der.* From slang British term "bobbies," meaning policemen.

∞**bolero toque** (bow-ler'-oh toke) Woman's small draped hat of fabric or fur, with black trimming extending up over the crown, worn in 1887.

∞**bollinger** Man's hat, worn from 1858 to late 1860s, having bowl-shaped crown with knob in center and narrow circular brim. First worn by British cab drivers, later adopted by gentlemen for country wear. Also called *hemispherical hat.*

bonaid See under HEADWEAR: BLUEBONNET.

∞**bongrace** (bohn-gras') 1. Stiffened oblong woman's headcovering with drapery in back; worn in 16th and early 17th c. over a coif. 2. Pendant flap in back of French hood, which was brought up over crown and fastened so as to project forward over forehead. Also called *burn grace.*

bongrace #1

bonnet 1. Sometimes generic for headcovering; however, is more specifically applied to headwear for women, children, and infants that fits over the back and top of head and ties with strings under the chin. Bonnets were first worn in the Middle Ages. Women's bonnets of the 18th and 19th c. usually had a crown and a brim and were primarily an outdoor garment. Bonnet-style headcoverings predominated until about 1870, after which they were less fashionable. Rarely worn since 1920s except by babies and young girls. 2. See under HEADWEAR: BLUEBONNET.

bonnet #1 with bavolet c. 1850

∞**bonnet à bec** (bon-neh' ah beck) Woman's early 18th-c. bonnet that covered top of head and had a peak over the forehead. Lower edge touching the hair was called the *papillon.* Also called *bonnet en papillon* (bon-neh' on pah-pee'-yon).

bonnet babet See under HEADWEAR: BABET BONNET.

bonnet en papillon See under HEADWEAR: BONNET À BEC.

∞**bonnet rouge** (bon-neh' rooje) Red wool peaked-top cap, symbol of liberty, worn by patriots in French Revolution of late 18th c. *Der.* French, "red bonnet." Also called *liberty cap.*

∞**bosses** Decorative snoods of gold or linen covering thick coils of braided hair arranged at each side of face with a coverchief, or veil, over entire headdress. Worn from late 13th to end of 14th c. **Templers** were a 15th c. style of ornamental bosses that conceal the hair. Sometimes connected by band above forehead, sometimes part of headdress. Also spelled *templettes, temples.*

∞**boudoir cap** (boo'-dwar) Soft, lace-trimmed cap with gathered crown and ruffled edge worn over woman's hair in bedroom in 19th and early 20th c.

∞**Bourbon hat** (boor'-bon) Blue satin hat decorated with pearls in a fleur-de-lis pattern. Popular in 1815 to celebrate Napoleon's defeat at Waterloo and the return of King Louis XVIII, a member of the Bourbon royal family, to the throne.

∞**bourrelet** (boor'-lay) (*birlet, burlet*) Padded sausage-shaped roll worn by men and women for headdress, or as base of headdress during 15th c.

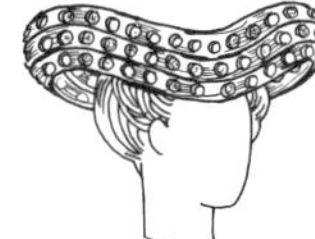
bourrelet 15th c.

bowler See under HEADWEAR: DERBY.

breton (breh'-ton) Woman's off-the-face hat made with medium-sized, rolled-back brim worn on back of head. Copied from hats worn by peasants of Brittany, France.

breton

bridal veil Traditionally, a length of white net, lace, tulle, or silk illusion reaching to waist, hips, ankles, or floor in back. Chest length in front and worn over face during wedding—turned back after ceremony.

brim See under introduction to HEADWEAR.

∞**broadbrim** Wide-brimmed, low-crowned hat worn by members of the Society of Friends, called Quakers. "Broadbrim" therefore became a nickname for Quakers.

brow band Ribbon, fabric, beaded band, or braid of hair around head worn low on forehead.

bubble beret See under HEADWEAR: BERET #3.

bubble hat Puffed-out felt or straw hat, usually stiff rather than soft, made with tiny brim in early 1960s. Worn perched on top of head over bouffant hairstyles. Also called a *dome hat.*

bucket hat Casual hat made of fabric that has moderate-sized, sloping brim that may be stitched in concentric circles and is attached to flat-topped, slightly cone-shaped crown.

bully-cocked See under HEADWEAR: COCKED HAT.

∞**bumper** 1. Cap worn in the Netherlands by children, fitted at back of head, with wide thick roll of yarn around the face for protection. Also see child's PUDDING under HEADWEAR. 2. Hat with a BUMPER BRIM (see under HEADWEAR).

bumper brim Thick rolled-back brim, surrounding various styles of crowns. Used in various widths on different styles of hats.

burlet See under HEADWEAR: BOURRELET.

∞**burnet/burnette** 17th-c. hood or headdress.

burngrace See under HEADWEAR: BONGRACE.

busby Tall cylindrical black fur or feathered military hat with cockade at top of center front. A bag-shaped drapery hangs from crown and is draped to the back. Worn by Hussars and certain guardsmen in the British army.

bush hat Large-brimmed Australian-type hat worn turned up on one side. Worn in Australia and in Africa for safaris, also worn as part of uniform by Australian soldiers in World War II. Also called *caddie* or *caddy*.

bush hat

bustle back Puffs of ribbon or bows at back of hat, popular in 1930s.

∞**butterfly cap** Woman's small lace cap wired in shape of a butterfly, worn perched above forehead with lappets, jewels, and flower trimmings frequently added for court wear. Worn in 1750s and 1760s. Also called *fly cap.*

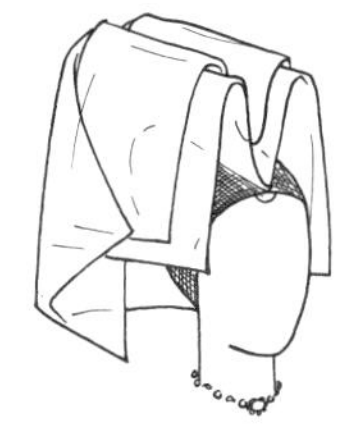
butterfly headdress

∞**butterfly headdress** 16th-c. term for a 15th-c. towering headdress made of sheer gauze pieces, wired to stand out like wings, and supported by a fez-shaped cap. Worn after this period by an order of nuns in Normandy, France.

∞**bycocket/bycoket** 1. High-crowned hat with a wide brim peaked in front, and turned up in back worn by men in the Middle Ages. 2. Similar hat called a *student bycocket* worn by Italian students in mid-20th c.

cabas (kah-bas') Version of PHRYGIAN CAP (see under HEADWEAR), made of beaver or velour, draped across forehead to conceal hair and ornamented in back. Created by New York milliner Sally Victor in 1956.

∞**cabriole headdress** (kab'-ree-oll) Rare fashion of about 1755, lasting only a few years, consisting of a miniature coach-and-six, or post chaise, worn by women on head instead of a cap. Coach was made of gold thread with six dappled-gray horses made of blown glass. Also spelled *caprioll. Der.* French, "two-wheeled carriage."

∞**cabriolet bonnet** (kab-ree-o-leh') Large bonnet, popular from the late 18th to mid-19th c., made with brim extending forward, framing the face like a carriage top, but cut away in back to show hair. *Der.* French, "two-wheeled carriage."

∞**cache-peigne** (cash payn) Snood of net and ribbon worn by women to hold hair back, in the 1850s and 1860s. *Der.* French, "hide-comb."

caddie/caddy See under HEADWEAR: BUSH HAT.

cadogan net See under HEADWEAR: SNOOD.

∞**cake hat** Man's soft felt hat of 1890s with a low oval crown creased in manner similar to ALPINE HAT (see under HEADWEAR).

∞**calash/calèche** (ka-lash') Large hood worn from 1720 to 1790 and revived 1820 to 1839, made with hinged arches of whalebone or cane covered with fabric in manner similar to folding top of convertible car. Stands away from head, protecting bouffant hairstyles. *Der.* After hood of "French carriage" called *calèche.*

calash

calotte (ca-lot') 1. A SKULLCAP (see under HEADWEAR) frequently made of leather or suede with a small matching projection like a stem on center top. 2. See under CLERICAL DRESS. 3. Woman's small skullcap worn in 1940s and 1950s, sometimes with large jeweled pin. 4. A cap worn by schoolboy, called a *beanie* (see HEADWEAR: SKULLCAP).

∞**camargo hat** (kam-are'-go) Small woman's evening hat with brim raised in front; worn in mid-1830s. *Der.* After Marie Ann de Cupis Camargo (1710–1770), celebrated dancer.

∞**camelaurion** (kamel-loh'-ree-yon) Coronet with closed crown, worn by Roman Caesars and by Byzantine emperors.

campaign hat Broad-brimmed field hat with high crown first worn by Union soldiers in Civil War and later issued to entire U.S. Army. Worn by soldiers in World War II with four dents in top of crown. Same as MOUNTIE'S HAT (see under HEADWEAR).

canotier See under HEADWEAR: BOATER.

cap Headcovering that fits more snugly to the head than a hat, frequently made with a visor-type front. Usually made of felt, leather, or fabric and worn for sports or informal occasions. In the 16th c., caps were worn by servants and apprentices; in the 19th c., gentlemen began to wear caps in the country or for sports, but not in town. From 15th to 19th c., ladies wore caps indoors. After the mid-19th c., indoor caps were worn only by female servants and the elderly. See under HEADWEAR: DAY CAP. *Der.* Latin, *cappa,* "a hooded cloak."

cap

cape hat Woman's half-hat made by attaching felt or fabric capelet to a springy metal clip that crosses the head from ear to ear, letting capelet fall over back of head.

capeline (cap-leen′) ∞1. See under ARMOR. ∞2. Second half of 18th c., woman's feather-trimmed wide-brimmed hat. ∞3. Hood with attached cape worn in 1863 by women in rural areas. 4. Wide, floppy-brimmed hat with small round crown worn since 1920s.

cap of maintenance Cap carried on a cushion before British sovereigns in coronation processions; sometimes used for mayors. Usually made of scarlet velvet with ermine trim and symbolizing high rank. Also called *cap of dignity* and *cap of estate.*

∞**capote** (kah-poat′) Popular bonnet of 1830s with stiff brim framing the face, soft gathered crown, and ribbon bows tied at side or under chin. By 1890, worn mostly by older women.

∞**capot-ribot** (ka-poh′ ree′-bow) Black velvet hat with long "curtain" (or veil), hanging below shoulders at sides and back. Popular in France after Napoleonic campaign in 1798.

∞**capuche** (cap-poosh′) 1. Sharp-pointed, pyramid-shaped hood worn by an order of monks, the Capuchins. 2. See under HEADWEAR: CAPUCHIN. 3. Woman's hood attached to cloak worn in 17th c. 4. Woman's silk-lined sunbonnet of mid-19th c.

∞**capuchin** (kap′-yoo-shen) (*capuchon, capucine, capuche*) 1. Hood worn outdoors in 16th, 17th, and 18th c. 2. Hood and shoulder cape or long cloak, sometimes lined in colored or striped silk, called a *redingote* (red′-in-gote), worn by women in 18th c. for traveling. *Der.* From *capuche,* "cowl worn by Capuchin monks of Franciscan order."

∞**capuchon** (ka-poo-shon′) 1. See under HEADWEAR: CAPUCHIN. 2. Tiny bonnet made of flowers. Worn in 1877.

capulet (cap-yew-let′) Small hat conforming to shape of head and placed back from brow, sometimes with cuffed brim in front. *Der.* For cap worn by Juliet Capulet, heroine of Shakespeare's play *Romeo and Juliet.*

∞**caravan** Small type of collapsible bonnet of 1765 similar to the CALASH (see under HEADWEAR). Made of semi-circular hoops that, when opened, drop a veil of white gauze over the face.

carnaby cap See under HEADWEAR: NEWSBOY CAP.

∞**Caroline hat** Man's hat made of Caroline beaver, imported from Carolinas in the British colonies, worn in England from 1680s to mid-18th c.

cartwheel hat Woman's hat with extra-wide stiff brim and low crown frequently made of straw.

cartwheel hat

casque (cask) Hat shaped like a helmet. *Der.* French, "helmet."

∞**casquette** (kass-ket′) 1. Cap with visor, similar to military officers' caps, adapted for women's headwear. 2. Woman's straw cap worn in 1863 and 1864 similar to a GLENGARRY (see under HEADWEAR) with additional short brim in front and in back. Trimmed with black velvet ribbon and ostrich feathers.

∞**castor** Hat made entirely of beaver fur, popular in 17th and 19th c. If rabbit fur was added, it was called a **demi-castor.** The 17th-c. trade term for a man's castor hat in the 17th century was **codovec.**

∞**cater cap** (kay-ter) Used in 16th and 17th c. to describe a square cap worn at universities, now called *mortar-board.* See under ACADEMIC COSTUME.

∞**caudebec** (kawd′-ee-bek) An imitation beaver hat made of felt worn from end of 17th throughout 18th c. Also called *cawdebink* or *cordybeck hat.*

∞**caul** (kol) 1. Mesh cap that encloses the hair and is often the work of a goldsmith. Frequently called a *fret* in medieval times. Also see under HEADWEAR: BOSSES and CRISPINE. Usually worn by unmarried girls and by women of high status during the medieval period. 2. See under WIGS AND HAIRPIECES. 3. In 18th and 19th c. used to describe soft crown of bonnet or cap.

caul #1

cavalier hat 1. A wide-brimmed velvet hat trimmed with ostrich plumes. 2. Brimmed hat with one side turned up worn by Theodore Roosevelt and his Rough Riders in Spanish-American War.

∞**ceryphalos** (ser-rif-ah′-los) Wide headband or fillet worn by women in ancient Greece.

chaffers See under HEADWEAR: ENGLISH HOOD.

chain hat Decorative close-fitting cap made with lengths of chain—some linked together, others dangling. Decorative item of body jewelry introduced in the late 1960s.

chapeau (cha-po′) (French) Hat or cap.

chapeau à la charlotte See under HEADWEAR: CHARLOTTE.

∞**chapeau bras** (sha-po′ bra) 1. Man's flat, three-cornered hat, evenly COCKED (see under HEADWEAR) or crescent-shaped, made expressly to be carried under arm; from 1760s to 1830s in France, England, and United States. By 1830, generally called *broken hat.* Also see under HEADWEAR: OPERA HAT. 2. Woman's crush bonnet, or CALASH (see under HEADWEAR), that folded small enough to be carried in handbag or under the arm. Worn to concerts and opera in early 19th c. England. *Der.* French, "arm-hat."

chapeau claque (sha-po′ klack) See under HEADWEAR: OPERA HAT.

∞**chapeau cloche** Small-crowned hat with wide, drooping brim worn by women in 1860s to protect face from the sun.

chapel cap Small round cap that fits on the back of the head, sometimes lace-trimmed, matched to choir robes, and worn by women of choir for church services.

chapel veil Small circle of lace or tulle, frequently edged with a ruffle, worn by women over top of head while inside a church. Also called *chapel cap.*

∞**chaperon** (shap′-er-ohn) **1.** Used as general designation for a hood during the Middle Ages. Worn largely by men, but also occasionally by working-class women. **2.** Anglo-French term for a fitted hood cut in one piece with a shoulder cape (called a *gole, collet, gorget,* or *guleron*), which was worn from the late 12th c. until the mid-15th c. The hood had a long pendant tail called a **liripipe** (lir′-ee-peep) in 14th c. **3.** Draped version of the chaperon popular in the 15th c. in which the cape was rolled and tied with the extended tail of the hood to form a turbanlike headress. **4.** Woman's soft hood in the 17th c. Also spelled *chaperone, chaperonne.* Also called *cappuccio.*

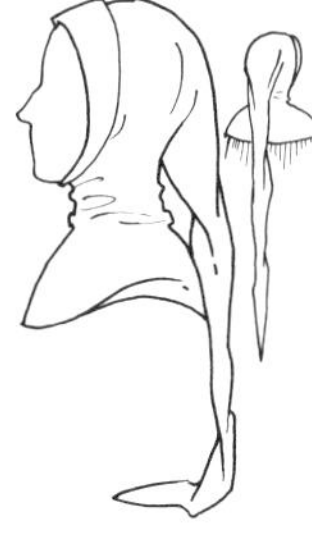

chaperon #2 with liripipe

∞**chaplet** **1.** Originally a garland of flowers for the head worn by Anglo-Saxon men and women on festive occasions. **2.** In 15th c. such a garland was worn only by a bride. **3.** Circlet, or metal band set with gems, worn by both men and women in 14th, 15th, and 16th c. Also called a *coronal of goldsmithry.* **4.** In late 14th and 15th c., a headband of twisted silk or satin wound around a padded roll. **5.** A short rosary or set of beads worn on the neck in the 17th c.

∞**charlotte** Very large-brimmed hat with lace ruffle at edge, worn drooping over forehead, sometimes worn over a lacy cap. Crown richly decorated with wide loops and bows of ribbon. Worn in mid-1780s. *Der.* Named for Queen Charlotte of England (1744–1818), married to George III of England. Style later returned to popularity somewhat modified in late 19th c. and early 20th c. Both styles also called *chapeau à la charlotte.*

∞**charlotte corday cap** Indoor cap worn during the day in 1870s, made with puffed muslin crown gathered into a band, sometimes had a ruffle around edge, sometimes with lappets. *Der.* Named for Charlotte Corday, who assassinated Marat, a leader of the French Revolution.

chechia Adaptation for women in the late 1930s and early 1940s of a felt hat with a tassel—similar to a fez but more peaked in shape—that was worn by Algerian and Moroccan children.

cheek wrappers See under HEADWEAR: DORMEUSE.

chef's hat Tall, white, full-crowned fabric hat starched to stand up stiffly. Set into the headband with one hundred pleats, which originally indicated that the chef could cook eggs one hundred ways. Also called *hundred pleater.* The more important the chef—the taller the hat.

chignon cap Small cap made in a variety of colors and fabrics worn over the chignon in the 1930s and 1940s. Popular again in the 1960s and 1970s—usually made of crocheted wool—and called a *bun-warmer* or *bun snood.*

chignon strap Band of ribbon fastened to woman's hat that passes around back of head and under the chignon to hold hat firmly. Worn in the 1860s and 1870s, again in the 1940s and 1950s.

chimney-pot hat See under HEADWEAR: TOP HAT.

∞**chin stays** Ruffles of tulle or lace added to bonnet strings forming a frill when tied under chin in the 1830s. Synonym: *mentonnieres* (men-ton-yehr′).

∞**chip bonnet** Coarse, inexpensive straw bonnet made of strips or shavings of wood, or woody material, imported from Italy and used for millinery in the 19th c.

chou (shoo) (pl. *choux*) Soft, crushed-crown hat similar to MOBCAP (see under HEADWEAR). *Der.* From the French, "cabbage."

chukka hat (chuh′-ka) Domed hat with small brim copied from hats worn by polo players. Similar to, but not as high as, English policeman's hat. *Der.* Named for divisions of polo game called chukkars.

circumfolding hat See under HEADWEAR: OPERA HAT.

claque See under HEADWEAR: OPERA HAT.

∞**clara bow hat** Trademark for various styles of felt hats for women in late 1920s. The beret and cloche styles were the most popular. *Der.* Named after Clara Bow, famous movie star of the 1920s.

∞**clarissa harlowe bonnet/hat** Pictured in 1857 as a wide-brimmed, lace-trimmed hat with drooping sides and a small rounded crown with large ostrich plume placed so it curved from the crown over the back brim of hat. In 1879, described as a bonnet made of leghorn straw (see HEADWEAR: LEGHORN HAT) with a large brim lined with velvet, worn tilted on the forehead; popular until 1890s. *Der.* From heroine in novel *Clarissa, or the History of a Young Lady,* by Samuel Richardson, published in 1747–48.

clip hat See under HEADWEAR: BICYCLE-CLIP HAT.

cloche (klohsh) Deep-crowned hat with very narrow brim or brimless, fitting to the head closely, almost concealing all of the hair. Worn pulled down almost to eyebrows, fashionable in 1920s and again in 1960s. *Der.* French, "bell."

cloche

∞**coal-scuttle bonnet** Bonnet of mid-19th c. with a large, stiff brim with peak in center front. *Der.* Shaped like the scoop called a *scuttle* that was used to pick up coal and put it into the fire.

∞**cocked hat** **1.** Man's hat with wide brim worn from late 17th to early 19th c.. To avoid weather sag and deterioration, it became the fashion to turn up brim, which was sometimes fastened with buttons and loops to crown—first one side, then two sides, and eventually three sides forming a tricorne. Many variations developed, each involving individual details. Various styles include: (1) **bully-cock,** an 18th-c., broad-brimmed, three-cornered cocked hat; (2) **continental hat,** a three-cornered hat with a wide, upturned brim worn with the point placed at center front. Worn by the Continental Army during the American Revolution. Rank of officers was denoted by various colors of cockades worn on the left side of the hat; (3) **denmark cock,** a man's three-cornered hat of the second half of the 18th c. with three sides of the hat turned up, the back higher than the front; (4) **dettigen cock,** a man's cocked hat of the 18th c. with the brim turned up equally in three sections; (5) **kevenhuller cock,** man's three-cornered hat worn from 1740s to the 1760s, cocked with the front forming a peak and turned up higher in back. (6) **monmouth cock,** a broad-brimmed hat of the second half of the 17th c. turned up or cocked in back. Also see under HEADWEAR: TRICORNE. **2.** Contemporary hat inspired by any of the historic versions of a cocked hat.

cocked hat

∞**cockle hat** Hat trimmed with a scallop shell, worn by pilgrims returning from the Holy Land during the Crusades in the 11th to 13th c. *Der.* French, *coquille,* "shell."

∞**coffer headdress** Woman's small, box-shaped headdress of 14th c. usually worn over top of hair with coiled braids over the ears.

coif (kwaf) (*quoif*) **1.** White headdress worn by nuns of some orders under the veil. ∞**2.** From 12th to 15th c., linen head-covering similar to a baby's bonnet, tied under chin. Art of the period shows it to have been worn by individuals from many levels of society and by soldiers and knights under metal helmets. By the 16th c. it was more likely to be worn by the aged and the learned professions. Coif may be a modern term applied to this headwear. ∞**3.** From 16th to 19th c., an undercap worn mainly by women. In the late 16th c. and early 17th c. the cap was sometimes embroidered, with sides curved forward to cover the ears. These were called *cheeks-and-ears.* Similar caps were called *orrelets,* or *round-eared caps.* **4.** Also see under HEADWEAR: BIGGIN.

coif #2
13th c.

commander's cap See under HEADWEAR: ASTRONAUT'S CAP.

commode ∞**1.** A silk-covered wire frame of the late 17th and early 18th c. that was used to support the high FONTANGES headdress (see under HEADWEAR). Also called *mont la haut* (mont lah hoh) and *palisade.* **2.** English name for the fontages headdress.

∞**commodore cap** Flat-topped cap with a visor, fashionable for women for boating and sports, including bicycling, in 1890s. Similar to a YACHTING CAP (see under HEADWEAR).

communion veil A sheer net, elbow-length veil worn by girls for first Communion in the Catholic Church.

conductor's cap Cap with crown shaped like a pillbox with visor-shaped brim, frequently trimmed with braid around the crown and an insignia in front. Worn placed straight on forehead by train conductors.

conical Asian hat **1.** Chinese hat made of straw that may take many forms—mushroom-shaped with knob at top, bowl-shaped, conical flared shape, and a flared shape with a peak in the center. All are made of bamboo, palm leaves, or straw, and stand away from the head, forming almost a parasol against the sun. **2.** Copies of the above styles made in felt and straw for general wear. Was once referred to by the now derogatory term *coolie hat* (*der.* Chinese "kuli," an unskilled worker). Also known as a *sedge hat, rice hat,* or *paddy hat.*

continental hat See under HEADWEAR: COCKED HAT.

conversation bonnet See under HEADWEAR: POKE BONNET.

∞**copotain** (ko-poh-tan') Man's or woman's hat with a high conical crown rounded at top and medium-sized brim usually turned up at the sides and back. Made of beaver, fur, or leather trimmed with wide band. First mentioned in 1508, but very fashionable from 1560 to 1620. Revived in 1640s to 1665; then called the **sugarloaf hat** due to its resemblance to a loaf of sugar. Also called *pantile.* Also spelled *copatain, copintank, coppintanke, copytank, coptank.*

copotain or sugarloaf hat

cornet (*cornette*) **1.** See under HEADWEAR: HENNIN. ∞**2.** Dark-colored velvet cap similar to a BONGRACE (see under HEADWEAR) worn from 17th to 19th c. ∞**3.** Day cap with rounded caul; tied under the chin, in first half of 19th c. (see under HEADWEAR: CAUL #1). **4.** Synonym for MORTARBOARD (see under ACADEMIC DRESS).

coronet (kor'-o-net) **1.** Crown that denotes rank below that of sovereign. Nobility of Great Britain have seven different styles of crowns—for prince of the blood, younger son, nephew, duke, marquis, earl, viscount, and baron. **2.** Band or wreath worn by women on the head like a TIARA (see under HEADWEAR). ∞**3.** Open crown worn by nobility in 14th c. Also spelled *coronal.*

cossack forage cap Visored cap with soft crown set on band worn toward back of head rather than pulled down on forehead. Made in napped suede fabric in natural, black, or loden green. Adapted from caps worn by Russian Cossacks and accepted for general wear by men and women in the late 1960s. Also see under FORAGE CAP.

cossack hat Tall brimless hat of fur worn by Russian horsemen and cavalrymen. Copied for man's winter hat in the United States and England in 1950s and 1960s.

∞**cottage bonnet** Straw bonnet fitting head closely with brim projecting beyond the cheeks, worn from 1808 to 1870s. Early styles were worn over a cap. Later styles had upturned pleated brim with satin lining.

∞**couel** British turban headdress of 15th c. in red for commoners, and black for nobility.

∞**counter fillet** Late 14th and early 15th c., the fillet or band securing a woman's veil.

Courrèges hat (Koor'-rej) Fashion helmet shaped similar to World War I aviator's helmet. Introduced in 1964 by French couturier André Courrèges as a result of universal interest in astronauts.

∞**coverchief/couverchief/couverchef** Norman term meaning **head rail,** a draped Saxon headcovering made of different fabrics and colors worn by women of all classes from medieval times to the 16th c.

cowboy hat Large, wide-brimmed felt hat with crown worn creased or standing up in cone shape with the brim rolled up on both sides and dipping in front. Sometimes with hatband of leather and silver. Worn in the United States by Western cowboys to shade face and neck. Also called **ten-gallon hat** when extra tall and uncreased. Also see under HEADWEAR: SOMBRERO and STETSON®.

cowboy hat: ten-gallon type

∞**coxcomb/cockscomb** Hood trimmed with strip of notched red cloth at the apex worn by licensed court jesters in 16th and 17th c.

∞**crants** (*craunce, graundice*) Garland of flowers or chaplet made of gold and gems worn by women from medieval times to 18th c.

∞**crisp** A woman's VEIL (see under HEADWEAR) in the 16th c.

∞**crispine** (kris'-pihn) An extra band at the forehead used during the late 14th c. to keep the elaborate net (see under HEADWEAR: CAUL or FRET) in place. A veil draped over the crispine and caul was referred to as a **crispinette** (kris'-pin-ett).

crispinette See under HEADWEAR: CRISPINE.

crocheted cap (kro-shade') Any type cap that is hand-crocheted. Styles vary—some are helmet-shaped—others made like TAMS (see under HEADWEAR). Some styles are trimmed with metal or plastic PAILLETTES attached at intervals.

crosscloth ∞1. Triangular KERCHIEF of 16th and 17th c. worn by women with a COIF or CAUL (see under HEADWEAR) tied under chin or at back of head. Frequently embroidered to match the coif. **2.** A brow band worn in bed to prevent illness, or as a beauty aid to remove wrinkles. Worn by men and women from 16th to 18th c. Also called *forehead cloth.* Also see under FRONTLET.

crown **1.** See under introduction to HEADWEAR. **2.** Circlet of precious metal and gems worn by kings and queens. **3.** Bridal headpiece worn with veil. **4.** A garland or wreath worn on the head as an ornament or sign of honor.

crown hats Hats of African inspiration that are round, flat-topped, and sometimes have leather medallions with maps of Africa in the colors of African and West Indian countries. Worn by African Americans in late 1980s and 1990s.

crusader hood Snug-fitting hood cut in one piece with a small shoulder cape. Originally made of chain mail, and later copied in knits for winter sportswear.

crusher hat Comfortable man's snap-brim felt hat that can be made into a compact roll to fit in pocket or pack for travel. Introduced about 1900 and popular in the 1920s and again in the 1980s and after.

∞**cumberland hat** Man's hat with 8″-high tapered crown and small brim turned up at the sides, worn in 1830s. Also called *hat à la William Tell.*

∞**curch** (*kerche*) Untrimmed, close-fitting woman's cap worn in Colonial America.

∞**cushion headdress** Large padded roll worn as headdress by women in first half of the 15th c.

dandy hat Woman's high-crowned, roll-brimmed hat decorated with jet embroidery, feathers, and a veil. Introduced by New York milliner, Sally Victor, in mid-1950s.

davy crockett cap Coonskin (raccoon fur) cap with tail of animal hanging down back. Worn in Colonial America by woodsmen and pioneers and named after David Crockett, frontiersman and politician, who fought and died at the Alamo, in Texas, in 1836. Popular for young boys in 1950s and 1960s after wide exposure on television programs, at which time the term was copyrighted. Trademark now applies to a wide variety of apparel and other products.

∞**day cap** Muslin cap worn by adult women indoors and sometimes under bonnets outdoors in the 18th and 19th c. By the second half of the 19th c., only elderly women continued to wear these caps.

day cap, first half of 19th c.

deerstalker Checked or tweed cap with visor on both front and back and ear flaps that can be buttoned or tied to top of crown, worn from 1860s on. Associated with pictures of Sherlock Holmes, the fictional detective created by Sir Arthur Conan Doyle. *Der.* Originally worn in England for hunting, including "stalking deer." Also called *fore-and-after.*

deerstalker

demi-castor See under HEADWEAR: CASTOR.

demi-coronal See under HEADWEAR: TIARA.

denmark cock See under HEADWEAR: COCKED HAT.

derby American name for a hat, called a **bowler** in England; it was first worn about 1860, made of hard felt with a domed crown and narrow, stiff brim rolled up on the sides. Usually black, but brown and fawn colors were worn with NORFOLK JACKET (see under COATS AND JACKETS). *Der.* The British version was named for the hatter William Bowler, about 1850 to 1860, although shape dates from 1820s. The American version was named for Earl of Derby and an English horse race called the Derby; pronounced *darby* in England.

derby or bowler

desert fatigue cap Visor cap of cotton poplin made with soft crown set on wide band, worn with top crushed down at sides. Copied from German forage cap worn in World War II and accepted for general wear in late 1960s.

diadem (dy'-ah-dem) **1.** A crown. **2.** Decorative headdress resembling a crown.

∞**diadem cap** (dy'-ah-dem) Bathing cap of 1870s, usually of oiled silk, shaped like a shower cap with a band and upstanding ruffle in front and ties under the chin.

∞**diadem fanchon bonnet** (dy'-ah-dem fan'-shon) Lace and velvet bonnet of late 1860s with brim forming a halo. Made with two sets of bonnet strings—one tied under CHIGNON (see under HAIRSTYLES) in back, the other trimmed with RUCHING—loosely tied under the chin.

diamanté headband (dya-mahn-tay') Band of fabric set with artificial sparking jewels (e.g., rhinestones) and worn around head, low on forehead during Edwardian period (1890–1910) and in late 1920s.

∞**diana vernon hat/diana vernon bonnet** Wide-brimmed, shallow-crowned straw bonnet of the late 1870s with one side of the brim turned up and trimmed with a rosette. Wide streamers came from underside of brim to tie under the chin. *Der.* Named for the heroine of *Rob Roy,* 1817 English novel by Sir Walter Scott.

dink/dinky See under HEADWEAR: SKULLCAP.

∞**directoire bonnet** (dir-eck'-twa) Bonnet tied under the chin, fitting close over the ears, with a high, flaring front brim. Worn in late 1870s through early 1880s. Inspired by hats worn during the French DIRECTOIRE PERIOD (1795–1799), but not known by this name at that time.

∞**dolley madison hood** Lace-trimmed opera hood resembling a DUST CAP (see under HEADWEAR) with a deep ruffle of lace falling around the face and neck. Worn toward back of head and secured under chin with broad ribbon ties. Popular at end of 19th c. Also spelled *Dolly. Der.* Named after Dolley Madison, wife of James Madison, president of the United States from 1809 to 1817.

doll hat Miniature hat worn in different ways at different time periods. In the late 1930s, pushed forward on the head and held on with an elastic band around back of head. Popular after being worn by Jacqueline Kennedy when she was First Lady in early 1960s, when it was attached to the back of head with combs or pins and sometimes had a veil. Reintroduced in 1984 to perch on the front of the head in various shapes—square, round, etc.

dome hat See under HEADWEAR: BUBBLE HAT.

doo rag Headcovering with the appearance of a head scarf tied in the back with long, hanging tail. Usually made from brightly colored fabrics or leather.

∞**dorelet** (dor-reh'-lay) (*dorlet*) Woman's hair net ornamented with jewels, so called in the Middle Ages.

dormeuse/dormouse (dor-muse') Ribbon-trimmed white cap with a puffed crown and falling lappets (see under HEADWEAR) trimmed with lace, called *wings,* popularly known as *cheek wrappers.* Worn in the house by women in second half of 18th c. Also called a *french nightcap.*

dressmaker's brim Hat brim, usually on a fabric hat, that has closely spaced rows of machine stitching or stitched tucks around the brim.

drum major's hat Very tall hat with chin band, frequently made of fur in black or white, worn by the leader of a band or drum major for parade functions. Similar to BEARSKIN CAP (see under HEADWEAR).

dunce cap Tall conical cap, sometimes marked with a D, formerly worn in school by students who failed in their lessons. Sometimes wrongly called FOOL'S CAP (see under HEADWEAR).

dunstable Hat of plaited straw originally made in Dunstable, England.

∞**dust cap** Cap made of handkerchief or circular piece of fabric hemmed on outer edge and gathered by elastic, worn by women or maids for housework from 19th to early 20th c.

dutch-boy cap Cap with visor and soft, wide crown usually made of navy blue wool.

Dutch cap Cap worn by women and girls in Volendam, Holland, made of lace or embroidered muslin fitted to the head with a slight peak at the crown and flaring wings at sides of face. Made fashionable by Irene Castle, famous ballroom dancer in 1920s. Sometimes used as bridal cap. Also called *Dutch bonnet.*

earmuffs 1. Two disks of wool, fur, felt, or other fabric worn to keep the ears warm in winter. Disks may be fastened to a strap that goes overhead and ties under the chin, or fastened to a springy metal band that fits over top of the head. 2. A pair of flaps on sides of a cap that may be turned up and buttoned at top of cap, or left down to cover the ears.

Easter bonnet Another name for an Easter hat. May be any type of hat, not necessarily tied under the chin. Also see under EASTER PARADE.

∞**egham, staines, and windsor** Nickname used in early 19th c. for three-cornered TRICORNE hat (see under HEADWEAR). *Der.* From geographical location of three English towns that form a triangle on map.

eight-point cap Policeman's cap, or utility cap, with soft crown and a stiff visor in front. Crown is made by sewing together eight straight-edged wedges of fabric, making an octagon-shaped crown.

∞**elastic round hat** Patented collapsible hat of 1812, which could be flattened by releasing steel spring and carried under the arm. Forerunner of the *gibus* (see under HEADWEAR: OPERA HAT).

∞**empire bonnet/empire cap** (em'-pire or ohm-peer') Small outdoor bonnet of 1860s, shaped like a baby's cap with no veil or curtains in back.

engineer's cap Round cap with visor worn by railroad workers, usually of blue-and-white striped cotton. The crown is box-pleated onto the band. Adopted in 1960s by young people for sportswear.

english cottage bonnet See under HEADWEAR: BIBI BONNET.

∞**english hood** Woman's headdress worn from 1500s to 1540s, sometimes made of black fabric wired to form a peak or gable over the forehead with long velvet lappets at side and the back draped in thick folds over the shoulders. When these lappets were embroidered, they were called **chaffers** (chaf'-ers). After 1525, the back drapery became two long pendant flaps. Also called *gable* and *pediment headdress,* by 19th-c. writers.

English hood

envoy hat Man's winter hat similar to COSSACK HAT (see under HEADWEAR), with leather or fur crown and fur or fabric edge. Popular in late 1960s.

ermine cap See under HEADWEAR: LETTICE CAP.

eton cap Close-fitting cap with a short visor, modeled after those worn at Eton College in England. Popular in fabrics to match coats for young boys in the United States in 1920s and 1930s.

eugénie hat (yoo-je'-nee) Hat worn by actress Greta Garbo in 1930s film titled *Romance.* The style, a small hat tipped to one side with a large feather, was similar to one worn by the Empress Eugénie of France in a photograph that may have served as an inspiration for this very popular hat style of the 1930s that has been revived from time to time.

eugénie hat

∞**fanchon** (fan-shon') Small, lace-trimmed head scarf, or the lace trimming on sides of an outdoor bonnet or day cap; first worn in the 1830s.

∞**fanchon cap** (fan-shon') Small indoor cap of tulle or lace with side pieces covering the ears, worn by women from 1840s to 1860s.

∞**fantail hat** Three-cornered hat with wide brim, cocked or turned up at sides, with point in front; the back, somewhat-shaped semicircular, resembled a fan. Worn in the last quarter of 18th c. by men and women for horseback riding.

fascinator A type of headpiece that is mounted on a band or hairclip. Colorful, elaborate, fanciful, and highly ornamental this headwear was particularly evident at the wedding of Prince William of England and Catherine Middleton in 2011.

fashion helmet Any helmet designed as a fashion item rather than for protection. May be made of leather, fabric, fur, plastic, or other materials. Types include *Courrèges, Paco Rabanne, Pucci,* and *chain helmets.*

fatigue cap U.S. armed forces cap, usually made of twill fabric in style similar to ENGINEER'S CAP (see under HEADWEAR).

fedora Felt hat with medium-sized brim and high crown, with lengthwise crease from front to back. Originally worn by men but now also styled for women with turned-up back brim. *Der.* Popular for men after Victorien Sardou's play *Fedora* was produced in 1882. Now a classic men's hat style.

fedora

fez 1. Red felt hat shaped like truncated cone with long, black, silk tassel hanging from center of crown worn by Turkish men until 1925; also worn in Syria, Palestine, and Albania. Also worn by the "Shriners," an auxiliary order of the Masons. 2. Basic shape, without tassel, copied for women's hats in the West. *Der.* Named for town of Fez in Morocco.

fillet 1. Narrow band tied around the hair, usually as a brow band, worn from 13th to 19th c. ∞2. Stiffened band of linen worn with the BARBETTE, FRET, or both in 13th and 14th c. (see under HEADWEAR). 3. See under HEADWEAR: HEADBAND # 1 and #2.

∞**fitzherbert hat** Modified form of BALLOON HAT (see under HEADWEAR), with wide oval brim and low crown of puffed fabric, worn by women in mid-1780s.

∞**flandan** (flahn′-dahn) A PINNER or LAPPET (see under HEADWEAR) fastened to woman's day cap, as it was called in the 17th c.

Flemish hood See under HEADWEAR: BEGUIN.

flight deck cap See under HEADWEAR: ASTRONAUT'S CAP.

∞**flower-pot hat** Man's hat of 1830s, with crown shaped like a truncated cone or upside-down flower pot, with large turned-up brim. Also called *turf hat.*

fly cap See under HEADWEAR: BUTTERFLY CAP.

fold-up hat Straw sun hat with pleated brim and crown that folds to a 6″ roll for carrying in pocket or purse.

∞**follow-me-lads** Long ribbon streamers that hung from back of girl's bonnet; popular in the 1850s and 1860s.

∞**fontanges** (fawn′-tanjz) **/fontange** Woman's starched, pleated, lace-and-ribbon headdress placed on top of upswept hairstyle in late 17th and early 18th c. Said to have originated about 1679 when Marie Angélique de Scoraille de Roussille, la Duchesse de Fontanges, a favorite of Louis XIV, was out riding with the king and used her lace and jeweled garter to fasten back her hair, which had become disarranged. Also called *tower headdress* and *high head.* The COMMODE (see under HEADWEAR) was used to support the headdress.

fontanges

∞**fontanges hat** (fawn′-tanjz) Tiny hat covering crown of head trimmed with lace, ribbon, and flowers with a sheet veil or curtain in back. A band of ribbon, edged with fluting, went under the chin. Featured in *Godey's Magazine* in 1876.

fool's cap Of three types: (1) forward-curved peaked cap with donkey's ears; (2) a cockscomb in place of peak and without ears; (3) two hornlike peaks at sides of head. Bells were added to each style. Also called *jester's cap.* Also see under JESTER'S COSTUME.

football helmet Molded plastic helmet that conforms closely to the head, covering the ears. Made with nose guard, consisting of curved plastic strips attached to sides, and decorated with symbols indicating team. Worn by all contact football players.

forage cap 1. Cap with a visor adapted from the military for small boys in first half of 19th c. Made with circular felt crown, headband stiffened with cane, a tassel from center of crown, and sometimes glossy black leather straps under the chin. 2. Small cap similar to a KEPI (see under HEADWEAR), formerly worn by soldiers in U.S. Army.

fore-and-after See under HEADWEAR: DEERSTALKER.

∞**foundling bonnet** Small, soft-crowned, stiff-brimmed bonnet of 1880s usually made of plush and fastened with ties under chin.

∞**frelan** (*freland, frelange*) Woman's BONNET and PINNER (see under HEADWEAR) worn together in the late 17th c.

French beret See under HEADWEAR: BERET.

∞**French hood** Woman's headdress, consisting of a small bonnet over a stiffened frame, worn at back of head and trimmed with RUCHING. Front border was curved forward to cover the ears and had two ornamental gold bands or BILLIMENTS. A back flap either enclosed the hair or was folded forward over head, projecting above forehead (see under HEADWEAR: BONGRACE). Fashionable from 1521 to 1590 and worn by some until 1630.

French hood c. 16th c.

French sailor hat Large navy blue or white cotton TAM (see under HEADWEAR), stitched to stiff navy blue headband and trimmed with red pompon at center of crown. Originally worn by French seamen pulled down on forehead with top exactly horizontal.

∞**fret** Mesh snood or skullcap made of gold mesh or fabric worked in an openwork lattice design and sometimes decorated with jewels. Worn by women from the 13th to early 16th c. Also called a *caul.*

frigate cap Utility visored cap of mid-20th c. with flat top slanting toward back. Made of water-repellent, black, silky rayon, with cord and buttons on front for trim. Copied from caps worn by merchant seamen of the 19th c.

∞**frontlet** Decorative BROW BAND worn in medieval times under a COVERCHIEF or VEIL. Also worn in 16th and early 17th c. with COIF or CAUL. (See under HEADWEAR.)

funnel hat Brimless, tall, conical hat of felt or fabric worn by women in the 1930s and 1940s.

∞**gable bonnet/hat** Woman's hat of 1884 with front brim angled like a Gothic arch.

gable headress See under HEADWEAR: ENGLISH HOOD.

gainsborough hat Large, graceful, brimmed hat worn from late 1860s to 1890s and copied periodically since. Made of velvet, straw, or beaver, frequently turned up on one side and trimmed with ostrich plumes. *Der.* Named after the 18th-c. British painter Gainsborough, who painted many portraits of ladies in this type of hat, including portrait of *Duchess of Devonshire.*

∞**galatea hat** (gal′-ah-teh-ah) Child's hat of plaited straw with sailor crown and turned-up brim worn in 1890s.

∞**galea Roman soldier's helmet** A Roman soldier's helmet with cheek plates and a curvature at the back of the helmet to protect the neck.

Garbo hat Slouch hat worn so frequently by Greta Garbo in the 1930s that it is sometimes called by her name. See under HEADWEAR: SLOUCH HAT. Also see under GARBO, GRETA.

garden hat ∞1. Woman's hat of 1860s, made of muslin with flat top cut in oval shape. Ruffles or long pieces of muslin hung down to protect the wearer from the sun. Hat was frequently made with ribbon trim. 2. Large-brimmed floppy hat of horsehair or straw worn in 1920s and 1930s for afternoon teas and garden parties. 3. Large-brimmed straw hat currently worn when gardening to protect face from the sun.

garrison cap See under HEADWEAR: OVERSEAS CAP.

gaucho hat (gow-cho) Wide-brimmed black felt hat made with medium-high flat crown. Fastened under chin with leather thong. Originally worn by South American cowboys, it was adapted for women in late 1960s and worn with GAUCHO PANTS (see under PANTS). Also called *sombrero córdobes* (som-brer′-oh kor-dob′-ehs). *Der.* Spanish "cowboy" of Argentina, Chile, and Uruguay.

German helmet Metal helmet made with small visor and a spike on the top decorated with large gold eagle on front. Worn by Germans in World War I and adopted by teenage boys in the late 1960s. Also called a *pickelhaube.*

gibus See under HEADWEAR: OPERA HAT.

glengarry cap Military cloth cap creased to fold flat like an OVERSEAS CAP (see under HEADWEAR) usually with tartan band at edge, regimental badge at side front, and two black ribbon streamers in back. Part of the uniform of Scottish Highland regiments, and adapted for sportswear by women and small boys in mid-19th c. *Der.* After Glengarry, a valley in Inverness-shire, Scotland.

gob hat See under HEADWEAR: SAILOR HAT.

∞**goffered veil** Linen headdress, with fluted or GOFFERED frill surrounding the face, worn in the 19th c. Has back drapery to shoulders, worn from 1350 to 1420. *Nebula headdress* is a 19th-c. synonym.

gondolier's hat (gon-doh-leer′) Straw hat with a medium-sized brim and a shallow, slightly tapered crown with a flat top. Wide ribbon trims the crown and long streamers extend down the back; the color of the ribbon once denoted length of service. Worn formerly by gondoliers of Venice, Italy. Often purchased as a tourist souvenir by visitors to Venice.

∞**granny bonnet** Child's bonnet of early 1890s, with ribbon ties under the chin, broad flaring brim, and gathered conventional crown decorated with ribbons. *Der.* Styled after the bonnets that grandmothers wore.

greek fisherman's cap Soft cap of denim or wool with crown higher in front than in back. Elaborately trimmed with braid on visor and at seam where visor meets crown. Styled in black wool, blue denim, or white and worn for sportswear or boating in 1980s by both men and women.

hair net Fine, cap-shaped net worn over the hair to keep it in place. Sometimes made of knotted human hair and nearly invisible. Also made of chenille, gold, or silver threads and worn as decoration. Also see under HEADWEAR: SNOOD.

halo hat See under HEADWEAR: PAMELA.

hard hat Protective covering for the head. Made of metal or hard plastic in classic PITH HELMET shape or similar to a baseball BATTER'S CAP (see under HEADWEAR). Held away from the head by foam lining to absorb impact. Worn by construction workers and others subject to work hazards. In late 1960s, the term "hard hat" took on political connotations when U.S. construction workers expressed their sentiments against peace advocates.

harlequin Hat with brim, wide at sides and cut straight across front and back, worn in 1938. *Der.* From *Harlequin,* a part played by an actor in 16th- to 18th-c. Italian comedies called *commedia dell'arte.*

harvest hat Believed to be the name given to the first straw hats worn by farmers in the United States.

hat Sometimes generic for headwear; however, it more specifically applies to headwear that consists of a crown and a brim and that usually does not tie under the chin. A decorative accessory or one worn for warmth, hats can be made of felt, straw, fur, fabric, leather, or synthetic materials. The Greek PETASOS (see under HEADWEAR: PETASOS #1) was among the earliest brimmed hats. Medieval hat styles included the COPOTAIN (see under HEADWEAR), and until c. 1660 men wore hats indoors as well as outdoors, and in church. Women did not generally wear hats, except for traveling, until after the late 16th c., when they wore either hats or bonnets outdoors and for church. From the late 1950s, bouffant hairstyles, and later the use of wigs and falls, made it difficult to wear hats. Although hats have been periodically fashionable since then, they are worn much less frequently than in the past.

hat à la william tell See under HEADWEAR: CUMBERLAND HAT.

∞**hat cap** Day cap worn under a hat mainly by women in the 18th c. Also called *undercap.*

hat pin Straight pin from 3″ to 12″ long with bead or jewel at top. Used by women to secure their hats in late 19th through early 20th c., becoming less common after hair was bobbed in the 1920s.

havelock 1. Cloth covering for military cap extending to shoulders in back in order to protect the neck from sun.

Der. Named for Sir Henry Havelock, British general in India. **2.** See under HEADWEAR: AUTOMOBILE CAP.

headband **1.** Strip of leather, cord, or fabric bound around the head horizontally across the forehead. Also called a *brow band.* **2.** Band worn over top of the head from ear to ear as an ornament or to keep hair in place since ancient times. **3.** Band at bottom edge of hat crown.

head rail See under HEADWEAR: COVERCHIEF.

head wrap In 1980s, a scarf, bandanna, ribbon, or piece of fabric worn in carefree manner around the head to frame the face or as a BROW BAND (see under HEADWEAR).

∞**heart-shaped headdress** Rolled woman's headdress worn between 1420 and 1450, forming a heart-shaped peak in center front. Raised on sides to show netting coming down over the ears. Usually worn with a long veil. The style was called a **miter** by 19th-c. writers.

helmet Protective covering for the head worn particularly by armed forces, primarily to prevent injury, as well as for various sports. First worn by Greeks and Romans with feathered crests; *chain mail* was used during the Crusades; cast metal used from 14th c. on for knights' helmets, which usually had a visor. In the late 1950s, space helmets were introduced for astronauts, and in the 1960s helmet-shaped hats were introduced as a fashion accessory. Also see under ARMOR: BURGONET and MORION.

hemispherical hat See under HEADWEAR: BOLLINGER.

henley boater See under HEADWEAR: BOATER.

∞**hennin** (hen'-in) Woman's tall, steeple-shaped headdress worn in Burgundy during the second half of 15th c. Supported by a wire frame and worn tilted back with a long, sheer veil hanging from tip down to floor, or caught up as drapery at waist. SUMPTUARY LAWS regulated the size of these hats. Princesses could wear hats a yard high; however, those of noble ladies could be only 24″ or less. Also called *steeple headdress* and *corner. Der.* From an old French word meaning "to inconvenience," a reference to the inconvenience such a headdress would cause.

hennin, 2nd half of the 15th c.

∞**heuke** (hyuke) (*hewke, heyke, hewk*) Veil enveloping wearer to knees or ankles—sometimes with the top stiffened by wire—worn over head forming a cage. Worn in Flanders in 16th and 17th c.

high hat See under HEADWEAR: TOP HAT.

hijab A veil worn by Muslim women in the presence of nonrelated males; it covers the hair and neck.

hive bonnet See under HEADWEAR: BEEHIVE HAT #1.

homburg Man's hat of rather stiff felt with narrow rolled brim and lengthwise crease in the crown, worn since 1870s on for formal occasions. Made fashionable by Prince of Wales, later Edward VII, who visited Bad Homburg in Germany many times. Revived after President Dwight Eisenhower wore one to his inauguration in 1952. *Der.* Homburg, Prussia.

homburg

hood **1.** Preliminary, shaped piece of FELT or straw from which the milliner works. Has a high, rounded, nondescript crown and an extra-large floppy brim. **2.** Accessory worn on the head and sometimes the shoulders that is frequently attached to a jacket or coat. Differs from a hat in that it has no specific shape and usually covers the entire head, sometimes tying under the chin. Popular item for winter wear, it is made in all types of fabrics and fur. Although there are a great variety of styles, there are no specific names for these items. Worn since the 11th c., but replaced generally by caps in 1860s and 1870s, and for winter sportswear in the 1920s and 1930s. Regained popularity in the late 1960s.

∞**horned headdress** Headdress consisting of two horns extending horizontally at either side of face or curved upward. A veil was draped over top and hung down the back. Worn from 1410 to 1420, and, rarely, to 1460.

horned headdress 15th c.

hundred pleater See under HEADWEAR: CHEF'S HAT.

hunt cap Cap cut in six segments with small visor, elastic chin strap, and button on center top, sometimes of cloverleaf shape. Worn with riding habit, it is sometimes made with a plastic shell covered with velvet or velveteen and a padded lining.

hunt derby Stiff protective DERBY (see under HEADWEAR) made with reinforced strong plastic shell covered with black felt worn with riding habit.

hunting cap Bright-orange, visored cap, sometimes fluorescent, enabling the hunter to be seen in the woods.

∞**Jenny Lind cap** Crocheted band that crossed the crown of the head and came down over ears and around to the back, where it fastened. Sometimes made of scarlet and white wool. Worn as a woman's MORNING CAP in late 1840s and early 1850s. *Der.* Copied from style worn by Jenny Lind (1820–1887), famous coloratura soprano called the "Swedish Nightingale."

∞**joan** Woman's small, close-fitting indoor cap shaped like baby's bonnet and tied under chin with narrow frill of muslin or lace around face. Worn from 1755 to 1765. Also called *Quaker cap.*

jockey cap Visored cap with crown usually of bicolored sateen cut in gores, similar to BASEBALL CAP (see under

HEADWEAR) but with deeper crown, worn by racetrack jockeys. Similar caps worn by women in mid-1960s.

juliet cap SKULLCAP (see under HEADWEAR) of rich fabric worn for evening or with wedding veils. May also be made entirely of pearls, jewels, or chain. *Der.* Medieval costume of Juliet in Shakespeare's play *Romeo and Juliet.*

kepi High-crowned, flat-topped, visored cap frequently worn with HAVELOCK (see under HEADWEAR) in back as protection from sun. Worn by French Foreign Legion and French general and statesman Charles de Gaulle. Also called *Legionnaire's cap.*

kerchief 1. In current usage, a large triangle of cloth, or square folded in triangular fashion, worn as a headcovering or around the neck. Also see under SCARVES: KERCHIEF and NECKERCHIEF. ∞2. Covering for the head from medieval times to end of 16th c., when it may also have been spelled *karcher, kercher, kercheve, kersche.* In 16th and 17th c., called a *head rail.* See under HEADWEAR: COVERCHIEF.

kevenhuller hat See under HEADWEAR: COCKED HAT.

∞kiss-me-quick Popular name for tiny bonnet fashionable in late 1860s.

∞lamballe bonnet (lam-bahl') Saucer-shaped straw bonnet of mid-1860s, worn flat on head with sides pulled down slightly and tied under chin with large ribbon bow. Some had lace LAPPETS (see under HEADWEAR), others had small veils in back called "curtains."

∞langtry hood Detachable hood on woman's outdoor garment of 1880s with a colored lining. *Der.* Named after actress Lillie Langtry.

lappets Long, ribbon-like strips of fabric that extend from a headdress. Particularly used in the 18th c. and 19th c. to refer to such strips, often lace trimmed, when they hang at sides or back of an indoor cap.

leghorn hat/leghorn bonnet Woman's hat or bonnet in leghorn straw, a fine, smooth, straw braid plaited with thirteen strands. Made from the upper part of wheat stalks grown near Livorno, a town in Tuscany, Italy. Fashionable at intervals since latter half of 19th c. *Der.* Named for place of export for the straw, Livorno, Italy. The British anglicized the name of the city to "Leghorn."

Legionnaire's cap See under HEADWEAR: KEPI.

lettice cap/bonnet ∞1. Woman's outdoor cap or bonnet of triangular shape that covered the ears, as it was called in the 16th c. Made of lettice, a fur resembling ermine. 2. In 16th and 17th c., a man's nightcap of lettice fur worn to induce sleep. Also called *ermine cap* or *miniver cap.*

liberty cap 1. See under FRENCH REVOLUTION STYLES. 2. See under HEADWEAR: BONNET ROUGE. 3. See under HEADWEAR: PHRYGIAN CAP.

liripipe (*liripipium, lirapipe, liripoop*) ∞1. Long pendant tail of the CHAPERONE (see under HEADWEAR), a hood worn in 14th and 15th c. 2. Part of a hood worn by university graduates from 1350 to 15th c. Also called *tippet.*

long hood See under HEADWEAR: PUG HOOD.

∞Louis XV hat Woman's hat of mid-1870s with large, high crown and wide brim turned up on one side. Fastened to crown with velvet bows and trimmed elaborately with ostrich feathers. *Der.* Named for Louis XV of France (1710–1774).

∞lounging cap Gentleman's at-home cap, worn in mid-1860s, made in pillbox or dome shape with silk tassels fastened at center. Also called *Greek lounging cap.*

Lunardi See under HEADWEAR: BALLOON HAT.

∞mafors Long, narrow veil worn by women from 6th to 11th c. that usually covered head and draped over shoulders.

∞mameluke turban (mama-luke') White, satin, woman's turban of 1804 trimmed with one large ostrich feather, with the front rolled back like a hat brim over a dome-shaped crown. *Der.* Mamelukes were originally non-Arab slaves brought to Egypt, later trained as soldiers. Ruled Egypt from 1250 to 1517 and remained powerful until 1811 under Turkish viceroys. The Mameluke army was defeated by Napoleon Bonaparte during his Egyptian campaign in 1798.

∞mandarin hat Woman's black velvet PORK-PIE HAT (see under HEADWEAR) of early 1860s with feather trim over the back of the flat crown. Design inspiration may have come from an ancient Chinese court hat with wide, flaring, upturned brim and decorative button at crown (indicating rank of wearer), made of fur and satin for winter and decorated with a peacock feather.

mantilla (man-til'-ah) Large, oblong, fine lace veil, usually in rose pattern of black or white, worn wrapped over head and crossed under chin with one end thrown over shoulder. In Spain and South America, frequently worn to church, instead of a hat. Popular after it was worn in early 1960s by U.S. first lady, Jacqueline Kennedy.

∞marie stuart bonnet/cap Bonnet with heart-shaped peak or brim projecting over center of forehead, popular from 1820 to 1870, especially for widows. A derivative of the ATTIFET headdress (see under HEADWEAR) worn by Mary, Queen of Scots, also called Mary Stuart (or Stewart) (1542–1587).

∞marie stuart hood Separate hood of 1860s with heart-shaped, peaked brim in front that extended over the face with crown cut round and gathered at edge. Tied with ribbons under chin and lavishly trimmed with RUCHING, embroidery, braid, and ribbon.

∞marin anglais bonnet (mar'-ahn an-glayz') Woman's bonnet worn on the back of the head like a child's sailor hat in 1870s. Trimmed with ribbon and feathers and tied under chin. *Der.* French, "English sailor cap."

∞**marmotte bonnet** (mar′-mowt) Tiny bonnet of early 1830s with narrow front brim similar to BIBI BONNET. See under HEADWEAR.

∞**marmotte cap** (mar′-mowt) Triangular handkerchief, placed on back of head and tied under chin, worn indoors by women in early 1830s.

∞**marquis** (mar-kwiss′ or mar-kee′) A three-cornered hat worn by women.

∞**mary, queen of scots cap** Indoor cap worn by women, mainly matrons and widows, from 1750s to 1760s. Made with a heart-shaped peak in center front edged with beads, may have side frills and lappets. Also called *Mary cap.*

matador hat (mat-ah-door) Hat shaped like the top of a bull's head—rounded over forehead with two projections like bull's horns covered with black tufts of fabric, with the center of crown of embroidered velvet. Worn by bullfighters in Spain and Mexico.

∞**mazarin hood** (maz′-ah-rhan) Woman's hood worn in the last quarter of the 17th c. *Der.* Named after the Duchesse de Mazarin, niece of Cardinal Mazarin (1602–1661), minister to Louis XIV.

∞**mecklenburg cap** Turban-style indoor cap worn by women in 1760s. *Der.* Named after Charlotte of Mecklenburg, who married George III of England in 1761.

mentonnières (mahn-toe-nyehr′) See under HEADWEAR: CHIN STAYS.

merry widow hat Very wide-brimmed hat, sometimes a yard across, frequently of velvet and ornately trimmed with ostrich plumes. *Der.* Named for 1905 light opera *The Merry Widow,* with music by Franz Lehár.

∞**milan bonnet** (mee-lan′) Man's cap of first half of 16th c., usually black with soft puffed crown. Rolled-up brim was sometimes slit on the sides and trimmed with crimson satin lining pulled through slashes.

milkmaid hat See under HEADWEAR: BERGÈRE HAT.

miner's cap Stiff cap with short, duck-billed visor and battery-powered light attached to front of crown.

∞**mistake hat** Woman's hat with tall, flat-topped crown and brim cut in blunt point in front and turned up. Back brim was turned down. Worn on the back of the head in 1804.

∞**miter** 1. Woman's headband worn in ancient Greece. 2. See under HEADWEAR: HEART-SHAPED HEADDRESS.

∞**moabite turban** (mo′-ab-ite) Woman's crepe turban draped in many folds and trimmed with an aigrette feather on one side. Worn tilted to back of head in early 1830s.

mob cap Woman's indoor cap of 18th and 19th c. made of white cambric or muslin with gathered crown and ruffled edge forming a bonnet. Had side LAPPETS (see under HEADWEAR), called *kissing strings* or *bridles,* which tied under the chin.

mob cap 18th c.

mod cap Cap similar to NEWSBOY CAP (see under HEADWEAR), popular in the United States in the mid-1960s.

molded felt A felt HOOD, as referred to in the hat industry, which was made into hat shape by placing over a wooden block shaped like a head. See under HEADWEAR: HOOD #1.

∞**monmouth cap** Man's knitted cap with high, rounded crown and small turned-down brim worn by soldiers, sailors, and civilians. Listed as necessary item for new settlers in America. Most common in 17th c., although also worn from 1570s to 1625. Made at Monmouth and Bewdley in Worcestershire, England. Also called *bewdley cap* and worn by country folk as late as 19th c.

monmouth cock See under HEADWEAR: COCKED HAT.

∞**montespan hat** (mon-tes-pan′) Woman's small, round, velvet evening hat of 1843 with brim turned up in front, trimmed with plume. *Der.* Named for Marquise de Montespan (1641–1707), mistress of Louis XIV of France.

montgomery beret Military cap, a bit larger than the conventional BASQUE BERET (see under HEADWEAR: BERET) but set on a band like a Scottish *tam-o-shanter* and decorated with regimental insignia. Popular after being adopted by field marshal Bernard Law Montgomery, 1st Viscount Montgomery, commander of British ground forces in World War II.

mont-la-haut See under HEADWEAR: COMMODE.

∞**morning cap** Dainty cap of muslin, lace, tulle, and ribbon worn on the back of the head indoors in the morning by women from 1820s to end of 19th c. Also called a *breakfast cap.*

mortarboard See under ACADEMIC COSTUME.

motorcycle helmet Molded plastic helmet with foam lining worn when riding a motorcycle. Usually has a large dark-colored plastic shield that snaps on to protect eyes and face.

motoring veil See under HEADWEAR: AUTOMOBILE VEIL.

Mountie's hat Wide-brimmed hat with high crown creased into four sections with a small peak at the top. Similar to one of the U.S. Army hats worn with dress uniforms during World War I. Worn by state policemen, Forest Rangers, and by the Royal Canadian Mounted Police.

∞**mourning bonnet** Any black bonnet worn to complete a mourning costume—especially in the 1870s and 1880s. An off-the-face bonnet, sometimes with a heart-shaped brim; it was made of black silk, lavishly trimmed with RUCHING and ribbon, and tied under the chin. The veil was arranged over the face or allowed to hang down the back.

mourning veil Semi-sheer black veil to the shoulders, usually circular, sometimes edged with wide band of black fabric worn under or over hat at funerals or during periods of mourning.

∞**mousquetaire hat** (moose-ke-tare′) **1.** Wide-brimmed hat usually trimmed with three ostrich plumes. Also called *Swedish hat. Der.* From hats worn by French musketeers or royal bodyguards of Louis XIII in 17th c. **2.** Brown mushroom-shaped woman's straw hat edged with black lace hanging from the brim worn in late 1850s.

∞**muffin hat** Man's fabric hat with round flat crown and narrow standing brim used for country wear in 1860s.

∞**muller cut-down** Man's hat of 1870s, made like top hat with crown cut to half the height. *Der.* Named after English murderer whose hat led to his arrest in 1864.

mushroom hat Woman's straw hat with small round crown and downward-curved brim, shaped like the cap of a mushroom. Worn in 1870s and 1880s, trimmed with ribbons, flowers, and birds. Worn again in early 1900s and in the 1930s and 1940s usually made of felt.

napkin-cap Man's 18th-c. house cap or plain NIGHTCAP (see under HEADWEAR: NIGHTCAP #2) worn at home when wig was removed.

∞**neapolitan bonnet** (nee-a-poll-i-tan) LEGHORN BONNET of 1800 (see under HEADWEAR) trimmed with straw flowers and matching ribbons attached at the crown and loosely tied over the chest. *Der.* Greek, *Napolis,* "old town," present-day Naples.

neapolitan hat (nee-a-poll′-i-tan) Sheer, lacy, conical hat made in Naples of horsehair braid. Later, any hat made of this braid. *Der.* City in which it originates: Naples.

nebula headdress See under HEADWEAR: GOFFERED HEADDRESS.

∞**necked bonnet** Lined or unlined cap with wide flap fitted around back of neck, worn by men in first half of 16th c.

newsboy cap Soft fabric cap with flat, bloused crown and visor that sometimes snaps to the crown. Formerly worn by newsboys and made famous by child actor Jackie Coogan in silent films of the 1920s. Revived in exaggerated form in 1960s and 1970s. Also popular since the beginning of the 21st c. May be referred to by various names (e.g., Carnaby, bebop, soul, applejack cap).

nightcap **1.** Plain, washable cap worn in bed by men and women from earliest times, sometimes made like stocking cap of knitted silk with tassel on top. In 19th c. called a *jellybag.* Also see under HEADWEAR: BIGGIN #2. ∞**2.** 14th- to mid-19th-c. skullcap with upturned brim, worn indoors by men when wig was removed. **3.** See under HEADWEAR: NAPKIN-CAP. **4.** See under HEADWEAR: MOB CAP.

man's nightcap 18th c.

∞**night coif** (kwaf) Woman's cap worn with NEGLIGEE costume or in bed in 16th and 17th c. Frequently embroidered and usually worn with FOREHEAD CLOTH (see under HEADWEAR: CROSSCLOTH #2).

∞**norwegian morning cap/norwegian morning bonnet** Woman's cerise and white-striped Shetland wool, knitted, kerchief-shaped head covering of 1860s. Tied under the chin with a ribbon and trimmed with bows over crown and back of the head.

nurse's cap White, stiffly starched, fabric cap received by nurses at graduation. At one time, but no longer, worn pinned to the crown of the head when dressed in uniform and on duty in hospitals. Each school of nursing had an individual style of cap.

∞**obi hat** Woman's hat of 1804 with high, flat-topped crown and narrow brim rolled up in front. Ribbons come over crown and brim of hat, tying under chin.

∞**octagonal hat** Cap shaped like a TAM (see under HEADWEAR) made of six wedges stitched together, forming an octagonal-shaped crown. Sometimes made of two contrasting fabrics and usually trimmed with two short streamers hanging in back. Popular for girls and young women in mid-1890s.

open-crown hat Woman's hat made without a crown—may be of the HALO or TOQUE hat type (see under HEADWEAR).

∞**opera hat** **1.** Small TRICORNE hat carried under the arm rather than worn from mid-18th c. on. Also called *chapeau bras.* **2.** Bicorne hat worn from 1800 to 1830 with a crescent-shaped brim front and back that could be compressed and carried under the arm. Also called a *military folding hat.* **3.** Man's tall silk hat with collapsible crown worn formerly for full dress occasions. Also worn by ringmasters, magicians, and performers. Differs from a TOP HAT (see under HEADWEAR) by being completely collapsible and made of dull, rather than shiny, fabric. Also called a **gibus** (jy-bus) and made with sides containing metal springs that snapped open to hold it upright. *Der.* From Antoine Gibus, who invented the hat in 1823, patented in 1837. Similar styles were called *chapeau claque, circumfolding hat,* and *elastic round hat.*

∞**oralia** (or-ahl′-yuh) (*orales*) Early medieval term for pointed veil. By first quarter of 14th c., known as *cornalia* or *cornu. Der.* Latin, "veil."

∞**orrelet** (or-let′) (*oreillett, orillette, orilyet*) Term used in later half of 16th c. for hanging side pieces of woman's coif that covered ears. Also called *cheeks-and-ears.* See under HEADWEAR: COIF #3.

overseas cap Flat-folding cloth cap of khaki or olive drab fabric worn by men and women in the armed services. Has a lengthwise pleat from front to back in center of crown to enable it to fold flat. Worn overseas in World War I and II. Also called *garrison cap.*

Paco Rabanne hat (pak′-oh rah′-bahn) Unusual cap fitted to conform to the head and covered with tiny diamond-shaped mirrors linked together. Introduced in late 1960s and named for French couturier Paco Rabanne.

padre hat Shovel-shaped hat with turned-up brim on the sides and long, square-cut brim in front and back. Worn by some orders of Catholic priests. *Der.* Italian, "father."

painter's cap Lightweight, duck-billed, fabric cap made with a round, flat-topped crown. Sometimes imprinted with school name, team name, or resort on front of crown. *Der.* From cap worn by house painters.

palisade See under HEADWEAR: COMMODE.

pamela ∞1. Straw bonnet worn from 1845 to late 1860s, made of a "saucer-shaped" piece of straw or fabric placed on top of the head. Fastened with bonnet strings that bent it into a U-shape around the face. Trimmed on top with foliage, flowers, or feathers. 2. Continued to be a basic hat style with a rounded crown and wide brim and now often called a *halo hat.*

pamela or halo hat

panama hat 1. Hat made of fine, expensive straw obtained from the leaves of the *jipijapa* plant, handwoven in Ecuador. Very popular at the end of 19th and beginning of 20th c. Worn in different styles from 1855 on. A large panama hat was worn by the Prince of Wales in 1920s at Belmont Park, Long Island, where more than 50,000 people were gathered, thus reviving the wearing of panama hat. 2. By extension, any man's straw summer hat regardless of type of straw.

Panama hat

pancake beret See under HEADWEAR: BERET.

pantile See under HEADWEAR: COPOTAIN.

papillion See under HEADWEAR: BONNET À BEC.

parachute hat See under HEADWEAR: BALLOON HAT.

∞**Peruvian hat** Woman's rain hat made from plaited palm leaves, worn in early 19th c.

∞**petasos** (pet′-ah-soss) 1. Felt hat with a large floppy brim and nondescript crown worn in ancient Greece when traveling. Also worn in ancient Rome. 2. Close-fitting, winged cap as seen in representations of Roman god, Mercury. Also spelled *petasus.*

Peter Pan hat Small hat with brim extended in front and turned up in back. Made with a conical crown trimmed with long feathers. *Der.* Named after the hat worn by actress Maude Adams in 1905 when starring in J. M. Barrie's play *Peter Pan.*

phrygian cap/phrygian bonnet (frij′-ee-an) 1. Cap with high, rounded peak curving forward with lappets hanging at sides, sometimes made of leather. Worn in ancient Greece from 9th to 12th c. and copied from 18th c. on as BONNET ROUGE (see under HEADWEAR). 2. See under PILEUS #2.

pickelhaube See under HEADWEAR: GERMAN HELMET.

picture hat Hat with large brim framing the face, frequently made of straw. Also see under HEADWEAR: LEGHORN HAT.

∞**pileus** (pi′-lay-uss) **/pilleus** 1. Ancient Roman skullcap worn at games and festivals. 2. Felt brimless cap with peak folded over, similar to PHRYGIAN CAP (see under HEADWEAR), worn by freed Roman slaves. Also see under PILOS. *Der.* Latin, "skullcap."

pillbox hat Classic, round, brimless hat that can be worn forward or on the back of the head. Introduced in late 1920s and worn since with slight variations. *Der.* From small, round pillboxes formerly used by chemists or druggists.

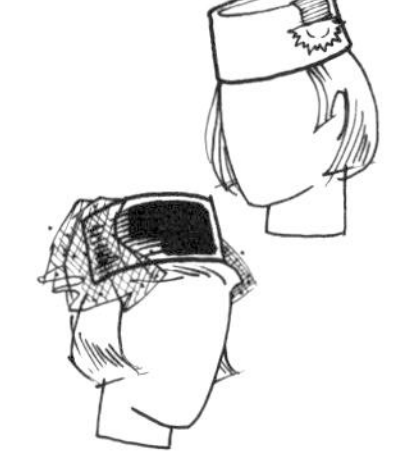
pillbox hat

pilos (pi′-los) Conical cap worn by Greek peasants or fishermen, derived from those worn by ancient Greeks and Romans, similar to PILEUS (see under HEADWEAR). *Der.* Latin, "skullcap."

∞**pinner** A lappet, or strip of fabric hanging from a woman's indoor cap, when worn pinned up; and, by extension, term for cap itself in 17th to mid-18th c.

∞**pipkin** Woman's small hat, worn about 1565 to 1600, made with flat crown pleated into narrow brim. Usually trimmed with a narrow jeweled band and feathers. Also called *taffeta pipkin.*

pith helmet See under HEADWEAR: TOPEE.

planter's hat Wide-brimmed, white or natural, handwoven, straw hat with high, dented crown, banded with dark ribbon. Worn by Southern gentlemen in the U.S. and popular for women in late 1960s.

plug hat See under HEADWEAR: TOP HAT.

∞**poke bonnet** Bonnet of 19th c. made with very wide brim slanting forward from small crown to frame and shadow the face. Also called *poking bonnet.* When made with rolled brim—one side extending beyond the cheek, the other side rolled back from face, it was called a **conversation bonnet,** a style worn in 1803.

∞**polish toque** Woman's hat of mid-1860s somewhat similar to *pillbox,* trimmed in front with foliage and in back with a large bunch of velvet ribbon loops.

∞**polka** Woman's cap of cream-colored tulle with crocheted edges appliquéd with lace floral designs, with LAPPETS (see under HEADWEAR) covering ears, and tied under chin.

polo hat See under HEADWEAR: CHUKKA HAT.

pork-pie hat 1. Classic, snap-brim, man's hat, flat on top with crease around edge of crown, made of fabric, straw or felt. Worn in 1930s and copied for women in the 1940s. Still a basic hat for men. ∞2. Introduced in 1860s as a hat for women made of straw or velvet with a low, flat crown and turned-up, narrow brim.

pork-pie hat #1

∞**postboy hat** Woman's small straw hat of 1885 styled with high, flat crown and narrow brim sloping down all around. Trimmed with plume in front and worn perched on top of head.

postillion (pohse-til′-yohn) Hat with tall, tapered crown and narrow brim, usually beaver, worn by women for riding. *Der.* From clothes worn by *postillions,* "men on horseback accompanying carriages."

pot hat See under HEADWEAR: TOP HAT.

prayer veil Small, triangular, lace veil worn instead of hat for church services.

profile hat Woman's hat with brim turned down sharply on one side, silhouetting the profile, popular in late 1930s.

Pucci hat (pooch′-ee) Transparent plastic bubble with cutout for the face that stands away from the head to keep hair from blowing. Designed by Emilio Pucci, Italian couturier, as part of wardrobe for airline stewardesses.

∞**pudding** Small, round, padded cap or padded band worn by infants and small children to serve as shock absorber in a fall. Synonym: *bumper.*

pudding 17th c.

∞**pug hood** Woman's soft hood of 18th c. with pleats radiating from back where it fitted the head. Made with or without an attached cape. Usually black with colored turned-back lining and tied under the chin with matching ribbons. Same as *short hood.* A **long hood** was similar, but with long tabs on the sides to facilitate tying under the chin.

∞**pultney cap** Woman's heart-shaped indoor cap of 1760s with wired peak, worn on the back of the head.

puritan hat Black, stiff, tall-crowned man's hat with medium-wide straight brim trimmed with wide black band and silver buckle in center front. Worn by Puritan men in America in early 17th c. and copied for women in 1970s.

∞**Quaker bonnet** Small, close-fitting, undecorated woman's bonnet with a puffed crown and stiff brim tied under the chin. Made in same fabric as the dress (often gray) or in straw, and worn over a ruffled white muslin cap. In 17th through 19th c. prescribed for women of Quaker faith by the Society of Friends.

Quaker cap See under HEADWEAR: JOAN cap.

∞**Quaker hat** 1. TRICORNE hat with open cock and tall crown, worn in 18th c. 2. Hat with large, slightly rolled brim, low crown, and no ornamentation worn in the 19th c. by Quaker men.

∞**quartered cap** Boy's cap with flat, circular crown divided into four segments and attached to stiff band. Made with or without a visor from mid-18th to mid-19th c.

rain bonnet Accordion-pleated plastic covering for head that ties under chin. Folds up to fit in purse when not in use.

rain hat Any waterproof hat worn in the rain. Some hats are made of vinyl and styled with a high crown and a floppy brim. Also see under HEADWEAR: SOU′WESTER.

∞**ranelagh mob** Woman's cap of 1760s made with a KERCHIEF (see under HEADWEAR) folded diagonally and placed over the head with two long ends tied under chin. The ends were pulled back and pinned or left to hang down.

ranger's hat See under HEADWEAR: MOUNTIE'S HAT.

Red Baron helmet See under HEADWEAR: AVIATOR'S HELMET.

∞**red crown** Outward-flaring crown with long extension up back worn by kings of Upper Egypt in ancient times. When kingdom became united both the *red crown* and the WHITE CROWN (see under HEADWEAR) were worn together.

∞**reticulation** (re-ti′-cu-lay-shun) Decorative netting holding hair on either side of face worn with horned headdress by women in 15th c. See under HEADWEAR: CAUL #1.

Rex Harrison hat Man's snap-brim hat of wool tweed with narrow brim and matching tweed band. Popular after being worn by actor Rex Harrison in his role as Professor Henry Higgins in the musical *My Fair Lady* in 1956.

rigid frame hat A hat base made from buckram, a coarse cotton or linen fabric, that has been heavily sized with glue. The shape, made to a specific head size, is meant to be covered with fabric.

robin hood hat Hat with high peaked crown, brim turned up in back, down in front, and trimmed with one long feather. *Der.* From hat in illustrations of books about Robin Hood, legendary British outlaw of the 12th c.

∞**roll** Circular pad made when converting the man's chaperon into a hat, as it was referred to in the 15th c. Also see under HEADWEAR: BOURRELET.

roller Hat with close-fitting crown and narrow, curved brim worn rolled up or with the front turned down. Popular for women and girls in 1930s and 1940s, revived in early 1970s.

∞**round-eared cap** Woman's white, cambric or lace, indoor cap worn from 1730s to 1760s. It curved around face and was finished with a ruffle. The shallow back was pulled together with a drawstring. Sometimes with side LAPPETS (see under HEADWEAR) pinned up or tied loosely under chin. Sometimes called *coif.*

∞**roundlet** 1. The 15th-c. roll of the CHAPERONE, as it was called in the 17th c.; worn with a stuffed roll encircling the head and tail, called a **becca,** which was a long strip of fabric hanging forward that was sometimes worn slung over the shoulders. This style was very popular in the reign of Henry VI of England and was also called a **berretino.** 2. Man's small, round hat of the 18th c. with attached streamer for carrying it over shoulder.

∞**rubens hat** High-crowned woman's hat of 1870s and 1880s with brim turned up on one side, sometimes trimmed with feathers and bows. *Der.* Named for hats painted by Flemish master Peter Paul Rubens (1577–1640).

∞**safari hat** Lightweight straw or fabric hat shaped somewhat like a shallow soup dish with medium-sized brim. Hat is somewhat similar to a TOPEE (see under HEADWEAR) with a shallower crown. Worn to deflect heat in warm weather. *Der.* Shape of hat is similar to those worn on African hunting trips called "safaris."

sailor hat 1. Hat worn by naval enlisted personnel made of white duck fabric with gored crown and stitched upturned brim worn either on the back of the head or tilted over the forehead. Also called *gob hat* and *tennis hat.* 2. Woman's straight-brimmed hat with shallow flat crown worn since 1860s. Very popular in 1890s for sportswear and bicycling and worn intermittently since. 3. Popular hat for small boys in the 1880s, sometimes embroidered with fictitious name of a ship on a ribbon band at the base of the crown, similar in style to the brimless FRENCH SAILOR HAT (see under HEADWEAR).

sailor hat #1

Saint Laurent hat Cap designed by French couturier Yves Saint Laurent in 1966, made of leather studded with nailheads, and styled similar to World War I aviator's helmet.

Salvation Army bonnet High-crowned, black, straw bonnet with short front brim raised off forehead to show a pale-blue lining. Has dark-blue ribbon around crown and ties under chin; worn by women of the Salvation Army, a religious and charitable organization.

scarf cap Long, tubular, knitted or crocheted scarf with opening for head in one end, similar to STOCKING CAP (see under HEADWEAR).

scarf hat 1. Woman's soft fabric hat made by tying a scarf over a lining or base, sometimes shaped like a PILLBOX HAT (see under HEADWEAR), and sewed in place. 2. A triangular piece of colorful print or plain fabric quilted on long side. Worn with quilted part in center front and tied on the head like a KERCHIEF (see under HEADWEAR).

∞**scoop bonnet** Bonnet popular in 1840s with wide, stiff brim shaped like a flour scoop attached to soft crown. *Der.* From old-fashioned "flour scoop."

scottie A brimless hat styled somewhat like the GLENGARRY (see under HEADWEAR) with narrow recessed crown. Veiling, ribbon, or feathers are sometimes placed on top toward the back.

∞**sempstress bonnet** Woman's bonnet of 1812 with long, wide ribbons crossing under chin and brought up to top of crown, where they tied in a bow.

service cap Army cap worn with dress uniform, made with a stiff, round, flat top and stiff visor of leather or plastic.

∞**shade** Piece of knitted or woven fabric usually attached to a hatband and arranged to fall over the back of the head and neck to prevent sunburn. Worn by women in 1880s.

shako (shay'-ko) Cylindrical, stiff, tall cap with attached visor. Top is sometimes tapered, sometimes flared, with feather cockade in front. Worn by marching bands, it was adapted from a style of military cap worn formerly. Also see under HEADWEAR: DRUM MAJOR'S HAT.

shepherdess hat See under HEADWEAR: BERGÈRE HAT.

shoe hat Hat designed by Elsa Schiaparelli in the 1930s that looked like a woman's shoe. This design was reflective of the designer's interest in SURREALISM.

shoe hat 1930s

shower cap Plastic or waterproof cap, usually shirred into an elastic band, worn to keep the hair dry while taking a shower.

∞**silk hat** High, cylindrical-shaped hat with flat top and silk-plush finish used by men on formal occasions and with formal riding dress by men and women. Invented by John Hetherington, a haberdasher of London, provoking a riot when first worn by him on January 15, 1797. He was charged in court for "breach of peace" for frightening timid people. Hat subsequently became the TOP HAT (see under HEADWEAR) in 1830.

skimmer SAILOR HAT or BOATER (see under HEADWEAR), with exaggerated shallow crown and wide brim.

skullcap Gored cap, usually made in eight sections, which fits tightly to crown of the head, often part of ecclesiastical garb or national costume. A **beanie** is a skullcap cut in gores to fit the head. Worn by children and by freshmen students as a part of hazing by upperclassmen, this is also called a *dink* or *dinky.* A **yarmulka** (yahr-muhl'-kuh) is a skullcap made of plain, embroidered, beaded, or crocheted fabric that is worn by Orthodox

Jewish males for day wear and in the synagogue. Worn by other Jewish men for special occasions and religious services. Also see under HEADWEAR: CALOTTE and CLERICAL DRESS: CALOTTE.

sleep bonnet Any net, snood, or cap worn to bed to protect hairstyle.

slouch hat Woman's hat similar to a man's FEDORA (see under HEADWEAR), made with a flexible brim that may be turned down in front. Also called a GARBO HAT (see under HEADWEAR).

slouch hat

snap-brim hat Man's or woman's hat with the brim worn at several different angles according to the preference of the wearer. Also see under HEADWEAR: REX HARRISON HAT.

snood Hairnet made from chenille, mesh, or other material worn at the back of the head and nape of neck to confine the hair—sometimes attached to a hat. In 15th and 16th c., nets decorated with pearls and jewels were worn. During the Second Empire (1852–1870) snoods of chenille or fine silk cord decorated with steel beads were worn over the CHIGNON (see under HAIRSTYLES). A **cadogan net** was a popular snood in late 1870s and early 1880s—particularly for young women and girls—that was sometimes made of knotted silk yarn, worn over crown of head, and enclosed the hair that hangs down the back. Also spelled *catagan.* Snoods are revived periodically.

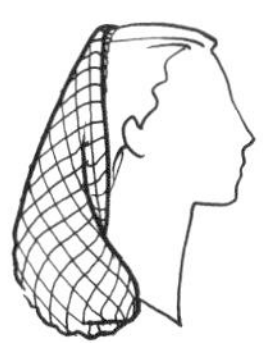
snood

sombrero (som-brer′-oh) Mexican hat with a tall, slightly tapered crown and large upturned brim. Worn in Mexico by laborers in straw and by wealthier citizens in felt lavishly trimmed around the edge, sometimes with silver lace. Also worn in Spain and the southwestern United States, where it is made of felt and somewhat similar to a *ten-gallon hat. Der.* Spanish, *sombre,* "to shade."

sombrero córdobes See under HEADWEAR: GAUCHO HAT.

soul cap See under HEADWEAR: NEWSBOY CAP.

sou′wester/southwester Rain hat made with a dome-shaped sectioned crown and broad stitched brim—larger in back. Originally made of yellow oiled silk—now made of any waterproof fabric for children's rainwear and for fishermen. *Der.* First worn by fishermen in New England where a wind from the southwest portended rain.

space helmet Helmet made of molded plastic covering the head and neck completely and fastening to collar around the top of the space suit. Front section is made of see-through plastic with mirrorlike reflective finish.

∞**splyter-hat/splinter hat** Hat made of braided split pieces of straw rather than whole rounded stalks, as it was called in the 16th c.

∞**spoon bonnet** Small-crowned bonnet of early 1860s with brim narrow at sides and projecting upward above forehead in elliptical shape.

Statue of Liberty visor Headband with seven spikes and visor in front worn during "Liberty Weekend" in 1986 in celebration of the renovation of the Statue of Liberty in New York harbor.

steeple headdress See under HEADWEAR: HENNIN.

∞**stephane** 1. Decorated, crescent-shaped headdress worn in ancient Greece and Rome by brides, or as a badge of office or wreath used as a symbol of victory. 2. Ancient Greek term for anything that encircles the head; a *coronal, diadem,* or the brim of a helmet. 3. Crown sent by Byzantine emperors to other monarchs and important dignitaries.

Stetson® Brand trademark for a man's hat manufacturer of all types of hats, but often used to mean a wide-brimmed, Western-style hat, especially the COWBOY style (see under HEADWEAR).

stocking cap A knitted or crocheted cap with a long pendant tail worn hanging down the back or side, frequently with a tassel on the end. Also called *toboggan cap.*

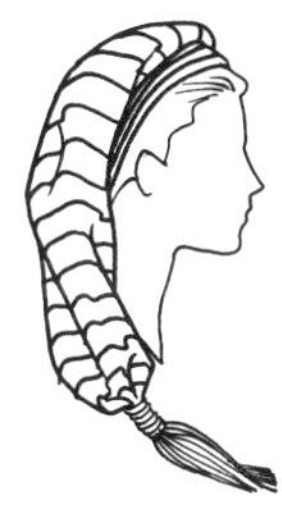
stocking cap

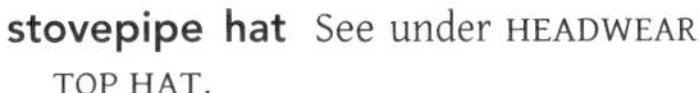

stovepipe hat See under HEADWEAR: TOP HAT.

stroller Casual, mannish, felt hats worn by women for town and spectator sports in 1930s and 1940s.

sugarloaf hat See under HEADWEAR: COPOTAIN.

sun bonnet Wide-brimmed fabric BONNET (see under HEADWEAR: BONNET #1) tied under chin, especially worn by infants and children for protection against the sun. Often made with pockets into which pieces of cardboard or other firm material could be slipped in order to provide stiffness to the brim. Originally worn by early pioneers on western treks across the United States for protection against the sun. Revived for Centennial celebrations throughout the United States.

swagger hat Informal sports hat, often made of felt, with medium-sized brim turned down in front. Popular in 1930s and 1940s for men and women.

sweatband 1. Band, usually made of sheepskin leather, placed around the inside of a man's hat where crown joins the brim, to protect hat from sweat. 2. A stretch terrycloth band worn around the head during exercise to absorb sweat.

tam/tam-o-shanter 1. "Tam" is a shortened form of the Scottish "tam-o-shanter" used in the United States. It is a flat cap made in several ways: (1) made out of two circles of fabric—one complete and one with hole cut in center—sewed together at the outer edge; (2) crocheted

tam

with pompon on top for trim; (3) made out of piece of circular molded felt and also called a BERET (see under HEADWEAR). 2. Genuine Scottish tams are frequently made out of long, shaggy, striped wool fabric and cut in segments so that stripes form a pattern on the top. Usually larger than other tams with a pompon at center of crown. *Der.* From the name of the main character of Scottish poem written by Robert Burns about 1791 called "Tam O'Shanter."

tea-cozy cap Cap introduced in late 1960s that fits head closely to cover hair completely. *Der.* Quilted, padded cover for teapots used to keep the tea hot at the table.

templers/temples/templettes See under HEADWEAR: BOSSES.

ten-gallon hat See under HEADWEAR: COWBOY HAT and SOMBRERO.

∞**terai hat** Riding hat of fur or felt with red lining, shaped somewhat like a DERBY (see under HEADWEAR), with large brim that had a metal vent in the crown. Made from two hats sewed together at edges of brims, and worn by British women, and sometimes men, in tropical climates since 1880s.

∞**thérèse** (ter-eece') /**teresa** Large hood, held out with wire, designed to go over tall bonnets and hairstyles. Worn in France from mid-1770s to 1790, later with an attached shoulder cape.

∞**three-storeys-and-a-basement** Amusing name given to woman's hat of 1886 with very high crown.

∞**thrum** 1. Short tufts of wool left on loom after fabric is cut away, knitted into workmen's caps in the United States and England in 18th c. 2. Long-napped felt hat worn in 16th c. Also called a *thrummed hat.*

tiara (tee-ar'-ah) Curved band, often of metal set with jewels or flowers, worn on top of woman's head from ear to ear, giving effect of a crown. Sometimes used to hold a wedding veil. Also called *demi-coronal.*

∞**tilbury hat** Man's small hat with high, tapered, flat-topped crown and narrow, rounded brim worn in 1830s.

toboggan cap See under HEADWEAR: STOCKING CAP.

topee/topi Tropical helmet shaped more like a hat with a wide brim, originally made of cork ½″ thick. Worn particularly in the jungles as a protection from the sun. Does not fit close to the head, because constructed with an air space between head and helmet. Also called *pith helmet. Der.* Name refers to European cork.

top hat Man's tall hat made of shiny silk or beaver cloth with narrow brim. Differs from an OPERA HAT (see under HEADWEAR) in that the latter is always collapsible and made of dull silk. Term used since about 1820 for a high-crowned hat with a flat top and narrow brim, sometimes slightly rolled at the sides. Also called a **chimney-pot hat** from the 1830s, when it replaced the beaver hat. After this it was made by felting rabbit hair on top of silk and applying steam and pressure to make a smooth and shiny surface. Also see under HEADWEAR: SILK HAT. Also called *plug hat* (American term for top hat), *pot hat, stovepipe hat* (because of its resemblance to a stove pipe), or *topper.*

top hat

topper See under HEADWEAR: TOP HAT.

toque (tok) 1. A basic hat type that has a high crown and is generally brimless or may have a very small brim. Can be made in various shapes, often turban-like. ∞2. Woman's coif or head scarf worn in the 16th and early 17th c.

toque #1

∞**toquet** (toe-ket') Woman's small, draped, evening hat worn on back of head in 1840s. Made of satin or velvet with small turned-up brim in front and trimmed with ostrich feather.

toreador hat (tor-ayah'-dor) 1. See under HEADWEAR: MATADOR HAT. ∞2. Woman's hat of the 1890s with flat, shallow, circular crown made of felt or straw and worn tilted. Inspired by the opera *Carmen,* starring Emma Calve.

∞**torsade** (tor-sahd') Coronet of pleated velvet or tulle with long LAPPETS (see under HEADWEAR) worn for evening by women in 1864.

touring cap Leather or fabric cap with snap-down visor, frequently treated for water repellency. Popular in the 1980s, it is copied from earlier cap worn when "touring" in early 20th-c. automobiles.

∞**trafalgar turban** British woman's evening turban of 1806, embroidered with Admiral Nelson's name. *Der.* Named for British naval victory near Cape Trafalgar, off Spanish coast, in 1805.

∞**trencher hat** Woman's silk hat with triangular brim coming to point above forehead, worn in first decade of the 19th c.

tricorne (try'-korn) (*tricorn*) Variation of the COCKED HAT (see under HEADWEAR), turned up to form three equidistant peaks with one peak in center front, as it was called in the 19th c.

tricorne

∞**trilby** Man's soft felt hat with supple brim worn from 1895 on. *Der.* Inspired by George du Maurier's 1894 novel *Trilby.* The following year, *Trilby* was made into a play in which Beerbohm Tree played the character Svengali, in this type of hat.

trooper cap Man's or boy's cap of leather or leatherlike plastic, with fur or pile lining and a flap around sides and back. Flaps can be folded down to keep ears warm or up to reveal lining. *Der.* Originally worn by state police or "troopers"; now used by mail carriers, police officers, etc.

trucker's cap A mesh cap, collected by truck drivers from the stops along their routes; similar to baseball caps, but stiffer with a higher crown.

turban 1. Man's headdress of Moslem origin consisting of long scarf of linen, cotton, or silk wound around the head; sometimes with one loose end hanging down, or decorated with a jewel in center front. Sometimes consists of fabric wrapped around a FEZ (see under HEADWEAR) with crown showing. 2. Adaptation of this draped hat for women has become a classic style.

turban #2

∞**turkey bonnet** Man's or woman's tall cylindrical hat without a brim, as it was referred to in the 15th and 16th c. Introduced to Italy, France, and England from the East. Woman's style was shaped like inverted flower pot with veil from crown passing under chin. Also called *turkey hat.*

∞**tutulus** (toot-too′-luss) Tall, cone-shaped hat worn by ancient Etruscan women with or without upturned brim across the front.

Tyrolean hat See under HEADWEAR: ALPINE HAT.

∞**ugly** (British usage) Collapsible brim worn from late 1840s to mid-1860s over a *bonnet* as a sunshade to protect weak eyes or when traveling. Made of series of cane half-hoops covered with silk. When not in use, folded up like a *calash.*

umbrella brim Brim of woman's hat set in *umbrella pleats,* opens out to resemble an umbrella.

∞**under cap** 1. Indoor cap made like a skullcap worn under hat by elderly men in 16th c. 2. Woman's indoor cap usually shaped like a COIF (see under HEADWEAR: COIF #3) worn under outdoor hat from 16th to mid-19th c.

∞**valois hat** (val-wa′) Velvet or beaver hat with brim of equal width all around worn by women in 1822.

veil 1. Decorative accessory usually made of lace, net, tulle, or sheer fabric placed on the head and usually draped down the back. May also drape over the face and shoulders. 2. Piece of net or tulle attached to a hat. Introduced in medieval times and called a *coverchief.* From late 18th to end of 19th c. a piece of net, lace, or gauze worn attached to an outdoor bonnet or hat worn by women. Arranged to cover part of or the entire face or draped to back as trimming. From 1890s veils extended to the chin. Worn intermittently since, mostly as trim. Particularly worn in 1930s, 1940s, and 1950s.

visor Stiffened part of a semicircle attached to a headband or to front of a cap to protect eyes from the sun. Also called *bill.*

∞**vulture-winged headdress** An Egyptian queen's headdress with two wings hanging down on either side of the face with the uraeus, or cobra design of the sacred asp, usually attached to center front. The vulture wings are a symbol of protection used by the Egyptians.

watch cap Knitted cap, fitting closely over head with turned-up cuff, made of navy-blue wool yarn. Worn by sailors on watch, for other work duty, or as a replacement for white duck hat. Adapted in other colors for sportswear by men, women, and children.

watch cap

∞**watteau hat** (wat-toe′) Small hat for the seashore, shaped like an upside-down saucer, worn by women in 1866. Trimmed with ribbons radiating from crown to edge of brim. Sometimes had a rosette with attached streamers on right side. *Der.* Named for the artist WATTEAU.

welding cap Cap similar to a baseball cap but with a relatively short VISOR (see under HEADWEAR).

wellington hat Tall beaver hat worn by men in the 1820s and 1830s with a crown at least 8″ high and flared at the top. *Der.* Named for the first Duke of Wellington, British military hero who defeated Napoleon in the Battle of Waterloo in 1815.

western hat High-crowned hat with a flat top and wide brim frequently trimmed with a leather thong pulled through holes that are punched at regular intervals around the crown. Has a leather adjustable strap worn under the chin to secure the hat or permit it to hang down the back. Similar to GAUCHO HAT (see under HEADWEAR).

∞**white crown** Crown of ancient Upper Egypt made in tall, cylindrical shape tapered in at top and ending with a knob. When Egypt became united, this crown was worn together with the red crown of lower Egypt.

∞**wide-awake** Man's 19th-c., broad-brimmed, low-crowned hat of felt or other material used for country wear.

∞**widow's peak** Small cap wired in heart-shaped form with peak in center of forehead. Originally worn by Catherine de Medici as a widow's bonnet and much worn by Mary, Queen of Scots. Also see under HEADWEAR: MARIE STUART BONNET.

wig hat Soft hat, often crocheted, that fits tightly around the face but blouses in the back. Some hats are covered entirely with feathers, some with flowers. No hair shows from beneath the hat. Popular in mid-1960s.

william penn hat Medium-sized brim with high-rounded crown worn forward on the head. Introduced in late

1960s. *Der.* Similar to hat worn by William Penn (1644–1718) when he colonized Pennsylvania.

wimple 1. Cloth worn to cover the chin of a woman in the Middle Ages. During the 14th c., it gradually became a part of the customary dress of widows, who wore it with a dark hood and veil. It also became a part of the habits of some orders of nuns. Also called a *barbe.* ∞2. Gauze veil of 1809 worn with evening dress.

wind bonnet Lightweight, fold-up covering for head made of net, point d'esprit, or chiffon to protect hair.

World War I helmet Cast metal helmet, with a shallow crown and narrow brim, that did not cover the ears or conform to the shape of the head, held on by a chin strap.

World War II helmet Cast metal helmet conforming closely to the shape of the head with slightly upturned edge. When worn in battle, sometimes covered with a piece of multicolored fabric for camouflage.

yachting cap Cap, usually white, with flat crown and black or navy-blue visor, decorated with yacht-club emblem. Styled similar to a naval officer's cap, and also worn by yacht-club members on boats.

yarmulka See under HEADWEAR: SKULLCAP.

∞yeoman hat Woman's fabric hat with puffed crown gathered into wide band, sometimes with upturned brim worn with WALKING DRESS from 1806 to 1812.

zucchetto See under CLERICAL DRESS: CALOTTE.

---

head wrap See under HEADWEAR.

heart breaker See under HAIRSTYLES: CRÈVE-COEUR and LOVE LOCK.

heart-shaped cut See under GEMS, GEM CUTS, AND SETTINGS.

heart-shaped headdress See under HEADWEAR.

†heather effect Appearance of fabric achieved by blending dyed fibers with white fibers to produce a mottled appearance. First made in lavender tones similar to the flowers of the heather plant, but now made in many different colors.

†heat setting Process used to set, by applying heat and pressure, permanent pleats or creases in fabrics made of manufactured fibers such as nylon, polyester, and acetate.

heat transfer printing See under PRINTING.

hedebo See under EMBROIDERIES AND SEWING STITCHES.

hedgehog See under HAIRSTYLES: COIFFURE À L'HÉRISSON.

heel 1. See under FOOTWEAR. 2. See under HOSIERY.

heel horn See under FOOTWEAR: A.T.P.

heelless hose See under HOSIERY.

heel lift See under FOOTWEAR: HEEL.

heels See under FOOTWEAR.

heely See under FOOTWEAR.

heliodor See under GEMS, GEM CUTS, AND SETTINGS.

heliotrope See under GEMS, GEM CUTS, AND SETTINGS: BLOODSTONE.

helmet See under HEADWEAR.

hem See under CLOTHING CONSTRUCTION DETAILS.

hematite See under GEMS, GEM CUTS, AND SETTINGS.

hemispherical hat See under HEADWEAR: BOLINGER.

hemming stitch See under EMBROIDERIES AND SEWING STITCHES.

†hemp A coarse, strong, lustrous fiber from the stem of the hemp plant. Cultivation of hemp plants is illegal in the U.S. because the plant is from the same family as marijuana; however, sale of hemp fabrics and fibers is legal, and the fiber is used for making apparel.

hemstitch/hemstitching See under EMBROIDERIES AND SEWING STITCHES.

henley boater See under HEADWEAR: BOATER.

henley neckline See under NECKLINES AND COLLARS.

henley shirt See under SHIRTS.

henna 1. Orange-colored dye, one of the earliest dyes discovered; comes from the plant by the same name. Egyptians used it to dye their fingers to the first joint, simulating our nail polish. Also used on toes in some Eastern countries in early days. Used to dye fabrics in primitive times. 2. Basic hair dye or rinse. 3. An orange color.

hennin See under HEADWEAR.

henrietta jacket See under COATS AND JACKETS.

Henry II collar See under NECKLINES AND COLLARS.

Henry IV collar See under NECKLINES AND COLLARS.

hense lynes/henselyns See under DOUBLET.

hercules braid See under BRAIDS.

herigaut See under GARDE-CORPS.

hérisson See under HAIRSTYLES.

Herkimer diamond See under GEMS, GEM CUTS, AND SETTINGS.

herl See under FEATHERS.

herlot See under HARLOT.

heroin chic Applied to fashion advertising and magazine photography style of the late 1980s and 1990s in which models appear emaciated, pale, and unkempt, with large circles under their eyes; an appearance likened to that of hard-drug addicts.

herringbone Pattern made of short, slanting parallel lines adjacent to other rows slanting in reverse direction, creating a continuous V-shaped design like the bones of a fish. Used in tweeds, embroidery, and in working of fur skins.

herringbone chain See under CHAIN #1.

herringbone stitch See under EMBROIDERIES AND SEWING STITCHES: CATCH STITCH and HERRINGBONE STITCH.

†herringbone weave Chevron pattern produced in a fabric by using the twill weave for several rows in one direction, then reversing the direction. Usually made of yarns of two colors in yarn-dyed woolen fabric with thick yarns producing a large pattern. Also called *broken twill weave.*

hessian boot See under FOOTWEAR.

heuke See under HEADWEAR.

heuse See under FOOTWEAR.

hickory stripe See under PRINTS, STRIPES, AND CHECKS.

hidden rivets jeans Jeans with rivets hidden inside the pockets, manufactured by Levi Strauss between 1937 and about 1960.

high button shoe See under FOOTWEAR: BUTTONED SHOE.

high cut See under FOOTWEAR.

high fashion Apparel of advanced design available from innovative designers and/or firms. It is usually expensive.

high hat See under HEADWEAR: TOP HAT.

Highland dress Traditional man's costume of Scots Highlander, consisting of KILT; PLAID over one shoulder fastened by brooch; scarlet jacket; wide belt with SPORRAN attached (see under HANDBAGS AND RELATED ACCESSORIES); feather bonnet or GLENGARRY CAP (see under HEADWEAR); plaid-top socks; and buttoned gaiters over shoes. Costume was forbidden by law from 1747 to 1782. Also see under introduction to PLAIDS AND TARTANS.

Highland suit Boy's suit of 1880s and early 1890s consisting of jacket, kilt, GLENGARRY CAP (see under HEADWEAR), and plaid socks copied from *Highland dress.* Also called a *Scotch suit.*

highlights See under HAIRSTYLES.

high-rise pants See under PANTS.

high-rise waistline See under WAISTLINES.

high tech fabrics/hi-tech fabrics Fabrics made from manufactured fibers with special performance characteristics (e.g., water repellency, strength, stretch, heat resistance). Such fabrics have been used for fashion goods, especially in the area of clothing for active sports. Also called *high-performance fibers.*

hijab See under HEADWEAR.

hikers See under FOOTWEAR: HIKING BOOT.

hiking boot See under FOOTWEAR.

∞hiking costume Dress worn by women in 1890s consisting of serge or lighter-weight bloomers, pleated or gathered at the waist and pulled down below the knee. Worn with a tight-fitting Eton-type jacket with large lapels; a white shirt; man's necktie; serviceable shoes with flat heels worn with PUTTEES (see alphabetical listings) or high-top laced boots to below the knee; and hat similar to a cowboy hat with high uncreased crown and wide brim. Worn for mountain climbing and hiking.

himation

∞himation (he-matt′-ee-own) Greek mantle in the form of a rectangular shawl, 3½ to 4 yards long and about 1½ yards wide that was worn alone or over a tunic by men and women in ancient Greece. Made of wool or linen—usually white with border—it was usually draped over the left shoulder and wrapped under the right arm; sometimes one end was pulled over the head.

hinged bracelet See under JEWELRY.

∞hip bags Slang term of 1883 for the folds of skirt forming PANNIERS at hips. Also called *curtain drapery* in the U.S. and *pompadour* in England.

hip boot See under FOOTWEAR.

hip buttons See under CLOSURES.

hip-hop A style of dancing associated with rap music that began in the Bronx in New York City. **B-boys** (break boys) of 1970s (their female followers were called **flygirls**) developed an athletic dance style. When this music and dance became part of the mainstream in the 1980s, fans imitated styles worn by B-boys and flygirls and wore bright, baggy clothes, football or baseball shirts, baseball caps turned backward, and high running shoes with untied shoe laces, designer sportswear, athletic shoes, and large-scale gold jewelry. In the 1990s, mainstream fashion designers such as TOMMY HILFIGER incorporated hip-hop styles into their lines, and hip-hop influences permeated styles worn by the young. Around 2001, fans of rap music began to wear clip-on covers for their teeth, called **fronts** or **grills,** made of gold and set with diamonds or other gems. When a person wearing these devices smiled, it was said that his or her smile had **bling.**

hip-hugger Low-slung pants, skirt, or belt worn below normal waistline, resting on hip bones, as known contemporarily. See also under PANTS, SHORTS, SKIRTS, and UNDERGARMENTS.

hip length See under LENGTHS.

hippie *adj.* Describes the style associated with people who were known by this name. Derived from the mid-1960s name for or reference to a young person who defied established customs and adopted an unconventional mode of dress (e.g., long uncombed hair, aged blue jeans, miscellaneous tops, fringed jackets, strings of beads, symbolic pendants, pouch bags, bare feet, or sandals). The hippie style of dressing started a trend toward ethnic fashions and unusual mixtures of dress. See under HANDBAGS AND RELATED ACCESSORIES: SQUAW BAG and JEWELRY: HIPPIE BEADS.

hippie style

hip-rider swimsuit See under SWIMWEAR.

hipster brief See under UNDERGARMENTS: HIP-HUGGERS.

hipsters 1. See under PANTS: HIP-HUGGERS. 2. Fans of bebop music, played by Dizzy Gillespie in the 1940s, who wore berets, colorful, wide scarves, sunglasses, and GOATEES (see under BEARD). 3. Ongoing subculture of 20–30 year olds who value independent thinking as it relates to politics, art, creativity, and fashion.

hi-rise girdle See under UNDERGARMENTS: GIRDLE.

historic dress See under COSTUME #3 and DRESS #1.

his and hers *adj.* Descriptive of garments that look alike but that are specifically made, one for a man, the other for a woman; distinct from "unisex look," where garments were actually interchangeable. Popular for pajamas during the 1950s. During the late 1960s, popular for all types of clothing, particularly pantsuits with matching vest, caped coats, shirts, and sweaters. Also see under UNISEX.

hive bonnet See under HEADWEAR: BEEHIVE HAT #1.

H-line Straight silhouette, or dress, marked by a low horizontal belt or seam and called *H* by Paris designer Christian Dior in 1957.

hobble skirt See under SKIRTS.

hobnailed boot See under FOOTWEAR.

hobo See under HANDBAGS AND RELATED ACCESSORIES.

hockey skate See under FOOTWEAR.

hogger/hoker See under FOOTWEAR: OKER.

holbein stitch See under EMBROIDERIES AND SEWING STITCHES: DOUBLE-RUNNING STITCH.

holbein work See under EMBROIDERIES AND SEWING STITCHES.

Hollywood-top slip See under UNDERGARMENTS.

holoku (hoh-low′-koo) Traditional Hawaiian garment derived from the EMPIRE DRESS (see under DRESSES) styles worn by American missionary women when they arrived in Hawaii in the early 1880s. Hawaiian royalty asked the missionaries to make them dresses, and the resulting gowns were altered slightly to accommodate the relatively larger size of the Hawaiians, as well as the difference in the local climate. The full-length garment had a YOKE from which the dress fell in a loose fit, a high neck, and long sleeves. Over the years these garments have changed somewhat as fashions changed, but retain these basic lines in either more or less fitted versions and are still worn for formal occasions by women of Hawaiian descent.

holster pocket See under POCKETS.

holy work/hollie work See under EMBROIDERIES AND SEWING STITCHES.

homburg See under HEADWEAR.

home fashions Textile products used for home-end uses such as towels, bedding, draperies, and table linens, and which exhibit style changes over time in response to changing fashion trends.

home party See under PARTY PLAN.

†homespun Fabrics made from handspun yarns and woven on a hand loom. Most are plain weave, loosely constructed, heavy wool fabrics made of coarse, uneven yarns. Contemporary versions are now made with automatic looms from manufactured and wool blends and imitate the texture and appearance of the handmade fabrics.

†honeycomb Any fabric that forms a series of recessed squares similar to a waffle and is made either in a honeycomb weave or knit. Cotton fabrics are frequently called *waffle-cloth.* They are sometimes erroneously called *waffle piqués.*

honeycomb stitch See under EMBROIDERIES AND SEWING STITCHES.

honiton gossamer skirt See under UNDERGARMENTS.

honiton lace See under LACES.

hood See under HEADWEAR.

hooded heel See under FOOTWEAR.

hooded seal See under FURS: HAIR SEAL.

hook and eye See under CLOSURES.

hook-and-loop closure See under CLOSURES: VELCRO®.

hoop bracelet See under JEWELRY: BANGLE BRACELET.

hoop earrings See under JEWELRY: GYPSY EARRINGS.

hoop petticoat See under UNDERGARMENTS: HOOPS.

hoops See under UNDERGARMENTS.

hoop skirt See under SKIRTS.

hoover apron See under APRONS.

Hope Star See under GEMS, GEM CUTS, AND SETTINGS.

Hopi bracelet See under JEWELRY.

†hopsacking A broad classification of fabrics made in loosely constructed plain weave of coarse, uneven yarns. The fabric was originally found in sacks made from coarse undyed jute or hemp, into which hops were put during harvesting. Made in cotton, spun rayon, and manufactured fibers. Coarse varieties also called BURLAP.

∞hoqueton/houqueton See under ARMOR: ACTON.

horizontal integration The production by a business of products competitive with other products it makes. For example, a knitted fabric producer that makes various types of knitted fabrics. Also see under VERTICAL INTEGRATION.

horned headdress See under HEADWEAR.

horn rims See under EYEWEAR.

horsehair † 1. Hair fiber obtained from the mane or tail of a horse. 2. Fabric made from this fiber used in combination with mohair, linen, cotton, and other fibers woven in an openwork weave. Used for interfacing in suits, coats, and also for stiffening.

horsehair braid See under BRAIDS.

horsehide See under LEATHERS.

horseshoe Term for U-shape, used as neckline or yoke on blouses, sweaters, and dresses.

horseshoe collar/horseshoe neckline See under NECKLINES AND COLLARS.

horseshoe jumper See under JUMPERS.

hose See under HOSIERY.

HOSIERY

Knitted item of wearing apparel covering the foot and/or leg. Includes apparel also called STOCKINGS and SOCKS (see under HOSIERY). For forerunners of knitted hosiery, see under CHAUSSES and CHAUSSEMBLES in the alphabetical listing. A machine for knitting stockings was invented in the late 1500s, and the inventor presented Queen Elizabeth I with a pair of knitted silk stockings. Hosiery was made from cotton, linen, wool, and silk yarns. Among the innovations in the development of hosiery were "flesh-colored," or beige, silk hosiery in the 1920s, the introduction of NYLON hose in 1940, textured hose in the 1960s, and PANTYHOSE (see under HOSIERY) in the 1960s. Synonym: HOSE (see under HOSIERY). *Der.* Anglo-Saxon *hosa.*

all-in-one pantyhose See under HOSIERY: PANTYHOSE.

all-sheer pantyhose Sheer nylon pantyhose made with no reinforcements. Also called *sheer pantyhose.*

ankle-length hosiery Sock-length hosiery made out of conventional nylon yarn. Worn by women with full-length slacks or pants.

ankle sock Short sock reaching only to the ankle; may be worn turned down or have elastic top on the cuff. Introduced for women in 1920. This caused a sensation when they were first worn in Forest Hills, New York, for an amateur tennis match in 1931 by Mrs. Fearnley-Whittingstall. Worn today by women and children and infrequently by men. Also called *anklet.* Also see under HOSIERY: BOBBY SOCK.

ankle sock

anklet See under HOSIERY: ANKLE SOCK.

anti-embolism stocking A stocking specially constructed with graduated compression that aids blood flow and prevents blood clots from forming. Also called *surgical stockings.*

argyle socks Sock knitted in a diamond pattern of several colors by hand or on a jacquard loom. Heel, toe, and top areas are of solid color while the other part is of a multicolored, diamond-patterned plaid. *Der.* Tartan of Duke of Argyle and Clan Campbell of Argyll, a county in West Scotland. Also spelled *argyll, argyl.*

Art Deco hose Hose printed with geometric designs derived from Art Deco styles, which underwent a revival in the late 1960s. *Der.* French, *art decoratif,* "decorative art."

Art Nouveau hose Stylized single or multiple printed designs placed on the calf or climbing the leg, usually on opaque or colored hose, based on Art Nouveau designs. An innovation of the late 1960s. *Der.* French, "new art."

astrolegs hose Hose imprinted with signs of the zodiac, introduced in the late 1960s.

athletic sock See under HOSIERY: SWEATSOCK.

bed sock Knit sock worn when sleeping to keep foot warm. Often hand-knit in a variety of fancy stitches. Also called *foot warmer.*

bikini pantyhose Pantyhose with low-slung top for wear with bare-midriff dresses, hip-hugger skirts, or low-slung pants.

blazer sock Boys' and girls' socks decorated with bands of color. Similar in effect to competitive stripes on knit shirts.

bobby sock Ankle sock, usually with turned-down cuff, worn by children and so universally popular with female teenagers during 1940s and 1950s that young girls were called "bobby soxers."

bodyshaper pantyhose See under HOSIERY: PANTYHOSE.

boot That part of pantyhose or stocking that extends from the panty or welt to the toe.

∞boot hose Long stockings of coarse linen with flared tops. The tops sometimes had decorated borders made of gold or silver lace, ruffled linen, or fringed silk, which were called **boot hose tops.** When made with no foot, fitted with a strap under arch of foot, and laced through eyelets at top to connect with breeches, they were called **stirrup hose.** Worn by men from mid-15th to 18th c. to protect silk stockings under heavy boots. Also called *boot stocking.*

boot hose tops See under HOSIERY: BOOT HOSE.

bootie See under FOOTWEAR: BOOTIE #2.

checkerboard hose Hose knitted in a checked design with some squares sheer and some opaque, or knitted in two colors.

clocked hose Hose or stockings that have designs running part way up the sides of the legs. First worn in the 16th c. and intermittently since. Designs may be knitted in or embroidered on after hose are knitted.

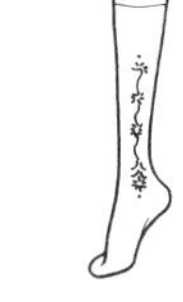
clocked hose

control pantyhose See under HOSIERY: PANTYHOSE.

Courrèges flower sock See under HOSIERY: KNEE-HI SOCK.

crew sock Heavy sock extending to lower calf with foot knitted in plain stitch, upper part with rib stitch. Originally white and worn for rowing and other sports. Now made in colors, especially for men and boys.

cushion-sole sock Sock worn for active sports knit with a special sole that keeps the foot from blistering—often a layer of cotton and stretch-nylon terry cloth. Frequently given a special finish to help protect the foot from fungus, bacteria, and odor.

detachable pantyhose Three-piece pantyhose made with patented bands on panties to attach replacement stockings.

dress sock Man's sock in lightweight, silky type, nonbulky yarns in conservative colors.

electric sock Heavyweight knee-high sock, usually made of a combination of fibers, with a specially designed heating element operated by a battery held on by strap around the leg. Worn by spectators at winter sports events. Trademarked by Timely Products Corp. and called *Lectra-Sox®.*

english rib sock Man's sock knit with a wide rib or wale and a narrow depression between the wales (see under WALE #2).

fancies Men's socks in multicolor designs.

finger band In all nude pantyhose, a reinforcement just under the waistband to protect against fingernail punctures.

fishmouth toe Method of closing a nonreciprocating toe (see under HOSIERY: RECIPROCATED CONSTRUCTION) in which the seam runs parallel to the bottom of the foot rather than across the top of the toe.

fishnet hose Openwork hose in a diamond-shaped pattern.

flat-knit hose See under HOSIERY: FULL-FASHIONED HOSE.

footsock/footie Sock that ends below the ankle bone. When these socks have a pompon sewn on at the back, they may be called **poms.**

foot warmers See under HOSIERY: BED SOCK.

full-fashioned hose Hose that are knit in flat pieces and seamed up the back, leaving fashion marks where knitting is increased or decreased. Also called *flat-knit hose.*

garter belt hose Hose attached to two elastic strips that connect at waistline to an elastic band around waist.

glitter hose Hose made of shiny yarn—some made with metallic yarn that reflects silver, gold, and copper tones. Introduced to wear with mini dresses in the 1960s. Also called *glimmer, silver, gold* or *metallic hose.*

gold hose See under HOSIERY: GLITTER HOSE.

gym sock See under HOSIERY: SWEATSOCK.

half-hose Standard-length stocking for men that ends halfway between the ankle and the knee.

heel Portion of the hose that fits the heel of the foot.

heelless hose Hosiery without a double reinforcement at the heel.

hose Synonym for STOCKINGS (see under HOSIERY) and HOSIERY (see under introduction to HOSIERY). Current usage suggests that hose tends to be used when referring to the more transparent and decorative varieties of hosiery, while "stockings" is used for heavier varieties of a more utilitarian nature.

jacquard hose (ja-kard') Hosiery knit on a jacquard knitting machine that permits much variation in colors and patterns. Argyle and herringbone designs are examples of jacquard patterns. Popular in the 1920s for children, and fashionable since.

jeweled pantyhose Sheer pantyhose with embroidery at ankle trimmed with rhinestones. Introduced in 1986.

knee-high hose Hose of conventional nylon yarn or of nylon and SPANDEX that come to just below the knees and are finished at the top with elastic. First made in beige and worn when dresses were long, now worn with various types of pants and after the 1980s featured in black, white, and colors. Sometimes abbreviated to *knee-hi.*

knee-hi sock Sock that reaches to below the knee. Worn by boys in early 1900s with knickers and accepted for girls in 1920s and 1930s and after. Adopted by teenagers and adult women in the 1960s as the popularity of the MINI increased. Featured by the French couturier Courrèges in his collection in 1965. In 1967 he introduced a variation called the **Courrèges flower**

knee-hi sock

sock (coor-rej′), a dainty feminine sock coming to several inches below the knee usually styled in white with lacy top, embroidered with flowers. Also called *knee sock, trouser sock.*

knee sock See under HOSIERY: KNEE-HI SOCK.

lace hose Hose made of knitted lace in rose, Chantilly, and Spanish lace patterns. Introduced in 1960s and popular for children and women in 1980s.

lace pantyhose Pantyhose made of patterned stretch lace in openwork styles.

legwarmer Knitted covering for legs extending from the ankle to the knee or above. Originally worn by ballet and toe dancers when exercising, and in the 1980s became a fashion item.

legwarmer

lisle hosiery (lyle) Socks and hose made of cotton LISLE YARN, smooth, lustrous cotton yarn. Nearly as fine as silk, usually white, brown, or black, lisle hosiery was worn by men, women, and children throughout 19th and early 20th c. until replaced by silk in 1920s and nylon in 1940s. Revived in the 1960s when longer opaque socks were popular. See under HOSIERY: OPAQUE HOSE. *Der.* Early spelling of Lille, France.

mesh hose Nylon hose knit with a milanese stitch, forming tiny diamond designs that make hose run-resistant. See under MILANESE KNIT.

metallic hose See under HOSIERY: GLITTER HOSE.

mini-pane hose See under HOSIERY: WINDOWPANE HOSE.

mock seam Hosiery industry term for seam sewed into circular-knit hose to give appearance of FULL-FASHIONED HOSE (see under HOSIERY).

neats Solid-color socks ornamented with small, evenly spaced designs such as dots.

neon sock Ankle- or knee-length sock styled with ribbed top in extremely bright colors of 100% nylon.

nonreciprocated See under HOSIERY: RECIPROCATED CONSTRUCTION.

novelties Women's hosiery that has unusual patterns, designs, or coloring.

nude heel Women's pantyhose or nylon stockings that have no reinforcement at the heel. Popular for wear with backless or sling-back shoes.

nylons Now synonymous with women's hose because of the almost universal use of NYLON in dress hose for women. Trademarked nylon yarn was introduced in 1939, making possible a much more sheer type of hose that was also more durable than the silk hosiery worn previously. In great demand during World War II, nylon hosiery became a "black market" item.

opaque hose/opaque pantyhose (oh-pake′) Textured or plain hose or pantyhose that are not sheer and come in all colors. Opaque nylon pantyhose are 40 DENIER or more in weight.

over-the-knee socks Sock or stocking with an elastic top that reaches above the knee. Elastic top holds up the stocking without a garter.

pantyhose Hosiery, made with textured and sheer nylon yarns, that follows the design of tights, having stockings and panties cut in one piece. In 1958 the firm called Société de Bonneterie De Tergnier in France patented a brand of sheer pantyhose called *mitoufle* (mitt-oof′-luh) (or tights). Mary Quant, British designer, also was influential in trying to find a suitable hose and girdle combination for wear with her short-skirted dresses of early 1960s. Pantyhose were introduced in the United States about 1963. First made in sizes for tall, medium, and petite heights, and later made in larger sizes, pantyhose were introduced for men in fall 1970. In the mid-1980s, interest in unusual pantyhose was revived and currently they are made in many patterns, colors, and textures. Those pantyhose with a knitted-in panty of heavier-weight nylon or cotton are known as **all-in-one pantyhose. Control pantyhose** are those in which the panty portion is knit of nylon and stretch yarns (see under ELASTOMERS) to provide the control of a lightweight girdle. **Bodyshaper pantyhose** are control pantyhose with the control section extending to cover the thighs in addition to abdomen and hips. Also see under HOSIERY: TIGHTS.

pantyhose

patterned hose Hosiery woven in a design, usually on a Jacquard knitting machine, e.g., point d'esprit, checkerboard, and argyle hose.

Peds® Registered trademark for a broad range of hosiery products of varying types and uses. Also see under HOSIERY: SOCKLET.

point d'esprit hose (pwan des-pree′) Netlike, machine-manufactured hose of cotton or nylon with some of the holes made solid to form a decorative pattern.

poms See under HOSIERY: FOOTSOCK.

proportioned hose Hosiery designed to fit different types of legs (e.g., extra-long, full above-the-knee, long, short, and average).

quarter socks Socks, shorter than ankle length, made of acrylic and nylon with colored terry knit top in colors.

reciprocated construction In the making of a stocking, which begins at the top and moves toward the toe, a semicircular or "reciprocating" motion of the machine shapes a pocket for the heel. A toe may also be formed.

A **nonreciprocated** stocking has no shaped heel or toe. (See under HOSIERY: TUBE SOCK and FISHMOUTH TOE.)

replaceable legs Waist-length garment in which one or both legs can be replaced. Made either as a separate panty to which legs attach at the bottom or as two separate legs, each with a half panty and a full waistband.

ribbed hose Textured hose, knit with vertical wales.

∞**rollups** Man's stockings pulled up over knee of breeches and folded over in wide band. Worn in late 17th to mid-18th c. Also called *rollers, rolling stockings,* or *hose.*

run See under RUN.

run-resistant hosiery See under RUN RESISTANT.

sandalfoot hose Hosiery with no reinforcement at the toe. Popular for wearing with open-toed shoes or sandals.

sandalfoot pantyhose Sheer pantyhose with no reinforcements at toes or heels. May have an opaque panty portion, or be sheer to the waist.

sanitary sock An athletic sock, usually white, worn under STIRRUP HOSE (see under HOSIERY) as part of an athletic uniform.

seamed hose 1. Full-fashioned hose with a seam up the back, originally made by the flat-knit process and sewed together. Popular type of hose generally worn until the 1960s, when textured yarns were invented with more "stretch," making it possible to make well-fitting hose without the seam. By 1968, very few seamed hose were sold. Reintroduced in 1970s but made in circular knits usually with black lines up the back.

seamed pantyhose Conventional pantyhose with black seam up the back.

seamless hose Circular-knit hose without seam in back. See under CIRCULAR KNIT.

sheer hose Nylon hose made with a fine or low denier yarn, thus making them more translucent. **Ultra-sheer** hose are made with exceptionally fine yarns; **day sheer** or **business sheer** hose are less sheer and more durable.

sheer pantyhose See under HOSIERY: ALL-SHEER PANTYHOSE.

silver hose See under HOSIERY: GLITTER HOSE.

slipper sock Crocheted or knit sock attached to soft, moccasin-type sole.

slouch sock Anklet with shirred tricolored top, made of acrylic and stretch nylon, designed to be pushed down and gathered around the ankle.

sneaker sock Type of SOCKLET (see under HOSIERY) that is shaped higher in front to conform to laced instep of the sneakers. Worn instead of sock for the bare-legged look.

socklet Very low-cut sock, usually lightweight and not visible above pumps or other shoes, styled to keep feet comfortable while maintaining bare-leg look in summer. PEDS® (see under HOSIERY) is a trademark for the first widely available socklet made in a number of fibers and styles.

socklet

socks Now generally applied to knitted coverings for the foot and part of the leg that end somewhere around the ankle or above. Also see under HOSIERY: STOCKINGS. *Der.* from the Latin *soccus,* which was a soft Roman shoe that covered the foot and ankle.

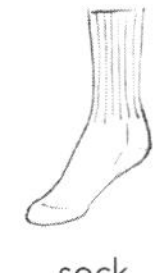
sock

stay-up hose Regular hose knitted with a special top that holds the hose up without garters. Also called *stretch top.*

stirrup hose 1. Hosiery in which the foot portion is fashioned without a heel or toe but which has a strap that fits under the instep of the foot. Often this construction is part of an athletic uniform. 2. See under HOSIERY: BOOT HOSE.

stocking Generally applied to knitted coverings for the foot and most of the leg. The distinction between socks and stockings is not entirely clear-cut, although socks are generally thought of as shorter and stockings as longer. *Der.* From a type of leg covering called STOCKS that was worn in the 15th and 16th c. and covered the foot and leg, extending to the waist. The upper section was called the "upper stocks" and the lower section, the "lower stocks." When the garment was eventually divided into two separate parts in the 16th c., the lower part, which extended to the knee or above, became known as a stocking.

stocking

stretch hose Hosiery made with textured nylon stretch yarns. When such hose are not on the leg, they look very small.

stretch socks Socks knitted with textured yarns. Made so flexible that one size usually fits any size foot. Also made for men, women, and children.

support legwear Hosiery for men or women knitted of stretch nylon combined with spandex yarns to provide support to the muscles and veins of the legs. These fabrics keep pressure on the blood vessels so they will not dilate. This improves the circulation and prevents leg fatigue. They are made as hose and pantyhose for women and socks or stockings for men.

surgical stocking See under HOSIERY: ANTI-EMBOLISM STOCKING.

suspender tights Stockings that are permanently attached to a GARTER BELT (see under UNDERGARMENTS). **Mock suspender tights** are made to look like suspender tights, being sheer from the top of the hose to a simulated garter belt, although they are constructed like PANTYHOSE (see under HOSIERY).

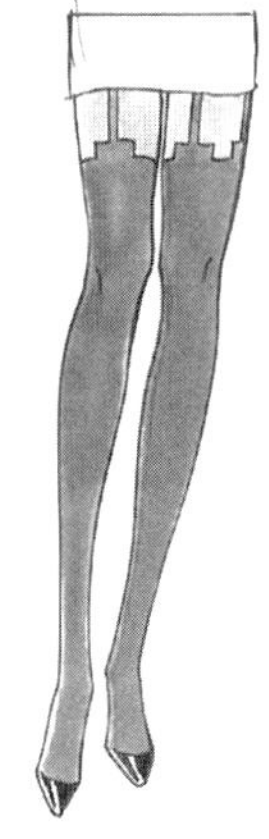
mock suspender tights

sweatsock Sock made of combination of fibers (e.g., wool, acrylic, cotton, sometimes with cushioned sole). When this type of sock was first worn, it was always white and made of coarse cotton yarns that stretched out of shape easily. The cotton versions were known as **gym socks,** which were worn instead of wool socks for active sports and gym classes, because of their washability. Blends now make these socks more washable and shape retentive. Usually they have a ribbed top and plain foot. Also called *athletic sock.*

tattoo pantyhose Very sheer pantyhose with legs painted in twining floral designs that appear, at a distance, to be tattooed on the leg.

textured hose Any style of hose patterned with thicker and thinner sections (e.g., lace, striped, or windowpane hose). First introduced by Rudi Gernreich in 1964 and later shown by other couturiers such as Givenchy in 1969.

thermal sock Heavy boot-length sock worn for winter activities; made of fibers with good insulating qualities.

thigh highs Nylon or nylon and spandex stockings that end at the top of the thigh and usually have elastic lace tops.

tights Knitted pants and stockings made in one piece, usually of opaque textured yarns. Worn originally by athletes and dancers, later worn by children. In the early 1960s worn primarily by women and girls as a substitute for hose. In 1980s also worn with leotards for dancing, exercising, etc.

toelet Hosiery designed to cover only the toe portion of the foot. Worn with heelless shoes such as mules or clogs.

trouser sock See under HOSIERY: KNEE-HI SOCK.

tights

tube sock Calf- or knee-length sock made of stretch yarn that does not have a knitted-in heel or toe.

ultra-sheer pantyhose See under HOSIERY: SHEER HOSE.

U seams Pantyhose in which one leg is sewn to the other with a continuous U-shaped seam, As a result, they have no crotch.

welt That part at the top of a stocking that is reinforced so that it is strong enough to fasten a support device. It may be a separate piece of fabric that is machine sewn to the top of the stocking, or may be knitted in heavier yarn and folded double.

windowpane hose Textured hose made in geometric squares in thin and thick sections. Heavier part looks like the frame of a window, and the more sheer section looks like the glass. **Mini-pane** hose have smaller squares. Made in white, black, and all colors (e.g., shocking pink, chartreuse, and orange). Popular in the mid-1960s.

---

hostess *adj.* Describes informal apparel worn at home while entertaining. Also called *at-home wear.* See under SLEEPWEAR AND LOUNGEWEAR: HOSTESS CULOTTES and HOSTESS ROBE.

hot mask See under MASKS.

hot pants/HotPants See under SHORTS.

hounds' ears See under CUFFS.

hound's-tooth/houndstooth check See under PRINTS, STRIPES, AND CHECKS.

∞**houppelande** (hoop'-land) **1.** Man's voluminous outer robe of late 15th and 16th c., introduced by Richard II of England, made with high funnel-shaped neckline—later V-shaped. Sleeves were long, full, and ornamented with DAGGING at edge or of BAGPIPE SLEEVES (see under SHOULDERS AND SLEEVES) or other full sleeves. Varied from thigh length to trailing on the ground when worn as ceremonial robe. A short houppelande with embroidery on both sleeves was known as a **haincelin** (ayn-cell-ihn) and named after Haincelin Coq, jester of Charles VI of France. **2.** Woman's dress worn from late 14th through the 15th c. with fitted bodice, V-neckline with REVERS (see under NECKLINES AND COLLARS), and dickey, or scooped neckline. Sleeves were long and tight-fitting or voluminous with fur lining. Frequently trained in back and so long in front that skirt had to be lifted when walking.

houppelande #2

hourglass silhouette The shape of a woman's dress that has a full bust, pinched-in waist, and full, curving hips, a shape not unlike that of an hourglass. Shown at SILHOUETTE.

housecoat See under SLEEPWEAR AND LOUNGEWEAR.

housedress See under DRESSES.

housel See under FOOTWEAR: HEUSE.

house slipper See under FOOTWEAR.

housse See under GARNACHE.

howling bags See under PANTS.

HTSUS See under HARMONIZED TARIFF SCHEDULE FOR THE UNITED STATES.

huarache (wa-rach-ee) See under FOOTWEAR.

hubbard blouse See under BLOUSES AND TOPS.

huckaback embroidery See under EMBROIDERIES AND SEWING STITCHES.

huckaback stitch See under EMBROIDERIES AND SEWING STITCHES.

Hudson Bay sable See under FURS: MARTEN.

Hudson seal See under FURS.

hug-me-tight See under VESTS.

huke See under HUQUE.

hula skirt See under SKIRTS.

human hair wig See under WIGS AND HAIRPIECES.

hundred pleater See HEADWEAR: CHEF'S HAT.

hungarian embroidery See under EMBROIDERIES AND SEWING STITCHES.

hungarian point See under EMBROIDERIES AND SEWING STITCHES: FLORENTINE EMBROIDERY.

∞**hungarian suit** A boy's belted double-breasted tunic, worn from late 1860s with a small turned-down collar and fastened on the side in a double-breasted manner. Trimmed with braid down the side front, on the flapped pockets, and cuffs. Worn with matching full or fitted trousers to below the knees with JOCKEY BOOTS (see under FOOTWEAR).

hunt *adj.* 1. Describes clothing and accessories used by equestrians when hunting on horseback. See under ACTIVEWEAR: HUNT BREECHES; COATS AND JACKETS: PINK COAT; and HEADWEAR: HUNT CAP and HUNT DERBY. 2. Characterizing the overall appearance, popular around 1984, created by wearing, for daytime or evening, either full attire or individual items of apparel worn when riding or for a formal fox hunt (e.g., jodhpurs or stirrup pants in tweeds or flannels with a stock shirt or any other type blouse; derby worn with stock tie, weskit (sometimes with sleeves), pleated trousers, and a full-length coat similar to a CHESTERFIELD; a narrow midi-length skirt with side slit worn with boots and hacking or velvet jacket).

hunter's pink See under COATS AND JACKETS: PINK COAT.

hunter watch See under WATCHES.

hunting calf British term for REVERSE CALF. See under LEATHERS.

hunting cap See under HEADWEAR.

hunting necktie See under TIES.

hunting plaid See under PLAIDS AND TARTANS.

hunting shirt See under SHIRTS.

hunting stock See under TIES.

hunting vest See under VESTS.

∞**huque/huke** Man's flowing outer garment, worn throughout 15th c., generally calf length—sometimes longer or shorter—slashed up sides, and fur-trimmed around edges. Sometimes slashed up front and back for ease in riding horseback.

hurluberlu See under HAIRSTYLES.

huseau See under FOOTWEAR: HEUSE.

Hush Puppies® See under FOOTWEAR.

husky sizes Boys' sizes—8 to 20—cut with more generous proportions.

hussar boots See under FOOTWEAR.

hussar jacket See under COATS AND JACKETS.

hyacinth See under GEMS, GEM CUTS, AND SETTINGS.

ice cube heel See under FOOTWEAR.

Icelandic sweater See under SWEATERS.

ID/identification bracelet See under JEWELRY.

igloo mitt See under GLOVES AND GLOVE CONSTRUCTION.

†ikat (ee'-kat) **1.** A method of yarn dyeing in which selected areas are treated in some way so the dye will not penetrate. This may be done by selectively applying a substance that resists dye penetration, the preferred method at present, or knotting or tying the yarn at various places. **2.** Fabrics woven from ikat yarns. The resulting design has a pattern that can range from definite to blurry or indistinct in appearance. *Der.* Malayan, *mengikat,* "to tie, bind, knot, or wind around." Also see under PRINTS, STRIPES, AND CHECKS: WARP PRINT.

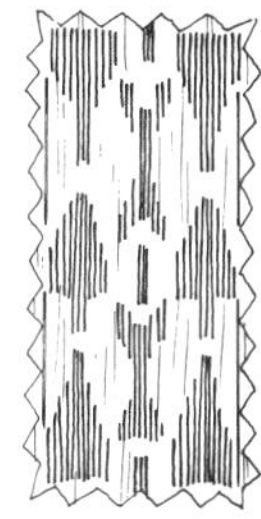
ikat fabric

I.L.G.W.U. Abbreviation for INTERNATIONAL LADIES' GARMENT WORKERS' UNION. See under UNION OF NEEDLETRADES, INDUSTRIAL, AND TEXTILE EMPLOYEES (UNITE).

illuminants The various light sources (incandescent, sunlight, fluorescent) that must be considered in color matching.

image The perception customers have of a company's brand and products.

imbecile sleeve See under SHOULDERS AND SLEEVES.

imitation gems See under GEMS, GEM CUTS, AND SETTINGS.

imitation leather Fabrics such as drill, sateen, and duck that have been coated, dyed, and embossed to simulate leathers such as alligator, snakeskin, or lizard. Coatings used include rubber, pyroxlin, nitrocellulose compounds, or vinyl resins. Also see under LEATHERETTE, NAUGAHYDE, and PLEATHER.

imitation moleskin See under MOLESKIN FABRIC.

imitation pearls See under GEMS, GEM CUTS, AND SETTINGS: PEARL.

imperial **1.** See under COATS AND JACKETS. **2.** See under BEARD.

imperial skirt See under UNDERGARMENTS: HOOPS.

import **1.** *n.* Merchandise bought offshore and brought into another country to sell. **2.** *v.* The act of importing.

importer/packager Company that arranges with foreign contractors for the development and manufacture of full lines of apparel. The lines are sold to U.S. retailers to sell as private label merchandise.

impulse buying Consumer purchasing of goods with little or no planning.

∞inchering Taking measurements of a person in order to make a garment, as it was called in the 18th c.

∞incroyable bow (an-kwai'-ab-leh) Large bow of lace or transparent, lightweight silk worn at the neck by women in 1889 with revival of DIRECTOIRE costume.

incroyable coat See under COATS AND JACKETS.

incroyables See under DIRECTOIRE # 2.

incrustation **1.** Set-in piece of embroidery, lace, or trimming on women's and children's garments. **2.** Covered or studded with gems.

independent buying office A firm with retailers as clients that performs such services as buying goods, forecasting trends; assists with finance, personnel, advertising, and promotion; may consult on a variety of issues, including the manufacture of private-label merchandise. Also called *salaried* or *fee buying office.*

independent store A retailing unit that is not part of any chain of stores.

Indian **1.** *adj.* Describes articles of clothing and accessories copied from or inspired by North American Native American tribes. **2.** *adj.* Describes styles from the Indian subcontinent in southern Asia.

Indian beadwork See under AMERICAN INDIAN BEADWORK.

Indian embroidery See under EMBROIDERIES AND SEWING STITCHES.

Indian gown/Indian nightgown See under BANYAN.

Indian handbag See under HANDBAGS AND RELATED ACCESSORIES: SQUAW BAG.

Indian headband See under HEADWEAR: AMERICAN INDIAN HEADBAND.

Indian lamb See under FURS: LAMB.

Indian meditation shirt See under SHIRTS: MEDITATION.

Indian moccasin See under FOOTWEAR: MOCCASIN.

indian necktie See under TIES.

Indian print See under PRINTS, STRIPES, AND CHECKS.

Indian wedding blouse See under BLOUSES AND TOPS.

indie fringe See under HAIRSTYLES.

†indigo Blue dye made since earliest time from stems and leaves of *Indigofera tinctoria, Indigofera anil*; was used to dye the denim from which "blue jeans" were made; however, currently, other dyes are used as well.

indispensible See under HANDBAGS AND RELATED ACCESSORIES: RETICULE.

induction cut See under HAIRSTYLES.

industrial mask See under MASKS.

industrial zipper See under CLOSURES: ZIPPER.

ineffibles See under INEXPRESSIBLES.

∞inexpressibles Late 18th- and early 19th-c. polite term for men's BREECHES or TROUSERS. Also called *ineffibles, don't mentions, nether integuments, unmentionables,* and *unwhisperables.*

infanta style (in-fahn'-tah) Costumes as in paintings by Velásquez of Philip IV of Spain's daughter showing extremely wide VERTUGALE (see under FARTHINGALE). Used as inspiration for evening gowns by *Lanvin* in the 1920s and *Balenciaga, Givenchy,* and *Castillo* in 1950s. Also see under GUARDINFANTE.

infinity scarves See under SCARVES.

informal habit See under ACTIVEWEAR.

initial cost estimate Approximation of the cost of a new style. Developed from the cost of materials, FINDINGS, labor, shipping, and any import duty required.

initial ring See under JEWELRY: SIGNET RING.

inlay See under FOOTWEAR.

inner-vest jacket See under COATS AND JACKETS.

innerwear Underwear or lingerie, as called in the garment trade.

innocente See under SACK #1.

inseam **1.** The seam in pants and trousers, from the crotch to the hem. Since the waist location of pants, particularly for women, changes with fashion, the inseam measurement provides a more accurate length guide for the development of patterns. **2.** See under GLOVES AND GLOVE CONSTRUCTION.

inseam pocket See under POCKETS.

†insertion Trimming made in straight bands and set between pieces of fabric in a garment. Especially popular from 1890 to 1910 when bands of beading, embroidery, braid, or lace were often set in between rows of tucks and ruffles. Used particularly on white lawn dresses, blouses, petticoats, and drawers. Also see under EMBROIDERIES AND SEWING STITCHES: INSERTIONS.

insert thumb See under GLOVES AND GLOVE CONSTRUCTION.

inside pocket See under POCKETS.

insole See under FOOTWEAR.

instant sunglasses See under EYEWEAR.

instep See under FOOTWEAR.

∞instita (in-stee'-tah) The distinctive dress of a Roman matron. Costume historians differ as to precisely what it was. Some consider it to have been a flounce or narrow ruffle on the lower edge of a Roman matron's STOLA, while others identify it as the *stola* itself and describe it as a dress suspended from sewed on straps.

insulated *adj.* Describes a garment constructed to protect against the cold. Materials used to insulate include down, foam, fiberfill, wool, and sheepskin. See under COATS AND JACKETS: INSULATED JACKET; FOOTWEAR: INSULATED BOOT; and GLOVES AND GLOVE CONSTRUCTION: INSULATED GLOVE.

intaglio See under GEMS, GEM CUTS, AND SETTINGS.

†intarsia (in-tar'-sea-ah) A knitting technique that incorporates one or more contrasting colored yarns to create design motifs or patterns in a solid block of knit fabric, e.g., argyle or fair isle patterns.

intellectual property Creations of human intelligence that have commercial value for which exclusive rights are recognized by law. Intellectual property includes inventions, literary and artistic works, symbols, names, and images that are protected by copyright, trademark and patent law.

†intelligent textiles Intelligent textiles not only sense stimuli, but can react and respond to environmental conditions or stimuli. Stimuli/responses may be thermal, chemical, mechanical, electric, or magnetic in nature.

interactive kiosk Computerized unit in retail stores that allows customers to ascertain whether the company has a particular size or item in stock. If the kiosk is programmed for placing orders, the customer can place an order and have the product delivered to the store or to their home.

interchangeable bag See under HANDBAGS AND RELATED ACCESSORIES.

†interfacing Canvas of linen, linen and hair, unbleached muslin; crinoline fabric; or nonwoven fabric, which is sewn or fused to either the garment or facing of a garment to strengthen areas of stress, give body and/or retain the shape of garment parts. Called INTERLINING in manufacturing.

interior product displays Showing merchandise in locations such as countertops, showcases, ledges, aisles, or at point of purchase or in open selling displays, and closed-island displays. Such displays help customers locate merchandise and may provide examples of how the merchandise is used or worn.

†interlining 1. Fabrics used between the lining and the outer fabric of a coat, collar, or suit to give shape to the garment. Best types have permanent stiffening that will survive dry cleaning or laundering (e.g., tailor's canvas, linen canvas, or nonwoven fabrics). Unbleached muslin and crinoline fabric are used in less expensive garments and will not wash or clean satisfactorily. Same as INTERFACING. 2. Open-weave woolen or cotton fabric used between the lining and outer fabric in a winter coat to give warmth.

†interlock Knit made on a machine having alternate units of short and long needles. Thicker than plain rib knits with good lengthwise elasticity, firm texture, and less tendency to curl at the edges. Similar to JERSEY but both the face and back of the fabric look alike.

International Ladies Garment Workers Union See under UNION OF NEEDLETRADES, INDUSTRIAL, AND TEXTILE EMPLOYEES (UNITE).

international market A market that could be located anywhere in the world. Paris, London, Milan, and Tokyo are just of few of the larger international markets. See under DOMESTIC MARKET and REGIONAL MARKET.

international source/sourcing Buying goods from or manufacturing goods in countries other than the U.S. (see under IMPORT, DOMESTIC SOURCE/SOURCING, SOURCING). As the number of imports in the fashion industry rises, international sourcing plays a significant role in the related businesses.

in the white See under LEATHERS.

intimate apparel Category name for lingerie and underwear.

inventory 1. *n.* A current record made by a product developer, manufacturer, or retailer of its goods or stock. 2. *v.* To generate such a record.

inverness 1. See under COATS AND JACKETS: INVERNESS COAT. 2. See under CAPES, CLOAKS, AND SHAWLS: INVERNESS CAPE.

inverted frame See under HANDBAGS AND RELATED ACCESSORIES.

inverted heel See under FOOTWEAR.

inverted leg-of-mutton sleeve See under SHOULDERS AND SLEEVES.

inverted pleats See under CLOTHING CONSTRUCTION DETAILS and SKIRTS.

inverted-T/-Y embroidery See under EMBROIDERIES AND SEWING STITCHES: MATHILDE EMBROIDERY.

invisible necklace See under JEWELRY: FLOATER NECKLACE.

invisible zipper See under CLOSURES: ZIPPER.

irene castle bob See under HAIRSTYLES.

irene jacket See under COATS AND JACKETS.

Iribe (1883–1935) Paul Iribarnegaray, a Parisian illustrator and designer who was an important figure in artistic and fashionable circles of Paris in the early 20th c. In 1908, he illustrated *Les Robes de Paul Poiret,* a limited edition of the couturier's oriental fashions. His original and imaginative style influenced fashion illustrations. Also see under LEPAPE.

†iridescent fabric Any fabric made with yarns of one color in the lengthwise direction and another color crosswise. Reflects both colors in the light, e.g., chambray.

iridium See under JEWELRY.

irish crochet lace See under LACES.

†irish knit Hand-knit in traditional patterns usually including cables, popcorn, and other unusual stitches. Knit on large needles with natural wool yarns (without the oil removed from yarn). Used for Irish fishermen's bulky sweaters imported by the U.S. for general sportswear in 1950s and 1960s. Also, similar knits of manufactured yarns imitating the authentic Irish knits. Also see under SWEATERS: FISHERMAN'S SWEATER.

†irish linen Fine quality of linen fabric woven from flax grown mainly in Northern Ireland. Uses: handkerchiefs and apparel.

Irish mantle See under CAPES, CLOAKS, AND SHAWLS: BRATT.

irish point lace See under LACES: YOUGHAL LACE.

∞irish polonaise See under DRESSES.

irish stitch See under EMBROIDERIES AND SEWING STITCHES: BRICK STITCH.

irish tweed See under DONEGAL TWEED.

ironed hair See under HAIRSTYLES.

iron ring See under JEWELRY.

∞isabeau bodice Black or colored silk, woman's evening bodice of 1869, ending at the waistline with a wide ribbon sash having long ends and large bow in front. Made with low square neckline, short puffed sleeves, and trimmed with two lace ruffles.

∞isabeau corsage (is-ah-bow' kor-saj') Bodice worn in mid-1840s made like a jacket, with the front cut away just below the hips. Also had a high neckline with a falling collar; long sleeves with open short oversleeve below each shoulder; and was trimmed with horizontal bands of *galloon lace,* braid, and silk buttons.

isabeau sleeve See under SHOULDERS AND SLEEVES.

∞**isabeau style dress** See under DRESSES.

isabella (the) See under CAPES, CLOAKS, AND SHAWLS.

∞**isabella peasant bodice** Close-fitting decorative corselet bodice decorated with long strands of beads hanging down from waistline. Worn over a dress in early 1890s.

isabella skirt See under UNDERGARMENTS: HOOPS.

∞**italian bodice** Corselet bodice laced up the front with straps over shoulders, flat fitted collar, and embroidery in front. Worn over a blouse in early 1870s.

italian cloak See under CAPES, CLOAKS, AND SHAWLS.

italian collar See under NECKLINES AND COLLARS.

∞**Italian corsage** Woman's low-cut BASQUE bodice of mid-1860s, laced up the front and worn over a blouse. PEPLUM was made up of decorative tabs. Sleeves of bodice were slashed and trimmed with bows of ribbons pulled through openings.

Italian farthingale See under FARTHINGALE.

italian heel See under FOOTWEAR.

Italian hose See under VENETIANS.

italian nightgown See under DRESSES: IRISH POLONAISE.

italian stitch See under EMBROIDERIES AND SEWING STITCHES: DOUBLE-RUNNING STITCH.

item-driven line/item line An apparel line that is designed to be sold as individual pieces, often in a variety of colors, as opposed to lines designed to be sold as coordinates.

item house Contractor that makes one specialized category of apparel or accessories. Examples: logo-printed T-shirts, baseball caps.

ivory 1. Hard, opaque substance—creamy white to pale yellow—from the tusks of elephants and other mammals, living and extinct (e.g., hippopotami, walruses, whales, warthogs, boars, and mammoths). Ivory from elephants is now in scarce supply because of over-hunting, and international restrictions have been imposed on trade in elephant ivory, in some other types of ivory from endangered animals, and in objects made from ivory. As a result, the horns and teeth of many animals, such as elk, are also called ivory and some nuts are used to produce **vegetable ivory.** Only antique ivory from restricted species that is more than one hundred years old and for which the buyer has documentation proving its age can be brought into the U.S. Carved for fans, jewelry, and other ornaments for many centuries. 2. The color of ivory—a creamy white.

ivy league *adj.* Descriptive of styles based on those first worn in the 1940s and 1950s by college men at Eastern universities that were members of the intercollegiate sports association called the Ivy League (Brown, Columbia, Cornell, Dartmouth, Harvard, University of Pennsylvania, Princeton, and Yale). The style consisted of a slim-cut suit jacket with natural shoulders, narrow lapels, and skinny sleeves; slim-cut pants. *Der.* The name was originally popular slang alluding to the old and ivy-covered buildings on these campuses. See under IVY LEAGUE SUIT; PANTS: IVY LEAGUE PANTS; and SHIRTS: IVY LEAGUE SHIRT.

ivy league style

ivy league suit Man's suit with natural shoulders, narrow lapels, three-button closing, and narrow trousers. Popular in 1950s, spreading from the eight Eastern college campuses in the Ivy League as reaction against exaggeratedly wide padded shoulders and wide trouser legs of the 1940s.

jabiru feathers See under FEATHERS.

jabot (zha-bo′) Ruffle of lace, embroidery, or sheer fabric made in a cascade (see CASCADE #1), attached to front of dress, blouse, or a cravat-like neckpiece (see TIES: CRAVAT). Popular in 18th c. for men and reintroduced for women in late 19th c., becoming trendy again in the 1930s, 1940s, and 1980s. Also see under BLOUSES AND TOPS: JABOT BLOUSE and NECKLINES AND COLLARS: JABOT.

jabot

jacinth See under GEMS, GEM CUTS, AND SETTINGS: HYACINTH.

jack See under DOUBLET.

jack boot See under FOOTWEAR.

jack chain See under JEWELRY.

jacket See under introduction to COATS AND JACKETS.

jacket bodice See under introduction to COATS AND JACKETS.

jacket dress See under DRESSES.

jacket earring See under JEWELRY.

Jackson, Michael See under MICHAEL JACKSON.

jack tar suit See under SAILOR SUIT.

jack tar trousers See under PANTS.

†jacquard (ja-kard′) 1. A system of weaving that, owing to a pattern-making mechanism of great versatility, permits the production of woven designs of considerable size. Invented by Joseph Marie Jacquard in France in 1801, the loom controls each lengthwise yarn separately by use of a pattern on a punched card or, in newer looms, by an electronic device. Some of the most widely used jacquard fabrics are BROCADE, DAMASK, and TAPESTRY. 2. Elaborately patterned knitted fabric produced on a knitting machine that makes a wide variety of stitches. 3. Fabrics made by jacquard weaving or knitting. See under HOSIERY: JACQUARD HOSE and SWEATERS: JACQUARD SWEATER.

jade See under GEMS, GEM CUTS, AND SETTINGS.

jadeite See under GEMS, GEM CUTS, AND SETTINGS: JADE.

Jaeger underclothes See under UNDERGARMENTS.

jagging/jags See under DAGGING.

jaguar See under FURS.

Jamaica shorts See under SHORTS.

jamb/jambe See under ARMOR: GREAVE.

jambeau See under ARMOR.

jamboy See under ARMOR: TONLET.

jammers See under SWIMWEAR.

janina stitch See under EMBROIDERIES AND SEWING STITCHES: ORIENTAL COUCHING.

Japanese *adj.* 1. Describes clothing and accessories, both traditional and contemporary, that are worn in Japan, many of which have been adopted in the Western Hemisphere. 2. Styles introduced by Japanese designers such as Rei Kawakubo and Issey Miyake in the 1980s that became a major fashion influence worldwide. Typical designs use few seams and are not fitted to the body—sometimes one size fits everyone. Although the basic Japanese kimono is not used, its "EASE" is borrowed. Emphasis is also on originality of fabrics, sophisticated colors, and dramatic simplicity. Most styles are bulky, such as the 1983 style of very full harem pants shirred in front from ankle to knee, worn with a big top that has large kimono-cut sleeves, or an oversized, knee-length coat of bulky fabric that is draped in front rather than buttoned. Some styles have asymmetric necklines, collars, and hems. 3. Style of the Japanese kimono as adapted by U.S. and European designers for dresses, robes, and sportswear. A style for negligées used since the 19th c.

Japanese style #2

japanese embroidery See under EMBROIDERIES AND SEWING STITCHES.

Japanese mink See under FURS.

Japanese parasol See under UMBRELLAS AND PARASOLS.

Japanese print See under PRINTS, STRIPES, AND CHECKS.

Japanese sandals See under FOOTWEAR: ZORI.

Japanese wrapper See under SLEEPWEAR AND LOUNGEWEAR.

Jap fox/Jap raccoon See under FURS: USSURIAN RACCOON.

jargon See under GEMS, GEM CUTS, AND SETTINGS: ZIRCON.

jasey (jay-see) See under WIGS AND HAIRPIECES.

jasmine gloves See under GLOVES AND GLOVE CONSTRUCTION: JESSAMY GLOVES.

†jaspé (jas-pay′) Cotton or cotton-blend fabric with narrow, woven stripes of color that shade from light to dark, or a knitted fabric with crosswise ribs, which achieve this effect.

jasper See under GEMS, GEM CUTS, AND SETTINGS.

Java lizard See under LEATHERS.

jazerant See under ARMOR.

jazz garter Elaborate, wide, round-elastic garter covered with colored satin and sometimes trimmed with lace rosettes. Worn for decorative effect with very short skirts in the late 1920s. *Der.* From jazz music of this era.

jazz oxford See under FOOTWEAR.

jazz suit Narrow-shouldered, tight-waisted, three-button jacket made with long 12″ center vent and vertical slashed pockets. Worn with pipe-stem pants by men in post–World War I era. *Der.* From jazz music of this era.

†jean Durable fabric made of carded yarns, primarily of cotton or cotton blend, in a twill weave. It may be bleached, dyed solid colors, or printed. Used in blue for overalls and work pants, such pants were given the name *blue jeans.* Uses: uniforms, slacks, shoe linings, and sportswear.

∞jeanette Women's necklace of 1836 made of a narrow braid of hair or velvet from which a small heart or cross is suspended.

jeans See under PANTS: BLUE JEANS.

jeggings See under PANTS.

jellaba See under SLEEPWEAR AND LOUNGEWEAR: DJELLABA.

jellies/jelly beans See under FOOTWEAR.

jellybag See under HEADWEAR.

jemmy See under COATS AND JACKETS: FROCK COAT.

jemmy boot See under FOOTWEAR.

jemmy frock See under COATS AND JACKETS: FROCK COAT.

Jenny Lind cap See under HEADWEAR.

Jenny Lind dress See under DRESSES.

jerkin **1.** See under DOUBLET. **2.** See under VESTS. **3.** Synonym for WAISTCOAT.

†jersey **1.** Classification of knitted fabrics that are made in a plain stitch without a distinct rib. These fabrics were originally made of wool but are now made of various natural and manufactured yarns, some textured. Also called *plain knit. Der.* From Isle of Jersey, off the coast of England, where it was first made. **2.** Synonym for knitted shirts worn by seamen, or for sport, from 1860s on—called *football jersey* in 1870s. **3.** See under JERSEY COSTUME. **4.** See under SHIRTS: KNIT SHIRT.

∞jersey costume Long, tight-fitted blouse, extending to the thigh, that was worn over a serge or flannel pleated skirt. Top was made of red or blue knitted silk or wool jersey. This fashion became popular around 1879 when worn by the beautiful **Lillie Langtry** (1852–1929)—famous British actress born on the Isle of Jersey, located in English Channel, who was also called the "Jersey Lily." Many other items of apparel were also named after her.

jessamy gloves See under GLOVES AND GLOVE CONSTRUCTION.

jester's costume An ensemble associated with court jesters of the Middle Ages and Renaissance that consists of a doublet and tights worn with a FOOL'S CAP (see under HEADWEAR) having bells attached to peak. Bells are also sometimes worn on garters below knee or attached to dangling sleeves. Usually the entire costume is of PARTI-COLORED fabric. See under HEADWEAR: FOOL'S CAP and HOSIERY: TIGHTS.

jet See under GEMS, GEM CUTS, AND SETTINGS.

jewel **1.** Precious stone that has been cut and polished—a gem. See under GEMS, GEM CUTS, AND SETTINGS. **2.** Natural or synthetic precious stone used as a bearing in a watch. See under WATCHES.

jeweled pantyhose See under HOSIERY.

jeweled watch See under WATCHES.

jewel neckline See under NECKLINES AND COLLARS.

JEWELRY

jewelry A purely decorative accessory (e.g., bracelet or necklace) made of precious or plated metal or of genuine or simulated stones mounted in precious or plated metals. Jewelry of less precious materials is called COSTUME JEWELRY (see under JEWELRY). Also see under JEWELRY: FASHION JEWELRY.

adjustable ring Ring, usually inexpensive, made with band with overlapping ends so that it can be fitted to any finger size.

Afro choker Necklace made of a strand of springy metal wound around the neck many times. *Der.* Copied from necklaces worn by Ubangi tribe in Africa. Also called *Ubangi necklace.*

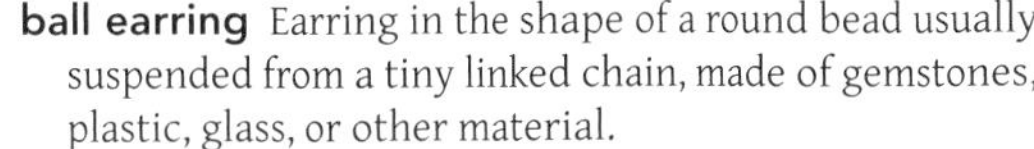

American Indian beads 1. Tiny opaque beads of various colors used to make necklaces and belts. Also used for embroidery on moccasins, headbands, belts, and other North American Indian clothes. 2. Shell beads used by North American Indian in 16th c. as money and called *wampum*. The amount of trimming on garments indicated wealth of individual.

American Indian necklace 1. Long, flat necklace made with tiny glass beads of various colors, usually woven on small loom. 2. Necklace of tiny colored beads worked in rope effect with North American Indian motif as center pendant, also made by North American Indian. North American Indian jewelry was popular in late 1960s and early 1970s.

amulet Small object believed to possess magical powers—a good-luck charm worn as protection against evil by primitive people and surviving to present time in various forms of jewelry.

ankh ring (angk) Gold or gold-finished ring made in the shape of the ankh, the ancient Egyptian symbol of life—a cross with a loop at the top.

ankle bracelet Ornament worn around the ankle; may be a chain or ID bracelet. Worn in Eastern countries and Egypt since earliest times. Also called *anklet*.

anklet See under JEWELRY: ANKLE BRACELET.

ansate cross See under ANKH.

ankle bracelet

armband Bracelet for the upper arm frequently made of a band of metal. Fashionable in matching sets with anklets in ancient Egypt and reintroduced in 1969.

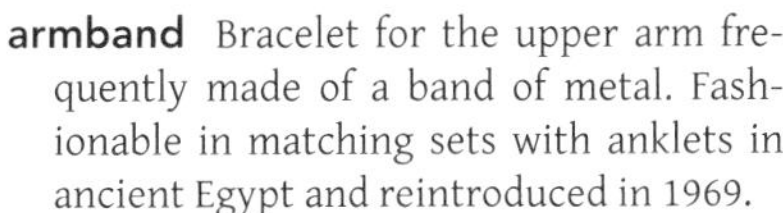

Art Deco earring Earring made in geometrical forms. Inspired by patterns of the 1920s shown in the 1925 Paris Exhibition and revived in the late 1960s. See under ART DECO.

aurora borealis crystal (aw-ror′-ah bore-ee′-al-is) Glass beads coated with a solution that causes them to reflect rainbow colors.

Austrian crystal Lead crystal made with 32 percent lead oxide, faceted and polished to give full spectrum light reflection in sunlight or artificial light. Usually colorless but may be coated on back to reflect a color (e.g., red or blue, or both colors if coated on both sides). Made in village of Innsbruck, Austria.

armband and bangles

baby bracelet Tiny beads with letters on them. Originally used in hospitals to spell out the name of the newborn child on a bracelet. Now used for personalized bracelets, barrettes, and necklaces.

ball earring Earring in the shape of a round bead usually suspended from a tiny linked chain, made of gemstones, plastic, glass, or other material.

bangle bracelet Narrow, round, rigid bracelet of metal, plastic, wood, or other material, worn singly or several at a time. Popular since 1900s and originally worn in sets that jingled when the arm moved. Also called *hoop bracelet*. Shown at JEWELRY: ARMBAND.

bar drop pin Long narrow pin made with attached pendants.

baroque pearls See under GEMS, GEM CUTS, AND SETTINGS: PEARL.

bar pin Long, narrow pin secured by back fastener the same length as the pin. Fashionable since early 20th c.

bayadere Seed pearl necklace made up of multiple strands twisted together.

bead/beads 1. One or more pieces of glass, plastic, wood, crystal, gem, or other material bored through the center and strung on leather, cord, thread, or chain to wear as necklace, bracelet, anklet, headband, or used for embroidery. Usually round but may be cylindrical, square, disc-shaped, pendant-shaped, oblong, etc. 2. A string of beads, synonym for necklace, made and worn since earliest recorded history. Egyptians used carved beads of lapis lazuli, amethyst, feldspar, and agate. Romans wore ropes of pearls. Manufacture of glass beads started in Venice in 14th c.

beaded necklace See under JEWELRY: AMERICAN INDIAN NECKLACE.

beggar beads Hand-carved ornamental gemstones in elongated shapes strung on necklace between gold beads. Stones include MOSS AGATES, GREEN JASPERS, BLOODSTONES, BROWN OR ORANGE CARNELIANS, and other nonprecious stones. (See specific stones under GEMS, GEM CUTS, AND SETTINGS.) Originally worn in India for good luck.

belly chain/waist chain Silver, gold, or other metal chain worn around the waist. Some **pierced belly chains** attach to a navel piercing.

∞**betrothal ring** 16th-c. ring, broken in half after wedding ceremony and halves given to bride and groom.

bib necklace Necklace fitting close to base of neck and extending in the shape of a child's bib. Sometimes made of linked metal, looking like a short, triangular scarf, sometimes made of several irregular strands of beads or chains arranged like a fringe.

bib necklace

birthstone necklace 1. Medium-length, fine-linked chain with individualized birthstones in the form of a bead placed about every three to four inches. Also see under

JEWELRY: DIAMONDS BY THE YARD. **2.** A short fine-linked chain with an attached pendant containing a colored gem representing an individual birthstone. Also see under GEMS, GEM CUTS, AND SETTINGS: BIRTHSTONE.

birthstone ring Ring set with a stone representing the birth month of the wearer (e.g., an amethyst for February). Also see under GEMS, GEM CUTS, AND SETTINGS: BIRTHSTONE.

body jewelry See under alphabetical listing and under JEWELRY: BODY PIERCING.

body piercing Making a hole somewhere on the body through which an item of jewelry can be fastened. Earlobes have long been pierced for the insertion of earrings, and in the late 1990s a fashion for piercing almost any part of the body spread, especially among young people. The jewelry for insertion in these openings is called **body jewelry.**

boot bracelet Linked bracelet, sometimes with dangling charms, worn either around the ankle or calf of the boot.

bracelet Decorative band or circlet worn on the arm, wrist, or ankle as an ornament. Made of metal, chain, plastic, wood, leather, or Lucite®, either in one piece or in links. *Der.* Latin, *bracum,* "arm."

bracelet ring See under JEWELRY: SLAVE BRACELET.

breastplate Solid metal bra or metal breast ornaments worn by women as body jewelry in late 1960s.

bridal set Matching engagement ring and wedding band.

bridge jewelry Category into which jewelers place several types of jewelry, including those made from silver, gold (14K, 12K, 10K), and less expensive stones; jewelry designed by artists using a variety of materials.

brooch See under JEWELRY: PIN.

bubble bracelet Oversized spherical beads, often hollow, popular for choker necklaces in 1950s and revived in mid-1960s.

bugle beads Long, tubular-shaped glass beads, often black, white, or silver, popular for trimming dresses from last half of 19th c. to present.

button earring Round, flat earring shaped like a button. Made in various sizes of materials such as imitation pearls, metal, wood, or plastic.

button earring

byzance (bi-zance′) Beads alternating with chain in long necklace with dangling ends similar to a rosary. Created by Christian de Gasperi (nephew of former prime minister of Italy) and given this name by Pierre Cardin in 1968 when it became popular at the Riviera resort of St. Tropez, France.

cameo See under GEMS, GEM CUTS, AND SETTINGS.

chain See under alphabetical listing.

chain bracelet One or more chains of varying width worn on the wrist.

chain necklace Necklace consisting of links of metal sometimes interspersed with gems or imitation stones. May be short or long and looped around neck several times. Worn at intervals since 16th c. and very popular during the late 1960s and 1980s. See alphabetical listing for types of CHAIN.

championship ring Ring presented to professional, scholastic, or amateur sports team members in recognition of the team's having won competitions.

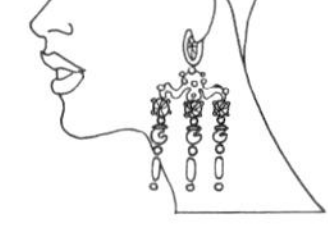
chandelier earring

chandelier earring Long, dangling, oversized earring made of metal or beads hanging like crystals on a chandelier.

changeable earring Earring usually made with a selection of colored plastic disks that may be snapped into metal circlet. Parts of the PEEK-A-BOO EARRING (see under JEWELRY) can also be interchanged.

charm Small amulet, usually of metal, consisting of all sorts of mementos (e.g., heart, disk, or zodiac signs worn on bracelet or necklace).

charm bracelet A metal (often gold or silver) chain bracelet on which one or more matching metal charms (e.g., disks, zodiac signs, or hearts) are hung, often to commemorate personal events.

charm bracelet

charm necklace **1.** Gold- or silver-toned chain worn around the neck with a cluster of metal objects attached in center front (e.g., hearts, initials, animals, sports motifs, some engraved with slogans or names). **2.** Young girls' plastic chain necklace with dangling miniature plastic replicas of keys, telephones, tennis rackets, roller skates, pencils, and other ornaments.

chasing Jewelry term for fine lines engraved on metals.

chatelaine (shat-len′) Pin worn on the lapel or chest with hook on back to secure a watch, or two decorative pins joined by a chain. Also called *fob pin. Der.* Keys worn at the waist on a chain by medieval mistress of the castle or "chatelaine," in French.

choker Necklace fitting snugly around base of neck, may be one or more strands of beads, a suede or ribbon band, or a dog collar.

choker

chute A single strand of pearls.

class ring High school or college ring, of individual design for each school, with class year included. Sometimes designed to accommodate large stones, crests, or individual initials. Also called a *school ring.*

clip Ornament similar to a pin but with spring clasp on back that snaps closed over the edge of fabric. Set with diamonds or rhinestones. Introduced in 1930s and 1940s.

clip-back earring Earring that fastens to the ear by means of a spring clip that snaps against back of the earlobe to secure it; an innovation of the 1930s.

cloisonné necklace 1. A medallion made of brass, enameled with luminous colors, and fired. Usually attached to a braided cord of silk, nylon, or polyester with an additional cord pendant hanging from base of medallion. 2. Necklace of beads with some of the beads being made in the cloisonné manner.

cluster earring Groups of pearls, gems, or beads fastened together to make a large earring.

cluster ring Type of ring set with many large and small stones grouped together. Sometimes made of precious stones, frequently diamonds.

cocktail ring Large showy ring, either a piece of costume jewelry or of fine jewelry, set with precious or semiprecious stones. Sometimes called *dinner ring.*

coiled bracelet Bracelet made from a long, gold- or silver-tone finished strip of metal, curled like a spring to fit the arm.

coin necklace Antique coin (e.g., a five-dollar gold piece, a silver dollar, an Indian head penny, or a buffalo nickel) worn on a chain around the neck, sometimes enhanced by a circlet of gold, silver, or other metal around edge.

collar necklace 1. Necklace shaped and fitted to the neck like a collar. Frequently of metal and popular in late 1960s. 2. Tiny beads interlaced to form a separate collar.

collar pin 1. Pin placed through holes embroidered into the points of shirt collars. 2. Stud first used in late 19th c. by men for attaching separate shirt collar.

costume jewelry Jewelry not made of genuine gems or precious metals. Introduction is credited to French couturier Gabrielle "Coco" Chanel, who showed imitation pearls, emeralds, and rubies for daytime in the 1920s—copies of her own real jewels. In the late 1970s new terms were introduced to describe costume jewelry. See under JEWELRY: FAUX JEWELS and FASHION JEWELRY.

cross See under alphabetical listing.

crusader's cross Name given in 1960s to a large MALTESE CROSS (see under CROSS) used as a pendant for a necklace. Also called *St. George cross.*

crystal bracelet Beads carved out of genuine transparent quartz. Popular from late 19th c. to about 1930s. Quartz is too cost prohibitive to be used today. Glass is usually substituted for genuine crystal.

cuff bracelet Oval-shaped, rigid bracelet styled with opening in back. May be wide or narrow and usually made of metal.

cuff link Decorative jewelry consisting of two buttons or disks, joined by a link or short chain, worn to close the FRENCH CUFF (see under CUFFS) of a shirt. May be metal, engraved, set with stones, or made in wide variety of materials. Worn originally by men and adopted by women. Also see under CLOSURES: CUFF BUTTON.

cultured pearls See under GEMS, GEM CUTS, AND SETTINGS: PEARL.

cut-steel beads Tiny faceted steel or other metal beads, similar in appearance to MARCASITE (see under GEMS, GEM CUTS, AND SETTINGS), popular in last half of the 19th and early 20th c.

damascene ring (dam′-ah-sehn) Blackened metal inlaid with fine gold-tone wire to form a delicate design.

damascening (dam′-ah-sehn-ing) Engraving steel, bronze, or iron, and filling up the incision with gold or silver wire. An inferior style of damascening can be made by etching the pattern on steel, then depositing gold or silver in the engraved lines electronically. *Der.* Named for Damascus, where the technique was formerly used.

decatur ring Gold band, similar to a wedding ring, with two inset bands of black enamel. Copied from ring given to Stephen Decatur, American naval officer, by Lieutenant Richard Somers in 1804 as a friendship ring. Original ring is in the Smithsonian Institution, Washington, D.C.

∞**devotional ring** Bronze, gold, or ivory ring with ten spherical projections around the band used in Middle Ages for saying the Apostles' Creed.

diamond bracelet Bracelet made of expensive metals (e.g., gold or platinum), set with many small faceted diamonds and other precious gems. Also worn as watch bracelet with diamond watch. Fashion started in 18th c. and very popular in late 19th and early 20th c.

diamond earring Earring made with single diamond attached to a post for pierced ears, sometimes designed with long strings of diamonds with larger stones set at the top. The former has been a popular wedding gift for the groom to give to the bride. Marie Antoinette, Queen of France in the late 18th c., had a famous pair of the latter type. Elaborate types of diamond earrings were popular from the 1920s on for evening wear.

diamond necklace 1. Any necklace made of genuine diamonds. May be single or large diamonds set in PAVÉ fashion in a band of precious metal, or diamonds set in precious metals and mounted in medallions linked together with chains of the same metal. **2.** Single large diamond suspended from a chain.

diamonds by the yard Chain of 18K gold interspersed with a diamond at intervals, sold by the yard. Worn wrapped around the neck, wrist, or waist. Introduced in 1974 by Elsa Peretti of Tiffany & Co., New York City. In 1984, sold for $2,500 per yard, depending on size of diamonds. Also made of rubies, emeralds, or sapphires.

dinner ring See under JEWELRY: COCKTAIL RING.

dog collar 1. Wide CHOKER (see under JEWELRY), similar to a dog's collar, often consisting of pearls or of a band of metal set with diamonds or rhinestones. Introduced in early 20th c., popular in 1930s, and again in 1960s at which time it was also called *throat belt.* **2.** Band of colored suede or leather worn tightly around neck, popular in early 1970s and since has been revived periodically as a fashion trend using different materials such as woven fabrics.

dome ring Ring with a high-rounded top, similar to a dome, usually set with many stones or made of metal.

door-knocker earring Elongated hoops hanging free from ear clips—may be interchangeable.

doublet Jewelry made of two pieces of glass or gems cemented together to form one large stone.

drop earring Any earring in which the lower part swings free. One of the earliest styles, and one that was popular for single genuine gemstones or pearls, was called a **pendant earring.**

duet pins Two pins worn together as a set.

ear band Earring with a dangling portion that clips on middle edge of an ear.

ear clip Synonym for JEWELRY: EARRING.

ear cuffs Decorative ear ornament that is attached to the ear by pinching it onto the ear without piercing.

earring Decorative jewelry accessory worn on the ear. Ear may be pierced and small wires or posts inserted. For unpierced ears, types include SCREW- OR CLIP-BACKS (see under JEWELRY). Mentioned in the Bible and visible on carvings of ancient monarchs, earrings have been worn by kings, nobles, and soldiers, as well as women since early times. Pirates have been depicted wearing one earring. Popular during the 16th and 17th c., earrings were worn by Henry III of France, and Charles I of England went to his execution wearing a drop pearl in his right ear. After this time, the fashion of earrings for men ended until the 1980s, whereas women have worn earrings from Biblical times to present. Mid-19th-c. earrings were also available in "sets" with matching necklace, brooch, and bracelet. In late 1950s, piercing of ears was revived, even for pre-school children. In early 1980s, double and triple piercing became a fashion with two and three sets of earrings being worn at the same time on either one or both ears. While in the 1960s earrings were often tiny, in the 1980s they became quite large and sometimes dangled to the shoulders. Also called an *ear clip.*

Egyptian collar Wide, flat necklace made in ancient Egypt of beads, shells, seeds, faïence, or semiprecious stones in various colors. Sometimes mounted in gold or made of papyrus or fabric with geometrical lotus designs embroidered in colored wool.

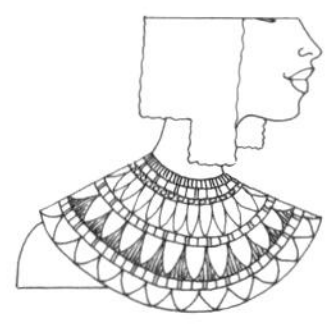
Egyptian collar

elastic bracelet Bracelet made of beads or sectional motifs of various types strung on elastic that slips over the hand.

engagement ring Ring given to a woman by a man signifying that they plan to be married—for many years a diamond SOLITAIRE (see under JEWELRY) was standard—now most any type of ring.

esclavage (ess-kla-vasj') A necklace composed of several rows of gold chain that falls in swags over the bosom, as it was called in the mid-18th c. *Der.* French, "slave."

eternity bracelet See under JEWELRY: SLAVE BRACELET.

eternity ring Full or half circlet of diamonds, rubies, or sapphires set in a narrow band of gold or platinum, sometimes given by husband to wife as a pledge of love on a special occasion (e.g., birth of a child or wedding anniversary). This tradition started in England in 1930s.

expandable bracelet Spring-link metal bracelet that stretches and needs no clasp. Since 1940s frequently used as watch bracelet.

facet See under GEMS, GEM CUTS, AND SETTINGS.

false doublet Stone made from two pieces cemented at the girdle (circumference of largest portion of faceted stone) in which a genuine stone makes up the crown or top, and a cheaper stone or glass is used for the pavilion or bottom part.

family ring Ring that is part of a set for all members of the family (i.e., father, mother, daughter, grandmother, etc.). Each ring may be of a different size and shape, but all rings incorporate several birthstones representing birthdays of various members of the family.

fashion jewelry Since the1980s, refers to high-quality, expensive costume jewelry. Styles include pavé collars (see under GEMS, GEM CUTS, AND SETTINGS: PAVÉ), flashy brooches, lapel pins, necklaces, earrings, and hat pins made of imitation gems. Identical imitation of precious stone jewelry is called **paste.** See under JEWELRY: COSTUME JEWELRY, FAUX JEWELS, and PASTE.

faux jewels (foh) Fashion jewelry that it is obviously fake.

ferronnière (fehr′-ohn-yair′) 1. Delicate chain worn as band across the brow with single jewel hanging in center of forehead. Fashion originated by La Belle Ferronnière, a favorite of Francis I (1515–1547), as shown in a portrait attributed to Giovanni Boltraffio or Leonardo da Vinci. 2. Narrow brow band, with jewel in center, worn on the forehead with evening dress by women in the 1830s. Also called *La Belle Ferronnière.*

ferronnière

filigree (fill′-eh-gree) Ornamental metalwork for jewelry or accessories made of fine silver, gold, or copper wire intricately arranged—or similar pierced metal openwork.

filigree ring (fill′-eh-gree) Gold or silver wire twisted in a lacy intricate pattern to make a ring, usually protruding upward to make a dome.

fine jewelry Jewelry made solely from precious metals and precious and semiprecious stones.

floater necklace Necklace of beads or pearls strung on an almost invisible cord, such as nylon fishing line, so that the beads appear to "float" on the skin of the wearer. Also called *invisible necklace.*

fob pin See under JEWELRY: CHATELAINE.

fraternal ring Emblematic ring only used by members of fraternal organizations (e.g., Masons, Elks, and Knights of Columbus). Frequently made of gold or silver with an onyx setting on which gold, silver, and gemstone symbols of the organization are placed.

fraternity pin Pin selected and specially made for a college fraternity. Usually contains the Greek letters of the fraternity in gold on an onyx background. Sometimes a small guard chain is attached with individual symbol. Also see under JEWELRY: PLEDGE PIN.

free-form ring Contemporary ring that may be almost any shape other than the conventional round ring. Frequently made of a long piece of metal shaped to the finger but having the two ends lapped over each other, often made with gemstones at the ends. *Der.* From free-form sculpture.

freshwater pearls See under GEMS, GEM CUTS, AND SETTINGS: PEARL.

friendship bracelet See under JEWELRY: WOVEN FRIENDSHIP BRACELET.

friendship pin Tiny colored beads threaded on small safety pin and worn fastened to shoelaces. Exchanged as tokens of friendship or love, colors of the beads have various meanings (e.g., red, best friend; pink, sweetheart; green, enemy; purple, good friend; yellow, pal; blue, going steady). A school fad of the 1980s.

friendship ring An older term for a simple metal ring exchanged by good friends and worn for sentimental value. Formerly called a *talisman ring.*

fronts See under HIP-HOP and under JEWELRY: GRILLS.

gemel ring A ring fashionable in the Middle Ages that was really two identical rings joined together and worn together. Popular style had clasped hands on the front. Traditionally the rings were separated at betrothal—the man and woman each wearing one. After marriage the rings were joined together and worn by the woman. Later, triple and quadruple rings of this style were worn. Revived in the mid-1980s. *Der.* From the Italian word *gemelli,* or Latin, *gemini,* "twins." Also spelled *gemmel, geminal, gimmel.*

genuine pearls See under GEMS, GEM CUTS, AND SETTINGS: PEARL.

girdle See under GEMS, GEM CUTS, AND SETTINGS.

gold beads 1. 14K gold beads sometimes purchased one at a time and added to a chain for necklace. 2. Beads plated with gold. 3. Costume jewelry with different bases and gilt finishes.

gold filled Gold of 10 to 22 karats fused to a base metal (e.g., nickel, silver, or brass). Layer of gold should weigh at least 1/20 of the entire metal used. Gold of 1/10 18K means that it's 18 karat and represents 1/10 of the weight of the metal.

gold-plated Describes jewelry that has a thin surface of gold electrolytically plated to a base metal.

golds See under JEWELRY: GRILLS.

gold-washed Describes jewelry that has a thin coating of gold applied to a base metal by dipping or washing it in a solution of gold.

∞**gorget** (gorge-et′) Chain with crescent-shaped ornament worn around the neck by officers during 17th and 18th c. as a badge of rank.

grain See under GEMS, GEM CUTS, AND SETTINGS.

grills Metal removable jewelry worn over the front teeth, a style that originated with those participating in HIP-HOP culture in the 1980s and has continued. Also called *golds* or *fronts.*

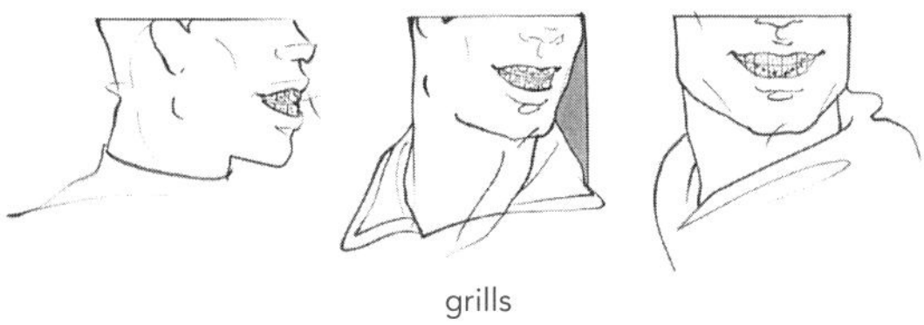

grills

gypsy earring Large hoop earring usually of brass or gold-colored metal, worn in pierced ear, inspired by plain brass circles worn by gypsies. For unpierced ears, hoop is suspended from a small button top that clips to the back of the ear.

∞**hair jewelry** Jewelry made with or from human hair. During the early 19th c., locks of hair from a deceased loved one were often incorporated into jewelry as a memento; however, by the latter part of the century, ready-made hair jewelry could be purchased.

hat pin See under HEADWEAR.

hinged bracelet Any bracelet with a hinge allowing it to open wide for removal.

hippie beads Beads adopted by hippies, an avant-garde group of young people in the United States in the mid-1960s. For necklaces, usually small beads worn in chest-length strands by both sexes. Influenced conventional men to adopt the fashion of wearing chains or medallion necklaces. Also called *love beads.* See under HIPPIE.

hoop bracelet See under JEWELRY: BANGLE BRACELET.

hoop earring 1. Circlet (or oval) of metal, plastic, or wood that swings free from a small button. Also see under JEWELRY: GYPSY EARRING. 2. Incomplete circlet that fastens around the earlobe. May be hinged and clip into place.

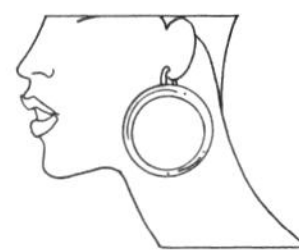

hoop earring

Hopi bracelet Narrow sterling silver cuff bracelet with symbols of Hopi Native American tribe in black. *Der.* From Hopi Indians of the southwestern U.S.

ID/identification bracelet Bracelet of large links attached to oblong metal plaque engraved with name or initials. First used by soldiers in wartime, later adapted for adults and children.

imitation pearls See under GEMS, GEM CUTS, AND SETTINGS: PEARL.

initial ring See under JEWELRY: SIGNET RING.

iridium (ih-rid′-ee-em) Metal frequently alloyed with platinum to make a more durable metal for use in jewelry.

∞**iron ring** Finger ring worn by ancient Romans, with gold rings being reserved for badges of civil and military rank.

∞**jack chain** Chain made of links like a figure eight, worn as an ostentatious decoration by men in 17th c.

jacket earring Earring consisting of post on which various shaped, separate pieces with holes in their tops may be interchanged by placing post through hole. "Jackets" may be in shape of shells, roses, hearts, butterflies, etc. Introduced in early 1980s.

jet jewelry See under GEMS, GEM CUTS, AND SETTINGS: JET.

kilt pin See under SAFETY PIN #3.

lampshade beads Short lengths of tiny strung beads hung in a fringe from a ribbon tied close to neck, worn in early 1970s. *Der.* Beaded fringe on lampshades popular in late Victorian era and 1920s.

∞**langettes** (lan-get′) 16th-c. string of beads.

lapel pin Woman's pin originally worn on the lapel of a suit. Almost all medium-sized pins are now called lapel pins.

lariat necklace 1. Long strand of beads or metal, sometimes ending in tassels, that is not fastened by a clasp. Worn looped into a knot or used as a slide so that the two ends hang free. 2. Man's short necklace (or tie) usually made of leather that has a silver slide and two ends tipped with silver hanging free.

lavaliere (lav-al-yer′) Pendant, sometimes set with precious stones, worn as a necklace on a fine chain. *Der.* Named after Louise de La Vallière, mistress of Louis XIV of France.

locket Chain necklace with a gold or silver disk that opens to reveal picture of loved one or lock of hair. Very popular from mid-19th to early 20th c. and still worn as a family keepsake.

love beads See JEWELRY: HIPPIE BEADS.

magnetic earrings Earrings that simulate the appearance of pierced earrings by using magnets on the front of the earring and on the back of the ear that hold the jewelry in place.

Mali bracelet Handmade bracelet made of leather approximately 1″ wide and decorated with very small European glass beads (called AMERICAN INDIAN BEADS in the U.S.; see under JEWELRY) in a variety of colors and designs. Introduced from the Republic of Mali in Africa in 1980s.

matinee-length necklace Bead necklace, usually of pearls or simulated pearls, 30″ to 35″ long.

medallion necklace Heavy chain necklace with large disk as a pendant, worn by women during various eras and introduced for men in late 1960s.

medic alert bracelet Bracelet worn to indicate blood type and/or allergies to certain drugs.

mesh bracelet Metal bracelet made of minute links or a continuous piece of woven metal. Used in gold for expensive watches and bracelets.

mizpah medallion necklace (miz′-pah) Large medallion with a quotation from Genesis cut in half in zigzag fashion to form "his" and "hers" medals worn on a chain.

mobile earring (mo-beel) Delicate wire drop earring like small mobile sculpture, carefully balanced so it is constantly in motion.

∞**mourning jewelry** Jet and black-enameled jewelry worn by women from the mid-19th through early 20th

c. instead of regular jewelry during a mourning period. Also see under JEWELRY: HAIR JEWELRY.

∞**mourning ring** Massive ring, frequently black—later blue—enamel, sometimes given to guests at funerals. Sometimes included portrait of deceased, emblems, motto (e.g., "be prepared to follow me"), or hair of the departed plaited in a design.

mouse jewelry ∞1. Bracelets, brooches, rings, and earrings made of metal and decorated with replicas of mice, worn by women during the 1880s. Bracelet consisted of a metal ring with three mice placed along the outer edge, their tails winding around the ring of metal. **2.** In the late 1960s and early 1970s, jewelry for children was made with enameled metal or plastic mice, usually to look like Mickey Mouse®, a Walt Disney creation.

∞**neck-chain** Decorative gilded brass or gold chain worn by men from Middle Ages to mid-17th c. Sometimes worn by travelers in Middle Ages who used a few links of it for money. For late 17th-c. variation, see under JEWELRY: JACK CHAIN.

necklace Decorative accessory worn around the neck. Frequently made of beads or chain and sometimes of real or imitation gems set in gold, silver, or other metals. Remains of prehistoric necklaces indicate that people wore necklaces made from a wide variety of materials, including seeds, nuts, shells, and the teeth and claws of animals strung on grass or thong. A TORQUE (see under JEWELRY) was a twisted metal collar or necklace worn by ancient Teutons, Gauls, and Britons of the Bronze Age. Egyptians wore amulets such as the SCARAB and the *utchat* (oot-shat′), a representation of a sacred eye. Greeks wore metal necklaces with a "fringe" of small vase-like drops of diamonds, sapphires, garnets, etc. Romans introduced the rope pearl necklace. From 16th c. on, heavy chains and all types of necklaces have been worn. In contemporary times, an expensive necklace is frequently a status symbol.

neck ring Single narrow band of springy metal worn as choker, sometimes with dangling ornament. An innovation of late 1960s.

necktie pin See under JEWELRY: STICKPIN.

nose chains Jewelry consisting of chains that are attached though piercings through the nose and the ears. Often part of the dress of those following GOTH styles.

nose piercing jewelery Jewelry attached to the nose through piercing. Piercings are made at the nostril, through the septum, and through the skin of the bridge of the nose.

nose rings Jewelry attached to the nose, usually by piercings at the nostril.

nose studs Jewelry attached to the nose by piercings.

nugget ring Ring with stone made from a piece of metal in its natural shape (e.g., a gold nugget).

opera-length necklace Necklace of beads, usually of pearls or simulated pearls, 48″ to 120″ long, usually worn wrapped twice around the neck. Originated in 1890s for wear to the opera or for other formal occasions. Also see under JEWELRY: ROPE NECKLACE.

oriental pearls See under GEMS, GEM CUTS, AND SETTINGS: PEARL.

∞**ouch** A collection of jewels, or a jeweled clasp or buckle, that was worn between the 13th and 15th c. Also spelled *nouch*.

parure (pah-roor′) Matched set of jewelry that may consist of a necklace, earrings, pin, or bracelet. *Der.* French, "adornment."

paste Highly reflective transparent types of flint glass faceted or molded to make imitation gems. One variety is called **strass,** named for Josef Strasser, a German jeweler. Used in making replicas of expensive jewelry. Also see under JEWELRY: FAUX JEWELS and FASHION JEWELRY.

pavé See under GEMS, GEM CUTS, AND SETTINGS.

peace ring Simple ring designed of metal with peace symbol consisting of a circle intersected with straight bar down the center and Y-shaped bars to the outer edge.

pearl beads PEARLS (see under GEMS, GEM CUTS, AND SETTINGS) all of one size or graduated in size. Usually strung on thread, often with a knot after each bead, made in a variety of lengths and worn in single strand or several strands. A classic fashion for many centuries.

peek-a-boo earring Earring for pierced ears with small object or stone showing where ear is pierced and three or four stones showing at lower edge of ear. The latter group is attached to back of earring.

pendant earring See under JEWELRY: DROP EARRING.

pendant necklace Ornament such as a locket, medallion, or single jewel suspended around neck from a chain, thong, or cord. Worn since the Renaissance.

pendant pin Pin with a clasp at back and a hook at center top so it can be worn on a chain, cord, etc., as a necklace or a pin.

∞**pendicle** Single pendant earring worn by men in 17th c.

perfume ring Large ring that is hinged under the stone so that solid perfume may be placed inside.

pierced earring Earring designed to be worn in pierced ears. A wire or post is inserted through the earlobe; should be made of gold or surgical steel rather than plated metals to prevent infection. Until the introduction of screw-back earrings, all types of earrings were made for pierced ears.

pierced-look earring Earring designed for unpierced ears. Has a delicate band of metal coming under the ear to the front giving the appearance that it goes through the ear.

pin Ornamental jewelry made with pin fastener on back that may have a safety catch. Made in all types of materials (e.g., gold, silver, plated metals, and frequently set with gems or imitation stones). In Anglo-Saxon, Greek, and Roman times used to fasten clothing. See under PENANNULAR BROOCH and FIBULA. Later became more decorative. Synonym for *brooch*.

plated As applied to jewelry—e.g., gold-plated—a thin film of precious metal applied to an inexpensive base metal—usually by electrolysis.

platinum Rare white metal used for mounting jewels, usually alloyed with 10 percent iridium to increase hardness.

pledge pin A pin given to those pledging to join a fraternity or sorority. Worn during the pledge period prior to initiation. When initiated, the member replaces the pledge pin with a fraternity or sorority pin as a symbol of membership.

∞**plummet** Pendant earrings, as they were called in the 17th c. See under JEWELRY: DROP EARRING and PENDICLE.

poison ring 1. Finger ring, worn from Roman period through the 17th c., that was designed to hold a dose of poison. Made in Roman times with the setting a mere shell and the poison behind it. Cesare Borgia's ring, dated 1503 and still in existence, has a small sliding panel that opened into a small cavity where the poison was placed. 2. Similar novelty item of the late 1960s, sometimes used to contain perfume.

posts See under JEWELRY: STUDS.

posy/poesy ring Plain gold band, sometimes with small decorative design in center, given as a love token. Inside was inscribed "let love endure" or "faithful and true." Popular in the 16th c., revived in the 1980s.

purity ring Ring worn by members of Christian sexual abstinence groups who have vowed to remain abstinent until they marry. Also known as *chastity ring* or *abstinence ring*.

puzzle ring Ring made up of interconnecting rings—the number can vary from three to twelve. Disconnecting the rings is a puzzle for the wearer to solve.

∞**regard rings** Rings worn in 16th c. set with stones having initials spelling out such words as L-O-V-E or name of the beloved.

religious medal A pendant necklace worn by Christians of various sects (e.g., the St. Christopher medal worn predominantly by Catholics).

rhodium White-colored metal of the platinum group used for plating jewelry.

ring Decorative jewelry worn on the finger, sometimes on the thumb, and infrequently on one of the toes. Before the mid-1960s, rings were worn on the third finger and the little finger. After this time, it was fashionable to wear rings on any of the fingers. This was a revival of styles of the 16th c., when many rings were worn and two rings were sometimes worn on the same finger. Since earliest times a ring has been a pledge or a seal of faith and also used as a stamp of authority. See under JEWELRY: DEVOTIONAL RING, FISHERMAN'S RING, GIMMEL RING, and POISON RING.

ring bracelet See under JEWELRY: SLAVE BRACELET.

rolling ring Bands of three circlets of gold in different colors of gold—rose, yellow, and white—interlocked to make a ring. Designed and made by Cartier since the 1920s. Also made with six interlocking circles.

rondella (rohn-del'-ah) Round, small metal disk that is placed between beads. It may be plain or ornamented with stones.

rope necklace Extra-long beaded necklace, usually of pearls, that may be wrapped around neck several times or worn long and knotted. Very popular in 1920s and fashionable since then.

safety pin An item of jewelry shaped like a utilitarian safety pin that may have beads hanging suspended from the long bar or decorating the head.

sautoir (so-twar') Pendant-type necklace with a dangling piece in front that may appear to be fringed at base. *Der.* French, woman's watch chain or a medal of honor worn around the neck.

scarab bracelet Bracelet made of several oval semiprecious stones (e.g., lapis lazuli or chalcedony) engraved to look like beetles, outlined in gold, and connected by gold links. *Der.* Ancient Egyptian sacred beetle. Also see under SCARAB.

scarf pin See under JEWELRY: STICKPIN.

school ring See under JEWELRY: CLASS RING.

screw-back earring Earring for unpierced ears, with screw behind the ear that can be tightened to hold it in place. An innovation of the early 20th c. that enabled people without pierced ears to wear earrings.

seed bead necklace Necklace in various styles that is made from very small beads.

seed pearls See under GEMS, GEM CUTS, AND SETTINGS: PEARL.

serpent ring Ring shaped like snake curled around the finger. Similar rings were worn in ancient Rome.

signet ring 1. Ring with large stone cut INTAGLIO (see under GEMS, GEM CUTS, AND SETTINGS). Formerly used to make an impression in sealing wax to seal letters. 2. Ring with king's seal used by ancient Egyptians.

silk pin See under DRESSMAKER PIN.

simulated pearls See under GEMS, GEM CUTS, AND SETTINGS: PEARL.

slave bracelet 1. Ring connected by a chain to a bracelet worn around the wrist. Also called a *bracelet ring,* a *ring bracelet,* and more recently an *eternity bracelet.* Originally copied from bracelets worn in Eastern countries for centuries. Popular in 1880s and the 1990s. 2. A *toe-ankle chain* is also called by this name.

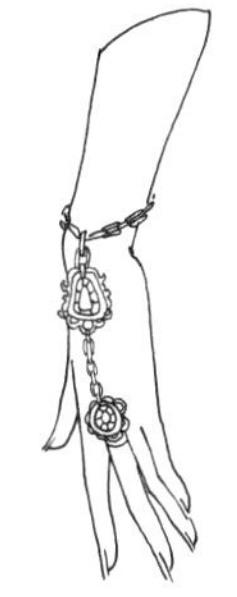
slave bracelet #1 or ring bracelet

sleeve bracelet Ornate bracelet worn around upper arm over full sleeve to make a double-puffed sleeve. Fashionable in England in late 1960s.

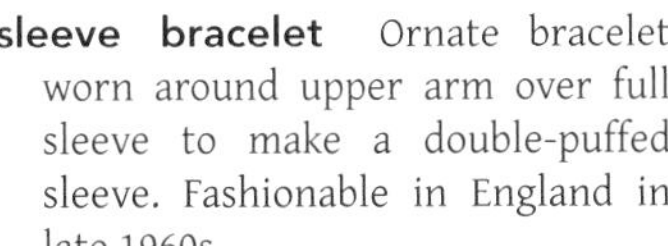

slide bracelet Bracelet with small piece of pierced metal through which fine flat chains are threaded. Needs no clasp as it is adjusted by pulling the chains. Popular in late 19th c. and revived by using antique watch chains in 1960s.

snake bracelet Metal bracelet in form of a serpent worn coiled around the arm. Worn by ancient Greeks and fashionable in 1880s and in late 1960s.

solitaire Ring set with a single stone, frequently a diamond, sometimes a pearl or another gem.

solitaire

sorority pin Similar to FRATERNITY PIN (see under JEWELRY) but worn by high school and college girls as an emblem of their club or sorority. See also under JEWELRY: PLEDGE PIN.

spoon ring The handle of a small sterling silver spoon molded to wrap around the finger to form a ring.

spring bracelet Beads strung on flexible wire in a spiral that expands to permit entry of hand.

squash blossom necklace Traditional necklace made of tiny pieces of turquoise set in sterling silver. Stones are mounted in a manner to imitate flowers with many petals. *Der.* Handcrafted by Zuni Native Americans of the southwestern United States. Some necklaces are in the collections of the Museum of Natural History and the Smithsonian Institution.

squash blossom necklace

Statue of Liberty earring Dangling earring with head of Statue of Liberty enclosed in a circle. *Der.* Inspired by the July 4, 1986, celebration in New York harbor of the restoration of the Statue of Liberty.

sterling silver Metal containing 92.5 parts silver and 7.5 parts copper, a standard set by law. Used for jewelry, it is "silvery" in color and lustrous. One of its disadvantages is that it tarnishes (darkens from exposure to chemicals in the atmosphere). This can be easily remedied with silver polish.

St. George cross See under JEWELRY: CRUSADER'S CROSS.

stickpin 1. Straight, stiletto-type pin with an ornamental top worn by a man to secure a four-in-hand necktie or ascot. Popular from late 19th c. to 1930s. Now *tie tacks* are more usually worn. Also called *scarf pin* and *tie pin.* 2. Same type of pin styled as a lapel pin for women.

stickpin

strass See under JEWELRY: PASTE.

studs 1. Earrings designed for pierced ears. One part of earring goes through the ear and back screws into the **post.** A basic type of earring for pierced ears. Some studs are secured by pushing a back piece onto straight post, where a notch in the post secures the back. 2. See under CLOSURES: STUD.

talisman ring (tahl'-iss-mahn) "Charm" ring worn in Ancient Greece and the Middle Ages to ensure the wearer good health, strength, wealth, and happiness. Worn in recent times as a pledge of friendship. Also see under JEWELRY: FRIENDSHIP RING.

tassel necklace Long, linked, chain necklace with cluster of as many as twelve short chains forming a tassel at the end.

∞**tethered studs** Man's evening jewelry of 1830s and 1840s consisting of three ornamental shirt studs joined with small chains.

throat belt See under JEWELRY: DOG COLLAR.

tie clasp/clip Jewelry consisting of a decorative metal bar, bent in half, that slides over a man's tie and behind his shirt front placket clipping the tie in place. May also have spring-clip back.

tie pin See under JEWELRY: STICKPIN.

tie tack Small ornament with a sharp-pointed back worn pierced through both parts of a man's necktie to hold them together. Back portion is usually screwed into a round metal stud.

toe-ankle chain Unusual ankle bracelet with chain attached to toe ring, worn in 1970. Also called SLAVE BRACELET (see under JEWELRY).

toe ring Any ring worn on one of the toes, usually the big toe. In 1967 plastic, papier-mâché, or felt rings were popular. Also see under JEWELRY: TOE-ANKLE CHAIN.

∞torque/torc (tork) An incomplete circle of metal that fit around the neck that was worn by the Celtic people of Western Europe. Some were ornamented by twisting or working the metal or inlaying colored enamel.

torsade Several strands of pearls, chains, or beads twisted together to form a single necklace.

Ubangi necklace See under JEWELRY: AFRO CHOKER.

utchat See under JEWELRY: NECKLACE.

washed gold Thin coating of gold applied to a base metal by dipping or washing it in a solution of gold salts.

watch bracelet Band, strap, or other device attached to wristwatch made of all types of metals, leather, plastic, or fabric that holds the watch on the wrist.

wedding band/wedding ring A ring used in wedding ceremony, traditionally a band of gold in any of various widths worn by both men and women on the third finger of the left hand. Although these rings have been worn since Egyptian times, they were not adopted by Christians until the second half of the 9th c. The plain gold band of modern times dates from the time of Mary Tudor and her marriage to Phillip II of Spain in 1554.

wedding band earring Wide gold hoop earring similar in style to a wide gold wedding ring.

wedding trio Woman's engagement ring and wedding band, along with the man's wedding band, similarly styled and sold together. Also see under JEWELRY: BRIDAL SET.

Wedgwood cameo A cameo, usually blue in color, with the head of a woman in raised design on the surface. Made by casting Wedgwood pottery material. Can be distinguished from cut cameos by the tiny air bubbles on the surface. *Der.* Made by the Wedgwood China Company in England.

wires Earrings for pierced ears that have a thin curved wire, usually gold, that passes through the ear. Usually dangling objects are attached to the wire or the wires may be worn separately.

worry beads Short string of beads, often made of semiprecious stones. Originally carried to move around in the hand by men in Middle Eastern countries, Greece, and Turkey when they were under stress. Popular in America in late 1960s. *Der.* From string of 33 beads used to count the 99 names of Allah during prayers in Muslim countries.

woven friendship bracelet Bracelet made from different colored strands of yarn woven, knotted, or plaited together.

wrist strap Wide band of leather buckled around wrist, usually trimmed with metal studs. Introduced in late 1960s.

zodiac necklace Any necklace, usually of the pendant type, with medallion engraved with a personal sign of the zodiac. Popular in late 1960s and early 1970s.

Zuni jewelry Beautiful exotic and unusual bracelets, pins, necklaces, and rings of sterling silver set with genuine turquoise gems. *Der.* Made by the Zuni, a Native American tribe inhabiting the largest of the Indian pueblos in western New Mexico.

zuni snake eye ring Sterling silver ring set with 25 turquoise stones, mounted 5 to a row in 5 rows, alternating with rounded silver beads. Copied from ring in the Smithsonian Institution. *Der.* Originally made by Zuni, Native Americans of the southwestern U.S.

---

jiffy dress See under DRESSES.

jiffy-knit sweater See under SWEATERS.

∞jigger button A button concealed under lapel on man's double-breasted coat that was used to fasten back a wide lapel, as it was called in the 19th c.

JIT Acronym for *just-in-time*. See under JUST-IN-TIME.

joan See under HEADWEAR.

∞joan-of-arc bodice Woman's tight-fitting bodice worn in 1875, reaching to hips and covered with jet or steel beads. Made with tight-fitting sleeves and ruffles at wrists.

jobber An agent in the apparel industry that sells CLOSE-OUTS and JOB LOTS or carries inventories of apparel immediately available to retailers.

job lot Odds and ends of remaining styles of which the manufacturer wants to dispose. Often made up of broken sizes, colors, and/or styles and if purchased as a group, can be bought for a considerable discount.

jocelyn mantle See under CAPES, CLOAKS, AND SHAWLS.

jockey *adj.* Describes apparel derived from or inspired by the clothing worn by professional jockeys in horseracing. See under ACTIVEWEAR: JOCKEY PANTS; FOOTWEAR: JOCKEY BOOT; HEADWEAR: JOCKEY CAP; SHIRTS: JOCKEY SHIRT; and VESTS: JOCKEY WAISTCOAT.

Jockey® shorts See under UNDERGARMENTS.

jockey silks Costume of racehorse rider who wears a colorful shirt and cap to designate stable that owns his horse. Also called *racing silks.*

jodhpur boot See under FOOTWEAR.

jodhpurs See under ACTIVEWEAR.

jogging shorts See under SHORTS: SWEATSHORTS.

jogging suit See under ACTIVEWEAR.

johnny collar See under NECKLINES AND COLLARS.

joinville See under TIES.

jornade See under COATS AND JACKETS: JOURNADE.

Joseph See under COATS AND JACKETS.

josephine knot Ornamental knot used for trimmings, which is made by looping two ribbons leaving the four ends hanging free.

journade See under COATS AND JACKETS.

jours See under LACES.

judo clothing See under ACTIVEWEAR: KARATE SUIT.

judo jacket See under ACTIVEWEAR: KARATE SUIT.

jugoslavian embroidery See under EMBROIDERIES AND SEWING STITCHES: YUGOSLAVIAN.

∞juive tunic See under DRESSES.

juliet *adj.* Descriptive of fashions thought to be similar to those that might have been worn by the heroine of Shakespeare's drama *Romeo and Juliet.* Often these styles derive from clothing used in popular films or theatrical presentations of the play. See under DRESSES: JULIET DRESS; FOOTWEAR: JULIET SLIPPER; HEADWEAR: JULIET CAP; SHOULDERS AND SLEEVES: JULIET SLEEVE; and SLEEPWEAR AND LOUNGEWEAR: JULIET GOWN.

juliet dress See under DRESSES.

jumbo curl See under HAIRSTYLES.

jump See under COATS AND JACKETS.

jumper coat See under COATS AND JACKETS: BEAUFORT COAT.

jumper dress See under DRESSES.

JUMPERS

jumper 1. A sleeveless garment, generally for women or children, worn over a sleeved blouse, sweater, or shirt. May be belted or beltless. Fashion terms for various jumper styles have developed and are generally formed by placing an adjective describing the apparel in front of the word "jumper." Examples: apron jumper, back belt jumper. 2. See under SWEATERS. 3. See under BLOUSES AND TOPS.

A-line jumper Jumper styled similarly to a sleeveless A-LINE DRESS (see under DRESSES); it can be worn with or without a blouse or shirt underneath.

bib jumper Jumper styled similarly to a skirt, with the front extending up to form a bib similar to the top of overalls. Straps are attached to the bib, extend over the shoulders, cross in the back, and attach to the skirt.

bib jumper

buckled jumper Bib-type jumper with two buckles placed at the neckline through which straps coming over the shoulder from the back are fastened.

buckskin jumper Jumper styled similarly to a sleeveless fringed AMERICAN INDIAN DRESS (see under DRESSES), fastened with a laced closing in center front.

coat-jumper Single- or double-breasted jumper styled similarly to a sleeveless COATDRESS (see under DRESSES).

horseshoe jumper Jumper made with a very low horseshoe neckline in front and back and large armholes. The straps that extend over the shoulders are cut in one piece with the skirt of the garment.

horseshoe jumper

painter's jumper Design inspired by painters' work clothes.

pantjumper 1. Jumper similar in structure to a sleeveless PANTDRESS, worn with or without a blouse. 2. Jumper worn over a long sleeved blouse combined with full-length pants.

pinafore jumper Similar to a BIB JUMPER (see under JUMPERS). Also see under APRONS: PINAFORE APRON.

sandwich-board jumper A jumper made by joining two oblong pieces of fabric at the shoulders and at the waistline. So called because it resembles a sign previously worn over the shoulder with advertising copy in front and back called a "sandwich-board sign."

shift jumper

shift jumper Jumper styled similarly to a sleeveless SHIFT dress (see under DRESSES); may be worn with or without a blouse.

suspender jumper Any jumper with straps extending over the shoulders usually hooked to waistband of the skirt. A popular style for young girls. Also see under SKIRTS: SUSPENDER SKIRT.

tunic jumper Thigh-length jumper worn over a blouse, usually made with matching full-length pants. Can be worn as a MINIDRESS (see under DRESSES) or as a PANTSUIT.

wrap jumper A jumper that fits over the head, wraps around the body, and ties in front or back. Also called *apron jumper.*

wrap jumper

jumper shift See under JUMPERS: SHIFT JUMPER.

jumper suit JUMPER DRESS (see under DRESSES) with matching jacket.

jumps Unboned bodice of 18th c. worn by women for comfort or during pregnancy.

jumpshorts See under SHORTS.

jumpsuit See under ACTIVEWEAR.

jumpsuit pajamas See under SLEEPWEAR AND LOUNGEWEAR.

jungle boot See under FOOTWEAR.

jungle print See under PRINTS, STRIPES, AND CHECKS.

junior petite sizes A size category that applies to garments cut with a junior fit for a shorter figure, 5′1″ to 5′3″ tall. Usually sized 1JP to 13JP. See JUNIOR SIZES.

junior sizes A size category cut to fit a young body with fewer curves, a smaller bust, and less definition between the waist and hips, 5′4″ to 5′5″ tall. Size nomenclature uses odd numbers typically 1 to 13. Due to its younger target market, styling tends to focus on trendy, casual clothes suitable for school, casual socializing, clubbing, and entry-level career wear.

jupe 1. See under SKIRTS. 2. See under DOUBLET. 3. See under COATS AND JACKETS.

jupon 1. See under DOUBLET. 2. See under SKIRTS. 3. See under UNDERGARMENTS: HOOPS. 4. See under COATS AND JACKETS: JUPE.

juppe See under DOUBLET.

justaucorps See under COATS AND JACKETS.

just-in-time (JIT) Manufacturing system designed to lessen costly inventories of textiles and apparel. Electronic communications allow suppliers to produce and supply materials to manufacturers "just in time" for production.

†jute A fiber from the stem of the jute plant, grown in Bangladesh, India, China, and Thailand. Soft, fine, lustrous, and pliable, it becomes weak and brittle when exposed to moisture. It is used in making fabrics such as BUCKRAM and BURLAP.

K Abbreviation for KARAT.

kabuki (ka-boo′-kee) *adj.* Describes clothing derived from or inspired by traditional costumes worn by actors in Japanese *kabuki theater.* See under DRESSES: KABUKI DRESS; SHOULDERS AND SLEEVES: KIMONO SLEEVE; and SLEEPWEAR AND LOUNGEWEAR: KABUKI ROBE.

kabuki dress (ka-boo′-kee) See under DRESSES.

kaffiyeh-agal (ka-fee′-yeh ah-gal) Headdress consisting of a large square of plain or striped cotton folded diagonally and placed on head. Sometimes has hanging tassels at corners and held by a circlet of twisted cord called **agal.** Worn by Arabs in Middle East. Also spelled *kaffiyah, kaffieh, keffiyeh, kuffieh.*

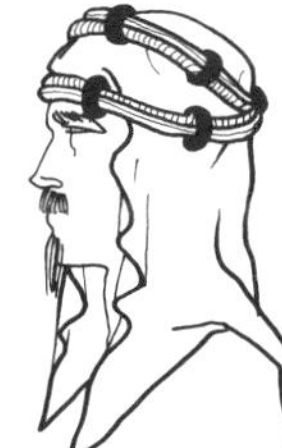
kaffiyeh-agal

kaftan See under CAFTAN.

∞kalasiris (kah-lah-seer′-iss) (*calasiris*) Egyptian garment sometimes inaccurately described as a long, tight-fitting, sheath-type dress, but based on the description of Herodotus, a Greek historian, more likely to have been a linen tunic. Also see under EGYPTIAN DRESS.

Kalgan lamb See under FURS: LAMB.

kalso See under FOOTWEAR.

∞kalyptra (ka-lip-tra) Sheer veil worn over head and face by women in ancient Greece.

kampskatcha slipper See under FOOTWEAR.

kangaroo See under LEATHERS and POCKETS.

kangaroo skirt See under SKIRTS.

kapa See under TAPA CLOTH.

Karaca sweater See under SWEATERS.

karakul See under FURS.

†karakul cloth (kar′-ah-kul) Heavyweight pile fabric, similar to ASTRAKHAN, woven in imitation of BROADTAIL LAMB or PERSIAN LAMB (see these terms under FURS).

karat Relates to the quality or fineness of gold, especially that used in jewelry. Gold of 24K is 100 percent gold with no alloys added; however, gold of this quality is too soft for jewelry. When alloys are added to gold, the resultant alloys are labeled as 12K, 14K, or 18K gold, meaning that 12/24, 14/24, or 18/24 of the metal is gold, the remainder is the alloy. The letter *K* is used as an abbreviation. Compare with CARAT, which is the weight of a gemstone.

karate clothing See under ACTIVEWEAR: KARATE SUIT. Also see under COATS AND JACKETS: KARATE JACKET and SLEEPWEAR AND LOUNGEWEAR: KARATE PAJAMAS.

∞karcher/ kercher/kercheve/kersche Medieval spelling of KERCHIEF. See HEADWEAR: KERCHIEF #2.

†kasuri Handwoven Japanese textile made by tie-dyeing yarns in a method similar to IKAT. Traditionally made of cotton with irregularly shaped white dots on a dark blue background. A technique often used by craftpersons for WEARABLE ART.

∞Kate Greenaway costume Children's dress, popular in 1880s and 1890s, inspired by illustrations of children in empire costumes drawn by Kate Greenaway, the popular British children's book illustrator of late 19th c. Typical costumes were made of lightweight fabric printed with flowers and styled with a high waistline, puffed sleeves, and ankle-length skirts trimmed with narrow ruffles, worn with ribbon sashes, PANTALETTES (see under UNDERGARMENTS) showing, and MOB CAPS or POKE BONNETS (see under HEADWEAR). These dresses were widely copied for children's wear through end of 19th c. and are still a fashion inspiration. *Der.* Named after the artist Kate Greenaway (1846–1901).

Kate Greenaway costume

Keds® See under FOOTWEAR: SNEAKERS.

keffieh See under KAFFIYEH-AGAL.

Kellerman, Annette See under SWIMWEAR: ANNETTE KELLERMAN.

Kelly bag See under HANDBAGS AND RELATED ACCESSORIES.

kemes/kemise/kemse See under UNDERGARMENTS: CHEMISE.

†**kente cloth** Fabric with woven or printed designs characterized by narrow, brightly colored bands with randomly placed geometric patterns. These fabrics are derived from traditional silk fabrics and their designs made by the Asante people of Ghana.

kente cloth

kepi See under under HEADWEAR.

kerchief 1. See under HEADWEAR. 2. See under SCARVES.

kevenhuller hat See under HEADWEAR: COCKED HAT.

keyhole neckline See under NECKLINES AND COLLARS.

key pocket See under POCKETS.

keystone markup See under MARKUP.

†**khaki** (ka-key) Fabrics of a dull, yellowish-tan color, whether serge, drill, or whipcords, fabrics are called by this name. Used for some military uniforms by a number of countries. *Der.* Hindu, "dust color or earth color."

kick pleats See under CLOTHING CONSTRUCTION DETAILS and SKIRTS.

kid/kidskin See under FURS; GLOVES AND GLOVE CONSTRUCTION: KID GLOVE; and LEATHERS.

kiddie couture The production of expensive clothing for children by well-known designers.

kidney belt See under BELTS.

kid seam See under GLOVES AND GLOVE CONSTRUCTION: FULL PIQUÉ.

Kikuyu See under HANDBAGS AND RELATED ACCESSORIES.

kilt See under under SKIRTS.

kiltie *adj.* Descriptive of clothing and accessories derived from those worn by Scots Highlanders. First adopted for boys in about 1880, revived at intervals, and fashionable since late 1960s. Elements include wearing of skirts cut like kilts, knee socks, TAMS (see under HEADWEAR), plaid fabrics, and GILLIES (see under FOOTWEAR), in imitation of Scots Highlanders' garb. Also see under FOOTWEAR: KILTIE FLAT and KILTIE OXFORD.

kiltie dress See under DRESSES.

kilt pin See under SAFETY PIN #3.

kilt pleat See under CLOTHING CONSTRUCTION DETAILS.

kimono (keh-mo′-no) 1. A traditional costume of Japan, either in dark colors for men or in bright colors and floral patterns for women, that is a loose, straight-cut cotton or silk robe made in various lengths and sashed at waist with a belt called an OBI (see under BELTS). Loose, straight sleeves are either cut on or set-in at right angles. Adapted for fashionable wear in the U.S. 2. See under SLEEPWEAR AND LOUNGEWEAR.

kimono #1

kimono dress See under DRESSES.

kimono sleeve See under SHOULDERS AND SLEEVES.

kiosk 1. A small structure, open on one or more sides, used to distribute merchandise or disperse information; found in shopping malls, airports, and other areas with high foot traffic. 2. A popular temporary format to test product in a retail setting before committing to a more traditional space. See also under POP-UP STORES, INTERACTIVE KIOSK.

kip/kipskin See under LEATHERS.

kipper See under TIES.

∞**kirtle** 1. A knee-length tunic with sleeves worn by men, from 9th to end of 14th c. 2. Full-length, sleeved garment worn by women from 10th to 16th c. as basic garment over the smock and under the gown. May appear as a synonym for COTE. 3. In the 16th c., applied also to an underskirt that is part of a dress, but by the mid-16th to mid-17th c., it was more likely to be called **half-kirtle** and, eventually, a PETTICOAT. 4. Short jacket worn in 18th and 19th c. 5. An outer petticoat worn when riding.

kiss curl See under HAIRSTYLES: GUICHE.

kiss-me-quick See under HEADWEAR.

kitsch Styles considered to be overly sentimental or pretentious. Also used as an adjective to describe such styles.

kit fox See under FURS: FOX.

kitten heels See under FOOTWEAR.

knapsack See under HANDBAGS AND RELATED ACCESSORIES.

∞**knee breeches** Garment worn on lower half of the body by men from 1570s to about 1820. Extending from waist to slightly below the knee, they fit the leg, bloused slightly below knee, where they fastened with a button on outside of leg. From end of 17th c. on, buckles were usually worn as closures.

∞**knee cop** See under ARMOR: POLEYN.

∞**knee-fringe** Fringe of ribbons around bottom edge of open-style breeches, worn by men from 1670 to 1675.

knee-high/knee-hi See under HOSIERY.

knee-high boot See under FOOTWEAR.

knee length See under LENGTHS.

knee pants See under PANTS: KNICKERS.

∞**knee-piece** 1. Upper part of BOOT HOSE (see under HOSIERY). 2. See under ARMOR.

knee sock See under HOSIERY: KNEE-HI SOCK.

∞**knee-string** Drawstring used in 17th and 18th c. for tightening breeches below knee.

knee warmers Pair of knitted cuffs that slip on over legs to cover knees and may be worn under or over hose in winter or when participating in active sports.

knickerbockers ∞1. Loose breeches gathered or pleated into buckled band at knee that were introduced for men about 1860, originally for country wear. ∞2. Worn by women for bicycling in early 1890s. Also called RATIONALS (see under ACTIVEWEAR). 3. Used by men for golf and sportswear in late 19th and early 20th c. Also see under PANTS: PLUS FOURS. 4. Short, full pants ending at the knee that were worn by young boys from 1860s to the early 1940s. Typically boys were dressed in short pants until school age, then in knickers until adolescence, and after this, in full-length, adult-style pants. In the early 20th c., boy's knee-length pants were usually called *knickers.*

knickers or knickerbockers #4

knickers 1. See under KNICKERBOCKERS. 2. See under UNDERGARMENTS. 3. See under PANTS.

knife pleats See under CLOTHING CONSTRUCTION DETAILS and SKIRTS: KNIFE-PLEATED SKIRT.

∞**knightly girdle** Decorative belt made of sections of metal joined together and buckled around hips with ornamental buckle in front. Worn only by nobility from about 1350 to about 1420.

†**knit/knitting** Process of making a fabric or an item of apparel by the interlacing of loops either by machine or by hand. A crosswise row of loops is called a **course,** while a vertical row is called **wale.** A great variety of stitches and yarns may be used to give textured effects and surface interest. Knitted stockings were introduced about 1530 when Queen Elizabeth I was presented with the first pair of knitted silk hose. Knits were used in colonial days but not widely used for clothing until late 1870s, when the JERSEY COSTUME was introduced by Lillie Langtry. Popular in handknits for sweaters for men from 1860s and women from early 20th c., in the 1920s, knits also became fashionable for women's dresses. Knits have also been important for lingerie and underwear since the 1880s. In the 1950s, double-knit fabrics, which gave knits better shape retention, were popular. Once a hand-process that could only be used for weft knits, mechanized knitting has added a wide variety of fabrics to the range of knits available. The two major divisions of knitted goods are **weft knits,** which interlock loops horizontally, and **warp knits,** which interlock loops vertically. Among the better known examples of weft knits that can be made by hand, are double knits, interlock knits, jersey, knitted fleece, terry, rib knits, and velour. Widely available warp knits are known by the name of tricot, raschel, Milanese, and simplex. Complex patterns can be achieved by the use of special knitting machines.

†**knit corduroy** Knitted fabric made to have the appearance of CORDUROY, a pile weave fabric.

knit cuff See under CUFFS.

knit density The number of stitches and rows in a measured area of fabric. A fabric that has 32 wales per inch and 44 courses per inch would have a density expressed as 32 x 44.

knit shirt See under SHIRTS.

knitted fur See under FURS.

knitted knickers See under SLEEPWEAR AND LOUNGEWEAR.

knitted velour See under VELOUR.

†**knitting yarn** MANUFACTURED or NATURAL FIBER yarn used for making knitted fabrics or garments either by hand or by machine.

knob toe See under FOOTWEAR.

knock-off An item of apparel copied from a more expensive item and generally manufactured from lower-priced components so it can sell at a lower price. Compare with LINE-FOR-LINE COPY and PIRACY.

knot 1. Interlacing of threads, cords, ribbons, and joining them together to fasten a garment or ends of a belt. 2. Ornamental tying together of two or more lengths of ribbon, fabric, or lace. 3. See under HAIRSTYLES: CHIGNON.

knot stitch See under EMBROIDERIES AND SEWING STITCHES: FRENCH KNOT.

knotted lace See under LACES.

knuckle curl See under FURS.

kodpeased doublet See under DOUBLET.

kojah mink See under FURS: MUTATION MINK.

kolbe See under HAIRSTYLES.

kolhapuri sandal See under FOOTWEAR.

kolinsky See under FURS.

∞**kolobion** (ko-low′-bee-on) Shirtlike garment worn by men in ancient Greece, opening at the side seam rather than along the top. **Colobium** is a Roman variation of this term.

∞**kolpos** (Greek) Blousing of fabric at waistline of the CHITON. A second belt, worn at hips, made a *double kolpos.*

Korean dress National dress of Korean women, which consists of the **ch'ima,** a high-waisted, pleated skirt; **chogori,** an extremely short jacket; and **chang-ot,** a full-sleeved cloak.

kothornus See under FOOTWEAR: COTHURNUS.

krakow See under FOOTWEAR: CRAKOW.

krepis See under FOOTWEAR.

krimmer See under FURS: LAMB.

L Letter designation for size LARGE, used along with EXTRA SMALL, SMALL, MEDIUM, and EXTRA LARGE for men, women and children. See under LARGE.

L-85, General Limitation Order Restrictions—enacted on March 8, 1942, during World War II, by U.S. government War Production Board—that placed limitations on the quantities of fabric that could be used for men's and women's clothing. Among the restrictions on womens' wear were limitations on length and circumference of women's skirts and jackets, numbers of pockets, width of belts; and for menswear, shorter jackets, no vests with double-breasted suits, and no cuffs on trousers. Items that were exempt from the ruling included bridal gowns, maternity dresses, and burial gowns.

lab coat See under COATS AND JACKETS: LABORATORY COAT.

lab dip Sample of a specified fabric dyed to match a color standard.

label Woven or printed attachment to the neck or interior seams of a garment that conveys information such as the manufacturer, size, care instructions, country of origin, whether the item was made by unionized workers, and the like. The newest form of labeling apparel is printing the information directly on the garment via heat transfer, eliminating the need for a sewn-in label. Custom of labeling started in early 1820s with men's tailored garments. Also see under HANGTAG and CARE LABEL.

La Belle Époque (eh-puck') Used by some fashion writers to refer to the period of time between 1871 and 1914, when peace prevailed in Western Europe. The upper classes led an active social life, and wealthy women patronized Parisian couturiers and wore elegant clothes. Also a period noted for progress in literature, the arts, and technology. *Der.* French, "the beautiful epoch." Also see under HAIRSTYLES: POMPADOUR.

La Belle Ferronière See under JEWELRY: FERRONIÈRE.

∞**labels** Two lappets of silk or fur that were part of the hood worn with academic costume in the 14th c.

laboratory coat/smock See under COATS AND JACKETS.

laced closing See under CLOSURES.

laced foundation See under UNDERGARMENTS.

lace glove See under GLOVES AND GLOVE CONSTRUCTION.

lace hose See under HOSIERY.

lace insertion Narrow lace finished with straight edges used on blouses, dresses, lingerie, and infants' dresses.

lace insertion

lace pantyhose See under HOSIERY.

lacer/lace/lacing Rounded or flattened string or thong often with reinforced tips of metal or plastic. Usually threaded through eyelets as a fastener for a laced closing on shoes or other apparel. Also called SHOELACE or SHOESTRING.

lacerna See under CAPES, CLOAKS, AND SHAWLS.

†LACES

†**lace** 1. Decorative openwork fabric made by hand or machine by looping, braiding, interlacing, knitting, or twisting of thread to form a pattern. Various elements of lace structure include bars called **brides** that may be used to join motifs; heavier outline thread called a **cordonnet** (kor-dohn-ay'); and **picots** (pee'-koh), small loops along the edge of lace. Lace is classified according to method. **Needlepoint** or **point lace** is handmade by outlining the design with a single linen or cotton thread on parchment paper, holding it with tiny stitches to be cut away later, then working the background entirely with a needle. **Pillow** or **bobbin lace** is handmade with small bobbins holding each yarn. A paper design is placed on a pillow, pins inserted, and yarns interlaced around pins to form a pattern. Designs may also be made separately and appliquéd to handmade net. **Tatting,** a knotted lace, usually narrow, is made by using thread that is wound on a small handheld shuttle. The fingers make small loops and knots to create patterns. Used for edging lingerie, handkerchiefs, etc. Lacemaking probably developed from CUT-WORK EMBROIDERY (see under EMBROIDERIES AND SEWING STITCHES) in the 15th c. and was an important industry for centuries. Distinctive techniques and patterns that developed in cities and regions were named for the locality. Lace became very popular for collars, cuffs, and ruffs in 16th c. and was fashionable in 17th and 18th c. for trimmings and

flounces. By early 19th c., John Heathcoat invented the BOBBINET machine and John Leavers started a factory to make lace by machine in England. First lace factory in the U.S. was started in Medway, Massachusetts, in 1818. Machine-made lace was used for shawls, parasols, collars, cuffs, and trimmings. In 20th c., lace was used especially for lingerie trim, collars, cuffs, and wedding veils. In the 21st c., most lace is made by machine in third world countries. **2.** See under CLOSURES.

needlepoint lace

bobbin lace

ajour See under LACES: JOURS.

alençon lace (ah-lan-sohn′) Fine handmade or machine-made needlepoint lace with solid designs on sheer net ground outlined with cordonnet. First made in 1665 and called *point de france,* later in 1678 called *point d'alençon. Der.* For town of Alençon, France.

allover lace Wide lace with repeat patterns extending entire width of fabric. Lace purchased by the yard used for clothing.

aloe lace (ah′-low) Tatting and bobbin lace made from ALOE fiber in the Philippines, Italy, South America, and the Barbados Islands.

angleterre, point d' See under LACES: POINT D'ANGLETERRE LACE.

antique lace Darned bobbin lace made by hand with heavy linen thread on knotted square net with large irregular or square openings. Also called *araneum, opus araneum,* and *spider work.*

antwerp lace **1.** Rare handmade bobbin lace similar to ALENÇON (see under LACES) with a vase or basket effect in design first made in 17th c. Also called *antwerp pot lace* or *potten kant.* **2.** All Belgian laces, including MECHLIN and BRUSSELS (see under LACES), made before 17th c.

appliqué lace (app-lee-kay′) Type of lace made by attaching previously made bobbin or needlepoint handmade designs to machine-made mesh ground. Also called *point d'appliqué.*

araneum lace See under LACES: ANTIQUE LACE.

argentan lace (ahr-jahn-tahn) Flat-patterned French needlepoint lace of ALENÇON type (see under LACES) but with bolder designs, larger mesh background, and no CORDONNETS (see under introduction to LACES). Popular for aprons, cravats, sleeve ruffles, and caps in 18th c. Also called *point d'argentan* or *point de france.*

armenian lace Hand- or machine-made knotted lace made in narrow widths with saw-toothed edge.

baby irish lace Narrow, fine, hand-crocheted lace originally made in Ireland.

baby lace Any narrow, fragile, dainty lace used to trim infants' garments (e.g., baby caps and baptismal gowns).

battenberg lace Lace made by applying a coarse linen battenberg tape to the lace design and attaching the tape with decorative linen stitches by hand or machine. Similar to RENAISSANCE LACE (see under LACES) but coarser.

bavarian lace Simple type of TORCHON LACE (see under LACES).

beading Narrow slotted lace, or embroidered bands, through which ribbon was threaded in the late 19th and 20th c.

beggar's lace Inexpensive type of TORCHON LACE (see under LACES). Also called *bisette.*

Belgian lace Classification for PILLOW LACES (see under introduction to LACES) with machine-made grounds from Belgium, including ANTWERP, VALENCIENNES, BRUSSELS, and MECHLIN LACES (see under LACES).

binche (bansh) Flemish bobbin lace similar to VALENCIENNES (see under LACES) with scroll floral patterns and snowflakes sprinkled on net ground. Used for cuffs and fichus since 18th c. *Der.* Named for town of Binche, Belgium.

bisette (bee-set′) Inexpensive, narrow, coarse bobbin lace of TORCHON type (see under LACES), made in France since 17th c. Same as *beggar's lace.*

blonde de fil See under LACES: MIGNONETTE LACE.

blonde lace Fine French bobbin lace with floral pattern on net ground, originally made of unbleached Chinese silk in Bayeux, Caen, and Chantilly; later bleached and dyed black or colors. Fashionable at French court from mid-18th to mid-19th c.

bobbinet (bob-in-ett′) Mesh fabric base for lace with hexagonal holes made by hand or machine.

bobbin lace See under introduction to LACES.

bohemian lace Bobbin lace characterized by tape-like designs on net ground. Originally handmade in Bohemia from old Italian patterns, now machine-made.

bone lace BOBBIN LACE (see under introduction to LACES) made by fastening threads to pillow by thin fish bones when pins were scarce in Elizabethan times.

bourdon lace (boor′-dohn) Machine-made, net lace with cord outlining pattern and outer edge.

breton lace 1. Lace made by embroidering with colored yarns on net, rather than weaving design, in imitation of ALENÇON LACE (see under LACES). 2. Net fabric with larger holes than BRUSSELS NET.

bridal lace 1. Contemporary industry reference for lace used to make a wedding dress, bridal trimming, and/or the bridal veil. 2. RETICELLA-type of lace (see under LACES) worn by brides of France and Spain in the 16th and 17th c. The designs consist of heraldic devices relating to owner. Also called *carnival lace.*

brides See under introduction to LACES.

bruges lace (broozh) Fine, GUIPURE (see under LACES), tape lace of bobbin-type, similar to DUCHESSE (see under LACES), but coarser. *Der.* For city of Bruges, Belgium.

brussels lace Needlepoint lace with cords outlining designs that are made separately and appliquéd to fine net. Once handmade, now largely machine-made.

brussels net Handmade BOBBINET (see under LACES), originally made in Belgium, with hexagonal holes, two sides of holes braided, the other four sides twisted. Also called *filet de bruxelles.*

buckingham lace Fine bobbin lace with simple pattern on a fine clear ground, worked all in one piece. *Der.* For Buckinghamshire, England, where it was first manufactured in 16th c. Also called *buckinghamshire lace.*

bullion (bull-yon′) Antique, heavy lace made of silver or gold thread in a simple design. Also called *bullion lace.*

burn-out lace See under BURN-OUT and under LACES: PLAUEN LACE.

carnival lace/carnaval lace See under LACES: BRIDAL LACE #2.

carrickmacross lace (kar-ik′-ma-cross) Two types of lace: (a) GUIPURE type with design cut from fine cambric or lawn and embroidered with fine needlepoint stitches connected by brides; and (b) APPLIQUÉ type with designs embroidered, then superimposed on machine net. See under LACES. *Der.* Made in or near Carrickmacross, Ireland, since 1820.

chantilly lace (shan-til′-ee or shon-tee-yee′) Delicate, fragile-looking bobbin lace first made by hand in early 18th c. Later made by machine with hexagonal mesh and a design of scrolls, branches, and flowers outlined with CORDONNETS (see under introduction to LACES). Made with a scalloped edge in white and used for contemporary bridal dresses. Also produced in black. Made in Caen and Bayeux during the last half of the 19th c., chantilly lace was very fashionable for shawls and parasols. *Der.* For town of Chantilly, France, where it was first made.

chenille lace (shen-eel′) 18th-c. French needlepoint lace made with hexagonal mesh and designs outlined in white chenille yarn. See under CHENILLE.

cluny lace (kloo′-nee) 1. Coarse bobbin lace, similar to TORCHON (see under LACES), usually made of heavy, ivory-colored linen thread in wheel or paddle designs. 2. Machine-made cotton lace of similar design.

colbertine lace (*colberteen, colbertan*) A coarse, French bobbin lace with a square mesh ground. Produced in France in 17th c. under royal patronage when Colbert was prime minister.

cordonnet See under introduction to LACES.

cork lace Older types of Irish lace, formerly made in Cork, Ireland. Includes flat needlepoint lace copied after Italian laces and YOUGHAL LACE (see under LACES).

Crete lace Silk or linen bobbin lace, usually made with geometrical designs on colored ground with colored chainstitch along the edge. Made in Crete.

crochet lace See under CROCHET.

damascene lace (dam-ah-seen′) Lace made with sprigs and braids of lace joined together by corded bars in imitation of HONITON LACE (see under LACES).

darned lace All filet-type lace made by pulling out groups of warps and fillings from fabric and inserting stitches with a needle. Background may also be reworked in buttonhole stitch. See under LACES: FILET LACE.

dentelle de la vierge See under LACES: DIEPPE POINT LACE.

dieppe point lace (dee-epp′) French bobbin lace similar to VALENCIENNES (see under LACES) but simpler, made in 17th and 18th c.; narrow variety is called **poussin** (poos-ahn′); wider type called **dentelle de la vierge** (dahn-tel′ de la veeairzh). *Der.* For town of Dieppe, France.

duchesse lace (do-shes′) Type of bobbin lace characterized by floral designs and a tape-like effect made with fine thread and much raised work. Designs are made first then connected by means of BRIDES (see under introduction to LACES) or bars. When joined together, it gives an allover look with irregularly shaped spaces between the designs. Frequently handed down from one generation to next for use on bridal dresses. Originally called *guipure de bruges.*

egyptian lace Knotted lace frequently made with beads placed between meshes.

fausse valenciennes (fowss va-lahn-see-enz′) Lace similar to VALENCIENNES (see under LACES) but not made in the city of Valenciennes.

fiber lace Delicate lace made of banana and aloe fibers.

filet de bruxelles See under LACES: BRUSSELS NET.

filet lace (fil-ay′) Hand-knotted lace with square holes frequently filled in with colored yarns in darning stitch. Also imitated by machine. Also called *darned filet lace.*

flouncing Lace wider than edging lace, used for ruffles or trimmings, with one straight edge, the other scalloped.

Usually made with one strong thread along straight edge that can be pulled to make gathers.

french lace Machine-made lace fabrics made in imitation of handmade French lace. Included are lingerie laces of the ALENÇON, CHANTILLY, and VALENCIENNES types (see under LACES) and couture laces used for garments, grouped into: (a) re-embroidered lace, (b) CHANTILLY of the fine type, (c) GUIPURE lace, (d) veiling and tulle. See cross-references under LACES.

greek lace See under LACES: RETICELLA LACE.

gros point (groh pwanh) Venetian needlepoint lace made in large designs with high relief work. Also called *gros point de venise* and *point de venise.*

ground The background of lace as opposed to the designs it supports or surrounds. Two types are used: net or mesh and bar.

guipure (ghee-poor′) **1.** Heavy tape lace characterized by large showy patterns in needlepoint or bobbin fashion worked over a coarse mesh ground. **2.** Lace with designs, with or without bars or brides, to hold pattern in place. **3.** Early name for gold and silver lace.

guipure de bruges See under LACES: DUCHESSE LACE.

hairpin lace Insertion-type lace with a looped edge made by winding the thread around a hairpin. Crochet hook is used to catch the threads together.

hamburg lace Heavy embroidered effect carried out on cambric or muslin fabric.

honiton lace (hon′-ih-ton) Bobbin lace, similar to DUCHESSE, made in England either with motifs made first and appliquéd to machine-made net ground, or lace with round heavy motifs made of fine braid joined together like GUIPURE. See under LACES. *Der.* From town of Honiton, Devonshire, England, where lace has been made since time of Queen Elizabeth I.

irish crochet lace Handmade lace characterized by raised designs of roses, shamrocks, or other patterns set against a coarse diamond-shaped mesh with heavy scalloped edge. Made in the chainstitch. Copied from needlepoint lace of Spain and Venice and made in Ireland originally. Later made in France, Belgium, China, and Japan. Popular for collars and cuffs in early 20th c.

irish point lace See under LACES: YOUGHAL LACE.

jours The fancy stitches used in needlepoint and bobbin lace for filling enclosed spaces.

knotted lace Lace made by hand-tied knots to form a mesh-like pattern, e.g., MACRAMÉ (see in alphabetical list) and TATTING (see under introduction to LACES).

lacis (lay-sis) Square-mesh net that is darned or embroidered; a forerunner of lace.

leavers (leevers) **/levers** Laces made on Leavers machine invented by John Leavers in 1813. First used in factories, particularly in Nottingham, England, and in the U.S., and by the 21st century used less in European and North American countries and more in countries where lower wages offer economic advantages.

lille lace (lihl) Fine bobbin lace of simple pattern outlined by heavy CORDONNETS (see under introduction to LACES) on net background with hexagonal holes, similar to MECHLIN LACE (see under LACES). First made in 16th c. *Der.* From town of Lille, France.

lyons lace (lee′-yon) MALINE-type lace (see under LACES) with pattern outlined in silk or mercerized cotton. *Der.* From British name for town of Lyons, France.

machine-made lace Any type of lace made by machine. See under LACES: LEAVERS LACE and NOTTINGHAM LACE. Most contemporary laces of all types are made by machine.

macramé lace See under MACRAMÉ.

maline lace (malines) (mah-leen′) **1.** Stiff bobbin lace with hexagonal mesh ground similar to MECHLIN LACE (see under LACES). **2.** Light Flemish laces before 1685.

mechlin lace (meck′-lin) Fragile bobbin lace with ornamental designs outlined with shiny cordonnets and placed on hexagonal net ground. Used in Regency and Louis XV period; greatest vogue about mid-18th c. *Der.* From city of Mechlin, Belgium, where it was made.

medici lace (med-ih′-chee) French bobbin lace, combining closed and open work, one edge finished in scallops similar to but finer than CLUNY LACE (see under LACES). Also spelled *Medicis* in France. *Der.* For noble Italian family in power from 14th to 18th c.

mignonette lace (min-yohn-et′) Narrow, light, fine, French bobbin lace made in linen thread and worked in small patterns on six-sided mesh ground that resembles tulle. Also called *blonde de fil.*

milan lace (mee-lan′) Type of bobbin lace, originally made with flat, tape-like, circular designs connected with BRIDES (see under introduction to LACES) or bars. Popular in 17th c. and earlier made of gold, silver, and silk thread. Later, elaborate designs such as flowers, animals, and figures were used on a mesh ground and made in shaped pieces for collars. *Der.* From Milano, Italy. Also called *milan point lace.*

moscow lace A copy of Italian lace made in Russia.

needlepoint lace See under introduction to LACES.

northamptonshire lace Bobbin lace with fine mesh ground imitating Flemish laces, similar to LILLE, VALENCIENNES, and BRUSSELS LACES (see under LACES). Made in England in 17th and 18th c. and popular in U.S. in 19th c.

nottingham lace **1.** Cotton lace made on nottingham machine. Has a V-shaped, mosaic-like pattern and is made in wide width. **2.** Originally a classification of machine-made laces made in Nottingham, England. Now used for laces made on nottingham machines anywhere. *Der.* From place of origin.

opus araneum See under LACES: ANTIQUE LACE.

orris lace (or-iss') 18th-c. lace of gold and silver. *Der.* From Arras, France. Also spelled *orrice.*

passement (pass'-mahnt) (French) In 16th c., all types of lace, finally developed into PASSEMENTERIE.

pillow lace See under introduction to LACES.

plauen lace (plow'-en) Lace made by BURN-OUT method—the design is embroidered by schiffli machine in a fiber different from the ground fiber, so when chemically treated, the ground dissolves, leaving lace. *Der.* From Plauen, Germany, where method was invented. Also called *st. gall* and *saxony laces.*

point d'alençon See under LACES: ALENÇON LACE.

point d'angleterre (pwanh donh'-gla-tare) Fine handmade BRUSSELS bobbin lace (see under LACES) with pattern of floral, bird, or geometrical motifs worked separately and applied to handmade mesh. Introduced into England and Belgium in 17th and 18th c. and used for collars, fichus, handkerchiefs, aprons, petticoats, fans, and to trim gloves. Revived in the 19th c. when applied to good Belgian lace, a coarse mixed Belgian lace or a type of tape lace.

point d'appliqué See under LACES: APPLIQUÉ LACE.

point d'argentan See under LACES: ARGENTAN LACE.

point d'esprit (pwanh des-pree') Open stitch used in GUIPURE lace (see under LACES) with loops forming a pattern on a mesh ground.

point de france Needlepoint lace similar to *venice* and *milan* laces of same era. Manufacture was encouraged by French government under supervision of Colbert, a state official who imported workers from Italy and started a factory in 1665 at alençon. Also see under LACES: ARGENTAN LACE.

point de gaze (pwanh de gahz) Belgian needlepoint lace with flower designs appliquéd on fine bobbin net, later cut away under the designs.

point de paris (pwanh de pa-ree') **1.** Narrow bobbin lace with hexagonal mesh and flat design. **2.** Machine-made lace similar to VAL LACE (see under LACES) with design outlined with GIMP (see under BRAIDS).

point de rose See under LACES: ROSE-POINT LACE.

point de venise (pwanh de ven-ees') Type of Venetian needlepoint lace made with padded, raised cordonnets, and edges of designs trimmed with many picots. By late 17th c. also made in France and England. Most sought-after lace by 17th-c. Cavaliers. Also called *gros point de venise.*

point lace Shortened form for NEEDLEPOINT LACE (see under introduction to LACES).

point noué (pwanh new-ay') (French) In lacemaking, a buttonhole stitch, the basis of all needlepoint lace.

potten kant lace See under LACES: ANTWERP LACE.

poussin lace See under LACES: DIEPPE POINT LACE.

princesse lace (pranh-sess') Imitation of DUCHESSE LACE (see under LACES), done in a fine, delicate manner with machine-made designs joined together or applied to net ground.

punto (puhn'-toe) Italian laces of 16th c. Also applied to Spanish laces. *Der.* Italian, "stitch."

renaissance lace (ren-ay'-sonse) Heavy, flat lace made with tape laid out in pattern and joined together in a variety of stitches. First made in 17th and revived in late 19th c. for fancy work and then called BATTENBERG LACE (see under LACES).

reticella lace (reh-tee-chel'-lah) First needlepoint lace made by cutting and pulling out threads, then re-embroidering. Developed from cutwork and drawn work done on linen. Early patterns were geometrical and connected by PICOT BRIDES (see under introduction to LACES) or bars. First mentioned in 1493 in an inventory of the Italian Sforza family possessions. Very fashionable in 16th c. and widely imitated; still made in Italy. Also called *greek lace, greek point, roman lace, roman point,* and *venetian guipure* (ghee-poor').

roman lace See under LACES: RETICELLA LACE.

rose-point lace Venetian needlepoint, similar to VENETIAN POINT (see under LACES) but finer and with smaller motifs of flowers, foliage, and scrolls. Has more design repeats and connecting brides, or bars, and is padded with buttonhole edges and a heavy cordonnet. Also called *point de rose.*

saxony lace See under LACES: PLAUEN LACE. *Der.* From Saxony, Germany.

shadow lace Machine-made lace that has flat surface and shadowy indistinct designs.

shetland lace Bobbin lace made of black or white shetland wool. Formerly used for baby covers and shawls.

spanish blonde lace Lace characterized by heavy pattern on fine net ground. Made in Catalonia and Barcelona or frequently imported from France to Spain for use in mantillas, scarfs, and flounces.

spanish lace **1.** Lace with a flat design of roses connected with a net background. Used for mantillas. **2.** Coarse pillow lace made with gold and silver threads.

spider work Coarse open bobbin lace, synonym for LACES: ANTIQUE LACE.

st. gall lace Swiss laces and embroideries, specifically PLAUEN LACE (see under LACES). *Der.* From St. Gallen, Switzerland.

stretch lace Machine-made lace of narrow or full width knitted with extra-core yarns that are elastic. Used in narrow width for hems; wider widths used for girdles and foundations.

tambour work See under EMBROIDERIES AND SEWING STITCHES.

tape lace A lace made of machine or handmade tape manipulated into a pattern either connected with bars or laid upon a net ground.

tatting See under introduction to LACES.

teneriffe lace (ten-err-eef') Lace with wheel designs made by winding thread around the top of a small spool about 2½″ in diameter, then working back and forth across the circle with a needle and thread. Made chiefly in the Canary Islands. Sometimes called *teneriffe work.*

toile (twal) In lacemaking, a pattern of lace as distinguished from the background. *Der.* French, "cloth."

torchon lace (tor'-shon) Coarse, inexpensive bobbin lace made of cotton or linen in simple fanlike designs. Can be made by machine. Also called BEGGAR'S LACE and BISETTE LACE (see under LACES).

valenciennes lace (va-lahn'-see-enz) Handmade French fine bobbin lace first made in time of Louis XIV. Distinguished by small floral and bow designs made in one with the ground of square, diamond-shaped, or round mesh. *Der.* From Valenciennes, France.

val lace Abbreviated form of VALENCIENNES (see under LACES). Usually applies to machine-made copies.

Venetian lace Many types of laces and embroidery from Venice including cutwork, drawn work, RETICELLA (see under LACES), raised point, and flat point.

venetian point lace Heavy needlepoint lace with floral sprays, foliage, or geometrical designs made in high relief by buttonhole stitches with motifs connected with BRIDES (see under introduction to LACES) or bars and decorated with picots. Originally made in Venice; later made in Belgium and other countries. Also called *venetian raised point.* Also see under LACES: POINT DE VENISE.

youghal lace (yoo-gahl') Irish, flat, needlepoint lace inspired by Italian laces, particularly Venetian types. *Der.* First made in Youghal, County Cork, Ireland. Also called *irish point lace.* Also see under LACES: CORK LACE.

---

lacet See under BRAIDS.

lace wig See under WIGS AND HAIRPIECES.

lacing studs See under CLOSURES: SPEED LACING.

lacis See under LACES.

Lacoste® See under SHIRTS.

ladder braid See under BRAIDS.

ladrine See under JEWELRY: LANDRINE and FOOTWEAR: LANDRINE.

La Goulue See under HAIRSTYLES: POMPADOUR.

laid embroidery See under EMBROIDERIES AND SEWING STITCHES: GIMPED EMBROIDERY.

laid stitch See under EMBROIDERIES AND SEWING STITCHES.

laisse-tout-faire See under APRONS.

Lake George diamond See under GEMS, GEM CUTS, AND SETTINGS.

lamb/lambskin See under LEATHERS and FURS.

lamballe bonnet See under HEADWEAR.

lamboy See under ARMOR: TONLET.

lame See under ARMOR.

†lamé (lah-may') Any textile fabric woven or knitted with metallic yarns to form either the background or the pattern. May be made in jacquard or rib weave. The metallic yarns are frequently coated with a fine polyester film that prevents tarnishing. *Der.* French, *lamé,* "leaves of silver or gold."

†laminated fabric A layered fabric structure in which the outer layer is joined to the backing fabric by either heat-sensitive foam or adhesive.

lampshade beads See under JEWELRY.

landing strip See under HAIRSTYLES: FLATTOP.

landlady shoe See under FOOTWEAR: WOOLWORTH® SHOE.

landrine See under FOOTWEAR.

∞langet (lahn-jay') **1.** A thong (see under THONG #2) or LACER used to fasten garments together in 15th c. Also see POINTS. **2.** Plume worn on a knight's helmet.

langettes See under JEWELRY.

langtry bustle See under UNDERGARMENTS: BUSTLE.

langtry hood See under HEADWEAR.

Langtry, Lillie See under JERSEY COSTUME.

∞languette (lan-get') Flat, tongue-shaped piece of cloth appliquéd as trimming on woman's cloak or skirt, either singly or in series. Especially seen from 1818 to 1822. *Der.* French, *langue,* "tongue."

lantern sleeve See under SHOULDERS AND SLEEVES.

lanyard Cord, usually braided in contrasting colors, suspended around neck or from belt to hold an accessory such as a whistle or pocket knife.

lapel See under NECKLINES AND COLLARS and WATCHES.

lapel pin See under JEWELRY.

lapidary Person who specializes in cutting of gems other than diamonds. Same as a *gem cutter.*

lapin See under FURS.

lapis lazuli See under GEMS, GEM CUTS, AND SETTINGS.

∞**la pliant** (la plee'-awnt) Invention of 1896 for holding out back of skirt by inserting steel strips in casings, eliminating the need for many petticoats. *Der.* French, "flexible."

lapped seam See under CLOTHING CONSTRUCTION DETAILS.

lappets 1. See under HEADWEAR. 2. See under CLERICAL DRESS: FANONS.

lapponica See under CAPES, CLOAKS, AND SHAWLS.

large Size used along with EXTRA SMALL, SMALL, MEDIUM, and EXTRA LARGE for men, women, and children in such categories as: gloves, girdles, knit shirts, nightgowns, pajamas, panty girdles, robes, shirts, sports jackets, and sweaters. Abbreviation is *L.*

lariat necklace See under JEWELRY.

last See under FOOTWEAR.

lasting boots See under FOOTWEAR.

latch buckle See under CLOSURES.

latchet See under FOOTWEAR.

†**latex** Rubber, in natural or synthetic liquid form, that may be extruded or cast to form core of ELASTOMERIC yarn. May be used bare or wrapped with another textile yarn.

lattice Decorative openwork made from crossed pieces of fabric, leather, or BIAS BINDING. Pieces are crossed at right angles to look similar to lattice work on old houses. Used for decorative trimming on clothing and shoes.

Laura Ashley® print See under PRINTS, STRIPES, AND CHECKS.

lava-lava See under PAREO.

lavaliere See under JEWELRY.

†**lawn** Sheer, lightweight, high-count cotton fabric made in a plain weave of fine combed yarns. May be dyed or printed, given a soft or a starched finish, and calendered (see under CALENDER).

∞**lawn-tennis apron** See under APRONS.

∞**lawn-tennis costume** Woman's fitted jacket and full skirt coming to boot tops made with bustle back. Sometimes embroidered with racquets and tennis balls at hem. Worn by women for playing tennis in the 1880s. See under ACTIVEWEAR for modern tennis clothing.

layaway Purchase of apparel through scheduled payment amounts on merchandise that is held by the store. When all the payments have been made, the customer takes ownership of the goods. With increases in Internet shopping, some stores now allow layaway purchases to be made online.

layered cut See under HAIRSTYLES.

layered/layered look The look of several garments worn one on top of the other, all of different lengths. Popular from the late 1960s, early 1970s, and 1980s and after. See under SKIRTS: LAYERED SKIRT.

layette Garments and accessories collected by prospective mother for a new baby.

lay figure A well-proportioned pose that can be slid under a page and used as a template to help control proportions and the location of garment details. See under CROQUIS.

laying off See under GLOVES AND GLOVE CONSTRUCTION.

layout In print design, refers to the placement of one motif relative to another, taking into consideration direction, repeat, coverage, and arrangement of adjacent motifs.

lazarine See under FOOTWEAR: LANDRINE.

lazy daisy stitch See under EMBROIDERIES AND SEWING STITCHES.

L.B.D. Abbreviation for "little black dress." See under DRESSES: BASIC DRESS.

LCD quartz watch See under WATCHES.

leading strings Narrow, ropelike cords attached at the shoulders of children's dresses in the 17th and 18th c. Used to guide child when learning to walk. Also called *tatas.* Also see under RIBBONS OF CHILDHOOD.

leaf See under NECKLINES AND COLLARS.

leased department Space within a large department store for a specialty department (such as fine jewelry, furs, shoes) so that it may provide special goods or services.

†**leatherette** Coated fabrics with the appearance of leather. Also see under FAUX LEATHER, NAUGAHYDE®, and PLEATHER.

leathering See under FURS.

leather jerkin See under COATS AND JACKETS: BUFF COAT.

leather look Classic tailored look of natural, sueded, or simulated leather used for coats, jackets, pants, skirts, or accessories. First introduced in 1920s for jackets, and in 1960s for coats, skirts, and pants. Not called by this name until 1968, when it started a trend toward the slick, shiny, or WET LOOK. Popular again in 1984 when it also included patchwork-leather patterns in various colors. Still used in merchandising items with a leather-like appearances. Also called *cuir savage.*

LEATHERS

leather Skin or hide of an animal with the hair removed and the grain revealed by process of tanning. Usually dyed and finished by **glazing,** a shiny finish applied to kidskin by using a glass roller; **buffing,** abrading with an emery wheel; **embossing,** impressing a design with engraved metal rollers to imitate another leather; or **sueding,** buffing on the flesh side to raise a slight nap. Sometimes split into several layers with top layer called the **grain,** others called **splits.** Leather has been used for footwear and garments since prehistoric times. Now used extensively for all types of apparel including coats, jackets, skirts, vests, pants, suits, handbags, shoes, and other accessories. Also used as trim on garments. Fabric and vinyl used as a substitute for leather must be labeled "man-made or manufactured materials." Real leather may be labeled "genuine leather." In LEATHERS category listing also see under ALUM, CHROME, COMBINATION, and VEGETABLE TANNING.

alligator Leather from alligators with characteristic markings of blocks, rectangles, and circles with cross markings between. Used for shoes, handbags, and belts. Law passed by Congress in 1970 prohibited use in the U.S., later rescinded and each state regulates the harvesting of alligators.

alligator-grained Alligator-skin pattern EMBOSSED (see under introduction to LEATHERS) or printed on cowhide, calf-skin leather, plastic, or imitation leather.

alligator lizard Leather from a large lizard with markings like grains of rice and elongated blocks, similar in appearance to hides of small alligators.

alum tanning Process used to produce soft, pliable, white leathers. Mainly used for gloves. Primary disadvantage is that the tanned leather is not washable.

antelope Rare, soft, velvety leather made from antelope or gazelle skins, usually SUEDED (see under introduction to LEATHERS). Used for fine shoes, bags, and jackets.

antelope-finished lambskin Soft finish applied to lambskin, calfskin, or goatskin in imitation of genuine antelope skin.

antique finish Finish applied to leather giving a shaded effect by dyeing, buffing, wrinkling, waxing, and oiling the surface to resemble old leather.

bark tanning See under LEATHERS: VEGETABLE TANNING.

bating Processing of skins and hides to reveal grain of leather after hair has been removed.

bend The best section of leather cut from a whole hide, as it is called in the leather industry.

boarded finish A finish applied to leather to make the grain of the leather more pronounced. Hand-processed by folding the leather with grain sides together and rolling it back and forth while pressing it with a cork board.

box calf Calf BOARDED (see under LEATHERS) in two directions to give it squared markings on the GRAIN side (see under introduction to LEATHERS).

bronzed leather Copper-colored kid or calfskin.

brush-dyeing Coloring of leather by placing skins flesh side down on metal table and applying dye to grain side with brush. Desirable for black kidskin gloves because the inside remains white.

buckskin 1. Deer or elk skins given a suede finish that creates a grain that appears similar to that of early skins cured by North American Indians. Second SPLITS (see under introduction to LEATHERS) of deerskin must be called *split deerskin* or *split buckskin.* 2. Sheepskin treated to resemble true buckskin.

buffing See under introduction to LEATHERS.

cabretta Fine, smooth, tight-grained leather made from Brazilian sheepskins used mainly for women's dressy gloves.

calf/calfskin Supple, fine-grained, strong leather from skins of cattle a few days to a few weeks old After being finished in many ways (e.g., GLAZED, SUEDED, BOARDED, EMBOSSED, WAXED, or made into PATENT LEATHER), the calfskin is used for shoes, handbags, belts, and wallets. Best qualities come from the U.S. See cross-references under introduction to LEATHERS.

capeskin Light, flexible, fine-grained leather made from skin of the South African hairsheep or from other hairsheep. *Der.* Frequently shipped from Capetown, South Africa.

carpincho Leather tanned from the skin of the capybara, a large South American rodent that lives near water. Often sold as pigskin and used mainly for sport gloves.

cattlehide Heavy leather, usually vegetable-tanned, from cow, bull, and steer hides. Used for shoe sole leather. Also called *cowhide.*

chamois (sha'-mee, or French, shah-mawh') Originally leather made from an Alpine goat or chamois; now undersplits of sheepskins that are oil-dressed and suede-finished are correctly called by this name. See under LEATHERS: CHAMOIS TANNING.

chamois tanning Treatment of hides by scraping the surface, saturating both sides with oil, and pounding the hide until the oil is absorbed. Also called *oil tanning.*

chicken skin Lightweight leather of unborn calves.

chrome tanning A mineral-type of tanning process for leather. Skins are placed in large revolving drums and are tanned in three to eight hours. The basic ingredients used are salts of chromium. This is the most used process today for tanning shoe uppers, handbags, belts, etc. Before being dyed, leather is a robin's-egg blue color.

combination tanning Leather tanned by using both CHROME and VEGETABLE TANNING methods (see under LEATHERS).

cordovan Durable—almost completely nonporous—leather, made from the shell of horse-butts (a flat muscle beneath the hide on the rump of the horse); used for uppers of fine men's shoes. It is given a characteristic waxy finish in black and reddish-brown colors. *Der.* Named for Cordoba, Spain, where tanning of leather was highly perfected under the Arabs.

cowhide See under LEATHERS: CATTLEHIDE.

crocodile Thick-skinned leather, from a large water reptile, characterized by black markings and a scaly, horny surface; very similar to ALLIGATOR (see under LEATHERS). American crocodiles are protected by the U.S. Endangered Species Act and by the Convention on International Trade in Endangered Species. These animals are considered endangered.

cross-boarded In the leather industry, skins processed to make grain more pronounced by folding leather in one direction, pressing with a cork arm board and rolling; then folding in opposite direction and repeating the process.

crushed leather Leather given a crinkled surface by hand boarding, machine boarding, or by embossing to produce an imitation of a boarded finish. See EMBOSSING under introduction to LEATHERS and LEATHERS: BOARDED FINISH. Also called *écrasé leather* (eh-kras-zay), French for leather crushed to reveal the grain.

deerskin See under LEATHERS: BUCKSKIN.

doeskin 1. Genuine doeskin is leather made by tanning female or male deerskins by the CHAMOIS PROCESS (see under LEATHERS) and then buffed to produce a SUEDED FINISH (see under LEATHERS). 2. Sheepskin or lambskin tanned by CHAMOIS or ALUM PROCESS (see under LEATHERS) and sueded. Should be called *doeskin-finished lambskin.*

écrasé See under LEATHERS: CRUSHED LEATHER.

elkhide CATTLEHIDE (see under LEATHERS) finished to look like elk leather—should be labeled *elk-finished cowhide.*

embossed See under introduction to LEATHERS.

fancy leather In the leather industry, leather having a natural grain or a distinctive pattern, e.g., alligator, lizard, and snakeskin. Also includes embossed effects simulating reptile patterns or leathers given a decorative finish, e.g., metallic kid.

fleshing Processing the skin side of hides, with a machine that has rollers fitted with sharp spiral knives, to remove excess skin and flesh making hide appear even in thickness.

formaldehyde tanning A bleaching process that can be added to chrome or chamois tanning. Necessary if white leather is to remain white after frequent laundering. See under LEATHERS: CHROME TANNING and CHAMOIS TANNING.

French antelope lambskin LAMBSKIN (see under LEATHERS), tanned in France, that has been given a lustrous suede finish to make it look like antelope skin.

french kid Originally KIDSKIN (see under LEATHERS) imported from France, now refers to any alum- or vegetable-tanned kidskin that resembles the original.

frog Leather with a distinctive grain and pattern made from the skin of a species of giant frog found in Brazil. Limited in availability and used for women's accessories and trimmings. May be simulated by EMBOSSING (see under introduction to LEATHERS) other leathers and called *frog-grained leathers.*

full grain/full top grain In the leather industry, the side of the skin or hide from which the hair has been removed.

galuchat (ga-lu'-chat) Leather made from tough outer layer of SHARKSKIN (see under LEATHERS). Used for handbags and novelty items.

ganges Leather embossed to imitate snakeskin.

glacé (gla-say') Shiny finish applied to kidskins by using a glass roller. Also called *glazed. Der.* French, "frozen."

glazé kid/glazed kid KIDSKIN (see under LEATHERS) given a very shiny surface by means of heavy rollers. *Der.* French, "shiny."

goatskin Leather made from the skin of the goat. Used for gloves, shoe uppers, and handbags. Also see under LEATHERS: KIDSKIN.

grain The markings that appear on skins and hides when the hair or feathers are removed. Pigskin shows small markings in groups of three. Ostrich skins show a rosette where the quill has been removed. See also under introduction to LEATHERS.

horsehide A fine-grained leather from horses and colts. Usually imported and used flesh side up with GRAIN (see under introduction to LEATHERS) used for inside surface of shoe uppers. Also see under LEATHERS: CORDOVAN LEATHER.

hunting calf See under LEATHERS: REVERSE CALF.

"in the white" Undyed and unfinished tanned leather.

Java lizard Lizard skins with black, white, and gray coloring. Imported from Java, Indonesia, and used for handbags, shoes, and belts.

kangaroo Durable, scuff-resistant leather made from kangaroo and wallaby hides. Similar to KIDSKIN (see under

LEATHERS) in appearance and imported mainly from Australia.

kid/kidskin Leather made from young goat skins. Used for women's shoe uppers, handbags, belts, and fine gloves.

kip/kipskin Pelts of young steers, cows, or horses that weigh between 15 and 25 pounds, as distinguished from skin or hide of older animals.

lambskin Leather made from skin of a young sheep.

lizard Reptile leather with pattern similar to grains of rice. Often named for place of origin in India and Java. Used for shoe uppers, handbags, belts, and ornamental trimmings.

mocha Fine-sueded glove leather made from skins of blackhead or whitehead sheep from Somaliland, Sudan, and Egypt. Used for women's fine gloves and shoes.

moroccan leather Fancy goatskins with a pebbly GRAIN (see under introduction to LEATHERS), often dyed red. Originally tanned in Morocco and mainly used for handbags and slippers. See under HANDBAGS AND RELATED ACCESSORIES.

nap finish Creation of a suede-like finish (see under LEATHERS: SUEDE) on the grain side of the leather.

nappa Glove leather from sheepskins or lambskins of domestic New Zealand or South American origin that have been tanned by CHROME, ALUM, or COMBINATION METHODS (see under LEATHERS).

nubuck An imitation deerskin made from cattle hide. See under LEATHERS: BUCKSKIN #1.

oil tanning See under LEATHERS: CHAMOIS TANNING.

ostrich Leather with a distinctive rosette pattern caused by removal of plumes from ostrich skins. Used for fine shoes and handbags.

patent leather Leather processed on the grain side to form a bright, hard, brittle surface. Done by degreasing, stretching on frames, coating with paint and linseed oil, then alternately baking in the sun and rubbing with pumice stone. VINYL is used to make imitation patent leather.

pebbled finish An embossed leather finish similar to tiny cobblestones or pebbles.

peccary Leather processed from the skin of the wild boar of Central and South America. Used mainly for pigskin gloves.

persians In the leather industry, hair-sheepskin leather tanned in India. See LEATHERS: SHEEPSKIN.

pigskin Leather made from the skin of the pig, which has groups of three tiny holes forming a distinctive pattern caused by removing the bristles.

pin seal High-grade skins from hair seal with fine pebbly grain. Imitated widely by embossing patterns on calfskin, cowhide, goatskin, and sheepskin, and then called *pin-grain calfskin, cowhide*, etc.

python Leather processed from skin of a large nonpoisonous snake with medium-sized scales and distinctive markings. Available in black and white, tan and white. It is sometimes dyed bright red, yellow, blue, and other colors. Used for handbags, shoes, and trimmings.

rawhide Leather in natural pale beige or yellowish color made from CATTLEHIDES (see under LEATHERS) not actually tanned but dehaired, limed, stuffed with oil and grease. Used mainly for thongs (see THONG #2).

reverse calf Calfskin finished with flesh side out, GRAIN side (see under introduction to LEATHERS) inside. Called *hunting calf* in England.

rosette Mark left on ostrich skin when quill is removed.

russian leather Leather tanned with birch bark, which has distinctive odor. Usually finished in brown and originally from Russia. Now used to refer to any similar brown calfskin.

saddle leather Natural tan leather made from vegetable-tanned STEERHIDES or CATTLEHIDES (see under LEATHERS) and used for tooled-leather handbags, belts, and saddles for horses.

sealskin Leather made from genuine Alaska fur seal hides. Rare, because the Alaska fur seal is protected by the U.S. government and by international agreements. Also see under LEATHERS: PIN SEAL.

shagreen (sha-green') Untanned leather of the shark and similar fishes usually dyed dark green or black and highly polished. Used in 18th and 19th c. for snuffboxes, medallions, and watch cases.

sharkskin Almost scuff-proof leather, made from the skin of certain species of sharks. The "outer armor," or SHAGREEN (see under LEATHERS), is removed before the skins are tanned. Used for shoes, belts, handbags, wallets, and cigarette cases. Also see under LEATHERS: GALUCHAT.

shearling Short, curly wool skins of sheep or lambs sheared before slaughter and tanned with the wool left on. Used for slippers, gloves, coats, and jackets, with the sueded flesh side out.

sheepskin Leather from sheep, characterized by more-than-average sponginess and stretchability, frequently sueded. Small skins with fine grain are called LAMBSKIN (see under LEATHERS). Used for shoes, handbags, coats, and jackets. Sheepskin tanned with wool left on is often used leather side out for coats and sport jackets. See under LEATHERS: SHEARLING.

side leather CATTLEHIDES (see under LEATHERS), too large to process in one piece, are cut down center back into two parts—each part is called a **side.** Used for sole leather or for shoe uppers and belts.

snakeskin Diamond-patterned leather with overlapping scales, processed from skin of a number of species of snakes (e.g., diamond-backed rattlesnake, python, cobra, or boa).

sole leather Heavy, stiff leather—usually CATTLEHIDE (see under LEATHERS)—used for the soles and built-up heels of shoes.

split One of several layers or cuts sliced from thick CATTLEHIDE with the grade of leather determined by the split: TOP-GRAIN is the smooth hair side of the skin; other splits have a rough surface, called **deep-buff,** split, and **slab.** The latter cuts mainly used to make SUEDE. See cross-references under LEATHERS.

split buckskin/deerskin See under LEATHERS: BUCKSKIN.

staking A means of making leather more pliable by passing it over a blunt metal blade.

steerhide Heavy leather from skins of castrated male cattle, usually used as SOLE LEATHER for shoes or to make SADDLE LEATHER (see under LEATHERS).

suede Leather, usually lambskin, doeskin, or splits of cattlehide (sometimes called REVERSE CALF, see under LEATHERS) that has been buffed on the flesh side to raise a slight texture. Sometimes buffed on grain side or on both sides of a split to cover small defects. Used for skirts, pants, jackets, vests, and accessories.

tanning The process of making leather from hides. Methods include: VEGETABLE TANNING with tannin, mineral tanning with CHROME or ALUM, CHAMOIS TANNING with oil, and artificial methods. See cross-references under LEATHERS.

top grain In the leather industry, the first SPLIT (see under LEATHERS) from grain side of leather. Used for shoes and handbags.

undersplit One of the underlayers of leather obtained when leather is SPLIT (see under LEATHERS).

vegetable tanning Tanning process that produces various shades of orange- and beige-colored leathers. Basic ingredients include vegetable products such as bark, leaves, nuts, tannic acid, and twigs. Great disadvantage is the length of time involved for tanning, which runs between four and six months.

vici kid 1. All GLAZÉ KID (see under LEATHERS). ∞2. Formerly a trade term for a chrome tanning process.

wallaby Leather made from the skins of small species of kangaroo family. Similar to KANGAROO LEATHER (see under LEATHERS) but sometimes finer grained.

---

leavers See under LACES.

Le Canned dress See under DRESSES.

lederhosen See under SHORTS.

le dernier cri (ler durn'-yer cree) (French) "The last word," meaning the utmost in fashion.

le dernier mode (French) "The latest fashion."

leek button See under CLOSURES.

∞**leg bandages/leg bindings** Strips of woolen cloth that were wound around the leg. Worn as a leg covering from ancient times in Northern Europe, adopted by Roman soldiers, and continued in use in the early Middle Ages. Considered to be a forerunner of STOCKINGS (see under HOSIERY).

legging Covering for leg and ankle extending to knee or sometimes secured by stirrup strap under arch of foot. Worn in 19th c. by armed services and by civilian men. See under PUTTEE and GAITER. Worn by women in suede, patent, and fabric in late 1960s.

leggings/leggins See under PANTS.

leghorn See under HEADWEAR.

Legionnaire's cap See under HEADWEAR: KEPI.

leg-of-mutton/leg-o'mutton sleeve See under SHOULDERS AND SLEEVES.

legwarmers See under HOSIERY.

legwear Any type of apparel worn on the legs. Examples: stockings, tights, socks. See under HOSIERY.

lei Hawaiian garland of flowers, frequently orchids, worn around the neck. Often presented to visitors on arrival in Hawaii or to individuals in celebration of important events such as birthdays, anniversaries, and the like.

leicester jacket See under COATS AND JACKETS.

leisure bra See under UNDERGARMENTS.

leisure suit Man's suit styled in knit or woven fabric in casual style with jacket similar to a shirt having a convertible collar, more "sporty" buttons, and sleeves with no cuffs or with single cuffs. Popular in the 1970s.

leisure suit c. 1970s

LENGTHS

length Point at which the lower edge of an item of apparel ends, (e.g. the hem of a coat, jacket, skirt, or dress). Dresses were generally floor, or at least ankle, length until World War I. In the late 1920s they were knee length; after which the fashionable length varied—at some times to the ankle, at others below the knee. In the

1960s, MINI skirts ended above the knee and vied in popularity with MAXI and MIDI lengths (see under LENGTHS). Since then, skirt length has become more a matter of personal choice rather than being dictated by fashion.

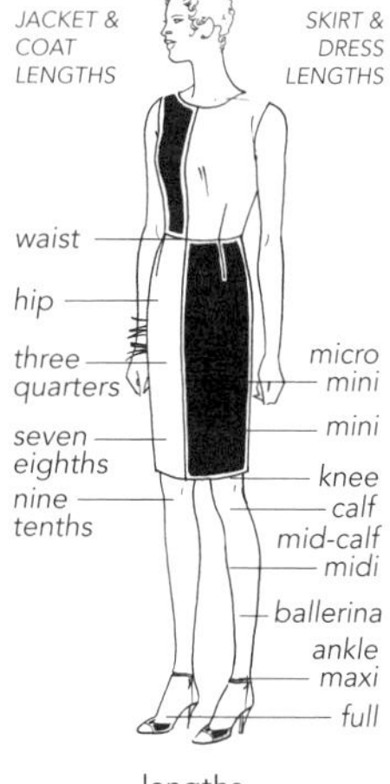

lengths

ankle length Length that clears the floor by a few inches, reaching to the ankle. Same as MAXI LENGTH (see under LENGTHS).

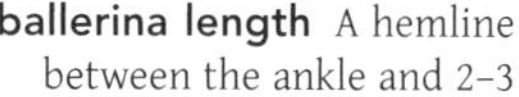

ballerina length A hemline between the ankle and 2–3 inches above the ankle. Valentina introduced the ballet-inspired look during the early years of World War II to work within wartime restrictions. Cycles in and out of fashion for bridal wear and evening wear, including prom dresses.

boy-leg *adj.* Describes a garment with a close-fitting leg that ends about halfway down the thigh.

calf length Hem of skirt, dress, or coat reaching below the knee at the widest part of the calf. Compare with MIDI LENGTH (see under LENGTHS), which is longer.

chapel-length train Hemline with back cut longer, ending in a short train of about one yard, primarily used for informal wedding dresses.

full length Hemline falling to the floor. Most dresses were this length until early part of the 20th c.

hip length Popular length for suit coats for men and women, ending at hip bone.

knee length Skirt or coat extending to the middle of the knee cap or to the top of the knee.

longuette Coined by *Women's Wear Daily* in January 1970, a name for the radically longer lengths on coats, skirts, and dresses reaching from below the knee to ankle length that were an abrupt change from the miniskirts of the late 1960s. Styles were introduced simultaneously in Paris and New York. *Der.* French diminutive for "long."

maxi length Garments that reach the ankles. Word coined in 1968. Ankle-length dresses were worn for day or evening, which was the first time since World War I that ankle-length dresses were worn as daytime dresses.

micro Hemline ending at the upper thigh. The micro length evolved as a more extreme and daring option to the mini length. This length is often worn over pants, leggings, or tights. Also used to refer to any very small piece of clothing.

midi length (mid′-ee) Hemline coming to the mid-calf of the leg. Coined in 1967 by *Women's Wear Daily. Der.* French, *midi,* "middy."

mini length (minn′-ee) Hemline ending at the mid-thigh, introduced in London by Mary Quant in 1964 and legitimatized by André Courrèges in his 1965 Paris collection. The length has had a fashion presence ever since, particularly with teens and young adults.

seven-eighths length Woman's coat length made several inches shorter than the dress or suit it covers. Popular for coats in the 1940s and 1950s and 1960s.

tea length Hemline ending at mid-calf to 3–4 inches above the ankle.

three-quarter length Woman's coat or jacket that reaches approximately halfway between hip and thigh.

waist length Jacket length reaching to the natural waistline. Fashionable length for suit jacket used at intervals since 1890s. Also a popular length for a jacket matched to a dress from the 1930s on.

waltz length Hemline ending at mid-calf. Often used to describe nightgowns and robes. Also see under TEA LENGTH.

Lennon specs See under EYEGLASSES.

†leno weave Open weave with two lengthwise yarns locking around each crosswise yarn in a figure-eight design. Also called *doup* and *gauze weave.* Marquisette is one of the most widely used leno-weave fabrics.

leopard See under FURS.

leopard print See under PRINTS, STRIPES, AND CHECKS: ANIMAL PRINT.

leotard See under ACTIVEWEAR.

leotard shirt See under SHIRTS.

Lepape (Georges) (1887–1971) An illustrator who studied at École des Beaux Arts and became famous when asked by Paul Poiret, Parisian couturier, to illustrate his publication *Les Chose de Paul Poiret* in 1911. After that, his fashion drawings were in demand by periodicals such as *Gazette du Bon Ton, Vanity Fair, Femina, Harper's Bazaar,* and *Vogue.* Did many covers for *Vogue* during the 1920s and early 1930s. Also designed sets and costumes for plays. He used bold color with original and inventive designs rather than naturalistic portrayals in his fashion illustrations. He was influenced by the *Ballets Russes* and famous artists of that time.

le smoking See under SMOKING SUIT.

letter/letterman sweater See under SWEATERS.

lettice See under FURS.

lettice cap/bonnet See under HEADWEAR.

letting-in See under FURS.

letting-out See under FURS.

lettuce edging See under CLOTHING CONSTRUCTION DETAILS.

lettuce ruff/lettice ruff See CABBAGE RUFF.

Letty Lynton dress See under DRESSES.

levers See under LACES: LEAVERS.

Levi's® See under PANTS.

Levi's 501s A lot or style number given to certain of Levi Strauss jeans in 1890 by the manufacturer. The original 501 jean has been modified over the years and adapted for women and represents Levi's classic signature jean style.

levite gown See under GOWN À LA LEVATINE.

∞**liars** Wire framework worn during latter half of 18th c. under a scarf, to give the effect of a larger bosom. Also called *menteurs* (mon′-tur) and *trompeurs* (trom′-puhr).

Liberty Trade name for products of Liberty Ltd., a London fabric manufacturer that produces cotton prints called LIBERTY PRINTS (see under PRINTS, STRIPES, AND CHECKS). Also produces a Liberty SATIN, a Liberty LAWN, and some silk fabrics. All have the trade name attached.

liberty cap See under HEADWEAR.

liberty stripes See under PRINTS, STRIPES, AND CHECKS: HICKORY STRIPES.

licensed goods Apparel or other products manufactured as a result of LICENSING.

licensing The legal granting of permission to use intellectual property rights, such as trademarks, patents, logos, or technology by the owner (licensor) to a product developer (licensee), in return for payment of royalties to the licensor who continues to own the rights to the original intellectual property.

life mask See under MASKS.

lifestyle The habits, attitudes, values, and tastes in combination with economic resources that characterize an individual's way of life.

lifestyle brand A brand's offerings that goes beyond the initial apparel product line to include other product categories.

lifestyle eyewear See under EYEWEAR.

lift See under FOOTWEAR.

light jack boots See under FOOTWEAR: JACK BOOTS #2.

ligne **1.** Canadian unit of measure equivalent to equaling ⅛ inch or 3,175 cm. **2.** French unit of measure for measuring narrow fabrics that has been replaced by the metric system.

lille lace See under LACES.

Lilly® See under DRESSES.

lily benjamin See under COATS AND JACKETS: BENJAMIN.

limerick gloves See under GLOVES AND GLOVE CONSTRUCTION.

limited marketing channel See under MARKETING CHANNEL.

limousine See under CAPES, CLOAKS, AND SHAWLS.

Lincoln lamb See under FURS.

Lindbergh jacket See under COATS AND JACKETS.

Linde Star See under DRESSES and GEMS, GEM CUTS, AND SETTINGS.

line See under COLLECTION.

linecloths, pair of See under UNDERGARMENTS.

line concept The mood, theme, and key elements that contribute to the identity of a line.

line development Translating trend information into actual sketches of styles.

line-for-line copy American interpretations of Parisian and Italian couture dresses made expressly for American stores. The retail dress buyer purchased a PROTOTYPE or pattern for the dress from the original designer in Paris and may have been given access to identical or very similar fabric; the dress was produced and sold in America at a slightly lower price than the original. A popular practice in the 1950s. Compare with KNOCK-OFF.

lineman's boot See under FOOTWEAR.

†**linen** **1.** Fibers of the flax plant that are used to make linen yarn. **2.** Fabrics made of linen yarns in many qualities and many weights. Crease-resistant finishes are frequently applied to linen fabrics. *Der.* French, *linge,* "linen."

line presentation Showing the proposed line of products to sourcing managers and technical design staff for selection of styles to include in the season's product line.

line sheet A chart used to track and market the current COLLECTION in-house and to retail buyers. It shows all available styles and includes names, colors, fabric, and size range.

lingerie (lan′-zha-ree) Women's underwear; sometimes called intimate apparel by the trade. *Der.* French, *linge,* "linen," as women's undergarments were originally of linen.

lingerie crepe See under FRENCH CREPE.

lingerie dress See under DRESSES.

lingerie hem See under CLOTHING CONSTRUCTION DETAILS.

lining Fabric, pile fabric, or fur used to finish inside of garment. The extra layer is used for warmth, to retain shape of outer layer, or for appearance. See under HALF LINING and ZIP-IN/ZIP-OUT LINING.

linked dress See under DRESSES.

lion's tail See under HAIRSTYLES.

lipstick A crayon-like stick of lip coloring, usually in a metal or plastic tube.

liquid embroidery See under EMBROIDERIES AND SEWING STITCHES.

liripipe See under HEADWEAR.

†lisle yarn (lyle) A two-ply cotton yarn made of long staple fibers that are combed, tightly twisted, and sometimes given further treatment to remove all short fuzzy fiber. Also see under HOSIERY: LISLE HOSIERY.

†list/listing See under SELVAGE.

list price The product developer's suggested retail price.

little black dress See under DRESSES: BASIC DRESS.

little bodkin See under PONYET #2.

little-boy shorts See under SHORTS.

little-girl look Fashions for adults, introduced by designers in 1960s, that imitated the dress of a 12-year-old girl with an undeveloped figure. Elements included above-the-knee skirts, knee-high socks for day and evening wear, and ankle socks worn with mary jane shoes.

∞Little Lord Fauntleroy suit Young boy's garment consisting of black velvet tunic and knee pants worn with wide sash. Blouse had wide, white, lace-trimmed collar and cuffs, and was worn with black stockings, pumps, and shoulder-length hair. Worn by boys in the U.S. from 1886 to 1914 for special occasions. *Der.* Inspired by popularity of book *Little Lord Fauntleroy,* by Mrs. Frances Hodgson Burnett, published in 1886.

Little Lord Fauntleroy suit

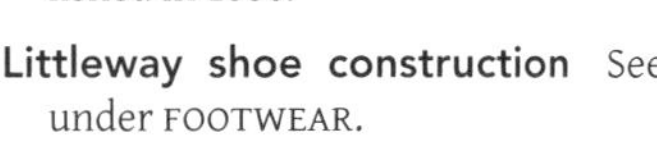

Littleway shoe construction See under FOOTWEAR.

Little Women dress See under DRESSES.

liturgical robe See under ROBE #2.

livery Characteristic clothes or uniform worn by servants, in the Middle Ages and after; servants' livery was made in the colors of the family crests of their employers. Worn today only for uses such as ceremonial events surrounding the British or other monarchies.

lizard See under LEATHERS.

†llama Fibers similar to ALPACA obtained from a member of the camel family, native to high altitudes in Andes mountains of South America. Fiber colors range from white, gray, and light brown to black. The outer coat of the animal is coarse while the underfiber is soft.

loafer See under FOOTWEAR.

locket See under JEWELRY.

lock stitch See under EMBROIDERIES AND SEWING STITCHES.

†loden cloth Dense, water-repellent coatings and suitings woven by people of the Tyrol, a section of Austria and Germany. Made of local wool in a deep olive-green color, sometimes with the addition of camel's hair, these fabrics are used for winter sportswear, skiwear, and coats.

†loft The resiliency of fibers.

logistics The coordination of all processes and people involved in the efficient distribution of raw materials and finished products from point of origin to point of consumption; focus on moving goods from place to place.

logo A graphic representation or symbol used by commercial businesses, organizations, or individuals to promote recognition of their company, organization, services, or products.

loincloth Under or outer garment consisting of a length of fabric wrapped around the hips and lower abdomen. Generally worn in cultures where clothing is draped rather than cut and sewn, such as ancient Egypt. Length may range from very short to ankle-length. Specific constructions vary. Some are shaped and worn like a triangular diaper, while others may consist of a long piece of fabric that goes between legs and is brought up and pulled under a belt in front and back with part of the fabric left hanging down in front and back. Synonyms: *breechcloth, breechclout.*

London Fog® See under COATS AND JACKETS.

London look See under BRITISH LOOK.

long and short stitch See under EMBROIDERIES AND SEWING STITCHES: BRICK STITCH.

long-bellied doublet See under DOUBLET.

long bob See under WIGS AND HAIRPIECES: BOB-WIG.

∞long clothes Dresses worn by infants from the second half of the 17th c. and after. Approximately 3 feet long, usually decorated with embroidery, the dress was worn with a matching petticoat. A style still used for modern christening dresses. Worn by children who could not yet walk, they were also called **carrying frocks,** while shorter dresses worn by children who could walk were known as **going frocks.**

long duvillier See under WIGS AND HAIRPIECES: DUVILLIER WIG.

long handles See under UNDERGARMENTS: LONG JOHNS.

long hood See under HEADWEAR.

long johns See under UNDERGARMENTS.

long john trunks See under ACTIVEWEAR.

long-leg panty girdle See under UNDERGARMENTS: GIRDLES.

long-line bra See under UNDERGARMENTS.

long-line bra slip See under UNDERGARMENTS.

long lock See under HAIRSTYLES: LOVE LOCK.

∞**long stocks/long stockings** Stockings attached at thigh to TRUNK HOSE worn by men in 16th and 17th c.

long-torso *adj.* Describes a garment with waistline placed near the widest part of the hips.

longuette See under LENGTHS.

look *n.* Used with descriptive adjectives to characterize the overall impression or appearance of a style or trend. This usage of the word began in 1947 with Christian Dior's NEW LOOK, a radical change in fashion. Since the 1950s, looks have been influenced by protest of the younger generations against traditional styles, social evolution, civil rights movements, and political events. Other looks evolved from clothes and accessories worn on stage, as well as movies and TV shows or from clothes and accessories worn by celebrities in the limelight (e.g., Jackie Kennedy Onassis and Princess Diana of England). Looks may not always be widely adopted, but general trends they represent often find their way into the mainstream of fashion, such as the vintage look or the androgynous look.

†**loom** A mechanical device on which cloth is woven. Looms may be hand operated (now used mostly for crafts) or automated for use in the textile manufacturing industry.

loo mask See under MASKS.

look book A digital or printed collection of images designed to promote the work of an illustrator, blogger, photographer, model, or brand. In fashion, a look book may be one of several elements used to promote a seasonal line to buyers, both in-store and online.

loop and button closing See under CLOSURES.

∞**looped dress** See under DRESSES.

Lord Byron shirt See under SHIRTS.

Lord Fauntleroy suit See under LITTLE LORD FAUNTLEROY SUIT.

lorgnette See under EYEWEAR.

Louis XIV sleeve See under SHOULDERS AND SLEEVES.

Louis XV basque See under COATS AND JACKETS.

∞**Louis XV bodice** Dress bodice of 1850s and 1860s made with long point in front tapering to waistline with a short PEPLUM in back. Had several rows of RUCHING around neck and a V-shaped neckline in front that was filled in with bows of ribbon. RUCHING also was used on the peplum and sleeves. *Der.* Similar to bodice worn by Marquise de Pompadour, mistress of Louis XV of France in mid-18th c.

Louis XV hat See under HEADWEAR.

Louis XVI basque See under COATS AND JACKETS.

louis heel See under FOOTWEAR.

lou mask See under MASKS: LOO MASK.

lounger See under FOOTWEAR.

∞**lounge suit** (British) A man's suit worn for informal occasions from 1860s on, consisting of lounging jacket, vest, and trousers all of same fabric.

loungewear See under introduction to SLEEPWEAR AND LOUNGEWEAR.

lounging cap See under HEADWEAR.

lounging jacket See under COATS AND JACKETS: SACK JACKET and SMOKING JACKET.

lounging pajamas See under SLEEPWEAR AND LOUNGEWEAR.

lounging robe See under SLEEPWEAR AND LOUNGEWEAR.

loup See under MASKS.

louvre sunglasses See under EYEWEAR.

love beads See under JEWELRY: HIPPIE BEADS.

∞**love knot** **1.** Decorative bow used in 16th c. tied across puffs in vertically slashed sleeves. **2.** Ornamental knot of ribbon originally worn as a love token. Made of intertwined loops of two or more cords, the knot originally symbolized constancy of true love.

love lock See under HAIRSTYLES.

∞**love ribbon** Gauze ribbon with narrow black-and-white satin stripes, formerly worn as a mourning band.

low cut See under FOOTWEAR.

∞**lower stocks** Stockings made of silk or wool cloth worn by men from mid-16th to 17th c. Also called *nether stocks;* formerly called *bas de chausses* (ba deh shos). Worn with upper stocks. See under CHAUSSE and TRUNK HOSE.

low rise/low-slung See under WAISTLINES.

low-rise jeans See under PANTS.

∞**lozenge front** Daytime dress bodice with front trimmed with strips of net, ribbon, and lace arranged in crisscross fashion to form a diamond-shaped pattern. Worn at the end of 18th and beginning of 19th c.;

similar to dresses worn by the Marquise de Maintenon, second wife of Louis XIV of France. *Der.* French, *lozenge,* "diamond shaped."

L-shaped lapel See under NECKLINES AND COLLARS: LAPEL.

luau pants See under PANTS.

Lucite® Trademark for transparent acrylic plastic material used for handbags, sandals, shoe heels, and jewelry.

lug sole See under FOOTWEAR.

lumberjack/lumber jacket See under COATS AND JACKETS.

lumberjack plaid See under PLAIDS AND TARTANS.

lumberman's overboot See under FOOTWEAR.

Lunardi hat See under HEADWEAR: BALLOON HAT.

lunar fashion/lunar look Clothing and accessories imitating those used by astronauts that were introduced after American astronauts landed on the moon July 20, 1969. During the same month Italian designers Baratta and Tiziani showed metallic jumpsuits. Parisian designer Cardin showed a moon cape. Spacesuits were introduced for children in imitation of the astronauts' suits. *Der.* Latin, *lundris,* "of the moon." For earlier interpretations of this same look, see under COSMONAUT LOOK.

lunchbox bag See under HANDBAGS AND RELATED ACCESSORIES.

lunette See under CRESCENT.

†Lurex® Trademark for a decorative metallic fiber and yarn made of aluminum-coated plastic to prevent tarnishing.

†luster The light reflected from the surface of a fabric, yarn, or fiber.

Lycra® See under SPANDEX.

lynx/lynx cat See under FURS.

†lyocell Regenerated cellulosic fiber made by a more environmentally friendly process than rayon. The Federal Trade Commission has designated lyocell as a generic fiber name but classified it as a subcategory of rayon.

lyons lace See under LACES.

lyons loops See under DRESSES: LOOPED DRESS.

mac See under COATS AND JACKETS: MACKINTOSH #2.

∞**macaroni** Name given to a fashionable man of George III's reign who belonged to the *Macaroni Club,* formed in 1764 with membership based on having traveled to Italy. Style of dress did not develop until 1770s and included the macaroni suit, which had a thigh-length, tight-fitting jacket with very tight-fitting sleeves; an extremely high, tight stock or cravat and collar, breast pocket for handkerchief; low flapped pockets; large nosegay on left shoulder; and breeches worn with hose of various colors. Shoes were low-cut with enormous buckles, and a tiny three-cornered hat was carried.

macaroni c. 1770s

macaroni collar See under MACARONI.

macaroni cravat See under MACARONI.

Macbeth tartan See under PLAIDS AND TARTANS.

macclesfield tie See under TIES.

MacDonell of Glengarry tartan See under PLAIDS AND TARTANS.

macfarlane See under COATS AND JACKETS.

MacGregor (Rob Roy) tartan See under PLAIDS AND TARTANS.

machine knitting See under KNIT.

machine-made buttonhole See under CLOSURES.

machine-made lace See under LACES.

Macintyre and Glenorchy tartan See under PLAIDS AND TARTANS.

mackinaw See under COATS AND JACKETS.

mackintosh See under COATS AND JACKETS.

MacPherson hunting tartan See under PLAIDS AND TARTANS.

†**macramé** (mak′-rah-may) Two, three, four, or more strands of cord, string, or yarn knotted in groups to form patterns. Craft used by sailors as a pastime, producing belts and ornaments. Revived in early 1970s by young adults to make neckwear, vests, belts, and other accessories. In 1980s, used for belts, handbags, and shoes. *Der.* Turkish *magramah,* "napkin" or "facecloth."

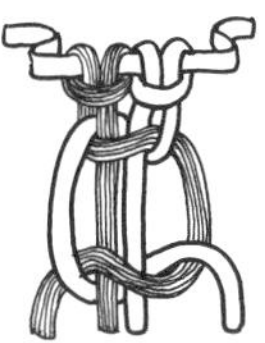

macramé flat knot

madeira embroidery See under EMBROIDERIES AND SEWING STITCHES.

made-to-measure See under CUSTOM-MADE and TAILOR-MADE.

†**madras** (mah-drass′) Shirt or dress fabric woven in a variety of structural patterns (e.g. stripes, cords, plaids, dobby, and Jacquard) from cotton or cotton blends, usually made with combed yarns and mercerized (see under MERCERIZATION). Stripes and plaids are yarn-dyed and may bleed. Sometimes this is considered an asset, as it tends to soften the sharp plaid effect. Such fabrics are called **bleeding madras.** *Der.* Imported from the city of Madras in India. See also under PLAIDS AND TARTANS.

mafors See under HEADWEAR.

magnetic earring See under JEWELRY.

magyar sleeve See under SHOULDERS AND SLEEVES.

maharatta tie (ma-ha-ra-ta) See under TIES: INDIAN NECKTIE.

mail See under ARMOR.

mail-coach necktie See under TIES.

maillot See under SWIMWEAR.

Maine hunting boot See under FOOTWEAR.

mainstream fashion Those trends adopted by the mass market at a particular point in time.

maintenon cloak See under CAPES, CLOAKS, AND SHAWLS.

maintenon coiffure See under HAIRSTYLES.

∞**maintenon corsage** (man-te-non) Woman's evening dress bodice of 1839 and 1840s, trimmed with ribbon bows down center front in ladderlike effect with lace ruffle at waist. *Der.* Named for the *Marquise de Maintenon,* mistress and second wife of Louis XIV of France.

maintenon toupet See under WIGS AND HAIRPIECES.

majorette boot See under FOOTWEAR.

major wig See under WIGS AND HAIRPIECES.

malacca cane See under CANE.

malachite See under GEMS, GEM CUTS, AND SETTINGS.

Mali bracelet See under JEWELRY.

Malimo® See under STITCH-BONDED FABRIC.

maline (mah-leen′) †1. Extremely fine, soft, silk, rayon, or cotton net with hexagonal holes used primarily for millinery. Sometimes used over feathers on hats to keep them in place. *Der.* Originally made in Maline, Belgium. 2. See under LACES.

Maltese cross See under CROSS #1.

mameluke sleeve (mama-luke) See under SHOULDERS AND SLEEVES.

mameluke tunic See under TUNIC À LA MAMELUKE.

mameluke turban See under HEADWEAR.

mamma shoe See under FOOTWEAR.

manbag See under HANDBAGS AND RELATED ACCESSORIES.

mancheron See under SHOULDERS AND SLEEVES.

∞**manchette** (mon-chet) Wrist ruffle of lace worn by women on afternoon dresses from 1830s to 1850s.

mandarin coat See under COATS AND JACKETS.

mandarin collar See under NECKLINES AND COLLARS: CHINESE COLLAR.

mandarin dress See under DRESSES: CHEONGSAM.

mandarin hat See under HEADWEAR.

mandarin jacket See under COATS AND JACKETS.

mandarin sleeve See under SHOULDERS AND SLEEVES: KIMONO SLEEVE.

mandilion/mandeville See under COATS AND JACKETS.

Mandinko See under HAIRSTYLES.

manikin See under MANNEQUIN.

maniple See under CLERICAL DRESS.

man-made fiber See under MANUFACTURED FIBERS.

mannequin (*manikin*) (man′-eh-kin) 1. A model of the human body, used to display clothes in department stores, etc. 2. A woman whose job is wearing clothes in FASHION SHOWS.

Manon robe See under DRESSES.

mant See under MANTUA.

man-tailored Applied to a woman's suit or coat to imply that the garment is tailored similarly to a man's suit, coat, or shirt, as contrasted with tailoring of the softer type used in DRESSMAKER SUITS. Sometimes made in men's wear fabrics. See also under COATS AND JACKETS.

manteau (man-tow) 1. See under CAPES, CLOAKS, AND SHAWLS. 2. See under MANTUA.

mantee See under COATS AND JACKETS.

mantelet See under COATS AND JACKETS: PARDESSUS and CAPES, CLOAKS, AND SHAWLS.

mantella 1. See under HEADWEAR: MANTILLA. 2. See under CAPES, CLOAKS, AND SHAWLS: MANTILLA.

mantelletta See under CLERICAL DRESS.

mantellone See under CLERICAL DRESS.

mantelot See under CAPES, CLOAKS, AND SHAWLS: MANTELET #4.

mantilla 1. See under HEADWEAR. 2. See under CAPES, CLOAKS, AND SHAWLS.

mantle See under CAPES, CLOAKS, AND SHAWLS.

mantlet See under CAPES, CLOAKS, AND SHAWLS: MANTELET.

mantlet matilda See under CAPES, CLOAKS, AND SHAWLS.

manto See under MANTUA.

mantón de Manila See under CAPES, CLOAKS, AND SHAWLS: SPANISH SHAWL.

∞**mantua** (man′-tu-a) Woman's overdress or gown, worn over underskirt that was made with a loosely fitted, unboned bodice joined to overskirt with long train. Split in front to expose petticoat, the front edges of the overskirt were sometimes looped up at the sides to create a draped effect. Worn on social or formal occasions from mid-17th to mid-18th c. Also called *mant, manteau, manto, manton,* and *mantua gown.*

mantua 1708

∞**mantua maker** 17th- and 18th-c. name for a TAILOR (a man) or DRESSMAKER (a woman).

†**manufactured fibers** Textile fibers that are not found in nature but are produced through various chemical processes. They may be classified as either **synthetic fibers,** which are created from chemical components (e.g., ACRYLIC, NYLON, POLYESTER, OLEFINS, SPANDEX) or as **regenerated fibers,** which are created by taking natural materials, such as wood chips or very short cotton fibers that cannot be used as textile fibers in their natural form but which can be chemically processed and reformed into useable textile fibers (e.g. RAYON, ACETATE, LYOCELL). Also called *manufactured fibers.*

Mao suit A suit first worn by Sun Yat-sen, the provisional president of the new Chinese republic in 1911 and later under the reign of Mao Zedong. The suit consisted of a straight-cut jacket made out of cotton with button closures and a mandarin collar. It was worn with loose-fitting cotton pants. See also under COATS AND JACKETS: MAO JACKET.

marabou See under FEATHERS.

marcasite See under GEMS, GEM CUTS, AND SETTINGS.

marcel wave See under HAIRSTYLES.

marguay See under FURS: SPOTTED CAT.

marguerite dress See under DRESSES.

marguerite girdle See under BELTS.

marie antoinette fichu See under SCARVES: FICHU #1.

marie antoinette skirt See under SKIRTS.

marie sleeve See under SHOULDERS AND SLEEVES.

∞**marie stuart bodice** Tight-fitting, boned, evening bodice ending in a deep point at waistline, worn in late 1820s. *Der.* Similar to bodice of dress worn by Mary, Queen of Scots, also called Mary Stuart (or Stewart) (1542–1587).

marie stuart bonnet/cap See under HEADWEAR.

marie stuart hood See under HEADWEAR.

marin anglais bonnet See under HEADWEAR.

marine gems See under GEMS, GEM CUTS, AND SETTINGS.

mariner's cuff See under CUFFS.

Marino Faliero sleeve See under SHOULDERS AND SLEEVES.

markdown Reduction of the retail price of an apparel item. Some markdowns are temporary, while others are permanent.

marker A precise arrangement of pattern pieces for cutting a specific garment style in a single size or combination of sizes from a spread of fabric.

market 1. The location where a buyer (representing the retailer) and a seller (representing the manufacturer), purchase or sell goods. The site may be a MERCHANDISE MART or TRADE SHOW or even refer an entire city. 2. A time when buyers and manufacturers come together, such as the spring market. 3. A reference to the customer base for a particular product, brand, or retailer. Also see under TARGET MARKET.

market calendar The schedule of dates and locations for trade shows and markets. Also see under MARKET WEEK.

market center A city that not only has marts and showrooms but is also a principal location for manufacturing and retailing industries (e.g., New York, Los Angeles, Dallas, Atlanta, Chicago).

market niche See under NICHE.

market week Any of the weeks of the year in which apparel companies show their fashion lines.

mark stitch See under EMBROIDERIES AND SEWING STITCHES: TAILOR'S TACKS.

markup/markon The amount of money added to the manufacturer's cost to determine the final retail sales price. A **keystone markup** doubles the cost of the merchandise; today markups may be significantly more in order to cover the costs of price promotions and steep markdowns.

†**marled** Made from MARL YARN.

marlotte See under COATS AND JACKETS.

†**marl yarn** Yarn, made from two or more different-colored strands of fiber or two or more different-colored yarns that produce mottled or HEATHER EFFECT in fabrics woven or knitted from this yarn.

marmot See under FURS.

marmotte bonnet See under HEADWEAR.

marmotte cap See under HEADWEAR.

marquis See under HEADWEAR.

marquise 1. See under GEMS, GEM CUTS, AND SETTINGS: MARQUISE CUT. 2. See under COATS AND JACKETS: MARQUISE MANTLE. 3. See under UMBRELLAS AND PARASOLS.

∞**marquise bodice** (mar-keez) Evening bodice of mid-1870s with low heart-shaped neckline forming two large scallops and trimmed with RUCHING or lace frill. Also called *bodice en coeur.*

marquise mantle See under COATS AND JACKETS.

†**marquisette** (mar-kee-set') Fine, transparent, netlike fabric with good durability. Made with cotton, silk, or manufactured yarns in the LENO WEAVE, which prevents the crosswise yarns from slipping. Used for evening gowns, cocktail dresses, and sheer blouses.

mart See under MERCHANDISE MART.

marten See under FURS.

martha washington fichu See under SCARVES: FICHU #1.

martha washington waist See under BLOUSES AND TOPS.

martingale belt See under BELTS: HALF BELT.

mary cap See under HEADWEAR: MARY, QUEEN OF SCOTS CAP.

mary jane/Mary Jane See under FOOTWEAR.

mary, queen of scots cap See under HEADWEAR.

∞**masher** An elaborately dressed DANDY of 1880s and 1890s. Also called *Piccadilly Johnny.*

masher collar See under NECKLINES AND COLLARS.

masher dust wrap See under COATS AND JACKETS.

masi See under TAPA.

MASKS

mask Covering for the face used as a disguise for Halloween or masquerades. Also worn as a protection for the face for active sports and industrial purposes. Some cultures use masks in rituals. Ancient Greeks used masks in the theater. In the 16th and 17th c., masks were used for purposes of disguise when going out on the street at night (see under MASKS: LOUP). In the American Colonial period, masks were fashionable for protection of face from the sun in the daytime.

∞**cache-laid** (cash lade) Mask worn in Paris to conceal a plain or unattractive face. Fashionable about 1650 during reign of Louis XIV. *Der.* French, "hide-ugly."

catcher's mask Mask made of wire or plastic covering the face that fastens with strap around the head. Worn in baseball games by the catcher to prevent facial injury.

chill mask/cold mask See under MASKS: HOT MASK.

domino Small mask covering upper half of the face, leaving the mouth exposed; worn for masquerades. Also called a *half-mask.*

domino

false face See under MASKS: RUBBER MASK.

fencing mask Protective mask of fine wire screening fitting over the face to prevent injury from foil when fencing.

half-mask See under MASKS: DOMINO.

hat mask Hat extending partway down over the face with cutouts for the eyes. Used for beach hats and for helmet-type hats in 1960s.

hot mask Mask shaped like a DOMINO (see under MASKS) that ties at back of head. **Chill mask** is used for puffy eyes, tension, or hangover; **heat mask** is used to relieve sinus pain and stuffy noses. Also called *cold mask.*

industrial mask Large fiberglass mask with clear, see-through window. Worn for soldering or doing dangerous industrial tasks.

life mask Mask similar to a surgical mask with carbon filter. Worn on the street as a protection against air pollution and smog.

∞**loo mask** (*lou*) Half-mask that concealed upper part of face, worn by women from mid-16th to early 18th c. as part of a costume for the stage or as a disguise. Also see LOUP and DOMINO under MASKS.

∞**loup** (loo) Black velvet mask worn during 16th and 17th c. by fashionable women on the street to protect the face from sun, rain, dust, and eyes of passing men. A full mask was worn in 16th c. as a fashion item or when riding. When not being worn, the mask hung from the belt by a string. Also see under MASKS: LOO MASK. *Der.* French, "wolf," because it frightened children. Also see under MASKS: DOMINO.

rubber mask Mask fitting over the entire head, worn for Halloween. Molded of LATEX and painted various colors in a realistic representation of characters from comic strips, cartoons, stories, films, politics, and television; grotesque and imaginary creatures; and animals. Also called *false face.*

scarf mask Fashion item of the early 1970s consisting of a scarf tied across the face that revealed only the eyes.

scuba mask See-through mask, covering eyes and nose, worn when swimming underwater or for scuba diving or snorkeling.

ski mask Knitted hood that fits snugly over the head and neck with openings for the eyes, nose, and mouth. Worn for skiing and various other winter sports, as well as in cold climates, to prevent frostbite. *Der.* Inspired by similar hoods worn in the mountains of Peru.

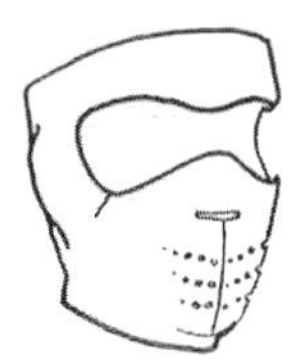

ski mask

sleep mask Soft, cushioned mask fitting closely to eyes and nose, made of black fabric with an elastic band fitting around head. Worn when sleeping in daylight to block out the light.

surgical mask Sanitized cloth mask tied over nose and mouth by physicians and nurses to prevent spread of germs to patients. Sometimes used outdoors by people affected by allergies or air pollution.

---

mass customization The adaptation of a garment style for a specific customer by using computer technology to adjust the fit to the customer's measurements or by offering options in fabric, styling, or proportion that tailor the product to a retailer's or customer's preferences.

mass market fashion Fashionable goods that are produced in large quantities, and sold at moderate prices to many consumers who follow fashion. Also see under FASHION CYCLE.

mass merchandiser Retailer that provides fashion for the MASS MARKET.

mass production The manufacture of large quantities of the same item of apparel.

master pattern See under SLOPER.

master's gown See under ACADEMIC COSTUME.

master's hood See under ACADEMIC COSTUME.

masstige The convergence of mass-market and prestige retailing.

matador hat See under HEADWEAR.

matador's jacket See under COATS AND JACKETS: BOLERO #2.

†matelassé (mat-lass-ay') Luxurious fabric with a blistered or embossed effect made on the JACQUARD or DOBBY loom in a double-cloth weave. Front and back of cloth are actually separate fabrics, which are fastened together with extra crepe yarns that form the raised pattern. Genuine matelassé will not become flat looking as the raised portion is woven in and is quite different from an inexpensive embossed design (see EMBOSSING). Made from many different fibers. Cotton may have a quilted effect, others a blistered effect. Uses: formal dresses, cocktail dresses, evening wraps, blouses, and robes. *Der.* French, "cushioned or padded." Also spelled *matellassé.*

maternity clothes Garments designed to be worn by pregnant women. See under BLOUSES AND TOPS: MATERNITY BLOUSE; DRESSES: MATERNITY DRESS; PANTS: MATERNITY PANTS; SKIRTS: MATERNITY SKIRT; and UNDERGARMENTS: MATERNITY SLIP.

maternity dress See under DRESSES.

mathilde embroidery See under EMBROIDERIES AND SEWING STITCHES.

∞matilda **1.** In the 19th c., a velvet decoration around hem of a woman's skirt. **2.** In the 1840s, a bouquet of flowers worn in the hair by women.

matinee **1.** See under SLEEPWEAR AND LOUNGEWEAR. **2.** See under BLOUSES AND TOPS: TEA JACKET.

matinee-length necklace See under JEWELRY.

matinee skirt See under UNDERGARMENTS: HOOPS.

matte finish (mat) A dull finish. Used in the textile industry to describe fabrics devoid of luster or reflective quality, as well as for makeup that has no shine.

mattress-ticking stripe See under PRINTS, STRIPES, AND CHECKS.

maud See under CAPES, CLOAKS, AND SHAWLS.

Mao jacket See under COATS AND JACKETS.

mauve diamond See under GEMS, GEM CUTS, AND SETTINGS.

maxi/maxi dress See under LENGTHS.

maxi coat See under COATS AND JACKETS.

maxi fall See under WIGS AND HAIRPIECES: FALL.

maxi skirts See under SKIRTS.

mazarin hood See under HEADWEAR.

Mazur plan A traditional model of management functions introduced in 1927 that divide retail activities into four areas: (1) merchandising, which is the buying and selling of goods and services for a profit. This includes the planning, pricing, and control of sales and inventory; (2) publicity, which is concerned with promotion and advertising, display, special events, and public relations; (3) store management, which involves the operations of the retail store, including selling, customer service, and all such physical concerns for the store such as maintenance and security; (4) accounting and control (finance), which is concerned with all the financial aspects of the business, including credit, collection, budgets, control, and bookkeeping.

McKay shoe construction See under FOOTWEAR.

M-cut collar See under NECKLINES AND COLLARS: LAPEL.

mechlin lace See under LACES.

mecklenburg cap See under HEADWEAR.

medallion **1.** See under JEWELRY. **2.** See under PRINTS, STRIPES, AND CHECKS. **3.** See under FOOTWEAR.

medic See under NECKLINES AND COLLARS and SHIRTS.

medic alert bracelet See under JEWELRY.

medici collar See under NECKLINES AND COLLARS.

medici dress See under DRESSES.

medici lace (meh-dee-chee) See under LACES.

medici sleeve See under SHOULDERS AND SLEEVES.

∞medici vest (meh'-dee-chee) Woman's fitted blouse of mid-1870s with double-puffed sleeves ending in three fluted ruffles at elbow and V-neck trimmed with a single pleated ruffle. Had a short BASQUE below the waistline with fullness in back. *Der.* Inspired by clothes worn by Marie de Medici, Queen of France c. 1600.

medieval *adj.* In a broad sense, usually refers to period of 500 to 1450; same as *Middle Ages.* For historic costume study the period is sometimes divided into these periods: *Byzantine* (400–1100), *Romanesque* (900–1200), *Early Gothic* (1200–1350), and *Late Gothic* (1350–1450).

meditation shirt See under SHIRTS.

medium Size used along with EXTRA SMALL, SMALL, LARGE, and EXTRA LARGE for men, women, and children for such items as sweaters, knit shirts, sport jackets, nightgowns, pajamas, robes, gloves, girdles, and panty girdles. Abbreviated as *M.*

medusa wig See under WIGS AND HAIRPIECES.

melanite See under GEMS, GEM CUTS, AND SETTINGS: ANDRADITE GARNET.

melee See under GEMS, GEM CUTS, AND SETTINGS.

melon sleeve See under SHOULDERS AND SLEEVES: BERET SLEEVE.

†melton Heavy, durable, coating fabric that looks somewhat like wool broadcloth and has a hand similar to felt. Originally made of heavy woolen yarns or wool crosswise and cotton lengthwise yarns. Now made in combinations including manufactured fibers. Compactness of the fabric makes it warm and protective against wind penetration. Used by the U.S. Armed Forces as well as for men's, women's, and children's coats and snowsuits. *Der.* Named for Melton Mowbray, a town in Leicestershire, England.

men's furnishings Merchandising term meaning "men's wear," especially when sold by a HABERDASHERY.

menswear *adj.* Characterizing a style of women's dress using menswear references for women's garments. including man-tailored blazers and coats; pinstriped suits; men's tailored dress shirts worn with neckties; tailored, cuffed trousers in silk and linen tweed; and well-cut jodhpurs worn with a Victorian blouse.

menswear style 1976

menteurs See under LIARS.

mentonnière See under ARMOR.

mentonnières See under HEADWEAR: CHIN STAYS.

menu vair See under FURS: VAIR.

Menzies black-and-white tartan See under PLAIDS AND TARTANS.

Menzies hunting tartan See under PLAIDS AND TARTANS.

†mercerization A finishing process that involves the application of caustic soda to cotton yarn, fabric, or thread, to increase luster, strength, and dyeability of the fabric. *Der.* Named for John Mercer, calico printer in Lancashire, England, who discovered this process in 1844.

merchandise mart A trade center with year-round showrooms and exhibition space for exhibiting and selling apparel lines to retail buyers. Dallas and Atlanta have permanent marts; in other cities, seasonal trade shows may be held in rented exhibition space so as to avoid the overhead of permanent showrooms.

†merino wool High-quality wool yarn made from fleece of merino sheep, which has short, fine, strong, resilient fibers and takes dyes well.

mermaid sheath See under DRESSES.

merry widow See under UNDERGARMENTS.

merry widow hat See under HEADWEAR.

merveilleuse See under DIRECTOIRE # 2.

mesh 1. Metal links joined together to form a flat, flexible unit. See under JEWELRY, BELTS, HANDBAGS AND RELATED ACCESSORIES and also ARMOR: MAIL. †2. Openweave, knitted, or woven fabric, such as LENO, producing a net or a screenlike effect. Also see under MILANESE KNIT.

mesh hose See under HOSIERY.

messenger bag See under HANDBAGS AND RELATED ACCESSORIES.

mess jacket See under COATS AND JACKETS.

†metallic cloth Any type of fabric made with metallic yarns or using metallic yarns in the crosswise direction and other yarns lengthwise. Formerly yarns such as silver tarnished, but now they may be coated with a fine film of polyester that resists tarnish. Used for blouses, formal wear, cocktail dresses, and knitwear.

metallic hose See under HOSIERY: GLITTER HOSE.

metallic yarn 1. See under LUREX®. 2. CORE YARN made by twisting thin metal foil around another yarn.

metal thread embroidery See under EMBROIDERIES AND SEWING STITCHES.

metternich sack See under COATS AND JACKETS.

mexican wedding boot See under FOOTWEAR.

Mexican wedding shirt See under SHIRTS.

Michael Jackson *adj.* Characterizing styles made popular by singer Michael Jackson, originally a member of the Jackson Five. He became famous as solo artist in 1983 and set the first record for winning eight Grammy awards. The styles he wore influenced fashion trends across the country and specific articles of clothing became "must-have" fashions for back-to-school students of all ages in September 1984. Elements included multi-zippered jackets, pants of polyurethane, white socks, and black loafers. Some students even copied his habit of wearing one white rhinestone-studded glove. Also see under COATS AND JACKETS: MICHAEL JACKSON JACKET.

micro See under LENGTHS.

micro dress See under DRESSES.

†microfiber Manufactured filament fiber that measures 1.0 denier per filament or less.

micromarketing The trend to market apparel to increasingly smaller, well-defined niche markets.

Middle Ages See under MEDIEVAL.

middleman An agent who oversees the handling of some part of the transfer of merchandise from the manufacturer to the retailer.

middy 1. Blouse worn by sailors in U.S. Navy. Extended to mean dress with top styled like a MIDDY BLOUSE (see under BLOUSES AND TOPS). Also see under MIDDY SUIT and DRESSES: SAILOR DRESS. 2. *adj.* Used to describe apparel or its elements similar to or derived from the sailor's middy top. See under BRAIDS: MIDDY BRAID;

NECKLINES AND COLLARS: SAILOR COLLAR; and SLEEPWEAR AND LOUNGEWEAR: MIDDY-TOP PAJAMAS.

∞**middy suit** Three-piece sailor suit for children introduced in the mid-1890s. Boy's suit had waist-length jacket with large sailor collar, close-fitting collarless blouse, and short or knee-length pants. Girl's suit had hip-length jacket with sailor collar, leg-of-mutton sleeves, and unpressed pleated skirt.

midi See under LENGTHS and SKIRTS.

midi coat See under COATS AND JACKETS.

midriff That part of a garment that covers the middle part of the torso between the chest and the abdomen.

midriff dress See under DRESSES.

midriff shirt See under SHIRTS.

midsole See under FOOTWEAR: SOLE.

mignonette lace See under LACES.

milan bonnet See under HEADWEAR.

†**milanese knit** (mil'-en-aze) Machine-made, warp knit with diagonal yarns at intervals giving run-resistant openwork effect. Used particularly for women's underpants and hose.

milan lace See under LACES.

Milan straw (mih-lan') Plaited straw using seven strands in each braid. Made from lower part of a type of wheat stalk, called *pedal straw,* grown near the city of Milan in the region of Lombardy, Italy.

military *adj.* 1. Characterizing clothes and accessories, inspired by military uniforms of officers and enlisted men, that often serve as a source of inspiration for designers. Frequently trimmed with brass buttons. See under BRAIDS: MILITARY BRAID; COATS AND JACKETS: MILITARY COAT, MILITARY FROCK COAT, and MILITARY TUNIC; NECKLINES AND COLLARS: MILITARY COLLAR; and TIES: MILITARY STOCK. 2. Descriptive of the late 1960s fad of wearing army jackets of previous wars and sometimes helmets for daytime wear. 3. Wearing of all types of military clothing and accessories by non-military personnel.

military folding hat See under HEADWEAR: OPERA HAT #2.

military heel See under FOOTWEAR.

milkmaid hat See under HEADWEAR: BERGÈRE HAT.

milkmaid skirt See under SKIRTS.

mille-fleurs (mihl-flhur) (French) Name for a pattern of tiny flowers. *Der.* French, "thousand flowers."

milliner 1. One who makes headwear for women. ∞2. In the 17th c., one who traded in goods from the city of Milan in Italy. This included trimmings, buttons, and small accessories including gloves.

millinery Covering for the head, generally for women. Synonym for HEADWEAR.

minaudiere See under HANDBAGS AND RELATED ACCESSORIES.

miner's cap See under HEADWEAR.

mini (minn'-ee) *adj.* Descriptive of a skirt length reaching to mid-thigh or the look of short, thigh-length skirts, fashionable in 1960s, that was later applied to any fashion item that is tiny or short. See under LENGTHS; COATS AND JACKETS: MINI COAT; HANDBAGS AND RELATED ACCESSORIES: MINI BAG and MINI-CLUTCH; HAIRSTYLES: MINI-BRAIDS; SHORTS: MINI-JEANS; SKIRTS: MINISKIRT; and UNDERWEAR: MINI-PETTI.

mini-clutch bag See under HANDBAGS AND RELATED ACCESSORIES: CLUTCH BAG.

mini-crinoline See under DRESSES.

minidress See under DRESSES.

mini fall See under WIGS AND HAIRPIECES: FALL.

mini-jupe See under SKIRTS: JUPE #1.

minimal bra See under UNDERGARMENTS: NUDE BRA.

minimalism A fashion movement, based on the 1960s art movement of the same name, that reduces designs to their most essential elements. The focus is on pairing shapes, fabrics, proportions, and colors that create harmony in the whole. It is exemplified by the likes of Jil Sander and Calvin Klein.

minimizer bra See under UNDERGARMENTS.

minimum orders The least amount of merchandise that must be bought from a vendor in order to place an order.

mini-pane hose See under HOSIERY: WINDOWPANE HOSE.

mini-pettipants See under UNDERGARMENTS: PETTIPANTS.

miniver See under FURS.

miniver cap See under HEADWEAR: LETTICE CAP.

mink See under FURS.

mi-parti See under PARTI-COLORED.

miranda pump See under FOOTWEAR.

miser's purse See under HANDBAGS AND RELATED ACCESSORIES.

misses sizes Women's garments cut for a well-proportioned adult figure about 5′5″ to 5′6″ tall, usually sizes 6 to 18.

mistake hat See under HEADWEAR.

miter 1. See under CLERICAL DRESS. 2. See under HEADWEAR. 3. See under CLOTHING CONSTRUCTION DETAILS.

mitons See under MOUFLES.

mitre See under HEADWEAR: MITER.

mittens See under GLOVES AND GLOVE CONSTRUCTION.

mitten sleeve See under SHOULDERS AND SLEEVES.

mitten-sleeve gown Infant's nightgown with drawstrings at the ends of the sleeves that covers a baby's hands to prevent scratching. In 1980s, the style was made with small mitten, with slit for hand, at end of sleeve.

mitts See under GLOVES AND GLOVE CONSTRUCTION.

mix and match/mix-and-match *adj.* Descriptive of the practice of wearing coordinated prints or plaids with plain-colored fabrics for blouses, skirts, jackets, pants, vests, etc. Popular style in the 1950s, which resulted in increased sales of "separates" in retail stores. In the late 1960s, generally described as "PUT-TOGETHER."

mixed suit Man's suit with contrasting jacket and pants. First popular in early 1930s, after which it developed into sport jacket and slacks look.

†mixture 1. Fabric woven with yarns composed of fibers dyed different colors. Fabric may also be made of yarns that vary in luster. Preferred term is **blend.** 2. U.S. manufacturers of manufactured fibers limit this term to fabrics with lengthwise yarn of one type yarn and crosswise yarn of another (e.g., a nylon warp with a rayon filling).

mizpah medallion necklace See under JEWELRY.

moabite turban See under HEADWEAR.

moat collar See under NECKLINES AND COLLARS: RING COLLAR.

mob cap See under HEADWEAR.

mobile earrings See under JEWELRY.

moccasin See under FOOTWEAR.

mocha leather See under LEATHERS.

mocha stone See under GEMS, GEM CUTS, AND SETTINGS: AGATE.

mockador See under MUCKINDER.

mock collar See under NECKLINES AND COLLARS.

mock pocket See under POCKETS.

mock safety stitch See under EMBROIDERIES AND STITCHES.

mock seam See under HOSIERY.

mock suspender tights See under HOSIERY: SUSPENDER TIGHTS.

mock turtleneck See under NECKLINES AND COLLARS and SWEATERS.

moctour See under MUCKINDER.

mod (British-English slang) A pseudo-Edwardian style, first adopted by the group of young men known as the TEDDY BOYS, and their girlfriends, around 1958. The *mods* opposed the ROCKERS, who wore leather jackets and other motorcycle gear. Mod styles included miniskirts for girls and somewhat longer, neat hair for men, along with Edwardian-style suits—exemplified by the dress of the Beatles singing group. Mary Quant, a British fashion designer with imaginative and unconventional designs, gained wide acceptance for her mod-look clothes. The new styles were sold in London on side streets such as King's Row and Carnaby Street—away from Savile Row and Bond Street, the home of traditional tailoring. In England, the concept of mod was somewhat different from that in the U.S. The British version consisted of close-cut hair, ankle-length skirts worn with granny boots, Edwardian suits, etc. *Der.* From word "modernist," meaning someone who appreciated the music of the times—the Beatles. Also see under CARNABY.

mod dress

†modacrylic Generic category of manufactured fiber made from acrylic resins and characterized by soft hand, warmth without bulk, resistance to moths and mildew, easy care, and high wrinkle recovery. Used for sweaters, other knitwear, and fur fabrics.

mod boot See under FOOTWEAR.

mod cap See under HEADWEAR.

mode (French) Fashion.

model 1. As used in America, a person who is paid to wear a garment in a fashion show or for a photograph. 2. (French) A garment.

∞model dolls/fashion dolls Full-sized or smaller dolls made of wax, wood, or fabric that, as early as the 14th c., served as a means of sending examples of the current fashions to various places to show styles. Initially they circulated only among the courts and royalty, but by the 18th c., they were available to all who could afford to pay a fee to see them. The word "doll" was not used until about 1750—previously they were referred to as *moppets* or *courier dummies.* They appeared in America in early 18th c., where they were called *little ladies* or *fashion babies.* In the 19th c., FASHION PLATES replaced the dolls.

model form See under DRESS FORM.

moderate-priced goods See under APPAREL PRICE RANGES.

modeste See under SKIRTS: JUPE #2.

modesty piece Piece of fabric inserted at the front of a dress in order to cover the cleavage of the bosom. Worn with décolleté bodices since the 18th c.

modiste (mow-deest') 1. (French) Milliner. 2. In Great Britain, a *dressmaker.*

modular production Apparel production system in which employees are organized into teams of seven to nine operators who are all able to carry out production tasks. The team is responsible for the construction of a complete garment. As a result, production is more flexible than it would be using a typical mass production system.

†mohair Fiber obtained from the hair of the angora goat or fabric made from that hair. The fiber is long, white, lustrous, and comparatively coarse. Durable and resilient, it is used for apparel, linings, coats, imitation furs, and knitting yarn. *Der.* Arabic, *mukhayyar,* "goat's hair."

Mohawk hairstyle See under HAIRSTYLES.

Mohs' scale See under introduction to GEMS, GEM CUTS, AND SETTINGS.

moile See under FOOTWEAR: MULE.

†moiré (mwa-ray') Stiff, heavy-ribbed fabric with a watered effect, made of silk or manufactured fibers. The design is applied with heated rollers that flatten some of the heavy crosswise yarns, thus changing the light reflection. The pattern is not permanent on silk, but is permanent if made with heat-sensitive fibers. Used for evening dresses, skirts, and women's coats. *Der.* French, "watered."

moiré pattern See under FURS.

mokadour/moketer See under MUCKINDER.

†mola appliqué (ap-plee-kay) A technique for making decorative textiles, associated with the indigenous Cuna women of Panama and Columbia. Created by tacking together two or more layers of fabric of the same size in different colors, designs are cut out of one or more of the uppermost layers to expose brightly colored lower layers. The edges of the cut fabric are turned under and stitched down to prevent raveling.

moldavian mantle See under CAPES, CLOAKS, AND SHAWLS.

molded boot See under FOOTWEAR.

molded dress See under DRESSES.

molded felt See under HEADWEAR.

mole See under FUR.

†moleskin fabric Durable cotton fabric with a suede-like nap in a satin weave made with coarse cotton yarns and a large number of crosswise yarns. Fabric should be called *moleskin fabric* to distinguish it from the fur of the same name. Used for sportswear and work clothes. *Der.* Arabian, *molequin,* "old fabric."

Mondrian dress See under DRESSES.

Mondrian, Piet (Mohn'-dree-yon, Peet) (1872–1944) Dutch painter who was an exponent of neoplasticism. Best known for his geometrics, which employed only vertical and horizontal lines intersecting to form compartments of color. From about 1921 on, his palette held only red, yellow, and blue colors, plus neutrals of white, black, and gray. His work served as the inspiration for dress designs of Yves Saint Laurent in fall of 1965, as well as styles imitating the Saint Laurent designs.

money belt See under BELTS.

money mitt See under GLOVES AND GLOVE CONSTRUCTION.

Mongolian lamb See under FURS: KARACUL.

monkey See under FURS.

monkey jacket See under COATS AND JACKETS.

monk's *adj.* Descriptive of apparel and accessories worn by monks in monasteries since early Christian times and subsequently to describe items derived from or inspired by their vestments.

monk's belt 1. See under BELTS. 2. See under CLERICAL DRESS.

monk's dress See under DRESSES.

monk shoe See under FOOTWEAR.

monk's robe See under SLEEPWEAR AND LOUNGEWEAR.

monmouth cap See under HEADWEAR.

monmouth cock See under HEADWEAR: COCKED HAT.

∞monobosom silhouette Shape of bodices worn in the first decade of the 20th c. The name derives from the way that garments are cut with a full, pouched front section that creates the impression of a single, large breast.

monobosom silhouette 1904

monocle See under EYEWEAR.

monofilament yarn Yarn consisting of a single strand of manufactured fiber. To be strong, this yarn must be large in diameter. Compare with MULTIFILAMENT YARN.

monogram One or more initials embroidered, printed, or engraved on a garment, accessory, or jewelry. Usually these will be the initials of the owner; however, sometimes the initials of the designer who created the garment may be used.

mono-kini See under SWIMWEAR.

monster shoe See under FOOTWEAR.

montague curls See under HAIRSTYLES.

∞montespan corsage (mon'-tes-pan') Tight-fitting woman's evening bodice of 1843 with deep, square-cut neckline and pointed waistline in front and back. *Der.* Named for Marquise de Montespan (1641–1707), mistress of Louis XIV of France.

montespan hat See under HEADWEAR.

∞**montespan pleats** (mon-tes′-pan) Large, flat, double or triple BOX PLEATS used at waistband of skirt. (See under CLOTHING CONSTRUCTION DETAILS.) Popular in 1859 and 1860s. *Der.* Named for Marquise de Montespan (1641–1707), mistress of Louis XIV of France.

montespan sleeve See under SHOULDERS AND SLEEVES.

montgomery beret See under HEADWEAR.

mont-la-haut See under HEADWEAR: COMMODE.

montpensier mantle See under CAPES, CLOAKS, AND SHAWLS.

mood board A collection of color swatches, fabric samples, and tear sheets of silhouettes that inspire a designer's work.

moonstone See under GEMS, GEM CUTS, AND SETTINGS.

moppet See under MODEL DOLLS.

moravian work See under EMBROIDERIES AND SEWING STITCHES.

morganite See under GEMS, GEM CUTS, AND SETTINGS.

morion See under ARMOR.

morning cap See under HEADWEAR.

morning coat See under COATS AND JACKETS: CUTAWAY.

morning dress **1.** Formal daytime attire for men consisting of striped pants, cutaway coat, ascot tie, and sometimes top hat. **2.** For women, see under DRESSES.

morning frock coat See under COATS AND JACKETS: FROCK COAT.

morning-glory skirt See under SKIRTS.

∞**morning gown** **1.** Long, loose dressing gown with a sash at the waist, worn indoors by men from 18th c. to 1830s. Similar to BANYAN. **2.** See under DRESSES: MORNING DRESS.

morning robe ∞**1.** Type of dress suitable for the boudoir or for informal occasions worn in last half of 19th c. by women. **2.** See under DRESSES: MORNING DRESS.

Moroccan handbag See under HANDBAGS AND RELATED ACCESSORIES.

moroccan leather See under LEATHERS.

∞**Morris bells** Tiny bells attached to leather or ribbon trim worn for Morris dancing in 16th-c. Tudor England. Bells were attached to ribbon-trimmed garters worn below knees, hatbands, sleeves, or special leggings. These bells became part of what was considered to be the traditional dress of court jesters.

Morris, William (1834–1896) Creator of printed and painted fabrics in intricate designs first produced in the 1870s. From 1881 until 1940, they continued to be made in a large workshop in Merton Abbey, England. These prints were used in fashionable clothing of women who were associated with the Arts and Crafts movement, which its proponents promoted as a replacement for prevailing Victorian styles. Morris was an artist, an architect, social reformer, and writer—instrumental in changing Victorian taste and launching the Art Nouveau movement.

mortarboard See under ACADEMIC COSTUME.

mosaic print See under PRINTS, STRIPES, AND CHECKS.

moschettos See under PANTS.

moscow lace See under LACES.

moscow wrapper See under COATS AND JACKETS.

moss agate See under GEMS, GEM CUTS, AND SETTINGS: AGATE.

∞**mother hubbard/mother hubbard wrapper** Comfortable, plain housedress or wrapper styled for girls in ankle length, full length for women. Usually made with a yoke, with buttons or ties down the front and fitted only at the yoke. Used for morning wear at home in late 19th and early 20th c. *Der.* Named for nursery-rhyme character who was shown in illustrations in a similar style.

mother hubbard
c. 1890

mother hubbard cloak See under CAPES, CLOAKS, AND SHAWLS.

mother-of-pearl Shiny, iridescent substance lining shell of the pearl oyster, abalone, or other mollusks. Also called *nacre* (nay′-cruh). Also see under CLOSURES: MOTHER-OF-PEARL BUTTON.

†**mothproofing** A special finish used on wool fabrics or clothing to make them resistant to moths. Can also be purchased in a spray can for use at home.

motifs See under PRINTS, STRIPES, AND CHECKS.

motorcycle *adj.* Describes clothing and accessories worn for motorcycling or items inspired by motorcycling clothes. Example: HEADWEAR: MOTORCYCLE HELMET.

motorcycle boots See under FOOTWEAR.

motorcycle jacket See under COATS AND JACKETS.

motoring veil See under HEADWEAR: AUTOMOBILE VEIL.

mouche (moosch) *Der.* French, "fly" or "speck." See PATCH #3.

∞**moufles** (moof′-lah) **1.** Fingerless gloves or mittens worn in Merovingian Period for hunting or working. **2.** Extensions of sleeves covering hand in the 14th c. Also called *mitons.*

∞**moulds** Men's DRAWERS (see under UNDERGARMENTS), padded with horsehair and other fibers, worn under wide trousers in England in latter half of 16th c. Also spelled *mowlds.*

mountain climbing boot See under FOOTWEAR: HIKING BOOT.

Mountie's hat See under HATS.

mountmellick work See under EMBROIDERIES AND SEWING STITCHES.

mourning bonnet See under HEADWEAR.

mourning clothes Clothing, usually black, worn for funerals or during the mourning period after the funeral. Etiquette for mourning was not well established until the end of the 15th c., although black had been recognized in Northern Europe as a symbol for grief since the 14th c. During 19th and early 20th c., custom prescribed not only colors and fabrics, but also stages and gradations of mourning. Men were required to wear a black armband. Widows had to wear **deep mourning,** black, crape-covered dresses worn with black accessories, for a year and a day. Other female relatives wore deep mourning for varying periods of time, depending on their relationship to the deceased. The next stage was **half mourning,** which usually consisted of black, gray, or purple costume with touches of white. See also under MOURNING CRAPE; JEWELRY: MOURNING JEWELRY; and HEADWEAR: MOURNING BONNET.

∞†**mourning crape/crepe** Black fabric, usually CRAPE, worn for funerals or for mourning, as it was referred to collectively. During the 19th and early 20th c., deep mourning or black was worn for six months to a year after the death of a close member of the family. *Half-mourning,* a purple or lavender color, was worn for six months longer.

∞**mourning garland** Willow hatband or garland of willow worn for mourning in the 17th c.

∞**mourning jewelry** See under JEWELRY.

∞**mourning knot** Armlet with attached bunch of black ribbons worn on left arm for mourning by men in 18th c.

∞**mourning ribbon** Black ribbon worn by men on the hat for mourning in the 17th c.

∞**mourning ring** See under JEWELRY.

∞**mourning scarf** Scarf of lawn about 3¼ yards long presented along with hatbands to principal mourners at funerals in 17th and 18th c.

∞**mourning tire** A MOURNING VEIL (see under HEADWEAR) worn by women in the 17th c.

mourning veil See under HEADWEAR.

mouse jewelry See under JEWELRY.

mousers See under FOOTWEAR and PANTS.

mousquetaire collar See under NECKLINES AND COLLARS.

mousquetaire cuff See under CUFFS.

mousquetaire gloves See under GLOVES AND GLOVE CONSTRUCTION.

mousquetaire hat See under HEADWEAR.

mousquetaire mantle See under CAPES, CLOAKS, AND SHAWLS.

†**mousseline** Transparent, lightweight fabric made in the plain weave and similar to chiffon. Often made of silk.

moustaches See under HAIRSTYLES: COIFFURE EN CADENETTE.

mouton-processed lamb See under FURS.

mowlds See under MOULDS.

mowle/moyle See under FOOTWEAR: MULE.

mozetta See under CLERICAL DRESS.

∞**muckinder/mockador** 1. A child's bib, as it was called from the early 16th to 19th c. 2. Handkerchief. Also spelled *mocket, mockete, muckender, muckiter,* and *muckinger.*

muff Warm tubular covering for the hands open at each end, frequently of fur or rich fabrics—usually round or oblong in many sizes—sometimes with concealed inner pockets. Carried by women as an accessory and usually matched to material of coat or trimming. Carried by men from second half of 16th to 19th c.

muff

muff bag See under HANDBAGS AND RELATED ACCESSORIES.

∞**muffettees** 1. Pair of small wrist muffs worn for warmth or when playing cards to protect wrist ruffles by both men and women in 18th and 19th c. 2. Pair of small muffs worn for warmth in mid-18th c., closed at one end and sometimes with separate stall for thumb. 3. Coarse mittens of leather or wool knit worn by old men in early 19th c.

muffin hat See under HEADWEAR.

muffler See under SCARVES.

muff's cloak See under COATS AND JACKETS.

mukluk See under FOOTWEAR.

mulberry silk Silk obtained from silkworms that are fed on leaves of cultivated mulberry tree.

mule See under FOOTWEAR.

muleta See under CAPES, CLOAKS, AND SHAWLS.

muller cut-down See under HEADWEAR.

mullet See under HAIRSTYLES.

Munro tartan See under PLAIDS AND TARTANS.

muscle shirt See under SHIRTS.

museum heel See under FOOTWEAR.

mushroom hat See under HEADWEAR.

mushroom pleats See under CLOTHING CONSTRUCTION DETAILS.

mushroom sleeve See under SHOULDERS AND SLEEVES.

musk apples/muskballs See under POMMES DE SENTEUR.

muskrat See under FURS.

†muslin Plain-weave cotton or cotton blend fabric, made in many weights, from very fine and sheer to coarse and heavy. Higher qualities have COMBED, mercerized yarns (see under MERCERIZATION) and may be either dyed or printed. Such fabrics are lustrous, long-wearing, washable, and soft to the touch. Coarser qualities have CARDED YARN, may have a variety of construction counts, and are used for sheets and pillowcases. Lightweight fabrics are used for summer dresses and blouses.

muslin pattern **1.** Complete garment made in an inexpensive fabric (e.g., muslin) usually draped on a dress form and, after muslin garment is finished, taken apart to provide a pattern for actual garment. **2.** Process used for fur designing. Also called a *toile* (twal).

mustache The hair on a man's upper lip. When it is allowed to grow, this hair may be shaved and trimmed into various shapes. One of the more common variations is the **walrus mustache,** which has long drooping ends hanging at either side of the mouth.

mustache

mutation mink See under FURS.

mu'umu'u (moo-oo'-moo-oo') Loose-fitting, full dress worn by Hawaiian native women that was adapted from chemises given to native women by missionaries in the early 19th c. to wear under the HOLOKU, a European-derived style of outerwear. Native women wore the garment for swimming and sleeping until the 1930s when it was made in Hawaiian floral-printed fabrics and adopted for street wear. By the post–World War II period, it was made in various lengths and its use had spread to the mainland, especially for loungewear. *Der.* Hawaiian, meaning *cutoff.*

mu'umu'u

∞nabchet 16th-c. slang for cap or hat.

nacre See under MOTHER-OF-PEARL.

†nacré velvet (nah-cray') Velvet fabric with an iridescent or changeable effect caused by using one color for the background yarn and another color for the pile. Used for evening wear.

NAFTA See under NORTH AMERICAN FREE TRADE AGREEMENT.

nailing See under FURS: STAPLING.

nameplate See under HANDBAGS AND RELATED ACCESSORIES.

†nanotechnology As it relates to textiles, the development of new textile and textile-related products through the use of **nanofibers**, defined as a fiber with a diameter of less than one micron. One example of nanotechnology is its use to form a barrier to substances with the potential to stain the fabric. Because of the small size of nanoparticles there is no sense of any change in the texture of the fabric.

†nap 1. Fiber ends, protruding on the surface of one or both sides of a fabric, which produce a fuzzy appearance and soft texture. Achieved by brushing the surface of a fabric with loosely twisted yarn. The nap may be brushed in one direction so that when cutting a garment with a nap, pieces of the pattern should be placed so that the nap runs in the same direction in all pieces. 2. In home sewing, any fabric that has either a nap or a PILE, which is formed by an extra yarn. Both require that all pattern pieces run in the same direction.

nap finish See under LEATHERS.

∞napkin Handkerchief used for the nose in 16th and early 17th c.

napkin-cap See under HEADWEAR.

∞napkin hook Ornamental hook of 17th c., attached to woman's waistband, used to suspend a handkerchief.

Napoleon *adj.* Descriptive of apparel derived from or inspired by the clothing of Napoleon Bonaparte (1769–1821) or clothing worn in the Napoleonic period. He was the first Emperor of France, and along with his wife, Josephine, influenced styles during and after his reign. See under COATS AND JACKETS: NAPOLEON COAT; TIES: NAPOLEON NECKTIE; NECKLINES AND COLLARS: NAPOLEONIC COLLAR; and FOOTWEAR: NAPOLEONS.

nappa leather See under LEATHERS.

nappe/napperon See under APRONS: NAPRON.

napping See under NAP.

napron See under APRONS.

narrow In retailing, describes an ASSORTMENT that consists of relatively few different styles.

narrowcasting See MICROMARKETING.

†narrow fabric Any nonelastic fabric such as tape, ribbon, or webbing, not more than 12″ wide, woven on narrow looms with selvages on both sides. Bias binding and seam binding are not included in this classification.

∞narrow goods Fabrics that were woven 27″ wide or less.

Nast, Condé (1874–1942) Publisher of *Vanity Fair* from 1913 to 1936 and of *Vogue* magazine, including English and French *Vogue,* from 1909 to 1942. President of The Condé Nast Publications Inc., which also published the *Vogue Pattern Book, Glamour,* and *House and Garden* during his lifetime. Other periodicals were acquired later.

National Press Week Semiannual event when newspaper fashion editors across the country were invited to New York by the *New York Couture Group* to see collections of Seventh Avenue designers. Idea originated with New York manufacturer Ben Reig in 1942. Over time, the event has evolved and is now called FASHION WEEK.

natural bra See under UNDERGARMENTS.

†natural fiber Fiber that is of animal, vegetable, or mineral origin, as opposed to manufactured fiber regenerated from natural materials or synthesized from chemicals (e.g., WOOL, LINEN, SILK, COTTON, HEMP, RAMIE, CASHMERE, and MOHAIR).

naturalistic print See under PRINTS, STRIPES, AND CHECKS.

naturally colored cotton Cotton that is used in its natural color. At present, commercially available colors are limited to shades of green and brown.

natural mink See under FURS.

natural shoulder See under SHOULDERS AND SLEEVES.

natural straw Straw made from any vegetable plant or tree grown in the soil (e.g, bark, coconut fibers, grass, hemp, or palm-tree fibers).

natural waistline See under WAISTLINES.

†Naugahyde® Trademark of U.S. Rubber Co. for a fabric with a vinyl resin coating on the face and knitted fabric back. The knitted back gives stretch to the vinyl. Used for handbags, shoes, and rainwear.

nautical *adj.* Describes items of clothing and motifs borrowed from navy uniforms or seamen's clothes, frequently using a red, white, and blue color scheme and symbols such as stars, chevrons, or stripes. In 1966, Saint Laurent showed clothes of this type. Used since the 1860s, particularly for boys' sailor suits, it is a classic style for yachting and boating as well as sportswear. Also see under BLOUSES AND TOPS: MIDDY BLOUSE.

Navajo Native American tribe of Southwestern U.S. living in Arizona and New Mexico, noted for metalworking in iron, copper, and silver; blankets woven in distinctive geometric designs; and for handmade silver jewelry often set with turquoise. The latter is not only a classic fashion in the Western states, but is also popular throughout the U.S.

neapolitan bonnet See under HEADWEAR.

neapolitan hat See under HEADWEAR.

neats See under HOSIERY.

nebula headdress See under HEADWEAR.

neck button See under CLOSURES.

neck-chain See under JEWELRY.

neckcloth 1. See under TIES. 2. See under SCARVES: NECKERCHIEF #2.

necked bonnet See under HEADWEAR.

neckerchief See under SCARVES.

neckerchief slide Ring of metal, plastic, or woven braid used to hold NECKERCHIEF (see under SCARVES) in place, e.g., those used by Boy Scouts or cowboys.

neck handkerchief See under TIES.

necklace See under JEWELRY.

NECKLINES AND COLLARS

neckline Contour or shape of clothing at neck, shoulders, or above the bust—ranging from high to low to strapless. Before the 20th c., garments designed and worn during the same time periods tended to have similar respective styles of necklines. Conversely, in the 20th c., a wide variety of different neckline styles were worn at the same time. However in both the 19th c. and 20th c., evening dresses have usually had low necklines.

collar 1. Separate piece attached to an item of clothing at the neckline in order to finish the neckline edge. May be made of matching or contrasting fabric, and may be trimmed with lace or embroidery. Shape may be flat, rolled, standing, or draped. Not to be confused with the neckline, it is an extra section attached to or turned over at neckline. 2. Separate costume element made of fabric, fur, leather, or other material that fits around the neck and is not permanently attached to the garment. Collars were not generally worn until the 15th c., when garments such as the HOUPPELANDE and DOUBLET were made with collars. Another early style of the 16th c. was the RUFF (see under NECKLINES AND COLLARS). Subsequently other styles appeared. Many new collar styles were introduced in the 20th c.

∞amazon collar Standing collar, similar to a CHINESE COLLAR (see under NECKLINES AND COLLARS), with gap in center front. Used on women's blouses in early 1860s and worn with a black ribbon necktie.

angled shawl collar Collar that follows the front opening of a TUXEDO jacket. The outer edge is square cut or "angled" at the waistline.

ascot neckline/ascot collar Long scarf, approximately 8′ wide, attached to center back of neckline. The ends are brought around to the front and looped over. Popular in the late 1920s, reintroduced in late 1960s, and popular since for both men and women. *Der.* Fashionable horse-racing spot Ascot Heath, England. Also called *stock neckline* and *stock collar.*

ascot neckline or collar

asymmetric collar Any collar that does not appear the same on both sides of center front (e.g., large collar with slanting line to one side appearing longer on one side); popular in the 1980s.

asymmetric neckline Any neckline that appears different on either side of center front, or closes to one side of center front of blouse or shirt (e.g., a slit at left side closed with a loop and button which, when opened, makes one lapel on right).

asymmetric neckline

attached collar Any collar that is permanently attached to the clothing for which it is made. From the early

19th c. to the early 20th c., men's shirt collars were separate, fastened with STUDS (see under JEWELRY) to the neckline in back and front and called DETACHABLE COLLARS (see under NECKLINES AND COLLARS).

ballet neckline/ballerina neckline (bal-lay') Wide, rounded neckline that falls below the collarbone and is similar to those of ballet practice clothing.

band 1. See under FALLING BAND. 2. See under CLERICAL DRESS: GENEVA BANDS.

band collar/banded collar Collar that stands up around neck and closes with buttons at front or back. A variant may also be turned down in either front or back. Also called *stand-up collar.* Also see under NECKLINES AND COLLARS: CHINESE COLLAR and NEHRU COLLAR.

banded neckline Narrow band attached to neckline and buttoned in front. Introduced in early 1980s, it looks somewhat like neckbands of shirts of the 1890s and early 1900s without the ATTACHED COLLAR (see under NECKLINES AND COLLARS).

barrymore collar DRESS SHIRT (see under SHIRTS) collar with long points in front, frequently worn with STRING TIE (see under TIES), that became popular after it was worn by the actor John Barrymore in 1930s.

bateau neckline (ba-toe') Boat-shaped neckline, wide from side-to-side over the shoulders but high in front and back. Popular neckline in 1930s and 1940s, and revived in 1980s. Also called *boat neckline. Der.* French, "boat."

bateau neckline

Ben Casey collar See under NECKLINES AND COLLARS: MEDIC COLLAR.

bermuda collar Woman's shirt collar that opens in front, is small and round, and lies flat. Its corners have a right-angle shape. Popular since 1940s, mainly on blouses.

bertha Large cape-like collar falling over shoulders and bodice of dress, introduced about 1839 as a lace ruffle encircling the décolleté neckline of evening dress. Fashionable in 1930s as a large cape collar, revived in 1980s. Spelled *berthe* when first introduced.

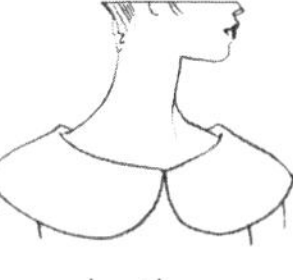

bertha

∞**bertha pelerine** (pel-er-een') Lace ruffle or BERTHA (see under NECKLINES AND COLLARS) open at the front where the ends extend down center front to waist. Worn in 1840s on low-necked dresses.

∞**betsie ruff** Small RUFF (see under NECKLINES AND COLLARS) worn around the neck, with dresses having either a high or low neckline in late Empire period.

bib collar Flat, rounded, or square collar fitting over top of dress or blouse and around neck like a child's bib. Also called a *plastron.* Popular in 1980s with pleating, embroidery, or lace around edge.

bib collar

biker collar A collar with a zipper that extends up the lapel, making the collar convertible; typically double-breasted.

bishop collar Large collar, rounded in front, extending almost to shoulder seams.

boat neckline See under NECKLINES AND COLLARS: BATEAU NECKLINE.

bolster collar Padded circlet worn around neck as a collar.

bow collar Flat, stand-up band, with extended ends, that is sewn to the neckline. The ends tie in a bow in front. Introduced in the late 1920s and continued in fashion ever since.

breakline The line on which the lapels of a collar turn back.

bumper collar Large fur collar that extends to edges of shoulders when worn flat. Becomes a high rolled collar when ends are hooked in center front. Popular on fabric coats of the late 1920s, early 1930s, and mid-1980s.

buster brown collar Medium-sized, stiffly starched, round, white collar first worn by boys in the beginning of the 20th c. and later adopted by women and girls. Often worn with a separate wide, soft bow tie. *Der.* Named for *Buster Brown,* a comic strip character, drawn by Richard F. Outcault in early 20th c.

butterfly collar Extremely large collar extending to sleeves at shoulders. Front hangs down in two points almost to waist with outer edge having scrolled effect to shoulders, creating the appearance of a butterfly's wings. An innovation of early 1980s.

button-down collar Shirt collar with pointed ends that are fastened to the shirt by small buttons. Popular collar of 1950s and 1960s for men and women, and part of preppy look introduced in 1980s.

button-down collar

byron collar Collar with large points and not much roll, similar to BARRYMORE COLLAR (see under NECKLINES AND COLLARS). *Der.* Named after English poet Lord Byron. Also called *Lord Byron collar* and *poet's collar.*

cabbage ruff See under NECKLINES AND COLLARS: RUFF.

cadet collar See under MANDARIN COLLAR.

caftan neckline Round neckline with slit down center front, frequently edged with embroidery, beading, or diamanté bands. Fashionable in late 1960s and adapted from the African CAFTAN.

camisole neckline Neckline cut straight across above the bust with straps over the shoulders. Also see UNDERGARMENTS: CAMISOLE.

cape collar Large circular-cut collar that extends over the shoulders and upper arms. Similar to a BERTHA (see under NECKLINES AND COLLARS), but can be used with high or low neckline. Also called *capelet collar.*

∞**capuchin collar** Continuous roll collar on a wrap-over front bodice with a V-neckline that was used with high-waisted dresses of the late 18th and early 19th c.

∞**carcaille** (kar-kai′) 15th-c. standing collar that flared upward to the ears. Used on HOUPPELANDE and POURPOINT (see under DOUBLET).

cardigan neckline Plain, round, collarless neckline on garment with a center front opening (e.g., cardigan sweater). *Der.* Named for the Seventh Earl of Cardigan, who needed an extra layer of warmth for his uniform during the Crimean War of 1854.

∞**cardinal pelerine** (pel-er-een′) Large lace BERTHA (see under NECKLINES AND COLLARS) that is open in center front, worn on evening dresses in 1840s.

carnaby collar Collar, usually white with rounded ends in front, worn on colored, printed, or polka dot shirt in mid-1960s. *Der.* Named after Carnaby Street, London, where MOD fashions originated.

carnival collar Collar made of wide loops of bright printed fabric arranged in an unstarched RUFF (see under NECKLINES AND COLLARS) as on a clown's costume.

cartwheel ruff See under NECKLINES AND COLLARS: RUFF.

cascade Circular-cut ruffle attached to neckline of blouse with a binding. The ruffle may extend to waistline in a straight or diagonal line.

cascade

cavalier collar Broad, flat, lace-edged collar falling over shoulders that is similar to collars worn by Cavaliers, partisans of Charles I, in early 17th c. Also called a *falling collar.*

∞**celluloid collar** Detachable shirt collar made of celluloid, a highly flammable plastic made of guncotton and camphor, that was popular for men in the early 20th c.

Chanel neckline A neckline that is framed or bound with a contrasting fabric or edged with a braid.

chelsea collar Medium-sized, flat, woman's collar with pointed ends that form a low V-neckline in front; popular in late 1960s. *Der.* For borough in southwest London where it originated.

∞**cherusse/cherusque** (sher-oose′) Starched lace standing border for low-cut necklines on women's gowns. Worn during the Revolutionary period in France and later at Napoleon's court in Empire period. Also called *collarette à la Lyon.*

chinese collar/chinese neckline Standing BAND COLLAR that extends up on neck, not quite meeting at center front. Also called *mandarin collar* or NEHRU COLLAR (see under NECKLINES AND COLLARS).

Chinese collar

choir-boy collar Flat collar with rounded ends in front, similar to PETER PAN COLLAR (see under NECKLINES AND COLLARS), only larger; worn over choir robes.

choker collar Tight band collar that stands up high on neck almost to chin and fastens in back. Often made of sheer material or lace, it is boned, and edged with a narrow ruffle. Fashionable from 1890 to 1910 and revived in mid-1960s and 1980s. Also called *Victorian collar.*

clerical collar See under CLERICAL DRESS.

∞**collaret/collarette** (kol-lar-et′) **1.** Woman's tiny separate collar of 19th c., specifically one made of lace, fur, or beads. **2.** RUCHING worn inside of high standing collar in the 16th c. **3.** In Colonial America, a ruff of ribbon ending in a bow.

collarette à la Lyon See under NECKLINES AND COLLARS: CHERUSSE.

comfort collar A feature sometimes used on formal shirts in which the collar button is attached to a small tab that slides in order to provide greater range of movement and comfort.

convertible collar Rolled shirt collar that, if worn open, forms small lapels. When worn fastened with small concealed button and loop, it fits close to the neck with no lapels and has the appearance of a DRESS SHIRT (see under SHIRTS).

convertible collar

cossack collar High-standing collar that closes on the side and is frequently banded with embroidery. Also called *Zhivago collar* (zhi-vah′-go) and *russian collar.*

cowl collar **1.** Large, draped collar, frequently cut on the bias, that extends nearly to shoulders in circular style. Popular in 1930s and revived in 1980s. **2.** Cowl collar that drapes to form a hood that can be pulled over head. Also called a *cowl hood. Der.* Inspired by a monk's habit.

cowl neckline Draped neckline falling in soft folds. Blouse or dress is usually bias cut for better drape. Popular style of the 1920s, 1930s, and 1980s.

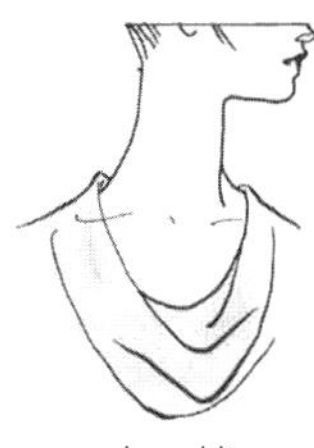
cowl neckline

crew neckline Round neckline finished with knit ribbing. *Der.* From neckline on crew-racing shirts.

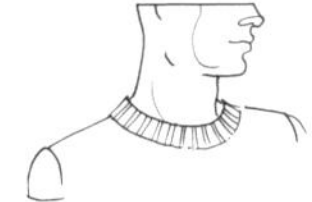
crew neckline

∞**cromwell collar** Wide turnover collar with front edges nearly meeting; worn by women in the 1880s. *Der.* Named for Oliver Cromwell, Lord Protector of England, from 1653 to 1658.

crossover collar A convertible collar with two large lapels that, when buttoned up to the neck, overlap.

crossover neckline See under NECKLINES AND COLLARS: SURPLICE NECKLINE.

décolleté neckline (day-kohl-tay') Any neckline cut very low. *Der.* French, "to bare the neck."

detachable collar 1. Made with tiny buttonholes at lower edge of collar so that it can be buttoned onto a dress or blouse. 2. A man's separate shirt collar usually fastened with a STUD (see under JEWELRY) in back and a collar button in front. Popular men's collar from early 1800s until 1920s and worn later with TUXEDO and FULL DRESS. Said to have been invented by Hannah Montague, wife of a blacksmith in the 1820s, who cut the collars off her husband's shirts and washed them separately—thus he could wear the shirt several times with a fresh collar. During the 19th and early 20th c., the collar became taller and stiffer until it reached 4″, as worn by President Herbert Hoover. The Cluett, Peabody & Co. of Troy, New York, promoted it as the *Arrow® collar* from 1905 to 1931. J. C. Leyendecker, an artist, created advertisements in which a handsome young man called the *Arrow Collar Man®* appeared. He was considered the idealized male, comparable to the GIBSON GIRL.

dog collar 1. Collar that fits tightly around base of neck or higher, sometimes used with HALTER NECKLINE (see under NECKLINES AND COLLARS). Also see NECKLINES AND COLLARS: CHOKER COLLAR. 2. From 1860s, a small, plain, standing collar that overlapped in front. Formerly called an *all-rounder.* Later a name given to CLERICAL COLLAR (see under CLERICAL DRESS), which buttoned in back.

dog-collar neckline See under NECKLINES AND COLLARS: HALTER NECKLINE.

dog's-ear collar Flat collar of medium size with long rounded ends. *Der.* Ends shaped like a spaniel's ear. Also called *spaniel's-ear collar.*

double collar Usually a large collar styled with two identical layers of fabric—one slightly larger than the other. May also be two layers with the upper one cut in an ASYMMETRIC style.

draped collar A collar in which the collar or lapel falls into soft folds rather than laying flat against the body.

draped collar

drawstring neckline Neckline with cord threaded through a casing that can be gathered and adjusted to create either a high or low neckline. Inspired by peasant styles. Introduced for little girls in the 1930s and used intermittently since.

dutch neckline See under NECKLINES AND COLLARS: SQUARE NECKLINE.

elasticized neckline Low neckline cut very wide and finished by turning fabric over a narrow band of stretched elastic, making a wide scooped neckline in front and back. Often used for nightgowns and blouses.

∞**elliptic collar** Patented DETACHABLE COLLAR (see under NECKLINES AND COLLARS) for man's shirt of early 1850s, with the front cut higher than the back. Could be fastened either in front or in back.

eton collar Stiffened boy's collar, similar to a man's shirt collar but twice as wide, with wide-spread points in front. Worn by underclassmen at Eton College in England until 1967. Also see under ETON SUIT in alphabetical listing.

∞**eugénie collarette** (yoo-je'-nee) Crocheted collar of late 1860s made in two-tone yoke effect, pointed in center back and front, and closed in center front with loops and buttons. *Der.* Named for EUGÉNIE, EMPRESS OF FRANCE.

fall The part of a collar that turns over the collar stand or onto the garment.

∞**fall/falling band** Large, flat, turned-down collar attached to the shirt, later made as a separate collar. Usually edged with lace and worn instead of a RUFF (see under NECKLINES AND COLLARS) by men and women from 1540s to 1670s.

fall or falling band

falling ruff See under NECKLINES AND COLLARS: RUFF.

falling tucker See under NECKLINES AND COLLARS: TUCKER.

∞**fan collar** Standing collar of Elizabethan times, shaped like an open fan and placed at back of neck. Usually lace edged, starched, and wired to stand up.

fichu Originally a sheer fabric or lace, triangular kerchief (see under SCARVES: FICHU) worn in late 18th and 19th c. with very low neckline. Reintroduced in 1968 as separate collar worn around neck, crossed in front, and tied in back of waist.

flat collars A category of collars characterized by laying flat against the garment with only enough stand to hide the seam where the collar is attached to the garment.

florentine neckline Wide, square neckline extending to shoulders and cut straight across front and back. *Der.* Inspired by Florentine paintings of the Renaissance.

flounce collar A circular ruffle attached to a neckline as a collar.

French ruff See under NECKLINES AND COLLARS: RUFF.

frizzle See under NECKLINES AND COLLARS: RUFF.

funnel collar Large, stand-up collar that stands away from the face. Generally, buttoned or zippered up the center front and used on heavy winter coats or jackets.

funnel neckline Neckline coming up high on the throat, cut in one with garment. Made with shoulder seams slanted upward toward neck in the shape of an inverted funnel.

funnel neckline

fused collar Collar for a man's shirt made by bonding the interlining with the right side of the collar using chemical or heat-sensitive adhesive, thereby making collar easier to iron and wrinkle-free.

∞**gladstone collar** Standing collar with sides flaring up toward cheeks. Worn with a wide black scarflike tie in latter half of 19th c. *Der.* Named for William Ewart Gladstone, prime minister of England at intervals between 1868 and 1894, during Queen Victoria's reign.

∞**gorget** (gorge-et') **1.** Small ruffle at neck of smock in 16th c. Also spelled *gorgette.* **2.** See under NECKLINES AND COLLARS: WHISK. **3.** High collar, cut low in front, worn by women in late 19th and early 20th c.

halter neckline Sleeveless front of garment that is held in place and leaves the back and shoulders bare. A strap around neck, drawstring at neck gathered and tied in a bow, or a band like a dog collar (see under DOG COLLAR #1.) may serve to hold the front.

halter neckline

henley neckline Round neckline made with ribbing and front placket opening. *Der.* From crew racing shirts worn at Henley, England.

∞**Henry II collar** **1.** Small, medium, or large collar standing up high on the neck in back and rolling over to form points in front. Larger collars had a shawl-collar effect in front. Worn by women in 1890s. **2.** Medium-sized RUFF (see under NECKLINES AND COLLARS) with a large ribbon bow and ends in front worn by women in 1890s.

∞**Henry IV collar** Standing collar around which are placed loops of ribbon that form a small RUFF (see under NECKLINES AND COLLARS) worn by women in 1890s.

horseshoe collar Flat collar extending approximately three-quarters to seven-eighths the distance around the neck with ends not quite meeting in center front.

horseshoe neckline Scooped neckline made low in front in shape of a horseshoe.

italian collar Collar cut in one piece with front of blouse or shirt, then faced and turned over.

jabot (zha-bo') Standing BAND COLLAR (see under NECKLINES AND COLLARS) with hanging ruffle attached to front of collar.

jewel neckline High, round neckline made with or without binding as a simple background for jewels.

jewel neckline

johnny collar Very small collar used for woman's or girl's shirt.

keyhole neckline High, round neckline made with wedge-shaped or keyhole piece cut out at center front.

lapel Turned-back front section of blouse, jacket, coat, or shirt where it joins the collar. Each side folds back to form REVERS (see under NECKLINES AND COLLARS) or lapels that are cut in various shapes. Names of the types are based on the shape of the point where the collar and lapel meet and they include: **cloverleaf**, both collar and lapel are rounded where they meet; **fishmouth**, with lapel cut slanted and collar end rounded; **L-shaped**, with lapel cut straight across a narrow rounded collar; **notched**, with lapel and collar cut slanted thereby creating a notch; **peaked**, with V-shaped ending at lapel and collar fitting into it. Other variants include an **M-cut collar,** a man's coat collar of first half of 19th c. with M-shaped notch at the lapel, a style worn for daywear that continued until 1870 for evening coats.

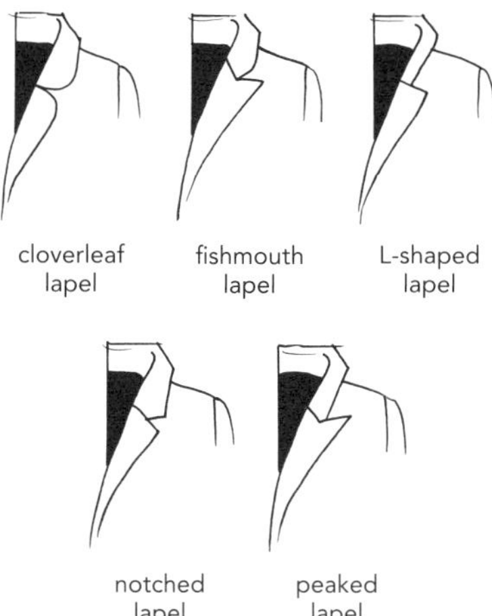
cloverleaf lapel
fishmouth lapel
L-shaped lapel
notched lapel
peaked lapel

leaf (British) Turned-down part of a *stand-fall* or *rolled collar.*

mandarin collar/mandarin neckline See under NECKLINES AND COLLARS: CHINESE NECKLINE. *Der.* the neckline used on the Chinese mandarin robes.

∞**masher collar** Extremely high collar worn by ultra-fashionable men in 1880s and 1890s.

M-cut lapel See under NECKLINES AND COLLARS: LAPEL.

medic collar Standing BAND COLLAR (see under NECKLINES AND COLLARS) fastened on the side with a single button. Made like those on a physician's white jacket that has a side closing. Popular after it was seen on *Ben Casey*, a popular television show in 1961. Also called *Ben Casey collar.*

medici collar (meh-dee-chee) **1.** Large, standing, fan-shaped collar, usually of net or lace, wired to stand up in back and sloping to join low square neckline in front. Worn by Marie de' Medici (1573–1642), second wife of Henry IV of France. Not given this name until the 19th c. when it was revived. ∞**2.** Smaller woman's standing collar of 1890s rolled over at top, sometimes nearly meeting in front.

medici collar #1

middy collar See under NECKLINES AND COLLARS: SAILOR COLLAR.

military collar Standing collar, high in front and hooked either in front or back (e.g., type used on cadet's uniform at U.S. Military Academy at West Point, New York).

moat collar See under NECKLINES AND COLLARS: RING COLLAR.

mock collar/mock-turtleneck collar Single unfolded fabric band that reaches a short distance up the neck that is made to simulate a TURTLENECK COLLAR (see under NECKLINES AND COLLARS).

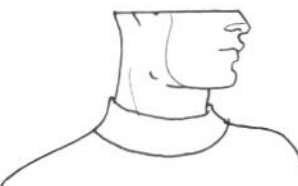
mock collar or mock turtleneck collar

∞**mousquetaire collar** (moose-key-tare') Medium-sized, turned-down collar, usually linen, with the front ends pointed. Fashionable for women about 1850. *Der.* From uniform of French musketeers or royal bodyguards of Louis XIII in 17th c.

napoleonic collar Collar that rolls up high on neck in back then turns over. Extends approximately three-quarters of the way around neck with wide lapels in front and double-breasted closing. *Der.* Named for *Napoleon Bonaparte* (1769–1821) as depicted by J. L. David, court painter.

∞**neck ruche** Woman's neckpiece of early 20th c. made of frilled MOUSSELINE, pleated, sewed to a ribbon, and worn around the neck with long hanging streamers of silk or ribbon in front.

∞**neck whisk** **1.** Small wired or stiffened, fan-shaped, man's, sheer standing collar worn inside standing collar of the doublet in late 16th c. **2.** Flat, round, man's collar with pointed ends open in front. Worn in Spain in 17th c.

Nehru collar/Nehru neckline (nay'-roo) Standing collar similar to Chinese collar but sometimes made with rounded ends in front. Copied from the costume of Jawaharlal Nehru, prime minister of India from 1950 to 1964. Also called *rajah collar.*

notched collar/notched lapel Tailored collar primarily for man's suit coat that has an indentation or "notch" cut out or formed where the lapel joins the collar.

∞**officer's collar** Woman's collar of mid-1880s with stiff standing band around neck, sometimes with frill of lace at neck. A tri-layered JABOT (see under NECKLINES AND COLLARS) with vandyked edges (see VANDYKING) was worn in center front.

off-the-shoulder neckline Low neckline, usually elasticized, extending around upper part of arms baring the shoulders, sometimes with straps, sometimes without. Frequently finished with a wide ruffle around the edge. Popular for evening gowns in 1930s and 1940s and used intermittently since for nightgowns, blouses, and evening dresses.

off-the-shoulder neckline

one-shoulder neckline Asymmetric neckline starting under one arm and continuing diagonally over opposite shoulder leaving one shoulder bare. Popular for evening dresses, swimsuits, and nightgowns. Also called *sling neckline.*

one-shoulder neckline

oval ruff See under NECKLINES AND COLLARS: RUFF.

∞**papillon collar** (pa-pi-yon') Small standing collar, decorated with pleated fabric in front to form a small butterfly, worn by women in late 1860s. Cuffs were also decorated with small pleated butterflies. *Der.* French, "butterfly."

partial roll A classification of collars characterized by a stand, typically at the back of the neck, that blends back to the neckline, allowing the collar to lay flat on the garment on the front; examples include shawl, notched, and convertible collars.

peasant neckline Low, round neckline gathered into a bias band or made with a drawstring. Sometimes worn in off-the-shoulder fashion. See under NECKLINES AND COLLARS: DRAWSTRING NECKLINE.

peggy collar Rounded collar with scalloped ends similar to PETER PAN COLLAR (see under NECKLINES AND COLLARS).

petal collar Collar made of several irregularly shaped pieces that look like petals of a flower.

peter pan collar Small, round, flat collar with rounded ends in front. Worn originally by children, later

peter pan collar

also adopted by women. *Der.* Copied from costumes worn in play *Peter Pan,* written by James M. Barrie in 1904.

∞**piccadilly collar** Man's detachable high wing collar of 1860s fastening to the shirt with a stud in front and a button in back. By 1895, collar was cut larger to allow a scarf to pass underneath.

∞**pierpont collar** (peer′-pont) Man's collar ending in sharp points extended over tie, worn in 1840s and 1850s. Also called *pinpoint collar.*

pierrot collar (pee-yehr-oh′) Small collar made of a double ruffle or ruff. *Der.* From costume of the comedy character in French pantomime called *Pierrot* (little Peter), especially the clown in opera *Pagliacci,* who wore a clown suit with this collar.

pilgrim collar Large round collar extending to the shoulder seams at sides and ending in two long points at center front. *Der.* Copied from early Pilgrim costume.

pin collar Shirt collar fitting high on neck made with an eyelet on each side of opening through which a special collar pin is inserted.

pinpoint collar See under NECKLINES AND COLLARS: PIERPONT COLLAR.

placket neckline Slit at neckline, bound with bias binding or made with a facing, sometimes in a contrasting color. Bias may continue around neck or a simple collar may be added.

placket neckline

plastron See under NECKLINES AND COLLARS: BIB COLLAR.

platter collar Medium to large, round collar with large rounded ends in front, worn flat on shoulders.

plunging neckline Neckline made with low V in center front, sometimes extending to the waist or below. Fashionable for extreme styles in the 1960s and continued in popularity since.

poet's collar See under NECKLINES AND COLLARS: BYRON COLLAR.

∞**polo collar** Man's white starched collar, worn in late 1890s, with points sloping toward shoulders. Could be worn either standing or turned down.

portrait collar An open V-necked collar with lapels wide enough to extend to the top of the sleeve, generally notched in the front and rounded in back.

portrait collar

∞**princess stock** High choker collar, usually made of shirred fabric with two bows extending at sides. When a PLASTRON (see under NECKLINES AND COLLARS: BIB COLLAR) was attached at center front neckline, collar was called *princess stock collarette.* Worn by women in mid-1890s.

puritan collar Square-cut, wide, flat, white collar, or FALLING BAND (see under NECKLINES AND COLLARS), that extends to shoulder seam. *Der.* Copied from early Puritan costume.

Quaker collar Collar made in the style worn by Quakers in the 17th and 18th c. that is generally white against a dark background with large square lapels on either side at the front. Also called *puritan collar.*

∞**rabat** (ra-bat′) **/rabbi** A linen and lace collar worn over the DOUBLET in 17th c.

rabato (rah-bah′-toe) **/rebato** ∞**1.** White collar wired to stand up at back of neck, worn with low-cut neckline by women from late 16th to mid-17th c. **2.** See under NECKLINES AND COLLARS: RUFF.

rajah collar/rajah necklines See under NECKLINES AND COLLARS: NEHRU COLLAR.

regency collar Similar to NAPOLEONIC COLLAR (see under NECKLINES AND COLLARS) but smaller in size.

revers (reh-veerz′) Another name for lapels, actually the facing of the lapels, which fold back to show the reverse side of the collar and lapels. See under NECKLINES AND COLLARS: LAPELS.

revers

ring collar Stand-away band that circles the neck at a distance about halfway to shoulder seam. Also called *moat collar* and *wedding-band collar.*

∞**robespierre collar** (robz-pee-yehr′) Man's coat collar worn about 1790, coming up high at back of neck and then turned down with jabot showing in front. Used on a double-breasted coat. *Der.* Named for Maximillien François Marie Isidore de Robespierre, French lawyer and revolutionist, executed in 1794.

rolled collar **1.** Collar extending upward from neckline and turning over, the roll higher at back than in front. **2.** Any shirt collar or other collar that has a roll to it making it stand up on neck, as differentiated from a flat collar that has no roll and lies flat at base of neck (e.g., NECKLINES AND COLLARS: NAPOLEONIC or CONVERTIBLE COLLAR). Called *stand-fall collar* in the 19th c.

rolled collar

roll neck A neckline used on sweaters that takes advantage of the tendency of a jersey knit to roll onto itself. May also be a design feature on cuffs and hems of knit garments when ribbing is not desired as a finish.

∞**rollpoint collar** Similar to wing collar but overturned point is not pressed down. Worn by men in late 19th and early 20th c.

roman collar See under CLERICAL DRESS: CLERICAL COLLAR.

∞**rosebery collar** Man's detachable collar of mid-1890s of white linen, 3″ high in back, with rounded points in front. *Der.* Named for Fifth Earl of Rosebery, British statesman, author, and prime minister, 1894–1895.

ruff Stiff white collar of varying widths, often edged in or made of lace, that projected from the neckline like a wheel around neck. Worn by men and women from 1560s to 1640s, the ruff was one of the most characteristic features of costume of this time period. After the ruff went out of fashion, it became another alternative that could be used as a collar and has appeared in fashion periodically since the 17th c. The earliest ruffs appear to have evolved from a small ruffle at the neckline of a shirt or chemise that became a separate item of clothing and could be of enormous width. Ruffs were made in one of the following ways: (a) gathering one edge of a band of fabric to the size of the neck to form a frill of deep folds; (b) round, flat pieces of lace without depth or folds, more like a wide collar; (c) several layers of lace placed one over the other; (d) open ruffs, almost a cross between a ruff and a collar that stood behind the head and fastened in front into a square neckline. Ruffs were supported either by starching or by a **supportasse** (sup-port′-tass) or **underpropper,** a wire framework used to tilt an enormous starched ruff up on back of neck. Also called a *rabato.* Named variations of ruffs included the **oval ruff,** a woman's large plain ruff, oval shaped rather than round, made with large PIPE ORGAN PLEATS (see under CLOTHING CONSTRUCTION DETAILS). Worn from about 1625 to 1650. The **cabbage ruff** was a large ruff falling in irregular folds, like leaves of a cabbage. Worn by men in early 17th c. Also called *lettuce ruff* or *lettice ruff.* The **vandyke** was a 17th-c. ruff edged with points of saw-toothed lace. A **cartwheel ruff** or **French ruff** was extremely large, starched, and set in regular convolutions and was worn from 1580 to 1610 and somewhat later in Holland. By contrast, the **frizzle** was a 17th-c. small ruff. The **falling ruff** was an unstarched ruff falling around the neck in unregulated folds. Worn in England from about 1615 to 1640 by men and women and by men in France during reign of Henry IV (who ruled from 1589 to 1610) and then called *fraise à la confusion.*

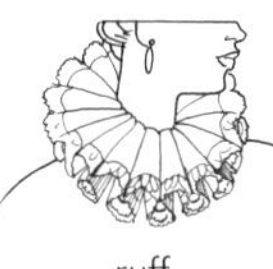
ruff

supportasse

russian collar See under NECKLINES AND COLLARS: COSSACK COLLAR.

sabrina neckline High, boat neckline fastened together at shoulders with spaghetti strings that are tied in bows. Originally designed by Edith Head and worn by Audrey Hepburn in film *Sabrina* in the 1950s.

sailor collar Large square collar hanging in back with front tapering to a V with dickey inserted. Trimmed with rows of braid and worn on MIDDY *blouses* by the U.S. Navy. Popular style since 1860s, especially for children. Also called *middy collar.*

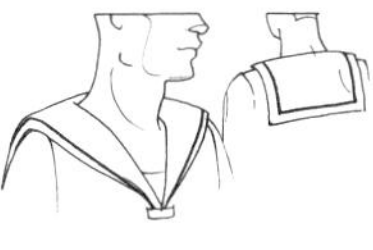
sailor collar

∞**santon** (sahn-tone′) Colored silk cravat worn with small RUFF (see under NECKLIINES AND COLLARS) by women in 1820s. Also called a *sautoir* (sew-twar′).

sautoir See under NECKLINES AND COLLARS: SANTON.

scallop neckline or collar A series of convex curves along the neckline of a garment or along the style line of a collar.

scarf tie A collar with ends that extend from the neckline which can be tied or looped as a design element.

scoop neckline Low curved neckline extending to shoulders or cut deep in front or back or both. Introduced for evening wear in late 1930s, used on daytime dresses since 1950s, and blouses since late 1960s.

separate collar **1.** Any collar not permanently attached to the garment with which it is worn (e.g., collars as worn with choir robes). **2.** See under DETACHABLE COLLAR.

shakespeare collar **1.** Standing collar of medium width, flaring away from face. Made of a curved pleated strip of stiffened lawn. *Der.* Similar to those shown in a portrait thought to be of 16th-c. dramatist, William Shakespeare. ∞**2.** Similar collar with longer points, sometimes trimmed with LACE and INSERTION, worn by women in mid-1860s. ∞**3.** Small collar with points turned down in front, worn by men from 1860s on.

shawl collar **1.** Collar that follows the front opening of garment. Cut in one piece or with seam in center back, it does not have separate lapels. It may be narrow or broad and can extend to waistline. Used on women's dresses, coats, sweaters, and men's tuxedos. See NECKLINES AND COLLARS: ANGLED SHAWL COLLAR. **2.** Women's blouse or dress collar made in one piece with low V-neck in front and hanging ends of frilly lace. Worn in early 1980s.

shawl collar #1

shirt collar Turned-down collar used on a man's or woman's shirt; specifically, a small collar fitting not too high on the neck, with medium-spread points (e.g., NECKLINES AND COLLARS: BUTTON-DOWN, CONVERTIBLE, PIN, TAB, SPREAD, and WING COLLARS).

sling neckline See under NECKLINES AND COLLARS: ONE-SHOULDER NECKLINE.

spaniel's-ear collar See under NECKLINES AND COLLARS: DOG'S-EAR COLLAR.

split mandarin collar Similar to mandarin collar, standing high on the neck. In mid-1980s called a *split mandarin* *collar* when it did not fasten at neckline and could be turned down to form lapels. See under NECKLINES AND COLLARS: CHINESE COLLAR.

spread collar Man's shirt collar made with a wide division between points in front.

spread collar

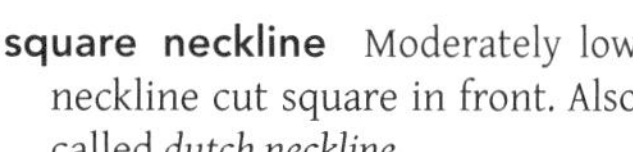

square neckline Moderately low neckline cut square in front. Also called *dutch neckline.*

stand The part of the collar that extends upward from the bodice and fits close to the neck.

stand-away collar Women's collar that does not hug the neck, usually of the roll-type and popular from early 1960s.

stand-fall collar See under NECKLINES AND COLLARS: ROLLED COLLAR #2.

standing whisk See under NECKLINES AND COLLARS: WHISK #2.

stand-up collar 1. See under NECKLINES AND COLLARS: BAND COLLAR. 2. Collar similar to a band collar extending higher on the neck and sometimes finished with a frill of lace or pleating. Widely used in the late 19th and early 20th c. and revived periodically.

stand-up collar #2

stick-up collar See under NECKLINES AND COLLARS: WING COLLAR.

stock collar/stock neckline See under NECKLINES AND COLLARS: ASCOT NECKLINE.

strapless neckline Boned or elastic bodice that requires no shoulder straps. An innovation in the 1930s and a basic neckline style since then that has been popular for evening wear as well as sportswear.

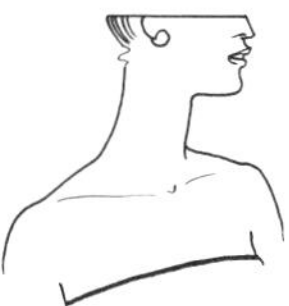
strapless neckline

style line The outer edge of a collar that defines its width and shape.

supportasse See under NECKLINES AND COLLARS: RUFF.

surplice collar (sir′-pliss) Flat pointed collar fastened to a SURPLICE NECKLINE (see under NECKLINES AND COLLARS). Used on a coat-style dress.

surplice neckline (sir′-pliss) Neckline of wraparound blouse, dress, or robe with one side lapping over other to form a V in center front. Introduced in 1920s and used since.

swallow-tailed collar Tailored collar with extremely long narrow points in front. *Der.* From resemblance to "the tail of a swallow."

sweetheart neckline Moderately low neckline with heart-shaped center front. Sides of neckline slant toward neck in front with back rounded. Introduced in 1930s and used intermittently since.

tab collar Shirt collar fitting high on the neck with a small flap or tab at the neckband that buttons or snaps to other side of shirt.

tab collar

talleyrand collar (ta′-lay-rahn) Collar standing up at back of neck and turned over, similar to ROBESPIERRE COLLAR (see under NECKLINES AND COLLARS). *Der.* Named after French statesman Charles Maurice de Talleyrand-Perigord, active in politics from 1775 to 1815.

∞**toby ruff** Woman's small RUFF of 1890 (see under NECKLINES AND COLLARS: RUFF), made of two or three layers of frills tied at the throat with ribbon.

trench collar/trench coat collar A one-piece collar with the appearance of a collar made in two sections (a collar and separate lapel) with the same appearance as a collar on a TRENCH COAT. See under COATS AND JACKETS.

∞**tucker** Narrow strip or frill of plain or lace-trimmed fabric, used by women from 17th c. to about 1830s, to fill in low décolletage. Also called *pinner* or *falling tucker* in 19th c. when it hung down over bodice. Also see under PARTLET #2 and SCARVES: CHEMISETTE.

turndown collar Any collar that folds over on the garment or on itself, as contrasted with standing-band or stand-up type. Also see under NECKLINES AND COLLARS: ROLLED COLLAR.

turnover collar Any collar that rolls and then turns over (e.g., NECKLINES AND COLLARS: CONVERTIBLE COLLAR).

turtleneck/turtleneck collar High-band collar, usually knitted, that fits very close to the neck and rolls over, sometimes twice. Introduced in the 1860s for men, popular in the 1920s and 1930s, and revived in the late 1960s for men, women, and children.

turtleneck collar

turtleneck convertible collar Turtleneck collar with zipper down center front so collar may be worn high on neck or unzipped to a V.

tuxedo collar Collar that rolls over and extends down entire length of front opening in women's jacket or coat with no fasteners. Name borrowed from shawl collar of men's dinner jacket. *Der.* So named in the 1920s after the country club at Tuxedo Park, New York. Also see TUXEDO in alphabetical listing

Ubangi neckline (yoo-bang′-ee) Extremely high choker-type neckline covering the entire neck. Sometimes made of fabric, sometimes of chain or springy wire wrapped around the neck. Popular in late 1960s. *Der.* Inspired by dress of women of the Ubangi tribe of Africa.

underpropper See under NECKLINES AND COLLARS: RUFF.

U-neckline See under NECKLINES AND COLLARS: HORSESHOE NECKLINE.

vandyke collar See under NECKLINES AND COLLARS: RUFF.

ventilated collar See under CLERICAL DRESS.

Victorian collar See under NECKLINES AND COLLARS: CHOKER COLLAR.

V-neckline Neckline cut down in front or in back to a sharp point resembling the letter V.

wedding-band collar See under NECKLINES AND COLLARS: RING COLLAR.

∞**whisk** 1. Wide, flat, lace-trimmed, or plain collar worn by women in 17th c., like FALLING BAND (see under NECKLINES AND COLLARS). 2. Standing lace collar called *standing whisk.*

wing collar 1. A tailored shirt collar with spread points. 2. Stiff man's collar fitting high around neck with turned-down points in front; sometimes worn with man's full dress or daytime formal wear. Worn by upperclassmen at Eton College until 1967. Also called *stick-up collar.* 3. Same type as above, introduced in 1980s of softer fabric, usually white on a colored shirt.

wing collar #2

∞**winker** Man's collar with extremely high points reaching nearly to eyes that was worn from 1816 to 1820.

wrap collar Collar that has one end pulled around to side of neck where it buttons, introduced in 1983.

∞**yoke collar** Square or V-shaped yoke, extending wide on the shoulders, to which two gathered ruffles are attached. Worn by women in mid-1890s with high choker collar at neck.

Zhivago collar See under NECKLINES AND COLLARS: COSSACK COLLAR. *Der.* From 1965 film of Boris Pasternak's novel *Dr. Zhivago,* depicting Russian Revolution of 1917.

---

neckpiece See under SCARVES.

neck ring See under JEWELRY.

neck ruche See under NECKLINES AND COLLARS.

∞**neckstock** Stiffly folded made-up cravat buckled in back, worn by men in 18th and 19th c. See under TIES: STOCK.

necktie See under TIES.

necktie pin See under JEWELRY: STICKPIN.

neckwear Accessories worn around neck exclusive of jewelry. Includes neckties, scarves, and collars.

neck whisk See under NECKLINES AND COLLARS.

needle 1. Small, thin spike, usually of polished steel, with one end pointed and an eye at the other end through which the thread is drawn for sewing. 2. A long implement without an eye that has a hook at one end used for knitting or for crocheting.

needlepoint 1. See under EMBROIDERIES AND SEWING STITCHES. 2. See under introduction to LACES.

needle tapestry work See under EMBROIDERIES AND SEWING STITCHES.

needle toe See under FOOTWEAR.

needle trades See under APPAREL INDUSTRY.

needleweaving See under EMBROIDERIES AND SEWING STITCHES.

negligée See under SLEEPWEAR AND LOUNGEWEAR.

negligée costume (neg-glee-zheh') Informal costume, worn primarily in privacy of home or bedroom. Usually a long, easy robe of supple material, ranging from simple cotton to elaborately trimmed silk. Worn by both men and women from 18th through 19th c. Developed into the TEA GOWN for women in last quarter of 19th c. *Der.* French, *négligée,* "neglected."

negligée shirt See under SHIRTS.

Nehru styles See under NEHRU under NECKLINES AND COLLARS and COATS AND JACKETS.

Nehru suit (nay-roo) 1. A suit with a high stand-up NEHRU COLLAR (see under NECKLINES AND COLLARS) introduced in 1967. Made in various fabrics for both men and women. 2. Woman's pantsuit with a tunic top made with nehru collar. Top may be worn separately as a dress. *Der.* Named after Jawaharlal Nehru, prime minister of India from 1950 to 1964.

Nehru suit #1

nelson See under UNDERGARMENTS: FRISK.

neon colors Very bright, vibrant colors similar to those produced by neon lights.

neon sock See under HOSIERY.

nephrite See under GEMS, GEM CUTS, AND SETTINGS: JADE.

net See under BOBBINET.

net embroidery See under EMBROIDERIES AND SEWING STITCHES: TULLE EMBROIDERY.

nether integuments See under INEXPRESSIBLES.

nether stocks See under LOWER STOCKS.

newgate fringe See under BEARD.

New Look Style introduced by couturier Christian Dior in Paris in 1947. The style—characterized by a rounded shoulder, tightly fitted waistline, curved hipline, and hemline that was almost six inches longer than prevailing styles—was a radical departure from the wartime styles. The fashion press called these changes the "New Look," the first time the word "look" had been used to describe an overall style.

newmarket coat See under COATS AND JACKETS: CUTAWAY.

newmarket frock See under COATS AND JACKETS: CUTAWAY.

newmarket jacket See under COATS AND JACKETS.

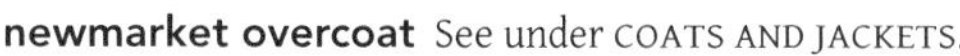

New Look

newmarket overcoat See under COATS AND JACKETS.

newmarket top frock See under COATS AND JACKETS.

newmarket vest See under VESTS.

New Romantics Media-coined name for young people of the late 1970s and 1980s, who, in reaction against PUNK fashions, wore clothing made in soft, extravagant fabrics, in dressy styles derived from historic fiction or futuristic or fantasy costumes.

newsbag See under HANDBAGS AND RELATED ACCESSORIES.

newsboy cap See under HEADWEAR.

New Wave Punk See under PUNK.

New York Couture Business Council, The An organization of manufacturers of ready-to-wear clothing serving as a trade council and mediating disputes between retailers and manufacturers. The promotional arm of this organization is called *The New York Couture Group* and was responsible for *National Press Week.*

neyge See under EDGE #2.

niced See under SCARVES: NYCETTE.

niche/niche marketing (neesh) Describes a narrowly defined group of customers and the practice of marketing to those customers. Needs of consumers in niches can be analyzed and apparel offered that appeals to this specific group.

nightcap See under HEADWEAR.

night clothes Apparel worn to bed. For full discussion of such apparel, see under SLEEPWEAR AND LOUNGEWEAR.

night coif See under HEADWEAR.

nightgown 1. See under SLEEPWEAR AND LOUNGEWEAR. ∞2. In the 18th c., a comfortable women's dress, without stays, worn either outdoors or indoors. Also see under MORNING GOWN.

nightgown/nightshirt See under SLEEPWEAR AND LOUNGEWEAR.

nightie See under SLEEPWEAR AND LOUNGEWEAR: NIGHTGOWN #1.

night rail See under SLEEPWEAR AND LOUNGEWEAR.

nightshift/nightshirt See under SLEEPWEAR AND LOUNGEWEAR.

Nike® waffle trainers See under FOOTWEAR.

nine-tenths length See under LENGTHS.

ninon coiffure See under HAIRSTYLES.

nipped waist See under WAISTLINES.

no bra *adj.* Descriptive of styles accompanying the *see-through styles.* Originally a sheer lightweight bra designed by Rudi Gernreich in early 1960s. Later by extension transferred to advocating of wearing nothing, or bikinis, under see-through clothes in late 1960s and early 1970s.

nomad *adj.* Descriptive of apparel inspired by clothing worn by nomadic tribes of Middle East countries. Unusual patterned fabrics, use of shearling and embroidered leather as exemplified by the AFGHANISTAN JACKET (see under COATS AND JACKETS) and vest popular around 1968.

nonreciprocated See under HOSIERY: RECIPROCATED CONSTRUCTION.

nonseasonal Products that sell at much the same rate throughout the year.

†nonwoven fabrics Interlocking or bonding of fibers (or both) by chemical, mechanical, thermal, solvent methods, and combinations to create a fabric.

norfolk jacket See under COATS AND JACKETS.

norfolk shirt See under COATS AND JACKETS.

norfolk suit ∞1. Little boy's suit with top styled like norfolk jacket with one or two box pleats in front and back, usually worn with a belt at waist that continues under pleats. Worn with KNICKERBOCKERS to above knee, buster brown collar, bow tie, and large off-the-face hat in early 1900s. 2. Man's suit with matching coat and pants, jacket styled in norfolk manner (see under COATS AND JACKETS: NORFOLK JACKET), worn from about 1912 to about 1930. Revived occasionally.

normandie cape See under CAPES, CLOAKS, AND SHAWLS.

North American Free Trade Agreement (NAFTA) Treaty that provides for the reduction and eventually elimination of trade barriers between Canada, Mexico, and the U.S.

North American Industry Classification System (NAICS) System of classifying firms by the type of product they produce. Introduced in 1997 and revised in 2003 to harmonize the gathering of statistical industry data by category in the U.S, Canada, and Mexico as a result of the NAFTA free trade agreement. NAICS replaced the Standard Industrial Classification (SIC) system used in the U.S.

northamptonshire lace See under LACES.

north-south bag See under HANDBAGS AND RELATED ACCESSORIES.

norwegian morning cap See under HEADWEAR.

nose chains See under JEWELRY.

nose piercing jewelry See under JEWELRY.

nose rings See under JEWELRY.

nose studs See under JEWELRY.

notch The triangular shape between the lapel and the collar, formed where the gorge line ends. Found in menswear and women's wear (see COLLAR in introduction to NECKLINES AND COLLARS). Markings cut into the seam allowance of pattern pieces to indicate how pieces should be matched up when they are joined together.

notched collar See under NECKLINES AND COLLARS.

notched lapel See under NECKLINES AND COLLARS: LAPEL.

nottingham lace See under LACES.

nouch See under JEWELRY: OUCH.

novelties See under HOSIERY.

†novelty fabrics Unusual yarn, print, pattern, weave, or knit that makes a fabric unique.

†novelty yarn Yarns made with unusual or special effects such as nubs, slubs, loops, or some other variation. The preferred term in the textile industry is now *fancy yarn.*

nubuck See under LEATHERS.

†nub yarn Yarn made with slubs or lumps, knots, or flecks of fibers at intervals—sometimes of different colors giving a mottled effect to the finished fabric.

nude bra See under UNDERGARMENTS.

nude heel See under HOSIERY.

nude *adj.* Characterizing styles that reveal large areas of the body or that use beige or natural-colored body stockings that simulate a nude effect. Introduced in 1966 by Saint Laurent and Cardin with sheer transparent dresses worn over nude-colored body stockings. Later in the 1960s, the body stocking was not worn and these clothes were described as "SEE-THROUGH."

nugget ring See under JEWELRY.

numeral shirt See under SHIRTS: FOOTBALL JERSEY/SHIRT.

nun's habit Apparel worn by nuns, women living in convents who devote their lives to their church. Many of these styles dated from the Middle Ages and usually consisted of a covered-up, ankle-length black dress, often with a white collar and belted with a long cord. Head and neck were wrapped in starched white cotton headdress like a WIMPLE (see under HEADWEAR), with the shape varying according to the convent or order and often covered by a long black veil. Many changes have been made in Roman Catholic nuns' habits since 1965, (e.g., simpler headdresses, shorter skirts, brown, navy, and gray colors added to conventional black color). Some orders have abandoned habits altogether, wearing conservative street dress instead.

nun's tucks See under CLOTHING CONSTRUCTION DETAILS.

Nureyev shirt See under SHIRTS.

nurse's cap See under HEADWEAR.

nurse's cape See under CAPES, CLOAKS, AND SHAWLS.

nutria See under FURS.

nycette See under SCARVES.

†nylon Generic fiber category established by the FTC for a MANUFACTURED FIBER composed of a long chain of chemicals called polyamides. Introduced in 1939 by DuPont and later produced by other manufacturers, nylon fabrics generally have a silky hand, strength, crease resistance, washability, and resistance to mildew and moths.

nylons See under HOSIERY.

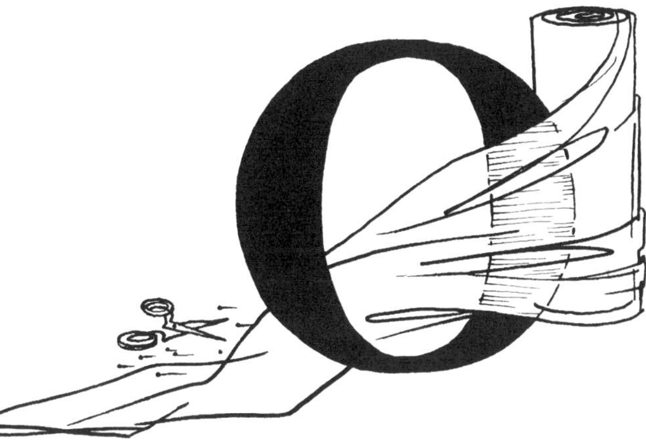

obi See under BELTS: OBI-STYLED SASH.

obi hat See under HEADWEAR.

oblong hoops See under UNDERGARMENTS: PANNIERS.

obsidian See under GEMS, GEM CUTS, AND SETTINGS.

ocelot (ah-seh-lot) See under FURS.

ocepa See under ANDEAN SHIFT.

ochy pant See under PANTS.

octagonal hat See under HEADWEAR.

octagon tie See under TIES.

odd priced Prices for goods that end with an odd number. Endings such as .95 or .99 often are assigned to sale merchandise, whereas .00 or easily divisible numbers are used for nonsale prices.

oegge See under EDGE.

off-color diamond See under GEMS, GEM CUTS, AND SETTINGS.

†off grain *adj.* 1. Descriptive of the condition in which lengthwise and crosswise threads in a fabric do not meet at 90 degrees. 2. Descriptive of a garment that is cut so that the grainline on the pattern piece is not parallel to the grain of the fabric, causing the garment to twist or hang crookedly.

officer's cape See under CAPES, CLOAKS, AND SHAWLS.

officer's coat See under COATS AND JACKETS: GUARDSMAN COAT.

officer's collar See under NECKLINES AND COLLARS.

off price *adj.* Merchandise or retailing of merchandise purchased at discount prices.

offshore In U.S. apparel trade, refers to countries other than the U.S. See INTERNATIONAL SOURCING and IMPORT.

offshore production Manufacturing of apparel in countries other than the U.S. while using specifications that U.S. companies provide.

off the peg See under READY-TO-WEAR.

off the rack See under READY-TO-WEAR.

off-the-shoulder See under NECKLINES AND COLLARS.

†oilskin 1. Waterproof fabric, frequently colored yellow, made by coating cotton with linseed oil. Used originally for raincoats worn by fishermen, sailors, and children. Fabrics that have been given waterproof finish. 2. Garments made of this or similar fabric (e.g., raincoats, pants, and jackets) worn by sailors in rainy weather.

oil tanning See under LEATHERS: CHAMOIS TANNING.

oker See under FOOTWEAR: COCKER.

old mine cut See under GEMS, GEM CUTS, AND SETTINGS.

†olefin (oh'-leh-fihn) Generic fiber category for a manufactured fiber composed of either polyethylene or polypropylene. Manufacturers prefer the term **polyolefin** (pol-ee'-oh'-leh-fihn). Polypropylene is used for some types of apparel, such as activewear products (e.g., knitted underwear and hosiery), and for outdoor sports in such products as wetsuits and biking shorts,

olive button See under CLOSURES.

oliver twist dress See under DRESSES.

∞oliver twist suit Little boy's suit worn about 1919 similar to a girl's OLIVER TWIST DRESS (see under DRESSES) except that the blouse was worn with knee pants buttoned to the blouse.

olivette See under CLOSURES: FROG.

olivine See under GEMS, GEM CUTS, AND SETTINGS.

Olympics Sporting contests held both in the winter and summer, every four years, with participants from around the world. The various types of athletic clothing worn for different sporting events frequently have an important influence on activewear. *Der.* From the games and festivals held in honor of the god, Zeus, on the plain of Olympia in ancient Greece, where a laurel wreath was presented to the victor.

†ombré (om'-bray) (French) "Shaded." Closely related tones of color with monochromatic shading from light to dark of single color (e.g., pale pink to red, or in several colors like a rainbow). Also see under PRINTS, STRIPES, AND CHECKS.

one-piece swimsuit See under SWIMWEAR.

one-shoulder backpack See under HANDBAGS AND RELATED ACCESSORIES.

one-shoulder dress See under DRESSES: TOGA DRESS.

one-shoulder neckline See under NECKLINES AND COLLARS.

one-size bra See under UNDERGARMENTS: STRETCH BRA.

on grain *adj.* 1. Descriptive of a fabric in which the lengthwise and crosswise threads of a fabric meet at 90 degrees. 2. Descriptive of a garment that is cut so that the grainline on the pattern piece is parallel to the grain of the fabric.

onion See under HAIRSTYLES: POMPADOUR.

online retailing See under ELECTRONIC RETAILING.

on order Goods ordered but not yet received.

onyx See under GEMS, GEM CUTS, AND SETTINGS.

opal See under GEMS, GEM CUTS, AND SETTINGS.

opaque *adj.* Descriptive of gems and fabrics through which no light passes. Compare with TRANSLUCENT and TRANSPARENT. See also under HOSIERY: OPAQUE HOSE/OPAQUE PANTYHOSE.

Op Art print See under PRINTS, STRIPES, AND CHECKS.

open-back shoe See under FOOTWEAR: SLINGBACK.

open buttonhole stitch See under EMBROIDERIES AND SEWING STITCHES: BLANKET STITCH.

open-crown hat See under HEADWEAR.

opening price point See under APPAREL PRICE RANGES.

open orders Those orders that allow a manufacturer to ship merchandise at some point other than a set delivery date. Such orders may specify a dollar amount to be purchased, but may not require specific styles, sizes, or colors.

∞**open robe** See under DRESSES.

open-shank See under FOOTWEAR.

open-to-buy (OTB) A calculation based on difference between merchandise a buyer plans to order over a specified period and what has already been ordered. The open-to-buy amount can be used by the buyer to adjust orders so as to maintain inventory and profitability.

open-toed shoe See under FOOTWEAR.

open-to-ship A calculation of the amount of merchandise needed to meet planned purchases.

open-welt seam See under CLOTHING CONSTRUCTION DETAILS: TUCKED SEAM.

open window display See under WINDOW DISPLAYS.

openwork Knitting, weaving, or embroidery in which threads are used in such a manner that holes in fabric give a lacy effect. See under EMBROIDERIES AND SEWING STITCHES.

opera *adj* Describes apparel and accessories of a type that might be worn to performances of operas or other formal public performances. See under CAPES, CLOAKS, AND SHAWLS: OPERA WRAP and OPERA CAPE; EYEWEAR: OPERA GLASSES; FOOTWEAR: OPERA PUMP and OPERA SLIPPER; GLOVES AND GLOVE CONSTRUCTION: OPERA GLOVE; and HEADWEAR: OPERA HAT.

opera-length necklace See under JEWELRY.

opossum See under FURS.

opus anglicum See under EMBROIDERIES AND SEWING STITCHES: ENGLISH WORK.

opus araneum See under LACES: ANTIQUE.

oralia See under HEADWEAR.

oreilles de chien See under HAIRSTYLES.

†**organdy** Light, sheer, cotton fabric with a permanently crisp feel. If made of manufactured fibers, it is crease resistant, but if made of natural fibers the fabric will wrinkle. Made in an open weave of fine, high-quality combed yarns, the fabric may be dyed, printed, or embroidered. Uses: dresses, collars, cuffs, millinery, aprons, interfacing, and neckwear.

†**organic cotton** Cotton grown without the use of pesticides and chemical fertilizers.

†**organza** Lightweight, thin, transparent fabric that is stiff and wiry. Made in the plain weave of manufactured filament or silk yarns, this fabric has a tendency to crush, but is easy to press. Used for dresses, millinery, trimmings, neckwear, and blouses.

oriental cat's eye See under GEMS, GEM CUTS, AND SETTINGS: CAT'S EYE.

oriental couching See under EMBROIDERIES AND SEWING STITCHES.

oriental pearls See under GEMS, GEM CUTS, AND SETTINGS: PEARL.

oriental stitch See under EMBROIDERIES AND SEWING STITCHES.

oriental wrapper See under COATS AND JACKETS: ZOUAVE COAT.

original design See under HAUTE COUTURE.

orle See under OURLE.

ornamental stones See under GEMS, GEM CUTS, AND SETTINGS.

orphrey See under CLERICAL DRESS.

orrelet See under HEADWEAR.

orris/orrice lace See under LACES.

Orsay, Count d' Alfred Guillaume Gabriel (1801–1852) (ore'-say) French society leader in Paris and London at the time of William IV who reigned from 1830 to 1837. A DANDY or arbiter of fashion, he is described as a wit, a sculptor, and a conversationalist, and his name is attached to fashions such as D'ORSAY SLIPPERS (see under FOOTWEAR) and D'ORSAY COAT (see under COATS AND JACKETS).

osbaldiston tie See under TIES.

osprey See under FEATHERS.

ostrich See under FEATHERS and LEATHERS.

otter See under FURS.

†ottoman Heavy, luxurious fabric with broad, flat, crosswise ribs or wales. Made from silk, acetate, rayon, cotton, or wool with crosswise cord yarns of cotton. Lengthwise yarns are finer, and more are used so that they cover the crosswise yarns completely on both sides. Uses: coats, evening wear, suits, and trimmings.

†ottoman ribbed knit Double-knit fabric with a pronounced wide crosswise rib.

ouch See under JEWELRY.

∞ourle A fur border that was used in the 13th and 14th c. Later spelled *orle.*

† outing flannel/outing cloth Light- or medium-weight, soft, fuzzy cotton fabric. Made with lightly twisted yarns that are napped to conceal the plain or twill weave completely. May be made in yarn-dyed stripes, piece-dyed, or printed. Uses: winter pajamas, nightshirts, and gowns.

outlet store Brand-owned stores that product developers use to broaden their customer base as well as sell excess goods, overruns, and irregulars at discounted prices.

outline stitch See under EMBROIDERIES AND SEWING STITCHES.

outré (oo'-tray) (French) *adj.* Exaggerated, strained, excessive.

outseam See under GLOVES AND GLOVE CONSTRUCTION: GLOVE SEAMS.

outsole See under FOOTWEAR: SOLE.

oval cut See under GEMS, GEM CUTS, AND SETTINGS.

oval ruff See under NECKLINES AND COLLARS: RUFF.

oval toe See under FOOTWEAR.

oval trunk hose See under BOULOGNE HOSE.

overalls See under PANTS.

overblouse **1.** See under BLOUSES AND TOPS. **2.** See under SWIMWEAR: OVERBLOUSE SWIMSUIT.

overboot See under FOOTWEAR.

overcast/overcasting See under CLOTHING CONSTRUCTION DETAILS: OVERCAST SEAM and EMBROIDERIES AND SEWING STITCHES.

overcoat See under COATS AND JACKETS.

overdress **1.** See under DRESSES: OVERDRESS #1 and #2. Also see under DRESSES: CAGE DRESS.

overlapped seam See under GLOVES AND GLOVE CONSTRUCTION: FULL PIQUÉ and CLOTHING CONSTRUCTION DETAILS: LAP SEAM.

overlay See under FOOTWEAR.

overplaid See under PLAIDS AND TARTANS.

overseam See under GLOVES AND GLOVE CONSTRUCTION.

overseas cap See under HEADWEAR.

overshirt See under SHIRTS.

overshoe See under FOOTWEAR.

oversized See under SHIRTS and BLOUSES AND TOPS.

overskirt See under SKIRTS.

overstocks See under STOCKS.

over-the-knee boot See under FOOTWEAR.

over-the-knee socks See under HOSIERY.

owl glasses See under EYEWEAR.

oxford See under FOOTWEAR.

oxford bags See under PANTS.

oxford button-overs See under FOOTWEAR.

oxford cap See under ACADEMIC COSTUME: MORTARBOARD.

†oxford cloth Men's shirting fabric made in a basket weave, sometimes 2 × 2 and sometimes 4 × 2. Yarns may be all COMBED YARN or all CARDED YARN with crosswise yarns coarser than lengthwise. Better grades are mercerized (see under MERCERIZATION). The fabric may be bleached, dyed, and exhibit yarn-dyed stripes or small fancy designs. *Der.* Originally produced by a Scottish firm along with fabrics labeled yale, harvard, and cambridge, which are no longer important.

oxford coatee See under COATS AND JACKETS: OXONIAN JACKET.

Oxford glove See under GLOVES AND GLOVE CONSTRUCTION.

oxford tie See under TIES.

oxonian boots See under FOOTWEAR.

oxonian jacket See under COATS AND JACKETS.

oxonians See under FOOTWEAR: OXONIAN BOOTS.

oxonian shoe See under FOOTWEAR.

P See under PETITE.

pac boot See under FOOTWEAR.

Paco Rabanne hat See under HEADWEAR.

padded bra See under UNDERGARMENTS.

padded sleeve See under SHOULDERS AND SLEEVES.

padding Any stuffing material used between two layers of fabric or leather to give a rounded effect to clothing or accessories. At present padding is used mostly for warmth in the form of DOWN for coats and jackets or FIBERFILL for shaping in bras.

padding stitch See under EMBROIDERIES AND SEWING STITCHES.

paddock boot See under FOOTWEAR.

paddock coat See under COATS AND JACKETS.

padre hat See under HEADWEAR.

paenula See under CAPES, CLOAKS, AND SHAWLS.

∞**page** Belt with long loop of ribbon, cord, or velvet placed in either side. Used to loop up overskirt of dress from 1850 to 1867. Compare with DRESS CLIP/DRESS HOLDER.

pageboy See under HAIRSTYLES.

pagoda parasol See under UMBRELLAS AND PARASOLS.

pagoda sleeve See under SHOULDERS AND SLEEVES.

paillette (pay-et') Spangle made of metal or plastic, usually a round disk larger than a SEQUIN. Used as trimming on evening clothes and handbags. *Der.* French, "speck or spangle."

painter's *adj.* Used to describe clothing and accessories derived from or inspired by the dress of painters. See under HEADWEAR, JUMPERS, and PANTS for examples.

pair of bodies See under UNDERGARMENTS.

paisley print See under PRINTS, STRIPES, AND CHECKS.

paisley scarf See under SCARVES.

paisley shawl See under CAPES, CLOAKS, AND SHAWLS: CASHMERE SHAWL #2.

pajama checks See under PRINTS, STRIPES, AND CHECKS.

pajamas See under SLEEPWEAR AND LOUNGEWEAR.

pajama set See under SLEEPWEAR AND LOUNGEWEAR.

pajama stripes See under PRINTS, STRIPES, AND CHECKS.

pakistani vest See under VESTS.

palasade See under HEADWEAR: FONTANGE.

palatine 1. See under SCARVES. 2. See under CAPES, CLOAKS, AND SHAWLS: TIPPET.

palatine royal See under CAPES, CLOAKS, AND SHAWLS.

palazzo pants See under PANTS.

paletot See under COATS AND JACKETS.

paletot-cloak See under CAPES, CLOAKS, AND SHAWLS.

paletot-mantle See under CAPES, CLOAKS, AND SHAWLS.

paletot-redingote See under COATS AND JACKETS: PALETOT.

paletot-sac See under COATS AND JACKETS: PALETOT.

palisade See under HEADWEAR: COMMODE.

palla See under CAPES, CLOAKS, AND SHAWLS.

pallatine See under SCARVES: PALATINE.

pallium 1. See under CAPES, CLOAKS, AND SHAWLS. 2. See under CLERICAL DRESS.

palmerston wrapper See under COATS AND JACKETS.

paltock See under DOUBLET.

paludamentum See under CAPES, CLOAKS, AND SHAWLS.

pamela See under HEADWEAR.

panache (pah-nash') Plume or erect bunch of feathers worn on hat—originally used on military helmets.

panama hat See under HEADWEAR.

pancake beret See under HEADWEAR: BERET.

panel dress See under DRESSES.

panel pantdress See under DRESSES.

panel print See under PRINTS, STRIPES, AND CHECKS.

panel skirt See under SKIRTS.

∞**panes** Fabric strips cut vertically in a garment or fabric strips fastened together so that spaces appear between them. Used from 1500 to 1650s as a decorative device on sleeves, DOUBLETS, TRUNK HOSE. Shown at DOUBLET.

A contrasting lining, a shirt, or chemise was visible between the panes or might be pulled out to make a puff. See under PULLINGS OUT. Compare with SLASHING.

panier/paniers See under UNDERGARMENTS.

paniers à bourelet See under UNDERGARMENTS: PANIERS.

paniers à coudes See under UNDERGARMENTS: PANIERS.

paniers anglais See under UNDERGARMENTS: PANIERS.

panne satin See under SATIN.

†panne velvet (pan-ay') VELVET that has had the pile pressed down in one direction giving it a glossy appearance. Originally made with wool or silk pile and raw silk ply yarns; later with silk ground and flattened rayon pile. Uses: dresses and sportswear.

pannier/panniers (pan-yehr') **1.** See under UNDERGARMENTS. **2.** Puff formed over the hip by looping up the outer skirt. *Der.* Latin, *panarium,* "a basket for bread."

pannier bag See under HANDBAGS AND RELATED ACCESSORIES.

pannier crinoline See under UNDERGARMENTS: BUSTLE.

pannier curls See under HAIRSTYLES.

pannier drape (pan-yehr') **1.** See under UNDERGARMENTS: PANNIER. **∞2.** In late 1860s, puff formed over hip by looping up the outerskirt of a dress. **∞3.** In 1880s, fullness of drapery on hips made by an extra piece of fabric attached to bodice or waistline draped over hips with remainder pulled to the back in polonaise style (see under POLONAISE #1). **∞4.** In World War I era, drapery over hips sometimes made in tunic effect or sometimes cut as part of the dress to give a PEG-TOP look.

pannier dress See under DRESSES.

pannier skirt See under SKIRTS.

pant- *adj.* As a prefix, refers to styles that became prevalent when pants became accepted women's clothing for the office, daytime, and evening wear in the late 1960s. Examples: pantdress, pantshift and pantgown, pantjumper, and pantsuit.

pantalettes **1.** See under UNDERGARMENTS. **2.** See under PANTS.

pantaloons **1.** For men: See under PETTICOAT BREECHES. **2.** See under PANTS. **3.** For women: See under UNDERGARMENTS: PANTALETTES.

pantdress One-piece garment that has some type of pants in place of a skirt.

pantgown Full-length pantdress suitable for formal occasions, popular in late 1960s and early 1970s. Sometimes made with accordion-pleated pants attached to a halter top.

panties See under UNDERGARMENTS.

pantile See under HEADWEAR: COPOTAIN.

pantjumper See under JUMPERS.

pantofle See under FOOTWEAR.

PANTS

pants **1.** Clothing for the lower torso made to fit around each leg, may be any length and width; some have cuffs, and some do not. In early times various styles were worn by Persian and Anglo-Saxon men and also women in China and Middle Eastern countries. Although not referred to as pants until late 19th c.—when first used as a colloquial term for items worn by men and boys—now it is a broad term that encompasses all types of TROUSERS and BREECHES worn by children and adults. SLACKS (see under PANTS) for women became popular in the 1930s after Hollywood stars such as Marlene Dietrich and Katharine Hepburn wore them. They were also worn in war plants during World War II. All types of pants became very popular for women in late 1960s when pants became acceptable for business, townwear, school, and evening wear. Since that time many different styles of pants have gone in and out of fashion periodically and a wide variety of shapes and cuts in pant styles are always available to women. **2.** See under UNDERGARMENTS.

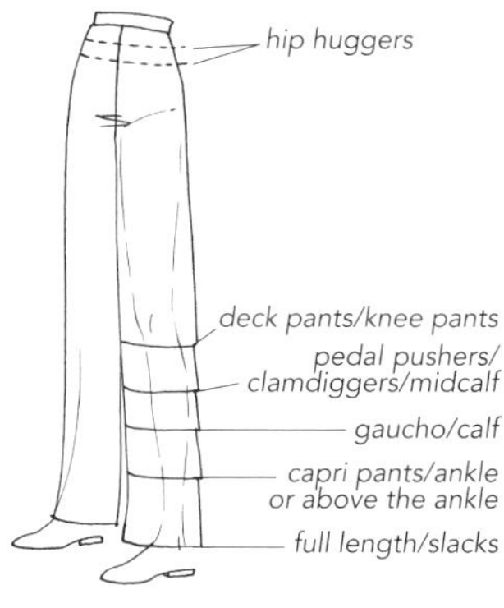

pant lengths

accordion-pleated pants See under PANTS: PARTY PANTS.

athletic pants See under PANTS: SWEATPANTS.

baggy pants Pants cut fuller through hips with legs tapering and becoming narrow at ankles. Term used originally for jeans in late 1970s, adopted for all types of pants in 1980s. Also called *baggies.*

bell-bottoms **1.** Pants cut with fullness on both the outer and inner seams to give a "bell" flare at the hem. Style most generally worn by

bell bottoms #1

young people in late 1960s and early 1970s and revived periodically. Also called FLARES (see under PANTS). **2.** See under PANTS: SAILOR PANTS.

bib-top pants See under PANTS: OVERALLS.

bleached jeans See under PANTS: BLUE JEANS.

bloomers **1.** Full pants of any length that are gathered at the end of the legs. Popularly worn under little girls' dresses in 1920s. **2.** Black, sateen, pleated bloomers worn for gym and camp by women from early 20th c. to late 1920s. *Der.* Name applied in 1851 to young ladies wearing rather narrow, ankle-length pants with elastic at the bottom in imitation of costume worn by AMELIA BLOOMER. Shown at BLOOMER COSTUME.

blue jeans Ankle-length pants traditionally made in faded blue or indigo denim. Originally worn by farmers and workmen, pants were styled with top-stitching, two hip pockets, two side pockets, a V-shaped yoke in back, and rivets reinforcing points of strain. In the late 1960s, adapted for the general public as fashionable casualwear with flared legs in same cut but made of many fabrics, including denim, bleached denim, printed fabrics, suede, stripes, corduroy, and even velvet. In the 1960s, **bleached jeans,** with their faded worn look, became popular, as were STONEWASHED or acid-washed jeans in the 1980s; this process produced an uneven color. In the 1970s, jeans with a small watch pocket added to carry money were accepted for school wear. Now a classic garment style, jean leg styles conform to the current mode. LEVI'S 501S represent the classic Levi's style which has evolved over time. See also under PANTS: LEVI'S. Also called *dungarees, Levi's, jeans, dude jeans,* and *designer jeans.* Also see under PANTS: BAGGY PANTS.

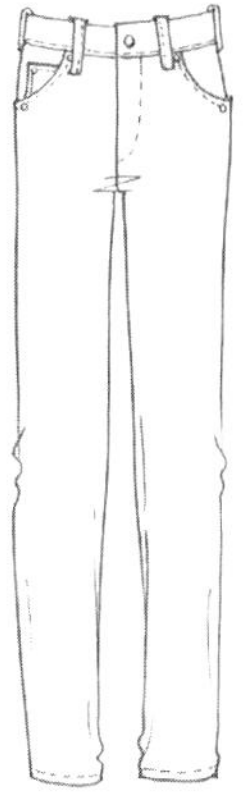
blue jeans

boot-cut pants Refers to the width at hem of pants—cut wide enough so that pant leg can be pulled over the outside of a pair of western boots.

boyfriend jeans/pants Pants with a relaxed fit through the thighs and rear as if a woman is wearing her boyfriend's pants.

breaker pants Straight-legged pants with zipper at side seam that shows contrasting lining when opened. May have zippered back pocket and grommet trim. *Der.* From break dancing, which requires a lot of movement.

breeches Pants reaching to below the knee, worn particularly for horseback riding. Also see under BREECHES. *Der.* From word "breech," plural of Old English *broc,* "leg covering." Also see under PANTS: HUNT BREECHES and ACTIVEWEAR: RIDING BREECHES.

cabin-boy breeches Tight-fitting pants laced below the knees worn for sportswear by women in the late 1940s. *Der.* Named after uniform worn by an employee on an ocean vessel who waits on officers and passengers.

camouflage pants A style of pants that is characteristically printed with greens and browns in an abstract pattern, first used by the military for safety, and adapted for general wear in around the 1980s. Originally used as camouflage wear for the Army because the colors of the fabric easily blended with scenery.

canary breeches See under ACTIVEWEAR: RIDING BREECHES.

capri pants (kap'-ree or kap-ree') **1.** Tight-fitting, three-quarter-length pants, with short slit on outside of leg. Worn in 1950s, revived after 2000. **2.** Tight-fitting, trademarked jeans, with slit on outside of leg, called *Capri®* *jeans.* Worn in 1980s. *Der.* Named for Italian resort, Island of Capri, where style first became popular.

cargo pants Any pants with CARGO POCKETS (see under POCKETS).

carpenter pants Pants style derived from pants traditionally worn by carpenters, which not only have front and back pockets, but also have a loop for a hammer and a pocket for tools on one leg.

chaps Covering for the legs worn over pants, made to cover the legs and a front girdle, but without a seat. Originally worn by cowboys, made of leather or shearling. Adopted by women as fashion item in the late 1960s. *Der.* Shortened form of Spanish word *chaparejas,* "undressed sheepskin."

chaps

charro pants (char'-row) Wide Mexican-inspired pants in midi length, similar to GAUCHO pants (see under PANTS). *Der.* Mexican, "rancher."

chinos Washable man's sport pants made of chino cloth, a durable, close-woven, khaki-colored cotton fabric. Popular in 1950s for sportswear and for schoolwear since the early 1960s. *Der.* Adapted from Army summer uniforms made of fabric that originally was purchased in China before World War I.

choori-dars (cho-ree'-dars) Pants with full-cut top and tight-fitting legs that are extra long and worn rumpled from knee down. Worn in 1960s, increasing in popularity in 1980s. *Der.* From pants worn in India called by the same name.

cigarette pant Straight, narrow pant for women that tapers to a narrow opening.

city pants Women's trousers considered suitable for wear in town as well as at home or for sportswear. Term coined by fashion industry newspaper *Women's Wear Daily* in 1968. Also see under SHORTS: CITY SHORTS.

clamdiggers/Clamdiggers® Trademark registered in 1946 by White Stag Manufacturing Co. for mid-calf slacks and snug-fitting calf-length pants. Originating from cut-off BLUE JEANS (see under PANTS), worn while wading to dig for clams. Adopted for sportswear in 1950s. At present the trademark applies to a wide variety of apparel.

continental pants Man's trousers styled with fitted waistband and no belt. Front pockets are placed horizontally or curved to waistband seam rather than placed in the side seams. Popular in late 1960s, the style originated in Italy.

cords/corduroys Jean-cut pants made from cotton corduroy fabric; more recent versions may include a percentage of Lycra.

∞cossacks Peg-top trousers made with double straps under the instep. Worn by men from 1814 to about 1850, these pants were adapted from the full trousers worn by Cossack soldiers in the entourage of the czar of Russia at a peace celebration in 1814.

crawlers Slacks for infants and also sizes 1 through 3, frequently made in bib-overall style of corduroy and other fabrics. Formerly called *creepers.*

creepers See under PANTS: CRAWLERS.

cropped pants Pants cut at varying lengths between ankle and knee. The most common type was cut just below the knee. Since 1984, newer versions have been full cut, longer, and sometimes pleated into the waistband or snug-fitting.

cuffed trousers See under PANTS: PRE-CUFFED TROUSERS.

culottes (ku-lotz') Pants of any length cut to look like a skirt. Worn from 1930s to 1940s and again in 1960s and very popular in the 1980s and after. In 1986 some culottes were worn knee-length in a pleated style, sometimes with a matching jacket. *Der.* French, *culotte,* "pants."

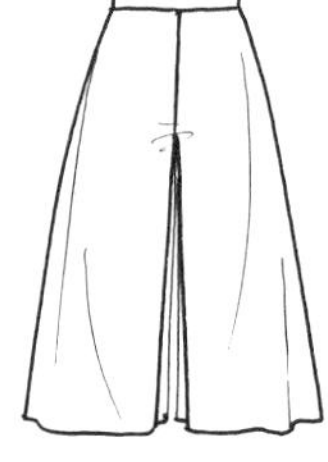
culottes

cut-offs See under SHORTS.

∞danish trousers Pants worn by young boys in 1870s that were calf-length and open at the hems. Also called *open-bottom trousers.*

deck pants Fitted pants ending below the knees; worn by men, women, and children particularly on boats in late 1950s and early 1960s.

designer jeans Jeans produced by well-known designers, after blue jeans became fashionable for men, women, and children for general wear at school and some offices. Noted designers such as Calvin Klein and Gloria Vanderbilt produced them in higher priced lines, usually attaching their names to the hip pocket and trademarking their product. Especially popular in the late 1970s.

dhoti (doe'tee) Pants with many gathers at waistband, made long between the legs and tapering to ankle. *Der.* From pants worn in India called by the same name. Also see alphabetical listing.

dirndl pants (durn'-del) Culottes or pants styled with gathers at the waistline, introduced in early 1980s. Sometimes made in seven-eighths length with large pockets in side seams and decorative braided belt.

drain-pipe trousers Pants with legs cut straight, having the same diameter for the length of the garment and with no crease.

drawstring pants Pull-on pants, usually of cotton, with drawstring at top. A unisex fashion of the late 1960s. Now a classic style. Also called *unisex pants.*

drop-front *adj.* Descriptive of pants fastened by two buttoned plackets on either side of the center front, allowing the front panel to drop down when unbuttoned. Used frequently on JODHPURS, other RIDING BREECHES (see under ACTIVEWEAR), and in the past on U.S. Navy seamen's pants. An earlier version of this section of pants was call the FALL.

∞ducks Trousers worn by men in late 19th c. made of DUCK fabric.

dude jeans Similar to WESTERN PANTS (see under PANTS). Also see under PANTS: BLUE JEANS.

dungarees Work pants or overalls named for the coarse blue fabric from which they are made. Also see PANTS: BLUE JEANS.

∞eelskin masher trousers Very tight trousers worn in mid-1880s by MASHER or DANDY. *Der.* Literally, "as tight as an eel's skin."

elephant-leg pants Trousers with extremely wide legs similar to HARLOW PANTS (see under PANTS). Introduced in late 1960s.

fatigues **1.** Pants of tough fabric worn by U.S. Army for work details. Also called *field pants.* **2.** Coveralls for work worn by Army men and WACS during World War II, sometimes made in olive drab or camouflage colors.

field pants See under PANTS: FATIGUES #1.

flares **1.** See under PANTS: BELL-BOTTOMS. **2.** Pants with slight flare at hem.

flat front pants Pants that are made without pleats or fullness in the front.

∞french bottoms 19th-c. term for men's trousers flaring at the hems.

frontier pants See under PANTS: WESTERN PANTS.

gaucho pants (gow'-cho) Wide, calf-length, women's pants, frequently made of leather, copied from pants worn by Spaniards as a part of Andalusian riding suit and adapted by South American cowboys; a fashion in the late 1960s. *Der.* Spanish, "cow-boy" of Argentina, Chile, and Uruguay. Shown at GAUCHO.

harem knickers Knee-length bouffant harem pants similar to BLOOMERS (see under PANTS), introduced in late 1960s.

harem pants Bouffant pants gathered into bands at the ankles, popular at-home fashion of late 1960s. *Der.* Copied from Near Eastern styles.

harem pants

harlow pants Trousers wide from hips to hem, introduced in late 1960s. *Der.* Copied from slacks worn in 1930s by Jean Harlow, a popular film star.

high-rise pants Pants that extend to above the waistline, as opposed to HIP-HUGGERS.

hip-huggers Low-slung pants of any style starting below the normal waistline, usually with belt resting on hip bones. First popular in mid-1960s. Also called *hipsters* and *low-slung pants.*

hipsters See under PANTS: HIP-HUGGERS.

∞**howling bags** (slang) Men's trousers made of colorful patterned fabrics worn in mid-19th c.

hunt breeches See under ACTIVEWEAR.

ivy league pants Type of men's trousers with "skinny" legs, usually without cuffs, cut somewhat shorter in length. Worn first by college men and introduced for general wear in 1950s. *Der.* From the group of eastern colleges called the Ivy League.

∞**jack tar trousers** Man's trousers, close-fitting at knees, flaring widely around ankles, and worn for yachting in 1880s. *Der.* "a sailor."

jeans See under PANTS: BLUE JEANS.

jeggings Very tight denim leggings similar in appearance to blue jeans. The name derives from a combination of the words "jeans" and "leggings."

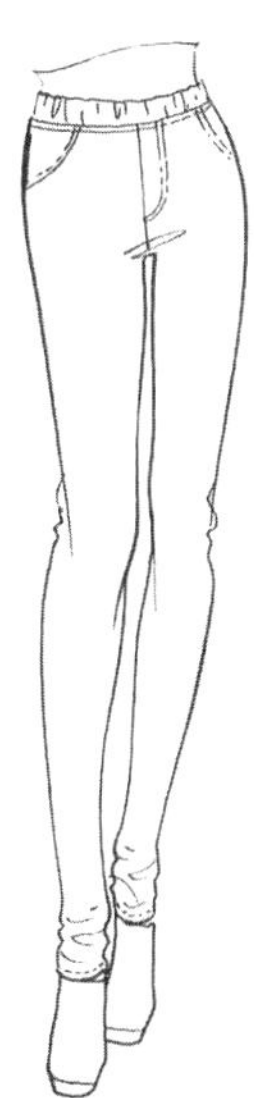
jeggings

jockey pants See under ACTIVEWEAR.

jodhpurs See under ACTIVEWEAR.

knee pants See under PANTS: KNICKERS.

knickers **1.** Pants of varying widths fastened below knee with buttons, buckles, or elastic; popular for boys in early 20th c. for school. Reintroduced in late 1960s for women and men. Worn for hiking and cross-country skiing. **2.** See under UNDERGARMENTS. *Der.* shortened form of word *knickerbockers.* Also called *knee pants.* Also see under KNICKERS and KNICKERBOCKERS in the alphabetical listing.

leggings **1.** Outer pants for children worn in cold weather and usually matched to a coat, making a leggings set. Made in any of several styles: with tight-fitting legs, sometimes cut like JODHPURS (see under ACTIVEWEAR) or full to the ankle where they are held by a knitted band. Also spelled *leggins.* **2.** Ankle-length, skintight pants made from thin Lycra spandex knit fabrics. Originally worn by dancers and entertainers in brilliant colors or in regular knits with LEOTARDS (see under ACTIVEWEAR) in place of tights for exercising. Adopted by women for general wear in place of pants after the 1980s. Some have stirrup straps (see under PANTS: STIRRUP PANTS) at foot.

Levi's® Trademark for type of DUNGAREES or BLUE JEANS (see under PANTS). Distinguishing characteristics are a label stitched to the outside on one hip pocket, also the placing of rivets at places of most strain, and patch pockets placed at hips. First made out of cloth used for sails—later DENIM was used—by Levi Strauss in California for miners prospecting for gold in 1840s. A distinctly American fashion, it developed into a multimillion-dollar industry, with many pairs exported yearly. The Costume Institute of the Metropolitan Museum in New York and the Smithsonian Institution in Washington, D.C., have included Levi's in their Americana collections. The trademark is also used for a wide variety of casual apparel.

low-rise jeans Pants designed to sit below or low on the hips; a rise of 4 inches to 7.5 inches (rise = distance from the crotch to the button at the waist).

low-slung pants See under PANTS: HIP-HUGGERS.

luau pants (loo-ow') Man's calf-length pants styled in colorful Hawaiian print. *Der.* From Hawaiian luau parties, where these pants were first worn.

maternity pants Pants worn by expectant mothers with either a cut-out section at top center front or a section of stretch fabric inserted over the abdomen.

∞**moschettos** (mos-ket'-tos) Pants similar to men's pantaloons (see under PANTS: PANTALOONS #2) of early 19th c. but fitted to leg and worn over a boot like GAITER (see under FOOTWEAR).

mousers Women's leather stocking pants reaching to waist, made of shiny wet-look leather with attached chunky-type shoes. Introduced by Mary Quant, British designer, in 1969.

ochy pant A pant with a front hip pocket opening that extends out from the body; popularized by Maria Cornejo.

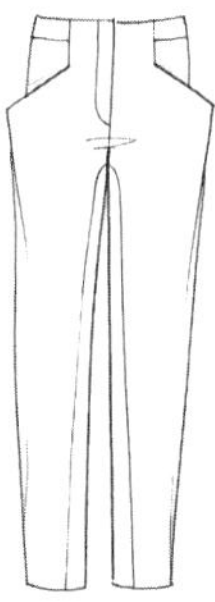
ochy pants

overalls Pants with a bib top and suspender straps over the shoulders that cross in back. Traditionally made in blue denim and worn by farmers. House painters and carpenters wore them in natural or white. See under PANTS: PAINTER'S PANTS. Also made of striped fabrics and worn by railroad workers. In late 1960s, styled in many fabrics for all occasions and worn by adults and children. Also called *bib-top pants* and *suspender pants.* **Pleated overalls** introduced in early 1980s are similar in style but cut all in one piece in front with much fullness at top, which was pleated into a band. *Der.* So called because originally worn over clothing.

overalls

oxford bags Men's long trousers with very wide cuffed legs. Popular in the 1920s, beginning at Oxford University in England and revived for men and women in early 1970s.

painter's pants 1. Natural-colored or white pants, styled with one or more loops on legs to hold brushes, originally worn by house painters. Adapted as a fashion item in late 1970s and worn for school and sportswear. Made in colors since 1980s. 2. See under PANTS: OVERALLS.

pajamas See under SLEEPWEAR AND LOUNGEWEAR.

palazzo pants (pah-latz'-zoh) Women's long, wide pajamas or culottes with voluminous flared legs and gathered waist. Worn for lounging or evening dress in the late 1960s and early 1970s.

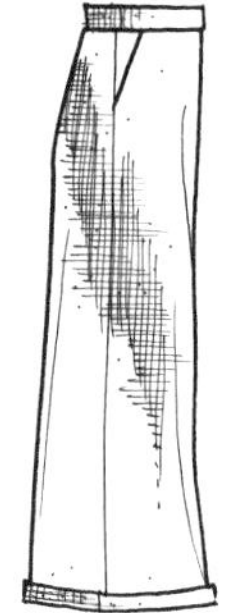
oxford bags 1920s

pantaloons 1. See under PETTICOAT BREECHES. ∞2. From 1790 to about 1850, tight-fitting pants. They ended at the calf, until 1817. Later they extended to ankles, with strap under the instep. Known as *tights* around 1840. 3. For women: See under UNDERGARMENTS: PANTALETTES.

parachute pants Straight-legged pants with zipper (of about 6″) from hem up leg to give tight fit at ankles. Three zip pockets are placed at side of leg, and another zip pocket on hip.

party pants Name adopted in late 1960s for women's pants and pajamas made in more elaborate fabrics and sometimes accordion-pleated. Styled to wear for dining and dancing in the evening.

pedal pushers Below-the-knee, straight-cut, women's pants, often cuffed. Popular during World War II for bicycling; reintroduced in 1980s.

peg-top pants 1. Pants pleated at the waistband and narrow at the ankles. ∞2. Man's trousers wide and pleated at top, tapered on lower leg, and close fitting at ankles. Popular from 1857 to 1865 and revived in 1892.

∞**Petersham cossacks** Trousers worn by men from 1814, modified in 1820s, and worn into the 1830s. Very bouffant and worn spread out over the foot, drawn in with ribbon tied in bows on outside of leg and worn with flounces at ankles. Also called *Petersham trousers. Der.* Named for Viscount Charles Petersham.

plain-front pants Trousers without pleats at the waistband so that the front is smoothly fitted.

plain-front pants

pleated-front pants Trousers with pleats at waistband in front, giving more fullness through the hips.

pleated overalls See under PANTS: OVERALLS.

plus fours Full baggy knickers worn for golf and other sports in the 1920s. They became stylish after they were worn by DUKE OF WINDSOR, then Prince of Wales. Generally combined with patterned wool socks and BROGUES (see under FOOTWEAR). Reintroduced for men in late 1960s. *Der.* When first introduced, the length of these knickers was 4 inches longer than typical knicker length. See under KNICKERBOCKERS.

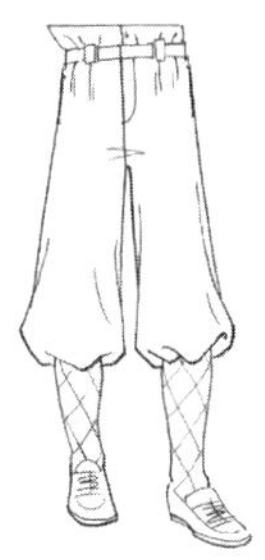
plus fours 1920s

pre-cuffed trousers Men's trousers sold in various lengths (e.g., 27″, 29″, and 31″ for inside seam), with cuff already finished. As contrasted with trousers bought with unfinished hems, tailored to length, and finished in retail store workroom.

proportioned pants Men's or women's pants for which customers are given a choice from among three or four different named pant lengths. The names and specific lengths will vary somewhat from manufacturer to manufacturer. Most men's pants are sold by waist measurement and inseam length, but some may be designated as short, regular, or long. Women's pants are more likely to be sold by proportion such as petite, average, and tall sizes.

pull-on pants Stretch pants with an elasticized waistband that do not have a placket.

push-up jeans JEANS (see under PANTS) made with spandex that lift and shape the buttocks of the wearer.

∞**railroad trousers** Men's trousers with horizontal or vertical stripes, worn from late 1830s to 1850.

riding breeches See under ACTIVEWEAR.

sailor pants Worn by sailors—navy blue during winter and white during summer. Now made in conventional style with zip closing. Originally made in bell-bottom style with drop-front closing having thirteen buttons representing the thirteen original states. Seven buttons went across horizontally with three additional buttons extending vertically at each side. Also called *bell-bottoms.*

see-through pants Women's pants of sheer fabric or lace worn over bikini pants—a style of the late 1960s.

seven-eighths pants Any style pants coming to just below the calf of the leg.

shorts See under SHORTS.

show breeches See under ACTIVEWEAR: HUNT BREECHES.

skant Women's full-length pants that have a short, skirt-like layer that is open at the side and attached at the waist.

skinny jeans Blue jeans cut with very narrow legs, frequently made of stretch denim worn literally "skintight."

ski pants See under ACTIVEWEAR.

skort See under SKIRTS.

slacks Loose-cut casual pants that are not part of a suit. In the 1930s, when women first began wearing pants for leisure activities, these garments were generally called *slacks* rather than pants. Synonym: *pants.*

∞**spring-bottom trousers** Trousers worn in the 1870s and 1880s that flare at the ankles.

stirrup pants Pants, usually made in a narrow style, having an extension under the instep that can be worn inside or under the shoe.

stovepipe pants Tight-fitting pants with narrow legs of the same width from knees down. Worn by men from 1880 until 1920, reintroduced in mid-1960s, popular in 1980s, and revived periodically.

straight-cut pants Pants straight cut from knee down. See under PANTS: STOVEPIPE PANTS.

∞**strapped trousers** Man's trousers fashionable from 1820s to 1850s made with one or two straps under the instep.

stretch pants Pants made from knitted stretch fabric that conform closely to the body, very popular from 1950s to mid-1960s. In 1980s, popular for jeans made of stretch denim.

surfers Close-fitting pants extending to knee, popular in early 1960s. *Der.* Introduced for beachwear and surfboard riding in California.

suspender pants 1. See under OVERALLS. 2. Children's pull-on pants with straps made of same fabric as pants.

sweatpants Pants of cotton knit with fleece backing to absorb moisture. Worn by athletes before and after exercising. Also called *warmup pants.*

tapered pants Full-length pants with legs becoming narrower toward the ankle, popular in early 1960s and 1980s and periodically since, depending on whether wider or narrower pants are fashionable.

tights 1. See under HOSIERY and UNDERGARMENTS. 2. See under PANTS: PANTALOONS.

toreador pants (tor-ay-ah-door') Tight-fitting, below-the-knee pants patterned after those worn by Spanish bullfighters, popular for women in late 1950s and early 1960s.

track pants Flat-front, straight-leg running pants with an elastic waist; often designed with side zippers or snaps on the outer seam so athletes can remove their pants without taking off their shoes.

trousers Synonym for all full-length pants. The word origin is uncertain; most likely it derives from the Irish word for a garment similar to BREECHES. By the 17th c., they had been used as protective garment worn over breeches; and in the 18th and 19th c. they were loose-fitting pants worn particularly by sailors, soldiers, and town workers. By the 19th c., the term came to have the modern meaning of pants. *Der.* From *trouse,* a variation of *trews.*

turkish trousers See under PANTS: HAREM PANTS.

∞**turnip pants** Bicycling knickers that could be turned down to become full-length pants, worn in 1890s.

∞**turn-ups** Man's cuffed trousers first worn in House of Commons in 1893, as they were called in Great Britain.

tuxedo pants 1. Men: Conventional black trousers, usually with narrow satin stripe down each side, worn with TUXEDO JACKET (see under COATS AND JACKETS) and CUMMERBUND (see under BELTS) for semiformal wear. 2. Women: Pants made with gathers at waistline, worn with a cummerbund, and introduced in 1980s.

unisex pants See under PANTS: DRAWSTRING PANTS.

warmup pants See under PANTS: SWEATPANTS and ACTIVEWEAR: WARMUP #2.

western pants Low-waisted, slim-fitting pants made of denim or gabardine, characterized by double-stitched seams and rivets placed at points of strain. Often with pockets opening at both top and side, producing right-angle front flaps that are buttoned at the corners. Also see PANTS: BLUE JEANS. Originally worn by ranchers and cowboys in American West. Popular for general wear since mid-1960s. Also called *dude jeans* and *frontier pants.*

white flannels Slacks made of white wool, especially flannel, worn by men in 1980s. Reminiscent of those worn from 1890s through 1930s for sportswear with striped blazer and straw hat.

work pants Durable full-length trousers with patches at knees, triple-stitched main seams, and rivets at points of strain. Worn by auto mechanics and other workmen. Styled with watch pocket, tool pockets, and hammer loop on the legs. Made of durable, washable fabric.

wrapped-leg pant A pant designed with extra fabric from the side seam extending across the front leg; extension may begin at the hip or further down the leg. Also called *petal pant*.

yoga pants Pants made of a fabric with give to allow the wearer to flex, bend, and move.

zippered pants Straight-legged pants with one zipper from waist to ankle and second zipper from waist to upper thigh on each leg. Snap tabs hold pants tightly at ankle.

---

pants boot See under FOOTWEAR.

pantshift Simple pantdress cut like a shift dress—made with pants instead of a skirt.

pants liner See under UNDERGARMENTS.

pantskirt See under SKIRTS.

pantsuit A woman's suit with pants instead of a skirt, styled for town wear and evening wear, introduced in the mid-1960s. Some are of traditional styling with jackets. Others are composed of a thigh-length tunic and pants. Some formal pantsuits are styled in elaborate fabrics. Also made with matching vest or coat and with various types of pants including knickers.

pantsuit

panty See under UNDERGARMENTS: PANTIES.

panty dress See under DRESSES.

panty foundation See under UNDERGARMENTS.

panty-girdle See under UNDERGARMENTS: GIRDLE.

pantyhose See under HOSIERY.

pantyslip See under UNDERGARMENTS.

pantywaist See under UNDERGARMENTS.

paperbag waistline See under WAISTLINES.

paper-doll dress See under DRESSES.

paper dress See under DRESSES.

paper pattern Dress pattern made in various sizes and sold by pattern companies such as Vogue, Butterick, McCalls, and Simplicity to individuals for home sewing. At first, paper patterns were not made in sizes, but offered to subscribers of magazines such as *Harper's Bazaar* in supplements. Patterns for eighteen garments were sometimes placed on one large sheet of paper. Pieces for each pattern were made with different types of lines (e.g., ... or ______). To make a pattern, women copied these lines with a tracing wheel on tracing paper and enlarged the pattern to the proper size. Ebenezer Butterick invented patterns in various sizes in 1872. These were sold through fashion magazines such as *The Delineator* and *Demorest's Magazine*.

†paper taffeta Crisp, lightweight taffeta fabric.

papier-mâché/paper-mâché (pap'-yeh mah-shay'/pay'-per mah-shay') Lightweight material molded of combination of tissue paper, bits of newspaper, or paper pulp fastened together with glue or various binders. May be painted and shellacked. Used for jewelry, particularly bracelets, beads, and pins in late 1960s. *Der.* French, "chewed paper."

papillion See under HEADWEAR: BONNET À BEC.

papillon collar See under NECKLINES AND COLLARS.

papillotte comb See under HAIR ACCESSORIES.

parachute hat See under HEADWEAR: BALLOON HAT.

parachute pants See under PANTS.

parachute sleeve See under SHOULDERS AND SLEEVES.

paradise feather See under FEATHERS: BIRD-OF-PARADISE FEATHER.

parament (pah-rah'-ment) ∞**1.** Early name for a FACING (see under CLOTHING CONSTRUCTION DETAILS). **2.** See under CUFFS. ∞**3.** Trimming used on GOWN À LA FRANÇAISE in 18th c., usually a long, decorated band, wider at hem. **4.** Synonym for an ornamental ecclesiastical vestment.

parasol See under introduction to UMBRELLAS AND PARASOLS.

parasol a la Pompadour See under UMBRELLAS AND PARASOLS: MARQUISE.

parasol fan See under FANS: COCKADE FAN.

parasol skirt See under SKIRTS.

parchment calves See under FALSE CALVES.

pardessus See under COATS AND JACKETS.

pareo (pah-ray'-o) Rectangular piece of colored printed cloth worn as a skirt or loincloth as the principal item of clothing for men and women of Polynesia. Adaptations popular in the U.S. as beach fashion in 1950s and after. Also called *lava-lava*.

pareo

paris, point de See under LACES.

parka See under COATS AND JACKETS.

partial roll See under NECKLINES AND COLLARS.

parti-colored Bicolored garment divided vertically, with each side made of a different color—or striped on one side, plain on the other. Popular from mid-14th to mid-15th c. for hose and clothing. When hose were different colors, they might be called *pied hose.* Synonym: *mi-parti.*

parti-colored clothing

∞**partlet/parlet** (part′-let) **1.** Decorative covering for upper part of chest and neck showing under low-cut doublet worn by men in first half of 16th c. **2.** Fill-in for low-cut *bodice* worn by women in 16th and 17th c. Also called *chemisette* and *tucker.*

party *adj.* Describes clothes made to be suitable for parties. See under SLEEPWEAR AND LOUNGEWEAR: PARTY PAJAMAS and PANTS: PARTY PANTS.

party plan Sale of apparel to invited customers at a party in the home of a host or hostess. Also called *home party.*

parure See under JEWELRY.

pashm See under CAPES, CLOAKS, AND SHAWLS: CASHMERE SHAWL.

†**pashmina** (pash-mee′-nah) Synonym for CASHMERE; used in the 1990s and after to promote fine-quality cashmere apparel.

passé/passé de mode (pass-ay′) (French) "Out of fashion," "unfashionable." Generally used in English simply as *passé.*

passement See under LACES.

passementerie (pas-mahn′-tree) Trimmings, e.g., heavy embroideries, braid, tinsel, beads, lace, and gimp, used as edging in 19th c.

paste See under JEWELRY.

paste setting See under GEMS, GEM CUTS, AND SETTINGS.

pasties See under UNDERGARMENTS.

patch **1.** Extra piece of fabric sewed or bonded by heat to clothing for mending a tear or for decorative effect (e.g., suede elbow patches on sweaters and knee patches on blue jeans). **2.** Insignia sewed to sleeve of uniform to indicate rank. **3.** From 1590s to end of 18th c., a decorative cutout of black silk or velvet shaped like moon, star, etc., applied to the face. Placement of patch denoted the wearer's mood (e.g., the "coquette" was placed on the lip; the "roguish" was placed on the nose; the "impassioned" was placed at the corner of the eye). From 1702 to 1714, in England, the patch indicated the political party of the wearer. Also called *beauty spot* or *mouche.* **4.** Flesh-colored pieces of cotton, affixed to the face with adhesive, used to cover blemishes in early 20th c., were known as *court plasters. Der.* From cutouts of black silk or velvet adhered to the face by ladies of the English and French courts beginning in late 17th c.

patches #3 17th c.

patch box Small box carried by women in 17th c. to hold various types of decorative cutouts called PATCHES (see under PATCH #3) that were applied to face.

patch pocket See under POCKETS.

patchwork A method of sewing small pieces of various colors and patterns together to form a fabric or quilt.

patchwork apparel Small pieces of various-colored prints and plain colors sewed together to make the fabric from which dress or other garment is cut. Became high fashion when introduced by Saint Laurent in 1969. Old antique American patchwork quilts were found and used to make coats and skirts. Also featured in leather of different colors and patterns in 1980s. From this style, printed fabrics evolved that were made to have the appearance of actual patchwork. *Der.* From *patchwork quilt*—a country craft practiced in the U.S. since colonial days.

patchwork apparel

patchwork print See under PRINTS, STRIPES, AND CHECKS.

patent Registration of an idea, product, or process with the U.S. patent office so that it is excluded from use by others for a period of 17 years. A description of the invention is published and once the patent expires, it becomes part of the public domain.

patent leather See under LEATHERS.

patio dress See under DRESSES.

patlet See under PARTLET.

patrol jacket See under COATS AND JACKETS.

∞**patte** (pat) Earliest form of lapel, resembling a narrow collar with tabs, worn on GARNACHE in 13th and 14th c. Also called *paw.*

patten See under FOOTWEAR.

pattern book Large volume issued regularly (and updated) by the publisher of paper patterns for home sewers, showing all of the designs available. Available where patterns are sold for convenience of customers. Also called *counter book.*

pattern design system (PDS) Computer system used to create and store new garment and pattern styles.

pattern grading Creating a set of pattern pieces for each of the sizes listed on the garment specification sheet from the production pattern pieces made in the sample size for a style.

patterned hose See under HOSIERY.

pauldron See under ARMOR.

paultock See under PALTOCK.

pavé See under GEMS, GEM CUTS, AND SETTINGS.

pavilion See under GEMS, GEM CUTS, AND SETTINGS.

paw 1. See under PATTE. 2. See under FURS.

paw crosses See under FURS: CROSSES.

PCM See under PHASE-CHANGE MATERIALS.

peace ring See under JEWELRY.

peace symbol Circle or oval enclosing a vertical staff with two bars projecting at about a 60-degree angle down to left and right from center of staff. Introduced in 1960s by opponents of U.S. involvement in Vietnam War. Often displayed on rings and medallions.

peacock feather See under FEATHERS.

peacock revolution Beginning in 1967, radical changes in men's wear from the conventional type of clothing (i.e., the gray flannel three-button suit worn with buttoned-down shirt and necktie) to clothing of a more relaxed, more creative, unconventional type. New styles accepted for men's wear included turtleneck knit shirts, Nehru jackets, flared pants, Edwardian coats, medallion necklaces, rings, perfumes, wider color ranges, and less conservative hairstyles.

peacock revolution

pea jacket/coat See under COATS AND JACKETS.

peaked lapel See under NECKLINES AND COLLARS: LAPEL.

peaked shoe See under FOOTWEAR: CRAKOW.

pear cut See under GEMS, GEM CUTS, AND SETTINGS.

pearl See under GEMS, GEM CUTS, AND SETTINGS.

pearl beads See under JEWELRY.

pearl button See under CLOSURES.

pearl dress See under DRESSES.

∞**peasant bodice** Woman's bodice of mid-1880s worn over a blouse. It laced up the front, reaching the bustline, and had straps extending over outermost edge of shoulder.

peasant apparel Clothing that is adapted from or inspired by European peasant dress originally worn for festive occasions by peasants in various countries. Although each region had its own distinctive style, peasant dress came to be thought of as having full skirts gathered at the waist, full puffed sleeves, and drawstring neckline trimmed with embroidery. Sometimes an apron or black-laced CORSELET (see under BELTS) was added. See under BLOUSES AND TOPS: PEASANT BLOUSE; COATS AND JACKETS: PEASANT COAT; NECKLINES AND COLLARS: PEASANT NECKLINE; SHOULDERS AND SLEEVES: PEASANT SLEEVE; and SKIRTS: PEASANT SKIRT.

peascod-bellied doublet See under DOUBLET.

†**peau de soie** (po de swah') Heavyweight satin with a fine filling ribbed effect on the reverse side made of silk or manufactured fibers. Piece-dyed and given a dull luster—better grades are reversible. Used for shoes, dresses, evening gowns, and wedding dresses. *Der.* French, "skin of silk."

pebbled finish See under LEATHERS.

peccary See under LEATHERS.

pedal pushers See under PANTS.

pediment headdress See under HEADWEAR: ENGLISH HOOD.

pedlar dolls See under MODEL DOLLS.

Peds® See under HOSIERY.

peek-a-boo Any part of a garment that has been cut out to reveal skin or underwear.

peek-a-boo earrings See under JEWELRY.

peek-a-boo-waist See under BLOUSES AND TOPS.

peeptoe See under FOOTWEAR: OPEN-TOED SHOES.

peggy collar See under NECKLINES AND COLLARS.

peg-top Apparel with fullness through hips that tapers to hem. See under PANTS: PEG-TOP; SHOULDERS AND SLEEVES: PEG-TOP SLEEVE; and SKIRTS: PEG-TOP SKIRT.

peigne josephine See under HAIR ACCESSORIES.

peignoir See under SLEEPWEAR AND LOUNGEWEAR.

pelerine See under CAPES, CLOAKS, AND SHAWLS.

pelisse See under COATS AND JACKETS.

∞**pelisse-robe** See under DRESSES.

∞**pellison** (pel'-iss-ohn) Fur-lined outer tunic or gown for men and women worn between the 14th c. and 16th c. Also called *pilch.*

†**Pellon®** A nonwoven fabric used for interlining and made by fusing natural fibers and man-made fibers together. Retains its shape through laundering and dry cleaning. Uses: interlining in collars and facings.

pelt See under FURS.

peltry See under FURS: PELT.

pembroke paletot See under COATS AND JACKETS.

penang lawyer See under CANES.

∞**penannular brooch** A moveable pin set on a ring that was used to fasten clothing from 11th through 13th c. A Medieval metal brooch used to fasten cloaks or capes that consisted of ring with an open space or break and a nail-shaped, sharp pin that fit into the open break area. When compared with the ANNULAR BROOCH this type of closure was more effective in holding the fabric in place.

pencil pocket See under POCKETS.

pencil stripe See under PRINTS, STRIPES, AND CHECKS.

pendant An ornament that hangs or dangles. See under JEWELRY and WATCHES.

pendant cuff See under CUFFS.

pendicle See under JEWELRY.

penny loafer See under FOOTWEAR: LOAFER.

pentes See under SKIRTS.

peplos See under CHITON.

peplum (pep′-lum) Extension of bodice of dress that comes below waistline, sometimes pleated, sometimes flared. Can be made in one piece with bodice, cut separately and joined to bodice by a seam or attached to a belt. Popular in mid-1860s, 1890s, and revived periodically in the 20th c. Also see under BLOUSES AND TOPS: PEPLUM BLOUSE.

peplum c. 1950s

∞**peplum basque** (bask) Woman's dress of mid-1860s with peplum attached to belt. Peplum was usually short in back and front with long hanging ends at sides.

∞**peplum bodice** Bodice of evening dress, worn in 1870s, cut with long side panels draped to form *panniers* at hips.

peplum dolman See under COATS AND JACKETS: DOLMAN.

peplum dress See under DRESSES.

peplum rotonde See under CAPES, CLOAKS, AND SHAWLS.

peplum shirt See under SHIRTS.

†**percale** Plain-weave, lightweight fabric made in a great variety of qualities. Originally produced using cotton, better qualities now use blended yarns of polyester staple with the cotton. Finest qualities are high count and made with combed yarns. Other percales are of low count, made of carded yarns, and sized to add body to the fabric. All types may be dyed or printed.

perdita chemise See under DRESSES.

perfecto jacket See under COATS AND JACKETS.

perfs/perforations See under FOOTWEAR: PERFORATIONS.

perfume ring See under JEWELRY.

peridot See under GEMS, GEM CUTS, AND SETTINGS.

periodic inventory The counting of merchandise at specified time periods. Apparel retailers often do these counts twice a year, in July and January.

periwig See under WIGS AND HAIRPIECES.

permanent/permanent wave See under HAIRSTYLES.

permanent markdown See under MARKDOWN.

permanent press See under DURABLE PRESS.

perpetual inventory A continuous record of incoming and outgoing merchandise. See under POINT OF SALE.

perruque á l'enfant See under WIGS AND HAIRPIECES.

∞**perruquier** (per-uke′-yay) Person who arranged and set wigs in the 18th c.

Persian lamb See under FURS.

Persian paw See under FURS.

persians See under LEATHERS.

personal flotation device See under VESTS: FLOTATION VEST.

personalized garments Apparel items, produced in single or limited quantities, that are decorated with photographs or other applied designs unique to the person or organization for whom they are made.

personal shopper A retail store employee in an upscale store who works with individual customers to help them select apparel.

peruke See under WIGS AND HAIRPIECES: PERIWIG.

Peruvian hat See under HEADWEAR.

petal collar See under NECKLINES AND COLLARS.

petal hem See under CLOTHING CONSTRUCTION DETAILS.

petal sleeve See under SHOULDERS AND SLEEVES.

petasos See under HEADWEAR.

∞**petenlair/pet-en-l'air** (pet′-en-lair) Dress worn by women from 1745 to 1770s, made with separate thigh-length bodice with fitted STOMACHER front, full back, and elbow-length sleeves. Worn with long petticoat to make a dress. Also called *French jacket.*

peter pan collar See under NECKLINES AND COLLARS.

Peter Pan hat See under HEADWEAR.

Peter Thomson dress See under DRESSES.

∞**petersham** Strip of firmly woven ribbon placed in the interior of a woman's bodice that fastened around her waist in order to keep the bodice from shifting while it was worn. First used about 1870. Often had the name of the designer or manufacturing firm woven into the ribbon.

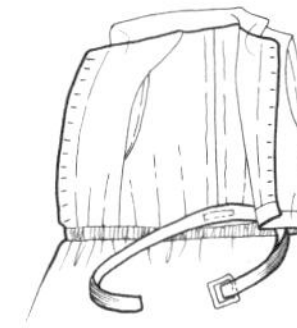
petersham belt on the interior of a dress c. 1880

petersham cossacks See under PANTS.

petersham frock coat See under COATS AND JACKETS.

petersham greatcoat See under COATS AND JACKETS.

Petersham, Viscount Charles (1780–1851) Fashionable figure from Regency period to 1850, classified between an eccentric and a true DANDY, for whom various items of men's clothing and fabrics were named (e.g., Petersham cossacks, Petersham frock coat, and Petersham greatcoat).

petit casaque See under POLONAISE.

petite 1. Size range for women who are below-average height—usually sized from 0 to 16. Junior petite sizes for short-waisted women run from 1 to 13. 2. Smallest size, along with SMALL, MEDIUM, and LARGE for pantyhose, bodysuits, and nightgowns. Abbreviated *P.*

petit point See under EMBROIDERIES AND SEWING STITCHES.

∞**petits bonshommes** (peh′-tee bon-zohm′) Bands of fabric with several ruffles—often of lace—used to edge sleeves of gown (e.g., gown à la française from early 1720s to 1780s).

petti Prefix used to mean little or small.

pettibockers See under UNDERGARMENTS.

petticoat 1. See under UNDERGARMENTS. ∞2. Skirt of a dress in the 17th and 18th c.; not the underskirt. ∞3. Waist-length underdoublet worn by men from last half of 15th to end of 16th c. Also called a *waistcoat.*

petticoat breeches and cannons c. 1660

petticoat bodice See under UNDERGARMENTS.

petticoat breeches A knee-length, divided skirt, similar to modern CULOTTES, cut so full that it looked like a skirt. Fashionable court fashion for men in England and France in 1660s and 1670s, made pleated or gathered to waistband. Trimmed with ribbon loops at waistband and near hem on sides and sometimes worn with CANNONS. Worn as livery for "running footmen" until mid-18th c. Also called *Rhinegraves.*

petticulottes See under UNDERGARMENTS.

pettipants See under UNDERGARMENTS.

pettiskirt See UNDERGARMENTS: PETTICOAT.

pettiskirt brief See under UNDERGARMENTS.

petti-slip See under UNDERGARMENTS.

PFD Acronym for PERSONAL FLOTATION DEVICE. See under VESTS: FLOTATION VEST.

†**phase-change materials (PCMs)** Substances that store, release, and absorb heat as they oscillate between solid and liquid form. Based on technology originally developed for the U.S. space program, phase-change materials are now finding applications in textiles for apparel. Fiber, fabric, and foam with built-in PCMs store the warmth the body creates and then release it back to the body as it needs it. The dynamic process is ideally suited for activities where the level of physical activity of the body and the outside temperature is constantly changing.

pheasant feather See under FEATHERS.

Philippine embroidery See under EMBROIDERIES AND SEWING STITCHES.

photographic print See under PRINTS, STRIPES, AND CHECKS.

phrygian cap See under HEADWEAR.

physical wig See under WIGS AND HAIRPIECES.

piano shawl See under CAPES, CLOAKS, AND SHAWLS: SPANISH SHAWL.

pianta bag See under HANDBAGS AND RELATED ACCESSORIES.

picadill/Piccadilly See under PICKADIL.

piccadilly collar See under NECKLINES AND COLLARS.

pick See under FILLING.

∞**pickadil** Notched edge on sleeve, bodice front, or neck opening worn from late 16th through early 17th c. Also spelled *piccadill, pickardil, Piccadilly. Der.* From Piccadilly, a street in London.

pickdevant See under BEARD.

∞**pickelhaube** See under HEADWEAR: GERMAN HELMET.

picot (pee′-ko) †1. A row of small loops woven along selvage of ribbon or a part of the edge design on lace (see under introduction to LACES). 2. Machine-made edge on fabrics produced by cutting through center of *hemstitching,* each edge becoming a picot edge. See under EMBROIDERIES AND SEWING STITCHES: HEMSTICH. 3. Run-resistant loops on edge of the welt (see under WELT #2) in hosiery. 4. See under CLOTHING CONSTRUCTION DETAILS: PICOT HEM.

picot stitching See under EMBROIDERIES AND SEWING STITCHES.

picture hat See under HEADWEAR.

†piece goods Fabric sold by the yard. Piece-good departments in retail stores sell fabrics by the yard to customers for home sewing. In the early days of retailing, few ready-made dresses were sold, so this department was one of the largest in the store. Also called *yard goods.*

pied hose See under PARTICOLORED.

Piedmont gown See under SACK #1.

pierced earrings See under JEWELRY.

pierced-look earrings See under JEWELRY.

piercing See under JEWELRY: BODY-PIERCING.

pierpont collar See under NECKLINES AND COLLARS.

∞Pierrot (pee-ehr-oh′) Close-fitting, low-necked bodice, extending to slightly below the waist worn with a matching flounced skirt from 1780s to 1790s.

pierrot cape See under CAPES, CLOAKS, AND SHAWLS.

pierrot collar See under NECKLINES AND COLLARS.

Pierrot costume (pee-ehr-oh′) Clown suit worn by the comedic character in French pantomime called *Pierrot* (Little Peter) and interpreted by the Italian clown *Pagliacci* in Leoncavallo's opera. Face is whitened, the suit loose and baggy similar to clown suit, most often white with large buttons or pompons on the jacket front. Usually worn with slippers with pompons and tall hat.

Pierrot costume

pigeon-wings See under WIGS AND HAIRPIECES.

pigskin See under LEATHERS.

pigtails See under HAIRSTYLES.

pigtail wig See under WIGS AND HAIRPIECES.

piked shoe See under FOOTWEAR: CRAKOW.

pilch ∞1. Close-fitting, fur-lined outergown worn by men and women during winter from 14th to 16th c.; later worn by clergy in drafty churches. 2. See under PELLISON.

†pile Cut or uncut loops of yarns that stand erect on fabric to form all or part of the fabric surface. Either lengthwise or crosswise yarns can be used to produce this thick, soft surface. May be uncut, as in terry cloth, or cut as in VELVET, VELVETEEN, and CORDUROY.

pileolus See under CLERICAL DRESS.

pileus See under HEADWEAR.

pilgrim collar See under NECKLINES AND COLLARS.

pillbox hat See under HEADWEAR.

pilleolus See under CLERICAL DRESS: PILEOLUS.

pilleus See under HEADWEAR: PILEUS.

†pilling Tendency of woven fabrics and knits, especially wool and synthetic fibers, to form surface nubs or bunches of fibers from rubbing during normal wear and washing. Pilling is caused by loosely twisted yarns unwinding and interlocking with each other.

pillow lace See under introduction to LACES.

pillow-slip dress See under DRESSES.

pilos See under HEADWEAR.

pilot coat See under COATS AND JACKETS: PEA JACKET.

pilot shirt See under SHIRTS: EPAULET SHIRT.

∞pilot's suit Woman's early, two-piece aviatrix suit of 1912 made with knee-length knickers, fitted blouse with long, full sleeves at wrist and high neckline with attached hood. Worn with bulky knee-length socks, high laced boots, and gauntlet gloves. Costume was designed by Harriet Quimby, who, on April 16, 1912, was the first woman to fly across the English Channel.

†pima cotton Fine-quality long-staple cotton raised in Arizona, Texas, New Mexico, and California, a variety of American-Egyptian cotton. *Der.* From Pima County, Arizona.

pin 1. See under STRAIGHT PIN. 2. See under JEWELRY.

pinafore Sleeveless garment like an apron worn over dress by women and children since latter half of 19th c. as protection against soiling. See under APRONS.

pinafore

pinafore dress See under DRESSES.

pinafore heel See under FOOTWEAR.

pinafore jumper See under JUMPERS.

pinafore swimsuit See under SWIMWEAR.

pince-nez See under EYEWEAR.

pinchbeck Alloy, composed of five parts copper and one part zinc, used for pins and buckles cast with a surface design and then plated with a thin layer of silver or gold; frequently set with colored glass or paste. *Der.* From invention of Christopher Pinchbeck, London watchmaker, about 1700.

pincheck See under PRINTS, STRIPES, AND CHECKS.

pin collar See under NECKLINES AND COLLARS.

pin curl 1. See under HAIRSTYLES. ∞2. Term used from 1840 to 1860s for curl pinned on to underside of bonnet. Also called *pin-on curl.*

pin dot See under PRINTS, STRIPES, AND CHECKS: DOTS.

pin-in bra See under UNDERGARMENTS.

pink coat See under COATS AND JACKETS.

pinked See under CLOTHING CONSTRUCTION DETAILS.

pinking †1. Unhemmed border of fabric cut with saw-toothed edge to prevent raveling by using special pinking scissors or shears that have saw-toothed blades. Also see under CLOTHING CONSRUCTION DETAILS: PINKED. ∞2. Decorative effect made by cutting short slits to form a pattern in shoes or garments, in late 15th to 17th c. Also called *pouncing.* 3. See under FOOTWEAR: PINKING.

pinner 1. See under HEADWEAR. 2. See under NECKLINES AND COLLARS: TUCKER.

pinning blanket See under BARROW #2 and LAYETTE.

pin-on curl See under PIN CURL.

pinpoint collar See under NECKLINES AND COLLARS: PIERPONT COLLAR.

pin seal See under LEATHERS.

pinson/pinsnet See under FOOTWEAR.

pinstripe See under PRINTS, STRIPES, AND CHECKS.

pin tucks See under CLOTHING CONSTRUCTION DETAILS: TUCK.

pinwale See under CORDUROY.

pinwale piqué See under PIQUÉ.

piped buttonhole See under CLOSURES.

piped pocket See under POCKETS: BOUND POCKET.

pipe-organ pleats See under CLOTHING CONSTRUCTION DETAILS: GODET.

∞**pipes** Small rolls of clay pipe heated and used to tighten curls of man's wig in 17th and 18th c. Also called ROULETTES.

piping See under CLOTHING CONSTRUCTION DETAILS.

pipkin See under HEADWEAR.

†**piqué** (pee-kay') Group of durable fabrics characterized by corded effects either lengthwise or crosswise. Plain piqués in the U.S. are made with lengthwise cords similar to BEDFORD CORD, by which name they could more properly be called. **Pinwale piqué** is a variation with smaller ribs. Piqués made in England have cords in the crosswise direction. **Waffle piqué** is made in a HONEYCOMB pattern. **Bird's-eye piqué** has a diamond-shaped pattern that is a woven-in dobby pattern. **Embroidered piqué** is plain piqué that has been embroidered with the SCHIFFLI MACHINE (see under EMBROIDERIES AND SEWING STITCHES). All types are used for dresses, blouses, pants, sportswear, handbags, and neckwear.

pique devant See under BEARD.

piqué embroidery See under EMBROIDERIES AND SEWING STITCHES.

piqué seam See under GLOVES AND GLOVE CONSTRUCTION: FULL-PIQUÉ and HALF-PIQUÉ.

piracy Stealing of an idea for a dress by making sketches of it. Punishable as a crime in France, where dress designs are protected by the French government, it is not considered a crime in the U.S. unless the design is patented. Viewers at couture showings are permitted to mark their programs, but not permitted to make sketches.

pith helmet See under HEADWEAR: TOPEE.

pixie crop See under HAIRSTYLES: PIXIE HAIRCUT.

pixie haircut See under HAIRSTYLES.

pizzazz/pizazz (pih-zazz') Coined in 1930s to express the quality of audaciousness or daring; credited by the fashion magazine *Harper's Bazaar* to students at Harvard University.

p.j.'s Abbreviation for PAJAMAS. See under SLEEPWEAR AND LOUNGEWEAR.

P.K. seam See under GLOVES AND GLOVE CONSTRUCTION: FULL-PIQUÉ.

∞**placard/plackard** (placcard, placart, placate) 1. Chest piece or stomacher, used to fill in gap made by open neckline of man's DOUBLET in late 15th to mid-16th c. 2. From mid-14th to early 16th c.: Front panel of woman's open-sided SURCOAT, often trimmed with fur and embroidery. Compare with PLASTRON #2.

placket See under CLOTHING CONSTRUCTION DETAILS.

placket neckline See under NECKLINES AND COLLARS.

PLAIDS AND TARTANS

plaid 1. Pattern woven of various colored yarns in stripes of different widths running at right angles to form blocks. *Der.* From Scottish fabrics woven to designate different clans. See under PLAIDS AND TARTANS: TARTAN. 2. Fabric design printed or woven of yarns dyed in various colors. Bands of color of different widths run both horizontally and vertically, crossing at right angles to form a series of boxes which may be slightly longer lengthwise.

tartan Each clan in Scotland has adopted a specific plaid fabric in individual colors used for the KILT, or short pleated skirt worn by men, and the *plaid,* a drapery worn hanging from the shoulders, across back, and tucked into belt. Although Scots are reported to have used stripes as early as the 5th c. and were fond of "mottled" fabrics, the real origin of the tartan is controversial. Various historians mention plaids as early as 1594 and 1645, but it was not until early 18th c. (1703) that they began to emerge as a clan symbol that designated a place of residence. After the defeat of Bonnie Prince Charles in 1747, plaids were banned by British law. Revived in 1822, when George IV visited Scotland—from that time on there were specific tartans for each clan. The better-known tartans are described in this category. *Der.* Believed to have come from Flemish word *tiretaine.*

argyle plaid Plaid made with various-colored diamond-shaped designs—usually a larger diamond pattern of dark or light lines is superimposed over other solid-colored diamonds. Popular in 1920s, 1940s, and revived in the late 1960s. *Der.* Tartan of Duke of Argyle and Clan Campbell of Argyll, a county in West Scotland. Also spelled *argyll, argyl.*

Balfour plaid A tartan cloth pattern identifying the Balfour clan, whose modern design was created by Peter MacDonald of Crieff, Perthshire, Scotland.

Balmoral tartan (bahl-mor′-al) Predominantly gray tartan with two narrow black stripes and one red stripe grouped together and running vertically, with two red stripes running horizontally plus wider stripes of black and gray used in both directions.

Black Watch tartan A tartan of very dark blue and green squares with wide and narrow black lines in both directions and no overplaid. Worn by members of the Black Watch, a Scottish regiment.

blanket plaid Plaid of a very large design, with dark-colored ground and lighter overstripes or white ground and colored overstripes, used originally in woolen and cotton blankets.

Bruce tartan Tartan of bold red plaid crossed by dark green stripes of various sizes, forming a central box consisting of four green boxes outlined with narrow green stripes. Large yellow and white overplaid encloses the design.

Buchanan tartan Tartan of intricate bold plaid consisting of dull green bands combined with red, orange, green, and yellow checks arranged in squares, having a fine overplaid of white and black.

buffalo checks See under PRINTS, STRIPES, AND CHECKS.

Burberry plaid Beige, red, and black plaid named after Thomas Burberry, a mid-19th-century British tailor who specialized in waterproof gabardine raincoats lined in this plaid. The plaid is now used in a wide variety of garments and accessories. See under COATS AND JACKETS: BURBERRY RAINCOAT.

Cameron tartan Predominantly bright red tartan with four dark green stripes crossed at right angles, making a central section of sixteen blocks of green. Yellow overplaid outlines each pattern.

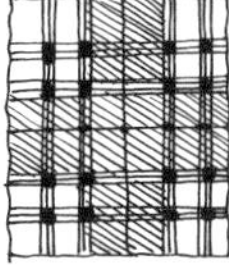
even plaid

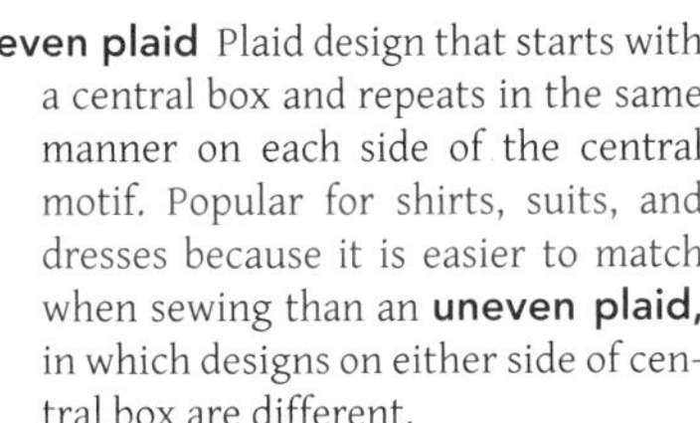

even plaid Plaid design that starts with a central box and repeats in the same manner on each side of the central motif. Popular for shirts, suits, and dresses because it is easier to match when sewing than an **uneven plaid,** in which designs on either side of central box are different.

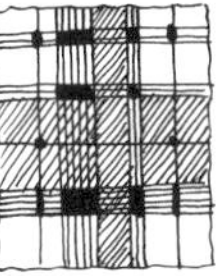
uneven plaid

Frazer tartan Similar to the CAMERON TARTAN (see under PLAIDS AND TARTANS) but smaller in size, with navy and green stripes crossing at right angles, making a central section of sixteen navy and green blocks. Also includes an overplaid in white.

gingham plaid Plaid of woven design in a cotton fabric made with stripes and boxes of various sizes in three or more colors. Gingham with only two colors is called a *gingham check.* Fabrics used for aprons, dresses, and shirts. Also see under GINGHAM.

glen plaid See under PLAIDS AND TARTANS: GLEN URQUHART PLAID.

Glen Urquhart plaid Plaid of woven design that pairs small checks with larger checks, made with similar-colored yarns in warp and filling in a combination of subdued color and white. Used particularly for men's worsted suits. Also called *glen plaid* or *glen check. Der.* Named for Glen Urquhart, a valley in Inverness-shire, Scotland.

hunting plaid Everyday version of Scottish clan's tartan made in subdued colors to blend with landscape, in contrast to dress plaid worn on ceremonial occasions.

lumberjack plaid Distinctive plaid similar to a BLANKET PLAID (see under PLAIDS AND TARTANS) but smaller in size. Usually combines tones of green and tan on a beige background. *Der.* From early plaids used for jackets by lumbermen.

Macbeth tartan A complicated-patterned tartan made with cobalt-blue ground and colored stripes in red, yellow, green, and black, some outlined in white.

MacDonell of Glengarry tartan Tartan of dark green and navy ground crossed with narrow red lines of two widths, making a smaller design than most tartans. Has a large overplaid in white.

MacGregor (Rob Roy) tartan Tartan that exhibits a combination of vivid red blocks and wide black bands in a small block design.

Macintyre and Glenorchy tartan Tartan of red ground crossed with medium-sized bands of green and navy running vertically and horizontally with narrow bands of green and blue in between—making a square pattern with large overplaid of light blue.

MacPherson hunting tartan Tartan of bold black block alternating with gray and beige blocks, and outlined with two narrow red stripes with bright blue stripe between them.

madras plaid (mad-dras′) Plaid made from East Indian woven cotton in multicolor crossbar patterns with red. May bleed after washing to produce a blurred effect. Also see under MADRAS.

Menzies black-and-white tartan Similar in design to MENZIES HUNTING TARTAN (see under PLAIDS AND TARTANS) but woven only in black and white.

Menzies hunting tartan Tartan of predominantly wide blocks of solid green alternating with red blocks divided into checks by green bands—other blocks are striped.

Munro tartan Tartan of vivid red ground, plaided in dark green and navy, with fine yellow lines running in both directions at intervals.

†overplaid Lines of another color superimposed over a plaid or a checked design.

Ramsay tartan Tartan of brilliant-red ground with wide black bands in both directions and double lines in white overplaid. Also has fine purple stripes running in both directions. Dates back to the 17th c.

Rob Roy tartan See under PLAIDS AND TARTANS: MACGREGOR TARTAN.

Royal Stewart (Stuart) tartan Similar to STEWART DRESS tartan (see under PLAIDS AND TARTANS) with bold-red ground and central box of nine squares of red outlined with green, black, and blue bands. Fine navy lines run through center of boxes, with fine white and yellow overplaid.

shepherd's plaid/shepherd's check See under PRINTS, STRIPES, AND CHECKS.

Stewart (Stuart) dress tartan Tartan that has a central box containing nine red squares outlined by wide black bands, alternating with white blocks, and green-, red-, and black-striped blocks with fine yellow-and-white alternating stripes defining the squares.

Stewart hunting tartan Tartan of very dark blue or green ground crossed at right angles with black bands, making a central section of sixteen blocks. An overplaid of red and yellow outlines the pattern.

tartan See under introduction for category PLAIDS AND TARTANS.

tattersall plaid Plaid consisting of narrow lines in two alternating colors, crossed to form a checked design on a plain, light-colored ground, often uses red and black lines on white ground. *Der.* Named after Richard Tattersall, British horseman and founder of Tattersall's London Horse Auction Mart, established in 1776. Also called *tattersall check.*

uneven plaid See under PLAIDS AND TARTANS: EVEN PLAID.

windowpane plaid See under PRINTS, STRIPES AND CHECKS: WINDOWPANE CHECKS.

---

plain-front See under PANTS.

plain hem See under CLOTHING CONSTRUCTION DETAILS.

plain knit 1. See under JERSEY #1. 2. See under EMBROIDERIES AND SEWING STITCHES: PLAIN KNITTING STITCH.

plain seam See under CLOTHING CONSTRUCTION DETAILS. Also see under EMBROIDERIES AND SEWING STITCHES: PLAIN KNITTING STITCH.

†plain weave Weave in which one crosswise yarn passes over the first lengthwise yarn, then under the next lengthwise yarn, and continues across the width of the fabric to pass over one yarn and under another. In the next row, the crosswise yarn passes under the first lengthwise yarn, then over the next lengthwise yarn, and so on. In the third row, the pattern of the first row is repeated. The resulting interlacing of yarns is like a checkerboard pattern. Synonym: *tabby weave.*

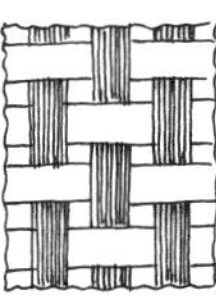
plain weave diagram

plait (plate) 1. *n.* See under HAIRSTYLES: BRAIDS. 2. *v.* To weave three or more strands into a single strip or braid, e.g., bands of straw for hats or ribbons for trimming. 3. Old spelling of PLEAT. See under CLOTHING CONSTRUCTION DETAILS.

planter's hat See under HEADWEAR.

plastic patent Simulated or imitation PATENT LEATHER (see under LEATHERS) made from a vinyl compound that is durable and will not split or crack like genuine patent. May have a crushed surface or be embossed with a design, e.g., alligator or snakeskin. Used for shoes and handbags and in lighter weights for jackets, coats, and trimmings. Popular from 1960s on.

∞plastron (plas′-tron) 1. See under ARMOR. 2. Front center portion set into a woman's dress, usually made of a contrasting fabric for a decorative effect. Used in the 19th through the mid-20th c. and revived in the 1980s when a lacy and frilly version was called a *gilet.* In earlier centuries also called a *placard* or *stomacher.* 3. See under NECKLINES AND COLLARS: BIB COLLAR. *Der.* French, "breastplate."

plate See under ARMOR.

plated See under JEWELRY.

plates See under FURS.

platform See under FOOTWEAR: PLATFORM SANDAL, PLATFORM SHOE, and PLATFORM SOLE.

platina See under FURS: PLATINUM FOX.

platinum 1. See under JEWELRY. 2. Very pale, silvery blond, popular shade of hair in 1930s and 1940s.

platinum fox See under FURS.

platter collar See under NECKLINES AND COLLARS.

platypus toe See under FOOTWEAR.

plauen lace See under LACES.

playsuit See under SHORTS: JUMPSHORTS and ACTIVEWEAR.

playwear Fashion business designation of casual clothing worn by children for playing.

pleat/pleated 1. See under CLOTHING CONSTRUCTION DETAILS. 2. Apparel that utilizes pleats in its construction. See under PANTS: PLEATED-FRONT PANTS and PLEATED OVERALLS and SHORTS: PLEATED SHORTS.

pleather A slang term for faux leather made from plastic. A polyurethane or PVC film is applied to a woven or knit base fabric. Pleather is less expensive and lighter in weight than leather; those made with polyurethane can be dry cleaned and are porous, allowing them to breathe when used in apparel applications. See also NAUGAHYDE, LEATHERETTE, and FAUX LEATHER.

pledge pin See under JEWELRY.

†plissé (plee-say') Lightweight cotton with a pebbly surface given a creped appearance by applying caustic soda with rollers, thereby causing the fabric to shrink in those areas, while the untreated areas remain the same size. The result is a crinkled appearance. Pressing will remove the crinkle. Uses: pajamas, nightgowns, and children's clothing. Also known as *crinkle crepe* and *plissé crepe.*

plucking See under FURS.

pluderhose See under TRUNK HOSE.

plug hat See under HEADWEAR.

plug/plugged oxford See under FOOTWEAR: BUSTLE.

plumage See under FEATHERS.

plume See under FEATHERS.

plumet petticoat See under UNDERGARMENTS: BUSTLE.

plummet See under JEWELRY.

∞plumpers Lightweight, thin, round balls of cork or wax used by women inside mouth to make cheeks look rounder from late 17th to early 19th c.

plunge bra See under UNDERGARMENTS.

plunging neckline See under NECKLINES AND COLLARS.

plus fours See under PANTS.

plus sizes Sizes in women's apparel that are at the upper range of sizes manufactured. Generally, retailers place sizes 14 and above in this category.

†ply yarn A number of individual yarns, or singles, twisted together to form a heavier yarn.

Pocahontas dress See under DRESSES: AMERICAN INDIAN DRESS.

pocketbook Synonym for *handbag.* See under introduction to HANDBAGS AND RELATED ACCESSORIES.

pocket handkerchief See under HANDKERCHIEF.

pocket hoops See under UNDERGARMENTS: PANNIERS.

POCKETS

pocket Piece of fabric shaped to fit either on the outside or inside of clothing. Used for decorative purposes or to carry small articles, e.g., handkerchiefs or coins. From 15th c. on, small pouches were worn fastened to the belt. Men: In mid-16th c., pockets were added to TRUNK HOSE; by end of the 16th c., added to BREECHES. Waistcoat pocket introduced in early 17th c. In late 17th c., flaps were added to coat and waistcoat pockets. Women: 18th-c. tie pockets were worn suspended from waist under dress and reached by means of placket holes. In 19th c., a pouch called a *railway pocket* was worn under the dress and reached by a slit in the dress. By the 1840s small pockets were put into the waistline seams of dresses, and from midcentury on, pockets were put in dresses and shirtwaists.

angled pocket See under POCKETS: HACKING POCKET.

bagge Leather pocket worn under breeches in 16th c.

bellows pocket Outside pocket made with center BOX or INVERTED PLEAT (see under CLOTHING CONSTRUCTION DETAILS) that expands when pocket is used. Type of pocket used on BUSH JACKET (see under COATS AND JACKETS) and SAFARI dress. Also called *safari pocket.*

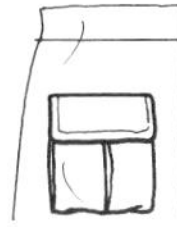
bellows pocket

besom pocket See under POCKETS: WELT POCKET.

bound pocket Interior pocket made with slit finished like a bound buttonhole on outside, providing access to inner concealed pocket. Also called *piped, slash, slit pocket.* Also see under POCKETS: WELT POCKET.

breast pocket Man's pocket placed on left side of chest on suit coats and overcoats.

cargo pocket Large patch pocket used on shorts and pants. Curved top of pocket extends to waist and forms a loop through which belt is pulled.

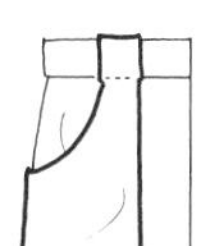
cargo pocket

change pocket See under POCKETS: TICKET POCKET.

circle pocket See under POCKETS: ROUND POCKET.

continental pocket Pocket cut away at the top, usually in a curved manner, used on men's western or continental trousers. Also called a *western pocket.*

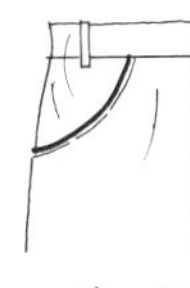
continental pocket

double-besom pocket See under POCKETS: WELT POCKET.

double-entry pocket Pockets that may be entered from the top or side.

flapped-besom pocket See under POCKETS: WELT POCKET.

flap pocket Pocket with separate piece of material covering the opening. May be of BOUND, WELT, or PATCH POCKET type (see under POCKETS).

fob pocket Small horizontal WELT POCKET (see under POCKETS) near waistband of man's pants, designed to hold pocket watch. Popular from 17th c. until the 1920s, when wristwatches began to be fashionable. Also called *watch pocket.*

front hip pocket A pocket formed by cutting a style line into a garment at the hip and then facing that style line to form a pocket opening. Typically found on the front of jeans and men's trousers. Also called *western pockets* by some sources.

hacking pocket Flap pocket placed on an angle used on jackets and coats, especially on hacking jackets.

half-moon pocket Curved, semicircular, bound pocket used primarily on cowboy shirts. Usually reinforced at ends with embroidered arrowheads. Also called a *smile pocket.*

holster pocket Novelty pocket shaped like a gun holster, used on sportswear.

inseam pocket A pocket sewn into a seam.

inside pockets Such pockets as BOUND, WELT, and FLAP are inside or interior to the garment exterior.

kangaroo pocket 1. Extra-large pocket placed on center front of garment (e.g., a sweatshirt). 2. Any extra-large pocket.

kangaroo pocket #1

key pocket Small patch pocket sewn inside of larger right-front pocket in jeans-style pants, just large enough for a key or a few coins.

mock pocket Flap sewed on outside of garment to suggest a real pocket.

patch pocket Pocket stitched on outside of garment, either made plain or with a flap.

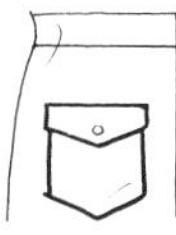
patch pocket

pencil pocket Zip pocket placed on upper sleeve of sport coat or SNORKEL JACKET (see under COATS AND JACKETS), used to hold small items or a pencil.

piped pocket See under POCKETS: BOUND POCKET.

∞**railway pocket** Flat bag with side opening tied on with tape around waist and reached by slit in skirt. Worn by women under dress when traveling, from late 1850s. A later version of the TIE POCKET (see under POCKETS).

round pocket Full, circular patch pocket bound around the edge with opening in the center, top, or side for access. Also called a *circle pocket.*

safari pocket See under POCKETS: BELLOWS POCKET.

∞**salt-box pocket** In 1790s, a man's narrow, rectangular, flapped waistcoat pocket.

seam pocket Pocket inserted in seam of skirt, dress, or pants that is not visible from outside.

slash pocket See under POCKETS: BOUND POCKET.

slit pocket See under POCKETS: WELT POCKET.

smile pocket See under POCKETS: HALF-MOON POCKET.

ticket pocket (British) In the tailoring business, a small pocket, usually flapped, placed above regular pocket on right side of a man's suit coat or overcoat. Introduced in late 1850s for a railroad ticket and used at intervals since. Also called *change pocket.*

∞**tie pocket** Large pocket sewn to a ribbon, cord, or string that tied around the waist and was used by women in the 18th and early 19th c. to carry necessary items. Often made with two pockets, one on each side of the dress. Was generally worn under the skirt and reached through a slit. When skirts were looped up and the petticoat visible, they might be worn under the petticoat. Sometimes embroidered, early American examples are frequently made of patchwork scraps of fabric. Also called *work pockets.*

tie pockets 1774

vest pocket Welt pocket placed on side chest of waistcoat or vest, originally used to carry a pocket watch. In the Louis XV period a fashion for men to carry two watches (one was often not real) required that a pocket be made on either side of the garment. Also called a *waistcoat* or *watch pocket* or FOB POCKET.

waistcoat pocket See under POCKETS: VEST POCKET.

watch pocket See under POCKETS: FOB POCKET and POCKETS: VEST POCKET.

welt pocket An inset pocket with the lower lip finished by an upstanding welt that may be from ⅜″ to 1″ wide. Usually a breast pocket placed on the left front of a man's suit coat or overcoat. May be called **besom pocket** (bee′-zum) by tailors or if both edges have welts, a **double besom** pocket. If a flap is added, it is called a **flapped besom.** Also called *slit pocket.* Also see under POCKETS: BOUND POCKET.

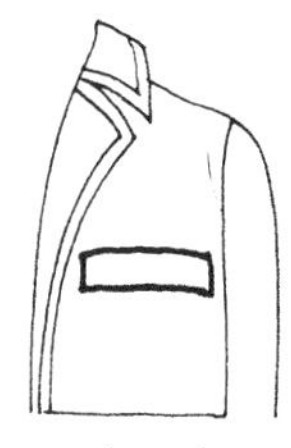
welt pocket

western arrowhead pocket A bound pocket that is curved with arrowhead appliques or tacks on either end, used on shirts and dresses to convey a western look.

western pocket Synonym for POCKETS: CONTINENTAL POCKET.

work pocket See under POCKETS: TIE POCKET.

zip pocket Any pocket closed with a zipper; used particularly on sportswear.

pocket siphonia See under COATS AND JACKETS: SIPHONIA.

pocket square See under HANDKERCHIEF.

pocket T-shirt See under SHIRTS.

pocket watch See under WATCHES.

poet's collar See under NECKLINES AND COLLARS: BYRON.

poet's shirt See under SHIRTS: LORD BYRON.

point Shortened form for NEEDLEPOINT. See under EMBROIDERIES AND SEWING STITCHES and introduction to LACES.

point d'alençon See under LACES: ALENÇON LACE.

point d'angleterre See under LACES.

point d'appliqué See under LACES: APPLIQUÉ LACE.

point d'argentan See under LACES: ARGENTAN LACE.

point d'esprit (pwan des-pree') †**1.** Netlike, machine-made fabric of cotton or nylon that has some of the holes made solid to form a decorative pattern. Uses: evening gowns and veiling. First handmade in France in 1834. Compare with BOBBINET. **2.** See under LACES. **3.** See under HOSIERY.

point de france See under LACES.

point de gaze See under LACES.

point de paris See under LACES.

point de rose See under LACES: ROSE-POINT LACE.

point de venise See under LACES.

pointing See under GLOVES AND GLOVE CONSTRUCTION.

point lace See under introduction to LACES.

point noué See under LACES.

point-of-purchase display Merchandise displayed so that it can be handled and self-selected by the customer.

point of sale (POS) Computer program that allows retailers to track inventory and sales. Usually this is done at the cash register (the "point of sale"). Because sales data are captured instantly, they can be relayed to the vendor for automatic reordering as part of the QUICK RESPONSE system.

∞**points** Cords with metal tips used to fasten garments together from 15th to mid-17th c. (e.g., TRUNK HOSE attached to DOUBLET). Also see under LANGET #1.

point shoe See under FOOTWEAR: TOE SLIPPER.

poison ring See under JEWELRY.

poke ∞**1.** Large pouch used as pocket in late 16th and early 17th c. **2.** Still used as a colloquial term for any kind of a bag in the southern U.S. *Der.* French, *poche,* "bag" or "pocket."

poke bonnet See under HEADWEAR.

poker chip button See under CLOSURES.

pokey See under HANDBAGS AND RELATED ACCESSORIES.

∞**poking sticks** Term used in 16th c. for heated bone, wood, or metal sticks used to set pleats of a RUFF (see under NECKLINES AND COLLARS).

polarized glasses See under EYEWEAR.

†**Polartec®** Napped, knit polyester fabric made from recycled soda bottles. Used extensively for cold-weather ACTIVEWEAR because of good insulation qualities.

poleyn See under ARMOR.

police boot See under FOOTWEAR.

polish boot See under FOOTWEAR.

†**polished cotton** Most any plain-weave cotton fabric, e.g., SATEEN, CHINTZ, given a glazed finish to make it shiny and lustrous. Some finishes are permanent, particularly those of the resin-type. If the finish is made by starching and ironing with a hot roller, it is not permanent. Uses: blouses, dresses, and sportswear.

polish greatcoat See under COATS AND JACKETS.

polish jacket See under COATS AND JACKETS.

polish mantle See under CAPES, CLOAKS, AND SHAWLS.

polish toque See under HEADWEAR.

polka **1.** See under COATS AND JACKETS **2.** See under HEADWEAR.

polka dot See under PRINTS, STRIPES, AND CHECKS: DOTS.

polo *adj.* Describe clothing copied from or inspired by clothes worn for polo, a game played on horseback with long-handled wooden mallets and a ball. Periods of the game are called *chukkas.* Distinctive polo clothing has been much copied for sportswear. See under BELTS: POLO BELT; COATS AND JACKETS: POLO COAT; HEADWEAR: CHUKKA HAT; NECKLINES AND COLLARS: POLO COLLAR; and SHIRTS: POLO SHIRT.

polo shirt dress See under DRESSES: T-SHIRT DRESS.

polonaise (pol-on-nays') **1.** Has come to refer to any overskirt pulled back and looped up at the sides to form a large drape or puff. Seems to appear first in the second half of the 18th c. when it was described as a boned bodice and overskirt looped up by drawstrings at hips and back to form three large puffs, thereby revealing the petticoat or underskirt. Worn over a separate ankle-length or trained skirt, sometimes contrasting in color, or with one skirt plain and the other striped. Disappeared from use when the silhouette narrowed at the end of the century, then revived again in the second half of the 19th c. Also called a *gown à la polonaise* and *robe à la polonaise.* The French name **petit casaque** (pe-tee' ca-sack') was also used in 1870s for polonaise dress. *Der.* Named after

polonaise #1
18th c.

a Polish national dance and also the music for such a dance. **2.** See under CAPES, CLOAKS, AND SHAWLS. **3.** See under COATS AND JACKETS.

polonese frock See under POLONAISE #1.

†polyester Generic fiber name for manufactured fibers made of acids and alcohols derived from petroleum. The wide variety of fabrics made from these fibers are easy to care for, resilient, retain their shape, and are often blended with other fibers.

polyethelyne See under OLEFIN.

polyolefin See under OLEFIN.

polypropylene See under OLEFIN.

∞pomander (poh'-man-der) A ball of fragrant herbs and/or flowers, or the case in which these were carried. Examples of pomanders include **pommes de senteur** (pohm duh sahn'-ture), small balls of gold or silver filigree set with precious stones used to hold scent, carried or hung from belt from 1500 to 1690s (also called *musk apples, pound-box, musk balls*), and **pouncet box,** consisting of a dry-scent box that contained fragrant herbs and flower petals and was carried during the late 16th c. *Der.* French, "perfumed apples."

pommel slicker See under COATS AND JACKETS.

pommes de senteur See under POMANDER.

pompadour **1.** See under HAIRSTYLES. **2.** See under HAIR ACCESSORIES: POMPON. **3.** See under HIP BAGS.

pompadour bag See under HANDBAGS AND RELATED ACCESSORIES.

∞pompadour bodice (pohm'-pah-dure) Bodice for daytime dress worn in the 1870s, having a low square neckline, and tight, elbow-length sleeves, trimmed with lace or ruffles. Worn as part of the POLONAISE in 1870s. See POLONAISE #1. *Der.* Named for Marquise de Pompadour, mistress of Louis XV of France.

pompadour hairstyle See under HAIRSTYLES.

Pompadour, Marquise de (pohm'-pah-dure, mar-kees' deh) (1721–1764) Born Jeanne Antoinette Poisson. Mistress of Louis XV of France (from 1745 to 1764), who had great influence over him. Promoted the arts during this period. Paintings of her by Boucher epitomize the beautiful costume of this era. Many items of fashion have been named after her. Examples: POMPADOUR HAIRSTYLE (see under HAIRSTYLES), POMPADOUR BAG (see under HANDBAGS AND RELATED ACCESSORIES), POMPADOUR BODICE, and POMPADOUR SLEEVE (see under SHOULDERS AND SLEEVES).

pompadour sleeve See under SHOULDERS AND SLEEVES.

pompeian silk sash See under BELTS.

pompey See under WIGS AND HAIRPIECES: PHYSICAL WIG.

pompon/pompom **1.** Round ball of cut ends of yarn used as trimming. **2.** See under HAIR ACCESSORIES. **3.** See under HAIRSTYLES: TOP KNOT.

poms **1.** A measure of yarn or thread dyed to a specific color used to communicate color predictions. **2.** See under HOSIERY: FOOTSOCK.

poncho See under CAPES, CLOAKS AND SHAWLS.

†pongee (pon-gee') Light- to medium-weight, rough-textured, silk fabric made from wild silk and usually left in natural color. Originally hand-loomed in China, later machine made. Warp yarns are finer than the filling, causing a slight rib formed by the uneven texture of the yarn. *Der.* Chinese, *penchi,* "woven at home."

pony See under FURS.

∞ponyet **1.** Sleeve of DOUBLET that covers the lower part of arm, frequently of different fabric from upper sleeve. Worn from 14th to 16th c. Also spelled *poynet.* **2.** Long pin with decorative head worn by men in 17th c. Also called *little bodkin.*

ponytail See under HAIRSTYLES.

†poodle cloth Knitted or woven fabric characterized by small curls over the entire surface. Similar to ASTRAKHAN fabric but made with looser curls like the coat of a poodle dog.

poodle cut See under HAIRSTYLES.

poodle skirt See under SKIRTS.

poor-boy *adj.* Descriptive of mid-1960s style of shrunken casual clothing based on a typical style worn by newsboys in early 20th c. Examples: poor-boy dresses, sweaters, and NEWSBOY CAP (see under HEADWEAR).

poor-boy shift An elongated version of the poor-boy sweater. Also see under SWEATERS: POOR-BOY SWEATER.

popcorn stitch See under EMBROIDERIES AND SEWING STITCHES.

Pope, Virginia (1885–1978) Fashion editor of the *New York Times* beginning in 1933. She changed fashion reporting by seeking news in the wholesale markets of New York; encouraged young American designers; and originated the Fashion of the Times fashion show in 1942, which featured clothes from American designers. In 1955, became fashion editor of *Parade* magazine. She also held the Edwin Goodman chair, established by Bergdorf Goodman, at Fashion Institute of Technology. Cosmopolitan, statuesque, and beautifully dressed, in her later years she became the grande dame of American fashion.

†poplin Medium-weight durable fabric with crosswise rib effect made with cotton or blends of cotton and polyester. Better qualities use combed yarns in both directions. A water-resistant or water-repellent finish may also be applied to fabrics used for raincoats. Also used for sportswear, pants, shorts, blouses, dresses, and men's shirts.

popover See under DRESSES.

porcupine hairstyle/headdress See under HAIRSTYLES.

pop-up stores Temporary retail spaces that typically appear in vacant space, drawing crowds and offering unique merchandise, only to disappear or morph into something else weeks or up to a year later.

porc-epic See under HAIRSTYLES: PORCUPINE HEADDRESS.

pork-pie hat See under HEADWEAR.

port canons See under CANNONS.

∞**porte-jupe pompadour** (port-zhupe pohm′-pah-dure) Belt worn under a dress in 1860s that was made with eight suspenders that fastened to the hem of the skirt with loops that enclosed buttons. When a tab at the front of the device was pulled, the skirt raised in much the same way as a modern Venetian blind. Also called *dress elevator.*

porte-monnaie See under HANDBAGS AND RELATED ACCESSORIES.

portfolio 1. A sampling of work done by an artist or designer used to illustrate their skills to a potential employer. A fashion portfolio might include mood or concept boards, illustrations with color chips and fabric swatches, embellishment designs, and photographs of finished garments or collections. 2. A container used to hold and organize samples of an artist or designer's work.

port of entry Location in the U.S. with customs offices through which import of goods is authorized. Oakland, CA; Los Angeles, CA; New York, NY; and Miami, FL, are major entry ports.

portrait collar See under NECKLINES AND COLLARS.

posh British slang term meaning rich or luxurious, derived from the acronym for preferred quarters on ships sailing between Britain and India. *Der.* "Port Out, Starboard Home," i.e., the shady side of the ship.

posts See under JEWELRY: STUDS.

postboy hat See under HEADWEAR.

poster dress See under DRESSES.

postiche See under WIGS AND HAIRPIECES: WIGLET.

∞**postillion** (poce-till′-yun) 1. See under HEADWEAR. 2. Dress bodice extending below back waistline, usually with pleats or ruffles that flare outward. Worn by women in latter half of 19th c. Also called *postillion basque* (bask). *Der.* From clothes worn by *postillions,* which is the French word used to refer to men on horseback accompanying carriages.

postillion basque See under POSTILLION.

postillion coat See under COATS AND JACKETS.

postillion corsage See under BALMORAL BODICE.

posts 1. See under UNDERGARMENTS: PASTIES. 2. See under JEWELRY: STUDS.

posy/poesy ring See under JEWELRY.

pot derby See under HEADWEAR: DERBY.

pot hat See under HEADWEAR: TOP HAT.

potholder vest See under VESTS.

potten kant lace See under LACES: ANTWERP LACE.

pouch 1. See under HANDBAGS AND RELATED ACCESSORIES. ∞2. Bag or purse of 12th to 16th c. worn suspended from gentleman's belt, often with dagger thrust through the pendant strap.

pouf See under HAIRSTYLES: BOUFFANT.

pouf au sentiment See under HAIRSTYLES.

pouf, le A wide, puffy skirt with a light, airy appearance; made in both short and longer styles around 1985, and created by Christian Lacroix, designing for Patou.

le pouf 1987

poulaine/poulain See under FOOTWEAR: CRAKOW.

pouncet-box See under POMANDER.

pouncing See under PINKING #2.

pound-box See under POMANDER.

pourpoint See under DOUBLET.

poussin lace (poo-sahn) See under LACES: DIEPPE POINT LACE.

∞**powdering jacket/gown** A loose wrap worn by men in 18th c. to protect clothing while the wig was being powdered. Also see under FACE CONE.

power suit/power dressing Used in the late 1980s and 1990s for a man's or woman's tailored suit worn for business.

poynet See under PONYET.

prairie *adj.* Describes styles introduced in early 1970s in imitation of dresses worn by pioneer women. Elements included long dresses, usually of calico-like printed fabric, styled with two-gored skirts and bodices with high neckline and long sleeves. In 1980s shown in full skirts with ruffle at hem and Victorian-styled collars. *Der.* From dresses worn by American settlers moving westward in mid- and late 19th c. Also see under SKIRTS: PRAIRIE SKIRT.

prayer veil See under HEADWEAR.

precious stone See under GEMS, GEM CUTS, AND SETTINGS.

pre-cuffed trousers See under PANTS.

predatory pricing Illegal pricing of a product below cost, the intent being to drive out any competition. Selling goods at a loss at the end of season to clear out old merchandise is not considered predatory pricing.

preliminary line sheet Internal catalog of projected styles in a line as used by a company while developing a line.

prepack An assortment of merchandise in certain quantities of sizes and/or colors of one or more styles chosen according to a manufacturer's or retailer's direction.

preppy *adj.* Descriptive of a style of dress, inspired by clothing worn by students at private, preparatory schools, which emphasizes well-known trademarks from high-quality brands; classics such as Ivy League shirts, wool and cashmere sweaters, A-line skirts, conventional-style pants in fabrics such as chino, wool, and corduroy; and shoes such as oxfords, loafers, or classic pumps in expensive leathers.

preppy style, 1950s

pre-Raphaelites A society of artists founded in England, c. 1850, that encouraged painting in a style they felt was characteristic of work done in the period before the time of the Italian Renaissance artist Raphael. They encouraged women associated with the movement to abandon corsets and hoopskirts. Later in the century, the clothing in which they painted women also influenced AESTHETIC DRESS.

prestige pricing Pricing method based on the assumption that customers are willing to pay a higher price for products that are perceived to be special in terms of aesthetics, name recognition, quality, value, or service.

prêt-à-porter (pret-ah'-por-tay') Ready-to-wear clothes. Many haute couture designers produce special, less expensive, prêt-à-porter lines of clothing in addition to their custom-made lines. *Der.* French, "ready to be carried away."

pre-walkers See under FOOTWEAR.

price discrimination Selling by a vendor of identical merchandise at different prices to two or more retailers. Laws prohibit price discrimination.

price point A range in which a category of apparel products must be priced in order to be competitive; a product's price point relates to the customer to which the product is meant to appeal, the product's quality level, and the product styling. Price points in the apparel industry may be designated as falling into one of the following categories that form a continuum of prices from low to high: **discount, mass market, moderate, better, contemporary, bridge**, and **designer**.

prime pelt See under FURS.

prince albert coat See under COATS AND JACKETS.

prince of wales jacket See under COATS AND JACKETS.

prince of wales shoe See FOOTWEAR: GILLIE.

prince rupert See under COATS AND JACKETS.

princess chemise See under UNDERGARMENTS.

princess coat See under COATS AND JACKETS.

princess dress See under DRESSES.

princesse lace See under LACES.

princess slip/princess petticoat See under UNDERGARMENTS.

princess stock See under NECKLINES AND COLLARS.

princess-style dress

princess style Basic cut for women's clothing characterized by continuous vertical panels, shaped to body through torso without waistline seam. Used in dresses, coats, and slips, since 1860s. Called AGNÈS SOREL STYLE and ISABEAU STYLE in early 1860s. French form, *princesse.*

princess waistline See under WAISTLINES.

†printing Reproducing a design on fabric in color either by mechanical means or by hand. The most common methods currently in use in the textile industry are **roller printing,** using as many as 16 engraved metal rollers, and **rotary screen printing,** using perforated, round, metal screens. Hand-printed designs often used in crafts include those made by BLOCK PRINTING and SCREEN PRINTING (see under PRINTS, STRIPES, AND CHECKS). Prints may be applied as overall, repeat patterns, border designs, or in large panel designs. Most countries have traditional prints native to their land. **†Heat transfer printing** or **thermal transfer printing** is a method to transfer designs from rolls of paper to fabrics. Designs are preprinted on paper with special dyes that transfer onto fabric when they are brought together in a heat transfer printing machine. The process is most effective on polyester, nylon and acrylic and is not suitable currently for fabrics with low softening points.

PRINTS, STRIPES, AND CHECKS

†print A design applied to a fabric by means of a mechanical or hand method of PRINTING. See entries below for named types of prints and print designs.

stripes 1. Bands of color or texture of varying widths, making a design in a fabric, either printed on or woven in; may go in horizontal, vertical, or diagonal direction. 2. Narrow bands of braid, bias binding, ribbon, or fabric applied in rows.

check A fabric design composed of alternate squares of colors in various sizes usually alternating with white. Design may be similar to checkerboard or any other block design that is geometrical and repeats regularly. A checked pattern may be woven or printed.

abstract print A pattern or motif not related to natural or real objects. May emphasize line, color, or geometric forms.

abstract print

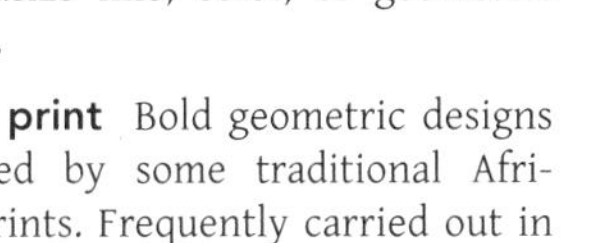

African print Bold geometric designs inspired by some traditional African prints. Frequently carried out in browns, blacks, and whites.

allover print Print covering the entire surface of the fabric from selvage to selvage in a repeat design. Compare with PRINTS, STRIPES, AND CHECKS: BORDER PRINT or a PANEL PRINT.

American Indian print Bold, stylized, geometric designs from North American Indian sources carried out in bright colors.

animal print Designs imprinted on fabrics in imitation of fur of the leopard, giraffe, ocelot, tiger, or zebra. Used on cotton, jersey, or on MODACRYLIC pile fabric to resemble furs. Popular since the mid-1960s.

apron checks A gingham fabric made in even checks of white and a color, designated as 4 × 4 or 8 × 8, according to number of yarns used in each check. Originally a fabric used for aprons, by extension, a type of check.

Art Deco print Small geometric prints, frequently outlined in black, inspired by *Exposition International des Arts Décoratifs et Industriels Modernes,* Paris, 1925; reintroduced in the late 1960s. *Der.* French, *art décóratif,* "decorative art."

Art Nouveau print Designs emphasizing curved, waving lines; stylized natural forms of plants, animals, and women; and a strong sense of motion. Inspired by early 20th-c. French art movement called *Art Nouveau.* First revived in late 1960s and seen occasionally since. *Der.* French, *nouveau,* "new art."

awning stripe Wide, even bands of one or more bright colors and white, woven or printed on coarse canvas. Formerly used for window awnings, now copied in lighter fabrics for sportswear.

aztec print Designs based on Mexican Indian, geometric motifs in bright colors usually banded in black.

†bandanna print (ban-dan'-nah) Designs, usually in black and white on a red or navy-blue background, in imitation of bandanna handkerchiefs. *Der.* Indian, *bandhnu,* "method of tie-dyeing cloth."

†batik print (baa'-teek) Designs, usually in dark blue, rust, black, or yellow, copied from Indonesian technique of painting with WAX before dyeing. Also see BATIK.

batik print

bayadère stripe (by-yah-deer') Horizontal stripes of varying widths in brilliant colors of red, green, blue, and gold. Also called *gypsy* or *Romany stripes. Der.* Hindu, "dancing girl."

∞bend Synonym for *stripe* in Middle Ages.

blazer stripe Inch-wide bands of one or several colors alternating with white. *Der.* From striped patterns of some blazer jackets.

block print See under PRINTS, STRIPES, AND CHECKS: BLOCK PRINTING.

†block printing Method of hand-printing fabric by cutting separate wood or linoleum blocks for each color in relief, then inking and printing individual colored blocks. Also called HAND-BLOCKED PRINT.

bookbinder print Designs copied from multicolored abstract, swirled, and wood-grain designs, formerly used on endpapers of expensively bound books.

border print Print designed so that one selvage forms a distinct border used at the hem of a dress or shirt or worked into the garment in some other way.

buffalo checks Heavy fabrics made with large square blocks in contrasting colors, often red and black, that are used for shirts or outerwear.

burnt-out print See under BURN-OUT/BURNT-OUT in alphabetical list.

calico print Allover print usually of tiny naturalistic sprigs of flowers on a colored background of red, blue, yellow, or black.

calico print

camouflage print A print pattern designed to help soldiers and hunters blend into the environment.

candy stripe Narrow bands of red on white background, imitating peppermint candy sticks.

chalk stripe Narrow lines of white, widely spaced, frequently used on gray, navy, or black flannel—a classic for men's business suits.

check See under PRINTS, STRIPES, AND CHECKS.

checkerboard checks Even squares of two colors alternating to form a row. Succeeding rows alternate between colors. *Der.* From resemblance to a checkerboard. Also called *even checks.*

chiné See under PRINTS, STRIPES, AND CHECKS: WARP PRINT.

coin dots See under PRINTS, STRIPES, AND CHECKS: DOTS.

competition stripe Brightly colored single or cluster stripes across front of garment borrowed from competitive-sports uniforms (e.g., football jerseys).

coverage The amount of ground or background in a print that can be seen after the motif is placed in repeat. See under PRINTS, STRIPES, AND CHECKS: REPEAT.

discharge print Design made on piece-dyed fabric by applying with copper rollers chemicals that dissolve and remove the dye in the design area. A white polka-dot design on a navy ground can be made in this manner.

dots Round spots used as a pattern in regular rows or a random arrangement (e.g., **coin dots,** which are larger than a dime; **pin dots,** which are as small as the head of a pin).

double ombré stripe (om-bray') Stripes of two colors shaded from light to dark, usually run horizontally, either printed or woven.

duplex print Fabric with same design printed on both sides to imitate a woven pattern.

engineered print Patterns designed with a particular end use in mind so that the length of each pattern repeat relates to the shape that will be cut from it, e.g., a silk scarf.

even checks See PRINTS, STRIPES, AND CHECKS: CHECKERBOARD CHECKS.

express stripe Twill weave fabric made with even stripes of blue and white running lengthwise. Originally used for janitors' uniforms, caps, and railroad workers' overalls. *Der.* From overalls worn by railroad workers.

fleur-de-lis (flur deh lee') French, stylized, lily design used in heraldry and part of the coat-of-arms of France's former royal family. Often used in formal repeat designs.

fleur-de-lis

†flocked print Design made by applying adhesive to fabric in a pattern and affixing tiny fibers. Frequently used to make border prints or flocked dotted Swiss. See under FLOCKING #2.

floral print Any design using flowers in either a natural or stylized manner (e.g., a daisy, a rose, or sprigs of flowers arranged together in repeat design).

geometric print 1. Circles, oblongs, squares, triangles, or other geometrical forms used in a printed design. 2. Print with background broken up by using a repeat design of rectangular forms, then imprinting another design within each unit.

geometric print #1

gingham checks Yarn-dyed checks of 1″, ½″, ⅛″, or ¹⁄₁₆″, made in a color alternating with white. Also called APRON CHECK (see under PRINTS, STRIPES, AND CHECKS). Also see under GINGHAM #1.

glen check/Glen Urquhart check See under PLAIDS AND TARTANS.

granny print Small floral print similar to a calico print. *Der.* Named after prints formerly worn by grandmothers for housedresses at the turn of the 20th c.

gun-club checks A three-color, double-check design consisting of a large check over a smaller one used in wool and worsted fabrics.

gypsy stripe See under PRINTS, STRIPES, AND CHECKS: BAYADÈRE STRIPES.

hairline stripe See under PRINTS, STRIPES, AND CHECKS: PINSTRIPES.

hand-blocked print See under PRINTS, STRIPES, AND CHECKS: BLOCK PRINTING.

hand-painted print Not a print at all, but rather a pattern painted directly on fabric.

hand-screened print See under PRINTS, STRIPES, AND CHECKS: SCREEN PRINTING.

harlequin check (har'-leh-kin) Check made of medium-sized, diamond-shaped colored motifs alternating with white.

hickory stripe Lengthwise stripes, usually blue and white with the blue two times the size of the white, woven in a denim-type fabric. Fancy hickory stripes are white stripes of varying widths on a blue ground. Also called *liberty stripes* and *victory stripes.* Originally used for janitors' uniforms and work clothes, now used for sportswear.

hound's-tooth/houndstooth checks Irregular colored ½″ to 2″ check that has the appearance of a square with points at two corners. Consists of yarn-dyed, twill weave colored checks that alternate with white. *Der.* From resemblance to pointed dog's tooth.

ikat See under PRINTS, STRIPES, AND CHECKS: WARP PRINT.

Indian print Either a hand-blocked print or a batik print as long as it originates in Madras or another city of India. Frequently made with inferior dye that *bleeds*, or runs, when the fabric is washed.

Japanese print Typically a scenic print featuring pagodas, foliage, and mountains, in a repeat design. Fabric is frequently used to make garments in the KIMONO style.

jungle print Designs using animals found in the jungle, e.g., leopards, tigers, and lions.

kente cloth print Fabric printed to imitate woven KENTE CLOTH.

Laura Ashley® print Provincial, small floral designs, typically Victorian, copied from antique designs and printed on cotton fabrics and wallpapers. Originally used for home furnishings, now used for clothing as well. Trademarked by Laura Ashley of England.

Liberty® print Trademark of Liberty, London, for wide range of printed fabrics. The best known are small, multicolored floral designs.

liberty stripe See under PRINTS, STRIPES, AND CHECKS: HICKORY STRIPES.

mattress-ticking stripe See under PRINTS, STRIPES, AND CHECKS: TICKING STRIPES.

medallion print Repeat round or oval design sometimes connected with realistic swags of foliage.

mosaic print Print introduced in early 1970s made by tiny square blocks of color arranged in a manner imitating a Byzantine mosaic.

motifs Design elements that create patterns when used in repetition.

naturalistic print Representation of flowers, shrubs, trees, and birds, arranged in a realistic manner in a repeat design.

ombré stripe Bands of color either woven or printed, usually composed of monochromatic tones of one color running from light to dark.

Op Art print Design, basically geometric, in which lines are "bent" or "warped" to give optical illusion, (e.g., a checkerboard design formed with some curved lines and squares not all of equal size). *Der.* Became popular in 1964 after an exhibit of Op Art paintings at the Museum of Modern Art in New York City.

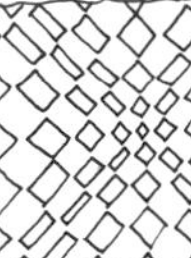

Op Art print

†paisley print Allover design featuring a design shaped like a teardrop, rounded at one end and with a curving point on the other. Frequently features rich colors with bold designs outlined in delicate tracery and swirls. A printed version of the pattern used in a PAISLEY SHAWL (see under CAPES, CLOAKS, AND SHAWLS: CASHMERE SHAWL #2.)

paisley print

†pajama checks DIMITY woven with coarser yarns at intervals in both warp and filling, forming a checked design. Used for men's underwear in 1920s and 1930s.

†pajama stripes Broad, boldly colored stripes used for PAJAMAS (see under SLEEPWEAR AND LOUNGEWEAR).

panel print A large design intended to be used in one length without repeating (e.g., one panel used for front—one for back of a dress). Usually made with hand-screened process and expensive.

patchwork print A print designed to mimic a patchwork quilt design. Design is printed on fabric, not made with "patches."

pencil stripe Vertical stripes as wide as a pencil line, with wider stripes of background color in between.

†photographic print 1. Large design covering entire front of the garment and reproduced in such a manner as to look like a black-and-white photo. Such prints have included pictures of Beethoven and Bach imprinted on sweatshirts; rockets, tigers, and pictures of movie stars imprinted on the front of a T-shirt-type dress. 2. Prints made by coating a photosensitive dye on fabric, then printing a design from a photographic negative.

pincheck Check made of very tiny squares.

pin dots See under PRINTS, STRIPES, AND CHECKS: DOTS.

pinstripe Very narrow stripes, the width of a straight pin, woven or printed in vertical stripes placed close together, either white stripes on dark ground or vice versa. Also called *hairline stripes.*

psychedelic print (sy-keh-dell'-ik) Unconventional designs done in extremely vibrant, full-intensity colors (e.g., chartreuse, fuchsia, and purple in bizarre combinations forming flowing patterns on the fabric). *Der.* Inspired by the hallucinations seen when under the influence of the drug LSD.

Pucci print (poo'-chee) Design introduced by Emilio Pucci, an Italian couturier, which is highly original and difficult to imitate. Pattern is abstract and composed mainly of brilliant, unusual color combinations outlined in black, usually printed on knitted fabric. White space is also utilized, but the distinguishing feature is the use of exciting color combinations. *Der.* Prints are inspired by medieval and late Renaissance designs still used in flags and costumes of the famous Palio in Siena.

rainbow stripe Full range of the spectrum hues arranged in bands on the fabric; a multistriped effect made by weaving or printing.

regimental stripe Wide, even, colored stripes on plain dark background. Used for men's tie fabrics. *Der.* Taken from insignia on British military uniforms in which colors of stripes identify the regiments.

registration The precise alignment of colors in a multicolored pattern.

repeat The process of adapting a pattern to the printing tools of the industry so it will print continuously along the length and width of the fabric.

†resist printing Method of printing fabric by first applying design to fabric with chemical paste that will not take dye, and then dying the fabric. When chemical is removed, design is left white against colored background, e.g., white polka dot on navy ground.

†roller print A printing process that utilizes a steel cylinder with an outer layer of copper, into which a design is etched. Each color in the print requires a separate engraved copper roller.

roman stripe Horizontal stripes, varied in size and color, grouped together with no contrast in background.

romany stripe See under PRINTS, STRIPES, AND CHECKS: BAYADÈRE STRIPES.

satin stripe Satin-woven stripes alternating with bands of plain fabric.

screen printing Printing process in which a design for each color is etched on separate pieces of pure dye silk or MANUFACTURED FIBER enclosed in wooden frames. Fabric to be printed is stretched on a long table; each screen is placed individually over the fabric; and paint, applied with a squeegee, is pushed through the etched sections. Process produces especially vibrant colors and unusual designs. When made using silk fabric, called *silk-screen printing.*

shadow stripe Indistinct narrow stripes, all in tones of one color family, woven vertically (e.g., navy, light blue, and gray-blue used together).

shepherd's check Small-checked fabric pattern usually made of black and white or of white and another color. Made in a TWILL WEAVE of fine- to medium-quality yarns. Originated from a checked length of fabric about 4 yards long and 1½ yard wide worn in a draped manner by Scottish shepherds in Scotland. Also called *shepherd's plaid.*

signature print A print that incorporates a logo or pattern that is associated with a particular brand and protected as intellectual property.

silk-screen print See under PRINTS, STRIPES, AND CHECKS: SCREEN PRINTING.

stenciled print Design made by using cardboard or metal cutouts over fabric, spraying paint or roller printing over them. The uncovered portions absorb the color and form the pattern.

stripes See under introduction to PRINTS, STRIPES, AND CHECKS.

stylized print Ideas presented in an abstract, rather than naturalistic, manner, reducing the objects to a design.

tablecloth check Large checkerboard check, 1–3″ in size, usually in red or blue alternating with white. *Der.* Originally used for tablecloths.

tattersall Fabric with an overcheck, approximately one-half-inch square made with colored lines in both directions, on a white or contrasting ground. Also called *tattersall checks.* Sometimes called *tattersall plaid.* Uses: vests, sport shirts, and coats. *Der.* Named after Richard Tattersall, English horseman, founder of Tattersall's London Horse Auction Mart established in 1776. Also see under PLAIDS AND TARTANS and VESTS.

tesselation The organization of information needed to render the appearance of three-dimensional objects.

ticking stripes Narrow, woven, dark-blue stripes, sometimes spaced in pairs, on a white ground made in a twill weave. *Der.* Originally a heavy fabric called *ticking* used to cover mattresses, now used for sport clothes and copied in lighter weights and other colors for clothing.

tie-dyed print Handmade print created by gathering the fabric and tying at intervals, then immersing in dye that does not penetrate the tied areas. When untied, reveals a pattern of irregular designs. Method originated in Dutch East Indies and became popular as a handicraft in the U.S. in late 1960s and after. Used on pants, knit shirts, dresses, and even furs. Also imitated commercially using other methods. Called *bandanna* in India.

victory stripe See under PRINTS, STRIPES, AND CHECKS: HICKORY STRIPE.

wallpaper print Tiny floral stripes alternating with plain-colored stripes, frequently of pastel colors. *Der.* Made in imitation of 19th-c. wallpaper.

warp print Design printed on warp yarns before fabric is woven, producing a watered effect with fuzzy edges. Also called *chiné* and *ikat.*

warp print

windowpane check Dark horizontal and vertical bars crossing over light background, giving effect of a window divided into small panes. Also called *windowpane plaid.*

---

priscilla apron See under APRONS.

private buying office The buying office of an individual retail firm. Also called *store-owned buying office.* Compare with ASSOCIATED BUYING OFFICE and INDEPENDENT BUYING OFFICE.

private label/private label brand Apparel, produced under some degree of control by a retailer, that has a retailer's label on the product. Unlike STORE BRANDS, private label merchandise may carry not only the store's name, but also names other than that of the store.

prix seam See under GLOVES AND GLOVE CONSTRUCTION.

product data management (PDM) Computer system that joins computer to computer, and also people to people by way of e-mail. This speeds up the product development cycle and reduces the time it takes to bring products to market.

product development See under APPAREL PRODUCT DEVELOPMENT.

production cutting A system of cutting large numbers of apparel pieces by laying fabric open across its entire width and for a specified length, then stacking fabric in multiple layers with the marker (see under PRODUCTION MARKER) resting on the top. Cutting is done either by computer or by using hand-cutting machines.

production marker Full-size master cutting layout not only of the pattern pieces for a specific style, but also for all the sizes specified for production.

production planning Function that links merchandising decisions with design and technical decisions in order to plan the activities related to making that product.

production sample Garment that reflects the exact product expected to come off of a production line. The final stage before the product goes into full production.

production specs Instructions for producing quantities of a product in the manufacturing environment, rather than an individual prototype garment.

production yardage The amount of fabric needed to fulfill a production order as opposed to yardage purchase to work up into a sample garment or product.

profile hat See under HEADWEAR.

progressive bundle system See under BUNDLE SYSTEM.

progressive lens See under EYEWEAR.

∞**promenade dress** See under DRESSES.

promenade skirt See under UNDERGARMENTS: HOOPS.

promotional markdowns Temporary reductions in retail price when an item first is marketed to the public.

promotional orders Purchases from vendors at lower-than-usual prices that can be sold at lower prices to the customer.

promotional pricing Offering apparel at reduced prices for a temporary period of time.

pronged setting See under GEMS, GEM CUTS, AND SETTINGS.

proportioned See under HOSIERY and PANTS.

prospector's shirt See under SHIRTS.

protos See under PROTOTYPE.

prototype A sample garment made for a new style that will go into a manufacturer's or designer's current line. Generally made in new or in a facsimile fabric. If made in muslin, the prototype is usually called a TOILE.

prussian collar coat See under COATS AND JACKETS.

psyche knot See under HAIRSTYLES.

psychedelic print See under PRINTS, STRIPES, AND CHECKS.

psychographics The study of the social and psychological factors that constitute consumers' lifestyles, including reference groups, life stage, activities, personality, attitudes, level of class consciousness, and motivation.

Pucci hat See under HEADWEAR.

Pucci print See under PRINTS, STRIPES, AND CHECKS.

pudding See under HEADWEAR.

pudding basin cut See under HAIRSTYLES: BOWL CROP.

puff 1. *v.* To make full, to enlarge. ∞2. *n.* A V-shaped gore of thin fabric that filled in space at back of waistband of men's trousers in the 19th c. Lacing was used to close gap, and fabric was pulled out through laces. 3. Also see under SHOULDERS AND SLEEVES: PUFF SLEEVE.

puffball skirt See under SKIRTS.

puffs 1. See under HAIRSTYLES. 2. See under PULLINGS OUT.

pug hood See under HEADWEAR.

pullayne See under FOOTWEAR: CRAKOW.

pullback See under SKIRTS.

pull-down cutting See under GLOVES AND GLOVE CONSTRUCTION.

pulled fabric work/pulled thread embroidery See under EMBROIDERIES AND SEWING STITCHES: PUNCH WORK and DRAWN FABRIC WORK.

∞**pullings out** Decorative effect used from 16th through mid-17th c. made by drawing out colored lining fabric or an undergarment through PANES or SLASHES in the outer garment, e.g., the DOUBLET, TRUNK HOSE, or sleeves. Also called *puffs.*

pullman slipper See under FOOTWEAR.

pull-on/pullover A garment without full-length opening so that it must be pulled over the head or feet, e.g., a pullover sweater as opposed to a cardigan, which buttons up the front. See under BLOUSES AND TOPS: PULLOVER; GLOVES AND GLOVE CONSTRUCTION: PULL-ON; PANTS: PULL-ON PANTS; SHIRTS: PULLOVER; SHORTS: PULL-ON SHORTS; SWEATERS: PULLOVER; and PULL-ON GIRDLE under UNDERGARMENTS: GIRDLE.

pultney cap See under HEADWEAR.

pump See under FOOTWEAR.

punched See under FOOTWEAR: PERFORATIONS.

punch work See under EMBROIDERIES AND SEWING STITCHES.

punk *adj.* Descriptive of fashion originating in London in the late 1970s, which served as both a demand for attention and a protest against the establishment by working-class teenagers, who were largely unemployed. Their goal was to scare and frighten their elders, who responded with feelings of rage, guilt, compassion, and fear. The style was characterized by pasty white makeup, blackened eyes, and much lipstick; hair was cut short and dyed or painted startling colors (e.g., red, yellow, orange, green, or lavender). Clothing included black leather jackets, stud-decorated jeans, and T-shirts printed with vulgar messages or pornographic pictures. Clothing was torn and soiled, held together by safety pins. Favorite accessory was a bicycle or dog chain worn around the neck, sometimes used to fasten

punk style

one leg to the other. Punk women wore hot pants, skirts with side slits, tight sweaters, and spike-heeled sandals. American version called **new wave punk** was an exaggerated theatrical look not associated with the working class. Look included ripped shirts, leather clothing, and extreme hairstyles (e.g., Mohawk, and wild, spiky, or frizzy hair dyed in patches of various colors; e.g., blue, orange, pink). Worn mainly by rock entertainers and their followers. *Der.* From punk rock music, popular in late 1970s and after. A spinoff of the punk movement was **cyberpunk,** which combined elements of punk style with futuristic fantasy and technological decoration. Along with black leather, rubber, and PVC (polyvinyl chloride plastics), they wore accessories made from cables and circuit boards. **Steampunk** originated in the 1980s and 1990s; it represents a blending of victorian, medieval, goth, or gypsy historical garb re-imagined with the knowledge of contemporary technology. Also see under HAIRSTYLES: PUNK HAIR.

punto lace See under LACES.

†pure-dye silk Soft, lustrous, high-quality silk fabric from which the gum, or impurities, have been removed. So called because less than 10 percent (15 percent for black goods) metallic salts have been added to give the fabric more weight. Pure-dye silk has a very good affinity for dye and may be printed, dyed, or screen-printed. Also see under WEIGHTED SILK.

puritan See under NECKLINES AND COLLARS and HEADWEAR.

purity ring See under JEWELRY.

†purl knit A weft knit fabric in which the knitting machine can form stitches on both the front and back of the fabric so that both sides of the fabric can have the same appearance.

purl stitch See under EMBROIDERIES AND SEWING STITCHES.

purse Synonym for HANDBAG. See under introduction to HANDBAGS AND RELATED ACCESSORIES.

push money See under SPIFFS.

push-up bra See under UNDERGARMENTS.

push-up jeans See under PANTS.

put-on See under WIGS AND HAIRPIECES.

puttee (putt-ee′) **1.** Legging worn by U.S. Army in World War I consisting of long strip of khaki-colored wool fabric; about 4″ wide, wrapped around leg from ankle to knee. **2.** Legging worn by U.S. Army made of shaped pieces of fabric or leather, usually closed with buckles, similar to GAITER. Also see under LEGGINGS.

put-together *adj.* Characterized by the use of separate items such as blouse, pants, and skirt, plus jewelry and accessories worn by each person in an individual manner rather than a formula for conformity. Popular in late 1960s and after.

puzzle ring See under JEWELRY.

†PVC Acronymn for POLYVINYL CHLORIDE, the chemical material from which **vinyon** fiber is composed. Vinyon is a manufactured fiber that is no longer manufactured in the U.S. and has limited use in consumer products.

PVC jacket See under COATS AND JACKETS.

PXM See under GLOVES AND GLOVE CONSTRUCTION.

pyjamas British variant of PAJAMAS. See under SLEEPWEAR AND LOUNGEWEAR.

pyramid coat See under COATS AND JACKETS.

pyramid heel See under FOOTWEAR.

python See under LEATHERS.

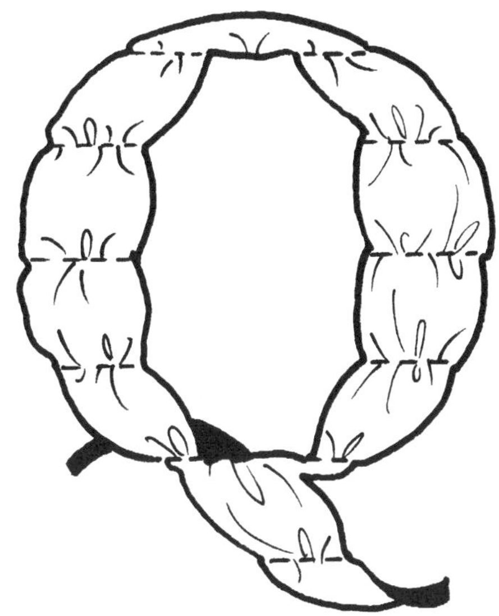

†qiviut (kay′-vee-ut) Underwool of the domesticated musk ox. Spun into yarn, this fine, soft fiber is knitted into a variety of apparel by Eskimo women in Alaska. Sold to tourists and by mail order.

QR See under QUICK RESPONSE.

quail-pipe boot See under FOOTWEAR.

∞quaintise See under ARMOR: COINTISE.

Quaker bonnet See under HEADWEAR.

Quaker cap See under HEADWEAR: JOAN.

Quaker collar See under NECKLINES AND COLLARS.

Quaker hat See under HEADWEAR.

quality assurance Inspection of the quality of products before and/or after production in order to be sure that they conform to specified quality standards.

quarter See under FOOTWEAR.

quartered cap See under HEADWEAR.

quarter socks See under HOSIERY.

quartz See under GEMS, GEM CUTS, AND SETTINGS.

quartz crystal watch See under WATCHES.

quatrefoil (kat′-rah-foyl) Geometrical four-lobed design derived from heraldry.

queen size Large-sized women's wear; particularly used for pantyhose.

queue (kew) See under HAIRSTYLES.

queue de lion (kew de le-ohn) See under HAIRSTYLES: LION'S TAIL.

queue-peruke See under WIGS AND HAIRPIECES.

†Quick Response (QR) Phrase coined for use in the American textile industry to describe streamlining of manufacture and delivery of apparel to retailers. A key component of Quick Response is ELECTRONIC DATA INTERCHANGE.

QR code A two-dimensional barcode designed to have its contents read at high speeds by QR scanners and smart phones.

quiff See under HAIRSTYLES.

quill See under FEATHERS.

∞quilling Trimming made of narrow, fluted fabric, used in 19th c.

quill work Decorative designs made on fabric and leather by North American Indians using porcupine quills.

†quilting Technique of joining together layers of fabrics, sometimes with BATTING or other filling between. Made by hand or machine, topstitching in crisscross lines, in diamonds, or in other patterns. Heat-sensitive manufactured fibers may be quilted electronically, with heat being used to fuse the layers together. Used to provide added bulk or warmth (e.g., quilted petticoats worn as underskirts in 18th and 19th c.). Used for robes, raincoats, sport jackets, coats, handbags, and linings.

∞quintise See under ARMOR: COINTISE.

quirk See under GLOVES AND GLOVE CONSTRUCTION.

quissionet See under UNDERGARMENTS: CUSHIONET.

quizzing glass See under EYEWEAR: MONOCLE.

quoif See under HEADWEAR: COIF.

quota A limit set on the quantity of textile fibers, yarns, fabrics, manufactured products, and the like that can be imported into a country in a specified period of time. Since 2005 when new international trade agreements went into effect such quotas have been eliminated.

rabat 1. See under CLERICAL DRESS. 2. See under NECKLINES AND COLLARS.

rabato See under NECKLINES AND COLLARS.

rabbi See under NECKLINES AND COLLARS: RABAT.

rabbit See under FURS.

raccoon 1. See under COATS AND JACKETS. 2. See under FURS.

raccoon dog See under FURS: USSURIAN RACOON.

racing *adj.* Describes items of apparel and accessories derived from or inspired by clothing worn for various forms of competitive racing (e.g., foot racing, auto racing, and horse racing). See under COATS AND JACKETS: RACING JACKET; FOOTWEAR: RUNNING SHOE; and GLOVES AND GLOVE CONSTRUCTION: ACTION GLOVE.

racer-back bra See under UNDERGARMENTS.

racing silks See under JOCKEY SILKS.

rack trade Apparel industry colloquialism for manufacturers who design, produce, and market belts to retailers.

†raffia (raf'-ee-uh) Fiber from species of Madagascar palm used for making hats, bags, and fabrics.

rag business/rag trade Slang used to refer to APPAREL INDUSTRY.

raglan boot See under FOOTWEAR.

raglan cape/raglan coat See under COATS AND JACKETS.

Raglan, Lord (1788–1855) Fitzroy James Henry Somerset, British general in Crimean War. After losing an arm in the Charge of the Light Brigade in 1854, had a coat designed with special sleeve, later called RAGLAN SLEEVE (see under SHOULDERS AND SLEEVES).

raglan sleeve See under SHOULDERS AND SLEEVES.

rail 1. See under SCARVES. 2. See under SLEEPWEAR AND LOUNGEWEAR: NIGHT RAIL. 3. See under HEADWEAR: COVERCHIEF.

railroad trousers See under PANTS.

railway pocket See under POCKETS.

railway stitch See EMBROIDERIES AND STITCHES: CHAIN and TRICOT STITCHES.

raiment Poetic or archaic term for clothing.

rain *adj.* Describes apparel intended for use in rainy weather. See under CAPES, CLOAKS, AND SHAWLS: RAIN CAPE and PONCHO #3; COATS AND JACKETS: RAINCOAT; FOOTWEAR: RAIN BOOT; HEADWEAR: RAIN BONNET and RAIN HAT.

rainbow stripe See under PRINTS, STRIPES, AND CHECKS.

rain dress See under DRESSES.

rain or shine coat See under COATS AND JACKETS.

rainwear Clothing and accessories that are waterproofed or water-repellent.

rainy daisy skirt/rainy day skirt See under SKIRTS.

raised embroidery See under EMBROIDERIES AND SEWING STITCHES.

rajah collar See under NECKLINES AND COLLARS: NEHRU.

rajah jacket See under COATS AND JACKETS.

†ramie Strong, soft, lustrous fiber, somewhat similar to linen from inner bark of *ramie* plant, formerly imported from China. Used for dress goods and hats. Also called *rhea* or *China grass.*

Ramillies wig See under WIGS AND HAIRPIECES.

Ramsay tartan See under PLAIDS AND TARTANS.

ranch coat See under COATS AND JACKETS.

ranch mink See under FURS.

rand See under FOOTWEAR.

ranelagh mob See under HEADWEAR.

ranger's hat See under HEADWEAR: MOUNTIE'S HAT.

rap See under HIP-HOP.

∞raphael body Woman's fitted bodice worn from late 1850s through mid-1860s with a low square neckline. Sometimes worn with a high-necked CHEMISETTE (see under BLOUSES AND TOPS) underneath and a matching skirt.

rapolin See under BRAIDS.

ra-ra skirt See under SKIRTS.

†raschel knit Type of warp knitting done on a special Raschel machine that can produce a wide variety of complex knit patterns, including lacelike effects.

rash guard See under SWIMWEAR.

rasta dreadlocks See under HAIRSTYLES: DREADLOCKS.

rasta styles Clothing adopted by reggae musicians of the 1970s and 1980s and their followers that consisted of practical jackets and trousers worn with a T-shirt of red, gold, and green (the colors of the Ethiopian flag) and a large knitted TAM (see under HEADWEAR) placed over hair dressed in DREADLOCKS (see under HAIRSTYLES).

rat See under HAIR ACCESSORIES.

ratcatcher See under SHIRTS.

†ratiné (rat'-in-ay) Spongy, rough, nubby-surfaced fabric loosely constructed in a plain weave. The appearance results from the use of ratiné yarn with nubs or knots at intervals. In better quality fabrics, the ratiné yarn is used in both directions. In less expensive variations, it is used only in the crosswise direction. *Der.* French, "frizzy" or "fuzzy."

rationals See under ACTIVEWEAR.

rat-tail braid See under BRAIDS.

rat-tail comb Comb for the hair with fine teeth and a long, pointed handle used for shaping curls.

rattan 1. Flat, reedlike stem from tropical palm woven to form basket handbags and other items. 2. See under CANE.

ratting See under HAIRSTYLES: BACK-COMBING.

rave Refers to clubs where the young danced all night—often in warehouses—that appeared first in late 1980s in Britain and then spread to other countries. The illegal drug Ecstasy became associated with some of these clubs, and some fatalities did result. Styles associated with raves included athletic shoes and T-shirts with smiley-face logos. Boys wore baggy jeans, T-shirts, and hooded sweatshirts, similar to HIP-HOP styles. Girls wore CROPPED TOPS (see under BLOUSES AND TOPS), HOT PANTS (see under SHORTS) and MINIDRESSES. Hats, jewelry, and whistles, used to accompany the music, were designed to attract attention.

rawhide See under LEATHERS.

†raw silk Silk fiber reeled from cocoon while still containing the gum or sericin that gives it a rough, slightly sticky feel. Often used to make women's summer suits.

†rayon GENERIC FIBER name for manufactured cellulosic fibers regenerated from short cotton fibers or wood chips. First produced by Count Hilaire de Chardonnet in 1889, it was worn at Queen Victoria's funeral in 1901. Known as "artificial silk" until 1927, after which the name rayon was used. Characteristics include a silky hand, shiny, lustrous appearance, good dye absorbency, and good draping qualities. Disadvantages include poor wrinkle recovery and a tendency to shrink. Used for lingerie, dresses, blouses, and shirts. *Der.* French, "ray of light."

razor-back bra See under UNDERGARMENTS.

razor bob See under HAIRSTYLES.

razor cut See under HAIRSTYLES.

ready-to-wear (RTW) Apparel that is mass produced in standard sizes. Records of ready-to-wear industry tabulated in U.S. Census of 1860 included hoop skirts, cloaks, and mantillas. In 1890, shirtwaists and wrappers were added; and, after 1930, dresses were also included. In French, called *prêt-à-porter* and in the U.K., *off the peg.* Also called *off-the-rack.*

rebato See under NECKLINES AND COLLARS: RABATO.

rebozo See under CAPES, CLOAKS, AND SHAWLS.

∞rebras (ray-brah') *adj.* Describes apparel or accessory that was turned back to reveal lining of coat, upturned brim on hat, or cuff of glove; from the 13th to 17th c., e.g., REVERS (see under NECKLINES AND COLLARS).

rècamier hairstyle See under HAIRSTYLES.

Rècamier, Madame (ray'-cahm-ee-ay) Jeanne Françoise Julie Adelaide (1777–1849), famous beauty of Napoleonic era. Painted by both David and Gérard, famous French artists of her time. Her mode of dress and hairstyles were widely imitated.

reciprocated construction See under HOSIERY.

reclaimed wool See under RECYCLED WOOL.

†recycled manufactured fibers Those fibers produced from post-consumer recycled products. One example is POLYESTER made from recycled soda bottles.

†recycled wool Under the amendments of 1980 to the Wool Products Labeling Act of 1939: (1) wool fiber that was pulled apart from yarn or fabric that was never used by the ultimate consumer or (2) wool fiber from yarn, fabric, or products used by consumers. This term replaced the terms **reclaimed wool, reused wool,** and **reprocessed wool**. Only wool that has never been used before can be called **wool, new wool,** or **virgin wool.**

Red Baron helmet See under HEADWEAR: AVIATOR'S HELMET.

red crown See under HEADWEAR.

red fox See under FURS.

redingote (red'-in-gote) 1. Ensemble consisting of a dress with matching or contrasting full-length coat. *Der.* French, "mannish woman's frock coat" or English, "riding coat." 2. See under COATS AND JACKETS.

reductions A lowering of the retail price of merchandise to encourage its sale so that new goods can replace older items. MARKDOWN, MARKUP, cancellation, and **discount** are all types of reduction used by retailers.

reefer See under COATS AND JACKETS.

regalia (re-gale′-yah) Clothing established by custom for a particular social or professional rank, position, or organization.

regard rings See under JEWELRY.

regatta shirt See under SHIRTS.

Regency costume 1. Period of English history during the regency of the Prince of Wales, 1811–1820, for George III. Noted for fashions of the DANDY and BEAU BRUMMELL (see in alphabetical listings). 2. *adj.* Describes apparel inspired by or derived from Regency Period styles. See under COATS AND JACKETS: REGENCY COAT and NECKLINES AND COLLARS: REGENCY COLLAR.

regenerated fibers See under MANUFACTURED FIBERS.

regimental stripe See under PRINTS, STRIPES, AND CHECKS.

regional market A market (see under MARKET #1) that serves U.S. retailers in a geographical region. Examples include Atlanta, Dallas, and Los Angeles.

registration See under PRINTS, STRIPES, AND CHECKS.

regular The ordinary size range for clothing as opposed to special sizes (e.g., regular boys' sizes as opposed to slim or husky).

regular orders Those orders placed in season for goods that are part of the usual line of a manufacturer's products.

regular pricing Prices normally charged for products.

relationship merchandising A trend for department stores to emphasize presentation, customer service, and inventory of the right products for their target market, so that they can differentiate themselves from other competing stores.

religious medal See under JEWELRY.

†remnant 1. Short length of fabric remaining after yardage has been cut off a bolt or roll of fabric. Too short to make an entire garment, these pieces are typically sold at a special prices. 2. Short lengths of fabric left at mill after winding bolts to be sold at retail. Also called *mill ends.* 3. Short lengths of lace or trimming sold at reduced prices.

remote displays Product displays not located in the actual store but placed in locations where they can alert potential customers to the store and its merchandise.

renaissance lace See under LACES.

reorders Orders for additional quantities of a product previously purchased by the retailer.

†rep Fabric with closely spaced crosswise ribs that may be made from a variety of fibers. Used for neckties and women's wear.

repeat See under PRINTS, STRIPES, AND CHECKS.

replaceable legs See under HOSIERY.

rep stitch See under EMBROIDERIES AND SEWING STITCHES.

reprocessed wool See under RECYCLED WOOL.

rerebrace See under ARMOR.

reserve wig See under WIGS AND HAIRPIECES.

resident buying office (RBO) An organization with offices at the MARKET that offer consultation services and procure merchandise for retailers. The two major types of resident buying offices are INDEPENDENT BUYING OFFICES and PRIVATE BUYING OFFICES.

†resist dyeing Piece-dyeing process in which some of the yarns are treated with chemicals or covered with some water-resistant substance. These yarns remain undyed while other, untreated yarns, take the dye, resulting in a two-toned fabric. Also see under PRINTS, STRIPES, AND CHECKS: RESIST PRINTING.

resist printing See under PRINTS, STRIPES, AND CHECKS.

retailer Individual or firm that sells merchandise to the public. In the fashion industry, that merchandise would be apparel and related products.

retail store/direct market brand Brand name on merchandise that is the same as the retailer (e.g., Gap, L.L. Bean).

reticella lace See under LACES.

reticulation See under HEADWEAR.

reticule See under HANDBAGS AND RELATED ACCESSORIES.

retro *adj.* Descriptive of a return to the fashion look of earlier decades (abbreviated use of the word "retrospective"). Used when fashions from past are updated and used as current styles. Sometimes the date is attached (e.g., *retro-thirties, retro-forties, retro-fifties*).

retro style of 2013 based on 1920s Great Gatsby-inspired garment

returns to vendor (RTV) Return of goods to a manufacturer by a retailer.

reused wool See under RECYCLED WOOL.

revers (ri-veerz) See under NECKLINES AND COLLARS.

reverse calf See under LEATHERS.

reverse glove See under GLOVES AND GLOVE CONSTRUCTION.

reverse guiche See under HAIRSTYLES: GUICHE.

reverse heel See FOOTWEAR: INVERTED HEEL.

reversible clothing Any item of clothing made so that it can be worn on either side. Usually of different color, pattern, or style on reverse side. Popular for capes, ponchos, vests, and coats. See under COATS AND JACKETS and VESTS.

reversible fabric Any fabric that may be used on either side (e.g., DOUBLE CLOTH or CREPE-BACK SATIN).

Rex Harrison hat See under HEADWEAR.

Reykjavik sweater See under SWEATERS: ICELANDIC SWEATER.

rhea See under RAMIE.

rhea feathers See under FEATHERS.

rhinegraves See under PETTICOAT BREECHES.

rhinestone See under GEMS, GEM CUTS, AND SETTINGS.

rhinestone button See under CLOSURES.

rhodes work See under EMBROIDERIES AND SEWING STITCHES: PUNCH WORK.

rhodium See under JEWELRY.

rhumba/rumba *adj.* Descriptive of clothing inspired by or derived from Latin or South American dance costumes, usually using ruffles. See under DRESSES: RHUMBA DRESS; SHOULDERS and NECKLINES: RHUMBA SLEEVE; and UNDERGARMENTS: RHUMBA PANTIES.

rhumba dress See under DRESSES.

†rib 1. Corded effect in fabrics caused by use of heavier yarns in either a lengthwise or crosswise direction (e.g. BENGALINE, GROSGRAIN, OTTOMAN, or FAILLE or on the diagonal by weaves such as TWILL). 2. Individual strip of metal that forms part of frame of umbrella (e.g., there are usually six to sixteen ribs in an umbrella). 3. See under RIB KNIT.

∞riband (rib′-and) 1. The border of an item of apparel, from 14th to 15th c. 2. Narrow band of decorative material or silk from 16th c.

ribbed hose See under HOSIERY.

†ribbon Long, narrow strip of fabric woven with selvages on both sides. May be made of heat-sensitive fiber and then sliced into narrow strips with heated knives that fuse the edges. Used mainly for trimming and for tying hair. Made in a variety of weaves: (a) cross-ribbed, called GROSGRAIN; (b) with looped edges, called PICOT; (c) cut-pile surface, or VELVET (sometimes satin-backed); (d) SATIN; very narrow pink or blue satin is called BABY RIBBON.

ribbons of childhood c. 1690

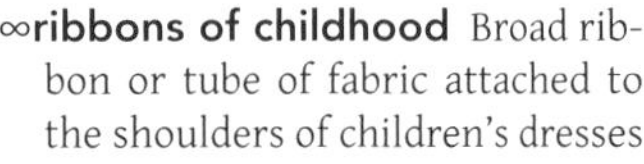

∞ribbons of childhood Broad ribbon or tube of fabric attached to the shoulders of children's dresses in the 17th and 18th c. Some costume historians consider these to be the same as LEADING STRINGS, however others consider them to be a stylized form of medieval hanging sleeves that were retained in the dress of upper-class children as a symbol of childhood.

†rib knit Knitted fabric that shows alternate lengthwise rows of ribs and wales on both sides. (See under RIB #1 and WALE #2.) More elastic, heavier, and durable than plain knitting. Used frequently on cuffs and necklines of sweaters and sport jackets.

rib-tickler Short top that just reaches to ribcage—similar to BARE MIDRIFF top. Also see under SWIMWEAR: RIB TICKLER SWIMSUIT.

rice braid See under BRAIDS.

rich peasant ***adj.*** Characterizes designs from the late 1960s, made in midi-length, of elaborate prints or plain-colored silks, velvets, and rich fabrics ornately decorated with colorful embroidery and rich bands of braid. Yves Saint Laurent, Oscar de la Renta, and Giorgio Sant'Angelo designed many clothes of this type.

rickrack See under BRAIDS.

ridicule See under HANDBAGS AND RELATED ACCESSORIES: RETICULE.

riding *adj.* Describes apparel used for or derived from clothing worn for the sport of horseback riding. See under ACTIVEWEAR: RIDING BREECHES, RIDING HABIT, RIDING SKIRT, and RIDING SMALLS; COATS AND JACKETS: RIDING COAT; and FOOTWEAR: RIDING BOOTS.

∞riding coat dress Woman's dress, cut in coat style, worn from 1785 to 1800, with buttons down front, large collar and lapels, long tight sleeves, and skirt with slight train.

riding stock See under TIES: STOCK.

rigid frame hat See under HEADWEAR.

rimless glasses See under EYEWEAR.

ring See under JEWELRY.

ring and pin See under ANNULAR BROOCH and PENANNULAR BROOCH.

ring bracelet See under JEWELRY: SLAVE BRACELET.

ring buckle See under CLOSURES.

ring collar See under NECKLINES AND COLLARS.

ringlets See under HAIRSTYLES.

ring purse See under HANDBAGS AND RELATED ACCESSORIES: MISER'S PURSE.

ring scarf See under SCARVES.

ring tops/bottoms See under SWIMWEAR.

ring watch See under WATCHES.

ripple cape See under CAPES, CLOAKS, AND SHAWLS.

ripple skirt See under SKIRTS.

rise Distance from crotch to top of waistband in pants; e.g. HIP-HUGGER PANTS (see under PANTS) have a low rise.

robe 1. Informal clothing usually styled like a loose coat; may be sashed, buttoned, zipped, or hang loose. Worn over pajamas or nightgown, at the beach, or for informal entertaining at home. Current meaning of the word is a shortened form of the word BATHROBE or DRESSING ROBE. See individual entries under SLEEPWEAR AND LOUNGEWEAR. 2. Ceremonial garment made in long, loose, flowing style (e.g., academic robe, clerical robe, or coronation robe). 3. During Middle Ages, a long, loose flowing gown or tunic worn as an outer garment. 4. From 1817 to 1830, an outer garment or wrap; synonym for the PELISSE (see under COATS AND JACKETS). *Der.* Originally the robe meant all furniture and personal effects belonging to a person. Later it meant his or her collection of clothes; still later a GOWN. 5. *v.* To put on a garment. Generally used in donning a ceremonial garment.

robe à la française See under GOWN À LA FRANÇAISE.

robe à l'anglaise See under GOWN À L'ANGLAISE.

robe à la Piedmontese See under SACK #1.

robe à la polonaise See under POLONAISE #1.

robe battante See under SACK #1.

∞robe de chambre (robe de sham'-bra) 1. A man's informal style of dressing intended for occasions other than court functions, receptions, and ceremonies in the 17th c. Considered a DESHABILLÉ style of dress. 2. A woman's dress suitable for informal occasions or in the boudoir, worn in the 19th c. Also called a *breakfast wrapper* in 1880s.

robe de style 1920s

robe de style See under DRESSES.

∞robe gironnée (jir-own-nay') Loose-fitting dress worn in 15th c. with PIPE-ORGAN PLEATS (see CLOTHING CONSTRUCTION DETAILS: GODET PLEATS) at waistline.

robe redingote See under DRESSES.

robes of state See under CORONATION ROBES.

robespierre collar See under NECKLINES AND COLLARS.

robe volante See under SACK #1.

∞robin front 19th-c. bodice with trimming from shoulder to waist forming a deep V.

∞robings/robins Wide, flat trimmings used in 18th and 19th c. around neck and down front of woman's bodice, sometimes continued down sides of open overskirt.

robin hood hat See under HEADWEAR.

Rob Roy tartan See under PLAIDS AND TARTANS: MACGREGOR TARTAN.

∞roc Loose-fitting gown of the late Middle Ages, of which the bodice is cut with a round neckline from which a cascade of gathers or pleats falls at the very center of the front and back. Worn unbelted, the gown was made with either long or short sleeves and worn over an underdress that is sometimes visible at the neck or sleeves. Most often seen in Flemish and German art.

roc 2nd half 15th c.

roccelo See under CAPES, CLOAKS, AND SHAWLS: ROQUELAURE.

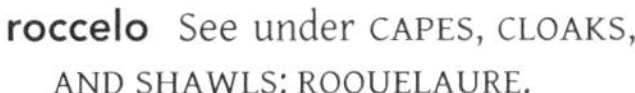

rochet See under CLERICAL DRESS.

rock crystal See under GEMS, GEM CUTS, AND SETTINGS.

rocker *adj.* Descriptive of styles associated with tough young British men in late 1950s; mixture of storm trooper and motorcyclist costume with crash helmet, tight jeans or DRAIN-PIPE TROUSERS (see under PANTS), black leather jacket, and knee-length boots or short boots with high heels. Rockers liked rock-and-roll music and admired Elvis Presley, movie star and singer, imitating his hairstyle.

rocklo See under CAPES, CLOAKS, AND SHAWLS: ROQUELAURE.

rococo embroidery See under EMBROIDERIES AND SEWING STITCHES.

roculo See under CAPES, CLOAKS, AND SHAWLS: ROQUELAURE.

rodeo suit See under ACTIVEWEAR.

roll 1. See under HEADWEAR. 2. See under HAIR ACCESSORIES.

rolled collar See under NECKLINES AND COLLARS.

rolled hem See under CLOTHING CONSTRUCTION DETAILS.

roller See under HEADWEAR.

roller blades See under FOOTWEAR.

roller print See under PRINTS, STRIPES, AND CHECKS.

rollers See under HOSIERY: ROLLUPS.

roller shoes See FOOTWEAR: HEELY.

roller skate See under FOOTWEAR.

roll farthingale See under FARTHINGALE.

rolling ring See under JEWELRY.

rolling stockings/hose See under HOSIERY: ROLLUPS.

rollio See under ROULEAUX.

roll line The foldline where the collar fall turns over the stand. See under NECKLINES AND COLLARS: COLLAR.

roll neck See under NECKLINES AND COLLARS.

rollpoint collar See under NECKLINES AND COLLARS.

roll sleeve See under SHOULDERS AND SLEEVES: ROLL/ROLL-UP SLEEVE.

roll-up 1. See under CUFFS. 2. See SHOULDERS AND SLEEVES: ROLL/ROLL-UP SLEEVE.

rollups See under HOSIERY.

roman collar See under CLERICAL DRESS: CLERICAL COLLAR.

romanian embroidery See under EMBROIDERIES AND SEWING STITCHES: HOLBEIN WORK.

romanian stitch See under EMBROIDERIES AND SEWING STITCHES: ORIENTAL COUCHING.

roman lace See under LACES: RETICELLA LACE.

Roman leggings See FEMORALIA.

roman stripe See under PRINTS, STRIPES, AND CHECKS.

romantic 1. *adj.* Descriptive of feminine styles for women, and sometimes men, often decorated with lace, frills, and ribbon and made in soft fabrics. 2. Styles associated with the Romantic period (c. 1820–1850) in art, literature, and music in Western European and American culture.

romantic *adj.* Descriptive of a design tendency for rilly, fluffy ruffles, choker-necked Victorian blouses, and softer fabrics in 1967 after the rigid lines and geometric look of the Courréges style. Also see under NEW ROMANTICS and EDWARDIAN.

romany stripes See under PRINTS, STRIPES, AND CHECKS: BAYADÈRE STRIPES.

romeo hairstyle See under HAIRSTYLES.

romeo slipper See under FOOTWEAR.

romper cover-up See under SWIMWEAR.

rompers 1. Bloomer-type short pants introduced for children's playwear during the World War I period. 2. Similar styles for adult women in one-piece sport suits or in sleepwear consisting of shirt and shorts or bloomers, joined by waistline seam. 3. See under SLEEPWEAR AND LOUNGEWEAR.

rondella See under JEWELRY.

∞**ropa** A woman's outer gown, made either sleeveless or with sleeves, that fell from the shoulders, unbelted in an A-line to the floor. Originating in Spain in the first part of the 16th c., it then spread throughout Europe.

ropa 2nd half 6th c.

roped chain See under CHAIN #1.

rope necklace See under JEWELRY.

roquelaure See under CAPES, CLOAKS, AND SHAWLS.

rosary String of beads arranged on a chain with a pendant cross. Used by Roman Catholics for counting the prayers of the Rosary.

rosebery collar See under NECKLINES AND COLLARS.

rose cut See under GEM, GEM CUTS, AND SETTINGS.

rose-point lace See under LACES.

rose quartz See under GEMS, GEM CUTS, AND SETTINGS.

rosette (ro-zet′) 1. Ornament arranged like a rose—usually ribbon arranged in standing loops or flattened into a formal pattern. Used to trim shoes in 17th c. and since then to trim dresses and hats. See under SHOE ROSES. 2. See under FURS. 3. See under LEATHERS.

rotary screen printing See under PRINTING.

rotonde See under CAPES, CLOAKS, AND SHAWLS.

rouche See under RUCHING.

Rough Rider shirt See under SHIRTS.

∞**rouleaux** (roo-low′) Tubular-shaped trimming stitched at regular intervals to make puffs of fabric. Used around hems of women's skirts in the 1820s. Also called *rollio.*

roulettes See under PIPES.

∞**round dress/round gown** In 18th to mid-19th c., a full-length dress that did not open at the front to show a petticoat. Sources differ as to whether these gowns did or did not have TRAINS. Also called a *closed robe* or *closed gown.*

round-eared cap See under HEADWEAR.

round hose See under TRUNK HOSE.

roundlet See under HEADWEAR.

round pocket See under POCKETS.

round seam See under GLOVES AND GLOVE CONSTRUCTION: OVERSEAM.

rowle See under HAIR ACCESSORIES: ROLL.

∞**roxalane bodice** Low-necked bodice of late 1820s, trimmed with wide pleated folds meeting at an angle at the waistline. Bodice had a central bone that held pleats in place.

roxalane sleeve See under SHOULDERS AND SLEEVES.

∞**roxburgh muff** Woman's muff carried in 1816, made of swansdown fabric sometimes gathered at intervals and trimmed with bands of white satin.

royal george stock See under TIES.

Royal Stewart tartan See under PLAIDS AND TARTANS.

RTV See under RETURNS TO VENDOR.

RTW Abbreviation for the READY-TO-WEAR clothing industry.

rubber boot See under FOOTWEAR.

rubber mask See under MASKS.

rubbers See under FOOTWEAR.

rubber shoe/rubber moccasin See under FOOTWEAR: DUCK SHOE.

rubens hat See under HEADWEAR.

rubicelle See under GEMS, GEM CUTS, AND SETTINGS: SPINEL.

ruby See under GEMS, GEM CUTS, AND SETTINGS.

ruby keeler shoe See under FOOTWEAR.

ruching (roosh'-ing) **1.** Trimming made by pleating a strip of lace, ribbon, net, fine muslin, or silk so that it ruffles on both sides, and then stitching through the center of pleating. Also spelled *rouche, ruche.* **2.** Contemporary usage also applies to clothing with large rippled areas formed by gathers.

ruching #1

ruff See under NECKLINES AND COLLARS.

ruffle Strip of cloth, lace, or ribbon gathered along one edge or cut in a curve to produce a ripple. Used to trim neckline, wrist, or hem of apparel. Also see under FLOUNCE.

rug See under WIGS AND HAIRPIECES.

rugby shirt See under SHIRTS.

rugby shorts See under SHORTS.

rumba See under RHUMBA.

rump furbelow See under UNDERGARMENTS.

run A flaw that may develop in jersey knit fabrics (see JERSEY #1), especially hosiery, when a stitch breaks and the stitches connected to it unravel vertically. Also called a *ladder* because the flaw has the appearance of a ladder.

running shoe See under FOOTWEAR.

running shorts See under SHORTS: ATHLETIC SHORTS.

running stitch See under EMBROIDERIES AND SEWING STITCHES.

run proof In hosiery and knits, items made with specially interlocked stitches that withstand runs.

†**run resistant** In hosiery and knits, stitches with locked or displaced loops that inhibit runs but do not prevent them.

Russell, Lillian (1861–1922) American singer and actress noted for her spectacular costumes—having had fitted, narrow waistlines, full bosoms, and hips—as well as for her large hats. She represented the fashion ideal at the turn of the 20th c.

Russian blouse See under BLOUSES AND TOPS: COSSACK BLOUSE.

∞**Russian blouse suit** **1.** For boys: A long belted blouse with box pleats in front, sometimes made with a sailor collar, sometimes with a turndown collar. Worn with knickers that came below the knees. **2.** For girls: A long overblouse, sometimes with Russian styling, worn over a full circular skirt during the early 20th c.

russian braid See under BRAIDS: SOUTACHE BRAID.

russian collar See under NECKLINES AND COLLARS: COSSACK COLLAR.

Russian crown sable See under FURS: SABLE.

russian embroidery See under EMBROIDERIES AND SEWING STITCHES.

russian leather See under LEATHERS.

russian shirtdress See under DRESSES.

russian-style dress See under DRESSES.

Russian styles **1.** Clothing and accessories copied from those worn in pre-Revolutionary Russia. See under BLOUSES AND TOPS: COSSACK BLOUSE; NECKLINES AND COLLARS: COSSACK COLLAR; HEADWEAR: COSSACK HAT; SHIRTS: COSSACK SHIRT; and ZHIVAGO. **2. russian** *adj.* Descriptive of a fall-winter 1976–77 collection of Russian style dresses—evening dresses had long sleeves and tight-fitting bodices to a little below hips; usually made in black with bouffant gathered skirt in colored satins (e.g., red, green). A coat with high waistline made of elaborate gold brocade was also shown with fur Russian cossack hat from Saint Laurent. Also see under ZHIVAGO.

S.A. 1. Abbreviation for SEVENTH AVENUE, an allusion to New York City garment district, coined by trade newspaper *Women's Wear Daily.* 2. Sex appeal, as exemplified by glamorous Hollywood film stars in the 1940s.

sabaton See under ARMOR.

sable See under FURS.

sabot See under FOOTWEAR.

sabot sleeve See under SHOULDERS AND SLEEVES.

sabot-strap shoe See under FOOTWEAR.

sabrina neckline See under NECKLINES AND COLLARS.

sack/sac/saque/sack gown ∞1. Various styles of women's dresses, in the 16th to the 18th c. In the 16th c. seems to have referred to a loose-fitting gown for country wear. It is mentioned in *Pepys' Diary* in 1669, but its lines are not clear. Much used in the 18th c., this dress was fashionable in France at beginning of 18th c. (about 1704) and popular until 1755. Popular in England from 1720 to 1780. Its main feature was the full back or **sack-back** (called a WATTEAU BACK in the 19th c.) with two large box pleats stitched from neckband to shoulders and then hanging free to make a full skirt. In its earliest form, it was unbelted and loose in front and back from shoulder to floor and was also called *robe battante* (bah-tahnt'), *robe volante* (voh-lahnt'), or *innocente* (ahn'-oh-sahnt). From 1720 to 1730 the bodice was fitted at sides and front, loose in back. After 1750, the skirt was split up the front to reveal an underskirt. From 1770s pleats in back were sometimes stitched to the waist as in ROBE À L'ANGLAISE, or loose as in ROBE À LA PIEDMONTESE or *Piedmont gown.* The **Brunswick gown**, worn from 1760 to 1780, was sack-backed with a front-buttoned bodice and long sleeves and also known as the *German gown.* Also called *Adrienne.* ∞2. Woman's or child's loose-fitting jacket of 1896. 3. See under DRESSES: CHEMISE.

sack #1, 18th c.

sack-back See under SACK #1.

sack coat See under COATS AND JACKETS: STROLLER.

sack dress See under DRESSES: CHEMISE.

sack jacket See under COATS AND JACKETS.

sack overcoat See under COATS AND JACKETS.

sack suit Man's single-breasted, daytime suit of early 20th c. Made with unfitted long jacket that has wide shoulders. Pants were cut wide in legs and at hems. The earliest example of the modern business suit.

sack suit

sacque (sack) 1. See SACK. 2. Layette item of late 19th and early 20th c. for an infant. Styled like a small jacket usually having ribbon ties for closing. 3. See under SLEEPWEAR AND LOUNGEWEAR: DRESSING SACQUE.

saddle See under FOOTWEAR; HANDBAGS AND RELATED ACCESSORIES; SHOULDERS AND SLEEVES; and EMBROIDERIES AND SEWING STITCHES.

saddle coat See under COATS AND JACKETS: POMMEL SLICKER.

saddle leather See under LEATHERS.

saddle shoulder See under SHOULDERS AND SLEEVES.

saddle stitch See under EMBROIDERIES AND SEWING STITCHES.

saddle-stitched seam 1. See under GLOVES AND GLOVE CONSTRUCTION: SADDLE-STITCHED SEAM. 2. See under FOOTWEAR: SADDLE SEAM.

safari *adj.* Describes garments and accessories adapted from, or similar to, the BUSH JACKET (see under COATS AND JACKETS) and other clothes worn in South Africa by hunters on safaris. In 1967 Dior restyled the bush jacket—a belted hunting jacket buttoned down the front, with two bellows pockets with flaps on chest, and two toward the hem—for daytime wear. In 1980s this style resurfaced with the popularity of the film *Out of*

safari dress

Africa, 1986, starring Meryl Streep and Robert Redford. *Der.* From name for an African hunting trip. See under BELTS: SAFARI BELT; HANDBAGS AND RELATED ACCESSORIES: SAFARI BAG; HEADWEAR: SAFARI HAT; POCKETS: BELLOWS POCKET; and SHIRTS: SAFARI SHIRT.

safeguard 1. See under SKIRTS: FOOT-MANTLE. 2. See under APRONS. 3. See under SWADDLING CLOTHES.

safety glasses See under EYEWEAR.

safety pin 1. Utilitarian elliptical pin with covered head to sheath the point, introduced from Denmark in late 1870s. 2. Similar-shaped pin used on front of kilt. Also called *kilt pin.* 3. See under JEWELRY.

safety shoe See under FOOTWEAR.

safety stitch A category of machine stitches used for sewing seams consisting of a single-needle chain stitch and a three-thread over-edge stitch formed simultaneously.

safety toe See under FOOTWEAR.

sagum See under CAPES, CLOAKS, AND SHAWLS.

†sailcloth Durable canvas fabric made in a rib weave. When made in medium weight in cotton or a cotton blend, it is used for sportswear.

sailor *adj.* Since 1860s, descriptive of clothing and accessories inspired by uniforms worn by British, French, and U.S. Navy. See under HEADWEAR: SAILOR HAT; NECKLINES AND COLLARS: SAILOR COLLAR; PANTS: SAILOR PANTS; SCARVES: SAILOR SCARF; SHORTS: SAILOR SHORTS; and TIES: SAILOR'S TIE and SAILOR'S REEF KNOT.

sailor dress See under DRESSES.

sailor suit Boy's suit, introduced in 1860s, that was inspired by French and British sailors' uniforms. It consisted of MIDDY BLOUSE (see under BLOUSES AND TOPS) with braid-trimmed square collar in back, plus either baggy KNICKERS or DANISH TROUSERS (see under PANTS). Called a *jack tar suit* when made with bell-bottom trousers (younger boys wore knickers) in 1880s and 1890s. Has continued as a popular children's style.

sailor suit

Saint George cross See under JEWELRY: CRUSADER'S CROSS.

Saint Laurent hat See under HEADWEAR.

salaried buying office See under INDEPENDENT BUYING OFFICE.

sallet See under ARMOR.

Sally Jess bag See under HANDBAGS AND RELATED ACCESSORIES.

salon de couture (koo-ture') Haute couture designer's showroom.

salon dresses A department store designation for expensive dresses made by well-known designers sold in a special room in department stores. Dresses are not hung on view in salesroom but brought out by salespeople and sometimes shown on live models.

salt-box pocket See under POCKETS.

Salvation Army bonnet See under HEADWEAR.

samarra/samarre See CHAMARRE.

sam browne belt See under BELTS.

sample cut Fabric of three to five yards in length obtained by the apparel manufacturer from a textile mill to use for making a PROTOTYPE garment.

sample garment A garment made to test the design and fit of a pattern before it goes into production.

sample sewer/sample hand A person with excellent sewing skills who constructs the PROTOTYPE garment using equipment and production processes similar to those that would be used in the manufacturing process.

sample size Body measurements from which the full size range of a garment is developed.

sample yardage Fabric purchased for design exploration.

sandal See under FOOTWEAR.

sandalfoot hose/sandalfoot pantyhose See under HOSIERY.

sandwich-board jumper See under JUMPERS.

†Sanforized Trademark formerly appearing on fabrics subjected to treatments that provided residual shrinkage of no more than one percent, despite repeated laundering.

sanitary sock See under HOSIERY.

∞sans culottes (sahn koo-lowt') Nickname for those opposing the monarchy during the French Revolution (i.e., those who wore trousers—the common people—instead of BREECHES, worn by the aristocrats). *Der.* French, literally "without breeches."

santon See under NECKLINES AND COLLARS.

sapphire See under GEMS, GEM CUTS, AND SETTINGS.

sapphirine See under GEMS, GEM CUTS, AND SETTINGS: SPINEL.

sard See under GEMS, GEM CUTS, AND SETTINGS: CARNELIAN.

sardinian sac See under COATS AND JACKETS.

sardonyx See under GEMS, GEM CUTS, AND SETTINGS.

sari (sah'-ree) (*saree*) Woman's outer garment consisting of a long length of cotton, silk, or manufactured-fiber fabric wrapped around the waist and pleated at the side to form a skirt. One end is thrown over shoulder or used to cover the head. Worn with bare midriff blouse called a CHOLI (see under BLOUSES AND TOPS). Western adaptations of the garment have been worn since the early 1940s.

sari

sarong/sarong dress See under DRESSES, SKIRTS, and UNDERGARMENTS.

sarong swimsuit See under SWIMWEAR.

sash See under BELTS.

∞**sash ring** Large ring on a chain suspended from a belt at the hip in late 1860s. Overskirt was pulled through ring to drape the skirt.

Sassoon hairstyle See under HAIRSTYLES.

satchel See under HANDBAGS AND RELATED ACCESSORIES.

†**sateen** Smooth, glossy cotton fabric made in the SATEEN WEAVE (see under SATIN WEAVE) with floating crosswise yarns on the right side, given a lustrous finish, and used mainly for linings. Formerly spelled *satine.*

sateen weave See under SATEEN.

†**satin** Smooth, lustrous, silk fabric woven with floating yarns in the warp in many variations: (a) woven with a crepe back and called CREPE-BACK SATIN; (b) finished to be rather stiff in texture and called panne satin; (c) finished with a dull-nubbed surface (see NUB YARN) and a satin back and called antique satin. Usually made of FILAMENT YARNS. *Der.* Name derived from *Zaytoun,* now Canton, China, from which fabrics were shipped in the Middle Ages.

satin back See under CREPE-BACKED SATIN.

satin-backed ribbon See under RIBBON.

satine See under SATEEN.

satin-faced crepe See under CREPE-BACKED SATIN.

satin stitch See under EMBROIDERIES AND SEWING STITCHES.

satin stripe See under PRINTS, STRIPES, AND CHECKS.

†**satin weave** A basic weave in which the lengthwise, and sometimes the crosswise yarns, float over five to eleven yarns before interlacing. As a result the surface has a smooth feel and a lustrous appearance. When floats are in the crosswise direction, fabric is called *sateen,* and this construction is sometimes called a †**sateen weave.**

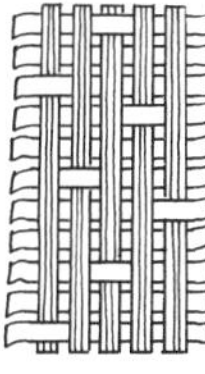
satin weave

sauna suit See under ACTIVEWEAR.

sausage curl See under HAIRSTYLES.

sautoir (sow-twar) 1. See under JEWELRY. 2. See under NECKLINES AND COLLARS: SANTON.

Savile Row Street in London's West End where many of the finest men's custom tailoring shops have been located since Henry Poole & Co. opened in 1843. They cater to wealthy internationals, stressing quality and conservatism.

saw-toothed hem See under CLOTHING CONSTRUCTION DETAILS.

saxony lace See under LACES: PLAUEN LACE.

scabilonians See under UNDERGARMENTS.

scaling hose See under TRUNK HOSE.

scallop 1. The shell of a mollusk, used in ornamentation. See HEADWEAR: COCKLE HAT. 2. One of series of curves or circle segments—like one edge of the scallop shell—forming an ornamental edge on fabric, lace, or garment edges. See under CLOTHING CONSTRUCTION DETAILS: SCALLOPED HEM.

scallop #2

scallop neckline See under NECKLINES AND COLLARS.

scalpette See under WIGS AND HAIRPIECES.

scarab (skar'-ab) A beetle, regarded as the symbol of immortality by the ancient Egyptians, used in stylized designs on fabrics or carved from gemstones with inscriptions on the undersides. Semiprecious stones carved with scarabs are still used in rings and bracelets, and were especially popular in the United States in the late 1940s.

scarab bracelet See under JEWELRY.

scarborough ulster See under COATS AND JACKETS.

scarf cap See under HEADWEAR.

scarf hat See under HEADWEAR.

scarf mask See under MASKS.

scarf pin See under JEWELRY: STICKPIN.

scarf slide See under NECKERCHIEF SLIDE.

SCARVES

scarf (pl. *scarfs* or *scarves*) 1. Decorative or utilitarian accessory worn draped around the shoulders and neck or over the head for warmth or adornment. May be square, oblong, or triangular, and made of knitted, crocheted, or woven fabric. 2. A decorative sash worn diagonally from shoulder to opposite hip, like a BALDRICK. 3. See under TIES.

antoinette fichu See under SCARVES: FICHU #1.

apache scarf (ah-patch'-ee or ah'-pash) Man's small square or triangular scarf introduced in late 1960s for wear instead of a necktie. Worn knotted or pulled through a slide. *Der.* French slang for gangster or thug, especially as depicted by French nightclub dancers. The French word taken from the southwest American Indian tribe, thought to be very fierce.

ascot scarf Oblong scarf, frequently white, lapped over and worn loosely around the neck by men and women. Reintroduced in late 1960s by Yves Saint Laurent, the Paris couturier, who emblazoned it with his initials, making it a status symbol. *Der.* Named for a scarf worn at Ascot Racecourse in England. Shown at TIES: ASCOT.

babushka (bah-boosh′-ka) Triangular- or square-shaped scarf, folded diagonally, worn draped over head and tied under chin in manner of Russian peasant woman. *Der.* Russian, "grandmother." So called because it was worn by older Russian immigrants to the United States. Also called a *kerchief.*

∞**bachlick** Woman's FICHU (see under SCARVES) of CASHMERE edged with SWAN'S DOWN, with a hoodlike point finished with tassel in back. Worn over daytime dresses in late 1860s.

bandanna (ban-dan′-nah) Large, square, cotton handkerchief of either red or blue, with distinctive black-and-white design. Worn in late 19th and early 20th c., tied around the head or neck by workmen and later adopted in all colors for wear with sport clothes.

∞**bandelet** (ban′-duh-let) Any type of scarf in the 16th c.

bayadère (by-yah-deer′) Long narrow scarf of silk or lace worn in early 19th c. *Der.* Costume of Indian *bayadère* or "dancing girl."

blue billy Neckcloth made of blue fabric with white polka dots; introduced by the fighter William Mace and worn from about 1800 to 1820.

boa (bow′-ah) Round, narrow, long scarf worn since 1829, and especially fashionable in 1890s, 1920s, and 1970s. Made of feathers, pleated silk, fur, or swansdown. Also called *french boa.*

boa

∞**breast kerchief** Scarf worn under doublet or gown, wrapped around neck and shoulders for warmth, in late 15th to mid-16th c.

∞**buffon** (boof′-own) (*buffont*) Woman's large scarf or neckerchief of gauze or fine linen draped around neck, shoulders, and puffed out over the chest. Sometimes supported by wire framework in 1780s. Also spelled *buffont.*

buffon

calligraphic scarf Letters of the alphabet arranged to form a pattern in much the same manner a picture is "drawn" on a typewriter by using Xs and other characters. Introduced in late 1960s.

charlotte corday fichu See under SCARVES: FICHU #1.

∞**chemisette** (shem-ee-zet′) Scarf or FICHU (see under SCARVES) of cambric, tulle, or muslin fabric worn as fill-in for low-necked gown in 18th and 19th c. Also see under PARTLET and NECKLINES AND COLLARS: TUCKER. Also called a *chemise tucker.*

∞**chin cloak** From about 1535 to 1660s a synonym for MUFFLER or SCARF (see under SCARVES). Also called *chin clout, chin cloth,* and *chinner.*

comforter Woolen scarf worn around the neck in cold weather, so named from 1840 on.

designer scarf Scarf made in an elaborate design using beautiful or unusual colors. In the late 1960s, it became popular to print the name of a famous company or designer on the pure silk scarves, which were then called **signature scarves.** The fashion started in Paris with Balenciaga, Dior, and Saint Laurent—and spread to Italy and U.S. as a status symbol for most prestigious designers.

dog collar scarf Triangular or oblong scarf folded to go around neck twice, bringing ends back to the front where they are knotted or looped over.

écharpe (eh′-sharp) Synonym for SCARF. *Der.* French, "scarf."

fanchon See under SCARVES: HALF HANDKERCHIEF.

fascinator Large long woolen scarf made in a lacy knit worn over the head or around the shoulders by women. First fashionable in the early 1890s and worn at intervals since.

feather boa See under SCARVES: BOA.

∞**fichu** (feesh′-u) 1. Neckwear usually consisting of a large square of muslin folded diagonally to form a triangle and worn in the 18th c. As time progressed, became more elaborate—shaped to fit the neck, trimmed with ruffles, lace, and RUCHING. Frequently fastened or tied in front with hanging ends. Continued to be worn until about 1871. Variations in the style were often named after women of the 17th and 18th c. and included the **antoinette fichu** or *marie antoinette fichu* (1850s), draped around the neck and crossed at the waistline to form two long cords that fall to the hips; the **charlotte corday fichu** (mid 1860s), made of grenadine trimmed with a ribbon threaded through a wide hem, which crossed in front, and tied in back; **fichu lavalliere** (fish-u la-va-leer) (1868), with sides not crossed in front and fastened with a button. Named after the Duchesse de La Vallièré, a mistress of

fichu #1

King Louis the XIV; **martha washington fichu** (mid-1890s), large and draped, extending to shoulders with pointed ends fastened by a rosette of lace in front, and two wide ruffles of lace extended around the edge (*Der.* An adaptation of style worn by Martha Washington, wife of the first U.S. president, George Washington). *Der.* French, "handkerchief." **2.** A triangle of net edged in lace worn in early 19th c. as a capelet.

fichu lavalliere See under SCARVES: FICHU #1.

∞**fichu menteur** (feesh′-u mahn-ture′) Scarf worn by women in 1780s at neck of coat or low bodice. Draped so it puffed out to increase apparent size of bust. Also see under SCARVES: BUFFON.

∞**flea fur** Fur scarf made of any small animal with head, tail, and paws attached to a jeweled muzzle and chain. Worn by women during late 16th c. as decoy for obnoxious insects. *Der.* From fact that "fleas" were attracted to it. Also called *Flohpelzchen* (flow-pelz′-ken).

Flohpelzchen See under SCARVES: FLEA FUR.

∞**folette/follette** (fall-et) Loose scarf or FICHU (see under SCARVES) in triangular shape of soft light-colored fabric, worn during first half of 18th c. Ends were tucked into neckline of bodice.

foulard scarf (foo-lahr′) **1.** Scarf of silk twill, called FOULARD, often made with small designs printed on plain ground. Originally imported from India.

∞**fraise** (fraze) **1.** Embroidered muslin scarf, folded across the chest and kept in place by an ornamental pin, worn by women in 1836 with a carriage dress. **2.** Fashionable neckpiece worn by women from about 1877 to 1885. Had a FRILLING or RUCHING around a high neckline which continued down front of dress nearly to waistline, trimmed with bow and frilled at edges.

french boa See under SCARVES: BOA.

fur scarf Neckpiece made of several skins of a small animal such as *mink* or one large fox skin complete with head, tail, and paws. Popular in the 1930s in black, platinum, or silver fox. In the late 1940s and early 1950s made of MINK, SABLE, FISHER, KOLINSKY, and BAUM MARTEN (see under FURS). A fashion revived in 1973, continuing into 1980s and periodically since.

∞**galatea fichu** (gal-ah-tay′-ah feesh′-u) Large ruffled FICHU (see under SCARVES) of mid-1890s with unpressed vertical pleats ending at center front waistline in a point and two ruffles around the outside edge.

hacking scarf Long oblong scarf doubled and placed at back of neck. Both ends are then pulled through loop and hang down in front. *Der.* Long scarf, originally 72″, worn by four-in-hand coach drivers in Old England; popular at Oxford and Cambridge Universities in England in 1931 when it was worn by Prince of Wales, becoming a fad for U.S. college students in 1932.

∞**half handkerchief** Neck or headscarf worn by women in 18th and early 19th c. made of decorative fabric in triangular shape. From 1830s on, called **fanchon.**

infinity scarf A long scarf in which the ends have been sewn together so that it can be looped several times around the neck.

kerchief Scarf worn as head or neck covering, usually a square folded into triangle with crossed ends fastened on chest. Also called *neckerchief.* Originally spelled *kerchner, kercheve, karcher.* See under SCARVES: NECKERCHIEF.

mantilla See under HEADWEAR.

martha washington fichu See under SCARVES: FICHU #1.

muffler **1.** Long scarf approximately 12″ wide; usually knitted or woven of plaid or plain-colored wool, silk, or rayon. Worn from 19th c. to present. Fashionable for men when made out of FOULARD, tie silk, and white silk for evening wear from 1920s to 1940s. **2.** See under SCARVES: CHIN CLOAK.

neckcloth See under SCARVES: NECKERCHIEF #2.

neckerchief **1.** Triangular scarf, either cut in shape of a triangle or a square folded diagonally, worn by men and women in late 1960s and early 1970s. Worn from 19th c. on by cowboys instead of a necktie. Also worn by Boy Scouts with their uniforms. ∞**2.** Late 14th to early 19th c., a square or oblong of fabric folded around the neck and worn by women. Called a *neckcloth* prior to the 16th c. ∞**3.** A large silk *cravat* worn by men and women, as it was sometimes called in the 19th c.

neckpiece BOA or SCARF (see under SCARVES), usually of fur.

∞**nycette** (*niced*) Light scarf worn at neck in late 15th and early 16th c.

paisley scarf **1.** Square or oblong scarf made with paisley designs that are shaped like teardrops, rounded at one end and with a curving point, and delicate tracery, done in rich reds, rusts, beiges, and browns. Usually made in an allover design. **2.** Unusual scarf featuring a shell design with elongated blocks around edge, Paisley print inside, and plain, cream-colored center sprinkled with a few designs. Comes in 18″ × 62″ size and is copied from shawl in National Museum of American History's costume sollection of the Smithsonian Institution.

∞**palatine** (pal′-ah-tyne) Fill-in or small scarf of tulle worn around the neck to cover the low neckline of dresses of mid-17th c. *Der.* Named after Elizabeth-Charlotte, Princess Palatine (Liselotte), who tried to induce more modesty in dress at the French court. Also spelled *pallatine.*

∞**rail** Folded *neckerchief* worn like a shawl around neck by women from late 15th to late 17th c. See under SCARVES: NECKERCHIEF # 2.

ring scarf Oblong scarf with ends stitched together to form a circle. Worn with jewelry to form a collar on a dress in early 1950s.

sailor scarf Square NECKERCHIEF (see under SCARVES) folded diagonally, worn under sailor collar, and slipped through loop front of blouse or tied in a knot. Also called *sailor tie.*

∞**shade** Sheer scarf of lace, net, or gauze worn by women over the bosom of a low-necked bodice. Sometimes had a small ruff attached at the neck. Worn from latter half of 18th to early 19th c.

signature scarf See under SCARVES: DESIGNER SCARF.

∞**solitaire** Narrow, colored scarf, worn by women in mid-1830s, loosely tied with ends hanging to knees—usually worn with a white dress.

souvenir scarf Large, square scarf imprinted with scene, picture, symbol, or words depicting a special place, e.g., Miami, Paris. Usually bought by tourists to remind them of a special holiday spent at that place.

stock Oblong scarf worn loosely lapped over rather than tied. During 1968 introduced to be worn instead of *neckties* by men. Also see under TIES.

stole **1.** Long, wide scarf, often fringed at ends, and made of fabric, knit, or fur; worn since 19th c. as woman's wrap. **2.** Long, wide scarf matched in fabric to woman's dress worn with bare-top dress in 1950s, especially in the evening.

stole

∞**sultana scarf** Scarf of oriental colors worn in mid-1850s that tied below waistline with long hanging ends.

∞**tasseau** (tass-oh') Triangular scarf, usually black, used to fill in the low-bodice neckline worn by women in the late 15th c. Also called *tassel. Der.* Latin, *tassa,* "clasp."

∞**thérèse** (ter-eece) Scarf of light gauze fabric often worn over an indoor cap in the 1770s and 1780s.

∞**zendado** (zehn-dah'-doh) Scarf, usually of black fabric, covering head and falling to waist in front, where it tied. Fashionable in France and Venice in second half of 18th c.

---

scarf tie See under NECKLINES AND COLLARS.

scavilones See under UNDERGARMENTS: SCABILONIANS.

∞**schenti** (shen'-tee) Ancient Egyptian man's garment with the appearance of a skirt that ranged in length from above the knee to the ankle. Styles varied over time; some were pleated at center front. Often they were worn with an elaborate belt. Also spelled *shendot, shenti, shendyt, skent.* Shown at EGYPTIAN STYLES.

schiffli embroidery (sif-lee) See under EMBROIDERIES AND SEWING STITCHES.

schlappen See under FEATHERS.

Scholl's® exercise shoe See under FOOTWEAR: DR. SCHOLL'S EXERCISE SANDALS.

school bag See under HANDBAGS AND RELATED ACCESSORIES.

school ring See under JEWELRY: CLASS RING.

school sweater See under SWEATERS: LETTER SWEATER.

scissoring See under SLASHING.

scoop bonnet See under HEADWEAR.

scoop neckline See under NECKLINES AND COLLARS.

scooter shorts/skirt See under SHORTS and SKIRTS: SKORT.

†**Scotchgard®** Registered trademark of Minnesota Mining and Manufacturing (3M) for a fluoride-based finish used on fabrics to repel grease and water stains.

Scotch plaid Yarn-dyed fabrics woven in plaids that represent the various clans of Scotland. See under introduction to PLAIDS AND TARTANS: PLAID #1.

Scotch suit See under HIGHLAND SUIT.

scottie See under HEADWEAR.

Scottish Highlander costume See under HIGHLAND DRESS.

scrambled eggs See under HEADWEAR: ASTRONAUT'S CAP.

scratch wig See under WIGS AND HAIRPIECES.

screen print See under PRINTS, STRIPES, AND CHECKS.

screen print top See under BLOUSES AND TOPS.

screw-back earrings See under JEWELRY.

scrub suit/scrubs Pants and tunic top with round or V-neck and short or long sleeves. Worn with matching pants. Adapted from garments worn by physicians when operating on patients, now used for casual wear by men.

scrub suit

scrunchy See under HAIR ACCESSORIES.

scuba mask See under MASKS.

scuba suit See under ACTIVEWEAR: WETSUIT.

scuff See under FOOTWEAR.

sculptured hair See under HAIRSTYLES.

sculptured heel See under FOOTWEAR.

scye (sigh) See under ARMHOLE.

sea bag See under HANDBAGS AND RELATED ACCESSORIES: DUFFEL BAG.

seal/sealskin 1. See under FURS: FUR SEAL and HAIR SEAL. 2. See under LEATHERS.

seam See under CLOTHING CONSTRUCTION DETAILS.

seam allowance Extension between the rows of stitching forming a seam and the edges of the fabric.

seam binding/seam tape See under CLOTHING CONSTRUCTION DETAILS.

seamed hose/pantyhose See under HOSIERY.

seamless bra See under UNDERGARMENTS.

seamless hose See under HOSIERY.

seamless knit See under CIRCULAR KNIT.

seam pocket See under POCKETS.

seamstress Synonym for DRESSMAKER.

sea otter See under FURS.

season Refers to the time of year for which garments are designed to be shipped, sold, and worn. In womenswear there are generally six seasons per year; there may be fewer seasons in menswear and childrenswear.

seasonal goods Merchandise that has its best sales during either the fall or spring season.

seasonal line A division or firm's overall collection of garments that will be offered for sale at a given time.

secondary line A less-expensive version of a design originated by a manufacturer and sold by that manufacturer in different markets, different stores, and to a different group of customers than the original design.

seconds Merchandise with slight flaws that is sold at lower prices.

secrete See under SKIRTS: JUPE #2.

seed bead necklace See under JEWELRY.

seed embroidery See under EMBROIDERIES AND SEWING STITCHES.

seed pearl See under GEMS, GEM CUTS, AND SETTINGS: PEARL.

seed stitch See under EMBROIDERIES AND SEWING STITCHES.

†seersucker Medium-weight fabric made with lengthwise crinkled stripes alternating with plain woven stripes. Puckering is achieved by releasing the tension at intervals on the lengthwise yarns. Effect is permanent and will not wash out.

see-through *adj.* Descriptive of fashion started by American designer Rudi Gernreich in 1964 with sheer blouses over bare skin. In 1966, sheer dresses with bands of glitter at strategic places, usually worn with body stockings underneath, were shown by Paris designers Pierre Cardin and Yves Saint Laurent. In 1968 transparent blouses were seen, and by the late 1960s, there were transparent voile shirts for men. These fashions were part of a general trend toward greater acceptance of nudity. Also see under BLOUSES AND TOPS: SEE-THROUGH BLOUSE; PANTS: SEE-THROUGH PANTS; and SHIRTS: SEE-THROUGH SHIRT.

seggard See under SKIRTS: SAFEGUARD.

seint See under CEINT.

self-covered Descriptive of belts and buttons that are made in fabric that matches the garment on which they are placed. See under BELTS: SELF-COVERED BELT and CLOSURES: COVERED BUTTON.

self-edge See under SELVAGE.

self sash See under BELTS: SELF-COVERED BELT.

self-winding watch See under WATCHES.

selham See under CAPES, CLOAKS, AND SHAWLS: BURNOOSE.

sell through A percentage computed from a comparison of the number of items sold to the number of items purchased from a particular line. A higher percentage would indicate a more successful line.

seloso A long, flowing African dress worn by women, similar to the BUBA (see under DRESSES), introduced in 1969.

selvage/selvedge (sehl'-vudge) A narrow, tightly woven band on either edge of fabric parallel to the warp that prevents fabric from raveling, used since 14th c. Originally called *self-edge.* Also called *list* and *listing.*

semi cut See under FOOTWEAR.

semiformal suit Suit appropriate for semiformal occasions. For men, a tuxedo or dinner jacket is required. For women: any type of dressy suit or dress made in a more elaborate style or fabric that would be suitable for semiformal dinners, dances, or weddings.

semiprecious stones See under GEMS, GEM CUTS, AND SETTINGS.

sempstress bonnet See under HEADWEAR.

señorita See under COATS AND JACKETS.

separate collar See under NECKLINES AND COLLARS.

separates In retailing, sportswear items—shirts, blouses, sweaters, and pants—designed to wear in combination with other items from same line.

sequin (sea'-qwin) Small, shiny, iridescent disk of metal or plastic pierced in the center and sewn on garments in a decorative design or in rows to cover a portion or the entire surface. Often used for evening dresses or sweaters. Also see under PAILLETTE.

serape See under CAPES, CLOAKS, AND SHAWLS.

†serge (serj) Suiting fabric made in an even twill with worsted yarns. Occasionally some woolen yarn is used to provide greater softness. Generally piece-dyed and given a clear finish that becomes shiny with wear. Uses: suits, skirts, and pants. *Der.* Latin, *serica,* "silk," indicating it was first a silk fabric; later Italian, *sergea,* "cloth of wool mixed with silk," probably appearing as early as the 12th c.

serpentine belt See under BELTS.

serpentine skirt See under SKIRTS: MORNING-GLORY SKIRT.

serpent ring See under JEWELRY.

serviceability Integrated measure of a product's utility that includes wear life, ease of care, safety.

service cap See under HEADWEAR.

set The smooth fit of a garment that hangs from the body with no unwanted wrinkles.

set-back heel See under FOOTWEAR.

set-in 1. See under SHOULDERS AND SLEEVES. 2. See under WAISTLINES.

set-in thumb See under GLOVES AND GLOVE CONSTRUCTION.

setting See under GEMS, GEM CUTS, AND SETTINGS.

set-under heel See under FOOTWEAR.

seven-eighths See under LENGTHS and PANTS.

seven-fold tie See under TIES.

seventeen-jeweled watch See under WATCHES.

Seventh Avenue Nickname for garment district of New York City, roughly from 34th to 40th streets and from Avenue of the Americas (6th Avenue) to 9th Avenue, where much of American READY-TO-WEAR is produced. Abbreviated *S.A.*

sew To join together by hand or machine stitching.

sew by A sample garment sewn and submitted to the apparel manufacturer for approval by a contractor. Sewn production goods are compared to the sample to check quality. Also called a *counter sample.*

sewing machine Machine for stitching that was first patented in the 1830s in France and in the United States in the 1840s. Use of sewing machines in making Civil War uniforms helped to demonstrate their usefulness, and home use expanded in the postwar period. Through innovative manufacturing and marketing, I. M. Singer captured much of the growing market for sewing machines, which were responsible for much of the rapid growth of the READY-TO-WEAR garment industry.

shade 1. Hues with black added to darken (e.g., navy blue is correctly called a "shade of blue"). However, light blue with white added is called a "tint of blue." 2. See under SCARVES. 3. See under HEADWEAR.

shades See under EYEWEAR.

shade sorting Grouping shades together for distribution to specific customers or regions. Shade sorting of finished goods is a function of quality management.

shadow See under EMBROIDERIES AND SEWING STITCHES, LACES, and PRINTS, STRIPES, AND CHECKS.

shadow-panel slip See under UNDERGARMENTS.

shag See under HAIRSTYLES.

shagreen See under LEATHERS.

shahtoosh Exceptionally soft, fine, and rare wool taken from a Tibetan antelope, the chiru, which is an endangered species. The animals must be killed in order to obtain their wool, and it is illegal in the U.S. to buy or sell products made from this fiber. Shahtoosh shawls sell for as much as $15,000 on the black market.

shaker knit A heavyweight rib-knit fabric, used for sweaters. Developed by members of the Shakers, an American religious sect.

shakespeare collar See under NECKLINES AND COLLARS.

Shakespearean costume See under ELIZABETHAN STYLES.

shakespeare vest See under VESTS.

shako (shay-ko) See under HEADWEAR.

shale See under CAPES, CLOAKS, AND SHAWLS.

shallow Characterizes a merchandise assortment that has styles in relatively few sizes and colors.

sham See under SHIRTS: HALF SHIRT.

shamew See under CHAMARRE.

sham hanging sleeve See under SHOULDERS AND SLEEVES: HANGING SLEEVE.

shandoots See under FOOTWEAR.

shank See under FOOTWEAR.

shank button See under CLOSURES.

†shantung (shan-tung') Medium-weight fabric woven with irregular, elongated slubs (see SLUB YARN) in the crosswise direction caused by yarns of uneven diameter throughout. Originally made of TUSSAH silk yarn that varied in thickness, texture is now imitated with yarn of various fibers. Used for dresses, sportswear, and a wide variety of items.

shapewear See under UNDERGARMENTS: BODYSHAPERS.

†sharkskin 1. Worsted fabric woven in a TWILL WEAVE with alternating black and white yarns in both directions to give a grayed effect. Characteristic feature is the smooth, sleek, clear finish. Used for men's suits. 2. Lightweight acetate (sometimes rayon) sharkskin uses filament yarns in a plain, basket, or sometimes jacquard weave to get a smooth, sleek appearance. Usually made in white but sometimes dyed, used for sportswear and uniforms. 3. See under LEATHERS.

shave coat See under SLEEPWEAR AND LOUNGEWEAR.

Shaver, Dorothy President from 1946 to 1959 of Lord & Taylor, a specialty store in New York City, one of the first women to hold such a position. A backer of American designers during World War II, when French couture was in eclipse. An important person in the development of clothing design in the United States.

shawl See under introduction to CAPES, CLOAKS, AND SHAWLS.

shawl collar See under NECKLINES AND COLLARS.

shawl-collared cardigan See under SWEATERS: CARDIGAN.

shawl tongue See under FOOTWEAR: TONGUE.

shawl waistcoat See under VESTS.

sheared raccoon See under FURS.

shearing 1. See under FURS. †2. Textile process of clipping nap of fabric to desired length.

shearling 1. See under FURS. 2. See under LEATHERS. 3. See under COATS AND JACKETS.

sheath See under DRESSES.

sheath skirt See under SKIRTS.

sheath swimsuit See under SWIMWEAR.

sheepskin See under LEATHERS and COATS AND JACKETS.

†sheer 1. *adj.* Describes any fabric that is fine and transparent or semitransparent. 2. See under HOSIERY.

shell See under BLOUSES AND TOPS; FOOTWEAR: SKIMMER; SWEATERS; TIES; and ZIP-IN/ZIP-OUT LINING in alphabetical listing.

shell cameo See under CAMEO.

shell lining Lining for only part of a coat or jacket, similar to a HALF-LINING. Also see under ZIP-IN/ZIP-OUT LINING.

shell stitch See under EMBROIDERIES AND SEWING STITCHES.

shenti/shendot/shendyt See under SCHENTI.

shepherdess hat See under HEADWEAR: BERGÉRE HAT.

shepherdess heel See under FOOTWEAR: MUSEUM HEEL.

shepherd's check/shepherd's plaid See under PRINTS, STRIPES, AND CHECKS.

sheriff tie See under TIES.

sherte See under UNDERGARMENTS.

†shetland 1. Soft suiting fabric made of fine wool from Shetland sheep of Scotland. Usually woven in HERRINGBONE WEAVE, Shetland, refers to the type of wool used. 2. Knitted fabric or item such as a sweater, made from Shetland wool. Also see under LACES and SWEATERS.

†shibori (she-bor′-ee) Japanese fabric ornamentation technique often used by artists to create WEARABLE ART. Made by stitching gathers into fabrics before dyeing. After dyeing the stitched areas may be released to display complex patterns in the areas protected by the stitching.

shift See under DRESSES and UNDERGARMENTS: CHEMISE.

shift jumper See under JUMPERS.

shigra See under HANDBAGS AND RELATED ACCESSORIES.

shillelagh See under CANE.

shingle See under HAIRSTYLES.

shirring See under CLOTHING CONSTRUCTION DETAILS.

shirt button See under CLOSURES.

shirt collar See under NECKLINES AND COLLARS.

shirt-drawers See under UNDERGARMENTS.

shirtdress See under DRESSES.

shirt front A man's backless false shirt, which had a complete front but tapered into a band in back and buttoned in center back of collar, worn since 1860s. Also see under CLERICAL DRESS: CLERICAL FRONT.

†shirtings Fabrics traditionally used for men's shirts, and now for women's shirts as well, such as broadcloth, chambray, madras, oxford, and poplin.

shirt-jac See under SHIRTS.

SHIRTS

shirt 1. Clothing for the upper part of the body that is usually more tailored than a blouse. May be closed in front or back or pulled on over the head; some are worn tucked in while others are worn outside of the lower garment. For women and girls: worn with pants, skirt, shorts, jumper, or suit, and buttoned right over left. For men and boys: worn with pants, shorts, or suit and buttoned left over right. Worn since early Middle Ages, the shirt originally slipped on over the head, was worn next to the skin, and was considered an undergarment. Collarless at first, a neckband was added in the 14th c.; a standing collar in the 15th c.; and embroidery, frills, and lace in 17th and 18th c. Innovations of the 19th c. included shirts that buttoned down the front and removable collars and cuffs. Usually white, although colors, including pink, were introduced in mid-19th c.; printed shirts with white collars in 1860s; and stripes in the late 19th c. In the 20th c., the white shirt became the standard for wear with business suits until the 1960s, when colors were accepted. The attached collar gained popularity in 1920s, and today detachable collars are seen only rarely—for formal wear. 2. In 1890s, a summer blouse worn by women. See under BLOUSES AND TOPS: SHIRTWAIST. In 1920s and 1930s, shirts became popular for sportswear for women.

Afghanistan wedding tunic/shirt 18th c.-style, velvet tunic-blouse, lavishly decorated with gold embroidery, worn in early 1970s by men in the United States in both original and copied styles.

A-line or trapeze shirt A shirt that flares out from above or below the bust. Also referred to as a *fit and flare shirt.*

aloha shirt See under SHIRTS: HAWAIIAN SHIRT.

apache shirt (ah-patch'-ee) Overblouse or tuck-in shirt of pullover type. Neckline is cut in low V, sometimes laced, sometimes with ITALIAN COLLAR (see under NECKLINES AND COLLARS). Sleeves are sometimes long, full, and gathered into band at the wrist. *Der.* Named for North American Indian tribe of the southwestern U.S.

A-shirt See under SHIRTS: ATHLETIC SHIRT.

athletic shirt Sleeveless shirt with large armholes and scooped neckline, worn for track and active team sports, copied for men and women in 1960s and early 1970s. Also called TANK TOP or *A-shirt.* Also see under UNDERGARMENTS.

athletic shirt

baby-doll shirt A shirt body that is softly gathered to a yoke that ends just above or below the bust.

barong tagalog (ba'-rohn teh-gah'-log) Man's overblouse-type shirt worn in the Philippines for informal occasions. Made with no buttons and a vent at the neckline of fine sheer fabric and frequently trimmed with embroidery; introduced for casual wear in United States in late 1960s. Sometimes called *barong.*

baseball shirt/baseball jersey Knit shirt with three-quarter-length RAGLAN SLEEVES (see under SHOULDERS AND SLEEVES) that are usually made in contrasting color to the body of the shirt. May have a round neckline bound with contrasting color or slit neckline with buttons. Became popular in 1980s. *Der.* From shirt worn by major league baseball players under uniforms.

basque shirt (bask) Striped, wide CREWNECKED (see under NECKLINES AND COLLARS) shirt popular in the 1930s.

Ben Casey shirt See under SHIRTS: MEDIC SHIRT. *Der.* Named for television series *Ben Casey,* popular in early 1960s.

big shirt See under SHIRTS: OVERSIZED SHIRT.

big T-shirt Extremely large mini-skirt length shirt with placket neckline, tailored collar, and all-in-one sleeve. Worn as a beach cover-up. Can also be worn as a mini-dress or tunic over pants. Also called *oversized shirt.*

bodyshirt 1. Shirt fitted by shaping side seams to conform to body lines, introduced in early 1960s. Also called *tapered shirt.* 2. Long shirt with rounded tails worn by girls over short shorts in 1960s. 3. Woman's leotard or bodysuit combination often made with a snap crotch. Introduced in 1960s in stretch fabrics. Also see under SHIRTS: LEOTARD SHIRT.

bodyshirt #3

boiled shirt See under SHIRTS: FORMAL SHIRT #3.

bosom shirt 1. Man's formal white shirt with starched bib front. ∞2. Shirt worn in late 19th and early 20th c., made with collar and bib front of shirt fabric and rest of shirt of an inferior fabric, sometimes knitted.

bowling shirt Shirt designed to be worn by men and women for bowling—personalized with name of individual on front and team name on back.

bush shirt See under SHIRTS: SAFARI SHIRT.

button-down shirt See under SHIRTS: IVY LEAGUE SHIRT.

calypso shirt (kal-ip'-soh) Tailored collar or V-neck shirt that ties in center front, giving a bare-midriff effect. *Der.* Style of music characteristic of the West Indies, where shirt was originally worn.

camp shirt Conventional front-buttoned shirt with a notched collar. Usually made of woven cotton and polyester blends in solid colors, prints, or blocks of color.

camp shirt

cardigan shirt Collarless, front-buttoned shirt with round or V-neckline that is identical to cardigan sweater but usually made in lighter-weight knits. *Der.* Named for the Seventh Earl of Cardigan, who needed an extra layer of warmth under his uniform during the Crimean War in 1854.

cartoon T-shirt Conventional T-shirt with round neck, short sleeves, and screen printed with slogan or cartoon.

cavu shirt Long-sleeved man's sport shirt, popular from 1940 to 1950, with single pocket on the left and pointed collar. Closed diagonally from under collar almost to right side seam.

chemisette See under SHIRTS: HABIT SHIRT.

chukka shirt See under SHIRTS: POLO SHIRT.

clerical shirt See under CLERICAL DRESS.

coat shirt Shirt that buttons down front like a coat. Introduced in the U.S. in 1890s for men; now the conventional-type shirt. Formerly all shirts were pullover placket style.

competition-striped shirt Sport shirt designed with wide, colored stripes alternating with white. Also see under SHIRTS: RUGBY SHIRT.

∞**corazza** (kor-ats′-zah) Man's shirt with close-fitting sleeves, buttoned down the back, tapered to fit the body and worn from 1845 on. Usually made of cambric or cotton.

cossack shirt 1. Russian-type shirt with standing collar and neck placket placed to one side. Often made with braid trimming at neck, down front, and at cuffs. 2. Similar style with TURTLENECK (see under NECKLINES AND COLLARS) called **turtleneck cossack shirt**.

cowboy shirt Shirt with a convertible collar sometimes worn with a NECKERCHIEF (see under SCARVES) or a STRING TIE (see under TIES), often closed with GRIPPER CLOSURES (see under CLOSURES). May have pockets in front and a V-shaped yoke in front and back that is sometimes made of contrasting fabrics. Originally worn by cowboys in the western U.S. and now worn by men, women, and children in all parts of this and some foreign countries. Also called a *western shirt.*

cowboy shirt

C.P.O. Navy-blue shirt of lightweight wool worn by chief petty officer in U.S. Navy, made with buttoned front and patch pockets. Adapted for civilian wear, sometimes in wool plaids, and worn open as a jacket over shirt or T-shirt by men, women, and children in late 1960s and after.

crew-neck shirt Plain pullover knit shirt, usually made with short sleeves and a CREW NECKLINE (see under NECKLINES AND COLLARS). *Der.* From knit shirts worn by members of a "crew" of a racing shell.

dandy shirt Shirt with lace or self-ruffles down front and at cuffs, popular in late 1960s for women and worn with dinner suits in evening by men. *Der.* From shirts worn by BEAU BRUMMELL and other 18th- and 19th-c. dandies.

denim shirt A shirt made of lightweight denim or blue chambray fabric, often cut with a western fit and details.

∞**dishrag shirt** Net shirt that first became popular on the French Riviera in the 1930s. Loosely knitted man's sport shirt with placket closing at neck worn in 1930s. *Der.* Resemblance of knit to knitted dishrags of that period.

double tee A layered look with one T-shirt or other garment worn over another; can be harmonious or contrasting colors or textures to create different visual impact. The hem of one layer may be longer than the other for emphasis.

drawstring shirt Hip-length shirt with drawstring at bottom giving a bloused effect. Designed to be worn over a bathing suit and frequently made of terrycloth or cotton knit. Introduced in 1940s and 1950s and still used.

dress shirt 1. Traditional buttoned-down-the-front shirt usually worn by men with a necktie and a traditional suit. Made in tuck-in style with TAB, SPREAD, BUTTONED-DOWN, or PIN COLLAR (see under NECKLINES AND COLLARS) and with conservative sleeves with SINGLE or FRENCH CUFFS (see under CUFFS). Popular for men since 1920s, when it replaced shirt with separate collar. Originally made in woven cotton, now made in cotton/polyester blends and in fine knitted nylons and polyesters. 2. See under SHIRTS: FORMAL SHIRT.

dueling shirt Man's full-sleeved shirt of slip-on type sometimes worn with long stock around the neck. *Der.* Named after full-sleeved shirts shown in movies depicting era of *The Three Musketeers.* Similar to SHIRTS: FENCING SHIRT.

∞**emperor shirt** A country gentleman's shirt of red flannel worn in the 1850s and 1860s.

epaulet shirt (ep′-ah-let′) Shirt possessing long sleeves, buttoned front, convertible collar, patch pockets with bellows pleats, and buttoned-down flap. The characteristic feature is a separate epaulet tab on each shoulder with button near neckline. Also called *pilot shirt.* Shown at EPAULET.

extra-long knit shirt T-shirt to knee or below, styled with ribbed or placket neckline in plain or striped fabric worn with below-the-calf matching skirt.

fencing shirt Unisex shirt with large, full sleeves and pointed collar, frequently laced at neck. *Der.* Similar to those worn in old swashbuckling movies by Errol Flynn and Tyrone Power. Similar to SHIRTS: DUELING SHIRT.

fiesta shirt (fee-ess′-tah) Man's white cotton sport shirt trimmed with a wide band of eyelet embroidery down either side of front. Popular vacation wear from Acapulco, Mexico, in late 1960s. Also see under SHIRTS: MEXICAN WEDDING SHIRT.

fishnet shirt Round-necked, raglan-sleeved shirt made of a loose, openwork, diamond-shaped knit. Designed to keep warm air next to skin, but allow perspiration to evaporate. Undershirt originally used by Norwegian army made of 100 percent cotton for protection against 0-degree cold and 90-degree heat.

fit and flare shirt See under A-LINE OR TRAPEZE SHIRT.

flannel shirt Shirt of colored or plaid flannel fabric with one or two patch pockets and conventional or convertible neckline. Worn originally by woodsmen, later for sports (e.g., hunting). From early 1960s popular in lighter-weight washable fabrics for general wear. In the early 1980s a lining might be added and shirt was frequently worn as a jacket.

football jersey/football shirt 1. Knit shirt with round neck, long or short sleeves set on dropped shoulders, and large numerals printed on front and back. Copied from shirts worn by football players and popular for children and teenagers in 1960s. Also called *numeral shirt.* 2. In early 1980s and after made with very long dropped shoulders in short rib-tickler style of mesh fabric. ∞3. Shirt worn for football games in 1870. Made with long sleeves of knitted jersey with horizontal stripes.

formal shirt 1. Man's conventional white shirt with pleated front, WING COLLAR, and long sleeves, usually finished with FRENCH CUFFS. Worn with TUXEDO JACKET and black BOW TIE or TAILS and WHITE TIE. See cross-references under NECKLINES AND COLLARS, CUFFS, COATS AND JACKETS, and TIES. 2. A similar man's shirt styled with ruffles made in white or colors. Fashionable particularly for weddings or semiformal wear since late 1960s. ∞3. Formerly a shirt with highly starched bib front and detachable stiff starched collar and called a *boiled shirt.*

formal shirt #1

full tee Shirt cut out of a circular piece of fabric gathered into waistband in front and back and stitched at the sides to form deep dolman-like sleeves. Finished with a wrapped peplum below waistline. Design originated with Paris couturier Pierre Cardin in mid-1980s.

guayabera shirt (gwah-ya-bare′-a) 1. Lightweight overshirt made with convertible collar, short sleeves, and four large patch pockets. Has two sets of pin tucks in front running from small shoulder yokes to hem, and three sets of pin tucks in the back from yoke to hem. Small, white pearl buttons are used for the front closing, pocket flaps, and at the top and bottom of the sets of tucks. Copied from shirts worn by the well-dressed businessmen in pre-Castro Havana. 2. Another style is similar with embroidered stripes down front instead of tucks styled for men and women. *Der.* Shirt worn in Cuba by guava-tree growers.

∞**habit shirt** 1. Linen shirt with standing collar, ruffled front, and wrist ruffles. Worn under a vest as part of woman's RIDING HABIT (see under ACTIVEWEAR) in 18th and 19th c. 2. Shirt worn as fill-in under low necklines in early 19th c. Also called *chemisette.*

∞**half shirt** Man's short shirt, with decorated panel down front, worn over plain or soiled shirt from 16th to 18th c. Also called *sham.*

Hawaiian shirt Man's sport shirt printed with colorful Hawaiian floral or other local designs. Made with a CONVERTIBLE COLLAR (see under NECKLINES AND COLLARS) and worn outside of trousers. Appears to have been introduced in the late 1930s for local wear, adopted by tourists and military men stationed in Hawaii, and gradually more widely seen on the mainland after World War II. In 1951, President Harry Truman appeared on the cover of *Life* magazine in a Hawaiian shirt. Continues to be a staple wardrobe item in Hawaii and is periodically very popular on the mainland as well. Also called *aloha shirt.*

Hawaiian shirt

henley shirt Lightweight knit shirt with buttoned PLACKET (see under CLOTHING CONSTRUCTION DETAILS) at neckline, made in striped or plain knits with contrasting lining at placket and around ribbed neck. Popular in early 1960s and has become a classic knit shirt style for men, women, and children. *Der.* Copied from shirt worn originally by rowers in crew races at Henley, England. Also see under SHIRTS: WALLACE BEERY SHIRT.

henley shirt or Wallace Beery shirt

hunting shirt Bright-red wool shirt worn by hunters so they are visible for long distances in woods.

ivy league shirt Traditional shirt with buttoned-down collar, front buttoned, and styled with a YOKE in back with a loop at center of yoke. Worn first by college men in the 1950s and later by girls and boys. *Der.* Named for the group of northeastern colleges called the Ivy League.

jersey See under SHIRTS: KNIT SHIRT.

jockey shirt Woman's shirt with contrasting colored inserts, similar to JOCKEY SILKS. Introduced as sportswear in late 1960s after first woman was accepted as a professional jockey.

knit shirt Sport shirt made of knitted fabric usually in pullover style. First introduced in mid-19th c. and called a **jersey**. Made of worsted wool and so called because the fabric was first knitted on the Isle of Jersey, off the coast of England. Early shirts were worn for football, rowing, and for other sports. In 1920s worn for tennis. In 1930s knit shirts with placket necklines and convertible collars were introduced for casual wear at resorts for men. In the 1950s and 1960s and after, knit shirts increased in popularity for men, women, and children due to improvements in knitting and acceptance of less formal style of dress.

Lacoste® An internationally recognized trademark used extensively on apparel as well as other goods. Originally identified the knit shirts manufactured by La Chemise Lacoste of Paris, marked with a small alligator symbol on left front. The shirts were designed of piqué knit with the shirttail being slightly longer in back so that it would not pull out when worn during active sports. *Der.* René Lacoste, an international tennis champion, nicknamed "*le Crocodile*" by French sportswriters in the 1920s. Lacoste had his friends in a textile company produce a new style of short-sleeved cotton knit shirt that he designed and sold to replace the uncomfortable long-sleeved woven shirts then worn by tennis players. He adopted the alligator symbol as the logo for knit shirts of this design because of his nickname.

leotard shirt (lee′-ah-tard′) Fitted shirt with a long tail that snaps between the legs making a leotard-type garment.

Lord Byron shirt Shirt with full sleeves and long, pointed collar worn open at neck in shape of a V. Popular in 1920s and late 1960s. Also called *poet's shirt. Der.* Named for Lord George Gordon Byron, early 19th-c. English poet.

medic shirt White shirt-jacket with standing-band collar and shoulder closing worn by members of medical profession. Also called *Ben Casey shirt.*

meditation shirt Loose, open-sleeved, pullover tunic, usually made of Indian printed cotton or of solid colors and banded with embroidery around slit neck, across shoulders, and at hem. *Der.* Part of late 1960s ethnic trend inspired by eastern gurus.

Mexican wedding shirt Tailored shirt of a crisp white fabric, usually made with wide bands of embroidery down either side of front and on collar, popular in Acapulco, Mexico, for men and women in late 1960s. *Der.* Inspired by shirts worn by Mexican peasant grooms at weddings. Also see under SHIRTS: FIESTA SHIRT.

midriff shirt Shirt for women cut to just below bustline, revealing rib cage. Often improvised from a conventional shirt by tying the tails in a knot under the bosom.

muscle shirt 1. A tight-fitting knitted shirt usually made in black or dark color, banded with white around the neck, short sleeves, and on underarm seams. Popular in late 1960s. 2. Later version is sleeveless with rib-knit band around upper arm. Made in white and colors with printed designs or words on front. *Der.* Fitted tightly to reveal "muscles" of upper arm.

∞**negligée shirt** (neh′-glee-zheh) Man's shirt, either white or striped, with white, stiff, separate collar and white cuffs. Worn from early 1900s to about 1925.

nightshirt See under SLEEPWEAR AND LOUNGEWEAR.

numeral shirt See under SHIRTS: FOOTBALL SHIRT.

Nureyev shirt (noor-ay′-ef) Shirt with long, full sleeves gathered in bands at wrists and a low, round neckline finished with bias binding, popular in late 1960s. *Der.* Named for Rudolf Nureyev (1938–1993), ballet performer who defected from his native Russia to the West in 1961.

overshirt Any shirt styled to be worn outside of trousers or skirt rather than tucked in.

oversized shirt Shirt cut extra large and extra long, usually made with button closing and convertible collar. Also called *big shirt.*

peplum shirt A shirt with a short overskirt attached at the waist.

pilot shirt See under SHIRTS: EPAULET SHIRT.

pocket T-shirt Simple knit shirt worn for sports with crew neck and tiny rounded pocket on left breast.

poet's shirt See under SHIRTS: LORD BYRON SHIRT.

polo shirt A knitted shirt with PLACKET NECKLINE and collar (see under NECKLINES AND COLLARS) usually made with short sleeves and originally used when playing polo in 1920s, then introduced for men's sportswear in the 1930s. Now a classic shirt style.

polo shirt

prospector's shirt Shirt worn next to the skin made of knitted silk fabric that insulates. Similar in style to WALLACE BEERY knit shirt (see under SHIRTS).

pullover Any light-knit shirt without neck placket or fastening (e.g. SHIRTS: T-SHIRT or FOOTBALL SHIRT).

∞**regatta shirt** (re-gaht′-tah) Man's cambric or oxford striped shirt with plain front. Worn as informal summer wear in 1840s.

Rough Rider shirt Khaki shirt buttoned down the front and made with standing collar, breast pockets with flaps, and epaulets. *Der.* Similar to shirts worn by Theodore Roosevelt, Leonard Wood, and their volunteer cavalry regiment in Cuba during Spanish-American War in 1898.

rugby shirt Knit shirt with broad stripes in two contrasting colors with small, white, rib-knit collar and cuffs. The PLACKET NECKLINE (see under NECKLINES AND COLLARS) closed with a zipper or buttons. *Der.* So called in imitation of shirts worn in Great Britain when playing rugby.

rugby shirt

safari shirt African-inspired shirt introduced by Dior in mid-1960s for women. Styled with lapels, buttoned center-front closing, and four large pockets—usually of bellows type. Same as *bush shirt. Der.* Named after an African hunting trip.

see-through shirt 1. Woman's shirt of transparent fabric worn without undergarments. Introduced by Parisian couturier Saint Laurent in spring 1968 and popularly accepted in 1969 and 1970. Presented by Rudi Gernreich in 1964 for "at-home" wear but not called by this name at that time. Also called *see-through blouse.* 2. Voile and sheer fabric shirts as worn by men in the late 1960s and early 1970s.

sham See under SHIRTS: HALF SHIRT.

shirt-jac Front-buttoned shirt worn outside the trousers for sportswear. May have side slits, FLAP POCKETS (see under POCKETS), and sometimes worn open over another shirt or knit shirt. *Der.* Combination of words "shirt" and "jacket."

skivvy Knit shirt, copy of undershirt worn by sailors, made with bound neckline and tiny placket opening in front.

Often used in the plural, **skivvies**, to refer to men's underwear. *Der.* Scot-Gaelic, *skivvy* or *skivvies*, slang for sailors' underwear.

sport shirt 1. Any type of shirt worn without a necktie by a man. At first a woven-fabric shirt with a CONVERTIBLE COLLAR (see under NECKLINES AND COLLARS) worn outside or tucked in trousers, popular in mid-1930s. Now any shirt, other than a DRESS SHIRT (see under SHIRTS), whether it is woven or knitted. 2. Tailored or knitted shirt worn by women as sportswear since 1940s.

stock-tie shirt Plain shirt with ASCOT NECKLINE (see under NECKLINES AND COLLARS). Also called *stock-tie blouse* and *flip-tie blouse.*

sweatshirt Long-sleeved, fleece-backed, cotton-knit pullover or zipped-front knit shirt made with rib-knit CREW NECK (see under NECKLINES AND COLLARS), rib-knit cuffs, and rib-knit waistband. Sometimes has attached hood and often worn with matching sweatpants, as a SWEATSUIT (see under ACTIVEWEAR). Originally worn after exercising to prevent chilling. In late 1960s adopted for jogging. Became more popular in 1980s and after for school and sportswear, sometimes with cartoon pictures, slogans, or name of school or club printed on front or back.

tank top Similar to ATHLETIC SHIRT (see under SHIRTS), but styled in colors. Also see under BLOUSES AND TOPS.

tapered shirt See under SHIRTS: BODYSHIRT #1.

tchamir (cha-meer) Moroccan shirt or overblouse with heavily embroidered caftan neckline. Imported as a current style in late 1960s for men and women in black with white embroidery and white with multicolored embroidery.

tee See under SHIRTS: T-SHIRT/TEE SHIRT.

tee shirt See under SHIRTS: T-SHIRT/TEE SHIRT.

thermal shirt A T-shirt-like garment designed to retain body heat in cold temperatures through its close to the body fit, texture, and fiber content. It may be made of nylon, polyester, bamboo, cotton, wool, or a blend; a waffle weave helps to trap body heat. Intended as a base layer for cold weather dressing; high-tech fabrics help to wick moisture away from the body.

Tom Jones shirt Pullover shirt made with STOCK-TIE (see under TIES: STOCK), yoke, full body, and full sleeves with ruffled wristband gathered into dropped shoulders. Some adaptations omit yoke and have slit neckline with pointed collar. *Der.* Inspired by costumes worn in *Tom Jones,* 1963 film of Henry Fielding's novel, about an 18th-c. hero.

T-shirt/tee shirt Originally a white undershirt worn by men with round neck and set-in sleeves, this knitted pullover sport shirt is now made in any color, frequently screen-printed with names, slogans, or cartoons. In early 1980s became so popular that some were trimmed with lace, embroidery, and ruffles. The name in 1980s was extended to include simple woven blouses. Also see under DRESSES: T-SHIRT DRESS. Shown at UNDERGARMENTS: T-SHIRT.

tuxedo shirt 1. See under SHIRTS: FORMAL SHIRT #1 and #2. 2. Woman's version made with bib front frequently tucked, becoming popular in the early 1980s. Sometimes worn with a black bow tie and a version of the man's tuxedo jacket. Also called *tuxedo blouse.*

unisex shirt Shirt designed to be worn by a man or woman. Has no buttons and is usually laced at neckline.

Wallace Beery shirt Narrow, rib-knit, HENLEY-style shirt for men and women with self-binding at neck and buttoned placket closing. (See under SHIRTS: HENLEY SHIRT.) Copied after government surplus underwear. *Der.* Called by this name because a shirt of this type was sometimes worn by the Hollywood actor Wallace Beery in films of the 1930s.

western dress shirt Elaborately decorated western shirt worn by cowboys for important rodeos. May be trimmed with fringe, elaborate embroidery, leather, beads, or sequins. Also see under SHIRTS: COWBOY SHIRT.

western shirt See under SHIRTS: COWBOY SHIRT.

wrap shirt A shirt that encircles the body by wrapping rather than buttoning. Variations include a surplice wrap or a silhouette that has tie extensions that wrap around the body.

Zhivago shirt See under SHIRTS: COSSACK SHIRT. *Der.* Inspired by costumes worn in *Dr. Zhivago,* 1965 film of Boris Pasternak's novel, set in Revolutionary Russia in 1917.

∞**zouave shirt** (zoo'-ahv) Back-buttoned shirt with small banded collar with small, standing frill and long, full, puffed sleeves. Decorated down the front with a panel, sometimes made of sheer gathered fabric crossed by bands of lace and trimmed with lace at cuffs and neck. Worn by women under zouave jacket in 1860s. *Der.* Arabic, Zouaova, a Kabyle tribe, Berbers living in Algeria or Tunisia.

---

shirt sleeve See under SHOULDERS AND SLEEVES.

shirtwaist See under BLOUSES AND TOPS.

shirtwaist dress See under DRESSES.

shoe/shoes See under FOOTWEAR.

shoe buckle See under CLOSURES.

shoe button See under CLOSURES.

shoe cloth Any fabric used in making of fabric shoes, shoe linings, or any other part of the shoe. SILK, COTTON, WOOL, and MANUFACTURED FIBERS are all used to make fabrics such as BROCADE, TAPESTRY, SLIPPER SATIN, FAILLE, nylon MESH (see MESH #2) CREPE, and SHANTUNG. Many of these fabrics are used to make white dyeable shoes. Better shoes are lined with leather, while DRILL and similar fabrics are used for less-expensive shoes.

shoe hat See under HEADWEAR.

shoehorn A curved piece of plastic, wood, metal, or other firm material over which the foot can slide, making it easier to put on a pair of shoes.

shoelace 1. Synonym for shoestring since 19th c. When jogging-type shoes became popular, shoelaces became more decorative and included such woven designs as small hearts, animals, or strawberries. Also called a *lacer.* 2. See under TIES: BOLO TIE.

∞**shoe rose** Large ornamental rosette of lace or ribbon, frequently jeweled, used by men and women to trim shoes in 17th c. Sometimes also used on garters and hat bands.

shoestring Lace for tying a shoe. At first not acceptable to society—some invitations stated that shoe buckles were required—but fashionable by the end of 17th c. when made of ribbon. Since mid-19th c., SHOELACE has been more commonly used.

shoestring tie See under TIES.

shooting coat See under COATS AND JACKETS.

shopping goods Merchandise, such as most apparel, that is more carefully assessed before purchase than CONVENIENCE GOODS.

shopping the market Investigating retail fashion trends that may influence an upcoming line.

shortalls See under SHORTS: BIB SHORTS.

short bands See under CLERICAL DRESS: GENEVA BANDS.

short bob See under WIGS AND HAIRPIECES: BOB-WIG.

short hood See under HEADWEAR: PUG HOOD.

∞**short gown** Garment similar to a jacket or overblouse worn with a skirt by working class and rural women of the 18th and early 19th c.

short gown 18th c.

shortie/shorty See under COATS AND JACKETS, GLOVES AND GLOVE CONSTRUCTION, and SLEEPWEAR AND LOUNGEWEAR.

shortie pajamas See under SLEEPWEAR AND LOUNGEWEAR.

short markup A markup that creates a retail price less than double the cost of the goods to the merchant. Also see under MARKUP.

short paletot See under COATS AND JACKETS: YACHTING COAT #1.

short-range forecasting Determining the demand for new styles and fashion trends through research and estimating when, what, and how much should be manufactured.

SHORTS

shorts 1. Two-legged garment ending above, at, or slightly below the knee that is mainly worn by adults and children for sportswear. Worn by little boys from late 19th c. but not called by this name until 1920s. See under PANTS: KNEE PANTS. In early 1930s worn by children and adults for camping. In 1933 worn by Alice Marble for a professional tennis match. Later became generally accepted for tennis and sportswear for women. In 1940s became a children's-wear item—an alternative to dresses and rompers. In 1950s Bermuda shorts were accepted by men for leisure and city wear but not for business. In the late 1980s accepted for school wear and accepted as day wear but not for business. In 1986 the shorts suit was introduced with jackets matched to various types of shorts worn with contrasting tops giving the appearance of a minidress. 2. See under UNDERGARMENTS: BOXER PANTS #2.

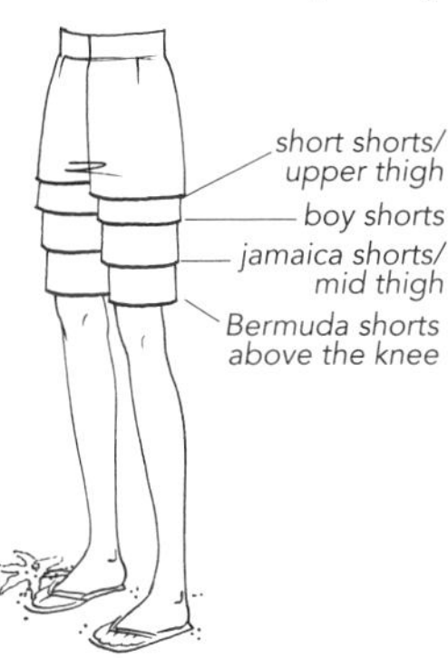

variations in shorts lengths

athletic shorts Pull-on, cotton-twill, men's shorts with elastic top worn for gym and exercise. Also called *exercise shorts, running shorts,* and *track shorts.*

balloon shorts Wide shorts set into waistband with large pleats and gathered at the legs into wide bands. Similar to PANTS: BLOOMERS.

bermuda shorts Just-above-the-knee shorts that fit close to leg. First worn with knee socks as streetwear by men on the island of Bermuda, introduced in the United States in early 1950s, as sportswear for women, later adopted by men for summer casual wear both in country and in town. Also called *walking shorts.*

bib shorts Women's and children's shorts made with a bib top and straps over the shoulders attached to pants at the back of waist. Popular for women in 1940s, again in

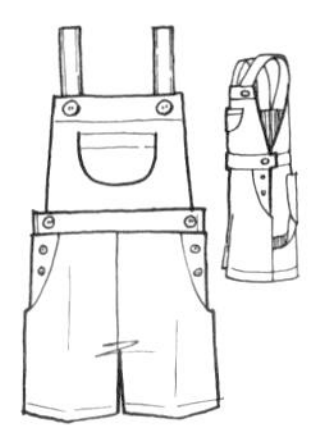

bib shorts or shortalls

1960s, and in 1980s and after. For women and children in the 1980s and after the word **shortall** (a combination of the words "shorts" and "overalls") was used for this type of shorts.

bike shorts 1. Thigh-length shorts of durable fabric with fitted waistband, inside drawstring, and zip-fly closing with button at waist. Cut to fit snugly, but not to restrict movement, seat has an extra lining of terry cloth with back cut higher to prevent shirt from pulling out. Also have specifically designed pockets on sides of legs for wallet and maps. 2. Tight-fitting shorts knitted with SPANDEX. *Der.* Shortened form of word *bicycle.*

bike shorts

bloomer or bubble shorts Shorts with full legs, gathered at the lower edge; attributed to Amelia Bloomer.

board shorts Swim trunks worn by surfers, cut low on the hips with a hemline that falls anywhere from mid-thigh to right below the knee. Also see under SWIMWEAR.

body shorts Woman's tight-fitting shorts cut to top of leg, like leotards, with horseshoe-shaped straps in front and back. Worn with a knit shirt for dancing and exercising.

boxer shorts 1. Shorts made with elastic in a casing around waist, similar to those worn by prizefighters. Worn as underwear and for sportswear. 2. See under UNDERGARMENTS: BOXER SHORTS.

camp shorts 1. Shorts with large patch pockets on the front and back. Belt is run through tunnel loops formed by tops of pockets. Also called *trail shorts.* 2. Any shorts worn at a summer camp by children and counselors, sometimes of a required style or color constituting a uniform.

camp shorts

cargo shorts Thigh-length shorts similar to CAMP SHORTS with two very large patch pockets in front—extending almost to hem and up and over belt in a tunnel loop; has one large box-pleated pocket in back with buttoned flap. Usually made in twill fabric in a blend of polyester and cotton.

city shorts Coined in 1969 by fashion-industry newspaper *Women's Wear Daily,* for women's tailored shorts worn instead of skirt with matching jacket for town wear.

combat shorts Military in origin, these loose shorts are characterized by loops and large pockets on the legs, designed to hold and make accessible equipment that needs to be carried.

cut-offs Full-length pants, often BLUE JEANS (see under PANTS), cut off above knee and fringed. Fad among teenagers in early 1960s. Became so popular that stores began selling this style of shorts.

cut-offs

daisy dukes Jean shorts with a minimal inseam and a raw-edge hem. Made popular by the 1979 TV show *The Dukes of Hazzard.*

dhoti shorts (doe'tee) Thigh-length shorts with many gathers at waistband that hang longer between the legs. *Der.* From Indian loincloth of the same name.

drawstring shorts Pull-on shorts fastened with a drawstring at the waist similar to short pajama pants, introduced in late 1960s.

exercise shorts See under SHORTS: ATHLETIC SHORTS.

hip-huggers Low-slung shorts resting on hips rather than coming to waistline.

hot pants Slang usage coined by fashion-industry newspaper *Women's Wear Daily* in early 1971 to describe women's short shorts made of luxury fabrics and leather, and worn with colored tights and fancy tops as evening wear and on city streets.

hot pants

Jamaica shorts Shorts ending at mid-thigh, shorter than Bermudas. *Der.* Named for shorts worn in resort areas on island of Jamaica.

jogging shorts See under SHORTS: SWEATSHORTS.

jumpshorts JUMPSUIT with legs reaching to knee or above, worn in late 1960s. Similar to style worn in 1930s and 1940s called a PLAYSUIT (see under ACTIVEWEAR).

lederhosen (laid-err-hose'-en) Leather shorts usually made with bib top, originally a Tyrolean style, adopted for children and young people in the United States in late 1960s. *Der.* German plural of *Lederhose,* from *leder,* "leather" and *hose,* "trousers."

little-boy shorts Short-length shorts made with turned-back cuffs. Popular in early 1960s for sportswear and bathing suits.

mini-jeans Very short shorts made by cutting off BLUE JEANS (see under PANTS). Introduced in late 1960s.

playsuit See under SHORTS: JUMPSHORTS and ACTIVEWEAR.

pleated shorts 1. Woman's shorts styled to resemble a short skirt with inverted pleats in front and back and knife pleats in between. 2. Shorts with several small, unpressed pleats in front for added fullness.

pull-on shorts Shorts made with an elasticized waistband.

rugby shorts Thigh-length shorts precisely cut for unrestricted leg movement with elastic waistband only over hips, inner drawstring, lap-over closing with fly-front, and double-stitched side pockets. Made in colors and white of strong cotton twill. *Der.* Inspired by British shorts worn when playing rugby.

running shorts See under SHORTS: ATHLETIC SHORTS.

sailor shorts 1. Shorts that fasten up back with lacings made with square buttoned flap closing in front like *sailor pants.* 2. Woman's shorts with a zipper at front or side and a decorative, but not functional, lacing in back.

scooter shorts Shorts made with a panel attached in front, making them appear like a skirt. Also called a *scooter skirt.* Also see under SKIRTS: SKORT.

shortalls See under SHORTS: BIB SHORTS.

short shorts Very brief shorts.

shorts suit Suits accepted for city wear with longer jackets and shorts ending above-the-knee in a variety of styles.

skort See under SKIRTS.

suspender shorts Any style shorts worn with suspenders of felt, fabric, or other material. Style was inspired by Tyrolean costume. Also see under SHORTS: LEDERHOSEN.

sweatshorts Pull-on shorts made of cotton fleece fabric, used for running and jogging in warmer weather. Also called *jogging shorts.*

tear-away shorts Shorts with side snaps that can be pulled open very quickly.

tennis shorts Conservative type of shorts, traditionally white, worn for playing tennis and general sportswear. Colored shorts were promoted in the late 1960s, but white was still first choice on the courts. Originally women players wore skirts but when length of skirts got longer in the 1930s, Señorita de Alvares played in a below-the-knee divided skirt in 1931, and in 1933 Alice Marble appeared in the above-the-knee shorts. Tennis shorts are currently available in a wide range of colors and styles, and white is still much used.

track shorts See under SHORTS: ATHLETIC SHORTS.

trail shorts See under SHORTS: CAMP SHORTS and CARGO SHORTS.

trunks Man's brief loose shorts worn (originally over tights) for swimming, boxing, and track.

walking shorts See under SHORTS: BERMUDA SHORTS.

western shorts Shorts styled like dungarees with zipper fly in front, patch pockets on hips, and tight-fitting legs. Popular in late 1960s.

---

short shorts See under SHORTS.

shorts suit 1. See under ACTIVEWEAR. 2. See under SHORTS.

shorty glove See under GLOVES AND GLOVE CONSTRUCTION.

shot cloth/shot silk See under CHANGEABLE EFFECT.

shotten-bellied doublet See under DOUBLET.

shoulder bag See under HANDBAGS AND RELATED ACCESSORIES.

shoulder belt See under BELTS: SAM BROWNE BELT.

shoulder cop See under ARMOR.

shoulder dart See under CLOTHING CONSTRUCTION DETAILS.

∞**shoulder heads** (British usage) Shoulder straps of low-cut dresses used from 17th c. on.

∞**shoulder knot** 1. Ribbon loops, sometimes jeweled, worn by men on right shoulder from 1660 to 1700. 2. 18th-c. decoration used on footman's livery. 3. One of a pair of detachable flaps, decorated with braided metallic cord insignia, worn on the shoulder by commissioned and warrant officers of the U.S. Armed Forces to designate rank.

shoulder pad Triangular-shaped or rounded pad, filled with wool, cotton, synthetic foam, or MANUFACTURED FIBER, tacked to the shoulder seam of clothing such as coats, dresses, and blouses so as to create the illusion of broad or square shoulders. Introduced in late 1930s and also popular in 1940s and again since 1980s.

SHOULDERS AND SLEEVES

shoulder Manner of cutting an item of apparel in order to achieve a desired fit over the shoulder. Variations of fit across the shoulder were often achieved through the cut of the SLEEVE. In most early historical periods, shoulders of garments followed normal body lines; however, in the late 15th c., shoulder lines began to show greater variations as sleeves were less likely to be cut in one with the garment. Periods of considerable shoulder width occurred in the late 15th and the 16th c., in the 1830s, 1890s, 1930s and 1940s, and the 1980s and 1990s. These effects were often aided by the use of padding placed in sleeves or at the shoulder of the garment.

sleeve That part of an item of clothing that covers the arm. In early times sleeves were cut as part of the main garment pieces. In the late Middle Ages, clothing construction techniques became more sophisticated and sleeves were cut separately and set into the armhole of the garment. In 16th and 17th c., sleeves were puffed, padded, or slashed (see SLASHING); in 18th c., women wore plain, elbow-length sleeves ending in ruffles, and coat sleeves for men were made with large turned-back cuffs. In early 19th c., sleeve styles varied a good deal, with short, puffed sleeves worn by women being especially popular and tailored plain set-in sleeves for men. Sleeves of the 1830s were enormous; after 1845, they subsided, with a dropped shoulder being achieved by setting the sleeve well below the shoulder. By the 1870 to 1890 period, armhole placement returned the shoulder, and by 1890s, sleeves grew huge once more. Sleeves of the 20th c. showed considerable variation, but rarely did daytime clothing have extremely large sleeves.

all-in-one sleeve Sleeve with no armhole. Front and back of bodice and sleeve front and back are cut in one piece. The pieces are sewn together down the inside and outside of the arm. Resembles the BATWING SLEEVE and KIMONO SLEEVE but not cut as full under the arm. May be combined with a RAGLAN or SET-IN SLEEVE with the front cut in either manner and the back cut all-in-one. See cross-references under SHOULDERS AND SLEEVES.

∞**amadis sleeve** 1. Sleeve with tight cuff, buttoned at the wrist, worn in 1830s. 2. Revived in 1850s when the sleeve was buttoned to elbow and the upper sleeve was full and pleated into armhole. *Der.* Said to have originated by an opera singer to cover her unattractive arms.

angel sleeve Any type of long flowing sleeve. May fit smoothly into the armhole or be gathered. Sometimes split up outer arm to shoulder like a HANGING SLEEVE (see under SHOULDERS AND SLEEVES).

∞**angel sleeves** Long square panels from shoulders reaching nearly to floor. Used on women's mantles of 1889.

baby-doll sleeve Another name for a tiny PUFFED SLEEVE (see under SHOULDERS AND SLEEVES).

∞**bagpipe sleeve** Full sleeve gathered like a pouch on outer side of arm, ending in wide band at wrist. Worn in 15th c. by men and women primarily in the garment called the HOUPPELANDE. *Der.* From shape of Scottish bagpipe.

balloon sleeve Very large puff sleeve extending to elbow set into a regular armhole and frequently made of crisp fabrics. Popular in 1890s and since for evening and wedding dresses.

banded sleeve Full sleeve bound in to fit the arm at intervals, thereby creating a series of puffs.

barrel sleeve Sleeve that fits at armhole and at wrist but is full at the elbow.

batwing sleeve Long sleeve cut with deep armhole almost to waist, made tight at wrist, giving winglike appearance when arm is extended. A variation of the dolman sleeve. See under SHOULDERS AND SLEEVES: DOLMAN.

∞**bellows sleeve** Full sleeve, gathered into cuff at wrist, with vertical slit from upper arm to below elbow; could be worn as short hanging sleeve in 14th and 15th c.

bell sleeve Sleeve made narrow at the top, set into normal armhole, and flaring at lower edge like a bell. Introduced in the second half of 19th c.

bell sleeve

beret sleeve Short sleeve, often used on evening dresses; made from two circles of fabric seamed at outer edges with holes cut in centers for armhole and arm and typically lined to stand out stiffly. Popular from 1820 to 1850 and again in 1930s. Also called *melon sleeve.*

∞**Bernhardt sleeve** Long, fitted sleeve made with a point extending over the hand; worn in the latter part of 19th c. *Der.* Named after Sarah Bernhardt, a famous French actress of the period.

bishop sleeve 1. Full sleeve set into normal armhole and gathered into band at wrist. 2. Sleeve of similar design that gradually increased in fullness from the upper arm to the wrist, where it was gathered into a cuff and the sleeve fullness created a puffed area that hung down from the wrist. Worn in the 1850s this version was called **full bishop.** 3. In the 1890s a sleeve of the similar design contained less fabric and was called **small bishop.**

bishop sleeve #1

∞**boot sleeve** Man's coat sleeve with BOOT CUFF (see under CUFFS); popular from 1727 to about 1740.

∞**bouffant mécanique** (boo-fant′ mek-can′-eek) Sleeve created by hidden spring attached to corset neckline and projected into sleeve to extend it, worn in 1828.

bracelet sleeve Three-quarter-length, fitted, cuffless sleeve, allowing a bracelet to show.

∞**brassart** (brass′-are) 1. (French) In the 15th c. part of the sleeve extending from wrist to elbow attached by ribbons to upper sleeve called MANCHERON (see under SHOULDERS AND SLEEVES) 2. Fur-lined half-sleeve.

butterfly sleeve Wide flaring sleeve set in smoothly at armhole, extending to elbow or wrist, giving a caped effect.

button-tab sleeve A long, convertible, roll-up sleeve. Sleeve is rolled up and fastened by attaching a button on the exterior to a buttonholed tab sewn on underside of sleeve.

∞**cannon sleeve** Woman's padded and boned sleeve, large at shoulder and tapering to wrist, giving appearance of shape of a cannon. Used in women's gowns from about 1575 to 1620. Also called *trunk sleeve.*

cape sleeve 1. Shoulder cut in shape of a cape with the sleeve set-in at a dropped shoulder-line to give more freedom of movement. Used on sport jackets in mid-1980s. 2. Circular or semicircular piece placed over each shoulder and stitched to the blouse, giving a caped effect over each arm. 3. Flared piece of fabric cut to extend to neck in raglan style. Introduced in 1920s and featured in late 1960s for cape coats (see under COATS AND JACKETS: CAPE COAT #2).

cape sleeve #1

cap sleeve

cap sleeve Small extension cut on the front and back sections of a blouse that covers the shoulder. Has a seam at the shoulder and under the arms fastening front and back of garment together but no set-in sleeve. Popular in the 1940s and worn at intervals since. In the 1980s, flat turn-over cuffs were sometimes added to this type of sleeve.

∞**caroline sleeve** Woman's daytime dress sleeve worn in 1830s, full from shoulder to elbow and fitted to wrist.

cartwheel sleeve Short sleeve composed of two circles joined together around the outer edge. One circle fits into armhole, the other fits around the arm. Copied from the BERET SLEEVE (see under SHOULDERS AND SLEEVES). Also called *circle sleeve.*

∞**cased sleeve** Woman's long sleeve of about 1810 to 1820, made from sections of fabric alternating with bands of lace insertion.

∞**Cavalier sleeve** Sleeve slashed and fastened along outer edge by ribbon bows, full at shoulder, and close-fitting on forearm, used on women's daytime dresses in 1830s. Modeled after the sleeves of dresses and jackets of the 1600s in England by those supporting King Charles II during the English Civil War.

circle sleeve See under SHOULDERS AND SLEEVES: CARTWHEEL SLEEVE.

cornet sleeve (kor'-net) Close-fitting sleeve ending in a trumpet-shaped flounce.

demi-gigot (demee' jhee'-goh) Sleeve, tight from wrist to elbow, but full at shoulder and upper arm. Worn from 1825 to 1830, revived in early 1890s and again by young designers in England and Scandinavia in the early 1970s. *Der.* French, "half leg-of-mutton."

∞**demi-sleeve/demi-maunch** Full, elbow-length sleeve of 16th c.

dolman or batwing sleeve

dolman sleeve Sleeve fitted at wrist but cut with deep armhole so that it somewhat resembles a cape from the back. So called because it looks somewhat like sleeve in original DOLMAN coat (see under COATS AND JACKETS). Also called *batwing sleeve.*

double-puffed sleeve Full sleeve with band around arm that divides it into two puffs. In 1960s, a bracelet was sometimes worn around upper arm over full sleeve to give same effect.

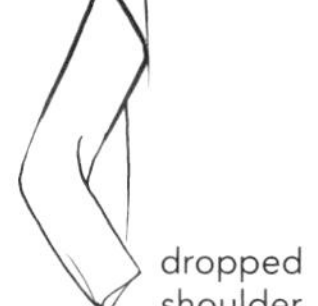
dropped shoulder

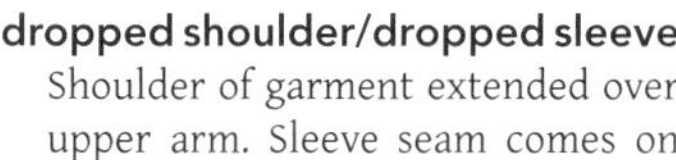

dropped shoulder/dropped sleeve Shoulder of garment extended over upper arm. Sleeve seam comes on the upper arm rather than at the natural armhole. Style was very popular from 1835 to 1870, used occasionally since, becoming fashionable again in the mid-1980s.

∞**du barry sleeve** Double-puffed sleeve, one puff above elbow and another below, worn in mid-1830s. *Der.* Named for Comtesse du Barry, Marie Jeanne Bécu (1746–1793), the last mistress of King Louis XV of France.

∞**eelskin sleeve** Tight-fitting, lace-trimmed sleeve worn by women in the 17th c.

elbow-length sleeve Any sleeve that stops at elbow. Popular length used for dresses in 1940s and 1960s.

∞**elephant sleeve** Large sleeve of early 1830s usually made of sheer fabric; full at the shoulder, hanging down somewhat in the form of an elephant's ear, and close-fitting at the wrist.

epaulet sleeve (ep'-oh-let) Sleeve with yoke across top of shoulder cut in one piece with sleeve. It is decorated with an epaulet (ep'-oh-let), which is a wide, flat band extending along top of shoulder to sleeve seam and is frequently trimmed with braid. *Der.* Borrowed from military uniforms. See under EPAULET.

extended shoulder/extended sleeve Plain shoulder seam extending down over arm to form a cap sleeve of longer length. Very popular in 1980s.

false hanging sleeve See under SHOULDERS AND SLEEVES: HANGING SLEEVE #2.

∞**farthingale sleeves** Sleeves cut wide above and narrow below that are held out with wire, reed, or whalebone. Worn in late 16th and early 17th c. by men and women.

fitted sleeve Full-length, bracelet-length, or three-quarter-length sleeve cut to fit the arm closely and set into the normal armhole.

flange shoulder Extension of shoulders over armhole seam. Top sometimes made by using a wide band at edge, sometimes by making a deep pleat in front of blouse at the shoulders.

foresleeve Sleeve covering the arm from wrist to elbow. Also see under SHOULDERS AND SLEEVES: HALF SLEEVE.

French gigot sleeve See under SHOULDERS AND SLEEVES: LEG-OF-MUTTON SLEEVE.

∞**French sleeves** Detachable sleeves worn by men in England in second half of 16th c.

funnel sleeve See under SHOULDERS AND SLEEVES: PAGODA SLEEVE.

∞**gabrielle sleeve** (ga-bree-el') **1.** Type of sleeve used in SPENCER jackets (see under COATS AND JACKETS) and dresses in 1820s and early 1830s. Made with a small oversleeve or epaulet at shoulder, full to elbow, narrowed to wrist, and ending in a deep cuff. **2.** Sleeve composed of series of puffs extending from shoulder to wrist worn from late 1850s to 1870s.

∞**half sleeve** 1. Protective sleeve covering the sleeve on forearm, held on by an elastic garter. Worn in early 20th c. particularly by clerical workers. 2. Sleeve covering forearm made of richer material than rest of garment, attached by lacings. Worn from late 14th to mid-17th c. Also called *foresleeve.*

handkerchief sleeve Sleeve made with square piece put over shoulder in such a manner that it falls in points like a handkerchief.

∞**hand sleeve** Lower part of sleeve, in the 16th c.

hanging sleeve 1. Any long sleeve with an opening in the sleeve at the shoulder, at the upper arm, or at the elbow through which the arm can be put. The remainder of the sleeve hangs down at the back of the arm. Sometimes made open from upper arm to wrist with a cuff. Also see under SHOULDERS AND SLEEVES: ANGEL SLEEVE. ∞2. **Sham hanging sleeve** or a **false hanging sleeve** is a variant in which a long hanging pendant piece of fabric is attached to a short sleeve or set in the armhole in back. This piece sometimes reached ankle length (1560s to 1630s). In 17th and 18th c., pendant fabric became more like a ribbon streamer. See under RIBBONS OF CHILDHOOD.

hanging sleeve #1

∞**imbecile sleeve/idiot sleeve** Very full, balloon sleeve set in at a dropped shoulder and gathered to narrow cuff at wrist. Worn from late 1820s to mid-1830s. Also called *sleeve à la folle. Der.* Named after the garments used to confine patients in insane asylums, which had very large sleeves.

imbecile sleeve

∞**inverted leg-of-mutton sleeve** Woman's sleeve of early 1900s with tiny darts at shoulder, close-fitting at upper arm, bouffant on lower arm, and a tight-fitting cuff. Compare with LEG-OF-MUTTON (see under SHOULDERS AND SLEEVES).

∞**isabeau sleeve** (Iz-ah-bow') Triangular-shaped sleeve of 1860s with one point at the shoulder and widening to wrist. Used as an oversleeve with ENGAGEANTES (see under entry #2) on dresses, on the PARDESSUS (see under COATS AND JACKETS), and on the MAINTENON CLOAK (see under CAPES, CLOAKS, AND SHAWLS).

juliet sleeve Long sleeve with short, puffed top, fitted on lower arm. *Der.* Named after heroine of William Shakespeare's tragedy *Romeo and Juliet.*

kabuki sleeve See under SHOULDERS AND SLEEVES: KIMONO SLEEVE.

kimono sleeve 1. Wide sleeve cut in one piece with front and back of the garment and seamed down outer- and underarm like a Japanese KIMONO. Also called *kabuki sleeve* and *mandarin sleeve.* 2. A 1984 version of kimono sleeve was made with wide hanging piece under the arm, tapering to close-fitting at wrist.

kimono sleeve #1

lantern sleeve Sleeve, plain at top and wrist, that balloons out halfway between the wrist and the elbow. Cut in two pieces with a seam going around the sleeve at the fullest part.

leg-of-mutton sleeve/leg-o'-mutton sleeve Sleeve with full top gathered or pleated into armhole and tapered to wrist where it looks like a regular sleeve. Size may vary—in 1895, very full sleeves requiring a yard or two of fabric were popular. Also called a *French gigot sleeve,* which derives from French, for "leg of lamb." Shown at TAILOR-MADE.

∞**Louis XIV sleeve** Women's oversleeve, flared as it descends from the shoulder and edged with rows of fluting. Worn with undersleeve or ENGAGEANTES in 1850s. *Der.* Named after Louis XIV, who ruled France from 1639 to 1715.

∞**magyar sleeve** (mag'-yar) Name assigned by costume historians to a sleeve worn in the 13th c. that was cut in one with the body of the garment with additional fullness under the arm. Similar to BATWING SLEEVE (see under SHOULDERS AND SLEEVES).

∞**mameluke sleeve** (mam'-eh-luke) Full sleeve finished with a large cuff of thin fabric used in daytime dresses of the late 1820s. *Der.* Mamelukes were originally slaves brought to Egypt, later trained as soldiers. Ruled Egypt from 1250 to 1517 and remained powerful until 1811 under Turkish viceroys.

∞**mancheron** (man-cher-own') 1. Late-15th- and early-16th-c. half sleeve, reaching from elbow to shoulder, lower part of sleeve called *brassart.* Two parts held together with pins and ribbons. 2. 16th-c. false sleeve attached only at shoulder and worn hanging down back. 3. Very short oversleeve, similar to a large EPAULETTE, worn by women in the 19th century. Replaced by word *epaulette* in 1860s.

∞**mandarin sleeve** See under SHOULDERS AND SLEEVES: KIMONO SLEEVE.

∞**marie sleeve** Full sleeve tied at intervals to form several puffs. Worn from about 1813 to mid-1820s and revived in the early 1870s—then called the *Marie Antoinette sleeve.*

∞**Marino Faliero sleeve** (mar-ee'noh fahl-yer'-oh) Full hanging sleeve of first half of 1830s secured with ribbon band at elbow, and long point hanging to wrist. *Der.* After drama of the same name written by Lord Byron.

∞**medici sleeve** (meh′-dee-chee) Full sleeve, puffed to elbow and tight from there to wrist, worn by women in 1830s. *Der.* Inspired by clothes worn by Marie de' Medici, Queen of France, c. 1600.

melon sleeve See under SHOULDERS AND SLEEVES: BERET SLEEVE.

∞**mitten sleeve** Woman's tightly fitted sleeve of lace or net reaching to the knuckles; used in the early 1890s in theater and dinner dresses.

∞**montespan sleeve** (mon′-tes-pan) Woman's puffed sleeve of early 1830s made with upper part caught in band at elbow and lace VANDYKE ruffle falling down from the band. *Der.* Named for Marquise de Montespan (1641–1707), mistress of Louis XIV of France.

∞**mushroom sleeve** Woman's short sleeve pleated into the armhole with the lower edge trimmed with lace. Used in evening dresses of the mid-1890s.

natural shoulder Follows body lines with sleeve set in at natural armhole without padding. Fashionable for men's suits in 1950s and 1960s.

padded sleeve Pads sewn inside garment to make shoulder appear broader. Introduced for women in 1930s by Schiaparelli and also popular in mid-1980s.

pagoda sleeve (pah-gode′-ah) Funnel-shaped outer sleeve flaring at wrist, falling over a puffed undersleeve. *Der.* Named for the shape of a Far Eastern temple's flaring roof. Also called *funnel sleeve.*

pagoda sleeve

parachute sleeve Long, full sleeve made without a cuff with the lower edge gathered to a lining cut shorter than the sleeve.

peasant sleeve Full sleeve gathered at top and bottom. May be either short and puffed or long and full.

∞**peg-top sleeve** Sleeve worn by men from 1857 to 1864, full at shoulder and tapered to wrist. A modified form of the LEG-OF-MUTTON SLEEVE (see under SHOULDERS AND SLEEVES).

petal sleeve Short sleeve curved at hem and overlapping to give a petal-shaped effect in front.

∞**pompadour sleeve** (pohm′-pah-dure) Adaptation in 1830s and 1840s of elbow-length sleeve edged with ruffle worn by the Marquise de Pompadour, mistress of Louis XV of France.

puff or puffed sleeve

puff/puffed sleeve Short sleeve gathered, either at the armhole or at the cuff band or both, producing a rounded shape. Popular in 1920s and 1930s, revived in late 1960s, and still used for babies and children's wear.

raglan sleeve Sleeve that extends to neckline, set in by seams slanting from underarm front and back. Used since mid-1850s. A variation is made with an additional seam down outside of arm called a **three-seamed raglan.** **Saddle sleeve** or **saddle shoulder**, another raglan variation, has a shoulder with small yoke made by not bringing the raglan sleeve to the neck in a point, but by widening it so that it is 3–4″ in width at the neck, thus forming a "saddle" over the shoulder. *Der.* Lord Raglan, or Fitzroy James Henry Somerset, British general in Crimean War, who, after losing an arm in the Charge of the Light Brigade in 1854, had a coat designed with a special sleeve.

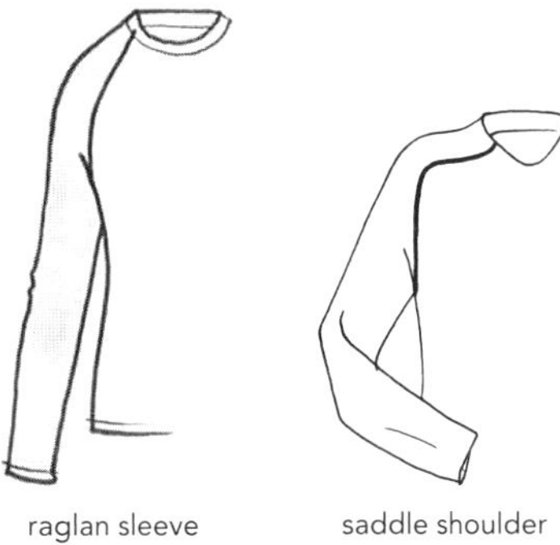
raglan sleeve   saddle shoulder

rhumba sleeve Barrel-shaped sleeve covered with rows of small horizontal ruffles. *Der.* From shirts worn by men dancing South American rhumba.

roll/roll-up sleeve Sleeve, approximately elbow length, finished only with a narrow hem, designed to be folded—or rolled up—at least twice in lieu of a cuff. Popular for women's tailored shirts in 1950s and 1960s, an outgrowth of earlier fad for wearing long sleeves folded up in this manner.

∞**roxalane sleeve** (rok-so-lane′) Bouffant sleeve worn from the late 1820s on made by tying a fringed band around a long full sleeve above the elbow—dividing it into two puffs.

∞**sabot sleeve** (sa-boh′) **1.** Sleeve used on 18th-c. dresses, tight-fitting to elbow, flared below elbow, and trimmed with ruffles. **2.** Sleeve with single or double puff above elbow used on women's evening dresses from late 1820s to 1836. Also used from 1836 to 1840 on day dresses and then called *victoria sleeve.*

saddle shoulder/saddle sleeve See under SHOULDERS AND SLEEVES: RAGLAN SLEEVE.

set-in sleeve Any type of sleeve which is sewed into an armhole.

sham hanging sleeve See under SHOULDERS AND SLEEVES: HANGING SLEEVE #2.

shirt sleeve Tailored wrist-length sleeve made with FLAT-FELLED SEAMS (see under CLOTHING CONSTRUCTION DETAILS) and set smoothly into the armhole. Sometimes has one or two small unpressed pleats where it joins the cuff. Basic sleeve for men's shirts since late 19th c. and may have SINGLE or FRENCH CUFF (see under CUFFS)—women's style may have a band at cuff.

slashed sleeve See under SHOULDERS AND SLEEVES: SPANISH SLEEVE.

sleeve à la folle See under SHOULDERS AND SLEEVES: IMBECILE SLEEVE.

∞**sleeve hand** In 17th-c., an opening in sleeve through which hand is thrust.

∞**sling sleeve** Sleeve cut in one with upper part of garment like a cape, frequently with attached horizontal piece of fabric, similar to a *sling,* on which to rest the arm. Worn by women in mid-1880s and used in sling-duster coat.

∞**spanish sleeve** Puffed sleeve, with vertical slashes revealing colored silk lining, worn by women from 1807 to 1820 and in late 1850s and 1860s. Also called a *slashed sleeve.*

suit sleeve Sleeve cut in two pieces—one for under the arm and one for the top of the arm. Cut to allow for the bend at the elbow, it is generally used for tailored suits for men and women. A popular style in the 1850s for women's dresses.

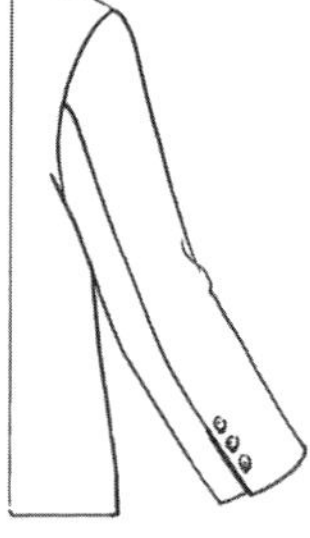
suit sleeve

∞**sultana sleeve/sultan sleeve** Full hanging sleeve (see under SHOULDERS AND SLEEVES: HANGING SLEEVE #1) of late 1850s slit open down outside. Sometimes fastened with ribbons around upper and forearms.

three-quarter sleeve Sleeve ending between elbow and wrist.

three-seamed raglan sleeve See under SHOULDERS AND SLEEVES: RAGLAN SLEEVE.

Tom Jones sleeve Full sleeve, gathered into cuff or ruffle, used on men's shirts, sometimes set into dropped shoulder. *Der.* Named for style of shirts worn in 18th c. made popular by costumes worn in 1963 film of Henry Fielding's 1749 novel *Tom Jones.*

trumpet sleeve Sleeve fitting into natural armhole, falling straight to elbow where it flares in the shape of a trumpet.

trunk sleeve See under SHOULDERS AND SLEEVES: CANNON SLEEVE.

tulip sleeve Set-in sleeve with bell shape made in several pieces like petals on a flower.

∞**venetian sleeve** Full sleeve of late 1850s fitting into armhole, slashed nearly to shoulder, worn by women over puffed undersleeves.

victoria sleeve See under SHOULDERS AND SLEEVES: SABOT SLEEVE.

∞**virago sleeve** (veer-ahg'-goh) Puffed sleeve worn by women in first half of the 17th c. made with many panes that are tied together at intervals to the wrist. Sometimes tied only at elbow and wrist, making two large puffs.

virago sleeve

∞**wearing sleeves** In 17th c., sleeves worn on the arms as compared with hanging sleeves (see under SHOULDERS AND SLEEVES: HANGING SLEEVES #1).

∞**shoulder wing** Decorative projection at shoulder attached at armhole seam like a wing covering the POINTS (laces) by which the sleeve is fastened to the armhole. Worn from 1545 to 1640 by both men and women.

show 1. See under COATS AND JACKETS. 2. See under ACTIVEWEAR: HUNT BREECHES.

showcase displays Display of merchandise in glass cabinets. When used for expensive items, such display cases are usually locked. See under CLOSED ISLAND DISPLAY.

shower *adj.* Describes clothes designed to be worn in the shower. Examples: HEADWEAR: SHOWER CAP and FOOTWEAR: SHOWER SHOE.

showing horn See under SHOE HORN.

showroom Location where manufacturers or designers present their current lines to retail buyers.

showrooming The habit of customers to shop brick-and-mortar stores to assess the quality and fit of a desired garment and then make their purchase online in order to take advantage of lower prices.

shrink See under SWEATERS.

†**shrinkage control** Fabrics woven and finished with processes that make them have less tendency to reduce their dimensions after washing and dry cleaning.

shrug See under SWEATERS.

∞**Sicilian bodice** The upper part of an evening dress of mid-1860s made with square décolletage and four knee-length panels attached—two in front and two in back—giving tunic effect. See TUNIC #2.

sicilian embroidery See under EMBROIDERIES AND SEWING STITCHES: SPANISH EMBROIDERY #2.

∞**side** From the 15th to 16th c. it was synonymous with "long" (e.g., a "side gown" is a long gown).

∞**side boards** Slang for side whiskers.

side bodies In tailoring, the two side pieces in the back of a man's coat. The seams that join these side panels to the center back piece curve outward at the shoulder blades, ending at the armhole seams. This construction gives better fit and flexibility than a one- or two-piece back and was used from 1840s on.

side braid See under HAIRSTYLES.

sideburns See under HAIRSTYLES.

side-channel frame See under HANDBAGS AND RELATED ACCESSORIES: FRAME.

side-gore shoe See under FOOTWEAR.

side-laced shoes See under FOOTWEAR: SIDE-LACED OXFORDS.

side leather See under LEATHERS.

sideless surcote See under SURCOTE.

side parted See under HAIRSTYLES.

side placket See under CLOTHING CONSTRUCTION DETAILS: PLACKET.

side pleats See under CLOTHING CONSTRUCTION DETAILS: KNIFE PLEATS.

signature Practice started by Parisian couturiers in late 1960s of using their own name printed on scarves and handbags. See under HANDBAGS AND RELATED ACCESSORIES and SCARVES: DESIGNER SCARF.

signature prints A trademarked print that incorporates a logo, brand name, or pattern that is recognized by consumers as related to a particular brand.

signature stores Stores that are owned and managed by a wholesale product developer used to build brand image, test new styles, and learn more about their customer preferences.

signet ring See under JEWELRY.

silhouette Contour or outline as shown in solid black on a white background. Similar to a black shadow cast on a white wall. Once, widely used to indicate trend in length and general outline of garments for the coming seasons. *Der.* Named after French author and statesman Étienne de Silhouette (1709–1767), who first made portraits in black with no background details.

hourglass silhouette

†**silk** Fiber obtained from the cocoon of the silkworm. Noted for its resiliency, elasticity, strength, and luster. Often used to make luxurious fabrics.

silk hat See under HEADWEAR.

†**silk illusion** Very fine net, similar to TULLE, used for wedding veils.

silking See under GLOVES AND GLOVE CONSTRUCTION: POINTING.

silk pin See under DRESSMAKER PIN.

silk ribbon embroidery See under EMBROIDERIES AND SEWING STITCHES: ROCOCO EMBROIDERY.

silk-screen printing See under PRINTS, STRIPES, AND CHECKS: SCREEN PRINTING.

silver fox See under FURS.

silver hose/pantyhose See under HOSIERY: GLITTER HOSE.

silver-streakers The population group age 50 and over.

simar (si-mar′) **1.** See under COATS AND JACKETS. **2.** See under CLERICAL DRESS.

†**simplex knit** A reversible warp-knit, double-faced fabric with the same appearance on both sides. Used for gloves.

simulated gems See under GEMS, GEM CUTS, AND SETTINGS.

simulated pearls See under GEMS, GEM CUTS, AND SETTINGS: PEARL.

single-breasted Conventional closing for suits, jackets, blouses, and coats. Abbreviated *S.B.* May be closed with buttons that are aligned down center front of garment. Lap is not as great as in a DOUBLE-BREASTED closing.

single cuff See under CUFFS.

single-hand system A garment production method, used primarily for couture or very high-priced, limited production apparel and for sewing PROTOTYPES, in which one sewer makes an entire garment. Compare with BUNDLE SYSTEM.

†**single yarn** Refers to one strand of yarn. When two single yarns are twisted together the result is a two-ply yarn. Also see under PLY YARN.

siphonia See under COATS AND JACKETS.

siren suit British one-piece COVERALL worn during World War II. Designed for fast dressing in case of emergencies signaled by air-raid sirens.

Siwash sweater See under SWEATERS: COWICHAN SWEATER.

size migration A situation in which one woman typically fits into a range of three or more sizes, depending on the manufacturer and cut of the garment.

size specification Measurements at particular locations on a garment that are established by the manufacturer for each of the sizes in which the style will be made.

size standards The amount of proportional increase or decrease in garment measurements that a ready-to-wear apparel company requires for each of the sizes it produces.

sizing 1.Measurements of body used as guide for cutting garments to fit a variety of body types. †2. Nonpermanent finishing process applied particularly to cotton fabrics to increase weight, crispness, and luster by means of starch, gelatin, oil, and wax. When done at home or in a commercial laundry, the process is called **starching**.

skant See under PANTS.

skate shoes See under FOOTWEAR: HEELY.

skating See under FOOTWEAR and SKIRTS.

skating dress See under DRESSES.

skating skirt See under SKIRTS.

†skein (skane) Unit by which knitting yarn is sold, usually comes packaged in loosely coiled form. Also called a *hank*.

skeleton skirt See under UNDERGARMENTS.

∞skeleton suit Boy's suit worn from 1790 to 1830, consisting of a short, tight jacket and ankle-length trousers buttoned to the jacket at waist.

skeleton suit

skeleton waterproof See under COATS AND JACKETS.

ski clothing See under ACTIVEWEAR: SKI PANTS and SKI SUIT; COATS AND JACKETS: SKI JACKET; FOOTWEAR: SKI BOOT; SLEEPWEAR AND LOUNGEWEAR: SKI PAJAMAS; and SWEATERS: SKI SWEATER.

ski mask See under MASKS.

skimmer 1. See under DRESSES. 2. See under FOOTWEAR. 3. See under HEADWEAR.

skinny jeans See under PANTS.

skin-on-skin process See under FURS: WORKED IN THE ROUND.

skirt-belt See under BELTS.

SKIRTS

skirt 1. Lower part of dress or long garment without *legs*, the section below the waistline. Dresses can be made with separate skirts and bodices or with skirt and bodice joined by a waistline seam. After the late Middle Ages, it became customary in the Western world for women to wear only garments with skirts and for men (unless their professions required wearing robes) to wear BIFURCATED GARMENTS, a practice that ended only in the 20th c. 2. Separate item of clothing starting above, below, or at natural waistline. 3. Lower part of a coat or jacket, particularly in Great Britain.

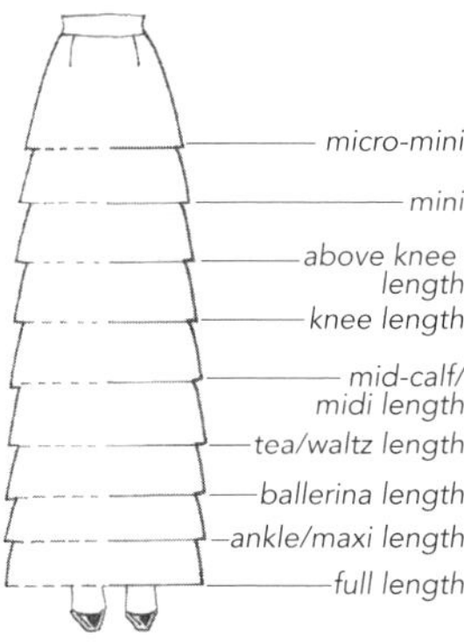

skirt lengths

accordion-pleated skirt Skirt made from a full circle of fabric with pressed-in pleats that are wider at the hem and taper to waistline, giving a flare to skirt. When the body is in motion, pleats flare at the hem like the bellows of a half-open accordion. Introduced in late 1880s by Loie Fuller for "skirt dancing" and popular at intervals since. Also called *sunburst-pleated skirt* or, in a usage of the 1880s, a **sunray skirt.**

A-line skirt Slightly flared skirt introduced in the early 1960s. In silhouette, it appears like the letter *A*.

A-line skirt

asymmetric skirt Any skirt that differs on either side of an imaginary line drawn down the center front. Sometimes has ruffles or flounces attached diagonally across center front from waist to hip; frequently has an ASYMMETRIC hemline.

baby skirt Short, flared, or pleated skirt worn over bathing suit or playsuit during 1930s and 1940s.

∞ballet skirt Tiered skirt of evening dress, worn in 1880s, made with three or four layers of tulle in a variety of lengths attached to a silk foundation. Top layer was sprinkled with stars, pearls, or beetle wings.

balloon skirt See under SKIRTS: BUBBLE SKIRT.

bell skirt Skirt usually gathered at waistline, making it full over hips and flared at hem. Popular from the 1830s to late 1860s and sometimes worn with crinoline or hoops underneath. Popular for evening gowns.

bell skirt

bias skirt Any skirt cut on the diagonal or bias of the fabric. The bias cut was introduced by Madeleine Vionnet in 1920s, was popular through the 1930s, and worn at intervals since.

bouffant skirt (boo-fahnt') Any full skirt; more specifically, a gathered skirt.

box-pleated skirt Two flat folds meeting underneath to form box pleats that extend around the waist, alternating with inverted pleats. Popular in 1940s and 1950s, and at intervals since.

broomstick skirt Full skirt that, after washing, is tied tightly with a string around a broomstick. When dry, it contains vertical ridges or wrinkles. Popular in the 1940s and somewhat revived in the late 1960s.

bubble skirt Skirt gathered to small waistline, ballooning out and tapered in at hem, popular in 1950s. Also called *balloon skirt, tulip skirt.* Shown at DRESSES: BUBBLE DRESS.

bustle-back skirt Any skirt with puffed fullness, ruffles, or large bow in the center back. In the late 1860s skirt fullness was pulled to the back, however, skirt remained full. During the late 1870s skirt became slim with accent in back. In mid-1880s, skirt was full with large bustle. Style was somewhat revived in the 1930s, 1940s, and 1980s. Typically used for evening or bridal gowns.

carwash skirt A skirt with split panels like those at a carwash.

circle/circular skirt Skirt made by cutting a semicircle out of a piece of fabric folded lengthwise. The selvages are then joined to make a full circle. Popular for skating and general wear in the 1930s, it has remained a basic type of skirt, becoming very popular in mid-1980s.

∞**cornet skirt** Woman's skirt of early 1890s cut straight and fitted in front, with back cut on the bias with small train. Also called *french skirt.*

crinoline See under UNDERGARMENTS.

culottes (koo-lotz′) Skirt divided into two sections so that it is actually a pair of pants but looks like a skirt when not in motion. Also called *split skirt, pantskirt, divided skirt, scooter skirt,* or *skort. Der.* French, *culotte,* "knee breeches"; *des culottes,* "trousers." Shown at PANTS: CULOTTES.

dance skirt Short skirt worn over leotard and tights by dancers for practicing.

∞**Directoire skirt** (dir-eck′-twa) Skirt cut in seven gores worn from late 1880s through early 1900s. The back four gores were lined, stiffened, and fluted into PIPE-ORGAN or GODET PLEATS (see under CLOTHING CONSTRUCTION DETAILS)—the hem being four to six yards wide around. A name patented for this style by *The Delineator* magazine.

dirndl (durn′-del) Full, gathered skirt. The style derives from Tyrolean peasant costume originating, and still worn, in the Austrian and Bavarian Alps.

dirndl

divided skirt 1. See under SKIRTS: CULOTTES. ∞2. Wide trousers that hang like a skirt, introduced in England in 1882 by Lady Harberton for bicycling. Same as *pantskirt* or *culottes.*

draped skirt Any skirt with additional fullness, pleated or gathered into one side seam, or forming a drapery that hangs down.

dropped skirt 1. Skirt set on a low waistline; also called a *torso skirt.* ∞2. Skirt made separate from the lining, as it was called in late 19th and early 20th c. Both are attached to the same seam at waist.

∞**eel skirt** Woman's gored skirt of late 1890s cut on the bias, fitting very snugly over the hips, and flared slightly from the knees to hem.

empire skirt Straight skirt starting at a high waistline under the bust. Originated in *Empire period* (1804–1815), and worn at intervals since.

evening skirt Any type of separate skirt worn for a formal or semiformal occasion.

∞**featherbrush skirt** Daytime skirt of sheer material, with overlapping flounces below knees, worn in 1898.

fishtail skirt Skirt with additional stitched-on, free-hanging panel in front or back, simulating the tail of a fish.

flying panel skirt Complete skirt made with an extra panel, attached at the waistline, that hangs free. Basic type skirt for dresses in 1940s and 1950s and revived with pants-type dress of late 1960s.

∞**foot-mantle/fotemantle** 1. An outer, or extra, woman's skirt, worn in American Colonial days to keep dress clean when riding horseback. 2. An overskirt worn by countrywomen when riding horseback in the 14th c. Called a *safeguard* from 16th to 18th c.

french skirt See under CORNET SKIRT.

friponne See under SKIRTS: JUPE #2.

full skirt Any skirt made with several widths of fabric; may be cut in a complete circle, made with many gores, or gathered.

gathered skirt Skirt made straight with panels of fabric sewed together, shirred (or gathered) at the top, and attached to a waistband or bodice of dress. Popular at intervals since 1830.

godet skirt (go-day′) A triangular piece of fabric inserted upward from the hem of the skirt to give more fullness. Popular in 1930s and used occasionally since.

godet skirt

gored skirt Skirt that fits through the waistline and flares at the hem. May be made of from four to twenty-four shaped sections. Dates from 14th c. and much used in 19th c. Very popular in the late 1860s, mid-1890s, early 20th c., 1930s, 1940s, and now worn as a classic skirt style.

gored skirt

granny skirt Full-length, gathered skirt usually with a ruffle at hem introduced in 1960s. *Der.* Worn by a young girl in imitation of skirt worn by her grandmother, or "granny."

handkerchief skirt Skirt with hemline cut to fall in points as if made of handkerchiefs. Popular in 1920s, 1960s, and 1980s and after.

harem skirt Draped skirt with hem gathered, turned up, and fastened to lining. Worn in the Near East and introduced to the West by Paris designer Paul Poiret in 1912. Revived periodically.

hip-hugger skirt Any skirt, usually belted, that rides low on hips below the natural waistline, popular in late 1960s and later.

hobble skirt

∞hobble skirt Woman's skirt rounded over hips, tapered to ankle so narrowly that walking is impeded. Fashion designed by Paris designer *Paul Poiret* about 1912. For a variation, see under SKIRTS: PEG-TOP SKIRT.

hoop skirt A skirt held out with crinoline, a stiffened underskirt, or hoops. May be bell-, cone-, or pyramid-shaped. Very fashionable from 1850 to 1870 and worn at intervals since, particularly for evening and bridal gowns.

hula skirt Mid-calf-length skirt, made of long grasses fastened together at low waistline, worn in Hawaii for hula dances performed for tourists. Copied in plastic strips for costumes.

inverted pleated skirt Skirt made by bringing two folds of fabric to a center line in front and/or back. May be cut straight at sides or be slightly flared. Has been a basic type of skirt since 1920s.

∞jupe (zhoop) **1.** French word for skirt. A **mini-jupe** is a miniskirt. Used in 1960s as a synonym for skirt. **2.** A late 17th-c. woman's skirt, sometimes in three layers: *modeste* on top, *friponne* in middle, and *sècrete* underneath.

jupon (zhoo'-pown) Woman's *underskirt* that contrasted or matched fabric of bodice, worn between 1850 and 1870.

kangaroo skirt Maternity skirt designed by Elsie Frankfurt in early 1940s with a circular cutout in center top front. This portion was not filled in with stretch fabric as in later maternity skirts.

kick-pleated skirt Straight skirt with only one pleat in either front or back to make walking easier. Popular when narrow silhouettes are worn.

kilt Scottish skirt made in wraparound style. Center front is plain with KNIFE PLEATS (see under CLOTHING CONSTRUCTION DETAILS) starting at side front and wrapping around to other side or front. Hanging end may be fringed and fastened with a large decorative safety pin. Originally worn by Scots Highlander men in various tartans. See also under PLAIDS AND TARTANS: TARTAN. Copied for children and women at times since the 1860s.

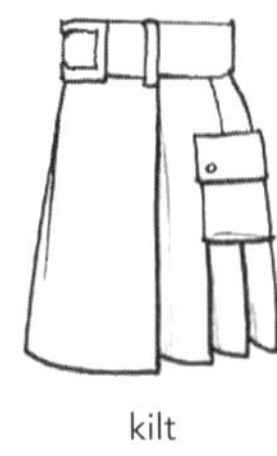
kilt

knife-pleated skirt **1.** Skirt made with single pleats about 1″ wide all going in the same direction completely around the skirt. **2.** Skirt made with single pleats starting from a center *box pleat* and going around to center back, where they form an INVERTED PLEAT (see under CLOTHING CONSTRUCTION DETAILS). Both are basic types of skirts introduced in the 1920s. Also popular in 1940s and late 1960s and after when heat-set pleating was introduced.

layered skirt Skirt made of tiers in varying lengths, placed one on top of the other.

∞marie antoinette skirt (mah'-ree an-twan-ett') Skirt worn since 1895 made with seven gores—three in front, four in back—with two back panels pleated in large BOX PLEATS (see under CLOTHING CONSTRUCTION DETAILS) stitched down to hips, making the skirt 4–6 yards wide at the hem. Named for Marie Antoinette (1755–1793), wife of Louis XVI of France.

maternity skirt Skirt with either a cut-out section at top center front or a section of stretch fabric inserted over the abdomen, worn by expectant mothers. Until the 1990s, maternity wear was designed to obscure the figure changes taking place during pregnancy, and some maternity dresses consisted of loose fitting tops worn over maternity skirts.

maxi skirt Ankle-length daytime skirt, popular with women in late 1960s as reaction against miniskirts.

midi skirt (mid'-ee) Skirt with hem halfway between ankle and knee, below the widest part of the calf. Introduced by designers in 1967 as a reaction to very short miniskirts.

∞milkmaid skirt From 1885 to 1895, a double skirt with plain overskirt gathered and pulled up on one side by cord or loop at waistband to reveal a striped underskirt.

mini-jupe See under SKIRTS: JUPE #1.

miniskirt Extremely short skirt, any length from 4 to 12″ above the knee. Popular for day and evening in the 1960s, credited to London designer Mary Quant.

modeste See under SKIRTS: JUPE #2.

morning-glory skirt Gored skirt of early 20th c., fitted through hips, then flaring in trumpet fashion. Also called *serpentine skirt.*

overskirt 1. A second skirt or drapery often looped up or split at sides, front, or back. Also an entire skirt of a sheer fabric constructed over a more opaque underskirt. 2. See under POLONAISE #1.

panel skirt See under SKIRTS: FLYING PANEL SKIRT.

∞**pannier skirt** (pan-yehr′) 1. Skirt extended at the sides but frequently narrow from front to back. Popular in the 18th c. and again in the 1870s. 2. Skirt with an overskirt draped at the hips to form puffs, popular in the 1850s and 1860s, and again in the 1880s. Also called a *pannier puff.*

pantskirt Synonym for *culottes, split skirt, skort, divided skirt,* and *scooter skirt.* All popular since mid-1960s.

∞**parasol skirt** Skirt cut with many gores, stitched in same manner as seams in a parasol. Worn by women in late 19th and early 20th c.

peasant skirt 1. Full gathered skirt that may be trimmed with bands of embroidery; plain gathered skirt; or skirt worn with an embroidered apron. 2. In the 1960s, referred to skirt decorated with bands of embroidery rather than style of skirt. *Der.* Adopted from national costume of European countries.

peg-top skirt 1. Basic skirt cut full at the waistline with darts, gathers, or small unpressed pleats used at waistline. From hips to hem, skirt tapers inward, becoming very narrow at hem. Sometimes made with center front seam with each panel rounded at hem. Usually made with a KNIFE PLEAT (see under CLOTHING CONSTRUCTION DETAILS) or slit on center back seam. Popular in 1950s and 1960s, used occasionally since. 2. Skirt made with fullness from waistline to hips, tapering narrowly to hemline. Popular about 1912 to end of World War I and revived at intervals since. *Der.* Name borrowed from boy's cone-shaped spinning top.

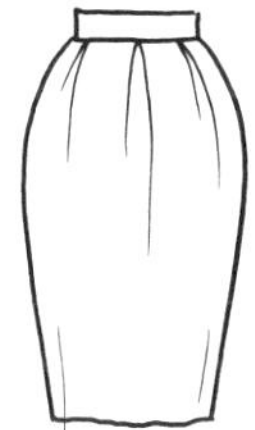

peg top skirt #1

∞**pentes** (pahn) Distinctive woman's skirt of mid-1880s cut in two layers. The overskirt was draped to reveal an underskirt trimmed with alternating silk and velvet strips that were pyramid-shaped and graduated in size.

poodle skirt Full circle skirt very popular with adolescents of the late 1940s and early 1950s that was often made of felt and decorated with an appliquéd poodle dog. Revived in the 1990s.

poodle shirt

prairie skirt Flared skirt, gathered at the waistband with one or two ruffles at the hem, made in plain or calico-patterned fabrics. *Der.* Adapted from skirts worn by women traveling west on the wagon trains.

puffball skirt Christian Lacroix design of 1986 that resembled a short, puffed-out ball of fabric. Similar to the MINI-CRINOLINE (see under DRESSES).

∞**pullback** Skirt of 1880s, with the fullness drawn to the back and draped.

∞**rainy daisy skirt/rainy day skirt** Tailored, ankle-length walking skirt fashionable from about 1902. Also worn for roller-skating. *Der.* A nickname given to women who were members of the "Rainy Day Club" and wore skirts of this type.

ra-ra skirt Style of the 1980s derived from the skirts worn by cheerleaders, which were mid-thigh length with full flounces or tiers.

∞**ripple skirt** *Gored* skirt worn in 1890s sometimes with as many as eleven gores. Fitted snugly over hips but flared at hem to a width of six yards or more. Lined with horsehair stiffening and pressed to hang in rounded PIPE-ORGAN PLEATS (see under CLOTHING CONSTRUCTION DETAILS).

safeguard See under SKIRTS: FOOT-MANTLE.

sarong (sar-ong′) Wrapped skirt, usually made of bold floral-print cotton, used as beach cover-up. Popular after actress Dorothy Lamour wore one in film *Hurricane,* late 1930s. *Der.* Copied from Indonesian native dress.

scooter skirt See under SKIRTS: SKORT.

secrete See under SKIRTS: JUPE #2.

sheath skirt Straight skirt with no flare. Usually has a kick pleat or slit in back or side to facilitate walking. Popular style in the 1950s and early 1960s and revived when straight skirts are fashionable.

skating skirt Very short, full, circular skirt. First popular in late 1930s after films by Norwegian-American ice-skater Sonja Henie.

skort Miniskirt with shorts, popular in late 1960s and after. Also called *scooter skirt. Der.* Combination of words "skirt" and "shorts."

slit skirt Straight-lined skirt with slashes on each side seam to knee or thigh. Copied from styles worn by Chinese and Vietnamese women. Also see under CHEONGSAM.

split skirt Synonym for *pantskirt, divided skirt,* and *culottes.*

square-dance skirt Full skirt with large ruffle at hem. Popular in rural areas for square dancing and barn dances.

squaw skirt Full skirt, set with tiny pleats, which may have horizontal embroidered bands at intervals and a ruffle at hem. Originally worn with embroidered blouse by American Indian women. In late 1960s, accepted for general wear by other women.

straight skirt Any slim skirt without fullness.

St. Tropez skirt Ankle-length, full skirt made with diagonal bands of various printed and plain-colored fabrics—may be as many as eight different fabrics used.

sunburst-pleated skirt See under SKIRTS: ACCORDION-PLEATED SKIRT.

sunray skirt See under SKIRTS: ACCORDION-PLEATED SKIRT.

suspender skirt Any skirt with attached suspenders. Frequently worn by young girls.

swing skirt Flared skirt, circular or cut in gores, fitted at hips with a wide flare at the hem. Popular in the late 1930s and at intervals since. Very popular in mid-1980s.

swirl skirt Skirt made from bias-cut strips of multicolored fabrics that were often from India.

∞**tablier skirt** (tab-lee-eh') Skirt worn from 1850s to 1870s with decorated free hanging panel in front, suggesting an apron. Sometimes trimming was applied directly to skirt. *Der.* French, "apron."

∞**tie-back skirt** Skirt with a train pulled back and looped to form puffs at sides by means of a drawstring inserted through tapes. Produced a silhouette that was flat in front and puffed at back and hips. Worn from mid-1870s through early 1880s.

tiered skirt Straight-lined skirt with a series of flounces cut either in circular style or on the straight of the material. Each flounce is usually cut larger than the previous one. Popular in the 1840s, 1860s, 1930s, and at intervals since.

torso skirt Pleated or gathered skirt attached to a yoke at hips.

∞**trouser skirt** Tailored skirt, split at side front to reveal matching bloomers attached at waistline. Worn from 1910 to 1920 by avant-garde women.

trumpet skirt Straight skirt that flares at the hem like an inverted trumpet. The flare is created either by cutting greater fullness at the hem or by attaching a large circular flounce.

trumpet skirt

tulip skirt See under SKIRTS: BUBBLE SKIRT.

tunic skirt Double-layered skirt with the overskirt cut shorter than the underskirt. Originally introduced in the 1850s as a ball dress with an upperskirt trimmed with lace and an underskirt with a deep flounce. Popular in slim style in the 1880s, 1910 to 1920, and worn intermittently since.

tunic skirt

umbrella-pleated skirt Circular-cut or gored skirt with widely spaced pleats, similar to accordion pleats only larger, simulating folds in an umbrella.

underskirt Simple, basic skirt over which an overskirt, or drapery, hangs.

∞**waterfall back** Skirt of mid-1880s worn over bustle made with series of cascading puffs down center back. Fullness was held in place with series of drawstrings inside dress.

wrap skirt A skirt, open from waist to hem, that wraps around the body and fastens with buttons or ties, usually lapped across the front or back.

yoke skirt Skirt with small fitted piece, sometimes straight, pointed, or scalloped attached at waistband. Lower part of skirt attached to yoke may be gathered or gored. Yoke may be placed at front or back of skirt, or both.

∞**zouave skirt** (zoo'-ahv) Style of the 1860s made by gathering the full skirt at the hem and attaching it to an inside lining to make it appear like baggy trousers worn by the French Zouaves. *Der.* Arabic, Zouaova, a Kabyle tribe, one of the Berbers, living in Algeria or Tunisia.

---

skirt supporter See under UNDERGARMENTS.

skivvies See under UNDERGARMENTS.

skivvy 1. See under UNDERGARMENTS. 2. See under SHIRTS.

skoncho See under CAPES, CLOAKS, AND SHAWLS.

skort See under SKIRTS.

SKU See under STOCK KEEPING UNIT.

skullcap See under HEADWEAR.

skunk See under FURS.

slacks See under PANTS.

∞**slammerkin** Loose-fitting, unboned gown worn at home in the morning without hoops by women from 1730 to 1770. If worn outdoors, hoops were added. Also called *trollopee.*

slant/slanted toe See under FOOTWEAR.

slap-sole See under FOOTWEAR.

slashed sleeve See under SHOULDERS AND SLEEVES: SPANISH SLEEVE.

slashing In the 15th and 16th c., slits deliberately made in clothing that enabled a garment underneath or contrasting lining to be pulled through. Slashes could be any length and run in any direction of the cloth, unlike PANES, which were vertical. Used on DOUBLETS sleeves and TRUNK HOSE. Also called

slashing on 16th c. doublet

scissoring, chique-tades, and *creves.* Called *blistered* during late 16th and 17th c.

slash pocket See under POCKETS: BOUND POCKET.

slave bracelet See under JEWELRY.

sleep bonnet See under HEADWEAR.

sleep bra See under UNDERGARMENTS: LEISURE BRA.

sleepcoat See under SLEEPWEAR AND LOUNGEWEAR.

sleep mask See under MASKS.

sleep set See under SLEEPWEAR AND LOUNGEWEAR.

sleep shorts See under SLEEPWEAR AND LOUNGEWEAR.

SLEEPWEAR AND LOUNGEWEAR

sleepwear Clothing used for sleeping or for preparing to go to bed.

loungewear Clothes designed to be worn primarily at home when relaxing or entertaining.

baby-doll nightgown Bouffant, hip-length nightgown made with short puffed sleeves and matching bloomers. Usually made of sheer fabric and popular in 1940s and 1950s.

baby-doll nightgown

baby-doll nightie A short, feminine nightgown or negligee that may feature bra cups to support the bust and is often sold with matching panties. It is frequently trimmed with lace, ruffles, bows, or ribbons to project a romantic, feminine image.

baby-doll pajamas Very short, micro-mini or mini-length pajamas consisting of a tent-shaped top, usually gathered into the neckline or yoke, worn with brief panties.

bare-midriff pajamas Two-piece pajamas with a brief top worn by women since late 1960s for lounging or sleeping.

bathrobe **1.** Wraparound robe usually styled with long sleeves, a shawl collar, and held closed with a sash. Worn by men, women, and children, popular styles are often made of plaid fabrics, plain wool, velour, fleece, or terrycloth. **2.** Synonym for various types of robes.

bathrobe #1

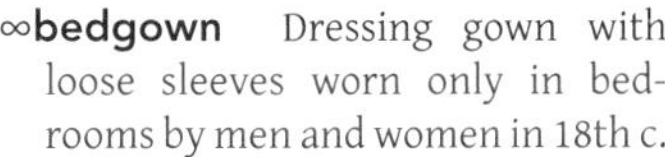

∞bedgown Dressing gown with loose sleeves worn only in bedrooms by men and women in 18th c.

bed jacket Waist-length jacket worn when sitting up in bed for breakfast or when recuperating from an illness. May match or contrast with nightgown. Popular in 1920s and still used.

blanket sleepers Children's winter pajamas made in two pieces or in one piece with front buttoned or zippered, of napped fabric similar to that used for blankets.

breakfast coat Contemporary name for BRUNCH COAT or DUSTER (see under SLEEPWEAR AND LOUNGEWEAR).

brunch coat Knee- or mid-calf-length, front-buttoned robe often in printed cotton worn in the daytime at home, popular since 1950s. Also called *duster* or *breakfast coat. Der.* Named for meal combining "breakfast" and "lunch."

brunch coat

bubble cover-up Loose-fitting, mini-length, blouson-type gown gathered below hips into wide band, forming a very short shirt.

bunny suit Form-fitting knitted jumpsuit buttoned or zippered down the front and made in footed-pajama style. Sometimes made in wide crosswise stripes of red and white.

caftan See under alphabetical listing.

∞chinese lounging robe Full-length lounging robe with standing chinese collar, full kimono sleeves flaring at wrist, and closing to one side in Chinese manner. Worn by women in early 1900s.

chinese pajamas Hip- or thigh-length jacket with side seams slashed to waist, mandarin collar, and closing—sometimes diagonal with frogs; worn with straight-legged pants. *Der.* From work garments worn in China by men and women.

coat-style pajamas Classic pajama style made like a single- or double-breasted coat with tailored convertible collar, frequently trimmed with piping, and worn with drawstring or elastic-top pants.

cocoon Luxurious hip-length robe with large batwing sleeve and blouson back with the open front usually banded in a contrasting color.

cossack pajamas Pajamas consisting of pants and a tunic top that closes at side front with standing-band collar. Introduced in 1930s and revived in late 1960s.

culotte pajamas (koo-lot′) Floor-length pajamas with wide legs, resembling a long dress, worn for dining in mid- and late 1960s and early 1970s. Also called *hostess culottes* and *party pants.*

djellaba (jel-ah′-bah) Loose garment, sometimes hooded, derived from Moroccan man's cloak. It was popular in 1960s, along with the CAFTAN, and is still worn by women as a housecoat or hostess robe.

dorm shirt Above-the-knee nightshirt made of knitted fabric and styled like a T-shirt.

Dr. Denton Sleepers® Trademark of Denton Mills, Inc., for one-piece knitted pajama, originally worn by children, that had covered feet, buttoned down the front, and with buttoned drop seat. Similar style now worn by adults called a BUNNY SUIT (see under SLEEPWEAR AND LOUNGEWEAR). This trademark is still active.

dressing gown/dressing robe **1.** Men: Generally used for a man's bathrobe that is usually lined and styled in a silk, rayon, or nylon fabric. Made in wraparound style with long shawl collar and sash. **2.** Women: Voluminous wraparound robe worn in the boudoir.

∞**dressing sacque/dressing sack** Short, loose, hip-length woman's jacket worn in boudoir in late 19th and early 20th c.

duster See under SLEEPWEAR AND LOUNGEWEAR: BRUNCH COAT.

flannel nightgown Full-length winter nightgown made of cotton FLANNEL or a blend of cotton and polyester. Frequently styled with a square or round yoke accented with a ruffle.

flannel nightgown

flashy nightshirt Low, scoop-necked, raglan-sleeved, above-the-knee nightshirt made with curved hem split at sides. Made of sweatshirt gray polyester knit. Similar to FLASHDANCE knit shirt (see under BLOUSES AND TOPS).

footed pajamas One- or two-piece child's sleeping garment with attached slipper-like coverings for the feet with soles often made of nonskid plastic.

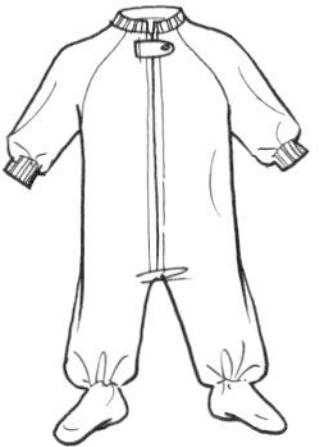
footed pajamas

french maid sleeper Provocative two-piece pajamas consisting of a lace-trimmed sheer top, styled like a French maid's apron, with bikini panties worn underneath.

granjamer Granny-style top with yoke, a placket neckline, and ruffle trimming worn with matching pants in 1960s for sleeping.

granny gown High-necked, long-sleeved, full-length gown made with ruffle-trimmed yoke, no waistline seam, and sometimes a ruffled flounce at hem. *Der.* Worn by a young girl who copied styles worn by her grandmother, or "granny."

grow sleepers Children's pajamas with several rows of snaps at waist that extend the garment's length as the child grows taller.

happi coat (*happie*) Hip-length jacket made in kimono style of brightly printed fabric, copied from knee-length jackets worn by Japanese laborers. Frequently with printed medallion on back in imitation of original Japanese jackets, which had symbol of employer on the back. Used in the U.S. as beach coats from 1950s to 1960s.

harem pajamas Very full trousers gathered at ankle, which may be paired with tunic or Oriental bolero. Fashionable for at-home wear in late 1960s.

hostess culottes See under SLEEPWEAR AND LOUNGEWEAR: CULOTTE PAJAMAS.

hostess robe Full-length robe fastening in front, frequently with zipper, made in elaborate fabrics and worn for entertaining at home. Also called *hostess gown* or *hostess coat.*

housecoat Informal robe worn at home. See under SLEEPWEAR AND LOUNGEWEAR: BRUNCH COAT and LOUNGING ROBE.

∞**Japanese wrapper** Woman's lounging robe of early 20th c. made in wraparound style with long, wide sleeves and a square yoke. Styled after a Japanese KIMONO (see under SLEEPWEAR AND LOUNGEWEAR).

juliet gown Nylon gown, usually made full length with a high or Empire waistline. May be lace-trimmed, have tiny puffed sleeves, and have ruffle at hem.

jumpsuit pajamas Fitted pajamas in one piece, usually buttoned or zipped at center front; similar to BUNNY SUIT but lacking feet (see under SLEEPWEAR AND LOUNGEWEAR).

kabuki robe (kah-boo′-kee) Short-length man's or woman's wraparound robe styled like a KIMONO (see under SLEEPWEAR AND LOUNGEWEAR) and closed with a sash.

karate pajamas (kah-rah′-tee) Two-piece pajamas styled like a KARATE COSTUME, with pants and Japanese-type wrap top, introduced in late 1960s and early 1970s.

kimono (keh-mo′-no) Type of robe cut like the Japanese kimono with KIMONO SLEEVES (see under SHOULDERS AND SLEEVES) and generally made in a scenic or floral printed fabric reminiscent of Japan. Sometimes closed with frogs rather than buttons. Very popular in the early 19th c. and used continually since. Shown at KIMONO.

knitted knickers One-piece, sleeveless, knitted pajamas with fitted top, round neck, and pants shirred at hem making a ruffle below the knee.

lounging pajamas Full-length pajamas cut in tunic or one-piece style. Legs are wide and long, giving the appearance of a skirt when not in motion. Introduced in the 1930s and used for lounge- and beachwear. Reintroduced in mid-1960s for evening or entertaining at home. Also called *hostess pajamas.*

lounging robe Any woman's robe, often a long one, worn informally at home for relaxation.

∞**matinee** (mah-tin-ay′) 1. A hooded PARDESSUS (see under COATS AND JACKETS) worn with morning dress in early 1850s. 2. Another name for a *tea jacket* worn in 1890s and early 20th c. 3. Lace-trimmed simple jacket to hips worn only in the boudoir from about 1915 to 1930s.

middy-top pajamas Man's two-piece pajamas styled with a slip-on top having no buttons. So named because of the resemblance to a MIDDY BLOUSE (see under BLOUSES AND TOPS).

monk's robe Full-length, flowing robe with bell sleeve, frequently made with a hooded cowl neckline and a rope belt. *Der.* Inspired by a monk's habit.

negligée (neg-glee-zheh′) Flowing informal woman's robe of delicate fabric with trimming of lace, ruffles, etc., often worn with a matching nightgown.

nightgown 1. An item of apparel, styled similar to a dress, worn by men, women, and children for sleeping. Sometimes abbreviated to *gown* or *nightie.* Also called a *sleeper.* Meaning of the word and use of the item dates from the early 19th c. ∞2. From the 16th to the 19th c., an informal coat for men cut on contemporary lines which could be worn outdoors as well as indoors. See BANYAN in alphabetical listing.

∞**night rail** (*night rayle*) 1. A nightgown, as it was once called. 2. Loose-fitting dress or robe made of plain, drab-colored fabric worn in the morning by women in Colonial America. 3. Woman's shoulder cape of lawn, silk, satin, or lace. Worn from 16th to early 18th c. as boudoir jacket or in bed.

nightshirt #1

nightshift/nightshirt 1. Sleeping garment worn by both men and women. Frequently made in "his or hers" style like a man's shirt in mini-, knee-, or calf-length, usually with rounded hem and a slash at side seams. Formerly worn by men and boys before introduction of pajamas about 1880. ∞2. Mid-1980s versions for women made in tank top, shirt, or T-shirt styles which can double as day wear.

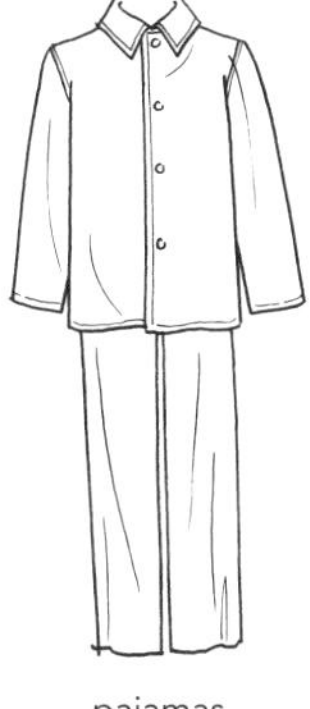
pajamas

pajamas/pyjamas One- or two-piece item of apparel originally designed for sleeping; later for lounging; and in late 1960s for entertaining, evening parties, and dining out. The word "pajamas" is often abbreviated to "pj's." Originally introduced around 1880 from India for men to wear for sleeping instead of nightgowns. Introduced for women for sleeping in mid-1920s. Popular for lounge- and beachwear in the late 1920s and 1930s. *Der.* Hindustani "pajama," which came from the Persian words *pai,* "leg," and *jaman,* "a garment."

pajama set Tailored pajamas with a matching robe styled for men or women.

party pajamas/party pants Type of pajamas, pants, or culottes with styling suitable to wear for dining and dancing. Also called *hostess pajamas* or *culotte pajamas.*

peignoir set

peignoir (pane′-war) Feminine type of robe made in a sheer or elaborate fabric only intended for the boudoir; usually made with a matching nightgown, in which case it is called a **peignoir set**. *Der.* French, *peignoir,* "to comb," as it was originally worn when combing the hair.

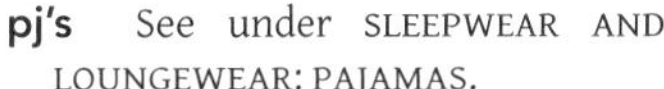

pj's See under SLEEPWEAR AND LOUNGEWEAR: PAJAMAS.

rompers One-piece pajamas styled like a jumpsuit with short legs. Usually knitted, sometimes made of terry cloth.

shave coat Man's knee-length wraparound bathrobe frequently matched to pajamas.

shortie Mini-length gown.

shortie pajamas

shortie pajamas Two-piece pajamas with legs coming to knee. Worn primarily in summer by both men and women.

ski pajamas Any two-piece pajamas styled with full legs gathered into knitted cuffs at the ankles.

sleepcoat Sleepwear top styled like a man's pajama top but longer in length.

sleep set Two-piece seductive sleepwear consisting of jacket or camisole-type top worn over brief bikinis. Top can also double for streetwear.

sleep shorts Man's pull-on shorts, sometimes with two piped pockets, worn for sleeping.

slip gown Bias-cut full-length gown made with no waistline seam, but with a slip-like top with V-neck and narrow shoulder straps. Sometimes made of satin with matching jacket.

slouch gown Thigh-length gown of knitted fabric, styled like a long sweatshirt with a band at hem.

tailored pajamas Any pajamas not excessively decorated or trimmed, usually finished with piping.

teddy One-piece sleep garment with low-cut, wrap-style front, high-cut legs, and elasticized waistline; sometimes with a short skirt. Often made of nylon satin or georgette trimmed with lace or ruffles. Can also be worn as an undergarment. See under UNDERGARMENTS: TEDDY.

toga nightgown Gown styled with one shoulder or with conventional top and one or both sides split to hips. Introduced in the late 1960s. *Der.* From draping of Roman toga.

∞**toilet/toilette** (twa-let') (*twillet*) In 18th c., loose *wrapper* worn by women while having hair arranged.

travel coat Nylon jersey robe that packs easily and does not wrinkle.

T-shirt pajamas Two-piece pajamas with a knitted T-SHIRT top (see under SHIRTS).

tunic pajamas Two-piece pajamas styled with a long overblouse top. Also see under SLEEPWEAR AND LOUNGEWEAR: COSSACK PAJAMAS.

twillet See under SLEEPWEAR AND LOUNGEWEAR: TOILET.

watteau wrapper (wa-toe') Fitted, full-length dressing gown worn by women in the 1880s and 1890s. Sometimes did not meet in front and tied together with sash at waistline. Had characteristic double or triple box pleats in back, sometimes ending in a train. Robes with this style back are revived periodically. *Der.* Named for the artist WATTEAU.

wraparound robe Any robe made in wraparound style.

∞**wrapper** 1. A woman's dressing gown worn in the boudoir and in bed in the 18th c. 2. Synonym for WRAPAROUND ROBE.

---

sleeve See under introduction to SHOULDERS AND SLEEVES.

sleeve à la folle See under SHOULDERS AND SLEEVES: IMBECILE SLEEVE.

sleeve bracelet See under JEWELRY.

sleeve button See under CLOSURES.

sleeve hand See under SHOULDERS AND SLEEVES.

sleeveless blouse See under BLOUSES AND TOPS.

sleeve string See under CLOSURES: CUFF STRING.

∞**sleeve tongs** Ornamental metal tongs used to position large sleeves inside coat sleeves in mid-1890s.

sleevings See under TRUNK HOSE.

slicked-back hair See under HAIRSTYLES.

slicker See under COATS AND JACKETS.

slide See under FOOTWEAR.

slide bracelet See under JEWELRY.

slide fastener See under CLOSURES: ZIPPER.

slingback shoe See under FOOTWEAR.

slingback thong See under FOOTWEAR: THONG SANDAL #2.

sling-duster See under COATS AND JACKETS.

sling neckline See under NECKLINES AND COLLARS: ONE-SHOULDER NECKLINE.

sling pump See under FOOTWEAR: SLINGBACK SHOE.

sling sleeve See under SHOULDERS AND SLEEVES.

slip 1. See under UNDERGARMENTS. ∞2. 17th-c. lining for semitransparent dresses. ∞3. A man's white piqué edging for a morning vest called a WHITE SLIP in the late 19th c.

slip-blouse See under UNDERGARMENTS: BLOUSE-SLIP.

slip-dress See under DRESSES.

slip gown See under SLEEPWEAR AND LOUNGEWEAR.

slip-on/slip over 1. See under PULLOVER. 2. See under GLOVES AND GLOVE CONSTRUCTION and FOOTWEAR.

slippage †1. In textiles, defects in the fabric due to shifting of yarns. Occurs because fabric is poorly constructed. 2. In sewing, shifting of yarns at seams of a sewed garment.

slipper See under FOOTWEAR.

†**slipper satin** Lustrous, stiff satin fabric or made in brocaded effect. Used for formal gowns and shoes.

slipper socks See under FOOTWEAR and HOSIERY.

slip-shoe See under FOOTWEAR.

slip stitch See under EMBROIDERIES AND SEWING STITCHES.

slit Slashed opening in front of clothing used since 14th c. to facilitate entry. When used at back of jacket, called a *vent.* See under POCKETS and SKIRTS.

slit trank See under GLOVES AND GLOVE CONSTRUCTION.

slivings See under TRUNK HOSE.

∞**slop** 1. Short jacket worn by men in 14th and early 15th c. over a DOUBLET. 2. See under FOOTWEAR. 3. Cloak or nightgown worn by men and women in first half of 16th c. 4. Laborer's SMOCK worn by men in 18th and 19th c. Also see SLOPS.

sloper Basic pattern for a garment section, without style lines or seam allowances, developed from a dress form, live model, specific measurements, or manufacturer's specifications. Used to develop original patterns and create new designs. Also called *standard pattern, foundation pattern, block pattern,* and *master pattern.*

∞**slops** 1. See under TRUNK HOSE. 2. Used until late 18th c. for sailor's trousers carried in a sea chest or "slop chest." 3. From 17th to 19th c., ready-made or old clothes and also for the bedding and supplies sold in stores known as "slop shops."

slot seam See under CLOTHING CONSTRUCTION DETAILS.

slouch See under HEADWEAR, SLEEPWEAR AND LOUNGEWEAR, and HOSIERY.

†slub yarn Yarn that has thicker areas alternating with thinner ones. When used as crosswise yarns in shantung and other fabrics, it produces an uneven appearance with elongated thickened places at intervals.

small Size used along with EXTRA SMALL, MEDIUM, LARGE, and EXTRA LARGE for men, women, and children in such categories as sweaters, knit and sport shirts, sport jackets, nightgowns and pajamas, robes, gloves, girdles, and panty girdles. Abbreviated *S.*

∞smallclothes Men's breeches used from 1770 to mid-19th c., as they were referred to politely.

small falls See under FALL #1.

small slops See under TRUNK HOSE.

smart textiles Materials and structures that can sense environmental conditions or stimuli.

smile pocket See under POCKETS: HALF-MOON POCKET.

smock 1. Long-sleeved, loose-fitting garment fastened down front or back and meant to protect clothes while wearer is working. 2. See under UNDERGARMENTS: CHEMISE.

smock #1

smock blouse See under DRESSES.

smock dress See under DRESSES.

∞smock-frock 1. In the 18th and 19th c., a man's knee-length, loose-fitting homespun gown worn by farmers. Sometimes made with a sailor collar, or yoke. Usually smocked in various patterns indicating the place of residence of the worker. Also called *smock.* 2. In 1880s, a women's garment cut like a farmer's smock.

smocking See under EMBROIDERIES AND SEWING STITCHES.

smock top See under BLOUSES AND TOPS.

smoking jacket See under COATS AND JACKETS and SMOKING SUIT.

smoking suit Woman's lounging suit with jacket styled similar to man's smoking jacket, usually combined with matching velvet pants. Introduced in late 1960s, and attributed to Saint Laurent, Paris couturier. Also called *le smoking.*

smoky quartz See under GEMS, GEM CUTS, AND SETTINGS.

snail button See under CLOSURES.

snake bracelet See under JEWELRY.

snakes See under HAIRSTYLES: LOVE LOCKS.

snakeskin See under LEATHERS.

snap See under CLOSURES and UNDERGARMENTS: SNAP PANTS.

snap-brim hat See under HEADWEAR.

snap pants See under UNDERGARMENTS.

sneaker See under FOOTWEAR.

sneakerization The process of transforming an inexpensive commodity product or a product that has lost its cachet into a cutting-edge specialty product through the use of technology or an update of the product's aesthetics. Examples include Nike athletic shoes or the Burberry plaid.

sneaker sock See under HOSIERY.

snip slip See under UNDERGARMENTS.

snood See under HEADWEAR.

snorkel coat/jacket See under COATS AND JACKETS.

snowboarding suit See under ACTIVEWEAR.

Snow, Carmel White (1888–1961) Fashion editor who worked for *Vogue* magazine from 1921 in fashion department. Made editor of American *Vogue* from 1929 to 1932. In 1932 she became fashion editor of *Harper's Bazaar*—later becoming editor until her retirement in 1957. A personality of wit, intelligence, and strong views, she was tiny and well dressed in Parisian clothes. She had an instinct for fashion today and what would come tomorrow. Awards include 1941, Neiman Marcus Award; 1949, French Legion of Honor; 1954, Italian Star of Solidarity. Author with Mary Louise Aswell of *The World of Carmel Snow.*

snow leopard See under FURS.

snowmobile boot See under FOOTWEAR.

snowmobile gloves/mitts See under GLOVES AND GLOVE CONSTRUCTION.

snowmobile suit See under ACTIVEWEAR.

snowsuit See under ACTIVEWEAR.

snuggies See under UNDERGARMENTS.

soccus (pl. *socci*) 1. See under FOOTWEAR. 2. See under CAPES, CLOAKS, AND SHAWLS.

socklet See under HOSIERY.

sock lining See under FOOTWEAR.

socks See under HOSIERY.

∞sock suspenders (British usage) Men's garters (see under GARTER #2), introduced in 1895, to hold up calf-length socks. Consisted of a band of elastic with attached garter clip.

socq See under CAPES, CLOAKS, AND SHAWLS: SOCCUS.

soft dressing Loosely-fitted clothing made from soft fabrics that drape well.

soft goods Fashion and textile merchandise (e.g., dresses, lingerie, coats, household textiles), as contrasted with **hard goods** (e.g., home appliances, hardware, or furniture).

solaret See under ARMOR: SOLLERET.

solar powered apparel See under ELECTRONIC TEXTILES.

sole See under FOOTWEAR.

solea See under FOOTWEAR.

sole leather See under LEATHERS.

solers See under FOOTWEAR.

solitaire 1. See under JEWELRY. 2. See under TIES. 3. See under SCARVES.

solleret See under ARMOR.

sombrero See under HEADWEAR.

sombrero córdobes See under HEADWEAR: GAUCHO HAT.

sontag See under CAPES, CLOAKS, AND SHAWLS.

Sorel, Agnès (1422–1450) Mistress of Charles VII of France (who rules from 1444 to 1459), called "La Dame de Beauté" (Lady of Beauty), wore jewel-studded robes, was the first commoner to wear diamonds, and made the king a waistcoat embroidered with pearls and precious stones. Acted as a model for the financier and merchant Jacques Coeur, who brought linen, silken gowns, sables, and pearls from the Orient. Painted by French artist of the time Fouquet. Many 19th-c. fashions were named after her. Examples: AGNÈS SOREL COIFFURE (see under HAIRSTYLES), AGNÈS SOREL CORSAGE, and AGNÈS SOREL DRESS (see under DRESSES).

sorority pin See under JEWELRY.

∞**sorquenie/soucanie** (sor-ken-ee') Woman's TUNIC worn from 13th to 19th c., fitted tightly over bust.

sortie de bal See under CAPES, CLOAKS, AND SHAWLS.

soucanie See under SORQUENIE.

soul cap See HEADWEAR: NEWSBOY CAP.

soul patch See under BEARD.

soulette See under FOOTWEAR.

source The vendor or supplier that sells products necessary for the production and distribution of products in the textile, apparel, or retail industries.

sourcing The process of determining how, where, and when the materials required for textile and apparel products will be purchased.

soutache (soo-tash) See under BRAIDS.

soutane See under CLERICAL DRESS: CASSOCK #1.

Southern Colonel tie See TIES: STRING TIE.

souvenir scarf See under SCARVES.

sou'wester/southwester See under HEADWEAR.

sovereign purse See under HANDBAGS AND RELATED ACCESSORIES.

space blanket See under CAPES, CLOAKS, AND SHAWLS.

space clothes Since the entrance of the United States into the space program in the 1960s, the development of clothing and accessories for astronauts has been essential. New fabrics have been designed that withstand extremes of heat and cold. Velcro® was introduced for use on soles of booties and floor of space cabin to keep astronauts feet on the floor when in weightless condition. French and U.S. designers were inspired by space clothes. For examples see under HEADWEAR: COURRÈGES HELMET; COSMONAUTS; and LUNAR.

†**space-dyed yarn** Yarns colored or dyed various colors at intervals. When woven into a fabric, they produce a random design.

space helmet See under HEADWEAR.

Space® shoe See under FOOTWEAR.

spaghetti sash See under BELTS.

spaghetti strap Very narrow strap with cord inserted to produce a round effect, similar to a strand of spaghetti.

∞**spaier** Vertical slash in garment, similar to a slit, used to reach pocket on inner garment in Medieval time.

spair See under FALL #1.

†**spandex** Generic fiber name for manufactured fibers, composed largely of segmented polyurethane, which are stretchable, lightweight, and resistant to body acid. Used for girdles, foundations, and bras, for bathing suits, and to make stretchable fabrics. Spandex is not used alone, but in combination with a wide variety of other fibers.

spangle Synonym for SEQUIN or PAILLETTE.

spaniel's-ear collar See under NECKLINES AND COLLARS: DOG'S-EAR COLLAR.

Spanish See under LACES and CAPES, CLOAKS, AND SHAWLS.

spanish blackwork See under EMBROIDERIES AND SEWING STITCHES: BLACKWORK.

spanish blonde lace See under LACES.

∞**spanish breeches** Narrow, high-waisted, below-the-knee breeches worn by men from 1630s to 1645 and from 1663 to 1670. Loose at hems, trimmed with rosettes, buttons, and ladder-like trim. Hooked to doublet lining and similar to SMALL SLOPS (see under TRUNK HOSE) but longer. Also called *Spanish hose.*

spanish cloak See under CAPES, CLOAKS, AND SHAWLS: ITALIAN CLOAK.

Spanish comb See under HAIR ACCESSORIES.

spanish embroidery See under EMBROIDERIES AND SEWING STITCHES.

spanish farthingale See under FARTHINGALE.

∞**Spanish flounce** Deep, gathered ruffle joined to hem of short skirt worn in late 19th and early 20th c.

spanish heel See under FOOTWEAR.

Spanish hose See under SPANISH BREECHES.

spanish jacket See under COATS AND JACKETS.

Spanish kettledrums See under TRUNK HOSE.

spanish lace See under LACES.

spanish shawl See under CAPES, CLOAKS, AND SHAWLS.

spanish sleeve See under SHOULDERS AND SLEEVES.

spats See under FOOTWEAR.

spatterdashes See under FOOTWEAR.

spec page/spec sheets A document used to describe in great detail what an apparel product looks like, how it is made, ad what it should be made of. Also contains sketches, notes on design, colors, materials, etc., and any references needed for design components.

spec/specification In fashion illustration, a sketch of clothing, without a human figure, that comes in various garment measurements.

special order An order for an item for a specific customer.

specialty goods BRAND-name merchandise.

specialty store Retail establishment that sells a specific type of merchandise (e.g., children's clothes, women's apparel).

specification buying Development and purchase by a retailer of private label merchandise by working directly with the sewing contractor rather than by going through an apparel manufacturer.

specification libraries Collection of a firm's previously developed style, pattern, and measurement specifications that can be recalled and reused within specification packages for new styles.

specification package Series of forms that define a garment, including a design sheet with a flat of the garment, a measurement sheet, a piece reference sheet, an assembly sheet, and a cost sheet. Also called *spec package.* Also see under TECH PACK.

spectacles/specs See under introduction to EYEWEAR.

spectator pump See under FOOTWEAR.

speed lacing See under CLOSURES.

spencer See under COATS AND JACKETS.

spencer cloak See under CAPES, CLOAKS, AND SHAWLS.

spencerette See under COATS AND JACKETS.

∞**spencer waist** Woman's fitted blouse with a band at the waistline, worn in 1860s and 1890s.

∞**spere/speyer** PLACKET, in the late 16th and 17th c. (see under CLOTHING CONSTRUCTION DETAILS).

Sperry Topsiders® See under FOOTWEAR.

spider work See under LACES.

spiffs Incentives to motivate salespersons to sell particular items. Spiffs are provided by vendors and are sometimes called *push money.*

spiked shoe See under FOOTWEAR.

spike heel See under FOOTWEAR.

spike-tail Slang for man's SWALLOW-TAILED COAT (see under COATS AND JACKETS).

spiky hairstyle See under HAIRSTYLES.

spinel See under GEMS, GEM CUTS, AND SETTINGS.

†**spinning** 1. Process of twisting fibers together to form a yarn. 2. The formation of manufactured fibers by extruding the liquid fiber material through a spinneret, a metal disk with holes, into a medium (air or liquid) that causes the fiber to solidify.

spitalfield tie See under TIES.

spit-boot See under FOOTWEAR.

spit curls See under HAIRSTYLES.

SPF See under SUN PROTECTION FACTOR.

splinter-hat See under HEADWEAR: SPLYTER-HAT.

split See under LEATHERS.

split buckskin See under LEATHERS: BUCKSKIN.

split falls See under FALL #1.

split mandarin collar See under NECKLINES AND COLLARS.

split skirt See under SKIRTS.

splyter-hat See under HEADWEAR.

∞**spoon back** Circular folds of drapery formed at back by the overskirt of a walking dress, worn in the 1880s.

spoon bonnet See under HEADWEAR.

spoon ring See under JEWELRY.

sporran See under HANDBAGS AND RELATED ACCESSORIES.

sport jacket See under COATS AND JACKETS.

sports bra/Sport Bra® See under UNDERGARMENTS.

sport set Two or more items of sportswear made to match or contrast and sold as a set (e.g., bathing suit with cover-up, top with shorts or skirt, twin sweaters and skirt, child's bloomers with pinafore).

sport shirt See under SHIRTS.

sports sandals See under FOOTWEAR.

sport suit Clothing designed to be worn for specific sports, e.g., a suit used for horseback riding, exercising, scuba diving. Using specialized clothing when participating in active sports began with the introduction of hunting clothing at the end of the 18th c. Since then, special clothing has developed for most sports. See under ACTIVEWEAR for specific styles used in various sports.

sportswear 1. Originally designated clothing worn for tennis, golf, bicycling, bathing, ice-skating, yachting, and hunting in 1890s. See SPORT SUITS. 2. By the 1920s and 1930s used for casual wear for leisure time and when participating in spectator sports (e.g., sweaters, skirts, blouses, pants, and shorts). 3. In the post–World War II period, sportswear has become synonymous with casual wear and is worn for day or evening and even for work in some businesses. Clothing worn for active sports is designated as ACTIVEWEAR. This has occurred primarily in the U.S. due to the adoption of less formal lifestyles by Americans. It has been stated that sportswear is the primary American contribution to the history of costume.

spotted cat See under FURS.

spread collar See under NECKLINES AND COLLARS.

spreading Unwinding large fabric rolls onto cutting tables and stacking the fabric in layers prior to cutting garment pieces.

spreading machines Equipment designed for SPREADING fabric smoothly prior to cutting.

spring-bottom trousers See under PANTS.

spring bracelet See under JEWELRY.

spring heel See under FOOTWEAR.

springy pelts See under FURS: BUCKY PELTS.

square See under NECKLINES AND COLLARS and FOOTWEAR: SQUARE TOES.

square-bottom channel frame See under HANDBAGS AND RELATED ACCESSORIES: FRAME.

square cut See under GEMS, GEM CUTS, and SETTINGS: EMERALD CUT.

square-dance skirt See under SKIRTS.

square dancing dress See under DRESSES.

square hoops See under UNDERGARMENTS: PANNIERS.

square neckline See under NECKLINES AND COLLARS.

square setting See under GEMS, GEM CUTS, AND SETTINGS.

squash blossom necklace See under JEWELRY.

squaw *adj.* Describes clothing influenced by garments worn by North American Indian women. *Der.* The word "squaw" is what European settlers called North American Indian women, but the word was not used by North American Indians. See under BLOUSES AND TOPS: SQUAW BLOUSE, FOOTWEAR: SQUAW BOOT, HANDBAGS AND RELATED ACCESSORIES: SQUAW BAG and SKIRTS: SQUAW SKIRT.

squaw dress See under DRESSES.

squirrel See under FURS.

stacked heel See under FOOTWEAR.

stadium See under FOOTWEAR and COATS AND JACKETS.

staking See under LEATHERS.

stand See under NECKLINES AND COLLARS.

Standard Industrial Classification (SIC) codes U.S. Office of Management and Budget codes used to identify U.S. business establishments according to their general types of business activity. Both manufacturers of products such as apparel and various types of retailers are included.

standard pattern See under SLOPER.

standards A shortened term for STANDARD SPECIFICATIONS.

standard specifications Defines levels of performance that products must meet in order to be considered acceptable for use.

stand-away collar See under NECKLINES AND COLLARS.

stand-fall collar See under NECKLINES AND COLLARS: ROLLED COLLAR #2.

standing whisk See under NECKLINES AND COLLARS: WHISK #2.

St. Andrew's cross See under CROSS.

stand-up collar See under NECKLINES AND COLLARS.

†staple fibers Natural or manufactured fibers that are short and must be spun in order to form a yarn. Compare with FILAMENT FIBERS.

staples See under BASICS.

staple yarn See under YARNS.

stapling See under FURS.

starcher See under TIES.

starching See under SIZING.

star ruby/star sapphire See under GEMS, GEM CUTS, AND SETTINGS.

startup See under FOOTWEAR.

Statue of Liberty 1. See under HEADWEAR: STATUE OF LIBERTY VISOR. 2. See under JEWELRY. 3. See under HAIRSTYLES.

staurolite See under GEMS, GEM CUTS, AND SETTINGS: FAIRY STONE.

stay See under CLOTHING CONSTRUCTION DETAILS.

∞**stay hook** Small ornamental hook attached to bodice in 18th c. to hold a watch. Also called *breast hook* or *crochet* (see under CROCHET #2).

stays See under UNDERGARMENTS.

stay-up hose See under HOSIERY.

steeple headdress See under HEADWEAR: HENNIN.

steerhide See under LEATHERS.

steinkirk See under TIES.

stem stitch See under EMBROIDERIES AND SEWING STITCHES.

stenciled print See under PRINTS, STRIPES, AND CHECKS.

stenciling Applying dye to fur or fabric by painting through a cut-out stencil (e.g., used to make pile fabric look like leopard). In late 1960s and early 1970s applied to sheared mink and all kinds of fur and fur fabrics to simulate giraffe, tiger, leopard, jaguar, and zebra. Practice continued after this time.

step cut See under GEMS, GEM CUTS, AND SETTINGS.

stephane See under HEADWEAR.

step-in dress See under DRESSES.

step-ins See under UNDERGARMENTS.

step-in shoe See under FOOTWEAR: SLIP-ON SHOES.

sterling silver See under JEWELRY.

stertop See under FOOTWEAR: STARTUP.

Stetson™ See under HEADWEAR.

Stewart dress and hunting tartan See under PLAIDS AND TARTANS.

st. gall lace See under LACES.

St. George cross See under JEWELRY: CRUSADER'S CROSS.

stickpin See under JEWELRY.

stick-up collar See under NECKLINES AND COLLARS: WING COLLAR.

stiletto (stil-let'-o) ∞1. Narrow, pointed stick used in ancient Greece as a hairpin. 2. Pointed instrument similar to a large needle used to punch holes in embroidery. 3. See under FOOTWEAR.

stirrup hose See under HOSIERY.

stirrup pants See under PANTS.

stirrup tights See under ACTIVEWEAR: AEROBIC ENSEMBLE.

stitch One complete motion of a threaded needle or other implement (e.g., a knitting needle or crochet hook), which, when used in a series, results in such decorative or utilitarian work as sewing, embroidering, knitting, crocheting, or tatting. May be made by hand or machine with thread, yarn, embroidery floss, string, straw fiber, or other material. For names of specific types of stitches, see under EMBROIDERIES AND SEWING STITCHES category.

stitch-bonded fabric Fabrics constructed by binding together yarns or fabric webs with stitches like those made in knitting. The earliest trademark name for this process is Malimo®.

stitch class Nomenclature that divides commercial stitches into six classes or groups based on their complexity, configuration, and the type of machine that is required to form the stitching.

stitchdown shoe construction See under FOOTWEAR.

stitches See under EMBROIDERIES AND SEWING STITCHES.

stock 1. See under SCARVES and TIES. 2. From about 1590, the word *stock* was occasionally used as a synonym for stocking (see under HOSIERY). 3. Leather, as it is called in shoe manufacturing. 4. Synonym for MERCHANDISE.

stock collar/neckline See under NECKLINES AND COLLARS: ASCOT.

stocking See under HOSIERY.

stocking bodice See under BLOUSES AND TOPS.

stocking boot See under FOOTWEAR.

stocking cap See under HEADWEAR.

stocking purse See under HANDBAGS AND RELATED ACCESSORIES: MISER'S PURSE.

stocking shoe See under FOOTWEAR.

stock keeping unit (SKU) Unit designation for inventory and record-keeping purposes that is based on style, color, size, and any other information that needs to be tracked. Only those items identical in style, color, etc., would belong to a particular SKU.

stock on hand The stock currently available in a retail store.

∞**stocks** Garment originally styled like tights. Worn on the legs from 1400 to 1610, stocks evolved into two separate pieces. The upper part was known as trunk hose or *overstocks, haut de chausses,* or *upper stocks;* lower part was often called *bas de chausses, lower stocks, nether stocks, hose,* and later STOCKINGS (see under HOSIERY). Also see under CHAUSSE and CHAUSSEMBLES.

stock-tie blouse/shirt 1. See under BLOUSES AND TOPS. 2. See under SHIRTS.

∞**stola** (stow'-la) Ancient Roman garment denoting a married, free woman. It was apparently worn as an outer layer over an undertunic and probably resembled the Doric *chiton* of ancient Greeks, being sleeveless and either pinned at the shoulder or suspended from straps. See under INSTITA. Shown at CAPES, CLOAKS, AND SHAWLS: PALLA.

stole 1. See under SCARVES. 2. See under CAPES, CLOAKS, AND SHAWLS: FUR STOLE. 3. See under CLERICAL DRESS.

∞**stomacher** 1. An ornamental chest piece worn by men under a V- or U-shaped doublet from late 15th to early

16th c. **2.** In women's dress, a heavily embroidered or jeweled V-shaped panel over chest, extending down to point over stomach, held in place by busks. Either a part of the dress or a separate plastron (see PLASTRON #2) worn with low-cut décolletage from late 15th c. to 1770s. **3.** Same type of inserted front panel made of shirred fabric used on dresses in first half of 19th c. Also see under COTTAGE FRONT.

stone marten See under FURS.

†stonewashed *adj.* Descriptive of fabrics or garments that have been treated to produce certain color and/or texture effects by tumbling them with pumice stones or other abrasives that may have been soaked in bleaching chemicals. Where the stones come into contact with the fabric, abrasion occurs and color is removed. Synonyms include *acid washing, distressing, frosting, ice washing, snow washing, super washing,* and *white washing.*

store brand Goods that carry the name of the retailer who not only sells but also produces and names them. See under PRIVATE LABEL.

store-owned buying office See under PRIVATE BUYING OFFICE.

storm See under FOOTWEAR: STORM BOOTS and COATS AND JACKET: STORM COAT.

storm flap See under CLOSURES.

storm rubbers See under FOOTWEAR.

stormsuit See under ACTIVEWEAR.

stovepipe hat See under HEADWEAR.

stovepipe pants See under PANTS.

straight-cut pants See under PANTS.

straight pin Functional device consisting of a sharp, pointed shaft with flattened head used to pin pattern to fabric when cutting out a pattern, to pin cut out pieces together before sewing, or to serve as temporary fastening. Used since the 14th c., pins were scarce and sold only on January 1 and 2. Originally heads were hammered on top, after 1830 made in one piece. Also see under DRESSMAKER PIN.

straights See under FOOTWEAR.

straight skirt See under SKIRTS.

strapless See under UNDERGARMENTS, NECKLINES AND COLLARS, BLOUSES AND TOPS.

strapless dress See under DRESSES.

strapless slip See under UNDERGARMENTS.

strapped trousers See under PANTS.

strap seam See under CLOTHING CONSTRUCTION DETAILS.

strass See under JEWELRY: PASTE.

straw A vegetable substance or a synthetic imitation used for hats, bags, shoes, and trim. Natural straw comes from dried stems of grains such as barley, oats, rye, and wheat, from stems and stalks of other plants, from leaves, and from bark. Straws may be woven into bodies of hats or made into narrow "straw braid," which is stitched together in a circular manner to make a hat. Also used for handbags, particularly of the basket type. Sometimes used for shoes.

streaking A fad popular during the winter of 1973–74 for running across a college campus or other public place nude except for shoes and possibly a hat. "Classic" college streaker's costume consisted of knit ski mask and tennis shoes.

street style Fashions that originate with or are inspired by clothing worn by individuals, usually young, rather than with the fashion industry, although the contemporary fashion industry draws inspiration from street style.

†stretch **1.** Classification of fabrics of various types: (a) Knitted fabrics that stretch because of the elasticity of the knit. (b) Fabrics made with TEXTURED YARNS that have been crimped or curled. Such yarns give more resiliency and elasticity to fabrics and clothing (e.g., knit shirts, sweaters, and dresses). (c) Fabrics given special finishes that provide increased resiliency and elasticity. (d) Fabrics woven with yarns made from ELASTOMERS. **2.** *adj.* Descriptive of apparel that exhibits the ability to extend in length or width from its original size. See under BLOUSES AND TOPS: STRETCH TOP; FOOTWEAR: TOTES; HOSIERY: STRETCH HOSE and STRETCH SOCK; LACES: STRETCH LACE; PANTS: STRETCH PANTS; UNDERGARMENTS: STRETCH BRA and GARTER BRIEF; and WIGS AND HAIRPIECES: STRETCH WIG.

†stretch knit fabrics Fabrics knitted with textured or stretch yarns. Also see under STRETCH.

†stretch woven Woven fabric that has at least 20 percent stretch in either the lengthwise or crosswise direction or both.

strike off A full repeat of a print or yarn-dyed fabric in the specified colors and on the specified fabric or a computer-aided design (CAD) copy with a color key of all colors that appear within the print submitted for approval before production.

strike through Condition when adhesives on interfacings show through to the surface of the garment during pressing.

string bikini **1.** See under UNDERGARMENTS. **2.** See under SWIMWEAR: BIKINI.

string tie See under TIES.

stripes See under introduction to PRINTS, STRIPES, AND CHECKS.

stroller 1. See under COATS AND JACKETS. 2. See under HEADWEAR.

∞**strophium** (strof′-ee-uhm) 1. A band of fabric worn by women in Ancient Rome to support their breasts. 2. See under HEADWEAR: CHAPLET. *Der.* Greek *strophos,* "a swaddling band."

structural design 1. Design style used by dress designers for lines of dress that are concerned with the functional design of the dress (e.g., a zipper down the back of the dress, pleats to provide fullness) as contrasted with decorative elements of the design. †2. In textiles, a fabric, motif, or pattern achieved by weaving rather than surface treatment (e.g., fabric woven on a JACQUARD loom).

St. Tropez skirt See under SKIRTS.

stud See under CLOSURES.

student bycocket See under HEADWEAR: BYCOCKET.

studs See under JEWELRY.

stump work See under EMBROIDERIES AND SEWING STITCHES.

style 1. *n.* In fashion, an individual and distinctive type of dress, coat, blouse, or other item of apparel or accessory. 2. *v.* **style, styling** Usually used with "to" (e.g., "to style a line"). Used by a manufacturer when making or selecting the specific types of apparel for seasonal collections. 3. *n.* Flair that is specific and individual; "to have style," meaning to have a certain unique fashion sense.

style line See under NECKLINES AND COLLARS.

style number A coded number (usually four digits) assigned by the apparel manufacturer to a specific garment style that indicates the season/year for the style and other style information. In this way the manufacturer can keep track of the style throughout development, marketing, and production.

style sheet Document in which a merchandiser describes the construction and fabric of garments for import so that duty rates and quota classifications can be established by the U.S. Customs offices.

style show See under FASHION SHOW.

style tribe Coined by sociologist Ted Polhemus to describe groups of individuals, usually young, who identify with a particular subcultural group and adopt fashions that proclaim their membership in that group (e.g. HIPPIE, MOD, PUNK, GOTH). These fashions may influence current fashions. Also see BOTTOM-UP THEORY OF FASHION CHANGE.

stylists Refers to designers who tend to adapt the ideas of others rather than creating totally original garments.

stylized print See under PRINTS, STRIPES, AND CHECKS.

styrtop See under FOOTWEAR: STARTUP.

subclassification (subclass) Category that identifies a group of merchandise within a CLASSIFICATION (e.g., eveningwear) that is closely related in styling, such as full-length or short.

subcultural styles Clothing styles originated, developed, or modified by members of groups that reject the values and mores of the dominant society. Such groups have existed in America since the founding of the European colonies, often based on religious ideals. In the post–World War II period, numerous youthful subcultures have developed that have adopted distinctive styles of dress. Some of these styles may influence high-fashion designers. For examples see TEDDY BOYS, MOD, PUNK, HIP-HOP, GOTH, RAVE.

substrate An underlying material on which inks, dyes, or paints are applied.

suburban coat See under COATS AND JACKETS: CAR COAT.

suede See under LEATHERS.

†**suede cloth** Knitted or woven fabric of wool, cotton, or rayon having a nap on one or both sides. Used for suits, coats, vests, pants, and sportswear in imitation of genuine *suede.*

sugarloaf hat See under HEADWEAR: COPOTAIN.

suit Two, three, or more items of apparel, either of matching or contrasting fabric, designed to be worn together. For women, generally consists of a jacket and skirt or pants. For men, usually consists of trousers and jacket made in single- or double-breasted style, sometimes including a vest. When the suit consists of a jacket, vest, and trousers for men or a jacket, skirt, and trousers for women, it is called a **three-piece suit.** DOUBLET and HOSE, in 16th and 17th c. Current meaning of the word suit dates from late 19th c. For some specific styles, see under DITTO SUIT, ETON SUIT, LITTLE LORD FAUNTLEROY SUIT, SAILOR SUIT, TAILOR-MADE, and ZOOT SUIT.

suitcase bag See under HANDBAGS AND RELATED ACCESSORIES.

suit dress See under DRESSES.

†**suiting** As defined broadly, any fabric used for men's and women's suits. Includes worsteds and woolens, and manufactured fibers and blends made in a variety of weaves and patterns that have no specific name but tailor well.

∞**suit of knots** From 17th to mid-18th c., a set of matching bows, used to trim a dress or to wear in the hair.

∞**suit of ruffs** Matching neck and wrist ruffs, worn by men and women from 1560 to 1640.

suit sleeve See under SHOULDERS AND SLEEVES.

suit slip See under UNDERGARMENTS.

suit vest See under VESTS.

sultana scarf See under SCARVES.

sultana sleeve See under SHOULDERS AND SLEEVES.

∞**sultane** (sul-tane′) **1.** Dress worn in the late 17th c. and again in the 1730s and 1740s, trimmed with buttons and loops. Worn for traveling. In 18th c., it was a dress with short ROBINGS, a stomacher (see under STOMACHER #2), and a plain back. **2.** PRINCESS-STYLE daytime dress of late 1870s with scarf elaborately draped to one side.

sultane jacket See under COATS AND JACKETS.

sumptuary laws (sump′-too-air-ee) Laws restricting the ownership and use of luxury goods to certain social and/or economic classes. Such laws were frequently applied to clothing and its ornamentation, but were rarely obeyed or much enforced.

sun bonnet See under HEADWEAR.

sunburst-pleated skirt See under SKIRTS: ACCORDION-PLEATED SKIRT.

sunburst pleats See under CLOTHING CONSTRUCTION DETAILS: ACCORDION PLEAT.

sunburst tucks See under CLOTHING CONSTRUCTION DETAILS.

Sunday clothes/Sunday best In the 19th and early 20th c., clothing worn especially for church and special occasions, as opposed to WORK CLOTHES.

sundress See under DRESSES.

sunglasses See under EYEWEAR.

†**Sun Protection Factor (SPF)** A number that indicates the ability of a sunscreen or fabric to protect the skin from the harmful effects of the sun. The higher the SPF number, the greater the ability to block ultraviolet (UV) radiation. An SPF of 15 is recommended as a minimum to block out most UV radiation.

sunray skirt See under SKIRTS: ACCORDION-PLEATED SKIRT.

sunshade See under introduction to UMBRELLAS AND PARASOLS: PARASOL.

sunsuit See under ACTIVEWEAR.

supermodel Fashion models who have gained individual recognition by the press and public. The publicity they gain and images of them on, as well as off, the RUNWAY may serve to influence fashion trends.

∞**super tunic** Overgarment made with or without sleeves. From 9th to end of 14th c., worn by men and women. In the 13th and 14th c., more likely to be called a SURCOTE.

supportasse See under NECKLINES AND COLLARS: RUFF.

support legwear See under HOSIERY.

†**surah** Lightweight, soft, silky fabric made in a twill weave of silk or manufactured yarns. May be woven in yarn-dyed plaids, printed, or dyed in solid colors. Used for dresses, scarves, neckties, and blouses.

surcingle belt See under BELTS.

∞**surcote/surcoat** (ser′-koht) Outermost tunic, so called in the 13th and 14th c., worn by men and women over an undertunic, or COTE. There were both knee-length and long versions for men and long versions for women. Some had wide or bell-shaped sleeves, while others were sleeveless and known as **sideless surcotes.** Shown at COTE. Synonyms: *cyclas, super tunic.*

surface interest Texture or appearance of the face or outer side of a fabric that is noteworthy in some way.

surfers See under PANTS.

surfer hair See under HAIRSTYLES.

surfing suit See under ACTIVEWEAR: WETSUIT.

surf trunks See under SWIMWEAR.

surgical mask See under MASKS.

surgical stocking See under HOSIERY: ANTI-EMBOLISM STOCKING.

surpied See under FOOTWEAR: SOULETTE.

surplice **1.** See under CLERICAL DRESS. **2.** See under NECKLINES AND COLLARS. **3.** See under CLOSURES: WRAP CLOSING.

∞**surplice bodice/surplis front** (sir′-pliss) A day bodice, worn in 1881; the top of the dress wraps rather than buttons up to close. May be plain or pleated at shoulders and waistband.

Surrealism (sur-re-al-iz′-ihm) Movement in art and literature starting in the 1930s that was greatly influenced by psychoanalysis. Art has a "dreamlike" quality, which suggests the expression of the subconscious and reflects the imagination uncontrolled by reason. Salvadore Dali is one of the main exponents of this style. Designers such as Elsa Schiaparelli were much influenced by the Surrealists.

surtout See under COATS AND JACKETS.

suspenders **1.** Detachable straps of elasticized fabric passed over shoulders and clipped or buttoned to trousers or skirt front and back. Called *braces* by the British. **2.** (British Usage) Woman's garters for stocking attached to corset called a *suspender garter.* **3.** Shoulder straps on bodice or bib top. Also used to describe apparel with shoulder straps. See under JUMPERS: SUSPENDER JUMPER; PANTS: SUSPENDER PANTS; SHORTS: SUSPENDER SHORTS; and SKIRT: SUSPENDER SKIRT.

suspender tights See under HOSIERY.

suspender trimming See under BRETELLES #1.

sustainable design Design that takes into account the effects of textile and apparel production on the environment and seeks to eliminate negative impacts.

∞**swaddling clothes/swadding bands** Narrow strips of fabric wrapped around infants as their earliest clothing. Thought to make their bones straight and strong, the practice existed since ancient times and ended only in the early 19th century. Also called *safeguard, sweathbands,* and *swathing band.*

swaddling clothes

swag Draped folds of fabric used on women's gowns in latter part of 18th c. Any similar ornamentation.

swagger 1. See under COATS AND JACKETS. 2. See under HEADWEAR.

swagger pouch See under HANDBAGS AND RELATED ACCESSORIES.

swallow-tailed 1. See under NECKLINES AND COLLARS. 2. See under COATS AND JACKETS.

swanbill corset See under UNDERGARMENTS.

swan's down See under FEATHERS.

†**swatch** In textiles and sewing, a small sample of fabric.

Swatch See under WATCHES.

swathing band See under SWADDLING CLOTHES.

sweatband See under HEADWEAR.

sweatclothes See under ACTIVEWEAR.

sweater blouse See under BLOUSES AND TOPS.

sweater clasp Two decorative clasps connected with a short chain used to hold a sweater together at the neckline.

sweater coat See under COATS AND JACKETS.

sweater dress See under DRESSES.

sweater-for-two See under SWEATERS.

sweater girl In 1940s slang, a name that referred to shapely film stars who wore tight pullover sweaters that emphasized the bosom.

sweater-knit clothing Apparel knitted and styled in the same manner as a sweater. See under BLOUSES AND TOPS: SWEATER BLOUSE; COATS AND JACKETS: SWEATER COAT; and VESTS: SWEATER VEST.

SWEATERS

sweater Clothing for the upper part of the body worn either as an outer garment or under a coat or jacket. Hand- or machine-made by knitting or crocheting in a wide variety of patterns. The sweater first appeared as the jersey, in mid-19th c. In early 1890s, turtleneck jerseys were introduced. Later a collar was added and the jersey was worn for golf and sports. In the 1920s, accepted by students and later widely adopted for general wear. At first only made of wool, washability was improved when new yarns (e.g., acrylic and nylon) came onto the market in the 1950s and 1960s.

Aran Isle sweater Pullover with round or V-neck knit in traditional Irish designs including raised cable knit and interlaced vertical diamond-shaped patterns. *Der.* Named for island off coast of Ireland where sweaters of this type were originally made. See SWEATERS: FISHERMAN'S SWEATER.

argyle sweater (ar'-gyle) Distinctively patterned sweater made in several colors to produce diamond-shaped designs, either knit by hand or machine, often matched to socks. Popular in 1920s and 1930s, and revived in late 1960s. See under PLAIDS AND TARTANS. *Der.* Tartan of Duke of Argyle and Clan Campbell of Argyll, a county in west Scotland. Also spelled *argyll, argyl.*

argyle sweater

award sweater See under SWEATERS: LETTER SWEATER.

aztec sweater Long, bulky, coat sweater with shawl collar closed with matching sash. Usually made in white with predominantly black jacquard-knit Aztec Indian motifs running in wide bands across chest, below waist, and around upper arm and wrist.

beaded sweater Woman's sweater with decorative beading, sometimes of seed pearls, often worn for evening in 1940s and 1950s, and worn at intervals since.

big easy sweater Extra-large, long sweater. One style is made in lacy bouclé knit with extended shoulder making a short sleeve in loose-fitting style with rib-knitted hem.

blazer sweater Single or double-breasted jacket-type sweater with collar that is styled similarly to BLAZER JACKET (see under COATS AND JACKETS).

bolero sweater (bo-lehr'-oh) Short sweater only extending to the waist or above, styled with rounded ends in front and no fasteners. *Der.* A Spanish dance costume worn for dancing the bolero, a lively Spanish dance; also the music for this dance.

blazer sweater

cable sweater Knit sweater in which the effect of a heavy cord (a cable) is produced by crossing groups of knitting stitches over each other. Shown at SWEATERS: PULLOVER and FISHERMAN'S SWEATER.

cardigan sweater Coat-style sweater known by various names. **Classic cardigan** is made with CREW NECK (see under NECKLINES AND COLLARS), ribbed cuffs and hem, closed with pearl buttons. **Belted cardigan** is usually made in longer length, sometimes in NORFOLK style (see under COATS AND JACKETS). **Shawl collar cardigan**, also called *tuxedo sweater*, is made with a SHAWL COLLAR (see under NECKLINES AND COLLARS) and no buttons. Another type of cardigan is the COAT SWEATER (see under SWEATERS). *Der.* Named after Seventh Earl of Cardigan, who needed an extra layer of warmth under his uniform during the Crimean War in 1854.

cardigan sweater

cashmere sweater Sweater in any style knitted of yarn spun from the hair of the CASHMERE goat. Extremely soft and luxurious, usually imported from England or Scotland. See under CASHMERE.

coat sweater Cardigan-style sweater, usually made in a longer style with or without a ribbed waistband. Frequently styled with a long V-neck and buttons. From 1930s to 1960s, usually restricted in usage to men or older people. In 1980s worn by adults and children.

Cowichan sweater (koo'-ih-chan) Sweater using North American Indian pattern—black on white or gray background—made by Cowichan Indians of Vancouver Island. Used in the late 1940s and early 1950s and revived in early 1970s. Also called a *Siwash sweater.*

cowl-neck sweater Pullover sweater with extra-large, rolled collar that forms a cowl drapery, popular in 1980s and after.

crew-neck sweater Pullover sweater with a round rib-knit neck. *Der.* Named for knit shirts worn by members of college rowing teams, or "crews."

dolman sweater Pullover sweater with BATWING SLEEVES and with ribbing at waist. In early 1970s worn with a belt—in 1980s became loose and full with ribbed band at waist. Also see under SLEEVES: DOLMAN.

embroidered sweater Sweater that is knitted first and then decorated with embroidery, usually in large floral allover designs in many colors, as compared with a jacquard-knit sweater where the design is part of the knit.

Fair Isle sweater Sweaters, both pullovers and cardigans, imported from Fair Isle off the coast of Scotland. Characterized by soft HEATHER EFFECT and bright-colored knit in traditional patterns. Name also applied to sweaters imitating this style. Popular since the 1920s when worn by Duke of Windsor, at that time Prince of Wales, as a short-waisted sweater with V-neck, worn instead of a vest.

Fair Isle sweater

fanny sweater Long coat sweater coming to below the hips with ribbing or sash at waistline, introduced in early 1970s and still worn.

fatigue sweater Slip-on sweater made in firm rib knit with long sleeves, small V-shaped yoke, round turnover collar, and five-button closing. Originally worn in World War II and restyled in cotton for men and women in 1980s.

fisherman's sweater Bulky hand-knit sweater made of natural color and water-repellent wool, in characteristic patterns, including wide cable stripes, bobbles, seed stitch, and other fancy stitches—imported from Ireland. Popular in early 1960s and widely imitated in MANUFACTURED FIBER yarns. *Der.* From Irish fishermen who wear hand-knit sweaters in a pattern indicating locale in which they live.

fisherman's sweater

Icelandic sweater Hand-knit sweater in traditional designs made in natural-colored wool of browns, blacks, whites, and grays. Fleece is from the rare heath sheep. Rich in lanolin, the wool is said to be almost entirely water repellent. Designs consist of bands around the neck in yoke fashion copied from beaded collars worn by Icelandic Eskimos. Also called *Reykjavik sweater.*

jacquard sweater (ja-kard') Sweater knit by machine with an elaborate design in many colors. May be made of a geometrical repeat pattern or one large design, such as a deer, either on front, back, or both sides of sweater. Popular type of sweater for winter.

jiffy-knit sweater Sweater hand-knit of bulky yarn on very large needles that takes only a few hours to knit. Popular in late 1960s.

jumper (British usage) Pullover sweater.

Karaca sweater (ka-rah'-kah) Turtleneck pullover sweater with elaborate Turkish embroidered panel down center front and lines of embroidery down sleeves. Imported from Black Sea region.

letter sweater Bulky coat sweater with service stripes on upper sleeves and school letter on chest. Formerly given to varsity sports team members in high schools and colleges, now copied for general sportswear. Also called *award, letterman, school,* or *varsity sweater.*

letter sweater

mock turtleneck sweater See under SWEATERS: TURTLENECK SWEATER.

poor-boy sweater Ribbed, knit sweater made with high, round neck or turtleneck. Revived in the mid-1960s. *Der.* From type of sweater worn by newsboys of the early 20th c.

pull-on sweater See under SWEATERS: PULLOVER.

pullover Sweater with round, crew, or V-neck pulled on over the head as contrasted with a cardigan or coat sweater, which opens down the front. Also called *pull-on* or *slip-on sweater.*

pullover sweater with cable pattern

Reykjavik sweater *Der.* Capital of Iceland. See under SWEATERS: ICELANDIC SWEATER.

school sweater See under SWEATERS: LETTER SWEATER.

shawl-collared cardigan See under SWEATERS: CARDIGAN.

shell Sleeveless, collarless pullover sweater usually made in solid colors, worn instead of blouse. Introduced in 1950s.

Shetland sweater Originally a sweater knit of fine worsted yarn from the Shetland Islands off the coast of Scotland. Usually made in classic styles, in a medium-sized plain jersey knit stitch. By extension, name now used for same type of sweater made in MANUFACTURED FIBER yarns.

shrink Waist-length sweater sometimes made with ribbing from below bust to hem, sometimes sleeveless, sometimes has short sleeves. *Der.* Entire sweater looks as if it "shrunk" when washed.

shrug 1. A cropped knit cardigan that does not quite meet at the center front with short or long sleeves. 2. Short-sleeved sweater baring midriff with long V-neckline and fastened with one hook under the bust.

shrug #1

Siwash sweater See under SWEATERS: COWICHAN SWEATER.

ski sweater Classification of elaborately patterned sweaters made in jacquard knits in many colors either domestically or imported, particularly from Norway, Sweden, Switzerland, or Iceland. Worn outdoors for skiing and sometimes indoors for after-ski wear. Also see under SWEATERS: ICELANDIC SWEATER.

slip-on See under SWEATERS: PULLOVER.

sweater-for-two Extremely wide sweater made of stretch acrylic with wide horizontal strips. Designed with two necks, a sleeve on each side, and a single slit for arms in center. A fad of the early 1960s, worn by two people for warmth at football games.

sweater set Two sweaters made to be worn together—one usually of short-sleeve PULLOVER type and the other in CARDIGAN style. Also called *twin set.*

sweater set or twin set

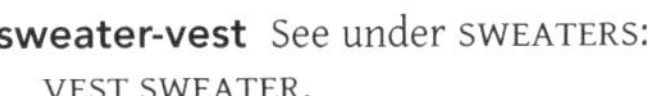

sweater-vest See under SWEATERS: VEST SWEATER.

tennis sweater Pull-on, long-sleeved sweater sometimes made in cable knit. Usually white and trimmed with narrow bands of maroon and navy blue at V-neck and wrists. Worn since 1930s.

tennis sweater

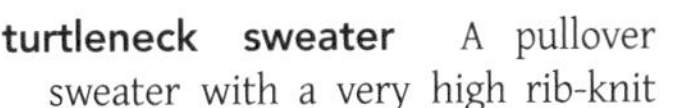

turtleneck sweater A pullover sweater with a very high rib-knit roll collar that folds over twice to form a flattened roll around the neck. **Mock turtleneck** may fold only once or be knitted double to give turtleneck effect without folding.

tuxedo sweater See under SWEATERS: CARDIGAN.

twin set See under SWEATERS: SWEATER SET.

undershirt sweater Pullover with tank top, similar to man's undershirt, sometimes tunic length. Popular in early 1970s.

varsity sweater See under SWEATERS: LETTER SWEATER.

vest sweater Sleeveless, coat-style sweater made double- or single-breasted with a V-neck. Also called a *sweater-vest.*

wraparound sweater Hip-length, cardigan-type sweater with one side lapping over the other, held closed with a matching rib-knit sash.

vest sweater or sweater-vest

---

sweater set See under SWEATERS.

sweater-vest See under SWEATERS: VEST SWEATER.

sweath-bands See under SWADDLING CLOTHES.

sweat jacket See under COATS AND JACKETS.

sweatpants See under PANTS.

sweatshirt See under SHIRTS.

sweatshirt dress See under DRESSES.

sweatshop Slang for a clothing manufacturing plant where workers were paid low wages and worked long hours under unfavorable conditions. Such establishments were common at the turn of the century and have been found again in recent years in large metropolitan areas where undocumented workers are willing to work under poor conditions.

sweatshorts See under SHORTS.

sweatsock See under HOSIERY.

sweatsuit See under ACTIVEWEAR.

Swedish hat See under HEADWEAR: MOUSQUETAIRE HAT.

swedish weaving/Swedish darning See under EMBROIDERIES AND SEWING STITCHES: NEEDLEWEAVING.

sweeper See under DUST RUFFLE.

∞**sweet coffers** In Elizabethan times, boxes used by women to hold cosmetics.

sweetheart neckline See under NECKLINES AND COLLARS.

swim bra See under UNDERGARMENTS.

swimdress See under SWIMWEAR.

SWIMWEAR

Garments for recreational bathing that originated about 1865 and consisted of knee-length dresses and ankle-length pants in woven fabric might most accurately be called **bathing dress.** The encumbering nature of these garments meant that women could do little more than get wet; they could not swim. Around 1880, a combination garment was made in one piece with top, pants, and skirt. Bathing dress grew less and less voluminous and by the mid-1920s terminology changed, with **bathing suits**, such as the ANNETTE KELLERMAN SUIT and TANK-TOP suits, being accepted for the beach. From then until about 1940 all bathing suits were made of knitted fabrics, preferably wool jersey, and by the late 1930s two-piece suits and elasticized bathing suits were adopted. DRESSMAKER-type suits of woven fabric were popular in the 1940s and the first BIKINIS appeared at Mediterranean resorts. Men's bathing suits of the turn of century consisted of one-piece striped jersey suits with knee-length legs, sometimes short-sleeved. By the 1920s, men were wearing sleeveless knit tops and trunks and by the late 1930s, only trunks. After about 1950, the general category of apparel for swimming was more likely to be called **swimwear** and the individual garments, **swimsuits.** See under SWIMWEAR: ANNETTE KELLERMAN SUIT, TANK SWIMSUIT, DRESSMAKER SWIMSUIT and BIKINI.

Annette Kellerman One-piece knit bathing suit with short sleeves, knee-length pants, and a high, round neck. Originally worn under an outer bathing dress by women from late 19th c. to 1920s. Named for Annette Kellerman, the swimmer who first wore it without the bathing dress on top in early 20th c. Similar suits were worn for everyday sportswear during the summer of 1987.

apron swimsuit See under SWIMWEAR: PINAFORE SWIMSUIT.

asymmetric swimsuit Swimsuit that has a strap over only one shoulder.

bandeau swimsuit (band oh') Elasticized strapless swimsuit for women, cut straight across top, usually made without a skirt, popular in 1980s and after.

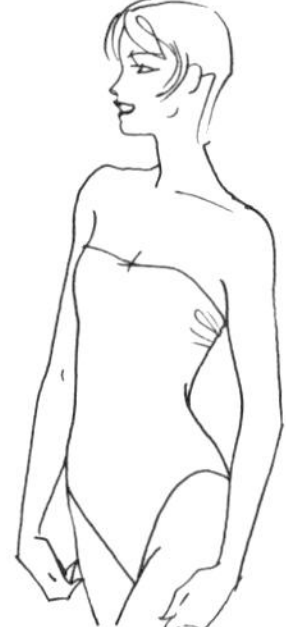

bandeau swimsuit

beach coat Cover-up worn over a bathing suit, styled to match or contrast with bathing suit. Frequently made of terrycloth, sometimes of lace fabric. Also called *beach toga.*

beach wrap-up Large square or rectangle of fabric frequently of terrycloth, wrapped around the body in various ways for protection after swimming or as fashion beachwear item.

bikini (bih kee' nee) 1. Two-piece swimsuit introduced in 1946 by designer Jacques Heim, who called it the *atom* because of its small size. Soon after, a version was advertised as "smaller than the atom." The name was eventually changed to bikini after Bikini Atoll, a small coral island in the Pacific where atomic tests were made from 1946 to 1956. Worn on Riviera beaches but not accepted on U.S. public beaches until the early 1960s. By the 1980s these suits became still smaller and a number of variations had developed. These were: **string bikini**, consisting of a minimal halter bra with bikini panties worn low on hips and made of two triangular-shaped pieces attached to an elastic band or string ties; **teardrop bikini**, made up of bikini pants worn with a teardrop bra composed of two tiny triangles with straps at neck and around the body; **tankini** (tan'-kee-nee), a woman's bathing suit with a tank top and a bikini bottom; **corset bikini**, a top that looks like an underwire bra and a bikini bottom; **camikini**, with a camisole top and a bikini bottom. 2. Man's very brief swim trunks.

bloomer swimsuit Swimsuit made with bouffant pants gathered into elastic bands at legs that was fashionable in 1940s and also in the 1960s, particularly for little girls. Also see under BLOOMER.

blouson swimsuit (blue-zone') One- or two-piece swimsuit of which the top extends below the natural waistline in a bloused effect. The top usually has a built-in bra. Fashionable in the 1960s, then revived in 1980s and after.

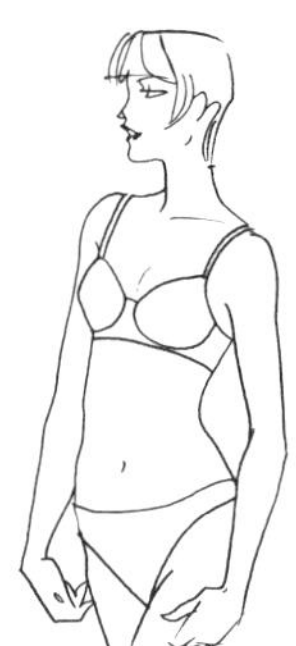

bikini #1

string bikini

tankini

bloomer swimsuit 1950s

board shorts Swim trunks that end a short distance above the knee. Developed for men for surf boarding, presently they are also worn by women. Also see under SHORTS.

boxer shorts swimsuit Man's swim trunks with thigh-length legs and elastic waistband, styled similarly to shorts worn by prizefighters and frequently made with three contrasting stripes down side.

boy shorts swimsuit Girl's two-piece swimsuit designed with shorts or cuffed shorts and brief top.

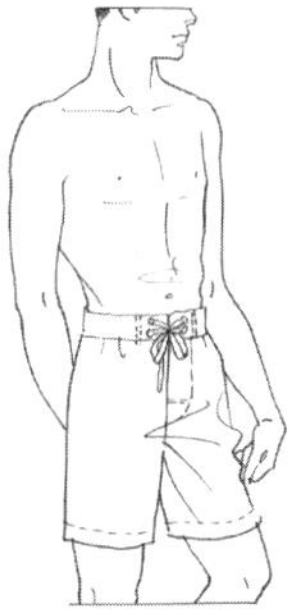
boxer shorts swimsuit

boy shorts swimsuit

briefers Very short swim trunks worn by men and boys that are made of elastic or knitted fabric. By the 1980s, these were often cut like bikini bottoms.

burqini Bathing dress worn by Muslim women that covers the entire body except for the face. It generally consists of a knee-length, long-sleeved tunic worn with long pants and a headscarf. The garment is made in a wide range of colors; fabrics are those used for other swimwear.

cabana set (ca-bahn'-ya) Swimsuit and short-sleeved jacket for men and boys with trunks and jacket cut out of the same fabric or made in contrasting fabrics designed to be worn together. *Der.* Spanish, *cabaña,* "a small tentlike shelter placed on the beach."

burqini

cabana set

camikini See under SWIMWEAR: BIKINI.

convertible swimsuit Women's bikini or two-piece swimsuit with under and upper sides made from different fabrics in order that the sides can be reversed, thereby providing two different-appearing swimsuits.

corset bikini See under SWIMWEAR: BIKINI.

∞**crab-back bathing suit** Man's swimsuit worn in 1920s and 1930s that had a top cut out very wide at armholes and a second cutout near waistline.

cutout swimsuit Fitted maillot-type of swimsuit with cut-out sections that might be located at any place, including sides or center front. Sometimes fishnet is inserted in cutouts or laces may connect the cutout parts. Introduced in mid-1960s.

cutout swimsuit

drag suit Shorts and/or shirts worn over a bathing suit by athletes who want to increase their strength by swimming against the drag produced by the fabric against the water.

dressmaker swimsuit Any swimsuit made of knitted or woven fabric and styled with a skirt. Sometimes shirred across back with elastic thread. A basic type of swimsuit since the 1940s.

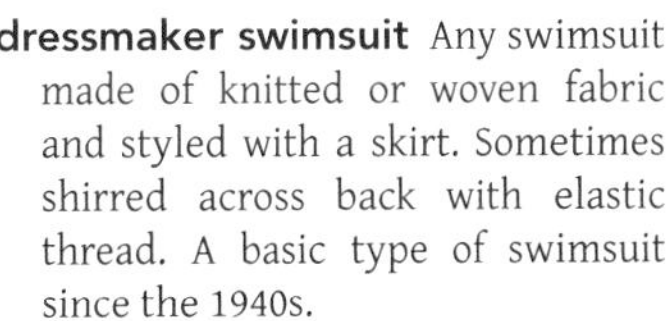

dressmaker swimsuit

Gay 90s swimsuit Two-piece, circular-striped, knitted suit with knee-length pants and hip-length short-sleeved top. Offered for sale in late 1960s, it imitated jersey suits of the 1890s.

hip-rider swimsuit Two-piece swimsuit for women that has pants or skirt cut low enough to show the navel; an innovation in the 1960s.

jammers Swim suits resembling biking shorts that are made of nylon and spandex and are often worn for racing by athletes for competitions. These suits are designed to reduce water resistance, thereby increasing swimming speeds.

long john trunks Man's swimsuit made with rope sash and just above-the-knee knit pants with wide stripes alternating with bright red, green, or black. *Der.* Worn in imitation of boxing trunks worn by late John L. Sullivan (1858–1918), heavyweight boxing champion (1882–1892).

maillot (my'-yo) Classic, one-piece, knitted or jersey swimsuit without a skirt, form-fitting and usually backless. Sometimes with detachable strap tied around neck or buttoned to back of suit. Popular since 1930s and very popular in 1980 and after with high-cut legs. *Der.* French, *maillot,* "tight garment."

mono-kini Woman's TOPLESS SWIMSUIT (see under SWIMWEAR). Introduced by Rudi Gernreich in 1964.

one-piece swimsuit Any swimsuit for women or children made all in one piece. Sometimes has an attached skirt.

overblouse swimsuit Woman's two-piece bathing suit that consists of brief trunks and a separate blouse. Often has a tank-top neckline and unfitted waist.

mono-kini topless swimsuit | overblouse swimsuit | pinafore or apron swimsuit 1970

pinafore swimsuit Bikini swimsuit with an extra pinafore that fits tightly over bust and has a free-hanging skirt curving from sides up to center back, revealing the bikini pants underneath. Also called *apron swimsuit.*

rash guard A wet suit-like garment of lighter weight for warmer weather that protects swimmers from rashes and abrasion produced by water and/or sand, and from ultraviolet light.

rib tickler swimsuit Two-piece, bare midriff suit for women, made in knits or woven fabrics.

ring tops/bottoms A bikini-type swimsuit ornamented with rings. The fabric of the bottom of the suit is pulled through rings that create a draped effect over the top of the leg. At the top in front the left and right sides of the top are fastened to the decorative ring, which serves to join them.

romper cover-up A garment worn over a bathing suit that resembles a one-piece child's romper suit. See under ROMPER #2.

sarong swimsuit (sar-ong') Dressmaker-type swimsuit with rounded ends on wrap skirt that drapes to one side. *Der.* Copied from dress designed by Edith Head for Dorothy Lamour for film *Hurricane* in 1937, similar to Indonesian dress.

sarong swimsuit

sheath swimsuit Similar to a maillot with a tiny skirt panel added in front, but not in back, usually made of stretch fabric. Classic style since the late 1930s.

sheath swimsuit

string bikini See under SWIMWEAR: BIKINI.

surf trunks Man's swim trunks, longer in length than regular trunks, with a hip pocket for surfboard wax. Introduced in the late 1960s.

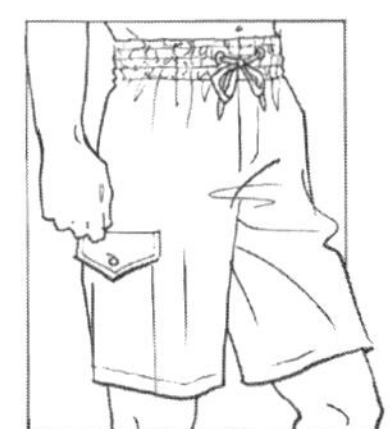

surf trunks

swimdress Swimsuit that looks like a micro-mini–length dress. Synonym: *bathing dress.*

tank swimsuit Classic maillot swimsuit without skirt made with scooped neck and built-up straps. *Der.* Early indoor swimming pools were called "tanks."

thong swimsuit Bikini or other swimsuits cut to reveal as much of the buttocks as possible while covering the crotch.

topless swimsuit Swimsuit that starts below bust or at waist held up by two straps from the back meeting in a V in center front. Introduced by American designer Rudi Gernreich as the MONO-KINI (see under SWIMWEAR) in 1964. Forbidden on most U.S. beaches but started topless waitress style in California nightclubs.

tank swimsuit

trunks Synonym for men's or boy's swimsuits.

tunic swimsuit Two-piece swimsuit cut like a dress with straight lines, slashed on the side seams with panties worn underneath.

---

swing *adj.* Descriptive of a garment that is cut to hang free or to "swing" away from the body. Examples: swing blouse, swing dress, swing skirt.

swinger bag/swinger clutch See under HANDBAGS AND RELATED ACCESSORIES: CONTOUR CLUTCH.

swing skirt See under SKIRTS.

swirl skirt See under SKIRTS.

swiss belt See under BELTS: CORSELET BELT.

∞**swiss bodice** Sleeveless velvet bodice worn with SWISS BELT (see under BELTS: CORSELET BELT), placed over sleeved blouse in late 1860s.

swiss dress See under DRESSES.

swiss embroidery See under EMBROIDERIES AND SEWING STITCHES: MADEIRA EMBROIDERY.

swiss girdle See under BELTS: CORSELET BELT.

switch See under WIGS AND HAIRPIECES.

syglaton See under CYCLAS.

sylphide parasol See under UMBRELLAS AND PARASOLS.

syndicated buying office A RESIDENT BUYING OFFICE owned and operated by a retail conglomerate, an organization that unites a number of different independently operated retail stores that may be located in various parts of the United States.

synthetic fiber See under MANUFACTURED FIBERS.

synthetic fur Soft pile fabric made to imitate fur. Also called **fake fur**. Both terms are misnomers, as the word "fur" should not be used. The correct term would be "furlike fabric."

synthetic gem See under GEMS, GEM CUTS, AND SETTINGS.

synthetic straw Manufactured fibers or materials used to make straws. See under STRAW.

T 1. Abbreviation designating *tall* size range. See under TALL. 2. Abbreviation designating *toddler* sizes. These range from 1T to 4T. See under TODDLER.

tab See under CLOSURES.

∞tabard (tab′-erd) 1. Overgarment constructed with loose front and back panels and short, winglike sleeves, sometimes with heraldic coat-of-arms embroidered on back. Worn by heralds for tourneys and by knights over armor from 13th to 16th c. 3. See under CAPES, CLOAKS, AND SHAWLS.

tabard #1

tabbed closing See under CLOSURES.

†tabby weave See under PLAIN WEAVE.

tab collar See under NECKLINES AND COLLARS.

table See under GEMS, GEM CUTS, AND SETTINGS: BRILLIANT CUT.

tablecloth check See under PRINTS, STRIPES, AND CHECKS.

table-cut gloves See under GLOVES AND GLOVE CONSTRUCTION.

tablet mantilla See under CAPES, CLOAKS, AND SHAWLS.

tablier skirt See under SKIRTS.

∞tablion (tab-lee-ohn′) Elaborate decorative oblong of gold embroidery on both the front and back of the Byzantine Imperial robes and on the PALUDAMENTUM (see under CAPES, CLOAKS, AND SHAWLS). Worn by the Emperor Justinian and his wife, Theodora, during the Byzantine period. High court officials wore a purple tablion on a white mantle. Depicted in mosaics in a church in Ravenna, Italy.

∞tabs In 19th c., loose-hanging pieces of fabric with a border of square or round edges forming a peplum or used as trimming. See under VANDYKING and TURRET BODICE.

tack See under EMBROIDERIES AND SEWING STITCHES.

†taffeta (taf′-et-tah) Crisp fabric with a fine, smooth surface made in plain weave with a small crosswise rib. Originally made in silk, now also made in manufactured filament fibers. *Der.* Persian *tuftah,* "fine, plain-woven silk fabric."

taffeta pipkin See under HEADWEAR: PIPKIN.

tagboard A heavyweight, durable paper, used in the fashion industry for pattern pieces. Also called *oaktag* or *hard paper.*

taglioni See under COATS AND JACKETS.

taglioni frock coat See under COATS AND JACKETS.

tail coat See under COATS AND JACKETS: SWALLOW-TAILED COAT.

tailleur (tay-yure′) French for tailored costume—a suit. *Der.* French, "tailor" or "cutter."

tailor 1. *n.* Person who makes either men's or women's clothes, mends clothing, or does alterations. Originally men did all of the commercial clothing production of menswear, coats, and suits, especially those made of wool. 2. *v.* To fit clothing for one individual; to fashion a garment.

tailored *adj.* Describes an item of apparel that is relatively plain and without decoration and which depends on the line and fit of the item for style. Those dresses, coats, and suits that are the opposite of tailored (i.e., have softer lines, more trimming, and are more elaborate) may be described as **dressmaker**. See under BLOUSES AND TOPS: TAILORED BLOUSE; CLOSURES: WORKED BUTTONHOLE; SLEEPWEAR AND LOUNGEWEAR: TAILORED PAJAMAS; and UNDERGARMENTS: TAILORED SLIP.

tailor-made 1. Garment made specifically for one individual by a tailor—customer's measurements are taken and several fittings are necessary. Also called *custom-made* or *custom-tailored.* ∞2. In the late 19th c., a woman's costume for morning or country wear, usually a suit consisting of a jacket and skirt made by a tailor rather than a dressmaker. Introduced by the designer Redfern in late 1870s.

tailor-made #2
1905

tailor's tack See under EMBROIDERIES AND SEWING STITCHES.

tails See under FULL-DRESS SUIT.

taj toe See under FOOTWEAR.

talisman ring See under JEWELRY.

tall 1. Men's size corresponding to a chest measurement of 38–48″ and a height of 5′11″–6′2½″. Also see EXTRA TALL. 2. Women's size range corresponding to a height of 5′8″ to 6′.

talleyrand collar See under NECKLINES AND COLLARS.

tallien redingote See under COATS AND JACKETS.

tallith (tal′-ith or tal′-iss) Prayer shawl, worn by Jewish men after age 13. Made with tassels called TSITSITH, usually blue, attached at the four corners. Believed to have been derived from Roman *pallium.* Took various shapes throughout the ages. Modern tallith is made of wool or silk in white with black or blue stripes. Silk types vary from 54″ to 90″ long and 32″ to 72″ wide. Woolen type is larger and made with two lengths joined together. Narrow silk ribbon covers place where it is pieced. At the neck is the **ata,** a narrow ribbon or band woven with silver or gold thread. Also spelled *tallis.* Also see under ARBA KANFOTH.

tallow-top cut See under GEMS, GEM CUTS, AND SETTINGS: CABOCHON #2.

talma See under CAPES, CLOAKS, AND SHAWLS.

talma lounge See under COATS AND JACKETS.

talma overcoat See under COATS AND JACKETS.

tam See under HEADWEAR.

tambour farthingale See under FARTHINGALE.

tambour work See under EMBROIDERIES AND SEWING STITCHES.

tam-o-shanter See under HEADWEAR.

tango shoe See under FOOTWEAR.

tankini See under SWIMWEAR: BIKINI.

tank suit See under SWIMWEAR: TANK SWIMSUIT.

tank top See under BLOUSES AND TOPS and SHIRTS.

tanning See under LEATHERS.

tanuki See under FURS.

tanzanite See under GEMS, GEM CUTS, AND SETTINGS.

†tapa cloth (tah′-pah) Fabric made from fibers of the inner bark of the paper mulberry tree, *Brousonnetia papyrifera* or the tree *Pipturus albidus.* Fabric was made by natives in the South Pacific Islands by beating bark to form a weblike fabric. Before contact with the West, it was used for clothing by the natives of Pacific Islands and eastern Asia. Now made mostly for ceremonial dress and tourist items. In Hawaii called *kapa,* and in Fiji, called *masi.*

tape lace See under LACES.

tapered *adj.* Characteristically wider at the top and narrower at the bottom. See under HAIRSTYLES: TAPERED HAIRCUT; PANTS: TAPERED PANTS; and SHIRTS: BODYSHIRT #1.

†tapestry 1. Handwoven fabric with large, mostly pictorial designs. Not used for apparel, but as decorative hangings. 2. Heavy fabric, usually with a pictorial design, woven of multicolored yarns on a Jacquard loom in imitation of handwoven tapestries. A heavy fabric, it is used mainly for shoes, bags, and handbags. 3. See under EMBROIDERIES AND SEWING STITCHES.

tap panty See under UNDERGARMENTS.

tap shoe See under FOOTWEAR.

target marketing/customer segmentation Using demographic variables such as age, gender, income, education, marital status, religion, family size, life-cycle stage, ethnicity, and mobility—as well as psychographic information regarding lifestyle, hobbies, and interests—as a basis of identifying and marketing to a potential customer population.

tartan See under introduction to PLAIDS AND TARTANS.

tasar See under TUSSAH.

tasseau (tas-oh′) ∞1. Type of pin or clasp used to fasten a MANTLE (see CAPES, CLOAKS, AND SHAWLS: MANTLE #1) in late Middle Ages. 2. See under SCARVES. *Der.* Latin, *tassa,* "clasp."

tassel 1. Bundle of threads, bound at one end, hung singly or in groups as ornament on belts, hats, shawls, etc. 2. See under SCARVES: TASSEAU. 3. See under JEWELRY: TASSEL NECKLACE.

tassel-tie See under FOOTWEAR.

tassel-top loafer See under FOOTWEAR: LOAFER.

tasset See under ARMOR.

tatamis See under FOOTWEAR.

tatas See under RIBBONS OF CHILDHOOD.

tattersall See under PLAIDS AND TARTANS and PRINTS, STRIPES, AND CHECKS.

tattersall vest See under VESTS.

tatting See under introduction to LACES.

tattoo (ta-too′) 1. Permanent design made on skin by process of pricking and ingraining indelible pigment that has been practiced since prehistoric times. The name is of Polynesian origin. Tattooing has been a common practice of many aboriginal tribes. Adopted in the Western world and popular with sailors. Since the late 1990s being tattooed has become popular among those who consider tattooing a form of body art. **2.** Fashion fad in early 1970s of decorating body with transfer designs of ships, hearts, etc., imitating those tattooed on sailors' skin. Also see under BODY PAINTING and DECALCOMANIA.

tattoo pantyhose See under HOSIERY.

tau cross See under CROSS.

taure See under HAIRSTYLES: BULL HEAD.

tawning See under FURS.

tchamir See under SHIRTS.

tea apron See under APRONS.

tea-cozy cap See under HEADWEAR.

∞**tea gown** **1.** Long, informal hostess gown in pale colors worn from 1877 to early 20th c. Usually made of thin wool or silk, it might be loose-fitting and worn without a corset. **2.** Used in 1920s and 1930s to designate semiformal dress suitable for an afternoon tea or garden party.

tea gown #1 1891

tea jacket See under BLOUSES AND TOPS.

tea length See under LENGTHS.

tear-away shorts See under SHORTS.

teardrop bikini See under SWIMWEAR: BIKINI.

teardrop bra See under UNDERGARMENTS.

teasing See under HAIRSTYLES: BACK-COMBING.

tebenna See under CAPES, CLOAKS, AND SHAWLS.

tech drawing An abbreviation of "technical drawing," which is a flat, rather than three-dimensional, drawing of a garment that may also include drawings of close-up details of the garment.

technical flat See under FLAT.

techno Music style of the 1980s. Fans wore leather clothing and industrial accessories.

techno stretch Name given to high-tech fabrics that stretch. Often made from a blend of other fibers and SPANDEX.

tech pack Black-and-white flat sketch of a design and all technical information needed to make the corresponding apparel product. Also see under SPECIFICATION PACKAGE/SPEC PACK.

teck scarf See under TIES.

teddy **1.** See under UNDERGARMENTS. **2.** See under SLEEPWEAR AND LOUNGEWEAR.

teddybear coat See under COATS AND JACKETS.

Teddy boy Name given to tough, young, British youth from London in early 1950s who adopted styles consisting of exaggerated Edwardian jackets, high stiff collars, tight pants, pointed-toed shoes called WINKLE PICKERS (see under FOOTWEAR), long hair carefully greased and waved, and no hats. The result was a trend to an individualized style of dress worn as a protest against the establishment by working-class teenagers. Fashion came up from the streets rather than being set by designers. *Der.* Teddy is nickname for "Edward," or Edwardian fashions.

Teddy boy

Teddy girl Female counterpart of TEDDY BOYS, who also wore distinctive clothes in protest against traditional current fashions. Their preferred dress consisted of short tight skirts, high-heeled, pointed-toed shoes, and high beehive hairstyles.

teen bra See under UNDERGARMENTS.

teeny-bopper Name given to young girls, usually aged between 11 and 14, who follow fads in clothing and pop music popularized by young performers.

tee shirt See under SHIRTS: T-SHIRT and UNDERGARMENTS: T-SHIRT.

television shopping Television programs that offer retail merchandise that can be ordered by phone or e-mail.

templar cloak See under COATS AND JACKETS: CABAN.

temple See under EYEWEAR.

templers See under HEADWEAR: BOSSES.

temporary retailer See POP-UP STORES.

†**Tencel**® See under LYOCELL.

tendrils See under HAIRSTYLES.

teneriffe lace See under LACES.

ten-gallon hat See under HEADWEAR: COWBOY HAT and SOMBRERO.

tennis clothes/tennis dress See under ACTIVEWEAR and also see under FOOTWEAR: TENNIS SHOES; SHORTS: TENNIS SHORTS; and SWEATERS: TENNIS SWEATER.

†**tensile strength** The ability of a fiber or fabric to withstand strain and resist breaking. Used in textile testing.

tent Apparel with much fullness. See under DRESSES: TENT DRESS and COATS AND JACKETS: TENT COAT.

tent dress See under DRESSES.

tent stitch See under EMBROIDERIES AND SEWING STITCHES: CONTINENTAL STITCH.

terai hat See under HEADWEAR.

teresa See HEADWEAR: THÉRÈSE.

terms of sale In a purchase agreement between retailer and vendor, specifications for purchase that include details such as discounts, delivery, and transportation costs.

†terry cloth 1. Fabric made in the pile weave (see under PILE) with uncut loops and a background weave of PLAIN WEAVE or TWILL WEAVE. Usually made in cotton but now also made with manufactured yarns. Sometimes woven in plaid, dobby, or Jacquard patterns of two or more colors. May be yarn-dyed, bleached, piece-dyed, or printed. 2. A similar pile weave, knitted fabric is usually called *knitted terrycloth.* Both fabrics are used for shorts, jumpsuits, pants, beachwear, summer dresses, robes, and sport shirts.

tessellation See under PRINTS, STRIPES, AND CHECKS.

tête de mouton See under WIGS AND HAIRPIECES and HAIRSTYLES: COIFFURE À LA MOUTON.

tethered studs See under JEWELRY.

Teva® See under FOOTWEAR: SPORTS SANDAL.

Textile/Clothing Technology Corporation (TC)² An organization established by the textile and apparel industries and funded by industry and government to conduct research and educate apparel manufacturers, technologists, retailers, and educators about implementation and use of automated systems for manufacture and management in the textile and apparel industries. Among the outgrowths of its work are the concepts of AGILE MANUFACTURING, long-distance learning, and the VIRTUAL FACTORY.

†textile fabric Cloth made of textile yarns by weaving, knitting, lace making, braiding, netting, or felting. Also cloth made by bonding or nonwoven methods. *Der.* Latin, *fabrica,* "workshop."

†Textile Fiber Products Identification Act (T.F.P.I.A.) Federal law setting labeling requirements for clothing made of textiles, which requires generic fiber identification, fiber content by percentage, manufacturer identification, and designation of country of origin.

textured hose See under HOSIERY.

†textured yarn Manufactured continuous-filament yarns permanently heat-set in crimped manner, or otherwise modified to improve its handle, increase bulk, or increase elasticity.

theatre suit Woman's two-piece dressy suit suitable for late afternoon or evening. Made in two or three pieces with short jacket or regular-length coat. Were made in luxurious fabrics, trimmed with beading or fur. Popular from about the 1930s into the 1950s.

theme A concept or narrative that ties together a seasonal group of clothing (e.g., nautical, African).

theo tie See under FOOTWEAR.

Theory of the Leisure Class See under VEBLEN, THORSTEIN.

thérèse 1. See under HEADWEAR. 2. See under SCARVES.

thermal *adj.* Descriptive of garments made to provide insulation from cold. See under GLOVES AND GLOVE CONSTRUCTION: THERMAL GLOVES; HOSIERY: THERMAL SOCK; and UNDERGARMENTS: THERMAL UNDERWEAR.

thermal knit See under UNDERGARMENTS: THERMAL UNDERWEAR.

thermal shirt See under SHIRTS.

†thick and thin yarn Yarns of uneven size at intervals. When woven into cloth, they add interest.

†Thinsulate® A 60 percent polyolefin, 40 percent polyester microfilament insulation providing warmth equal to down or polyester insulations of close to twice the thickness. Does not absorb water.

thigh highs See under HOSIERY.

thirties *adj.* 1. Descriptive of an early 1930s style that featured long, lean, bias-cut dress with intricate drapery, unusual sleeves, and frequently V- or round necks. 2. In late 1930s, extremely broad shoulders were featured with small waistline and more tailored styles. Both of these styles have been revived by designers in the 1980s and 1990s.

thong 1. See under UNDERGARMENTS. 2. Narrow strip of rawhide or other leather used for a LACER, braided into a belt, or wound around foot and leg as a fastening for sandals. Also see under BELTS: THONG BELT and FOOTWEAR: THONG SANDAL.

thong swimsuit See under SWIMWEAR.

†thread Smooth, tightly twisted yarn made specifically for sewing.

†thread count The number of warp (lengthwise) threads per inch and the number of filling (crosswise) yarns per inch in woven cloth. For example a count of 68 × 72 would mean 68 warp threads by 72 filling threads. Also called FABRIC COUNT.

threads (British slang) Used by young "trendy" people in 1960s for mod clothes sold on Carnaby Street, London.

three-armhole dress See under DRESSES.

three-decker See under COATS AND JACKETS.

three-piece suit See under SUIT #1.

three-quarter See under LENGTHS and SHOULDERS AND SLEEVES.

three-quarter cut See under FOOTWEAR: SEMI-CUT.

three-seamed raglan sleeve See under SHOULDERS AND SLEEVES: RAGLAN SLEEVE.

three-seamer See under COATS AND JACKETS.

three-storeys-and-a-basement See under HEADWEAR.

thrift-shop dress See under DRESSES.

throat See under FOOTWEAR.

throat belt See under JEWELRY: DOG COLLAR.

thrum See under HEADWEAR.

tiara 1. See under HEADWEAR. 2. See under CLERICAL DRESS.

ticket pocket See under POCKETS.

†ticking Sturdy, durable fabric woven in a close satin weave or a twill weave with soft filling yarns. Originally used for covering pillows and mattresses, now used for sport clothes and pants.

ticking stripes See under PRINTS, STRIPES, AND CHECKS.

tie-back skirt See under SKIRTS.

tie clasp/clip See under JEWELRY.

tied closing See under CLOSURES.

tie dyeing Hand method of coloring a fabric by tying strings tightly around puffs of fabric and dipping the fabric into a dye bath to get a two-color design. Repeating the process by covering other areas and using different dye colors can add even more colors. Designs are usually circular with feathered or blended edges. A technique originating in Indonesia and popular in the 1920s mainly for scarves. Revived in 1960s and periodically since then for blue jeans, T-shirts, dresses, and furs. Also see under PRINTS, STRIPES, AND CHECKS: TIE-DYED PRINT.

tie fabrics See under TIE SILK.

tie pin See under JEWELRY: STICKPIN.

tie pocket See under POCKETS.

tiered skirt See under SKIRTS.

tiers Several layers of ruffles or bias-cut sections placed one above the other and overlapping. Used mainly on skirts, full sleeves, or pants.

TIES

tie Long band made in various widths of double-thick fabric or rounded braid worn around the neck under the shirt collar and tied in various ways. May be made of fabric, suede, leather, and beads. A shortened form of the word **necktie,** the term came into use about 1820 but did not entirely replace the term "cravat" used earlier. Originally worn only by men, women adopted ties in 1890s to wear with the shirtwaist. Since 1930s, the fashionable width has varied.

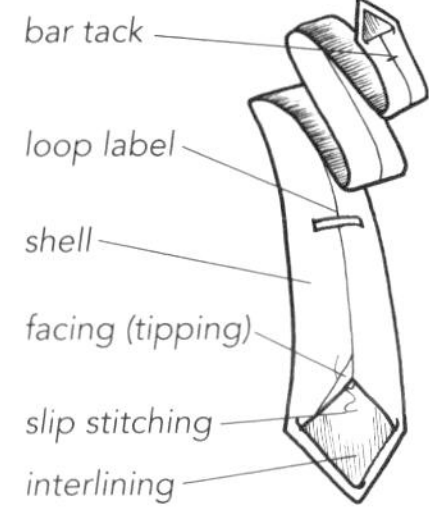

necktie

apron The wide ends at the front and back of a contemporary necktie.

ascot 1. Wide necktie worn looped over and held in place by scarf pin. The ends are cut diagonally. Introduced in 1876 and worn since with a CUTAWAY (see under COATS AND JACKETS). 2. Scarf looped under the chin. *Der.* Fashionable horse-racing spot, Ascot Heath, England. Also see under SCARVES: ASCOT.

ascot #1

∞ballroom neckcloth Man's pleated, starched evening neckcloth crossed over in front with ends secured to suspenders on either side. Fastened with an elaborate brooch in center front; worn in 1830s.

band bow Pre-tied bow tie on an adjustable-sized band that fastens around the neck.

bar-shaped tie FOUR-IN-HAND TIE (see under TIES) with ends that are parallel and of the same width.

∞batswing tie Man's bow tie cut with wide flaring ends, worn c. 1896.

∞belcher handkerchief Blue neckerchief with large white polka dots, each centered with a dark blue eye; worn by men in first half of 19th c. *Der.* Named for Jim Belcher, a fighter during English Regency period who originated style—other neckwear of the era was very formal.

∞bib cravat Man's wide neck piece, in shape of a bib, usually lace edged and held on by colored CRAVAT STRING (see under TIES); popular at end of 17th c.

black tie 1. Man's black BOW TIE (see under TIES) worn with dinner jacket or tuxedo, for semiformal occasions. 2. Denotes type of dress expected at a semiformal occasion. "Black tie" indicates a tuxedo is required for men.

boater tie Man's FOUR-IN-HAND TIE (see under TIES), shorter than average, made with extra-large knot, and usually with square-cut ends. Introduced in late 1960s from England.

bolo tie/bola tie Western-type tie of heavy rounded braid with metal-tipped ends, fastening with an ornamental slide. Also called *shoelace tie.*

bolo tie

bootlace tie See under TIES: STRING TIE.

bow tie 1. Man's tie, square-cut or with shaped ends, tied in a bow under the chin. Originally introduced in late 19th c. and worn with FULL DRESS since. See under TIES: BLACK TIE and WHITE TIE. 2. Man's tie, already tied in

bow tie #1

a bow, which clips to the collar. **3.** Short bow tied by hand on the front of a woman's dress or blouse.

butterfly bow tie Bow tie with top and bottom edges that narrow at the middle of the tie to make the center about half the width of the ends. Ends may be either square or pointed. Contrast with TIES: CLUB BOW TIE.

∞**byron tie** Short, narrow string necktie made of silk worn in the 1840s and 1850s *Der.* Named for LORD BYRON.

∞**chaconne** (shak-kon') Ribbon CRAVAT (see under TIES: CRAVAT #2) tied with ends dangling over chest. Named for dancer Pecourt, who, in 1692, danced a chaconne with his cravat tied in this manner. *Der.* Name of 17th-c. dance.

clip-on tie Tie, pre-tied in a knot like a four-in-hand or a bow tie, that is fastened to the collarband by a metal clip.

club bow tie Bow tie in which the top and bottom edges are straight. Ends are either square or pointed. Contrast with TIES: BUTTERFLY BOW TIE.

cravat **1.** Sometimes used as a synonym for a man's wide necktie worn with morning coat and pin-striped trousers. ∞**2.** Lawn, muslin, or silk NECKCLOTH (see under TIES) with ends tied in a bow or knot in center front, worn from 1660 to the end of the 19th c. Sometimes worn with starched collar.

cravat #2 c. 1800

∞**cravate cocodes** (kra-vat' ko'-kod) Large bow-tied CRAVAT (see under TIES) worn by women about 1863 with a HABIT SHIRT (see under SHIRTS).

∞**cravat strings** Piece of colored ribbon worn on top of the cravat and tied in a bow under chin. Later a ready-made bow placed behind the loosely tied CRAVAT (see under TIES). Worn by men from 1665 to 1680s.

∞**cremona cravat** (kre-mo'-nah kra-vat') Plain ribbon CRAVAT (see under TIES) edged with gathers, introduced for men in 1702 after the battle of Cremona, Italy.

∞**de joinville teck** Pre-tied man's silk or satin necktie of 1890s that was made narrow around the neck and wide like a STOCK (see under TIES) in front. It fell in graceful folds with wide, squared, fringed ends.

four-in-hand tie Long necktie that goes around the neck with one end looping over the other end twice and is then pulled through loop, making a slip knot. Usually made of bias-cut fabric or knit, narrow in the center back and wider at the ends. Worn continuously since the 1890s in varying widths. Also worn by women with tailored suits.

∞**hunting necktie** Man's broad, high necktie worn from 1818 through 1830s with three horizontal pleats on each side angled toward center front. Worn with ends brought to front, tied, and hidden by coat.

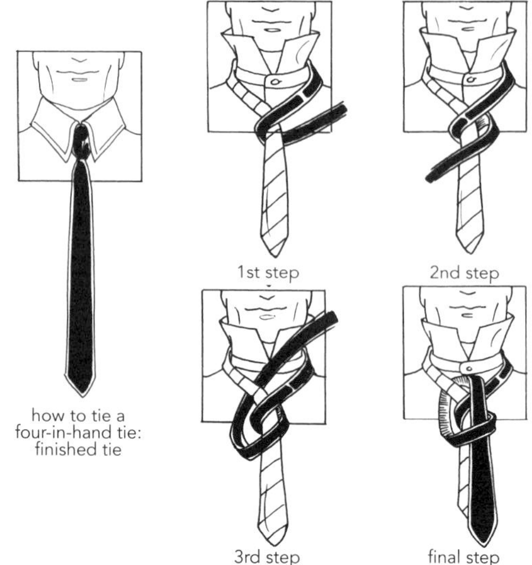

how to tie a four-in-hand tie

∞**hunting stock** **1.** Man's long scarf folded double, wrapped twice around neck, and tied. Worn instead of necktie for sports in 1890s. **2.** Type of wide tie or STOCK (see under TIES). Worn folded over once to fill in neckline of jacket. Used by equestrians when riding in hunt field or show ring.

∞**indian necktie** Muslin CRAVAT (see under TIES) worn by men from 1815 to 1830s, secured in front with a sliding ring. Also called a *maharatta tie* (mah-har'-attah).

∞**joinville** Men's neckwear of mid-1840s to mid-1850s made by tying a 5″ wide scarf around neck in a bow. Usually had square-cut fringed ends.

kipper Necktie 4 or 5″ wide with ends like a bow tie, usually of striped or patterned fabric. Introduced from England in late 1960s.

macclesfield tie (mak'-liz-feld) Necktie made from silk fabric of a type produced in Macclesfield, England. Fabric has small DOBBY WEAVE patterns.

maharatta tie See under TIES: INDIAN NECKTIE.

∞**mail-coach necktie** Man's large scarf, sometimes a cashmere shawl, loosely folded twice around neck, tied in knot in front with ends falling over chest like a waterfall. Worn as NECKCLOTH (see under TIES) from 1818 to 1830s by dandies. Also called *waterfall necktie.*

∞**military stock** Man's made-up NECKCLOTH (see under TIES), frequently of black corded silk edged with kidskin, stiffened with cardboard or leather, and tied or buckled in back. Worn from mid-18th to mid-19th c.

∞**napoleon necktie** Man's medium-wide necktie first worn circa 1818, in violet color; passed around neck, crossed over chest, and ends tied to suspenders or continued around to tie at back of neck. *Der.* Reported to have been copied from necktie worn by Napoleon on his return from Elba. By 1830 it was called a *corsican necktie.*

∞**neckcloth** Any type of man's neckwear or CRAVAT wrapped around neck, as worn from 1660 to the mid-19th century. See under TIES: CRAVAT and STOCK.

neckerchief See under SCARVES.

∞**neck handkerchief** Synonym for man's NECKTIE or CRAVAT in 18th and 19th c.

necktie See under introduction to TIES.

∞**octagon tie** Man's pre-made scarf or cravat worn from 1860s on with long wide piece of fabric folded to form an X in front and attached to a narrow band fastening at back of neck with hook and eye.

∞**osbaldiston tie** (os-bald-dis'-stun) Necktie tied in front with a barrel-shaped knot worn by men from 1830s through 1840s. Also called *barrel knot tie.*

∞**oxford tie** Straight, narrow necktie worn in 1890s by men with informal lounge suit and by women with shirtwaist.

regimental striped tie See under PRINTS, STRIPES, AND CHECKS: REGIMENTAL STRIPES.

rep tie/repp tie See under REP.

∞**royal george stock** Man's black velvet STOCK (see under TIES) worn in 1820s and 1830s, made with satin over the velvet at base of neck and tied in bow in front.

∞**sailor's reef knot** Common double knot or square knot used on sailor ties in U.S. Navy. Used for men's neckties from 1870 on, most fashionable in 1890s.

sailor tie Large square scarf of black silk folded diagonally and worn under square SAILOR COLLAR (see under NECKLINES AND COLLARS) and either tied in sailor knot or pulled through strap on front of MIDDY BLOUSE (see under BLOUSES AND TOPS). Formerly worn by U.S. Naval enlisted personnel and adopted by women and children in late 19th c. and after to wear with middy blouse.

scarf 1. Extremely large CRAVAT (see under TIES) worn by men in 1830s that spread over shirt front and fastened with a decorative tie pin. 2. Trade name for late-19th-c. necktie that was narrow in back and had wide hanging ends. 3. Also see under SCARVES: SCARF #1.

seven-fold tie Unlined tie made from an outer fabric that is folded over itself seven times. As a result, no lining is required; however, due to the cost of such ties, they are now relatively rare.

shell Outside fabric of a necktie.

sheriff tie See under TIES: STRING TIE.

shoelace tie See under TIES: BOLO TIE.

∞**shoestring tie** Man's extremely narrow necktie of 1850s, tied in bow in front or fastened by pulling ends through a small ring. Also see under TIES: BYRON TIE.

∞**solitaire** Necktie worn with man's bagwig from 1730s to 1770s, tied in various ways (e.g., in a bow under chin and pinned in place, or loosely knotted with free hanging ends).

Southern Colonel tie See under TIES: STRING TIE.

spitalfield tie (spit'-ahl-field) Necktie made from silk fabric of a type produced in the Spitalfield section of London, England. Fabric has a small, overall pattern that looks like a mosaic. It is usually made in a DOBBY WEAVE.

∞**starcher** Man's starched cravat of 19th c.

∞**steinkirk** Long, lace-edged cravat loosely knotted under the chin that was pinned to one side or left hanging. The ends were pulled through a buttonhole. Worn by men from 1692 to 1730 and by the unfashionable until 1770. Women wore it with their riding habits. *Der.* From the Battle of Steinkirk in 1692, when soldiers were surprised in battle before they could tie their cravats.

steinkirk

∞**stock** Man's ready-made neckcloth, sometimes stiffened with pasteboard, that fitted high on the neck and fastened in back with strings or buckles. Usually white or black, the stock sometimes had a bow at the front. At first a part of military dress, civilians soon adopted it, and it was worn from about 1735 to end of 19th c.

stock

string tie Necktie, usually not more than one inch wide, often black, worn in a bow with ends hanging down. Also called *bootlace tie, Southern Colonel tie,* and, in Britain, *sheriff's tie.*

∞**teck scarf** Man's wide necktie of 1890s somewhat shorter than average. Tied in *four-in-hand-knot* with ends cut straight across or ending in center point with slanted sides. Also see under TIES: DE JOINVILLE TECK.

white tie 1. Man's white bow tie worn for formal occasions, traditionally with tails, usually hand tied. 2. Denotes the most formal style of men's dress in Western culture consisting of a white tie, tails, waistcoat, and wing collar shirt for men, and a formal gown for women.

windsor tie 1. Regular man's necktie tied in four-in-hand style with a more complicated knot that is larger. *Der.* Called a *Windsor knot* after Duke of Windsor, who made it popular in early 1920s. 2. Large, flowing bow tie worn by men in 1870s and 1880s.

---

tie shoe See under FOOTWEAR.

†**tie silk** Fabrics used for making neckties and scarves. Usually distinguished by small designs or stripes and

woven in narrower widths than other fabrics. Since neckties are now made of fabrics with all types of fibers including cotton, polyester, and nylon, the term *tie fabrics* is more accurate.

tie tack See under JEWELRY.

Tiffany setting A simple pronged setting used for diamonds and large stones. See under GEMS, GEM CUTS, AND SETTINGS.

tiger's eye See under GEMS, GEM CUTS, AND SETTINGS.

tights 1. See under PANTS: PANTALOONS. 2. See under HOSIERY. 3. See under UNDERGARMENTS.

tilbury hat See under HEADWEAR.

tinsel yarn Metals such as gold, silver, aluminum, or copper cut into fine strips and used alone or made into core yarn for use in brocades and glitter fabrics.

tint Hues with white added to lighten (e.g., light blue and white added is called a "tint of blue"). Also see SHADE.

tippet (tip'-it) 1. A long, narrow strip of fabric that hangs from a sleeve, hood, cape, or other areas of a garment. A particularly notable example is often shown hanging from sleeve of the COTEHARDIE, a medieval garment. Shown at COTEHARDIE. 2. See under CAPES, CLOAKS, AND SHAWLS.

tipping 1. See under FURS. 2. See under HAIRSTYLES.

tire See under HEADWEAR: ATTIRE #2.

†tissue Descriptive of lightweight, semitransparent fabric (e.g., tissue gingham, tissue taffeta).

titus coiffure/wig See under HAIRSTYLES.

toboggan cap See under HEADWEAR: STOCKING CAP.

toby ruff See under NECKLINES AND COLLARS.

toddler Size range from 1 to 4 for very young children. Abbreviated *T*.

toe See under FOOTWEAR.

toe-ankle chain See under JEWELRY.

toelet See under HOSIERY.

toe ring See under JEWELRY.

toe rubbers See under FOOTWEAR.

toe slippers See under FOOTWEAR.

toe spring See under FOOTWEAR.

∞**tog** Coat, in the Middle Ages. *Der.* Shortened form of *toga.*

∞**toga** Ancient Roman outer garment worn only by male Roman citizens age 16 or older. In its earliest form, it consisted of large, semicircular mantle of white wool that was draped over the left shoulder, across the back, under the right arm, and over the left shoulder again, leaving the right arm free. By the time of the Roman Empire, it had become more oval. The upper section was folded over, creating a sort of draped area at the front called the **sinus.** Although the traditional toga, called a **toga pura** (poor-ah') or **toga virilis,** was white and undecorated, there were a few significant variations. (1) The **toga praetexta** (pray-tex'-ta) had a purple border several inches wide and was worn by children of the nobility (sons until age 16 and girls until age 12) and certain adult magistrates and high priests. (2) The **toga pulla** (pooh'-lah) was black or dark colored and worn for mourning. (3) The **toga picta** was purple with gold embroidery and was assigned on special occasions to victorious generals or other distinguished persons. (4) The **toga trabea** (trah-beh'-ah), probably multicolored and striped, was worn by augurs (priests who predicted the future) and important officials. (5) The **toga candida** (kan-dee-dah'), lightened to an exceptional white, was worn by candidates for office. The word "candidate" derives from this practice.

toga

toga dress See under DRESSES.

toga nightgown See under SLEEPWEAR AND LOUNGEWEAR.

toggle See under CLOSURES.

toggle coat See under COATS AND JACKETS: DUFFEL COAT.

togs (slang) Clothing, especially fancy garments.

toile (twal) 1. (French) MUSLIN pattern for a garment. Also see under PROTOTYPE. 2. See under LACES. *Der.* French, "cloth."

toilet/toilette (twa-let') ∞1. In the late 19th-c., referred to a woman's entire costume (e.g., afternoon toilette). 2. Process of a woman dressing (e.g., combing her hair, applying her makeup). Used especially in 19th and early 20th c. 3. See under SLEEPWEAR AND LOUNGEWEAR.

tolerance A range of acceptable variations from the dimensional measurements called for in the SIZE SPECIFICATIONS. Tolerance is stated as a + or – in inches or metric dimensions.

Tom Jones Film version (1963) of Henry Fielding's novel about an 18th-c. hero that inspired clothes in mid-1960s. See under SHIRTS: TOM JONES SHIRT and SHOULDERS AND SLEEVES: TOM JONES SLEEVE.

tongue See under FOOTWEAR.

tonlet See under ARMOR.

tooled leather See under BELTS and HANDBAGS AND RELATED ACCESSORIES.

top 1. See under category heading BLOUSES AND TOPS. 2. See WIGS AND HAIRPIECES: TOUPÉE.

topaz See under GEMS, GEM CUTS, AND SETTINGS.

topazolite See under GEMS, GEM CUTS, AND SETTINGS: ANDRADITE GARNET.

top boot See under FOOTWEAR: JOCKEY BOOT.

topcoat See under COATS AND JACKETS.

topee/topi See under HEADWEAR.

top frock See under COATS AND JACKETS.

top grain See under LEATHERS.

top hat See under HEADWEAR.

topknot See under HAIRSTYLES.

topless *adj.* Descriptive of women's styles that bare the body to the waist. In 1964 Rudi Gernreich introduced the sensational TOPLESS SWIMSUIT (see under SWIMWEAR). Women who attempted to wear it on American beaches were arrested, although it was accepted on the beaches of France. Topless style was accepted in nightclubs for dancers and waitresses.

topline See under FOOTWEAR.

topper 1. See under HEADWEAR: TOP HATS. 2. See under COATS AND JACKETS.

tops See under BLOUSES AND TOPS.

topsider See under FOOTWEAR: SPERRY TOPSIDER.

top-stitch See under EMBROIDERIES AND SEWING STITCHES.

topstitching/topstitched seam See under CLOTHING CONSTRUCTION DETAILS.

†topweight Fabric suitable for such garments as blouses and shirts.

toque 1. See under HEADWEAR. 2. See under HAIR ACCESSORIES.

toquet See under HEADWEAR.

torchon lace See under LACES.

toreador *adj.* Descriptive of apparel inspired by or derived from the dress of Spanish bullfighters called toreadors. See under COATS AND JACKETS: TOREADOR JACKET; HEADWEAR: TOREADOR HAT; and PANTS: TOREADOR PANTS.

torque See under JEWELRY.

torsade 1. See under HEADWEAR. 2. See under JEWELRY.

torso *adj.* Descriptive of apparel that fits the body tightly from neck to hips. See under DRESSES: TORSO DRESS; BLOUSES AND TOPS: TORSO BLOUSE; and SKIRTS: TORSO SKIRT.

torso dress See under DRESSES.

torsolette See under UNDERGARMENTS: BUSTIER.

tortoiseshell 1. An attractive, brown, speckled material, obtained from the shell of the hawksbill turtle, which was prized for its attractive appearance. Its widespread use as a decorative material in such objects as hair ornaments, eyeglass frames, jewelry, and other trimmings caused the turtle to be hunted to near-extinction and use of the natural material has been banned. Very good imitations of genuine tortoiseshell are now made of plastic and used in similar applications. 2. Pattern similar to genuine tortoiseshell used for printed fabrics and plastic eyeglass frames or other accessories.

tortoiseshell glasses See under EYEWEAR.

tote See under HANDBAGS AND RELATED ACCESSORIES.

totes See under FOOTWEAR.

toupée See under WIGS AND HAIRPIECES.

touring cap See under HEADWEAR.

tourmaline See under GEMS, GEM CUTS, AND SETTINGS.

tournure See under UNDERGARMENTS: BUSTLE.

tournure and petticoat See under UNDERGARMENTS: BUSTLE.

tournure corset See under UNDERGARMENTS.

tow coat See under COATS AND JACKETS.

tower See under WIGS AND HAIRPIECES.

toyo (toe-yow') Hat-body material made of cellophane-coated rice paper of fine quality produced in Japan (Okinawa) and Taiwan.

track See under FOOTWEAR and SHORTS: ATHLETIC SHORTS.

track pants See under PANTS.

trade association Nonprofit organization that does any or all of the following: conducts research for an industry, promotes the interests of an industry, or provides educational services on behalf of member companies from that industry. Examples include the American Textile Machinery Association, National Retail Federation, or the Embroidery Trade Association.

trade discounts and allowances A percentage subtracted from the suggested retail price or list price that is given to retailers to arrive at the tentative purchase price or wholesale price charged to a retailer by the manufacturer.

trademark Any word, name, or symbol that has been adopted and used by the owner to identify a product and distinguish it from others. When trademarks have been registered they may not be used for the same type of product by any other individual or firm and are written with the symbol ® or ™.

trade name A name that a business assigns to a product for purposes of identification in promotion and commence. Trade names have no legal protection, unlike registered TRADEMARKS.

trade show Exposition sponsored by trade associations, apparel marts, and/or promotional companies that allows companies to promote their newest products to prospective customers.

trafalgar turban See under HEADWEAR.

tragedy mask Mask with corners of mouth turned down, used in Greek theater.

trail shorts See under SHORTS: CAMP SHORTS and CARGO SHORTS.

train Elongated back portion of woman's skirt that lies on the floor and is pulled along behind by wearer. Worn for formal evenings, especially in late 19th and early 20th c., and traditionally a part of bridal gowns. Dates from Middle Ages, when length of train worn only at court indicated rank.

trainer heels See under FOOTWEAR: KITTEN HEELS.

training bra See under UNDERGARMENTS: TEEN BRA.

tramezza stitched welting See under FOOTWEAR.

trank See under GLOVES AND GLOVE CONSTRUCTION.

transformation See under WIGS AND HAIRPIECES.

transition lenses See under introduction to EYEWEAR.

translucent *adj.* Describes the quality of being semitransparent, as applied to gems and fabrics.

transparent *adj.* Describes gems and fabrics through which light passes so that object behind may be seen clearly.

∞**transparent dress** Dress worn during the last quarter of the 17th c. consisting of a layer of lace over a complete dress of gold or brocade. Lace was usually black *point d'Angleterre.*

†**transparent velvet** Lightweight velvet that reflects light, thereby changing color to be somewhat iridescent. Has excellent draping qualities. Usually made with rayon pile, and given a crush-resistant finish.

trapeze dress See under DRESSES.

trapeze top See under BLOUSES AND TOPS.

trapunto (tra-poont′-oh) Type of quilting in which design is outlined and then stuffed from the back of the fabric to achieve a raised or embossed effect.

travel bag See under HANDBAGS AND RELATED ACCESSORIES: FLIGHT BAG.

travel coat See under SLEEPWEAR AND LOUNGEWEAR.

traveling bag See under HANDBAGS AND RELATED ACCESSORIES.

traveling wig See under WIG: CAMPAIGN WIG.

trench coat See under COATS AND JACKETS.

trench collar/trench coat collar See under NECKLINES AND COLLARS.

trenchdress See under DRESSES.

trencher cap See under ACADEMIC COSTUME: MORTARBOARD.

trencher hat See under HEADWEAR.

trend See under FASHION TREND.

trend research Determining current directions for color, fabric, and fashions by reading the fashion press, subscribing to trend forecasting services, SHOPPING THE MARKET, and otherwise keeping up with the latest fashion developments.

†**triacetate** (try-ass′-eh-tate) Manufactured fiber regenerated through chemical treatment from wood chips or very short cotton fibers. Used for wearing apparel. Relatively little triacetate is produced at present, none in the U.S.

Triangle Shirtwaist Fire A fire at the New York City women's garment manufacturing shop, Triangle Waist Co., on March 25, 1911, that took 146 workers' lives. Public opinion was consequently aroused to demand reforms for fire protection, better working conditions, sanitation, and unionization.

trickle-across theory of fashion change A theory that explains how digital technology has democratized fashion by making runway styles available for all to see before they appear in stores and giving lower-priced brands a window of opportunity to knock off runway looks, offering similar looks at lower prices in the same season.

trickle-down theory of fashion change The theory that fashion changes result from the initial adoption of new and innovative styles by the upper socioeconomic classes and the subsequent imitation of these styles by lower socioeconomic classes. Compare with BOTTOM-UP THEORY OF FASHION CHANGE.

trickle-up theory of fashion change A theory that explains the phenomenon of street fashions that originate with avant-garde consumer groups rather than a designer or product developer. These unique looks are put together from items found in resale stores and at flea markets and army surplus stores.

tricorn/tricorne See under HEADWEAR.

†**tricot** (tree′-co) 1. Warp-knit fabric made with two sets of yarns characterized by fine vertical WALES on the face and crosswise ribs on the back. When made with one set of yarns, it is called **single-bar tricot. Two-bar tricot,** made with yarns crossing, is run-resistant. Also called *double warp tricot, glove silk.* **Three-bar tricot** has an openwork effect. Manufactured fibers are used—with acetate tricot used frequently for backing on bonded knits. 2. See EMBROIDERIES AND SEWING STITCHES: AFGHAN STITCH. *Der.* French, *tricoter,* "to knot."

tricot stitch See under EMBROIDERIES AND SEWING STITCHES: AFGHAN STITCH.

trifocals See under EYEWEAR.

trilby See under HEADWEAR.

trim Decorative material, surface treatment, or detail such as buttons, braids, and lace, that are used to embellish a garment.

triple-needle toe See under FOOTWEAR: NEEDLE TOE.

triple stitchdown See under FOOTWEAR: STITCHDOWN SHOE CONSTRUCTION.

triplex See under HANDBAGS AND RELATED ACCESSORIES.

tri-suit See under ACTIVEWEAR.

trollopee See under SLEEPWEAR AND LOUNGEWEAR: SLAMMERKIN.

trompe l'oeil (trump' loy) Descriptive of embroidery and painting that create an optical illusion; also applied to dress and clothing. *Der.* French, "to fool the eye."

trompeurs See under LIARS.

trooper cap See under HEADWEAR.

†tropical suiting Lightweight fabric, originally used for men's summer suits, now used for suits for all seasons. Usually tightly woven of highly twisted yarns.

†tropical worsted Lightweight WORSTED FABRIC (see WOOLEN) made in an open weave to permit circulation of air. Finished by removing surface fibers to give a clear finish. Packs well and is popular for dresses and suits for cooler days in the summer.

trousers See under PANTS.

trouser skirt See under SKIRTS.

trouser sock See under HOSIERY: KNEE-HI SOCK.

trouses/trowses See under UNDERGARMENTS.

∞trousses (trouz) French TIGHTS (see under HOSIERY) worn by pages and knights of king's order in 17th c.

trucker's apron See under APRONS.

trucker's cap See under HEADWEAR.

trumpet *adj.* Describes garments or garment parts that flare out at the bottom. Their shape is like that of the musical instrument the trumpet. See under DRESSES: TRUMPET DRESS; SHOULDERS AND SLEEVES: TRUMPET SLEEVE; and SKIRTS: TRUMPET SKIRT.

trumpet dress See under DRESSES.

∞trunk hose A garment related to both BREECHES and CHAUSSE. About mid-16th c., chausses were divided into two parts—the upper part then being called *haut de chausses,* and subsequently called *trunk hose* or **upper stocks.** At the same time the term BREECHES was used synonymously with trunk hose, these being a man's garment covering the legs to the middle of the thigh or to the knee. The designation of trunk hose was generic, and many variations existed. Some were tight, others were loose-fitting or heavily padded with BOMBAST. Often they were PANED. Padded trunk hose included **barrel hose** that were cut very full and stuffed with horsehair or other materials and worn by men between 1570 and 1620. **Gregs** (also spelled *gregues*) were first worn in last quarter of 16th c. and were usually slashed to reveal the lining and elaborately trimmed with gold and silver. Synonyms: *gallygaskins, gally-gascoynes,* or *gaskins.* **Round hose** were described as onion-shaped and padded. In English colloquial usage of the time, round hose were sometimes called *Spanish kettledrums.* **Boulogne** (boo-lawn'-yah) **hose** was an English term for round or oval trunk hose worn from 1550 to 1660. Frequently PANED and worn with CANIONS, after 1570, they were also called *bullion-hose* or *French hose.* **Venetians,** worn from 1570 to 1620 and most fashionable in 1580s, were pear-shaped, often padded, and fastened below knee by garter-ribbons. When tightly fitted, they were called **venetian galligascoines, galligaskins,** or **chausses en tonnelet** (sho sawn ton-leh'). Also called *trusses* and *Italian hose.* When voluminous throughout, they were called **Venetian slops. Slops** or **slivings** were knee-length, unpadded trunk hose, worn during second half of 16th and early 17th c. Those large at the top, without a band at hem, and reaching just to knees were known as **small slops** and required for Cambridge University students in England from 1585 to about 1610. Other types included **scaling hose** or *scalings,* similar to Venetians, popular in latter half of 16th c. **A pair of buffins,** was an English colloquial term for men's trunk hose similar to slops that were worn in 16th c. **Pluderhose** were German and Swiss unpadded trunk hose worn in latter half of 16th c. Characterized by broad slashes with loose silk linings protruding, they were also called *almain hose* and *german hose.*

trunk hose: melon-shaped, c. 1572

trunk hose: venetians, c. 1582

trunks 1. See under ACTIVEWEAR. 2. See under TRUNK HOSE. 3. See under UNDERGARMENTS. 4. See under SHORTS.

trunk show A show of a complete apparel line in a retail store that is presented for customers and/or store personnel by a vendor or designer. In this way, even if the store has not chosen to buy the entire line, customers and salespersons can become familiar with the line.

trunk sleeve See under SHOULDERS AND SLEEVES: CANNON SLEEVE.

∞truss *v.* To tie up, used from 14th c. to about 1630. Phrase "to truss the points" meant to fasten HOSE to TRUNK

HOSE and DOUBLET by means of POINTS (lacers), which ended in decorative metal tip called an AGLET.

trusses See under TRUNK HOSE.

T-shirt 1. See under SHIRTS. 2. See under UNDERGARMENTS. 3. See under SLEEPWEAR AND LOUNGEWEAR.

T-shirt dress See under DRESSES.

tsitsith (*zizith*) (zit-zith′) Tassel, usually blue, worn on prayer shawl called TALLITH or on the ARBA KANFOTH by Jewish men.

T-strap See under FOOTWEAR.

tube See under UNDERGARMENTS: TUBE BRA; HOSIERY: TUBE SOCKS; and BLOUSES AND TOPS: TUBE TOP.

tubular knit See under CIRCULAR KNIT.

tuck/tucks See under CLOTHING CONSTRUCTION DETAILS.

tucked seam See under CLOTHING CONSTRUCTION DETAILS.

tucker See under NECKLINES AND COLLARS.

tudor cape See under CAPES, CLOAKS, AND SHAWLS.

tuft Variant of POMPON; a cluster of threads or fibers tied together to form a ball.

tulip *adj.* Describes apparel or parts of apparel that are shaped like the tulip flower. See under SHOULDERS AND SLEEVES: TULIP SLEEVE and SKIRTS: BUBBLE SKIRT.

†**tulle** (tool) Fine, sheer, net fabric made of silk, nylon, or rayon with hexagonal holes. Used unstarched for wedding veils and millinery and starched for ballet costumes. In the 18th c., all hexagonal netlike fabrics were called by this name. *Der.* First made in 1768 in England by machine; in 1817, a factory was opened in the city of Tulle, France.

tulle embroidery See under EMBROIDERIES AND SEWING STITCHES.

tunic 1. *n.* Simple garment worn since ancient times that is T-shaped with openings for the head and arms. Lengths can vary. 2. *n.* Garment that ends somewhere between the hip and the calf and is designed to be worn over another garment such as pants, skirt, bloomers, or dress. 3. *adj.* Used to describe a garment similar to a tunic. See under DRESSES: TUNIC DRESS; SWIMWEAR: TUNIC SWIMSUIT; BLOUSES AND TOPS: TUNIC BLOUSE; JUMPERS: TUNIC JUMPER; SKIRTS: TUNIC SKIRT; and SLEEPWEAR AND LOUNGEWEAR: TUNIC PAJAMAS.

tunic #1

∞**tunic à la mameluke** (mah′-meh-luke′) Woman's knee-length tunic with long sleeves fashionable at beginning of 19th c. Later called *tunique à la juive.* Inspired by Napoleon's Egyptian campaign, 1798. *Der.* Mamelukes were originally slaves brought to Egypt in 19th c., later trained as soldiers. Ruled Egypt from 1250 to 1517 and remained powerful until 1811 under Turkish viceroys.

∞**tunic à la romaine** (ro-main′) Tunic, worn by women in late 18th c., that was full-length, high-waisted, long-sleeved, and made of gauze or lawn.

tunic dress See under DRESSES.

tunnel loops Loops of matching fabric placed at waistband of pants or skirt for belt to pull through. Loops may be 1″ to 3″ wide—larger than regular belt loops.

tunnel waistline See under WAISTLINES: DRAWSTRING WAISTLINE.

turban See under HEADWEAR.

turkey bonnet See under HEADWEAR.

turkey gown ∞1. Long, black velvet gown bordered with lynx and decorated with 77 gold- and black-enameled buttons made for Henry VIII, who ruled England from 1515 to 1548. 2. Long gown open in front with long narrow sleeves slit above elbow so arm could come through, remainder of sleeve hung down. Worn since 1530s, becoming style for Puritan ministers.

turkish polonaise See under DRESSES: IRISH POLONAISE.

turkish trousers See under PANTS: HAREM PANTS.

turnaround time The lead time required for making, dyeing, and finishing fabric in order to meet the delivery date determined by the production schedule.

turndown collar See under NECKLINES AND COLLARS.

turned-back cuff See under CUFFS.

turned-shoe construction See under FOOTWEAR.

turnip pants See under PANTS.

turnover Describes how many times stock is sold and replaced within a period of time.

turnover collar See under NECKLINES AND COLLARS.

turn-ups See under PANTS.

turquoise See under GEMS, GEM CUTS, AND SETTINGS.

∞**turret bodice** Bodice with peplum, cut in square tabs below waistline, popular in early 1880s.

turtleneck See under NECKLINES AND COLLARS and SWEATERS.

turtleneck convertible collar See under NECKLINES AND COLLARS.

turtleneck cossack shirt See under SHIRTS: COSSACK SHIRT.

†**tussah** (tuss′-ah) (*tasar, tusser, tussas, tussus*) Coarse, irregular silk, from wild Asian silkworms, used to make PONGEE and SHANTUNG. The silkworm, the fiber, the yarn, and also

the fabric made from the yarn are all called by this name. *Der.* Hindu, *tasar,* from the Sanskirt *trasara,* "a shuttle."

tutu 1. Ballet dancer's costume designed in 1832 by Eugene Lami for Maria Taglioni, a great Italian ballerina of the Romantic period. Consisted of a tight-fitting, bare-shouldered bodice worn with a bell-shaped, sheer, white gathered skirt reaching midway between knee and ankle. 2. Multilayered very short skirt of NET or TULLE. Pale pink *tights* were worn underneath and pale pink satin *ballet slippers* were worn with both versions.

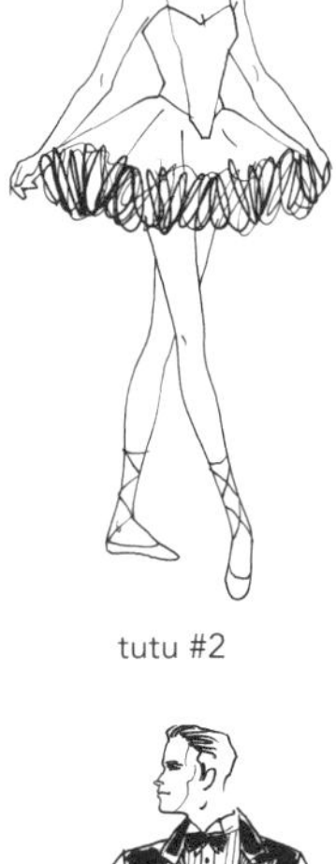
tutu #2

tutulus See under HEADWEAR.

tuxedo 1. See under COATS AND JACKETS. 2. Man's semiformal, fingertip-length jacket and pants made with satin or faille lapels and side stripes on pants. Made in black or midnight blue in winter, white jacket with dark pants in summer. Since the 1960s, sometimes made in other colors or plaids. Worn with CUMMERBUND (see under BELTS) and black BOW TIE (see under TIES). Abbreviated as *tux.* Also called *black tie.* The origin of this tailless dinner jacket are unclear. It appears that the Prince of Wales may have been the first to wear the jacket around 1865. Its name in American usage derives from the wearing of the style by residents of an upperclass enclave, Tuxedo Park, NY, around 1886. 3. *adj.* Describes garments like those worn with a tuxedo or that derive from the tuxedo style. See under BLOUSES AND TOPS: TUXEDO BLOUSE; COATS AND JACKETS: TUXEDO JACKET; FOOTWEAR: TUXEDO PUMP; NECKLINES AND COLLARS: TUXEDO COLLAR; PANTS: TUXEDO PANTS; SHIRTS: TUXEDO SHIRT; and SWEATERS: TUXEDO SWEATER.

tuxedo #2

†tweed Made in plain, twill, or herringbone weave in various weights for coats, jackets, and suits. *Der.* Scottish, *tweed,* meaning "twill," because they were at first hand-loomed in homes along the Tweed River in Scotland. See under COATS AND JACKETS: TWEED JACKET.

tweens Apparel targeted to appeal to preteen girls and younger teen customers that is age-appropriate and without sexual overtones. Also referred to as *tween market.*

twenties bob See under HAIRSTYLES: BOB.

twenties /twenties style See under FLAPPER.

twillet See under SLEEPWEAR AND LOUNGEWEAR: TOILET.

twill fabric/twills Fabrics made with the TWILL WEAVE.

†twill weave Basic weave characterized by diagonal wales (see WALE #1) produced by staggering the points of intersection of lengthwise and crosswise yarns. Wales generally run upward from left to right, called **right-hand twill,** or from lower right to upper left, **left-hand twill.** Both make a firm, durable fabric (e.g., DENIM, TICKING, SERGE, and GABARDINE).

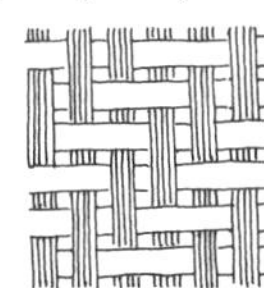
right-hand twill weave diagram

twin set 1. See under BLOUSES AND TOPS. 2. See under SWEATERS: SWEATER SET.

two-bar tricot See under TRICOT.

two-ply yarn See under SINGLE YARN.

two-sided line stitch See under EMBROIDERIES AND SEWING STITCHES: DOUBLE-RUNNING STITCH.

two-way stretch foundation See under UNDERGARMENTS.

tye 1. See under WIGS AND HAIRPIECES. 2. See under APRONS.

tying contract Illegal practice in which retailers are required to buy unwanted merchandise in order to be able to purchase desired other merchandise.

Tyrolean (tee-roll'-ee-an) *adj.* Describes the type of dress worn by natives of Austrian Tyrol and Bavarian region, including DIRNDL SKIRTS (see under SKIRTS), embroidered vests, and aprons worn by women; LEDERHOSEN, knee socks, and feather-trimmed felt ALPINE HATS (see under HEADWEAR), worn by men. These styles have inspired specific items of fashionable dress such as dirndl skirts and Alpine hats. *Der.* Named for alpine region in Austria and Bavaria called the "Tyrol."

Tyrolean hat See under HEADWEAR: ALPINE HAT.

Ubangi See under JEWELRY and under NECKLINES AND COLLARS.

Ugg boot See under FOOTWEAR.

ugly See under HEADWEAR.

ulster See under COATS AND JACKETS.

†ultrafine fiber Manufactured filament fiber that measures 0.01 denier per filament or less.

ultra-sheer pantyhose See under HOSIERY: SHEER HOSE.

ultrasonic sewing Sewing accomplished by special machines using ultrasonic sound waves that create heat as a result of vibrations that fuses heat-sensitive fabrics together without the use of needles and thread. Advantages: eliminates use of needles and thread, also eliminates seam slippage.

†Ultrasuede® Registered trademark for luxury suedelike fabric made of 60 percent polyester and 40 percent nonfibrous urethane in a porous sheet material. Used in a wide variety of apparel.

umbrella brim See under HEADWEAR.

umbrella drawers See under UNDERGARMENTS.

umbrella-pleated skirt See under SKIRTS.

umbrella pleats See under CLOTHING CONSTRUCTION DETAILS.

UMBRELLAS AND PARASOLS

umbrella Accessory used as a protection against the rain or sun; a round, flat, or convex plate-like fabric canopy, originally served to shade the person beneath from the sun. It had six to sixteen collapsible ribs mounted at the top of a handle. In early Egyptian, Assyrian, Indian, and African civilizations and in the Catholic Church throughout the Middle Ages, this device was a sign of rank. By the early 16th c., it had also become a fashionable novelty to protect against the sun. Occasional mention is made in the early 17th c. of the umbrella as protection against rain, however it was only at the end of that century that waterproof umbrellas came into widespread use. By 1800 a distinction was made in English usage between an umbrella, which was waterproof and used against rain, and a **parasol,** which was a sunshade and often highly decorative. Parasols were very important accessories throughout the 19th c. and into the early 20th c., after which they gradually went out of fashion while the utilitarian umbrella continued to be used against the rain. *Der.* from the Italian *umbra,* meaning shade. Parasol derives from *para,* against, *sol,* the sun.

bell umbrella Dome-shaped umbrella of transparent plastic or of fabric with a transparent plastic window that is deeper than most umbrellas and therefore protects the face. Also called a *bell-shaped umbrella* or a *dome umbrella.*

∞carriage parasol Small parasol intended to be carried and used when riding in a horse-drawn carriage. It had either a folding or short handle. Compare to UMBRELLAS AND PARASOLS: WALKING PARASOL.

carriage parasol

coquette parasol See under UMBRELLAS AND PARASOLS: MARQUISE.

dome umbrella See under UMBRELLAS AND PARASOLS: BELL UMBRELLA.

∞en tous cas (on too′ kah) Nickname for a parasol, which could also be used as an umbrella, carried about 1870. *Der.* French, "in any case."

fan parasol See under UMBRELLAS AND PARASOLS: MARQUISE.

∞gamp 19th-c. slang for umbrella. *Der.* Named after Mrs. Sarah Gamp, a character in Charles Dickens's 1843 novel *Martin Chuzzlewit.*

∞gingham 19th-c. colloquial usage for an umbrella. So called because the less expensive types were made out of gingham fabric.

Japanese parasol Parasol or umbrella made of brightly colored glazed paper with bamboo ribs. Also made of oiled silk for wet weather.

∞marquise (mar-keez′) Parasol with a hinge at the top that allowed the top to be tilted in different directions. Also called *coquette* (kok-ett′) or *fan parasol* or, in the 1850s, *parasol à la Pompadour. Der.* Thought to have been invented by the Marquise de Pompadour, mistress of King Louis XIV of France.

pagoda parasol Parasol cover shaped like the roof of a Chinese temple (pagoda).

parasol See under introduction to UMBRELLAS AND PARASOLS.

parasol à la Pompadour See under UMBRELLAS AND PARASOLS: MARQUISE.

∞**sylphide parasol** (syl-feed′) Patented in 1844, this parasol had a spring at the end of the handle that allowed the shade to be closed by the hand holding it. It had a metal shaft, whalebone ribs, and a handle and point of carved ivory. The cover was usually made of silk taffeta fringed with lace.

∞**walking parasol** Parasol with a long stick or handle that was meant to be carried while walking. Compare to UMBRELLAS AND PARASOLS: CARRIAGE PARASOL.

walking parasol

---

umbrella tote See under HANDBAGS AND RELATED ACCESSORIES.

umbril See under ARMOR: BURGONET.

†**unbleached muslin** Coarse, heavily-sized cotton utility fabric woven in a plain weave of carded yarns and sold in the unbleached or gray state (see GRAY GOODS). Used by fashion designers when draping garments on DRESS FORMS. After garment is designed, it is taken apart and the muslin pieces are used as a pattern. Also used for interfacings in low-quality suits and coats.

underarm dart See under CLOTHING CONSTRUCTION DETAILS: DARTS.

under cap See under HEADWEAR.

under cut See under HAIRSTYLES: BOWL CUT.

underdrawing A well-proportioned pose that can be slid under a page and used as a template to help control proportions and the location of garment details. Also called *lay figure.*

underfur See under FURS.

underlap (extensions on closures) Extension beyond the edge of the bottom layer of a garment that provides additional space for a button or other closure without affecting the finished size of a garment.

underlining Lining variation in which the outer shell fabric and the lining are layered together before the garment is constructed. Used to stabilize shell fabrics or make the shell fabric opaque.

UNDERGARMENTS

undergarment Item of apparel worn under the outer garments. These garments serve many functions. They may protect the outer clothing from being soiled or provide a more comfortable layer between the skin of the wearer and the outer clothing. Those garments serving this purpose are usually made from soft, washable fabrics. Undergarments may serve to give shape to the outer garments either through constricting the body or providing support to the clothing. It is not unusual for several layers of undergarments to be worn at the same time. Although generally unseen, parts of undergarments may sometimes be a visible element of the costume. Also called *underwear.*

all-in-one See under UNDERGARMENTS: FOUNDATION.

∞**amazon corset** English corset worn for riding in mid-19th c. Made with elastic lacings that shortened the garment by three inches when a hidden cord was pulled.

∞**apollo corset** Waist cincher stiffened with whalebone, worn by both men and women about 1810. When worn by English dandies of Regency period (1810–1820), sometimes called a *brummell bodice* or *cumberland corset.*

athletic shirt/A-shirt Man's sleeveless undershirt with low, round neckline, also worn for gym and sports.

backless bra Bra made with cups but no back. Elastic straps fasten at shoulder and at bottom of bra. These are worn crossed in back, brought around waistline, and hooked in center front. Shoulder straps may be unhooked and fastened at back of neck in halter style.

∞**balmoral petticoat** Colored petticoat, originally red with wide decorative black band mitered to form squared half frames, which projected below a looped-up outer skirt, worn in mid-1860s.

band briefs Short underpants finished at the legs with knitted bands. Also called *band-leg panties.*

bandeau slip See under UNDERGARMENTS: BRA-SLIP.

band-leg panties See under UNDERGARMENTS: BAND BRIEFS.

bare bra Bra constructed of a framework of straps with sewn-in uplift bands. There is no fabric over upper part of breasts.

∞**bearer** Padded roll worn under the back of a skirt by women from second half of 17th and early 18th c. Similar to a BUSTLE (see under UNDERGARMENTS).

∞**bell hoop** Dome-shaped, hoop-skirt petticoat popular in England from about 1710 to 1780. Also called *cupola coat.*

bias slip Slip cut on the diagonal of the fabric. This creates a closer fit, as the fabric stretches to conform to the movements of the body. Introduced in the 1920s, popularized in the 1930s, and a classic since.

bias slip

bikini brief Man's brief, low-rise underwear made in all colors and styles of knit cotton or manufactured fiber yarns.

bikini brief

bikini panties Below-the-navel brief underpants introduced in early 1960s, modeled after BIKINI SWIMSUIT (see under SWIMWEAR).

bloomers Full panty with thigh-length leg gathered into elastic. Popular since 1920s for little girls and worn by older women until c. 1930s. *Der.* Named for Amelia Jenks Bloomer, early-19th-c. American reformer who wore full, gathered pants instead of a skirt when lecturing. Also see under BLOOMER COSTUME.

blouse-slip Combination slip and blouse with top cut like a blouse and lower part serving as a slip under the skirt. Also called *slip-blouse.*

bodice See under UNDERGARMENTS: PAIR OF BODIES.

body briefer 1. Two-way stretch garment made in panty style without garters for hose. Usually made in SPANDEX powernet, sometimes with lace inserts for bra. 2. Lace-trimmed garment styled like a TEDDY (see under UNDERGARMENTS) with high-cut legs made of lightweight stretch fabric and with a V- or camisole-type top.

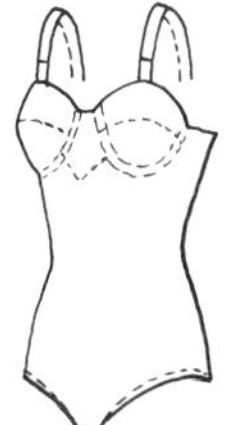
body briefer #1

bodyshapers Fashion business designation of the undergarments designed to control and support the figure. Also called *shapewear.*

boned foundation Foundation garment in which thin metal or plastic strips called "bones" have been inserted for stiffening in order to make a firm garment with more control. *Der.* So called because these bones were originally made of whalebone. Also see under CLOTHING CONSTRUCTION DETAILS: STAY #1.

bouffant petticoat (boo-fahnt') Any full petticoat made with gores or ruffles for wearing under a wide-skirted dress.

bourrelet See under UNDERGARMENTS: BUM ROLL.

boxer pants Women's and children's loose-legged underpants of pull-on type.

boxer shorts Somewhat loose-fitting, short underpants worn by men and boys. Originally made of woven fabric but now also made in knits. *Der.* Similar to men's shorts worn for the sport of boxing.

boxer shorts

bra/brassiere Bra is shortened form of word *brassiere,* a word first used in 1905 for a shaped undergarment worn by women to mold and support the breasts. Cup sizes range from AA–JJ with double letter sizes for A, F, G, H, and J. Usually consists of two cups held in place with straps over the shoulders and elastic in center back. Also called a *bandeau* (band-oh'), although a bandeau was usually made without darts or other shaping. Also see under UNDERGARMENTS: DEBEVOISE BRASSIERE.

bra cups Component used to provide shape and support to the bustline of garments such as swimsuits and evening gowns

braies See in alphabetical listing.

bra-slip Slip made with a fitted top. One garment replaces two—the bra and the slip. Popular in 1960s and after. Also called *bandeau slip.*

briefs 1. Woman's or girl's very short underpants, sometimes made of control-stretch fabric. 2. Tight-fitting short knitted underpants worn by men and boys.

brummell bodice See under UNDERGARMENTS: APOLLO CORSET.

built-in bra Bra used in swimsuits and sundresses as a part of the structure of the clothing.

built-up slip Slip, made with U-neckline, deep armholes, and wide straps. May be worn as lining for a sheer dress.

∞**bum roll** Padded roll worn around the hips to hold the skirt out into the French farthingale style, a fashion of the 16th and early 17th c. See under FARTHINGALE. Also called *bourrelet* (bour'-lay).

bum roll c. 1600

bustier (boo-ste'-yay) One-piece support garment that is a combination bra and waist cincher. Reaches to a few inches below the waist or to the hips. Frequently made without straps and with or without removable garters, it has flexible boning and is sometimes lace trimmed. Also called *torsolette.*

bustier bra (boo-ste'-yay) Tight-fitted strapless bra usually waist length and often laced up the front. Sometimes used for the top of a dress.

bustle (bus'-sel) Pad, cushion, or arrangement of steel springs creating a rounded projection below the waist at the back of woman's dress. Although not called *bustle* until about 1830, skirts with back fullness had been worn earlier and were called by names such as *bum roll, cork rump, frisk, nelson, cushion pad, cushionet,* or *rump furbelow,* which are defined under the category of UNDERGARMENTS. Bustles that resembled a small pad and tied around the waist were worn from the 1830s to the 1850s but were not used with hoopskirts in the 1850s and 1860s. By 1870, bustles were once again used to support back fullness. Initially, they tended to use hoops and back fullness, as in the **crinolette** (krin-o-let'), a smaller form of woman's CAGE PETTICOAT (see under UNDERGARMENTS: HOOPS) with steel half-hoops only in back and having CRINOLINE or HORSEHAIR ruffles forming a bustle in the back. They were worn from late 1860s to 1870s and revived in 1883. The **eugénie petticoat** (yoo-je′-nee), worn in the early 1870s, was made full length in back and a little below the waist in front. Semicircular steel *hoops* in the back and *bustle* held out skirt in the back. (*Der.* Named for Eugénie, Empress of France [1853–1871].) A **pannier crinoline** was an underskirt in 1870s for extending the dress that combined a CAGE PETTICOAT with a BUSTLE. Also called *Thomson's pannier crinoline.* The **crinoline and tournure** was a stiffened petticoat with bustle added in back worn under dresses in late 1860s. A **plumet petticoat** was a narrow, back-buttoned petticoat of 1870s with ruffles forming bustle at back and continuing to form a detachable train. The term **tournure** (toor-nure′) was applied either to a bustle of early 1870s made from six rows of horsehair ruffles mounted on a calico foundation stiffened with whalebone and attached to a band around the waist that tied in front; or, during a short period around 1876 to 1882, it was applied to a foundation piece that hung down back from waist, with ruffles at hem to hold out the train of a dress. It had ties to fasten in front at intervals. In the **tournure and petticoat,** a bustle was combined with petticoat. Worn from about 1875 to 1885, some were made all in one piece and some with buttons and buttonholes at hip-level so that the tournure or bustle could be used separately or removed. Bustles returned in the 1880s and were seen until the 1890s. Large bustles included the **haut ton** (oh′ ton), a patented bustle of the late 1880s made of three pendant spirally-coiled springs with small pad at back of waist. It was secured by a belt around the waist that fastened in the front. The **langtry bustle** was a patented, lightweight, collapsible bustle, worn in late 1880s and was made of a series of semicircular hoops fastened to a *stay* on either side. (*Der.* Named after actress *Lillie Langtry.*) As bustles diminished in size in the late 1800s, these smaller types developed: **cushion pad,** a tiny bustle stuffed with horsehair worn in late 19th c.; and the **figure improver,** a small bustle worn by women in the 1890s. Throughout the period from 1849 to the 1880s, **dress improver** was a polite term for bustle. Another synonym was *tournure.* Since 1900, back fullness in skirts has appeared occasionally, particularly for evening dress, but never again have skirts had the extreme fullness of the 19th c. bustle styles.

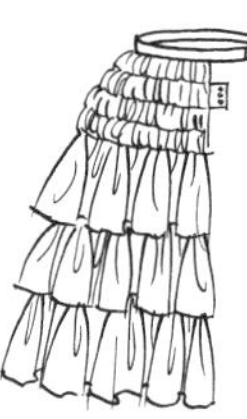

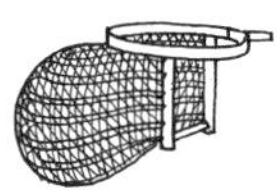

bustles

B.V.D.'s® See under UNDERGARMENTS: ENVELOPE COMBINATION.

cadoro bra Decorative metal bra worn with scarf or bikini underneath, consisting of metal cups, frequently filigreed, held on with chains. Introduced in late 1960s as an item of body jewelry.

cage See under UNDERGARMENTS: HOOPS.

cage-americaine See under UNDERGARMENTS: HOOPS.

cage empire See under UNDERGARMENTS: HOOPS.

cage petticoat See under UNDERGARMENTS: HOOPS.

camisa See under UNDERGARMENTS: CHEMISE.

camise See under UNDERGARMENTS: CHEMISE.

camisette (ka-mee-sett′) Minimal support foundation with a natural bra top made close-fitting to hips with long attached garters. Sometimes worn with bikini underpants.

camisole (kam′-ih-sole) 1. Short underbodice or vest with built-up straps worn over corset or stays. Introduced in early 1800s. Also called *chemise, corset cover,* and *petticoat bodice.* 2. For lingerie, used to describe a waist-length, gathered, straight-cut top with straps, trimmed with lace or embroidery. Worn with a petticoat under a sheer blouse in late 19th and early 20th c. 3. Contemporary, sleeveless undergarment that is worn under a sheer blouse. It can be made in many different styles and lengths that can range from waist to hip.

camisole #3

camisole slip (kam′-ih-sole) Slip with a lace or embroidered top to be worn under a sheer blouse—often cut straight across at neckline with wide straps.

cami-tap set See under UNDERGARMENTS: TAP PANTY.

capri-length panty-girdle See under UNDERGARMENTS: GIRDLE.

chemise (shem-eze′) (synonyms and alternate spellings used at various times: *camise, camisia, cames, kemes, kemise, kemse, robe linge*) Linen garment worn next to the skin by men and women in Middle Ages. Made with long sleeves, it was straight-hanging and as long as the garment that was worn over it. By 14th c. a man's chemise was called *shirt* or *sherte* and a woman's chemise, a *smock.* In 17th c. called *shift,* and by the late 18th c. the term *chemise* came back into English from French and continued in use in the 19th c., at which time it was generally made of cotton or linen, had a low round neck, was short-sleeved, about calf-length, and sometimes trimmed with lace and embroidered.

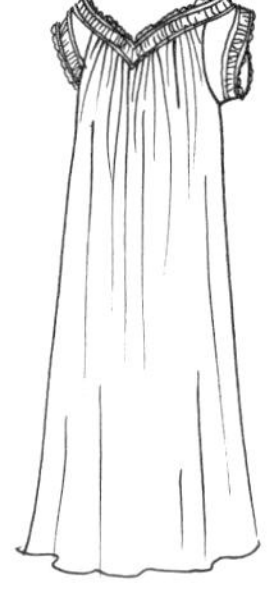

chemise c. 1900

chemise slip Thigh-length slip of the late 1960s, it hangs straight and is not fitted.

∞**colobium** (ko-loh'-bee-um) Type of undertunic or undershirt worn in ancient Rome and during the Middle Ages; also called a *sherte* by Anglo Saxons.

combinations 1. Underwear in which two garments (e.g., chemise and drawers or chemise and petticoat) are combined to make one. Introduced in the mid-19th c. 2. In 1920s, name for a UNION SUIT for women. See under UNDERGARMENTS.

combination c. 1920s

contour bra Rounded bra padded with fiberfill or foam.

control-brief See under UNDERGARMENTS: GARTER BRIEF.

control pants BRIEFS, LONG-LEG PANTY, GIRDLE, or PANTS LINERS (see under UNDERGARMENTS) knitted with elastomeric yarns (see under ELASTOMER) to provide support.

∞**cork rump** Bustle of late 18th c. made in shape of a crescent and stuffed with cork.

corps à baleine See under UNDERGARMENTS: CORPS PIQUÉ #2.

∞**corps piqué** (cor pe-kay') 1. Quilted camisole with a busk of varnished wood used as stiffening, first worn in France. 2. In 17th and 18th c., a tightly laced underbodice stiffened with whalebones and held on with shoulder straps. Same as French *corps à baleine* (cor ah bah-lehn').

corselet (kors-let') Foundation with firm support achieved by boning, power-net side panels, and front panel of no-stretch nylon taffeta. Sometimes has an inner belt that hooks separately to help flatten abdomen. Bra top is often of nylon lace with *marquisette* (mar-kee-set') lining and adjustable shoulder straps. Foundation is fastened by hooks underneath zipper and has six garters. Appearing first in America in 1921 and then spelled *corsellette.* Also see alphabetical listing.

corset Woman's one-piece sleeveless and often strapless garment for shaping the figure. Earlier versions laced shut, while in late 19th and 20th c. corsets often closed with hooks. Term comes into use in the 19th c. and is synonymous with STAYS (see under UNDERGARMENTS). The shape of the corset changes with the current fashionable silhouette. From 1820s to 1930s generally it is a heavily boned, rigid garment. Since 1940s made of lighter-weight elasticized fabrics and more likely to be called a GIRDLE OR FOUNDATION garment (see under UNDERGARMENTS). For named varieties see under UNDERGARMENTS: AMAZON CORSET, CORSET À LA NINON, DEMI-CORSET, EMPIRE STAYS, FOUNDATIONS, and SWANBILL CORSET.

corset

∞**corset à la ninon** (ah lah nee-non') Lightweight corset reaching to hips that laced up the back and was designed to wear under empire style dresses in 1810.

corset cover See under UNDERGARMENTS: CAMISOLE #1.

∞**criardes** (kree-ards) Underskirt of gummed linen puffed out at the sides, forerunner of panniers. *Der.* French, "crying or scolding" because the petticoat creaked as the woman walked.

crinolette See under UNDERGARMENTS: BUSTLE.

crinoline (krin'-oh-lyn) 1. Stiffened petticoat intended to hold out a bouffant skirt—may be made of stiff nylon, either plain or ruffled. ∞2. Underskirt, worn in 1840s and 1850s, made of stiff fabric called *crinoline.* Horsehair was often incorporated into the fabric to provide stiffening. 3. Term applied to any underskirt with hoops that support a full skirt. See under UNDERGARMENTS: HOOPS.

crinoline and tournure See under BUSTLE.

crossover bra Bra with reinforced straps, usually of elastic, that form an X in center front.

cuff-top girdle See under UNDERGARMENTS: GIRDLES.

culotte slip (kul-lot') Slip styled like wide underpants cut knee length or shorter.

cumberland corset See under UNDERGARMENTS: APOLLO CORSET.

cupola coat See under UNDERGARMENTS: BELL HOOP.

∞**cushionet** BUSTLE (see under UNDERGARMENTS) worn with the FARTHINGALE from 1560 to 1630s that raised the back of a skirt. Also spelled *quissionet.*

cushion pad See under UNDERGARMENTS: BUSTLE.

dance set See under UNDERGARMENTS: STEP-INS.

DeBevoise brassiere (deh bev-waz' brah-zeer') Sleeveless, low-necked, upper body undergarment, similar to a *corset cover,* reaching to waistline with a point in front and boned to support the bosom. Patented by the DeBevoise Company in Newark, NJ, in early 1900s. Although the firm used the name *brassiere,* it was only in its later models that it produced a garment more like a contemporary bra.

décolleté bra (deh-coll'-eh-tay) Low-cut bra for wear with low necklines.

demi-bra Half bra that exposes upper part of breasts, for wear with low necklines. Also called *half bra.*

∞**demi-corset** Short corset worn by women in 1830s and 1840s.

dickey Late 18th- and early 19th-c. name for under-petticoat worn by women.

dirndl petticoat (durn'-del) Petticoat flitting smoothly over hips then expanding to gathered fullness to hem. Sometimes made with tiers or ruffles. *Der.* From Austrian Tyrol full-skirted peasant costume.

double-zipper foundation Easy-to-get-into foundation garment with one zipper extending from under arm to below waist, a second zipper on opposite side extends from thigh to waistline.

drawers Underpants. *Der.* Name likely derives from the act of drawing a garment over the lower part of the body and comes into fairly widespread use in the 16th c. Although *drawers* was applied to both men's and women's undergarments, they were not universally worn by women until the 19th c. Although currently still a general term for underpants, by the early 20th c., it has been replaced to a large extent by names for specific kinds of underpants.

∞**dress improver** See under UNDERGARMENTS: BUSTLE.

elastic-leg brief Short panty finished with elastic around the leg rather than a band.

empire jupon See under UNDERGARMENTS: HOOPS.

empire petticoat See under UNDERGARMENTS: HOOPS.

∞**empire stays** (em′-pire or ohm-peer′) Short, high-waisted corset, forerunner of the bra, laced in back for wear with high-waisted EMPIRE DRESSES in the 1890s (see under DRESSES).

∞**empress petticoat** Evening petticoat substituted for the cage petticoat in mid-1860s. Made in gores to fit tightly at the waist and spread to eight yards at the hem, forming a train a yard long and finished with a full gathered flounce beginning at the knees.

∞**envelope combination** Man's *undershirt* and *drawers* combined into one garment—a type of loose-fitting UNION SUIT (see under UNDERGARMENTS)—with open double fold in the back. Worn in the 1920s and 1930s, **B.V.D.**® was the best-known trade name for this garment.

eugénie petticoat See under UNDERGARMENTS: BUSTLE.

evening petticoat Narrow, ankle-length petticoat made with slash in center front or slashes on side seams.

evening slip Slip made to be worn under an evening dress with the cut of the back of the slip and the length conforming to the dress worn over it.

false hips See under UNDERGARMENTS: PANNIERS.

∞**Ferris waist** Trade name for PANTYWAIST (see under UNDERGARMENTS).

figure improver See under UNDERGARMENTS: BUSTLE.

fishnet underwear Lightweight 100-percent-cotton string yarn in netlike weave, acting as an insulator against zero temperatures and 90-degree heat. Originally worn by Norwegian explorers and Norwegian Army. Worn by athletes and by general public as sportswear in 1970s and 1980s.

∞**flannel petticoat** Infant's and woman's winter petticoat worn for warmth under fancy petticoats from 1870s to early 1920s. Usually made of wool flannel, sometimes of cashmere. Also called a *flannel skirt.*

flared-leg pants Longer underpants that flare and hang loose on the leg. Introduced in the 1920s.

foundation Undergarment combining a bra and girdle in one piece to mold the figure. Made with or without straps over the shoulders and optional supporters for the hose. Frequently made with alternating panels of flexible elastic fabric and nonstretch fabric. Also called *all-in-one.* Formerly called a *foundation garment* from about 1920 to early 1980s. Evolved from the CORSET (see under UNDERGARMENTS).

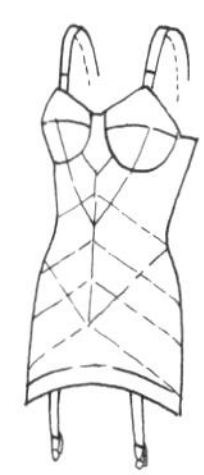
foundation

four-gore slip **1.** Slip with no waistline, cut in four panels with two side seams, one seam down center front, and another in center back. **2.** Slip with a plain top, a waistline seam, and a four-gored flared skirt made to wear with bouffant dresses.

french bra Bra that fits under bust as an uplift but has no cups, worn with low-necked dresses for natural look.

french cinch Short, girdle-like garment designed to accentuate a small waist, starts at the ribs and stops above the hips with or without long garters. Consists of a wide strip of fabric with six or eight vertically placed *bones* or *stays* that hook in front or made of ELASTOMERIC fiber. One version designed by Marcel Rochas, Paris couturier, in 1947 was called a **guepiere** (geh-pih-yair′). Also called *waist-cincher.*

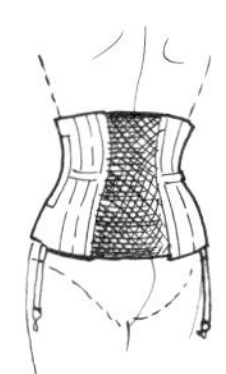
french cinch

∞**french drawers** Flared, knee-length underpants lavishly trimmed with lace, ruffles, and INSERTION at the hems. Set on a band at waist with ties or buttons in back to adjust the size. With split crotch, called *open,* or with seam sewed, called *closed.* Made of fine cambric, lawn, or muslin and worn in late 1890s and early 1900s.

∞**french panties** Short, flared, lacy underpants made of silk and cut with wide legs, worn in 1920s.

∞**frisk** Small BUSTLE worn on the exterior of the skirt by women from 1815 to 1818 to produce the grecian bend posture. Also called *nelson.* See under UNDERGARMENTS: BUSTLE.

front-closure bra A bra that closes in the front, usually with hooks and eyes, sometimes has built-up straps.

garter belt Elasticized band that fits either around the hips or waist, with four or six elastic garters attached to hold up hose. Some are styled like a girdle to give added support. Some are lacy and considered sexy when worn over tiny bikini underpants.

garter belt

garter briefs Short underpants with attached supporters to hold up stockings.

∞**gertrude** Infant's slip worn in early 20th c. styled with round neck, built-up shoulders, and sometimes long in length. Also called a *gertrude skirt.*

girdle Undergarment worn by women and girls designed to mold the lower torso and sometimes the legs. May be flexible two-way stretch or one-way stretch elastic with nonstretchable fabric panels and made with or without garters. Ends anywhere from hip- to ankle-length; when it is called a **long-leg panty-girdle,** made with longer legs to eliminate bulges. **Hi-rise girdle** extends above the waistline, and the **cuff-top girdle** is a pull-on zippered girdle that extends above waistline with wide band of elastic at top. **Pull-on girdle** is made without a zipper or other opening and is pulled on over the hips like panties. **Panty-girdle** has a closed crotch, resembling panties, and comes in lengths from hip joint to ankle. **Capri-length panty-girdle** is a very long two-way stretch panty girdle extending about 4″ below knees. Girdles were introduced in the 1930s as a rigid support garment but contemporary versions range from rigid support to, more commonly, support by means of elastic fabrics.

girdle

guepiere See under UNDERGARMENTS: FRENCH CINCH.

half bra See under UNDERGARMENTS: DEMI-BRA.

half-slip Straight-cut slip beginning at the waist. Introduced in 1940s, becoming a classic substitute for a regular slip. In contemporary terminology also called a *petticoat.* See UNDERGARMENTS: PETTICOAT.

haut ton See under UNDERGARMENTS: BUSTLE.

hip-huggers Low-slung underpants starting at hip bone level, intended to be worn with hip-hugger pants and bare-midriff dresses.

hi-rise girdle See under UNDERGARMENTS: GIRDLE.

Hollywood-top slip Slip with a fitted V-shaped top, introduced in 1920s. Previous to this time, slips were cut straight across in front or made with wider built-up straps. Patterns for this slip were produced and sold by the Hollywood Pattern Company.

∞**honiton gossamer skirt** (hon′-ih-ton) Lightweight summer petticoat of 1850s made with strips of fabric attached to a waist belt by means of several vertical tapes as far as the hips where three circular ruffles of fabric were attached.

hoop petticoat See under UNDERGARMENTS: HOOPS.

hoops A framework consisting of round or oval circles (shaped like a hoop) of whalebone, wire, or cane used to extend the skirt. Used in the 16th c. as part of the structure of the FARTHINGALE, in the 18th c. when they were called PANNIERS (see under UNDERGARMENTS) and in the 19th c. when they were called *hoops* or CRINOLINES (see under UNDERGARMENTS). Revived in 1950s, hoops are now sometimes worn with evening or bridal gowns. Fashionable in the 19th c. from c. 1857 to 1870, hoops usually consisted of a full-length petticoat made with a series of circular bands gradually increasing in size from top to hem. The hoops could be sewn into a petticoat or, as in the so-called **cage petticoat** or **hoop petticoat** or **skirt supporter,** held in place with vertical tapes making the skirt flexible enough to permit one to sit down. The following were among the most widely used named types of hoops: **cage empire** Made with graduated hoops of steel, shaped into a slight train in back, worn under a ball gown from 1861 to 1869. Also called *cage* or *artificial crinoline* and *skeleton skirt.* **cage-americaine** Hoop-skirt petticoat worn from 1862 to 1869, the upper part made of hoops connected with vertical tapes and lower part covered with fabric. **Empire jupon** (ohm′-peer zhu-pon) Gored petticoat, very full at the hem where two or three steel hoops were inserted, worn under the *empire dress* of 1867 instead of the *cage petticoat.* Also called *empire petticoat.* **Imperial skirt** Patented cage-type hoop skirt of late 1850s with as many as 32 hoops hung on fabric strips to provide a flexible, lightweight crinoline. **isabella skirt** Underskirt worn in late 1850s with three small hoops extending one-third of the distance from waist to hem. The remainder of skirt was made with three widely spaced hoops with quilted fabric between. **matinee skirt** Woman's lightweight patented hoop skirt of 1859 made by inserting 11 lightweight hoops into a petticoat. **promenade skirt** Petticoat of 1850s with steel hoops set into muslin worn to support dress. **skirt supporter** Patented elliptical metal hoop of late 1850s with two moon-shaped wire metal cages inserted within the hoop—one on either side. Fitted over woman's petticoat just below the waistline to hold out a full skirt.

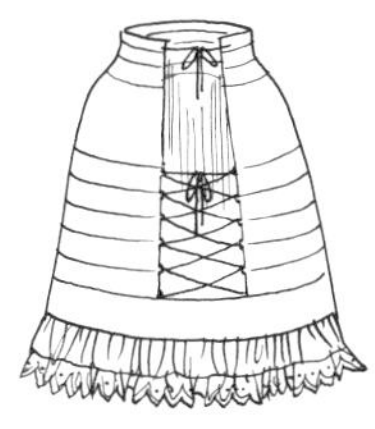

hoops

imperial skirt See under UNDERGARMENTS: HOOPS.

isabella skirt See under UNDERGARMENTS: HOOPS.

Jaeger underclothes (yay′-ger) Type of wool UNION SUIT (see under UNDERGARMENTS) made with hygienic principles in mind. Introduced for men and women by a German, Dr. Gustave Jaeger, in 1880s.

Jockey® shorts Trademark for knitted BRIEFS (see under UNDERGARMENTS).

knickers Woman's below-the-knee-length underpants, originating in 1890s. English term still current and synonymous with any type of underpants.

laced foundation Foundation closed by lacing through eyelets, an early method of fastening still used in some support-types of foundations.

langtry bustle See under UNDERGARMENTS: BUSTLE.

leisure bra Lightweight unconstructed bra, often of stretch lace, designed to be worn at home or when sleeping. Also called *sleep bra.*

∞**linecloths, pair of** Linen DRAWERS (see under UNDERGARMENTS) worn by men in the 15th c.

long handles See under UNDERGARMENTS: LONG JOHNS.

long johns Slang for UNION SUIT or THERMAL UNDERWEAR (see under UNDERGARMENTS) with long legs. Also called *long handles.*

long-leg panty-girdle See under UNDERGARMENTS: GIRDLE.

long-line bra Bra that fits the bust or rib cage, extends to waist or below. Worn with girdle to eliminate waistline bulges. Sometimes boned and wired to be worn without straps.

long-line bra-slip A long-line bra attached to a petticoat or half-slip.

maternity slip Slip with an elastic panel at midsection in the front worn by pregnant women.

matinee skirt See under UNDERGARMENTS: HOOPS.

merry widow Bra and short girdle combined into a minimal support garment. Made of elastic power-net, some versions are made in a lacy pattern with a ruffle and hose supporters at lower edge.

merry widow

minimal bra See under UNDERGARMENTS: NUDE BRA.

minimizer bra A bra designed to reduce the bust area by compressing the breasts. Minimizer bras are designed with a fuller cup and higher sides than the cup of other styles to eliminate spillover.

mini-petti Mid-thigh-length petticoat. Introduced in late 1960s for wear with MINISKIRTS.

mini-pettipants See under UNDERGARMENTS: PETTIPANTS.

natural bra See under UNDERGARMENTS: NUDE BRA.

nelson See under UNDERGARMENTS: FRISK.

nude bra Bra made of lightweight nude-colored fabric with no bones, wires, or padding. Also called *natural bra* or *minimal bra.*

oblong hoops See under UNDERGARMENTS: PANNIERS.

one-size bra See under UNDERGARMENTS: STRETCH BRA.

padded bra A bra with fiberfill, cotton, or gel added to the cup to enhance the size and definition of the bust and eliminate nipple definition, providing a more fashionable silhouette.

∞**pair of bodies** Stays or corset worn in the 17th c. stiffened with whalebone, steel, or wood—frequently padded. Sometimes called a *bodice.*

∞**panier/paniers** (pan-yehr') French spelling for hoops worn to extend skirts. Worn in France from about 1718 or 1720 until the French Revolution, the earliest styles were *en coupole* (domed-shaped) and *en guéridon* (round-shaped). **Paniers à coudes** (pan-yehr a could) were French paniers of late 1720s that extended wide at the sides and were narrow from front to back. (*Der.* French, "elbows," because the woman's elbows could be rested on them.) Toward the middle of the 18th c., paniers were made in two pieces to create a skirt that was wide from side to side. **Paniers à bourelet** (pan-yehr a boor-lay) was a French panier hoop petticoat with a thick roll at the hem to make the skirt flare. By 1750 half paniers, (called *pocket hoops* in England) were worn only for court functions while **considerations,** lightweight panniers worn to extend sides of dresses thereby eliminating need for petticoats, were worn for other occasions. **Paniers anglais** (pan-yehr' ong'-glaze) was the French name for the English hoop petticoat. This term and the term *pannier* (English spelling) were rarely used in England in the 18th c. Also see under UNDERGARMENTS: PANNIERS.

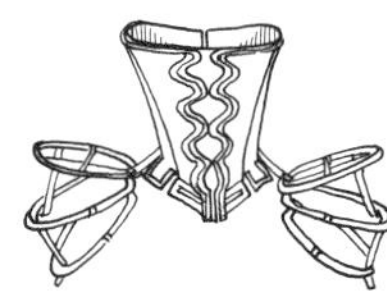
paniers

paniers à bourelet See under UNDERGARMENTS: PANIERS.

paniers à coudes See under UNDERGARMENTS: PANIERS.

paniers anglais See under UNDERGARMENTS: PANIERS.

pannier crinoline See under UNDERGARMENTS: BUSTLE.

pannier/panniers (pan-yehr') Structure of metal, cane, wire, or wooden hoops for extending a woman's dress at both sides at hip level. Popular from about 1720 to 1789 in France. The word *pannier* (English spelling of the French word *panier*) was seldom used in England, where this garment was called "hoops." Present-day costume historians, however, tend to call all 18th c. hoops by the name *panniers* or *paniers.* **Oblong hoops** was a British term used from 1740s to 1760s for panniers on women's gowns that were flattened from front to back and projected sideways over hips and were sometimes hinged to permit passage through narrow doorways. Synonyms were *square hoops* and *false hips.* **Pocket hoops** (British usage), were very small panniers popular in early 1720s, when side hoops were coming into fashion, and in the 1770s, when the style was waning. Also refers to petticoat popular from late 1860s to 1880s. *Der.* Latin, *panarium,* "a basket for bread," so-called because they looked like baskets perched on the hips. Also see under UNDERGARMENTS: PANIERS.

∞**pantalettes** (pan-tah-let') Women's and girls' underpants with long, straight legs ending in ruffles, tucks, and embroidery, which showed below the hem of the dress. From early 1800s to 1840 worn by women and until 1865 by girls. James Monroe's daughter, Maria Hester, is said to have been first person to wear pantalettes in Washington, D.C., in 1807 (she would have been about eight years old). Also called *pantaloons* when worn by women. [PANTALOONS (see under PANTS) for men were an outergarment.]

pantaloons 1. For women, see under UNDERGARMENTS: PANTALETTES. 2. For men, see under PANTS: PANTALOONS.

panties Women's and children's underpants; garments worn under outer clothing covering torso below the waist. Word came into popular usage in the 1930s. Previously called *drawers.* In the 1980s, some types of briefs and underpants were higher cut, revealing all of the leg. The word "underpants" is used in reference to men's and boys' underwear. Also called PANTY.

pants Synonym for PANTIES and UNDERPANTS (see under UNDERGARMENTS).

pants liner Tight-fitting control underpants coming over the knee to the calf or the ankle and worn under pants for a sleek fit.

panty-girdle See under UNDERGARMENTS: GIRDLE.

pantyslip Short petticoat with underpants attached at waistband; a popular style for little girls.

∞**pantywaist** Child's cotton undergarment worn in late 19th and early 20th c. consisting of fitted sleeveless top button-down front. Made with buttons around waistline to attach panties. Also had elastic tabs or garters to hold up long stockings suspender garters. Also called *underwaist* and sold under the trade name *Ferris waist.*

pasties 1. Cups for the breasts that have no straps or back, fastened in place with adhesive. Also called *posts.* 2. Small decorative coverings that adhere over nipples, worn by dancers.

∞**pettibockers** Ankle-length, silk-jersey pantaloons worn as underwear by women in early 20th c.

petticoat Undergarment for a woman or girl similar to a slip, but starting at the waist. Depending on the overgarment, it may be full or narrow, lace-trimmed or tailored, and long or short. Originally called an *under-petticoat,* from 16th to 18th c., to distinguish it from *petticoat,* as used in 17th and 18th c. when it referred to the outer, visible skirt of a dress. Current usage dates from the 19th c. Current synonym: *pettiskirt.*

petticoat bodice ∞1. Petticoat joined by waistline seam to sleeveless bodice, worn from about 1815 until 1890. 2. In 1890, a type of corset cover. See under UNDERGARMENTS: CAMISOLE.

petticulottes (pet-tee-koo-loht') Short petticoat and underpants combined in one garment that has flared legs and an inverted pleat in center front and back, frequently lace-trimmed. Also see under CULOTTES #3 in alphabetical listing.

pettipants Long, dress-length underpants made of plain or bright-colored knits with ruffles and lace trimming, introduced in late 1960s. Also came in mini length, called *mini-pettipants.*

pettiskirt See under UNDERGARMENTS: PETTICOAT.

pettiskirt brief Combination petticoat and short underpants joined by elastic waistband.

petti-slip Same as HALF-SLIP or PETTICOAT (see under UNDERGARMENTS).

pin-in bra Two bra cups fastened together in the center with a piece of elastic and with two tabs at the sides for pinning to clothing.

plumet petticoat See under UNDERGARMENTS: BUSTLE.

plunge bra Bra with deep V-shaped open section in front, separated cups are attached to a band; worn with plunging necklines.

pocket hoops See under UNDERGARMENTS: PANNIERS.

posts See under UNDERGARMENTS: PASTIES #1.

∞**princess chemise** Woman's undergarment with corset cover and petticoat made in one piece with no waistline seam. Sometimes lavishly trimmed with lace at neckline, armholes, and hem. Worn in late 19th and early 20th c.

princess slip/princess petticoat Slip made in fitted panels from top to hem having no waistline seam, may be flared or straight cut. Called *princess chemise* in 1870s.

promenade skirt See under UNDERGARMENTS: HOOPS.

pull-on girdle See under UNDERGARMENTS: GIRDLE.

push-up bra Bra with low-cut front and removable foam bust pads to raise the breasts.

racer-back bra A bra characterized by a T-strap down the center back allowing for maximum movement of the back and arms without strap slippage. Racer-back bras hide straps under sleeveless and halter style bodices.

rhumba panties Little girls' panties with several rows of ruffles across the seat. *Der.* From ruffled costume worn for South American dance.

∞**rump/rump furbelow** Stuffed pad forming a bustle worn in the late 18th c.

Sarong (sar-ong') Formerly a trademark for a girdle, popular in the 1950s, with a lapped front giving it an appearance similar to a SARONG.

∞**scabilonians** (sca-bill-own'-ee-ans) Man's underpants worn in latter half of 16th c. Also spelled *scavilones.*

seamless bra Bras with molded bra cups made of a single piece of fabric eliminating seams and stitching that might show through; ideal to wear under clothes that are tight or made of clingy knits or sheer fabrics. Seamless bra technology can be applied to many types of bras including minimizer, sports, or underwire bras.

shadow-panel slip Slip made with an extra layer of fabric in a panel in front or back to diffuse the light when worn under a sheer dress or skirt.

∞**sherte** Chief male undergarment worn by men from 12th to 16th c., forerunner of modern shirt, which was considered an undergarment until the 20th c. Usually called *chemise* until 14th c. Also called *camise.*

shift See under UNDERGARMENTS: CHEMISE.

∞**shirt-drawers** Man's combination undershirt and underpants worn in 1890s.

skeleton skirt See under UNDERGARMENTS: HOOPS.

skirt supporter See under UNDERGARMENTS: HOOPS.

skivvies/skivvy Slang for a man's underwear, usually referring to shorts and top. *Der. skivy,* a sailor's term for an undershirt.

sleep bra See under UNDERGARMENTS: LEISURE BRA.

slip 1. Undergarment, beginning above the bust, worn by women and girls usually held in place with shoulder straps. Length is long or short in relation to the dress worn on top. Current meaning of the word dates from the early 19th c. ∞2. 18th c. type of corset cover.

slip-blouse See under UNDERGARMENTS: BLOUSE-SLIP.

smock See under UNDERGARMENTS: CHEMISE.

snap pants Waterproof panty for infants with snaps at the crotch.

snip slip Slip finished with three rows of hemstitching around bottom. One or more rows may be cut off to adjust length.

snuggies Knee-length or over-the-knee underpants made of knitted cotton, worn for warmth with matching tank-top undershirt.

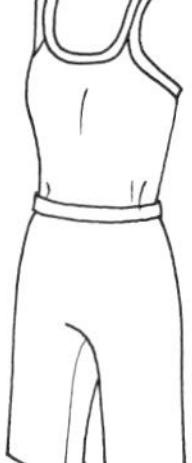
snuggies

sports bra A bra with built-up straps, coming over shoulders forming a crablike shape in back, secured by an elastic band around the body. Worn for active sports.

sports bra

square hoops See under UNDERGARMENTS: PANNIERS.

∞**stays** Corset made very rigid with iron or whalebone. Made like a bodice laced up back with scoop neckline in front, higher in back, with shoulder straps set wide in front.

step-ins Woman's underpants with widely flared legs and narrow crotch, popular in 1920s and 1930s. Also called DANCE SET in the 1920s.

strapless bra 1. Bra constructed so that it stays in place without straps over the shoulders. Popular since 1940s using boning or wire cups. 2. See under UNDERGARMENTS: LONG-LINE, TUBE, and WIRED BRAS.

strapless slip Bra-top slip made with elastic, boning, and detachable or no straps.

stretch bra Bra made of fabric knitted with spandex. Elastic straps permit great freedom of movement. Often made in only one size, sometimes in pullover style with no fastening. Also called ONE-SIZE BRA.

stretch brief/control brief Stretch panty or girdle with detachable garters offering light control.

string bikini Minimum underpants consisting of two small triangular pieces attached to a band of elastic worn low on the hips.

suit slip Slip with white top and dark skirt worn under dark suit and sheer or white blouse.

∞**swanbill corset** Back-laced woman's corset of mid-1870s with long metal bone in front that curves outward over lower abdomen.

swim bra Molded cups, attached or separate, used inside a bathing suit to shape the bosom.

tailored slip Slip made with cording, appliqué, or tucks as trim, rather than lace. Popular in 1940s, revived in early 1970s and after.

tap panty Panty styled like short shorts with a slight flare at hem. May be made of satin or floral print with lace-trim. Frequently made with matching camisole and then called *cami-tap set.*

teardrop bra Minimal bra with triangular cups; looks like the upper part of a bikini swimsuit.

teddy 1. Straight-cut garment of 1920s, combining a CAMISOLE (see under UNDERGARMENTS) with short slip or long vest with underpants. Wide strap is attached to the front and back at the hem, thus making separate openings for each leg. 2. As revived in late 1960s and 1980s and since, becoming a one-piece tight-fitting minimal garment with a low-cut front and back and high-cut leg openings.

teddy #1

teen bra Bra with shallow cups designed for the young girl whose breasts are not fully developed. Also called *training bra.*

tee-shirt See under UNDERGARMENTS: T-SHIRT.

thermal underwear Long-sleeved undershirt and long-legged pants or one-piece UNION SUIT (see under

UNDERGARMENTS) made of knitted cotton, wool, blends of these fibers, or polypropylene for winter, particularly for sports.

thong Rudi Gernreich design of 1975 for what was variously described as "a virtually bottomless bathing suit" or a "glorified jockstrap" cut to reveal as much of the buttocks as possible while covering the crotch. Now a common cut for underwear.

tights 1. Underpants and stockings knit in one piece, worn originally by athletes, circus performers, and dancers in late 19th c. with a LEOTARD. Now worn by women and children in variety of natural or manufactured fiber knits in many colors for all occasions. 2. LEOTARD with legs and sometimes feet added. 3. Women's and girl's below-the-knee underpants made fine-ribbed knit in either black or white, worn in early 20th c.

torsolette See under UNDERGARMENTS: BUSTIER.

tournure See under UNDERGARMENTS: BUSTLE.

tournure and petticoat See under UNDERGARMENTS: BUSTLE.

∞**tournure corset** (toor-nure′) Laced foundation garment with straps over shoulders and hip-length underskirt of stiff fabric intended to hold out the skirt. Worn in late 1850s over the CHEMISE (see under UNDERGARMENTS).

training bra See under UNDERGARMENTS: TEEN BRA.

∞**trouses/trowses** (trouz) Underpants or drawers worn by Englishmen under the TRUNK HOSE in 16th and 17th c.

trunks Loose-fitting underpants cut similar to men's shorts.

T-shirt/tee shirt Originally a man's undershirt with short sleeves and high round neck, forming a T-shape, usually made in white cotton knit. Adapted for sportswear by men, women, and children. Also see under SHIRTS: T-SHIRT/TEE SHIRT.

T-shirt

tube bra Strapless circular stretch bra with no closing; must be put on over the head.

two-way stretch foundation Stretch garment made of SPANDEX with a satin panel in front.

∞**umbrella drawers** Women's wide bell-shaped DRAWERS of late 19th and early 20th c., trimmed with tucks, insertion, and lace.

underpants Garment for lower half of the body with separate space for insertion of each leg. Made in many different styles. Also see under UNDERGARMENTS: PANTIES.

∞**under-petticoat** Term for skirt of white cambric, flannel, or poorer quality fabric worn under dress skirt or under hoops from 16th through 18th c.

undershirt 1. Man's knitted shirt, usually white cotton, with U-neckline continued into built-up straps, or with short sleeves and crew or V-neckline, worn underneath outer shirt or sweater. See under UNDERGARMENTS: ATHLETIC SHIRT and T-SHIRT. 2. Woman's knitted garment usually of cotton or cotton and wool, shaped like a man's undershirt. 3. Infant's knitted wool or cotton shirt, in four styles: (a) double-breasted, fastened with grippers; (b) high-necked cardigan-style, usually with long sleeves; (c) similar to man's undershirt; (d) sleeved, with lapped shoulders that stretch to permit easy passage over head. Also called *vest.*

underwaist See under UNDERGARMENTS: PANTYWAIST.

∞**under-waistcoat** Undergarment worn by men in last half of 18th c. for warmth. Usually made of flannel.

underwire bra A bra that incorporates a semicircular strip of metal, plastic, or resin sewn into the seam under the cup from the center gore to the armpit in order to lift, separate, shape, and support the bust. Underwire bras were first patented in 1893.

union suit One-piece knitted undergarment buttoned up center front, introduced in 1880s and made with short or long legs, short or long sleeves, and a drop seat. Worn for warmth. Worn by all ages until 1940s, now mainly used under ski or other winter sports' clothing. Long-legged underwear is often nicknamed *long johns* or *long-handles.* Also see under UNDERGARMENTS: JAEGER UNDERCLOTHES, ENVELOPE COMBINATION, and THERMAL UNDERWEAR.

union suit

vest 1. Woman's undershirt usually made of knitted rayon or nylon styled with built-up straps or a CAMISOLE top (see under UNDERGARMENTS). 2. See under UNDERGARMENTS: UNDERSHIRT #3.

V-top Upper part of slip or other undergarment cut in the shape of a deep V.

waist-cincher See under UNDERGARMENTS: FRENCH CINCH.

waist watcher Wide band, reaching from ribs to top of hips, made of spongy stretch fabric secured with VELCRO®. Worn by men and women to pull in the waist and as an aid in reducing the size of the waistline.

wired bra Bra with fabric-covered wire under or over the breasts to give added support; often strapless.

zipper foundation Foundation with zipper placed in center front rather than at side.

zippered girdle Girdle usually made of two-way stretch and nonstretch panels closed with zippered placket for firmer support.

underground fashion Clothes in bizarre colors and extreme shapes worn in 1965 by avant-garde people who attended private showings of unconventional "underground movies" of the day shown in beatnik-type bars and coffee houses.

underlap (extensions on closures) Extension beyond the edge of the bottom layer of a garment that provides additional space for a button or other closure without affecting the finished size of a garment.

underlining Lining variation in which the outer shell fabric and the lining are layered together before the garment is constructed. Used to stabilize shell fabrics or make the shell fabric opaque.

underpants See under UNDERGARMENTS.

under petticoat See under UNDERGARMENTS.

underpropper See under NECKLINES AND COLLARS: RUFF.

undershirt See under UNDERGARMENTS.

undershirt dress See under DRESSES.

undershirt sweater See under SWEATERS.

underskirt 1. See under UNDERGARMENTS: SLIP or PETTICOAT. 2. See under SKIRTS.

undersleeve See under ENGAGEANTES.

undersplit See under LEATHERS.

∞**undervest** British usage from 1840s for undershirt. See under UNDERGARMENTS: UNDERSHIRT #1.

underwaist See under UNDERGARMENTS: PANTYWAIST.

under-waistcoat 1. See under VESTS. 2. See under UNDERGARMENTS.

underwear See under introduction to UNDERGARMENTS.

underwire bra See under UNDERGARMENTS.

∞**undress** Ordinary or unceremonial dress for man or woman as contrasted with formal wear. Term used in 18th and 19th c., particularly in England. Also see NEGLIGÉE COSTUME.

U-neckline See under NECKLINES AND COLLARS: HORSESHOE NECKLINE.

uneven plaid See under PLAIDS AND TARTANS: EVEN PLAID.

uniform 1. Any specific type of apparel required for wear by the armed forces of any country; for a specialized occupation, by a school, or for competitive team sports such as baseball, football, and hockey. Probably originated in antiquity with costumes worn by personal bodyguards of monarchs. Worn by the Greek and Roman armies and since then by armed forces throughout the world. 2. Worn throughout history to denote status or trade of an individual. See under BLUE-APRONED MEN. 3. Worn as LIVERY, particularly in France and England.

Union Nationale Artisanale de la Couture et des Activitiés Connexes See under FÉDÉRATION FRANÇAISE DE COUTURE, DU PRÉT-À-PORTER DES COUTURIERS ET DES CRÉATEURS DE MODE.

Union of Needletrades, Industrial, and Textile Employees (UNITE) Labor union formed by a merger in 1995 of the Amalgamated Clothing and Textile Workers Union and the International Ladies Garment Workers Union (ILGWU). **UNITE HERE** now also represents the industrial laundry industry, gaming, airport, and hotel workers. The ILGWU was founded in 1900 and was famous for the militancy of its early organizational drives, fight against sweatshop conditions, housing, educational, cultural programs, and medical services to members. David Dubinsky, elected president of the union in 1932, remained in office for 34 years and became a major figure in U.S. politics.

union suit See under UNDERGARMENTS.

unisex fashions Garments designed so that they may be worn by either men or women. Included shirts laced at the neckline, pants with drawstrings, and double-breasted jackets with buttons and buttonholes on both sides so they could be buttoned to the right or left. Introduced in 1968, it became a popular style, particularly with young people. In the 1980s, popular for sweatsuits and sweaters. Items were featured both in department stores and boutiques. Also see under HIS AND HERS. See under PANTS: DRAWSTRING PANTS and SHIRTS: UNISEX SHIRTS.

unisex garments

unitard See under ACTIVEWEAR.

UNITE See under UNION OF NEEDLETRADES, INDUSTRIAL, AND TEXTILE EMPLOYEES.

United States Customs Service U.S. Department of Treasury agency responsible for the administration of import-export regulations and the implementation of tariff duties, quotas, and labeling requirements.

unit production system (UPS) Garment manufacturing system in which garments are transported on a conveyer belt or overhead system to a sewing operator who performs one or more sewing operations, then forwards the garment to the next workstation for the next construction step.

Universal Product Code (UPC) Standard for bar-coded information on products that allows rapid optical scanning and computerized control of products. Used in management of textile and apparel merchandise and especially in QUICK RESPONSE and JUST-IN-TIME systems.

university coat See under COATS AND JACKETS: ANGLE-FRONTED COAT.

university vest See under VESTS.

unmentionables/unwhisperables See under INEXPRESSIBLES.

UPC See under UNIVERSAL PRODUCT CODE.

updated classics Apparel items that are derived from some classic style (examples: chemise, shirtwaist, cardigan, blazer) and changed in some way to give them a more contemporary appearance.

updo See under HAIRSTYLES.

upper See under FOOTWEAR.

∞**upper garment** British usage from 17th c. for outer garments such as a cloak, cassock, or gown that indicated dress of a gentleman.

upper stocks See under TRUNK HOSE.

UPS See under UNIT PRODUCTION SYSTEM.

upsweep See under HAIRSTYLES.

Ural emerald See under GEMS, GEM CUTS, AND SETTINGS: ANDRADITE GARNET.

urchin cut See under HAIRSTYLES: GAMIN.

usage The number of yards of fabric required to make a particular garment style.

U seams See under HOSIERY.

Ussurian raccoon See under FURS.

utchat See under JEWELRY: NECKLACE.

utility boot See under FOOTWEAR: BOOT.

vair See under FUR.

val/valenciennes lace See under LACES.

vallancy See under WIGS AND HAIRPIECES.

valois hat See under HEADWEAR.

vambrace See under ARMOR.

vamp See under FOOTWEAR.

vampire hair See under HAIRSTYLES.

vamprey See under FOOTWEAR: VAMP.

vandyke 1. *adj.* Describes items of clothing inspired by or copied from clothing in portraits by early 17th-c. Flemish artist, Sir Anthony Van Dyke. 2. See under NECKLINES AND COLLARS: RUFF. 3. Lace-bordered handkerchief.

vandyke beard See under BEARD.

vandyking Decorative trims or lace constructed with a pronounced V or saw-toothed edge.

vandyking

vane See under introduction to FEATHERS.

vanity 1. Small metal or plastic case, carried in woman's handbag, typically for carrying face powder and sometimes rouge or other cosmetics. 2. See under HANDBAGS AND RELATED ACCESSORIES.

vanity sizing The practice of increasing the measurements represented by a size to make the customer feel better about themselves.

varens See under COATS AND JACKETS.

vareuse See under COATS AND JACKETS.

variegated Having an unevenly colored, spotted, or streaked appearance.

varsity jacket See under COATS AND JACKETS: BASEBALL JACKET.

varsity sweater See under SWEATERS: LETTER SWEATER.

vasquine See under BASQUINE.

vassar blouse See under BLOUSES AND TOPS.

V-back bra See under UNDERGARMENTS: SPORT® BRA.

Veblen, Thorstein (1857–1929) American economist whose book *The Theory of the Leisure Class* (1899) has been influential in the study of fashion. He argued that socioeconomic status was communicated by the **conspicuous consumption** of luxury goods such as costly and fashionable dress worn by the well-to-do. An additional status symbol, **conspicuous leisure**, made it clear that by wearing apparel that was so confining or so delicate that they could not do physical labor, the wives and children of wealthy men were reflecting an affluence that did not depend on lower-status manual labor. In 1973, Quentin Bell in his *On Human Finery* added a third status symbol, **conspicuous outrage**, that was evident in very expensive dress that was non-functional or contrary to expectations for new apparel (e.g., the purchase of antique or vintage blue jeans that are torn.)

vegan accessories Made from non-animal products.

vegetable ivory See under IVORY.

vegetable tanning See under LEATHERS.

veil/veils See under HEADWEAR.

†veiling Nets of various sizes made in different constructions to form open-weave fabrics that are used for trimming on hats.

Velcro® See under CLOSURES.

veldtschoen construction See under FOOTWEAR.

†velour (ve-loor′) Soft, velvety, thick fabric with a cut pile brushed in one direction. It may be made of various fibers and yarns. Originally a woven fabric, now made by either weaving or knitting. Uses: coats, warm-up suits, knit shirts, and dresses.

†velvet A fabric with a short, closely woven pile created from extra lengthwise yarns. Usually the pile is cut to create a soft, rich texture; however, sometimes patterns are created by cutting some of the pile yarns and not others. Uses: dressy clothing and evening wear.

†velveteen Cut-pile cotton or cotton blend fabric in which the pile is made with an extra crosswise yarn. The pile is not more than ⅛″ high and the most durable of these fabrics have twill woven background. Uses: dresses, suits, and sportswear.

vendeuse (vahn-duze') (French) Saleswoman employed at a couture house in Paris.

vendor The individual or company from which raw materials or finished goods are purchased. Synonyms: *source, supplier*.

vendor-induced incentives Inducements provided by a vendor to a retailer or store personnel (see SPIFFS) that will influence the sale of the vendor's products. These can include such services as training, TRUNK SHOWS, educational material, and contests.

vendor-managed retail inventory Programs developed between a vendor and a retailer in which retail sales and stock data are reviewed by the manufacturer and additional merchandise is provided as required.

vendor marking Provision of and attaching by the supplier of hangtags, labels, and price tags.

vendor matrix A list provided by the retail company to its buyers of approved suppliers. Also called *key resource list*.

venetian-blind pleats See under CLOTHING CONSTRUCTION DETAILS.

venetian cloak See under CAPES, CLOAKS, AND SHAWLS.

Venetian lace See under LACES.

venetian ladder work See under EMBROIDERIES AND SEWING STITCHES.

venetian point lace See under LACES.

venetians See under TRUNK HOSE.

venetian sleeve See under SHOULDERS AND SLEEVES.

venetian slops See under TRUNK HOSE.

venise, point de See under LACES.

vent Used since 15th c. to indicate vertical slit in garment, usually from hem upward. May be seen, for example, in coats, gloves, jackets, shirts, and suit coats.

ventail See under ARMOR.

ventilated collar See under CLERICAL DRESS.

verdugale/verdugalle/verdugado/verdugo See under FARTHINGALE.

∞**veronese cuirasse** (ver-o-naze'-eh kwe-rass') Wool jersey knit bodice laced up the back that was fashionable in 1880s.

∞**veronese dress** (ver-o-naze'-e) Daytime dress of 1880s with knee-length, PRINCESS-STYLE, woolen tunic ending in deep points over silk underskirt with large box pleats around hem.

Veronica Lake hairstyle See under HAIRSTYLES.

vertical integration The combining under the management of one company a number of production stages that might formerly have been done by different companies. For example, a textile industry firm might produce fiber, spin yarns, weave fabrics, and manufacture apparel.

vertically worked See under FURS.

vertugale (*vertugadin, verdugale, verdyngale, vertugade, vertingale*) See under FARTHINGALE.

vest See under introduction to VESTS.

∞**vestee** Woman's decorative front or half vest attached around neck and by ties around waist. Worn under a jacket instead of a blouse in 19th c. Also called *chemisette*.

vestido See under VESTS.

vestments 1. Items of wearing apparel worn particularly for ecclesiastical services and by clergy. See under introduction to CLERICAL DRESS. 2. Ceremonial or official robe.

vest pocket See under POCKETS.

VESTS

vest 1. An item of apparel extending to the waist or below that is similar to a sleeveless jacket. Usually worn over a blouse or shirt and sometimes under a suit jacket. Also called a *waistcoat* and *weskit*. ∞2. An accessory worn by women as a fill-in for a low neckline or as a substitute for a blouse in 19th and early 20th c. 3. See under UNDERGARMENTS.

adjustable vest Man's front-buttoned vest that fits around the neck, halter-style, and is held on by a band around the waist fastening in center back with a buckle. Worn by men with formal wear (e.g., dinner jacket or tuxedo).

afghanistan vest Vest made of curly lamb tanned and worn with smooth embroidered skin side out, showing edges of curly lamb. An ethnic fashion popular in the late 1960s. *Der.* Copied from vests worn by men in Afghanistan.

∞**bag-waistcoat** Man's vest, full in front and bloused to form a pouch, worn in 1883.

∞**benjy** (ben'-gee) (British usage) Slang expression used in the 19th c. for a man's waistcoat or vest.

buckskin vest Garment made of sueded deerskin or sheepskin, frequently laced rather than buttoned, trimmed with self fringe at hem and shoulders. Style popular in America since colonial days.

clayshooter's vest Sleeveless vest with belted back, leather piping, and large side pockets; suitable for sportswear as well as shooting mark or clay pigeons. Main feature is a quilted leather pad at shoulder to absorb recoil of gun. Vest features a secret pocket for holding wallets and keys.

down vest Quilted vest fastened with snaps, toggles, or a zipper that is interlined for warmth with down quilted between the lining and outer fabric. Popular in late 1970s and after for general outerwear.

down vest

electric vest Vest with a lining that reflects 80 percent of body's heat. Special built-in, electric heating system operated by batteries in a zipper pocket that power heating units in the vest's front and back. Depending on the setting the vest can be kept warm for up to a full day.

fisherman's vest Waist-length vest usually made of khaki-colored cotton duck worn over other clothes when fishing. Has many pockets—two larger zip or snap pockets near hem, and small pockets on chest to stow gear when fishing.

flotation vest Lightweight, flexible vest with zip front made with shell of tear-resistant nylon filled with polyethylene foam, quilted together in wide vertical panels. Worn for all recreational boating activities as a life-saving device. Synonyms: *PFD, personal flotation device.*

∞**french opening vest** Man's vest of the 1840s cut low enough to reveal a large part of the shirt front.

∞**french vest** Man's high-buttoned vest of the 1860s with small lapels not turned over.

∞**gilet** (zhee-lay′) Vest or short waistcoat worn by men in the 1850s and 1860s.

∞**golf vest** Man's knitted, wool, single-breasted vest of mid-1890s made with braid-trimming, without a collar, and with three pockets—one on each side plus watch pocket.

hug-me-tight Knitted or quilted vest with V-neck buttoned down front. Usually worn by older people under coats for extra warmth.

hunting vest Front-buttoned sportsman's vest worn over a hunting shirt. Made of cotton duck fabric with large rubber-lined game pocket.

jerkin 1. Contemporary synonym for *vest, waistcoat,* and *weskit.* First made in buckskin by American colonists. ∞2. Man's sleeved jacket worn over doublet, sometimes laced or buttoned up front, sometimes sleeveless with shoulder wings; worn from late 15th through 16th c.

∞**jockey waistcoat** Straight-hanging man's vest or waistcoat with a low standing collar, similar to Chinese collar. Worn from 1806 and revived in 1880s.

∞**newmarket vest** Plaid or checked vest, buttoned high, made with or without flapped pockets, worn by sportsmen in mid-1890s.

pakistani vest Fitted vest with long, gold-braided, shawl collar, fastened in front with invisible hooks, and elaborately trimmed around edges with wide gilt braid, mirrors, and tassels. Originally called *pakistani wedding vest*—part of trend toward ethnic fashions in late 1960s.

personal flotation device See under VESTS: FLOTATION VEST.

PFD Acronym for personal flotation device. See under VESTS: FLOTATION VEST.

potholder vest Handmade, sleeveless, crocheted vest made with built-up straps over the shoulders and crocheted "granny squares" in front and back.

reversible vest Any vest that can be worn on either side. Different fabrics are used on each side (e.g., plain and plaid or corduroy and paisley print).

∞**shakespeare vest** Man's single- or double-breasted vest of mid-1870s, with narrow lapels and a turndown collar similar to shakespeare collar. See under NECKLINES AND COLLARS: SHAKESPEARE COLLAR #3.

∞**shawl waistcoat** 1. Man's vest with shawl collar worn in the 19th c. 2. Man's vest, sometimes cut from a fabric with a printed or woven design, typically used for shawls. 3. A man's vest that may be made from a woman's shawl or a similar-style garment.

shawl waistcoat #1 c. 1830s

suit vest Matching or contrasting vest sold with a man's suit. Usually styled with V-neck, six buttons, and two or four pockets. The back is made of lining material and has an adjustable belt. Sometimes designed for women and children.

suit vest

sweater-vest See under SWEATERS: VEST SWEATER.

tattersall vest Man's vest in small checked fabric, designed as single-breasted with six buttons, no collar, and four flapped pockets. Worn by sportsmen in mid-1890s and later worn with riding habit or with man's sport coat. *Der.* Named after Richard Tattersall, British horseman, founder of Tattersall's London Horse Auction Mart established in 1776.

under-waistcoat Man's short sleeveless vest worn under the waistcoat, introduced in 1790, fashionable in contrasting fabrics from 1825 to 1840. Still worn in England for men's formal wear as waistcoat with WHITE SLIP.

∞**university vest** Double-breasted waistcoat of early 1870s made with sides cut away from lowest button and fashionable with UNIVERSITY COAT (see under COATS AND JACKETS: ANGLE-FRONTED COAT).

waistcoat/weskit See under introduction to VESTS.

white vest Vest worn by men for dress under a SWALLOW-TAILED COAT (see under COATS AND JACKETS). It is cut low in front, showing the formal shirt and white tie.

vestsuit Pants and vest designed to be worn together. A full-sleeved blouse or shirt is worn underneath the sleeveless vest. Popular in 1960s.

vest sweater See under SWEATERS.

Vibram® See under FOOTWEAR.

vici kid See under LEATHERS.

VICS See under VOLUNTARY INTER-INDUSTRY COMMUNICATIONS STANDARDS COMMITTEE.

Victoria (1819–1901) Queen of Great Britain (from 1837 to 1901), married Albert of Saxe-Coburg-Gotha, who took the title of Prince Consort. She assumed the British throne when only eighteen and reigned for sixty-four years. Styles in fashion and the arts that are derived from or inspired by those popular during her reign are called **victorian.** Period was noted for conservative social values and excessively decorated designs. See under BLOUSES AND TOPS: VICTORIAN BLOUSE; NECKLINES AND COLLARS: CHOKER COLLAR; and SHOULDERS AND SLEEVES: SABOT SLEEVE.

victorian See under VICTORIA.

Victorian long purse See under HANDBAGS AND RELATED ACCESSORIES: MISER'S PURSE.

victorine See under CAPES, CLOAKS, AND SHAWLS: PALATINE ROYAL.

victory stripes See under PRINTS, STRIPES, AND CHECKS: HICKORY STRIPE.

†**vicuña** (vi-koon′-yah) Hair fiber from the vicuña, a species related to the llama; it is one of the softest fibers known. Colors range from golden chestnut to deep fawn. Despite attempts to domesticate the animals, most of the fiber must still be obtained by hunting and killing them. The Peruvian government limits the number of animals that can be hunted, therefore the fiber supply is very limited and very expensive.

∞**video catalog** A catalog reproduced on a videocassette or disk that was sent to customers. A precursor to online shopping, customers viewed the catalog on a VCR and could telephone the retailer to place orders.

∞**vinaigrette** (vin-ay-gret′) Small bottle attached to a metal chain carried by women or attached to a handbag in 19th c. Used to hold an aromatic (e.g., vinegar or smelling salts used to revive women if they felt faint).

vintage fashions Clothes and accessories from another era refurbished and sold in department stores or specialty shops (e.g., Victorian, Edwardian, and Twenties dresses—plus items such as beaded bags and antique jewelry). Called by this name in 1980s. Formerly called FLEA MARKET and *attic* fashions.

vintage Hollywood hair See under HAIRSTYLES.

vinyl Manufactured material that is a tough, flexible, shiny, elastic, nonporous plastic and can be made to be colored or transparent. Used for fabric coating and to produce materials resembling leather for boots, capes, gloves, raincoats, shoes, etc.

vinyl raincoat See under COATS AND JACKETS.

†**vinyon** See under PVC.

∞**violin bodice** Long bodice, reaching to the knees in back, worn over a dress, in 1870s. Made in PRINCESS STYLE with violin-shaped dark fabric inset in the back.

virago sleeve See under SHOULDERS AND SLEEVES.

virtual factory System of garment production controlled from a central computer. Electronic communications technologies make it possible for different stages of production to be completed in various locations. For example, designs may be created in one location, construction in another, and the product shipped to yet another.

virtual Internet site Imaginary environment, designed and developed by a participant, in which an **avatar**, a character representing the site developer, can participate in fashion by wearing apparel designed by the participant for the avatar or by acquiring apparel from designers who make items available online.

visa In international trade, a document provided by an exporting country that specifies country of origin of a product.

†**viscose rayon** (vis′-kos) Rayon fiber regenerated through the viscose process from wood pulp or cotton fibers too short to be spun. This process produces pollutants that are hard to eliminate; therefore, production of fiber made using the viscose process has ceased in the U.S. (Other less-polluting processes are used to make some rayon fabrics. See under LYOCELL.) The fiber is used for a wide variety of apparel because it drapes well, can be dyed or printed in attractive colors and patterns, and is comfortable to wear; however, if not given special finishes, it has a tendency to shrink and to wrinkle.

visite See under CAPES, CLOAKS, AND SHAWLS.

∞**visiting dress** Used throughout the 19th c., a woman's costume worn especially for making calls in the afternoon. Also called *visiting costume* and *visiting toilette.*

vison European name for *mink.* See under FURS: MINK.

visor 1. See under HEADWEAR. ∞2. See under ARMOR.

visual merchandising The visible environment of a retail store that contributes to the promotion and sale of merchandise. Included are the exterior appearance of the store, window displays, interior décor, signage, lighting, and displays of merchandise.

†**Viyella** (vy′-ella) Formerly trademarked lightweight British fabric originally made of a yarn blended of 50 percent cotton and 50 percent wool. Now made in sev-

eral weights and weaves and in varying blended proportions of cotton and wool. Uses: Shirts, dresses, pajamas, and underwear. Also called *Viyella flannel.*

V-neckline See under NECKLINES AND COLLARS.

V-shape Overall style characterized by broad shoulders and an oversized top tapering to a narrow skirt at the hem. Shoulders and DOLMAN (or BATWING) sleeves (see under SHOULDERS AND SLEEVES) were sometimes cut in one piece so that sleeves virtually terminated at the elbow and sloped into the side seam at waist. Other styles were made with extended padded shoulders and large armholes usually with sleeves of generous proportions. Introduced in 1983 and sparking a trend of wide and full-cut clothing.

V-shape style c. 1980s

Vogue Fashion magazine, first published as a weekly in December of 1892, and subsequently became a bimonthly in 1910. Arthur Baldwin Turnure was its founder and publisher. Bought by Condé Nast in 1909. Published in French and British editions, both in France and Great Britain in the 1920s. Edna Woolman Chase was the editor from 1914 until 1951. Now published monthly in over a dozen countries.

†voile (voyle) Lightweight, open-weave fabric made of tightly twisted combed yarns that give it a crisp and wiry feel. Originally made only of cotton but now popular in blends of cotton/polyester. Uses: dresses, blouses, and some men's shirts.

volendam cap See under HEADWEAR: DUTCH CAP.

Voluntary Inter-Industry Communications Standards Committee (VICS) Formed in 1986 by retailers and manufacturers in the textile and apparel industries to develop standardization of electronic data communication, including the use of UNIVERSAL PRODUCT CODE system and electronic data interchange formats.

Vreeland, Diana Dalziel (1906–1989) Dynamic fashion authority who went to work for *Harper's Bazaar* in 1937, becoming fashion editor after only six months. Left to become associate editor of *Vogue* magazine in 1962 and served as editor-in-chief until 1971. After that, she acted as consulting editor to *Vogue* and consultant to the Costume Institute of the Metropolitan Museum of Art, where she supervised outstanding exhibitions including subjects such as *Balenciaga, American Women of Style, The Glory of Russian Costume, Vanity Fair,* and *Yves Saint Laurent.*

V-top See under UNDERGARMENTS.

vulcanized shoe construction See under FOOTWEAR.

vulture-winged headdress See under HEADWEAR.

W Large-size pictorial fashion magazine that covers American and couture fashions, fashionable personalities, social events, and other articles of particular interest to women. Published monthly by Condé Nast.

wadded hem Hem that has been padded with wide band of CORDING. Used in 1820s and used occasionally on contemporary dresses and robes.

wadded hem

wadding Loosely connected fibers in sheet form used for shoulder pads in coats and suits. Also see under FIBERFILL.

waders See under FOOTWEAR.

†waffle cloth/waffle pique Cotton fabric made in a honeycomb weave. See HONEYCOMB.

waist 1. Narrowest part of the torso. 2. See under BLOUSES AND TOPS. 3. See under FOOTWEAR.

waistband 1. Band of fabric, usually faced and interfaced, seamed to waistline of skirt or pants and fastened to hold garment firmly around waist. 2. See under WAISTLINES: SET-IN WAISTLINE.

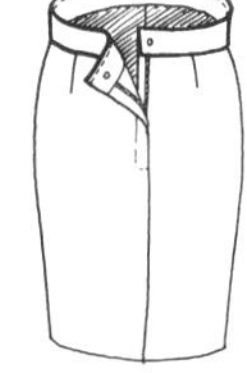

waistband #1

waist chain See under JEWELRY: BELLY CHAIN.

waist-cincher See under UNDERGARMENTS: FRENCH CINCH.

waistcoat 1. Synonymous with VEST in contemporary styles (see under introduction to VESTS). Other synonyms include jerkin and weskit. ∞2. From 16th c. to 1668, a man's garment either worn for warmth under the DOUBLET—it was waist-length, quilted—or worn to complete a costume, and then made of decorative fabric. Also called a petticoat. ∞3. From 1668 on, a man's undercoat cut along the same lines as the outer coat. It was made either with or without sleeves until 1750, after which waistcoats were sleeveless. Gradually became shorter in the 18th c., becoming waist-length in 1790. Predominantly single-breasted until 1730s, then more likely to be double-breasted in 1780s and 1790s, with both styles common in the 19th c. ∞4. 17th-c. woman's bodice buttoned in front and worn with a dress. ∞5. Latter half of the 18th c., woman's clothing similar in style to a man's waistcoat of the same date, worn with a riding habit. 6. See under UNDERGARMENTS. ∞7. In 1851, elaborately brocaded outergarment worn by women with a CARRIAGE DRESS. ∞8. In 1880s and 1890s, a fill-in VESTEE worn by women with a suit or TAILOR-MADE costume. Also see under VESTS.

waistcoat paletot See under COATS AND JACKETS.

waistcoat pocket See under POCKETS: VEST POCKET.

waist length See under LENGTHS.

WAISTLINES

waistline 1. Place on the torso where the belt is located. 2. Horizontal seam joining the top and skirt of a dress if the garment is made in two pieces. Waistlines are not necessarily located at the anatomical waist.

cinched waistline Waistline pulled in very tightly, usually with a wide belt.

corselet waistline (kors'-let) Pulled in waistline usually made by wearing a wide belt that generally laced in the front and was frequently used on peasant-style dresses.

directoire waistline See under WAISTLINES: EMPIRE WAISTLINE. *Der.* Named for DIRECTOIRE period in France (1795–1799).

drawstring waistline Waistline with a cord or belt drawn through a casing, heading, or beading, to gather the fullness when tightened and tied in a bow or knot. Also called *tunnel waistline.* Also see under WAISTLINES: PAPERBAG WAISTLINE.

drawstring waistline

dropped waistline Waistline seam placed below the natural waistline.

elasticized waistline A waistline used for pull-on pants, skirts, and dresses that may be made in three ways: (1) Elastic inserted through a casing. (2) Elastic sewn to the garment fabric. The elastic is stretched to the size of the fabric, sewn down with two or more rows of stitching, thereby causing the fabric to gather. (3) Elastic stitched directly to

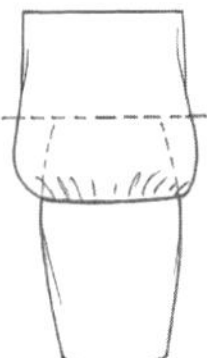

dropped waistline

the fabric at a waistline; used mainly for dresses with a waistline seam, for panties, and for half-slips.

empire waistline (em′-pire or ohm-peer′) High-waisted effect with seam placed directly under bust. This was the predominant waistline placement from the late 18th c. to 1820s during Empire and Directoire periods in France and has been popular periodically since then for women's dresses, coats, and lingerie. It derives from attempts to imitate the styles of the ancient Greeks and Romans.

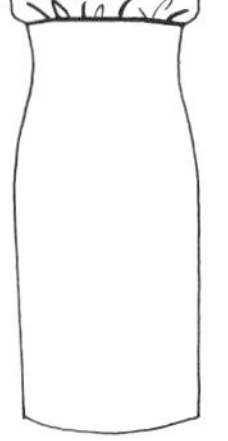
empire waistline

high-rise Used to describe any waistline higher than the natural waistline.

low-rise/low-slung Used to describe any waistline placed below the normal waistline, usually for hip-hugger skirts or pants.

natural waistline Belt or seam placed at narrowest part of the torso; the anatomical waistline.

nipped waist Narrow waistline making a marked contrast with the areas of the body above or below the waist. If not a natural anatomical feature, can be achieved with corseting.

paperbag waistline Made by inserting a drawstring through a casing placed far enough below the top edge of the garment in order to create a small stand-up ruffle around the waist. Introduced in early 1980s and used for pants, shorts, and skirts. Contemporary variations may be made by pleating or gathering the waist area of a skirt or pants and topstitching a band across the pleats or gathers to form a stand-up ruffle.

paperbag waistline

princess waistline Fitted waistline with no waistline seam. Garment is cut in panels from neck to hem and fitted by shaping the vertical seams. First appeared in the 1860s and popular periodically ever since. *Der.* Claimed to have been introduced about 1860 by French couturier Charles Frederick Worth in a morning dress for Empress Eugénie, hence the name "princess."

set-in waistline Horizontal panel of fabric used at waistline of dress, fitted between top and skirt, making two seams—one at or below normal waistline and one higher.

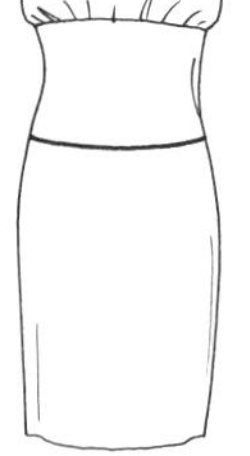
set-in waistline

tunnel waistline See under WAISTLINES: DRAWSTRING WAISTLINE.

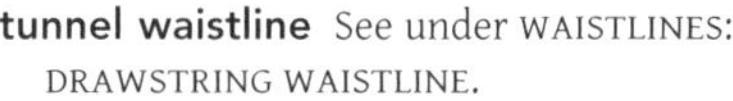

waist watcher See under UNDERGARMENTS.

†wale 1. In textiles, a ridge in woven fabric running either vertically (e.g., in Bedford cord and corduroy); crosswise in faille; or diagonally in twills (e.g., gabardine and whipcord). 2. In knitting, used in latter half of 19th c. and after to describe row of loops or stitches running lengthwise.

walking coat See under COATS AND JACKETS.

walking costume/walking dress See under DRESSES: PROMENADE DRESS.

walking parasol See under UMBRELLAS AND PARASOLS.

walking shoe See under FOOTWEAR.

walking shorts See under SHORTS: BERMUDA SHORTS.

walking stick See under CANE.

walking suit 1. Woman's three-quarter-length coat, sometimes fur-trimmed, worn with a matching skirt; and often made of tweed. ∞2. Woman's suit, worn in 1901, with skirt just brushing the ground.

wallaby See under LEATHERS.

Wallace Beery shirt See under SHIRTS.

walled toe See under FOOTWEAR.

wallet See under HANDBAGS AND RELATED ACCESSORIES.

wallpaper print See under PRINTS, STRIPES, AND CHECKS.

walrus mustache See under MUSTACHE.

waltz length See under LENGTHS.

wamus See under COATS AND JACKETS.

wardrobe 1. All the clothing belonging to an individual. ∞2. A room where clothing was kept in the 15th c. 3. Since 19th c., a piece of furniture used to contain clothing.

warehouse retailer Retailer who combines showroom, warehouse, and retail operations together so as to reduce operating expenses and to offer apparel at discount prices.

warmup jacket/warmup pants See under ACTIVEWEAR: WARMUP.

†warp/warp yarns Lengthwise direction in fabric, or yarns that run lengthwise, parallel to SELVAGE.

†warp knitting A form of knitting done by machines in which each needle is fed by a separate yarn; warp knitting is the fastest means of knitting fabric. Warp knits are characterized by loops that interlace vertically.

warp print See under PRINTS, STRIPES, AND CHECKS.

warranty/warrantee Written document that ensures the life of a product for a specific period of time. See under GUARANTEE.

wash-and-wear 1. See under DURABLE PRESS. 2. See under HAIRSTYLES.

washed gold See under JEWELRY.

watch bracelet See under JEWELRY and WATCHES: BRACELET WATCH.

watch cap See under HEADWEAR.

watch chain A decorative chain attached to a man's pocket watch, often embellished with seals or emblems. When watch is worn in vest pocket, chain may be pulled through vest buttonhole and end tucked into pocket on opposite side.

watch coat See under COATS AND JACKETS.

WATCHES

watch Timepiece usually carried in pocket or worn on a band at wrist. A fashionable accessory since 16th c. when it was usually carried in a pocket. In late 19th c., women wore watches that dangled from pins. The wristwatch was developed before World War I. In 1960s and 1970s, watches were worn with novelty straps and face designs and considered to be costume jewelry. There have been many technical developments in recent decades including watches powered by small replaceable batteries, and self-winding, waterproof, and shock-resistant watches. Digital watches have digital displays that not only show date, time, and seconds, but may also be designed with alarms and other technical features that remember appointments, read pulses, and tell the temperature.

alarm watch Wristwatch that rings at a set time; sometimes the alarm is musical and thus called *musical alarm watch.*

analog watch Watch that has moving hands and numbers of the hours visible on its face and tells time by the position of the hands on the face of the clock.

ankle watch Large watch with wide band worn strapped to the ankle.

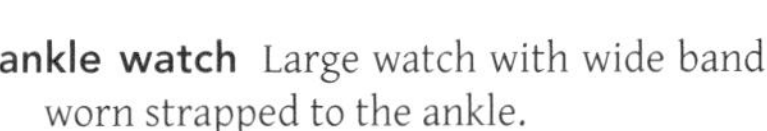

analog watch

bangle watch See under WATCHES: BRACELET WATCH.

bracelet watch Watch with an ornamental band; face of the watch is sometimes covered with a small, hinged piece of metal. Frequently set with stones, it is both a decorative bracelet and a watch. Also called *bangle watch.*

bracelet watch

calculator watch Watch that, in addition to giving the time in eight different time zones of the world, has a stopwatch, an alarm, and the functionality to perform mathematical problems.

calendar watch Watch that also shows month and day of year in addition to indicating time.

cartoon watch Children's watch with trademarked cartoon characters; popular since 1930s (e.g., Mickey Mouse®, Star Wars® characters, and Smurfs®).

chatelaine watch (shat'-eh-lane) Watch suspended from a lapel pin. Popular in 19th and early 20th c. and revived intermittently. Also called a *lapel watch. Der.* Keys worn at the waist on a chain by medieval mistress of the castle or "chatelaine."

chatelaine watch

chronograph A watch with features such as a perpetual calendar and moon phase repeater that has dials which glow in the dark.

chronometric watch Watch equipped with aviation computer to calculate speed, distance, conversion of miles into kilometers or knots, and fuel consumption. Used when flying, auto racing, and boating. First used by space pioneers in flight of May 1962.

diamond watch **1.** Wristwatch that has a dial decorated with diamonds and other precious gems. Introduced in the 1920s, the watchband was made with diamonds set in a platinum band. **2.** In the 1960s, semiprecious gems (e.g., CARNELIAN, ONYX, or TURQUOISE; see under GEMS, GEM CUTS, AND SETTINGS) were used for the face with diamonds set around the edge.

digital watch A watch that shows the time in hours, minutes, and seconds in numbers that constantly change, rather than having a dial with hands pointing to the time.

digital watch

fashion watch Watch that is a decorative accessory as well as a functional one. In the 1950s, bracelet, pendant, and ring watches were designed, some set with jewels, others in antique mountings. Previous to this, women owned one watch—now they may own several and wear them as jewelry.

go-go watch Watch that snaps into very interchangeable, colorful bands, matching or contrasting with the costume. Introduced in 1966, they were at first considered a fad but later influenced the introduction of larger-sized watches and watchbands for women.

hunter watch Large gold pocket watch with hinged cover protecting the face.

jeweled watch A watch in which the metal movements have gemstone tips that prevent wear and tear, thereby prolonging the life of the watch. Seventeen jewels will produce a serviceable watch; a 23-jewel watch will outlive its owner by many years.

lapel watch See under WATCHES: CHATELAINE WATCH.

LCD quartz watch Digital watch that displays time and date by Liquid Crystal Display (LCD); powered by a small replaceable battery. Liquid Crystal Display presents information by using very small segments, called pixels, that modulate light to create visual display of information in products ranging from watches to LCD televisions.

pendant watch Watch suspended from a chain worn around the neck. May be decorated on the back and worn on either side or made with a hinged cover. Made in all shapes and sizes in antique, as well as modern designs and in LCD calendar watches.

pocket watch Man's watch worn either in the vest pocket or in a small watch pocket in the trousers. First worn during Louis XIV period. Sometimes two watches were worn in small pockets of the waistcoat. By the 1840s, women were wearing pocket watches in small pockets set into the waistline of dresses. Pocket watches remained popular until the introduction of the wristwatch in the late 1800s.

pocket watch

quartz crystal watch A watch in which an electric current from a battery is sent to a very small quartz crystal that vibrates at exact, predicable rates. As a result such watches are very accurate and reliable.

ring watch Watch in ring style—popular in 1960s and 1980s, sometimes decorated with stones and made with hinged cover. Other very simple styles were made of lucite.

self-winding watch A wristwatch that winds automatically as a result of the movement of the wrist.

seventeen-jeweled watch Fine watch that uses genuine or imitation rubies and sapphires at points of friction inside the case. Originally stones were genuine, but now synthetic stones are more frequently used.

Swatch Trade name for a Swiss watch developed in the early 1980s that was intended for the lower-priced market niche, which had been lost to Japanese companies in the 1960s and 1970s. As part of this approach, Swatch watches also intended to revive interest in ANALOG WATCHES at a time when DIGITAL WATCHES predominated. After a successful launch, it quickly gained popularity and became fashionable after its introduction in 1983.

waterproof watch A watch in a sealed case that prevents the entrance of water.

wristwatch Watch worn on the wrist. Introduced in the late 1800s and gaining in popularity before World War I. Made in all sizes and types of faces, and sometimes with interchangeable bands. Some are set with diamonds and called DIAMOND WATCHES (see under WATCHES).

wristwatch wardrobe Women's watch sold with several interchangeable watchbands in several colors.

---

watch fob Short chain, ribbon, or charm, frequently engraved with initials, attached to man's pocket watch. Named for the trouser pocket in which the watch is carried, called a *fob pocket* (see under POCKETS).

watch pocket See under POCKETS: FOB POCKET and VEST POCKET.

waterfall See under HAIRSTYLES.

waterfall back See under SKIRTS.

waterfall necktie See under TIES: MAIL-COACH NECKTIE.

†waterproof *adj.* Descriptive of clothing, usually of rubber, plastic, or heavily coated fabric, that cannot be penetrated by water, especially boots and coats. Also see under WATER RESISTANT/REPELLENT.

waterproof cloak See under CAPES, CLOAKS, AND SHAWLS.

waterproof watch See under WATCHES.

†water resistant/repellent *adj.* Describes clothing of fabric or leather treated to shed water easily and dry quickly—not entirely WATERPROOF.

water wave See under HAIRSTYLES: FINGERWAVE.

watteau back (wa-toe') Style used for the back of a dress, jacket, coat, or dressing gown with box pleats called WATTEAU PLEATS, used since latter half of 19th c. (see under CLOTHING CONSTRUCTION DETAILS). Pleats started at the neckline and were stitched down usually to the shoulders, from which point the fabric of the back fell to the hem. This style appears most often today in dressing gowns. *Der.* Named for the artist Watteau, who portrayed such dress in his paintings. Not a term contemporaneous with the original style, when it was called a *sack back.*

watteau back

∞watteau body (wa-toe') Daytime dress bodice, worn in early 1850s to mid-1860s, having a low square neckline trimmed with ruffles and elbow-length sleeves. Bodice did not meet in front and was fastened with a ribbon lacing, exposing a *chemisette* worn underneath. *Der.* Named for the artist Watteau who portrayed such dresses in his paintings.

watteau cape See under CAPES, CLOAKS, AND SHAWLS.

watteau coat See under COATS AND JACKETS.

watteau dress See under DRESSES.

watteau hat See under HEADWEAR.

Watteau, Jean Antoine (Wa-toe', Jhan An-twan') (1684–1721) French artist who painted many scenes showing women in early 18th-c. dresses. The SACK DRESS, with box pleats set in at the neckline or yoke, was a prominent style of the time, and in 19th-c. fashion terminology, these pleats became known as WATTEAU PLEATS (see under CLOTHING CONSTRUCTION DETAILS) and imitations of the sack dress, WATTEAU DRESSES (see under DRESSES). See also under WATTEAU BACK.

watteau pleat See under CLOTHING CONSTRUCTION DETAILS.

watteau wrapper See under SLEEPWEAR AND LOUNGEWEAR.

wearable art Beginning as a trend in the 1970s, a garment created as a unique work of art. Fiber artists combine a variety of techniques such as crocheting, knitting, handweaving, embroidery, appliqué, layers, slashing, and special dyeing techniques. They also use feathers, beads, and ribbons.

wearable technology (intelligent clothing, smart clothing) Apparel and accessories that are made with built-in technological elements that can be used to support electronic devices such as cellular telephone chargers or design features that enable color changes or temperature control.

wearing sleeves See under SHOULDERS AND SLEEVES.

wear testing A variation of style testing often used as an important research tool, particularly in the active sportswear category, for which performance is a key criterion of purchasing decisions.

weasel See under FURS.

†weave 1. *n.* Method or pattern in which the lengthwise yarns, placed on the loom first, are interlaced with crosswise yarns to make a fabric. There are three basic weaves: PLAIN WEAVE, TWILL WEAVE, and SATIN WEAVE. All other woven fabrics use some variation or combination of these weaves. 2. *v.* To construct a fabric by weaving on a mechanized or hand loom.

webbed belt See under BELTS.

wedding band 1. See under JEWELRY. 2. See under NECKLINES AND COLLARS: RING COLLAR.

wedding-band collar See under NECKLINES AND COLLARS: RING COLLAR.

wedding dress See under DRESSES.

wedding garter Decorative garter, usually blue satin trimmed with lace, worn by brides. The tradition is to toss it away at the reception to an unmarried man. The custom derived from 16th to 18th c. practice, when young men wore pieces of a bride's garter in their hats. Also called *bride's garter.*

wedding ring/wedding trio See under JEWELRY.

wedding veil See under HEADWEAR: BRIDAL VEIL.

wede See under WEED.

wedge 1. See under HAIRSTYLES. 2. See under FOOTWEAR: WEDGIES, WEDGE HEEL.

wedge dress See under DRESSES.

wedge heels See under FOOTWEAR.

wedgies See under FOOTWEAR.

Wedgwood® cameo See under JEWELRY: CAMEO.

∞weed (*wede, weyd*) Clothing of any type from medieval times to 16th c., after which meaning of the word was limited to mourning garments of black plus veils to cover the head, usually worn by widows and then called **widow's weeds.** *Der.* Old English, *waed,* "garment or clothing."

weekender Woman's three- or four-piece suit including coordinated pants, skirt, jacket, and blouse suitable for weekend trips.

weepers ∞1. Muslin armbands or hatbands worn by mourners in 18th and 19th c. Usually black but sometimes white if deceased was a young girl. 2. See under FEATHERS.

†weft See under FILLING.

†weft knitting Knitting that uses one continuous yarn across a row of loops or a course; weft knitting can be done by hand or machine and can produce flat or circular fabric. The three general categories of weft knitting are single knits, purl knits, and rib knits.

weight belt See under BELTS.

†weighted silk/weighting Silk fabric having metallic salts, called *weighting,* added to it in the finishing process to give the fabric more body so that it drapes better. Since 1938, legislation has required that weighted silk must be identified if fabric has been weighted more than 10 percent for colors or 15 percent for black fabrics. Weighting was used in excessive quantities in many silk fabrics of the late 19th and early 20th c., which caused many of these fabrics to split and crack. This damage cannot be repaired or prevented. Compare with PURE DYE SILK.

welded seam See under CLOTHING CONSTRUCTION DETAILS: FUSED SEAM.

welding cap See under HEADWEAR.

wellesley wrapper See under COATS AND JACKETS.

wellington boot See under FOOTWEAR.

wellington hat See under HEADWEAR.

wellington styles Men's fashions of the early 19th c. named for the first Duke of Wellington, British military hero who defeated Napoleon in the Battle of Waterloo in 1815. Specific style was a single-breasted overcoat that buttoned to waist, had a full skirt to knees with no waistline seam, a center back vent, side pleats, and hip buttons. Worn with narrow pantaloons with slits from ankle to calf and closed with buttons, boots, a tall, flared-top beaver hat, and sometimes a cape.

welt 1. See under FOOTWEAR. 2. See under HOSIERY. 3. Since the 6th c., a border around edge of garment, either for decorative purposes or to reinforce edge. Also see under POCKETS and CLOTHING CONSTRUCTION: DETAILS.

weskit Synonym for WAISTCOAT and VEST (see under introduction to VESTS).

weskit dress See under DRESSES.

western *adj.* Descriptive of styles worn by western U.S. cowboys, styles disseminated around the world by movies set in the old western frontier in the U.S. Tight jeans, high-heeled boots, cowboy shirts, and western hats of various styles were accepted for city wear in the late 1960s and periodically since then. See under COATS AND JACKETS: WESTERN JACKET; FOOTWEAR: COWBOY BOOT; HEADWEAR: WESTERN HAT; PANTS: WESTERN PANTS; POCKETS: CONTINENTAL POCKET; SHIRTS: COWBOY SHIRT and WESTERN DRESS SHIRT; and SHORTS: WESTERN SHORTS.

western style

western arrowhead pocket See under POCKETS.

western suit 1. Man's or woman's suit with jacket cut longer and more fitted through waistline, worn with straight-legged pants. Reminiscent of styles of the American West in late 19th c. 2. A suit for formal occasions styled with similar lines, called a **western formal.**

wet look Descriptive of shiny, glistening fabrics—sometimes of CIRÉ satin—worn for pants, jackets, and shirts, c. 1968 and after. Frequently black with a high amount of reflection from the shiny surface, the impetus for these styles came with the adoption of black leather motorcycle jackets in 1950s. Resurfaced in the 1980s in bold, neon colors (e.g., red, chartreuse, and light pastels of pink, lavender, and lime). Also called *cuir savage look.* Also see under LEATHERS.

wetsuit See under ACTIVEWEAR.

weyd See under WEED.

whalebone Pliable hornlike strips called **baleen,** obtained from the16th c. to the mid-19 th c., from upper jaws of certain whale species. Used for stiffening bodices of women's dresses and under bodices called *stays,* which were the forerunners of CORSETS. Was replaced by lightweight steel when it became available in the 19th century.

wheel farthingale See under FARTHINGALE.

whipcord Medium- to heavyweight-worsted fabric with a diagonal wale caused by the steep twill weave. Yarns are hard-twisted and fabric is given a hard finish to make the weave very distinct. Also made of cotton, wool, manmade fibers, or blends. Used for men's and women's suits, coats, riding habits, and uniforms.

whip stitch See under EMBROIDERIES AND SEWING STITCHES.

whisk See under NECKLINES AND COLLARS.

white belt See under ACTIVEWEAR: KARATE SUIT.

white bucks See under FOOTWEAR: BUCK OXFORD.

white crown See under HEADWEAR.

white fitch See under FURS: FITCH.

white flannels See under PANTS.

white fox See under FURS.

white mink See under FURS: MINK.

∞**white slip** Narrow border of white piqué along front edges of man's waistcoat, correctly worn only with MORNING COAT (see under COATS AND JACKETS: CUTAWAY). A fashion introduced by Edward, Prince of Wales, in 1888.

white tie 1. Used to designate men's full evening dress. Compare with BLACK TIE. 2. See under TIES.

white tie and tails See under FULL-DRESS SUIT.

white vest See under VESTS.

white walls See under HAIRSTYLES: FLATTOP.

whitework See under EMBROIDERIES AND SEWING STITCHES.

whole fall See under FALL #1.

wholesale brand A brand created under a proprietary label and sold for distribution to a variety of retailers that also carry other wholesale brands. Also see under BRAND.

wholesale price The price charged by the apparel manufacturer for goods. This price is based on the cost to the manufacturer of producing the goods, plus profit.

wholesaler The individual or company that sells goods in relatively large quantities to a retailer or, less often, directly to consumers. The wholesaler may be a manufacturer or a MIDDLEMAN.

wholesale selling (contact selling) Sales directly to consumers by a manufacturer.

wicking The passage of moisture through or along the structure of a textile. A factor in evaporation of perspiration in some activewear.

wide-awake See under HEADWEAR.

wide wale Ribbed or corded fabrics with wider than average ribs (e.g., wide wale corduroy, wide wale piqué).

widow's peak 1. Hairline characterized by a point in center of forehead. 2. See under HEADWEAR.

widow's weeds See under WEED.

wifebeater See under BLOUSES AND TOPS.

wig hat See under HEADWEAR.

wiglet See under WIGS.

WIGS AND HAIRPIECES

wig 1. Hair, human or artificial, mounted on an elastic net cap or foundation of bands (called **capless wig**) worn stretched over head to conceal natural hair or baldness and styled in conventional cuts and colors or in fancy arrangements and colors as fashion fad. 2. Historically, human or artificial hair worn from early Egyptian times and becoming a status symbol of royalty and upper classes through 18th c. Considered a secret device to conceal baldness in 19th and early 20th c.

hairpiece Additional pieces of hair, either human or synthetic fibers, worn when elaborate hairstyles demand extra hairpieces or to fill in where hair is thin or missing.

Afro wig Very curly, short-haired wig that fits over the hair, often back-combed so that hair stands on end. Introduced in 1968 when African styles were very influential in fashion.

bag See under WIGS AND HAIRPIECES: BAGWIG.

∞**bagwig** Man's 18th-c. wig, styled with hair pulled back and stuffed into a square black silk bag tied with bow at nape of neck. Also called *coiffure en bourse, crapaud,* or *bag.*

barrister's wig White wig—with smooth top and sausage curls over ears and a small pigtail tied with ribbon in back—worn by British trial lawyers.

beach wig Modacrylic wig sometimes attached to a bathing cap or made in amusing shapes. Worn instead of beach hats at the shore or the swimming pool.

bench wig Tightly curled wig with flaps that hang down over the ears. Worn by British judges when they sit in court, on the "bench."

∞**binette** (bin-ett') Wig of late 17th c., worn by Louis XIV, of the full-bottomed type (see under WIGS AND HAIRPIECES: FULL-BOTTOMED) with three hanging locks of hair; designed by Binet, a wigmaker.

∞**bob-wig** 18th-c. man's informal wig without a queue, a long braid in back; a **long bob** covered back of neck, **short bob** ended at nape of neck.

∞**bourse** (*boorce*) (French) A rarely used reference to the black silk bag of a BAGWIG, used in the 18th c. (see under WIGS AND HAIRPIECES). *Der.* French, "bag." Also see under WIGS AND HAIRPIECES: MAJOR WIG.

brigadier wig See under WIGS AND HAIRPIECES: MAJOR WIG.

∞**brown George** A man's brown wig said to look like coarse brown bread, as colloquially used in the late 18th c.

brutus wig See under HAIRSTYLES: BRUTUS.

∞**buckled wig** 18th-c. man's wig with tightly rolled sausage curls arranged horizontally near ears. *Der.* French, *bouclé,* "curl."

∞**cache-folies** (cash fo-lee') Short-haired wig or supplementary curls were worn by women in Paris in the early 19th c. to cover the short hairstyles that were popular at the time of the French Revolution.

∞**campaign wig/campaigne wig** Wig of bushy, wavy hair with center part and three ends tied together when traveling. Worn by European soldiers from 1675 to 1750—after that considered old-fashioned. Also called *traveling wig.*

catogan wig/cadogan wig See under WIGS AND HAIRPIECES: CLUB WIG.

∞**caul** (kol) Late 17th- and 18th-c. foundation on which wig was made.

∞**cauliflower wig** Short-bobbed wig with tight curls all over, worn by coachmen in latter half of 18th c.

∞**caxon** Man's wig—usually white or pale yellow and sometimes black—styled with curls down the back and tied with a black ribbon. Worn as an undress, or informal, wig by professional men in 18th c.

∞**club wig** Man's wig with broad, flat, club-shaped QUEUE (see under HAIRSTYLES) turned under and tied with black ribbon. Sometimes ribbon came around to front and tied in bow under chin. Worn from 1760 to 1790s. Much favored by the MACARONI in 1770s. Also called *cadogan* or *catagan club wig.*

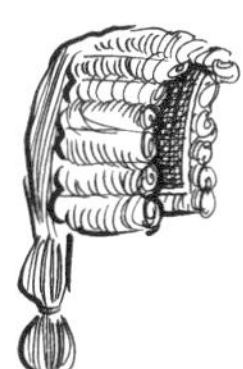
club wig

∞**coiffure en bourse** (on boorce) See under WIGS AND HAIRPIECES: BAGWIG. *Der.* French, "bag."

∞**corkscrew wig** Wig of various lengths of hair that falls in "corkscrew" fashion.

crapaud See under WIGS AND HAIRPIECES: BAGWIG.

crinière wig (kre-nyair') Wig cut in Dutch boy style, with bangs in front, and made of red, yellow, blue, etc., in synthetic hair or modacrylic fibers. Introduced in Paris by Courrèges, spring 1969.

∞**cue peruke** (kue per-uke') Wig with hanging queue and a long braid in back, fashionable in the 18th c.

∞**cut wig** A man's small, plain wig without a queue and a long braid in back, fashionable in the 18th c.

∞**duvillier wig** (doo-vee-yay') Man's wig, worn about 1700, dressed high on top of head with long, shoulder-length hair. Named after a French *perruquier* or wigmaker. Also called *long duvillier, falbala wig,* or *furbelow wig.*

∞**Egyptian wig** 1. Long black wig worn by ancient Egyptians with straight bangs, square cut at bottom, and often with intricate braiding interspersed with gold links. Wig was made on a framework that elevated it from the head, creating protection from the sun.

2. Colored short wigs in layered styles, blue or red, worn by ancient Egyptians.

falbala wig See under WIGS AND HAIRPIECES: DUVILLIER WIG.

fall Long, straight hairpiece fastened to head with ribbon headband or pinned in place so that it hangs down over natural hair. Popular in late 1960s. Purchased by length; short length fall is called a *mini fall;* shoulder-length fall is called a *maxi fall.*

fall

∞fantail wig Man's wig of early 18th c. with QUEUE (see under HAIRSTYLES) hanging loose in many small curls in back.

foretop See under WIGS AND HAIRPIECES: TOUPEE #2.

french wig See under WIGS AND HAIRPIECES: FULL-BOTTOM WIG.

∞frizz-wig/frizze Man's wig, closely crimped all over, worn from 17th to 19th c. Also called a *frizze* or *frizzle.*

∞front (17th-c). Hairpiece consisting of a fringe of false hair, worn on the forehead.

∞frouze/fruz (frooz) Curled, false hair or wig worn to conceal baldness in the 17th and early 18th c.

full-bottom wig Extremely large man's wig with center part, small SAUSAGE CURLS (see under HAIRSTYLES) all over, and long locks on shoulders. Worn from 1660 to early 18th c. on formal occasions by lawyers and learned professional people. Still worn by judges in Great Britain in 21st c. for ceremonial occasions. Also called *French wig.* Also see under WIGS AND HAIRPIECES: BINETTE.

full-bottom wig

furbelow wig See under WIGS AND HAIRPIECES: DUVILLIER WIG.

hair extensions Human hair or synthetic hair that supplements thin hair and can be attached with clips that are part of the hairpiece or may be integrated by pulling the supplement through existing hair.

hairpiece See under introduction to WIGS AND HAIRPIECES.

human hair wig Imported genuine-hair wig that reacts like regular hair, therefore is harder to care for, must be set more often, and is more expensive than synthetic wigs.

∞jasey (jay'-zee) Late 18th- and 19th-c. man's wig made of worsted jersey yarn.

lace wig Worn by individuals whose hair loss may be moderate to severe, these wigs create the appearance of hair growing from the scalp. Fibers are tied by hand to a fine poly-silk mesh base. Placed at the front of the head and extending to the crown of the head, the hair appears to come from a natural hairline.

long bob See under WIGS AND HAIRPIECES: BOB-WIG.

∞maintenon toupet (mant-non' too-pay') Band of false curls attached to ribbon that tied at nape of neck. Worn by women in mid-1860s, pulled over the forehead to imitate the hairstyle worn by the Marquise de Maintenon. Also called *toupet Maintenon.* Also see under HAIRSTYLES: MAINTENON COIFFURE. *Der.* Named for the *Marquise de Maintenon,* mistress and second wife of Louis XIV of France.

∞major wig Man's hairpiece consisting of a *toupée* with two *corkscrew curls* tied at the nape of neck to make a double *queue* in back. Originally a military style, but adopted by civilians and worn during latter half of 18th c. British English usage for a French **brigadier wig.**

maxi fall See under WIGS AND HAIRPIECES: FALL.

∞medusa wig (meh-doo'-sa) Woman's wig of early 19th c. made of many hanging *corkscrew curls. Der.* From the Greek mythical Gorgon, Medusa, slain by Perseus.

mini fall See under WIGS AND HAIRPIECES: FALL.

∞periwig/peruke Synonyms for wig, used in 17th and 18th c.

∞perruque á l'enfant/perruque naissante (pe-rook' ahl an-fant'/pe-rook' nay-sant') Man's wig of 1780s with tiny curls over most of the head, larger horizontal curls above ears and neck, and long queue (a braid) hanging down back.

∞physical wig Short wig, brushed back from forehead, bushy at sides and back, worn by professional men during latter half of 18th c., replacing FULL-BOTTOM WIG (see under WIGS AND HAIRPIECES). Also called *pompey.*

∞pigeon-wings Man's hairstyle or wig with single or double horizontal curls over the ears, smooth at top and sides, worn from 1750s to 1760s. Wig also called *pigeon-winged toupée* or *aile de pigeon.*

∞pigtail wig Wig with a queue (a braid) worn by men in 18th c., interwoven with black ribbon, tied with ribbon bow at nape of neck, and smaller bow at end of queue.

pompey See under WIGS AND HAIRPIECES: PHYSICAL WIG.

postiche See under WIGS AND HAIRPIECES: WIGLET.

put-on Thick hairpiece, sometimes 18″ long, made of modacrylic matched to hair. May be worn in a multiplicity of styles (e.g., PONYTAIL, double BRAID, BUN, CHIGNON, EMPIRE CONE, and FRENCH TWIST) (see under HAIRSTYLES).

∞queue-peruke (kew pe-ook') Man's small wig worn from 1727 to 1760 with fluffed or curled sides and long ends tied back with black bow to make a QUEUE (see under HAIRSTYLES).

∞Ramillies wig/Ramilet wig/Ramille wig Man's wig of 18th c., puffed at sides with long, tapered, braided queue (a braid) tied with black ribbon at end and nape of neck, or looped up and tied only at neck. *Der.* Named for English victory over French in Ramillies, Belgium, in 1706.

reserve wig Man's short-haired wig worn to cover long hairstyle in 1969 to 1970 by men enrolled in Army Reserves. *Der.* So called because men wearing the wig were in the U.S. Army Reserves.

rug Slang for a wig or hairpiece.

∞**scalpette** (scal-pet') A woman's hairpiece composed of extra curls attached to an invisible net worn on top of head, in mid-1870s.

∞**scratch wig/scratch bob** Man's BOB WIG (see under WIGS AND HAIRPIECES) worn from 1740 to end of 18th c. made with one long hanging curl, covering only back of head. Arranged with the natural hair brushed over top of wig. Also called *scratch bob.*

short bob See under WIGS AND HAIRPIECES: BOB-WIG.

stretch wig Comfortable, cool wig with synthetic hair attached to elastic bands running around and over the head in crisscross fashion.

switch Long hank of false hair that may be braided in a plait and worn as a CORONET or twisted into a CHIGNON (see under HAIRSTYLES).

∞**tête de mouton** (tate deh moo'-tone) Woman's short curly wig worn in Paris from 1730 to about 1755. *Der.* French, "sheep's head." Also see HAIRSTYLES: COIFFURE A LA MOUTON.

top See under WIGS AND HAIRSTYLES: TOUPÉE #2.

toupée (too-pay') **1.** Man's small, partial wig used to cover baldness. ∞**2.** From 1730 to end of 18th c., front roll of hair on man's wig. Also called *toupet, foretop,* and *top.*

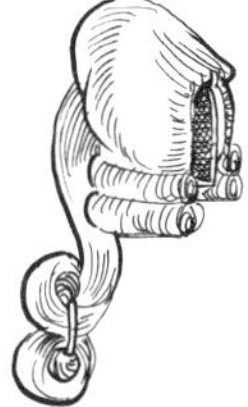

toupée #2

∞**tower** False curls, worn by women above the forehead from 1670s to 1710, usually with the FONTANGES headdress (see under HEADWEAR). *Der.* French, "tour."

∞**transformation** A natural-looking wig or hairpiece worn by women in the early 20th c.

traveling wig See under WIGS AND HAIRPIECES: CAMPAIGN WIG.

∞**tye** Man's tied-back wig, in the 18th c.

∞**vallancy** (va-lan'-see) Extremely large wig, worn in 17th c., that shaded the face.

wiglet Small hairpiece worn on the top of the head and usually combed into bangs. Worn as an aid for thinning hair by both men and women. Also a fashion item. Also called *postiche* (pos-teesh').

---

wilderness boot See under FOOTWEAR.

wild mink See under FURS.

wild silk See under TUSSAH.

william penn hat See under HEADWEAR.

wimple See under HEADWEAR.

wind-blown bob See under HAIRSTYLES.

wind bonnet See under HEADWEAR.

windbreaker See under COATS AND JACKETS.

window displays An important element of VISUAL MERCHANDISING. Traditional store window displays have solid backings and are called **closed displays.** They are visible when the store is open or closed. **Open displays** are common displays in malls that enable the viewer to see directly into the store through the display.

windowpane See under PRINTS, STRIPES, AND CHECKS and HOSIERY.

windsor knot/tie See under TIES.

wing collar See under NECKLINES AND COLLARS.

∞**wings** Decorative pieces projecting upward from shoulders of a doublet or dress, sometimes in shape of padded rolls or crescents sewn into the armhole seam, used from mid-16th to mid-17th c. Also called *shoulder wings.*

wing-tip See under FOOTWEAR.

winkers See under NECKLINES AND COLLARS.

winkle pickers See under FOOTWEAR.

Winnie See under COTY AMERICAN FASHION CRITICS' AWARD.

WIP See under WORK IN PROGRESS.

wired bra See under UNDERGARMENTS.

wires See under JEWELRY.

witchoura mantle See under CAPES, CLOAKS, AND SHAWLS.

wolf See under FURS.

wolverine See under FURS.

women's petites Sizes designed for a shorter figure of larger girth, generally with a fuller torso, and shorter sleeves and hemlines, in comparison to the misses category.

women's plus Sizes designed for the adult woman of average to above average height who is fuller and more mature, especially in torso girth, than the misses category figure.

women's sizes Women's garments in sizes for heavier figure than those included in MISSES SIZE range; even-numbered bust sizes range from 38 to 50.

Women's Wear Daily (WWD) Daily newspaper published by Fairchild Fashion Media, a division of Condé Nast Publications, which covers the apparel, retail and textiles industries, including menswear, footwear, cosmetics and beauty, and social news about fashion celebrities, among other industry topics.

wooden button See under CLOSURES.

†woof See under FILLING.

†wool 1. Animal fiber from fleece of sheep or lambs. Fabrics made from wool are warm, resilient, absorbent, and easily dyed. Disadvantages include tendency to shrink, and poor resistance to moths (unless treated). May be knitted, woven, or felted, which is possible because of a microscopic structure of scales on the surface of the fibers. May also be blended with other fibers. Used extensively for outerwear, suits, skirts, and dresses. 2. As defined by the WOOL PRODUCTS LABELING ACT of 1939, fibers not only from sheep and lambs, but also angora goats (see under MOHAIR) or CASHMERE goats; ALPACA, LLAMA, CAMEL, or VICUÑA.

†woolen Yarns or woven or knitted fabrics made from wool fibers that are not combed but may be carded two or three times to produce CARDED YARNS. **Worsteds** are made from COMBED and CARDED YARNS. Generally, woolens have more textured surface and are softer than worsteds. Finishing processes for woolens frequently include napping or brushing as the fabrics have a fuzzy warm HAND rather than a smooth hand as do worsteds. Spelled *woollen* in England.

Wool Products Labeling Act Law passed by Congress in 1939 and currently stating that products containing wool must be labeled for the consumer as either **wool, new wool,** or **virgin wool**—all of which have never been used before—or **recycled wool**—which may either have been made into products, returned to the fibrous state, but never used before, or used by consumers and returned to the fibrous state. Contents of the various types of wool must be properly stated on a label for the customer by percentage. If content is less than 5%, it need not be labeled. (Law has been amended several times.)

woolworth shoe See under FOOTWEAR.

work apron See under APRONS.

work clothes Apparel of sturdy fabric used by factory workers and other laborers (e.g., shirts, pants, overalls, coveralls, and jackets, usually made of denim, drill, chino, or duck).

worked buttonholes See under CLOSURES.

worked in the round See under FURS.

work in progress (WIP) The total amount of merchandise currently being constructed at a garment factory.

workout suit See under ACTIVEWEAR: AEROBIC WEAR.

work pants See under PANTS.

work pocket See under POCKETS: TIE POCKET.

World Trade Organization (WTO) Organization that succeeds the GENERAL AGREEMENT ON TARIFFS AND TRADE (GATT) in regulating international trade in all areas, including textiles and apparel.

World War I helmet See under HEADWEAR.

World War II helmet See under HEADWEAR.

Worldwide Responsible Apparel Production (WRAP) An independent, nonprofit organization dedicated to the certification of lawful, humane, and ethical manufacturing throughout the world.

worry beads See under JEWELRY.

worsted See under WOOLEN.

woven friendship bracelet See under JEWELRY.

wrangler Western U.S. name for a cowhand.

Wrangler® Trademark for a brand of western pants, jackets, and other clothing and accessories.

wrap 1. *v.* To drape an outer garment around the body in various ways. 2. *n.* A garment put on when going out of doors (e.g., a shawl, scarf, cloak, or mantle). Use of the word in this way is not as popular as it was in former years. 3. *adj.* In contemporary usage, a shortened form of the word *wraparound,* used to describe garments that wrap. See under BLOUSES AND TOPS: WRAP BLOUSE and WRAPPED TOP; CLOSURES: WRAP CLOSING; and JUMPERS: WRAP JUMPER.

wraparound *adj.* Describes apparel and accessories that are not closed with fasteners, but lapped over and held with sashes that are knotted or tied in a bow. Also see under COATS AND JACKETS; EYEWEAR; SLEEPWEAR AND LOUNGEWEAR; SWEATERS; and SKIRTS: SARONG and WRAP SKIRT.

wrap collar See under NECKLINES AND COLLARS.

wrap cufflinks Cufflinks made with extra band extending around outside of cuff, connecting the two parts.

wrap dress See under DRESSES.

wrapped-leg pant See under PANTS.

wrapper 1. See under SLEEPWEAR AND LOUNGEWEAR. 2. See under COATS AND JACKETS. 3. See DRESSES: HOUSEDRESS.

wrap-rascal See under COATS AND JACKETS.

wrap shirt See under SHIRTS.

†wrinkle resistance Ability of fabric to resist creasing. Many fabrics made from manufactured fibers are resistant to wrinkling. Special finishing processes can be used on fabrics that wrinkle to make them more crease resistant.

wristband Strip of fabric, usually double, seamed to the lower edge of a sleeve and fastened around the wrist. Also see under CUFFS.

wrist length See under GLOVES AND GLOVE CONSTRUCTION.

wristlet See under HANDBAGS AND RELATED ACCESSORIES.

wrist strap See under JEWELRY.

wristwatch/wristwatch wardrobe See under WATCHES.

WTO See under WORLD TRADE ORGANIZATION.

WWD See under *WOMEN'S WEAR DAILY.*

X-ray dress See under DRESSES.

---

yachting *adj.* Descriptive of apparel that derives from or was inspired by items worn for the sport of boating. See under YACHTING COSTUME; COATS AND JACKETS: YACHTING COAT and YACHTING JACKET; and HEADWEAR: YACHTING CAP.

∞**yachting costume** Ensemble for women popular in 1890s for yachting and other sports, including canoeing and boating. Frequently consisted of a full-length two- or three-piece suit with nautical influence or MIDDY BLOUSE (see under BLOUSES AND TOPS) worn with a straw sailor hat or commodore cap. (See under HEADWEAR: SAILOR HAT #2 and COMMODORE CAP.)

†**yard** Unit of measurement used in the U.S. comprising 36″ or 3′, equivalent to 91.44 centimeters, used to measure fabric.

yard goods Fabric sold by the yard at retail stores for sewing. Also called *piece goods.*

yarmulka See under HEADWEAR: SKULLCAP.

†**yarn** Fibers twisted together tightly enough for weaving purposes. The two basic types are **staple yarn,** made from short fibers (e.g., cotton or wool carded to lie parallel, then twisted); and continuous **filament yarn,** comprised of strands of indefinite length used singly or several filaments twisted together.

†**yarn-dyed** *adj.* Describes fabric that is woven or knitted from yarns dyed before the fabric is constructed.

†**yarn number** A measurement that reflects the fineness of a yarn, expressed either indirectly or directly. The systems used vary from place to place but in general indirect measurement tends to be used for spun yarns and lower numbers indicate heavier and thicker yarns while higher numbers indicate finer yarns. Direct measurements tend to be used for filament and manufactured fibers and lower numbers indicate finer yarns while higher numbers indicate thicker yarns. The international system of yarn measurement is called the Tex System and is a direct yarn numbering system.

yellow diamond See under GEMS, GEM CUTS, AND SETTINGS: FANCY DIAMOND.

yeoman hat See under HEADWEAR.

yoga pants See under PANTS.

yoke **1.** Portion of garment fitted across the shoulders—in front, back, or both—to which the lower front and back sections are attached. **2.** Fitted top of a skirt to which the lower part of the skirt may be attached by means of GATHERING, SHIRRING, GORES, or PLEATS (see under CLOTHING CONSTRUCTION DETAILS). **3.** *adj.* Describes apparel that incorporates a yoke. See under BLOUSES AND TOPS: YOKE BLOUSE; NECKLINES AND COLLARS: YOKE COLLAR; and SKIRTS: YOKE SKIRT.

yoke at neckline

∞**york-tan gloves** See under GLOVES AND GLOVE CONSTRUCTION.

∞**york wrapper** See under DRESSES.

youghal lace See under LACES.

yugoslavian embroidery See under EMBROIDERIES AND SEWING STITCHES.

yuppies A nickname applied to young, upwardly mobile professionals who work in fields such as the law and business. *Der.* Derived from the first letters of *y*oung *up*wardly mobile.

---

zebra See under FURS.

zeitgeist (zite'gaist) (German) "The spirit of the age." Used in English to refer to the thought and feeling of a particular period of time.

zendado See under SCARVES.

Zhivago/Zhivago influence (zhi-vah'go) Clothes inspired by those worn in the 1965 film *Doctor Zhivago,* based on the novel by Boris Pasternak, which was set in Revolutionary Russia in 1917. Introduced by Dior in 1966–67, this look featured Russian-inspired clothing and accessories such as a Russian-type overblouse with high-standing collar closing at the side rather than center front. Coats were usually midi length and often lavishly trimmed with fur at neck, sleeves, and hem. Boots were also featured. See under BLOUSES AND TOPS: ZHIVAGO BLOUSE; COATS AND JACKETS: ZHIVAGO COAT; NECKLINES AND COLLARS: COSSACK COLLAR; and SHIRTS: ZHIVAGO SHIRT.

Zhivago-influenced style 1960s

Zhivago dress See under DRESSES: RUSSIAN SHIRTDRESS.

zigzag stitch See under EMBROIDERIES AND SEWING STITCHES.

zip-in/zip-out lining Completely removable lining inserted into a coat by means of a zipper around the coat facing. It starts at one side of the hem, runs up side, across back neckline, and down the other side to make a dual-purpose coat. Also called a *shell.*

zip-off coat See under COATS AND JACKETS.

zipper 1. See under CLOSURES. 2. *adj.* Describes apparel in which a zipper is a prominent feature. See under PANTS: ZIPPERED PANTS; UNDERWEAR: ZIPPER FOUNDATION; and ZIPPERED GIRDLE.

zip pocket See under POCKETS.

zircon See under GEMS, GEM CUTS, AND GEM SETTINGS.

zizith See under TSITSITH.

zodiac signs Symbols of various constellations that are used in astrology. These signs sometimes appear as ornaments in apparel. See under JEWELRY: ZODIAC NECKLACE.

zone (zo-knee) ∞1. A piece, used in 1770s and 1780s, that filled in an open area of the bodice of a dress. The shape corresponded to that of the exposed gap. 2. See under BELTS.

zootie See under ZOOT SUIT.

∞**zoot suit** First adopted by teenaged boys of either Mexican American or African American heritage (sources disagree) and associated with the popularity of jitterbugging (a dance style) in the early 1940s, this extreme form of the sack suit was long with excessively wide shoulders and long, wide lapels. Trousers were pleated at the waist and tight at ankle. The outfit was worn with a wide-brimmed hat, and an extra-long key chain dangling from a watch pocket with attached keys placed in side pocket of pants and was one of the first styles to originate at the lower end of the socioeconomic ladder. Those who adopted these styles were known as **zooties.**

zoot suit 1942

zori See under FOOTWEAR.

zorina See under FURS: SKUNK.

∞**zouave** *adj.* Descriptive of fashions inspired by or adapted from the costumes of Algerian troops that fought as part of the French army in the 1830s. During the American Civil War, a regiment called the Zouaves fought for the North and adopted, in part, the costume of the French Zouave troops. The term appears in fashion as early as the 1840s and as late as the 1890s. See under ZOUAVE PUFF; ZOUAVE UNIFORM; COATS AND JACKETS: ZOUAVE COAT, ZOUAVE JACKET, and ZOUAVE PALETOT; HANDBAGS AND RELATED ACCESSORIES: ZOUAVE POUCH; SHIRTS: ZOUAVE SHIRT; and SKIRTS: ZOUAVE SKIRT.

∞**zouave puff** (zoo ahv') Single or double horizontal puffs at the back of the skirt, a style of the 1870s to 1880s. *Der.* Arabic, *Zouaova,* a Kabyle tribe, one of the Berbers, living in Algeria or Tunisia.

∞**Zouave uniform** (zoo-ahv') 1. Colorful oriental uniform consisting of a waist-length, unbuttoned navy-blue jacket worn over a navy-blue blouse (both trimmed in red), combined with below-the-knee red trousers styled like harem pants; short black boots; leggings; a sash of light blue; and a green-and-red turban with a blue tassel. Worn by French infantry soldiers in Algeria, a military corps originally composed of Algerians noted for their strength and courage. 2. Member of a military group, particularly some volunteer regiments in American Civil War, who wore a similar uniform that is same style but may vary in color *Der.* Arabic, *Zouaova,* a Kabyle tribe, one of the Berbers, living in Algeria or Tunisia.

zucchetto See under CLERICAL DRESS: CALOTTE.

Zuni jewelry See under JEWELRY.

zuni snake eye ring See under JEWELRY.

appendix: designers

Abboud, Joseph (ah-bood') *American designer* (1950–)
Born in Massachusetts to Lebanese parents, Joseph Abboud's mother was a seamstress and his great-grandfather owned Australia's largest tailored clothing company. He began working at Louis of Boston while in college, where he gained a strong retail background. He joined Ralph Lauren in 1981 as a sales representative at Polo/RALPH LAUREN and eventually joined the design team. In 1986, he started his own label. He was the first to win the Council of Fashion Designers of America (CFDA) Award for Best Menswear Designer two years running—in 1989 and 1990. He sold his trademarks and the rights to his name to JA Apparel in 2000; he left the company in 2005. In 2007 he launched a new line called Jaz.

Aberra, Amsale (ahm-sah'-leh) *American designer* (1955–)
Born in Ethiopia, Amsale Aberra immigrated to the United States to pursue a degree at the Fashion Institute of Technology in New York. She worked as an assistant designer at Harvé Bernard for two years after her graduation. While planning her own wedding in 1985, she became frustrated at the lack of simple and sophisticated bridal gowns; she launched a small bridal business out of her New York apartment, advertising in the want ads. The label grew quickly and expanded to include dresses for the bridal party and evening wear. She is considered one of the top designer bridal resources in the world.

Ackermann, Haider *French designer* (1971–)
Born in Bogota, Colombia, Ackermann moved to Belgium in 1994 to study at the Royal Academy of Fine Arts in Antwerp. He worked as an intern for John Galliano and as an assistant to Wim Neels, his former teacher, before launching his own label in 2000 and showing his first collection in Paris for Fall/Winter 2002/2003. He is influenced by global cultures and their dress codes; his silhouettes are typically asymmetric with a modern, urban energy. He is known for his ability to drape in jersey, suede, and leather.

Acra, Reem (ak-ra, ree-m) *American designer* (active 1997–)
Born in Beirut, Lebanon, Akra studied at the American University of Beirut and then came to the United States to attend the Fashion Institute of Technology in New York, finishing her studies at ESMOD in Paris. A leader in luxury bridal and evening wear, her designs draw inspiration from varied cultures and her travels around the world. She launched her first bridal collection in 1997; her designs feature classic silhouettes with intricate beadwork and embroidery. In 2002, she launched an evening wear collection and in 2008 her first ready-to-wear collection.

ADAM (Adam Lippes) *American designer* (1972–)
Lippes began his career at Polo Ralph Lauren and then Oscar de la Renta, where he was quickly promoted to Global Creative Director. He launched a basics collection in 2004 under the label adampluseve, which evolved into ADAM + EVE and finally ADAM. The line has become a full-blown sportswear line that utilizes some of the finest cotton, cashmere, and wool available.

Adolfo (Adolfo Sardiña) *American designer* (1933–)
Born in Havana, Cuba, Adolfo began his career as a milliner in New York in 1948. Gradually, he added clothing to his line, then later switched entirely to apparel. Design interests include: menswear, active sportswear, and accessories.

Adri (Adrienne Steckling-Coen) *American designer* (1930–2006)
After studying at Parsons School of Design in New York, Adri worked first at B. H. Wragge, then ANNE FOGARTY, after which she opened a small business for ready-to-wear and leisure wear. She established Adri Clotheslab, Inc., in 1983. She has said she believes that styles should evolve naturally from one collection to the next so that clients can collect, add to, and mix them freely from season to season.

Adrian, Gilbert (Adrian Adolf Greenberg) *American designer* (1903–1959)
Adrian designed for Metro-Goldwyn-Mayer Studios (1923 to 1939), then opened a couture and high-priced ready-to-wear retail business in Beverly Hills in 1941. It closed in 1948, and he continued in wholesale until 1953. Characteristics he was noted for included exaggeratedly wide shoulders on tailored suits; dolman sleeves; dramatic animal prints on sinuous black-crepe evening gowns; asymmetric lines; diagonal closings; and huge ruffle-topped sleeves.

AF Vandevorst *Belgian designers* (An Vandevorst [1968–] and Filip Arickx [1971–])
Graduates of the Royal Academy of Fine Arts in Antwerp, An Vandevorst worked as an assistant to Dries Van Noten; Arickx worked for Dirk Bikkembergs as a teenager and entered the service after graduation. They established their label in 1997. Their design style exudes a slouchy confidence, sexy in its intellectual cool. They use a medical-style red cross as their logo.

Agnès B (Agnès Andrée Marguerite Troublé) *French designer* (1941–)
After graduating from the École des Beaux-Arts in Versailles and doing an editorial stint at *Elle* magazine, Agnès B worked as an assistant to Dorothée Bis and as a freelance designer for several clothing firms before going into business for herself in the early 1970s. Her designs were a reaction to what she saw as clothes that were too dressy and too trendy. She is known for laid-back sportswear and accessories for women, men, and children.

Alaïa, Azzedine *French designer* (1935–)
Born in Tunis, Tunisia, Azzedine Alaïa studied sculpture at the École des Beaux-Arts of Tunis. While in art school he worked for several dressmakers. In 1957 he went to Paris, where he worked for Christian Dior, Guy Laroche, and THIERRY MUGLER. For a time, he supported himself as an au pair, while making clothes for his fashionable young employers and their friends. It wasn't until 1980 that he presented his first ready-to-wear collection. He utilizes elasticized fabrics and tapes to create clothes that are seamed, molded, and draped to define and reveal a woman's curves, yet are never vulgar.

Alfaro, Victor *American designer* (1965–)
Born in Mexico, Victor Alfaro immigrated to the U.S. and graduated from the Fashion Institute of Technology in 1987. After working as an assistant to Mary Ann Restivo and Joseph Abboud, he established his own label in the early 1990s, specializing in evening wear. In 1995 he received the CFDA Award for new fashion talent. In 2000 he launched the VIC diffusion line. After taking a break from fashion for a few years, he signed a licensing agreement with department store the Bon-Ton in 2008 to create an exclusive line for their stores. That relationship ended in 2012.

Allard, Linda *American bridge designer* (1940–)
Educated at Kent State University, Allard has worked for Ellen Tracy since her graduation in 1962. Assistant designer until 1964, she then assumed the position of design director, and in 1984 her name was added to the label. Her designs have been described as "career clothes that are up-to-the-minute but not over the top."

Amies, Hardy *British designer* (1909–2003)
London born, Amies worked at London couture house Lachasse from 1934 to 1941 and for House of Worth in London during World War II. Opening his own house in Savile Row in 1948, he specialized in tailored suits, coats, and cocktail and evening dresses. He started designing menswear in 1959. Considered forward thinking in his contemporary clothes, which included pant suits for women; wide yachting pants; and casual classics.

Anthony, John (Gianantonio Iorio) *American designer* (1938–)
Born in New York, Anthony worked at Devonbrook and with Adolph Zelinka before opening his own business on New York's Seventh Avenue in 1971. He was known for designs in natural fabrics, cardigan sweaters with pants, mannish shirts and ties, pullovers with skirts, dramatic easy pants, and gala dresses in soft satins with sequins and in sheer wool.

Aquilano Rimondi (Tommaso Aquilano and Roberto Rimondi) *Italian design team* (active 2004–)
Tommaso Aquilano and Roberto Rimondi met in 1998 while both were working at Max Mara. In 2004, they founded their first brand, 6267. They received the Who Is on Next Award in 2005; the resulting press allowed them to show at Milan Fashion Week. In 2008, they were appointed creative directors for Gianfranco Ferré; that same year they launched the Aquilano Rimondi label.

Armani, Giorgio *Italian designer* (1934–)
Born in Italy, Armani worked for seven years as assistant buyer for a large Italian department store and then went on to design menswear for the Cerutti group. His first menswear collection in 1974 attracted attention for his unconstructed blazer. Working on women's wear in 1975 and after and using fine tailoring techniques, he became known for easy and uncontrived shapes; and masculine cuts with feminine qualities in exquisite Italian fabrics in neutral colors such as beige, black, gray, and taupe. His business includes boutiques, accessories, and perfumes for men and women. Designs under the Emporio label offer his creations at affordable prices.

Ashley, Laura *British designer* (1925–1985)
Born in Wales, Ashley formed a company in 1953 to sell household linens. She began selling simple smocks, aprons, and dresses as well in 1969. By the late 1960s, Laura Ashley retail outlets had been established in the United Kingdom and abroad.

Azrouel, Yigal (as-roo-elle', yee-gal') *American designer* (active 1998–)
Israeli-born Azrouel received no formal training in fashion. He launched his line in 1998 in New York. He is known for his modern draped silhouettes in high-quality fabrics. His customers respond to his effortless feminine chic and urban sophistication inspired by art, culture, nature, architecture, and his travels.

Badgley Mischka (badge'-lee meesh'-ka) *American design team* (Mark Badgley [1961–] and James Mischka [1960–])
Mark Badgley and James Mischka met at Parsons School of Design where they both graduated with BFA degrees in fashion design. Both became design assistants, Badgley for Jack Rogers and Donna Karan, and Mischka went to Yves Saint Laurent and Willi Smith. They teamed up in 1988 to form their own company specializing in beaded evening wear. The company was purchased in 1992 by Escada. They have since expanded their focus to include day wear, separates, and bridal gowns. In October 2004, the company was acquired by Iconix Brand Group.

Bailey, Christopher *British designer* (1971–) See under BURBERRY.

Balenciaga, Cristóbal (bal-lawn-see-ah'-gah) *Spanish-French couturier* (1895–1972)
After copying a Paris suit for a rich marquesa at age 14, he left his home in Spain to study clothing design. He opened his own house in Paris in 1937 and was immediately successful. His career continued until his retirement in 1968. A partial list of his innovations includes: revolutionary semifit jacket, 1951; middy dress evolving into chemise, 1955; cocoon coat; balloon skirt; short-front, long-back flamenco evening gown; bathrobe-wrap coat; pillbox hat. In the late 1950s and early 1960s, Balenciaga designed gowns inspired by the post-cubist and abstract-expressionist painters of the period.

Balmain, Pierre (bal'-man, pee-yair') *French couturier* (1914–1982)
After studying architecture, Balmain designed at Molyneux from 1934 to 1939, then was assistant to Lucien Lelong from 1940 to 1945. He opened a new house in 1945, which was an immediate success. He was known for wearable, elegant clothes, which changed little from season to season; safe daytime classics; extravagant evening gowns. The house continued with other designers after his death.

Banks, Jeffrey *American designer* (1955–)
Educated at Pratt Institute and Parsons School of Design in New York, Jeffrey Banks began his career as assistant to Ralph Lauren, and then to Calvin Klein. He also designed for Alixandre, Concorde International, Merona Sport, and Nik Nik. He launched menswear and boy's labels under his own name in 1980. In 1988, Japanese investor Tomio Taki bought one-third interest in a joint venture with Banks, allowing Banks more time to design. Following a hiatus ending in 1998, Banks became design director of the Johnnie Walker menswear collection and creative design director for several Bloomingdale's labels. He is known for his penchant for plaid and classic silhouettes.

Banton, Travis *American designer* (1894–1958)
After World War I, Banton trained as a designer with LUCILE and Madame Frances. He went to Hollywood in 1924 and in the 1930s designed all of Marlene Dietrich's costumes. At the same time he was designing for several studios, he ran his own couture business for private clients.

Barnes, Jhane *American designer* (1954–)
Jhane Barnes established her own company in 1977, known for unconstructed, beautifully tailored menswear in luxurious and original fabrics. She is an innovator in computerized textile technology and committed to environmental sustainability.

Barrett, Neil *British designer* (1965–)
Barrett attended Central Saint Martins and the Royal College of Art. He worked for Gucci and then Prada Uomo before joining the Belgian luggage company Samsonite, where he designed a menswear collection intended for travelers. Primarily known for his "haute utilitarian" menswear, his first capsule collection for women appeared in Milan in January 2000. Barrett designs for less-than-perfect bodies and is known for using innovative modern fabrics. In 2003, he was named creative director for Puma.

Barrie, Scott *American designer* (1946–1993)
Born in Italy, Barrie attended Philadelphia Museum College of Art and the Mayer School in New York. He began designing in 1966, selling to small boutiques and eventually to Henri Bendel and Bloomingdale's. He established his own company, Barrie Sport, in 1969, known for skinny evening dresses in matte jersey with high slits and modern draping. In the early 1980s, Barrie moved to Milan and designed for the house of Krizia.

Bartlett, John *American designer* (1963–)
A menswear designer known for giving familiar pieces a fresh, young look by altering the scale and proportions and using unexpected mixes of texture and pattern. After graduating from Harvard with a B.A. in Sociology, he went on to the Fashion Institute of Technology to study menswear, where he received the Bill Robinson Award. He worked for Willi Smith, Bill Robinson, and Ronaldus Shamask before establishing his own label in 1992. In spite of winning two CFDA Awards in 1994 and 1997, he struggled to build a financially viable business. In 1997, he went to Milan and became the creative director of Byblos and in 2000 launched a new John Bartlett global collection under an agreement with Byblos sister company Genny. In 2009, he accepted an invitation to develop a menswear collection for Liz Claiborne.

Bartley, Luella *British designer* (1974–)
Bartley launched the Luella label in 1999 after a successful career as a journalist and fashion editor for British *Vogue.* She projected a whimsical girly/punk aesthetic, which appealed to a young adult customer. In 2001, she expanded distribution to Milan and New York. Target chose her as their debut guest designer for their Go International designer collaboration strategy in 2006. The brand ceased trading in 2009 when they lost funding.

Beckham, Victoria *British designer* (1974–)
Victoria Adams rose to fame in the late 1990s as part of the all-girl pop group the Spice Girls; she was dubbed "Posh Spice." After the group split she continued to make headlines as a model and style icon. She married British footballer David Beckham in 1997. Her fashion career

began when she designed a limited edition line of jeans for Rock and Republic in 2004; later she launched her own denim brand, dVb Style. In 2008, she launched the Victoria Beckham ready-to-wear line, which received positive press and is carried by specialty stores such as Bergdorf Goodman and Saks Fifth Avenue.

Beene, Geoffrey *American designer* (1927–2004)
Born in Haynesville, Louisiana, Beene studied design in New York and Paris. From 1949 to 1957 he designed for Samuel Winston and Harmay and joined Teal Traina in 1958, where his name was put on the label. He opened his own business in 1962 and became known for these characteristics: simplicity, emphasis on cut and line, dressmaking details, and unusual fabrics. In late 1960s, his business expanded to include furs, swimwear, jewelry, scarves, menswear, and a boutique collection, *Beene Bag,* in 1970, as well as a variety of licensed products.

Bérard, Christian (bayr-ard) *French artist, decorator, and costume designer* (1902–1949)
An illustrator for *Vogue* in the 1930s whose influence extended far beyond his artwork, Bérard was in great demand for his aesthetic and technical advice. He designed scenery and costumes for many theater productions by his good friend Jean Cocteau.

Biagiotti, Laura *Italian designer* (1943–)
Biagiotti graduated from Rome University with a degree in archaeology before going to work at her mother's clothing company, where she began producing clothes for other designers. Her first collection under her own label appeared in Florence in 1972. Soon afterward she bought a cashmere company and developed her reputation as a superb knitwear designer for both men and women. She collaborates with her daughter, Lavinia Cigna.

Bikkembergs, Dirk *Belgian designer* (1959–)
A graduate of the Royal Academy of Fine Arts in Antwerp, German-born Bikkembergs is part of the wave of talented designers to come out of Belgium since the early 1980s. He worked at various Belgian fashion firms before collaborating with a Belgian shoe manufacturer to design a collection of men's shoes in 1986. Men's clothing and then knits followed before his first full collection shown in Paris in 1988. He showed his first women's collection in 1993. His design philosophy is to make enduring fashion that will not be quickly dated.

Blahnik, Manolo *American designer* (1943–)
After completing his studies, Blahnik came to London in 1971. He opened a shoe store in Chelsea (London) in 1973 and in New York in 1979. He is known for "ornate, romantic, exotic shoes in luxurious materials."

Blass, Bill *American designer* (1922–2002)
Blass studied at Parsons School of Design in New York in the early 1940s and was employed sketching sportswear for David Crystal. After World War II, he designed for Anna Miller & Co. Miller merged with Maurice Rentner, Ltd., in 1958 and Blass was head designer and eventually vice president, and then owner, after which the company name changed to Bill Blass Ltd. Noted for women's classic sportswear and glamorous evening wear, the firm's design interests include: rainwear, men's clothing, Blassport women's sportswear, loungewear, scarves, automobiles, uniforms for American Airlines flight attendants, and chocolates. Blass sold his business and retired in 1999. The firm continues with Lars Nilsson as designer.

Bohan, Marc *French designer* (1926–)
Bohan worked with Molyneux, Piguet, and Madeleine de Rauch from 1945 to 1953 before opening his own business in 1953. He sold it in the same year and worked for Patou for a short time and freelanced for Originala in New York until 1958. In late 1958 he joined house of Dior, replacing Yves Saint Laurent, and continued as chief designer of couture and ready-to-wear for the Dior line until 1989.

Boss, Hugo *German design group*
Boss originally made his firm's name in menswear, but by 2000 they were also doing women's clothing. Known for tailored suits and trim shirts that utilize feminine fabrics and touches.

Branquinho, Veronique (bran-kee-no) *Belgian designer* (1973–)
A graduate of the Royal Academy of Fine Arts in Antwerp, Branquinho worked briefly for several commercial labels before opening her own business in 1997. Her designs were featured at Colette, a concept store that promotes what it considers to be the best designer collections for men and women each season, and attracted both favorable press and orders. She prides herself on putting her own signature on current trends. Her own label included garments and accessories for ladies and men using the highest quality fabrics, with a focus on fit. She closed her own label in 2009 but continues to design for other labels, including Delvaux and Camper.

Brooks, Donald *American designer* (1928–2005)
Brooks studied fine arts at Syracuse University and at Parsons School of Design in New York. Noted for uncluttered day clothes in clear, unusual colors, careful detailing, his own designed dramatic prints, and romantic evening costumes. He also designed costumes for stage and screen. Design interests included: furs, swimwear, menswear, shoes, costume jewelry, wigs, and bed linens.

Browne, Thom *American designer* (1965–)
Thom Browne began his career with Brooks Brothers in 2006 where he designed a high-end unisex collection for the outlet called Black Fleece. Later, a job in a Giorgio Armani showroom landed him a high profile position for Club Monaco, owned by Polo Ralph Lauren. He launched the Thom Browne label in 2001, declaring war on casual Friday with his narrow-cut suits (sometimes in plaid) paired with high-water pants or shorts.

Bruce *American design team* (Daphne Gutierrez [1972–] and Nicole Noselli [1972–])
The Bruce design team met while studying at Parsons School of Design in New York and began their collaboration soon after graduation in 1995. They design clothes unique to the wearer, with details and shaping

devices that require a closer look. They are known for their skillful pattern cutting, and exacting execution. They took a break between 2004 and 2007 but made a comeback in 2008.

Bui, Barbara (boo′-ee) *French designer* (1957–)
A self-taught designer of French-Vietnamese origins, Bui studied literature and theater. With her partner, William Halimi, she opened a boutique named Kabuki to sell her designs. The store was later renamed Barbara Bui. Her collections include suits, dresses, furs, evening wear, separates, bags, and shoes in a style that balances the masculine and feminine. Her global customer has a strong, confident point of view.

Burberry *British designer label* (founded in 1856)
A British luxury fashion house founded in 1856 by Thomas Burberry. Burberry distributes fashion clothing, accessories, and fragrances for men and women. Many of their products feature the brand's trademark tartan plaid, created in the 1920s, in tan, red, and black. The plaid was first used as a lining in the label's iconic trench coat. The company distributes apparel under the labels Burberry Prorsum, Burberry London, and Burberry Brit. Christopher Baily is the chief creative officer.

Burch, Tory *American designer* (1966–)
Contemporary designer Tory Burch launched her line in 2004. She offers easy, classic, 1960s-style silhouettes. A well-known New York socialite and mother, she studied art history at the University of Pennsylvania and then worked in PR for Ralph Lauren and Vera Wang before establishing her own firm, which appeals to a cross section of independent, fashion-conscious women much like herself.

Burrows, Stephen *American designer* (1943–)
After studying at Philadelphia Museum College of Art and The Fashion Institute of Technology, Burrows and classmate Roz Rubenstein opened a boutique in 1968. Hired the next year by Henri Bendel, Burrows concentrated on design. He worked for Bendel off and on, taking some time out to design for private customers and the theater. He returned to Bendel, doing a collection of evening dresses and separates in the 1990s.

Byblos *Italian design label* (founded in 1973)
Founded in 1973 as a division of Genny SpA, designers have included Versace (1977–1979); Guy Paulin (1979–1981); Alan Cleaver and Keith Varty (1981–1996); Richard Tyler (1997–2000); Richard Bartlett (2000–2002); Federico Piaggi, Greg Myler, and Stefano Citron (2003–2006); and Manuel Facchini (2007–2013).

Callot Soeurs (kal′-o sir) *French couture house* (1895–1935)
This firm was founded in 1895 as a lace shop by three sisters. From 1916 to 1927, it became one of the great Paris dressmaking houses and was famous for delicate lace blouses; gold and silver lamé; Renaissance patterns; much chiffon, georgette, and organdy; and rococo flower embroidery. It closed in 1937.

Capasa, Ennio *Italian designer* (1960–)
A graduate of the Milan Academy of Fine Arts in 1972, Capasa worked for Yohji Yamamoto, where he learned to drape, cut, and sew before launching his own label in 1986, Costume National, based on the title of an antique book on French uniforms. His silhouettes are close to the body, yet relaxed. He designs clothing, accessories, and scents for both men and women that appeal to a global audience, but are often under the radar of mainstream press. His C'N'C label is a secondary line of avant-garde streetwear.

Capraro, Albert *American designer* (1943–)
After graduating from Parsons School of Design, Capraro worked for Lilly Daché and then Oscar de la Renta before establishing his own designer ready-to-wear label in 1975. He was a favorite designer of First Lady Betty Ford. He closed his business in 1985, but continued to design for private clients and an exclusive line for the specialty store Martha, until it closed.

Capucci, Roberto (ca-puch′-ee) *Italian designer* (1930–)
Capucci first showed independently in Rome in 1952 at age 21. Moved to Paris in 1962; then reopened in Rome in 1969. Known for masterful handling of drapery, imaginative cutting, no extra ornamentation, tapered-pants jumpsuits, halter-neck hostess gowns, balloon drapes, huge bubble skirts, kimono and dolman sleeves, and sculptured forms. Also designed children's wear, knits, furs, footwear, and millinery.

Cardin, Pierre (kar-dahn′, pee-air′) *French designer* (1922–)
Born in Venice, Cardin grew up in St. Étienne, France. He studied architecture in Paris and designed costumes for Cocteau's movie *La Belle et la Bête* ("Beauty and the Beast"). His work history included PAQUIN, then SCHIAPARELLI, and head of the workroom at DIOR in 1947. He opened his own house in 1950 at age 25. A success by 1957, Cardin introduced many innovations for women and was called revolutionary for his metal body jewelry, unisex astronaut suits, helmets, batwing jumpsuits, and tunics over tights. He started designing menswear in 1958 and was considered a leader in field of couturiers designing for both sexes. He was the first Paris couturier to sell his own ready-to-wear, designed by André Oliver, to department stores. He entered into a trade agreement with the People's Republic of China in 1979 for the establishment of factories to produce Cardin clothes.

Carnegie, Hattie *American designer* (1889–1956)
Born in Vienna, Carnegie worked in New York from 1909 to early 1950s. She took her name from that of Andrew Carnegie, "the richest man in the world." Starting in 1909 as Carnegie–Ladies' Hatter, the firm became Hattie Carnegie, Inc., in 1918 and expanded into resort shops, wholesale business, factories, jewelry, and cosmetics. Designer of made-to-order and ready-to-wear for society and movie stars, Carnegie was influential throughout the 1930s and 1940s. She was noted for the "little

Carnegie suit." Among the noted designers who worked for her were NORMAN NORELL, JAMES GALANOS, PAULINE TRIGÈRE, and CLAIRE MCCARDELL.

Cashin, Bonnie *American designer* (1907–2000)
Cashin specialized in comfortable country and travel clothes in wool jersey, knits, tweeds, canvas, and leather, and believed in functional layers of clothing, which she coordinated with her own designs of hoods, bags, boots, and belts that were influenced by her collection of ethnic fashions and fabrics. Considered one of the most innovative of American designers, she also designed for stage, ballet, and motion pictures. From 1953 on, she freelanced for sportswear houses and did bags for Coach. She started the Knittery in 1967, which made limited-edition collections of hand knits.

Cassini, Oleg (cass-ee′-nee) *American designer* (1913–2006)
Born in Paris, raised in Italy, Cassini came to the United States in 1936. He designed for films and in New York and was selected by Jacqueline Kennedy as her official designer while her husband was president in the 1960s. He was known for sheath and A-line dresses and men's turtlenecks.

Castiglioni, Consuelo *Italian designer* (1959–)
Consuelo Castiglioni married into a family known as one of the premier suppliers of top-quality fur pelts to designer labels such as Fendi and Prada. The business was suffering from the anti-fur movement of the early 1990s, which led Castiglioni to design a small fur collection in 1993 called Marni; she showed it during Milan Fashion Week. Her first collections drew little press, but in 1999, she presented a colorful hippie collection of patchwork coats, tie-dyed crushed velvet dresses, and multicolored fur jackets that found critical acclaim. The fashion house has since split off from the fur business and is known for its use of luxurious materials such as cashmere, silk, and fur.

Castillo, Edmundo *American designer* (1967–)
A footwear designer for Sergio Rossi.

Cavalli, Roberto *Italian designer* (1940–)
After attending the Academy of Art in Florence, Italy, Roberto Cavalli decided to apply his painterly techniques to textiles rather than canvas. He patented a leather printing technique and is known for textile innovations in the denim category, including the use of stretch denim and sandblasting. Cavalli's first collection in 1970 featured printed leather evening gowns. He achieves an exotic, but bohemian glamour by mixing wild prints and applying them to seductively cut silhouettes. He began applying his design philosophy to denim in 1988 and launched his Just Cavalli denim label in 2000. He has also designed co-branded collections for H&M and Target Australia. His designs have been worn on stage by entertainers such as Jennifer Lopez and Christina Aguilera.

Cerruti, Nino (che-roo′-tee) *Italian designer* (1930–)
Cerruti's family owned a textile business, which Nino Cerruti took over after his father's untimely death. Intent on taking the business in a more modern direction, he began designing menswear in 1957 and moved the ready-to-wear business to Paris. Over the years, the company has offered menswear, women's wear, jeans, accessories, and fragrances, but the label is best known for its classic wool suits, which have been featured in movies such as *Bonnie and Clyde, Pretty Woman,* and *Basic Instinct.* Early in his career, Giorgio Armani honed his craft under Cerruti. Cerruti retired in 1996 and the company hired a succession of designers and creative directors but none seemed to have the right fit. The company was sold to the Italian corporation Fin.part SpA in 2000 and then to U.S. private equity firm MatlinPatterson in 2006. Cerruti continues to be involved in the family textile business.

Cesarani, Sal *American designer* (1939–)
Born to Italian immigrant tailors, Cesarani graduated from the High School of Fashion Industries and the State University of New York. He honed his color sense and knowledge of merchandising working for Paul Stuart, a prestigious men's store, and went on to work at Polo Ralph Lauren and Stanley Blacker. He launched Cesarini Ltd. in 1976 with a focus on menswear. Relying on his traditional tailoring background, he approaches modern trends in a classic way.

Chalayan, Hussein (sha-lie′-on) *British designer* (1970–)
Born in Nicosia, Cyprus, Hussein Chalayan and his family moved to the U.K. where he enrolled at London's Central Saint Martins College of Arts and Design. He apprenticed with a Savile Row tailor. His eccentric 1993 graduation collection featured silk dresses, which he had buried in his garden and dug up again; the avant-garde London boutique, Brown's, bought the collection in its entirety and featured it in their windows. Regarded as one of fashion's most experimental and innovative designers, he is known for creating interactive showpieces such as a frockcoat that builds itself (Fall, 2007); a coffee table that morphs into a skirt (Fall 2000); a dress with wings that mimics an airplane (Spring 2000); and pieces that can be folded into an envelope (Spring 2000). He is quick to point out that his collections also include real clothes inspired by art, architecture, politics, nature, and sculpture. His designs have been worn by Bjork and Lady Gaga.

Chanel, Gabrielle "Coco" (shan-ell′) *French couturière* (1883–1971)
Chanel started with a hat shop in 1913. She opened her own couture house in 1914 and closed it after World War II. In 1954, she reopened again, hardly changing her original concept of simple wearability. Her business consisted of the couture house, textile and perfume laboratories where Chanel No. 5 originated, and a costume-jewelry workshop. In the 1960s, her trademark suit—braid-trimmed, collarless jacket, patch pockets, and knee-length skirt in soft Scottish tweeds—was worn with multiple gold-chain necklaces with fake jewels; chain-handled quilted handbags; beige-and-black slingback pumps; flat, black hair bows, and a gardenia. She died in the midst of preparing a collection in January 1971.

The House of Chanel continued, directed by a succession of designers. Ready-to-wear was added in 1975, with Philippe Guibourgé as designer. KARL LAGERFELD has since taken over design responsibilities for both couture and ready-to-wear.

Chanin, Natalie *American designer*

Natalie Chanin began working in the fashion industry in 1988 in New York and later moved to Europe, working as a stylist and costume designer in film and photography. When she returned to the U.S. she launched Project Alabama with a series of business partners. The label gained a cult-like following for their one-of-a-kind garments made from up-cycled T-shirts, which were hand-stitched by local women using quilting techniques from the rural South. The company ceased operation in 2006 due to local laws about using contract sewers. Natalie Chanin went on to launch Alabama Chanin using the same techniques, but restructuring the manufacturing to comply with state labor laws. The company has grown to the point that they can no longer rely on up-cycled T-shirts; instead they use 100 percent organic cotton.

Chéruit, Madeleine (share'-oo-eet) *French couturière* (c. 1860s–unknown)

One of first women leaders of haute couture, Cheruit took over the house of Raudnitz (founded in 1873). She was first to launch simple, almost severe models in contrast to fussy clothes of the time. Not a designer, she was a critical editor of her house's designs. Louise Boulanger designed for her; PAUL POIRET sold her sketches at the beginning of his career. Cheruit retired in 1923, although the house continued until 1935, when it was taken over by SCHIAPARELLI.

Chloé *French design label* (founded in 1952)

Chloé was founded in 1952 by Gaby Aghion, an Egyptian-born Parisian, and her business partner Jacques Lenoir. The Chloé label represented the first designer ready-to-wear business merging the quality of haute couture with the postwar demand for accessible, stylish clothing. The label has been designed by KARL LAGERFELD, MARTINE SITBON, STELLA MCCARTNEY, PHOEBE PHILO, Paulo Melim Andersson, Hannah MacGibbon, and Clare Waight-Keller. The label is known for its romantic femininity.

Chung, Doo-Ri *Korean American designer* (1973–)

Doo-Ri Chung graduated from Parsons School of Design in 1995; she worked for Banana Republic and Geoffrey Beene, where she spent six years and eventually rose to the position of head designer. She began her own label in 2001 out of her family's basement. Her designs are avant-garde but not trend-driven. In 2012, she left her namesake label and in 2013 was named creative director of Vince.

Claiborne, Liz *American designer* (1929–2007)

Born in Brussels, Belgium, Claiborne grew up in New Orleans, then studied painting in Belgium and France. In 1949, in a design contest held by *Harper's Bazaar,* she won a trip to Europe to design and sketch. On her return to the United States she worked as a fit model, sketcher, and assistant to Tina Leser, and others, at Youth Guild. With her husband Arthur Ortenberg as business manager, she established Liz Claiborne, Inc., in 1976. Their original interests in sportswear expanded into designs for dresses and children's wear. The business has grown so that her function became largely as editor of the work of other designers. Their philosophy: simple and uncomplicated designs of mix-and-match separates with easy natural look; sensitive use of color; technical knowledge of fabrics; and moderate price range. She and her husband retired from the company in 1989. After considerable downsizing, the company was renamed Fifth & Pacific Companies, Inc. in 2012.

Clark, Ossie *British designer* (1942–1996)

Ossie Clark was one of the top designers for English film and rock stars in the 1960s. Known for being in touch with music, art, politics, film, and photography, he dressed the likes of Julie Christie and Brigitte Bardot. One of the first to put celebrity friends in the front rows of his fashion shows and helped to popularize King's Road with his shop, the Quorum.

Clements Ribeiro *British designers* (Suzanne Clements [1969–] and Inacio Ribeirio [1963–])

Suzanne Clements and Inacio Ribeiro trained and met at Central Saint Martins College of Arts and Design in London, graduating with honors in 1991. Their first collection under the Clements Ribeiro label was in October 1993 and featured crisp separates in cotton pique, hand-painted silk chiffon, and textured linen. They were known for uncluttered exuberant designs, featuring bold colors. They also designed for Cacharel for a time.

Cole, Anne *American designer* (1930–)

Born into the family that founded Cole of California swimwear company, Anne Cole joined the firm in 1951, after college. She worked her way up from mailroom to posting orders to representing the company at trunk shows. Her father sold the company in 1960 and Anne Cole left the company, but then went back to establish Cole's New York office and become stylist and company spokesperson. The Anne Cole Collection was launched in 1982 and is the expression of Anne Cole's swimwear philosophy—that swimwear should reflect current fashion trends but always enhance the appearance of the wearer. She is credited with introducing the tankini.

Cole, Kenneth *American designer* (1954–)

Kenneth Cole worked in his family's shoe business before launching his own company, Kenneth Cole Productions. The company expanded beyond shoes for men and women to offer clothing for men, women, and children, as well as luggage, accessories, and fragrance. He is known for his creative entrepreneurship, his socially conscious advertising, and active participation in causes, as well as for his urban fashion vibe.

Combs, Sean John *American designer* (1969–)

The fashion design firm Sean John was founded in 1998 by rap artist Sean John "Puffy" Combs (also known as P. Diddy and Diddy) to fill a void he saw in well-made, sophisticated urban menswear. The line quickly expanded into a global brand. The label has been nominated five times for excellence in design. He has been credited with bringing the suit back into fashion.

Comme des Garçons (comb-day garr-sawn') *Japanese label* (1942)

A label launched by Rei Kawakubo in 1969, Comme des Garçons is known for its rule-breaking, anti-fashion aesthetic. She thumbed her nose at traditional rules of patternmaking to create voluminous silhouettes with peculiarly placed details. She is one of the original deconstructionists. Both Junya Watanabe and Tao Kurihara have been mentored at Comme des Garçons.

Connolly, Sybil *Irish designer* (1921–1998)

Connolly worked for Bradley's, a London dressmaker, in 1938, and returned to Ireland at start of World War II and worked as buyer for Richard Alan in Dublin. She was discovered in the early 1950s by Carmel Snow of *Harper's Bazaar* magazine and the Fashion Group of Philadelphia, who were visiting Dublin. In 1957 she came to the United States with a collection of one-of-a-kind designs and Irish fabrics. She then formed her own firm with a ready-to-wear boutique. Known for evening gowns with horizontally mushroom-pleated handkerchief-linen skirts and ruffled blouses, finely tucked linen shirts, Carrickmacross lace, iridescent Donegal tweeds, Aran Island white, homespun, striped linen dish-toweling fabric.

Conran, Jasper *British designer* (1959)

Jasper Conran is the son of Sir Terrence Conran, founder of Conran's Habitat stores. He went to school at Parson's School of Design in New York. He returned to London, and in 1978 he produced his first independent show, becoming a member of London Designer Collections the next year. His designs are characterized by fine tailoring and thoughtful details executed in fine fabrics.

Cornejo, Maria *American designer*

Maria Cornejo was born in Chile, raised in Manchester, England, and graduated from Ravensbourne College in London in 1984. She worked for Fiorucci, Joseph, and Jigsaw before opening her own label, Maria Cornejo Collection. Her current label, Zero + Maria Cornejo, offers designs with a minimalist quality that are seldom symmetrical or sharply tailored, but offer her customers a relaxed, quirky, and feminine point of view.

Costa, Francisco *American designer* (1961–)

Francisco Costa's family operated a successful apparel business in his native Brazil. He moved to New York at age 21 and enrolled in classes at FIT. After his graduation, he worked for five years with Oscar de la Renta, and then moved on to Tom Ford for Gucci, where he served as senior designer for evening wear and custom client designs. Costa was handpicked by Calvin Klein to be his successor as creative director of the Calvin Klein Collection for women in 2002. He designs for women who are sexy, independent, and confident. He brings an increased complexity to Calvin Klein's minimal aesthetic. (See under KLEIN, CALVIN.)

Courrèges, André (koor-rej', awn-dray') *French designer* (1923–)

Born in France, Courrèges joined BALENCIAGA and worked there 1952 to 1960. He opened his own house in 1961 with a focus on impeccably tailored suits and roomy coats. He sold his business to L'Oreal perfume company in 1965, retired for a year, dressing only private clients, then returned in 1967 with surprising see-through dresses, Cosmonaut suits, knee socks, and knit catsuits. By 1972, his designs were using feminine ruffles, the color pink, and softer fabrics in evening gowns and loose pants. In 1983, Itokin, a Japanese group, purchased 65 percent of his couture firm from L'Oreal. Widely licensed, the label appeared on products around the world.

Crahay, Jules-François *French designer* (1917–1988)

Crahay started his own fashion house in 1951, but closed within a year and became chief designer at Nina Ricci from 1954 to 1964. He went to Lanvin as head designer in 1964; retired in 1984. Known for young, uninhibited, civilized, soignée clothes. One of first to glamorize pants as evening wear.

Daché, Lilly (da-shay') *American designer* (1904–1989)

Leading milliner in the United States from mid-1930s to early 1950s, Daché was born in France. She apprenticed at Reboux in Paris for four years. After coming to New York in 1924, she worked as a milliner and opened a small shop where she molded hats on customers and established her reputation. By 1949, she was designing dresses to go with her hats, gloves, hosiery, lingerie and loungewear, wallets, and jewelry; and by 1954 she had added perfume and cosmetics. Styles for which she is remembered include draped turbans, half-hats, war-workers' visor caps, colored snoods, romantic massed flower shapes, and, in 1949, a wired strapless bra. She closed her business in 1969.

Daryl K (Daryl Kerrigan) *Irish American designer* (1964–)

Daryl Kerrigan studied fashion in Dublin and moved to New York in 1986. She began her career in fashion working in thrift stores and as a wardrobe consultant on films, which informs her design aesthetic. She established a design studio in 1991 known for low-slung leather pants and lean T-shirts produced under the Daryl K label. She was approached by French luxury label Céline and did some consulting for Tommy Hilfiger, which led her to sell her company to an investment firm in 2000. The deal collapsed. She collaborated with Barneys New York to create an in-store boutique in 2005, which gave her the financial footing to expand. She has reopened her original space on New York's Bond Street, where she sells her Daryl K and lower-priced Kerrigan lines.

Deacon, Giles (dee-kin) *British designer* (1969–)

Giles Deacon attended Central Saint Martins College of Arts and Design in London to study art, but quickly gravitated to fashion. He worked for Jean-Charles de Castelbajac,

Louis Vuitton, Marc Jacobs, and French Connection; he debuted his own line, Giles, in 2004. His designs are beautifully constructed with edgy embellishments and interesting fabrics. He tries to maintain a more affordable luxury price point.

de Castelbajac, Jean-Charles (cass′-el-bai-jack) *French designer* (1950–)

Morocco native Castelbajac's family moved to France when he was five. At age 18 he was working with his mother in her clothes factory. Castelbajac designed for Pierre d'Alby, and after 1974 opened his own retail shop. He is best known for blanket plaids, canvas, quilting, and rugged coats.

de la Renta, Oscar (deh lah ren′-tah) *American designer* (1932–)

A native of the Dominican Republic, de la Renta studied art in Spain after which he worked for BALENCIAGA'S couture house in Madrid for twelve years. He spent four years with Castillo at Lanvin-Castillo Paris; then came to Elizabeth Arden in 1963. A partner in Jane Derby in 1965, he was soon operating under his own label, Oscar de la Renta, Ltd., for luxury ready-to-wear. Noted for his use of opulent fabrics such as taffetas and tulle with sequins for sexy, romantic evening clothes and sophisticated and feminine day wear, his design interests include: signature perfume introduced in 1977 and another in 1983; boutique lines, swimwear, wedding gowns, furs, jewelry, bed linens, and loungewear. He became creative director for Balmain, becoming the first American designer to head a French couture house.

Dell'Olio, Louis (del ohl′-yoh) *American designer* (1948–)

Dell'Olio received the Norman Norell Scholarship to Parsons School of Design, where he won the Gold Thimble Award for coats and suits at graduation in 1969. He assisted Dominic Rompollo at Teal Traina from 1969 to 1971; was designer at Giorgini and Ginori divisions of Originala from 1971 to 1974; and became co-designer with DONNA KARAN for Anne Klein & Co. in 1974. He was sole designer for Anne Klein from 1985 until 1993. His philosophy has been described as a modern, sophisticated interpretation of classic Anne Klein sportswear; using easy shapes in beautiful fabrics. He also designs furs for Michael Forrest.

Demeulemeester, Ann *Belgian designer* (1961–)

Deconstructionist designer who emerged in the 1980s and had significant success in the 1990s. An avant-garde designer, she is considered to be on the cutting edge of fashion but at the same time produces wearable designs.

Dennis, Pamela *American designer* (1960–)

Pamela Dennis made her mark as an evening wear designer in the 1980s and 1990s. Without formal training, she launched her business after taking silk fabric to a tailor and asking that he make a dress to her specifications for a wedding. The dress was a hit and resulted in a request to borrow it for a commercial. This inspired her to launch her business. Her clothes are characterized by simple shapes in luxurious fabrics. In 2000, she sold her business to an investor, with the hope of expanding distribution to a more accessible price point. The move proved disastrous and she left the company, losing the rights to design under her own name.

de Rauch, Madeleine (de rok′) *French couturière* (1896–1985)

Renowned sportswoman of the 1920s who wanted proper sports clothes for herself and for her friends who played tennis and golf, skied, and rode horses, de Rauch started a business called "House of Friendship by Mme. de Rauch" in 1932. Aided by two sports-minded sisters, she made beautiful, wearable, functional clothes, adaptable to many types of women. The firm closed in 1973.

Dessès, Jean (des-say′, zhon) *French couturier* (1904–1970)

Born in Alexandria, Egypt, of Greek ancestry, Dessès studied law in Paris; aimed at diplomatic service but switched to fashion design in 1925. After 12 years working for Jane, he opened his own house in 1937. Designing directly on the dress form, he draped the fabric himself. He was inspired by ethnic and historic garments, especially those from Greece and Egypt. His admiration for American women led him to make a lower-priced line for them in 1950, which he called "Jean Dessès Diffusion." This marked the beginning of the ready-to-wear trend in French couture. He gave up couture in 1965 because of ill health and returned to Athens, where he ran a boutique until his death.

Dior, Christian (dee-or′, chris′-ti-ahn) *French couturier* (1905–1957)

After initially aiming at a diplomatic career, Dior operated an art gallery from 1930 to 1934. By 1938, he was sketching hat designs for AGNÈS; and designing for PIGUET, and then for LUCIEN LELONG in 1941. He opened his own house in 1947, after which he launched the revolutionary New Look, an ultra-feminine silhouette; yards of material in an almost ankle-length skirt, with a tiny waist, snug bodice, rounded sloping shoulders, and padded hips. During the next ten years, he devised his own inner construction to shape dresses into the *H*, *A*, and *Y* lines. From 1948 to 1951, the business added perfumes, scarves, hosiery, furs, gloves, and men's neckties, as well as a young, less-expensive line, "Miss Dior." Having become a vast international merchandising operation, the House of Dior continued after his death in 1957, under designing leadership of his assistant, YVES SAINT LAURENT (1957 to 1960). The label was later designed by MARC BOHAN (1958 to 1996), and JOHN GALLIANO (1996–2011); and Raf Simons (2012–).

Dolce and Gabbana (dohl-chay′ and gahb-bah′-nah) (Domenico Dolce [1958–] and Stefano Gabbana [1962–]) *Italian designers*

Italians Domenico Dolce and Stefano Gabbana formed a fashion consulting studio in 1982. They opened D&G in 1985, when they showed their first women's collection. By 1987 they had added knitwear; in 1989, beachwear; and in 1990, menswear.

Dorothée Bis *French knitwear house* (1960s)
A chain of Paris trend-setting boutiques from the 1960s, run by designer-buyer Jacqueline Jacobson and husband, Elie, Dorothée Bis is credited by some with starting hot pants fad in 1969. Also remembered for long pants tucked into Tibetan boots; see-through knits; mid-calf coats over mini-skirts; skinny cardigans and scarves; knickers; sweetheart necklines; shrunken-crochet berets; dolman-sleeved jacquard knits. Their trademark shop display—a life-size rag doll slumped in chair.

Doucet, Jacques (doo-she', zhak) *French couturier* (c. 1860–c. 1932)
One of the first couture houses in Paris in mid-19th c.; the founder was the grandfather of Jacques, who started his career as a dress designer after the Franco-Prussian War (1870). A competitor of Worth, Doucet favored 18th-c. styles and much lace. His apprentices included Madeline Vionnet and Paul Poiret. In 1928, firm joined Doeuillet to become Doeuillet-Doucet.

Drécoll (dreh'-caul) *French couture house* (founded in 1900)
One of most prestigious couture houses in Paris from 1900 to 1925, Drécoll's designer was Austrian Mme. de Wagner, who bought the name from Baron Christophe Drécoll, a well-known Belgian dressmaker in Vienna. Designs were architectural, with elegant lines, and often black and white or two colors. Drécoll sent a mannequin to the races in the first harem skirt in 1910. Her son-in-law took over business in 1925. Her daughter, Maggy, formed her own couture house under name Maggy Rouff in 1929.

Dsquared2 *Canadian-born Italian designers* (Dean Caten [1965–] and Dan Caten [1965–])
These identical twins started their business in Milan in 1991 merging their rugged American style with Italian craftsmanship and fine tailoring. Using lots of leather and denim and black, their designs are edgy and ironic.

Duke, Randolph *American designer* (1958–)
After studying at the University of Southern California and at the Fashion Institute of Design and Merchandising in Los Angeles, he began his career as a swimwear designer. He relocated to New York, where he opened a shop and established a wholesale label. The wholesale business closed in 1992. In 1996, he became creative director for the newly resuscitated Halston label. After leaving Halston, he launched Randolph Duke, an evening wear collection that he sells at specialty stores such as Neiman Marcus, and a less-expensive collection that he sells on the QVC shopping channel and the Home Shopping Network.

Eiseman, Florence *American children's wear designer* (1899–1988)
Eiseman began to sew as a hobby following birth of her second son in 1931, and she continued making clothes for her children and her neighbors' children. After samples of her work were shown to Marshall Field, Chicago, an initial $3,000 order gave birth to a clothing firm selling across the United States and abroad. Hallmarks were simple styles, children not dressed as adults, fine fabrics, excellent workmanship, and high prices.

Elbaz, Alber *French designer* (1961–)
Alber Elbaz was born in Morocco and grew up in Tel Aviv, Israel, where he graduated from the Shenkar College School of Fashion and Textiles. He worked on Seventh Avenue in New York for a while before being introduced to Geoffrey Beene, who hired him as a design assistant. After seven years with Beene, he moved to Paris as the designer for Guy Laroche. After bringing that brand back to life he was hired as the head women's wear designer at Yves Saint Laurent Rive Gauche. He was replaced by Tom Ford when Saint Laurent was bought by Gucci, and worked briefly for Krizia in Milan before being hired as the creative director for Lanvin in 2001. His classic shapes in flattering colors get their appeal from interesting pattern cutting and the use of deconstructed details. He partnered with H&M in fall of 2010 to do a co-branded collection.

Ellis, Perry *American designer* (1940–1986)
Ellis earned a B.A. from William and Mary and an M.A. in retailing from New York University. At first a sportswear buyer, he began designing for Portfolio division of Vera in 1975. Perry Ellis Sportswear, Inc. was established in 1978 and Perry Ellis menswear in 1980. His philosophy: Fashion should not be taken seriously and individuals should not be overly concerned with clothing. He used natural fabrics; hand-knitted sweaters in silk, cotton, and cashmere, designed furs, shearling coats for men and women, shoes, legwear, scarves, Vogue patterns, sheets, towels, and blankets for Martex.

Emanuel, Elizabeth *British designer* (1953–)
Elizabeth and David Emanuel designed the wedding dress for Diana, Princess of Wales. They attended Harrow School of Art and Royal College of Art before opening their own ready-to-wear firm in 1977. In 1979, they decided to focus on custom-made apparel; they closed their doors in 1990 when their marriage dissolved. After working as a costume designer, Elizabeth Emanuel launched a new bridal/couture/ready-to-wear business in 1999; her business was acquired and the label renamed "Art of Being."

Erté (Romain de Tirtoff) *Russian designer* (1892–1990)
Erté studied painting in Russia before moving to Paris to study at Académie Julian, where he took a new name based on the French pronunciation of his initials R. T. (air-tay). He got a job in Paris as a sketcher for Paul Poiret and went on to design costumes for the opera and theater. From 1914 into the 1930s, he produced illustrations and covers for various magazines, including *Harper's Bazaar.* He designed costumes for the Folies Bergère and the Ziegfeld Follies, as well as for movies including *The Mystic, Ben Hur,* and *La Bohème.*

Escada *German design house* (founded in 1976)
Escada was founded in 1976 in Munich, Germany, by Wolfgang and Margaretha Ley, with Margaretha as chief designer until her death in 1992. She believed that creativity must be balanced by strong market appeal. Her

collections were characterized by exciting color and fabric combinations combined with strong, bold silhouettes. The company was acquired and distributes the apriori, BiBA, cavita, and Laurel lines, as well as Escada.

Etro (Gimmo Etro) *Italian design house* (founded in 1968)
Established by Gimmo Etro as a family business, Etro is known for its colorful, luxurious textiles for haute couture and ready-to-wear. In 1981, a paisley collection was introduced, which became the basis for the brand's signature look in textiles. In the 1990s, the company launched a ready-to-wear label. It continues to distribute a women's wear line, designed by Veronica Etro, and a menswear line, designed by Kean Etro; both are known for their sharp tailoring juxtaposed with brightly printed patterns on luxury fabrics.

Fath, Jacques (fat, zhak) *French couturier* (1912–1954)
Fath opened his own house in 1937, stayed open during war, and for next 17 years was immensely successful, designing elegant, flattering, feminine, sexy clothes. He also operated a boutique for perfume, stockings, scarves, and millinery. He is remembered for hourglass shapes, swathed hips, plunging necklines, full-pleated skirts, wide cape collars, and stockings with chantilly-lace tops. After his death in 1954, his wife carried on his business until 1957.

Fendi (fen'dee) *Italian fur house* (founded in 1918)
Founded in 1918 by Adele Fendi, the house specialized in furs, handbags, luggage, and ready-to-wear. In 1954, after she was widowed, Signora Fendi ran business with five daughters: Paola, Anna, Franca, Carla, and Alda. She died in 1978, and her daughters and granddaughters continued to run the business. KARL LAGERFELD was hired in 1962 as designer, and he introduced new, unusual, and neglected furs such as squirrel, badger, fox, as well as some unpedigreed species. Innovative design techniques such as furs woven in strips, unlined, lined with silk, and the double *F* initials designed by Lagerfeld have become international symbols in design.

Féraud, Louis *French designer* (1921–1999)
Louis Féraud founded a couture house in 1950, in Cannes, France, where he catered to movie stars coming to the Cannes Film Festival. By the 1960s, he moved to Paris and started a ready-to-wear line that was sold at Saks Fifth Avenue and Harrods, among others. He was inspired by the colors of South America, which also inspired his painting. He died of Alzheimer's disease in 1999; his company was bought by Escada.

Ferragamo, Salvatore (fer-ah-gah'-moh) *Italian shoe designer* (1898–1960)
An Italian shoemaker, Ferragamo immigrated to California in 1923. He opened a cobbler's shop in Hollywood and, in 1936, a business in Florence, Italy. By the time of his death, he had ten factories in Great Britain and Italy. He is said to have originated the wedge heel, platform sole, and transparent Lucite® heel. The business was carried on by his daughters, Fiamma and Giovanna, and his son Ferruccio, with an emphasis on elegant, ladylike, conservative styling, with comfortable fit. The Ferragamo name appears on handbags, scarves, luxury ready-to-wear sold in boutiques in Europe and the United States, and in major U.S. specialty stores.

Ferré, Gianfranco (fer-reh') *Italian designer* (1945–2007)
Ferré studied architecture in Milan, worked with a furniture designer, and then became known for accessories design by 1970. He designed sportswear and raincoats on a freelance basis in 1972 and established his own firm in 1974. His expertise in architecture combined with fine tailoring techniques made him one of the top European designers during his lifetime.

Ferretti, Alberta *Italian designer* (1950–)
Alberta Ferretti's mother owned an atelier where she learned her trade. By the age of 18, she had her own boutique and showed her first collection in 1974. She began showing at Milan Fashion Week in 1981. Her modern, feminine silhouettes are often made of gossamer fabrics such as chiffon, gazar, or georgette. She sees her designs as an extension of a woman's unique personality. In 1989, she launched a denim line, which morphed into a diffusion-priced ready-to-wear line, Philosophy di Alberta Ferretti.

Fisher, Eileen *American designer* (1950–)
In 1984, Eileen Fisher began designing sportswear pieces, which she presented at the New York Boutique Show. She took orders and sourced the production, and her company grew into an important bridge label. She is known for comfortable, loose-fitting separates in natural fabrics with a focus on texture rather than pattern. She is committed to fair trade and sustainability issues.

Fogarty, Anne *American designer* (1919–1980)
A designer of junior-size dresses between 1948 and 1957 for Youth Guild and Margot, Inc., and at Saks Fifth Avenue from 1957 to 1962; the designer established Anne Fogarty, Inc. in 1962. She is remembered for "paper-doll" silhouette of 1951, a revival of crinoline petticoats under full-skirted, tiny-waisted shirtwaist dresses; the "camise," a chemise gathered from a high yoke in 1958; lounging coveralls; and slim Empire dress with tiny puffed sleeves. In early 1970s, she showed a peasant look with ruffled shirts and long skirts with ruffled hems, and hot pants under a long quilted skirt. She had completed a spring/summer collection of sportswear and dresses at the time of her death.

Ford, Tom *American designer* (1961–)
Ford made his runway debut in 1998 and had a very quick success. By 2001, he was doing men's and women's collections for YSL and Gucci, where he was responsible for turning around a company that had been in decline. After resigning from Gucci in 2004, he launched the Tom Ford Brand in 2005, which distributes menswear, eyewear, and beauty products.

Fortuny, Mariano (Mariano Fortuny y Madrazo) (for-too'-nee) *Italian designer* (1871–1949)
Fortuny was an innovator, inventor, photographer, stage designer, textile and dress designer. Famous for his

long, slender, mushroom-pleated silk tea gowns, he is most famous for the design called the Delphos Gown, which was seen first in 1907. His clothes were considered classics all through the 1930s, and are now rare collector's items.

Galanos, James (gal'-ahn-oss) *American designer* (1929–)
Galanos studied fashion in New York. He worked at ROBERT PIGUET in Paris from 1947 to 1948, along with MARC BOHAN. After returning to the United States, he eventually started his own business in Los Angeles in 1951. His first New York show in 1952 launched him on to a spectacular career. Known for luxurious day and evening ensembles and a total look for collections including hats, shoes, hosiery, accessories, hair, and makeup.

Galitzine, Princess Irene (gahl-it-zeen') *Italian designer* (1916–2006)
Russian-born Galitzine was educated in Italy and England, studying art in Rome. She worked for SORELLE FONTANA for three years, then started her own import business in Rome in 1948. First showing her designs in 1959, she introduced silk palazzo pajamas in 1960. Also known for at-home togas, evening suits, tunic-top dresses, lingerie, bare-back or open-sided evening gowns, and decorative striped stockings. Her house closed in 1968, but she revived her couture collection in 1970 and showed sporadically for several years after that.

Galliano, John (gahl-ee-ahn'-oh) *French couturier* (1960–)
Galliano finished his training in 1983 and showed his first collection in 1984. He quickly established himself as a skilled technician and imaginative designer. He moved from avant-garde creations to more sophisticated styles. Named head designer at GIVENCHY in 1995, he remained only a few seasons before moving to the House of DIOR in 1996. In 2011, he was arrested for making anti-Semitic remarks in a Paris bar; he was fired after the incident and went into rehab. In the fall of 2013, at the urging of Anna Wintour, he worked with Oscar de la Renta on his fall collection.

Gaultier, Jean-Paul (gol-tee-yeh') *French designer* (1952–)
Gaultier presented a collection of designs to his mother and grandmother at age 13, and at 15 invented a coat with bookbag closures. In 1970, he sent his design portfolio to PIERRE CARDIN, who hired him as design assistant for two years. He also worked for Jacques Esterel and JEAN PATOU. He presented his first ready-to-wear collection with silhouettes contrary to the current designs. Inspired by London street dressing, Gaultier mixes fabrics and shapes that are unusual and controversial.

Genny *Italian design label* (founded in 1961)
Arnoldo Girombelli launched the Genny label, naming it after his eldest daughter. He also founded the Byblos label in 1973 and the Complice label in 1975. The Genny label was a launching pad for many young designers, including Gianni Versace, Claude Montana, Keith Varty and Alan Cleaver, Dolce & Gabbana, Christian LaCroix, Rebecca Moses, John Bartlett, Richard Tyler, and Josephus Thimister.

Gernreich, Rudi (gern'-rike) *American designer* (1922–1985)
Born in Vienna, Austria, Gernreich immigrated to California in 1938. He specialized in dramatic sport clothes in striking color combinations and cut, bathing suits, underwear, and hosiery—usually coordinated for total look. Remembered for maillot swimsuits with no bra and bare suits with deeply cut out sides in the mid-1950s; the topless swimsuit and see-through blouses in 1964; "no-bra" bra in skin-color nylon net; knee-high leggings patterned to match tunic tops and tights in 1967; wrap-tied legs and dhoti dresses in 1968. He announced in 1968 that he was taking sabbatical from his fashion career and never returned to fashion design.

Ghesquière, Nicolas (1971–)
After an internship with designer Agnès B., Ghesquière got his first couture job with GAULTIER at age 21. At the same time, he was doing some freelance designing of knitwear. In the mid-90s he joined Balenciaga, and in 1997 was made creative director. Suzy Menkes said his collections for Balenciaga explore shape, volume, and embellishment in a way that seems totally new, yet reflect in an abstract way the iconic house he represents. Ghesquière and the house of Balenciaga parted ways in late 2012.

Gigli, Romeo *Italian designer* (1949–)
Gigli was trained as an architect and launched his own company in 1983. His design style focused on definitive shapes, soft draping, and a preference for asymmetry—silhouettes that came alive on the body. He was known for his rich palette and use of luxurious fabrics.

Marithé + François Girbaud *French ready-to-wear design team* (founded in 1965)
This French sportswear label was established in 1965 by the team of François and Marithé Girbaud. They designed clothes for both men and women with a functional urban vibe and subtle complexity. They were pioneers in developing denim washes.

Givenchy, Hubert de (zhee-von'-she, u-bare') *French designer* (1927–)
Givenchy studied at École des Beaux Arts in Paris. At age 17, he started designing at FATH, then at PIGUET and LELONG, and spent four years with SCHIAPARELLI. He opened his own house in 1952 at age 25. Noted for clothing of exceptional workmanship, masterful cuts, and beautiful fabrics, his ready-to-wear was distributed worldwide through his Nouvelle Boutique. Licensing agreements include sportswear, men's and women's shirts, leathers, hosiery, furs, eyeglasses, home furnishings. He retired in 1995. Designers who succeeded him included JOHN GALLIANO, ALEXANDER MCQUEEN, and, in 2001, Julien MacDonald.

Gn, Andrew *French designer* (1966–)
A graduate of Central Saint Martins, Gn began his career as assistant designer to Emanuel Ungaro. In 1996, he started his own line, with manufacturing facilities in Italy and France. In 1997, he worked briefly as the artistic director of Balmain's ready-to-wear collection.

Gottex *Israeli label* (founded in 1957)
A swimwear company founded in 1957 by Lea Gottleib, who headed their design team until 1998. Gottleib's vision was to design swimwear that could be worn from the pool to the bar or restaurant. They are known for introducing textile innovations, including the use of the hard-cup bra in swimwear.

Graham, Gary *American designer* (1969–)
Gary Graham launched his label in 1999. His first collection featured a historically inspired silhouette made of garment-dyed, quilted silk organza. He is known for his sophisticated craftsmanship characterized by his use of deconstruction and his unique draped silhouettes.

Grès, Alix (gray, ah-leex') *French couturière* (1903–1993)
Grès was originally a sculptress before starting to design women's clothes. She served an apprenticeship at Premet, then started working independently under the name of Alix Barton in 1934, and showed in a house called Alix until 1942, at which time it was closed by the Germans. After World War II, using her married name, Grès, she reopened. Noted for superb craftsmanship; statuesque Greek-draped evening gowns; bicolor pleated jersey gowns with crisscrossed string belts; cowled black jersey day dresses; asymmetric drapes; bias-cut caftans; loose topcoats with hoods and batwing sleeves; at-home wear and beachwear. She sold her house in 1984.

Griffe, Jacques *French designer* (1910–1994)
Jacques Griffe got his start with an internship at the House of Vionnet from 1936 to 1939. After serving in the military, he started his own line in 1951, applying the lessons he had learned regarding the relationship of pattern cutting to fabric and drape.

Gucci (goo'-chee) *Italian leather house*
This family business in Italy established in 15th c. by ancestors of the current head, Dr. Aldo Gucci, has been manufacturing and retailing luggage and leather accessories since 1906. In 1969, they started to show collections of apparel for men and women. Known for the walking low-heeled loafer with metal harness-bit ornament across the vamp, tack-room hardware, and red-and-green canvas stripes used in luggage and accessories, the GG signature on bags and apparel has become a status symbol and is sold in a chain of Gucci shops throughout the world. Family court battles caused the firm difficulties, but the company was revitalized in 2000 by Tom Ford, who resigned in 2005. He was replaced as creative director by Frida Giannini.

Gurung, Prabal *American designer* (active 2003–)
Born in Singapore to Nepalese parents, Prabal Gurung interned with Donna Karan, worked for 2 years with Cynthia Rowley, and was the design director at Bill Blass for 5 years before launching his own label in 2010. His goal is to create clothes that make women look beautiful rather than following the latest trend. He partnered with Target for a co-branded capsule collection in the spring of 2013.

Hall, Kevan *American designer* (active 1982–)
Kevan Hall launched Kevan Hall couture in 1982. From 1998 to 2000, he served as the creative director of Halston, where he helped to revitalize the brand. In 2002, he launched Kevan Hall Collection; his designs exude a purity of style achieved through fine tailoring and sensuous draping.

Halston (Roy Halston Frowick) *American designer* (1932–1990)
Halston studied at Chicago Art Institute. He worked for LILLY DACHÉ in New York, and designed hats for Bergdorf Goodman from 1959 to 1968, where he made news with the pillbox hat he designed for Jacqueline Kennedy to wear at the inaugural ceremony in 1961. He started his own business on East 68th Street in 1968 for private clients and opened a ready-to-wear firm, Halston Originals, in fall 1972. His formula could be described as: casual throwaway chic, using superior fabrics for extremely simple classics such as a long cashmere dress with a sweater tied over shoulders; long, slinky halter-neck jerseys; wraparound skirts and turtlenecks. Though Halston died in 1990, the House of Halston continues under other designers.

Hamnett, Katharine *British designer* (1947–)
Katherine Hamnett graduated from Central Saint Martins and is best known for her political T-shirts and ethical business philosophy. Her collections prioritize sustainable fabrics and fair trade labor.

Hardwick, Cathy *American designer* (1933–)
Born in Seoul, Korea, Hardwick came to the United States at 21 and opened a boutique in San Francisco. She freelanced for Alvin Duskin and other firms, then moved to New York in 1960s. There she opened Cathy Hardwick & Friends in 1972. Her philosophy: clean-cut, fluid, sensuous clothing; comfortable and useful as well as fashionable. She has also designed tableware for Mikasa and bed linens for Burlington Industries.

Harp, Holly *American designer* (1939–1995)
An important designer of the 1970s, Harp set up a boutique on Sunset Boulevard in 1968 where she translated the hippie counterculture look into designer apparel, which eventually sold in specialty stores on Fifth Avenue, including Henri Bendel and Saks Fifth Avenue. Matte jersey and chiffon were two of her signature fabrics.

Hartnell, Sir Norman *British designer* (1901–1979)
Hartnell opened a dress shop with his sister in 1923, then his own house in 1930, which became the largest couture house in London and famous as dressmaker to the British Court. He is known for coronation gowns for Queen Elizabeth II in 1953; lavishly embroidered ball gowns, fur-trimmed suits, and city tweeds.

Head, Edith *American designer* (1897–1981)
A costume designer who spent much of her career with Paramount Pictures. She designed for Mae West, Dorothy Lamour, Barbara Stanwyck, and Audrey Hepburn, among others. She also designed costumes for the opera,

uniforms for the Coast Guard and Pan American Airlines, and a line of printed fabrics.

Heim, Jacques (heym′, zhak) *French designer* (1899–1967)
Paris-born son of Isadore and Jeanne Heim, who had founded a fur house in 1898, Jacques built this house into a world-famous couture establishment. Starting in 1923 and continuing for the next 40 years, he reflected trends rather than creating them. Known as the designer of the first bikini in 1945, he also had success with youthful clothes in his boutique, Heim Jeunes Filles. After his death, his son assumed direction of the firm.

Herman, Stan *American designer* (1930–)
Designer for a number of companies, Herman has done work in hat design for John-Fredericks, at Mr. Mort (1961–1971), for Henri Bendel, Youthcraft-Charmfit, Slumbertogs, and uniform houses. He has been active in the Council of Fashion Designers of America since 1967 and has served in leadership positions in this organization. He has been quoted as saying, "Fashion is one of life's nourishments which, like good food, must be grown each season to remain fresh."

Hermès (air-mes′) *French design house*
Thierry Hermès, saddle- and harness-maker, opened a shop in 1837 in Paris, adding sporting accessories, toilet articles, boots, scarves, and jewelry. Couture began in 1920 under Emile Hermès; closed in 1952, however, the firm continues to make women's and men's ready-to-wear, as well as leather products; it is famous for both the Kelly bag and the Birkin bag, for which there are waiting lists. Hermès added a women's ready-to-wear line under the creative direction of Martin Margiela (1997–2003), Jean Paul Gaultier (2004–2011), and Christophe Lemaire (2011–present).

Herrera, Carolina *American designer* (1939–)
Herrera established her firm in 1981. She did her first fur collection for Revillon in 1984, and in 1996 produced a lower-priced ready-to-wear line called CH. She makes clothes to order for some private clients and is known for her elegant clothes.

Hilfiger, Tommy *American designer* (1952–)
Born in Elmira, New York, where he opened a retail business, the People's Store, in 1969. By 1979, Hilfiger had moved to New York and showed his first signature collection in 1984. He has been described as making "Main Street America designs" and caters to the youth culture with designs reflecting pop music and team sports. His clientele is very loyal.

Horn, Carol *American designer* (1936–)
Horn studied fine arts at Boston and Columbia Universities and started designing junior sportswear for Bryant 9 and Benson & Partners. She opened her own company, Carol Horn Sportswear, in 1983. Clothing is uncontrived shapes made of natural fabrics and moderately priced.

Irene *American designer* (1900–1962)
Irene (full name, Irene Lentz) designed for both film and ready-to-wear. She began by dressing Hollywood celebrities for their private lives and they, in turn, influenced the studios to contract her for their on-screen wardrobes.

J. Mendel *American design firm* (founded in 1870)
J. Mendel was established in 1870 by Joseph Breitman as a furrier in Paris. Giles Mendel moved the company to New York City in the 1990s and expanded the company into women's wear as a diversion from the protests of animal rights groups.

Jacobs, Marc *American designer* (1963–)
After managing his own firm from 1986 to 1988, Jacobs joined Perry Ellis, then showed under his own name after 1994. Considered a design prodigy, he was immediately successful in building a reputation as a highly original young designer. He became artistic director at Louis Vuitton in 1997.

James, Charles *American couturier* (1906–1978)
Born in England, James moved to Chicago and eventually operated dressmaking salons in London and Paris in the 1930s and his own custom-order business in 1940s and 1950s. Rated by his peers: "A genius . . . daring innovator in the shape of clothes . . . more of an architect or sculptor . . . independent, stormy, unpredictable, contentious." Acknowledged as an equal by the Paris couture in 1947, he is remembered for new techniques for dress patterns; new dress forms; elaborate, bouffant ball gowns in odd mixtures of colors and fabrics; batwing oval cape-coat; intricately cut dolman wraps and asymmetric shapes. He retired from couture design in 1958 to devote himself to sculpture and painting.

Mr. John *American millinery designer* (1906–1993)
Born John Pico John in Munich, Germany, where his mother was a millinery designer, Mr. John came to New York in 1929 and designed millinery for house of Mme. Laurel. After he formed John Fredericks with a partner, Fred Fredericks, in 1929, and subsequently started his own firm, Mr. John, Inc., in 1948. Most successful in the 1940s and 1950s, the heyday of hats, he is remembered for forward-tilted doll hats, glorified Stetsons, scarf-attached hats, skullcaps held by tight face veils, wig hats, huge flower or bushy fur toques. His business closed in 1970, although he continued designing for private clients.

Johnson, Betsey *American designer* (1942–)
Graduate of Syracuse University, Johnson started as guest editor for *Mademoiselle* magazine, where she made sweaters for editors. These were seen by the owner of Paraphernalia boutiques, who gave her a job designing. She was one of the first American designers to design anti–Seventh Avenue fashions in early 1960s. With friends she started a boutique, Betsey, Bunky & Nini, in 1969. Her body-conscious clothes range from swimwear to bodysuits, tight pants to dance dresses. Betsey Johnson, Inc., established in 1978, manufactures sportswear, bodywear, and dresses, and operates a number of retail stores.

Joop, Wolfgang *German designer* (1944–)
A German journalist and freelance designer, Joop showed his first fur collection in 1978. By 1981, he added Joop!

ready-to-wear, and in 1987, Joop! jeans. In 2000, he left his own company, which continues without him.

Julian, Alexander *American designer* (1948–)
Born and raised in Chapel Hill, North Carolina, where his father was in retailing, Julian designed his first shirt at 12; managed his father's store at 18; and owned the shop at 21. In 1975, he moved to New York, where he designs his own fabrics, interpreting traditional themes with wit and imagination. Licenses include: men's, women's, and children's wear; hosiery; home furnishings and decorative fabrics; small leather goods; and pocket accessories.

Ka, Paule *French designer label* (founded in 1987)
This French brand was launched in 1987 by Serge Cajfinger, the company's founder, president, and stylist. An admirer of Jackie Kennedy, Audrey Hepburn, and Grace Kelly, the clothes offer discreet luxury in the finest fabrics for alluring, elegant women.

Kahn, Robin *American jewelry designer* (1947–)
Born in London, Kahn came to the United States at five years of age; graduating from the High School of Art and Design and Parsons School of Design. Trained with goldsmiths at the Haystack Mountain School of Crafts, he went on to design accessories for PIERRE CARDIN, OSCAR DE LA RENTA, and Kenneth J. Lane, and one-of-a-kind pieces for Bloomingdale's. He founded Robin Kahn, Inc., in 1978. His forms are bold, clean, and elegant; and he designs directly from metal, utilizing brass, copper, and bronze; he also uses ebony, turquoise, ivory, and lapis, as well as leather cording and taffeta.

Kamali, Norma *American designer* (1945–)
Born Norma Arraez and raised in New York, Kamali graduated from the Fashion Institute of Technology in 1964 with a major in fashion art. In 1969, with her husband, Eddie Kamali, she opened a tiny basement shop selling imports primarily from England and her own designs. Expanding in 1974, she began designing suits and lace dresses. In 1978, after a divorce, she established a boutique and company called OMO (On My Own). She is known for her swimwear designs and for her distinctive use of silk parachute fabric, sweatshirt fleece, snap tape, and giant removable shoulder pads, which gave her designs a unique look througout the 1980s.

Kane, Christopher *British designer* (1982–)
Christopher Kane received his MA from Central Saint Martins, where he received the coveted Harrod's Design Award. He launched his own label in 2006 with his sister Tammy. He's designed three capsule collections for Topshop and one for Versus. The brand was purchased in 2013 by PPR.

Karan, Donna *American designer* (1948–)
Donna Karan attended Parsons School of Design, but after her second year dropped out to work with ANNE KLEIN, where she became associate designer in 1971; then head designer following Klein's illness in 1974. She asked former Parsons classmate LOUIS DELL'OLIO to co-design the Klein collection. In 1983, she launched a less-expensive line, Anne Klein II. She and her husband, Stephan Weiss, founded Donna Karan, New York, with the support of Takihyo Corporation, Japan, Anne Klein's parent company. Very successful, the firm has many divisions, including those for men and accessories. Design principles include the classic mix-and-match sportswear concept.

Kawakubo, Rei *Japanese designer* (1942–)
Born in Tokyo, Japan, Kawakubo graduated from Keio University in Tokyo with a major in literature. After working in the advertising department of a textile firm and as a freelance stylist, she established Comme des Garçons Co., Ltd., in 1973. She first showed in Tokyo in 1975, then went on to introduce menswear in 1978 and knitwear in 1981. In 1981, she showed for first time in Paris, after which she established offices in Paris (1982) and New York (1986). Originally designing exclusively in black and gray, she currently adds some touches of color. Designs are often asymmetrical in shape and made of cotton, linen, or canvas, with tears and slashes in the designs.

Kelly, Patrick *American-born French designer* (1954–1990)
An African American designer who moved to Paris and began selling his flamboyant designs at street fairs and flea markets. In 1984, an investor provided him with a workshop and showroom, and his business took off. His whimsical designs often featured mismatched buttons, fringe, humorous patterns, and/or riotous colors.

Kenzo (Kenzo Takada) *French designer* (1945–)
A trendsetting French ready-to-wear designer from early 1970s and after, Kenzo came to Paris from Japan in 1965. He opened his own boutique, Jungle Jap, in 1970. His designs were widely distributed in the United States and he opened Kenzo-Paris boutique in New York in 1983, then in 1984 went on to produce Album by Kenzo for The Limited. Designs are based on traditional Japanese clothing and made in spirited combinations of textures and patterns. Kenzo retired in 2000, but the firm continues under other designers.

Khan, Naeem *Indian-born American designer* (1958–)
After moving to the U.S., Khan apprenticed for Halston. He launched his own line in 2003, designing clothes for Beyoncé, Eva Longoria, and Michelle Obama. His dresses, gowns, and chic separates often feature hand-embroidery that reflects his cultural heritage.

Khanh, Emmanuelle (kahn, e-man-u-el) *French designer* (1938–)
Khanh entered the fashion world as mannequin for GIVENCHY. She began designing inexpensive ready-to-wear, sold in Paris and London boutiques, as a rebellion against haute couture. Attracting publicity in 1963 as a pioneer of the new wave of dress that swept the Paris streets as MARY QUANT's did in London, she is remembered for dog's ear collars, droopy revers on long, fitted jackets, loose cravat closings on coats and suits. She reflected a contemporary approach to individuality symptomatic of the 1960s, and continued to design in the 1970s and after.

Kieselstein-Cord, Barry *American jewelry designer* (1943–)
Kieselstein-Cord studied at Parsons School of Design, New York University, and the American Craft League. He did his first jewelry collection for Georg Jensen around 1972. By early 1980s, his designs sold around the United States, as well as abroad. In 1984, his collection included accessories in precious metals and rare woods.

Kleibacker, Charles *American designer* (1921–2010)
Charles Kleibacker came to design after working for the chanteuse Hildegarde, who brought him to Paris and exposed him to haute couture. He worked as an assistant to Antonio Castillo at the House of Lanvin before returning to New York where he designed for Nettie Rosenstein before opening his own salon. Inspired by Madeline Vionnet, he was known as the master of the bias cut.

Klein, Anne *American designer* (1923–1974)
Klein has been called the all-American designer of classic sportswear for the woman 5′4″ and under and was responsible for transforming "junior" clothes from fussy, little-girl-type clothes to sleek, sophisticated fashion clothing. In 1948, with her first husband Ben Klein, she organized the firm Junior Sophisticates, where she was the designer from 1951 to 1964. Anne Klein & Co. was formed in 1968 with her second husband. She is remembered in the 1950s for nipped waist, full skirt; unbelted chemise; "little boy" look; and use of white satin with gray flannel. In the 1960s, it was for classic blazers, shirtdresses, long midis, leather gaucho pants, Western and American Indian accessories, Turkish rug coats, and hot pants; and in the 1970s she was interested in nongimmicky, interrelated wardrobe of jackets, sweaters, pants, and skirts, and slinky, hooded jersey dresses for evening. The firm continued after her death in 1974, first with DONNA KARAN and LOUIS DELL'OLIO as co-designers, and later with Dell'Olio as sole designer.

Klein, Calvin *American designer* (1942–)
Klein attended High School of Art and Design and graduated from the Fashion Institute of Technology in 1962. With friend Barry Schwartz he formed Calvin Klein Ltd. in 1968. His designs include: women's and men's ready-to-wear, sportswear, blue jeans, furs, women's undergarments in designs similar to traditional men's undershirts and briefs, bed linens, cosmetics, skin care products, fragrances, and pantyhose. He also has a "couture" collection exclusively for Bergdorf-Goodman. His clothing is simple and refined and based on sportswear principles; uses luxurious natural fabrics as well as leather and suede in earth tones and neutrals.

Koos (Koos Van Den Akker) *Dutch-born American designer* (1939–)
Koos Van Den Akker was born in Holland and attended school in Paris, where he was chosen for an apprenticeship at Christian Dior in 1963. In 1968, he moved to New York and launched a string of stores; in the 1970s he had a wholesale business for a time. He is known for his painterly mixes of colors, patterns, and textures. Bill Cosby helped to give his sweaters cultlike status when he wore them on his sitcom.

Kors, Michael *American designer* (1959–)
A New York native, Kors studied at Fashion Institute of Technology. In 1978, he designed and merchandised a collection for Lothar's, a New York retail store. By 1981, he was showing his own collection of luxurious and precisely cut sportswear. He joined Céline as creative director in 1997 and continues in the early 2000s to create his own line in New York and the Céline line in Paris.

Krakoff, Reed *American designer* (active 1996–)
Reed Krakoff began his career at ANNE KLEIN, RALPH LAUREN, and TOMMY HILFIGER before joining Coach in 1996, where he rose to president and executive creative director. In 2013, he gave up his role at Coach to devote his full attention to his concurrent role as designer for his namesake line of ready-to-wear, handbags, and shoes, with a focus on sportswear that juxtaposes utility and femininity.

Krizia See MANDELLI, MARIUCCIA.

Lacroix, Christian (lah-cwa′) *French designer* (1951–)
Lacroix studied art history at Montpellier University; and in 1972 studied at L'École du Louvre in Paris. Working first as a museum curator, then as an assistant at Hermès in 1978, and at Guy Paulin, he turned to the study of fashion design in Japan. After he returned to Paris, he designed for JEAN PATOU from 1981 to mid-1987, then opened his own couture and ready-to-wear business in mid-1987. He is known for dramatic styles, often theatrical and worn with fantastic accessories. His ready-to-wear is somewhat less extreme than his couture clothes.

Lagerfeld, Karl *French designer* (1939–)
Born in Hamburg, Germany, in 1939, Lagerfeld arrived in Paris in 1953. He worked for BALMAIN from 1954 to 1957, then in 1963 for Chloé, an upscale ready-to-wear house where he became sole designer in 1972. From 1982 he designed for CHANEL while continuing with Chloé, left Chloé in 1984 for Chanel and to begin a collection under his own label. He designed a sportswear collection specifically for the United States in 1985. He also designs furs and sportswear for FENDI. Lagerfeld creates highly original designs that are quite wearable and always interesting. He is exceptionally prolific.

Lam, Derek *American designer* (1966–)
Derek Lam's Chinese American parents ran a garment-manufacturing business in San Francisco that specialized in wedding dresses. He attended Parsons School of Design and went to work for MICHAEL KORS. Lam launched his own line in 2003. He prefers fabrics that hold their shape rather than mold to a woman's body. In addition to his own line he serves as creative director for Tod's ready-to-wear and accessories.

L.A.M.B. (Gwen Stefani) *American designer* (1969–)
L.A.M.B. is an acronym for Love Angel Music Baby; the brand distributes collections of clothing, handbags, shoes, and fragrances designed by singer Gwen Stefani and expresses her personal style and aesthetics. She is

influenced by movie star glamour and modern street wear.

Lane, Kenneth Jay *American jewelry designer* (1932–)
Lane studied at the University of Michigan and graduated from the Rhode Island School of Design in 1954. While working on the promotion staff at *Vogue* magazine, he met Roger Vivier, shoe designer, and spent part of each year in Paris working with him. He went to work for Delman shoes as assistant designer; then to Christian Dior Shoes as associate designer. At the same time, in 1963, he made some jewelry pieces that were photographed by fashion magazines and bought by some stores. He used his initials K. J. L. and by 1964 was designing jewelry full-time. He likes to see his costume jewelry worn with jewelry made of real gems.

Lang, Helmut *Austrian-born American designer* (1956–)
Helmut Lang is a self-taught designer/artist. He opened a made-to-measure shop in Vienna when he was about 20. He closed that shop in 1984 and moved to Paris, where he showed his first runway collection in 1986. In 1997, he moved to New York. His Helmut Lang label for men and women is known for its contemporary urban silhouettes and unconventional use of new materials. In 2005, Lang resigned from the label, which is now owned by Link Theory Holdings.

Lanvin, Jeanne (lahn-vahn', zhon) *French designer* (1867–1946)
Lanvin apprenticed at 13 and started as a milliner in 1890. Designing children's clothes for her daughter and friends led to the establishment of her own business in Paris, where she remained for nearly 50 years. Remembered for *robes de style* of 18th- and 19th-c. flavor, wedding gowns, fantasy evening gowns with metallic embroideries, tea gowns, dinner pajamas, dolman wraps, and capes. Her peak years were between World Wars I and II. She died at the age of 79, but the house continued under the directorship of her daughter Comtesse Jean de Polignac. After a succession of designers, the couture operation ended in 1992.

Lapidus, Edmond (Ted) *French designer* (1929–2008)
After an apprenticeship with Dior, Lapidus started his own label in 1951. He gained prominence in the 1960s when he persuaded Twiggy to wear a suit and tie rather than a miniskirt, and he designed the white suit that John Lennon wore on the cover of the *Abbey Road* album. He was considered a pioneer of the unisex look, putting military epaulets on both male and female clothing and helping to make blue jeans mainstream.

Laroche, Guy (lah-rosh', ghee) *French designer* (c. 1923–1989)
Son of a French cattle-farming family near La Rochelle, Laroche dabbled in hair styling and millinery; worked for three years on Seventh Avenue, eight years with JEAN DESSÈS in Paris. He showed his first collection in fall of 1957, mostly coats and suits. His greatest fame came during the early 1960s. At the time of his death, the firm had expanded into ready-to-wear, and licensing agreements (intimate apparel, furs, luggage, sportswear, rainwear, dresses, blouses, sunglasses, accessories, fragrances). He is remembered for back cowl drapes; short puffed hems for evening; schoolgirl dresses; and loose lines in soft coats.

Lars, Byron *American designer* (1965–)
After studying at FIT, Lars worked for Kevan Hall and Ronaldus Shamask, among others. He launched his own label in 1991, which was critically acclaimed. He became especially well known for his shirts. A licensing debacle sullied the brand's value in specialty stores such as Saks Fifth Avenue and he disappeared for several years. In 1997, he designed a line of African American Barbie dolls with flamboyant fashions to match for Mattel Corporation. Anxious to get back to designing for real women, he launched the Beauty Mark label in 2001 with a focus on tailored feminine shirts for women.

Lauren, Ralph *American designer* (1939–)
In 1967, Lauren persuaded a menswear firm to handle made-by-hand silk neckties he had designed, thereby establishing the Polo neckwear division. Lauren was contracted to design the Polo line of menswear for Norman Hilton. In 1968, a separate company was established that produced a total wardrobe for men. Lauren introduced women's ready-to-wear made of Harris tweeds, camel's hair, and silk in 1971; followed by Polo boy's wear; Western wear; Ralph Lauren for Girls; a less expensive men's line; Polo University Club for college students and young businessmen; and Roughwear, a rugged outdoor collection. Licenses include: men's and women's ready-to-wear, including men's robes, swimwear, and furnishings; and small leathers, furs, scarves, fragrances, cosmetics, skin care, luggage, and home furnishings.

Léger, Hervé (also known as Hervé Leroux) *French designer* (1957–)
The Léger label was known for its instantly recognizable, body-enhancing bandage dresses. Hervé Léger worked as an assistant to Karl Lagerfeld at Fendi and then Chanel before launching his own label in 1985 with the help of Maryll Lanvin at the House of Lanvin. His bandage dresses gave him international recognition in 1992. In 1999, his company was acquired by BCBGMaxAzria Group; he lost control of his company and the rights to his name. He worked designing ready-to-wear, swimsuits, and hosiery for Wolford, and worked and then launched a new line in 1999 under the name Hervé Leroux, where he developed a new concept for draped jersey dresses.

Lelong, Lucien (leh-lohn', luce-yen') *French couturier* (1889–1958)
One of the great names in couture of the 1920s and through the 1940s, Lelong was famed for elegant, feminine clothes of refined taste and lasting wearability. The couture house was organized by his parents in 1886. Lucien was born in 1889, and founded his own business in 1919. Not a designer himself, he was an inspiration to a distinguished atelier of workers, including CHRISTIAN DIOR, PIERRE BALMAIN, HUBERT DE GIVENCHY, and

Jean Schlumberger. He started Editions department of ready-to-wear, forerunner of boutiques, in 1934. He was responsible for revitalizing couture after World War II. He retired in 1947 because of ill health.

Lepore, Nanette *American designer* (1958–)
Nanette Lepore's family placed a high value on art. After graduating from FIT in New York, she worked in the Garment District before opening her own label in 1992. Her collections are colorfully patterned and described as gypsy-like and free-spirited.

Leroy See ROY, HIPPOLYTE.

Lesage, François *French embroidery designer* (1929–2011)
Lesage inherited Maison Lesage from his father, Albert, managing it through the latter half of the 20th c. He forged relationships with both ready-to-wear and couture houses when other embroidery houses were disappearing. He sold Maison Lesage to Chanel in 2002; Chanel has been acquiring artisan houses to ensure their continued survival.

Leser, Tina *American designer* (1910–1986)
Leser studied at the School of Industrial Art and Academy of Fine Arts, Philadelphia, and at the Sorbonne, Paris. From 1936 to 1942, she lived in Hawaii, where she designed and sold her own hand-blocked floral prints in play clothes. She returned to New York in 1942 and was associated with Edwin H. Foreman, Inc. (1943 to 1952), after which she established Tina Leser, Inc., in 1952. Retired in 1964, but returned to design from 1966 to 1982, Leser is remembered for sarong play clothes; water-boy pants; painted and sequined cotton blouses; wrapped pareo skirt with bandeau top; costume jewelry in cork, coral, and shells; and travel-inspired Mexican, Haitian, Japanese, Indian fabrics, used in original trousers, easy cover-up tops, and long at-home robes. She is credited with making the first dress from cashmere.

Lhuillier, Monique (loo-lee-ay) *American designer* (1971–)
Born and raised in the Philippines, Lhuillier moved to Los Angeles and enrolled at the Fashion Institute of Design and Merchandising. She launched an upscale bridal company with her husband after designing her own bridal dress and the dresses for her bridal party. She expanded into evening wear in 2001 and ready-to-wear in 2003. Her silhouettes are dramatic but soft, often with a juxtaposition of fabric textures.

Lim, Phillip *American designer* (1973–)
Lim launched his own label, 3.1 Phillip Lim, in 2005 with his friend and business partner Wen Zhou; both were 31 years of age at the time. He opened his first store in Soho in 2007. In 2008, he created a limited-edition line for The Gap. His design philosophy is to design real clothes that people wear—pretty, but cool and chic without the high prices of designer brands.

Lowe, Annie Cole *American designer* (1898–1981)
Born in Alabama, Lowe learned dressmaking from her mother. When Lowe was still a child, she and her mother moved to New York. Her mother died and Lowe took over her mother's seamstress work. She was the first African American to pursue a degree in fashion design at S. T. Taylor School. In 1951, she had a chance meeting with Jacqueline Bouvier, who ordered several dresses. Lowe designed Bouvier's wedding dress as well as ten other dresses for various members of her wedding party. She later opened a boutique in Saks Fifth Avenue where she was known for her use of trapunto.

Lucile *British designer* (1863–1935)
Lucile was the most successful London-based couturiere of her time; both Molyneux and Travis Banton worked for her. She set up a dressmaker's shop with her mother in the 1890s. After marrying Sir Cosmo Duff-Gordon, she was soon dressing London's grandest ladies. She opened salons in New York in 1910 and in Paris in 1912.

Mabille, Alexis *French designer* (1977–)
Alexis Mabille discovered fashion while wandering the museums of Lyon and exploring his family attic. He received a diploma from Paris's École Chambre Syndicale de la Couture Parisienne in 1997, followed by apprenticeships with Ungaro and Nina Ricci. From there he joined the Christian Dior team, where he stayed for nine years. In 2005, he launched a unisex clothing line, impasse 13, and Treizor, an accessories line specializing in bowties. He made his debut at Paris Haute Couture Fashion Week in 2008, where he decorated his collection with 1,500 bows—a signature fetish. His style is described as flamboyant, frivolous, and eccentric.

Macdonald, Julien *British designer* (1971–)
Julien Macdonald began experimenting with knitwear techniques when he studied for his B.A. in fashion textiles. He obtained an M.A. from the Royal College of Art, again focusing on knits. After graduation he went to Chanel as a knitwear designer. He launched his own company in 1997. In 2001, LVMH recruited him to be Alexander McQueen's successor at Givenchy. He stayed at Givenchy until 2004 while continuing to design his own line. Aside from knits he is known to love glitz and sequins.

Mackie, Bob *American designer* (1940–)
After studying art and design in Los Angeles, Mackie worked as a sketcher for Jean Louis and EDITH HEAD, as well as for Ray Aghayan, his future partner. Mackie and Aghayan designed costumes for such celebrities as Marlene Dietrich, Carol Burnett, Barbra Streisand, and Cher, and were nominated several times for Academy Awards for costume design. In mid-1980s, Mackie was successful with a ready-to-wear collection emphasizing glamorous evening clothes.

Mainbocher (man-bow-shay′) *American couturier* (1890–1976)
Born Main Rousseau Bocher in Chicago, he studied art at Chicago Academy of Fine Arts, and then in New York, Paris, and Munich. After World War I, Mainbocher supported himself as a fashion illustrator for *Harper's Bazaar* and *Vogue* and became a full-time fashion journalist in 1922 before opening his own salon in Paris in 1929. He left Paris at the outbreak of World War II and opened

a couture house in New York in 1939, which closed in 1971. He was noted for the Duchess of Windsor's wedding dress in 1936; Wave (Women in the Navy) uniform in 1942; and the Girl Scout uniform in 1948. Among his ideas, which were widely copied, were print-bordered and lined sweaters to match dresses, beaded evening sweaters, tweed dinner suits with delicate blouses, and embroidered apron evening dresses.

Malandrino, Catherine *French-born American designer* (active 1980s–)

After graduating from Esmod, Catherine Malandrino worked in Paris with Dorothée Bis, Louis Féraud, EMANUEL UNGARO, and in the 1990s she was the designer at the French label *Et Vous*. She currently designs under her own contemporary label based in New York.

Mandelli, Mariuccia *Italian designer* (mahn-dell'-ee) (1933–)

Founder in 1954 with her husband, Aldo Pinto, of the design firm Krizia, she won excellent reviews for her first show in 1957, and business boomed. She had learned dressmaking in a friend's shop growing up. Schooled as a teacher she began making skirts and then dresses in 1951. Her clothes have been described as "young and original with a sense of fantasy." In the early 1970s, they established a knitwear company Kriziamaglia, which became known for animal sweaters—at each collection a different bird or beast is emphasized. Introduced hot pants in 1960s. Designs include children's wear, a boutique line, and fragrances. Greg Myler, GIAMBATTISTA VALLI, ALBER ELBAZ, and Jean-Paul Knott have all designed for the label, but Mandelli remains the creative vision. The label is known for fashion that is adaptable to any lifestyle and culture with an eye for new materials.

Marant, Isabel *French designer* (1967–)

Isabel Marant came by her fashion instincts naturally—her mother was a designer. She started sewing at age 15. After graduation, she apprenticed at Michel Klein. She launched her own line of accessories and jewelry and shortly thereafter expanded into apparel under the label Twen. Her early collections focused on jersey and knitwear; that line later morphed into the Isabel Morant label. She also designs a diffusion line, Etoile. She believes in clothes that are a mix of bohemian and minimalism with prices at the more affordable end of the designer market.

Marchesa *British designers* (Georgina Chapman [1976–] and Keren Craig [1976–])

The Marchesa label was launched in 2004, merging Georgina Chapman's draping and design experience with Keren Craig's textile creations. The label specializes in high fashion evening wear with an eclectic aesthetic.

Margiela, Martin *Belgian designer* (1957–)

After studying at the Academy of Fine Arts in Antwerp, Margiela went to Paris in 1984 to work for Jean Paul Gaultier. He presented his first collection under the label Maison Margiela in 1988, making clothes of recycled materials and employing deconstruction techniques. He named his label Maison Margiela, giving credit to the team of hands required to complete a collection. He designed for Hermès from 1997 to 2003.

Marni *Italian design house* (founded in 1994)

Marni was launched in 1994 by Consuelo Castiglioni as an offshoot of her husband's family fur business. The label is known for its quirky femininity achieved through unusual combinations of bright colors and bold patterns.

MaxMara *Italian designer label* (founded in 1951)

Established in 1951 by Achille Maramotti, this company distributes under a variety of labels, with MaxMara women's wear at the core. The brand is particularly well known for its outerwear but also designs a full range of sportswear. The brand employed Karl Lagerfeld, Jean-Charles de Castelbajac, Dolce & Gabbana, and Narciso Rodriguez early in their careers.

Maxwell, Vera *American designer* (1903–1995)

Maxwell worked first with sportswear and coat houses Adler & Adler and Max Milstein before opening her own business on Seventh Avenue. She believed in a classic approach to go-together separates in finest quality Scottish tweeds, wool jersey, raw silk, Indian embroideries, etc. She was inspired by men's Harris tweed jackets and gray flannel Oxford bags. She continued to work until early in 1985, when she closed her business. In 1986, she designed a collection of dresses, coats, and sportswear for the Peter Lynne Division of Gulf Enterprises but retired again soon after.

McCardell, Claire *American designer* (1905–1958)

After studying at Parsons School in New York and in Paris, McCardell worked for Robert Turk, Inc., as a model and assistant designer in 1929, then in 1931 went with Turk to work at Townley Frocks, Inc. where she remained, except for two years with HATTIE CARNEGIE, until her death at the age of 52. Considered the top all-American designer of 1940s and 1950s, she specialized in practical clothes for the average working girl. Credited with originating the "American Look" (i.e., the separates concept inspired by travel needs), she was responsible for many firsts: the monastic dress with natural shoulders and tied waist; harem pajamas; the "Popover," a surplice-wrapped housedress; kitchen dinner dress; bareback summer dress; long cotton Empire dress with tiny puffed sleeves; diaper-wrap one-piece swimsuit; shoulder bolero over halter dress; balloon bloomer playsuit; signature spaghetti belts; ballet slippers for street.

McCartney, Stella *British designer* (1971–)

Daughter of former Beatle Paul McCartney and a graduate of London's Central Saint Martins College of Arts and Design, this designer worked at LACROIX in Paris at age 15. Her first major success was at Chloé in 1997 at age 25. In 2001, she left Chloé and started her own label.

McClintock, Jessica *American designer* (1930–)

Jessica McClintock learned to sew from her grandmother, who was a patternmaker and seamstress. In 1969, she invested $5,000 in a California company called Gunne Sax. She has built that company into a multifaceted operation that expresses her personal style of blending femininity and old-fashioned allure.

McFadden, Mary *American designer* (1938–)

After a varied career that included director of public relations for Christian Dior–New York from 1962 to 1964, editor of *Vogue* South Africa, and work on both the French and American *Vogue* staffs, she sold three tunics she had designed from Chinese and African silks she had collected to Henri Bendel. The silks were hand painted using resist techniques with oriental colorings. Mary McFadden, Inc., was formed in 1976 and she became known for her designs made of unique fabrics using fine pleating and quilting with ropes wrapping the body. Designs include: lingerie and at-home wear, Simplicity Patterns, scarves, eyewear, furs, shoes, bed and bath linens, and upholstery fabrics.

McQueen, Alexander *British designer* (1969–2010)

An art school graduate in 1992, McQueen began his design career by working in Savile Row, for Romeo Gigli, and for Koji Tatsuno. He showed under his own label in 1994, and after GALLIANO left GIVENCHY, he assumed its design leadership. By 2001, he had returned to showing under his own name. He has been called "Britain's bad boy of fashion" because of his dramatic confrontational styles and his sometimes rude personal style. McQueen committed suicide in 2010. The label is now designed by his friend and assistant, Sarah Burton, who designed the Duchess of Cambridge's bridal gown.

Miller, Nicole *American designer* (active 1982–)

After studying at Rhode Island School of Design and in Paris, Miller opened her own business in 1982. She has been described as "a technical master with an astute fashion sense." She makes women's and menswear and is especially known for creative use of prints and graphics in her designs.

Missoni (miss-oh'-nee) *Italian designer* (Rosita [1932–] and Ottavio [Tai] [1921–2013])

Married in 1953, Rosita and Tai Missoni launched their label with four knitting machines. Originally they hired freelance designers such as Emmanuelle Khanh and Christiane Bailly to style their line, but eventually Rosita took over the design of the clothing and Tai the design of the knit fabrics. In the early 1990s, they handed over creative control to their daughter Angela. The label is characterized by their trademark knit fabrics, particularly the Missoni zigzag, which they pair with stripes, geometrics, and abstract florals, primarily executed as knits. Styles are so classic that their designs are difficult to date.

Miyake, Issey (me-ya'-key, ee-see) *Japanese designer* (1938–)

Born in Japan, Miyake moved to Paris in 1965 to study at the Chambre Syndicale de la Couture Parisienne. Work history included being an assistant at GUY LAROCHE and GIVENCHY from 1966 to 1968 and work with GEOFFREY BEENE in 1969. Miyake Design Studio and Issey Miyake International in Tokyo opened in 1970. He showed in Paris for the first time in 1973; established a company in Europe in 1979 and in the United States in 1982. He combines Japanese attitudes of fashion with exotic fabrics of his own designs. Miyake retired in 1997, but his firm continues under other design leadership.

Mizrahi, Isaac (miz-rah'-hee) *American designer* (1961–)

Formed his own business in 1987 after working for PERRY ELLIS, Jeffrey Banks, and CALVIN KLEIN. Mizrahi specialized in luxury sportswear for women, and also for men starting in 1990. Although his designs were considered inventive, using unexpected colors and fabrics, his business ran into difficulty and closed in 1998, after which he went into television and designed for films and theater.

Molinari, Anna *Italian designer* (active 1977–)

Anna Molinari learned to sew from her mother. She established her Blumarine label in 1977, which originally focused on knitwear, but later expanded into a full range of women's wear focused on edgy romanticism. Her company also distributes a secondary label, Miss Blumarine (geared to a younger customer) launched in 1987, and Ana Molinari (a more upscale label), launched in 1995. Molinari handed over the design responsibilities to her daughter Rossella Tarabini, who subsequently opted to leave the company. It is now designed by Tarabini's design team.

Molyneux, Edward (mohl-ee'-noo) *French couturier* (1891–1974)

Born in Ireland, Molyneux was an aristocrat, sportsman, officer in the Duke of Wellington Regiment, and an art student. He started at 17 as a designer, working in London, Chicago, and New York until 1914. He opened his own house in Paris in 1919, where he designed well-bred, elegant, fluid clothes, and is remembered for purity of line in printed silk suits with pleated skirts; timeless, softly tailored navy blue suits, and coats. He left Paris during World War II, but returned in 1949, adding furs, lingerie, millinery, and perfumes to his lines. Because of ill health, turned over Paris house to Jacques Griffe in 1950. Persuaded to reopen in Paris, January 1965, as Studio Molyneux; he brought first ready-to-wear collection to the United States in 1965, but this venture was not successful and he retired again.

Montana, Claude *French designer* (1949–)

In order to earn money to stay in London on a trip there in 1971, Montana designed papier-mâche jewelry encrusted with rhinestones. He stayed for a year, then returned to Paris, where he went to work for a leather firm before establishing himself in his own business. Characteristics of his designs are: bold, well-defined shapes. He joined LANVIN in 1989, leaving them in 1992 to continue his own business.

Mori, Hanae (moh'-ree, hah-nah) *Japanese designer* (1925–)

Mori opened a small boutique in Tokyo, where her designs attracted members of the Japanese film industry. She designed costumes for films in 1955, and after opening another shop, went on to develop multimillion-dollar international business. Since 1977, she has shown her couture collection in Paris. Her ready-to-wear sells in fine stores around the world; her boutiques in many countries sell sportswear and accessories. She uses unusual and beautiful fabrics, with especially huge flowers, butterflies, and classic Japanese feminine motifs. Styles are Western with Oriental details; best known for evening or at-home entertaining wear.

Moschino, Franco (mos-keen'-oh) *Italian designer* (c. 1950–1994)

After studying fine arts, Moschino was hired as a sketcher with VERSACE in 1971. He went on to design for Cadette from 1977 to 1982, then worked under his own label from 1983 until his death. He was known for "wearable, sexy clothes with a sense of humor." The label continues with other designers.

Mouret, Roland *French designer* (1962–)

Roland Mouret withdrew from fashion school, preferring to learn through real-life experience. He worked for several magazines before going to work for Jean Paul Gaultier's menswear collection. In 1998, he launched his own line, known for its seductive silhouettes and austere sexuality. He took a two-year hiatus from design in 2006 after creative differences with his financial backers. He returned to the catwalk in 2008 under the RM Roland Mouret label.

Mugler, Thierry *French designer* (1946–)

Mugler made his own clothes as a teenager. His early endeavors include work for the Strasbourg ballet company, as well as window-dressing for Paris boutiques. He moved to England in 1968 and then on to Amsterdam before returning to Paris two years later. His first collection in 1971 was shown under the label Café de Paris, and by 1973 he designed under his own label. Characteristics include broad shoulders and well-defined waists, and the presentations of his lines are often startling and theatrical.

Muir, Jean *British designer* (1928–1995)

Muir started her career as a sketcher at Liberty, designed for six years at Jaeger, and then under her own label for Jane and Jane in 1962. She established Jean Muir, Inc., in 1966 and opened the Jean Muir Shop in Henri Bendel department store, New York, in 1967. Characteristics were: soft, classic tailored shapes in leathers or soft fabrics.

Mulleavy, Kate See RODARTE.

Mulleavy, Laura See RODARTE.

Natori, Josie *American designer* (1947–)

Born in the Philippines, Natori became a successful investment banker. She moved into the fashion world in the second half of the 1970s and became known for luxurious lingerie and evening wear.

Norell, Norman *American designer* (1900–1972)

Norell was the son of haberdashery store owner in Indianapolis. He came to New York in 1919 to study at Parsons School of Design, and his early career included theatrical and movie designing; and working for Charles Armour and Hattie Carnegie from 1928 to 1940. A partnership in the firm Traina-Norell (1941–1960) followed. He formed his own company, Norman Norell, Inc., in 1960 after Traina's death. Described as the top American designer on Seventh Avenue, the "Dean of the fashion industry," "the American Balenciaga," Norell was known for precision tailoring, dateless purity of line, conservative elegance in the finest imported fabrics. He is also remembered for trouser-suits for town and travel, widely flared day skirts, straight wool jersey chemises, slinky sequined sheaths, the sailor look. The firm continued for a short time after his death, under GUSTAVE TASSELL.

Ohne Titel *American designer label* (founded in 2006)

Flora Gill and Alexa Adams launched Ohne Titel (German for "untitled") in 2006. Both are graduates of Parsons and began their career working for Karl Lagerfeld. The Ohne Titel line is known for its crafty techniques, such as macramé and crochet, incorporated into futuristic silhouette.

Oldfield, Bruce *British designer* (1950–)

Bruce Oldfield launched his namesake label in 1975 making ready-to-wear for European and U.S. specialty stores. He began making couture clothes in 1978, for clients including Diana, Princess of Wales. In 1984, he opened his first store. Today, he continues to make bridal wear and custom garments in London.

Oldham, Todd *American designer* (1961–)

A self-taught designer, Oldham worked for a time in the alterations department of a Ralph Lauren Polo boutique. After going into business in Dallas, he moved to New York, where he made women's shirts. His first designer collection showing was in 1990. Since then he has added work as a design consultant for other firms. His clothes have been described as "a mixture of the commercial with the offbeat."

Olive, Frank *American millinery designer* (1929–1995)

Olive studied art and fashion in Milwaukee and Chicago; went to California to try costume design. Arriving in New York in the early 1950s, he was hoping to design for the theater, but was advised by NORELL, who reviewed some of his sketches, to design hats. He apprenticed, sold fabrics, worked in the Saks Fifth Avenue custom hat department, then established his own firm, where he distributed three hat lines: "Counterfits," for the mass market; "Frank's Girl," a moderate-priced line; and "Frank Olive" designer label. He also designed hats for private clients.

Oliver, André *French designer* (1932–1993)

Born in Toulouse; graduated from École des Beaux Arts in Paris, Oliver joined PIERRE CARDIN in 1955, designing menswear. Eventually he created ready-to-wear for both men and women. His association with Cardin continued as artistic director of Cardin couture with total artistic control, sharing design responsibilities with Cardin, until Oliver's death.

Olsen, Ashley and Mary-Kate *American designers* (1986–)

Fraternal twins Mary-Kate and Ashley Olsen began acting at the age of nine months on the ABC sitcom *Full House.*

Growing up in Hollywood, they were exposed to fashion at an early age. They began with a licensing deal with Walmart for a line of clothes geared to girls sizes 4 to 14 in 2001. This was followed by their appearance as models in a Badgley Mischka ad campaign in 2006. They launched their first owned label, The Row, in 2007, which competes at the designer ready-to-wear price point. That same year they launched a contemporary line, Elizabeth and James, named for their sister and brother and inspired by vintage finds and their own wardrobes.

Owens, Rick *American-born French designer* (1962–)

Rick Owens is originally from Southern California, but he now works and shows in Paris. He dropped out of design school and began his career working for various design houses in Los Angeles. He launched the Rick Owens label in 1994, and while it received critical acclaim, he worked mainly under the radar. In 2003, he moved to Paris, where a picture of Kate Moss wearing one of his fitted distressed leather jackets appeared in *Vogue Paris.* That catapulted him into the global spotlight. He is known for his understated luxury and sees his collections as an evolution of his design aesthetic. He is a master at juxtaposing light with dark, hard with soft, structure with draping. He shows two menswear collections and two women's wear collections a year and does not advertise.

Özbek, Rifat *Turkish-born British designer* (1953–)

After arriving in England in 1970, he studied fashion at Central Saint Martins College of Arts and Design. He worked in Italy for a time before returning to London to design for Monsoon, a made-in-India line. He launched his own line in 1984, showing out of his apartment. In 1991, he moved his business to Milan, where he showed until 1994; he then began showing in Paris. His designs frequently took inspiration from contrasting Eastern and Western cultures. Most recently he has worked as an interior designer.

Panichgul, Thakoon (Chiang Rai) *American designer* (1974–)

Thakoon Panichgul began his fashion career as a merchandiser for J. Crew. From there he went to work for *Harper's Bazaar* magazine. While there, he took some tailoring classes at Parsons School of Design and at the age of 29 started his label, Thakoon. His clothes are characterized by a sophisticated but minimal style, heavily influenced by his Eastern heritage. He has designed capsule collections for Nine West and the Gap.

Paquin, House of (pak-ann') *French couture house* (1891–1956)

Founded by Mme. Paquin and her banker husband, the House of Paquin was synonymous with elegance in the first decade of 20th c. Mme. Paquin was the first woman to achieve importance in haute couture. Remembered for: fur-trimmed tailored suits, furs, lingerie; evening dresses in white, gold lamé, and pale green; blue serge suits trimmed with gold braid and buttons; and fine workmanship. No two dresses were alike, and the firm was the first to take mannequins to the opera or to the races to show their designs. They also founded the first foreign branch of a couture house in London in 1912, and later in Madrid and in Buenos Aires. Mme. Paquin retired in 1920 after selling the firm. She died in 1936.

Parnis, Mollie *American designer* (1905–1992)

Born in New York City, Parnis was one of the most successful women designers on Seventh Avenue. She began her career in 1939 as designer for Parnis-Livingston (with husband, Leon Livingston), specializing in flattering, feminine dresses and ensembles for the well-to-do woman over 30. Her boutique collection was designed by Morty Sussman until his death in 1979. Mollie Parnis Studio collection, aimed at a younger woman, was organized in 1979. At end of 1984 she dissolved her firm to become a "part-time" consultant at Chevette Lingerie, owned by her nephew. She returned to work full-time and produced her first loungewear collection for Chevette, Mollie Parnis at Home, for fall 1985.

Patou, Jean (pa-too', zhon) *French couturier* (1887–1936)

One of the great names in couture of 1920s to 1930s, Patou brought glamour and showmanship to fashion. He was more of a businessman than designer, specializing in ladylike, elegant, and uncluttered country-club clothes. Having opened in 1914, the firm was interrupted by World War I, then reopened in 1919 in a shop called Parry. After the whole first collection was bought by an American, he started a new business as Jean Patou. Remembered for the sensation caused in 1929 when he lengthened skirts to the ankle and revived a natural waistline and for long simple gowns to go with important jewels. After his death in 1936, the house remained open under Raymond Barbas with series of resident designers, among the best known of which were: MARC BOHAN (1953–1956), KARL LAGERFELD (1960–1963), and CHRISTIAN LACROIX (1982–1986).

Pedlar, Sylvia *American lingerie designer* (1901–1972)

Pedlar studied at Cooper Union and Art Students League to be a fashion artist. She founded Iris Lingerie in 1929, and designed there for 40 years. She is remembered for reviving the peignoir and matching long-sleeved gown, the Istanbul harem-hem gown, the toga nightdress, short chemise-slip, lace-trimmed silk gowns—sometimes doubling as evening dresses. She retired in 1970.

Peretti, Elsa *American jewelry designer* (1940–)

Born in Florence, Italy, Peretti earned a diploma in interior design and worked for an architect. After coming to New York and working for several design firms, she designed a few pieces of silver jewelry in 1969 that were used by SANT'ANGELO and HALSTON. She joined Tiffany & Co. in 1974. Her well-known designs include: heart-shaped buckles, silver horseshoe-shaped buckle on a long leather belt (also designed in horn, ebony, and ivory); pendants in the form of small vases; small, open, slightly lopsided heart pendant that slides on a chain; diamonds-by-the-yard. She has designed a refillable rock crystal bottle for her perfume sold by Tiffany, as well as desk and table accessories.

Philo, Phoebe *British designer* (1973–)
Phoebe Philo grew up in England and attended Central Saint Martins College of Arts and Design. In 1997, she joined Chloé as assistant to her friend Stella McCartney, who was then creative director. When McCartney left Chloé in 2001, Philo assumed her position. Her designs had a modern edge that appealed to the younger customer that McCartney had cultivated. Philo was named creative director of Céline in 2008 after two-year break to stay home with her children.

Piana, Pietro Loro *Italian design label* (founded in 1924)
Pietro Loro Piana founded a luxury textile business in Italy in 1924, focusing on creating the finest raw materials, particularly cashmere and wool. The firm expanded into ready-to-wear and accessories that utilize their fine materials.

Piazza Sempione *Italian luxury label* (founded in 1991)
The mission of Piazza Sempione is to create an exclusive clothing and accessories line for women that combines textile technology with the excellence of Italian craftsmanship. The company was founded by the husband and wife team, Roberto Monti and Marisa Guerrizio.

Piguet, Robert (pee-geh') *French couturier* (1901–1953)
Born in Switzerland, Piguet came to Paris at age 17 and studied design with Redfern and POIRET. He opened his own house in 1933, using freelance designers. Great couturiers of the future worked for him: GIVENCHY at age 17 and DIOR in 1937, who said Piguet taught him "the virtues of simplicity . . . how to suppress." JAMES GALANOS worked for him for three months without pay. Known for refined simplicity of black-and-white dresses, afternoon clothes, tailored suits with vests, fur-trimmed coats, especially styled for petite women. He closed his house in 1951.

Pilati, Stefano *French designer* (1965–)
Stefano Pilati interned with Nino Cerruti at age 17. His first job was working for a velvet manufacturer, where he quickly assumed responsibility for designing their entire line. In 1993, he was hired by Giorgio Armani as an assistant menswear designer. He left Armani in 1995 to head up research and development at Prada; he was eventually promoted to assistant designer for Miu Miu in 1998. In 2000, he began working at Yves Saint Laurent as design director under Tom Ford; when Ford left YSL, Pilati took over the creative director position. In 2012, Pilati announced that he was leaving YSL; later that year, it was announced that he would join Ermenegildo Zegna as their design director.

Pinto, Maria *American designer* (1957–)
Maria Pinto graduated from the school of the Art Institute of Chicago with a degree in fine arts; she also studied at Parsons and FIT in New York. She worked as an assistant to Geoffrey Beene for two years before launching her own line of accessories in 1991. She eventually based her business in Chicago doing custom designs for the likes of Oprah Winfrey. Michelle Obama wore a Pinto sheath dress on the night her husband won the Democratic presidential nomination in 2008. In spite of all of the positive press, she shuttered her business in 2010.

Poiret, Paul (pwar-ay') *French designer* (1879–1944)
Poiret was the son of a Parisian cloth merchant. While apprenticed to an umbrella-maker, he sold sketches to couturiers and was first employed in couture by DOUCET in 1896. After spending a short period at the house of WORTH, he opened his own house in 1904. Known as "King of Fashion" from 1904 to 1924, Poiret developed a passion for theatrical costuming and was known for his original ideas and strident colors, for banning the corset, and shackling legs with the harem and hobble skirts. His work is remembered for extreme Orientalism, the minaret skirt, kimono-sleeved tunics, exotic embroidery, barbaric jewels, and eye makeup. He was the first to travel (1912) to foreign capitals with an entourage of 12 live mannequins. After World War I, he refused to change his exotic image, so he faded from the fashion scene. He died in Paris after years of poverty and illness, having left his mark on the taste of two decades.

Posen, Zac *American designer* (1980–)
Zac Posen interned with Richard Martin at the Costume Institute of the Metropolitan Museum of Art, where he developed a passion for the work of MADELEINE VIONNET. He studied at Central Saint Martins College of Arts and Design in London. He moved back to New York and interned with Nicole Miller and started designing gowns for private clients. His designs frequently utilize the bias cut, exuding a modern femininity, which makes them popular with Hollywood celebrities. His first runway show was in 2002. In 2004, Sean "Diddy" Combs became an investor. He also designs a diffusion line under the label Z Spoke.

Potter, Clare *American designer* (1902–1999)
One of the first group of all-American designers honored by Dorothy Shaver at Lord & Taylor in late 1930s. A graduate of Pratt Institute, she majored in portrait painting and then entered the fashion field designing embroidery. Formed her own business on Seventh Avenue under the name Clarepotter during 1940s and 1950s, and under the name Potter Designs Inc. in 1960s. She also had a wholesale firm, Timbertop Inc. She was known for making classic sport, at-home, and dinner clothes. She was noted for unusual color combinations, refinement of cut, and no extraneous trimmings.

Prada, Miuccia (prah'-dah, mee-uch'-ee-ah) *Italian designer* (1950–)
Granddaughter of a leather shop proprietor in Milan, Prada opened her ready-to-wear business in 1989. She has been known both for high-quality clothing and for leather accessories. Miu Miu is a secondary line for Prada, named after Miuccia Prada's nickname and designed after her personal wardrobe.

Proenza Schouler (pro-en-za skool-er) *American designers* (Lazaro Hernandez [1979–] and Jack McCollough [1979–])
Hernandez and McCollough met in 1999 when they were both attending Parsons School of Design. Hernandez

interned at MICHAEL KORS and McCollough at MARC JACOBS. Their senior collection was a collaboration using fabric donated by Kors. It was so impressive that Barney's bought it for the store. They founded their company in 2002 with a mission to provide classic silhouettes with a twist for grown-up women.

Pucci, Emilio (poo'-chee) *Italian designer* (1914–1992)
An aristocrat (Marchese Pucci di Barsento) living in Florence, Pucci was discovered as designer of his own ski clothes by an American photographer in 1947. The following year he designed skiwear for Lord & Taylor, New York. He opened a workshop in Florence in 1949, and by 1950 had a couture house under the name Emilio, with boutiques throughout Italy. He was known for brilliant heraldic prints on sheer silk jersey, made into clinging chemises, at-home robes, tights; signature scarves and dresses; resort shirts in designs from Sienese banners, Sicilian, or African motifs; the "capsula" (jumpsuit tapered to cover feet with soft boots). His house closed after his death in 1992 but reopened again in 2001.

Pugh, Gareth (pyoo) *British designer* (1981–)
Pugh attended Central Saint Martins College of Arts and Design, and his London Fashion Week debut was in 2005 as part of the Fashion East Collective. His first solo show was in 2006. He has worked with Topshop on two co-branded collections. He is one of the bad boys of the British fashion scene.

Pulitzer, Lilly *American designer* (1932–2013)
Socialite living in Palm Beach, Florida, when, in 1960, she designed and sold a printed-cotton shift called a "Lilly," which grew into nationwide fashion in the 1960s and 1970s. She also designed a child's version called "Minnie," print slacks for men, and "sneaky Pete" nightshirts. Ruffled hems and short sleeves were added to basic Lilly in 1970s. Her company was liquidated in mid-1980s.

Quant, Mary *British designer* (1934–)
Quant is credited with starting the Chelsea or Mod Look in the mid-1950s and making London the most influential fashion center at that time. Among the items she was associated with were body stockings, hot pants, the layered principle of dressing, and spirited, unconventional clothes. By 1967, she started the miniskirt revolution, introduced denim, colored flannel, vinyl in "kooky" (her word) clothes, with 1920s flavor. Within ten years, she had made a less expensive line, Ginger, joined huge U.S. department-store chain J. C. Penney Co.; and designed for Puritan's Youthquake promotion in the United States.

Rabanne, Paco (rah-bahn') *French designer* (1934–)
Born in San Sebastian, Rabanne was the son of BALENCIAGA's head dressmaker. After studying architecture, he moved into designing plastic accessories and opened a store in Paris in 1966 at age 32, causing a sensation with his metal-linked plastic-disk dresses, sun goggles, and jewelry made of plastic in primary colors. He continued the linked-disk principle in fur-patched coats; leather-patch dresses; masses of buttons laced with wire, strips of aluminum, and pioneered in fake-suede dresses in 1970; knit-and-fur coats; and dresses of ribbons, feathers, or tassels linked for suppleness.

Reboux, Caroline (reh-boo') *French millinery designer* (1837?–1927)
Reboux founded the most prestigious millinery house in Paris, both during the late 19th c. and later in the 1920s and 1930s. She created hats for leading actresses and aristocracy. After her death in 1927, her house continued leadership under Mme. Lucienne, making the head-fitting felt cloche the status symbol of fashion for many years. Noted for profile brims, dipping low on one side; forward-tilt tricorns; open-crown lamé turbans; flower bandeaus.

Redfern, House of *British couture house*
London house established in 1841 by Englishman John Redfern, dressmaker for Queen Victoria and the aristocracy. Responsible for jersey suit made for Lillie Langtry, "The Jersey Lily," in 1879. Known for sober, elegant, dark-blue tailored suits, the house of Redfern also designed the first woman's uniform for the International Red Cross in 1916 and also originated elaborate theater costumes.

Reece, Tracy *American designer* (1964–)
Tracy Reese attended Parsons School of Design and went to work as a design assistant to Martine Sitbon. In 1987, she launched her own company making contemporary sportswear. Hit by the recession, she closed her doors and worked for a time at PERRY ELLIS for the Portfolio division until it closed. From 1990 to 1995, she was the design director at Magaschoni, a bridge label. Eventually she was able to relaunch her own company, Tracy Reese Meridian.

Rhodes, Zandra *British designer* (1940–)
Textile designer who graduated from the Royal College of Art in 1966; Rhodes was producing her own designs by 1969. Her textile innovations include: hand-screened prints on soft fabrics, Art Deco motifs, lipsticks, teddy bears, zigzags, big splashy patterns, and punk-inspired styles. She designed soft, butterfly dresses, slit-sided chiffons, edges cut by pinking shears.

Ricci, Nina (ree'-chee, nee'-nah) *French couturier* (1883–1970)
Born Marie Nielli in Turin, Italy; she married Louis Ricci, a jeweler. Ricci began her professional life at age 13 when she came to Paris to work as seamstress. By 1905, she was designing her own models on live mannequins. The firm Nina Ricci opened in 1932 and specialized in dresses for mature, elegant women and trousseaux for brides. Styles were graceful with superb detailed workmanship. She was one of the first designers to show lower-priced models in a boutique. Since 1945 the House has been managed by her son Robert Ricci, and after 1959, other designers created the styles.

Rochas, Marcel (ro-shass, mar-sell') *French couturier* (1902–1955)
Born in Paris, Rochas opened a couture house about 1924. He became popular after eight women appeared at same party wearing identical gowns of his design. His designs were full of fantastic ideas: special bird- and

flower-patterned fabric; combinations of as many as ten colors; lots of lace, ribbon, and tulle, and a feminine, square-shouldered, hourglass silhouette several years ahead of the New Look. In 1948, he invented new corset called guêpière, which cinched the natural waist. He had a boutique for separates and accessories and designed for films.

Rodarte (ro-dart-tay) *American designers* (Kate Mulleavy [1979–] and Laura Mulleavy [1980–])

Sisters Kate and Laura Mulleavy did not study fashion, but in 2005 they made the cover of *Women's Wear Daily* within days of showing their ten-piece debut collection of hand-sewn garments. They are known for their handcrafted designs that use interesting fabrics and techniques to create textural wearable art-style pieces.

Rodriguez, Narciso (rod-ree′-gez, nar-seeze′-oh) *American designer* (1961–)

Rodriguez came to public notice in 1996 when he designed the late Carolyn Bessette-Kennedy's wedding gown. He had worked for DONNA KARAN at ANNE KLEIN, and at CALVIN KLEIN, where he came to know Bessette-Kennedy. He was subsequently hired by Cerutti to do his own line, which is shown in Milan and also works for a Spanish leather house (Loewe). He is known for skillful tailoring and pretty, feminine designs.

Rodriguez, Robert *American designer*

Robert Rodriguez attended FIT where he received the Critics Award for Best Designer of the Year. His first job after graduation was working for CHRISTIAN DIOR under MARK BOHEN and Geri Gerald. He launched his own line in 2003 with business partner Nicola Guarno. His clothes appeal to women of a broad age range and are known for their feminine yet sexy feel, selling at the contemporary price point. He also designs a diffusion line, Robbi & Nikki.

Rose, Lela *American designer* (active 1993–)

Lela Rose attended Parsons School of Design, graduating in 1993. She worked with both Christian Francis Roth and Richard Tyler before launching her own line in 1998. Designing gowns for Jenna and Barbara Bush to wear to their father's presidential inauguration in 2001 brought increased visibility. Her signature style embraces casual luxury.

Rosso, Renzo *Italian designer* (1955–)

Renzo Rosso and his partners launched Diesel designer jeans in 1978. In 1985, Rosso bought out his partners and took creative control of Diesel. Under his direction, Diesel became a leader in denim technology and vintage washes. He is also President of OTB, the holding group of Maison Martin Margiela, Marni, Viktor & Rolf, Diesel, Just Cavalli, Vivienne Westwood, Marc Jacobs Men, and DSquared2, and the founder of the Only the Brave Foundation.

Rouff, Maggy *French designer* (1896–1971)

The daughter of the directors of the couture house Drècoll, Maggy Rouff followed her parents into fashion design becoming the director of Drècoll. When the house merged with Beer, she launched her own line, Maggy Rouff, where she designed tailored sportswear, as well as evening wear.

Rowley, Cynthia *American designer* (1958–)

Cynthia Rowley began sewing at age seven. She attended the Art Institute of Chicago, and after graduating moved to New York in 1983. She founded her namesake business in 1988 making flirty vintage-inspired women's ready-to-wear. She has since expanded into accessories, menswear, and home accessories.

Roy, Hippolyte (roy, ip-po-leet) or **Leroy** *French couturier* (1763–1829)

Known to history as Leroy, Hippolyte Roy was the son of a stagehand at the Paris opera. He was encouraged to become a tailor by Rose Bertin. After the French Revolution he switched to the Republican side and designed red, white, and blue patriotic dress. He became a virtual dictator of fashion for Empress Josephine and other women of the time. Directed by Napoleon to design luxurious dress to encourage French industry, Leroy reached the peak of his fame at Napoleon's coronation. He continued to work for Napoleon's second wife. His style never changed through the Directoire, Consulate, and Empire periods, although he claimed he never made two dresses alike.

Roy, Rachel *American designer* (1974–)

Rachel Roy was born in 1974. After moving to New York she worked as a stylist for magazines and music videos. She interned at the urban fashion label Rocawear, where she later became creative director. In 2005 she launched her own line, Rachel Roy, and in 2009, a diffusion line RACHEL, that she sold exclusively at Macy's.

Rucci, Ralph *American designer* (1957–)

Ralph Rucci attended the Fashion Institute of Technology; shortly after graduating, he launched his own line. In 1994, he launched Chado, named after a Japanese tea ceremony. Chado embraces an Eastern sensibility, and hand-crafted techniques. He uses the finest fabrics from Europe and incorporates his skill as a fine artist into his work. In 2002, he was invited by the Paris Chambre Syndicale to show his collection in Paris, the first American designer since MAINBOUCHER to receive that honor.

Rykiel, Sonia (rye-kel′) *French designer* (1930–)

Rykiel got her start by making maternity clothes for herself and designing for her husband's firm, Laura. She opened Sonia Rykiel Boutique in 1968 in the Paris department store Galeries Lafayette, and, soon after, her own boutique on the Left Bank. Known for tight, long sweaters; sheer gowns over body stockings; long, slit-sided day skirts; layered dresses and sweaters with thick, roll-back cuffs; and high-rise wide pants. Her liberated, unconstructed clothes range from folkloric fantasy to basic classics.

Saab, Elie *Lebanese designer* (1964–)

Elie Saab is a self-taught designer who grew up in Beirut; his family shuttled between Paris, Cyprus, and Lebanon when the civil war broke out. He opened his first atelier at the age of 18. He opened his Paris salon and showroom in 2000. In 2003, he was invited by the Chambre Syndicale to show his first haute couture collection in Paris. His heavily embellished gowns are cut close to the body and are popular with Hollywood celebrities.

St. John Knits *American designer* (founded in 1962)

St. John is a designer brand specializing in fine gauge knitwear for women. It was founded in 1962 by Robert and Marie Grey in Irvine, California. St. John Sport is a more casual line for a slightly younger customer.

Saint Laurent, Yves (sanh la-rahn', eve) *French designer* (1936–2008)

Saint Laurent won a prize for a fashion sketch in a design competition judged by DIOR, after which he was offered a position as assistant to Dior. From 1954 to 1957, he worked in the House of Dior, inheriting the top designing post at Dior's death in 1957. He opened his own house in 1961 and a series of prêt-à-porter boutiques called *Rive Gauche* in 1966. His interests expanded to designing menswear in 1974. Licenses using the famous YSL initials include: sweaters, bed and bath linens, eyeglasses, scarves, children's wear. Saint Laurent was considered the most influential modern designer for the sophisticated woman, one who successfully interpreted the contemporary moods of fashion. Among the specific styles for which he is remembered are the trapeze line, 1958, in his first Dior collection; pea jackets and blazers; chemises divided into Mondrian-blocks of bold color; sportive leather; city pants; military jackets; the nude look in see-through shirts and transparent dresses over nude body stockings in 1966; the fantasy of the rich peasants; smoking jackets; spencer jackets; the tuxedo look. Although Saint Laurent had turned over ready-to-wear design to others, he continued to do the couture collections until 2002, when he announced his retirement. He died in 2008. A major retrospective of his work was shown at the Petit Palais in Paris in 2010.

Sanchez, Fernando *American lingerie designer* (1930–2006)

Born in Spain, Sanchez studied at the École Chambre Syndicale de la Couture in Paris. He worked handling lingerie for CHRISTIAN DIOR and came to New York to work with the lines represented at Dior European boutiques. Sanchez also designed furs for Revillon for about 12 years, becoming known for such designs as the hide-out mink coat. In 1973, he opened his own lingerie firm. Known for: lace-trimmed silk gowns, camisole tops, boxer shorts, bikini pants, and for developing lingerie based on sportswear principles, in which he mixed color, fabrics, and lengths. He signed with Vanity Fair in 1984 to design a moderate-price line of sleep and loungewear.

Sander, Jil *German designer* (1943–)

A freelancer until her first women's collection was shown in 1973, Jil Sander entered a partnership with Prada in 1999. This connection ended by her leaving the firm in 2004. In 2009, she established a fashion consultancy and went to work for Uniqlo of Japan. In February of 2012, she returned to her namesake brand after RAF SIMONS departed for Dior. She is known for "luxurious minimalism."

Sant'Angelo, Giorgio (sant'-ahn-jell-oh, joar'-joh) *American designer* (1936–1989)

Trained as an architect and industrial designer, Sant'Angelo studied art in France with Picasso; came to the United States in 1962 and created cartoons for Walt Disney. After moving to New York in 1963, he freelanced as a textile designer and stylist and served as a design consultant. He founded Sant'Angelo Ready-to-Wear in 1966 and di Sant'Angelo, Inc. in 1968, and he designed ready-to-wear and separates under the Giorgio Sant'Angelo label. His clothes were a bit out of the ordinary (ethnic themes such as the gypsy look, American Indian, and Chinese; and a body stocking and bodysuit in brilliant bi- and tri-colors to match T-shirts and shorts); he maintained a couture operation for a roster of celebrities. He made a short-lived comeback in the mid-1980s and died in 1989.

Sarafpour, Behnaz (bay-naz sa-raf-poor) *American designer* (1969–)

Of Iranian descent, Sarafpour studied at Parsons School of Design. She went on to work for Anne Klein, Isaac Mizrahi, Narciso Rodriguez, Richard Tyler, and Barney's before launching her own line in 2001. She is known for her ladylike glamour expressed in classic A-line silhouettes and featuring bows, nipped-in waists, and understated florals and lace. She designed a co-branded line for Target's Go International campaign in 2006.

Scaasi, Arnold (ska'-zee) *American designer* (1931–)

Born Arnold Isaacs in Montreal, Canada, Scaasi adopted his name spelled backward for his design work. He studied at the École Chambre Syndicale in Paris, beginning his career as an apprentice with PAQUIN. Moving to New York, he worked as sketcher for CHARLES JAMES; then, in 1957, opened his own wholesale business and, in 1960, a ready-to-wear collection. Scaasi switched to couture in 1963 and returned to ready-to-wear, with Arnold Scaasi Boutique, in 1983. Known for spectacular evening wear in luxurious fabrics, often fur- or feather-trimmed, he appealed to glamorous actresses and socialites. He has also designed costume jewelry, men's neckties and sweaters, and furs.

Scherrer, Jean-Louis *French designer* (1936–2013)

Jean-Louis Scherrer worked for Dior and Louis Féraud before launching his own company. He was known for luxurious dresses with rich embellishment symbolic of Paris fashions in the 60s. He retired in 1992 after being fired from his own company after a buyout. The label was designed by Erik Mortensen and then Stéphane Rolland after he left; the house closed in 2008. He died in 2013 after a long illness.

Schiaparelli, Elsa (skap'-a-rell'-ee) *French couturière* (1890–1973)

Roman-born Schiaparelli was one of the most creative, unconventional couturières of 1930s and 1940s, an innovator whose clothes and accessories were startling conversation pieces. By 1929, she had her own business, *Pour le Sport,* in Paris, where she had spectacular success with avant-garde designs. As a result of her close friendship with surrealist artists, such as Dali and Cocteau, they contributed to her designs. She stopped designing in 1940 for the duration of World War II, spending the time in the United States and returning to Paris after liberation. She reopened in 1945, returning to natural shoulderline, stiff peplums, and timeless black dresses. Schiaparelli had a great flair for publicity and defied tradition by using aggressive colors and rough materials. She remained a consultant for companies licensed to produce stockings, perfume, scarves, etc., under her name after closing her business in February 1954.

Scott, Jeremy *American-born French designer* (1976–)
Nonconformist Jeremy Scott studied at Pratt Institute in New York and moved to Paris in 1995, where he launched his own line. Known as an avant-garde designer, he has made garments from Band-Aids, hospital gowns, and trash bags.

Scott, L'Wren *American designer* (1967–)
Born in Utah, L'Wren Scott left for Paris at the age of 18 to pursue modeling. She returned to the states and moved to California in 1994, where she established herself as a stylist. She met Mick Jagger in 2001 and they've been together ever since. In 2006, she launched a Little Black Dress Collection. She's been designing ever since.

Shamask, Ronaldus *American designer* (1945–)
A self-taught designer, Shamask has a strong architectural style. He began by working for private clients designing both interiors and clothing. Since 1986, he has designed both menswear and women's wear sold at high-end specialty stores such as Bergdorf Goodman and Neiman Marcus.

Simons, Raf *Belgian designer* (1968–)
Raf Simons graduated with a degree in industrial and furniture design in 1991. After working in furniture design for several years, he launched a menswear collection in 1995. In 2000, he shut down his company to take a sabbatical. The company reopened in 2001with a new backer. He was appointed head professor of the fashion department at the University of Applied Arts in Vienna, Austria in 2000, a position which he maintained through 2005. In June of 2005, the Raf by Raf Simons line was launched. That same year he was appointed creative director of Jil Sander. He announced his departure from that job in 2012; later that year, he accepted the job of creative director at Dior. He is inspired by the world around him, particularly rebellious youth cultures and traditional menswear. He is known for his modern proportions, clean construction, and interesting shapes.

Sitbon, Martine *French designer* (1952–)
Martine Sitbon spent time as a freelance designer and fashion consultant after graduation before starting her own line in 1984. By 1987, she was appointed creative director of Chloé, where she stayed for nine seasons. In 1998, she launched a menswear line, and in 2001, she was named director for women's wear at Byblos. In 2004, she launched Rue de Mail, named after the street where her showroom is located.

Slimane, Hedi (Edee Sli-man) *French designer* (1968–)
Slimane studied at L'École du Louvre; he was hired by YVES SAINT LAURENT and promoted to creative director for menswear one year later. In 1999, Gucci bought YSL and TOM FORD became creative director for the company. Slimane left Yves Saint Laurent and moved to CHRISTIAN DIOR as designer for Dior Homme. He did not renew his contract with Dior in 2007 and pursued his interest in photography. In March of 2012, Slimane was appointed creative director of Yves Saint Laurent; he officially changed the name of the label to Saint Laurent Paris that same year. He is best known for introducing the skinny silhouette for men.

Smith, Paul *British designer* (1946–)
Paul Smith started working in fashion at age 18 as a lowly gofer in a clothing warehouse, though what he really wanted to be was a cyclist. Those aspirations disappeared after a serious cycling accident. He returned to the clothing warehouse and became interested in fashion, where he was eventually promoted to menswear buyer. He opened a tiny menswear shop in Nottingham in 1970 carrying designers such as Kenzo, up until then not available outside of London. He studied fashion at night and gradually added his own designs to the merchandise in his shop. In 1976, he showed his first collection in Paris; he forged into women's wear in 1993. He is known for high quality, simply cut classics in interesting fabrics often infused with a splash of color, a floral print, or his signature multicolored prints.

Smith, Willi *American designer* (1948–1987)
Born in Philadelphia in 1947, Smith studied painting until 1965, when at 17 he went to New York with two scholarships to Parsons School of Design. While a student he freelanced as a sketcher; then left Parsons in 1968 to work in a knitwear firm. In 1976, Smith, as a designer and vice president, formed WilliWear Ltd., and WilliWear Men in 1978. Following his death in 1987, WilliWear Ltd. continued to produce the same type of clothing that prompted Smith at one time to say, "People want real clothes. I don't think people want to walk around looking like statements with their shoulders out to there."

Som, Peter *American designer* (1970–)
After majoring in art, Peter Som continued his studies at Parsons School of Design in New York; while there he did internships with Michael Kors and Calvin Klein. He debuted his namesake collection in the fall of 1999. From 2007 to 2008, he served as creative director of Bill Blass Ltd. and is credited with helping to save the brand. He resigned to concentrate on his own collection. He is credited with adapting the American sportswear tradition for the 21st c.

Spade, Kate *American designer* (1962–)
Kate Spade made her name as an accessory designer. In college she majored in journalism; after graduation she moved to New York and worked for *Mademoiselle* magazine, where she rose to the rank of senior fashion editor/head of accessories. It was that experience that led her to

create her own line of handbags. She launched the Kate Spade New York brand with her husband Andy Spade in 1993. In 2007, Fifth & Pacific (then named Liz Claiborne, Inc.) acquired the brand.

Sprouse, Stephen *American designer* (1953–2004)
Borne into a well-off family, Sprouse dropped out of school to take a job with Halston. After three years he left Halston to explore his own creative instincts. By the mid-1970s he worked as a band photographer and lived on the Bowery, a seedy neighborhood, in the same building as Blondie lead singer, Deborah Harry. He began making her stage clothes. His family loaned him money to launch his own fashion label. His collections sold quickly but he had poor business managers. He failed to launch a collection in 1986. Through the remainder of his life he designed several co-branded collections for Bergdorf Goodman, Barney's, and Target. Despite his short career he is remembered for bringing street culture to fashion with graffiti prints and psychedelic colors.

Stavropoulos, George (stav-row′-pole-us) *American couturier* (1920–1990)
Born in Greece and having studied dress design in Paris, Stavropoulos had a well-known custom salon in Athens from 1940 to 1960. He came to New York in 1961, opening a house there, and slowly built a reputation for unusually beautiful, classically simple clothes. He was known for draped, tiered, or pleated evening gowns, asymmetric folds, wrapped coats, kimono sleeves, floating panels, capes, bias jerseys.

Steffe, Cynthia (stef, sin-thi-a) *American designer* (1957–)
Cynthia Steffe studied at Parsons School of Design; while there she worked as a design assistant at DONNA KARAN and ANNE KLEIN & Co. In 1983, she went to work for Spitalnick, where they put her name on the label. She left in 1988 to form her own company. Her company was sold to Bernard Chaus in 1994 in order to facilitate greater growth. Steffe left the company in 2006, but two labels continue, Cynthia by Cynthia Steffe (luxury sportswear) and Cynthia Steffe black label (ready-to-wear and sportswear in luxury fabrics).

Stuart, Jill *American designer* (1965–)
Jill Stuart grew up in the Garment District; her parents owned the Seventh Avenue Boutique Mister Pants. At the age of 15 she designed a collection of handbags and jewelry that was displayed in Bloomingdale's windows. After studying at Rhode Island School of Design, she returned to New York, where she opened a boutique in 1988. In 1993, she launched her first Jill Stuart collection. The company remains privately owned.

Sui, Anna *American designer* (1955–)
After studying at Parsons School of Design, Sui worked for various sportswear companies. She sold some of her designs to Macy's and showed her first runway collection in 1991. She is known for eclectic styling and is very popular among the young.

Tadashi, Shoji *American designer* (active 1970s–)
Tadashi was born in Japan, where he studied art. He moved to the U.S. to attend college in Los Angeles. There he had the opportunity to work with Bill Whitten, who designed flamboyant stage costumes for the likes of Elton John, Stevie Wonder, and The Jacksons in the 1970s. After working for several other design firms, he established his own line of special occasion dresses in 1982.

Tahari, Elie *American designer* (1952–)
Elie Tahari is an Israeli designer of Iranian Jewish descent. He immigrated to the U.S. in 1971; with no formal training, he found a job cutting fabric for a company that made disco-themed apparel. He launched his own line of flirty dance dresses in 1974. By the 1980s, he had turned his attention to career wear. The company distributes under three labels: T Tahari, Tahari, and Elie Tahari. The label's career wear focuses on muted colors, featuring a sharp fit and unique details. The company expanded into menswear and women's bags and shoes in 2006. Tahari and his former business partner, Andrew Rosen, cofounded the Theory brand in 1997. Elie Tahari sold his share of that business in 2003.

Tam, Vivienne *American designer* (1957–)
Vivienne Tam grew up in Hong Kong and moved to New York, where she launched her first collection in 1982 under the label East Wind Code. She showed her first collection under her own name in 1993. She has helped to popularize stretch mesh knits in eastern patterns featuring dragons, peonies, and Buddhas.

Tassell, Gustave (tass-ell′) *American designer* (1926–)
Born in Philadelphia in 1926, Tassell studied painting at Pennsylvania Academy of Fine Arts. He did freelance designing in New York and had a small couture business in Philadelphia, planned window displays at Hattie Carnegie; then spent two years in Paris selling his sketches. He returned to the United States in 1956 and, with the help of JAMES GALANOS, opened his own firm in Los Angeles, California, where he became known for refined, no-gimmick clothes with stark, clean lines. After the death of NORELL, Tassell designed under the label, Norman Norell by Tassell. When Norell closed four years later, Tassell reopened his own business.

Taylor, Rebecca *American designer* (1969–)
Born in New Zealand, Taylor moved to New York after college and worked for Cynthia Rowley for six years before launching her own signature collection in 1996.

Theallet, Sophie *French-American designer* (1964–)
After studying at Studio Berçot in Paris, Theallet was hired by Jean Paul Gaultier and then joined Azzedine Alaïa for a decade before moving to New York. In New York she continued working freelance for Alaïa and did work for private clients before launching her own signature collection in 2007. Her designs exude a freedom of spirit—they are feminine and sensual with attention to materials and craftsmanship.

Theyskens, Olivier *Belgian designer* (1977–)
Theyskens dropped out of school two years into a five-year program, and began working on his first collection, which was shown in 1997. His sophisticated clothes in experimental shapes caught the attention of a variety of celebrities who are his clients; he was named creative director of Marcel Rochas in 2002 until the fashion division closed in 2006. That same year he was named artistic director for Nina Ricci; he stayed there until 2009. He is currently the creative director for Theory.

Tice, Bill *American lingerie designer* (1946–1995)
Tice arrived in New York in the mid-1960s after studying fashion design at the University of Cincinnati. He became designer for Royal Robes in 1968, for Sayour in 1974, and then for Swirl from 1975 to 1984. He introduced many at-home-wear concepts such as jersey float, quilted gypsy look, caftans, fleece robes, sundresses, sarongs, and quilted silk coats worn with narrow pants.

Thimister, Josephus *Belgian designer* (1962–)
After attending school in Antwerp he worked as an assistant to Karl Lagerfeld and then Jean Patou. In 1991, he was named director of luxury ready-to-wear for Balenciaga. In 1997, he launched his own label, Thimister. He is known for his military shapes and "broken elegance."

Thomass, Chantal *French designer* (1947–)
Chantal Thomass began designing her own clothes as a child, which her mother would then make. She married Bruce Thomass who had studied at the École des Beaux Arts, and together they founded a small fashion company under the label Ter et Bantine. The company grew and after selling dresses made of handpainted scarves to the Dorothée Bis boutique, they had enough capital to launch a Chantal Thomass line in 1975. The line evolved as Thomass passed through various life stages—she added maternity, then children's wear, and eventually focused on lingerie. They were bought by a Japanese group, World, in 1995; one year later Thomass was fired. She took time off from designing and worked as a consultant for Wolford and Victoria's Secret, among others. Under World, her label floundered and went into bankruptcy. In 1998, she regained the rights to her name and rebuilt her lingerie label.

threeASFOUR *American design team* (active 1996–)
Gabi Asfour, Adi Gil, and Angela Donhauser met in 1996 and became friends before launching their business in 1998, ASFOUR, along with Kai Kühne. Kühne left in 2005 and the brand name was changed to threeASFOUR. They presented their first collection in miniature in 2000 on wind-up hula dolls. They are known for creating an environment in which to show their seasonal collections and have a reputation for their outlandish business antics. Their clothes feature curved seams, circular patterns, asymmetry, and impeccable tailoring.

Tilley, Monika *American swimwear designer* (1934–)
Tilley, born in Vienna, Austria, earned an M.A. degree from the Academy of Applied Arts, Vienna. She came to the United States in 1957 and worked with JOHN WEITZ. She freelance designed skiwear and children's wear, and held design positions at White Stag, Cole of California, the Anne Klein Studio, Mallory Leathers, and Elon of California. She established Monika Tilley Limited in 1970 for swim- and beachwear, children's swimwear, at-home fashions, and intimate apparel. Tilley uses bias cuts, madras shirred with elastic, as well as a technique that angles the weave so that the fabric is molded against the body.

Toledo, Isabel *American designer* (1961–)
Cuban-born Toledo came to the United States as a child. She was an intern for Diana Vreeland at the Metropolitan Museum of Art before showing her first designs after 1985. She works with her husband, Ruben, a painter, sculptor, and fashion illustrator. She is considered to be a "hands-on" designer whose clothes have avante-garde appeal. She designed the dress and coat that First Lady Michelle Obama wore to Barack Obama's first inauguration in 2009.

Trigère, Pauline (tree-zher') *American designer* (1908–2002)
Born in Paris, Trigère came to New York in 1937. She worked as assistant designer to Travis Banton for Hattie Carnegie in late 1930s and started her own New York business in 1942 with brother, Robert. Specializing in coats, capes, suits, dresses, and accessories in unusual tweeds and prints, with intricate cuts to flatter mature figures, her licenses include: scarves, jewelry, furs, men's neckties, sunglasses, bedroom fashions, paperworks, servingware, and fragrance. Her trademark was the turtle, which turns up in jewelry, scarf, and fabric designs. She closed her business in 1993, but continued designing jewelry for some time.

Turk, Trina *American designer* (active 1995–)
Taught to sew by her mother at age 11, Turk came by her love for fashion early in life. Her first job after graduation was with Britannia Jeans in Seattle. She returned to California and designed prints for Ocean Pacific before launching her own brand in 1995. She is inspired by the multicultural mix and architecture of Los Angeles.

Tyler, Richard *American designer* (1948–)
Australian-born Tyler moved to California, where he began to work. He became known for outstanding tailoring. After a short time as designer for Anne Klein, he once again made California his base.

Ungaro, Emanuel (ung'-aro) *French designer* (1933–)
Born in France to Italian immigrants, Ungaro worked with BALENCIAGA from 1958 to 1963 and then spent two seasons with COURRÈGES. He showed his first collection in 1965. In 1960s, he was known for short, straight, structured dresses; high-waisted coats; diagonal seaming; A-line dresses; deeply cut-out armholes; shorts and blazers—clothes designed for his generation of women. By early 1970s he showed softer lines and luxury fabrics featuring flamboyant patterns and elegant draping in seductive, body-conscious silhouettes. These dresses became his signature. In 1996, Ungaro sold majority stake of his business to Salvatore Ferragamo SpA. In 1998, Ungaro lured GIAMBATTISTA VALLI from Krizia to

begin handing over the creative reins of the business. They worked side by side until 2004, when Valli left the label. In 2005, Ungaro sold the business and retired. The ready-to-wear label has continued under a variety of designers but never regained its original stature.

Valentino (Valentino Garavani) (val-enn-tee′-noh) *French and Italian couturier* (1932–)

Born in Italy, Valentino went to Paris at 17 to study at Chambre Syndicale de la Couture. After working for JEAN DESSÈS in 1950 and Guy Laroche in 1958, he opened his own house, Valentino, in Rome, 1959. His designs include ready-to-wear, couture, and menswear. He is noted for refined simplicity, elegantly tailored coats and suits—usually marked with his signature *V* in seams as well as in gilt *V*'s on belts, shoes, bags, and V's woven in hosiery and silk pants. Other design interests include: Valentino Piu for gifts and interiors; bed linens, drapery fabrics, table- and cookware.

Valli, Giambattista *Italian designer* (1966–)

After studying at Central Saint Martins, Valli went to work for Roberto Capucci in Italy. That job was followed by positions at Fendi and Krizia. In 1997, he moved to Paris to work for Emanuel Ungaro as his handpicked successor. They worked side by side until his contract expired in 2004. He launched his own line in 2005, combining things he learned at all of his previous employers. His style is based on line and silhouette. In July of 2011, he showed his first couture collection in Paris.

Valvo, Carmen Marc *American designer* (active in his own firm 1989–)

After college, Valvo spent a few years traveling Europe to absorb the culture and museums. He returned to the U.S. and enrolled at Parsons in New York. He returned to Paris to work as a ready-to-wear designer for NINA RICCI and later spent time at CHRISTIAN DIOR. In 1989, he launched his own line of evening wear and high-end cocktail dresses.

Van Noten, Dries (van-note′-ahn, drees) *Belgian designer* (1958–)

Born into a family of tailors, Van Noten continued the tradition attending the Royal Academy of Beaux Arts in Antwerp and working as a freelance designer for Belgian and Italian menswear labels. He launched his first collection under his own name in 1985. He opened his Antwerp boutique in 1989 and added menswear in 1991. He is known for the juxtaposition of opposites—simple with sophisticated, classic with modern, menswear elements with women's wear elements. He has a passion for fabrics and incorporates exclusive prints into every collection.

Varvatos, John (var-vay′-toes) *American designer* (1954–)

John Varvatos worked for Ralph Lauren and Calvin Klein before debuting his own fashion label in 1999. He is known for his menswear. In 2013, he joined NBC's *Fashion Star* caste as a celebrity mentor.

Vass, Joan *American designer* (1925–2011)

After attending Vassar and the University of Wisconsin, Vass spent her early career as a curator and an editor. Although she learned to knit at age five, she didn't translate that into designing until she was in her early fifties. She began a cottage industry to help women who needed an outlet for their skills in the early 70s. That grew into a non-profit company. She expanded into her own line of Joan Vass knits in 1977, selling sweaters, jackets, coats, and dresses made of novelty yarns and woven materials which sold at fine specialty stores. In the 1980s, she licensed her name for the Joan Vass USA line of sportswear separates, which consisted of mid-priced garments made of beautiful fine-gauge natural fibers.

Venet, Philippe (ven-eh′, feel-eep′) *French designer* (1929–)

Venet started learning tailoring at age 14. He worked two years at SCHIAPARELLI (1951 to 1953) and at GIVENCHY (1953 to 1962). He showed the first collection in his own house in January 1962. He is known for lean suits; rounded shoulders; round-back coats and curved seams. He also designed furs for Maximilian, and menswear and ready-to-wear collections. Although his house closed in 1996, the house of Venet continues to sell the perfume named for him.

Versace, Donatella (ver-sah′-chay, dohn-ah-tell′-ah) *Italian designer* (c. 1956–)

Donatella Versace was the muse and critic for her brother Gianni in the mid-1970s. He gave her her own label, Versu, which she has used as a vehicle to help launch new design talent. After his death, Donatella became the vice chairman and style and image director of the House of Versace. Initially, the house declined somewhat, but by 2000 it had undergone a resurgence, and Donatella Versace has since earned praise for her work.

Versace, Gianni (ver-sah′-chay, gee-ahn′-ee) *Italian designer* (1946–1997)

Born in Italy to a dressmaker mother, Gianni Versace studied architecture, but became involved in his mother's couture business, eventually becoming her buyer in the late 1960s. He worked as designer for prêt-à-porter firms such as Genny and Callaghan; then presented his first solo menswear collection in 1979. After that, he designed for women and established boutiques around the world. Designs included: accessories, leathers, furs, and fragrances for men and women; costumes for La Scala and the ballet. After he was killed, his sister Donatella assumed the direction of the house.

Viktor & Rolf *Dutch designers* (Viktor Horsting [1969–] and Rolf Snoeren [1969–])

Viktor and Rolf met while studying fashion at the Academy of the Arts in Arnhem, the Netherlands. They moved to Paris after graduation, interning at Maison Martin Margiela. They launched their first ready-to-wear collection in 2000 in Paris. In 2006, they partnered with H&M to do a co-branded collection. They have a reputation for shocking and challenging the fashion world by sculpting their silhouettes and distorting proportions.

Vionnet, Madeleine (vee-o-neh') *French couturière* (1876–1975)

One of the most creative fashion designers of the 20th c., Vionnet has been called the greatest technician of modern couture for her innovation of the bias cut. Born in Aubervilliers, France, she began dressmaking at an early age; trained in London and in Paris with Mme. Gerber at CALLOT and later at DOUCET. She opened her own house in 1912, closed during World War I, reopened in 1922, and closed permanently before World War II in 1940. Vionnet's designs were noted for classical drapery, wide-open necklines, easy over-the-head entrance, cowl or halter neck, handkerchief-point hems, faggoted seams, and Art Deco embroideries. She worked by draping and cutting designs on small wooden mannequins.

Vollbracht, Michael *American designer* (1947–)

After attending Parsons School of Design, Vollbracht was hired by Geoffrey Beene; two years later he moved to Donald Brooks. In 1978, he launched his own label, known for its bold graphic prints designed by Vollbracht himself. He closed the label in 1985. In 1999, Bill Blass retired and asked Vollbracht to help him on a retrospective of his work at Indiana University. Vollbracht authored the exhibition book. Just after the project was completed, Bill Blass passed away; Vollbracht was appointed creative director of Bill Blass where he stayed for five years. He retired in 2007 to pursue his art.

von Furstenberg, Diane *American designer* (1946–)

Born in Brussels, Belgium, Von Furstenberg obtained a degree in economics from the University of Geneva. In 1969, she came to the United States, where she started her career in fashion with a moderate-priced lightweight jersey wrap dress with surplice top and long sleeves. She left the fashion business in 1977, but returned in 1985 with day and evening wear based on her original wrap dress concept. Her business includes a wide variety of products including makeup and cosmetics, stationery, costume jewelry, furs, loungewear, handbags and small leather goods, raincoats, scarves, shoes, sunglasses, table linens, and wall coverings.

Vuitton, Louis (vwee'-ton, loo-ee') *Leather firm* (founded in mid-19th c.)

Vuitton was the founder of a firm that produces signature luggage with its yellow LVs and fleuron patterns on brown ground. First created for Empress Eugénie to transport her hoops and crinolines in mid-19th c., the family business is still producing luggage and leathers, making everything from wallets to steamer trunks. The firm has added lines of women's and menswear, for which MARC JACOBS was doing the designs in 2001.

Wang, Alexander *American designer* (1984–)

Alexander Wang attended Parsons School of Design in New York. While still in school, he launched a collection of primarily knitwear which he sold to stores from a suitcase. In 2007, he expanded into a first full women's collection. He received the CFDA 2008 Fashion Fund Prize, which gave him capital to expand his business. In 2008, he expanded to handbags. In 2009, he launched his diffusion line for women, T by Alexander Wang. A men's T line followed in 2010. He is known for his very urban designs, primarily in black. In 2012, he was appointed the creative director for Balenciaga.

Wang, Vera *American designer* (1949–)

Known for bridal gowns, Wang has been active and popular since the 1990s. Beginning as a fashion editor at *Vogue*, where she worked for 17 years, she moved to RALPH LAUREN, where she was designer and director for two years. She opened her own boutique in 1990, showed her first bridal line in 1992, and added evening dresses in 1993.

Watanabe, Junya *Japanese designer* (1961–)

After attending Bunka College in Tokyo, Watanabe apprenticed at Comme des Garcons under Rei Kawakuba. In 1992, he launched his own label. His collections change dramatically from season to season—one season futuristic, the next inspired by ethnic work wear; one season punk and the next peasant; one season poetic in white and the next somber in black. He is particularly known for his experimentation with techno fibers.

Weitz, John *American designer* (1923–2002)

Born in Berlin, Weitz came to the United States in 1940. His fashion career started with Lord & Taylor after World War II, where he made bulky sweaters and jeans. One of the most versatile pioneers in design of practical clothes for sports and specific lifestyles, he is known for women's sports clothes with menswear look; poplin car coats; hooded, zippered-up cotton jackets; pea jackets with white pants; town pants; strapless dress over bra and shorts. In the 1960s, he devised "ready-to-wear couture," chosen from sketches and swatches. With his contour clothes for men, inspired by Levi Strauss jeans, cowboy jackets, and fatigue coveralls, he was one of first American designers to show both menswear and women's wear and one of the first to license his work.

Westwood, Vivienne *British designer* (1941–)

A self-taught designer, Westwood first became known for antiestablishment styles. She showed in London in 1982, and also in Paris in 1983. Her 1985 "mini-crini" was especially influential. Her haute couture and ready-to-wear are considered to have influenced other designers. In recent years she has focused on British heritage and craftsmanship themes.

Wilkerson, Edward *American designer* (active 1984–)

Edward Wilkerson is the design director behind the bridge line Lafayette 148. After attending the Art and Design High School in Manhattan, he worked at ANNE KLEIN under DONNA KARAN and Louis Dell'Olio. He then studied fashion at Parsons School of Design and landed a job with CALVIN KLEIN. That was followed by a job at Donna

Karan, where he stayed for 15 years. In 1998, he joined the bridge label Lafayette 148, which had been established in 1996. He has helped to build the brand known for its career wear with attention to detail and fine fabrics.

Williamson, Matthew *British designer* (1971–)
Williamson graduated from London's Central Saint Martins College of Arts and Design; after graduation he worked briefly for ZANDRA RHODES, Marni, and Monsoon. He showed his first collection under his own label in 1997. In 2004, he was appointed creative director at the House of Pucci, where he stayed for three years. He continues to focus on his own label.

Worth, Charles Frederick *French couturier* (1826–1895)
Born in England, Worth went to Paris to work in 1845. He became famous in the 19th c. as dressmaker for Empress Eugénie and the ladies of the court of France's Second Empire. He is considered to be the founder of the industry of *haute couture.* In 1858, the house called Worth et Bobergh opened. It closed during the Franco-Prussian War (1870–1871), and reopened as Maison Worth in 1874 with assistance of Worth's sons, Jean Phillipe and Gaston. For 50 years the house of Worth was a fashion leader without rivals, dressing ladies of the courts and society all over Europe and America. Worth was the innovator in the presentation of gowns on live mannequins and was the first to sell models to be copied in the United States and England. After the death of Charles, the house continued under his sons and grandsons. It was sold in 1954 to PAQUIN.

Wu, Jason *American designer* (1983–)
Jason Wu had learned to sew, pattern, and sketch by the time he was 14. Schooled in Tokyo, Paris, and New York, he interned with Narciso Rodriguez. In 2006, with financial help from his parents, he launched his own label of ladylike fashions. In 2008, he was asked to design a sparkly evening gown for Michelle Obama. It turned out to be the gown that she wore to the inauguration ball, putting Wu on the map, and the First Lady wore another of his designs for the inauguration ball at her husband's second inauguration in 2013.

Yamamoto, Yohji (ya-ma-mo-to, yo-gee) *Japanese designer* (1943–)
Born in Japan, Yamamoto studied in Japan and later in Paris. He began designing in 1970, opened his own company in 1974 in Tokyo. He branched out with shows in Paris in 1981 and New York in 1982. His design has been described as having a "Japanese sensibility and tradition" behind it. Known for use of black fabrics, flat shoes, and layered loose garments, he does both women's and men's collections.

Yeohlee, Teng *Malaysian American designer* (1955–)
Born in Malaysia, Yeohlee left at age 18 for New York to study at Parsons School of Design. Two years later she sold her first five-piece collection to Henri Bendel. She founded her own label in 1981. Her work is minimal but dramatic in its impact, characterized by Eastern-influenced geometric and architectural forms. Although she designs a complete collection of women's wear, she is best known for her coats.

Zang Toi (Zang Toy) *Malaysian American designer* (1961–)
Born in Malaysia, Zang Toi left for Canada in 1980 and moved to New York shortly thereafter. He studied fashion at Parsons School of Design and went to work for Mary Jane Marcasiano. After five years with Marcasiano, he did some freelance work for Ronaldus Shamask before opening his own business in 1989. He combines an Asian palette and his taste for the exotic with classic American sportswear silhouettes. His clothes are spirited and young at heart.

Zoran *American designer* (1947–)
Zoran (born Zoran Ladicorbic) is a fashion minimalist who used solid-colored luxury fabrics to create architecturally shaped silhouettes. His early collections were based on squares and rectangles in silk crepe de Chine, cashmere, and other luxurious fabrics. His lines have evolved from there but maintain that geometric silhouette.